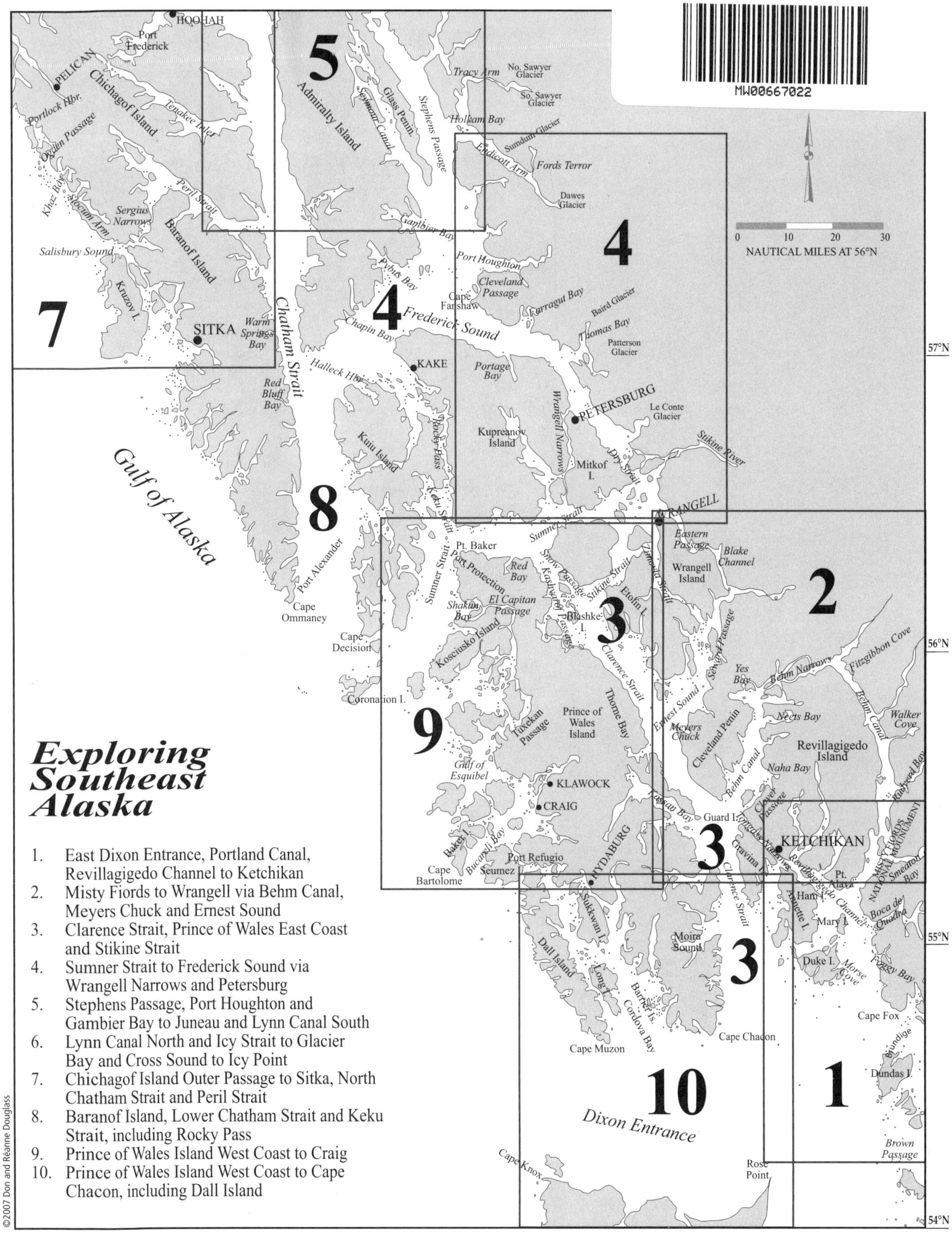


# Exploring Southeast Alaska

1. East Dixon Entrance, Portland Canal, Revillagigedo Channel to Ketchikan
2. Misty Fiords to Wrangell via Behm Canal, Meyers Chuck and Ernest Sound
3. Clarence Strait, Prince of Wales East Coast and Stikine Strait
4. Sumner Strait to Frederick Sound via Wrangell Narrows and Petersburg
5. Stephens Passage, Port Houghton and Gambier Bay to Juneau and Lynn Canal South
6. Lynn Canal North and Icy Strait to Glacier Bay and Cross Sound to Icy Point
7. Chichagof Island Outer Passage to Sitka, North Chatham Strait and Peril Strait
8. Baranof Island, Lower Chatham Strait and Keku Strait, including Rocky Pass
9. Prince of Wales Island West Coast to Craig
10. Prince of Wales Island West Coast to Cape Chacon, including Dall Island

Réanne Hemingway-Douglass

*The authors, Don and Réanne in the Research Vessel* Baidarka, *glide past the majestic arch at Boussole Bay—north of Cape Spencer.*

# *Exploring*
# SOUTHEAST ALASKA
## *Dixon Entrance to Skagway*

**2nd Edition**

**Don Douglass &**
**Réanne Hemingway-Douglass**

FINE EDGE
*Nautical & Recreational Publishing*

Anacortes, Washington

Editor: Linda Lewis, Ph.D.
Book Design: Melanie Haage
Graphics: Sue Athmann
Proofreader: Jan Hersey

Front cover photo by Frank Sjolie of the American Tug 41 *Emerald Lady* in front of the North Sawyer Glacier. Courtesy of Tomco Marine Group Inc., the builders of the American Tug.
Back cover center photo: Gary Luhm
Photos and sidebars in this book are the copyright of the individuals credited for the photo and/or sidebar and have been licensed for use in this book.
Front cover from Chart 17326
Back cover from Chart 17403

## Quotations from Canadian *Sailing Directions*

Quotations from the Canadian *Sailing Directions, Vol. 1* and *Vol. 2* are used with permission of the Canadian Hydrographic Service. Information from *Sailing Directions* is for illustrative purposes only and does not meet the CHS requirements; such information is not to be used for navigation. The appropriate *Sailing Directions* and CHS charts required under the Regulations of the Canada Shipping Act must be used for navigation.

## Important Legal Disclaimer

This book is designed to provide experienced skippers with planning information for cruising Southeast Alaska. Every effort has been made, within limited resources, to make this book complete and accurate. There may well be mistakes, both typographical and in content; therefore, this book should be used only as a general guide, not as the ultimate source of information on the areas covered. Much of what is presented in this book is local knowledge based upon personal observation and is subject to human error.

The authors, publisher and local and governmental authorities make no warranties and assume no liability for errors or omissions, or for any loss or damage of any kind incurred from using this information.

## Library of Congress Cataloging-in-Publication Data

Douglass, Don
Exploring Southeast Alaska : Dixon entrance to skagway / by Don Douglass and Réanne Hemingway Douglass. — 2nd ed.
p. cm.
Includes bibliographical references and index.
ISBN-13: 978-1-932310-24-5 (pbk., 2nd edition)
1. Pilot guides--Alaska--Alaska, Gulf of. 2. Pilot guides--Alaska--Alexander Archipelago. I. Hemingway-Douglass, Réanne. II. Title.

VK943.D65 2007
623.89'2297982--dc22 2007015794

ISBN 978-1-932310-24-5


Address requests for permission to:
Fine Edge, 14004 Biz Point Lane, Anacortes, WA 98221
www.FineEdge.com

Printed in the United States of America

# Contents



## Appendices and References

Réanne Hemingway-Douglass

Baidarka *exploring the upper reaches of Southeast Alaska—Cape Spencer*

# Foreword

## Professor Roderick Frazier Nash

The floor-to-ceiling map on the wall of the U'Mista Cultural Centre in Alert Bay, British Columbia, had to be over 15 feet high. It covered Puget Sound to Glacier Bay, and there was one of those little red "you are here" dots way down near the floor. It chilled my heart. That was back in the early 1990s and I was a week out of Anacortes, Washington, on my first cruise to Alaska. I had prepared as best I could with the information available at the time, but there in my face was the reality: a thousand miles to go, enormously complex coastline, myriad islands, few human settlements, current, wind, fog, rain—the whole maritime enchilada. Lots of decisions; lots of opportunities for wrong ones.

Sure, I had charts on that first trip, and now there are electronic charting miracles, but in a way, they only make Northwest boating more daunting. Where do you actually want to go on those wonderful charts? What I needed was a way to "get inside" the charts; advice on what they really meant for my voyage. As I walked tentatively down the hill to my boat and headed out into Queen Charlotte Strait, I thought about the value of a navigational psychologist, or just a hand to hold.

What I needed back then was exactly what you are holding right now. Think of it this way—you have just bought years of boating experience from two of the most accomplished explorers and map-makers in maritime history. Well over a thousand anchorages are precisely located and described in this book. It's based on primary research (the Douglasses have been everywhere!), and it is organized in an "open navigation" format. The old-style "recommended route" cruising guides were useful, but discouraged spontaneity. Don and Réanne know that wherever you go, "there you are"; and their book will help you with local knowledge everywhere in Southeast Alaska. They have done a lot of the physical and mental grunt work necessary for a voyage that is safe and special.

This book concerns part of the largest, most complex and most isolated cruising ground in the temperate latitudes of this planet. Thanks to glaciation and a rise in sea level over the last 15,000 years, there is a staggering amount of islands and radically varied coastline in Southeast Alaska. Settlements are few, far between and not accessible by motor vehicle. There is some logging and hydropower development in evidence, but the country swallows it up—we are talking about wilderness boating here. People are visitors who do not remain. There are outstanding opportunities for solitude; chances to interact with the biggest and wildest carnivores of land (grizzly) and sea (whales). You might even see an orca pick off a swimming wolf or grizzly!

Get off the main cruising corridors and you can go days and weeks without seeing another boat. Walk a few hundred yards into the rainforest and it is likely you are standing where no human has ever been. The ridges along the fiords are unclimbed. In general, the coastline looks the same as it did for the first Native peoples and for the Russian, Spanish and English seafarers. Forget about reaching a tow-boat service on Ch 16: Southeast, like all wilderness, puts a premium on self-reliance. If your idea of a lonely anchorage is Catalina Island on a weekday or Puget Sound in the off-season, you are in for a big—and potentially scary—but also exhilarating surprise. It's comforting under these circumstances to have this book close to your pilot station.

There are no trails, only wakes, on the water. Wilderness boating in a place like Southeast Alaska allows every mariner the chance to be a discoverer. Above all, this is an environment of personal exploration: a place to test your skill, your courage and your capacity for wonder. And the Douglasses will help you to—in Henry David Thoreau's words—"go confidently in the direction of your dreams."

*Authors' Note:*
Professor Roderick Frazier Nash, retired from the University of California, Santa Barbara, has cruised waters of the Inside Passage and Southeast Alaska for two decades. He is a creator of the field of environmental history and the author of such classics as *Wilderness and the American Mind* and *The Rights of Nature.* Over 15 years ago, Rod was instrumental in reviving Don Douglass's passion for the Inside Passage on a cruise from Juneau to Seattle on his Nordic Tug, *Forevergreen.*

Linda Lewis

*Kasnyku Falls in Waterfall Cove, Chatham Strait*

# Introduction

## Important Southeast Alaska Cruising Considerations

It is said that "Experience is what you get right after you needed it." We encourage you to carefully read this chapter. It will help you begin to build an invaluable base of experience and guide your use of this book.

Every summer, Southeast Alaska —called simply "Southeast" by Alaskans—draws a wide variety of pleasure craft, from solo kayakers, trailerable sport fishing boats, houseboats and small sailboats with outboards, to motorsailers, trawler-style cruisers and world-class yachts. They all head north through the Inside Passage to follow the path of Canadian geese, whales and salmon and, neither size, speed nor cost of a boat seem to have any correlation to the enjoyment or safety of their trip. Boaters who successfully cruise these waters all have certain values in common—they are well prepared and self-reliant, with the desire to explore this beautiful saltwater wilderness.

Réanne Hemingway-Douglass

*Research Vessel* Baidarka *in Berg Bay*

To help you plan your cruise, we include detailed route and anchoring information on every named—and many unnamed—anchor sites in Southeast, providing the vital "local knowledge" missing from charts and other sources. Our philosophy in our comprehensive guidebooks is this: in over 3,000 miles of pristine summer cruising in the Inside Passage, you are seldom more than one hour from a place where you can drop your hook to wait out the fog or chop or wait for the wind to die down or the tide to turn. You don't have to over-stress your boat or crew just to make it to a town 50 miles away.

There are all kinds of wonderful, intimate coves to explore—or to just enjoy a calm night's sleep. Some of them are along the ferry route; others are along the more scenic, remote routes. Some of the places or anchorages mentioned require advanced piloting skills or risk taking. Such places should be attempted only by qualified skippers who feel comfortable in accepting that type of risk. Any time a passage or an anchor site is too small or tricky, or other than you thought, turn around and return to a known safe place, or try another anchor site. By understanding your own abilities and interests and matching these to the almost unlimited outdoor opportunities found in Alaska, you will indeed experience a most rewarding adventure.

If you are a newcomer to cruising, we recommend that you prepare by consulting local experts—cruising instructors, yacht clubs, experienced Alaska boaters, commercial fishermen, the Power Squadron, the Coast Guard Auxiliary—and that you read many of the texts listed in the bibliography. There are also Internet sources that contain lots of cruising information. (See sidebar on p. xx: Internet Resources.) Make this the cruise of a lifetime. Plan now, and by all means, go!

## Planning Tips for Cruising to Southeast Alaska

1. For many boaters, cruising to Southeast Alaska is the dream voyage. It is a serious undertaking however, so you should test your vessel and crew well before you start your trip. The better you prepare your cruise, the bigger the dividends you'll reap in safety, comfort and enjoyment. A solid plan, executed with good judgment, minimizes potential surprises and has more to do with a successful voyage than the size or speed of your boat or the number of crew you have aboard.

2. Our suggested itineraries (see Appendix A) include information for trips all the way from the state of Washington, through British Columbia, to Southeast Alaska. These itineraries do not include layover days for bad weather or relaxation, so you should schedule such days. Fog—prevalent on the Inside Passage during late summer—may affect your travel time. Current, sea or weather conditions at Seymour Narrows, Yuculta and Dent Rapids, Johnstone Straits, Queen Charlotte Sound and Dixon Entrance may require you to alter your schedule. Chop caused by current flowing against a contrary wind can slow you down, too, so draw up plans for an alternative anchor site. If you pre-plot your route on detailed paper charts or electronic charts before you set out, it'll save you up to two hours each day.

3. Weather and anchoring conditions grow more challenging the farther north you go, and you will probably become more proficient at monitoring and forecasting local weather than you were at the start of your trip. For a safe and enjoyable cruise, remain flexible and don't become a slave to a schedule. Visit some of the more intricate coves and passages described in this book, but use good judgment. Turn around and head back to a known anchorage if you find you've exceeded your level of comfort or ability to cope. Of increasing importance, as you leave civilization behind, are oversized anchor gear (preferably chain rode), engine spares and knowledge in using such gear.

4. Newcomers to northwest cruising frequently undertake a series of preliminary cruises, first to British Columbia, then on to Southeast Alaska as they gain experience and have more time. Shake down cruises are also recommended, especially for owners of newly pur-

chased boats. Many people trailer their sport fishing boats to places such as Port Hardy, Bella Coola, Prince Rupert or to Southeast Alaska by ferry, which allows them to gain experience, one segment at a time.

Floatplanes that connect to a major airport can reach you within an hour almost anywhere along the Inside Passage. Consider picking up crew or guests along the route—they can be morale-boosters, bringing news from home or providing delivery of spare parts. (Note that any packages from the U.S. to Canada will have to clear Canadian Customs, which may delay delivery.) We generally pick up and drop off crew or guests two or three times on each of our north- and southbound trips (arrive in one port, but depart from another port), and we've been able to do this from many ports in Southeast Alaska without leaving anyone stranded overnight. This strategy maintains your journey's progress. A few owners even leave their cruising boats in Alaska with a caretaker during the winter and resume their voyage the following spring. (We suggest you check out Hoonah Harbor and Sitka for storing your boat.)

Don Douglass

*With the many floatplane companies available, your guests can fly into one location and out of another.*

5. If you're a newcomer to cruising and need some extra practice before you head for the Far North, plan some shakedown cruises in the greater Puget Sound in Washington or the Gulf Islands in British Columbia to test your boat, its equipment and crew. As you gain confidence, you can fine tune your plans. For Southeast Alaska trips, leave an itinerary, name of your boat and a detailed description of your boat with an associate back home with instructions to be followed in case you're overdue by a specified length of time. Be sure to continuously update your plans and timeline with your associate during your journey. (The U.S. Coast Guard in Southeast Alaska does not accept float plans.)

Linda Lewis

*Hoonah Harbor is a favorite marina for leaving your boat over the winter in Southeast Alaska.*

6. If you are inexperienced in running saltwater rapids, plan your trip to transit such areas in slack water on a Neap Tide (first and third quarters of the moon's monthly cycle), or when adjacent tidal differences are minimal. (Velocities

*A picture-perfect full moon tells you it is a Spring Tide, which means greater tidal ranges and faster currents.*

at neap tides are considerably less than those at spring tides.) This advice especially applies to narrow but important passages, like Sergius Narrows (in Peril Strait) on the way to Sitka, as well as for dinghy adventures, such as in the upper reaches of Very Inlet behind Foggy Bay.

7. You are likely to have difficulty obtaining parts, special tools and instruction manuals en route, so be sure to carry spares for any critical items. Even today, Sitka and Ketchikan are the only two places in Southeast where you can get a prop repaired. If you plan to approach glaciers at close hand, we recommend that you carry a spare prop. Haul-out facilities are quite limited, but many villages have useful tidal grids where you can check your hull or do your own work. (For tips on using haul-out grids, see the sidebar in Chapter 4: "Haul-out Grids in Southeast Alaska.")

8. A good quality, hard-bottom dinghy (such as aluminum or fiberglass) makes it possible for you to pull onto shores that are rocky and barnacle-encrusted. Seldom will you find sand beaches in Southeast Alaska, so a good dinghy is important if you want to explore the many secluded beaches and trails. We prefer an inflatable dinghy with a hard bottom (such as an RBI) because you will also add some safety in case of sinking. Don't tow any dinghy in windy weather or through chop if you want to keep it.

9. Don't hesitate to contact the U.S. Coast Guard via VHF radio for weather updates or alternate destinations if conditions deteriorate. Radio contacts with "buddy" boats, behind or ahead of you, can provide on-the-spot information and be a quick source of assistance if necessary. Be sure also to listen in to other VHF conversations and pick up a boat name you may not know but can hail for a report on the wind and sea-state they are currently experiencing. There is a real sense of community among boaters in these waters; participate in it and use it to your benefit.

10. Large-scale (large detail) charts, tide and current tables are required to be carried on board. Guidebooks and waypoint guides are useful, as well. Many chartbooks and marine atlases are out-of-date and of a scale useful only for planning a center-of-the-channel route. Unless you're on a marathon, you'll get most of your enjoyment travelling along the shore and poking your bow into intimate, secluded anchorages that require a more sophisticated level of navigational information.

Lay out your courses at least the day before a transit (using the largest-scale charts possible)—not after you have gotten underway. You need to be able to focus on looking out the window when you are underway. Situational awareness must be practiced at all times up here. Doing careful preliminary chart work makes you intimately familiar with the route's hazards and special requirements. When using your large-scale paper charts, use a yellow marker to highlight every rock and hazard that is within a quarter mile either side of your intended course. Use comparable hazard-highlighting methods with your electronic charts (such as alarm circles or electronic boundary lines).

Entering waypoints from guides or from other cruisers can be helpful, but you must examine the details of the course minutely and be responsible for your own course decisions. Then be ready to look out the window!

These are challenging waters to navigate, especially because Southeast Alaska's nautical charts are not as accurate as those along the lower Inside Passage. If you need to revisit your navigation skills, make it a priority. Do you really know what "cross track error" (XTE) means? And what "course made good" means? If these questions sit uneasily in your mind, you need a good review. If you are linking your GPS/electronic charting and autopilot together, these issues are paramount for you to understand.

Today, most of Southeast Alaska's cruisers use electronic charting methods. Chartplotters and PC-based electronic charting offer timesavings and ease of use. Electronic charting, however, comes with its problems, too. For example, "quilting" charts is the selected method for most users. But you need to use caution when the scales of the two charts being quilted are different; a seamless matching of chart edges is not always what you see on the screen. A prime example of this is in Keku Strait (Rocky Pass), where the mismatch occurs in exactly the most difficult stretch of the passage.

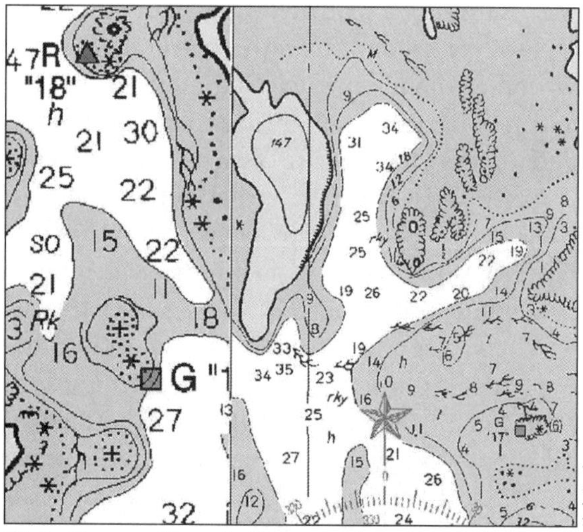

Linda Lewis

*Note the small-scale/large-scale mismatch in this electronic-chart-quilting example from Rocky Pass, near the Devils Elbow.*

Don Douglass

*Coauthor, Réanne, makes serious use of her paper chart in Rocky Pass.*

Along with GPS, electronic charting has contributed immeasurably to easier, safer journeys—*when used prudently*. You are advised to also carry paper charts for all of the waters you plan to travel. Those paper charts should be out, opened and stacked in the order of the day's passage. (It is also very helpful to be able to glance at them during the day for the "big-picture" context that is lost on computer screens.) You may not realize how dependent you are on electronic technology until your electronics go down. If your software freezes or your electronics fail and you don't have your paper charts instantly ready, you will literally be lost.

There is yet another reason for you to diligently use your paper charts. Southeast Alaska's charts frequently contain printed "Notes" about particular areas. These notes often contain critical information that is important for you to read. It is very easy for you to overlook the printed notes on the raster charts used with your electronic charting software, so we urge you to study your paper charts and get used to having them ready at hand.

11. Read the Sidebars placed throughout the book. They are based on personal experience and will give you many cruising tips. You will read short tales of cruisers who have gone before you and who share their joys and challenges with you. We tell you about how to work with haul-out grids in Southeast Alaska. Other cruisers present tips on how to stay clear of fishing nets along your route; how to meet some of the anchoring challenges in Southeast Alaska; how to have fun and stay safe with glaciers. Read the sidebars for the glories of whale watching, the Zen of carving totem poles and the soul-dancing experiences of Southeast Alaska.

12. Don't put off your cruise until everything is perfect. The docks are full of boaters who are forever planning their ultimate trip, but who never leave the harbor. All you need for a safe, satisfying and successful trip is a well-found boat, a good plan and careful navigation backed by a vigilant skipper and an alert crew. Set a date, and by all means, go for it. You won't regret it!

## How to Use this Book

Each of the following chapters in this book covers a separate cruising area, proceeding usually from south to north in the area of Prince Rupert, B.C., and Dixon Entrance, to north to Skagway and Glacier Bay, then north to south, following the west coast of Baranof Island to Cape Chacon. An area map at the beginning of each chapter contains most of the common routes and serves as a quick reference to the location of channels, passages and coves found within the text; the maps on the inside front and back covers provide a graphical overview of Southeast Alaska and the corresponding chapters.

Each geographical entry in this book follows the same user-friendly layout as the other titles of our *Exploring* series of guidebooks. The place name comes first, followed by the island or major body of water on which it is located, then general location and distance from a prominent place. NOTE: Mileage references for geographical locations are straight-line measurements, not the boat's course to or from.

Following the geographical entry is the nautical chart number(s) for that place, with the largest-scale chart mentioned first. We provide an entrance waypoint (the lat/long for the center of the preferred channel when approaching from seaward) and anchor position(s) we have personally used or recommend.

### Sample Layout Selection

**Anita Bay** (Etolin Island) — Place name (bay)

Anita Bay is 5 miles northeast of Whaletail Cove. — Distance from known point

Chart 17382 — Largest-scale chart listed first

Entrance: 56°14.27′ N, 132°22.82′ W

Anchor: 56°11.55′ N, 132°30.01′ W

> *Anchorage may be had near the head of the bay in 13 to 17 fathoms, mud and sand bottom*...(CP)

— Excerpts from official government publications (CP-*Coast Pilot*, SD-*Sailing Directions*)

Anita Bay indents Etolin Island almost to its west coast. Its upper end lies just 1.3 miles from the north tip of Burnett Inlet on Etolin Island's west side. The sharp 3,800-foot Virginia Peak, frequently bare of snow in the summer, lies just west of the entrance to Anita Bay, providing a scenic background to the anchorage. For larger boats, Anita Bay is the preferred anchorage in this area.

— Our own recorded local knowledge based on personal experience

Anchor in about 12 fathoms over sand with good holding.

— Describes in fathoms anchor position given above along with holding power

The horizontal datum on all the charts in Southeast Alaska is NAD 83, which is basically or very nearly the same as the GPS system default of WGS 84. All waypoint entries in this book are NAD 83 (WGS 84), except the insets on Chart 17372 for Rocky Pass (which are NAD 27).

*Please note:* If you are attempting to plot a fix from GPS coordinates onto an NAD 27 paper chart you will have to adjust for the difference in horizontal datum. This difference increases with latitude. See your paper-chart notes for the exact offset, as they differ from chart to chart.

Be alert when exiting from Prince Rupert to Dixon Entrance via Venn Passage. The paper chart for Venn Passage (3955) is based on NAD 27 horizontal datum. If your GPS is not also set to NAD 27 for this short passage, you can be longitudinally off-position by as much as 300–600 feet! Mariners using traditional paper-chart navigation methods must make this GPS adjustment themselves. A number of electronic charting systems automatically "convert" to the WGS 84 horizontal datum in areas where NAD 27 datum is encountered.

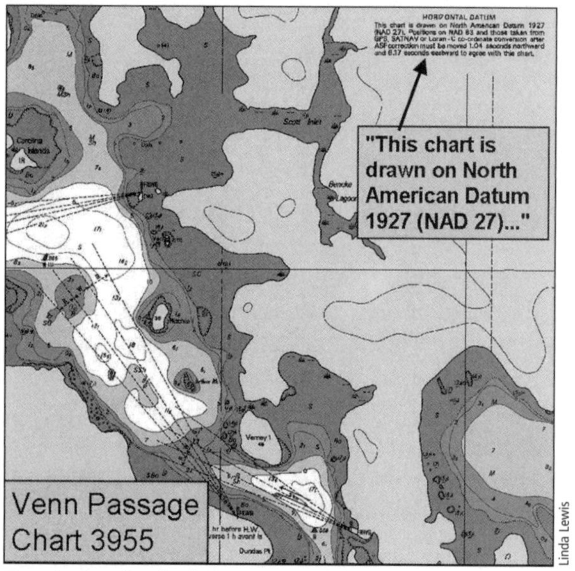


*Don't overlook the* notes *on charts; they provide important information.*

(Note that many charts throughout B.C. waters are based on NAD 27 horizontal datum). *A word of caution:* it has been reported by experienced mariners that *not all* electronic charting systems automatically adjust for horizontal datum. In addition, some vendors will tell you the electronic charts themselves have been adjusted for horizontal datum, while other vendors will tell you the software does the adjusting. Be prudent and check with *your* charting software vendor before you begin your cruise through the Inside Passage.

Be aware that in this book's schematic diagrams the route from an entrance waypoint to an anchor waypoint is normally *curvilinear,* so it can rarely be followed in a straight line; you must choose your cruising route by visual means and by using a depth sounder. If you were to blindly follow a straight-line course between the entrance and anchor waypoints, you may well find intervening land in your path!

As you head north, you will gain experience in judging what is a protected anchorage for you and your vessel, as determined by your unique circumstances. Some anchor sites are steep-to or have limited swinging room, in which case a stern tie to shore is required.

Text in indented italics is excerpted from the *U.S. Coast Pilot* or Canada's *Sailing Directions.* With this feature you have the official viewpoint (where it is available) as an extra source of information. (*Editor's caution:* Note that these are selected excerpts; for the complete text of each location see the actual *Coast Pilot* or *Sailing Directions.*)

The main body of our text describes the local knowledge we have discovered by personal observation or in conjunction with sources we believe to be reliable and knowledgable. If there is no text in italics, then the government publications are silent on this cove.

The last entry under each place-name is specific anchoring information for the anchor site waypoint identified at the heading and/or on the detailed diagram for that place. If you should find different conditions than those described, double-check your position on the chart and make your own judgment about suitability for the particular conditions. Conditions do change over the years, due to runoff, for example, and may have changed since last surveyed. Use caution and multiple sources of information to make anchoring decisions for your vessel.

Linda Lewis

Royal Sounder *at anchor next to their own private glacier in Reid Inlet, Glacier Bay National Park*

## Anchoring

Cruising in Southeast Alaska and along the waterways of the Inside Passage is all about anchoring: once you leave the marinas and fishing resorts of lower British Columbia, finding a safe, secluded anchor site is one of the challenges and pleasures of cruising.

Indispensable equipment includes a conventional, over-sized cruising anchor (not a lightweight folding version). The CQR and Bruce anchors are common favorites of recreational boaters in Southeast Alaska. On small boats, a boat-length of chain and good nylon rode works well. On yachts 40 feet or larger, generally all-chain rodes are used. We also carry a smaller lunch hook to use during temporary stops or to restrict our swinging room. For security in close quarters or in deep, steep-to anchorages, we sometimes use a stern-tie to shore. Although we usually prefer to swing on a single CQR anchor, in popular anchorages we try to minimize our impact by matching the mooring technique and swinging radius of other boats. Note that many larger vessels use an all-chain rode, which has a different turning radius than boats with mostly nylon rode. (Throughout this book the term "large" vessel generally refers to those 40 feet and over; the term "small" vessel refers to boats 30 feet and under.)

Choosing your anchor site carefully and setting your anchor well assures you of a good night's sleep, even when there are occasional downslope winds or williwaws. We have anchored in over 4,000 sites from Seattle to the Gulf of Alaska. The following rating system is based on our observations and experiences.

## Definitions Used for Holding Power

**Excellent—very good holding**
Anchor digs in deeper as you pull on it—the preferred bottom in a blow, but a rare find—usually thick, sticky mud or clay.

**Good holding**
Generally sufficient for overnight anchorage in fair weather—anchor digs in but may drag or pull out on strong pull. Common in mud/sand combinations or hard sand.

**Fair holding**
Adequate for temporary anchorage in fair weather, but boat should not be left unattended. Bottom of light sand, gravel with some rocks, grass or kelp or a thin layer of mud over a hard bottom. Anchor watch desirable.

**Poor holding**
Can be used for a temporary stop in fair weather only. Bottom is typically rocky with a lot of grass or kelp, or a very thin later of mud and sand—insufficient to properly bury anchor. Anchor watch at all times is recommended.

**Steep-to**
Depth of water may decrease from 10 fathoms to 1/2 fathom in as little as one boat length! (Approach at dead-slow recommended.) Use shore tie to minimize swinging and to keep anchor pulling uphill.

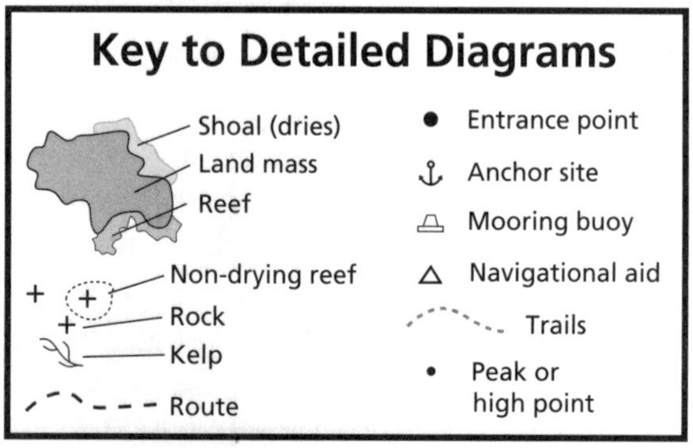


## Anchor Diagrams

We have included anchor diagrams for sites we feel would be helpful. These diagrams show simply the approximate routes we took, the typical depths we found and the places we anchored. *Please note* that these diagrams, which are non-representational and not to scale, do not include all known or unknown hazards and should always be used with caution and self-verification.

## Measurements and Other Conventions Used in this Book

Unless otherwise noted, the depths listed in the text or shown on diagrams are always given in fathoms, regardless of the measurement units on cited charts; depths are also reduced to approximate zero tide (mean lower low water). When you use the depth numbers on our diagrams, you should add the amount of tide listed in the tide tables. If there is a minus tide, you subtract the number from the depth number. Be sure you know how to correct times in the tide tables for the exact time you are there.

Bearings and courses, when given in this book by the authors, are generally magnetic and identified as such. (*Please note* that the bearings given in the *Coast Pilot* quotes throughout the book—in italics—are always stated in true bearings.) Courses are taken off the chart compass rose; they are approximate and are to be "made good." No allowances have been made for deviation, current or drift. Monitor cross track error if using GPS and "crab" as necessary to stay on proper track over ground. When compass cardinal points are used (e.g., NW or SE), these refer to true bearings and should be taken as approximate only.

Unless otherwise stated, distances are expressed in nautical miles and speed is expressed in knots. Scales on the diagrams are expressed in yards, meters and miles as noted and are approximate only. Time is given in four-digit, 24-hour clock numbers; all courses are given in three digits.

Latitude and longitude in the text are cited in degrees, minutes and decimal minutes to the nearest hundredth of a minute and are taken from the largest-scale chart available. (Seconds are not used.) These lat/longs are to be treated as approximate only. Many of the referenced charts are not accurate—nor can they be read accurately—to one-hundredth of a minute. We have approximated this last digit to provide as complete a picture as possible.

Spelling and usage of place names follows, as closely as possible, local tradition and the lead of the *U.S. Coast Pilot* and Canada's *Sailing Directions.* We have documented many small, unnamed coves and bays and, in each case, have tried to use local names. However, where we could find no reference to an anchor site, we used a new name that seemed appropriate.

## U.S. Customs Issues Crossing into Southeast Alaska from B.C.

Heading into Southeast Alaska, all boats (U.S. and foreign) must clear customs and obtain a clearance number. All persons on board must have a passport (regardless of age). Although this regulation does not go into effect until January 2008, in actual practice, Washington State and Ketchikan Customs officers expect you to have passports. Since regulations change frequently, boaters should check the U.S. Customs and Border Protection Website (www.cbp.gov/xp/cgov/travel) before making cruising plans.

Boaters need to clear customs before cruising in Alaska. You may wish to return to some areas (such as Misty Fiords) after you have cleared customs.

Most cruisers leaving British Columbia waters bound for Ketchikan do not want to (or cannot) make the long trip from Prince Rupert in one day. However, U.S. Customs and Border Protection does not permit anchoring without having cleared customs. If you anchor, you have touched land and may be subject to penalties.

There are several solutions to this Southeast Alaska challenge. One is to anchor as far north in British Columbia as possible (such as Brundige Inlet on Dundas Island), and make the transit all the way to Ketchikan the next day. Another alternative exists because the Ketchikan Customs office wants to facilitate recreational boater compliance with Customs regulations.

Ketchikan Customs has made Foggy Bay an approved site for an interim stop (with their prior approval) on the way to Ketchikan. They would like recreational cruisers to plan ahead and do the following:

1. Telephone the Ketchikan Customs office from Prince Rupert using a land line. U.S. cell phones do not work in Prince Rupert. (If you have a cell phone and cruise close to Cape Fox at the northeast edge of Dixon Entrance, you *may* be able to pick up a U.S. cell signal.)

2. Ask the Ketchikan Customs officer to approve anchoring in U.S. waters. Foggy Bay is their approved location for interim anchoring. They will ask you for specific information and give you permission to anchor.

3. You still must clear customs upon your arrival in Ketchikan. It is not permissible to take side trips until you do so. Ketchikan does not have a customs dock. Once you reach your destination marina, call customs from your cell or land line. Don't forget to post the clearance number in your window and record it in the ship's log. No one may leave or board the boat until clearance has been given.

4. Ketchikan has a 100 percent boarding policy for recreational boaters, which began in 2005. If every person on board your vessel has a NEXUS card (www.getnexus.com), Ketchikan Customs can choose to accept your NEXUS information by telephone and will likely give you a clearance number and elect not to board you.

If you enter U.S. waters and encounter serious weather that places your vessel and/or crew in danger or you have other mitigating circumstances, such as sea sickness and the like, that prohibit completing your journey to Ketchikan, contact the USCG via VHF radio. They will relay your request for permission to anchor to Ketchikan Customs. (The USCG does not routinely involve itself in customs issues.)

## Internet Resources

You will find references to Internet Websites throughout this book. *Please note* that Website addresses change over time or may not work. You are responsible for checking the timeliness and reliability of any information you find on a Website. See the sidebar "Internet Resources" on p. xx for some of these references related to: navigation, customs, weather and general Southeast Alaska cruising information.

While you are underway in Southeast Alaska, your ability to find a WiFi Internet connection

# INTERNET RESOURCES FOR SOUTHEAST ALASKA CRUISERS

Captain Linda Lewis

The Internet has become an invaluable resource in all walks of life, no less so for the Southeast Alaska cruiser. The addresses below are for Websites of interest on a variety of topics, beginning with the more technical navigation, customs, and weather sites, followed by Southeast Alaska cruising information. Numerous towns and harbors in Southeast Alaska also have Websites. The major locations are referenced throughout this book; use the search function in your browser for additional locations. Please remember that Website addresses and circumstances can change quickly.

## NAVIGATION, CUSTOMS, WEATHER RESOURCES:

### *U.S. Coast Pilot 8*—includes Southeast Alaska

Free download (Adobe PDF format). Put the files on your laptop and use word search to find your topics of interest. Look at the opening pages of each chapter for the chart catalog graphic for the area; this is an excellent way to see what charts are recommended for specific locations.
http://chartmaker.ncd.noaa.gov/nsd/cpdownload.htm

### Tides Predictions in Alaska

Online tide information is limited to a very few stations in Southeast Alaska. Be sure to dig deeper into the Reference Stations' sites for information on many Secondary Stations. http://tidesandcurrents.noaa.gov/station_retrieve.shtml?type=Tide%20Data&state=Alaska&id1=945&id2=946&id3=949

### Current Predictions in Alaska

A bit more online information exists for currents (than for tides) in Southeast Alaska. Again, dig deeper into the Reference Stations' sites for information on many Secondary Stations. Choose Alaska and year.
http://tidesandcurrents.noaa.gov/curr_pred.html

### Non-lateral Aid to Navigation in Southeast Alaska

This aid to navigation may be unfamiliar to you; review it here. http://www.uscgboating.org/safety/aton/non_lateral.htm

### *American Practical Navigator*—Bowditch

This is a highly regarded, technical navigation reference. Download for free; keep it on your laptop and use word search.
www.marineplanner.com/bowditch/bowditch.cfm

### NOAA Charts—Dates of Latest Editions

This is a wonderfully easy site to navigate and is your most up-to-date source of information for the latest editions of charts available and the latest corrections' dates. Most Southeast Alaska charts of interest to you are numbered in the 17xxx category.
http://chartmaker.ncd.noaa.gov/mcd/dole.htm

### Chart Catalogs by Region in Graphics Form

Select a specific Alaska region and see the chart outlines and numbers. Note: check the date of these catalogs carefully—they are frequently a bit old even at this online site.
http://nauticalcharts.noaa.gov/mcd/ccatalogs.htm#

### NOAA-approved site for Print-on-Demand Charts

Don't cruise to Southeast Alaska without paper charts. Buying a print-on-demand chart means you are getting the latest edition *and* the latest corrections to that chart—as of the time of purchase.
www.oceangrafix.com

### NOAA Free Downloadable Electronic Charts (ENCs)

To date, there are only 14 Southeast Alaska downloadable vector electronic charts available from NOAA; however, that number should steadily increase as NOAA builds its database. The downloadable raster electronic charts database appears to be complete. Be sure to check with your charting sofware company to determine whether you can install and use these NOAA charts with your software. (Ask specifically about the *version* of your software.) The chart number look-up process on the vector Website is tedious; the raster site is much easier to use, as the chart numbers are in chronological order. The download process for both is easy and your software's install routine should also be easy. The real plus with vector electronic charts is that they are corrected to the most current information available from Local Notice to Mariners.
For vector (S-57) downloads, go to: http://chartmaker.ncd.noaa.gov/mcd/enc/download.htm
For raster (BSB) downloads, go to: http//nauticalcharts.noaa.gov/mcd/Raster/download.htm

### *Chart No. 1—Symbols, Abbreviations & Terms*

Another free download, however you may find the paper version of Chart No. 1 much easier to use.
http://chartmaker.ncd.noaa.gov/mcd/chartno1.htm

### National Data Buoy Center

This site gives you the current-time wind speed and sea states at specific buoys. For example, to help you make choices about the timing of your Dixon Entrance crossing, look up: Station 46145—Central Dixon Entrance Buoy. (You don't even have to know the buoy numbers, just look at the graphic and pick the buoy in the vicinity; latitude and longitude is given for the buoy so you can verify location.) http://www.ndbc.noaa.gov/maps/Alaska.shtml

### National Dial-a-Buoy

This is an excellent *telephone* source for wind and wave measurements taken within the last hour at specific locations. Some stations also give barometric pressure, temperature, and weather forecast. Dial 888.701.8992 and enter a station name or a lat/long. Go to the website for intructions and station names.
http://www.ndbc.noaa.gov/dial.shtml

### U.S. Customs and Border Protection

Abundant information; a challenge to navigate. This is the site where you can purchase your "User Fee Decal" online. Customs information is changing all the time and even this Website does not keep up with the changes. (See notes below for the *Waggoner Cruising Guide* Website.) www.cbp.gov/xp/cgov/travel

### NEXUS Information

NEXUS is a mechanism for expediting your border crossings in both directions—between the U.S. and B.C. At press time, entering B.C. using the NEXUS clearance was still not possible. Be sure to call B.C. Customs before starting your cruise for the latest NEXUS status. There are many requirements, but NEXUS will likely become the method many cruisers will choose to simplify and speed up their interaction with customs. www.getnexus.com

### Weather—Southeast Alaska Marine Report

Printer friendly—low bandwidth; this is the same report you hear on your VHF radio weather channels.
http://pafc.arh.noaa.gov/pf.php?dir=marine

### Weather—Southeast Alaska Marine Report

Another online source for the exact report you hear on VHF radio weather channels.
http://www.weather.gov/om/marine/alaska.htm

### Mariner's Weather Guide—Alaska, Inside Passage

This (NOAA-produced) weather map shows you the location of every weather buoy or reporting station mentioned during your VHF weather report. It is very helpful to have this map in front of you when listening to the VHF weather report. This is a free, downloadable pdf file. A section of this map is printed in the introduction to this book.
http://pajk.arh.noaa.gov/info/brochures/mariners.pdf

## SOUTHEAST ALASKA CRUISING RESOURCES:

### Alaska Marine Highway

Ferry system information.
www.AKFerry.org

### General Alaska Resources

Location-by-location information; phone numbers; links to other Websites.
www.alaskajourney.com/southeast/index.html

### Recreation Areas and Parks Resource

National recreation and park areas.
www.dnr.state.ak.us/parks/boating

### FAQs About the Natural History of the Inside Passage

A wonderful site for reading about retreating glaciers, old growth forests, average rainfall, bald eagles, much more. Written by Herb Nickles, a Certified Alaska Naturalist.
www.insidepassagenews.com/AlaskaFAQ/index.html

### Fishing Vessels in Southeast Alaska—Pictures and Text

This site will show you what a purse seiner or a gill net vessel looks like, as well as explain their fishing methods. That information can help you in your efforts to avoid fish nets while underway.
http://cf.adfg.state.ak.us/geninfo/about/faq/cf_faq.php#PurseSeiners

### Information Bonanza for Southeast Alaska

Hosted by Captain Richard Friedman of Alaska Yacht Charters, this Website gives you links to multiple topics of interest, including history, geography, native cultures, national parks, climate, birds, trees, bears, whales, fishing, tsunamis, and more.
http://www.yachtexplorer.com/links.html

### Wildlife Notebook Series

Everything you could ever want to know about Alaska wildlife, from the Alaska Department of Fish and Game.
http://www.adfg.state.ak.us/pubs/notebook/notehome.php

### Sport fishing Information

Sport fishing regulations (by current year) for Southeast Alaska, from Alaska Department of Fish and Game.
http://www.sf.adfg.state.ak.us/statewide/regulations/seregs.cfm

*(Continued on next page)*

*(Continued from previous page)*

### Inside Passage News

A Website hosted by the authors of this book. You will find many boaters' experiences and interesting tips for cruising in Southeast Alaska, as well as many cruising planning maps and publications.
www.insidepassagenews.com

### Fine Edge Nautical & Recreational Publishing

This site has multiple publications of interest to Southeast Alaska cruisers, as well as cruisers who want to venture into waters world-wide. Fine Edge publishes the book you have in your hands.
www.fineedge.com

### Waggoner Cruising Guide

Although this Website focuses on cruising the Inside Passage from Washington through British Columbia as far as Prince Rupert, it is rich with information for cruisers ultimately headed for Southeast Alaska. There is no better online source for the most up-to-date, understandable information on U.S. and B.C. Customs issues for Inside Passage cruisers.
www.waggonerguide.com

### *Caveat about using Websites*

Please remember that Website addresses change over time and may not always work. You are responsible for checking the timeliness and reliability of any information you find on a Website.

from your boat will depend a great deal upon your geographical location (major ports) and even where your boat is moored in a particular marina. Important equipment variables include your WiFi adapter, the presence of an external antenna, and your distance from the provider's antenna. At press time, wireless Internet service providers are present in Ketchikan, Petersburg, Wrangell, Juneau, Hoonah and Sitka. When you find a provider online, you can create an account and purchase secured connection services for a fee, usually by varying time periods (hours, days, weeks).

Once you are in the marina, search for a WiFi connection using the "View Available Wireless Networks" tools in your computer's operating system. Just by opening your browser, the local provider may appear on a Web page with a listing of charges for using their service. You also may find a free or open "WiFi hotspot" you can piggy-back onto, but these connections are not secure and many find this action to be inappropriate.

Most of the wireless Internet companies are very regional. They usually provide services for their immediate geographical area only, although this is always changing. For instance, Seattle-based WiFi provider, BroadbandXpress, is in the process of implementing service programs for some of the marinas in Southeast Alaska; check www.bbxpress.net for details and system availability information.

Here is an extra communications tip: Try your cell phone whenever you are in the vicinity of a "MICRO" tower—as indicated on your nautical chart. We think cell equipment is being systematically added to these existing structures. You will be surprised how often you can get a signal while on the water. Examples: Cape Fox, Kake, outside the entrance to Baranof Warm Springs, outside Hoonah Harbor to about a mile away from the entrance to Glacier Bay National Park. Some people make their Internet connection via their cell phone.

## Rainforest Cruising Hazards

We have emphasized the wild and remote nature of the Inside Passage and the potential hazards to navigation—weather, remoteness (no VHF coverage in many areas) and lack of detailed, accurate charts and nav-aids. However, with adequate planning and skill you can minimize problems with these challenges.

One potentially serious and ubiquitous hazard needs special mention—encounters with floating jetsam or flotsam, especially floating logs and, in some cases, floating ice. Only constant vigilance by a skipper and crew can minimize this problem, for collision with a floating log can occur at any time and place in Northwest waters. Small, high-speed runabouts that collide with a log are frequently flipped over, with an occasional fatal result. Slower cruising boats with protected propellers or enclosed propellers tend to glance off or, sometimes, to roll up and over a log, with the most common damage occurring to the propeller, the drive train or the rudder. Exposed props are vulnerable to collisions with logs. Bending or breaking a prop means severe vibration or even flooding when the drive train or rudder is over-stressed.

Floating logs become a particular hazard after a storm when runoffs are heavy, during extreme spring tides when beach logs float free and in areas of active logging operations. Floating logs tend to bunch together in eddy currents or to spread out in a long line where tidal currents from different directions meet—such as in Wrangell Narrows. Long lines of floating logs and debris also are found where fresh water flows out from creeks and rivers on top of the saltwater.

Réanne Hemingway-Douglass

*Fend off bergie bits and proceed very slowly.*

When you pass through such areas, look for gaps in the lines of debris and head through these gaps with a slow approach, shifting into neutral and gliding through. Also, notice the quantity and age of logs on south-facing beaches, as this gives you an idea of the seriousness of these local hazards.

Of particular danger is a "deadhead"—also called a "sinker" or "black floater"—a vertical log, semi-submerged and bobbing up and down slowly with the chop of swells. Colliding with one of these deadheads can occasionally hole a vessel. Areas of icebergs also generate the same possibility for damage.

The best defense against collision with a log or an iceberg is to keep a constant watch on what's going on ahead. We cannot stress this enough! Use binoculars to check the route frequently and travel at a speed that clearly allows you to spot and avoid such potential threats. By the way, your binoculars are one of your most important navigation tools, so you should have good ones. Make sure yours have at least a 7 x 50 rating (magnification and field of vision). Ask your guests to bring their own binoculars for sightseeing purposes.

The decreased logging activity in Southeast Alaska has somewhat reduced the hazards of floating logs compared to decades ago, however, keep a watchful eye on the water in front of you.

Most of the boats we have seen with collision damage have been models with exposed and highly vulnerable shafts, props and rudders—particularly twin-engine, high-speed vessels. Displacement or semi-displacement hulls with an enclosed prop and rudder fair considerably better.

In Southeast Alaska, beyond the cities and major towns, damage to a prop usually means

Linda Lewis

*Birds don't stand on the water! Keep a vigilant watch for logs.*

flying in a new one and paying a substantial diving charge for its replacement. (As mentioned earlier, only Ketchikan and Sitka have propeller repair shops.) If you have an exposed prop or if you travel in areas of logging activity or icebergs, it's a good idea to carry a spare prop or the means for making your own repairs on a local tidal grid. The risks of colliding with a log are significant and the costs of repair are high! (See sidebar on how to use Haul-out Grids in Southeast Alaska.)

## Navigation on the Inside Passage

Navigation to Alaska through the Inside Passage consists largely of selecting appropriate point-to-point routes, avoiding any traffic, logs and flotsam, and reefs and rocks located along shore or occasionally in the middle of sounds or straits. You can usually spot these hazards visually, since even low clouds do not greatly interfere with visibility. A preset GPS waypoint route via paper or electronic charting is assuring, in case visibility decreases, and it also gives you a useful monitor on your progress and an idea of current, drift or distance remaining.

When you face lengthy crossings of open water, it's best to start very early in the morning after you've received a favorable weather report, and before the prevailing wind comes up. In such cases, where visible landmarks are too far away to be helpful, GPS-guided charting is useful to keep you on track and help you judge your progress.

Since most of the fiords and protected inside channels are steep-to, you can stay near the center of the channel to take maximum advantage of a favorable current, or follow the shore to pick up back eddies when currents are against you. In long channels that are open on both ends, such as Wrangell Narrows and Keku Strait (Rocky Pass), opposing currents meet midway through the passage and, with proper timing, you can ride the last of the flood upon entering and catch the first of the ebb on the "downhill" upon exiting.

With the exception of Wrangell Narrows, which has the highest concentration of buoys and aids to navigation anywhere, as you go north, you find fewer and fewer buoys and lighthouses. For those of you who like to get off the well-traveled commercial waterways, you can find areas in Alaska where you may go days or weeks without passing an aid to navigation, and your GPS receiver and electronic charting can offset this sparseness of nav-aids. GPS and electronic charting software have removed much of the guesswork of determining where you are at any given time, and we strongly recommend it.

Linda Lewis

*The march of the navigation aids in Wrangell Narrows*

## Global Positioning System (GPS)

Over the last decade, GPS has become a major factor in safe navigation of the Inside Passage, and particularly of Southeast Alaska. For old-timers who learned to navigate the hard way, it's an unbelievable tool with magic powers. In the hands of a trained skipper, a GPS receiver is easily worth two full-time navigational assistants on the bridge (one giving you accurate full-time positions, the other giving you steering, course headings, distance to go, drift, heading, distance made good).

In unfamiliar territory, GPS readings can verify your position. For cruisers who use electronic charting, the GPS-indicated position (in the form of your boat's icon) moves along the chart itself, giving you more freedom to watch outside the boat. In limited visibility you can use GPS readings to determine which direction to head and the distance to travel. But, while GPS and electronic charting are excellent navigational tools—essential for any boat on a tight schedule and a desirable tool for everyone else—you should use it only in conjunction with other means of navigation and allow for its limitations.

One of the specific limitations of GPS for the Southeast Alaska cruiser is the issue of GPS signal reception in this mountainous region; the other is the issue of GPS accuracy versus Southeast Alaska charts' accuracy. Both issues should be viewed as important limitations when cruising these waters.

Whether you have GPS equipment that is un-enhanced, DGPS-enhanced or WAAS-enhanced, you face an important GPS signal problem because Southeast Alaska is a mountainous area with many high-walled fiords. This kind of terrain results in a loss of GPS satellite signals on low orbits and signal refraction throughout these abundant high-mountain walls, resulting in transmission-induced errors. *These circumstances compromise your ability to rely heavily on your GPS.* Remember also that the GPS system as a whole is certainly not foolproof. As good mariners, you need to constantly use a multitude of sources of information. Look out the window and practice "situational awareness."

In Alaska you will also find many instances where the GPS and the chart do not agree. Your GPS latitude and longitude read one way, but your boat icon (or your position fix on your paper chart using the GPS figures) is near or sitting on land! What to trust? Of the two, in Southeast Alaska, it is more likely that the chart is inaccurate. That message is worth underscoring: Southeast Alaska charts are frequently small scale, based on old surveys (prior to a number of earthquakes and tsunamis), *and have many inaccuracies. Practice great caution.*

The important point is that in Southeast Alaska you cannot rely as heavily on chart accuracy and GPS signal as you do in urban waters. You need to be vigilantly looking out the window at all times and processing information from a variety of instruments and other sources. Practicing constant situational awareness is the only way to safely navigate these waters.

Don't wait until you're surrounded by a fog bank to program your route. It's too nerve-racking, and the chances of your making an error are greatly increased. Furthermore, you should maintain an adequate margin of safety in all GPS work, so you don't receive any nasty surprises.

GPS and electronic charting, like radar, require that you have adequate experience using it before you try to push its limits, so make a point to practice with your instruments in port, or in home waters. Ability to use GPS and electronic charting can be one of the more important skills you develop for safe navigation.

As a check on GPS signal data, especially in limited visibility, compare your depth sounder readings against the depths indicated on the charts for a given GPS lat/long. If the data differ very much, start asking questions and try to determine the answers. If nothing makes sense, slow down and head to deeper waters until you're sure of your data. Obviously, in tight situations, you should not rely on GPS alone, but should use traditional techniques—an alert bow watch, radar, a hand compass or binoculars with internal compass to track land reference points, and a depth sounder. Remember, a good pair of binoculars can be your best investment in most situations!

## U.S. Chart Symbols and Charts

To familiarize yourself with existing American chart* symbols and abbreviations, refer to *Chart No. 1 United States of America Nautical Chart (Symbols, Abbreviations and Terms).* There are commercial versions of *Chart No. 1* available and the U.S. government rendition is

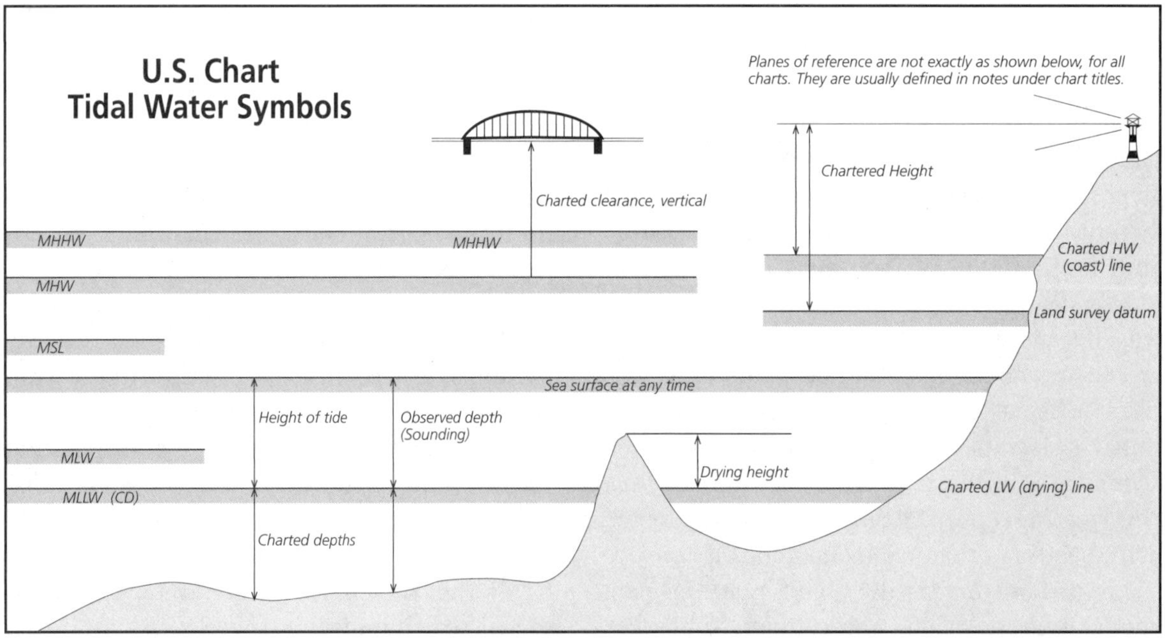

downloadable for free in PDF format at: http://chartmaker.ncd.noaa.gov/mcd/chartno1.htm.

This book recommends the charts you need for your cruise in Southeast Alaska. To investigate further and find the numbers of the charts for particular locations, go to the most current *NOAA Nautical Charts Catalog*, available for free at many boating stores. To find this online, go to http://nauticalcharts.noaa.gov/mcd/ccatalogs.htm#state and select Alaska. (Be watchful: both these online and free printed chart catalogs quickly become out of date.) Another strategy for looking at a graphic of charted areas is to turn to the opening pages of each chapter of the *U.S. Coast Pilot 8* for Alaskan waters. You will find the *most up-to-date* information on chart numbers and their latest editions and corrections dates by going to the NOAA "Dates of Latest Editions" Website, at http://chartmaker.ncd.noaa.gov/mcd/dole.htm.

In addition to traditional paper charts, Print-on-Demand (POD) paper charts are now available at many major marine stores or by ordering online (NOAA-approved site: www.oceangrafix.com). Their greatest advantage is the inclusion of the most recent chart corrections to date (at the time of their printing).

Most PC-based electronic software programs have proprietary charts available for use specifically with their program. (Let the buyer beware.) Companies emphasize many advantages for using their proprietary charts. The closer you are to the original raster image, government paper chart, the more accurate and reliable your data will be.

NOAA vector and raster charts are downloadable for free for some areas of the U.S. (This government database is a work-in-progress and not all Southeast Alaska vector charts may be available for download.) A real asset of downloading these free charts is that they are the most currently corrected NOAA charts (available as of the download date). The more recent versions of the major electronic charting software packages accommodate easy installation of these charts. At the NOAA Website, scroll down through the chart numbers until you find what you are interested in. The method for downloading the charts to your hard drive is easy. After download, install them in your charting software according to your product's instructions. The NOAA Website for free U.S. government chart download is http://chartmaker.ncd.noaa.gov/mcd/enc/index.htm.

Linda Lewis

*VHF reception becomes limited in steep-walled fiords and mountainous terrain.*

Many other U.S. government navigation-related documents are downloadable for free. Having the current edition of the *Coast Pilot* for Southeast Alaska on your laptop can be a real asset; the U.S. government's free, downloadable version is in (Adobe) PDF format, with its attendant easy word-search function. Go to http://nautical-charts.noaa.gov/nsd/cpdownload.htm for the most current edition of *U.S. Coast Pilot 8—Pacific Coast Alaska: Dixon Entrance to Cape Spencer.*

The same is true for the bible of navigation: *American Practical Navigator—Bowditch.* Numerous sites make this available. One download site can be found at www.marineplanner.com/bowditch/bowditch.cfm.

## Canadian Charts and Symbols

Exercise caution when leaving Prince Rupert, B.C., and crossing Dixon Entrance into U.S. waters. Be reminded: Canada's charts report depths in *metric* units. U.S. charts report depths in *fathoms.*

For B.C. waters, study *Canadian Chart 1 (Symbols, Abbreviations and Terms)* to familiarize yourself with Canadian Chart symbols. Canada does not make its publications or nautical charts available for free download.

## Alaska Weather

Contrary to its reputation among outsiders, Southeast Alaska enjoys a mild summer climate, although it does receive its fair share of rain—some places measure rain in feet rather than in inches. However, the summer season between May and early September usually brings periods of exceptionally beautiful weather. Each summer season is unique. However we have found weeks of from 90 percent rain and 10 percent sun to just the opposite. Horizontal visibility is generally good, unless you encounter fog. The North Pacific high usually brings mornings of calm seas and light breezes, which allow you to move toward your next destination before the afternoon prevailing breezes pick up and the "rippled" seas give way to 1- to 3-foot chop.

For those of you who would like temperature and precipitation graphical data, you can find more information in the "Summer Climate Guide to Southeast Alaska" at http://pajk.arh.noaa.gov/info/brochures/summer.pdf.

Sea conditions, along with fog, clouds and rain, are the main hazards. Tidal current opposing a wind can cause sharp, breaking seas, creating the most discomfort for a boat and its crew. Winds of 5 to 15 knots opposing a tidal current can cause the chop to double in height to the point where it starts to break. As the winds increase to near-gale force (20 to 30 knots) against an opposing current, seas build to a nasty, breaking chop that can become dangerous for small craft. Although these conditions are infrequent in summer, it is best to anticipate the weather and be prepared to seek shelter until conditions ameliorate. Also, if you plan your crossing of open waters in the early morning before prevailing winds come up, you can ensure a more comfortable crossing. This is particularly true of Dixon Entrance, Clarence Strait, Chatham Strait, Peril Strait and Lynn Canal.

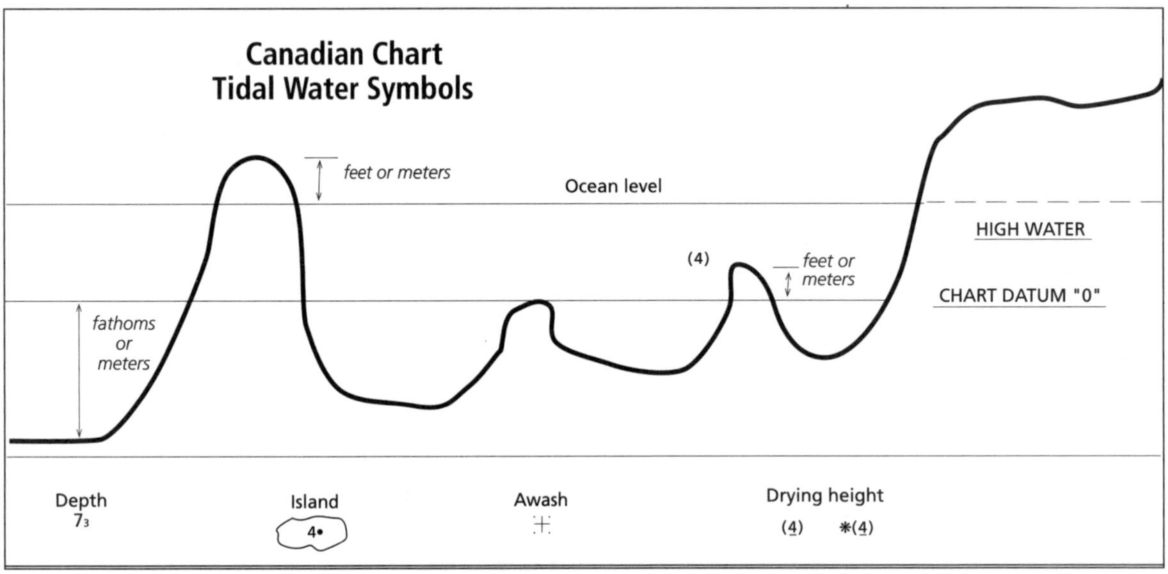

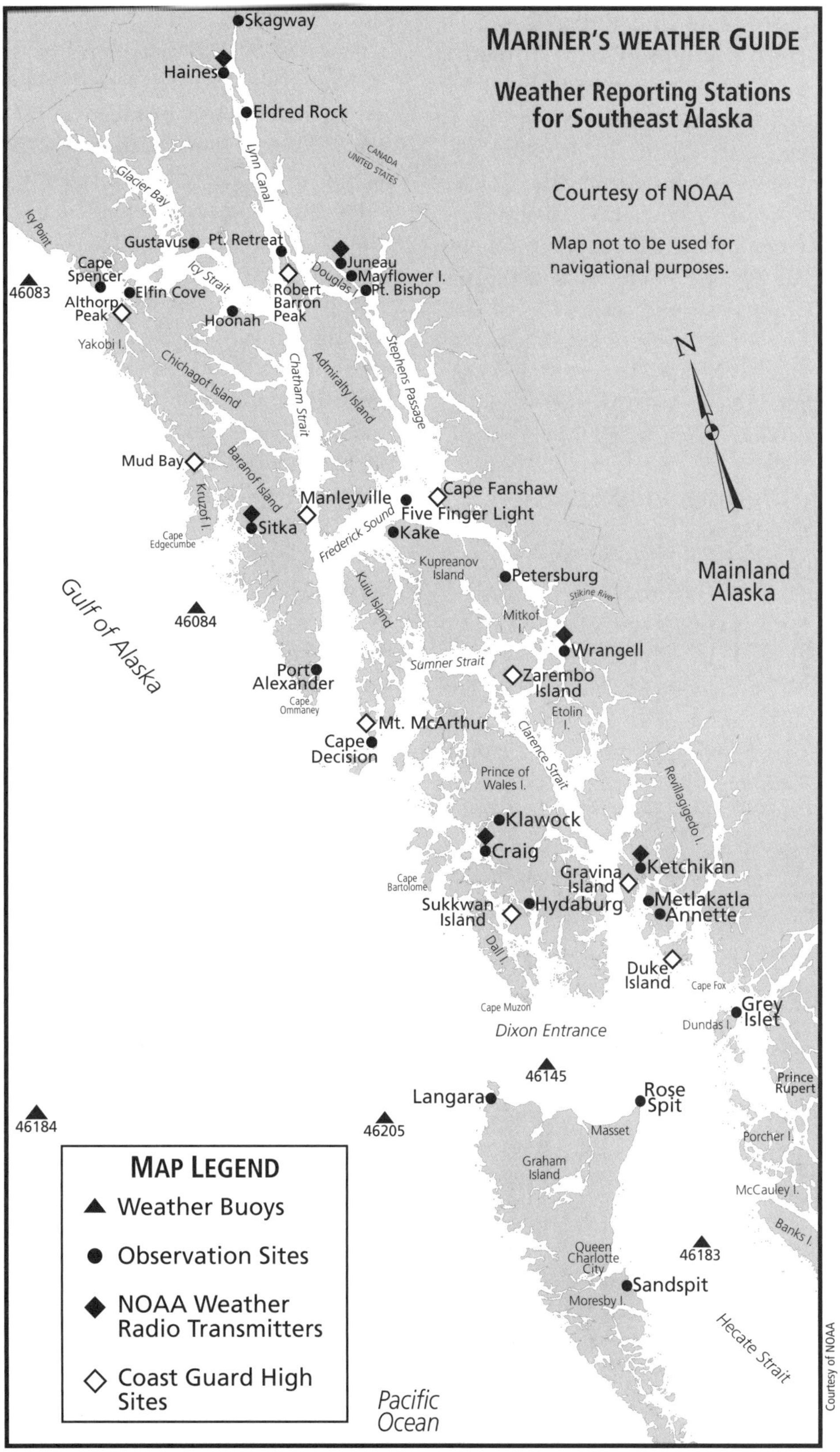
MARINER'S WEATHER GUIDE
Weather Reporting Stations for Southeast Alaska
Courtesy of NOAA
Map not to be used for navigational purposes.
MAP LEGEND
Weather Buoys
Observation Sites
NOAA Weather Radio Transmitters
Coast Guard High Sites
Skagway
Haines
Eldred Rock
Lynn Canal
CANADA
UNITED STATES
Glacier Bay
Icy Point
Gustavus
Pt. Retreat
Juneau
Mayflower I.
Pt. Bishop
Cape Spencer
Elfin Cove
Icy Strait
Douglas
Robert Barron Peak
Hoonah
Althorp Peak
46083
Yakobi I.
Chichagof Island
Chatham Strait
Admiralty Island
Stephens Passage
N
Mud Bay
Baranof Island
Manleyville
Cape Fanshaw
Five Finger Light
Kruzof I.
Sitka
Frederick Sound
Kake
Cape Edgecumbe
Kupreanov Island
Petersburg
Mainland Alaska
Stikine River
Gulf of Alaska
46084
Kuiu Island
Mitkof I.
Wrangell
Sumner Strait
Zarembo Island
Port Alexander
Cape Ommaney
Etolin I.
Mt. McArthur
Cape Decision
Clarence Strait
Prince of Wales I.
Revillagigedo I.
Klawock
Craig
Ketchikan
Gravina Island
Cape Bartolome
Sukkwan Island
Hydaburg
Metlakatla
Annette
Dall I.
Duke Island
Cape Fox
Cape Muzon
Grey Islet
Dundas I.
Dixon Entrance
46145
Prince Rupert
Langara
Rose Spit
46184
46205
Masset
Porcher I.
Graham Island
McCauley I.
Banks I.
Queen Charlotte City
46183
Sandspit
Moresby I.
Hecate Strait
Pacific Ocean
Courtesy of NOAA

## Weather Forecasts and Reports—Prince Rupert, B.C., and Dixon Entrance

Forecasts for Prince Rupert and Dixon Entrance are prepared and broadcast four times a day (at approximately 0400; 1030; 1600; 2130) by Environment Canada from the Pacific Weather Centre in Vancouver. These forecasts, which are rebroadcast 24 hours a day on continuous VHF weather channels and through repeater stations, can be heard with satisfactory reception all the way to Ketchikan. You can also receive B.C. marine weather forecasts by telephoning 604.664.9010. (Please see Appendix C for key VHF radio channels.)

## Weather Forecasts and Reports—Southeast Alaska

In Southeast Alaska, the marine weather forecast is issued by the National Weather Service (NWS) in Juneau at 0400 and 1600 for a 24-hour period, then repeated about every five minutes on VHF Weather Channel 1 or 2. This forecast is also repeated twice a day by the U.S. Coast Guard (morning and evening) and—during the summer—by Glacier Bay National Park. NWS transmitters are located in Haines, Juneau, Sitka, Wrangell, Annette Island (Ketchikan) and Craig. The working range of each broadcast station is only about 20 to 40 miles.

Linda Lewis

*Fog is ubiquitous in Southeast Alaska; hone your radar skills before you go.*

The mountainous terrain of Southeast Alaska limits VHF reception from these transmitters. However, in recent years, repeater stations have been installed at Robert Barron Peak, Althorp Peak, Mud Bay, Cape Fanshaw, Manleyville, Zarembo Island, Mt. McArthur, Sukkwan Island, Gravina Island and Duke Island. These new repeater stations considerably increase cruisers' ability to hear VHF weather transmissions in Southeast Alaska. Throughout the day, current observations are given for wind, temperature and barometric pressure at these repeater stations (land-based, therefore no sea state information) approximately hourly. If you have a cell phone connection, you can listen to these reports by telephoning 907.586.3997 or 800.472.0391.

It is critical to be able to identify the locations of the reporting stations that are named so quickly during the VHF transmission. We have included in this Introduction an excerpt of a very helpful map produced by NOAA: Mariner's Weather Guide—Gulf of Alaska Coastal Waters. This map indicates the location of each weather buoy or reporting station mentioned during the radio report. We recommend that you make a copy of the map, then insert it into a Mylar-type cover and keep it right next to your VHF radio to look at during the report. You can also download the map at the following Website: http://pajk.arh.noaa.gov/info/brochures/mariners.pdf.

The forecast covers the inside waters of Clarence Strait, Sumner Strait, Stephens Passage, Chatham Strait, Frederick Sound, Lynn Canal, Icy Strait, Cross Sound and Glacier Bay, as well as the outside waters from Dixon Entrance to Cape Fairweather.

Once you leave the main channels and venture out on your own, you're out of range of VHF weather broadcasts. Misty Fiords, Glacier

Bay, the west coast of Prince of Wales Island and a number of other places—perhaps half of Southeast—have little or no VHF broadcast reception and, in some areas, you may not even be able to rouse the Coast Guard on Ch 16.

However, you can get by quite well by making your own educated guesses, by contacting other boats to ask what conditions they're experiencing or by telephoning the number listed above where possible.

If you have an Internet connection, the National Data Buoy Center at http://www.ndbc.noaa.gov/maps/alaska.shtml provides information on the current-time wind and sea states at a few locations. Also click on "Meteorological Observations from Nearby Stations and Ships" for additional information. You will be particularly interested in Buoy 46145—Central Dixon Entrance (54°38' N–132°45' W) for planning your initial entry (from the Prince Rupert area) into Southeast Alaska across Dixon Entrance.

While on the Internet, you also can get a Southeast Alaska four-day weather forecast in text format. Go to the National Weather Service Marine Forecast site at http://www.weather.gov/om/marine/alaska.htm and click on your area of geographical interest under "Synopsis for Southeast Alaska Inside Waters."

## Semi-annual Weather Patterns: Spring and Summer

The weather in Southeast Alaska follows a general semi-annual pattern. Changes are associated with the building up or breaking down of the North Pacific High around the times of the spring and fall equinoxes.

Following the late winter storms, about March 21, the Pacific High begins to build up far off the western shore of Vancouver Island. This more or less permanent high-pressure zone deflects most summer lows into the Gulf of Alaska, where they either dissipate or take a varied path that affects Southeast weather. We recommend waiting until the Pacific High is well entrenched—generally early- to mid-May—before you head north of Dixon Entrance.

During the summer months, in times of stable high pressure, Southeast undergoes a daily pattern of diurnal micro-weather that is quite predictable. Nights are usually quite calm and quiet over the entire length of Southeast Alaska, with fog or low clouds moving on shore. In the afternoon, moderate northwest breezes pick up, dissipating the fog and clouds and creating 1- to 3-foot chop until evening, when conditions become calm again. During such periods, most weather stations report a high percentage of light winds with little or moderate precipitation—conditions that provide good cruising.

Although low pressure fronts do manage to evade the Pacific High and hit the West Coast, they usually occur at intervals of one to three weeks in Southeast Alaska. These fronts, which are usually announced by a falling barometer, a change in both the direction and intensity of the wind, as well as by clouds and precipitation, normally last just a day or two and are well forecast. It is best to remain in a sheltered harbor or cove during the approach of unstable weather.

Sometimes in Southeast, these fronts stall out and linger before picking up strength and heading north over the mountain. When this happens, their timing and path are less predictable than the fronts that occur farther south.

Although summer storms are not as intense as winter storms, they can still pack a dangerous wallop to small craft. Although gale force winds of up to 40 knots do occur, they are infrequent.

The farther north you go in Southeast Alaska, the lower the (barometric) pressure becomes, and the more the wind intensifies. Winds of 30 knots are not uncommon, and occasionally gale force winds occur in the summer. (From autumn to spring, gale force winds occur frequently.) In certain east-west channels, such as Peril Strait, Cross Sound, Icy Strait, Frederick Sound and Sumner Strait, you may experience strong easterlies at the very time a southerly is shrieking up the north-south channels. After the passage of the front, local channel winds generally reverse 180 degrees and blow hard for a day or two.

Take all these summer storms or deep, low-pressure fronts seriously by noting barometric pressure and monitoring weather broadcasts frequently. When you observe signs that a storm is developing or hear a report of an impending storm, head directly for an anchor site that offers protection from south or east winds, taking appropriate precautions for safety, such as maintaining sufficient swinging room and a well-set anchor. It is always a good idea to take bearings on fixed objects to detect if your anchor is dragging.

## Semi-annual Weather Patterns: Fall and Winter

Near the autumnal equinox (about September 21), the Pacific High begins to collapse and the first major low pressure fronts return, bringing foul weather and precipitation. Without the protection of a strong North Pacific High, about 10 to 20 low-pressure fronts per month affect Southeast Alaska. During some of these storms, barometric pressure drops as low as 960 millibars, bringing hurricane force winds of over 60 knots. In winter, prevailing winds are from the southeast, with heavy precipitation and high, dangerous seas. For this reason, we suggest that you head south of Dixon Entrance by early September and, if you're planning to continue south on the outside of Vancouver Island, it's a good idea to round Cape Scott by late August or early September to avoid being caught north of Brooks Peninsula in a series of lows. Although both the west and east coasts of Vancouver Island normally have fine weather in September and October, it's a good idea to head to protected waters south of Estevan Point or Chatham Point.

## Barometric Pressure and Wind Velocities

Wind velocity tends to occur in direct proportion to the barometric pressure gradient—the rate of rise or fall of pressure. Falling barometric pressure that descends 1 millibar per hour usually means strong winds of 20 to 30 knots; a drop of 2 millibars per hour means gales of 35 to 45 knots; a drop of 3 millibars per hour brings storm force winds of 50 to 60 knots. On the contrary, a rising barometer of 1 millibar per hour brings strong- to gale-force winds of 25 to 40 knots.

By noting barometric pressure hourly in your ship's log, or by using a recording barometer, you can visualize this gradient of pressure and prepare for expected wind and sea conditions.

## Wind Rotation

In the Northern Hemisphere, winds flow clockwise around a high-pressure cell and counterclockwise around a low-pressure cell. In other words, in the Northern Hemisphere, with the wind to your back, the low pressure is on your left, while the higher pressure is on your right. This simple test, and observation of the barometric pressure gradient, can give you an idea of the path of a storm cell and an idea of the strength and direction of upcoming winds. However, local topography can greatly affect the direction of the wind so, by studying the movement of clouds aloft, you can get a better idea of true wind direction and strength.

## Wind Direction and Cloud Cover

Winds that arrive in advance of a low-pressure front generally blow from the south or southwest, then back (counterclockwise) to the southeast as the front approaches. The strongest winds and highest seas usually occur just ahead of the low-pressure front. With the approaching front, clouds thicken and lower, taking on an ominous appearance;

*Wind opposing the current creates very difficult sea conditions.*

precipitation is heavy and may last for several hours or, in some cases, with the passage of a low-pressure front, the wind veers (moves clockwise), first to southwest, then to northwest. During the summer after the wind veers to its prevailing northwesterly direction, it may blow hard for a day or two, as if to send all the southern air back where it originated. We have experienced our lumpiest crossings of Dixon Entrance when we set out too soon after the barometer "bottomed out" and the wind veered to the west.

If high pressure over the interior sends strong outflow or arctic winds, with cold dry winds building from the northeast, along with a rising barometer, quickly seek shelter from down-channel winds and seas. (The eastern edge of Dixon Entrance, Portland Canal and Douglas Channel are notorious for such conditions.)

In addition, during times of strong runoff caused by heavy rainstorms or snowmelt, ebb currents tend to be quite strong and, in some cases, completely override the direction of the flood on the surface of the water. It's a good idea to stay put during the periods when strong currents oppose the wind.

## Micro-climatic Conditions

Since wind forecasts usually cover a wide general area and are given for the strongest winds expected, local winds—influenced by the topography of an area—may vary significantly from the forecast. We frequently hear stories of boats that stay put far more than they need to because of small craft warnings or high wind notices. Weather forecasts are conservative by nature. You won't hear one calling for a beautiful calm day; instead, it forecasts the worst weather expected to occur any time during that period.

*Corner wind* is the effect of increased wind speed when a wind blows past a headland, such as off Dundas Island or headlands facing the Gulf of Alaska. A corner wind is usually stronger than that experienced on either side of its land mass.

*Gap winds* (or funnel winds) are caused by a funneling effect between islands—such as the directional shift the wind makes to follow an inlet or channel or such as the increase in wind speed occurring in Peril Strait, Lynn Canal or Clarence Strait. When gap winds blow against tidal currents, they can cause dangerous, steep, breaking waves. These conditions occur on Baranof Island where outside inlets almost connect through a low pass to inlets on Chatham Strait.

*Lee effect* occurs along a steep shoreline where a turbulent and gusty offshore wind meets an opposing wind at the top of a cliff. Reversed eddies, along with onshore winds, may create confused, steep seas along the base of the cliffs.

During periods of light prevailing winds, *sea breezes* blow from sea toward land during the heat of the day (usually in the afternoon). In Dixon Entrance and Cross Sound, the prevailing inflow and afternoon sea breeze can combine to reach 30 to 40 knots. Sea breezes may contribute to the prevalence of moderately strong afternoon southerlies in north-south facing bodies of water such as Clarence and Chatham Straits, despite forecasts of light-to-moderate northwest winds over Southeast Alaska. These winds may intimidate a skipper new to the area who interprets them as winds that arrive in advance of a low-pressure front. Check your barometer to verify whether these south winds are prevailing afternoon sea breezes or a more serious change requiring you to seek alternative shelter.

*Land breezes* blow from land toward sea during the night and can be gusty, but—except for outflow winds—their velocity is usually less than that of a sea breeze. Both sea and land breezes die quickly, as does the chop they generate.

*Anabatic winds*, upslope winds caused by rising warm air, occur during the daytime in valleys and inlets.

*Katabatic winds*—downslope winds occurring at night (also known as williwaws) are caused by falling cool air. These winds, which are usually stronger than upslope winds, often blast down a fiord or the steep slope of a high, snow-laden ridge, giving you good reason to set your anchor well on an otherwise calm evening. Williwaws can reach frightening velocities when the sides of a fiord are steep and capped by ice or snow; they are usually of short, but intense duration and may affect just a small area. Since they are cyclonic in nature, the actual direction of a williwaw varies, and can frequently be seen whipping up chop or foam wherever it hits the water.

*Surge winds* are strong winds generated occasionally in the summer during periods of high barometric readings (1008 to 1012 millibars). These winds disturb the stable weather of the Pacific Coast and can surprise a cruising boat. Caused by a lee trough that forms off the coast during a period of prolonged thermal heating of the interior land mass, this phenomenon causes prevailing light easterlies adjacent to the coast, but it can cause gale force northwesterlies farther offshore. A more potentially dangerous condition called stratus surge occurs when a larger lee trough off northern California shoots north along the Oregon and Washington coasts, picking up speed as it surges, and bringing with it low clouds and fog. During a stratus surge, winds shift abruptly from light easterlies to southerlies of gale force or stronger; they can strike suddenly without much movement in the barometer, but they bring a sharp drop in air temperature. Local fishermen call these "fog winds" and, other than fog or low, dark stratus clouds from the south, there are no reliable signs of their approach. However, when such conditions do occur, they are usually forecast on the continuous weather broadcasts.

If you are in doubt about any weather forecast, or if you witness any unusual or rapid changes in prevailing conditions that could affect the safety of your boat, call the U.S. Coast Guard on Ch 16 at once and ask for a clarification or, if you need it, for their assistance. They would rather give you the information you need for a wise decision than risk a dangerous and costly rescue.

## Marine Fog

Marine fog—formed when warm Pacific air moves over relatively colder seas during late summer and early autumn—causes greatly reduced visibility a good part of the late summer, making navigation dangerous. At times in Southeast Alaska, visibility is even reduced to zero. Cruising boats without radar often find they have to wait until the fog burns off before they can move on. Fog can be forecast quite well as the dew point approaches the

Linda Lewis

*A bank of fog can await you just around the corner.*

temperature of the environment; local marine weather stations broadcast such conditions.

Marine fog frequently forms offshore, moves inland in early evening, remains all night, and then lifts or dissipates in the late morning. Many weather stations report the highest percentage of fog in their 7 a.m. observations, the least in their 4 p.m. observations. With the lengthened hours of daylight in summer, you can frequently get a late start after the fog lifts and still maintain your planned schedule.

During foggy periods, many sport fishing and commercial boats continue to fish, creating congestion and navigational hazards (or challenges!) for cruising boats, particularly near harbor entrances and across fishing grounds. It's a good idea when you approach congested areas to station an alert lookout on your bow and to listen carefully for fog horns, bells or the sound of other propellers. Remain especially alert in shipping channels. Ferry boats and other commercial high-speed craft rarely slow down, and there's nothing quite so alarming as hearing the horn of a large ship as it bears down on your little vessel. Good radar reflectors and radar sets are critical in these situations, as is bridge-to-bridge contact on VHF (Ch 13).

Today's "tag scanning" VHF radios allow you to monitor Ch 16, Ch 13, and the local Vessel Traffic Service channel simultaneously. The even newer Automated Information System (AIS) is a superb way to keep in touch with the positions of commercial vessels. (You must purchase an AIS receiver to obtain this information.)

Since the frequency of fog varies somewhat along the Inside Passage, with Dixon Entrance being strongly affected in late summer, we advise you to study the tables in the appendices of Canada's *Sailing Directions* and read the comments in *U.S. Coast Pilot.*

Radiation fog, primarily a problem in harbors and inlets, forms over land during the early mornings on windless days and generally dissipates after the sun or wind comes up. During prolonged spells of radiation fog, winds are usually (but not necessarily) light, and the seas are nearly flat.

When fog moves offshore during the day, it is called sea fog. Formed when winds are moderate, sea fog moves back onshore in the evening, and may persist as winds become stronger, lasting just a day, or continuing without a break for several days at a time.

## Rain

Rain—associated with the passage of a frontal system accompanied by low, dark clouds often lasting for several hours at a time—reduces visibility, although usually to a lesser extent than fog. Drizzle (fine precipitation) also occurs with the passage of a front. However, it sometimes persists between frontal systems. Rain showers cover a small area for short periods and fall from cumulus clouds, the heaviest usually occurring after a front has passed and cold northwesterly winds have set in.

Much of Southeast Alaska is located in a temperate rainforest zone. Rain is less pervasive in summer than in winter. North of Queen Charlotte Sound, B.C., rainfall averages 100 inches or more per year, peaking near Ketchikan, which has nearly 160 inches. In summer, we have experienced as few as two rainy days in a month in cruising from Anacortes, WA, to Juneau, AK, or as many as twenty.

## Sea Conditions

"Sea" is defined as that segment of a wave riding on top of the prevailing swell and caused by winds whose source lies outside the local region.

The ocean swells you encounter crossing Dixon Entrance can be alarming if you've sailed only on inside waters. Shoaling water (such as that found in Queen Charlotte Sound, B.C.) can cause the background swell to reach 3 or 4 meters. However, the length of such swell is generally about 100 yards, and while the swells may appear large, they are usually not threatening. However, if a strong ebb current meets a moderate southwest wind, the sea's swells are much closer together, causing an uncomfortable jostle, and a wet, hazardous crossing. These conditions may be confined to local areas—such as the east end of Dixon Entrance.

## Tides and Currents

The farther north you go, or the farther removed you are from the open ocean, the greater the tidal range. In general, human-powered kayaks and low-powered craft will need to pay close attention to tides and currents. Larger, faster vessels may be able to afford paying somewhat less attention.

In Glacier Bay and heads of remote inlets, an extreme tidal range of over 20 feet is not uncommon. As standard daily procedure, check tide tables and allow for changes in tide levels (as well as for their associated currents), especially when anchoring and transiting narrows.

Most electronic charting programs include tide and current tables. You should update your electronic tides and current data as you do your charts. NOAA has made several recalculations of their tables for Southeast Alaska, the latest in 2007. Three new current stations were added and 26 new secondary stations. Are *your* tides and current data up to date?

Having your electronics go down while in Southeast Alaska waters is always a possibility. Therefore, you should carry appropriate paper chart backups as well as tide and current tables. One hard-copy backup strategy is to use your (up-to-date) electronic tables in advance: call up the tide and current for locations and months of interest and make printouts before your trip starts.

The U.S. government (NOAA) no longer prints tide and current tables; private companies provide them using information from the National Ocean Service (NOS). For Southeast Alaska, look for *Tide Tables* [year] *West Coast of North and South America or Tidal Current Tables* [year] *Pacific Coast of North America and Asia. Note:* These books do not include corrections for Daylight Savings Time, which is a major headache; you must remember to *add one hour* to what you find in the book during DST.

Linda Lewis

*This Tlevak Narrows buoy is being towed by the current—situational awareness is critical.*

Only a very few Reference Stations for Southeast Alaska are found in Table 1 of these books (Ketchikan, Juneau, Sitka). If you don't look beyond Table 1, you will be missing lots of information for many other locations.

Look beyond Table 1 to "Table 2: Tidal Differences and Other Constants" in each book to calculate tides or currents (Table 2: Current Differences and Other Constants). Table 2 provides information on many additional locations (sometimes called secondary stations).

There is a way you can find and make a printout of many of the secondary stations found in Table 2. At the following NOAA online sites you will find tables for the "Differences" locations, by year and month. When you initially look at the site you see a very short list of reference stations; however, when you go inside each entry you will see many more options through the use of "Differences" (or secondary stations) data. For a tide example, Exchange Cove (a secondary station) in Clarence Strait (NW of Ketchikan) is listed in table form by days of the month; this is a convenient anchorage you might select on your way from Ketchikan to Wrangell Narrows.

*NOTE CAREFULLY* the *year (e.g.,* "tides07" or "currents07") in the following Website addresses for the most recent date. *CAUTION:* NOAA updates the tables by about December of each year for the following year. You are responsible for finding the year you are interested in.

## Tides

http://tidesandcurrents.noaa.gov/tides[year]/tpred2.html#AK

## Currents

http://tidesandcurrents.noaa.gov/currents[year]/cpred2.html#AK

One final word of caution. These tables are only predictions and may not be what you actually experience in a given location at a given moment. Be sure to use your eyes and learn to recognize the tide and current situation you are experiencing. Especially suspect is the accuracy of the timing of currents in Southeast Alaska. Slack water does not occur at times of high or low tide in restricted channels and lagoon entrances. Slack water at lagoon entrances is typically one to three hours *later* than outside waters. Outside of the major locations, such as Sergius Narrows, you will find many occasions in Southeast Alaska when the table says one thing and, as you look out the window, you are experiencing something very different. Take into account any nearby river run-off that may be affecting the area and/or the effects of any major weather systems. Remain vigilant and act accordingly.

## Steep Waves

Waves become steeper near shore, or when a current opposes the direction of the waves. It is this steepness that presents the most danger for small craft.

Dixon Entrance, Cross Sound and Peril Strait are areas known for strong tidal currents that can create steep, breaking waves. On the north side of Dundas Island in Dixon Entrance we have seen two-meter wind waves roughly double in height and steepen to the breaking point against an opposing ebb current of several knots. Strong outflow winds from Portland Canal, lasting several hours, frequently build up nasty chop that steepens to the breaking point on flood tides as far west as Dundas Island.

Linda Lewis

*Train your eye to roughly recognize the stage of the tide—such as the "low" tide at this island.*

A current flowing in the same direction as the wind has the opposite effect. The swell height is diminished and the period lengthened, cutting the steepness dramatically. When the current is unfavorable, it's a good idea to hole up for a few hours, rather than stressing your boat and crew unnecessarily.

Fortunately, the passages with significant exposure to ocean swells, or to the outlets of major fiords, are of rather short duration (a few hours in most cases). It's comforting for a crew to know that prevailing swells and seas die down quickly in protected waters and don't affect the coves where you anchor each night.

## Narrows and Rapids

Uncomfortable or dangerous seas also can be found in tidal narrows and rapids and across channel or inlet bars. Rips are turbulent agitation of the water caused by the interaction of currents and wind waves. In shallow water, irregular bottom rips can create short breaking waves. The entrance to Holkum Bay, Endicott

Arm and Tracy Arm are notorious examples of this.

Overfalls are areas of turbulent water caused by currents setting over submerged ridges or shoals. A severe overfall can produce a sharp rise or fall in water level and may even create whirlpools. Short, closely spaced, standing waves ("dancing waters") are also seen where currents meet. A small boat may be tossed from side to side in overfalls. Note the indications of rips and overfalls on the nautical chart and heed the warnings and instructions in Canada's *Sailing Directions* or the *U.S. Coast Pilot* when you transit such areas. Many narrows, such as Sergius Narrows, Hole in the Wall, Tlevak Narrows and others, have overfalls and turbulent water. Once again, try to plan your transit at or near slack water to reduce the effect of these overfalls and turbulent water.

Just as with tide tables, check your current tables daily. *Baidarka* finds it convenient to write down key tides and currents data on a small re-writeable tablet or post-it note that easily can be checked throughout the day or night. Always remain ready to react to the real conditions you experience rather than assuming the tables will be accurate. Predictions for major locations like Sergius Narrows are more likely to be accurate than less-travelled locations.

## Tsunamis

Tsunamis occasionally occur along the Alaska coast. These seismic sea waves are associated with earthquakes of magnitude 7 or higher on the Richter Scale, whose epicenters are within or border the ocean floor. Hazards of tsunamis to small boats come from strong currents (as much as ten times normal) that break moorings and drive boats ashore.

Tsunami warnings for the West Coast of North America in the U.S. are disseminated by the West Coast and Alaska Tsunami Warning Center (WCATWC) and broadcast by the USCG on channel 16. Any vessel in danger should clear harbor and head for open waters where the effect of the waves is reduced and navigation is less hazardous.

## Strategies for Coping with the Variables of Weather

To make your voyage more comfortable, here are additional practical tips.

1. Monitor weather broadcasts on VHF (or on continuous recordings by telephone) before you arrive in a critical area, and pay particular attention to the key area and the adjacent areas to give you an idea of the state and speed of an approaching front.

2. Monitor actual conditions at lighthouse and reporting stations to see if the forecast is indeed materializing. Since forecasts are given for the worst weather expected over a certain area during the period, you may frequently encounter lesser conditions on your actual route.

3. Track barometric pressure, wind direction and strength, cloud cover and sea conditions, and develop your own skills for monitoring and interpreting weather. Use every opportunity to check your findings against what is being reported and what you observe.

4. Maintain radio schedules with cruising boats ahead of you and monitor their inter-boat transmissions on working channels. Break in to ask for a report of local conditions from time to time.

5. Delay or advance your daily runs to arrive at critical passages when stable conditions are expected. We find that under normal conditions, starting early in the day (with due regard for favorable tidal currents) gives us an advantage before prevailing winds kick up. Be sure your boat is secure and shipshape before you leave.

6. Prepare alternative plans for safe anchorages in case the weather and seas exceed your

expectations or the crew becomes uncomfortable. Don't be afraid to implement these changes.

7. Through critical passages, talk with Coast Guard (via channel 16 and working channel 22A or VTS Traffic Control) about weather updates and solicit their observations if you need to, particularly if unexpected changes occur.

In conclusion, remember the quotation from the beginning of this Introduction: "Experience is what you get right after you needed it." Your voyage to Southeast Alaska may be just the first of a number of exciting experiences. There's a lifetime of exploring awaiting you there, and we hope that the serious topics we've covered here have given you the knowledge you need to keep you in your comfort zone and help you "get it right" *before* you need it. Happy cruising!

David Frisby

*Don Douglass, always ready to discover new territory*

Don Douglass

*Réanne Hemingway-Douglass, happy at the helm of* Baidarka*'s speedy dinghy*

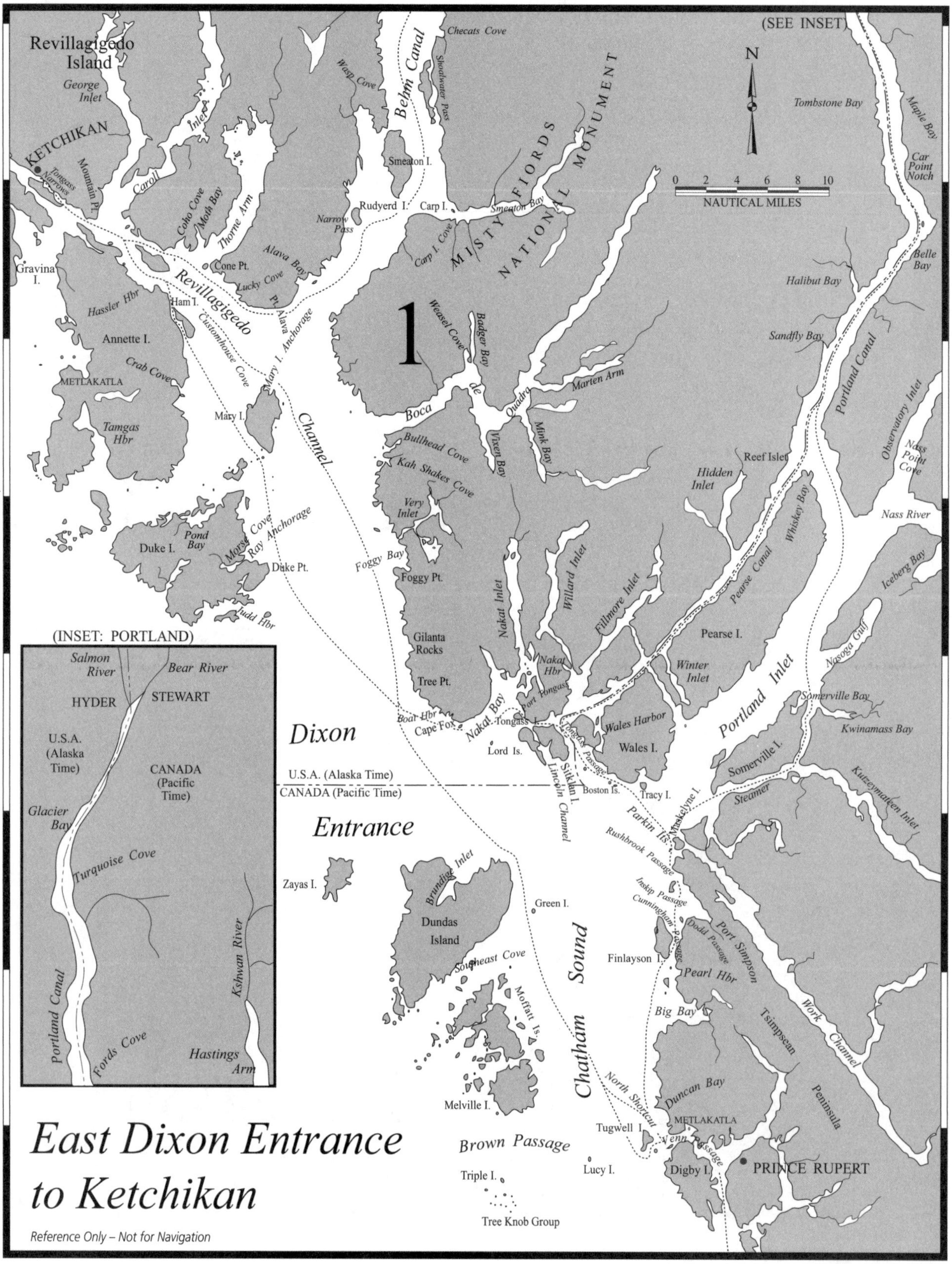
East Dixon Entrance to Ketchikan
Reference Only – Not for Navigation
1
(SEE INSET)
N
0 2 4 6 8 10
NAUTICAL MILES
30'
20'
10'
55°N
50'
40'
30'
20'
Revillagigedo Island
George Inlet
KETCHIKAN
Tongass Narrows
Mountain Pt.
Carroll Inlet
Coho Cove
Moth Bay
Thorne Arm
Gravina I.
Cone Pt.
Lucky Cove
Alava Bay
Pt. Alava
Revillagigedo Channel
Hassler Hbr
Ham I.
Annette I.
Customhouse Cove
Crab Cove
METLAKATLA
Tamgas Hbr
Mary I.
Mary I. Anchorage
Duke I.
Pond Bay
Morse Cove
Ray Anchorage
Duke Pt.
Judd Hbr
Checats Cove
Wasp Cove
Behm Canal
Shoalwater Pass
Smeaton I.
Narrow Pass
Rudyerd I.
Carp I.
Carp I. Cove
Smeaton Bay
MISTY FIORDS NATIONAL MONUMENT
Weasel Cove
Badger Bay
Boca de Quadra
Marten Arm
Bullhead Cove
Kah Shakes Cove
Vixen Bay
Mink Bay
Very Inlet
Foggy Bay
Foggy Pt.
Gilanta Rocks
Tree Pt.
Nakat Inlet
Willard Inlet
Fillmore Inlet
Nakat Hbr
Port Tongass
Boat Hbr
Cape Fox
Nakat Bay
Tongass I.
Lord Is.
Wales Harbor
Wales I.
Tongass Passage
Sitklan I.
Lincoln Channel
Boston Is.
Tracy I.
Tombstone Bay
Maple Bay
Car Point Notch
Belle Bay
Halibut Bay
Sandfly Bay
Portland Canal
Observatory Inlet
Nass Point Cove
Reef Islet
Hidden Inlet
Whiskey Bay
Pearse Canal
Nass River
Iceberg Bay
Pearse I.
Winter Inlet
Nasoga Gulf
Portland Inlet
Somerville Bay
Kwinamass Bay
Somerville I.
Steamer
Kutzeymateen Inlet
Dixon Entrance
U.S.A. (Alaska Time)
CANADA (Pacific Time)
Parkin Is.
Maskelyne I.
Rushbrook Passage
Inskip Passage
Cunningham Passage
Dodd Passage
Port Simpson
Zayas I.
Brundige Inlet
Dundas Island
Green I.
Southeast Cove
Moffatt Is.
Chatham Sound
Finlayson I.
Pearl Hbr
Big Bay
Tsimpsean Peninsula
Work Channel
Melville I.
North Shortcut
Duncan Bay
METLAKATLA
Tugwell I.
Venn Passage
Brown Passage
Lucy I.
Digby I.
PRINCE RUPERT
Triple I.
Tree Knob Group
(INSET: PORTLAND)
Salmon River
Bear River
HYDER
STEWART
U.S.A. (Alaska Time)
CANADA (Pacific Time)
Glacier Bay
Turquoise Cove
Kshwan River
Portland Canal
Fords Cove
Hastings Arm

# 1

# DIXON ENTRANCE, PORTLAND CANAL, REVILLAGIGEDO CHANNEL TO KETCHIKAN

## INTRODUCTION

Dixon Entrance—the gateway to Alaska's magnificent cruising wilderness—is the second of two main bodies of water to be crossed when cruising the Inside Passage to Southeast Alaska (or, as Alaskans say, "Southwest"), the other main body of water being Queen Charlotte Sound in British Columbia. Dixon Entrance marks the international boundary between the United States and Canada. Open to the prevailing swells and winds from the west, it also receives large flows of fresh water from the east and occasional high winds that can whistle down the inlets from the east. While the swells in Dixon Entrance originate in the Gulf of Alaska, they are frequently less noticeable than those in Queen Charlotte Sound. However, due to strong and confused tidal flows and complex wind and weather fronts, nasty chop or breaking waves can develop, so it is best to cross during a period of benign weather (stable barometer).

For the most direct route from Prince Rupert to Ketchikan, exit through Venn Passage, turn north in Chatham Sound and head for Revillagigedo Channel, passing the west side of Green Island. If the weather turns nasty or swells are uncomfortable, Brundige Inlet on Dundas Island provides good refuge at the south side of Dixon Entrance; on the north side, Foggy Bay, Judd Harbor or Morse Cove are good anchor sites. Most pleasure boats that cruise at slower speeds (5-9 knots) take two days to make the trip from Prince Rupert to Ketchikan, leaving near dawn on the first day and anchoring by noon before the chop builds up in Revillagigedo Channel. (Even faster boats should consider a two-day trip strategy because arriving in Ketchikan in the early afternoon will improve your chances for finding moorage.)

Linda Lewis

*Call Green Island Lighthouse for a real-time report on wind and sea state in Dixon Entrance.*

Linda Lewis

*Start your Dixon Entrance crossing from the very friendly Prince Rupert Rowing and Yacht Club.*

Northbound boats leaving from Prince Rupert that plan to anchor overnight in Alaskan waters should obtain permission from Ketchikan customs to anchor in Foggy Bay—the *only* designated anchorage. (U.S. cell phone connection may be possible at about Cape Fox.) Customs asks that you call during normal office hours to make your request (tel.: 907.225.2254).

There is no Customs dock in Ketchikan. Upon arriving at your moorage destination in Ketchikan, all boats (U.S. and foreign) must call the Customs office and obtain a clearance number before cruising in Alaska. You may wish to return to some areas of interest (such as Misty Fiords), but you can do so only after you have received your clearance number from Ketchikan Customs. All persons on board must have a passport. (Please see the Introduction of this book for more U.S. Customs details.)

During conditions of easterly outflow, winds in Portland Inlet, B.C., hugging the mainland shore and darting across from one secure anchorage to another allows you to escape the uncomfortable beam seas and chop near Green Island. This way you can move forward while other boats are still waiting in Prince Rupert for calm weather. On this route, rough water is reduced to about three miles across the entrance to Portland Inlet. Convenient layover sites can be found on either side of the inlet, allowing you to wait for an optimum crossing time.

If you want to hug the mainland shore, visit Khutzeymateen Grizzly Bear Reserve or head for the remote waters of Portland Canal, we find the following route to be the most protected.

Leaving Prince Rupert via Duncan Bay, from a point 0.25 miles west of buoy "D82," located 0.7 miles southwest of Ryan Point, head north (about 344° magnetic) for Slippery Rock light via the channel inside Hodgson Reefs. As you approach Slippery Rock, head for buoy "D86" at about 320° magnetic. From "D86," head for buoy "DK" at Sparrowhawk Rock off the south end of Finlayson Island, avoiding Ripple Bank and Escape Reefs in Big Bay. Pass north of buoy "DK" and turn directly for the white triangle on the mainland shore near Redcliff Point. When you have safely passed Pender Rock and Centre Rock, turn north (about 346° magnetic) into Cunningham Passage, passing east of Finlayson Island bound for buoy "D88" off Hankin Reef and the entrance to Dodd Passage, then to Port Simpson.

Réanne Hemingway-Douglass

Baidarka'*s brief encounter with long-distance paddlers off Cape Fox*

From Port Simpson, exit via Inskip Passage or Rushbrook Passage, and pass east of Parkin Islets to the west side of Maskelyne Island. The lee of Maskelyne Island is the last of smooth water until you cross Portland Inlet to the lee of Wales Island. If Portland Inlet looks forbidding, wait and watch from the south side of Maskelyne Island, or return to Port Simpson for shelter.

As you proceed farther north, you will notice more than just time zone and international boundary changes. The scenery is on a grander scale, the islands are higher, the channels deeper and the number of small, convenient anchorages decreases. The area around Ketchikan has some of the heaviest rainfall in Southeast Alaska, providing some of the most dense temperate rainforests on Earth.

When you cross northbound to Alaska, set your clocks back one hour to the Alaska time zone; southbound, advance your clocks an hour to Pacific Time. (Southeast Alaska *does* observe Daylight Savings Time.)

If you have the time before crossing into Southeast Alaska, a foray up British Columbia's Portland Canal will treat you to turquoise waters, waterfalls and gorgeous overhanging cliffs. Measured from Dixon Entrance to Stewart, this fjord—100 miles long—is perhaps the longest on the North American continent. Many of the inlets in the area, such as Observatory Inlet, have barely been surveyed and are a delight to explore. Hyder, Alaska, and Stewart, British Columbia, share an almost non-existent border at the head of this remote, isolated fjord. Largely pristine, and seldom visited, the canal named by Vancouver after William Bentinck, Duke of Portland, is deep, with sheer mountain sides. Anchorages—marginal at best and far apart—depend entirely on the weather. The farther north you go in Portland Canal, the more difficult it is to receive VHF weather reports or radio reception of any kind.

The international boundary between Canada and Alaska runs mid-channel through Pearse and Portland Canals, north to Stewart. Floating trees or flotsam, common past Fords Cove, call for caution. Between Blue Point and Glacier Cove, the water in Portland Canal is an unusually bright turquoise blue, becoming increasingly more opaque at the upper end of the canal, with underwater visibility very limited. Snowcapped peaks and hanging glaciers rise above Stewart, providing a lovely setting for the small community.

Narrower and more intimate than Alaskan fiords, Portland Canal generally has more benign weather in the summer and requires less challenging navigation. At its entrance and central section, you can receive weather broadcasts only on Ch 21B (on some receivers Weather Ch 8). North of Glacier Cove there is no reception. (See Stewart Marine Rescue under Stewart.) Locals report that upslope winds predominate in the summer, and downslope winds in the winter. The winds tend to die off as you near Stewart; this phenomenon becomes apparent near Hattie Island or a little farther north. Most summer nights are quiet and calm. Other than a few Stewart sport fishing boats, you are unlikely to see any other boats.

In Alaska, as in Portland Canal and other British Columbia fiords, VHF weather and Ch 16 (Coast Guard) coverage is spotty or nonexistent when you leave the express or ferry routes. Don't be surprised if, in Behm Canal and many other areas of Southeast Alaska, there is no VHF radio reception.

*Note:* For Portland Canal, we recommend the use of Canadian charts 3933, 3393 and 3794, which are more detailed than the U.S. charts; you may also want to use Chart 3994 for Pearse Canal and Chart 3960 for Tongass Passage.

It is important to remember, also, that charts for Alaska are in fathoms (1 fathom = 6 feet) rather than meters (1 meter = 3.28 feet). In addition, because of scale, Alaskan charts are not as accurate as the charts for British Columbia.

As you head north of Dixon Entrance, Port Tongass, Foggy Bay, Judd Harbor and Morse Cove—the first anchor sites you come to—afford good anchorage in most weather.

Port Tongass, a small harbor between Tongass Island and the mainland, is the site of an 1870 fort and an abandoned Tlingit community.

Note, however, that Ketchikan Customs will *only* give you permission to anchor in Foggy Bay; no other anchoring location is acceptable. Foggy Bay's best anchor site is within Very Inlet to its immediate north (see diagram). You should call Ketchikan Customs ahead of time for this permission, something

## Kaleidoscope Magic

Linda Lewis—Journal Notes—M/V *Royal Sounder*

All cruisers have their own favorite scenes of magic. For me, nothing is quite as mysterious and wonderful as seeing the land reflected in very still water at low tide. Nature is the supreme artist in these moments. I am the blessed observer. I have heard it said that native peoples were inspired to create totem poles by these same visions. When I turn my head to the side I can see the figures emerge.

When I was a child I had a kaleidoscope that I loved. Today, when I am on the water, I discover these images and know that I am privileged to see, first hand, nature's kaleidoscope magic.

*Totem pole imagery—turned upright the figures emerge*

*Land reflected in very still water at low tide*

*It's an alien, or an insect, or a cruiser gone bad*

Linda Lewis

*A bird in flight—or a stealth airplane when turned upright*

Linda Lewis

*A thick fog bank awaits these cruisers.*

that is best done while you are still in Prince Rupert. (You may find a cell phone signal as you pass close by Cape Fox.) Foggy Bay is worth at least a day's exploration. Paddling a kayak or quietly rowing your dinghy can give you the full sensation of a rainforest environment. This is the home of muskeg ponds, pools and lagoons and of cedar trees whose bark is the source of the deep brown water. Walking over land here is difficult and rubber boots are a necessity.

Ketchikan, the southern-most city in Southeast Alaska, is known as "Alaska's First City" because it is the first Alaskan port of call for northbound ships. The area is rich in Native history and a visit to Saxman, a Tlingit tribe village, two miles south of town, yields a peek at a workshop of local totem carvers. Ten miles north of Ketchikan, Totem Bight State Park features 14 magnificent totem poles relating the legends of the Tlingit and Haida peoples and a Raven Clan House. With a population of about 8,000, the community offers plenty of amenities, art events, festivals and sightseeing.

Thomas Basin (the location of the Ketchikan Yacht Club), Casey Moran (formerly City Floats and undergoing reconstruction at press time), or Bar Harbor are the most likely moorages for cruisers in Ketchikan. Those who want to be in the heart of the town amidst the hub-bub of cruise ships, tourists and Creek Street activities will choose Thomas Basin or Casey Moran Harbor. Cruisers who are looking for easy access to groceries, mall and laundromat—away from the crush—will choose Bar Harbor, just north of town.

## Venn Passage and Metlakatla Bay, B.C.

Venn Passage is 3 miles west of Prince Rupert.

Charts 3955 metric, 3958 metric
East entrance: 54°18.68′ N, 130°22.88′ W
South entrance (Metlakatla Bay): 54°18.40′ N, 130°30.40′ W

*Venn Passage, known locally as Metlakatla Passage, connects Metlakatla Bay to Prince Rupert Harbour. The passage should be used only by small vessels. Local knowledge is recommended. . . . Tidal streams in Venn Passage, between Dundas Point and Verney Island, attain 3 kn on the flood and ebb; the stream turns about 1 hour before HW.* (SD)

Although narrow and intricate with strong currents, Venn Passage is a good small-boat route to use from Prince Rupert to Chatham Strait; it greatly shortens the route to Chatham Strait for northbound boats. The passage is marked by a couple of ranges and several buoys. Be aware, however, that the buoys in Venn Passage are often dragged out of position after being hit by tows.

*Please note:* If you are using a GPS in conjunction with traditional paper charting methods, be alert when exiting from Prince Rupert to Dixon Entrance via Venn Passage. The paper chart for Venn Passage (3955) is based on NAD 27 horizontal datum. If your GPS is not also set to NAD 27 for this short passage, you can be longitudinally off-position by as much as 300–600 feet! (Electronic vector and raster charts have all been converted to the WGS 84 horizontal datum, so mariners using this

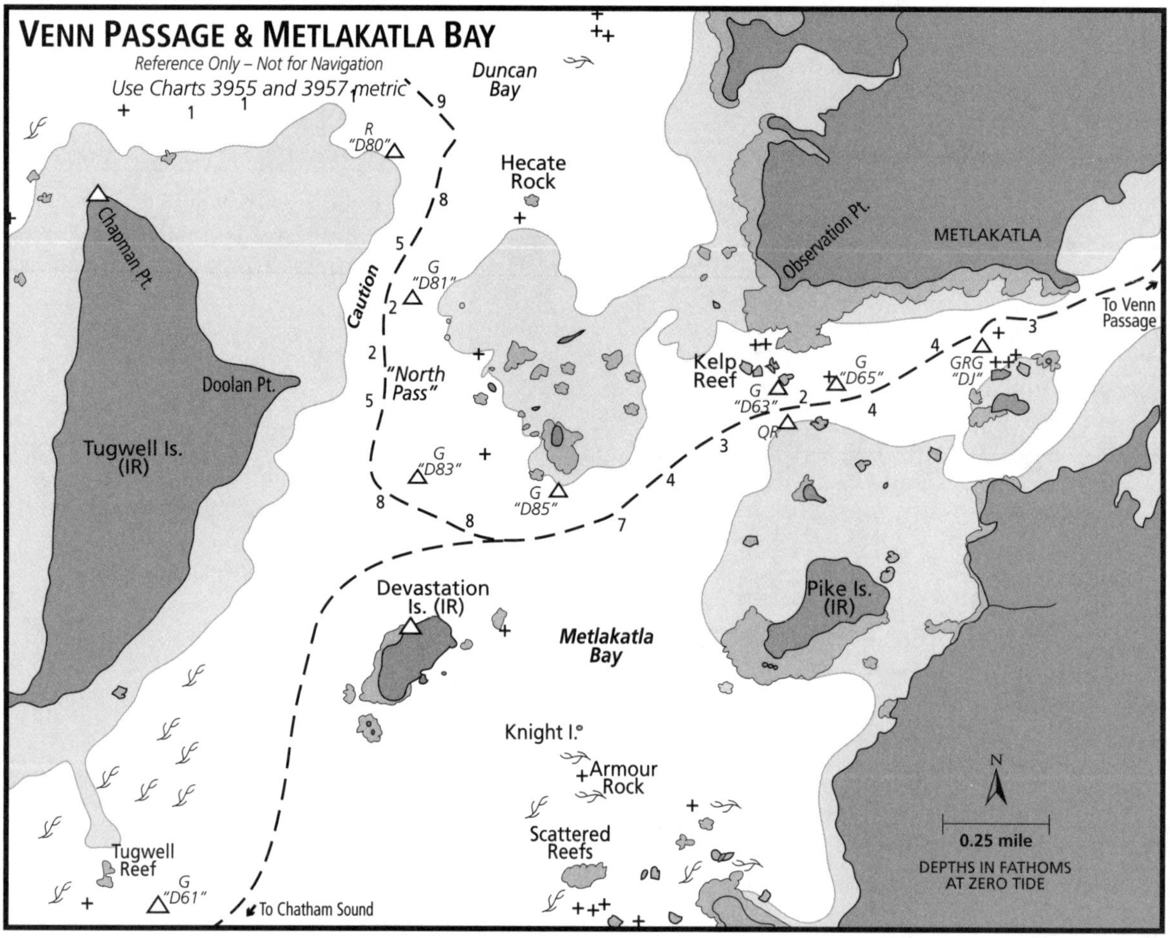



method do not need to alter their GPS.) Check with your electronic charting vendor to be sure this applies for your software.

Be sure of your route before attempting Venn Passage. Use Chart 3955 to identify turning points, and line up with the range marks (at the southeastern part of Venn Passage, in Shkgeaum Bay) and the three sector lights throughout the rest of Venn Passage. Notice that, as you transit from the Prince Rupert end of Venn Passage towards the Chatham Sound end, you will have the range marks and the sector lights *behind* you; this requires very careful helming skills.

The sector light, previously located in Shkgeaum Bay, was removed and replaced by standard range marks that are lit by yellow lights at night. When in narrow, critical passages (such as Venn Passage), be sure to check for recent chart corrections.

Both sides of the fairway have shoal water. Slow to no-wake speed when you pass the airport ferry dock at Du Vernay Point (where most locals slow down) and again off the Metlakatla float (where most locals do *not* slow down).

If you leave Prince Rupert near or ahead of high water, you have favorable current all the way to Green Island.

In summer, after a favorable weather forecast, there is frequently an early morning exodus (0400 to 0500 hours) of boats from Prince Rupert heading north. Venn Passage is heavily used by fishing vessels. Their skippers are not always in the most courteous of moods during this limited-space passage, so plan accordingly and be ready to give way a bit—safely.

## **Duncan Bay Shortcut** (west of Venn Passage)

Chart 3957, 3955; 1.6 mi W of Metlakatla float
Entrance (S) 54°19.70′ N, 130°29.40′ W
Entrance (N) 54°20.57′ N, 130°29.15′ W

*Please note:* When using paper Chart 3597 through the Duncan Bay Shortcut, the horizontal datum is WGS 84. If you are doing paper charting and used paper Chart 3955 through Venn Passage, your GPS was set for NAD 27. For the Duncan Bay Shortcut you will use paper Chart 3957 and you must re-set your GPS to WGS 84. Cruisers using electronic charting will find that their program makes the adjustments for these issues. (Check with your software vendor.)

Don't become buried in the chart. This is a *piloting* passage: look out the window. As you make the transit, watch your depth sounder and the many nav aids; they will provide good guidance for your passage.

By leaving the west end of Venn Passage and entering Duncan Bay, you can gain a half hour when northbound using a shortcut across the sand bar. We call this route "Duncan Bay Shortcut." Larger yachts (approximately 40 feet and over) may find this route too shallow and/ or narrow; however, smaller yachts can safely cross the bar during the upper half of most tides, staying close to the buoys and monitoring the depth sounder carefully. A professional skipper advises us that *at the appropriate tide*, vessels up to 80 feet with an 8-foot draft can also make this passage. Plan carefully and proceed cautiously.

Leaving Prince Rupert via Duncan Bay, from a point 0.25 mile west of buoy "D82," 0.7 mile southwest of Ryan Point, head north (about 344° magnetic) for Slippery Rock light via the channel inside Hodgson Reefs.

To enter the North Shortcut, turn north at buoy "D83" on the east side of Tugwell Island, due north of Devastation Island, and pass close on the west side of buoy "D81" that marks the shallow spot. Continue north and pass just east of red buoy "D80" as you enter Duncan Bay. Minimum depth on the bar is about 1½ fathoms at zero tide. However, the channel is narrow and subject to shoaling or shifting. On a north-bound route, do not cut west until 0.25 mile north of buoy "D80"—the Tugwell Island shoal extends well over a half-mile from shore. On a southbound route, red buoy "D80" is hard to see until you are fairly close; its position is about 54°20.48' N, 130°29.30' W.

On the Duncan Bay side, a large drying shoal extends well out from Tugwell Island, so avoid turning west too soon. Avoid the shoals 1.2 miles off Ryan Point, as well as Hodgson Reefs north of Duncan Bay. (To follow the mainland route north, please see the latter part of this chapter.)

## **Brundige Inlet** (Dundas Island)

Brundige Inlet is 5 miles northwest of Green Island Light.
Chart 3909 metric (inset)
Entrance: 54°36.86′ N, 130°50.73′ W
Anchor (bitter end): 54°35.30′ N, 130°53.50′ W

> *Brundige Inlet is entered east of Prospector Point. Fitch Island, 1 mile SW of Prospector Point, has a drying rock 0.1 mile west of it. A rock shoal, 0.6 mile SW of Fitch Island, lies in the middle of the fairway leading to the head of the inlet. . . . Anchorage for small craft can be obtained at the head of Brundige Inlet in 16 m (52 ft).* (SD)

Brundige Inlet, a narrow, 3-mile-long channel on the north side of Dundas Island, affords excellent shelter from all outside swells and chop. When you're anchored deep in the inlet, everything is still, and it's difficult to tell whether a tempest is blowing outside or not. The inlet has long been a favorite refuge for both north- and southbound cruising boats.

The only negative we've heard is the presence of pesky black flies when winds are slight or non-existent. However, we've been so thankful for this shelter after a rough crossing of Dixon Entrance that either we didn't notice the flies or else they weren't there. (There are no deer on Dundas Island because it is said that the black flies drain them of all their blood.)

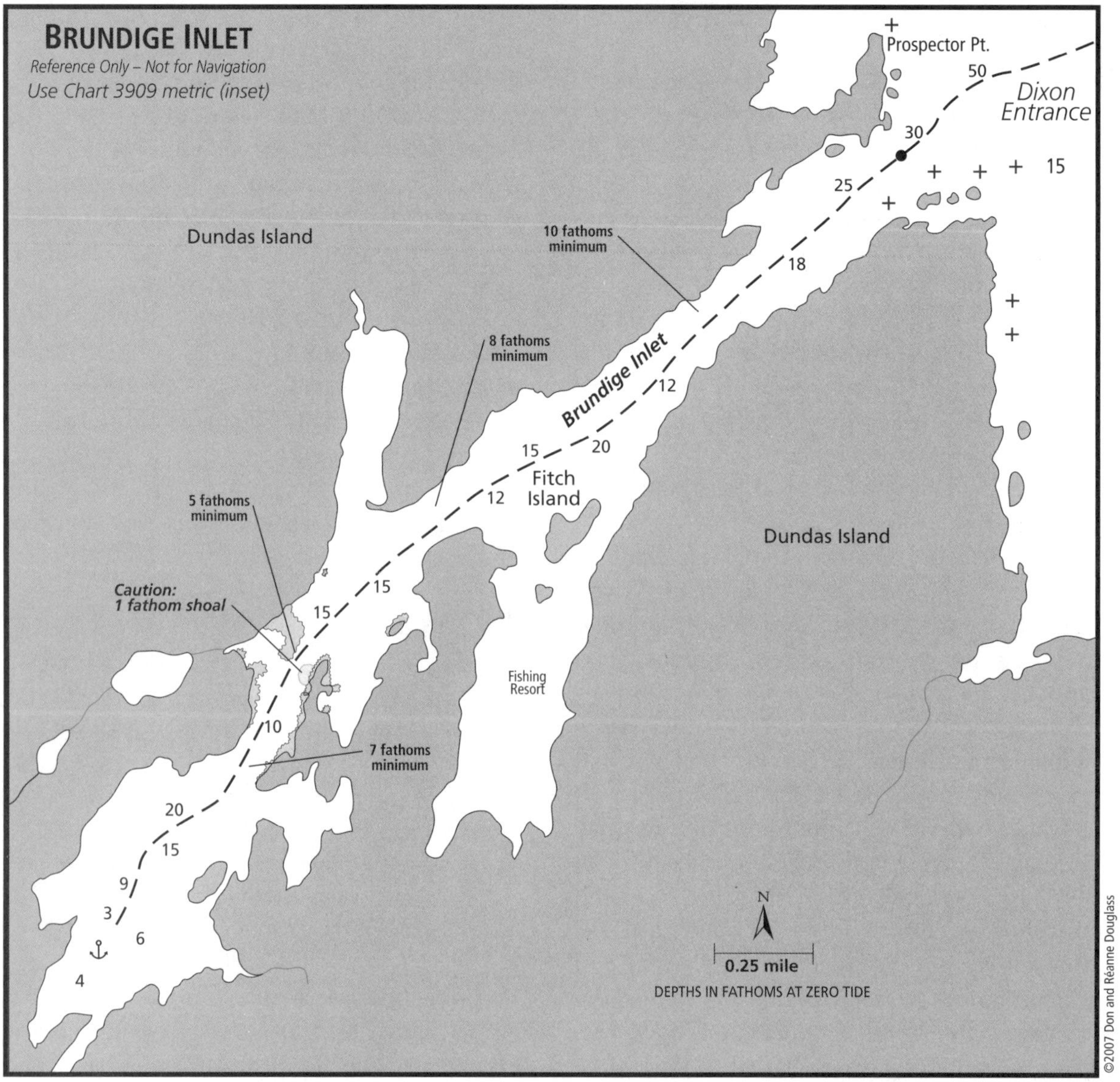


Although entering Brundige Inlet is not difficult, it is easy to overshoot the entrance; if you're arriving from the north, it helps to take a fix on Prospector Point. Stay mid-channel for the entire 3 miles, then favor the west shore at the beginning of the last narrows; there is a rock mid-channel with about 6 feet over it at zero tide. The entrance is quite narrow and Chart 3909 is helpful for entering.

We have anchored at the bitter end of the inlet and been perfectly comfortable during a major blow. There is shallower water and more swinging room on the south side of the lagoon south of Fitch Island.

Anchor (bitter end) in 4 to 6 fathoms over a mud bottom with very good holding.

## Mainland Route across East Dixon Inlet via Portland Inlet

(Recommended during periods of northeast outflow winds from Portland Inlet.)

When strong winds funnel down Portland Inlet and kick up a nasty chop in Chatham

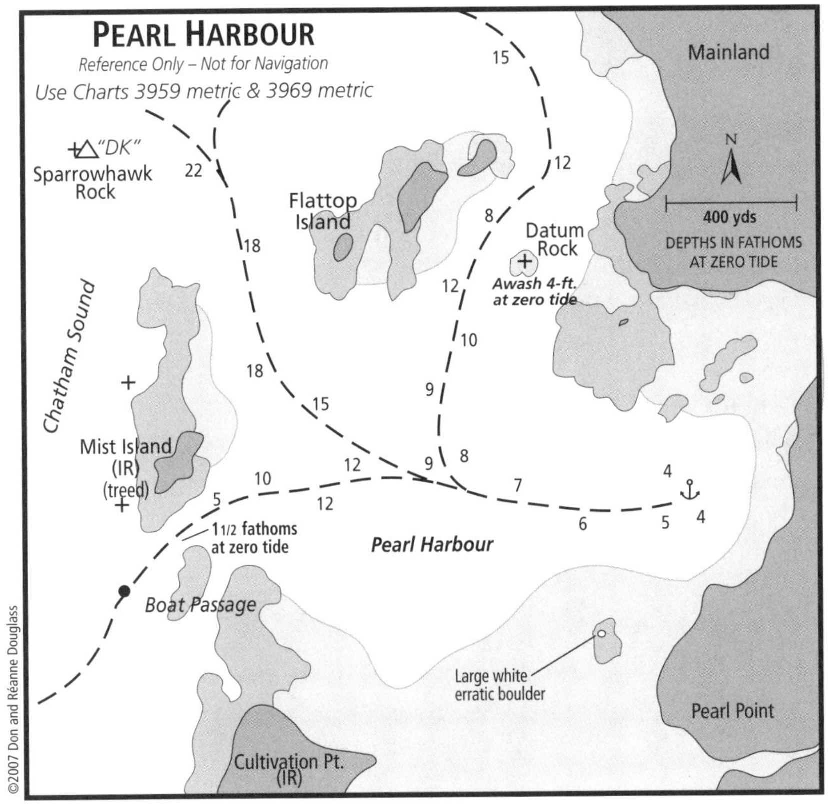


about 3 miles across the entrance to Portland Inlet. Convenient layovers can be taken on either side of the inlet to allow for an optimum crossing time.

## Pearl Harbour

Charts 3959 metric, 3963 metric
Entrance (Boat Passage): 54°30.16′ N, 130°28.30′ W
Anchor: 54°30.29′ N, 130°26.83′ W

*Good anchorage can be obtained near the middle of Pearl Harbour in 20 m (66 ft), mud. . . . Anchorage can also be obtained at Otter Anchorage, about 0.2 mile north of the NE end of Flat Top Islands, in 31 m (102 ft) mud.* (SD)

Very good protection from northeast winds can be obtained in the east side of Pearl Harbour. Several cruisers have reported to us that the Salmon Bight area in Big Bay—just South of Pearl Harbour—is also an excellent anchorage that is very well protected.

After clearing Sparrowhawk Rock, enter Pearl Harbour via the deep-water route on the west side of Flat Top Island. Small boats can use narrow Boat Passage, but the reef south of Mist Island must be identified and avoided. If passing north of Mist Island, be careful to avoid the drying spit to the north. Many boats have gone aground there, expecting the reef to terminate farther south. Stay close to Buoy "DK."

Anchor in the far east side of Pearl Harbour, due north of Pearl Point. The "pearl" in Pearl Point is a large glacial boulder 200 yards northwest of the point.

Anchor in 4 fathoms, sand and mud bottom, fair-to-good holding.

Sound and East Dixon Entrance, consider hugging the mainland coast for a smooth-water route. Although longer than the direct route, this route is more scenic and interesting. By staying in Port Tongass, you can divide your trip to Ketchikan into two easy segments. Rough water on this route is reduced to

*Public floats, Port Simpson (Lax Kw' Alaams)*

## Port Simpson (Lax Kw' Alaams)

Port Simpson is 15 miles northwest of Prince Rupert.

**Charts 3963 (inset), 3959**
**Breakwater light: 54°33.71′ N, 130°25.78′ W**

> *Port Simpson harbour, at the north end of Cunningham Passage, is fronted by Harbour Reefs and Birnie Island; it is one of the most spacious harbours on the north part of the British Columbia coast. The harbour is well sheltered from all but west winds and is easy of access, having no strong tidal streams.* (SD)

Port Simpson has three finger-floats for small boats on the south side of the breakwater, but the floats are frequently crowded with sport fishing and commercial boats. Avoid the shallow water east and south of the floats (see inset in Chart 3963). Fuel and propane are available on a part-time basis, good water can be obtained from a hose at the foot of the gangway; electricity is available for a reasonable fee. The village has a grocery store.

## Tongass Passage

Tongass Passage, between Sitklan and Wales islands, is 28 miles northwest of Prince Rupert.

**Chart 17437**
**Southeast entrance (0.3 mile east of Boston Islands): 54°42.10′ N, 130°32.72′ W**
**South entrance (0.54 mile northwest of Haystack Island): 54°43.50′ N, 130°37.72′ W**
**North entrance (mid-channel between Bartlett Point and Point Mansfield): 54°45.83′ N, 130°39.60′ W**

> *Tongass Passage . . . is a deep passage with steep shores that extends NW from Dixon Entrance. It bends to the NE off the entrance to Sitklan Passage, separates Wales Island from the mainland, and forms the W entrance to Pearse Canal. Tongass Passage is entered between Haystack Island . . . and Island Point . . . . Rocks awash are about 300 yards W of Haystack Island. From Bartlett Point . . . to Phipp Point . . . about 1 mile NE of Bartlett Point, a midchannel course will lead through deep water.* (CP)

Tongass Passage is the smooth-water route into Alaska that crosses the entrance of Portland Inlet and leads northwest into a narrow channel east of Boston and Proctor islands. The passage between these islands is clear and well protected. Both sets of islands have beautiful sandy beaches that provide excellent kayak haul-outs and campsites. The head of the bay, on the south end of Wales Island, offers protection from downslope winds from Portland Inlet. The south entrance between Island Point and Haystack Island is easier to enter in poor visibility.

Sitklan Passage can be followed to Port Tongass or Nakat Harbour.

## Lincoln Channel

Lincoln Channel, between Kanagunut and Skitlan islands, is 2 miles south of Port Tongass.

**Chart 17437**
**South entrance (0.5 mile east of Garnet Point): 54°43.12′ N, 130°40.27′ W**
**North entrance: 54°45.61′ N, 130°43.09′ W**

> [Lincoln Channel] *is very narrow at the N entrance with a controlling depth of 9 feet in midchannel. In the S part of the channel, about 0.2 mile N of the island in the bight, is a rock in midchannel with 3/4 fathom over it. A shoal with a depth of 1 fathom is about 0.5 mile N from Garnet Point, the S extremity of Kanagunut Island.* (CP)

Lincoln Channel can be used by small craft as a shortcut to Port Tongass. Anchorage can be found on the southwest side of the channel on the northwest side of the island labeled 260. The north end of the channel is very narrow and shallow with less than 10 feet in the fairway at low water. The bottom is clearly visible in the shallowest parts.

Lincoln Channel makes an interesting passage for shallow-draft boats; shelter can be found in the small west bight on the north side of the island just inside the south entrance. The head of the bight has the makings of a good campsite for kayakers. There is a log boom at 1 fathom.

The northeast side of the mid-channel islet has several fishing floats and a possible anchor site in southerlies. The north entrance has a flat bottom with kelp, and depths of

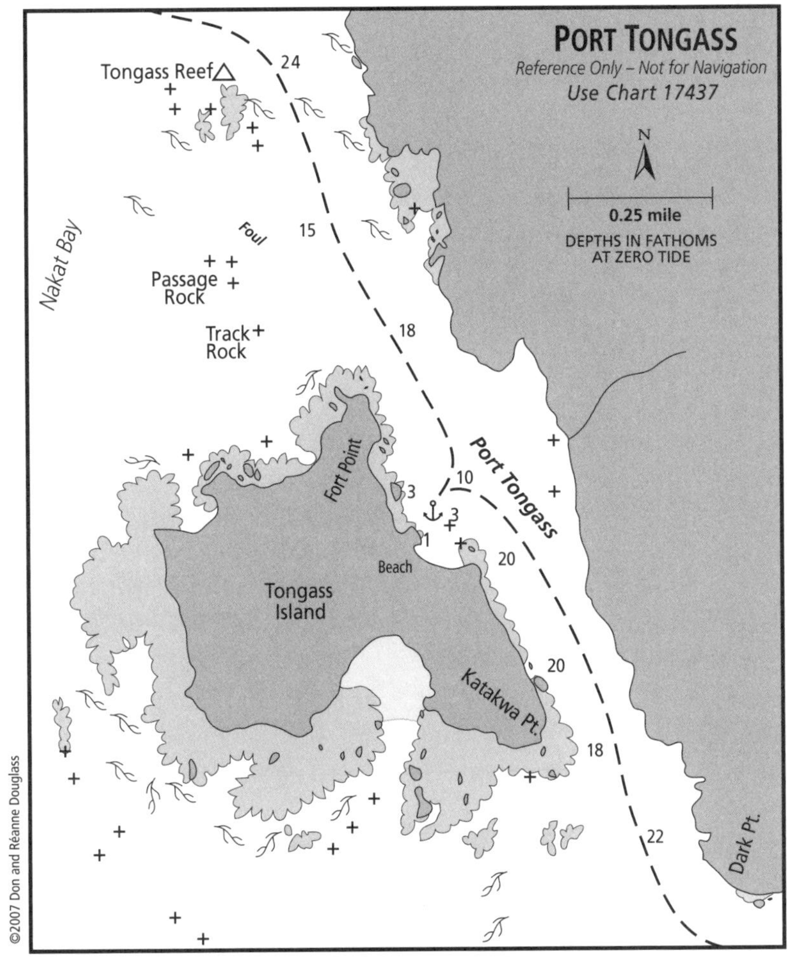


## Port Tongass

Port Tongass, on the east side of Tongass Island, is 3.8 miles east of Cape Fox.

Chart 17437
South entrance (0.09 mile west of Dark Point): 54°45.90′ N, 130°43.39′ W
North entrance (0.19 mile north of the Tongass Reef beacon): 54°47.40′ N, 130°44.68′ W
Anchor: 54°46.52′ N, 130°44.06′ W

*Port Tongass is a small harbor formed by the passage between Tongass Island and the mainland. Tongass Island is low and, except on the NE side, has ledges and submerged rocks that extend well out on all sides. A launch passage is immediately N of Tongass Island, but is tortuous and obstructed and should be used only with local knowledge.*

*The anchorage is 200 yards from the NE shore of the harbor, E of Fort Point in about 20 fathoms, hard bottom.*

*The N entrance between Tongass Reef and the mainland is the one recommended and is the best entrance for vessels approaching from W.* (CP)

about 7 feet at zero tide. The bottom is visible most of the way through the shoal area.

*Anchorage, Port Tongass*

The south shore of Tongass Island was once the site of a Tlingit village. The totems from the abandoned village were removed to Ketchikan in the 1970s. Most of the inhabitants had already moved to Saxman by the early 1900s. Fort Tongass, on the east side of the island—established in 1868 as a border station to prevent smuggling and to maintain peace among the tribes and traders—was abandoned in 1870. There are few signs of either the village or the fort, except for a few old bricks, scattered logs and old engine parts. The only residents of Port Tongass now are seals, loons and bald eagles.

There is a good landing beach of mud and

shell in front of the brambles filling the old fort site. The rocks on the north side of the cove hold a colony of giant barnacles, a variety that grows up to 4 inches in diameter! You can find protection from most winds except northerlies anchored near the landing beach.

A good walk from the fort site follows the shoreline around Katakwa Point to the former village. The rocks and reefs of the south side are full of shellfish, and the view to seaward is fantastic. Unless you have a war canoe to get through the reefs, do not approach the village site from the south.

Anchor off the beach in 2 fathoms, or as close as your draft allows. Eel grass grows along the 1-fathom line. By anchoring close-in you can avoid most of the current and find good holding. Ebb current flows southeast at one knot, with some back eddies in the cove. On the last of the flood that flows northwest at about 2 knots, small whitecaps develop off North Point and a slight swell is felt in the cove.

Anchor in 2 to 4 fathoms over a mud, sand, shell and grass bottom with good holding.

To regain the direct route to Ketchikan, head north from Port Tongass, rounding Tongass Reef, and turn southwest for Cape Fox. Cross Nakat Bay before resuming your northbound route to Revillagigedo Channel.

## Pearse Canal

Pearse Canal, which connects Tongass Passage to Portland Canal, is 32 miles north of Prince Rupert.

### Chart 17437

*Pearse Canal is about 25 miles long from Tongass Passage to its junction with Portland Canal off Tree Point, the N extremity of Pearse Island. The British Columbia shore is formed by Wales Island and Pearse Island, and the Alaska shore by Fillmore Island and the mainland.* (CP)

Pearse Canal, narrower and more sheltered than Portland Inlet, has interesting places to explore at its southern entrance.

Don Douglass

*First mate Réanne's work is never done.*

Réanne Hemingway-Douglass

*. . . But Captain Don plays on!*

## Wales Harbour

(Wales Island)

Wales Harbour is entered 0.5 mile south of Pearse Canal Island Light.

Chart 17437
Entrance (0.28 mile east of Phipp Point): 54°46.59′ N, 130°36.85′ W
Anchor: 54°45.27′ N, 130°34.50′ W

*Wales Harbour, on the British Columbia side of Pearse Canal, about 1.5 miles from Tongass Passage, affords good anchorage in 14 to 18 fathoms, soft bottom; its entrance is somewhat obstructed by islets and rocks, and only vessels with local knowledge should attempt to enter it. The usual anchorage is N of the larger island near the head of the harbor. In entering, follow the SW shore at a distance of about 200 yards until past the shoal in the entrance to the harbor.* (CP)

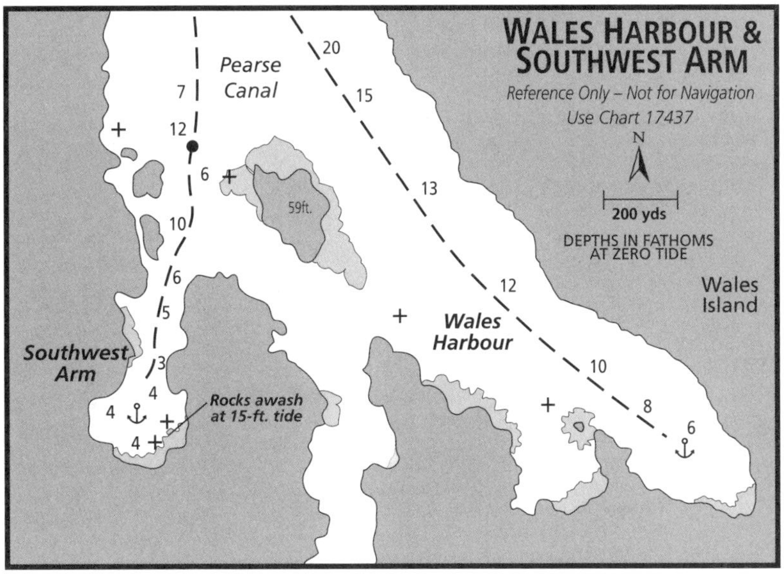




A small intimate anchorage can be found on the east side of an unnamed island southeast of Safa Islands. The south entrance is very narrow and should only be entered after you reconnoiter with a dinghy to ensure adequate depths. The anchorage is very well protected but it has limited swinging room and a shore tie should be used.

Anchor in 8 fathoms over mud and sand with good holding.

## Southwest Arm of Wales Harbour

(Wales Island)

The cove in the southwest arm of Wales Harbour is 1.6 miles southeast of Pearse Canal Island Light.

Chart 17437
Entrance (0.83 mile southeast of Safa Islands): 54°45.61′ N, 130°35.67′ W
Anchor: 54°45.27′ N, 130°35.79′ W

Anchorage can be found deep in the small basin in the southwest arm, avoiding the submerged rock on the east side of the basin. This intimate cove is shaped like a keyhole and offers very good protection from southerly weather. It has room for one or two boats over a flat bottom with steep-to, rocky shores.

Anchor in 4 fathoms over a soft bottom with good holding.

## Fillmore Inlet

Fillmore Inlet is 3.9 miles east of Port Tongass.

Chart 17437
Entrance (0.35 mile west of Pearse Canal Island Light): 54°47.06′ N, 130°37.19′ W

*Fillmore Inlet joins Pearse Canal on the Alaska side at the SW end of Fillmore Island, and separates that island from the mainland; it extends NE and is comparatively free to navigation, but there are numerous rocks and reefs close inshore. The narrow entrance beyond the group of islets at the head of this inlet leads into two consecutive basins, each of considerable size. The inlet has no value as an anchorage.* (CP)

## Willard Inlet

Willard Inlet is 2.3 miles northwest of Pearse Canal Island Light.

Chart 17437
Entrance (1.68 miles northwest of Male Point): 54°49.18′ N, 130°37.90′ W

*Willard Inlet is a narrow inlet that extends in a NW direction from the NW side of Fillmore*

*Inlet, about 1.5 miles N of Male Point, the SW extremity of Fillmore Island. It is very narrow at the entrance, and the currents have great velocity, forming swirls that extend well out from the mouth. The times of high and low water inside the inlet are about 1 hour later than at other places in the vicinity, and the rise and fall about 2 feet less. This inlet can only be entered at slack water and has no value as an anchorage.* (CP)

## **Regina Cove** (Fillmore Island)

Regina Cove is 2.1 miles northeast of Pearse Canal Island Light.

Chart 17437
Entrance 54°48.23′ N, 130°33.54′ W

*Regina Cove indents the S shore of Fillmore Island about 2 miles from Male Point. Anchorage is available in the center of the bay in 14 fathoms, mud bottom. A small shoal of 1-3/4 fathoms, with deep water surrounding it, is near midchannel about 0.2 mile off the entrance to the cove.* (CP)

Réanne Hemingway-Douglass

*Exploring the former U.S. Customs House, now on Canadian soil (Manzanita Cove)*

Regina Cove has an irregular bottom and many submerged rocks and is exposed to the south. It is not recommended for cruising vessels.

Wales Harbour and Winter Inlet are preferred anchorages in this region.

## Wales Passage

Wales Passage, between Pearse and Wales islands, is 1 mile southwest of Winter Inlet.

Chart 17437
South entrance (mid-channel between Swaine Point and York Island): 54°45.57′ N, 130°25.86′ W
North entrance: 54°49.64′ N, 130°29.52′ W

*Wales Passage . . . is free from midchannel dangers.* (CP)

When there's a blow in Portland Inlet or Pearse Canal, the water is generally smooth in Wales Passage. This passage frequently contains a number of crab pots marked by small floats.

## **Manzanita Cove** (Wales Island)

Manzanita Cove is 5 miles south of the entrance to Winter Inlet.

Charts 17437, 17427
Entrance: 54°45.67′ N, 130°26.20′ W
Anchor: 54.45.45′ N, 130°26.29′ W

*Manzanita Cove, on the west side of the south entrance of Wales Passage, is entered north of Swaine Point; it affords anchorage for small vessels.* (SD)

Manzanita Cove has a steep-to bottom with depths inconvenient for anchoring and no flat areas. The little nook on the south side, immediately west of Swaine Point, is protected in most weather and is useful for one or two small craft, using a stern-tie to shore.

At the head of the nook, you can see one of the four original stone masonry cabins built for the initial surveys of the Alaska border in 1896, under the direction of Captain Gaillard, U.S. Army Corps of Engineers. A stone plaque on the north corner of the ruined building says " . . . property, Do not Injure." The U.S.-Canada border was established north of Wales and Pearse islands by a later tribunal and, since then, someone has chiseled out the "US" in the stone marker. In contrast with the fairly well-maintained building that marks the Hyder-Stewart border, the roof, floor and door at this site are missing, and brush and moss have taken over inside its walls.

Anchor off the former U.S. Customs House in 6 fathoms, rocky bottom, poor holding, with a stern-tie to shore recommended.

## Wales Passage Cove (Pearse Island)

Wales Passage Cove, on the east side of Wales Passage, is 1.3 miles north of Manzanita Cove.

Chart 17437
Entrance: 54°46.79′ N, 130°25.77′ W
Anchor: 54°46.96′ N, 130°25.77′ W

Wales Passage Cove is what we call the small bay in Wales Passage, on the south side of Pearse Island. Temporary shelter may be found here when downslope winds are blowing in Portland Inlet. Depths in the cove are irregular, indicating a rocky bottom. Winter Inlet, just north, provides superior all-weather protection.

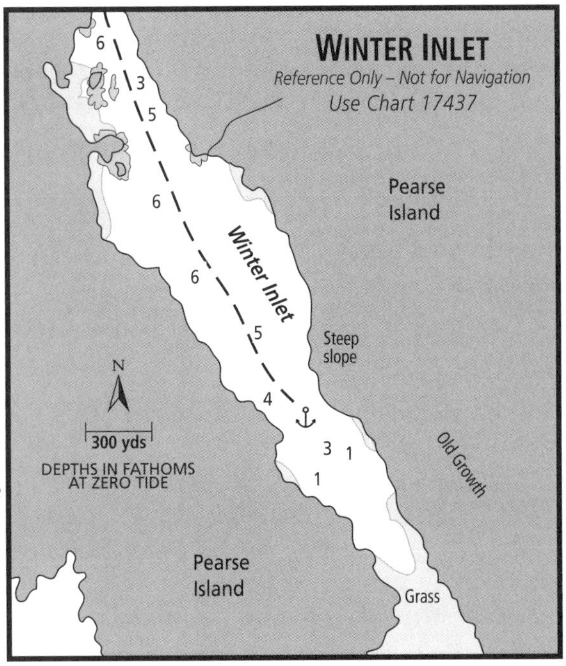




Anchor in about 6 fathoms over a largely rocky bottom with poor-to-fair holding.

## Edward Passage

Edward Passage is 1.6 miles west of the entrance to Winter Inlet.

Chart 17437
South entrance: 54°49.91′ N, 130°30.02′ W
North entrance: 54°52.06′ N, 130°31.94′ W

*Edward Passage separates Fillmore Island from the mainland N and connects Fillmore Inlet with Pearse Canal. The passage is narrow, foul, and only navigable by small craft with local knowledge.* (CP)

## Winter Inlet (Pearse Island)

Winter Inlet is 6.75 miles northeast of the entrance to Wales Harbour.

Chart 17437
Entrance: 54°50.50′ N, 130°27.67′ W
Anchor: 54°48.26′ N, 130°25.85′ W

*Winter Inlet, the entrance to which is about 1.3 miles NE of the N entrance to Wales Passage, indents the NW shore of Pearse Island. It affords secure anchorage for small craft; the holding ground is good and there is ample swinging room in the wider part. The N shore is bold, except where small sandspits make out at the mouths of streams. In entering, favor slightly the S shore until past the first spit on the N side, and then keep the N shore close aboard when passing the bight on the S side to avoid a reef that extends about 75 yards off a small wooded islet.* (CP)

Winter Inlet is one of the most well-sheltered anchorages east of Dixon Entrance. It is a long, scenic inlet and total protection can be found anywhere in reasonable depths past the small west shore islets with trees. Porpoises and seals like to play in the strong currents off the entrance. The creek outlet on the east shore has grassy margins, and the head of the inlet is a large grassy meadow.

Anchor in 3 to 5 fathoms over sticky black mud, small broken shells and wood debris; very good holding.

David Parker

*The majestic eagle rules Southeast Alaska*

## **Gwent Cove** (Pearse Canal)

Gwent Cove is 8.7 miles northeast of Winter Inlet.

**Chart 17437 (inset)**
**Entrance: 54°56.57′ N, 130°20.02′ W**
**Anchor: 54°56.55′ N, 130°20.25′ W**

*Gwent Cove, 0.6 mile north of Yelnu Islets, is the site of an abandoned cannery and ruined wharf.* (SD)

Gwent Cove, off the south entrance to Hidden Inlet, provides fair-weather anchorage directly in front of the old white cannery building with two smoke stacks. There is a 5-fathom flat area off the old wharf and small private float. The float is sometimes used as a sport fishing outstation.

The head of the cove shoals rapidly west of the wharf and, since the water is dark brown muskeg, you have no more than a foot or two of visibility through the water.

Anchor in 5 fathoms over sand and mud with shells; good holding.

## **Hidden Inlet** (Pearse Canal)

Hidden Inlet is 0.25 mile northeast of Gwent Cove.

**Chart 17437 (inset)**
**Entrance: 54°56.72′ N, 130°19.85′ W**
**Anchor: 54°57.14′ N, 130°20.27′ W**

*The entrance is less than 150 yards wide, and the tidal currents through it set with a velocity of 8 to 10 knots, forming swirls that extend well into Pearse Canal. The main body of the inlet is about 4 miles long, varying in depth from 30 to 73 fathoms, but there is only 2-1/2 fathoms at the entrance. It can be entered only at slack water, and is of no value as an anchorage.* (CP)

Hidden Inlet is located on the northwest side of Pearse Canal, 8 miles northeast of Winter Inlet. The entrance is narrow, set back from the canal, and is easy to miss. The tree-covered Yelnu Islets, 300 yards off the west shore, are a leading mark.

Enter the inlet on or near slack, staying mid-channel. The fairway is quite wide, but favor slightly west of center at the south entrance, and east of center in the narrows. The fairway has a fairly even bottom, bouncing between 3 and 5 fathoms. One hour after a low water of 6 feet, the flood current was 2 knots. Thirty minutes later, it had increased to 3-plus knots, with moderate turbulence forming.

Just beyond the narrows, on the west side of the inlet, is a grassy shore, off of which lies a 2- to 3-fathom shoal where temporary anchorage can be found. The bottom is rocky and there are kelp patches on either side of the beach area. The shores are steep, with rocky slabs, and high peaks can be seen nearby.

Anchor in 3 fathoms over a rocky bottom with kelp; poor holding.

## **Portland Canal**

Portland Canal, which forms the international boundary between Alaska and Canada for over 50 miles, terminates in Hyder, Alaska, and Stewart, British Columbia.

**Charts 17427, 17425**
**Entrance: (1.45 miles north of Tree Point): 55°03.47′ N, 130°11.54′ W**

*Portland Canal extends N from its junction with Pearse Canal and Portland Inlet at Tree Point. . . . The channel, clear and deep, has no dangers except for a rock awash, about 0.2 mile off the W* (Alaska) *shore, 2.3 miles above River Point.* (CP)

*Portland Canal, looking north at head*

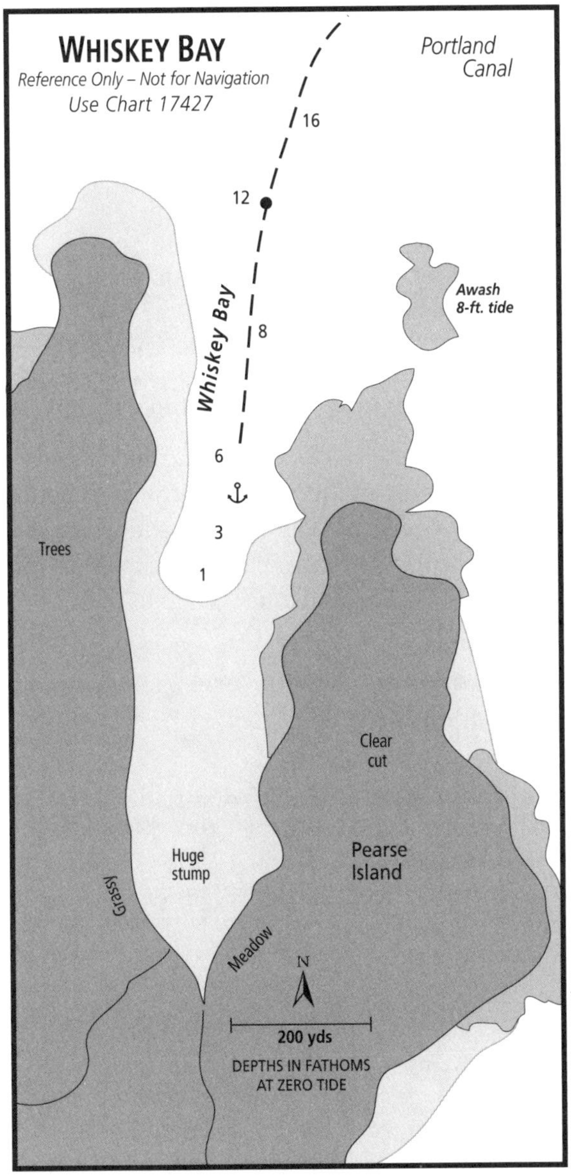


Portland Canal is a long, narrow fiord, perhaps the longest on the entire North American continent. When measured from Dixon Entrance to Stewart, it is more than 100 miles long. Its sides are sheer and steep and its waters are deep. This is a remote and isolated channel with a rugged wilderness appearance.

Anchorage is marginal at best and depends entirely on the weather. VHF weather reports are difficult to receive; VHF Ch 21B is useful in the central part of Portland Canal.

## **Whiskey Bay** (Pearse Island)

Whiskey Bay is at the north tip of Pearse Island, near the junction of Pearse and Portland canals.

Chart 17427
Entrance: 55°02.09′ N, 130°11.10′ W
Anchor: 55°01.93′ N, 130°11.15′ W

Whiskey Bay is a good lunch stop, or an overnighter if no downslope winds are expected. At the head of the bay is a grassy meadow with a huge stump; the shoreline has a constant slope, which can be used as a kayak haul-out. Upon entering, avoid the rocks awash on the east side of the bay and anchor in convenient depths.

Anchor in 4 to 6 fathoms over sand and mud with good holding.

## **Reef Island** (Portland Canal)

Reef Island is 3.0 miles northwest of Whiskey Bay.

Charts 17427
Anchor (south cove): 55°04.78′ N, 130°12.64′ W
Anchor (west Reef Island): 55°04.93′ N, 130°12.35′ W

> *Reef Island is close off the W shore, abreast Spit Point, at the entrance to Portland Canal.* (CP)

Reef Island, on the west side of Portland Canal, has two coves that provide some relief from downslope winds, but both are exposed to the south.

The south cove is steep-to and temporary anchorage can be taken in 6 to 8 fathoms off the drying beach near a drift tree with limbs still attached. Small craft can also find some protection directly west of Reef Island, off the stony beach, where there is a 100-foot-long tree lying onshore. The fairway on the west side of Reef Island has a minimum depth of about one fathom. There is a 1- to 2-fathom area in the passage between Reef Island and the shore. The level of the tree limbs indicates that the area is mostly free of chop. If you anchor in this passageway, a stern-tie to shore may be effective.

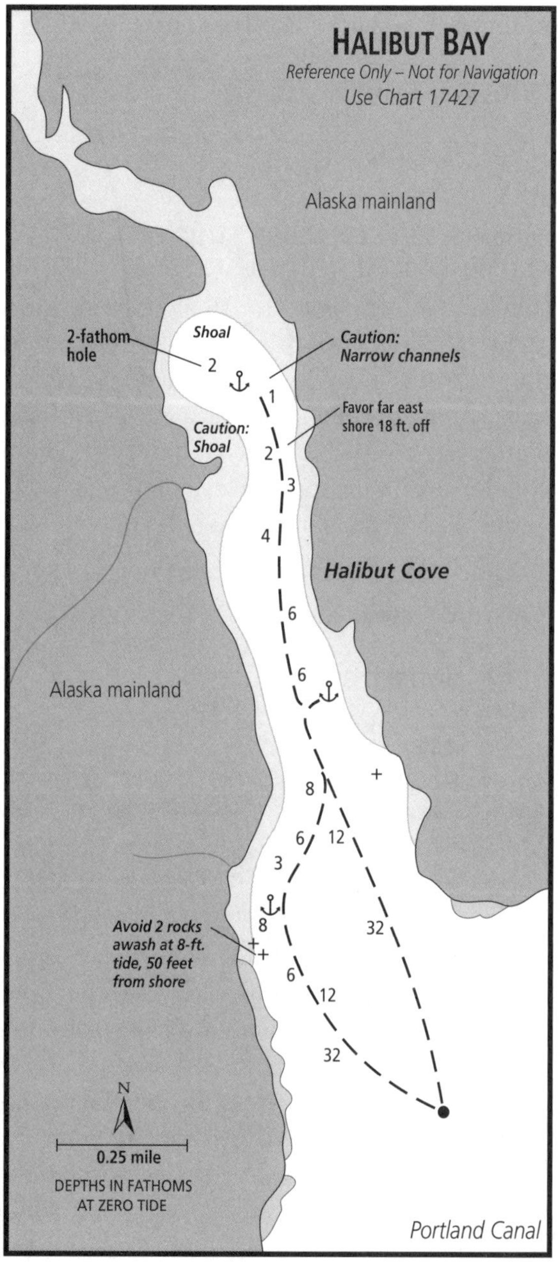




Anchor (south cove) in 6 to 8 fathoms. The bottom is sand, stones and iridescent seaweed; fair holding.

Anchor (west Reef Island) in about 3 fathoms, mixed bottom, predominantly sand; fair-to-good holding.

## **Sandfly Bay** (Portland Canal)

Sandfly Bay is 7.9 miles north of Whiskey Bay.

Chart 17427
Entrance: 55°09.52′ N, 130°09.07′ W
Anchor: 55°09.75′ N, 130°09.28′ W

> *Sandfly Bay, on the W shore abreast Dickens Point, 14.5 miles above Hidden Inlet, has no value as an anchorage.* (CP)

Some temporary protection from downslope winds can be found in scenic Sandfly Bay. It is a good place for small craft to anchor in fair weather only. Sandfly Bay is steep-to off the creek outlet. The foreshore slope on the west side of the bay is less steep, and its grassy margins have little driftwood to indicate severe weather or chop. Avoid the charted rocks near the east shore.

Anchorage can be found about 100 yards from the white granite rocks on the west shore, 50 yards south of the drying gravel flat. This spot can provide reasonable anchoring for one or two boats in fair weather. There is easy landing access.

Anchor in 3 to 5 fathoms over sand with fair-to-good holding.

## **Halibut Bay** (Portland Canal)

Halibut Bay is 11.6 miles northeast of Whiskey Bay.

Chart 17427
Entrance: 55°13.02′ N, 130°05.50′ W
Anchor (east shore): 55°13.73′ N, 130°05.69′ W
Anchor (west shore): 55°13.40′ N, 130°05.94′ W

> *Halibut Bay, free of hidden dangers, is on the W shore of Portland Canal, about 4 miles above Sandfly Bay. Its shores are generally bold, but on each side near the entrance are sandy beaches with shoals that extend 80 yards offshore and low grassy land running 100 yards back. Near*

*the head of the bay extensive flats, which bare, make out from the W shore almost all the way across leaving a narrow channel close to the E side, through which 5 feet can be carried to a narrow basin 2 to 4 fathoms deep and suitable only for small craft.*

*Halibut Bay affords anchorage for vessels in the middle of the bay in 10 fathoms, about 0.2 mile above Astronomical Point . . . where the anchorage is 450 yards wide; also 700 yards farther up abreast the N end of the sand beach on the E side, in 10 fathoms, where the anchorage is 300 yards wide.* (CP)

Halibut Bay affords the best protection between Whiskey Bay and Maple Bay or Fords Cove. Convenient anchorage can be found in the entrance on the east shore, just off a tiny creek and stony beach, or on the west shore between a small creek and the rocky point. While the bay is open to the southeast, most of the summer up- and downslope winds blow by the entrance.

In the inner bay, there is a 3-fathom hole north of the large creek. The passage to this hole is very shallow. We found as little as 2 feet in the fairway at zero tide, with rapidly shoaling flats on either side. There was a small float house moored to the west of this hole. In 1996, we found it necessary to travel within a few yards of the east wall until we were abeam the low point north of the west creek. We would not recommend inner Halibut Bay until it is more fully charted.

Anchor (east shore) in 8 fathoms over sand, gravel and stones with good holding.

Anchor (west shore) in 6 fathoms off a tiny creek over sand, gravel and stones with good holding.

## **Belle Bay** (Portland Canal)

Belle Bay is 17.5 miles northeast of Whiskey Bay.

Charts 17427, 17425
Entrance: 55°17.48′ N, 129°56.96′ W

*Belle Bay, the bight E of Hattie Island, does not afford anchorage.* (CP)

Belle Bay, which lies at the foot of a U-shaped valley, is steep-to, with depths dropping 45 degrees to 30 fathoms. Temporary protection from southerlies might be obtained at the south end of the beach with a stern-tie to the trees, or from northerlies at the far north end of the beach, with a stern-tie to the drift logs on shore. However, upwind chop blows into both sites, making them quite rolly. Belle Bay Creek flows from high lakes that lie just 1.5 miles from the lower end of Granby Bay in Observatory Inlet.

Temporary protection in southerlies may be possible off the northeast corner of Hattie Island, avoiding the charted rock.

## **Car Point Notch** (Portland Canal)

Car Point Notch is 19.4 miles northeast of Whiskey Bay.

Charts 17427, 17425
Position: 55°20.30′ N, 130°00.14′ W

*Car Point is on the E shore about 3.5 miles NW of Belle Bay.* (CP)

The head of the notch at Car Point holds a wonderful surprise—a stunning waterfall that tumbles vertically over somber, angular, gray- and rust-colored granite. Although we encountered many lovely cascades along the eastern shore of Portland Inlet, this one received raves from all the crew. As we approached the notch, the water grew calm and we were able to come within 10 feet of the waterfall. Ferns and delicate white flowers grow out of every small crevice, while hemlock and spruce sprout from unlikely vertical faces.

At the south end of Portland Canal, the water is tea-colored but it becomes progressively greener as you proceed northward.

## **Tombstone Bay** (Portland Canal)

Tombstone Bay is 23.25 miles northeast of Whiskey Bay.

Chart 17425
Float position: 55°24.36′ N, 130°03.30′ W

*Tombstone Bay, on the W side of Portland Canal about 7.5 miles above Hattie Island, affords a temporary anchorage for small craft in 8 fathoms near the head of the N bight.* (CP)

On the north side of Tombstone Bay there are overhanging cliffs from which hemlock and cedar grow. The bottom is steep-to with a rocky beach. This bight could offer shelter from north winds with an anchor placed close to the drying flat at its head.

The south end of Tombstone Bay is the watershed for an unnamed creek flowing from a perfect, U-shaped valley. On the north side of the south bight is a large steel ball with a 30-foot float attached. A house with its own dock and some small outbuildings is located along the shore of the creek and the float is probably private. Protection from southerly weather can be obtained here; however, avoid the charted rocks and the drying flat off the creek.

Anchor off the drying flat, in the vicinity of the float, in about 10 fathoms over an unrecorded bottom.

## **Maple Bay** (Portland Canal)

Maple Bay is 24.1 miles northeast of Whiskey Bay.

Chart 17425
Entrance: 55°25.36′ N, 130°01.17′ W
Anchor: 55°25.28′ N, 130°00.66′ W

> *Maple Bay . . . 8 miles above Hattie Island, affords fair anchorage for small craft, 300 yards from the S side, in 7 to 8 fathoms. In 1977, a rock awash was reported about 150 yards offshore on the S side of the bay near the entrance.* (CP)

Maple Bay lies 1.5 miles north of Tombstone Bay at the foot of Mt. Tourney. The bay offers good protection from southerlies if you tuck just inside Columbia Point on the south end, and moderate protection from northerlies behind Maple Point on the north end. Avoid the rocks near shore.

On our last visit, there were three mobile homes on log floats moored in the bay. An old cabin and pilings from a former pier are located at the north end of the bay. Several streams and waterfalls drop from snow fields on Mt. Tourney.

Anchor in 3 fathoms off the edge of the drying bank over stone and gravel with poor holding. Be sure to check the set of your anchor.

## **Fords Cove** (Portland Canal)

Fords Cove is 35.9 miles north of Whiskey Bay.

Chart 17425
Entrance: 55°37.80′ N, 130°06.02′ W
Anchor (small boats): 55°37.67′ N, 130°05.84′ W

> *Fords Cove, on the E shore just N of Green Islets, is a bight in the shore affording fair shelter from S winds but none from N winds. A rocky ledge, which partly bares, extends N about 75 yards from Green Islets. The S part of the cove is shoal for about 175 yards offshore. A fair anchorage with sufficient swinging room may be found in 13 fathoms, 0.2 mile from Green Islets and the same distance from the E shore. Small craft can anchor closer inshore.* (CP)

Fords Cove, directly west of the hanging glacier described above, affords good protection in southerly weather. Small boats can also anchor between the float and the sandy beach in 3 fathoms; larger boats can anchor just outside the float in 5 to 7 fathoms.

Anchor (small boats) in 3 fathoms over sand with very good holding.

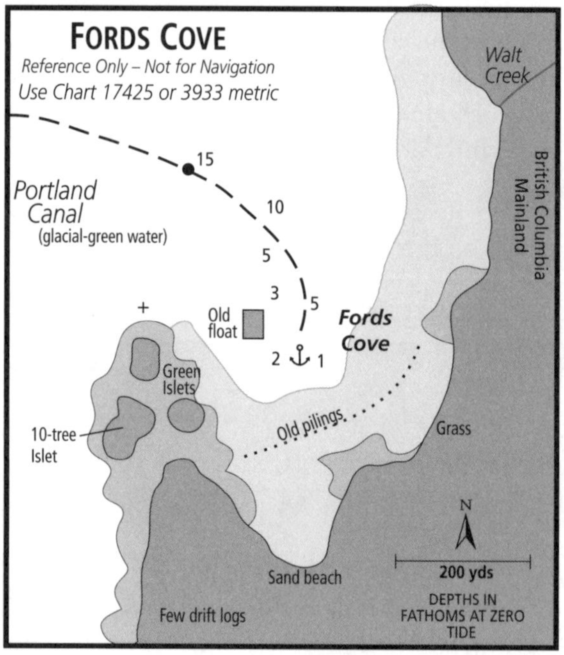

*Anchored safely in Glacier Cove*

## **Turquoise Cove** (Portland Canal)

Turquoise Cove is 43.5 miles north of Whiskey Bay.

Chart 17425
Entrance: 55°45.36′ N, 130°08.12′ W
Anchor: 55°45.20′ N, 130°07.97′ W

What we call "Turquoise Cove," on the east side of Portland Canal, 0.5 mile south of Round Point, can provide anchorage for one small boat only. It is out of the southerly chop and has good protection from most summer weather. The V-shaped cove is deep, with continuous shoaling to the small beach at its head. A stern-tie to shore is recommended.

You have a first-class view of high snowfields on the mountains to the west, and the color of the water is an exquisite light turquoise, thus our name for it. However, visibility through the water is only about a foot.

Anchor in the head of the cove in about 5 fathoms over soft silt with fair holding.

## **Glacier Cove** (Portland Canal)

Glacier Bay and Cove is 47.4 miles north of Whiskey Bay.

Chart 17425
Entrance: 55°49.13′ N, 130°07.55′ W
Anchor (east cove): 55°49.38′ N, 130°07.08′ W
Anchor (west bay): 55°49.44′ N, 130°07.61′ W

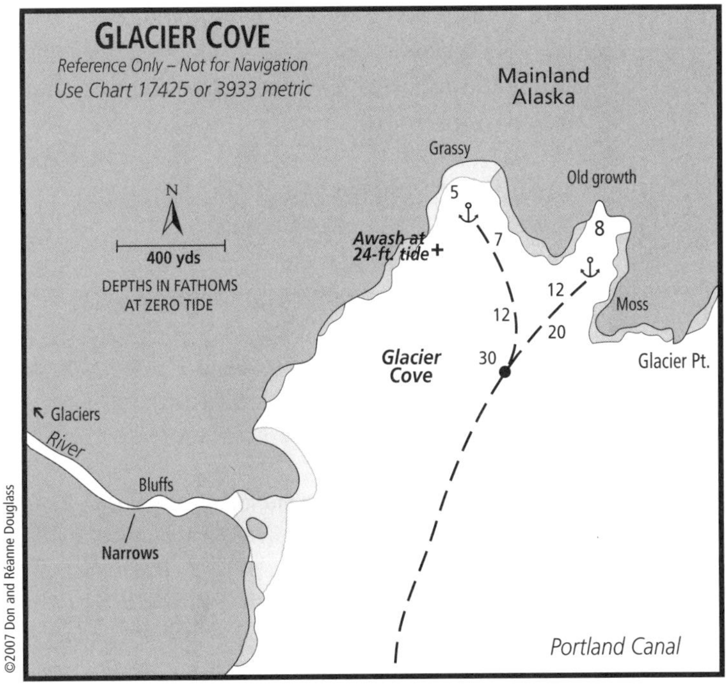


The large bay south of Glacier Point is known locally as Glacier Bay; we call it Glacier Cove, however, in order not to confuse it with Glacier Bay National Park. The cove has two possibilities for anchorage in stable weather or downslope winds. The easterly cove, just behind Glacier Point, is steep-to close to a rocky shore with room for one or two boats in about 7 fathoms. A stern-tie to shore can be used effectively here.

The western part of the bay is steep-to and more open, with swinging room for a number of boats. Water visibility is limited to about a foot due to glacier silt from the large glacier to the northwest. Both anchor sites are completely open to the south.

An unnamed river enters the south end of Glacier Cove through a 40-foot cleft in a 100-foot-high cliff. It's an impressive sight to view from a dinghy. *Caution:* shoal water exists a quarter-mile off the shore of the river, contrary to what is indicated on the chart. The waters here take a close second in beauty to Turquoise Cove.

Anchor (east cove) in 9 fathoms over sand or glacial silt, with fair holding.

Anchor (west bay) in 7 fathoms over sand or glacial silt, with fair holding.

## **Marmot Bay** (Portland Canal)

Marmot Bay is 51.5 miles north of Whiskey Bay.

**Chart 17425**
**Position: 55°53.09′ N, 130°00.41′ W**

> *There is a government landing float at Marmot Bay, 0.5 mile northeastward of Lion Point, with a depth of 18 feet alongside at the southern end and 9 feet at the northern end.* (CP)

Marmot Bay, on the Canadian side of Portland Canal, is 2 miles south of Stewart. Although it offers some protection from downslope winds, the bay is largely filled with log booms, float houses, and steel dolphins. Consider temporary moorage tied to the boomsticks. This is a place to stay only if fog develops and you have no radar, or if you don't want to approach Hyder or Stewart in poor visibility.

## **Hyder** (Portland Canal)

Hyder is 52.7 miles north of Whiskey Bay.

**Chart 17425**
**Float position: 55°54.22′ N, 130°00.64′ W**

> *Hyder, on the Alaska side of the boundary, is a community occupying the flats off the mouth of the Salmon River and extends up the valley. A 1,252-foot-long trestle with a small dock at its outer end extends SE over the mudflats from Eagle Point. . . . A 150-foot-long small-craft float with a seaplane float at its outer end extends SW from the dock; the community operates the floats. A small-boat harbor . . . is just NE of the trestle. A buoy marks the entrance to the harbor.*
>
> *Hyder, and Stewart, B.C., about 2 miles to the N, are connected by a shore road.* (CP)

Hyder advertises itself as the friendliest ghost town in Alaska. The Orthodox Church with its golden ornaments is the most attractive building in town. There are a couple of sourdough saloons. The town, with its pot-holed road, largely exists as a duty-free zone for Stewart residents, and a waypoint for Salmon Glacier, some 30 miles up the Salmon River. Ketchikan, Alaska, has the nearest customs and immigration facilities; there are none in Hyder.

The State of Alaska upgraded the Hyder floats in recent years, installed new pilings and a seaplane dock and has dredged the harbor. However, the area is still subject to shoaling and cruising boats are advised to enter at high tide; at low tide a boat may find its keel aground. There are no amenities at the floats.

Hyder's main attraction is its remoteness and one or two saloons where tourists go to get "Hyderized" (i.e., drunk)! A road connects the community to Stewart, approximately two miles to the north.

## **Stewart** (Portland Canal)

Stewart is 53.6 miles north of Whiskey Bay.

**Chart 17425**
**Entrance (Stewart Yacht Club public float): 55°55.20′ N, 130°00.47′ W**

> *Stewart, at the head of Portland Canal, is the northernmost deep-sea port in British Columbia. The principal industries are mining, logging and tourism. . . .*
>
> *Anchorage may be obtained off Stewart in 25 to 30 fathoms (46 to 55 m) over a soft mud bottom that provides good holding ground. The anchorage is exposed to the north and south winds that frequently draw through Portland Canal. Caution is require approaching the anchorage*

Réanne Hemingway-Douglass

*Stewart: public dock and yacht club floats*

> *because the drying flats to the north and west are steep-to and are covered except at the very lowest stages of the tide. . . .*
>
> *The public wharf, close NW of the bulk terminal* [not in use], *is 296 feet (90 m) long with depths alongside of 18 feet (5.6 m) at the south end and 30 feet (9 m) at the north end. . . .*
>
> *The public float, operated by the Stewart Harbour Authority, north of the public wharf, has 150 feet (46) m) of berthing space with a depth of 16 feet (4.9 m). The east end of the float is reserved for aircraft. Power is laid on the floats and they are protected by floating log breakwaters. The Stewart Yacht Club has two floats attached to the south side of the public float. . . . Fresh water is not available at any of the wharves or floats. Gasoline and diesel fuel can be obtained in town.* (SD)

The beautiful setting of Stewart and the upper canal make the lengthy cruise up Portland Canal worthwhile. The mountains become more precipitous, glaciers are more prominent, and waterfalls increase. As you approach the head of the canal and pass Marmot Bay, Bear Glacier comes into view, looming high above the town and its harbor. Stewart, like so many former logging and mining towns, is struggling to survive through tourism. Its attractions are Bear and Salmon Glaciers, Fish Creek Wildlife Viewing Area, fresh- or saltwater sport fishing and the town's similarity to the Arctic, which has drawn a number of filmmakers in recent years. Although most visitors arrive by automobile on Highway 37A, curious cruising boaters are beginning to wend their way up Portland Canal.

About 600 residents make their home in Stewart and they welcome visitors. The Stewart Yacht Club has a locked gate with a barbed wire fence, so if you wish to stay there, make prior arrangements by calling the Harbor Lights General Store at (tel. 250.636.2626). The floats have electricity but no other amenities (including water). It's just a short walk into town, where you can find provisions, post office, gift shops and an eatery or two. For weather conditions in the area, CBC broadcasts radio reports. However, you probably won't be able have reception until you're nearly to the end of the Portland Canal and can see for yourself.

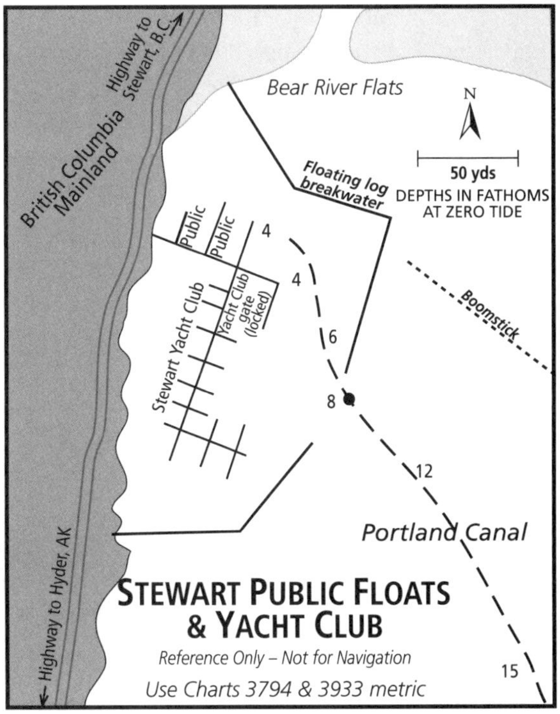

©2007 Don and Réanne Douglass

Stewart is connected by road to Hyder, Alaska, and the residents come and go freely. However, there is no U.S. Customs clearance in Hyder. Canadian Customs clearance is available by phone through Prince Rupert, but any vessels coming from Alaska should contact Prince Rupert ahead of time for the possibility of clearing in Stewart.

Long-term plans for improving the harbor are on the drawing boards as we go to press.

For additional information, contact the Stewart-Cassiar Tourism council at (tel. 866.417.3737) or see online the Stewart-Hyder Community Website: www.stewart-hyder.com.

# SOUTHEAST ALASKA

## Nakat Bay

Nakat Bay, immediately east of Cape Fox, is 9 miles north of Dundas Island.

Chart 17437
Southwest entrance (0.84 mile southeast of Fox Island): 54°45.27′ N, 130°49.45′ W

*Nakat Bay, making N between Cape Fox and Tongass Island, is the entrance to Nakat Inlet and the W approach to Port Tongass. The bay does not afford anchorage.* (CP)

Don Douglass

*Old boilers in Nakat Harbor gather moss.*

## Harry Bay

Harry Bay is 2.5 miles northwest of Port Tongass.

Chart 17437
Entrance (0.17 mile east of south point of Slim Island): 54°47.94′ N, 130°46.50′ W

*Harry Bay, on the NW side of Nakat Bay, is deep and exposed to the SE. Slim Island is close to the W shore at the entrance. A boat passage is between the island and the mainland, but the island shore must be kept close aboard, because the W half of the passage is foul.* (CP)

## Nakat Inlet

Nakat Inlet, northeast of Nakat Bay, is 4.7 miles northeast of Cape Fox.

Chart 17437
Entrance (0.16 mile west of Surprise Point): 54°49.13′ N, 130°44.06′ W
Anchor (8.3 miles north of Surprise Point): 54°57.41′ N, 130°45.06′ W

*Nakat Inlet extends in a N direction for about 8 miles. The shores are steep and heavily wooded to the water's edge. The main inlet is deep and affords no anchorage except near its head. The group of small, wooded islands near the head of the inlet provides shelter for small craft. Anchorage may be had in 8 to 13 fathoms. The inlet is clear of obstructions except near its head or close inshore.* (CP)

Anchorage can be found at the head of the inlet, northwest of three islets, off the drying sand flat.

Anchor in 8 fathoms over sand and mud.

## Nakat Harbor, Baidarka Arm

(Nakat Inlet)

Nakat Harbor is 2.8 miles northeast of Port Tongass.

Chart 17437
Entrance (southwest arm Nakat Harbor, 0.58 mile southeast of Surprise Point): 54°48.67′ N, 130°43.15′ W
Anchor (1.35 miles southeast of Surprise Point): 54°47.79′ N, 130°43.54′ W

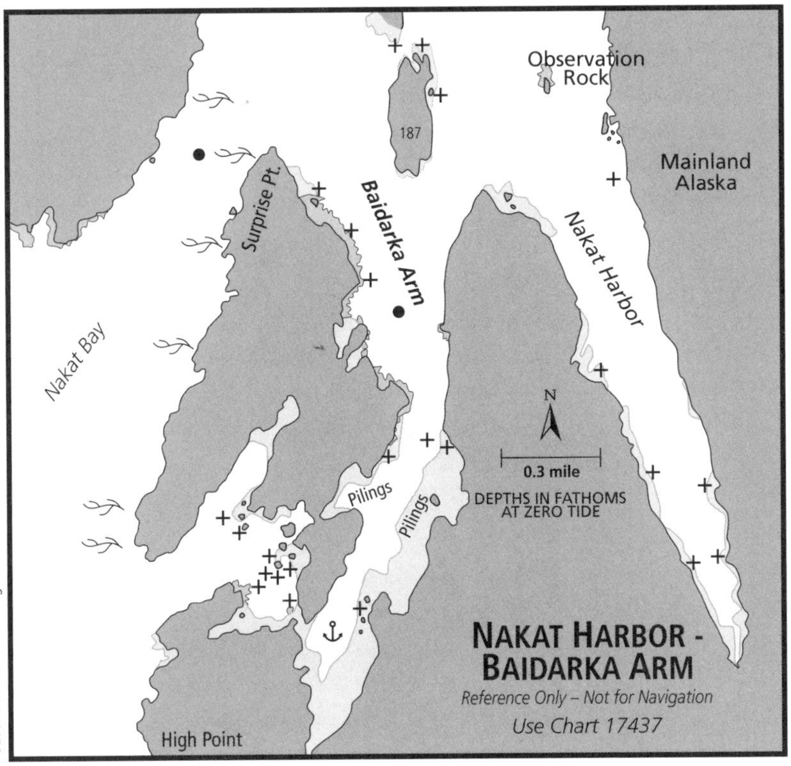




*Nakat Harbor makes off from the SE part of Nakat Inlet and is separated from it by a chain of wooded islands. . . . In the S part of the harbor, about halfway up the arm, off a small bight having a gravel beach, anchorage and shelter for vessels of moderate size may be found in 19 fathoms. The N arm of Nakat Harbor also has anchorage, but poor shelter.*

*The best channel for entering Nakat Harbor is SE of the southeasternmost islet of the chain separating it from Nakat Inlet.*

*Excellent anchorage may be had in 18 fathoms, mud bottom, in the SW arm of Nakat Harbor, about 0.6 mile SE of Surprise Point. Passage to the head of this arm is obstructed by a rock baring 3 feet in the middle of the constricted part of the arm. Small vessels should favor the W shore to avoid the rock and the extensive flats along the E shore. At high water the SW arm is connected with the small bight, about 0.7 mile N of the daybeacon on Tongass Reef, by a narrow passage that is obstructed by trees and is only navigable by small boats.* (CP)

The un-named arm in the southwest end of Nakat Inlet is what we call "Baidarka Arm." The lower two-thirds of this arm is shallow and constricted, however, excellent shelter from southeast weather can be found at the head of the arm.

The fairway is narrow and winding and an approach should be made slowly with a bow watch and using a depth sounder alarm. The small scale of the chart does not show all hazards. The first half of the fairway is 4 to 5 fathoms minimum; favor the west shore. The last third of the fairway is 2 to 3 fathoms; also favor the west shore. Because the depths change due to creeks flowing into the vicinity, you are on your own to identify the fairway and find your route to the anchorage. There is a dinghy passage at high water that can be used to enter Nakat Bay.

Anchor in 2 to 3 fathoms over soft brown mud with clam shells and twigs; very good holding.

## **Fox Island Cove** (Fox Island)

Fox Island Cove is 3.8 miles southeast of Tree Point Light.

**Charts 17437, 17434**
**Entrance: 54°45.83′ N, 130°50.40′ W**
**Anchor: 54°45.96′ N, 130°50.77′ W**

*A small boat channel between Fox Island and the cape is narrow and crooked, and should not be attempted without local knowledge. The channel has many piles and is used as a log storage area. A rock awash is about 500 yards ENE from the E tip of Fox Island, a small island about 0.2 mile off Cape Fox.* (CP)

Fox Island Cove—the small boat channel off Cape Fox—has provided comfortable anchorage in moderate weather for us. Although technically not a cove, when you are tucked inside, it has the feel of a cove. It makes a good lunch

## AVOIDING FISH NETS WHILE UNDERWAY

Linda Lewis and Dave Parker—M/V *Royal Sounder*

No one wants to have a "fishing-net-meets-prop" encounter. Good vigilance at the helm means being ever-watchful for fishing vessels with their nets deployed. OK, how do you know what vessels to look for? And what strategies can you use to spot and avoid the nets?

Although there are many types of fishing vessels in SE Alaska waters, the most likely ones a cruiser will encounter are gill netters and purse seiners, with the former being your biggest challenge.

Both vessels use a weighted net that extends down into the water from a "float line." Small, usually white, floats, which are only about six inches long, are dispersed along the float line. The small floats create a major challenge. Spotting them running along the water's surface can be very difficult, especially when the water is choppy or when you are looking into the sun.

Gill net fishing vessels are usually 30–40 feet long with a large drum on the stern to deploy and store the net. The float line, with its net hanging below it, is strung along the water in a more or less straight line, with one end remaining attached to the boat. Often after sitting awhile in the current, this line takes on a snake-like configuration along the top of the water. The "free" end of the float line usually has a large, orange, ball-shaped float. The goal is to avoid going between the fishing vessel and the orange float at the end of the net. When you see more than one gill netter in an area, you need to figure out which orange ball goes with which fishing vessel. Here's a tip we received from a fisherman: If you can't see enough of the float line to determine where it is coming from, very carefully head directly towards the big orange ball. As you get closer you will be able to determine what boat the net is leading from and steer a path to avoid it.

*This is how small the net-floats are—hard to spot in the water.*

*Gill netter's large orange ball—but where are the net floats?*

Purse seiners are larger vessels; about 50–60 feet long. They can be identified by the large "crane-like" power block used to winch the net onboard and there is always a skiff that helps set the net. The net is deployed in approximately a circle. This deployment (or "set") is usually done relatively close to shore. The proximity to shore and the (approximately) circular pattern of the set make these nets easier for the cruiser to spot.

The Alaska Deptartment of Fish and Game has a small brochure with pictures of these (and other) fishing vessels in PDF format that you can print out and carry with you on your boat. Go to: http://cf.adfg.state.ak.us/geninfo/about/faq/cf_faq.php#PurseSeiners.

*(Continued on next page)*

*(Continued from previous page)*

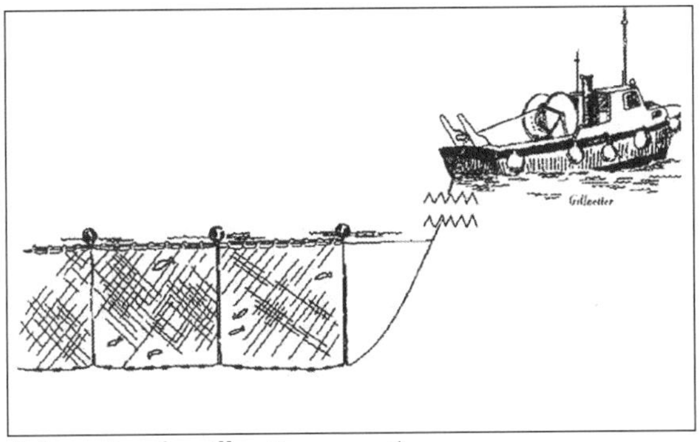

*Schematic of a gill netter operation*

*A small white line of floats snakes from the gill netting vessel to the large ball.*

*Schematic of a purse seiner operation*

*Purse seiner checking gear*

Photos: Linda Lewis

Schematics: Courtesy of Alaska Department of Fish and Game

stop and it is a favorite layover spot for kayakers doing the coast. Enter from the east, avoiding the charted mid-channel rock. The west entrance is chock-full of kelp that provides shelter in prevailing northwest winds.

Anchor on the north side of Fox Island in 2 to 3 fathoms over sand and mud with good holding.

## Boat Harbor

Boat Harbor is 1.2 miles southeast of Tree Point Light.

**Chart 17434**

**Position: 54°47.37′ N, 130°54.67′ W**

> *Boat Harbor, about 2.7 miles NW of Cape Fox, is a small cove forming a poor shelter for boats. It is badly exposed to SW. Two small wooded islets are at the entrance, and the best passage for small boats is between these islets. Near the middle of the N entrance is a rock that bares 5 feet.* (CP)

Temporary anchorage can be found near Boat Harbor; swells break on rocks both on the shore and offshore, giving the area an ominous appearance and making it very dangerous in foul weather. We do not consider Boat Harbor any kind of shelter from stormy weather and would push on to Foggy Bay to the north or Brundige Inlet to the south. In an emergency, head for Fox Island Cove, the small boat channel off Cape Fox described above, or the near perfect shelter found in Baidarka Arm of Nakat Bay, due south of Nakat Inlet.

## Revillagigedo Channel

Revillagigedo Channel connects East Dixon Entrance to Ketchikan.

Chart 17420
South Entrance (Tree Point Light brg 090°T): 54°48.20′ N, 131°01.35′ W
North Entrance (Potter Rock brg 090°T at 0.25 Nm): 55°18.09′ N, 131°35.11′ W

*Revillagigedo Channel and Tongass Narrows* (chart 17428) *are connecting bodies of water that have a combined length of about 53 miles from their junction with Dixon Entrance at Tree Point Light to their junction with Clarence Strait at Guard Islands Light. On their S side they connect with Clarence Strait through Felice Strait and Nichols Passage.*

*Revillagigedo Channel extends in a general NW direction from Dixon Entrance for about 40 miles to Tongass Narrows. . . . From its entrance to Bold Island, Revillagigedo Channel is broad and comparatively free of dangers. . . . Above Bold Island, the channel is narrow in places, but the principal dangers are marked by buoys and lights. No difficulty should be experienced in passing through in clear weather.* (CP)

## Tree Point

Tree Point is 10.4 miles north of Dundas Island.

Chart 17434
Tree Point waypoint (1 mile west of Tree Point Light): 54°48.17′ N, 130°57.81′ W

*Tree Point, low and timbered, has a rocky and steep-to shore. The shoreline from Cape Fox to Tree Point is very irregular and studded with many wooded islets and bare rocks. Because of the irregular bottom and inshore dangers this section of the coast should be given a berth of not less than 0.5 mile. The small bight at Tree Point affords no shelter from S seas.* (CP)

A shoal and foul area extending a half-mile or so offshore southeast of Tree Point causes the prevailing westerly swells to heap up. Keep well clear of the area in limited visibility. During fishing season, gill netters set an extensive series of nets close to Tree Point where there's excellent salmon fishing, so be alert for their nets. Between Cape Fox and Tree Point you can make faster time by staying west of the action and following the 40- to 50-fathom curve.

Réanne Hemingway-Douglass

*Cove at Gilanta Rocks*

## Gilanta Rocks

Gilanta Rocks are 2.75 miles northwest of Tree Point Light.

Chart 17434
Entrance: 54°50.89′ N, 130°56.84′ W
Anchor: 54°50.75′ N, 130°56.39′ W

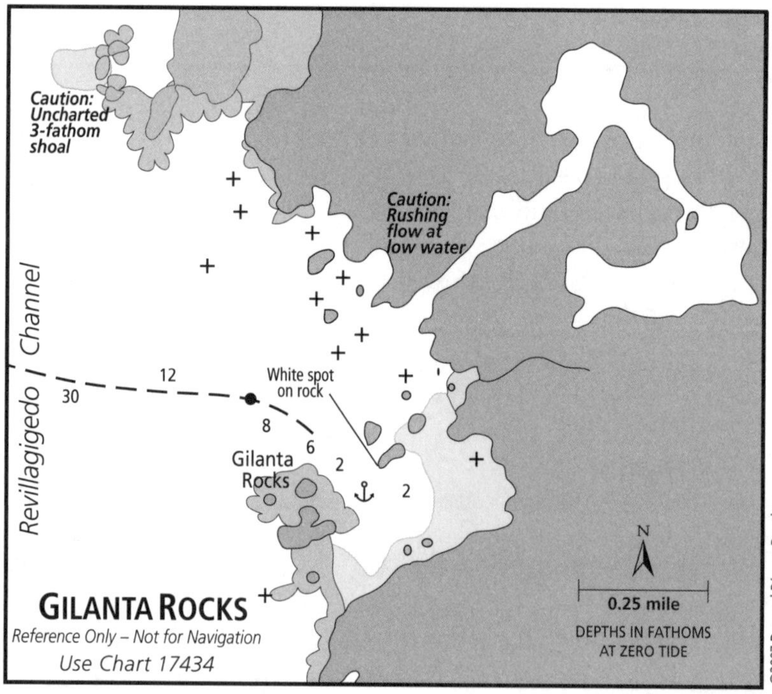

Behind Gilanta Rocks, there's an intriguing cove that makes a great lunch stop in fair weather. A lovely sand beach rings the cove, and old-growth forest is thick above the beach. According to Don's uncle who canoed the Inside Passage in 1936, this beach was the largest expanse he and his friends had come across since Puget Sound. At that time, there were also a number of totems still standing in the village site above the beach. The totems have long been removed to museums, but, as you explore the clearings behind the beach, you can imagine the marvelous culture that once thrived here.

Hike the beach, walk inside the forest or climb on the outlying rocks, but beware—we found fresh bear and wolf tracks on shore.

Enter from the north of Gilanta Rocks, passing close to a rock with white paint on its leading edge. There is good fair-weather anchorage anywhere from this rock to the sandy beach.

Anchor in 2 fathoms over sand and grass with fair-to-good holding.

## Foggy Bay, Outer Cove

Foggy Bay, Outer Cove is 7.9 miles north of Tree Point Light.

Chart 17434 (inset)
Entrance: 54°56.40′ N, 130°58.92′ W
Anchor: 54°56.00′ N, 130°56.86′ W

> *Foggy Bay is a wide indentation in the shore between Foggy Point and Kirk Point.*
>
> *The S part of the bay is used considerably by fishing boats and affords safe anchorage for small craft in its SE and E ends. . . . As practically all the dangers are covered at high tide, it is recommended that this bay be entered at low tide when the reefs are visible.* (CP)

Foggy Bay, the first and best anchorage north of Dixon Entrance, offers very good protection in most weather. Since its entrance is encumbered with rocks and reefs, you should always consult the inset on Chart 17434 before entering and use extreme caution.

Fishing boats use the outer cove in the southeast corner of Foggy Bay for convenient anchorage, and that site gets crowded at times. Most cruising boats head for the inner cove. Although it takes longer to enter and is more intricate, it offers complete shelter from all chop.

Some cruisers become complacent about their exit strategy for a harbor after experiencing a successful entry. Be particularly careful in Foggy Bay when making your exit from the inner cove when you plan to head north to Ketchikan. Plot your course from the Inner Cove to Revillagigedo Channel carefully to avoid the numerous rocks and reefs in the outer bay area. Exit Foggy Bay using the same course by which you entered it. Then, when you reach Revillagigedo Channel, turn north. This strategy will keep you away from the rocks and reef. In recent years, at least three cruising boats have hit these rocks with very serious consequences.

Note that the bay is called "Foggy Bay" for obvious reasons—be ready. Foggy Bay is also a favorite commercial fishing area. (See the sidebar in this chapter for tips on "Avoiding Fish Nets While Underway.") You should also anticipate the westerly swell from Dixon Entrance that you will encounter as you exit Foggy Bay and start your trip north in Revillagigedo Channel, a condition that will place you in beam seas if you head directly north. Particularly if you do not have stabilizers, you may have a much more comfortable trip if you proceed in a more westerly direction from Foggy Bay towards Duke Island, then turn north as you gain the protection of its lee shore.

*Special entertainment—throw a fish in the water and watch a nearby eagle swoop down to pick it up.*

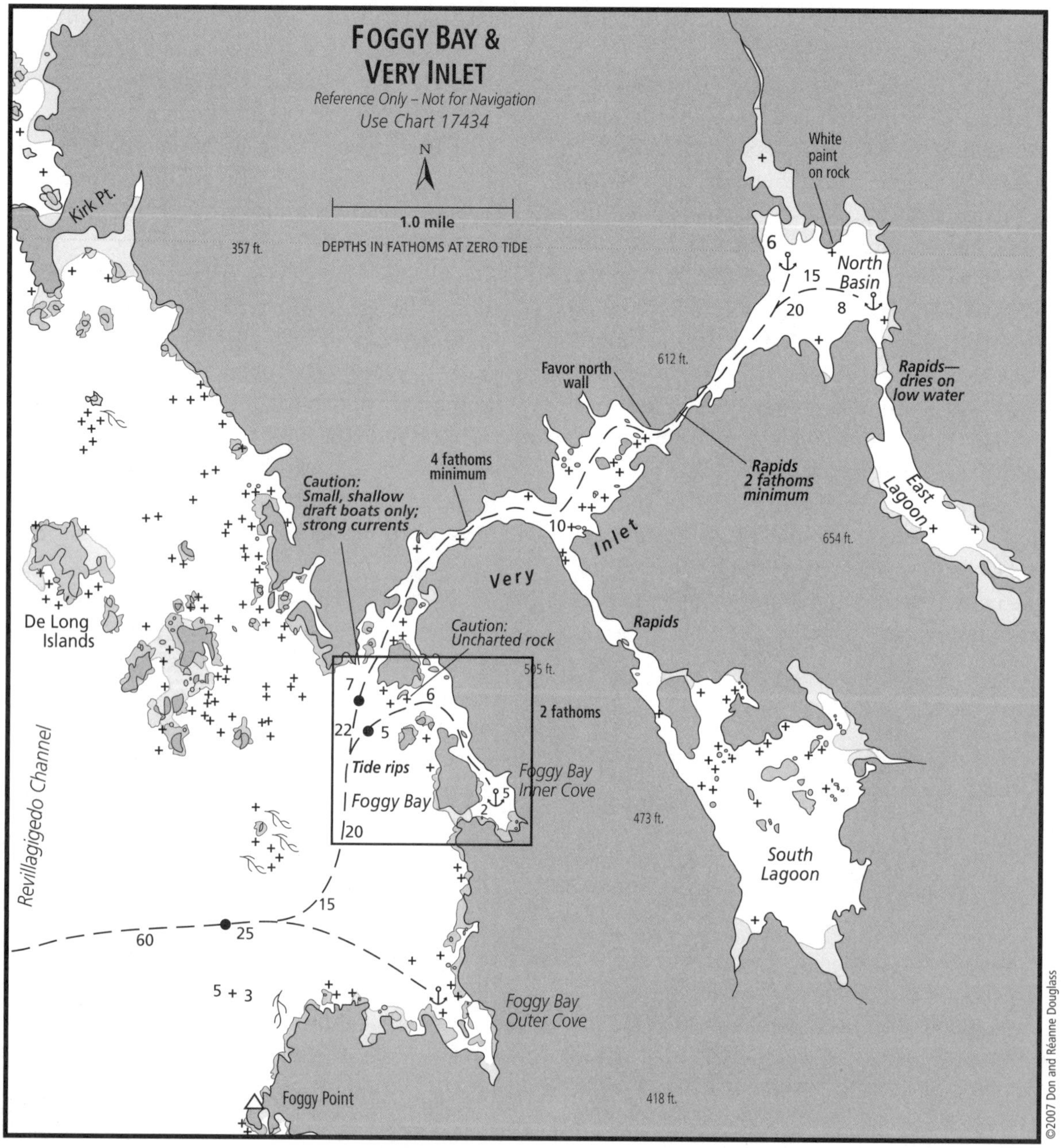


Anchor (Outer Cove) in 5 fathoms, deep in the southeast corner over mud and gravel with fair holding.

## Foggy Bay, Inner Cove

Foggy Bay, Inner Cove, is 8.8 miles north of Tree Point Light.

Chart 17434 (inset)
Entrance: 54°57.41′ N, 130°57.47′ W
Anchor: 54°57.00′ N, 130°56.48′ W

*Excellent anchorage for small craft can be had in the E head of Foggy Bay behind a large wooded island close to shore, about 1 mile SE of the entrance to Very Inlet. Use the N entrance as the S opening bares at half tide.* (CP)

After crossing Dixon Entrance, Foggy Bay's inner cove is a good place to unwind. The harbor on the far eastern side of the bay is well protected from all weather and receives no

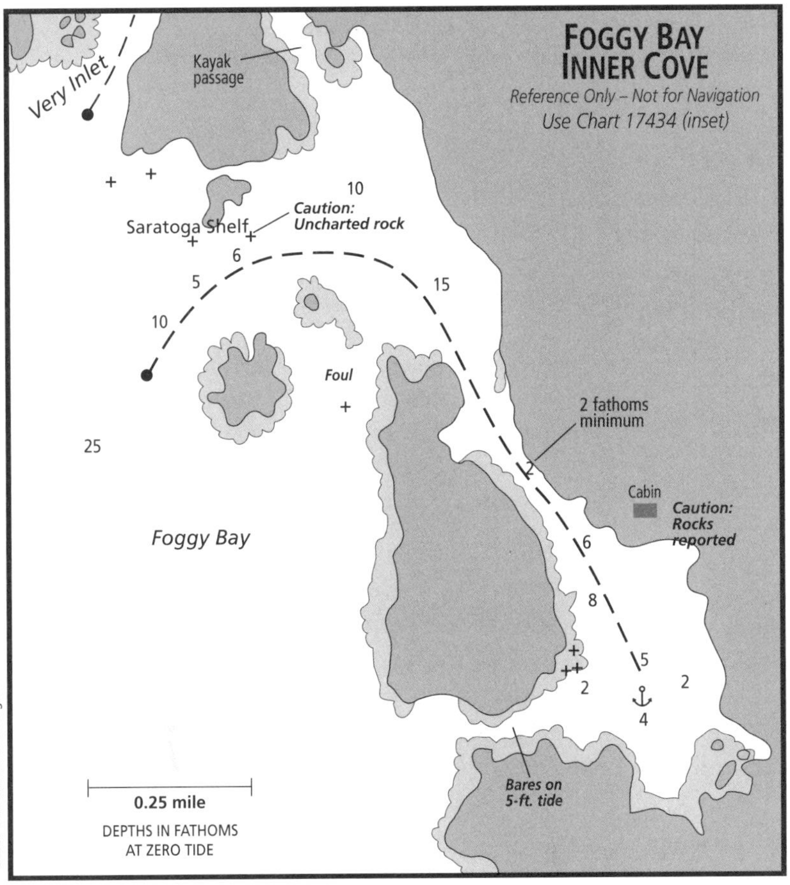



swell or chop. Rainforest surrounds the basin, and wildlife, including bear and little martens, poke about its shores searching for food.

Entrance to the inner cove is a bit tricky and requires a cautious approach with sharp lookouts. As you head northeast for the small, round island with tall cedar trees, avoid Saratoga Shelf on your port. An uncharted rock is located at 54°57.52' N, 130°57.24' W. (Leave this shelf well to your north.) Loop around the small island and the reef on its east side before turning south through a narrow, shallow channel. *Caution:* depths may be reported incorrectly on electronic charts. The protected anchorage lies behind the long ham-shaped island on the extreme east side of the bay. Note that there have also been uncharted rocks reported at the anchor site off the cabin.

Anchor in 4 to 6 fathoms over sand and mud with good holding.

## Very Inlet

Very Inlet is 9.5 miles north of Tree Point Light.

Chart 17434
Entrance: 54°57.63′ N, 130°57.69′ W
Anchor (North Basin, west side): 54°59.81′ N, 130°54.00′ W

*Very Inlet, a narrow arm that extends NE, has its entrance on the E side of Foggy Bay 2.2 miles N of Foggy Point. . . . The ebb current flows over the rapids in the narrowest part of the [first SE] branch for about 2 hours after low water. The passage has been made by a small vessel drawing 8 feet, but it should only be attempted at high-water slack. In entering, pass E of the ledge just within the opening.*

*At the head of Very Inlet is a small basin much used by fishing boats.* (CP)

Very Inlet is a good place for a day's exploration by small boat, dinghy or kayak, however the route is narrow and currents can be strong. Paddling quietly along the

Linda Lewis

*The narrow entrance to Foggy Bay's Inner Cove has been successfully maneuvered.*

rocks you may come face to face with a marten or two. This is a particularly good place to experience the full sensation of a rainforest environment.

We do not recommend Very Inlet for boats over 35 feet in length and then only under favorable conditions and with an experienced crew. We suggest checking it out by dinghy first before you enter. It is safest to pass through at high-water slack, which occurs after that of Ketchikan. If you're in a kayak or a canoe, it's easy to get caught inside and have difficulty getting out until the next tide, so keep an eye on the time.

Although the entrance to Very Inlet is narrow, good water is carried through to the north basin. The fairway tends to favor the north wall, especially in the turn before the rapids. The bottom is irregular and you can expect your depth sounder to bounce around. But we have encountered no particularly shoal area, unless you turn right too soon at the small islets midway through the inlet.

The rapids carries a minimum of about 4 fathoms, and the entrance the same or more. We know of boats with a 45-foot length that have explored as far as the north basin. The rapids before the inner cove can drop a foot or more on spring tides, so use caution. The north basin has room for several boats to anchor. The water is fairly deep, and we would suggest that the water is shallower for anchoring at the two places indicated in the diagram. Note the white paint on the rock in the north basin (used as a marker), and watch for bear on the east shore. You can also spot a marten or two along the rocky shore.

We do not recommend entering the south or east lagoons. The south lagoon is shallow and has a tricky passage. The east lagoon dries on low tides, and the current flows at a high rate.

Anchor (North Basin), as indicated, in 6 to 10 fathoms over mud and rocks with fair-to-good holding.

## Kah Shakes Cove

Kah Shakes Cove is 6.5 miles north of Foggy Bay.

Chart 17434
Entrance: 55°02.90′ N, 131°00.09′ W
Anchor (outer cove): 55°02.61′ N, 130°59.90′ W
Anchor (inner cove): 55°02.37′ N, 130°59.01′ W

> *Kah Shakes Cove, a bight about 2 miles SE of the entrance to Boca de Quadra, is a good anchorage for small craft. . . . Local knowledge is essential for entering and anchoring in the cove. About 12 feet can be carried through the entrance channel between the rocky islets. The cove has excellent holding ground in sticky mud.* (CP)

Kah Shakes Cove offers very good protection from southerly storms in picturesque surroundings. A fair-weather anchorage is located outside the narrow entrance, against the north side of the island west of Kah Shakes Cove. Enter the cove from the northwest; the southwest entrance is foul. Post an alert lookout on your bow, approach slowly, and follow a careful mid-channel course between the islets and rocks that nearly close the entrance.

If you are using passive stabilizers, be sure to raise them fully before entering or exiting the cove.

Minimum depth in the fairway is about 2 fathoms, and the bottom and underwater rocks are clearly visible. Avoid the mid-cove underwater rock, as well as the two rocks to the south end of the cove.

Anchor (outer cove) in 4 fathoms over sand with fair holding.

Anchor (inner cove) in 5 to 6 fathoms over mud with very good holding.

## Bullhead Cove

Bullhead Cove is 7 miles north of Foggy Bay.

Chart 17434
Entrance: 55°03.04′ N, 130°59.90′ W
Anchor: 55°03.33′ N, 130°58.89′ W

> *Bullhead* (Bull Head) *Cove, about 0.5 mile N of Kah Shakes Cove, affords anchorage, but*

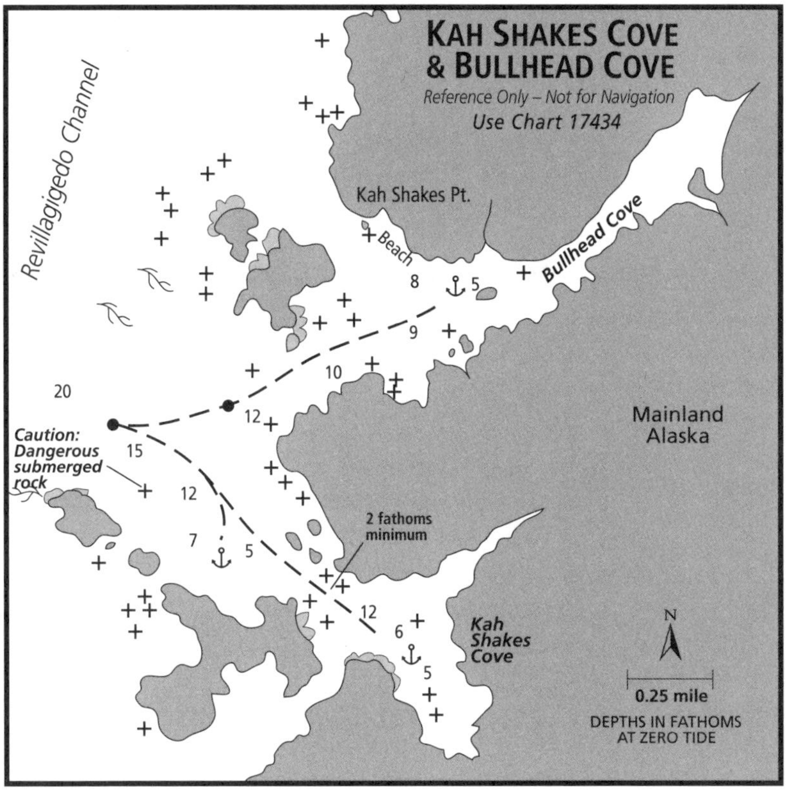



*requires local knowledge to enter. There is good holding ground in sand and mud; mooring piles have been driven in the cove. In 1976, it was reported that the mooring piles were no longer visible. The inner part of the cove is almost all bare.*

*Vessels too large to enter either Kah Shakes Cove or Bullhead Cove can find fair protection in the bight between the coves. The outer part of this bight is rough in heavy S weather; vessels should anchor as near the head as their drafts permit. The bottom is sandy.* (CP)

Bullhead Cove is another good anchorage offering very good protection in all but strong southwesterly weather. It has a fine beach on the south side of Kah Shakes Point and a deep inlet to explore by dinghy.

Bullhead is easier to enter than Kah Shakes and carries much more water. The fairway follows a mid-channel course, as indicated on the diagram. Avoid the numerous rocks en route to the anchor site. You can anchor on either side of the eastern island.

Anchor in 5 fathoms over sand and mud with good holding.

## Boca de Quadra

Boca de Quadra entrance is 6.8 miles southeast of Mary Island Light.

Charts 17434, 17427
Entrance (mid-channel between Kah Shakes and Quadra points): 55°04.64′ N, 130°59.33′ W

*Boca de Quadra has its entrance on the E side of Revillagigedo Channel between Kah Shakes Point and Quadra Point. . . . It extends NE to the flat that extends 0.8 mile from its head.* (See chart 17427.) *The sides are steep-to and densely wooded, and there are no outlying dangers.* (CP)

## **Weasel Cove** (Boca de Quadra)

Weasel Cove is 6.7 miles northeast of the Boca de Quadra entrance.

Chart 17434
Entrance: 55°08.52′ N, 130°49.80′ W
Anchor: 55°09.32′ N, 130°49.95′ W

*Weasel Cove indents the N shore . . . and affords anchorage in 17 to 19 fathoms, mud bottom, about 0.5 mile above the E point at the entrance. The entrance and anchorage are clear, but vessels must keep clear of the flat that extends 700 yards from its head.* (CP)

Anchor in 10 fathoms over a mud bottom.

## **Badger Bay** (Boca de Quadra)

Badger Bay is 7.0 miles northeast of the entrance to Boca de Quadra.

Charts 17434, 17427
Entrance: 55°08.53′ N, 130°49.22′ W

*Badger Bay, separated from Weasel Cove by a promontory, has 14 to 30 fathoms throughout its length, and there is a small flat at its head.* (CP)

## **Vixen Bay** (Boca de Quadra)

Vixen Bay is 6.4 miles east of the entrance to Boca de Quadra.

Charts 17434, 17427
Entrance (0.15 mile northwest of Gannet Island): 55°04.64′ N, 130°48.22′ W
Anchor (Gosling Island): 55°02.30′ N, 130°46.91′ W

> *Vixen Bay, entered SW of Kite Island, affords anchorage at the head about 2 miles above the entrance. In entering, the main channel is W of Gannet Island. Raven Island is close to the E shore, 1.3 miles from Gannet Island. Rocks, visible and submerged at various stages of the tide, are S of and near Raven Island.*
>
> *The anchorage is between the rocks off Raven Island and Gosling Island, which is at the head of the bay. A ledge extends 175 yards NW from the N end of Gosling Island. Local knowledge is essential in anchoring near the head of the bay.* (CP)

Anchor in about 5 fathoms.

## **Mink Bay** (Boca de Quadra)

Mink Bay is 2.8 miles northeast of the entrance to Vixen Bay.

Chart 17427
Entrance: 55°05.57′ N, 130°43.53′ W
Anchor: 55°05.11′ N, 130°43.80′ W

> *Mink Bay enters the S side of Boca de Quadra about 2 miles E of Kite Island, and has depths of 16 to 60 fathoms to near its head. Cygnet Island . . . is on the W side of the entrance. The narrow passage on the W side of the island is frequently used by small craft. A submerged rock is near midpassage about 100 yards S of the island. Grouse Rock, which bares, is about 0.2 mile S from Cygnet Island. . . . Anchorage may be found between Grouse Rock and Cygnet Island in 5-3/4 to 7 fathoms, off the old cannery site.* (CP)

Anchor in 5 to 7 fathoms in the west side passage.

## **Humpback Creek** (Mink Bay)

Humpback Creek is 0.8 mile north of the head of Mink Bay.

Chart 17427
Position: 55°02.06′ N, 130°41.52′ W

> *Humpback Creek enters from E about 0.8 mile from the head of Mink Bay and carries a flat halfway across the channel. . . . Above the flat is a secure anchorage, 0.3 mile wide, in 10 to 15 fathoms. A flat extends 700 yards from the head of the bay. Local knowledge is necessary to use this anchorage.* (CP)

Linda Lewis

*It's a male—see the narrow "arrowhead" profile on its underbelly?*

A mooring buoy and anchorage are reported to lie off the drying flat at Humpback Creek.

## **Marten Arm** (Boca de Quadra)

Marten Arm is 4.0 miles northeast of the entrance to Vixen Bay.

Chart 17427
Entrance: 55°07.01′ N, 130°42.61′ W

> *Marten Arm, entered about 1.5 miles N of the entrance to Mink Bay, has depths of 23 to 107 fathoms until near the flat that extends 0.7 mile from the head. The arm is clear but has no anchorage. Above Bactrian Point, the main NE arm of Boca de Quadra is too deep for anchorage.* (CP)

## **Duke Island**

Duke Island, on the north side of Dixon Entrance, is 8 miles west of Foggy Bay.

Chart 17434

> *Duke Island . . . between Clarence Strait and Revillagigedo Channel, is low and heavily wooded, and shows numerous round-topped hills. . . . The S and SW sides of the island should be avoided, as rocks and reefs extend about 7 miles offshore. Dangers are marked by kelp during the summer. . . . The farthest outlying dangers are Hassler Reef, West Rock, Club Rocks, Yellow Rocks, Barren Island, and a reported rocky shoal . . . about 4 miles W of West Rock.*

*Extreme magnetic disturbances, with differences of as much as 50° have been observed SE of Duke Island. The magnetic compass should not be relied upon within the area outlined in magenta on the charts.* (CP)

We like the isolation of Duke Island and find Judd Harbor and Morse Cove outstandingly secure anchorages.

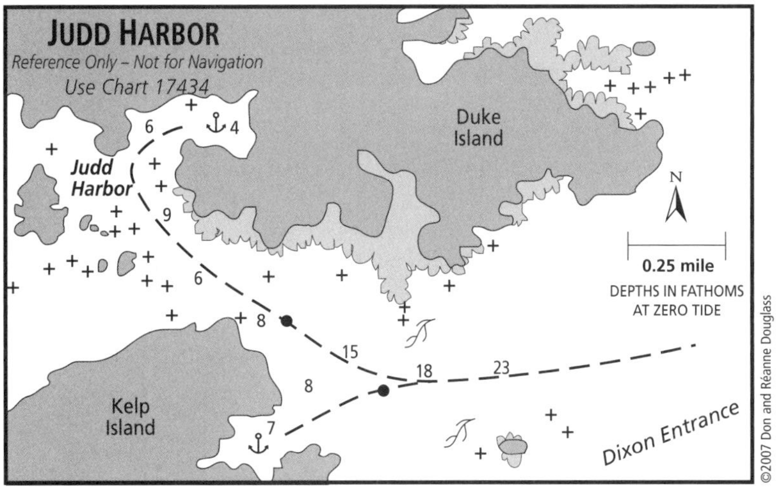


## Judd Harbor (Duke Island)

Judd Harbor, on the south side of Duke Island, is 13 miles northwest of Tree Point.

Chart 17434
Entrance (2 miles west of East Island Light): 54°52.49′ N, 131°15.27′ W
Anchor: 54°53.11′ N, 131°15.74′ W

*Judd Harbor . . . is N of the E end of Kelp Island. It offers excellent shelter with swinging room for vessels up to 175 feet long* (short scope).

*The best entrance is N of East Island. When abreast of the NE point of Kelp Island, steer midchannel toward the prominent point marking the W side of the entrance to Judd Harbor. When about to round into the bay give the point to the E a fair berth because of a submerged rock 130 yards off that point. Anchor in the center of the bay in 4 fathoms, sticky mud bottom. This anchorage is used extensively by fishing vessels during the fishing season and may be congested during that period.*

*Anchorage on the N side of Kelp Island, while good, is not recommended for use except for those with local knowledge, because the E entrance is shallow and the W entrance has numerous reefs. Currents through this passage are very strong at times.* (CP)

Pay close attention to Chart 17434 since numerous submerged rocks are on both sides of the fairway. The fairway carries 6 fathoms or more all the way into the anchorage. Kelp Island and the foul area on its north side give complete protection to Judd Harbor in all weather.

While this is an excellent anchorage, it is difficult to assess actual sea conditions outside the harbor. As always, be willing to weigh anchor and venture out, take a look and turn around and re-anchor if you don't like what you encounter.

Anchor in 4 fathoms over sand and mud with very good holding.

## Kelp Island Anchorage (Kelp Island)

Kelp Island Anchorage is 1.9 miles west of East Island Light.

Chart 17434
Entrance: 54°52.24′ N, 131°15.22′ W
Anchor: 54°52.15′ N, 131°15.58′ W

*Kelp Island Anchorage, a bight in the E end of Kelp Island, offers fair shelter for small boats. Anchorage is in 2 to 7 fathoms, rock and sand bottom. Piles have been driven along the S shore.* (CP)

Anchor in about 6 fathoms over rock and sand with fair holding if well set.

## Ray Anchorage (Duke Island)

Ray Anchorage is 9 miles west of Foggy Bay.

Chart 17434
Entrance: 54°56.25′ N, 131°12.86′ W

*Ray Anchorage, a bight in the E side of Duke Island, affords shelter from S winds, but the bottom is hard and the anchorage is open NE. Anchor about midway between the rocky patch in the entrance to Morse Cove and the point about 0.6 mile E, with the rocks bearing 277° in 10 to 22 fathoms, rocky and hard sandy bottom.* (CP)

## Morse Cove Adventure

Kris Jensen

I was on my way home to Ketchikan, with my dad aboard, in a new sailboat I'd bought in Anacortes, Washington. Although I was using your suggested "Ultra-Marathon" Itinerary [26-day trip], I had only 16-days to get back to work. (Not bad for a 5.5-knot cruise and never sailing at night!) Your book definitely played a large part in my enjoyment of this entirely too short trip, but I ran into a minor problem in Morse Cove on our next-to-last night.

My dad and I anchored overnight in Morse Cove (Duke Island) and, as we entered, I noticed the current was near 4 knots in the narrowest spot. I needed to plan my departure for near slack water the next morning to ensure I'd be able to push out against the current. Low tide on 22 June was a minus 3.75 feet at 0810 at Ketchikan, so I was concerned about the depth. My chart showed 1.25 fathoms near the rock but the diagram in your book showed 2 fathoms.

Hmmm. I figured I'd put down there at low slack and see if you were right, since I didn't want to hang around till high slack. If the chart was right I'd be right on the bottom; if you were right I'd have about 4 feet under the keel, no sweat.

So, in the morning, we head down the narrow passage just after 0800. Very quickly I notice we're moving faster than I'd like to and I throttle back. My dad is on the bow spotting the channel; the bottom is very visible as we slide by the rock. Kelp is visible all across the channel beyond the rock.

I aim for the thinnest spot. We run aground in gravel, sand and large rocks approximately 150 feet to seaward of the rock. The dink slams into the stern and fills about a quarter with water before it bounces back up and slides around to the side.

I get this great idea to spin the boat sideways and increase our drag and heel to—hopefully to lessen our draft and carry us over this high spot. Just 20 feet ahead deeper water is plainly visible. I allow the current to pull the rudder to one side and we slew quickly broadside to the current and heel approximately 20 degrees.

It feels like we're moving but it's just the rushing of the water against the hull. Yep, definitely stuck—the rudder is jammed hard over against a rock. I'm worried about it, so we stand on the bow waiting for slack water. My dad wonders aloud why we came down here at 0700 and I suddenly realize I forgot to change my watch over to Alaska time when we crossed the line! Arrggh!

We didn't see any bugs during the evening in Morse Cove. But now that we're sitting ducks, they descend in clouds as we wait on the bow. After significant loss of blood we say "screw the rudder" and run for the cabin.

At about 0815 (Alaska Time), the boat stands up and we wait for the tide to turn. Watching from the companionway hatch we see the tide reverse at 23 minutes after low slack in Ketchikan.

Now the concern is how fast the current will be running when there's enough water to float us out of the pocket our keel is now sitting in. I really don't want to be carried backwards by the current and find a big rock with my rudder.

As the current begins to flow and the boat rises, we're able to spin back around into the current with a shot of throttle against a hard-over rudder. Thirty minutes after slack we're lifted free, and I feel us slip backwards a few inches and bump another rock.

I pop the engine in gear and slowly motor forward against the current until the keel hits the sand again. I figure I'll hold it against the ground as long as possible and try to do a 180-degree turn if I can't outrun the current. Soon we're running at cruising RPM, which usually nets about 5.5 knots, and I have only a little throttle left.

My dad is up on the bow looking for a path through the rocks. He says it looks a little deeper to starboard once I get around this big rock. I back off the throttle about 3 RPM and we slide back a few feet and maneuver around a large rock. I have to go to full power to get moving forward again. Slowly, we crawl past the kelp and the large rocks toward deeper water. Finally our speed begins to increase over the ground and the depth finder has something to report.

So now, I can accurately report that on a minus 3.75-foot tide there is somewhat less than 4 foot 7 inches in the channel at Morse Cove, and it looks like the chart was closest!

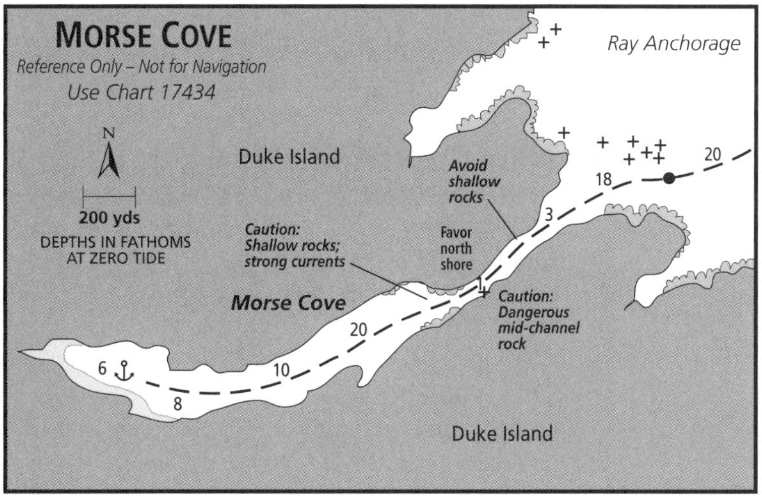


©2007 Don and Réanne Douglass

Ray Anchorage has a rocky shore and offers marginal anchorage. Protection from southerlies can be found along the south shore near the entrance to Morse Cove.

## **Morse Cove** (Duke Island)

Morse Cove, at the southwest corner of Ray Anchorage, is 10 miles west of Foggy Bay.

Chart 17434
Entrance: 54°55.78′ N, 131°13.90′ W
Anchor: 54°55.17′ N, 131°17.07′ W

> *Morse Cove, entered at the SW end of Ray Anchorage, is a landlocked harbor with varying depths and mud bottom. The entrance is very narrow and has a rock that bares 10 feet in the narrowest part, on the SE side of midchannel. The channel on the NW side of the rock is about 75 feet wide. Small craft with local knowledge can enter, preferably at low water. The entrance channel from Ray Anchorage is on the SE side of the rocky patch in its entrance. Rocks awash are between the rocky patch and the W shore.* (CP)

Morse Cove, one of our favorite anchor sites, is bombproof in all weather. The narrow entrance has rocks along its edges and a dangerous mid-channel rock. Favor the north shore as you pass through the narrows; the minimum depth in this section is about one fathom. Note that there are strong currents in the narrows on spring tides. (See the Morse Cove sidebar, p. 36.)

Once you have navigated the narrows, you enter a secure anchorage where you can spend a restful night or two. We once spent two days here with a curious Minke whale that awakened us early each morning with his blowing.

Anchor in 7 fathoms over mud and some gravel with good holding.

## **Reef Harbor** (Duke Island)

Reef Harbor is 3 miles north of Ray Anchorage.

Chart 17434
Entrance: 55°00.08′ N, 131°14.22′ W
Anchor: 54°58.78′ N, 131°15.15′ W

> *Reef Harbor is the indentation between Duck Islands, the reefs on the E, and the shore of Duke Island, S of Grave Point. . . . It has depths of 24 to 26 fathoms, mud bottom, but the swinging room is scant for the scope of chain required by this depth. Small craft may secure some protection from S weather by anchoring as close as size permits in the lee of Flag Point. Very small craft may use the wide part of the passage between the two largest of the Duck Island group, but this anchorage is not secure in S weather.* (CP)

Anchorage can be found at the head of the harbor with good protection from westerlies, but it is open to southeast weather, depending on tide level, with marginal protection from the submerged rocks.

Anchor in 10 fathoms.

## **Cat Passage**

Cat Passage lies between Duke and Dog islands on the south and Double Islands and Cat Island on the north.

Chart 17434
East entrance (0.29 mile north of Grave Point):
55°00.47′ N, 131°14.57′ W
West entrance (0.4 mile west of Double Islands):
55°00.01′ N, 131°19.34′ W

> *The best approach to Pond Bay is from Revillagigedo Channel through Cat Passage between Grave Point and three islets off the SE point of Cat Island. The best water leads about 0.3 mile*

*off Grave Point until up to a reef that extends SW from a small highwater island off the NE point of the entrance to the bay, thence it leads about midchannel. It is advisable for strangers to enter at low water and with caution. Rocks in depths of 4½ and 6 feet have been reported in the W end of Cat Passage.* (CP)

## **Pond Bay** (Duke Island)

Pond Bay is on the north side of Duke Island, 2 miles southwest of Grave Point.

Chart 17434
Entrance 54°59.78′ N, 131°17.39′ W
Anchor: 54°58.02′ N, 131°20.64′ W

*Pond Bay, SE of Dog Island between it and Duke Island, affords good anchorage when once inside, but is little used because of the dangerous approach. The entrance from Felice Strait and Dog Bay, W of Dog Island, bares about 2 feet. A 6-fathom passage leads N of Dog Island into Pond Bay, but it is obstructed by rocks and requires local knowledge to enter safely.* (CP)

Pond Bay offers very good protection in all weather. The best approach is through Cat Passage (see *Coast Pilot* description above).

Anchor in 6 fathoms over mud, shells, cobble and eel grass with fair-to-good holding.

## Danger Passage

Danger Passage (on the southwest side of Mary Island) connects Revillagigedo Channel to Felice Strait. The passage lies between Lane Island and Danger Island (and its associated reefs).

Chart 17434
East entrance (0.45 mile east of Lane Island): 55°02.07′ N, 131°12.19′ W
West entrance: 55°02.72′ N, 131°14.72′ W

*Danger Passage . . . is about 350 yards wide between the 3-fathom curves and suitable only for small craft. It is reported that the shoals in the passage are marked by kelp in the summer and fall.* (CP)

Danger Passage requires a curvilinear route to avoid the dangers southeast and west of Danger Island. It is possible that small vessels can use the narrow passage between Cat Island and Fripo Island with a minimum of 2 to 3 fathoms in the fairway; however, this passage is largely choked with kelp during the summer. Note that all dangers are marked by kelp.

## **Mary Island Anchorage** (Mary Island)

Mary Island Anchorage is 0.7 mile northwest of Mary Island Light.

Chart 17434
Entrance: 55°06.63′ N, 131°11.70′ W
Anchor: 55°06.46′ N, 131°11.73′ W

*Mary Island Anchorage is a bight in the N end of Mary Island between Point Winslow and Giant Point. It is a contracted anchorage with fair shelter from SE and SW winds, but more and better protection can be had in Custom House Cove. . . . Anchor in 12 to 15 fathoms, hard sandy bottom.* (CP)

Mary Island Anchorage, although a rather rocky site, is strategically located. We have taken refuge here in pea soup fog, but it offers protection from southerly weather only. There is a landing beach and campsite as noted in the diagram.

Entering is not a problem. Head due south, halfway between Point Winslow on the east and the islet to the west. Do not go deep into the cove—there is a reef and a rock awash at high water. Set your anchor well since the bottom is somewhat irregular.

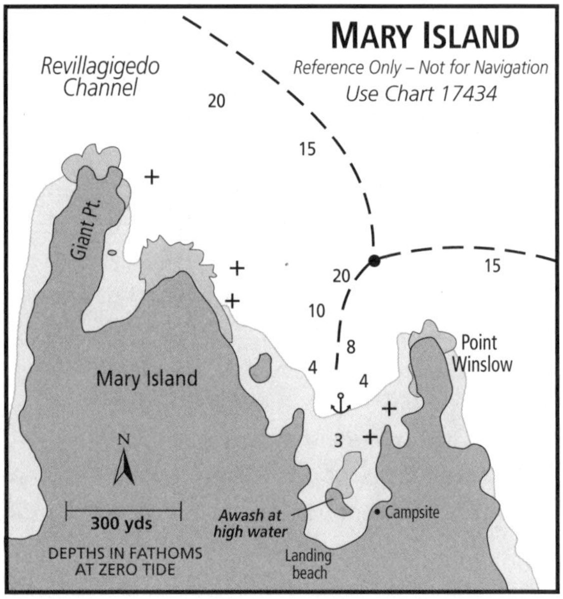

Anchor in 4 fathoms over sand and rock with fair-to-good holding.

## Felice Strait

Felice Strait joins Clarence Strait to Revillagigedo Channel. It lies between Duke, Dog, Cat, and Mary Islands on the southeast and Annette Island on the northwest.

Chart 17434
North entrance (1.5 miles west of Twin Islands Light): 55°08.54′ N, 131°15.67′ W
Southwest entrance (1.2 miles northwest of Percy Point and 1.7 miles southwest of Davison Point Light): 54°58.03′ N, 131°37.56′ W
Southwest entrance to Sealed Passage (2.7 miles southeast of Percy Point and 1.2 miles north of Bee Rocks): 54°54.60′ N, 131°34.50′ W
Northeast entrance to Sealed Passage (0.5 mile north of the north end of Vegas Islands and 0.9 mile southwest of Tamgas Reef): 54°58.73′ N, 131°26.73′ W

*Felice Strait extends from Sealed Passage to Revillagigedo Channel. . . . It offers the most direct route for vessels from the S end of Behm Canal, but is little used. There are several dangers, all charted. . . . No difficulty should be experienced in making the passage through the strait in daytime and with clear weather.*

*Currents in Felice Strait have considerable strength.* (CP)

## Customhouse Cove (Mary Island)

Customhouse Cove is 1.6 miles west of Mary Island Light.

Chart 17434
Entrance: 55°06.06′ N, 131°13.71′ W
Anchor: 55°05.69′ N, 131°13.68′ W

*Customhouse Cove is an indentation on the W side of Mary Island that affords good shelter during SE weather. The anchorage is in the middle of the cove, 300 yards from the bare ledges fringing the shore.* (CP)

Anchor in 4 fathoms.

## Village Island

Village Island is 2 miles north of Pond Bay and 6.3 miles southwest of Mary Anchorage.

Chart 17434
Entrance (0.3 mile west of the southwest tip of Cat Island): 55°01.15′ N, 131°17.43′ W
Anchor: 55°00.87′ N, 131°17.07′ W

*Village Island is low with a sand beach on all sides. During the summer, grass grows rankly around the old grave sites and decaying totem poles on the island.* (CP)

Village Island is a special place to visit, but it is poorly charted and cautious navigation is required.

Anchorage can be found 0.17 mile north of Village Island.

Anchor in 2 to 3 fathoms.

## Dog Bay (Dog Island)

Dog Bay is 3 miles east of Ryus Bay.

Chart 17434
Position: 54°59.06′ N, 131°20.45′ W

*Dog Bay, about 1.4 miles ENE of Niquette Harbor, is a small open bight with 33 fathoms at the entrance, 17 fathoms near the head, and 13 to 15 fathoms in the SE corner. Rocks are off the E and W shores.* (CP)

## Niquette Harbor (Duke Island)

Niquette Harbor, on the northwest side of Duke Island, is 1.5 miles east of Ryus Bay.

Chart 17434
Entrance: 54°58.68′ N, 131°22.96′ W
Anchor: 54°58.35′ N, 131°23.14′ W

*Niquette Harbor . . . is about 0.3 mile wide at the widest part. It extends about 0.5 mile in a SW direction, narrowing to an inlet that dries, about 0.5 mile long. A submerged rock is 100 yards off the E shore of the narrowest part of the entrance to the harbor, and a rock awash is opposite close to the W shore. Favor the W shore in entering. Anchorage for very small craft may be had in 4 to 6 fathoms in the bight within the entrance.* (CP)

Anchor in 5 fathoms.

## Ryus Bay (Duke Island)

Ryus Bay, on the northwest corner of Duke Island, is 6 miles south of Tamgas Harbor and 7 miles northwest of Judd Harbor.

Chart 17434 (inset)
Entrance: 54°58.37′ N, 131°25.51′ W
Anchor: 54°57.80′ N, 131°25.20′ W

*Ryus Bay is . . . about 1.4 miles E of Vegas Islands. It is easy of access and well-sheltered, and affords excellent anchorage for small craft in 10 fathoms, mud bottom.* (CP)

Enter Ryus Bay between Form Point and Goose Tongue Island. Anchor northwest of Roy Island at the south end of the bay.

Anchor in 8 fathoms over sand and shells with fair-to-good holding.

## Percy Islands

Percy Islands are 5 miles southwest of Tamgas Harbor and 5 miles west of Ryus Bay.

**Chart 17434**
**Anchor (northeast of island 270): 54°56.61′ N, 131°35.02′ W**

*Percy Islands are a large number of low wooded islands on the NW side of Sealed Passage. The passages between these islands are not navigable except for very small craft with local knowledge. Anchorage can be had either NE or SW of the southernmost island.* (CP)

## Harris Island

Harris Island, off the northwest tip of Hotspur Island, is 2.8 miles east of Point Davison Light.

**Charts 17435, 17434**
**Anchor (0.22 mile southeast of the Harris Island Light): 55°00.16′ N, 131°31.78′ W**

*Along the N shore of this island are considerable quantities of kelp that should be given a berth of at least 150 yards in rounding the island. Fair anchorage in 6 to 12 fathoms, sandy bottom, can be had 0.2 mile NE of Harris Island.* (CP)

Anchor in 3 fathoms over sand and shells with rocks and kelp. Fair holding.

## Tamgas Harbor (Annette Island)

Tamgas Harbor, on the southwest side of Annette Island, is 11 miles west of Mary Island and 25 miles northeast of Cape Chacon.

**Charts 17435, 17434**
**Entrance (0.32 mile west of Mule Rock Light and 0.35 mile east of Grass Rock): 55°01.30′ N, 131°31.39′ W**
**Anchor (0.35 mile northwest of Crab Point): 55°04.22′ N, 131°33.59′ W**

*Tamgas Harbor has its entrance about 1.5 miles N of Harris Island. It is a landlocked anchorage suitable for small and moderate-sized craft. . . . The depths are generally good except near the SW shore, which is shoal.*

*The best anchorage is in 6 fathoms in the middle of the basin, about 0.5 mile N of Crab Point, taking care to avoid the 2-1/2-fathom spot 0.4 mile NW of the point.*

*In entering Tamgas Harbor, pass about 500 yards W of Tamgas Harbor Entrance Light and keep the E shore close aboard, distant not over 300 yards until about abeam of Tent Point. Then follow a midchannel track into the harbor avoiding the shoals that extend off Crab Point and Yellow Point.* (CP)

For boating or emergency facilities, Tamgas Harbor is the closest major shelter to Cape Chacon and the lower part of Clarence Strait.

Anchor in 5 fathoms over sand with good holding.

## Kwain Bay (Annette Island)

Kwain Bay is 1 mile south of Crab Bay.

**Entrance: 55°05.50′ N, 131°21.68′ W**

*Kwain Bay and Crab Bay are on the E shore of Annette Island opposite Mary Island. The former affords fair anchorage for moderate-sized vessels and has an entrance S of the rocks in the center of the bay.* (CP)

Crab Bay is the preferred anchorage.

## Crab Bay (Annette Island)

Crab Bay is 9 miles northeast of Ryus Bay and 5.5 miles west of Mary Anchorage.

**Entrance: 55°06.49′ N, 131°21.30′ W**
**Anchor: 55°06.36′ N, 131°21.82′ W**

*Crab Bay is an excellent anchorage for small craft and is used considerably.* (CP)

Anchorage can be found at the south end of Crab Bay, protected by the reef that extends north from the peninsula. Avoid shoals on either side of the entrance when entering Crab Bay. The upper bay is interesting to explore by dinghy, but it is shoal and largely dries on low water.

Anchor in about 2 fathoms over sand and mud with very good holding.

## Cascade Inlet

Cascade Inlet lies on the east side of Annette Island.

Charts 17434, 17428
Entrance (1.1 mile south of Middy Point and 0.4 mile south of Ham Island): 55°09.47′ N, 131°21.19′ W

> *Cascade Inlet is a deep and narrow body of water between Ham and Annette Islands. A narrow, crooked boat passage connects the inlet at its head with Revillagigedo Channel; small craft can find fair anchorage in midchannel in the broadest part of this passage close to the W end of Ham Island.* (CP)

Avoid the dangerous rock which bares on a 1-foot tide, 0.45 mile southeast of the entrance waypoint to Cascade Inlet.

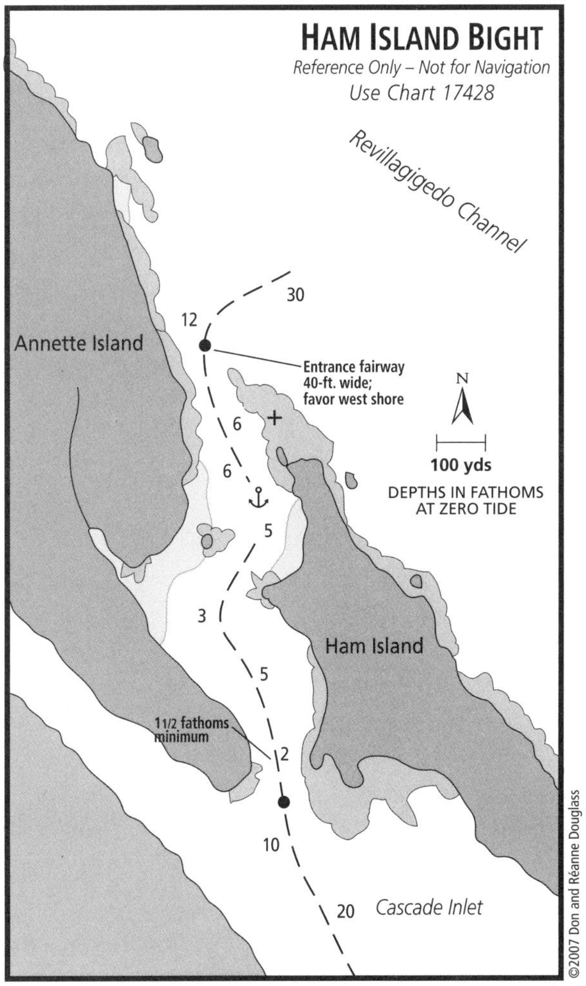


## Ham Island Bight (Ham Island)

Ham Island Bight is 2 miles southeast of Hassler Harbor.

Charts 17428, 17434
South entrance: 55°11.49′ N, 131°23.28′ W
North entrance: 55°11.95′ N, 131°23.23′ W
Anchor (south section): 55°11.68′ N, 131°23.33′ W

> *Ham Island, 2 miles W of Hog Rocks Light 13, is low and densely wooded. A deep channel is along the entire NE side of the island at an average distance from shore of 225 yards.* (CP)

We like the protection and intimate feeling of the channel between Ham Island and Annette Island, which we call "Ham Island Bight." Both the north and south bends allow you to get off to the side of the channel and find sheltered waters. You will experience some current here, so set your anchor well and maintain an anchor light—some small local fishing boats zoom through at high speed in the dark.

The north entrance requires that you avoid the long spit extending northwest from Ham Island, as well as the rocks farther north that extend 100 yards off the Annette Island shore. Favor the Annette shore until you are west of the north end of Ham Island.

Anchor in either bend in about 5 fathoms over sand with good holding.

## Nichols Passage

Nichols Passage is between Annette and Gravina Islands.

Charts 17432, 17434
South entrance (1.4 miles northwest of Hid Reef buoy R"2" and 1.8 miles south of Point McCartey Light): 55°05.00′ N, 131°42.47′ W
North entrance: (Potter Rock brg 090°T at 0.25: 55°18.09′ N, 131°35.11′ W

Nichols Passage connects the lower end of Chatham Strait to the south end of Tongass Narrows.

## Canoe Cove (Annette Island)

Canoe Cove is 3 miles north of Point Davison and 3 miles south of Cedar Point.

Chart 17434
North entrance (1.7 miles southeast of Hid Reef buoy R"2"): 55°03.15′ N, 131°38.14′ W
Anchor: 55°02.75′ N, 131°37.48′ W

*Canoe Cove indents the W shore of Annette Island about 3 miles S of Cedar Point. The cove is used by small boats and is entered through the N passage.* (CP)

When entering Canoe Cove, avoid the rocks and reefs on either side of the entrance. Anchorage can be found east of the two major islets.

Anchor in 4 to 6 fathoms. Bottom and holding are unrecorded.

## **Smuggler Cove** (Annette Island)

Smuggler Cove is immediately south of Cedar Point.

**Chart 17434**
**Position: 55°05.52′ N, 131°36.10′ W**

*Smuggler Cove . . . is open and exposed. In the upper part of the cove is a beach of fine clear sand 200 yards long.* (CP)

## **Port Chester** (Annette Island)

Port Chester, on the west side of Annette Island, is at the village of Metlakatla.

**Chart 17435**
**Entrance (small craft basin 0.3 mile west of Village Point): 55°07.87′ N, 131°35.07′ W**
**Entrance (small craft basin close southeast of City Pier): 55°07.76′ N, 131°34.23′ W**

[Port Chester] *is encumbered by numerous islands and reefs. . . . About 0.4 mile WSW of Gull Island is a rock awash at highest tides. Surrounding it and extending to the islet E are extensive ledges with bare heads. . . . Village Point, on the S side of the entrance to Port Chester, is low and sandy, with a gravel beach on the E side. W of Village Point are extensive reefs that bare to a distance of 0.2 mile offshore.*

*Metlakatla is a large native American community on the S side of Port Chester. A small-craft basin, protected by a breakwater, is close SW of the City Pier. . . . There is 1,100 feet of berthing space along the floats. The basin is under the control of the harbormaster who monitors VHF-FM channel 16 and can also be contacted by telephone at (907) 886-4646. A combination seaplane and small-boat float is on the NE side of Village Point.*

*Another small-craft basin, protected by breakwaters, is 0.3 mile W of Village Point.*

*Port Chester does not afford good anchorage. During SE gales, winds blow with great violence across it, and williwaws of 60 to 70 knots sweep down from Purple Mountains and across the anchorage.* (CP)

## **Sylburn Harbor** (Annette Island)

Sylburn Harbor is on the west side of Annette Island, 3.1 miles north of Metlakatla.

**Charts 17435, 17428**
**Entrance (0.73 mile northeast of Driest Point Light): 55°11.31′ N, 131°36.10′ W**
**Entrance (Japan Bay): 55°10.91′ N, 131°34.68′ W**
**Anchor: 55°10.62′ N, 131°35.68′ W**

*Sylburn Harbor is a small bay N of Driest Point, the S end of which affords fair anchorage for small craft in 7 to 18 fathoms. The easternmost branch of the harbor is known locally as Japan Bay. About the middle of the outer entrance to Sylburn Harbor is a large double-headed rock that is covered several feet at high water. Strangers entering the harbor are advised to wait for low water when the dangers are visible.* (CP)

A very narrow, shallow channel with one-half fathom or less in the fairway leads to the inner basin.

Anchor in 6 to 8 fathoms over sand and gravel with some rocks; fair holding.

## **Annette Bay** (Annette Island)

Annette Bay is 5 miles southeast of Ketchikan.

**Chart 17428**
**Entrance: 55°16.81′ N, 131°34.89′ W**
**Anchor: 55°15.25′ N, 131°31.55′ W**

*Annette Bay, at the NW end of Annette Island, is about 0.8 mile wide at the entrance and narrows to a small stream; it is about 3 miles long, has deep water and does not afford anchorage for vessels. Small craft can anchor near its head in 7 to 8 fathoms.* (CP)

Anchor in 8 fathoms over mud, shells and gravel with fair holding.

## **Dall Bay** (Gravina Island)

Dall Bay, on the west side of Nichols Passage, is 11.5 miles south of Ketchikan.

Charts 17432, 17434
Entrance: 55°09.41′ N, 131°43.02′ W
Anchor (between two islands): 55°09.33′ N, 131°44.86′ W
Anchor (small craft): 55°09.13′ N, 131°45.32′ W

*Dall Bay . . . about 1.5 miles N of Dall Head, has many dangers. . . . It offers good anchorage in 8 fathoms, mud bottom, between the two islands well inside the bay. There is also small-craft anchorage farther in, depth 3 fathoms, soft mud bottom. Local knowledge is essential for entering.* (CP)

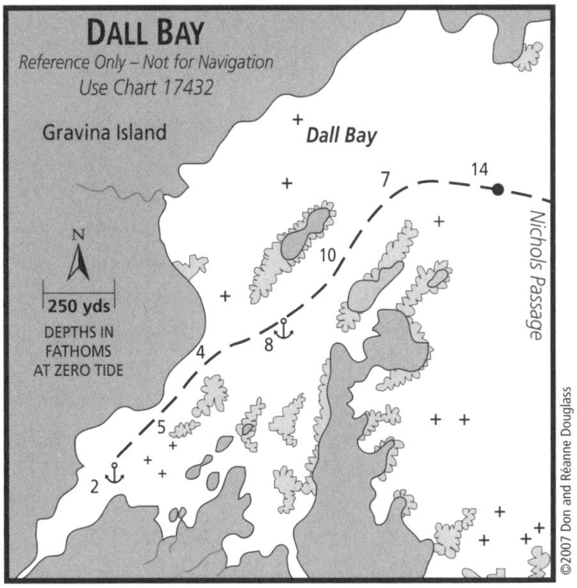


Dall Bay offers excellent protection for cruising boats; however, the narrow entrance is shallow and complex. It is best entered with Chart 17432.

Anchor (between two islands) in 8 fathoms.

Anchor (small craft) in 3 fathoms.

## **Seal Cove** (Gravina Island)

Seal Cove is 1.8 miles north of Dall Bay.

Charts 17428 (inset), 17434
Entrance: 55°10.53′ N, 131°43.16′ W

[Seal Cove] *has depths of about 30 to 40 feet, but is suitable only for small craft because of its narrow entrance. A reef, mostly bare at half tide, extends across the entrance, through which are two channels. The N one has a depth of 8 feet and a width of 75 yards, but it is full of boulders and dangerous. The S entrance is generally used. It is close to the S shore and has a depth of about 3 to 11 feet. The channel is narrow and has thick kelp and strong currents. Caution is advised when entering Seal Cove by the N or S entrance.* (CP)

Favor the Gravina Island shore to avoid the extensive rock and reef system in the entrance. Anchorage can be found anywhere in the bay over a flat bottom of 5 to 7 fathoms of sand, mud and lots of rocks with good swinging room. The cove is exposed to southeast winds but offers good protection in prevailing northwesterlies.

*Calm waters at Dall Bay*

## **Bostwick Inlet** (Gravina Island)

Bostwick Inlet is 4 miles north of Dall Bay.

Charts 17428, 17434
Entrance: 55°12.74′ N, 131°42.15′ W

[Bostwick Inlet] *affords no shelter in SE weather. The S shore is generally foul, and the upper part of the bay bares for 1.2 miles from the head. In entering, follow the N shore at a distance of about 0.2 mile.* (CP)

## **Blank Inlet** (Gravina Island)

Blank Inlet is 2 miles southwest of Blank Islands Light.

**Charts 17428, 17434**
**Entrance (0.6 mile southwest of Blank Islands Light): 55°15.73′ N, 131°39.28′ W**

> *Blank Inlet, about 4 miles N of Bostwick Inlet and W of Gravina Point . . . extends 3 miles NW into the shore of Gravina Island. It is open to the sea from Nichols Passage and affords no sheltered anchorage. Two rocks awash are almost in the center of the inlet.* (CP)

## **Blank Islands**

Blank Islands are 1.2 miles southwest of Gravina Point.

**Charts 17428, 17434**
**Entrance: 55°16.61′ N, 131°38.06′ W**
**Anchor: 55°16.45′ N, 131°38.51′ W**

> *Blank Islands, two in number . . . are near the N side of the entrance to Blank Inlet. The S shoreline is bare rock for 50 to 100 yards outside the trees, and the shore is bold. Small craft can find good anchorage in the bight on the N side of the islands.* (CP)

Anchor in 3 fathoms.

## **Black Sand Cove** (Gravina Island)

Black Sand Cove is 0.6 mile west of Gravina Point.

**Charts 14728, 17434**
**Entrance: 55°17.00′ N, 131°37.70′ W**
**Anchor: 55°17.06′ N, 131°37.98′ W**

Black Sand Cove affords protection from northwest winds only. The sizeable number of logs onshore indicates this cove is exposed to southeast winds.

Anchor in about 1 fathom.

## **Lucky Cove** (Revillagigedo Island)

Lucky Cove is 5.5 miles east of Hassler Harbor.

**Chart 17434**
**Entrance: 55°12.74′ N, 131°16.32′ W**
**Anchor: 55°12.70′ N, 131°16.10′ W**

> *Lucky Cove is a small indentation on the SW shore of Revillagigedo Island midway between Point Alava and Cone Island.* (CP)

Lucky Cove is a stopping place for local fishermen. Some temporary shelter can be found here from southeast weather. Anchor close to the drying mud flat in the lee of the small island. Note, however, that we found the cove marginal and uncomfortable when the wind shifted to the northwest in the middle of the night, and we had to proceed to Ketchikan under radar.

Anchor in about 10 fathoms on a somewhat steep-to sand and mud flat with fair holding.

## **Camp Cove** (Ham Island)

Camp Cove is 0.3 mile northwest of Middy Point.

**Charts 17428, 17434**
**Entrance: 55°10.41′ N, 131°20.05′ W**
**Anchor: 55°10.34′ N, 131°20.12′ W**

Camp Cove is a small cove suitable for anchorage in fair weather with limited swinging room. Bottom is rocky with poor holding.

## **Hassler Harbor** (Annette Island)

Hassler Harbor, on the northeast side of Annette Island, is 1.4 miles southwest of Bold Island Light.

**Charts 17428, 17434**
**Northwest entrance (0.7 mile northwest of Pow Island): 55°13.32′ N, 131°27.14′ W**
**East entrance (0.33 mile northeast of Pow Island): 55°13.13′ N, 131°25.22′ W**
**Anchor: 55°12.86′ N, 131°25.68′ W**

> *Hassler Harbor . . . affords excellent shelter with good holding ground for small craft in SE gales.* (CP)

Hassler Harbor is not one of our favorite anchorages. The east entrance is foul, although

Réanne Hemingway-Douglass

*Explosives storage ship at Hassler Harbor*

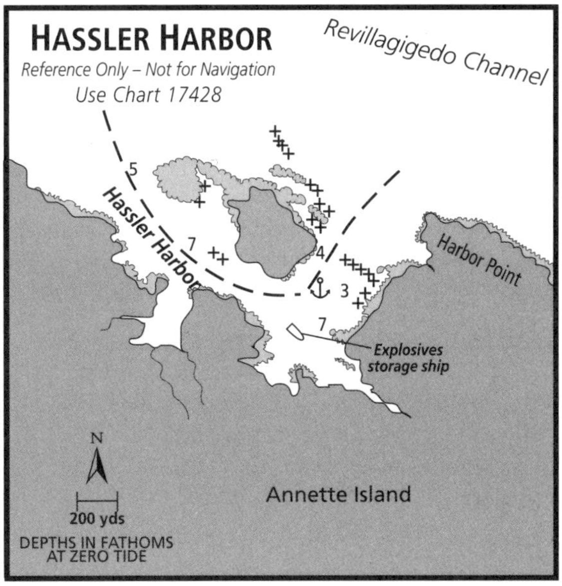




it is navigable by staying close to the Pow Island shore, 0.27 mile southwest of Harbor Point, to avoid a series of rocks extending from Annette Island. The harbor has a very irregular bottom, and we have experienced difficulty in getting a good anchor bite in the hard bottom. However, if a southeast gale were to spring up as we were heading south in Revillagigedo Channel, we would not hesitate to use it. We would use the north entrance and set our anchor very carefully. The hull of a large, wooden sailing ship anchored on the north side is used as a storage area for explosives, and vessels are warned to keep clear.

Anchor in 7 fathoms southeast of Pow Island over a hard bottom with poor-to-fair holding.

## **Nadzaheen Cove** (Annette Island)

Nadzaheen Cove is 1.7 miles northwest of Hassler Harbor.

Charts 17428, 17434
Entrance: 55°13.64′ N, 131°27.28′ W
Anchor: 55°13.81′ N, 131°28.33′ W

Nadzaheen Cove provides shelter from northwest winds but it is fully exposed to the southeast.

Anchor in 6 to 8 fathoms.

## **Thorne Arm** (Revillagigedo Island)

Thorne Arm extends northeast of Bold Island for 12 miles.

Chart 17428
Entrance (0.87 mile east of Round Island):
55°15.00′ N, 131°21.44′ W

> *Thorne Arm has its entrance E of Bold Island and W of Cone Island. . . . The arm is free from outlying dangers. . . . At the head of Thorne Arm in the cove E of Mop Point is a somewhat constricted anchorage in 18 to 20 fathoms, hard bottom. Anchorage can also be selected in the bight on the W side at the head between Snipe Island and Mop Point in 25 to 30 fathoms, soft bottom. Small craft may find shelter in the small cove NW of Snipe Island, between it and the adjoining small island. A midchannel course leads safely through the arm and to the anchorages.* (CP)

## **Coho Cove** (Thorne Arm)

Coho Cove, at the entrance to Thorne Arm, is 1 mile northeast of Round Island.

Chart 17428
Entrance: 55°15.80′ N, 131°22.11′ W
Anchor: 55°16.38′ N, 131°22.13′ W

> *Coho Cove, about 1.2 miles W of Moth Bay and opposite the E end of Bold Island, affords fair anchorage for small craft, although the depths are great. The best channel for entering is on the E side of the islet in the entrance.* (CP)

Anchor in 10 fathoms at the head of the cove.

## **Moth Bay** (Thorne Arm)

Moth Bay is 1.2 miles east of Coho Bay and 2 miles northeast of Round Island.

Chart 17428
Entrance: 55°15.96′ N, 131°19.83′ W
Anchor: 55°16.89′ N, 131°20.46′ W

> *In the middle of the entrance to the bay is a small wooded islet and about 325 yards NW from its northernmost extremity is a smaller islet with a rock about 50 yards to the SSW. The preferred channel leads E of the islets. . . . Small craft can find anchorage near the head of the bay in 12 fathoms, soft bottom.* (CP)

Anchor in the 12-fathom hole mentioned in *Coast Pilot.*

## Carroll Inlet (Revillagigedo Island)

Carroll Inlet extends 24 miles northeast of Mountain Point.

**Chart 17428**
**Entrance (0.83 mile northeast of Cutter Rocks Light): 55°17.76′ N, 131°30.19′ W**

> *Carroll Inlet has its entrance about 1.5 miles N of Spire Island Reef Light between Mountain Point and Carroll Point. The inlet extends N about 23 miles. California Head separates it from George Inlet.*
>
> *Mountain Point is an unincorporated settlement on the point.* (CP)

## California Cove (Carroll Inlet)

California Cove is 2.3 miles north of Carroll Point.

**Chart 17428**
**Entrance: 55°20.20′ N, 131°27.43′ W**

> *California Cove, on the W side of Carroll Inlet and immediately E of California Head, is a small open bight exposed to the S. The cove is deep except along the W shore. Two small wooded islets and a rock awash are close to the W shore.* (CP)

## Gnat Cove (Carroll Inlet)

Gnat Cove, on the east side of Carroll Inlet, is 5 miles northeast of California Cove.

**Chart 17428**
**Entrance: 55°23.06′ N, 131°19.98′ W**
**Anchor: 55°22.67′ N, 131°19.78′ W**

> *A fair anchorage can be had off the entrance to the cove in 17 to 18 fathoms, soft bottom. Foul ground extends 250 yards from the outer of two points at the S side of the entrance to the cove. Small craft can find good moorage inside the cove by rafting up to the anchored log booms of a log storage area on the NE side of Gnat Cove. Care should be taken, however, to avoid the mudflats that extend from the S shore and rock ledges that extend into the SW bight of the cove.* (CP)

Gnat cove is the best sheltered anchorage in Carroll Inlet. With the absence of log rafts, good anchorage can be found west of the islet on the south side of the bay. Avoid the mud flat and rock ledges as noted in *Coast Pilot.*

Anchor in about 7 fathoms over a mixed bottom, fair holding.

## Shelter Cove (Carroll Inlet)

Shelter Cove is 10 miles north of Gnat Cove.

**Chart 17428 (inset)**
**Position: 55°32.15′ N, 131°20.90′ W**

Some protection from upslope winds can be provided at Shelter Cove, tucked in between the east point and the drying mud flats in about 5 fathoms.

## George Inlet (Revillagigedo Island)

George Inlet extends 14 miles north of Mountain Point.

**Entrance (0.83 mile northeast of Cutter Rocks Light): 55°17.76′ N, 131°30.19′ W**
**Chart 17428**
**Entrance: 55°19.50′ N, 131°30.01′ W**

> *George Inlet . . . extends N about 12 miles and has deep water throughout. A former cannery and wharf are on the W side of George Inlet, about 3.5 miles above California Head. . . . The stub pilings of a former wharf remain close N of the present wharf; caution is advised in this area.* (CP)

## Herring Bay (George Inlet)

Herring Bay is 2 miles north of Mountain Point.

**Chart 17428**
**Float (0.5 mile south of Herring Bay): 55°19.13′ N, 131°31.20′ W**
**Position (Herring Bay): 55°19.51′ N, 131°31.27′ W**

> *Herring Bay . . . indents the W shore of George Inlet about 2 miles N of Mountain Point. In the small cove 0.5 mile S of Herring Bay, locally known as Hole-in-the-Wall, the city of Ketchikan maintains 493 feet of small-craft floats for vessels up to 40 feet. In 2002, 5 to 10 feet was reported alongside the floats. Marine supplies are not available in the cove; however, gasoline, diesel fuel, provisions and repairs can be obtained in Ketchikan.* (CP)

## Mahoney Bight (George Inlet)

Mahoney Bight is 8 miles north of Mountain Point.

**Chart 17428**
**Entrance: 55°25.28′ N, 131°30.27′ W**
**Anchor: 55°25.25′ N, 131°30.56′ W**

> *Mahoney Bight . . . is good shelter for small craft except during SE weather. Its entrance is*

> *clear of dangers, with 10 fathoms leading into the inner bight, which has depths from 5 to 11 fathoms, hard bottom.* (CP)

Anchor in 10 fathoms over mud with good holding.

## **Coon Cove** (George Inlet)

Coon Cove, on the east shore of George Inlet, is 10 miles north of Mountain Point.

Chart 17428 (inset)
Entrance: 55°27.33′ N, 131°29.40′ W
Anchor: 55°27.42′ N, 131°28.82′ W

> *Coon Cove . . . offers good anchorage in 13 fathoms, mud bottom, S of the small tree-covered islet off the N shore, and is the best shelter in the inlet in SE weather. It is entered on a midchannel course S of Coon Island.*
>
> *The upper part of Coon Cove is a tidal flat. The S extremity of the flat is marked by prominent pilings. Small craft may find more convenient anchorage in 7 to 9 fathoms, soft bottom, just S of the pilings.* (CP)

Anchor in 5 to 8 fathoms over mud with good holding.

## **Leask Cove** (George Inlet)

Leask Cove, on the west shore near the head of the inlet, is 3 miles northwest of Coon Cove.

Chart 17428 (inset)
Entrance: 55°30.08′ N, 131°30.77′ W
Anchor: 55°30.33′ N, 131°30.80′ W

> *Leask Cove . . . affords fair anchorage in depths of 10 to 15 fathoms, sand and gravel bottom, off the N shore of the cove. A prominent offshore rock, bare at all stages of the tide, is on the E side of the entrance. A shoal with a least depth of 2 fathoms is 400 yards NE of the W side of the entrance.* (CP)

Anchor in 10 fathoms over sand and gravel.

## **Bat Cove** (George Inlet)

Bat Cove is 3 miles north of Coon Cove.

Chart 17428 (inset)
Entrance: 55°30.17′ N, 131°30.16′ W
Anchor: 55°30.42′ N, 131°29.38′ W

> *Bat Cove, just E of Leask Cove, affords excellent shelter for small craft, with anchorage at the head in 10 to 11 fathoms, mud bottom. . . . Hold close to the rock* [mentioned in the Leask Cove reference] *when entering the cove to avoid a rock ledge, bare at low water, that extends one-third of the way across the entrance from Bat Point on the E side.* (CP)

Anchor in 10 fathoms over black mud with very good holding.

## **Tsa Cove** (George Inlet)

Tsa Cove, on the east shore of the inlet, is 2.5 miles northeast of Coon Cove.

Chart 17428 (inset)
Outer entrance (0.12 mile southwest corner of Granite Island): 55°29.97′ N, 131°28.92′ W
Inner entrance (in the narrow fairway between Granite and Bull islands): 55°29.89′ N, 131°28.49′ W
Anchor: 55°30.00′ N, 131°27.68′ W

> *Tsa Cove . . . is difficult to enter but affords good shelter and anchorage in 10 to 14 fathoms, mud and shell bottom. Small boats with local knowledge enter between Bull Island on the SW and Granite Island on the NE, holding close to the Granite Island shoreline to avoid shoals that extend from the numerous rock islets off the NE end of Bull Island.* (CP)

Anchor in 10 fathoms over black mud and shells with very good holding.

Réanne Hemingway-Douglass

*A typical sight along the cruise ship dock*

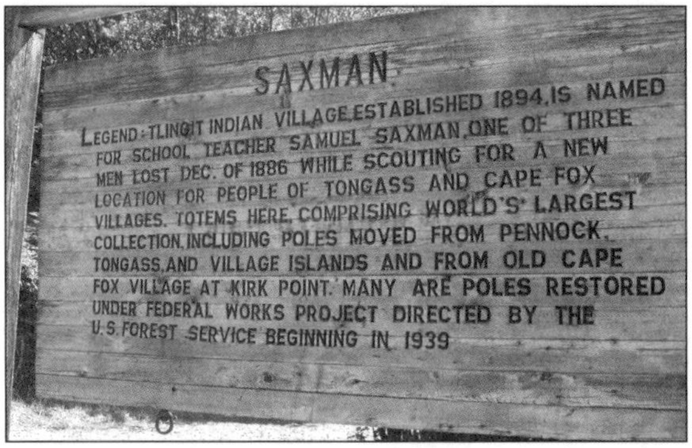


Réanne Hemingway-Douglass

*A sign at Saxman Park tells of the legend.*

Réanne Hemingway-Douglass

*The longhouse at Saxman Park*

Réanne Hemingway-Douglass

*One of the many faces on the totems*

Réanne Hemingway-Douglass

*Maintaining the totems with intricate care*

Réanne Hemingway-Douglass

*Creative, colorful totems fill the grounds.*

## Salt Lagoon (George Inlet)

The entrance to Salt Lagoon is 1 mile north of Tsa Cove.

Charts 17428 (inset), 17420
Position: 55°30.94′ N, 131°27.62′ W

*Small boats with local knowledge pass into Salt Lagoon* (chart 17420) *at the head of the inlet, but only at or near high water slack. The entrance is very narrow, with dangerous rapids at most stages of the tide.* (CP)

David Parker

*Tongass Narrows cruise ship traffic; one exiting and two at the dock in the distance.*

## Tongass Narrows

Tongass Narrows separates Gravina Island from Revillagigedo Island.

Charts 17428, 17430
Southeast entrance to East Channel (0.12 mile southwest of buoy N"2"): 55°18.49′ N, 131°35.42′ W
Southeast entrance to West Channel (0.20 mile southwest of buoy R"2"): 55°17.88′ N, 131°36.62′ W
Northwest entrance to West Channel (0.17 mile southwest of Pennock Reef buoy): 55°20.19′ N, 131°40.33′ W
Northwest entrance to East Channel (0.275 mile northeast of Pennock Reef buoy): 55°20.50′ N, 131°39.78′ W

*Tongass Narrows, a continuation of Revillagigedo Channel, extends NW to Guard Islands in Clarence Strait. The principal dangers are marked by buoys or lights, so that no difficulty should be experienced in passing through in clear weather.*

*The narrows is divided at its lower end by Pennock Island; the channel NE of the island is called East Channel locally, and the channel SW of the island, West Channel. Both channels are good for vessels of any draft. A lighted buoy marks the edge of a shoal making out from the SW side of West Channel. An isolated 9.3-fathom pinnacle rock . . . is about 0.5 mile SSE from the southernmost extremity of Pennock Island.* (CP)

Tongass Narrows is the main thoroughfare for large cruise ships that berth at Ketchikan. It is not unusual to find three of these huge ships tied up at the dock and they come and go frequently. An additional cruise ship may also be anchored in Tongass Narrows, just west of the cruise ships dock. Keep a careful ear and eye out for traffic and stay well to your side of the fairway.

## Saxman Village (Revillagigedo Island)

Saxman Village is 2.5 miles northwest of Mountain Point.

Charts 17430, 17428
Position: 55°19.12′ N, 131°36.08′ W

*Saxman is a small settlement in the bight indenting the SW shore of Revillagigedo Island N of Idaho Rock and about 2 miles SE of Ketchikan. The center of the settlement has a prominent group of totem poles.*

*A privately dredged basin protected on the S side by a breakwater is about 0.3 mile SE of Saxman. . . . The basin is the site of a privately operated barge and rail terminal.*

*The bight fronting Saxman N of Idaho Rock is used as a log raft storage area. Unlighted log rafts are frequently found close to shore in this area; caution is advised.* (CP)

## Ketchikan (Revillagigedo Island)

Ketchikan is on the south side of Revillagigedo Island and on the east side of Tongass Narrows.

Charts 17430, 17428

*Ketchikan (55°20.5′ N, 131°38.7′ W) on the SW side of Revillagigedo Island and on the E side of Tongass Narrows, is one of the most important cities in Alaska. It is 659 miles from Seattle via the Inside Passage; 79 miles from the sea at Dixon Entrance via Nichols Passage; 89 miles from Wrangell, and 220 miles from Juneau.* (CP)

Ketchikan, once a rough town full of miners and loggers, calls itself the First City, and not only is it the first port of call and the necessary customs clearance center as you enter from Canada, it is the busiest town in Southeast Alaska.

In summer, Tongass Narrows hums to the noise of cruises ships coming and going, tenders zooming southward to Misty Fiords and float planes taking off. Creek Street, which used to be the largest red light district west of the Mississippi, is full of smart boutiques, restaurants and Parnassus—one of the best bookstores for Alaskans in Southeast.

## Ketchikan

### Don Douglass & Réanne Hemingway-Douglass

Ketchikan is the first Alaskan stop for boaters heading north, hence the nickname, "the First City." Its population is less than 8,000, but the summer influx of visitors gives it a bustling atmosphere. It's a working community known for lots of salmon and totem poles but only one traffic light, which has changed in recent years. Bring rain gear—Ketchikan gets about 160 inches of "liquid sunshine" a year.

The community began with a Tlingit fishing village located at the mouth of Ketchikan Creek. That's a good place to orient yourself. From there, Ketchikan stretches out in both directions along the coast like the wings of an eagle.

The bridge at Steadman Street crosses the creek along which lies Ketchikan's most famous attraction, Creek Street. Pastel buildings, formerly brothels, now house gift shops, galleries and book stores. You can get a glimpse of the former occupants' lifestyle by taking the tour at Dolly's House Museum and Gift Shop at number 24.

Near the top of Creek Street is the Married Man's Trail, a leafy "back door" into the red-light district. Climb the mossy, wooden staircase for a view of the harbor, then come back down to Ketchikan Creek and see the salmon ladder. Cross the creek to visit the library where the Tongass Historical Museum is housed.

Inside, you'll peruse an eclectic mix of artistic and historical objects. There are bentwood boxes, tools, adornments, baskets, clothing, even a medical examination chair. You'll see the bullet-perforated skull of "Old Groaner," a massive bear brought down in 1935. And an assortment of photographs from the Victorian era to the present shows how the city and its people have changed.

Another hub of activity is the waterfront. The Ketchikan Visitors Bureau provides maps and bus schedules, and volunteers to answer your questions. Concessionaires can set you up with excursions and conveyances, including horse-drawn trolleys, Jeeps, kayaks, Harley-Davidson, and "duck tours" on amphibious vehicles.

The cruise ships dock here so there are lots of shops. But if shopping isn't your cup of tea, visit the spacious Southeast Alaska Discovery Center, a good place to learn about the Tongass rainforest and the Tlingit, Haida and Tsimshian cultures. Aside from its nature and wildlife exhibits, you can watch short videos of Alaskan residents talking about their lives and livelihoods.

Other attractions in town include the Totem Heritage Center with its collection of nineteenth-century totems and the Deer Mountain Tribal Hatchery and Eagle Center.

Two and a half miles southeast from Ketchikan is Saxman Native Village, a Tlingit community named for a teacher from Pennsylvania who drowned in 1886. You can see carving demonstrations and dance performances at the Beaver Clan House.

Ten miles northwest from the city is Totem Bight State Historic Park. See totems, a clan house and learn about cedar carving and other aspects of Native culture.

Pristine wilderness surrounds Ketchikan. Take a backcountry trip to see the abundant animal life—bears, wolves, martens, deer, minks—of Tongass National Forest, or a floatplane trip to Misty Fiords National Monument to see its glaciers, waterfalls and wildlife. Be sure to visit the Forest Service building located near the harbormaster's office at Bar Harbor. They have excellent literature on Southeast Alaska forests and a map of all the Forest Service buoys, floats and cabins.

For visitor information go to Ketchikan Visitors Bureau, 131 Front St., tel.: 907.225.4250 or 800.770.3300; Website: www.visit-ketchikan.com.

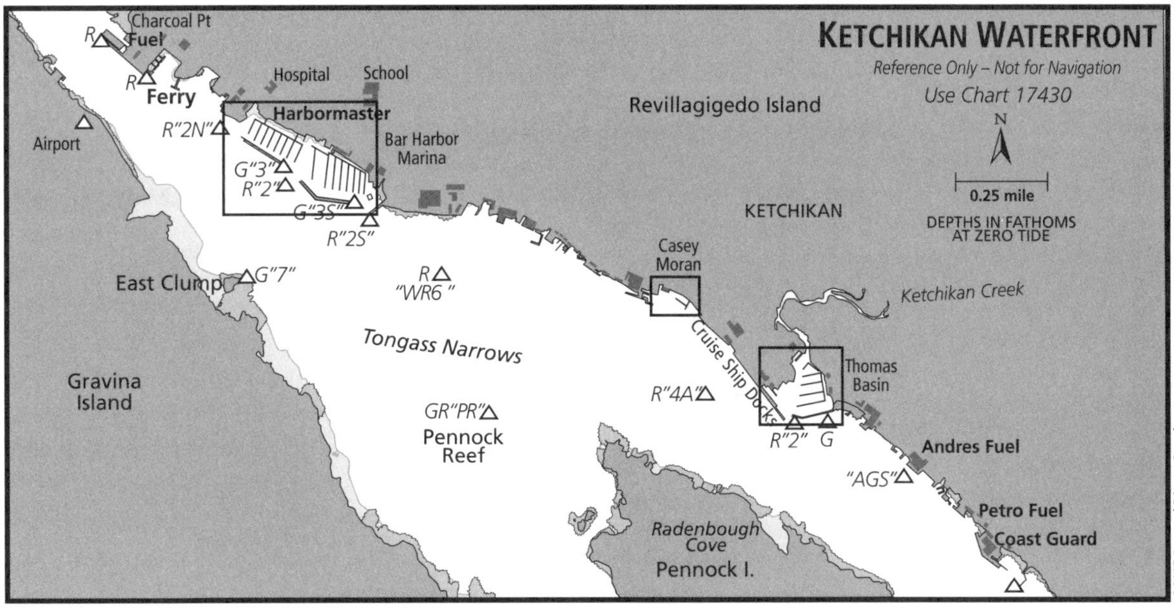


There are several possibilities for moorage in Ketchikan: Thomas Basin or Casey Moran Harbor, both in the center of town, or Bar Harbor, a mile north of town. Since the town floats tend to be crowded during summer, you may want to tie up for a just a few hours to do errands, then head to Bar Harbor, which has power, water, showers, a supermarket and shopping mall, and a laundromat. Call the harbormaster on Ch 73 for instructions on where to tie up.

For "super" yachts of virtually any size, another moorage option can be found at the full-service Doyon's Landing (400-foot dock), just south of the Coast Guard Station. Although expensive, it gives first-class service with ample power, fuel, Internet, covered ramps, a seaplane float and 24-hour security. Call on Ch 16 or telephone 907.225.1716. Website: www.doyonslanding.com.

*Watch for the small USCG base on your starboard as you approach downtown Ketchikan from the south.*

Within a short distance of Thomas Basin or Casey Moran Harbor you can find all services, as well as gift shops, art galleries and museums. Chief among the latter are the Tongass Historical Museum and the Totem Heritage Center. The Visitors Bureau, located at 131 Front Street along the quay, offers a wealth of brochures to help you decide what to visit. (Request their Walking Tour brochure.)

There are three markets on the north end of town. Alaskan & Proud to Be (known as A & P), three blocks south of the airport Ferry Terminal, will deliver you and your groceries to the harbor (tel.: 907.225.1279). A gigantic Safeway supermarket is located in the Plaza Mall Shopping Center, a block south of Bar Harbor Basin (tel.: 907.228.1900); pharmacy (tel.: 907.228.1960). Safeway allows you to take their grocery cart to your boat (via the easy south ramp access from Bar Harbor) and leave it at any dock cart

David Parker

*Two cruise ships in port but still room for one more; downtown Ketchikan.*

location where they will pick it up. For a fee of $5.00, the store will box your groceries and deliver them to your boat. WalMart is located north of Bar Harbor, on the bus line. When there is a cruise ship in harbor, WalMart provides a free van shuttle service that leaves from the waterside of the Southeast Alaska Discovery Center—near the cruise ship dock, downtown.

In the south end of town you can provision at Tatsuda's IGA (ice available) at the corner of Stedman and Deermount (tel.: 907.225.4125); they will deliver your groceries. (There is also a laundromat near Tatsuda's.) Tongass Trading Company, on the dock, has marine items and charts. For additional marine supplies go to Murray Pacific, 1050 Water Street (tel.: 907.225.3135), or Madison Marine (division of Madison Lumber and Hardware), 2557 Tongass (tel.: 907.225.9828).

Gasoline, diesel and propane are available south of town (near the Coast Guard base) at Anderes Oil, 900 Stedman (tel.: 907.225.2163), or Petro Marine, 1100 Stedman (tel.: 907.225.2106). Another fuel dock (with propane available) is located near Bar Harbor, north of the Alaska Ferry Dock (across from the airport). Propane is also available at White Pass Alaska, a mile south of town.

If you're picking up or letting off crew, Ketchikan has one of the most conveniently located airports (with an Alaska Airlines terminal), just across Tongass Narrows (north of Bar Harbor); city buses run from downtown to the Airport Ferry dock. In good weather, we tie up at the small float south of the terminal to await crew. The float adjacent to the terminal is reserved for the ferry and for float planes. Be alert to this very active Airport Ferry crossing as you cruise north out of Ketchikan.

The Ketchikan area provides you with your first opportunity in Southeast Alaska to query your computer for a Wifi hotspot. Try this while at any of the marinas mentioned below and you will probably bring up the site of an area-owned service provider. You can purchase varying amounts of time on a secured connection. (See the Introduction of this book for a more complete explanation.) Although there are cybercafés in Ketchikan, they are frequently packed with people (especially staff) from the cruise ships. (The Ketchikan Public Library used to provide computer time for visitors, however this is no longer true.)

Contact the Ketchikan area's harbormaster before entering Ketchikan on VHF Ch 73 (tel.: 907.228.5632) for a berth assignment. You can request the marina of your choice and the harbormaster will try to accommodate you; be sure to mention your AC power needs—especially if you want Bar Harbor. Be patient, this is a busy waterfront and you will likely be "hot-berthing"—meaning that you will be assigned to a slip that has been temporarily vacated, most likely by a fishing-vessel owner.

Customs clearance is available at any of the Ketchikan marinas. There is no designated "customs dock" in Ketchikan. Upon arrival at your destination marina, call the customs office from your cell phone or the nearest land line. (tel.: 907.225.2254, or after hours and Sunday: 907.225.2380) (See p. xix for a complete explanation, including anchoring options before reaching Ketchikan.) The *Coast Pilot* has excellent color pictures of Tongass Narrows, the Cruise Ship docks (with four ships in port), Thomas Basin and Bar Harbor marina (they label it Bar Point Basin).

*Aerial view, Thomas Basin, Ketchikan*

## **Thomas Basin** (Ketchikan Harbor)

Thomas Basin is 0.65 miles northwest of the Coast Guard Base.

Chart 17430
Entrance: 55°20.30' N, 131°38.59' W

> *Thomas Basin, the small-craft harbor off Ketchikan Creek, is protected on its W side by a log boom, and on the S side by a stone breakwater. The harbor is entered from the S through a 75-foot opening between the W log boom and the breakwater on the S; a light marks the entrance. . . . The city-operated floats in the basin have water and metered electricity; 80-foot and 65-foot grids are available. Fuel can be obtained at the facilities just N of the Coast Guard base.*
>
> *The basin is controlled by a harbormaster, who maintains an office at Bar Point Basin. . . . A 3-knot and "no wake" speed limit is enforced in the basin.* (CP)

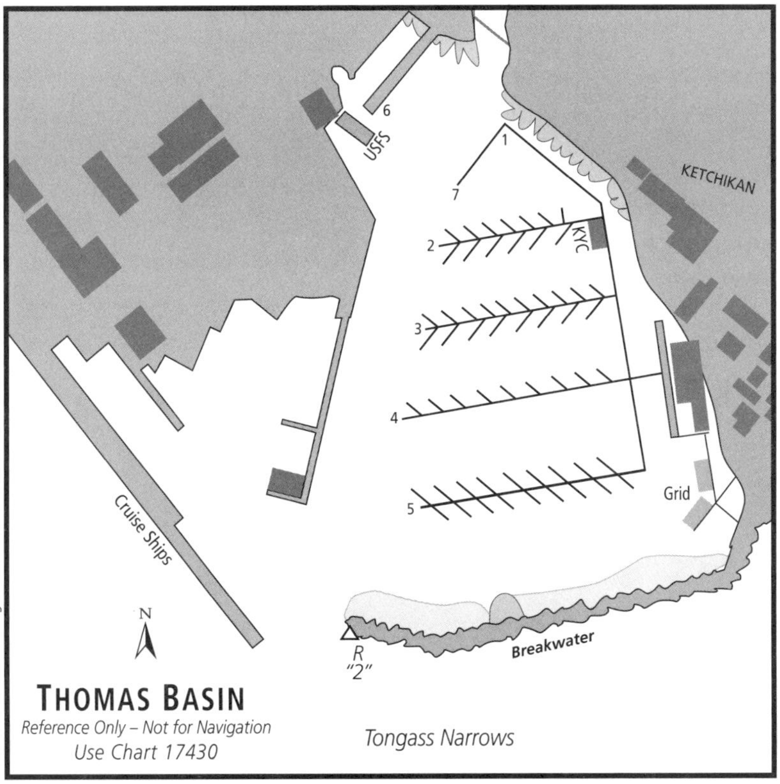


Thomas Basin may have accommodations for transients. Call the harbormaster on Ch 73 to inquire. Some of the docks have been upgraded and power pedestals have been installed with the goal of providing 50-amp power on all of the docks. Thomas Basin floats are often filled in the summer and you may have trouble finding space in this tight basin. *Note:* In heavy weather or high winds, it may be difficult for boats over about 36 feet to maneuver in the basin. Float number 2 is the Ketchikan Yacht Club transient float; if you can find space, tie up and check instructions on the outside of the club house.

Linda Lewis

*Thomas Basin puts you right in the heart of the downtown area and adjacent to the cruise ship docks.*

## **Ryus Float** (Ketchikan Harbor)

Ryus Float is 0.9 mile northwest of the Coast Guard Base.

Chart 17430
Float: 55°20.49′ N, 131°38.88′ W

> *Ryus Float: 525 yards NW of the entrance to Thomas Basin and immediately N of Ketchikan City Dock No. 1; 136 feet of berthing space; 25 to 30 feet reported alongside in 2002; limited to craft up to 80 feet long; 4-hour limit alongside for loading and unloading, and no vessels are permitted to tie-up when a cruise vessel is docked at Berth 2 Wharf.* (CP)

Ryus Float is an unloading zone, reserved exclusively for the use of cruise ship tenders and tour boats.

## **Casey Moran Harbor** (Ketchikan Harbor)

(On charts, labeled "City Floats")
Harbor is 1.1 miles northwest of the Coast Guard Base.

Chart 17430
Entrance: 55°20.63′ N, 131°39.18′ W

> [Casey Moran] *City Floats: 875 yards NW of the entrance to Thomas Basin; 1,151 feet of berthing space with depths of 20 to 80 feet reported alongside in 2002; limited to craft up to 90 feet long or as otherwise posted; water and metered electricity available.* (CP)

Casey Moran Harbor, formerly called City Floats, is conveniently located near the center of town. However, with the increase in cruise ship traffic and the noise of float planes taking off all day long, most cruising boats prefer the quieter Bar Harbor. Since the floats are crowded in summer, you may have to raft. But be forewarned that, if you raft on the outside of

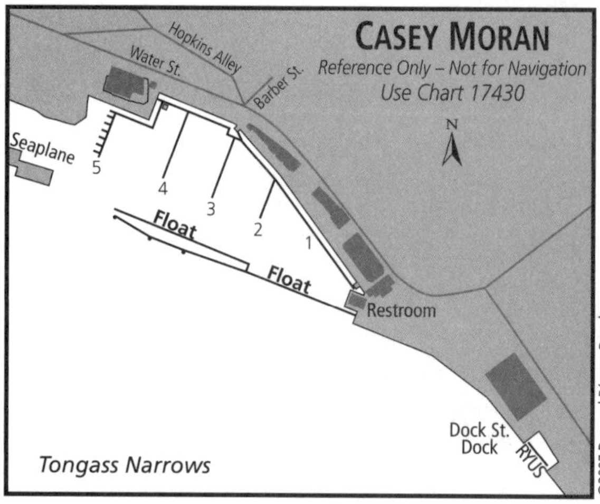

a fishing vessel, you may have to move early in the morning or late at night.

*Note:* As we go to press, Ketchikan is undertaking a plan for expansion of its cruiseship docks in Casey Moran (formerly City Floats). The floats will be reconfigured and two floating docks for cruise ships will be built outside the harbor. However, we have heard conflicting reports regarding whether this reconfiguration will in fact leave transient space for cruising boats. Inquire before you arrive in Ketchikan.

## **Bar Harbor** (Ketchikan Harbor)

The middle entrance to Bar Harbor is 2.25 miles northwest of the Coast Guard Base.

Chart 17430
East entrance: 55°20.87′ N, 131°40.75′ W
Middle entrance: 55°20.96′ N, 131°41.14′ W
West entrance: 55°21.11′ N, 131°41.43′ W

*Bar Point Basin, locally called Bar Harbor, is a small-craft harbor off Bar Point about 1.35 miles NW of Thomas Basin. . . . The harbor has three entrances which are marked by lights and daybeacons. The SE entrance is between the stone breakwater and the detached stone breakwater. The SW entrance is between the two detached floating breakwaters, and the NW entrance is N of the northernmost detached floating breakwater. . . . The city-operated floats in the basin have water and metered electricity. Fuel can be obtained at the oil facilities just N of the Coast Guard base.*

*The basin is under the control of a harbormaster, who maintains an office at the NE corner of the basin. Local regulations limit the maximum size of vessels using the basin to a length of 80 feet. A 3-knot and "no wake" speed limit is enforced in the basin.* (CP)

Bar Harbor is the main cruising-boat moorage in Ketchikan. Slips are assigned by calling the Ketchikan harbormaster on VHF Ch 73 (tel.: 907.228.5632). The Harbor has water and some

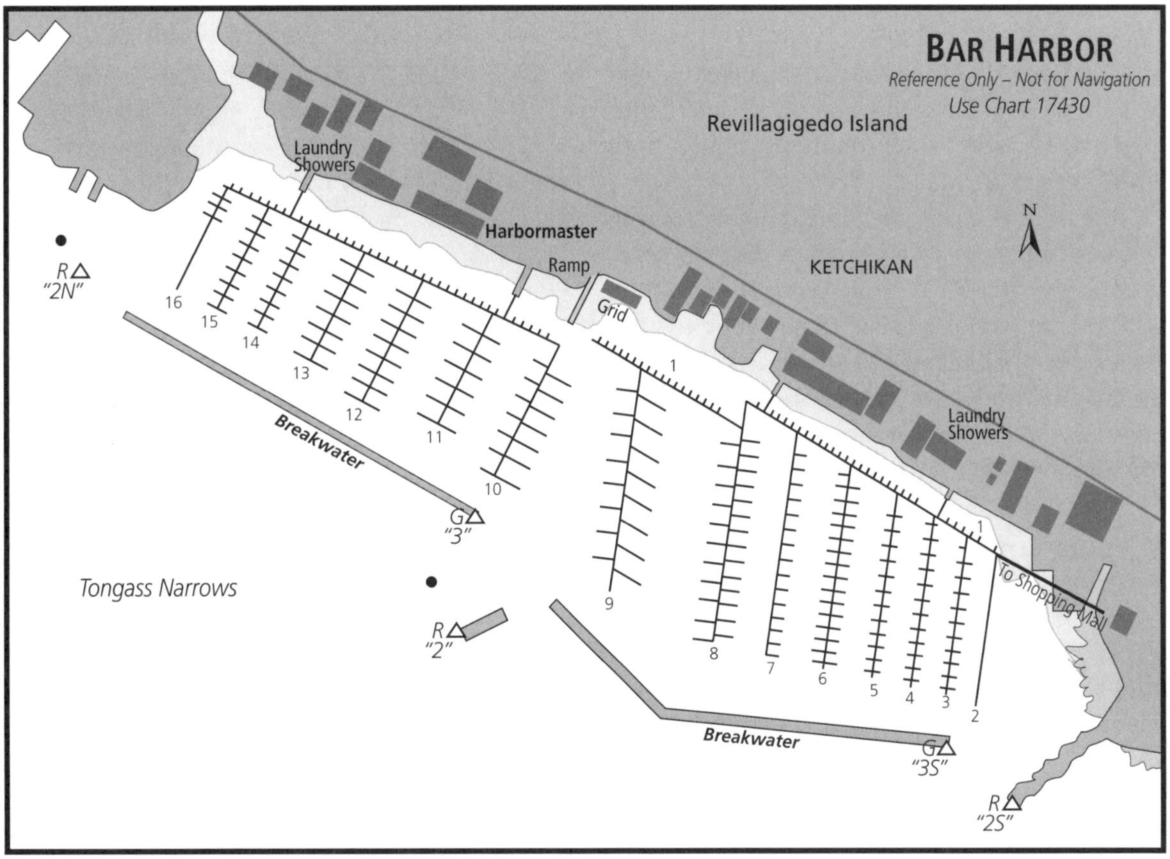

Linda Lewis

*Don't forget to watch for cruise ship traffic as you exit Ketchikan—fairway space can get tight.*

power (be sure to specify your needs when you inquire about a slip), showers and laundry and is close to supermarkets, liquor store and restaurants.

This large harbor is home to many fishing vessels and may provide your first up-close look at the real life of those who still work the sea. In fact, you are likely to be "hot-berthed" in a space that belongs to a fishing vessel that is out on the water. Take time to watch the labor and consider the long hours involved in the fishing life. It's a real education.

## Airport Small-craft Passenger Float
(Ketchikan Harbor)

Airport small-craft passenger float is 0.2 mile southeast of the airport tower and 0.7 mile northwest of Bar Harbor.

Chart 17430
Float: 55°21.27′ N, 131°42.24′ W

The small-craft float south of the passenger terminal is part of Seattle's old Lake Washington floating bridge.

Réanne Hemingway-Douglass

*Small boats can use the dock at the Ketchikan Airport to pick up their guests.*

## **Bald Headed Cove** (Pennock Island)

Bald Headed Cove is in the East Channel on Pennock Island and across from Saxman Village.

Chart 17430
Entrance: 55°19.01′ N, 131°36.72′ W

Bald Headed Cove is a small cove on the southeast side of Pennock Island.

## **Whisky Cove** (Pennock Island)

Whisky Cove, on the east side of Pennock Island, is across from the Coast Guard Base.

Chart 17430
Position: 55°19.73′ N, 131°37.95′ W

> *Whisky Cove* . . . [is] *about 0.45 mile S of Radenbough Cove.* (CP)

## **Radenbough Cove** (Pennock Island)

Radenbough Cove is immediately across from Thomas Basin.

Chart 17430
Position: 55°20.05′ N, 131°38.66′ W

> *Radenbough Cove* [is] *on the NE side of and about 0.5 mile S of the N end of Pennock Island. . . . Grids for vessels up to 30 feet long are available in the cove.* (CP)

## **Clam Cove** (Gravina Island)

Clam Cove is in West Channel, 0.9 mile south of Pennock Reef.

Chart 17430
Position: 55°19.50′ N, 131°39.77′ W

Clam Cove is a log booming area. Some shelter can be found from southeast weather close to the drying mud flats in the cove or in the unnamed cove 0.6 mile to the north. Both anchorages are temporary at best and subject to the wake of passing ships.

## **Ward Cove** (Revillagigedo Island)

Ward Cove is 3.3 miles northwest of Bar Harbor.

Chart 17428 (inset)
Entrance (0.25 mile east of East Island): 55°23.73′ N, 131°44.35′ W

> *Ward Cove, entered about 0.7 mile N of Peninsula Point, is on the N side of Tongass Narrows about 5 miles NW of Ketchikan. The cove is about 0.3 mile wide at the entrance, wider inside, and has steep shores. . . .*
>
> *Bolles Ledge, near the head and about 250 yards off the E shore, is covered by a least depth of 1.8 fathoms. A long log boom extends from the NE end of an inoperative pulpmill to the ledge. East Island is a wooded islet off the NW side of the entrance. A midchannel course leads safely into the cove, and there are no known dangers other than those mentioned.* (CP)

Ward Cove is the site of a large pulp mill and log storage area.

## **Refuge Cove** (Revillagigedo Island)

Refuge Cove is 3.8 miles northwest of Bar Harbor and 5.2 miles southeast of Guard Island.

Chart 17428
Entrance: 55°24.05′ N, 131°45.07′ W

> *W of Ward Cove and near the N side of Tongass Narrows is a group of islands . . . and rocks awash which are mostly surrounded by ledges. These small islands protect Refuge Cove from any swells that might be running in Tongass Narrows. The S side of the cove is clear. . . . A marina in the cove has floats with a total berthing capacity of 3,500 feet in length, and a reported depth of 40 feet alongside. The entrance to the cove is marked by a light and daybeacons. Water, electricity, gasoline, some marine supplies, storage, and a launching ramp are available.* (CP)

## **Mud Bay** (Revillagigedo Island)

Mud Bay is 4.1 miles southeast of Guard Island and 1.2 miles northwest of Refuge Cove.

Chart 17428
Position: 55°25.00′ N, 131°46.14′ W

> *Mud Cove, on the N side of the narrows . . . is shallow, with bare flats that extend 100 yards or more offshore. A boatyard is on the N side of the bay at the entrance.* (CP)

## **Guard Islands Light** (Tongass Narrows)

Guard Islands Light is at the northwest entrance to Tongass Narrows.

Chart 17428
Northwest entrance to Tongass Narrows (0.75 mile east of Guard Island Light): 55°26.75′ N, 131°51.54′ W

*Guard Islands, two in number, wooded, and close together, about 1.5 miles NW of Vallenar Point, guard the W entrance to Tongass Narrows. Guard Islands Light, 74 feet above the water, is shown from a white square tower on a rectangular building on the N island of the group.*

*About 0.3 mile SE of Guard Islands is a large kelp patch marking a reef covered 0.6 fathom. Passage can be made on either side of the reef, but Inside Passage, between the reef and Vallenar Rock and 0.6 mile wide, is preferred. An 8.5-fathom patch is near the middle of Inside Passage about 0.7 mile SE from Guard Islands Light.* (CP)

Linda Lewis

*The bright red and white* Empress of the North *is a uniquely designed cruise ship that will catch your eye.*

---

## Alaskan Eyes

**Don Douglass**

*Note:* In the days before Alaska became a state, most of the pink and chum salmon were taken from nets attached to floating fish traps anchored offshore. The traps were tended by watchmen who lived in a crude shack built on top of the float. These traps were outlawed after Alaska attained statehood.

It was July 1950, and I was a teenager fresh from the Lower 48. I had hired on for the summer season as an assistant watchman on a salmon fish trap. The trap, anchored off the southern tip of Revillagigedo Island, was tethered to shore by its 600-foot-long net, and it sat square in the face of whatever weather came blasting north from Dixon Entrance, a few miles away.

Since the trap tenders came just once a week to pick up the fish, other than fending off an occasional fish pirate and keeping up with maintenance, there wasn't a lot to do. I could spend my time rowing, fishing, diving, or—if the weather was lousy—reading.

One beautiful day, I had taken the 16-foot working skiff to a small bight a half-mile to the east and was free diving for king crab along the sandy bottom. I had

*(Continued on next page)*

*(Continued from previous page)*

managed to pull one up on my improvised hook before it slid off and scrambled quickly into the eel grass 20 feet below the drifting skiff.

I took a deep breath, preparing to dive after it, when I was stopped by the sight of a big rack of antlers bearing down on me. I grabbed the transom of the skiff, ready to hop out of the water as a five-pointer raced by, just twenty yards away, heading for the other end of the bight. Clearly, a bear or a pack of wolves had cornered the deer on one end of the spit, and he had decided to beat a fast retreat to the north side of the bight.

My heart pumped. This was my buck, and his rack would make a beautiful trophy. I quickly pulled myself into the skiff, and rowed in hot pursuit. Only two days to the opening day of hunting season: everything would be legal, I thought, if I could just catch him and keep him alive till then. Joe, my partner on the fish trap, would know how to dress the carcass, and instead of the canned and smoked stuff the trap owner provided, we could have fresh meat.

But I couldn't risk being caught with a poached deer—it would cost me my fishing license and summer income for college. How to pull it off?

First, I had to get him on board. Pulling alongside him, I looked at those horns and realized they're made for fighting males stronger and faster than I was. Trying to capture him with my bare hands was out of the question. Along with dreams of fresh meat, my courage waned.

But, wait! The skiff painter, twenty-five feet of rough manila line, might just make a lasso and even up my odds for a capture. A quick bowline-on-a-bight and I lassoed him, grabbed him by the horns, hauled him on board, tied his hoofs with the line, and rowed back to the trap.

Joe and I heaved "Big Deer"—as we soon named him—into our six-by-ten-foot shack, tied his thrashing feet to his antlers and settled down for a 48-hour wait.

That night, a southeast gale off Dixon Entrance came up and assaulted the 100-foot square trap with breaking seas. Two- to three-foot water spouts began shooting up between the cracks in the floor, wetting everything inside. Joe got nervous.

There was a shack on shore that provided shelter in case we had to evacuate the fish trap, but reaching it would be suicidal. Joe couldn't swim, and rowing the 600 feet to that rocky shore in these conditions was impossible.

The storm increased during the night, and Joe began talking to God. I stared out the small window, watching the breakers sweep across the trap. Then I spotted running lights. I figured it was a cruise ship; no small boat could make it through seas like this, tonight. I grabbed our powerful flashlight and began sending a slow SOS signal into the dark. Soon, a large local fishing boat pulled alongside and Joe and I were taken on board by the daring crew—good-hearted Ketchikan folk who were out raiding fish traps vacated due to the storm. (Later, we learned two lives were lost that night.)

The crew treated us for hypothermia, filling us with hot soup and booze as the boat shook and rolled at anchor in nearby Lucky Cove. Thirty-six hours later, they returned us to our fish trap which, amazingly, was still in one piece, with the deer now lying exhausted and passive in a corner.

Forty-eight hours had passed, and according to the plan, it was time to dispatch Big Deer. But he was a pitiful sight. In the pounding from the storm, and his efforts to escape, he had worn his skin raw. He couldn't move a muscle. He was beat, and he knew it was the end. He'd evaded a savage attack by bear, only to die by slow torture at the hands of his two-legged captors.

I couldn't escape his stare. His big, dark eyes, alert and beautiful, followed me everywhere. His brain processed my slightest move. And in that tiny room, there was no place to hide.

Finally, Joe looked at Big Deer and said, "Okay, this guy's history. I've got my knife. You get the gun, and let's move him outside for the slaughter."

My stomach tightened. My throat thickened. This was the biggest, easiest kill of my life but those big dark eyes kept watching my every move. Eyes pleading with me for a fair chance to do combat—man to man, like when I hauled him aboard the skiff—just one more chance. I couldn't pull the trigger on him. Not me. Not now. "No!" I told Joe. "We'll load him in the skiff, and I'll row him ashore."

I rowed him back to the bight, beached the skiff and searched the sand for fresh bear or wolf tracks. There weren't any.

I laid the buck gently on the sand and carefully untied his bindings. All the time he just kept staring at me, with those beautiful dark eyes. Finally, I stepped back 10 yards and said, "Go for it!"

He stood up slowly, wobbling like a newborn fawn. "Go for it!" I repeated. He glanced at me once more, shook himself and took off, leaping and bounding into the brush. And all I could see were those big dark eyes.

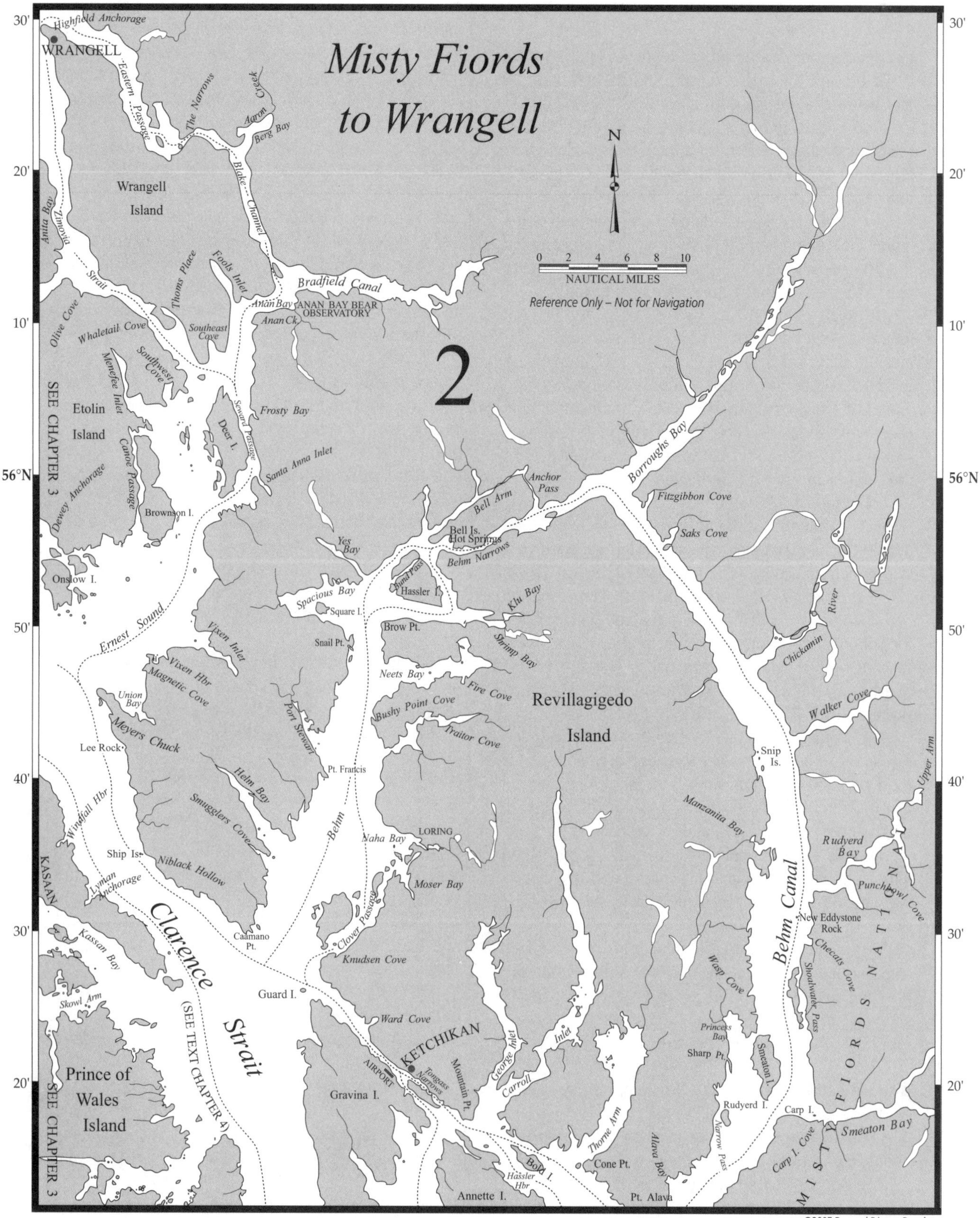

Misty Fiords
to Wrangell
2
N
0 2 4 6 8 10
NAUTICAL MILES
Reference Only – Not for Navigation
WRANGELL
Highfield Anchorage
Eastern Passage
The Narrows
Aaron Creek
Berg Bay
Blake Channel
Wrangell Island
Anita Bay
Zimovia Strait
Thoms Place
Fools Inlet
Bradfield Canal
Anan Bay
ANAN BAY BEAR OBSERVATORY
Anan Ck.
Olive Cove
Whaletail Cove
Southeast Cove
Menefee Inlet
Southwest Cove
SEE CHAPTER 3
Etolin Island
Canoe Passage
Seward Passage
Deer I.
Frosty Bay
Dewey Anchorage
Brownson I.
Santa Anna Inlet
Borroughs Bay
Anchor Pass
Bell Arm
Fitzgibbon Cove
Bell Is. Hot Springs
Behm Narrows
Saks Cove
Yes Bay
Onslow I.
Spacious Bay
Hassler I.
Square I.
Klu Bay
Ernest Sound
Vixen Inlet
Brow Pt.
Snail Pt.
Shrimp Bay
Chickamin River
Vixen Hbr
Magnetic Cove
Neets Bay
Fire Cove
Union Bay
Bushy Point Cove
Revillagigedo Island
Walker Cove
Meyers Chuck
Port Stewart
Traitor Cove
Lee Rock
Snip Is.
Pt. Francis
Upper Arm
Helm Bay
Windfall Hbr
Smugglers Cove
Behm
Manzanita Bay
Naha Bay
LORING
Rudyerd Bay
Ship Is.
Niblack Hollow
Moser Bay
Behm Canal
Punchbowl Cove
KASAAN
Lyman Anchorage
Clarence Strait
New Eddystone Rock
Caamano Pt.
Clover Passage
Checats Cove
Kassan Bay
Knudsen Cove
Wasp Cove
Shoalwater Pass
MISTY FIORDS NATIONAL
Guard I.
Skowl Arm
(SEE TEXT CHAPTER 4)
Ward Cove
KETCHIKAN
Princess Bay
George Inlet
Carroll Inlet
Sharp Pt.
Smeaton I.
Prince of Wales Island
AIRPORT
Tongass Narrows
Mountain Pt.
Gravina I.
Rudyerd I.
Carp I.
Smeaton Bay
Thorne Arm
Narrow Pass
Carp I. Cove
Alava Bay
Bold I.
Cone Pt.
Hassler Hbr
Annette I.
Pt. Alava
SEE CHAPTER 3
30'
20'
10'
56°N
50'
40'

# 2

# MISTY FIORDS TO WRANGELL VIA BEHM CANAL, MEYERS CHUCK AND ERNEST SOUND

## INTRODUCTION

The area from Ketchikan and Misty Fiords to Wrangell is often called the "banana belt" by native Southeasterners. Although the area gets a lot of precipitation, summer temperatures are usually mild, and wind and seas are less changeable and extreme than farther north. This region is popular with hunters, fishermen, miners and explorers of all kinds, and while it is rapidly becoming a tourist mecca, you still get a real sense of the frontier spirit once you venture away from the cruise ship port areas. In Ketchikan, itself, it is not uncommon to see three or four large cruise ships at the same time.

A circumnavigation of Revillagigedo Island via Behm Canal and a visit to hauntingly beautiful Misty Fiords National Monument gives you an excellent introduction to the rainforests and fiords of Southeast Alaska. Magnificent scenery and wildlife are the rewards for putting up with the rain that averages over half an inch per day. This area, known for its world-class salmon fishing, is remote and intensely beautiful; this is where you can immerse yourself in solitude and primitive surroundings and fish to your heart's content.

Located to the east and south of Revillagigedo Island, Misty Fiords National Monument, established in 1978, encompasses 2.2 million acres of unspoiled wilderness. You'll see beautiful, deeply cut fiords, glacier-fed streams and rivers and waterfalls that careen off 3,000-foot sheer cliffs, plummeting directly into the icy sea. This is an excellent spot to watch for Alaska's abundant wildlife—humpback whales, orcas, sea lions, bald eagles and, in August, spawning salmon.

Réanne Hemingway-Douglass

*Research Vessel* Baidarka *in Misty Fiords*

## Anchoring Challenges in Southeast Alaska

### Q & A with Brian Pemberton of NW Explorations

Most of us who dream of cruising our boat to Southeast Alaska have anchored our boats a fair amount. But we also know that the challenge of anchoring is different up there where the water is deeper, the bottom is rockier, the winds may be bigger and sometimes the williwaws come sweeping down from the mountains straining your boat hard against its anchor rode. You may feel the need for a little extra wisdom. Here are some words of guidance from an expert with lots of Southeast Alaska experience so you can feel better prepared. Brian Pemberton, of NW Explorations, a charter company in Bellingham, WA, has answers to some of the often-asked Southeast Alaska anchoring questions.

**Q:** *I'm nervous about my abilities to anchor in Southeast Alaska. It all seems so complex.*

**Brian:** A little apprehension is healthy but there is no reason to be nervous. Approach anchoring with a soft touch, with ease and gentleness. Anchoring has only one simple purpose: to the hold the boat.

You need to leave behind your preconceived notions about "only this type or weight of anchor is right," or "only this type and length of rode will be found on my boat," or "only certain types of secluded locations will be acceptable for putting my hook down," or "I must always be close to land."

**Q:** *But what do you mean? I thought there was a certain way to do this?*

**Brian:** Burst that balloon before you slip your lines. In truth, all of anchoring is about making choices based on the situation before you. The farther north you go, the more you must deal with anchoring "wherever you can find a place,"... and more likely than not, when you do find that place it will be deep and the wind may be blowing.

**Q:** *How deep is deep?*

**Brian:** At least 50 feet. Every Southeast Alaska cruiser needs to be prepared for anchorages at that depth, for anchorages with wind, big tidal ranges (~25 feet), and occasional 3-knot currents swirling through the anchorage.

**Q:** *Sounds intimidating. How should I prepare for those circumstances?*

Linda Lewis

*Rocks create anchoring challenges.*

**Brian:** It doesn't need to be daunting. Good planning will take you a long way.

**Q:** *I'd like to start with the anchor. What kind should I get and how heavy?*

**Brian:** I'm going to surprise you. An oversized, heavy anchor hanging off the end of your bow pulpit does not make good sense. That only adds weight to your bow and awkwardly extends the fulcrum point. An anchor is only one part in your ground tackle system. The more important picture is the combined weight of the anchor *and* the rode—usually chain for most Southeast Alaska cruisers.

**Q:** *OK, I'm hearing you: don't overdo the size of anchor for the boat. Do use chain (or a combination of chain*

*(Continued on next page)*

(Continued from previous page)

*and nylon). Tell me more. What anchor do you use on your boat?*

**Brian:** Now we're getting into one of boating's most passionate subjects: which anchor and how many pounds. Over-rated debate, folks. I'm not a passionate fan of one type of anchor over another. And I'm not in favor of oversized anchors.

**Q:** *Well what do you use on your boat?*

**Brian:** My boat is a 57-foot LOA [length overall]; I have a 60-pound CQR because I believe it is better in rocks. (My 60 lb anchor would be considered in the mid-range of what manufacturers recommend.) Some folks swear by the Bruce anchor. We have a Danforth for backup, which is best in mud.

**Q:** *If the anchor is not the star of the show, what is?*

**Brian:** The big picture is the combined setup of the anchor and its rode. In Southeast Alaska waters a long chain rode is as important a part of your ground tackle as is the anchor. It's all about getting weight down to the bottom of the ocean, laying it out in a nice line that parallels the bottom as much as possible, then "setting" the anchor into the bottom until it holds well, then taking the next steps.

**Q:** *Talk more about chain. What size, length?*

**Brian:** My 57-foot LOA boat has 400-foot BBB 3/8 chain (11,000-pound breaking strength) and 300 feet of 5/8 3-strand New England rope (12,200 breaking strength); total rode equals 700 feet. Between my 60-pound anchor and my 680 pounds of chain, I can withstand just about anything.

**Q:** *What about my smaller boat?*

**Brian:** If your LOA is ~42 feet, you probably use 5/16 chain (most cruisers have this size chain) which has a breaking strength of 7600 pound; your 1/2-inch nylon 3-strand has a breaking strength of 7500 pounds.

**Q:** *Why nylon? And isn't that little nylon rope a bit small for the job?*

**Brian:** That "little" rope has a 12,200-pound breaking strength. And here is why nylon is really important: it gives. nylon stretches 40 percent of its length under a load, thus protecting the set, ground tackle and pulpit. When the pull is reduced, the nylon returns to its original length, ready for the next stretch. The load of the boat isn't on your non-forgiving chain, but rather, on your resilient nylon.

Linda Lewis

*Kelp prevents an easy set.*

**Q:** *I'm convinced. Now what about the "Anchor Bridle" you like so much?*

**Brian:** The anchor bridle gets put in place after you have deployed and set your anchor and played out your desired scope. You start with an anchor chain grabber that gets placed on your anchor chain. The nylon line bridle comes off each side of the grabber and is led up through a convenient fairlead onto the deck of the boat. An anchor bridle should have a minimum of 15 feet of nylon line (use the same size as your nylon rode) on each side of the anchor chain grabber.

**Q:** *Seems like a lot of fuss to have a fancy bridle out there. Why am I doing this?*

**Brian:** It is critical to have an anchor bridle; the advantages are enormous. The entire load of the boat is

(Continued on next page)

*(Continued from previous page)*

shifted away from the pulpit that is sticking up high in the air (where we don't want the weight) to a lower spot on the boat (where we do want the weight), then through fairleads where the bridle lines can be well secured. An anchor bridle is especially critical if you have an all-chain rode. It may be the only stretch you have in your entire system.

**Q:** *So far this looks like a lot of money for ground tackle.*

**Brian:** A man whom I very much respect, Mr. Don Douglass, recommends that 5 percent of the value of your boat should go into ground tackle. I agree with him. How much is safety and security worth to you and your crew?

**Q:** *Well, now I'm equipped. Let's get to the anchorage and do something. Walk me through this.*

**Brian:** This is the time for making choices related to the situation you are in. Assess the weather, the wind (current and expected), tidal activity, other boats nearby, rocky bottoms, steep bottoms, very, very deep bottoms, little swinging room, scope issues, chance of wiliwaws, etc. Take a small cruise around your selected anchorage and look carefully. The Southeast Alaska charts are not as accurate as we wish they were. Look out the window; watch your depth sounder. Have a bow watch.

Think to yourself: here is what I have to work with, how can I optimize my situation? For example, if the weather makes you want to seek a "bomb-proof" anchorage, can you get there before dark? Or should you stay where you are and plan to let out much greater scope.

**Q:** *My anchor is in position to deploy; here we go.*

**Brian:** Hold it. Hold it. One more thing to think about: Windlasses draw enormous power. Consider turning your generator on before you start your anchoring maneuvers. It's a good idea to presume that it will take three tries to get a good set.

**Q:** *Three times! You can't be serious.*

**Brian:** Keep your power up; you won't be sorry. It's OK to take three times. This is not a contest; this is about getting a good set that will keep everyone on your boat safe and happy.

**Q:** *I'm really ready now.*

**Brian:** Do yourself a favor and don't dump your anchor and a large amount of chain over the front of the boat like you're trying to build a pyramid down there. Slowly lower your anchor until it touches the ground. Then ever so gently put your boat in reverse, paying out the chain as you idle or drift slowly backwards. Lay a nice trail of chain along the bottom of the ocean. At some point you decide to "set" your anchor. Easy does it. High powered boats should barely bump into reverse and come right back out.

**Q:** *How do I know it's set?*

**Brian:** When an anchor is set, as you are in reverse, the rode will raise up out of the water in a straight line, approaching parallel to the water. The rode (especially chain rode) becomes almost as stiff as a rod. One cruiser with chain suggests that you put your hand lightly on the chain and "listen" to the chain when you are testing for set and you're not sure. You can actually feel the chain bumping and klunking over rocks or fishtailing back and forth over eel grass or kelp if it is not set. If it is set, the chain rises up in that straight line and takes on the feel of a solid, stiff cable. If it's not set, letting out a little more rode and doing setting maneuvers again often does the trick.

**Q:** *I see. I have the chain laid out nicely, I have a good set, and I have let out appropriate scope for the circumstances—I hope.*

**Brian:** Remember that scope decisions are situational. If you anticipate a 50 plus knot gale, you need 7:1 scope. Those are the times you will be glad you have 350 feet of rode.

**Q:** *OK, I'm done now right?*

**Brian:** Not by a long shot. Put that anchor bridle in place as the final and important touch. You firmly attach the chain grabber to the chain, then you lead each line through its fairlead and secure it on a strong cleat or capstan. *Then*, don't forget the next critical step: You now let out additional chain until you have a nice big loop of chain hanging down. For example, if you are anchoring in 25 feet of water, after the bridle has been secured, let out another 50 feet of chain. That way the nylon rope of the bridle is taking all the strain and is doing so closer to the ground.

**Q:** *I think I'm ready to try it.*

**Brian:** Remember to have a soft touch. Don't be in a hurry. Be ready to make repeated tries, and sleep well!

Wrangell, the jumping off point to the goldfields up the mighty Stikine River, has the feel of old Alaska. Fewer cruise ships call at Wrangell and it's refreshing to enter a port full of working boats and a few pleasure craft. The Shakes Island longhouse and the petroglyphs along the beach make historic Wrangell a fascinating place to visit.

Anan Bear and Wildlife Observatory, 22 miles southeast of Wrangell, is well worth the stop. A short hike on a good boardwalk trail through the rainforest leads to a waterfall where the bear feed on migrating salmon.

David Parker

*Entering Rudyerd Bay from Behm Canal brings into view the dramatic wall in Punchbowl Cove; sharing this amazing sight with guests is an added pleasure.*

Three main cruising routes lead from Ketchikan to Wrangell: 1) the direct route used by larger vessels through Clarence and Stikine Straits (via Chichagof Pass); 2) the popular, more protected cruising route via Clarence Strait and Ernest Sound, Seward Passage and Zimovia Strait; and 3) the longer, more scenic, most protected of the three routes, which leads through Clarence Strait, Ernest Sound, Seward Passage, Blake Channel and Eastern Passage. This chapter deals only with the latter two routes. The first route through Clarence and Stikine Straits is detailed in Chapter 3.

## Behm Canal and Misty Fiords National Monument

Behm Canal borders the east, north and west sides of Revillagigedo Island; Misty Fiords National Monument extends along the east side of Behm Canal.

**Charts 17434, 17424, 17422, 17420, 17423**
**Southeast entrance (mid-channel between Point Alava and Point Sykes): 55°11.52′ N, 131°07.60′ W**
**Northwest entrance (mid-channel between Caamano Point and Point Higgins): 55°28.60′ N, 131°54.22′ W**

> [Behm Canal's] *E entrance, between Point Sykes and Point Alava, is about 5.7 miles NNE of Mary Island Light. The W entrance of the canal between Point Higgins and Caamano Point is about 2 miles N of Guard Islands Light; the distance from the E entrance to the W entrance through Revillagigedo Channel and Tongass Narrows is about 30 miles; the length of the canal from entrance to entrance is about 100 miles. The main channel of the canal is exceptionally free from dangers, with no submerged rocks or ledges that cannot be easily avoided by a stranger in clear weather.*
>
> *Naval restricted areas are in Behm Canal along the W side of Revillagigedo Island.* (CP)

Misty Fiords National Monument, which was established in 1978, encompasses 2.2 million acres. Although most of Misty Fiords is designated as wilderness, a portion within the Monument, including upper Smeaton Bay and the head of Boca de Quadra, was designated as non-wilderness to allow exploration and development of a potentially commercial molybdenum deposit at Quartz Hill. Hemlock, spruce and cedar grow on vertical granite slopes; numerous waterfalls tumble from snow-filled bowls; and gentle rain gives the area its misty appearance. Accessible only by float plane or boat, the Monument has rapidly become a popular destination for kayakers. Within the Monument, the U.S. Forest Service maintains

14 recreational cabins, a few mooring buoys, and some hiking trails. For more information, contact the Ketchikan—Misty Fiords Ranger District, 3031 Tongass, Ketchikan, AK, 99901 (tel.: 907.225.2148; fax: 907.225.8738). Website: mistyfiords.org.

For those cruisers whose schedule does not permit travel beyond Ketchikan, a circumnavigation of Revillagigedo Island via Behm Canal may be enticing. Taking side trips into Smeaton Bay, Rudyerd Bay and Walker Cove provides the most dramatic scenery of the circumnavigation. Finding anchorages along the way will require attention. Many cruisers with a time-limited schedule head south out of Ketchikan (after clearing customs), then north up Behm Canal past the landmark New Eddystone Rock and into Rudyerd Bay (about a 45-mile trip) and Punchbowl Cove. If you can make only one anchorage in Behm Canal, this would be the one to choose.

Throughout the Monument the fiords are steep-to and deep, and mud flats shoal rapidly at the head of the inlets, offering few possibilities for anchoring. Most of the anchor sites lie along the shore of Behm Canal, and many offer only marginal shelter. You may be able to pick up one of the public buoys, as noted in the text.

Within the Monument, you are out of reach of National Weather Service broadcasts from Annette Island.

The weather, as the name of the National Monument implies, is often overcast with frequent rain or drizzle (over 150 inches per year). Wind and chop are short-lived and benign, and because of the heavy fresh-water outflows, the current is largely a continuous ebb on the surface.

## Sykes Cove (Behm Canal)

Sykes Cove is on the east side of the southeast entrance to Behm Canal.

Chart 17434
Entrance: 55°12.04′ N, 131°04.82′ W
Anchor: 55°11.75′ N, 131°04.90′ W

Shelter from southerly winds can be found in Sykes on the north side of Point Sykes. Swinging room is limited.

Anchor off the beach at the head of the cove.

## Point Alava (Revillagigedo Island)

Point Alava, on the southern tip of Revillagigedo Island, is the south entrance to Behm Canal.

Chart 17434
Position (0.5 mile southeast of Point Alava): 55°11.11′ N, 131°10.58′ W

## Alava Bay (Revillagigedo Island)

Alava Bay, on the west shore of Behm Canal, is about 2.4 miles northeast of Point Alava.

Chart 17434
Entrance: 55°12.78′ N, 131°08.23′ W
Anchor: 55°13.52′ N, 131°09.13′ W

> *Alava Bay . . . is partly open to S weather. Depths in the main part of the W bight are 16 to 28 fathoms, but fair shelter for small vessels can be found close inshore in 6 to 10 fathoms, soft bottom. . . . The entrance to the W bight is constricted by a 1-1/2-fathom shoal in midchannel. . . . The E bight is clear, but too deep to afford anchorage.* (CP)

Fair-to-good shelter is found in the far west bight of Alava Bay during stable conditions, but there is little protection in a strong southerly blow. There may be a private buoy in the bight.

Anchor in 6 to 10 fathoms near the beach over mud bottom with fair holding.

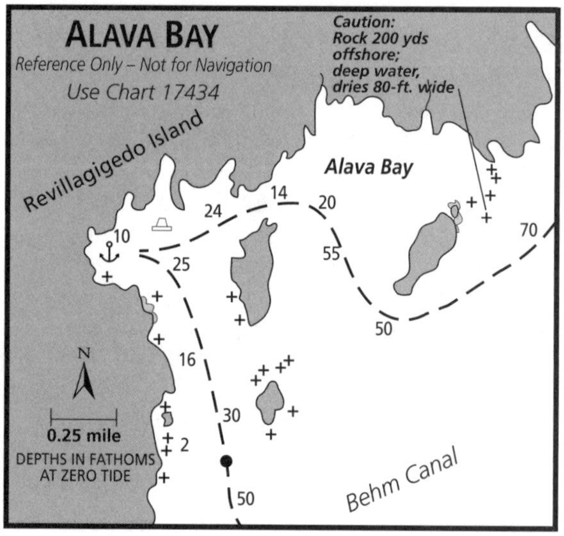

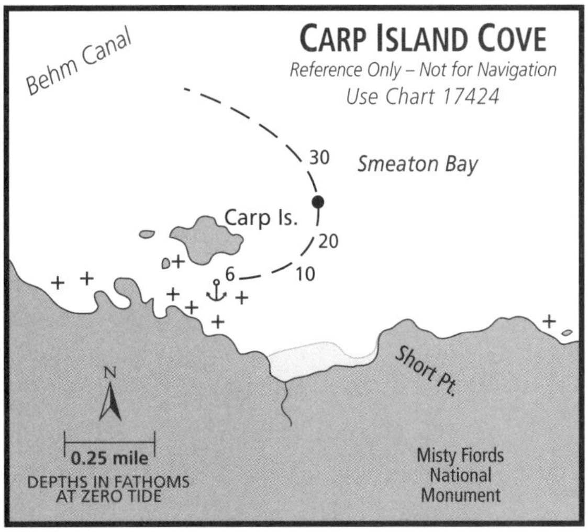



## Rudyerd Island, Narrow Pass
(Behm Canal)

Rudyerd Island and Narrow Pass are on the west side of Behm Canal, 8.5 miles northeast of Alava Bay.

Charts 17434, 17424
Entrance (north bight): 55°18.42′ N, 131°02.30′ W

> *The NE and SW shores of Rudyerd Island are very foul and should be given a wide berth. Small craft can find some shelter from SE blows in the two narrow bights at the N end of the island. Such craft have tied to the steep W shore of the W bight. The head of the W bight is shallow and rocky; in 1957 an anchored 50-foot cruiser grounded on a falling tide 100 yards from the S shore.* (CP)

A lee can be found on the north shore of Rudyerd Island from southerly storms. The water is steep-to and has very limited swinging room. We would prefer Sykes Cove to the south or Roe Point Cove and Carp Island to the east for convenience and comfort.

## Roe Point Cove (Behm Canal)

Roe Point Cove, on the east shore of Behm Canal, is 2.7 miles southeast of Rudyerd Island.

Chart 17434
Entrance: 55°14.69′ N, 131°00.26′ W
Anchor: 55°14.55′ N, 131°00.13′ W

> *The cove E of Roe Point, on the east shore, is a fair anchorage for small craft in 5 to 10 fathoms, soft bottom.* (CP)

## Carp Island Cove (Behm Canal)

Carp Island Cove is on the south side of the entrance to Smeaton Bay.

Charts 17434, 17424
Entrance: 55°17.99′ N, 130°52.85′ W
Anchor (south of island) 55°17.86′ N, 130°53.24′ W

> *. . . [B]etween Carp Island and Short Point, a vessel can lie in summer in 19 fathoms, hard bottom, protected from the summer winds. Small vessels may find shelter close to Short Point in 5 to 10 fathoms.* (CP)

The area off Carp Island is reported to be a very good crabbing area and it is a favorite summer anchorage for local cruising boats that anchor just south of Carp Island or on the shoal closer to Short Point. However, downslope or outflow winds (from the north) can make this a rough anchorage. One cruiser has reported to us that they found the bottom in this cove to be very rocky; they had to leave after repeated efforts to set their anchor failed.

Anchor in about 6 fathoms.

## Smeaton Bay (Behm Canal)

Smeaton Bay, on the east side of Behm Canal, is 9.8 miles northeast of Point Sykes.

Chart 17424
Entrance (Smeaton Bay, mid-channel between Nelson and Trollop): 55°18.56′ N, 130°53.49′ W
Entrance (Bakewell and Wilson arms, 6.6 miles east of Smeaton Bay entrance): 55°18.80′ N, 130°41.97′ W

> *Smeaton Bay enters Behm Canal from E . . . and E of the S end of Smeaton Island.*
>
> *Seven miles from the entrance, the bay divides into Wilson Arm and Bakewell Arm. A mining camp is on the S shore of Wilson Arm about 3.5 miles from the entrance.* (CP)

Smeaton Bay is the first of three majestic fiords cut deep into the mainland shore of Behm Canal.

## Sharp Point (Revillagigedo Island)

Sharp Point is 1.6 miles west of Smeaton Island.

Chart 17424
Entrance (cove west of Sharp Point): 55°20.55′ N, 131°01.78′ W
Anchor (cove 1.4 miles southwest of Sharp Point): 55°19.47′ N, 131°03.09′ W

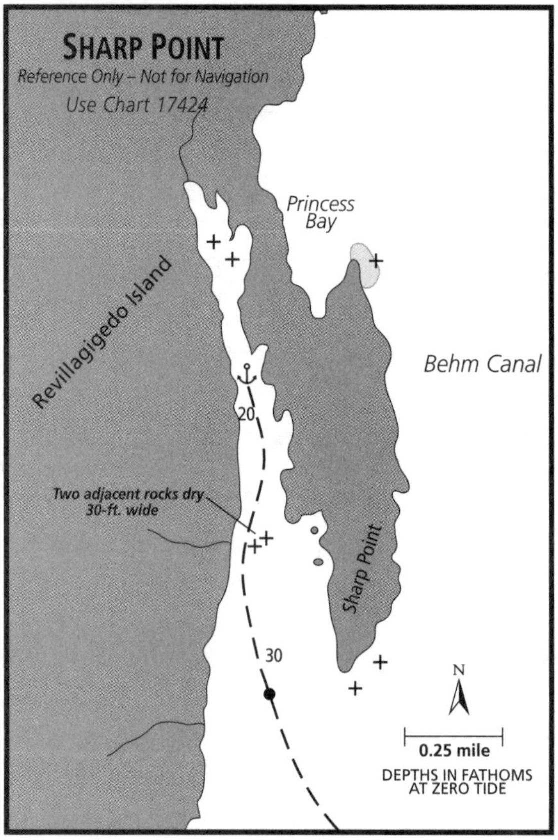




**Anchor (lee of Sharp Point): 55°21.03′ N, 131°01.82′ W**
**Entrance (cove 1 mile north of Sharp Point): 55°21.59′ N, 131°01.49′ W**
**Anchor: (cove 1 mile north of Sharp Point): 55°21.42′ N, 131°01.65′ W**

> *Small craft can find anchorage in the small bight in the W shore about 1 mile N of Sharp Point in 15 to 20 fathoms, hard bottom. This anchorage affords good protection from S and SE winds. Anchorage for small craft can be had in the bight to W of Sharp Point, depths ranging from 5 to 20 fathoms, hard bottom. In entering favor the W shore. Very small craft can find a land-locked anchorage in the bight on the W shore, about 1.5 miles SW of Sharp Point in 2 fathoms, soft bottom. . . . Enter only on a rising tide with local knowledge, and use extreme caution.* (CP)

Sharp Point provides anchorage in three nearby sites—one on the Behm Canal side of the peninsula, one on the bight and in the lee of Sharp Point immediately west and in the shallow cove 1.5 miles to the southwest. Each site is essentially uncharted and requires a careful approach. The mid-channel charted rock 0.25 mile northwest of Sharp Point is, in fact, two separate rocks. Anchor in depths as required. Swinging room is limited in all three sites.

## **Princess Bay** (Revillagigedo Island)

Princess Bay is 0.6 mile southwest of Wasp Point.

**Chart 17424**

> *Princess Bay, to the W of Smeaton Island, is open and exposed to the S. Deep water extends close to the shores, and depths in the bay are too great for anchorage. Short Pass, between the N end of Smeaton Island and Wasp Point, has a depth of 11 fathoms.* (CP)

## **Wasp Cove** (Revillagigedo Island)

Wasp Cove, on the west shore of Behm Canal, is about 3 miles north of Smeaton Island.

**Chart 17424**
**Entrance: 55°25.76′ N, 130°58.74′ W**
**Anchor: 55°25.64′ N, 130°59.21′ W**

> [Wasp Cove] *affords anchorage for small craft in 5 to 7 fathoms, soft bottom, free from obstructions.* (CP)

Wasp Cove is reported to provide good shelter in all but northeast winds.

Anchor in about 7 fathoms over soft bottom with fair-to-good holding.

## **Shoalwater Pass** (Behm Canal)

Shoalwater Pass, on the east side of Behm Canal, separates Winstanley Island from the mainland.

**Chart 17424**
**South entrance: 55°23.40′ N, 130°53.32′ W**
**North entrance: 55°27.96′ N, 130°54.17′ W**
**Anchor (USFS cabin): 55°27.07′ N, 130°54.32′ W**

> *Shoalwater Pass . . . is divided into two separate anchorages, the N one being the better of the two, with depths of 5 to 33 fathoms, mud bottom. The S anchorage has depths of 12 to 27 fathoms, mud bottom. Small craft can pass through the narrows between the anchorages at high water.* (CP)

There is a U.S. Forest Service cabin and float on Winstanley Island at the northwest end of the north anchorage. The shallow water in front of the cabin offers very good shelter from

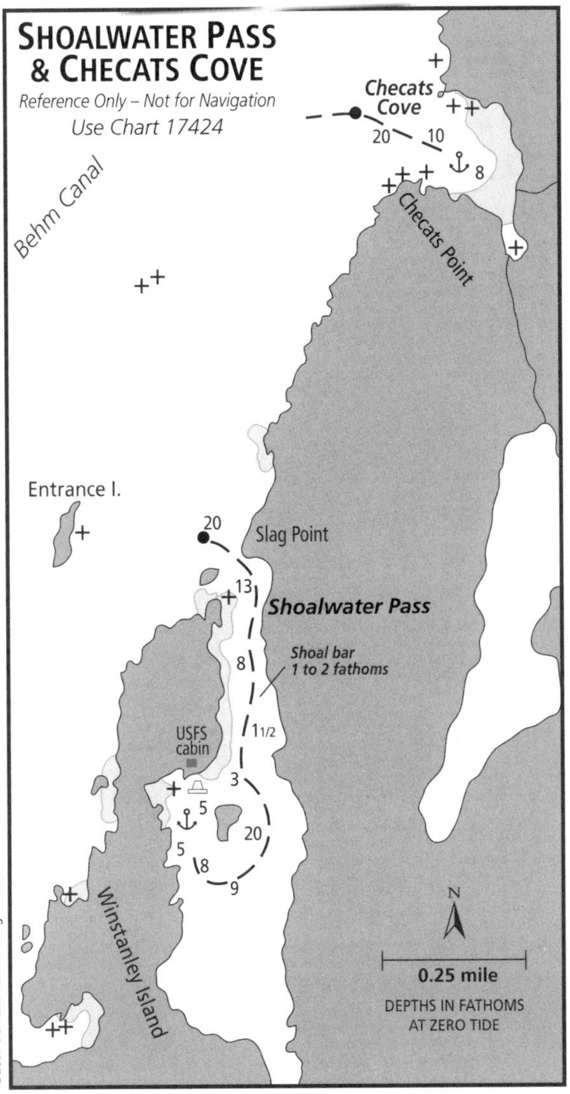


all winds. Enter from the north via Slag Point over a 1- to 2-fathom bar.

Anchor in 5 fathoms south of a U.S. Forest Service buoy over mud with good holding.

## Checats Cove (Behm Canal)

Checats Cove, on the east side of Behm Canal, is 2.1 miles southeast of New Eddystone Rock and about 1.7 miles northeast of Winstanley Island.

Chart 17424
Entrance: 55°29.37′ N, 130°53.01′ W
Anchor: 55°29.26′ N, 130°52.66′ W

> *The cove affords anchorage for small vessels, protected from S winds, in about 8 to 10 fathoms, mud bottom, about 100 to 200 yards N of Checats Point.* (CP)

Checats Cove offers good protection in a southerly blow and is easy of access.

Anchor in 8 to 10 fathoms over mud with good holding.

## Ella Creek Cove (Revillagigedo Island)

Ella Creek is 1.5 miles west of New Eddystone Rock

Chart 17424
Entrance: 55°30.09′ N, 130°58.97′ W

> *Ella Creek . . . empties into the small bight behind Ella Point on the W shore of Behm Canal. A mooring buoy is about 0.15 mile NW of Ella Point.* (CP)

## New Eddystone Rock (Behm Canal)

New Eddystone Rock is 2 miles northwest of Checats Cove.

Chart 17424
Position: 55°30.19′ N, 130°56.30′ W

> *New Eddystone Rock . . . is a remarkable shaft of rock, 230 feet high, rising from a sand shoal in the middle of the canal, with deep water surrounding it. It may be passed on either hand, keeping it at a distance of 0.5 mile to avoid the sand shoal. At the E extremity of the shoal is a small pinnacle rock that uncovers about 4 feet.* (CP)

New Eddystone Rock owes it name to George Vancouver, who found that it resembled the lighthouse rock off Plymouth, England. Have your camera ready: this 230-foot, dramatic rock is a much-photographed landmark along Behm Canal.

Jim Kyle

*New Eddystone Rock is a dramatic, 230-foot-high landmark in Behm Canal.*

## **Rudyerd Bay** (Behm Canal)

Rudyerd Bay is about 23 miles north of Point Sykes and 3.6 miles northeast of New Eddystone Rock.

**Chart 17424**
**Entrance (mid-channel between Louise and Eva points): 55°32.99′ N, 130°52.34′ W**

> *Rudyerd Bay, about 11 miles long, enters Behm Canal from E between Point Eva and Point Louise. . . . Two arms enter the bay from S; the lower . . . is 2.2 miles, and the upper arm about 7 miles, from the entrance.* (CP)

Rudyerd Bay with Punchbowl Cove is one of the main scenic attractions of Misty Fiords and well worth a complete tour. The high granite cliffs on the east side of Punchbowl Cove are covered with numerous waterfalls during rainy periods. Deeper inside Rudyerd Bay are a huge snow-filled bowl, overhanging gardens and waterfalls at every glance.

Linda Lewis

*The steep and muddy hike up to Punchbowl Lake is well worth it to see this amazing place.*

Linda Lewis

*The majestic wall at Punchbowl Cove*

## **Punchbowl Cove** (Rudyerd Bay)

Punchbowl Cove is 2.25 miles east of the entrance to Rudyerd Bay.

**Chart 17424**
**Entrance: 55°33.13′ N, 130°48.36′ W**
**Anchor: 55°31.59′ N, 130°46.86′ W**

> *. . . named Punchbowl Cove because of its precipitous sides. Temporary anchorage may be found close to the S shore near the head of Punchbowl Cove in 25 fathoms. A privately maintained mooring buoy is on the S side of the cove, about 0.3 mile from the head.* (CP)

The Punchbowl is the quintessential Misty Fiords. The 3,000-foot granite face on the east side of the cove is the scene depicted most often in pictures of Misty Fiords National Monument. A steep mud-and-boardwalk trail at the very southeast corner of the cove leads to gorgeous Punchbowl Lake. There are plenty of vantage points from which you can stop and admire the view. About a half-mile up the trail you will reach Punchbowl Creek Waterfall Overlook, which has breathtaking views. This hike might be better classified as a "scramble"; wear boots and be prepared to work. When you get your first glimpse of Punchbowl Lake, however, every minute of work will have been worth it. If you continue on to the lake you may be able to explore further in a USFS skiff with oars, available at no cost. A small USFS open-sided cabin offers a welcome lunch spot.

Use the buoy for a short stay, or seek anchorage a little south of the buoy, between the buoy and the shore over a deep, hard bottom avoiding rocks along the south shore.

Anchor in about 10-12 fathoms over rocky, hard, mostly mud bottom with fair holding.

## Rudyerd Bay, Upper Arm

The upper arm is about 4.8 miles from Punchbowl Cove.

Chart 17424
Entrance (upper arm): 55°35.82′ N, 130°42.56′ W
Position (Nooya Lake bight): 55°36.65′ N, 130°42.55′ W

> *An anchorage in 20 fathoms, hard bottom, is near the head of the upper arm and opposite a prominent landslide. Small craft can find temporary anchorage near the edge of the flats at the head of the bay and the head of the upper arm. Temporary anchorage may be had about 0.5 mile E of Point Louise and about 400 yards N of a small, but prominent landslide, in 18 to 20 fathoms, hard bottom. The bottom is very irregular.* (CP)

The far north arm of Rudyerd Bay shoals rapidly, offering little in convenient anchor sites. The sand and mud flats up-river are full of giant stumps and root systems. Crabbing is reported to be good in these cold waters, and you can sometimes see grizzlies combing the shores of the delta.

A private float used by tour boats has 12 fathoms at its south side and one fathom on its north. There is possible temporary anchorage off the outlet to Nooya Lake in 5 fathoms, but we have no record of the bottom. The south arm is reported to offer reasonable anchoring.

David Shuler

*Cascades in Misty Fiords*

## Manzanita Bay (Revillagigedo Island)

Manzanita Bay, on the west side of Behm Canal, is 3.5 miles northwest of the entrance to Rudyerd Bay.

Chart 17424
Entrance: 55°35.46′ N, 130°56.89′ W
Anchor: 55°34.82′ N, 130°57.60′ W

> *Manzanita Bay . . . affords good anchorage in 20 fathoms, soft bottom. . . . The anchorage is in the SE bight of the bay. . . . The Forest Service maintains a float in the small bight on the W side of Wart Point. Depths at the outer end of the float are reported to be 8 fathoms. The Forest Service also maintains a mooring dolphin off the mouth of Grace Creek, 4.7 miles N of Wart Point.* (CP)

Manzanita Bay, which provides significant shelter from southerly and northerly winds, is a good place to stay when visiting Rudyerd

Réanne Hemingway-Douglass

*Mossy granite, Misty Fiords*

Bay. The water is deep, however, and the drying mud flats are steep-to. *Cosmos* has anchored in the bight just west of Wart Point in 6 fathoms where they found a bottom of thin mud over rocks with good protection during a night of southerly winds.

A shore tie may be useful along the east shore of the cove.

Anchor in 6 fathoms over a bottom of thin mud and rock.

## **Snip Islands** (Behm Canal)

Snip Islands, on the west shore of Behm Canal, are 6 miles north of Manzanita Bay.

Chart 17424
North entrance: 55°41.78′ N, 130°57.89′ W
Anchor: 55°41.29′ N, 130°57.87′ W

> *Good anchorage for small craft can be had in the passage W of the islands in about 15 fathoms, sandy bottom. The S entrance is obstructed by a bar that bares.* (CP)

Snip Islands are west of Walker Cove. Southerlies blow right through here, the water is too deep and the sandy bottom too soft for convenient small-craft anchoring.

## **Walker Cove** (Behm Canal)

Walker Cove, on the east side of Behm canal, is 2.2 miles northeast of Snip Islands and 9.5 miles north of Rudyerd Bay.

Chart 17424
Entrance (mid-channel between Ledge and Hut points): 55°42.44′ N, 130°54.11′ W
Walker Cove buoy position: 55°43.90′ N, 130°45.29′ W

> *The shores of Walker Cove are very abrupt and in some places almost perpendicular. A summer anchorage can be made in midchannel on the inside of the bar at the entrance between Hut Point and Ledge Point in 10 to 20 fathoms.* (CP)

Walker Cove is a spectacular fiord at whose head lies a classic glacier-carved valley. Upon entering the cove, you pass a snow-filled bowl, high cirques, narrow snow-choked canyons and

Don Douglass

*Coauthor, Réanne, in Walker Cove*

a granite quarter-dome. Countless streams and dramatic waterfalls plunge down these granite walls to the saltwater from mile-high summits.

Except for its entrance bar of 5 fathoms, Walker Cove may be too deep for convenient anchorage by most pleasure boaters; however, Captain Brian Pemberton reports good holding in depths of 50-70 feet on either side of the buoy. We have used the buoy in the inner bay and spent a wonderful, quiet night after entering under radar.

Charter Captain Richard Friedman reports Walker Cove as one of his favorites for treating his guests to what he feels is one of the most beautiful anchorages in Southeast Alaska. He recommends one use a special anchoring technique for anchoring off the drying mud flats on the south side of the cove southwest of the buoy. Enter on a high tide. Drop the stern anchor over the mudflat area and run out to an area about 80 feet deep and drop the bow anchor. Winch back between the two anchors to an area where the depth is about 50 feet deep. The next day, depart on a high tide to retrieve the anchor on the mud flats.

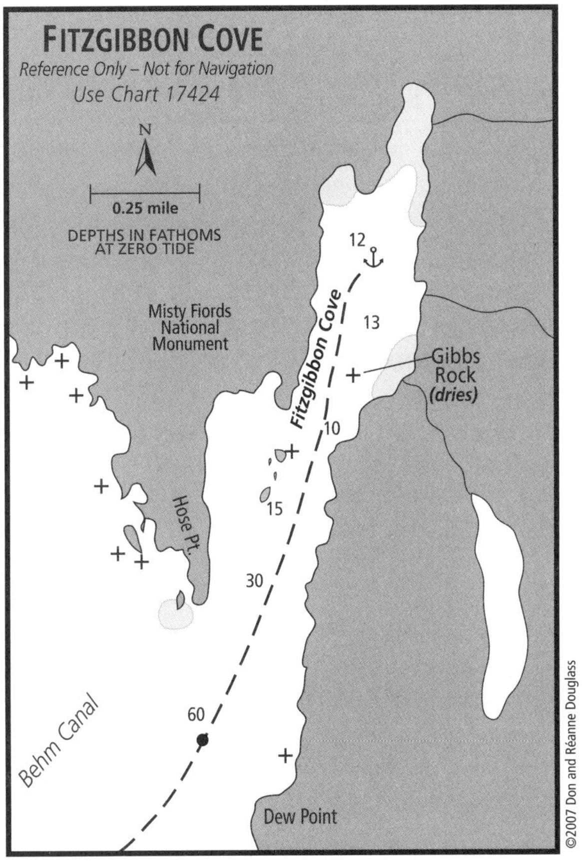


## **Chickamin River** (Behm Canal)

Chickamin River enters Behm Canal 5.8 miles northwest of the entrance to Walker Cove.

Chart 17424
Entrance: 55°47.53′ N, 130°58.86′ W

> *Small craft can find temporary anchorage near the edge of the flat.* (CP)

This place looks rather exposed to us, and because the water is an opaque green, you can't see any hazards. We prefer Snip Islands or Fitzgibbon Cove as anchor sites.

## **Portage Cove** (Revillagigedo Island)

Portage Cove is on the west side of Behm Canal, opposite the entrance to Chickamin River.

Chart 17424
Entrance: 55°46.31′ N, 131°02.47′ W

> *Portage Cove . . . bares. Depths of 3 to 8 fathoms can be found at the entrance, but these drop off quickly to deep water.* (CP)

## **Saks Cove** (Behm Canal)

Saks Cove is about 10 miles northwest of the mouth of the Chickamin River.

Chart 17424
Entrance: 55°55.80′ N, 131°08.74′ W

> *Saks Cove . . . affords anchorage near the N end.* (CP)

We found Saks Cove too deep for easy anchorage and recommend Fitzgibbon Cove. However, the deep waters of Saks Cove are reported to offer some fine hauls of prawns.

## **Fitzgibbon Cove** (Behm Canal)

Fitzgibbon Cove, on the northeast shore of Behm Canal, is 2.5 miles north of Saks Cove.

Chart 17424
Entrance: 55°57.81′ N, 131°11.58′ W
Anchor: 55°58.94′ N, 131°10.84′ W

> *The cove affords good anchorage about 0.2 mile above Gibbs Rock in 11 to 13 fathoms, mud bot-*

*tom. A submerged rock with 6 feet over it is 110 yards 300°* [true] *from Gibbs Rock.* (CP)

Set in a beautiful, remote location, Fitzgibbon Cove offers good shelter from all winds.

Entrance is made to the east of the islets and to the west of Gibbs Rock, which dries. The inner cove has plenty of swinging room over a deep, flat bottom.

Anchor in 12 fathoms over mud with good holding.

## **Burroughs Bay** (Behm Canal)

Burroughs Bay enters Behm Canal from the northeast, 2.4 miles northwest of Fitzgibbon Cove.

**Chart 17424**
**Entrance (0.8 mile northwest of Point Fitzgibbon): 55°59.63′ N, 131°13.86′ W**
**Klahini River USFS mooring buoy: 56°02.67′ N, 131.05.94′ W**

*The head of the bay and the mouths of both rivers are filled with flats. There is no secure anchorage. . . . Small craft can anchor near the edges of the flats. The depths at the head of the bay are gradually shoaling. The U.S. Forest Service maintains a mooring buoy here.* (CP)

## **Anchor Pass** (Behm Canal)

Anchor Pass, 5.9 miles west of the entrance to Burroughs Bay, separates the northeast end of Bell Island from the mainland.

**Chart 17422**
**South entrance: 55°57.58′ N, 131°24.04′ W**
**North entrance: 55°59.87′ N, 131°25.73′ W**

*The pass has good anchorage for small craft in the small cove just S of the restricted N entrance in 3 to 5 fathoms, soft bottom. The N entrance to Anchor Pass is shallow and rocky. The least depth of the shoalest reef, in the middle of the pass at its N end, is 1-1/2 feet.* (CP)

Anchor Pass has been the site of unfortunate small craft groundings.

## **Behm Narrows** (Behm Canal)

Behm Narrows separates Bell Island from Revillagigedo Island.

**Chart 17422**
**East entrance: 55°56.38′ N, 131°26.14′ W**
**West entrance (0.8 mile southeast of Snipe Point Light): 55°55.01′ N, 131°35.47′ W**
**Anchor (cove 0.5 mile south of Bell Island Hot Springs): 55°55.21′ N, 131°34.03′ W**

*The shores of the narrows are generally steep and heavily wooded. . . . Anchorage can be found in the bight on the N side of the narrows about 1.6 miles E of Snipe Point Light and about 0.5 mile S of Bell Island Hot Springs. The bight affords anchorage in about 14 fathoms, mud bottom.* (CP)

Exposed to westerlies and 100 feet deep, the bight mentioned above appears to be useful in fair weather only. In bad weather we would opt for Yes Bay.

Anchor in 14 fathoms over a hard bottom of unknown holding power.

## **Bell Arm** (Behm Canal)

Bell Arm separates the northwest shore of Bell Island from the mainland.

**Chart 17422**
**Entrance (0.5 mile north of Snipe Point Light): 55°56.01′ N, 131°36.92′ W**
**Anchor: 56°00.02′ N, 131°25.77′ W**

*Bell Arm . . . extends NE from Behm Canal and at its head is joined by Anchor Pass; it has good anchorage in the expansion at its head in 16 fathoms, soft bottom.* (CP)

Anchor in about 10 fathoms over sticky mud with very good holding.

## **Short Bay and Bailey Bay** (Bell Arm)

Short and Bailey bays are on the northwest side of Bell Arm.

**Chart 17422**
**Entrance (Short Bay): 55°58.60′ N, 131°30.92′ W**
**Anchor (Short Bay): 55.59.92′ N, 131°31.33′ W**
**Entrance (Bailey Bay): 55°56.24′ N, 131°37.30′ W**
**Position (Bailey Bay, mooring buoy): 55°58.05′ N, 131°37.23′ W**

*Short Bay and Bailey Bay are two small, narrow bays entering the NW side of Bell Arm. Short Bay, the E one, has good anchorage in 17 to 20 fathoms; a flat extends about 300 yards from its head. . . . Bailey Bay is an area of hot springs. A mooring buoy is on the W side of Bailey Bay about 1 mile from the head.* (CP)

Anchor (Short Bay) in about 15 fathoms.

## Blind Pass (Behm Canal)

Blind Pass separates Black Island from the northwest side of Hassler Island.

Chart 17422
Northeast entrance: 55°54.34′ N, 131°37.88′ W
Southwest entrance: 55°52.68′ N, 131°41.43′ W
Anchor: 55°53.04′ N, 131°40.91′ W

> *Blind Pass . . . is useless except as a small craft anchorage in the basin at the SW end of the pass. Because of rocks in this entrance, local knowledge is necessary in entering the basin. The pass is closed by a sandbar just NE of the basin.* (CP)

A small cove can be found on the south side with very good anchorage and protection. Enter north of the rocks, staying approximately 30 feet from shore until you reach the anchor site.

There is a gravel bar to the northeast up Blind Passage. It is not recommended to continue up the passage except by kayak.

Anchor in 5 fathoms.

## Convenient Cove (Hassler Island)

Convenient Cove is between the southwest end of Hassler Island and Gedney Island.

Chart 17422
Entrance: 55°51.91′ N, 131°41.89′ W

> *Convenient Cove . . . is too deep for anchorage.* (CP)

## Hassler Pass and Gedney Pass (Behm Canal)

Hassler and Gedney passes separate Hassler Island from Revillagigedo Island.

Linda Lewis

*Don't forget to bring thick gloves for working with the crab catch.*

Chart 17422
North entrance (Hassler Pass): 55°54.17′ N, 131°36.46′ W
South entrance (Hassler Pass): 55°51.10′ N, 131°34.58′ W
West entrance (mid-channel between Brown Point and Gedney Island): 55°50.68′ N, 131°42.69′ W

> *Hassler Pass and Gedney Pass . . . are broad and clear.* (CP)

## Shrimp Bay, Klu Bay (Revillagigedo Island)

Shrimp Bay is at the head of Gedney Pass; Klu Bay is at the head of Shrimp Bay.

Chart 17422
Entrance (Shrimp Bay): 55°50.33′ N, 131°30.98′ W
Entrance (Klu Bay): 55°50.10′ N, 131°27.99′ W
Anchor (Klu Bay): 55°50.56′ N, 131°27.20′ W

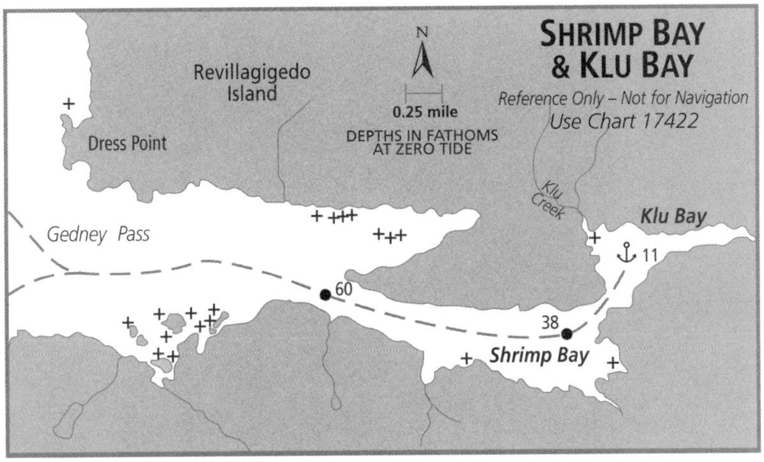



> *. . . [I]n Klu Bay is a good anchorage in 16 fathoms, soft bottom, suitable for vessels of moderate size. A private mooring buoy is on the W side of Klu Bay.* (CP)

Klu Bay, known locally as Echo Bay, comes highly recommended by Southeasterners who fish and crab here. It is well protected from all weather. In 1999, logging operations were being carried out along the south side of Shrimp Bay and in the Klu Bay watershed.

There are lots of eagles here and bear gather salmon along the creek bed.

Anchor off the drying flats of Klu Creek in 10 to 14 fathoms (if current logging operations allow it); soft bottom with fair-to-good holding.

## **Yes Bay** (Behm Canal)

Yes Bay, on the northwest side of Behm Canal, is entered between Bluff and Syble points.

Chart 17422 (inset)
Outer entrance: 55°53.13′ N, 131°44.54′ W
Yes Bay Resort: 55°54.86′ N, 131°47.56′ W
Inner entrance: 55°54.88′ N, 131°47.89′ W
Anchor (first basin southeast corner): 55°54.61′ N, 131°48.01′ W
Anchor (inner basin west of old tramway): 55°56.37′ N, 131°50.15′ W

*A fishing resort is on the N point of a narrow passage leading to the first basin, about 2.6 miles above the entrance to Yes Bay. Caution must be exercised in navigating the E end of this passage particularly in the vicinity of a wharf*

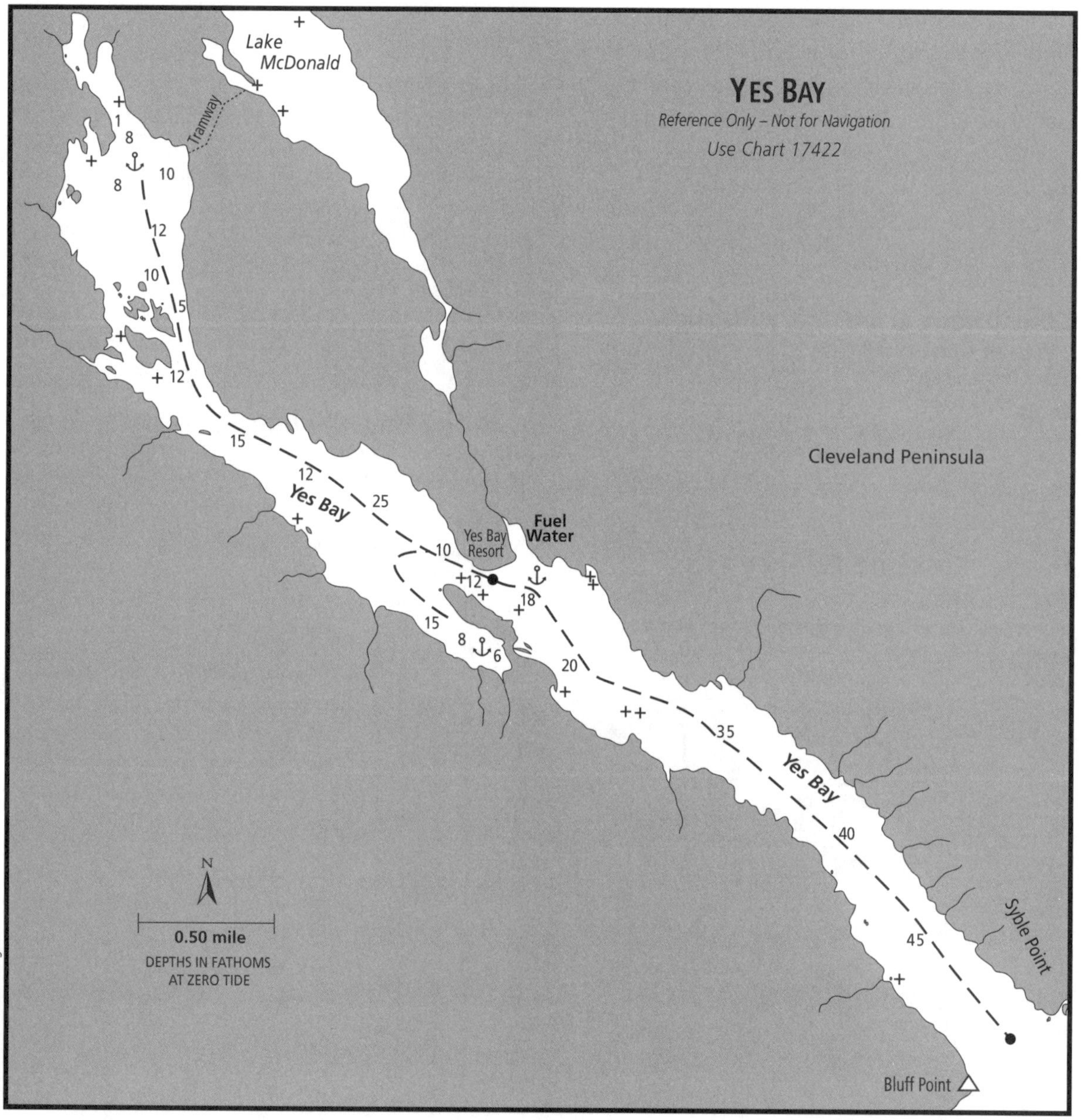

*which stood 300 yards E of the resort. No visible signs remain of the wharf.*

*The narrow passage . . . leads to the first basin where good anchorage can be had in 15 to 32 fathoms, mud bottom. A good small-boat anchorage in 8 fathoms is near the SE end of the first basin.*

*Care is required in navigating Yes Bay, and strangers should do so at low water. Enter in midchannel and then favor the N shore. In entering the first basin, pass about 35 to 40 yards SSW of the resort site and keep the N shore close aboard until the basin opens up. If going to the inner basin, keep about 100 yards off the N shore until up to the group of islands that separate the two basins. Here the channel narrows to about 75 yards because of a submerged rock with 3 feet over it, and a rock awash at low water, both of which are on the W side of the channel. In passing through this channel, keep the NE shore aboard about 30 yards. The inner basin is clear.* (CP)

Yes Bay, whose name derived from the Tlingit word for mussel (yas), has unbeatable shelter from all weather at the southeast end of the first basin. The first and second basins are seldom disturbed, and moss hangs heavy on the trees.

Yes Bay Lodge, which is open to the public, has fuel, water and telephone service, as well as a bar and dining room. During high season the lodge recommends that you call ahead for dinner reservations and availability of fuel (tel.: 907.225.7906). The lodge monitors VHF Ch 16. If you wish to stay at the lodge you can make reservations at 800.999.0784 (www.yes-bay.com). There is daily air service from Yes Bay to Ketchikan.

Entry to the outer bay is easy. To transit the first basin, you must pass directly off the lodge, hugging the shore closely and following the directions noted above in *Coast Pilot.* When you have cleared the narrow peninsula on the west side, round up and turn directly southeast until you're deep in the cove. There is not much swinging room at the head of the cove, but you shouldn't need a lot since anchor strain is rare.

David Parker

*You will never tire of seeing these glorious birds.*

If you are heading for the inner basin, follow the directions of *Coast Pilot* and anchor west of the old tramway to Lake McDonald.

Anchor in the first basin in 7 fathoms over mud with good holding.

## **Spacious Bay** (Behm Canal)

Spacious Bay is about 22 miles north of Caamano Point.

**Chart 17422**
**Entrance (1 mile north of Snail Point):**
**55°51.93′ N, 131°47.84′ W**
**Anchor: 55°51.28′ N, 131°50.94′ W**

*Good anchorage can be selected in the lee of Square Island, sand and mud bottom. A dangerous submerged rock has been reported about 0.4 mile NW of the island. The bights in the N shore of the bay are not recommended for anchorage.* (CP)

Inner Spacious Bay, which has easy access, provides good protection in settled weather. If southerlies are expected, consider the bight behind Snail Point, 1.9 miles to the southeast of Square Island. The west side of Square Island has a large, shallow area that provides convenient anchorage with good swinging room. Anchor 400 yards or more from shore to avoid the shoal.

Anchor in 2 to 4 fathoms over sand and mud with good holding.

## Snail Point Bight (Behm Canal)

Snail Point Bight, on the west side of Behm Canal, is 1.9 miles southeast of Square Island and 20.6 miles northeast of Caamano Point Light.

Chart 17422
Entrance: 55°49.45′ N, 131°46.78′ W
Anchor: 55°49.13′ N, 131°46.65′ W

> *On the W side of the point is a bight 0.5 mile long that affords good anchorage for small craft. A submerged rock with 3/4 fathom over it is in the middle of the bay, and small craft should favor the E shore until clear of this rock and proceed to the head of the bay for anchorage.* (CP)

Snail Point Bight offers good protection for one boat in southerly weather at the head of the bay.

Anchor in about 5 fathoms.

## Neets Bay, Fire Cove (Revillagigedo Island)

Neets Bay, on the east side of Behm Canal, is 19.2 miles northeast of Caamano Point.

Chart 17422
Neets Bay entrance (0.8 mile south of Chin Point): 55°46.48′ N, 131°42.15′ W
Fire Cove entrance (Fire Cove, 5.4 miles east of Neets Bay entrance): 55°46.58′ N, 131°32.23′ W
Anchor (Fire Cove): 55°46.30′ N, 131°32.44′ W
Rock Fish Cove position (2.7 miles east of Neets Bay entrance): 55°45.89′ N, 131°37.41′ W

> *The bay has no good anchorage. Small craft, however, can find fair shelter in the last cove (locally called Fire Cove) toward the head of the S side of the bay. Pass E of the small wooded islet and anchor E or S of it in 3 to 5 fathoms, sand bottom.* (CP)

Fire Cove, a popular getaway for local cruising boats, is very well protected from all weather and is reported to have excellent salmon fishing. A co-op fish hatchery is located in Neets Bay.

Anchor south of island in 4 fathoms over sand with good holding.

## Bushy Point Cove (Revillagigedo Island)

Bushy Point Cove is 16.6 miles northeast of Caamano Point Light.

Chart 17422
Entrance: 55°44.11′ N, 131°43.72′ W
Anchor: 55°43.80′ N, 131°43.40′ W

> *Bushy Point Cove, a small bay inside of Bushy Point, is too deep for anchorage except for small craft that anchor close to the beach at the head of the bay.* (CP)

Bushy Point Cove is easy to enter and offers good protection from south winds, but the bottom is undetermined.

## Traitors Cove (Revillagigedo Island)

Traitors Cove is about 2.5 miles southeast of Bushy Point Light and 15.1 miles northeast of Caamano Point.

Chart 17422
Entrance: 55°41.59′ N, 131°42.33′ W
Entrance (upper cove): 55°43.65′ N, 131°37.53′ W

> *About 300 yards W from the N point at the entrance is a reef that uncovers 6 feet. It presents a real danger to craft leaving or entering the cove by the N entrance.*
>
> *The cove should be avoided by strangers as the strong tidal currents and rocks make navigation dangerous. The upper part of the cove can be entered only by small craft at slack water, which is very short in duration; on the flood small craft should keep away from the narrow entrance to the upper cove as there is danger of being swept through by the force of the current.* (CP)

Traitors Cove derives its name from a skirmish Vancouver had with the natives in 1793.

## Marguerite Bay (Traitors Cove)

Marguerite Bay is on the south shore of Traitors Cove, about 2 miles from the entrance.

Chart 17422
Entrance: 55°42.24′ N, 131°38.97′ W
Anchor: 55°42.17′ N, 131°38.33′ W

> *Marguerite Bay . . . affords the only anchorage in the cove. Rocks are on both sides of the bight near its entrance, and a depth of 10 feet is found in midchannel at the entrance.* (CP)

There is a Forest Service Dock in the bay.

## Port Stewart (Behm Canal)

Port Stewart, on the west side of Behm Canal, is 13.3 miles north of Caamano Point.

Chart 17422
Entrance (0.3 mile east of two islets): 55°42.24′ N, 131°49.68′ W
Anchor: 55°43.62′ N, 131°51.21′ W

*A clear channel is between the easternmost and southernmost islets, but there are some off-lying rocks to avoid. The best entrance is N of the two islets.*

*Anchorage can be had in 16 fathoms, rock and mud bottom. . . . Small craft with local knowledge can find sheltered anchorage in 5 to 6-1/2 fathoms, mud bottom, in the land-locked bight in the N shore of Port Stewart, about 3.5 miles above Point Francis.* (CP)

Port Stewart was named by Vancouver in 1793 for John Stewart—master's mate on the *Discovery*—who drew the chart used in Vancouver's atlas. The landlocked basin on the north shore offers excellent protection for small craft. Care must be taken to avoid mid-channel rock and shoals. Chart 17422 is your best guide. The head of Port Stewart has been a major log booming operation.

Anchor in about 6 fathoms.

## Escape Point Bight (Revillagigedo Island)

Escape Point Bight, on the east shore of Behm Canal, is about 0.5 mile north of Escape Point.

Chart 17422
Anchor: 55°39.31′ N, 131°42.50′ W

*A small bight . . . is too deep for anchorage, although in good weather small craft anchor in the S end of this bight near Escape Point.* (CP)

## Naha Bay (Revillagigedo Island)

Naha Bay is 8.5 miles northeast of Knudson Cove.

Charts 17423 (inset), 17422
Entrance: 55°36.04′ N, 131°41.36′ W
Position (Loring): 55°36.01′ N, 131°38.04′ W
Anchor (0.2 mile southeast of Loring):
55°35.85′ N, 131°37.78′ W
Entrance (Roosevelt Lagoon):
55°35.28′ N, 131°37.08′ W

*Naha Bay . . . is a popular sports fishing and hunting area. The bay and its approaches are clear. Loring is a village on the N side near the head of the bay.*

*Public Float, Naha Bay*

*The usual anchorage is just below the ruins of an old wharf about 300 yards from the shore of the village, in 19 fathoms, mud bottom. The shore in front of the village should not be approached closer than 100 yards. Small craft can find anchorage in the small bay N of Dogfish Island where shelter is had from any SW squalls which occasionally strike with considerable force. . . . A State-maintained L-shaped small-craft float and a seaplane float joining it are at the head of the cove W of the wharf in ruins.*

*Roosevelt Lagoon is a body of brackish water that is connected to Naha Bay through a tiderace only at extreme high water. The passage is dangerous and should not be used without local knowledge.* (CP)

Naha Bay is the home of Loring, an early fish cannery and loading site for famous schooners bound for California with massive hauls of

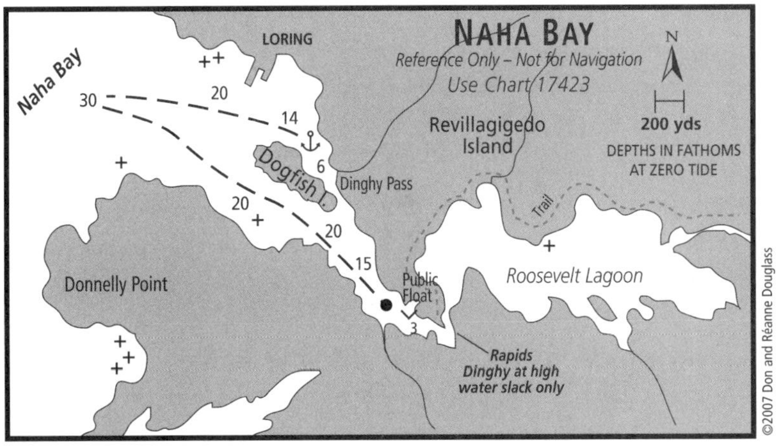

canned salmon. Loring has a few private residences with floats left from this former era. If you want to visit Loring, cruising vessels can find reasonable shelter 0.2 mile southeast of Loring in the lee of Dogfish Island as indicated in the diagram.

The attraction in Naha Bay is now Roosevelt Lagoon, with its nature trail, wildlife, and fishing. The lagoon is protected by a rapids that is safe to traverse only in a dinghy at, or near, high-water slack. The lagoon is a favorite place to watch for trumpeter swans, some of which are said to winter over here. Now endangered, their numbers have decreased greatly and visitors need to respect the birds' habitat. Bear and deer are plentiful along the lagoon trail and the river and lakes upstream to the east. During the late summer spawning salmon choke the rapids and the river's outlet.

The public float just west of the Roosevelt Lagoon rapids makes a great lunch or overnight stop. A good trail leads to the rapids and farther east along the lagoon. If the float is full, you can anchor in the rather deep water off the floats in mid-channel.

Anchor (Dogfish Island) in 6 fathoms over sand and some rock bottom with fair holding.

Anchor (off public float) in 8 to 12 fathoms over sand and rocky bottom with fair holding.

## **Moser Bay** (Revillagigedo Island)

Moser Bay entrance is 7.5 miles northeast of Knudson Cove.

Charts 17423 (inset), 17422
North entrance (between Moser and Cedar islands): 55°34.78′ N, 131°40.87′ W
South entrance (southeast of Stack Island): 55°33.88′ N, 131°41.41′ W
Anchor: 55°32.59′ N, 131°39.14′ W
Entrance (Long Arm): 55°34.22′ N, 131°39.48′ W

> *A reef makes off SE from Cod Point, the N point at the entrance to Long Arm.* (CP)

Anchorage can be found off the drying mud flat at the head of the bay. This area was used extensively for logging operations in the past and may have slash (logging debris) along the bottom.

Anchor in about 8 fathoms.

## **Moser Bay Bight** (Revillagigedo Island)

Moser Bay Bight is 6.6 miles northeast of Knudson Cove.

Charts 17423 (inset), 17422
Entrance: 55°33.66′ N, 131°40.71′ W
Anchor: 55°33.53′ N, 131°40.92′ W

> *Good anchorage for small craft is found in 7 fathoms in the small bight in the NW part of the bay.* (CP)

Shelter can be found on the west side of Moser Bay in a small bight just inside the entrance to the bay. The anchorage is close to the popular fishing grounds of Clover Passage immediately southwest. There may be floathouses in Moser Bay, cutting down on the solitude desired by cruising vessels.

Entering Moser Bay Bight, favor the southeast shore to avoid the islet and foul ground on the west side of the bight.

Anchor in 7 fathoms over an unrecorded bottom.

## **Clover Passage** (Behm Canal)

Clover Passage is 10 miles northwest of Ketchikan.

Chart 17422
North entrance (between Grant and Stack islands): 55°33.97′ N, 131°42.26′ W
South entrance: 55°28.53′ N, 131°49.70′ W

> *Clover Passage . . . is frequently used by vessels proceeding between Tongass Narrows and Naha and Moser Bays. It has several entrances from the N in deep narrow channels between Cedar and Moser Islands, Stack and Grant Islands, and a deep, wider entrance between Back and Grant Islands.* (CP)

Clover Pass Resort and Restaurant, near Survey Point is open in the summer and has moorage, gas, diesel, shower and laundry facilities, Internet access, a lodge, restaurant and small store. They also offer fishing charters. Monitors VHF Ch 16. Call the resort for more information (tel.: 907.247.2234).

## **Knudson Cove** (Revillagigedo Island)

Knudson Cove, on the southeast side of Clover Passage, is 2 miles northeast of Point Higgins.

Chart 17422
Entrance: 55°28.70′ N, 131°47.73′ W
Anchor: 55°28.53′ N, 131°47.78′ W
Float: 55°28.37′ N, 131°47.91′ W

> *Small craft use* [Knudson Cove] *as an anchorage. A depth of 4 fathoms is at the entrance. The 4-fathom area was reported to provide good anchorage in SE winds up to 35 knots. A daybeacon marks the W side of the entrance to the cove. Another daybeacon near the head of the cove marks a rock awash at half tide. A floating breakwater, marked on the NW end by a private daybeacon, is in the cove.*
>
> *The city of Ketchikan maintains small-craft floats with about 615 feet of mooring space on the E side of Knudson Cove near the head. . . . Local regulations limit the size of vessels using the floats to 65 feet in length.* (CP)

Knudson Cove has public and private floats and is used as a base of operation by the Clover Pass sport fishing fleet and for those who troll for its famous salmon. Although busy, it's a good place to run for cover when southeast gales kick up.

Knudson Cove marks the northwest entrance to Behm Canal. From here, it's a short return to Ketchikan for fuel and supplies.

## **Raymond and Wadding Coves** (Behm Canal)

Raymond Cove is 8.7 miles northeast of Caamano Point Light; Wadding Cove is 7.7 miles northeast of Caamano Point Light.

Chart 17422
Entrance (Raymond Cove): 55°37.48′ N, 131°52.13′ W
Entrance (Wadding Cove): 55°37.07′ N, 131°53.19′ W

> [Raymond Cove and Wadding Cove] *are useless as anchorages, and at low water there are extensive tidal flats of sand and gravel with some boulders.*
>
> *Mike Point is a low, rocky point separating Wadding and Raymond Coves. The point is foul and should be given a good berth.* (CP)

## **Helm Bay** (Behm Canal)

Helm Bay is 6.2 miles northeast of Caamano Point Light and 8 miles northwest of Knudson Cove.

Chart 17422
Entrance (0.75 mile northeast of Helm Bay Light): 55°35.34′ N, 131°54.74′ W
Float: 55°37.84′ N, 131°58.69′ W

> *Behind Forss Island, on the W shore, 3.3 miles in from the light, is a small cove at the head of which is a float with depths of 20 feet reported alongside. . . . Enter the cove from the N passing between two charted off-lying rocks.*
>
> *Anchorage is available in midchannel in 16 fathoms, mud bottom, about 1.2 miles above Forss Island, and in 21 fathoms, gravel and mud bottom, about 2 miles above the island. The latter is the better anchorage.* (CP)

Helm Bay appears to offer substantial protection. A small Alaska State float west of the north end of Forss Island is available for use by pleasure craft.

## **Smugglers Cove** (Behm Canal)

Smugglers Cove is 4.9 miles northeast of Caamano Point Light.

Chart 17422
Entrance: 55°34.53′ N, 131°56.10′ W
Anchor: 55°35.25′ N, 131°57.41′ W

> [Smugglers Cove] *is a fair anchorage for small craft, although local knowledge is necessary to clear the dangers. Extensive tide flats are at the head of the cove.* (CP)

## **Bond Bay** (Behm Canal)

Bond Bay is 1.8 miles northeast of Caamano Point Light.

Chart 17422
Entrance: 55°31.40′ N, 131°56.98′ W
Anchor: 55°31.77′ N, 131°57.20′ W

> *Bond Bay and the smaller indentations between Bond Bay and Caamano Point Light are used as temporary anchorages by the smaller fishing craft during the trolling season. The anchorages are exposed to SE and are not recommended because of the suddenness and great force with which the SE winds strike in this area.* (CP)

## CLARENCE STRAIT FROM KASAAN PENINSULA TO SUMNER STRAIT

Charts 17420, 17360

*Clarence Strait extends in a N direction from Dixon Entrance for 45 miles to Guards Islands and the W entrance to Tongass Narrows and Behm Canal, and thence in a NW direction for 67 miles to Sumner Strait. . . . At Zarembo Island the strait divides. The channel E of the island, called Stikine Strait, is the route taken by vessels to Wrangell and Wrangell Narrows; that W of the island, called Snow Passage, is used by vessels bound to Wrangell Narrows or W through Sumner Strait because it is more direct.* (CP)

### Caamano Point

Caamano Point is 4.5 miles northwest of Guard Island Light.

Chart 17420
Position (0.25 Nm south of Light): 55°29.67′ N, 131°59.00′ W

*Launches may find anchorage in any of the several shallow bights that indent the W coast of Cleveland Peninsula between Caamano Point and Lemesurier Point. These bights, however, are surrounded with many dangerous rocks, and their use during stormy weather is attended with extreme danger.* (CP)

Caamano Point—the southernmost tip of Cleveland Peninsula—is on the northeast side of Clarence Strait and the west side of the northwest entrance to Behm Canal.

Clarence Strait, northwest of Caamano Point, is a popular trolling area. Ebb currents are strong, however, and it doesn't take much of a southeast breeze to kick up a nasty chop. Cruising boats can pass inside Ship Island and get some shelter behind Lee Rock, but Meyers Chuck to the north or Lyman Anchorage on the west side of the strait offer better protection in a blow.

### Lee Rock (Clarence Strait)

Lee Rock is 2.5 miles south of Meyers Chuck.

Chart 17420

*Lee Rock, . . . 6.4 miles N of . . . Ship Island . . . is about 20 feet high and the westernmost of three rocky wooded islands at the entrance to a small cove. Anchorage may be made in the center of the cove, 0.2 mile from its head in 8 to 14 fathoms. Passage can be made between Lee Rock and the two E islands in 7 to 9 fathoms. There is no safe passage between the two E islands or between the islands and the shore. A reef 200 yards S of the easternmost island and 100 yards offshore bares 10 feet.* (CP)

There are two float houses moored in the small cove in the lee of Lee Rock. Since there is no large-scale chart of this area, you should enter the cove from the northwest, avoiding several rocks in the vicinity. With Meyers Chuck so close we would not recommend anchoring here except temporarily in fair weather.

Linda Lewis
*A lowering sky*

### Meyers Chuck (Meyers Island)

Meyers Chuck is 31 miles northwest of Ketchikan.

Chart 17423 (Union Bay Inset)
Outer entrance (0.26 mile southwest of inner entrance): 55°44.49′ N, 132°16.23′ W
Inner entrance: 55°44.55′ N, 132°15.80′ W
Public float: 55°44.37′ N, 132°15.48′ W
Anchor: 55°44.44′ N, 132°15.52′ W

*Meyers Chuck* [is] *a small harbor with good anchorage for small craft. . . . The harbor is entered between the light* [on the N side of Meyers Island] *and a buoy that marks the end of the reef that extends SE of the small island NNW of Meyers Island. . . . A seaplane float extends NW from the float near the approach pier. Care should be taken to avoid the reef that bares about 25 feet NW of the head of the approach pier.*

*A State-operated float with about 384 feet of berthing space . . . is at the NE side of the harbor. . . . A 56-foot boat grid is available just inside the State-operated float.* (CP)

Linda Lewis

*Meyers Chuck is a welcome stop both for cruisers and for float planes; watch for traffic.*

Meyers Chuck—a godsend for boats travelling along this part of Clarence Strait, which often kicks up a nasty chop—offers complete protection from almost all weather. Its narrow entrance can be a bit intimidating to first-timers but, once inside, all is calm.

Since the state float can be crowded during

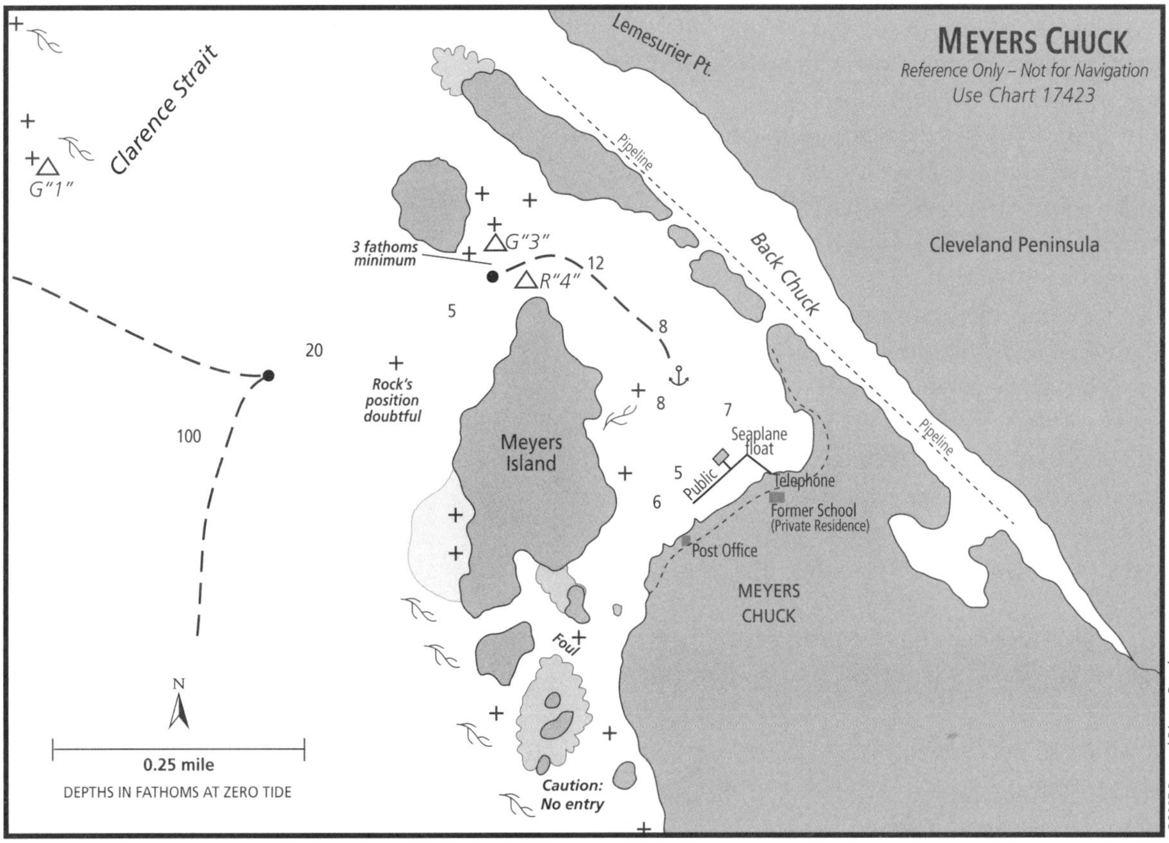

Linda Lewis

*The old Post Office at Meyers Chuck*

the summer, rafting is encouraged. Note that you can also be on the shore side of the float; just be sure to stay close to the float. There is untreated water on the float; check with locals before using it. (Drought conditions do exist in Alaska, believe it or not!)

There's usually room for several boats to anchor well off the float plane dock (no tie ups—this is in constant use).

The small settlement has a telephone, a small post office (across the bay from the float) and a lovely little gallery that sells locally-made crafts. Call the Gallery Girls (telephone numbers listed on the bulletin board above the float). A dirt trail that leads north from the float connects the home sites located along the island.

The entrance into Meyers Chuck is small and easy to miss. From Clarence Strait, watch for the two-second flashing xenon light on the microwave tower. The island north of the microwave tower is Meyers Island. The south side of Meyers Island is foul—do not enter there.

The entrance is on the north side of Meyers Island and is marked by G"3" to port and R"4" to starboard. Turn south immediately after clearing R"4."

Anchor off the float in 8 fathoms over a mixed bottom with good holding.

## ERNEST SOUND TO WRANGELL VIA ZIMOVIA STRAIT

Charts 17385, 17423 (inset)

**Ernest Sound southwest entrance (1.65 miles northwest of McHenry Ledge buoy): 55°48.26′ N, 132°19.81′ W**

*Ernest Sound . . . opens from Clarence Strait between Lemesurier Point and Onslow Point, with a width of about 4.5 miles between the points. Its general direction is NNE for about 25 miles to Point Warde; from this point, under the name of Bradfield Canal, it extends about 17 miles in a general E direction, with a width of about 1 mile. There are numerous small islands in the sound and two large ones, one on each side, about midway of its length.*

*From Ernest Sound two arms extend NNW and join N of the northernmost extremity of Wrangell Island near the mouth of Stikine River. The W arm is called Zimovia Strait. The S part of the E arm is called Blake Channel and the N part Eastern Passage. A passage to Wrangell through Ernest Sound, Blake Channel, and Eastern Passage is practicable and is sometimes used. Small craft use Zimovia Strait frequently.*

*The currents in Ernest Sound follow the general direction of the channel. The flood current sets N with an average velocity of about 1.7 to 2.1 knots. The ebb current sets S with about the same average velocity. At the junction of Bradfield Canal and Blake Channel, the joining of the tidal currents cause swirls. (See the Tidal Current Tables for daily predictions.)* (CP)

This route, the most popular cruising route between Ketchikan and Wrangell, offers better protection and is more attractive than the one through Stikine Strait. Follow instructions given in the prior section for Clarence Strait to Meyers Chuck, then turn northeast into Ernest Sound.

## **Union Bay** (Ernest Sound)

Union Bay, 1.5 miles east of Meyers Chuck.

**Charts 17423 (inset), 17385**
**Entrance (1.4 miles northeast of Lemesurier Point):**
**55°46.64′ N, 132°14.71′ W**

*The waters of* [Union Bay] *are deep, but there is anchorage with protection from S, on the E side of the head of the bay, in about 18 fathoms. The SW angle of the bay is foul for 0.2 mile offshore. The only danger, except near the shores, is a rock with a depth of 2-3/4 fathoms in the middle of the entrance and about 2.5 miles NNE of Lemesurier Point. At high water do not approach the head of the bay too rapidly as the points at the entrance to the lagoon are platforms of rock only 3 feet above high water and are not readily distinguished. Anchor in 18 fathoms, about 0.4 mile offshore, on the E side of the head of the bay, with the NE point at the entrance to the lagoon bearing about 140°.* (CP)

## **Magnetic Cove**

(Union Bay)

Magnetic Cove is 1 mile southwest of Vixen Harbor.

**Charts 17423 (inset), 17385**
**Entrance (3.3 miles east of Lemesurier Point): 55°46.93′ N, 132°11.29′ W**
**Anchor: 55°47.46′ N, 132°10.90′ W**

*For anchorage, fishermen use the cove behind the small islet . . . and the long cove behind Magnetic Point, about 1 mile N of the islet.*

*Small boats use the channel between Union Point, which is low and wooded, and the two islets S of it. An estimated current velocity of 3 knots sets S around Union Point on the ebb.* (CP)

"Magnetic Cove" is our name for the long narrow cove behind Magnetic Point. Landlocked and well protected from all weather, the cove has no signs of driftwood along its shore. Except for a float house with its commercial fishing boat moored alongside, this place is secluded and primitive, with old-growth forest and inquisitive resident seals. The name Magnetic Point comes from the observance of compass errors as high as 38° due to local underground magnetic disturbance.

The entrance to Magnetic Cove is quite narrow (about 80 feet) and there is a 3-foot bar in the center of the narrows. Time your passage at an adequate tide level, and avoid the tree trunk that extends about 40 feet from the east shore. This tree hides a rocky peninsula. The M/V *Sanctuary* found a rock 50 yards south that is estimated to be 2 feet above MLLW. Favor the west shore and use caution!

Anchor in 2 to 3 fathoms over very soft mud with good holding if your anchor is well set.

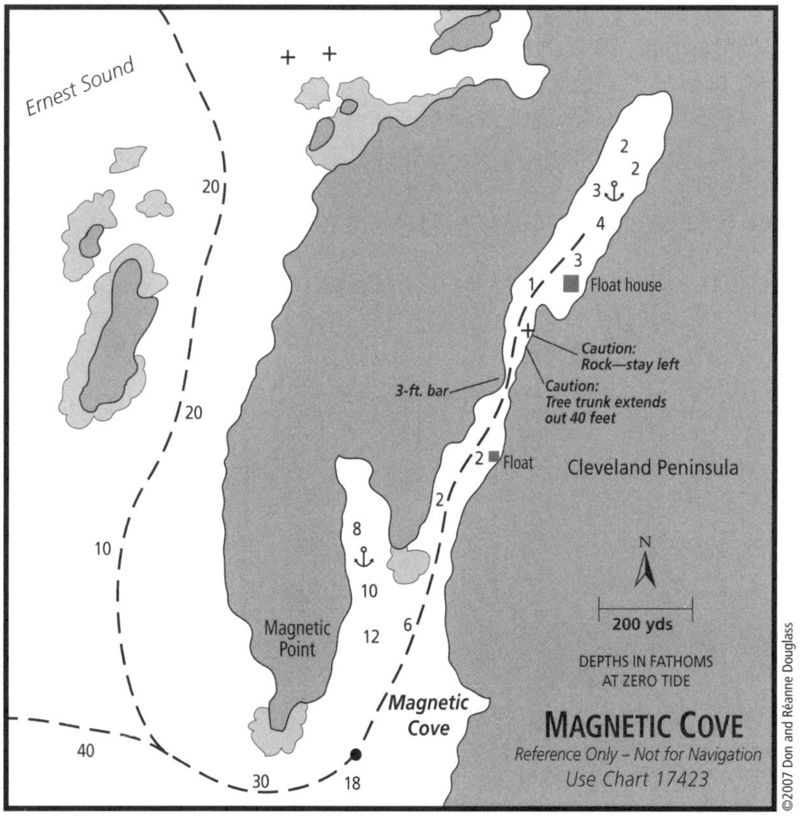

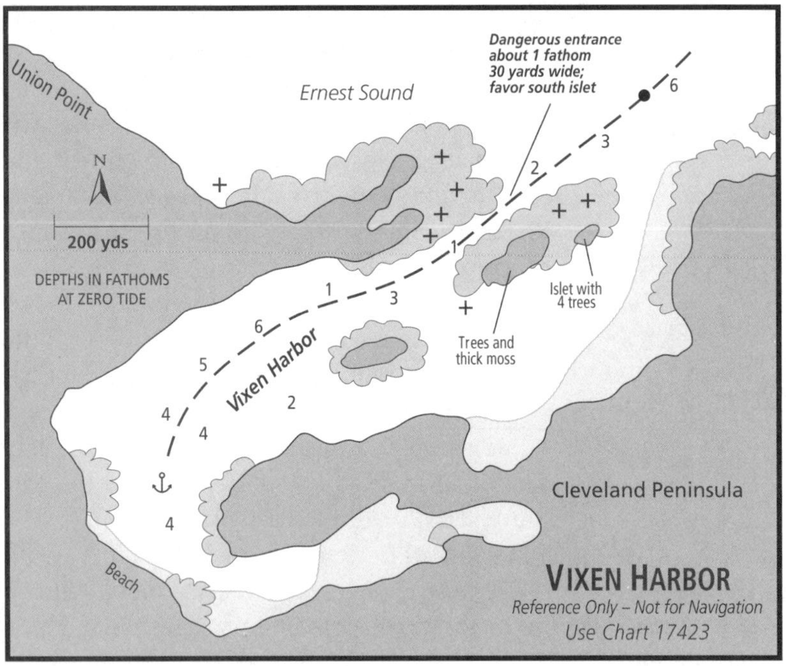




Vixen Harbor offers good shelter, and once you're inside it gives you a feeling of security. Birds and seals like this shelter, too!

We found entering Vixen Harbor more difficult than described in *Coast Pilot.* You should not enter it in foul weather, in poor visibility, or under radar. Dangerous reefs extend well off the point and off the three small islets. Because the reefs and rocks are dark in color and the water is murky (about 4 feet of underwater visibility), you have little warning if you veer off course. Slightly favor the islands on the south side of the entrance.

## Vixen Harbor (Ernest Sound)

Vixen Harbor is 5.5 miles northeast of Meyers Chuck.

Chart 17423 (inset)
Entrance (0.9 mile east of Union Point): 55°48.29′ N, 132°09.60′ W
Anchor: 55°47.90′ N, 132°10.31′ W

> *The entrance channel, about 100 yards wide, has depths of only 2 fathoms. In entering, proceed carefully to the N of and close to the small islands in the entrance. Temporary anchorage for larger craft may be had in 16 fathoms, sand and gravel, 0.4 mile N of the small island in the entrance.* (CP)

The entrance channel is quite narrow—we figure about 30 yards or less, not the 100 yards mentioned in *Coast Pilot*—and the depth is not 2 fathoms as noted! Chart 17423 (inset) seems to have it about right. As closely as we can determine, the channel has a minimum depth of about one fathom *or less* at zero tide!

The harbor bottom is mostly flat with room enough for several boats. There is a landing beach on the southwest side.

Anchor in 4 fathoms over soft, sticky mud and sand with very good holding.

*A friendly fisherman from Meyers Chuck, with his net extended*

## Vixen Inlet

Vixen Inlet is 6.5 miles northeast of Lemesurier Point.

Chart 17385
Entrance (0.9 mile northwest of Sunshine Island): 55°49.66′ N, 132°06.46′ W
Anchor: 55°48.26′ N, 132°02.77′ W

> *Vixen Inlet . . . has a small islet, Sunshine Island, in the middle of the entrance and a stream at the head. A reef makes out from the W side of Vixen Point and extends S about 1.2 miles. A reef with a least depth of 3/4 fathom, not marked by kelp, is in the middle of the entrance, 1.2 miles 284° from Sunshine Island.*

*In entering, the passage to the S of Sunshine Island is preferable. Round the S end at a distance of about 250 yards and select anchorage in depths of 11 to 15 fathoms. The inlet dries for a considerable distance from the head of the flats, dropping off sharply to 7 fathoms.* (CP)

Anchorage in Vixen Inlet can be found deep in the inlet off the drying mud flats.

Anchor in 7 to 9 fathoms over a mud bottom with fair holding.

## **Emerald Bay** (Ernest Sound)

Emerald Bay is 2.8 miles north of Vixen Point.

Chart 17385
Entrance: 55°53.45′ N, 132°02.81′ W

*Emerald Bay* [is] *open and exposed. . . . It is used by fishermen during E weather, but is a poor anchorage.* (CP)

## **Petersen Islands** (Ernest Sound)

Petersen Islands are 4.6 miles west of Easterly Island Light and 3 miles southwest of Brownson Island.

Chart 17385
South entrance: 55°52.98′ N, 132°13.76′ W

*Petersen Islands* [are] *separated by a narrow channel with a depth of 3 fathoms and having the appearance of a split island. . . .* (CP)

We have found temporary anchorage as a lunch stop at the scenic north end of the narrow channel mentioned above in *Coast Pilot.*

## **Canoe Passage** (Ernest Sound)

Canoe Passage separates Brownson Island from Etolin Island.

Chart 17385
South entrance: 55°55.26′ N, 132°12.88′ W
North entrance (0.3 mile southwest of Menefee Point): 56°02.38′ N, 132°10.37′ W
Anchor (north end): 56°02.42′ N, 132°12.63′ W
Anchor (tiny cove, 0.5 mile south of north narrows): 56°01.90′ N, 132°12.41′ W

[Canoe Passage] *separates Brownson Island from Etolin Island. It runs in a N direction, with depths too great for anchorage, until the narrows are reached about 2 miles from the N end, where the channel dries and in places is 100 yards wide. Pass E of a small islet at the N end of the narrows. A shoal makes out about 150 yards from the W shore, 0.4 mile S of the N end of the passage. Beyond this point midchannel depths are the greatest. At the N end of Brownson Island, the passage turns E, increases in width, and affords anchorage in 13 fathoms, sand bottom.* (CP)

David Parker

*Salmon lovers are everywhere.*

## **Seward Passage**

Seward Passage separates Deer Island from the mainland.

Chart 17385
Southwest entrance: 55°58.10′ N, 132°02.21′ W
Northeast entrance: 55°05.67′ N, 132°00.10′ W

*Seward Passage* [is] *deep and clear.* (CP)

## **Sunny Bay** (Seward Passage)

Sunny Bay is 12 miles northeast of Vixen Harbor.

Chart 17385
Entrance: 55°58.43′ N, 131°59.19′ W

*Sunny Bay and the small coves between Watkins Point and Point Santa Anna, about 3.2 miles to the ENE, are used by launches.* (CP)

Cruising boats can find better anchorage in Santa Anna Inlet than here in Sunny Bay.

## **Santa Anna Inlet** (Seward Passage)

Santa Anna Inlet is 18.5 miles northeast of Meyers Chuck.

Chart 17385
Entrance: 55°59.84′ N, 131°57.73′ W
Anchor: 55°58.64′ N, 131°56.04′ W

*Santa Anna Inlet is . . . about 2.7 miles NNE of Point Peters. A shoal area extends about 200 yards off the SW shore about 0.5 mile from the entrance. . . . Small craft will find good anchorage in 9 fathoms near the head of the inlet.* (CP)

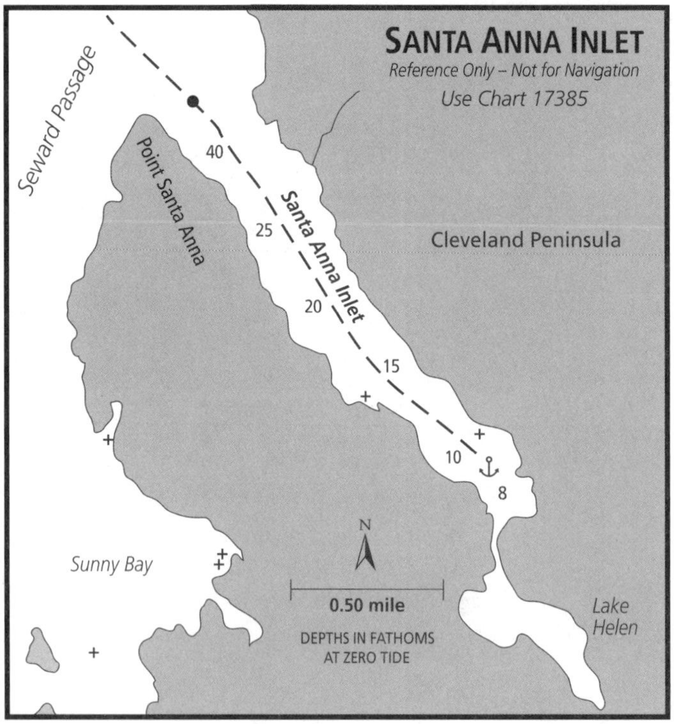




A loggers' cabin on the southwest shore near the log transfer site has been renovated by the USFS for use as a recreational cabin. There is also a USFS float in the bay. Anchor in the southwest corner just outside the narrows to the inner basin.

Anchor in 7 fathoms over sand and gravel with fair holding.

## **Fisherman Chuck** (Etolin Island)

Fisherman Chuck separates Menefee Point from Etolin Island north of Canoe Passage.

Chart 17385
North entrance: 56°03.45′ N, 132°11.16′ W
Anchor (0.16 mile south of north entrance); 56°03.27′ N, 132°11.16′ W

> [Fisherman Chuck] *is from 30 to 100 yards in width, has a depth of 14 fathoms at the N entrance, shoals to 2 fathoms 0.3 mile to the S, and thence to the S end is dry except at high water. It is used as an anchorage by fishermen.* (CP)

Santa Anna Inlet offers some of the most accessible, well-sheltered anchorage in Ernest Sound. Go deep into the inlet and anchor at its head off the outlet of Lake Helen. From Lake Helen at the head of the bay, it's only three miles overland to the upper basin in Yes Bay. (Locals report good crabbing here.)

Anchor in 8 fathoms over an unrecorded bottom.

## **Frosty Bay** (Seward Passage)

Frosty Bay, on the east side of Seward Passage, is 4.5 miles north of Santa Anna Inlet.

Chart 17385
Entrance: 56°04.05′ N, 131°58.76′ W
Anchor: 56°03.86′ N, 131°58.10′ W

> *Two rocks, bare at half tide, are about 150 yards N of the S point of the entrance. Fishing craft anchor in 7 fathoms in the SW part of the bay.* (CP)

Well protected and scenic, Frosty Bay is worth a visit if only to watch the seals (numbering about 40) that "hang out" on the partially submerged rocks off its west entrance.

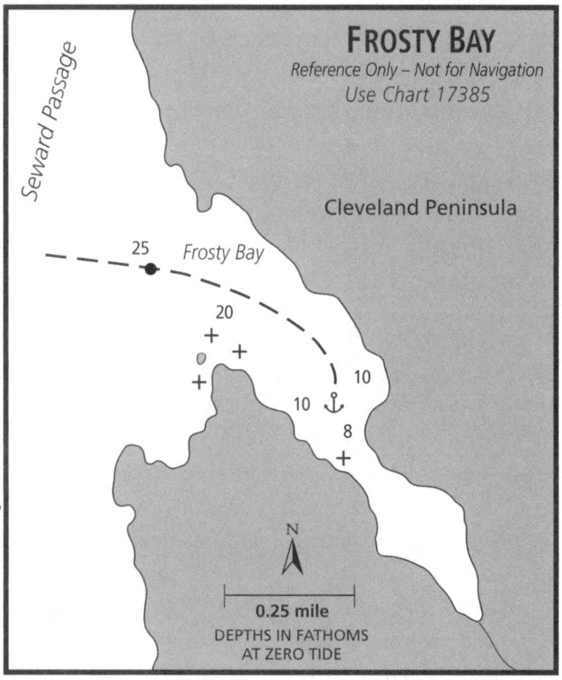

## Menefee Inlet (Etolin Island)

Menefee Inlet is 9 miles northwest of Santa Anna Inlet.

**Chart 17385**
**Entrance (0.6 mile northeast of Fisherman Chuck): 56°03.84′ N, 132°10.40′ W**
**Anchor: 56°07.51′ N, 132°14.35′ W**

> *Menefee Inlet . . . is deep to within 1 mile of the head, where three fair-sized streams empty. Anchorage may be had 1.2 miles from the head of the inlet in 14 fathoms, sand and mud bottom.* (CP)

## Southwest Cove (Etolin Island)

Southwest Cove is 10 miles southwest of Anan Bay.

**Chart 17385**
**Entrance (2.5 miles southwest of Found Island Light): 56°04.49′ N, 132°08.25′ W**
**Anchor (very small boats): 56°05.14′ N, 132°07.96′ W**

> *Southwest Cove, to the N of Bold Island, is too deep for anchorage. . . . Very small craft find anchorage back of the island on the E side of the cove.* (CP)

## Southeast Cove (Wrangell Island)

Southeast Cove is 6 miles southeast of Anan Bay.

**Chart 17385**
**Entrance (1.1 miles northeast of Thoms Point): 56°07.62′ N, 132°02.80′ W**

> *Southeast Cove . . . does not afford anchorage.* (CP)

## Fools Inlet (Wrangell Island)

Fools Inlet is 5 miles northeast of Zimovia Strait.

**Chart 17385**
**Entrance: 56°11.01′ N, 132°00.51′ W**
**Anchor (2.5 miles northwest of entrance, north of islets): 56°13.32′ N, 132°02.18′ W**

> *Mudflats bare 0.9 mile from its head, almost to two small islets. Anchorage may be had in 14 to 19 fathoms S of the S islet.* (CP)

## Zimovia Strait

Zimovia Strait lies between Etolin and Wrangell islands and connects Ernest Sound with the east end of Sumner Strait.

**Chart 17385 (inset)**
**South entrance: 56°06.06′ N, 132°05.42′ W**
**North entrance (Wrangell Harbor brg 013°T at 1.9 Nm): 56°26.31′ N, 132°24.09′ W**

> *Zimovia Strait . . . about 25 miles long, varies in width from about 0.4 to 2.5 miles, and furnishes a convenient route for small vessels bound from Ketchikan to Wrangell. The critical part of the passage is in The Narrows, in the vicinity of Button Island (56°12.06′ N, 132°15.17′ W), where the channel is tortuous, but marked by buoys, daybeacons, and lights.*
>
> *The flood current enters Zimovia Strait from both the N and S ends and meets near Village Islands. The approximate velocity of the current is 1.6 knots. Between Woronkofski Island and Wrangell Island, the ebb sets S and out through Chichagof Pass with a velocity of about 1.7 knots and the flood sets N with a velocity of about 1.7 knots.*
>
> *The channel in places is narrow and intricate, the depths are irregular, and local knowledge is desirable for safe navigation.* (CP)

Zimovia Strait, which divides Wrangell and Etolin islands, is a popular, smooth-water route between Ketchikan and Wrangell. More sheltered and attractive than Stikine Strait, it offers several anchor sites along its length. The eastern side of Etolin Island has an intricate shoreline, with narrow inlets and lagoons and steep-sided peaks that rise above 3,000 feet. The southern portion of the island lies within the South Etolin Island Wilderness. The island is almost split in two by Anita Bay and Mosman and Burnett inlets.

The strait is an intricate passage that requires careful navigating, particularly through Zimovia Narrows. The Narrows passes through the center of a once-flourishing tribal village, where you can still see evidence of places where the Natives cleared the beaches of rocks in order to land their canoes.

Follow the navigational aids as shown on Chart 17385 (inset), and you should have no difficulty. Pass north of Button Island and make the full jog to southwest before resuming your northwest heading.

## **Zimovia Cove** (Etolin Island)

Chart 17385; 1 mi NE of south entrance to Zimovia Strait
Entrance: 56°06.94′ N, 132°06.74′ W
Anchor: (cove) 56°06.76′ N, 132°07.53′ W

> *A small cove on the Etolin Island side of the channel . . . has depths of 18 fathoms 0.3 mile from the head, shoaling to 6 fathoms at the head.* (CP)

Good protection can be found near the head of the unnamed cove that we call "Zimovia Cove" on a flat shelf of 12 to 13 fathoms (zero tide) in the center portion of the cove. The north section of the cove may be shallower; however, the shore is steep-to. The shores of the cove show very few signs of stress.

Anchor in about 12 fathoms over fine brown sand and mud with very good holding. The cove has enough swinging room for several boats and it can be entered in the dark, but avoid charted rocks close to north shore.

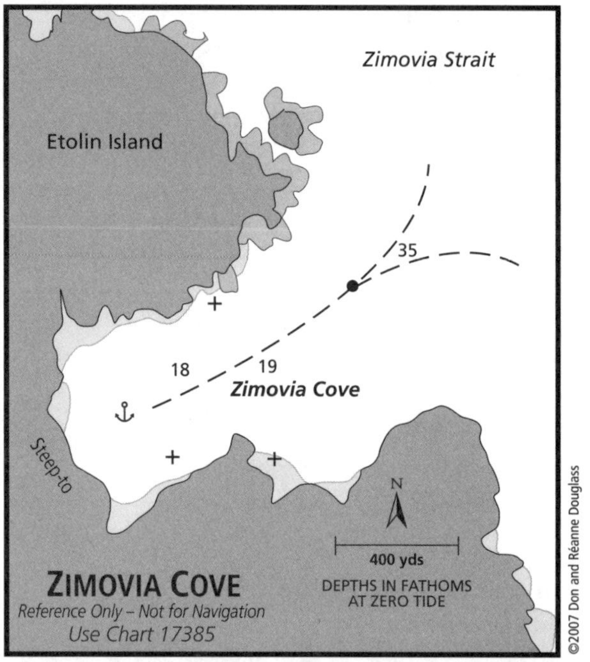


## **Thoms Place** (Wrangell Island)

Thoms Place is 3.5 miles from the south entrance to Zimovia Strait.

Chart 17385
Entrance: 56°09.64′ N, 132°07.37′ W
Anchor: 56°10.44′ N, 132°08.33′ W

> *Thoms Place, a cove on the Wrangell Island side of the channel . . . has two small wooded islets in the entrance. A group of islets is near the head close to the SW shore, and another close to the NE shore.*
>
> *In entering, pass between the entrance islets, where soundings vary from 6 to 10 fathoms. The channel between the E islet and the Wrangell Island shore is foul. The SW shore and the head of the cove are foul and should be given a wide berth.* (CP)

Thoms Place, an undeveloped state marine park, offers shelter in fair weather. The bottom is somewhat irregular, suggesting that it's rocky, but we have found mud holes where the bottom is level. Much of the shore is foul, so be careful in approaching it.

Anchor in 7 fathoms near the head of the bay over mud with good holding.

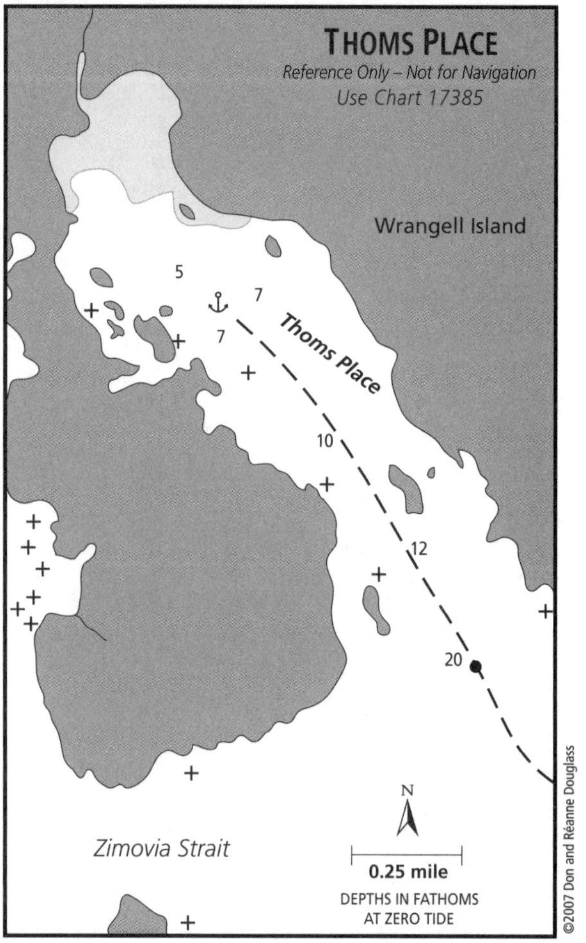

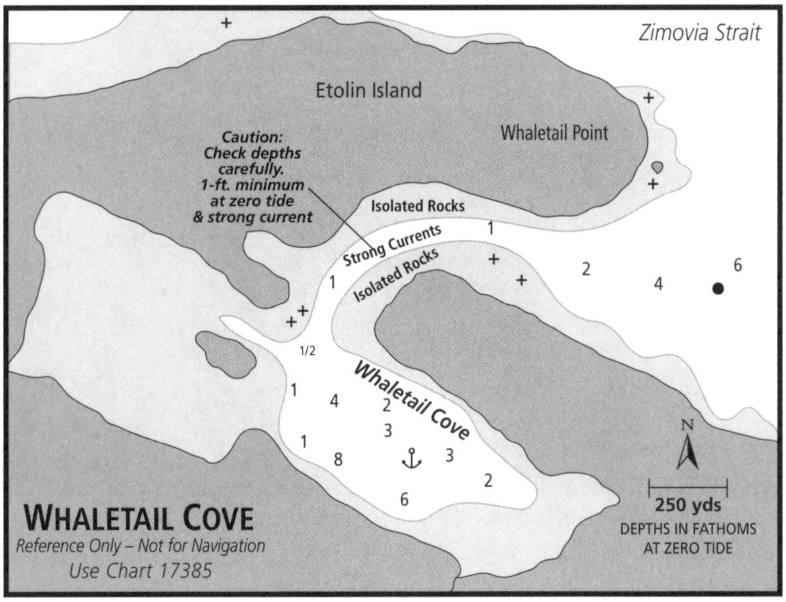




## Whaletail Cove (Etolin Island)

Chart 17385; 4 mi NW of Thoms Place
Entrance: 56°11.32′ N, 132°14.22′ W
Anchor: 56°11.06′ N, 132°14.85′ W

*Whaletail Cove, W of Trap Rock, has two branches; the entrance has a rock awash 6 feet in 56°11.19′ N, 132°14.32′ W, and then partially bares to the split. The W branch, which dries almost entirely, has a small island at its entrance. Depths of 1 to 7½ fathoms are found in the E branch, the greater depths are near the S shore. This branch shoals rapidly near the head.* (CP)

Small, completely landlocked Whaletail Cove has very good protection from all weather in its east branch. This anchorage is a challenge for small boats and can be entered only near high-water slack due to strong currents. *Caution:* The entrance, which is narrow, shallow and winding, has several uncharted, below-surface rocks, and it almost dries at zero tide. On approach, the entrance to Whaletail Cove is hidden and difficult to see due to the flat terrain. Use the inset on Chart 17385; electronic charting is also helpful.

Wait for adequate tide before you enter or exit; beware of the current which can carry a boat onto submerged rocks. When entering from Zimovia Strait, avoid Trap Rock to the east, which bares on a 6-foot tide; this large complex of rocks should be given a wide berth.

Anchor in the lower center of the east branch in 4 fathoms over sticky mud with very good holding.

## Olive Cove (Etolin Island)

Olive Cove is 2.5 miles west of Whaletail Cove.

Chart 17385
Entrance: 56°11.59′ N, 132°18.81′ W
Anchor: 56°11.41′ N, 132°18.95′ W

*Olive Cove is SSW of the Village Islands. . . . With local knowledge anchorage may be had off the entrance in 10 to 15 fathoms.* (CP)

Olive Cove, near the village sites in Zimovia Strait, is well protected from southerly weather. The cove largely dries at low tide. North of the cove there is a large vessel hard aground. The cove should be entered northwest of Village Island due to foul ground south of the island. Anchorage can be found off the entrance, short of the drying flat.

Anchor in 5 to 8 fathoms over sand with good holding.

## Anita Bay (Etolin Island)

Anita Bay is 5 miles northeast of Whaletail Cove.

Chart 17382
Entrance: 56°14.27′ N, 132°22.82′ W
Anchor: 56°11.55′ N, 132°30.01′ W

*Anchorage may be had near the head of the bay in 10 to 13 fathoms, mud and sand bottom. . . . A fish hatchery is in a small inlet along the NW shore of Anita Bay, 1.2 miles NW of the head of the bay at (56°12′07″N., 132°29′06″W). A log boom lies across the inlet, and a mooring buoy is 60 yards offshore of the log boom.* (CP)

Anita Bay indents Etolin Island almost to its west coast. Its upper end lies just 1.3 miles from the north tip of Burnett Inlet on Etolin Island's west side. The sharp 3,800-foot Virginia Peak, frequently bare of snow in the summer, lies just west of the entrance to Anita Bay, providing a scenic background to the anchorage. For larger boats, Anita Bay is the preferred anchorage in this area.

Anchor in about 12 fathoms over sand with good holding.

*Wrangell-Reliance Harbor*

## Shoemaker Bay Boat Harbor

(Wrangell Island)

Shoemaker Bay Boat Harbor is 3.5 miles southeast of Wrangell.

Chart 17384
Entrance: 56°25.01′ N, 132°21.22′ W

*The entrance channel is marked by lights. The stalls can accommodate 259 small craft, ranging from 20 to 62 feet with a 10-foot overhang. A new pier allows for small, tide dependent, hull repairs. Metered electricity is available upon request, and fuel can be obtained in Wrangell. A motel, restaurant and lounge, telephone service, and a large vehicle parking area are available in the immediate vicinity.* (CP)

Upgraded Shoemaker Bay Boat Harbor is located approximately 5 miles south of downtown Wrangell. The harbor has 250 slips for small and large commercial fishing and recreational vessels. There are also tidal grids, a hydraulic hoist, all-tide boat launch and a work float located at the harbor. Power, water, waste-oil collection and garbage collection are provided.

Rainbow Falls Trail takes off across the road from the harbor. It's an easy hike, worth doing. Since this harbor is part of a larger recreational complex (tent and RV camping), it also has a tennis court, park with shelter and playground.

*Wrangell, Alaska, welcomes cruisers with open arms.*

## Wrangell

(Wrangell Island)

Wrangell is 89 miles north of Ketchikan and 148 miles south of Juneau.

Chart 17384
Entrance (Wrangell-Reliance Harbor): 56°28.06′ N, 132°23.10′ W
Reliance Dock: 56°27.95′ N, 132°22.95′ W

*Anchorages. Wrangell Harbor affords shelter for vessels*

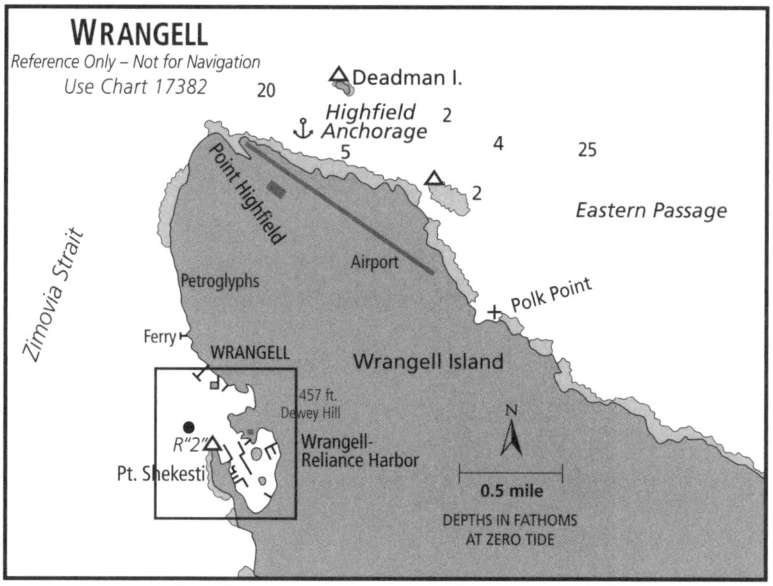




*only from offshore winds. During heavy SE winter gales Highfield Anchorage is sometimes used for better shelter. Good anchorage in strong SE weather has been found 0.8 mile off the NE side of Woronkofski Island in about 23 fathoms, mud bottom.* (CP)

*The City of Wrangell operates about 3,300 feet of float space in the mooring basin in the S part of the harbor, and about 1,900 feet of float space in the inner basin E of Shakes Island. Fresh water and electric power are available on all floats. A 65-foot grid is in the mud flats on the W side of the trestle connecting Shakes Island to Wrangell Island.*

*Two fuel facilities are on the SSW side of the harbor.* (CP)

In the past, it was difficult to find moorage in Wrangell-Reliance Harbor without rafting—sometimes three to four deep! Plans to improve Wrangell harbor area facilities are underway, with a phase-in plan for the new deep-draft Heritage Harbor in the bay south of Shekesti Point (at approximately °27.46' N, 132°23.18' W). At press time the breakwaters and entrance lights are in place.) As a part of phase one, the slips on fingers 2, 3 and 4 are scheduled to be completed by 2007.

Wrangell-Reliance Harbor will also be upgraded to accommodate more pleasure craft. You may be assigned a berth in any of the following locations (refer to diagram): Reliance Dock—the most likely (side-tie); Inner Harbor Floats, Standard Oil Float. Or you may be assigned to an area called the Summer Floats, located north of the harbor, on the north side of the Cruise Ship Dock (water is the only utility and the floats are subject to *very heavy* chop in heavy weather).

For a slip assignment, call the harbormaster on VHF Ch 16, switch and answer VHF Ch 10 (tel.: 907.874.3736). Harbor personnel are extremely helpful and they like cruising boats. ("They're good folks!" says the harbormaster). The

*The entrance to Wrangell-Reliance Harbor as viewed from the cruise ship dock area*

Reliance Dock has water, power, garbage and telephones; showers and laundromat can be found in town about 200 yards from the harbormaster's office. Heritage Harbor is expected to have full services. Two fuel docks—Wrangell Oil and Delta Western—are opposite the Reliance Dock.

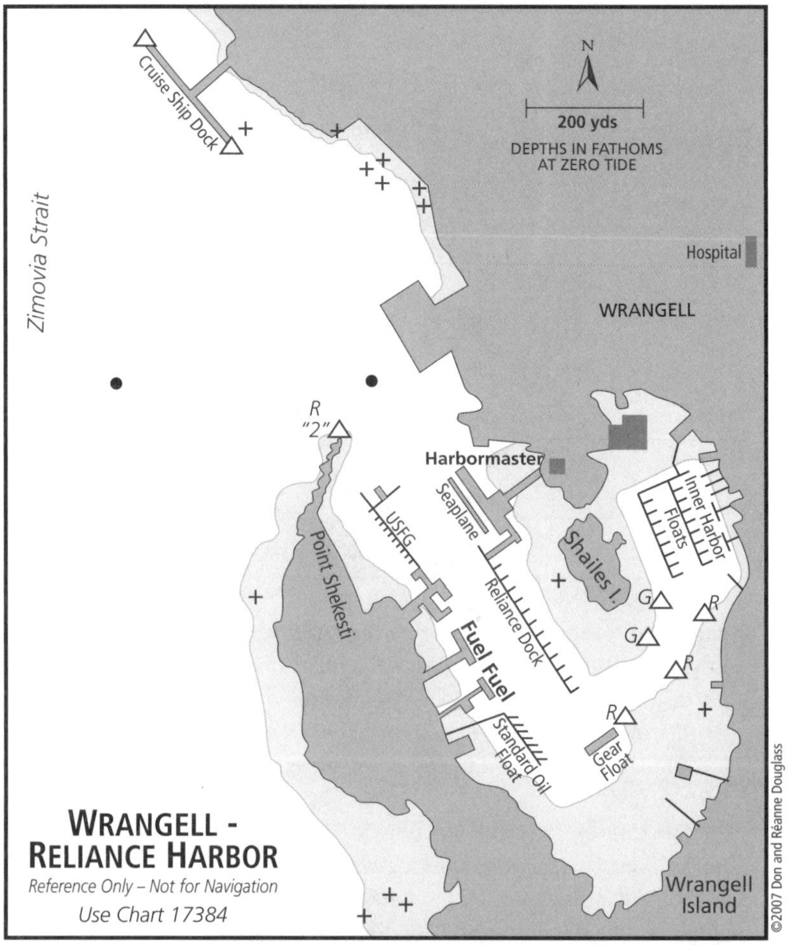


As well as the harbor improvements, the city has installed boat repair facilities with a 150-ton Travel Lift (located at the Marine Repair Center, across from the breakwater) and storage for vessels up to 50 feet. There is a tidal haul-out grid for vessels 45 feet and under within the harbor. The Float Plane Dock is located on your port as you enter the harbor.

For groceries and other supplies visit the following: City Market, Bob's IGA, Otteson's True Value and Sentry Hard-

*Rafting along the Reliance Dock (center of picture)*

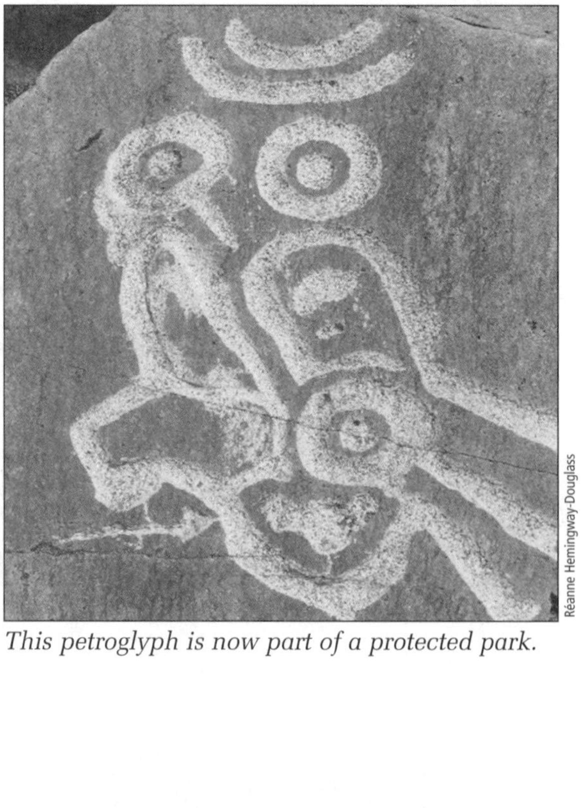


*This petroglyph is now part of a protected park.*

## Wrangell

Don Douglass and Réanne Hemingway-Douglass

Wrangell had its origins as Redoubt Saint Dionysius—a fort built by the Russians in 1834 to prevent encroachment by Hudson's Bay Company traders. In 1839, the Russians leased part of Southeast Alaska, including the fort, to the British who changed its name to Fort Stikine. Major trading went on between the Tlingits and the Hudson's Bay Company until 1849, when the fort was abandoned. After the U.S. purchase of Alaska, the Army established a military post here in 1867, naming the settlement Fort Wrangell. Boom-bust periods occurred regularly—with each gold strike—until the end of the nineteenth century.

Less sophisticated and more relaxed than other historic Southeast towns, Wrangell has the feel of the Alaska frontier and for that reason is one of our favorite ports of call. (In fact, residents say this is one of the few communities where people look you in the eye as they pass on the street!) Fewer cruise ships call here than at larger towns in Southeast, and it's refreshing to visit a port where skippers of working boats, barges, outboard skiffs and pleasure craft all communicate with one another in a friendly manner.

For visitors, attractions here include the Nolan Museum and Visitor Center (with a movie theatre)—a handsome addition to Wrangell; Chief Shakes House; Petroglyph Beach Park; picnic areas and some good hiking trails, as well as the Anan Bear and Wildlife Observatory, south of Wrangell. With the requirement of permits and the lack of convenient anchorage for cruising boats at Anan Creek, we suggest docking at Wrangell and taking one of the tour boats to see the bears. Also, if a raft trip on the Stikine River interests you, Stickeen Wilderness Adventures (tel.: 800.874.2085) and Alaska Vistas (tel.: 866.874.3006) offer tours. And if you just happen to need a "golf fix," you can find nine holes at the beautiful USGA Muskeg Meadows Golf Course, north of town (rentals available). When the sun shines, the view from the first tee rivals that of Pebble Beach, California. The Garnet Ledge in is no longer open for visits of any kind. The town also has a public swimming pool and a library with Internet service (sign up for your turn).

City of Wrangell Website: www.wrangell.com.

Réanne Hemingway-Douglass

*Muskeg Meadows Golf Course—where the view rivals that of Pebble Beach*

Réanne Hemingway-Douglass

*An example of crafts at Nolan Center in Wrangell*

Réanne Hemingway-Douglass

*Petroglyph faces*

Réanne Hemingway-Douglass

*The breakwaters at Wrangell's Heritage Harbor—south of Pt. Shekesti*

ware. All stores are within a short walking distance of Reliance Harbor. To carry heavy supplies to and from Heritage Harbor, you'll need transportation. Wrangell is serviced by air and the Alaska State Ferry (north of the cruise ship dock).

## BRADFIELD CANAL TO BLAKE CHANNEL AND EASTERN PASSAGE

Chart 17385

The most easterly of the three routes from Ketchikan to Wrangell, this is the longest, most protected and, for many, the most scenic. It follows Clarence Strait to Ernest Sound, Seward Passage to Anan Bay, then Blake Ch and Eastern Passage around the north tip of Wrangell Island to the town.

On this route, you can stop to take a hike at the Anan Bear and Wildlife Observatory, then experience the muddy glacier melt of the mighty Stikine River.

### Bradfield Canal

Bradfield Canal extends 13 miles east of Anan Bay.

Chart 17385
West entrance (0.5 mile northwest of Point Warde): 56°10.82′ N, 131°58.77′ W

> *The small cove W of* [Duck Point] *affords the best protection for small craft in the canal. The best anchorage is at the head of the cove in depths of 5 to 8 fathoms, soft bottom.*
>
> *The navigable channel of Bradfield Canal above Duck Point follows the N shore of the point, being restricted in one place to a width of 0.2 mile by a small islet which is passed on its S side. Beyond this point the canal continues 2 miles, where it ends in a broad flat off the mouths of two large streams.* (CP)

### Anan Bay (Bradfield Canal)

Anan Bay is 2.3 miles east of Point Warde.

Chart 17385
Entrance: 56°11.16′ N, 131°53.94′ W
Public float: 56°11.09′ N, 131°53.54′ W

> *Anan Bay, about 2.3 miles E of Point Warde, is an open bight on the S shore of Bradfield Canal.* (CP)

The Anan Bear and Wildlife Observatory—a protected bear and wildlife observation station in Anan Bay—is a real trip highlight for many Southeast Alaska cruisers; don't pass it by.

Anan Bay is located about 30 miles south of Wrangell. From Meyers Chuck head northeast into Ernest Sound then to Bradfield Canal, watching for Anan Bay on your starboard. Fed by Anan Creek, the Bay abounds with pink salmon that draw bears, eagles and seals, as well as humans who want to watch all this activity. From July 5 to August 25, a day-use permit (small per person fee) is required

Mike Youngblood

*Heed our caution: the anchorage at Anan Bay is temporary and an anchor watch should stay onboard.*

to visit the Anan Bear and Wildlife Observatory. A half-mile boardwalk follows the shoreline to a covered observation platform where you can watch black bears feeding near the falls. USFS guides (with firearms) greet you, give talks and answer questions. A maximum of 60 visitors per day is allowed. (An online reservation calendar at the Observatory Website allows you to see what dates are available and to enter your request.) No domestic animals are permitted on shore and no food or beverages, other than water. A small float off the USFS cabin is strictly reserved for cabin users.

## Respect the Bears!

Don Douglass & Réanne Hemingway-Douglass

Everyone has heard or has a story to tell about Alaska and her bears. For many cruising boaters, just spotting a bear can often be the highlight of the trip.

Black bears are the most common species and you will frequently see them prowling for trout at the mouths of the numerous streams that flow into the ocean. The smallest of the North American bears, black bears grow to about five feet long and weigh between 200 and 300 pounds, although some can reach 500 pounds. These bears are swift of foot and can run up to 25 miles per hour. They are skillful tree climbers and have a well-deserved reputation for being troublesome around campsites. They have often been known to bite (or maul) the hand that feeds them. (Don't try it!)

The brown bear (grizzly) roams Southeast Alaska and Kodiak and Afonak islands among others. They grow to be about eight feet long and weigh 350 to 500 pounds. They can anger quickly but usually don't attack unless threatened in some way. Known as *Silvertips* and *Grizzlies,* these bears use their long, curved claws for digging out ground squirrels and mice, the same claws that also become lethal weapons.

Bears are wild animals and people need to give them their proper respect. Boaters who disembark to sightsee on land need to be bear-conscious. National Park officials offer the following guidelines when entering bear territory:

- Use caution when near natural bear foods. Bears are attracted to areas where there are berries and nuts. Try to avoid these areas when these crops are in season.
- Stay away from carcasses. This is a great food source for a bear and bears will aggressively defend them.
- Watch for signs of bear. Tracks, fresh diggings and droppings may indicate that a bear is still in the area.
- Leave your dog on the boat. Dogs have been known to provoke a bear attack or even return to the unsuspecting owner with an angry bear in pursuit.
- Hike in a group. There is more safety in numbers. While hiking, make loud noises, whistle, sing, talk or carry noise makers. Most bears will leave you alone if they are aware of your presence. It's when you startle them that the trouble begins.
- If camping, always put away food in bear-resistant food storage facilities (when provided) or suspend food between two trees a minimum of 13 feet above the ground and three feet from the tree trunks.
- Avoid cooking or eating smelly foods as odors will attract bears. Bears may also be drawn to hair spray, soaps, toothpaste, shaving cream and cosmetics.
- Use a telephoto lens when photographing bears.
- Always keep children nearby and in sight.

## Anan Bay Bear and Wildlife Observatory

Linda Lewis—Journal Notes—M/V *Royal Sounder*

The opportunity to see bears, up close—in their own environment, was irresistible to the three mid-westerners on the boat. David stayed onboard to do anchor watch in Anan Bay, as recommended in the Douglass guide. The three of us spent a magical hour watching the bears in their world. We were able to feel safe (*we* were the ones enclosed) and see them in their own world. Anan Creek was so abundant with salmon it resembled a carpet. The bears would just reach in, pull out a fish and then feast on only the brain and roe. Then they would toss it aside for the eagles and ravens to clean up later. In all my trips to Southeast Alaska, this remains one of my most favorite experiences.

Courtesy of Forest Service

*The observatory includes a duck blind-type viewing area for a really up-close look.*

Linda Lewis

*Choices, so many choices*

Linda Lewis

*A selected salmon and the carcass pile*

Linda Lewis

*Anan Creek's carpet of salmon*

Réanne Hemingway-Douglass

*The bears get up close and personal at the observation platform at Anan Creek.*

For information and to apply for a permit, call the USFS Wrangell District at 907.874.2323 or check their Website: www.fs.fed.us/r10/tongass/.

And here is an extra tip from the Rangers. Even if the reservations calendar looks full, try calling at the last minute when you are nearby. Some unpublicized slots are left open until a few days before each date; or someone may have cancelled. You might be lucky.

Anchoring is possible for pleasure craft; however, the shoal along shore that drops steeply at a 45-degree angle into much deeper water as well as the sandy bottom make holding difficult; in addition, during good weather, a westerly swell sets up in the bay. If you do choose to anchor here, we strongly recommend that you leave a crew member aboard when you go ashore.

## Blake Channel

Blake Channel connects Ernest Sound with Eastern Passage and the east end of Sumner Strait; its south entrance is 3 miles northeast of Point Warde.

Chart 17385
South entrance (0.2 mile east of Blake Channel Light): 56°12.57′ N, 131°55.13′ W

> *Blake Channel* [is] *locally called Back Channel. . . .*
>
> *In Blake Channel the flood current sets NNW with a velocity of about 2.2 to 3 knots, and meets the flood current from Eastern Passage in the vicinity of The Narrows. The ebb current sets in the opposite direction with a velocity of about 2.2 to 3 knots.* (CP)

## Berg Bay (Blake Channel)

Berg Bay is 11 miles north of Anan Bay and 15 miles southeast of Wrangell.

Chart 17385
Southeast entrance: 56°21.15′ N, 132°00.39′ W
Anchor: 56°21.70′ N, 132°00.52′ W

> *Berg Bay . . . has depths of 5 to 11 fathoms to near its head and affords the best anchorage in Blake Channel. Vessels can enter on either side of the island in the mouth, but should give the island a good berth, and avoid a reef*

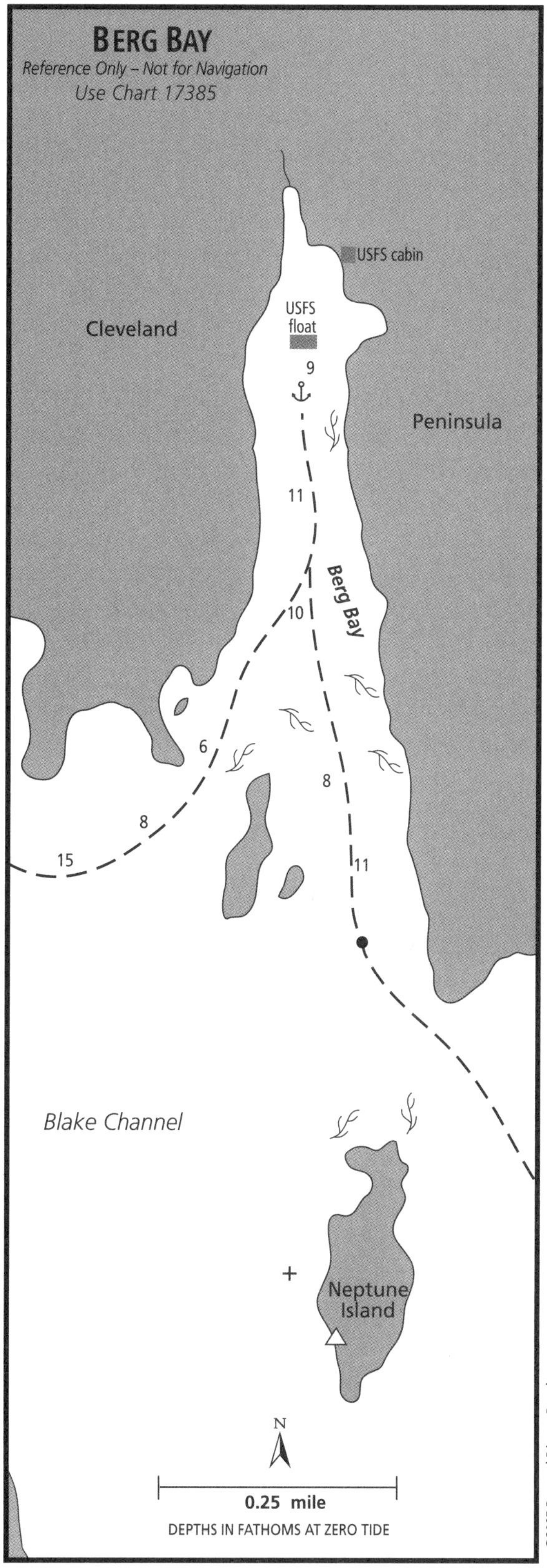

*that extends 0.1 mile N of the inner end of the island. . . . Other tributaries of Blake Channel and Eastern Passage shoal rapidly inside their entrances, and are not good anchorages.* (CP)

Berg Bay offers very good shelter in a chilly, remote alpine setting. As you proceed up Blake Channel, the water becomes a milky green, currents run strong, and the vegetation gets denser. There are permanent snowfields on the 5,000- to 6,000-foot peaks, less than 10 miles to the north.

From here you can explore the extensive outflow of Aaron Creek immediately east, being careful to avoid the numerous pilings in the log storage area.

Entry into Berg Bay can be made on either side of the islets as indicated in the diagram. The easterly route has deeper water. Anchor just south of the USFS float near the head of the bay next to the cabin. Avoid kelp and check the set of your anchor. There is a wonderful beach walk here and cruisers report great crabbing in this bay.

Anchor in 9 fathoms; silt and gravel with poor-to-fair holding.

## The Narrows

The Narrows, 12 miles northwest of the entrance to Blake Channel, connects Blake Channel with Eastern Passage.

Chart 17385
East entrance: 56°22.01′ N, 132°03.97′ W
West entrance: 56°21.75′ N, 132°07.36′ W

*The Narrows . . . is about 1.5 miles long and about 250 yards wide at its narrowest part. . . . The only dangers are a reef off the N point at the E entrance, and a rocky area with 3 to 4 feet over it at high water and marked by a light, on the S side of the channel just W of the narrowest part of the channel.* (CP)

In The Narrows, about 5 miles south of Wrangell, you can see a tidal bore and a definite demarcation line where the green water of The Narrows meets the chalky waters of the Stikine River. The water temperature immediately drops several degrees.

## Madan Bay (Eastern Passage)

Madan Bay is 5 miles northwest of Berg Bay.

Chart 17385
Entrance: 56°22.66′ N, 132°08.87′ W
Anchor: 56°24.09′ N, 132°10.28′ W

*Madan Bay . . . is deep and clear of dangers. It offers excellent anchorage for small craft N of the projecting point near its head on the W side in 7 fathoms, soft bottom. Large vessels may find anchorage in 12 fathoms, soft bottom, farther offshore and near the head of the bay.* (CP)

Cruisers enthusiastically report this anchorage as very protected and private.

## Highfield Anchorage (Wrangell Island)

Highfield Anchorage, at the north end of Wrangell Island, is 1.5 miles north of Wrangell Harbor.

Chart 17384
Anchor: 56°29.45′ N, 132°22.26′ W

*The anchorage is in 4 to 15 fathoms, fine sand and mud bottom. . .*

*Anchorage can also be had in 4 to 12 fathoms, fine sand and mud bottom, E from that area to directly N of Polk Point and about halfway between Deadman Island and the shore of Wrangell Island.*

*Light floating ice from Stikine River is encountered here in the spring, and countercurrents render a vessel very uneasy at times.* (CP)

After passing through the narrows (easier if you use the flood tide) and proceeding up Eastern Passage, you meet part of the muddy brown outflow of the mighty Stikine River. We once headed straight for the mud flats but lost our nerve when the water became totally opaque and the depth sounder began reacting to all the silt in the water.

Rounding the north tip of Wrangell Island, you can pass safely on either side of Simonof Island. The area south of Simonof Island, which is fairly shallow, provides refuge during southerly storms but it is used extensively for permanent anchorage by some local boats.

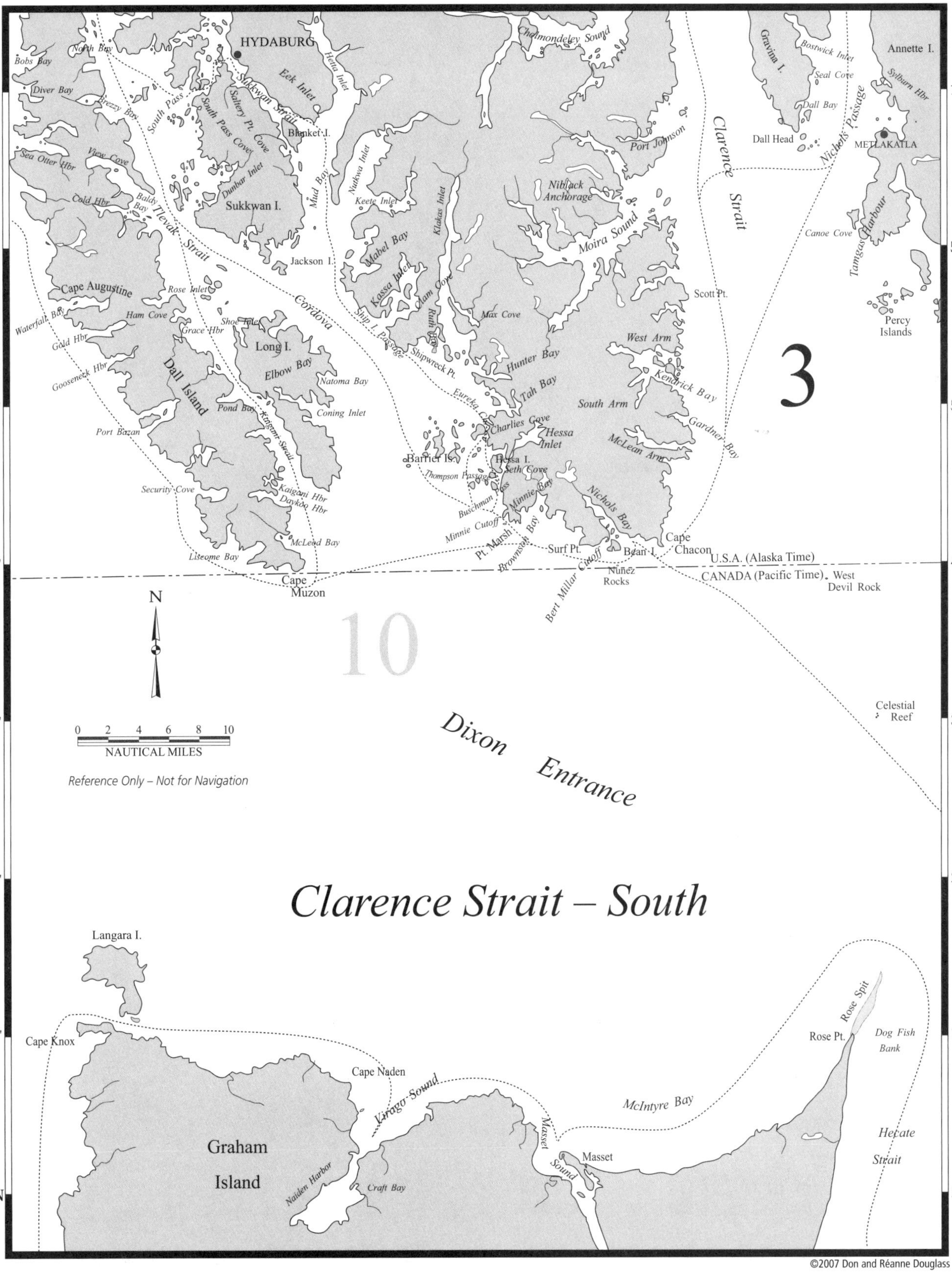
Clarence Strait – South
HYDABURG
METLAKATLA
Annette I.
Gravina I.
Bostwick Inlet
Seal Cove
Dall Bay
Dall Head
Sylburn Hbr
Nichols Passage
Tamgas Harbour
Canoe Cove
Percy Islands
Clarence Strait
Chomondeley Sound
Port Johnson
Niblack Anchorage
Moira Sound
Scott Pt.
West Arm
Kendrick Bay
Gardner Bay
South Arm
McLean Arm
Nichols Bay
Cape Chacon
Bean I.
Nunez Rocks
Bert Millar Cutoff
U.S.A. (Alaska Time)
CANADA (Pacific Time)
West Devil Rock
Celestial Reef
Bobs Bay
North Bay
Diver Bay
Brezzy Bay
South Pass
South Pass Cove
Saltery Pt. Cove
Sukkwan Strait
Eek Inlet
Hetta Inlet
Blanket I.
Mud Bay
Nutkwa Inlet
Keete Inlet
Klakas Inlet
Sea Otter Hbr
View Cove
Cold Hbr
Baldy Bay
Dunbar Inlet
Sukkwan I.
Tlevak Strait
Jackson I.
Mabel Bay
Kassa Inlet
Clam Cove
Max Cove
Hunter Bay
Tah Bay
Cape Augustine
Rose Inlet
Waterfall Bay
Ham Cove
Shoe Inlet
Grace Hbr
Gold Hbr
Long I.
Cordova
Ship I. Passage
Shipwreck Pt.
Elbow Bay
Natoma Bay
Gooseneck Hbr
Dall Island
Pond Bay
Coning Inlet
Kaigani Strait
Port Bazan
Eureka Channel
Charlies Cove
Hessa Inlet
Barrier Is.
Hessa I.
Seth Cove
Thompson Passage
Security Cove
Kaigani Hbr
Daykoo Hbr
Buschmann Pass
Minnie Bay
Minnie Cutoff
Pt. Marsh
Brownson Bay
Surf Pt.
McLeod Bay
Liscome Bay
Cape Muzon
3
10
N
0 2 4 6 8 10
NAUTICAL MILES
Reference Only – Not for Navigation
Dixon Entrance
Langara I.
Cape Knox
Cape Naden
Virago Sound
Graham Island
Naden Harbor
Craft Bay
Masset Sound
Masset
McIntyre Bay
Rose Spit
Rose Pt.
Dog Fish Bank
Hecate Strait
10'
55°N
50'
40'
30'
20'
54°N

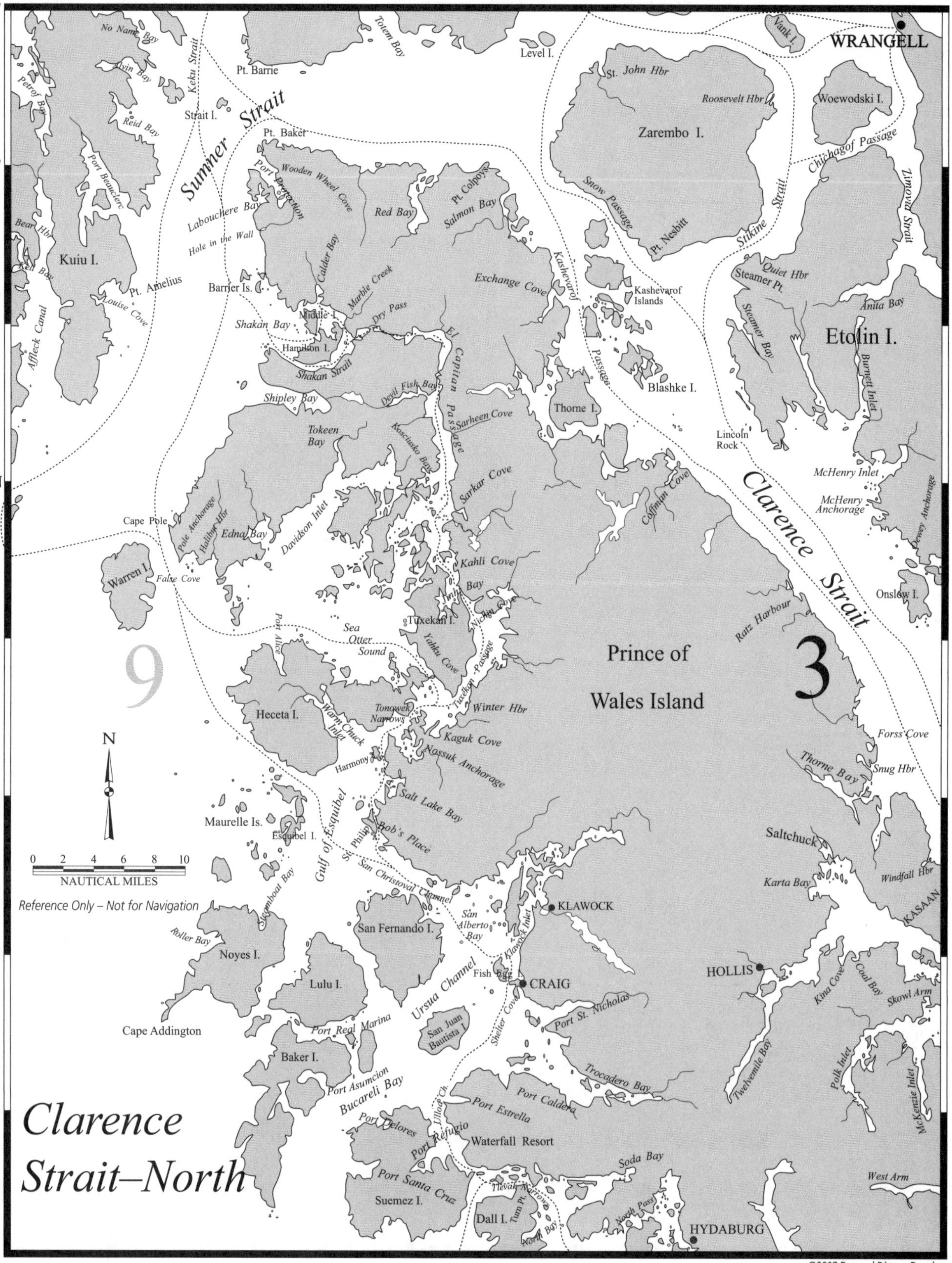
Clarence Strait–North
WRANGELL
Zarembo I.
Etolin I.
Prince of Wales Island
3
9
Kuiu I.
Warren I.
Heceta I.
Noyes I.
Lulu I.
Baker I.
San Fernando I.
Suemez I.
Dall I.
Tuxekan I.
Thorne I.
Blashke I.
Woewodski I.
Vank I.
Level I.
Strait I.
Pt. Barrie
Pt. Baker
Sumner Strait
Keku Strait
Totem Bay
No Name Bay
Alvin Bay
Petrof Bay
Reid Bay
Port Beauclerc
Bear Hbr
Bell Bay
Pt. Amelius
Louise Cove
Affleck Canal
Labouchere Bay
Hole in the Wall
Port Protection
Wooden Wheel Cove
Red Bay
Pt. Colpoys
Salmon Bay
Calder Bay
Marble Creek
Barrier Is.
Middle I.
Shakan Bay
Dry Pass
Hamilton I.
Shakan Strait
Shipley Bay
Devil Fish Bay
El Capitan Passage
Exchange Cove
Kashevarof
Kashevarof Islands
Kashevarof Passage
St. John Hbr
Roosevelt Hbr
Snow Passage
Pt. Nesbitt
Stikine Strait
Chichagof Passage
Zimovia Strait
Quiet Hbr
Steamer Pt.
Steamer Bay
Anita Bay
Burnett Inlet
Lincoln Rock
Clarence Strait
McHenry Inlet
McHenry Anchorage
Dewey Anchorage
Onslow I.
Tokeen Bay
Kosciusko Bay
Sarheen Cove
Sarkar Cove
Coffman Cove
Cape Pole
Pole Anchorage
Halibut Hbr
Edna Bay
Davidson Inlet
False Cove
Kahli Cove
Tinli Bay
Nichin Cove
Ratz Harbour
Port Alice
Sea Otter Sound
Yatuku Cove
Tuxekan Passage
Winter Hbr
Tonowek Narrows
Warm Chuck Inlet
Kaguk Cove
Nossuk Anchorage
Harmony
Forss Cove
Thorne Bay
Snug Hbr
N
Salt Lake Bay
Maurelle Is.
Esquibel I.
Gulf of Esquibel
St. Philip I.
Bob's Place
Saltchuck
0 2 4 6 8 10
NAUTICAL MILES
Reference Only – Not for Navigation
Steamboat Bay
San Christoval Channel
Karta Bay
Windfall Hbr
KASAAN
KLAWOCK
San Alberto Bay
Klawock Inlet
Roller Bay
Fish Egg
CRAIG
HOLLIS
Kina Cove
Coal Bay
Skowl Arm
Ursua Channel
Cape Addington
Port Real Marina
San Juan Bautista I.
Shelter Cove
Port St. Nicholas
Twelvemile Bay
Polk Inlet
McKenzie Inlet
Trocadero Bay
Port Asumcion
Bucareli Bay
Ulloa Ch.
Port Caldera
Port Estrella
Port Delores
Port Refugio
Waterfall Resort
Soda Bay
West Arm
Port Santa Cruz
Tlevak Narrows
Turn Pt.
North Bay
North Pass
HYDABURG
30'
20'
10'
56°N
50'
40'
30'
20'

# 3

# CLARENCE STRAIT, PRINCE OF WALES EAST COAST AND STIKINE STRAIT

## INTRODUCTION

Clarence Strait extends 100 miles north from Dixon Entrance to Sumner Strait where Kuiu, Kupreanof and Mitkof islands separate the southern part of Southeast Alaska from the northern part. We have made this area the subject of an entire chapter because we think it offers such outstanding cruising opportunities, yet it is in close proximity to Ketchikan.

The east coast of Prince of Wales Island, along the west shore of Clarence Strait, is worth serious exploration by cruising boats. Since boats entering Alaska from British Columbia must check in with customs at Ketchikan, they normally follow Revillagigedo Channel, bypassing some wonderful, little-known areas.

The southern part of Prince of Wales Island hides some jewels—complex inlets and sounds that are seldom visited. Kendrick Bay, Ingraham Bay, Moria Sound, Cholmondeley Sound, Kasaan Bay, Thorn and Tolstoi bays and Kashevarof Passage all have sheltered waters and solitary coves that rarely see the wake of pleasure vessels. To experience some remote wilderness that is not yet adequately charted and to test your pathfinding skills, this is a good place to start.

The islands along the east shore of Clarence Strait also have some little-known anchor sites worth exploring. Percy Islands on the south, Annette Island, the south shore of Gravina Island, and especially the west shore of Etolin Island and the Blashke Islands on the north, are excel-

Réanne Hemingway-Douglass

*Beachcombing provides many hours of pleasure for both photographers and collectors (Kasaan Bay).*

## Clothing in Southeast Alaska

Linda Lewis

My two favorite clothing words in Southeast Alaska are "fleece" and "layering". Along with silk or poly long underwear and waterproof outer wear, you have the main items you need to stay comfortable in this temperate-zone, rain-forest environment. Add boots for any dinghy expeditions and hiking. (Be Alaska savvy and get Xtra-Tuff—the 16" tall model; see: http://www.work-n-wear.com/shop. Then search on Xtra-Tuff.)

During June, July, and August, the temperatures range from the mid 40s (F) to mid 60s during daylight hours (as many as 18-20 hours), with an occasional gloriously sunny and warm (70s) day or two. It rains; some summers it really rains—a lot. Some summers it is wonderfully sunny for days at a time, repeatedly. You just never know. So you need the full range of clothing. A few shorts and sun tops, lots of long pants, t-shirts, long-sleeve shirts, warm socks, fleece jackets of all kinds, hats, gloves, and waterproof rain gear. For sailors: full foul-weather gear. For glacier viewing on the outside of your boat, pretend you're going snow skiing and dress accordingly.

Round this out with an inflatable PFD and you're ready to cruise in Southeast Alaska.

David Parker

*Clothing for glacier watching*

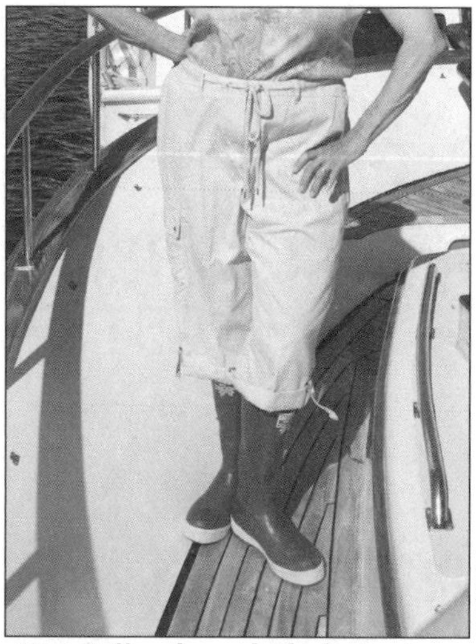

David Parker

*Xtra-Tuffs—the real Alaska boot*

Linda Lewis

*Don't forget the dog!*

David Parker

*Fleece, with layers, for comfort outside and inside*

Linda Lewis

*It really does get this warm and sunny—sometimes.*

Linda Lewis

*For most men, this is the uniform of the day.*

David Parker

*Sailing in full foul weather gear*

lent places you can poke around and explore while enjoying the world-famous salmon fishing. Be alert to the presence of commercial fishing vessels, which seem abundant in the area of Luck Point in Clarence Strait and in Kashevarof Passage. Stay vigilant to avoid their nets.

Clarence Strait, open to the southeast and northwest, has strong currents of several knots in certain areas and up to four knots in Snow Passage Narrows. (At the northwest corner of Prince of Wales Island in the vicinity of Point Baker—in Sumner Strait—currents up to four knots have been reported.) Clarence Strait is susceptible to southeast gales, which can quickly pick up to dangerous proportions with the passage of a weather front. A nasty chop develops in Clarence Strait any time a wind over 15 knots is blowing, especially against the strong outflowing ebbs at Behm Canal and Ernest Sound. It is best to cross the strait early in the morning when fair weather has been forecast. Once you are inside any of the major inlets or protected coves, chop or swells quickly die down.

## Clarence Strait South Entrance

### **Stone Rock Bay** (Prince of Wales Island)

Stone Rock Bay is 4.5 miles north of Cape Chacon.

Chart 17433
Entrance: 54°45.39′ N, 131°58.60′ W

> *Stone Rock Bay . . . is an open bight with deep water and irregular bottom. Foul ground extends off the entrance points, and there is a 5¼-fathom shoal midway in the entrance. Small fishing craft anchor close to shore, but the use of the bay as an anchorage is not recommended.* (CP)

### **Mallard Bay** (Prince of Wales Island)

Mallard Bay is 5 miles north of Cape Chacon.

Chart 17433
Entrance: 54°46.52′ N, 131°58.74′ W

> *Foul ground extends about 0.6 mile offshore from the point separating Stone Rock Bay and Mallard Bay.*
>
> *Fair weather anchorage may be had near the head of the bay in 15 fathoms, sandy bottom, with about 0.1 mile swinging room. Favor the N shore when entering.* (CP)

### **McLean Arm** (Prince of Wales Island)

McLean Arm is 6.5 miles north of Cape Chacon.

Chart 17433
Entrance: 54°47.71′ N, 131°57.15′ W
Anchor: 54°47.81′ N, 132°02.78′ W

> *The head of the arm has two branches. The W and larger branch affords anchorage in its widest part in 20 fathoms, sticky bottom, with swinging room for small vessels. A flat extends 0.1 mile from the head of this branch. Anchorage can be selected in about 17 fathoms at the entrance to the north branch, however it is less desirable, and care must be taken to avoid a ledge that bares, and extends about 250 yards E from the point dividing the two branches. . . . A small craft anchorage is close under the S shore about 3.2 miles inside the entrance.* (CP)

McLean Arm has easy access and offers the first reasonable shelter for small craft north of Cape Chacon.

Anchor in 3 to 5 fathoms over a mud and rocky bottom.

### **Gardner Bay** (Prince of Wales Island)

Gardner Bay is 8 miles north of Cape Chacon.

Chart 17433
Entrance: 54°49.44′ N, 131°57.37′ W
Anchor (nook): 54°49.46′ N, 131°59.11′ W
Anchor (head of bay): 54°49.64′ N, 131°59.93′ W

> *Gardner Bay . . . affords good anchorage, but its*

Réanne Hemingway-Douglass

*Entrance to Gardner Bay*

*narrow entrance restricts its use to small vessels only.*

*Fishing vessels and small craft frequently use the channel S of the outer islands and rocks. Midchannel courses suffice. Caution should be exercised when entering, because the dangers are unmarked. Anchorage in 13 fathoms, mud bottom, can be had in the basin at the head of the bay. The points at the entrance to the basin should be given a berth of about 150 yards.* (CP)

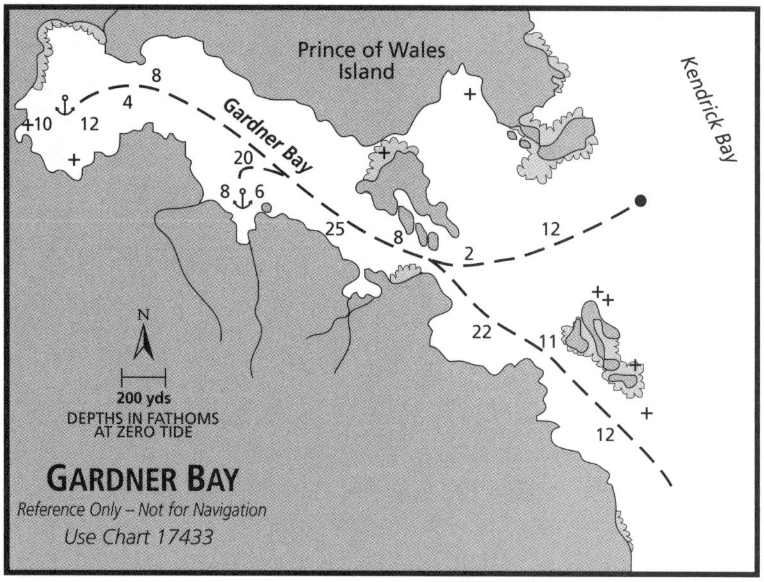


Gardner Bay is landlocked and offers very good shelter for small boats. Enter between two 1-fathom shoals marked by kelp or south of the outer islands. Stay mid-channel in either case. We prefer the small nook for one boat west of the islet and 0.4 mile west of the entrance narrows on the south side of the nook. Summer saltwater temperature is 65° F.

Anchor (nook south side) in 6 to 8 fathoms over sand and mud with good holding.

Anchor (head of the bay) in 10 fathoms over sand, mud and rocks with fair-to-good holding.

## Kendrick Bay (Prince of Wales Island)

Kendrick Bay is 10.5 miles north of Cape Chacon.

Chart 17433
North entrance: 54°54.00′ N, 131°58.05′ W
South entrance: 54°51.43′ N, 131°58.12′ W

Kendrick Bay offers cruising boats good protection in either the south or west arms. Entrance is south of the Kendrick Islands; avoid the reef located well within the entrance.

*You can find good anchorage in the small coves between Short and West Arms.*

## South Arm (Kendrick Bay)

South Arm is 2.5 miles west of the south entrance to Kendrick Bay.

Chart 17433
Entrance: 54°52.35′ N, 132°02.17′ W
Anchor: 54°50.44′ N, 132°03.43′ W

*South Arm is clear, and, near its head affords good anchorage for small craft.* (CP)

## Short Arm (Kendrick Bay)

Short Arm is 3 miles west of the south entrance to Kendrick Bay.

Chart 17433
Entrance: 54°52.39′ N, 132°02.47′ W

*Short Arm is clear of off-lying dangers except for an 8-fathom spot in the center of the arm, about 0.6 mile inside the entrance, and submerged rocks, about 0.3 mile from the head.* (CP)

Short Arm is too deep for convenient anchorage. The two small coves between Short and West arms offer anchorage to small craft, the first in 10 fathoms south of an uncharted 3-fathom shoal in the center of the cove. The second anchorage is tucked around the two-tree islet in the center of the cove in 10 fathoms over a soft-to-hard bottom. Watch for floating line across the head of the cove and uncharted 3- to 4-fathom shoals in the entrance.

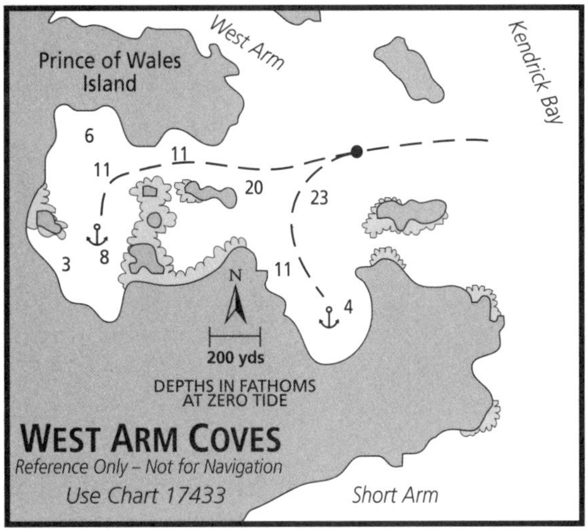




Anchor in 10 fathoms over mud and rocks with fair holding.

## West Arm (Kendrick Bay)

West Arm is 3.5 miles west of the south entrance to Kendrick Bay.

Chart 17433
Entrance: 54°53.23′ N, 132°03.28′ W
Anchor (first cove west of Short Arm): 54°53.78′ N, 132°03.15′ W
Anchor (third cove west of Short Arm): 54°52.89′ N, 132°04.03′ W
Anchor (head of West Arm): 54°53.97′ N, 132°06.31′ W

*West Arm is foul for a distance of 0.5 mile inside the entrance and should be entered preferably at low water. Enter S of the islets and proceed with caution. Good anchorage for small craft can be had near the head of the arm. . . .* (CP)

## Kendrick Islands

Kendrick Islands are at the entrance to Kendrick Bay.

Chart 17433
Entrance: 54°53.62′ N, 132°00.21′ W

*Small craft with local knowledge can enter Kendrick Bay from N by passing N of all the islands, between them and the main shore. Good anchorage and shelter for small craft can be found among the islands.* (CP)

The center island on the outside has potentially nifty anchorage for small craft at both its north and south shores, but the bottom is irregular, resulting in marginal holding.

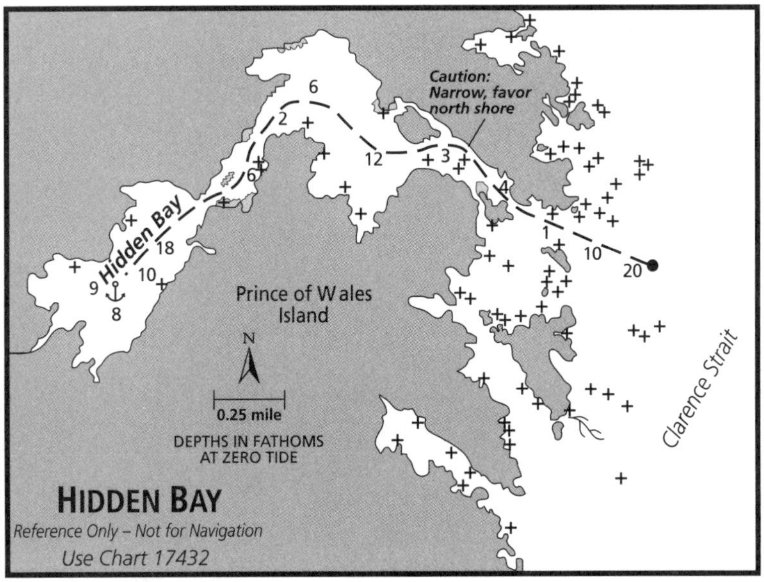




## Hidden Bay

(Prince of Wales Island)

Hidden Bay, on the west side of Clarence Strait, is 5 miles north of Kendrick Bay.

Chart 17432
Entrance: 54°56.08′ N, 131°57.73′ W
Anchor: 54°56.02′ N, 132°01.15′ W

*A depth of 1 fathom is in the entrance to the first narrows, and rocks are close to its S shore.*

*Depths of 5 to 21 fathoms were obtained in the first cove. . . . Depths in the second narrows range from 1 to 6 fathoms and ledges project from the SE shore. Depths in the inner cove range from 4 to 18 fathoms.*

*A stranger entering for the first time should select low-water slack when the reefs outside and the rocks in the entrance will be showing. The currents in the narrow part of the entrance are strong. Small craft may, with care, work their way to the entrance from the S back of the islands. The bay is suitable for small craft only.* (CP)

Hidden Bay, Ingraham Bay and North Arm of Ingraham Bay each have a special charm and wild qualities for the explorer, and it is difficult to pick a favorite. All are landlocked and protected by dangerous rocks and shoals with irregular bottoms until you are well inside. North Arm has the most straightforward entrance and takes less time and effort to enter, but it has poor holding. All three are influenced by currents, especially at spring tides. Keep in mind that these small-scale charts are not accurate.

Anchor (head of bay) in 7 fathoms over mud and shells with good holding and swinging room.

## **Ingraham Bay** (Prince of Wales Island)

Ingraham Bay is 2.2 miles north of Hidden Bay.

Chart 17432
Entrance: 54°58.40′ N, 131°58.62′ W
Anchor (south arm): 54°57.28′ N, 132°03.78′ W

*To enter the N arm, pass S of the two groups of rocky islets off its entrance. A narrow channel extends into the arm. . . .*

*The controlling depth in the narrows is 6 fathoms. Follow the trend of the channel leaving*

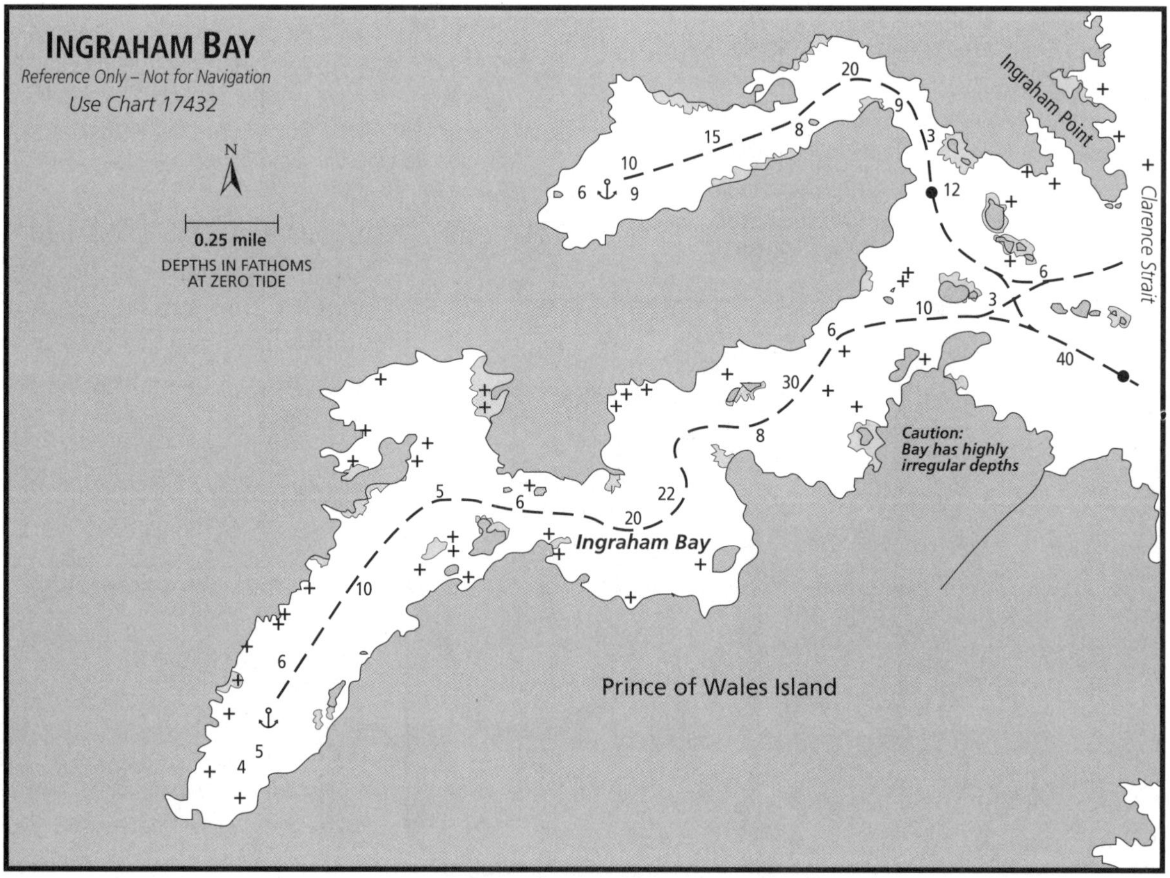

## About Salmon: Alaska's Famous Fish

Most people will agree that the best-tasting salmon comes from Alaskan waters. There are five species of wild Alaska salmon: the chum, pink, silver, sockeye, and King. Alaska salmon are active and thrive on the high levels of oxygen found in cold, rushing streams, estuaries and the upper levels of the ocean. The salmon spawn in fresh water and then migrate to the sea where they mature. Five to seven months after spawning the salmon fry emerge from the gravel where their parents had deposited and fertilized the eggs the previous fall. While some fry travel to sea immediately, others remain in the freshwater lakes and streams for a year or longer. As the fry migrate to sea they metamorphose to prepare for life in the saltwater. During this time of their life they are known as "smolt." In the estuaries where the fresh and salt water mix and the food is abundant, the smolt often double or triple their weight before heading west into the Gulf of Alaska or the Bering Sea.

Following is a brief description of the five species you may find in Alaska.

PINK—This is the smallest and most plentiful of the wild Alaska species. Most are between two and six pounds with the average weight around four pounds. Pinks can be found in all Alaskan streams from the Arctic to the Southeastern. Ocean-bright pinks are slim with silvery skin; semi-bright pinks have a distortion on their backs as the hump develops in the males. Dark bars are slightly apparent on the sides. Dark pink males have a pronounced hump and dark bars on the sides. Pink salmon has a delicate flavor.

CHUM—Most chums grow to be just over two feet long and weigh from 4–13 pounds. Eggs hatch in three to four months. The fry quickly move from their freshwater streambeds to the ocean. They spend three to five years in the salt water before returning home to spawn. Ocean-caught or bright Chums have silver sides and bellies with a dark, metallic, greenish-blue body. While they have no spots, fine, pale bars may be present on the sides. This is a delicately flavored, pink flesh fish with low-to-moderate fat content.

SILVER—Also known as Coho Salmon, Silvers are caught by troll and net fisheries. They are an attractive fish ranging from 25–35 inches and weighing two to 12 pounds. Silver fry stay in fresh water for a year before they turn into smolts. They spend 18-30 months growing in the ocean before they return to the streambeds of their birth. Ocean-caught or bright Silvers are dark, metallic blue on the back and upper sides. Small black spots may be evident on the back or on the top half of the tail. Pink skin or semi-bright Silvers have a slight pink or rose shading along the belly. Dark Silvers have a telltale red skin color with darker backs. Females may be darker than males; both have a pronounced hook of the nose. These salmon are most popular in restaurants because of their superior texture and pleasing orange-red flesh. Silvers make good smoked salmon.

SOCKEYE—Sockeye have a deep, red flesh and are one of the most abundant species of Alaskan salmon. They can grow to almost three feet and weigh up to 15 pounds. Eggs incubate from two to five months then the fry drift or swim to a nursery lake where they remain for one to two years. In their second or third spring they migrate to the sea. They return four years later to their original stream to spawn. Ocean-caught or bright Sockeye (also known as "blueback,") are deep, greenish-blue on their heads and back. Their sides are silver and they have a white belly. When mature they have a bright red back and green head with a pronounced line where the two colors meet at the gill plate. Sockeye flesh retains its deep red color when cooked. It has a high oil content, a moist texture and rich, complex flavor.

KING—The least abundant and most sought-after King (Chinook) Salmon ranges from 30–40 inches and from 5–40 pounds. Ocean-caught or bright Kings have silvery skin and scales and a deeper body than the other species. They have small, black spots on the back and upper sides and on the upper and lower halves of the silvery tail. The inside of a King's lower jaw is black. Most Kings return to their stream of origin after three to five years. King are prized for their red flesh, rich flavor, high oil content and firm texture. King salmon make up less than one percent of the total Alaskan salmon harvest.

*the small islet in the second narrows to the S and anchor in 10 fathoms, mud and sand bottom, in the bight at the head of the arm. This arm is suitable for small craft only.*

*The S arm is characterized by numerous rocks and reefs; the controlling depth in the entrance is 3 fathoms. With local knowledge 4 fathoms may be carried to the head where anchorage may be found for small craft in depths of 2 to 10 fathoms, with excellent holding ground in mud bottom. The chart should be the guide.* (CP)

Anchor in 4 fathoms over sticky mud with very good holding and swinging room.

## **North Arm of Ingraham Bay** (Prince of Wales Island)

North Arm of Ingraham Bay is one mile west of Ingraham Point.

Chart 17432
Entrance: 54°59.03′ N, 131°59.86′ W
Anchor: 54°58.99′ N, 132°01.80′ W

In fair weather, North Arm of Ingraham Bay can be entered or exited through the 6-fathom gap in the middle of the outer island chain. The arm is relatively easy to enter and is totally landlocked. It is very quiet within an old-growth cedar forest and has a tinge of a musty smell. There is room for several boats here and a grassy landing beach and kayak campsite. Contrary to the *Coast Pilot* we found the bottom hard.

Anchor in 7 to 10 fathoms with poor-to-fair holding.

## **Chichagof Bay** (Prince of Wales Island)

Chichagof Bay is 2.5 miles north of Ingraham Bay.

Chart 17432
Entrance: 55°01.58′ N, 131°59.05′ W
Anchor: 55°01.42′ N, 131°59.64′ W

*Chichagof Bay . . . has varying depths from 2-3/4 fathoms in the entrance to 4 fathoms near the shore. . . . A narrow inlet, with depths of 4 to 7 fathoms, extends 0.3 mile in a S direction from the SW corner of the bay. A depth of 1 fathom is in the middle of the entrance to the inlet.* (CP)

Chichagof Bay is a tiny, intimate bay with relatively good shelter protected by kelp beds and a small inlet. When entering, stay north until close to the east shore, then head southwest to the inlet. This anchorage has a safe feel to it and is close to Clarence Strait.

Anchor in 4 fathoms over sand with fair holding.

## **Moira Sound** (Prince of Wales Island)

Moira Sound, entered between Rip and Adams points, is 25 miles north of Cape Chacon.

Chart 17432
South entrance (Rip Point bearing 157°T at 0.4 Nm): 55°02.57′ N, 131°59.08′ W
North entrance (Moira Rock Light bearing 186°T at 0.6 Nm): 55°05.58′ N, 131°59.79′ W

*Moira Sound . . . divides into three separate arms.* (CP)

## **Rip Point Cove** (Moira Sound)

Rip Point Cove is 0.3 mile southwest of Rip Point.

Chart 17432
Entrance: 55°02.32′ N, 131°59.22′ W

*Rocks are on both sides of the* [cove] *entrance about 50 yards offshore. A rock is about 50 yards off the middle of the NW shore. Depths in the middle of the cove range from 9 to 21 fathoms; small-craft anchorage in 5 to 6 fathoms, fine sand bottom, may be had in the arm that extends S from the center of the cove.* (CP)

Rip Point Cove is not as bombproof as Menefee Anchorage 0.9 mile to the southwest.

## **Menefee Anchorage** (Moira Sound)

Menefee Anchorage is 1 mile west of Rip Point.

Chart 17432
Entrance: 55°02.07′ N, 132°00.81′ W
Anchor: 55°01.58′ N, 132°00.84′ W

*A secure anchorage can be found inside near the E shore, in the cove about 1 mile from the entrance directly S of the small cedar-covered island, in 6 to 10 fathoms, mud bottom. There is a rock awash near the middle of the cove.*

*At the head, North Arm divides into two fingers.* (CP)

Don Douglass

Rod Nash fishing in Moira Sound

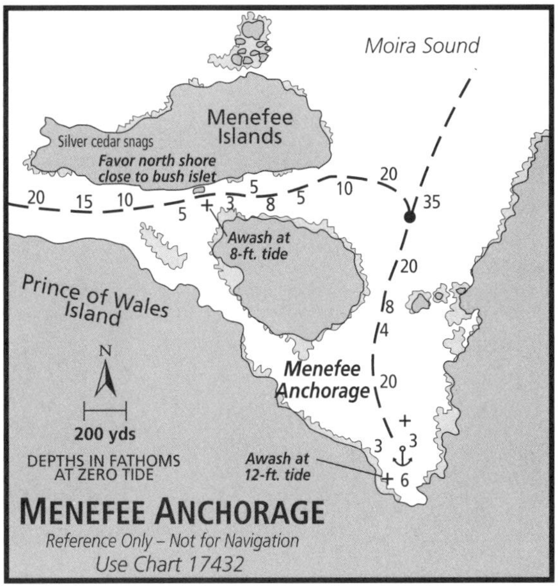

©2007 Don and Réanne Douglass

Menefee Anchorage is not at all as charted. We found the bottom to be highly irregular, with a 4-fathom shoal where the 25-fathom mark is! However, we found a neat 6-fathom hole near shore on the far steep-to south side that is bombproof if you use a stern-tie to trees.

Don Douglass

No net needed here; he lands this salmon by hand.

Don Douglass

Réanne and Rod are proud of this fish.

Anchor in a 6-fathom hole over a hard bottom and poor holding.

## **North Arm** (Moira Sound)

North Arm is 2.8 miles west of Moira Rock.

Chart 17432
Entrance: 55°04.65′ N, 132°04.89′ W

> *A secure anchorage can be found inside near the E shore, in the cove about 1 mile from the entrance directly S of the small cedar-covered island, in 6 to 10 fathoms, mud bottom.*
>
> *At the head, North Arm divides into two fingers.* (CP)

Fair Winds *of Ketchikan visiting Prince of Wales Island*

North Arm has some exceptional places to anchor and explore. Watch for unmarked shoals, but enjoy the great view of 3,500-foot Eudora Mountain to the west.

## **Moira Cove** (North Arm)

Moira Cove is 2.5 miles northwest of Moira Island.

Chart 17432
Entrance: 55°05.40′ N, 132°05.02′ W
Anchor: 55°05.30′ N, 132°04.77′ W

"Moira Cove" is what we call the small well-placed notch 1 mile inside the entrance to North Arm on the east shore. It is well sheltered and cozy. Avoid the long reef south of the islet.

Anchor in about 3 fathoms over sand, mud and some kelp with good holding.

## **Cannery Cove** (North Arm)

Cannery Cove is 3 miles northwest of the entrance to North Arm.

Chart 17432
Entrance: 55°06.92′ N, 132°08.49′ W
Anchor (1-fathom nook): 55°06.90′ N, 132°08.89′ W

> *Cannery Cove . . . affords good anchorage in 13 fathoms, and the small bight on the NW side of the cove has small-craft anchorage in 1-1/2 fathoms.* (CP)

## **Nowiskay Cove** (North Arm)

Nowiskay Cove is 3.5 miles northwest of the entrance to North Arm.

Chart 17432
Entrance: 55°07.35′ N, 132°08.70′ W
Anchor (head of bay): 55°07.62′ N, 132°08.99′ W

> *Nowiskay affords good small-craft anchorage in about 8 fathoms.* (CP)

Larger boats will find good protection from northwest winds at the head of Nowiskay Cove, but it is somewhat open to southeast chop. One or two small boats can find more complete shelter in the tiny west arm formed by a large submerged rock awash at high water.

Anchor (head of bay) in 8 to 10 fathoms over sand and gravel with fair holding.

Anchor (tiny cove) in 2 fathoms over sand and gravel with fair holding.

## **Clarno Cove** (North Arm)

Clarno Cove is 4 miles northwest of the entrance to North Arm.

Chart 17432
Entrance: 55°07.09′ N, 132°08.91′ W
Anchor: 55°07.53′ N, 132°10.63′ W

> *Craft entering this finger should favor the S shore, taking care to avoid the rock awash that is 240 yards (219 m) SE of the small islet off the N point at the entrance. By passing about 50 yards*

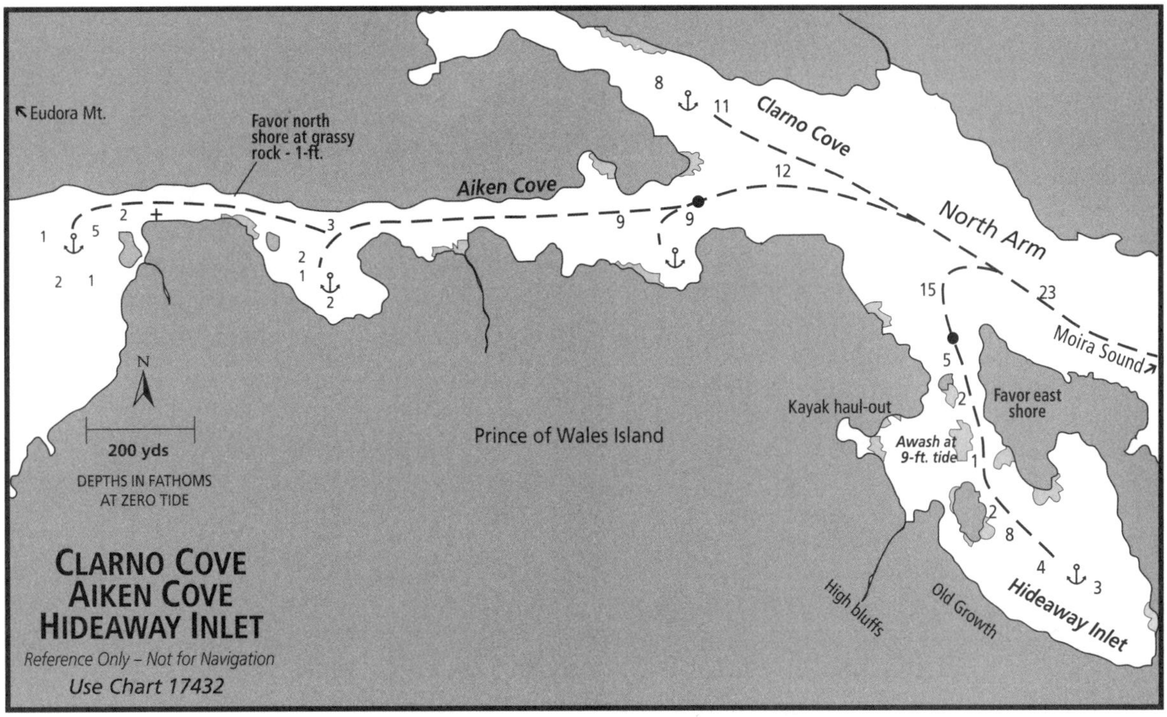




*off the S beach, a least depth of 10-1/4 fathoms can be carried into Clarno Cove, where good all-weather anchorage is available in about 12 fathoms, soft mud bottom.* (CP)

Anchor in 8 to 10 fathoms over mud with good holding.

## **Hideaway Inlet** (Clarno Cove)

Hideaway Inlet is on the south shore of Clarno Cove.

Chart 17432
Entrance: 55°07.26′ N, 132°10.07′ W
Anchor: 55°06.98′ N, 132°09.83′ W

Réanne Hemingway-Douglass

*A careful entry through Hideaway Inlet Narrows brings you to full shelter.*

Hideaway Inlet, the landlocked basin on the south side of Clarno Cove, is one of our favorites. Completely sheltered from all weather, it

Don Douglass

*Réanne with Hideaway Inlet in the background*

is quiet and peaceful and the entrance is narrow and shallow. Enter carefully and reap your rewards.

Anchor in four fathoms; sand and mud with good holding.

## **Aiken Cove** (North Arm)

Aiken Cove is 4.5 miles northwest of the entrance to North Arm.

Chart 17432
Entrance: 55°07.41′ N, 132°10.60′ W
Anchor (larger boats, 0.08 mile southwest of entrance): 55°07.36′ N, 132°10.70′ W
Anchor (leaping salmon, 0.45 mile west of entrance): 55°07.34′ N, 132°11.40′ W
Anchor (small boats, 0.75 mile west of entrance): 55°07.38′ N, 132°11.91′ W

*From Clarno Cove a narrow channel continues W into Aiken Cove, which is shoal and mostly bare except for a small area near the mouth where an anchorage can be found in about 9 fathoms. Favor the N shore in entering from Clarno Cove.* (CP)

Aiken Cove is a narrow inlet with quiet anchorage for small craft. We have used all three anchor sites and you may choose the one that suits you best. Enjoy the views of the high peaks of Eudora Mountain.

Anchor in 8 fathoms in outer anchorage; 2 fathoms in inner anchor sites in sand with fair holding.

---

## Bull Rails Instead of Cleats for Securing Dock Lines

Linda Lewis and David Parker—M/V *Royal Sounder*

We all know how to use cleats to secure our lines to the dock. But cleats aren't what you find in Southeast Alaska. What you'll find are Bull Rails—long pieces of timber on the dock. The Bull Rails require you to get off the boat, lead your line under the rail, then over the rail to tie off or run back to the boat. OK most of the time. But it can be a real problem when the currents are running, the wind is blowing, or the helm is making mistakes—or all of the above.

There is help for those times. We call it "The Hook." It is a device (a line with a hook) that can be thrown from the boat onto the dock, then drug back until it hooks the Bull Rail. Voila! You're attached to the dock long enough for you to get off and run secure dock lines. It's a life-saver in tough docking situations. We know of one line-handler who is disabled and uses the hook for every docking. It would also be useful if someone on your boat is injured or less nimble than usual. We highly recommend having it onboard.

For more information, contact: Interlock, LLC, 865 Lakispell Dr., La Conner, WA 98257 (tel.: 360.466.7408; Email: EZDOCKER@aol.com).

*Bull rail with a line that has been there for awhile*

*Unique way to secure lines to bull rails*

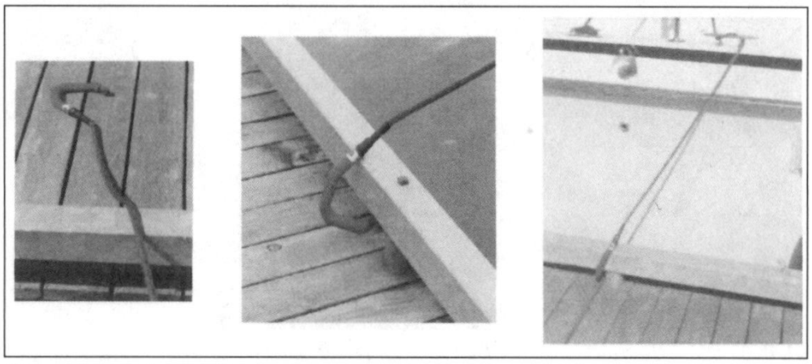

*"The Hook" is a big help getting a line to the dock.*

Réanne Hemingway-Douglass

*Eudora Mountain is your backdrop in Aiken Cove.*

Réanne Hemingway-Douglass

*Watch for dead heads that have become stuck in the bottom—like this one at Aiken Cove, complete with its own symbiotic tree.*

## **Niblack Anchorage** (Moira Sound)

Niblack Anchorage is 2.5 miles west of Moira Island.

Chart 17432
Entrance (south tip of Clare Island bearing 350°T at 0.08 Nm): 55°03.45′ N, 132°06.25′ W
Anchor: 55°03.93′ N, 132°08.60′ W

> *Niblack Anchorage . . . affords good protection in depths of 6 to 20 fathoms, mud bottom. . . . Safety Rock, grass covered and about 15 feet high, is in midentrance. A ledge that uncovers 5 feet is 400 yards S of Clare Island and 250 yards off the S shore. A rock, covered 9 feet, is 0.5 mile from the head of the anchorage and 0.1 mile from the S shore. Vessels entering Niblack Anchorage usually pass N of Moira Rock, Safety Rock, and the ledge S of Clare Island near the S shore of the anchorage.* (CP)

Good anchorage can be found northwest of Red Rock.

Anchor in 8 fathoms; sand and gravel with fair holding.

## **Clare Island Cove** (Niblack Anchorage)

Clare Island Cove is on the northeast shore of Niblack Anchorage.

Chart 17432
Entrance: 55°03.92′ N, 132°07.31′ W
Anchor (large boats): 55°04.00′ N, 132°06.83′ W
Anchor (small boats): 55°04.10′ N, 132°06.48′ W

Very good shelter can be found in what we call "Clare Island Cove." The north and west shores of Clare Island are very well protected. The inner basin has a mid-channel rock and reef and is suitable for small craft under appropriate conditions only.

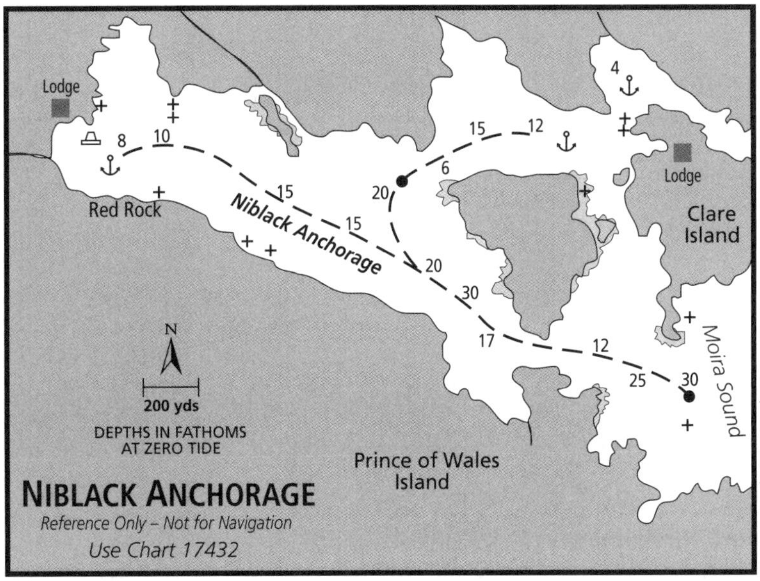

Réanne Hemingway-Douglass

*Private float at Niblack Anchorage*

Réanne Hemingway-Douglass

*Use Red Rock as a landmark at Niblack Anchorage.*

Large boats anchor in 12 fathoms over mud bottom. Smaller boats anchor (inner basin) in 4 fathoms over sand.

## **Kegan Cove** (Moira Sound)

Kegan Cove is 5.5 miles southwest of Moira Island.

Chart 17432
Entrance: 55°00.95′ N, 132°09.40′ W
Anchor: 55°01.25′ N, 132°09.97′ W

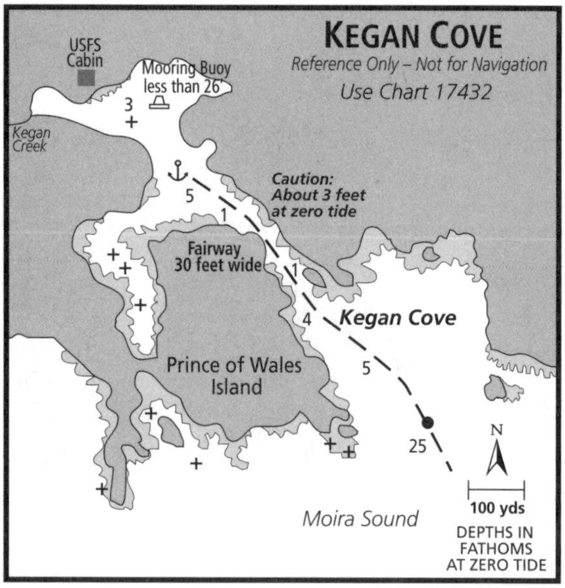


©2007 Don and Réanne Douglass

*The outer cove has fair anchorage in 8 to 12 fathoms, mud bottom. The inner cove . . . can be entered by boats drawing 5 feet, on the upper half of the tide. The W shoreline should be favored when entering. Excellent shelter and anchorage in 6-3/4 fathoms, mud bottom, can be had inside.* (CP)

Kegan Cove is a very small, intimate place and another of our favorites. It is suitable for smaller boats only when tide and currents allow transiting the tiny narrows. If in doubt, check it out by dinghy first. There is a USFS cabin on the creek and a small USFS buoy at the head of the cove.

Réanne Hemingway-Douglass

*Keep a careful bow watch as you enter Kegan Cove Narrows.*

Anchor in 5 to 7 fathoms over brown mud, sand and shells with very good holding.

## **Johnson Cove** (Moira Sound)

Johnson Cove is 4 miles southwest of Moira Island.

Chart 17432
Entrance: 55°00.74′ N, 132°05.92′ W
Anchor: 54°58.37′ N, 132°05.66′ W

> *Johnson Cove is about 2 miles long and indents the S shore of the sound. . . .* (CP)

Anchor in 6 fathoms over brown mud and small rocks with fair holding.

## **South Arm** (Moira Sound)

South Arm is 6 miles southwest of Moira Island.

Chart 17432
Entrance: 54°59.61′ N, 132°09.11′ W
Anchor: 54°56.00′ N, 132°12.25′ W

> *South Arm extends about 5 miles to the S and has numerous reefs that uncover at low water. Favor the E shore in entering. The S end of the arm affords good all-weather anchorage in about 6 fathoms.* (CP)

Anchor in 7 fathoms over sand and gravel with fair holding.

## **West Arm** (Moira Sound)

West Arm is 7 miles southwest of Moira Island.

Chart 17432
Entrance: 55°00.27′ N, 132°10.00′ W

> *West Arm has a length of 2.2 miles and then divides into two short arms, the N, known as Dickman Bay, the S as Frederick Cove.* (CP)

Pleasant temporary anchorage can be found among the islets on the south side of West Arm at the entrance to South Arm.

## **Dickman Bay** (West Arm)

Dickman Bay is 8 miles southwest of Moira Island.

Chart 17432
Entrance: 55°00.03′ N, 132°13.11′ W

There is no reference to Dickman Bay in the *Coast Pilot*. Both arms of Dickman Bay have small basins at their heads with very narrow and shallow entrances that appear to offer small craft an outstanding opportunity to explore and find solitude in a sheltered wild environment.

Réanne Hemingway-Douglass

*Old wooden ferry boat hard aground in Johnson Cove*

## **Frederick Cove** (West Arm)

Frederick Cove is 8.5 miles southwest of Moira Island.

Chart 17432
Entrance: 54°59.62′ N, 132°13.64′ W
Anchor: 54°58.85′ N, 132°18.02′ W

There is no reference to Frederick Cove in the *Coast Pilot*. Unfortunately, we have no local knowledge either, but the cove appears from a distance to have spectacular scenery with good anchorage at its head, favoring the north shore at the narrows, and pleasant temporary anchorage for small craft in two tiny coves northwest of the entrance point. Anchorage (head of bay) is reported in 6 to 8 fathoms over a soft bottom.

## **Port Johnson** (Prince of Wales Island)

Port Johnson lies between Adams Point and Wedge Islands.

Chart 17432
Entrance (Inner Point bearing 156°T at 0.2 Nm): 55°07.55′ N, 132°01.22′ W
Anchor: 55°07.22′ N, 132°06.04′ W

> *Port Johnson, a narrow deep inlet, . . . extends about 3.5 miles in a W direction. . . . There is good anchorage in 15 fathoms about 2.4 miles*

*above the entrance. . . . Anchorage in about 11 to 14 fathoms, but with limited swinging room, is at the head, and from this shore a trail through a divide leads to North Arm of Moira Sound.* (CP)

## **Dolomi Bay** (Port Johnson)

Dolomi Bay, on the north side of Port Johnson, is 1.3 miles west of Inner Point.

Chart 17432
Entrance: 55°07.40′ N, 132°03.15′ W

*The cove on the W side and near the head of the bay has a rock, covered 5 feet, near its center. Dolomi Bay is very restricted; the chart is the best guide.* (CP)

## **French Harbor** (Dutch Harbor)

French Harbor is 4 miles north of Moira Rock.

Chart 17432
Entrance (French Harbor): 55°08.45′ N, 132°00.66′ W
Entrance (Dutch Harbor): 55°09.31′ N, 131°59.70′ W

*French Harbor and Dutch Harbor are locally known small-boat anchorages behind Wedge Islands, 2 miles NE of the entrance to Port Johnson. They do not furnish good anchorages for strangers, and the approaches are rocky.* (CP)

These harbors are both really rock piles with many isolated rocks, reefs, kelp beds and channels that offer temporary anchorage in prevailing westerlies, but no serious protection or swinging room in southeast gales. Dutch Harbor is immediately north of French Harbor.

## **Cholmondeley Sound** (Prince of Wales Island)

Cholmondeley Sound is entered between Chasina Point and Skin Island.

Chart 17436
Entrance: 55°16.88′ N, 132°03.88′ W

*Its extreme length from the entrance . . . to the head of West Arm is about 16 miles; it has several arms, all of which are deep and bold . . . with steep-to rock shorelines. Cholmondeley Sound's tributaries have not been closely surveyed but are generally free from dangers. The currents in the sound are too weak or variable to be predicted* (CP)

Réanne Hemingway-Douglass

*Exploring Cholmondeley Sound*

Cholmondeley (pronounced "Chumly") Sound is another great sound on Prince of Wales Island. Like Moira Sound, it is a marvelous and remote place to explore and enjoy. Beware of the lack of truly accurate large-scale charts.

## **Chasina Anchorage** (Cholmondeley Sound)

Chasina Anchorage is 2 miles south of Skin Island Light.

Chart 17436
Entrance: 55°16.20′ N, 132°03.25′ W

*Chasina Anchorage . . . affords a lee only from E to S winds. Anchorage may be obtained on a rocky patch in about 9 fathoms with the NW corner of Chasina Island bearing 042° and Skin Island Light bearing about 338°; swinging room is about 250 yards.* (CP)

## **Lancaster Cove** (Cholmondeley Sound)

Lancaster Cove is 5 miles south of Skin Island Light.

Chart 17436
North entrance: 55°13.28′ N, 132°05.64′ W
South entrance: 55°12.72′ N, 132°05.85′ W

> *Lancaster Cove . . . affords good anchorage in 13 to 14 fathoms. . . . In 1959, a survey vessel used an anchorage about 150 yards S of the wooded island, in 12 to 20 fathoms, mud bottom, good holding ground.* (CP)

## **Kitkun Bay** (Cholmondeley Sound)

Kitkun Bay is 7 miles south of Skin Island Light.

Chart 17436 (inset)
Outer entrance: 55°12.76′ N, 132°08.92′ W
Inner entrance: 55°11.59′ N, 132°08.77′ W
Anchor (Inner Sanctum): 55°09.31′ N, 132°11.54′ W

> *Kitkun Bay has its entrance W of Babe islands, about 6 miles SW of Chasina Point and extends in a general SW direction from the S side of Cholmondeley Sound. The area was surveyed in 1961. Entrance to the N part of the bay should be made through the W of two channels. The least depth in midchannel is 3-1/2 fathoms. Entrance to the S part of the bay can be made through a narrow channel about halfway down the E shore of the N part of the bay. This channel is foul at the entrance; the foul area is marked by kelp. Currents in the channel and near the entrance are very strong, with tide rips near the entrance. The least depth in the narrowest part of the channel is 1-1/2 fathoms.* (CP)

Unfortunately, we have not been in Kitkun Bay yet, but it is on our list. The bay raises the definition of "landlocked" and "isolated" to a new and higher standard. We call the south basin the "Inner Sanctum."

## **Dora Bay** (Cholmondeley Sound)

Dora Bay is 7 miles southwest of Skin Island Light.

Chart 17436
Entrance: 55°13.85′ N, 132°13.21′ W

> *Dora Bay . . . may be used as an anchorage, but is not recommended.* (CP)

We have seen several inviting small coves along the shore of Dora Bay, but we have no local knowledge at this point.

## **Sunny Cove** (Cholmondeley Sound)

Sunny Cove is 7 miles southwest of Skin Island Light.

Chart 17436
Entrance: 55°14.93′ N, 132°14.79′ W
Anchor: 55°15.44′ N, 132°16.22′ W

> *Sunny Cove . . . with local knowledge affords anchorage for small craft. Vessels entering Sunny Cove should steer midchannel courses.* (CP)

It is reported that it never rains in Sunny Cove and that anchorage can be found in about 10 fathoms over sand and gravel with fair holding.

## **South Arm** (Cholmondeley Sound)

South Arm is 8 miles southwest of Skin Island Light.

Chart 17436 (inset)
Entrance: 55°14.65′ N, 132°16.92′ W
Anchor: 55°08.21′ N, 132°20.27′ W

> *South Arm is free of off-lying dangers as far as is known. Vessels entering should steer midchannel courses to the head of the arm to anchorage in 6 to 10 fathoms, soft bottom. Strong winds from Klakas Inlet draw through the low pass at the head of South Arm.* (CP)

## **West Arm** (Cholmondeley Sound)

West Arm is 8 miles southwest of Skin Island Light.

Chart 17436
Entrance: 55°15.01′ N, 132°17.92′ W
Anchor (1.5 miles west of confluence): 55°14.95′ N, 132°20.30′ W
Anchor (behind islet): 55°15.04′ N, 132°24.12′ W
Anchor (head of arm): 55°15.42′ N, 132°27.70′ W

> *Its S shore has two indentations, the first about 1.5 miles above the confluence of the two arms is small but furnishes shelter for small craft with anchor depths of 4 to 8 fathoms. The second indentation in the S shore is SSW of the most E of the chain of small wooded islets. Anchorage with ample swinging room may be had here behind the islet in 7 to 15 fathoms, soft bottom. . . . Anchorage may also be had in 7 to 15 fathoms, soft bottom, at the head of West Arm. This anchorage is exposed to strong winds drawing through the low pass from Hetta Inlet.* (CP)

Anchor (1.5 miles west of confluence) in 4 to 8 fathoms.

Anchor (behind islet) in about 10 fathoms over a soft bottom.

Anchor (head of arm) in about 10 fathoms off steep-to drying mud flat over a soft bottom.

## **Clover Bay** (Prince of Wales Island)

Clover Bay, between Clover Point and Anderson Point, is 1.5 miles west of Skin Island.

Chart 17436
Entrance: 55°18.12′ N, 132°07.52′ W

*Safe entry can be made on a course 245°, passing between the mid-channel rock and the rock off Anderson Point.*

*A small cove with depths of 12 to 21 fathoms, except for lesser depths along the edges, is to the N of King Island. . . . A bar with a midchannel depth of 1-3/4 fathoms stretches across the entrance to the cove from King Island to the rock off the point on the N shore. A ledge extends 50 yards NW of King Island within the cove.* (CP)

The cove north and west of King Island appears to offer shelter to small craft, but it is inadequately surveyed at this time.

David Parker

*An orca calf is escorted, probably by her mom and two aunts, on the south side of Kasaan Island.*

David Parker

*Playful orcas on the south side of Kasaan Island*

## **Kasaan Bay** (Prince of Wales Island)

Kasaan Bay, 47 miles north of Cape Chacon, is entered between Island Point and Grindall Island.

**Charts 17426, 17436**
**Entrance (High Island Light bearing 252°T at 1.1 Nm): 55°24.38′ N, 132°08.05′ W**

> *Kasaan Bay . . . extends about 17.5 miles NW to Karta Bay at its head. About halfway up the bay in the middle, are several islands. The shores of the bay and island are steep-to and heavily wooded. A high, steep mountain range extends along the N shore of the bay almost to the head. Fog often prevails in the S part of Clarence Strait, while it is clear in Kasaan Bay. During SE stormy weather, clouds and mist travel low along the N shore, while the S shore is generally free from low-flying scud. During SE storms the sea at the entrance to the bay is rough and treacherous for small craft. Temporary anchorage while waiting for the fog to lift may be had on an extensive bank, 0.6 to 1.2 miles S from Grindall Point in depths of 8 to 16 fathoms. All known dangers are shown on the chart. Midchannel depths are generally good.* (CP)

Kasaan Bay is a good example of the wonderful cruising opportunities along both coasts of Prince of Wales Island. If you remain in the Ketchikan area for long, be sure to visit the many scenic inlets found along this east coast. The M/V *Royal Sounder* reports seeing a spectacular half-hour display put on by a pod of Orcas making repeated passes along the southwest side of Kasaan Island in Kasaan Bay.

There is an extensive network of dirt roads on Prince of Wales Island. The Hollis area is the eastern ferry terminal for the roads on the island. The ferry terminal that used to be located near the Hollis dock has now been replaced by the ferry terminal located at 55°29.41' N, 132°37.19' W' in Clark Bay. Arrangements can be made for a rental car if you want to visit Craig, Hydaburg and Klawock. For information about the Alaskan Marine Highway or for reservations, call 800.526.6731; Website: www.AKFerry.org. There is a State float on the north of Kasaan Bay.

Kina Cove, described later in this chapter, is an example of the secure anchorages to be found in the area of Kasaan Bay.

## **Trollers Cove** (Kasaan Bay)

Trollers Cove, behind a chain of islands, is 1.4 miles west of Island Point.

**Chart 17426**
**Entrance: 55°22.52′ N, 132°12.84′ W**
**Anchor: 55°21.89′ N, 132°11.94′ W**

> *The cove has depths of 4 to 6 fathoms. It is considered a good small-boat anchorage and is used by those fishing on Twenty Fathom Bank. . . .*
>
> *Round the W island at a distance of about 125 yards and then follow a midchannel course to the S of the islands. Pass about 50 yards S of the S shore of the E island to avoid a rock awash that is about 100 yards S of the island. When abeam the SE end of the island, anchor in about 4 fathoms.* (CP)

Trollers Cove is inadequately charted but it does appear to offer good shelter in all weather.

## **Spiral Cove** (Kasaan Bay)

Spiral Cove is immediately west of Trollers Cove.

**Chart 17426**
**Entrance: 55°22.52′ N, 132°12.84′ W**

Spiral Cove appears to offer complete shelter inside the tiny basin. Like Trollers Bay it needs a large-scale chart.

## **Kluanil Island Cove** (Kasaan Bay)

Kluanil Island is 0.7 mile north of Spiral Cove.

**Chart 17426**
**Entrance: 55°23.07′ N, 132°13.65′ W**

Kluanil Island Cove appears to provide very good shelter in its small basin, but its entrance is poorly charted.

## **Skowl Arm** (Kasaan Bay)

Skowl Arm is the southern arm of Kasaan Bay.

**Charts 17426, 17436**
**Entrance: 55°26.13′ N, 132°16.47′ W**
**Position (Old Kasaan site): 55°25.93′ N, 132°22.30′ W**

> *On the N side, about 3.5 miles up the arm, is the abandoned Haida village of Old Kasaan. No evidence of the village remains; other than a few weathered totem poles and a few graves.*

*Scene of an abandoned Haida village at Skowl Arm*

> *The village site is part of Old Kasaan Village Historical Area, administered by the U.S. Forest Service. In front of the village site is a ledge, covered at high water, that extends about 100 yards offshore.* (CP)

This is a wonderful historical site worth a visit. Only the longhouse poles and some gravesites of the traditional Kasaan native site remain. The Haida totems were moved to a new park at Kassan, 6.5 miles northwest. Temporary anchorage can be found off the beach.

Anchor in 6 to 8 fathoms in sand and gravel with fair holding.

## **Saltery Cove** (Skowl Arm)

Saltery Cove is 2 miles southwest of Skowl Point.

Charts 17426, 17436
Entrance: 55°25.06′ N, 132°19.62′ W
Anchor: 55°24.21′ N, 132°19.68′ W

> *Saltery Cove is a small bay, about 1 mile long. . . . The channel E of the group of islands in the entrance is the one mostly used. A well-protected anchorage for small craft in about 4 to 9 fathom, mud bottom, is at the head of the cove.* (CP)

Saltery Cove has good southeast protection. There is a sport-fishing lodge in the cove. Notice the "retired mariner" sitting in a chair, 4 feet above high water on the mid-channel rock. Also note the sign on the float, "Ketchikan City Limits, Please Drive Carefully." Saltery Cove has an irregular bottom, so be sure that if you anchor here you are over sand or mud, not rocks.

Anchor in about 10 fathoms; sand, gravel, some rocks and kelp. Fair-to-good holding.

## **McKenzie Inlet** (Skowl Arm)

McKenzie Inlet is 3.7 miles west of Skowl Point.

Charts 17426, 17436
Entrance: 55°23.60′ N, 132°22.54′ W
Anchor: 55°19.92′ N, 132°21.74′ W

> *McKenzie Inlet . . . extends about 5 miles in a S direction. McKenzie Rock, bare, is about 0.5 mile W of Khayyam Point. . . ; there is no safe channel between. A dangerous submerged rock is immediately N of McKenzie Rock. . . . A rock, that uncovers 3 feet, and a rock awash immediately to the NW, are about 400 yards from the E shore, 0.5 mile S of McKenzie Rock.*
>
> *About 1 mile inside the entrance, the channel leads between East Sentinel Island and West Sentinel Island. . . . A careful midchannel course between the islands leads through safely; S of the islands the inlet is clear. There is good anchorage near the head of the inlet on the W side of Peacock Island, in depths of 7 to 10 fathoms, soft bottom.* (CP)

Anchor in 8 fathoms over sand and gravel with fair holding.

## **Paul Bight** (McKenzie Inlet)

Paul Bight is 1 mile west of McKenzie Rock.

Charts 17426, 17436
Entrance: 55°24.48′ N, 132°23.71′ W
Anchor: 55°24.36′ N, 132°24.15′ W

> *Paul Bight . . . affords anchorage for small craft in 3 to 5 fathoms. . . . In entering, favor the S point.* (CP)

## **Smith Cove** (Skowl Arm)

Smith Cove is 2 miles west of Kasaan Point.

Charts 17426, 17436
Entrance: 55°26.01′ N, 132°19.80′ W

> *Smith Cove . . . affords good anchorage in 10 to 20 fathoms, soft bottom. It should be entered with caution, taking care to avoid the rocks and shoals off the two small wooded islets at the entrance and inside the bay. In September 1998, a dangerous rock was reported in the E part of Smith Cove on the W side of the narrow channel about midway between the two islets in about 55°26.4′N., 132°19.8′W. A seaplane float is on the NW side of Smith Cove.* (CP)

Isolated shoals and rocks in Smith Cove require careful piloting and suggest an irregular rocky bottom.

## **Little Goose Bay** (Skowl Arm)

Little Goose Bay is 1.5 miles northeast of Goose Bay.

Charts 17426, 17436
Entrance: 55°25.00′ N, 132°27.73′ W

The head of Little Goose Bay has anchorage for one vessel with limited swinging room.

## **Polk Inlet** (Skowl Arm)

Polk Inlet, the west arm of Skowl Arm, extends west and south for 9.3 miles.

Chart 17426
Entrance: 55°25.12′ N, 132°28.08′ W

> *The entrance to the inlet is foul, and extreme caution must be exercised when entering.* (CP)

The entrance to Polk Inlet is encumbered with unmarked shoals and rocks which make for dangerous navigation when the current is flowing. Reconnoiter first before entering. Passage at slack water is advised. There are a series of small basins at the head of Polk Inlet, each with narrow, intricate entrances that appear to lead to good, sheltered anchorages at the bitter end.

## **Goose Bay** (Polk Inlet)

Goose Bay is 1.5 miles south of the entrance to Polk Inlet.

Chart 17426
Entrance: 55°23.74′ N, 132°29.22′ W

The head of Goose Bay appears to provide good shelter, but Polk Inlet entrance is notorious for difficulties.

## **Linney Bay** (Kasaan Bay)

Linney Bay is 0.6 mile west of Daisy Island.

Chart 17426
Entrance: 55°28.60′ N, 132°20.72′ W

> *A small cove, known locally as Linney Bay . . . is used regularly for storage of log rafts. Excellent shelter is afforded in all weather, but center depths and bottom do not favor good anchorage.* (CP)

## **Happy Harbor** (Kasaan Island)

Happy Harbor is on the northeast side of Kasaan Island.

Chart 17426
Entrance: 55°29.94′ N, 132°19.62′ W
Anchor: 55°29.65′ N, 132°20.08′ W

> *Anchorage for small boats is to be found in the landlocked inlet . . . in 7 to 10 fathoms* [sic], *soft bottom. This is called Happy Harbor locally. A shoal, covered 1-1/4 fathoms and marked by kelp, extends 300 yards N of a rock awash off the NE entrance point. After entering the narrow channel, favor the E side until through the entrance. The entrance is 2 feet deep, and caution is necessary in entering.* (CP)

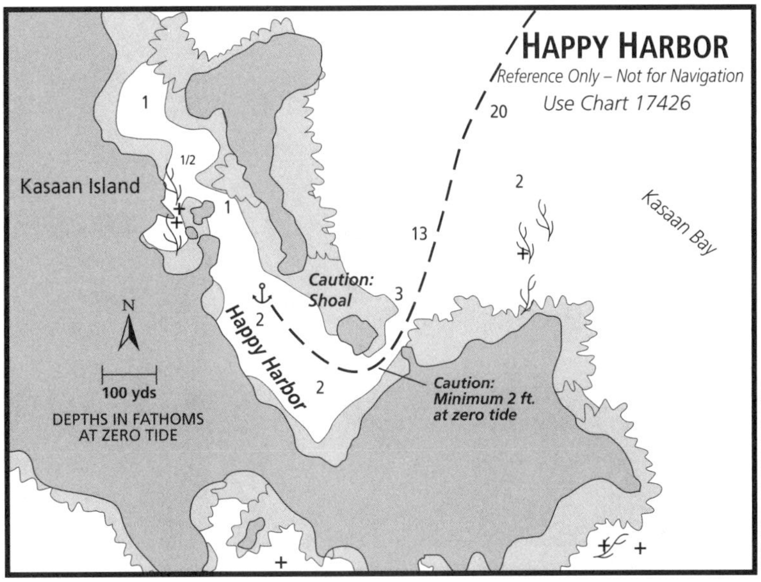

Happy Harbor is scantily charted and requires careful navigation. We find Happy Harbor worth the careful attention needed to enter it (two feet at zero tide), and we welcome its secure shelter.

Anchor in 2 fathoms over sand and mud with fair holding.

### **Kasaan** (Kasaan Bay)

Kasaan, a village on the north shore of Kasaan Bay, is 10 miles northwest of Grindall Island.

Chart 17426
Entrance: 55°32.14′ N, 132°23.91′ W

> *A state-maintained small-craft and seaplane float, with 224 feet of berthing space, is about 25 yards N of the cannery wharf.* (CP)

The totems and longhouse, a quarter mile from the Kasaan settlement, are a magical place. The trail to the Haida site leads northwest from the top of the floats past a half-dozen houses and trailers (pop. about 30). At the end of the cluster of homes, a well-groomed trail passes through a forest of second-growth trees. Along the way, new branches of spruce, hemlock and cedar spring from stumps of once hand-logged trees. The totems are attractively placed in various sites along a diverging path. A now-abandoned longhouse sits in a clearing at the end of the trail that looks out over Kasaan Bay. What charms a visitor is the lack of commercialization of the site, and we hope it remains that way.

*The float at Kasaan is at the right in this picture.*

The transient moorage is located on the south side of the docks; it is awash in heavy weather, not well maintained and is poorly connected to the next float, requiring an agile crossing—-wear good rain boots!

The M/V *Royal Sounder* confirms our praise and our cautions for this spot with this note: "After a wonderful walk to the totems and longhouse—one of our favorite walks in Southeast Alaska—we found out the hard way about the dock awash in heavy weather. The

*Use the transient float at Kasaan Bay cautiously; avoid it in heavy weather.*

Linda Lewis

*Kasaan Bay fish-shaped totem*

winds had picked up during our walk and we had to leave in a rush. Slipping the lines without slipping ourselves right off the docks was not easy; they were really bucking. We managed it without falling in and made a run for Kina Cove, where we were much happier."

Linda Lewis

*The Haida longhouse and totem at Kasaan Bay*

Réanne Hemingway-Douglass

*A magical walk through the quiet forest at Kasaan brings you to totems like this.*

## **Poor Man Bay** (Kasaan Bay)

Poor Man Bay is 1.3 miles west of Kasaan Village.

Chart 17426
Position: 55°32.75′ N, 132°26.02′ W

Poor Man Bay is too shoal for shelter.

## **Mills Bay, Lindeman Cove and Browns Bay** (Kasaan Bay)

Mills Bay is 4 miles northwest of Kasaan Village; Lindeman Cove is 5.5 miles northwest of Kasaan Village; Browns Bay is 6 miles northwest of Kasaan Village.

Chart 17426
Entrance (Mills Bay): 55°33.66′ N, 132°28.72′ W
Position (Lindeman Cove): 55°36.00′ N, 132°30.94′ W
Position (Browns Bay): 55°35.76′ N, 132°32.96′ W

Linda Lewis

*Rig a fish-cleaning device for your boat.*

*The head of Kasaan Bay is separated from the main part of the bay by a chain of wooded islands and affords secure anchorage in 5 to 8 fathoms. In heavy SE weather the NE part of this inner bay affords the only secure anchorage in 7 to 12 fathoms, soft bottom. The best entrance is between the fourth and fifth islands counting from E. This passage is 225 yards wide, but the channel is only 50 yards wide between the 3-fathom curves, with depth of 4 fathoms in midchannel.* (CP)

## **Karta Bay** (Kasaan Bay)

Karta Bay, at the head of Kasaan Bay, is 6 miles northwest of Kasaan Village.

Chart 17426
Entrance: 55°34.35′ N, 132°33.68′ W
Anchor: 55°34.03′ N, 132°34.53′ W

*Karta Bay, . . . about 2 miles NW of Sandy Point, affords good anchorage in 10 to 12 fathoms, with a clearance of about 430 yards. Mound Point, on the N side of the entrance to Karta Bay, is prominent. A 4-fathom shoal is about 1.1 miles ESE from the point. A number of shoals with less water over them are farther inshore in the direction of Sandy Point.* (CP)

Anchor in about 8 fathoms over a hard bottom with poor-to-fair holding.

## **Twelvemile Arm** (Kasaan Bay)

Twelvemile Arm extends southwest about 13 miles from near the head of Kasaan Bay.

Chart 17426
Entrance: 55°31.83′ N, 132°31.34′ W

*Midchannel courses lead in good water through Twelvemile Arm. Numerous rocky reefs at the points do not extend more than 60 yards offshore. In the middle of the arm, about 400 yards NNE from the first wooded islet at the head of the arm, is a small grass-covered islet that is just awash at extreme high tide. A rocky shoal that bares is 400 yards NNE from this islet and numerous patches of rocks that uncover 4 feet are between the islet and the W shore. Log booms and rafting grounds are reported to cover much of the head of Twelvemile Arm.* (CP)

## **Little Coal Bay** (Kasaan Bay)

Little Coal Bay is 1 mile east of Coal Bay.

Chart 17426
Entrance: 55°30.40′ N, 132°27.97′ W

Little Coal Bay is only useful for small boats in southerly weather. Coal Bay has more shelter and swinging room.

## **Coal Bay** (Kasaan Bay)

Coal Bay is 3.8 miles southwest of Kasaan.

Chart 17426
Entrance: 55°30.51′ N, 132°28.99′ W
Anchor: 55°29.87′ N, 132°29.51′ W

*Coal Bay . . . affords good anchorage in 15 fathoms except in N weather. . . .* (CP)

Anchor (head of bay) in about 6 fathoms.

## Kina Cove (Kasaan Bay)

Kina Cove is 0.5 mile west of Coal Bay.

Chart 17426
Entrance: 55°30.86′ N, 132°30.54′ W
Anchor: 55°29.60′ N, 132°31.23′ W

> *Kina Cove . . . affords good anchorage in 7 to 10 fathoms, 0.8 mile inside the entrance. In entering, follow a midchannel course. A reef is about 100 yards off the W shore about 0.1 mile S of the W point of the narrow entrance to the inner bay.* (CP)

This cove offers good protection from southerly winds and makes a good centrally located base from which to explore Kasaan Bay.

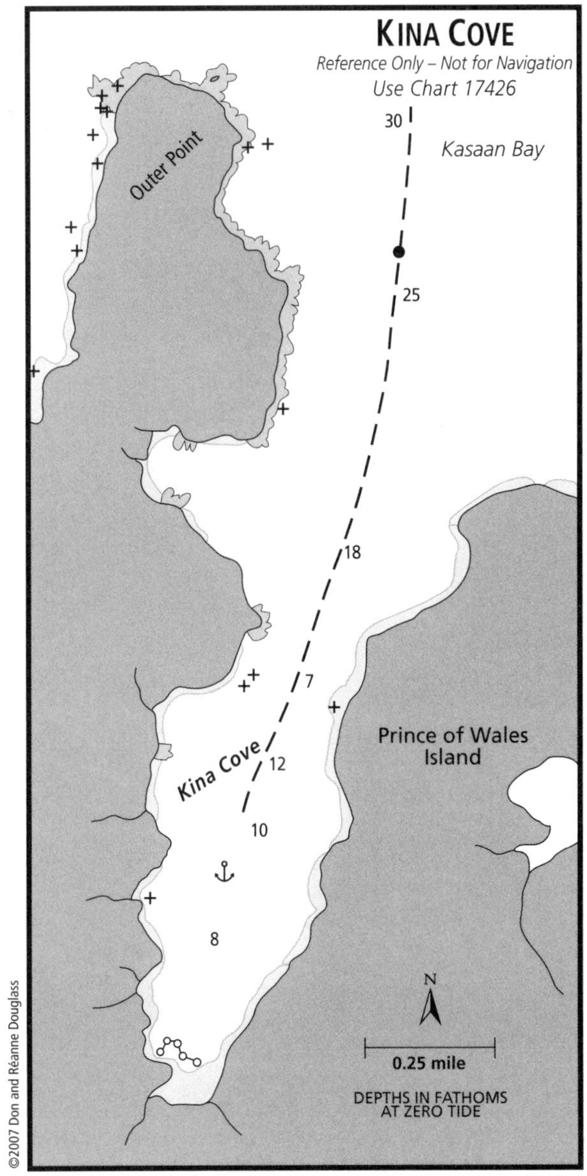


Anchor in 8 fathoms over mud with good holding.

## Nanny Bay (Twelvemile Arm)

Nanny Bay is 2.7 miles west of Kina Cove.

Chart 17426
Entrance: 55°30.07′ N, 132°35.12′ W

Nanny Bay is useful for temporary anchorage in fair weather.

## Twelvemile Bay (Twelvemile Arm)

Twelvemile Bay is 3 miles southwest of Kina Cove.

Chart 17426
Entrance: 55°29.01′ N, 132°34.34′ W

Twelvemile Bay has a shallow entrance, but appears to offer shelter for small craft from southeast winds near the head of the bay.

## Clark Bay (Twelvemile Arm)

Clark Bay is about 0.4 mile northwest of the northeast point of Loy Island.

Chart 17426
Entrance: 55°29.49′ N, 132°36.57′ W

> *A ferry terminal is in Clark Bay. . . . The terminal has berthing space, with dolphins, of about 235 feet, and a reported depth along side of about 25 feet.* (CP)

This ferry terminal has replaced the one near the Hollis dock. Roads from this terminal connect with Craig, Klawock and Hydaburg on the west side of Prince of Wales Island.

## Hollis Anchorage (Twelvemile Arm)

Hollis Anchorage is 10 miles west of Kasaan Island.

Chart 17426
Entrance: 55°28.44′ N, 132°38.46′ W
Anchor: 55°28.56′ N, 132°40.04′ W

> *Hollis Anchorage . . . affords good anchorage in 5 to 7 fathoms. The anchorage is somewhat constricted by a rocky ledge that extends W about 200 yards from the W end of the island on the N side of the entrance, and by the extensive flat*

*in the NW part of the anchorage that extends off the mouth of Maybeso Creek.*

*The approach channel to Hollis Anchorage has been cleared by a wire drag to a depth of 25 feet. The small arm . . . that extends NE has a controlling depth of 12 feet. The usable area of the arm is very limited and is suitable only for small vessels. The cleared 12-foot dragged area is only 45 yards wide at the entrance to the arm. The shoal area on the NW side of the arm extends with depths of 5 to 10 feet for two-thirds of the distance across the entrance.*

*Hollis is on the peninsula on the N side of the anchorage. A small-boat float, with a seaplane float at its SW end, and a surfaced launching ramp are near the SE end of the peninsula.* (CP)

It has been reported that the Hollis Dock is extremely small and is usually filled with local boats. The ferry dock noted on the chart is no longer operational; it has been converted to a launching ramp. Good holding was found in the anchorage, however entry should be carefully made. Not mentioned in the *Coast Pilot* notation above is the area of shoal water clearly marked on the chart (55°28.65' N, 132°39.21' W). The locals say that both visiting cruisers and some local boaters are caught unaware by this shoal every year.

## **Harris River Bay** (Twelvemile Arm, Kasaan Bay)

Harris River Bay, at the mouth of the Harris River, is 1.2 miles south of Hollis Anchorage.

Chart 17426
Entrance: 55°27.39′ N, 132°39.87′ W

*Harris River Bay . . . is bare, but at high tide small craft can cross into the river.* (CP)

## **Lyman Anchorage** (Prince of Wales Island)

Lyman Anchorage is 24.5 miles northwest of Ketchikan.

Chart 17426 (inset)
Outer entrance (0.5 mile northeast of Higgins Point): 55°32.88′ N, 132°17.28′ W
Inner entrance (0.1 mile northwest of Sawmill Point): 55°32.31′ N, 132°17.75′ W
Anchor: 55°31.94′ N, 132°17.97′ W

*Lyman Anchorage is . . . about 6.5 miles NW of*

Linda Lewis

*A true Alaska dog in Hollis*

*Streets Island. Its outer part is an open bight about 1 mile wide at its entrance. The inner harbor extends 0.6 mile to the SW from the head of the main bay, is about 200 yards wide, and has*

Linda Lewis

*The real world of Alaska—a one-man sawyering operation in Hollis*

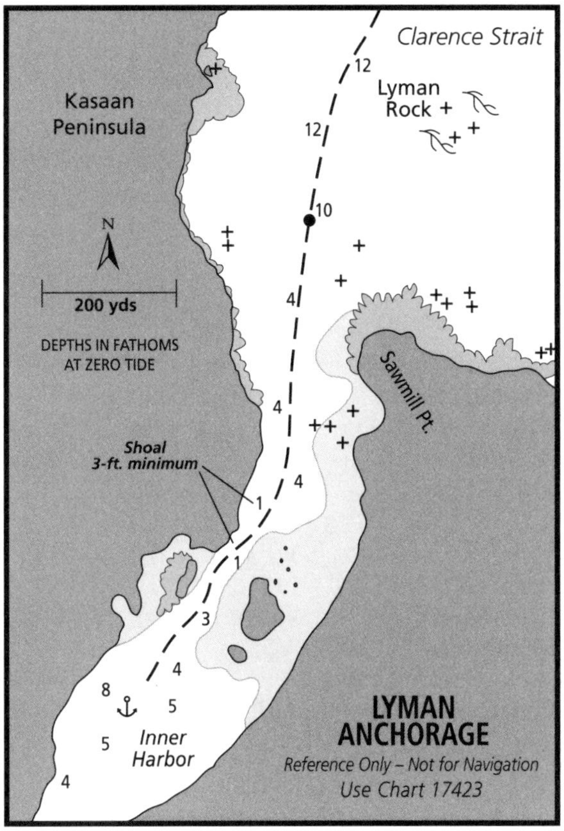




*a controlling depth of 1/2 fathom in its narrow approach. It offers excellent shelter in all weather for small craft in 4 to 5 fathoms, mud bottom.* (CP)

Lyman Anchorage is one of the most protected anchorages in this part of Clarence Strait. The 3-foot shoal at the entrance to the inner harbor can be traversed by most boats *only* on half-tide or more. Favor the west shore as indicated on the chart inset. Avoid Lyman Rock north of Sawmill Point, which is marked by extensive kelp.

Anchor in 6 fathoms over a soft bottom with fair-to-good holding.

## **Windfall Harbor** (Prince of Wales Island)

Windfall Harbor is 4 miles northwest of Lyman Anchorage.

Chart 17426
Entrance: 55°36.49′ N, 132°20.39′ W

*Windfall Harbor . . . is a narrow, crooked inlet that extends SW for about 1 mile. Its entrance is obstructed by rocks, reefs, and islands. It is a poor anchorage and should be avoided by all except small craft with local knowledge.* (CP)

We concur with the *Coast Pilot* that Windfall Harbor is a poor anchorage. Swinging room is quite restricted, the bottom is irregular with kelp, sand and rocks and poor-to-marginal holding. Although the harbor is well protected from swells, wind and chop, we would not recommend it for cruising boats.

## **Tolstoi Bay, West Cove** (Prince of Wales Island)

Tolstoi Bay is 23 miles northwest of Guard Island.

Chart 17423 (inset)
Outer entrance (mid-channel between Tolstoi Point and Tolstoi Island): 55°41.01′ N, 132°24.55′ W
Inner entrance: 55°40.21′ N, 132°25.70′ W
Entrance (West Cove): 55°39.07′ N, 132°26.45′ W
Anchor (West Cove): 55°39.39′ N, 132°26.81′ W

*On the W side of Tolstoi Bay about 1.2 miles S of the entrance is a small harbor marked by a wooded islet 150 yards offshore. The entrance is obstructed by an islet in midchannel and a rock that shows at low water off its E side, leaving a clear channel less than 100 yards wide on the NE side of the islet. The anchorage is in about 7-1/2 fathoms near the middle. In entering, pass S of the outlying wooded islet.*

*Near the E shore at the head of the bay is a wooded islet. . . . There is an anchorage in about 10 to 15 fathoms in midchannel W of the wooded islet, protected . . . except from N . . . making the anchorage uncomfortable. SW winds draw through with considerable force. A midchannel course leads to the anchorage.* (CP)

Tolstoi Bay, West Cove, the second cove on the west side of the bay, is tucked behind a wooded peninsula. The cove is well protected from moderate southeasterly winds and with minor chop during gale winds. We anchored *Baidarka* here in a near gale and although we felt gusts, we spent a comfortable night in 9 fathoms north of the islet that has a single dead tree on it.

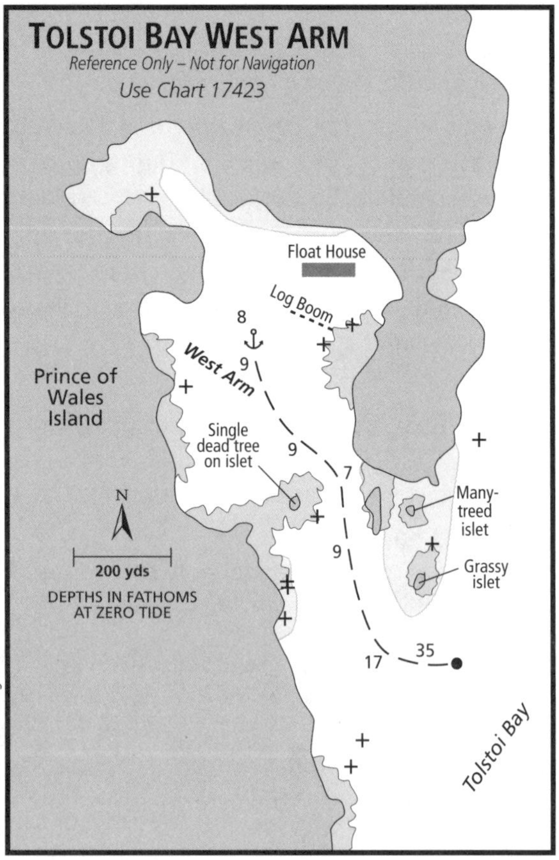


The entrance to the cove, which is somewhat restricted by rocks and the one-dead-tree islet, favors the peninsula side. The entrance fairway carries adequate depths, from 10 to 12 fathoms throughout, and the inner cove has good swinging room over a wide flat bottom. Beware of several old cables tied to trees on the shore—they may lie on the bottom, as well.

Anchor (West Cove) in about 9 fathoms over dry gray mud with fair-to-good holding.

## **Thorne Bay** (Prince of Wales Island)

Thorne Bay is 8 miles southwest of Meyers Chuck.

Charts 17423 (inset), 17420
Outer entrance (mid-channel between Tolstoi Point and Island): 55°41.01′ N, 132°24.55′ W
Inner entrance (0.27 mile west of Thorne Head Light "2"): 55°40.77′ N, 132°27.93′ W
Thorne Bay (narrows, west entrance): 55°39.81′ N, 132°29.75′ W
Public floats: 55°40.92′ N, 132°31.44′ W
Anchor (south bight): 55°39.69′ N, 132°28.37′ W

*Thorne Bay has its navigable entrance on the N side of a large island obstructing its mouth. . . . This area is thick with kelp; however, the kelp is towed under when the current runs strong.*

*Floating logs and deadheads may be encountered in the bay and off the entrance; caution is advised.*

*The bight S of the large island in the entrance to Thorne Bay affords a good anchorage in 14 to 20 fathoms.* (CP)

Thorne Bay, once the largest logging camp in the U.S., has become an attractive town with nice facilities for cruising boats. Incorporated in 1982 as the City of Thorne Bay, the town now has convenient services that include groceries, hardware, marine supplies, liquor store, post office and a medical clinic.

*The popular McFarland's Floatel in Thorne Bay may be able to provide moorage; call ahead.*

The town is serviced by the Hollis-Ketchikan Ferry.

The entrance to Thorne Bay is narrow and has strong currents. See *Coast Pilot* for detailed entrance instructions and study the inset on Chart 17423 to guide you.

Thorne Bay Harbor has extensive floats for transients with fuel, power (30 amp), water and pay telephone available. To contact the harbor, call the City of Thorne Bay at (tel.: 907.828.3380). The city monitors Channel VHF 16.

Réanne Hemingway-Douglass

*There is usually room for transients at the Thorne Bay floats.*

McFarland's Floatel, located southwest of the city, offers basket weaving classes attended by people from all over the United States. Although, they may, at times, have room for unregistered participants; please check ahead for special dinners and B & B reservations (tel.: 888.828.3335); Website: www.mcfarlandsfloatel.com.

Thorne Bay has a fairly flat bottom throughout its entire length. Cruising boats can anchor in 6 to 8 fathoms as desired; anchorage off McFarland's Floatel is also good.

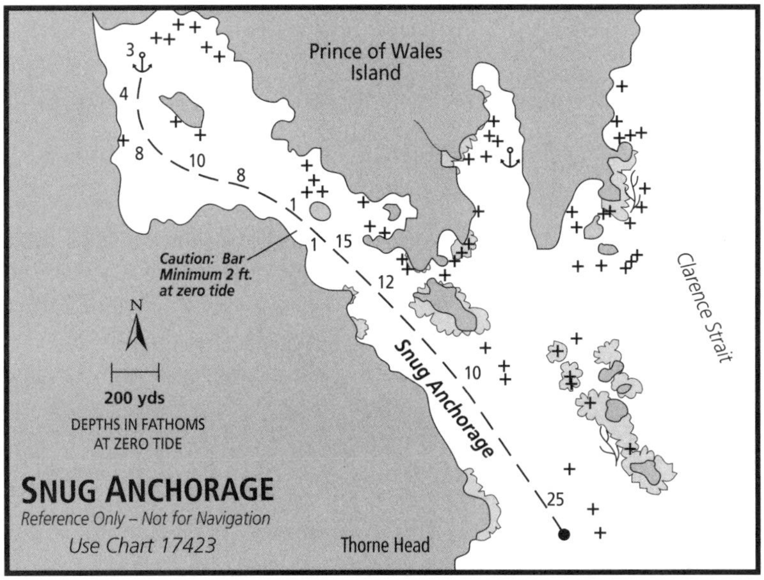



Anchor in 7 fathoms in the southern arm of Thorne Bay over mud with very good holding.

## **Snug Anchorage** (Prince of Wales Island)

Snug Anchorage is about 1 mile west of Tolstoi Island.

Charts 17423 (inset), 17420
Entrance (0.6 mile northeast of Thorne Head Light): 55°41.29′ N, 132°27.13′ W
Anchor (inner basin): 55°42.53′ N, 132°28.88′ W
Position (east cove): 55°42.38′ N, 132°27.31′ W

*In entering, pass S of the island off the entrance, then favor the W shore to avoid the rock awash that is about 300 yards S of an island off the N point of the entrance. . . . In the small cove E of Snug Anchorage, depths of 12 to 15 fathoms were found. Rocks are along the W side and near the head of this cove. Irregular depths indicate the necessity for caution in Snug Anchorage and the cove to the E.* (CP)

The entrance to Snug Anchorage, although tight and shallow, is well protected and secure in the north end of the anchorage.

Anchor in 3 to 16 fathoms at head of inner basin.

## **Forss Cove** (Prince of Wales Island)

Forss Cove is 2 miles northwest of Tolstoi Island.

**Chart 17420**
**Entrance: 55°43.50′ N, 132°26.84′ W**

*A midchannel course should be followed until about 150 yards before the entrance opens into the cove. The SE shore should then be favored to avoid a large reef and shoal area. Anchorage in 14 fathoms can be obtained 100 yards NW of the large island SW of the entrance. The N part of the cove has numerous reefs and shoal areas and should not be entered.* (CP)

## **Ratz Harbor** (Prince of Wales Island)

Ratz Harbor is 14 miles northwest of Meyers Chuck.

**Chart 17423 (inset)**
**Entrance (0.18 mile southwest of entrance light): 55°53.21′ N, 132°35.58′ W**
**Anchor (north): 55°53.23′ N, 132°36.03′ W**
**Anchor (south): 55°52.84′ N, 132°35.78′ W**

*Ratz Harbor . . . is a small anchorage that is little more than 0.5 mile long and 0.2 mile wide. It affords shelter from all winds except from N to NE, and these probably blow home with some force. Williwaws from the SE at times strike with great force in this anchorage. The NW point at the entrance is a ledge with an islet near the shore, and two heads, each with a single scrubby tree, near its SE end all connected at low water.*

*A careful midchannel course carries in clear. Depths of 4 to 11 fathoms were found at the entrance and 4 to 13 fathoms inside. The usual anchorage is in the middle of the S part of the harbor. There is a flat in the W indentation of the harbor, and a few stub pilings on the SE side of the harbor.* (CP)

Ratz Harbor, named "Gavan Rats" (after an individual) by Captain Tebenkov, then-Governor of the Russian-American colonies (1845–50), offers good protection from southerlies and prevailing northwesterlies. Although it has been used extensively in the past as a log staging and booming area, it is now quiet.

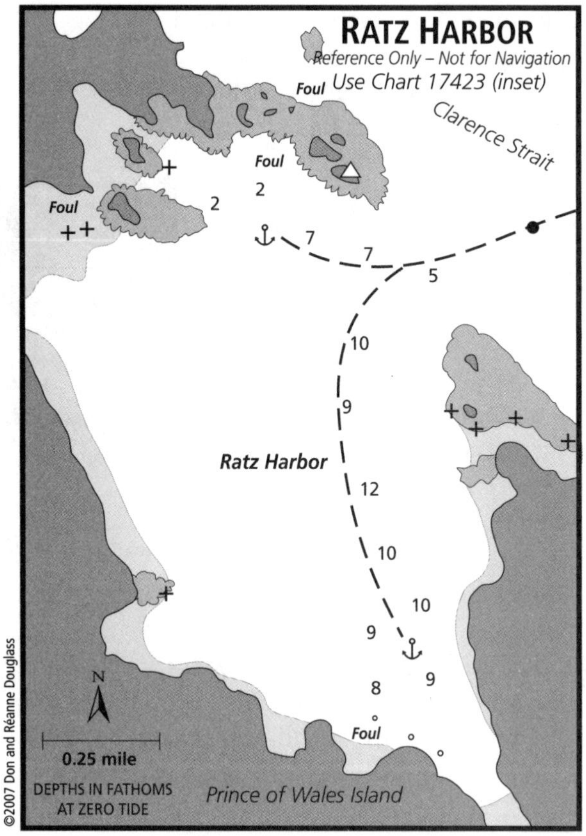


The entrance to Ratz Harbor has easy access over a 3- to 5-fathom bar marked by a flashing 4-second light. There is plenty of swinging room for a number of boats.

If southerlies are expected, anchor on the south side. After the front has passed, move to the north end, as indicated on the diagram.

Anchor (north) in 6 fathoms sticky mud with very good holding.

Anchor (south) in 9 fathoms over sticky mud bottom with good holding.

## **Dewey Anchorage** (Etolin Island)

Dewey Anchorage is on the south tip of Etolin Island just north of the entrance to Ernest Sound.

**Chart 17423 (inset)**
**Entrance (0.6 mile west of Gull Point, Onslow Island): 55°54.11′ N, 132°25.12′ W**
**Anchor (0.14 mile east of Carlton Island): 55°54.71′ N, 132°21.45′ W**

Linda Lewis

*A cruise ship in Clarence Strait passes the Ratz Harbor anchorage.*

*Dewey Anchorage, on the NE side of Clarence Strait opposite Ratz Harbor, can be used as a summer anchorage, but the bottom is irregular and rocky; there are several dangers in the entrance and the protection is poor. . . . The area between Center Island and the N shore of Dewey Anchorage is shoal and has a least depth of 21 feet.*

*Caution. There may be other dangers that are not charted.*

*Anchor 0.4 to 0.5 mile NNW of Carlton Island in 15 to 18 fathoms. Small craft can find better anchorage 0.5 mile E of Carlton Island in 15 to 18 fathoms.* (CP)

Dewey Anchorage provides temporary shelter when the chop of Clarence Strait kicks up. During southerly weather, a lee can be found on the northeast side of Carlton Island, using the inset on Chart 17423 as a guide.

Anchor in the lee of Carlton Island, as conditions warrant, in 6 fathoms over a bottom reported to be sand and shell; holding is unknown.

## McHenry Anchorage
(Etolin Island)

McHenry Anchorage is 7.5 miles northeast of Ratz Harbor.

**Chart 17360**
**Entrance (1.25 miles north of Double Island): 55°58.00′ N, 132°27.92′ W**
**Anchor: 55°57.94′ N, 132°26.46′ W**

[McHenry Anchorage] *is sheltered except from W, and small vessels can anchor in the SE part of the harbor with shelter from all winds.*

*To enter McHenry Anchorage, keep Avon Island aboard, distant 450 yards, and anchor in the middle . . . in about 8 fathoms; or a small vessel can follow a midchannel course and anchor 250 yards W of the wooded island in the SE end of the harbor in 5 to 7 fathoms.* (CP)

The inner basin of McHenry Anchorage is well sheltered in all but strong westerlies. Avoid rocks on south side of fairway and anchor in south center of basin.

Anchor in 6 fathoms.

## **McHenry Inlet** (Etolin Island)

McHenry Inlet is 2.5 miles north of McHenry Anchorage.

Chart 17382
Entrance: 56°00.42′ N, 132°28.33′ W
Anchor: 56°01.53′ N, 132°23.04′ W

> *Anchorage may be had in 12 to 19 fathoms beyond the turn in the channel.* (CP)

Anchor in about 13 fathoms.

## **Jadski Cove** (McHenry Inlet)

Jadski Cove is on the north side of McHenry Inlet.

Chart 17382
Position: 56°01.53′ N, 132°26.35′ W

> *Jadski Cove . . . has its entrance about 1 mile NE of Range Island. A depth of about 101⁄4 fathoms was found in the bight in the NW end of the cove, but the approaches are foul.* (CP)

## **Burnett Inlet** (Etolin Island)

Burnett Inlet is 5 miles northeast of Point Stanhope.

Chart 17382 (inset)
Entrance (0.25 mile southeast of Fawn Island): 56°03.01′ N, 132°29.25′ W
Anchor (Cannery Point): 56°04.16′ N, 132°28.87′ W

> *The small cove behind Cannery Point has depths of 6 to 7 fathoms in the middle, with swinging room of about 150 yards and is used by fishing craft for an anchorage.*
>
> *The depth of the inlet remains greater than 10 fathoms until about 1 mile S of the narrows. There are minimum depths of 1 fathom at the narrows, which is obstructed by kelp. The inlet above the narrows, about 3.5 miles above Deadman Island, is quite deep and clear. . . . There is a prominent waterfall on the E shore 3 miles above the entrance. The inlet is too deep for secure anchorage.* (CP)

Burnett Inlet has a very narrow entrance with high peaks on both sides. It is deep except for an area 4 miles north of Cannery Point where it has a minimum depth of 1-1⁄2 feet. Avoid the shoal on the north side of Cannery Point, which extends 100 yards from shore. There is a large basin 4 to 8 fathoms deep, 5.7 miles above Cannery Point.

Anchor in 6 fathoms over a hard bottom with fair holding.

*Endless vistas of beauty in Southeast Alaska offer opportunities for contemplation (Kasaan Bay).*

## **Mosman Inlet** (Etolin Island)

Mosman Inlet is 4 miles northeast of Point Stanhope.

Chart 17382
Entrance (mid-channel between Mosman Point and Fawn Island): 56°03.28′ N, 132°31.16′ W

> *A reef extends from the N end of the islet lying 1 mile NNW of Marble Point to the W shore. This reef obstructs the N approach to the coves on the W side of the entrance to the inlet. Above this area, the inlet is deep and free of obstructions.* (CP)

The islands to the north of Mosman Island appear to offer a number of potential anchor sites in the 4- to 6-fathom range; however, the channels between the islands have not been charted and this area remains ripe for exploration.

## Rocky Bay, Cooney Cove
(Etolin Island)

Rocky Bay, north of Point Stanhope, is 3 miles northeast of Point Stanhope Light.

Chart 17382
Entrance (1.3 miles southwest of Mosman Point): 56°02.46′ N, 132°33.83′ W
Entrance (Cooney Cove, 0.6 mile southwest of Mosman Point): 56°02.99′ N, 132°32.97′ W

> *Rocky Bay . . . is studded with rocky islets and rocks awash. . . . A rock with ½ fathom on it is 2.5 miles 060°* [true] *from Point Stanhope in 56°02′07″N., 132°32′31″W.*
>
> *Point Stanhope is the S extremity of a group of islands. . . . There are several available passages among these islands for small craft bound for Rocky Bay. Three Way Passage . . . leads close to several dangers, and requires local knowledge for its safe navigation.*
>
> *Cooney Cove is a narrow inlet to the NE of Rocky Bay. It is exposed to the S, the approach is foul, and there are rocks near the head.* (CP)

There may be anchorage available for small craft in about 10 feet of water at the head of Cooney Cove; however, the entrance fairway is not known at this time.

## Cove 2 Miles Southeast of Lincoln Rock (Etolin Island)

Cove 1.5 miles Southeast of Lincoln Rock is 6 miles east of Coffman Cove.

Entrance: 56°02.90′ N, 132°39.22′ W

> *There is an anchorage for very small craft in the cove, 2.6 miles NW from Point Stanhope. The channel that leads from the head of the cove to Rocky Bay bares in spots and is suitable only for boats drawing about 1 to 3 feet, with local knowledge and making passage at high water only.* (CP)

This unnamed cove, which is suitable for temporary anchorage only, allows exploration, via its northernmost entrance, of the labyrinth of islets and rocks of the unnamed bay to the east.

Réanne Hemingway-Douglass

*Anchor check; researching the character of the bottom.*

## Lincoln Rock (Clarence Strait)

Lincoln Rock is 4 miles northwest of Point Stanhope.

Chart 17382
Light: 56°03.42′ N, 132°41.85′ W

> *Lincoln Rock West Light . . . 58 feet above the water, is shown from a skeleton tower on a concrete base with a red and white diamond-shaped daymark on Lincoln Rock. A 35-foot white square tower on a house, 0.3 mile 062° from Lincoln Rock West Light, is prominent on an islet; it is the site of a former lighthouse.* (CP)

You can pass inside Lincoln Rock for a good look at the remains of a lighthouse that played an important role in earlier times, but which had difficulty resisting tempestuous winter storms. If you look carefully you will find the remains of a WWII bunker.

## **Johnson Cove** (Etolin Island)

Johnson Cove is 2.5 miles north of Lincoln Rock.

**Chart 17382**
**Entrance (0.3 mile north of south tip of Screen Islands): 56°05.52′ N, 132°41.93′ W**

> *Johnson Cove . . . offers anchorage for four or five small craft of less than 4-foot draft to those with local knowledge. Strangers should not attempt the entrance. Swinging room is limited by ledges on the NW side of the cove and shoal water toward its head.* (CP)

## **Coffman Cove** (Prince of Wales Island)

Coffman Cove is 26 miles northwest of Meyers Chuck.

**Chart 17401**
**Entrance (1.7 miles southeast of Beck Island Light): 56°01.55′ N, 132°49.80′ W**
**Public float: 56°00.67′ N, 132°49.95′ W**

> *Coffman Cove, protected on the N by Coffman Island, is close W of the unnamed cove and about 1.5 miles SSE of Beck Island. . . . Good anchorage for small craft may be had in the middle of the SE part of the cove in 8 to 10 fathoms, mud bottom, and a midchannel course will carry in safely.* (CP)

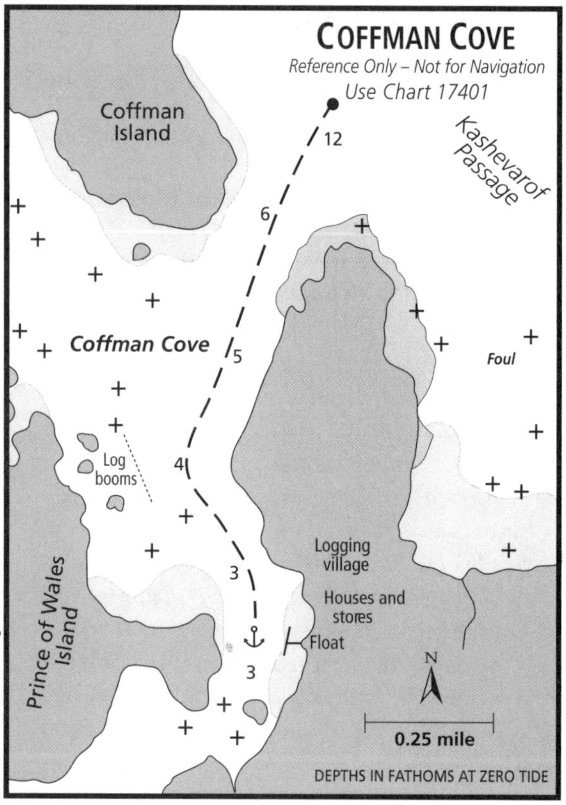

©2007 Don and Réanne Douglass

Coffman Cove, formally a logging camp, is now a small community with a general store that sells groceries and clothing. The public float is crowded, and the cove is filled with small sport fishing boats that come to the area to hunt and fish. Lake Bay and Barnes Lake to the west are popular areas for these sports.

Although the cove offers good shelter, watch out for work boats that come and go at all hours. The entrance is clear and a mid-channel course is advised. Anchorage can be found off the public float.

In 2006, a new inter-island ferry was initiated between Coffman Cove, South Mitkof Island and Wrangell. The one trip a day, round-trip service runs from mid-May to mid-September, four days a week. For information, phone 907.826.4848.

Anchor in 3 fathoms over a soft bottom with good holding.

## **Kashevarof Passage** (Clarence Strait)

Kashevarof Passage lies between the Kashevarof Islands and Stevenson, Thorne and Prince of Wales islands.

**Chart 17382**
**Southeast entrance (0.9 mile south of The Triplets and 1 mile southeast of Beck Island Light): 56°02.65′ N, 132°49.85′ W**
**North entrance (0.5 mile north of Fire Island): 56°14.54′ N, 133°03.47′ W**
**North entrance (0.5 mile east of Colpoys Light): 56°20.17′ N, 133°10.78′ W**

> *Kashevarof Passage and Snow Passage form the head of Clarence Strait and are the two passages connecting with Sumner Strait W of Zarembo Island. Kashevarof Passage is wide, but is beset with rocks, reefs, and shoals, with strong tidal currents and tide rips. . . . the dangers are shown on the charts. There are dangerous reefs and rocks, but passage can be had by following the chart closely. The pass is used extensively by small craft. Large vessels use Snow Passage . . .* (CP)

Réanne Hemingway-Douglass

Purse seiner bringing in its net, Clarence Strait

Kashevarof Passage is an alternate route to Snow Passage to the east; it is more protected and the velocity of its current is considerably less. This is also a route that lets you avoid the Snow Passage commercial traffic as well as putting you within easy reach of good anchorage in Exchange Cove.

You can follow Kashevarof Passage all the way to Point Colpoys (on the northeast corner of Prince of Wales Island) by carefully hugging the Prince of Wales coast for a smooth-water route. Proceed carefully, watching your charts and the waters around you for hazards. If your initial plan was to transit Snow Passage, don't change your mind along the way and try to take a route through the Middle Islands group south of Shrubby Island; in addition to the rocks and reefs, these passages can be choked with logs.

## **Lake Bay** (Stevenson Island)

Lake Bay is 1 mile southwest of Beck Island Light.

Chart 17401
**Entrance (0.3 mile southeast of Beck Island Light): 56°02.59′ N, 132°51.40′ W**
**Anchor (0.16 mile northwest of fishery float, 0.8 mile south of Keg Point): 56°01.25′ N, 132°55.70′ W**

> *Across the entrance and in the bay are detached islands and reefs and the best channel is from NE between Beck and Coffman Islands.* (CP)

The entrance to Lake Bay is filled with rocks and shoals. Use Chart 17401 as your guide if you want to enter it. Anchorage can be found mid-channel off the outflow of Lake Bay Creek, about 300 yards northwest of the buildings. This site offers good protection from southerlies, and is a good place to explore the lake and lagoons to the west. Watch for strong ebb currents and dangerous rapids south and west of Stevenson Island.

Anchor in about a 6-fathom hole over a bottom of sticky mud and shells with very good holding.

## **Whale Passage**

Whale Passage lies between Thorne Island and Prince of Wales Island.

Chart 17382
Southeast entrance (3.8 miles northwest of Beck Island Light): 56°03.89′ N, 132°58.16′ W
Anchor (northwest bay): 56°05.85′ N, 133°07.14′ W
Northeast entrance (2.7 miles southwest of Kashevarof Passage Light): 56°08.35′ N, 133°03.40′ W

> *This passage has many dangers and must be navigated with extreme caution.*
>
> *Shelter for small craft may be found on the N side of the passage near its S entrance in 5 fathoms, soft bottom, in the small cove just after passing between the two charted rocks directly off a small cabin near the beach. The bay that extends to the NW near the middle of the passage affords good anchorage with ample swinging room in about 4 to 10 fathoms, soft bottom. . . . An excellent anchorage for small craft in all weather may be found when headed N from the middle of Whale Passage, on the E side between the irregularly shaped wooded island and the shore of Thorne Island.* (CP)

Anchor in 6 to 8 fathoms over soft bottom.

## Blashke Islands

Blashke Islands lie between Clarence Strait and Kashevarof Passage; southwest entrance is 3.9 miles northwest of Beck Island Light.

**Chart 17382**
**Southwest entrance: 56°06.32′ N, 132°54.84′ W**
**Anchor (first basin): 56°07.31′ N, 132°54.86′ W**
**Anchor (second basin): 56°07.56′ N, 132°54.41′ W**

> *The Blashke Islands form a group of islands at the SE end of the Kashevarof group. All are wooded and separated by narrow foul channels. Rose Rock, Rose Island, Seal Rock, The Triplets, and Deichman Rock are on the foul ground to the SE.* (CP)

Blashke Islands—a complex of islands with unusual topography—can be useful to cruising boats because they are located just a day's cruise north of Ketchikan. The islands are part of the Kashevarof Islands which, to date, have not been documented for their endless cruising and fishing possibilities.

Numbering about 20 islands in all, the area is fun to explore by dinghy or kayak.

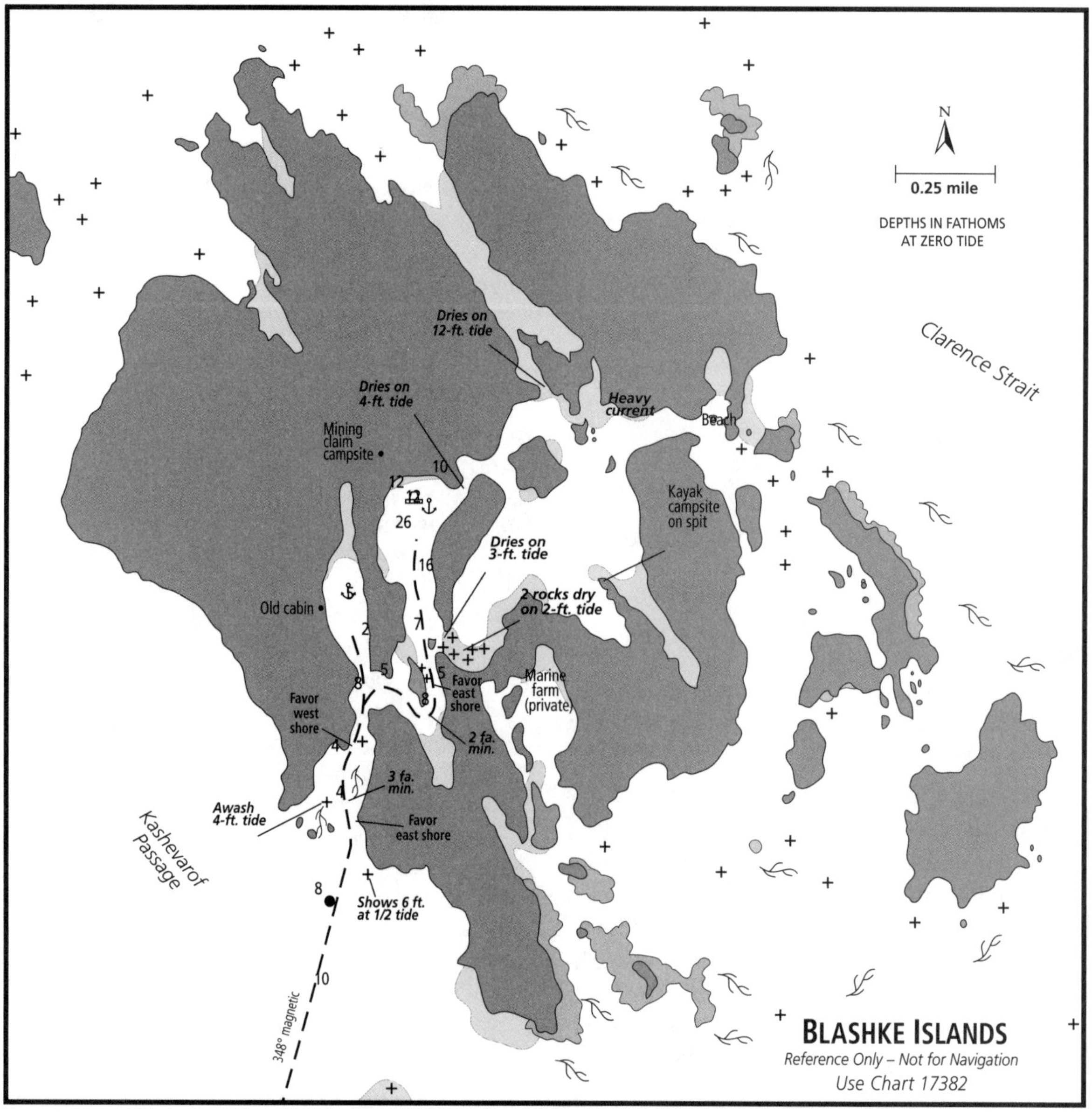

*This black bear became uneasy as the photographer came nearer.*

The complex is shaped like a giant set of molars that have opened slightly to create intricate waterways. Landlocked and isolated, the anchor sites shown on the diagram offer shelter and a solitude seldom found so near the Inside Passage route.

Small, old-growth trees line the shores, and just an occasional sign of visitors can be seen: we've found several shell middens, an empty bottle filled with a mining claim notice, and hunting campsites. Sitka black-tailed deer, marten, and eagles are locals here. A trail leads across the neck to an aquaculture operation in the south-facing cove; boaters are asked to respect the privacy of the site and not to "drop in."

The entrance to the Blashke Islands is intricate and somewhat difficult, and you must make a very slow approach, posting alert lookouts on your bow. Do not attempt to enter them in foul weather, limited visibility or by radar. The first narrows is about 100 feet wide, and the entrance to the second basin is even narrower. There are many rocks and shoals outside the islets, as well as along the narrow inside route. The bottom is irregular and the patterns of current are complex, due to the many different openings.

The Blashke Islands are poorly charted and the various electronic charts have large errors in this area. Do not be surprised if your chart plotter shows you cruising over land with errors as much as 200 feet in these narrow channels. Stay mid-channel, with an alert bow watch, and proceed slowly. Stop any time you are uncomfortable and do not continue until you are convinced it is safe to do so.

Pick your way carefully through the narrows, using the diagram as a general guide only. Beware: There may be some surprises!

When approaching from Kashevarof Passage to the southwest, we use a course of about 348° magnetic, crabbing as the wind or current requires. Avoid the rock and reef marked by a kelp patch a mile south of the entrance. Once inside the first narrows, work your way carefully into the two basins as indicated in the diagram.

There is a small exterior passage to the south of Blashke Islands that connects to Clarence Strait and hence to Wrangell. As you exit the Blashke Islands on a southbound trip, turn southeast 1/4 mile out and head for Rose Rock over a 9-fathom bottom. When you are halfway between the point on the south island and Rose Rock, turn east. From here, the bottom follows a 12- to 16-fathom curve, not the 39 fathoms as indicated on the chart.

Pass south of the rock located a half-mile southeast of the southernmost Blashke Island. This unnamed rock dries on about a 6-foot tide. As you approach this rock, depths are 37 fathoms for a short time before rising to an 8-fathom shoal southeast of the rock. East of here, you quickly reenter an area of 100 fathoms or more.

Within the Blashkes there is a private buoy at the head of the second basin. You can use the buoy, as we have, or anchor nearby towards the drying passage to the east. Entry into the large central basin is restricted to small craft because of the foul area at the west opening; the east opening has strong currents and is unsurveyed.

Anchor (first basin) in 5 fathoms over mud with good holding.

Anchor (second basin) in 12 fathoms over an unrecorded bottom.

## **Exchange Cove** (Exchange Island)

Exchange Cove, on the northwest side of Kashevarof Passage, is entered 12.1 miles northwest of Beck Island Light.

Chart 17382
Entrance: 56°13.03′ N, 133°03.46′ W
Anchor: 56°12.27′ N, 133°04.24′ W

> *Exchange Cove . . . is the largest sheltered anchorage in this vicinity. It has room for several small vessels and is well protected from all directions.* (CP)

Exchange Cove, which offers convenient and well-protected anchorage with lots of swinging room for a number of boats, makes an excellent base camp for exploring the islets of northern Clarence Strait. *Baidarka* has entered the cove several times at night using radar and electronic charting with little difficulty. Some electronic charts seem to have horizontal datum errors, so pay attention and post an alert lookout on entering.

When entering the cove, use the north entrance, off Kashevarof Passage, avoiding the rocks close to the west shore of Exchange Island. Find an appropriate anchoring depth prior to reaching the southern extreme of the island. The fairway seems to be a flat bottom with few rocks. The window south of Exchange Island is foul and useful for kayaks and tenders only. Do not overshoot the ground on the large mud flat at the head of the cove.

Anchor in 6 fathoms over soft mud and sand with very good holding and lots of swinging room.

## **Salmon Bay**

Salmon Bay is 2.5 miles southeast of Point Colpoys.

Chart 17382
Entrance: 56°18.28′ N, 133°08.81′ W
Anchor: 56°18.16′ N, 133°09.44′ W

> *Small craft can find sheltered anchorage in 1 to 3 fathoms near the head. It is extensively used as a harbor by local boats during certain seasons.*
>
> *The bays and coves to the S of Salmon Bay are almost dry at low water and have foul entrances. . . . Overfalls, currents, and rocks make the various entrances dangerous except at high water.* (CP)

Anchor in 1 to 2 fathoms over sand and mud with fair holding, restricted swinging room.

## **Snow Passage** (Clarence Strait)

Snow Passage is between Bushy and Zarembo islands.

Chart 17382
South entrance (1.0 mile southeast of Bushy Island Light): 56°15.73′ N, 132°56.57′ W
North entrance (1.0 mile northwest of Bushy Island Light): 56°17.32′ N, 132°58.64′ W

> [Snow Passage] *is a deep channel with foul shores and strong tidal currents. Snow Passage is largely used by vessels bound from or to Wrangell Narrows or between Clarence and Sumner Straits. . . . It is clear in midchannel, except for a shoal with a depth of 4-1/2 fathoms in the middle of the channel at the N end, 0.7 mile ENE of Round Island. . . .*
>
> *During spring tides, the passage may have a considerable number of drifting logs that may endanger vessels.* (CP)

Snow Passage is the narrow passage between the west shore of Zarembo Island and the many islands and islets found in the Kashevarof Islands to the west. Blashke Islands on the south to Scrubby and Bushy Islands on the north, offers some fine exploring and kayaking.

The passage is narrow, with strong currents, and is used frequently for northbound cruise ships that follow a route through Sumner Strait and then Chatham Straits. The currents in Snow Passage can be deceptive, and they are not laminar flow. Several cruising boats and single-handed boats have grounded here by not paying enough attention to circular currents, which have set them ashore.

This is a very good place to watch whales and sea lions cavorting and feeding in the upwelling currents and eddies.

Steamer Bay is the only easily accessible anchorage at the junction of Clarence Strait and Stikine Strait. Locals have reported good anchorage deep in the bay.

Gary Luhm

*A tufted puffin glides serenely by.*

## Clarence Strait North Entrance

Clarence Strait north entrance joins Sumner Strait west of Zarembo Island.

Chart 17382
North entrance (2.4 miles east of Point Colpoys Light): 56°20.30′ N, 133°07.38′ W

## Stikine Strait

Stikine Strait lies between Etolin and Zarembo islands.

Chart 17382
South entrance: 56°13.33′ N, 132°45.52′ W
North entrance (Point Ancon light brg 115°T at 0.9 Nm): 56°24.70′ N, 132°34.83′ W

> *Stikine Strait connects the N part of Clarence Strait with the E end of Sumner Strait and the waters off the mouth of Stikine River. The strait is broad and deep, and is generally used by vessels going to Wrangell, or following the Inner Passage from Clarence Strait to Wrangell Narrows. Both shores of Stikine Strait are free from dangers except at a few points, and all dangers are shown on the chart.*
>
> *In Stikine Strait the flood current sets N through the strait until met by the current from Stikine River W of Wrangell Harbor. Velocity of the current is about 2 knots.* (CP)

## Steamer Bay (Etolin Island)

Steamer Bay is 7.5 miles north of Lincoln Rock Light.

Chart 17382
Entrance (1 mile southeast of Mariposa Rock): 56°10.51′ N, 132°42.55′ W
Anchor: 56°09.04′ N, 132°40.80′ W

> *Steamer Bay, E of Point Harrington, affords anchorage at its head, but the holding ground is not good and SE winds draw with considerable force through Porcupine Creek. It is open to NW. . . . For a distance of about 2 miles from Point Harrington both shores of the bay have some rocks and ledges close inshore with the exception of a reef about 300 yards NW of the E shore near the U.S. Forest Service cabin, approximately 1.2 miles from the head.*
>
> *The bay is easy to access. . . Small craft may find better bottom by anchoring in 10 fathoms close to the E shore in a cove, just past the Forest Service cabin on the beach and S of Independence Island. A bare rock, 12 feet high is near the shore on the NE side of the basin.* (CP)

The bay 2 miles north of Steamer Bay—Kindergarten Bay—is strongly recommended for small craft.

Réanne Hemingway-Douglass

*Deep Bay offers a quiet anchorage toward the head of the bay.*

## **Kindergarten Bay** (Etolin Island)

Kindergarten Bay is 2 miles north of Steamer Bay.

Chart 17382
Entrance: 56°12.23′ N, 132°42.67′ W
Anchor (southeast of wooded islet):
56°12.19′ N, 132°41.15′ W

> *Kindergarten Bay . . . is used extensively as an anchorage for small craft. It is one of the best anchorages in the area and affords protection in all weather, although at times strong winds will blow down from the hills. It is reported that the N side of the bay appeared to be clear. . . . Mariners are cautioned to avoid a large rock, covered 4 to 6 feet at high tide, that was reported close SW of the largest islet near the head of the bay.* (CP)

Kindergarten Bay offers anchorage southeast of the wooded islet. As noted in the *Coast Pilot,* avoid the rock on the southwest side of the largest islet. The terrain at the head of the cove is very steep and may be subject to williwaws when winds have an easterly component.

Anchor in 5 to 10 fathoms.

## **Quiet Harbor** (Etolin Island)

Quiet Harbor is 2 miles northeast of Kindergarten Cove.

Chart 17382
Entrance: 56°14.29′ N, 132°39.86′ W
Anchor: 56°13.96′ N, 132°39.82′ W

> *Quiet Harbor is . . . about 2.5 miles S of Round Point, Zarembo Island. A well-protected and easily accessible anchorage, except in N wind, is reported to be about 400 yards from the head of the harbor in about 16 fathoms, mud and sand bottom.* (CP)

Quiet Harbor, true to its name, is out of the current that roars by outside, and offers good protection from all but north winds. However, depths are so great that unless you use a shore tie you won't have much scope.

Cruising boats can pass inside Molver Island, one mile to the east, where the water is half as deep and may offer very good anchoring opportunities, but the current is strong. Roosevelt Harbor, 9 miles to the north, is reported to offer protection from southerly winds.

## The Eyes Have It: Up Close on the Inside Passage

Roderick Frazier Nash—M/V *Forevergreen*

In the summer of 1990, Don Douglass and Réanne Hemingway-Douglass visited my wife, Honeydew, and me at our home in Crested Butte, Colorado, on the occasion of Don's induction into the Mountain Bike Hall of Fame. On our refrigerator, he noticed a snapshot of our then brand new Nordic Tug, *Forevergreen*. It was love at first sight, and we think the Douglass' first *Baidarka* was conceived that Colorado afternoon.

But before the birth of *Baidarka*, Don offered to crew for me on a southerly transit of the Inside Passage from Juneau to Anacortes in the fall of 1991. I was, of course, honored to have a seaman of Don's skill and vigilance on board, and his enthusiasm was worth at least two knots all the way!

The most memorable twenty-four hours of the trip began before we even reached the waters of Southeast Alaska, on September 3 in Graham Reach, south of Butedale, British Columbia. The Canoona River carries a substantial volume of water off Princess Royal Island, and its dramatic whitewater entrance into the ocean attracted our attention. I idled *Forevergreen* alongside a patch of kelp in forty feet of water and gave Don the wheel with a request to jog against the wind and current.

I tossed a three-inch, rubber-tailed jig with a light spinning outfit and twelve-pound-test line, hoping for a rockfish or ling cod for supper. I was disgusted when the line immediately snagged on the bottom, and I whipped the tip of the rod back and forth to free the lure.

But then I noticed a slow, steady pull of line from the reel. Impatiently, I called forward to Don to hold the boat in position. He replied, "Captain, we haven't moved a yard since you cast." And still the drag kept releasing line—no electricity, as with a big salmon—just pulse, pulse, pulse.

It finally dawned on me that something—a big something—was taking line into the deep water in the center of the channel. I couldn't turn the fish, so Don engaged the gears, and we went along for the ride. An hour later, we were a half-mile from the shoreside kelp bed, and I was exhausted from the pump-and-reel routine.

Finally, my second crew member, Scott, who was standing on the cabin roof shouted, "My God! You've hooked a Volkswagen!" Of course it was a halibut, normally the largest fish found in northern coastal waters. And this one was indeed huge.

Once the big fish surfaced, our problems began. The net—okay for salmon—looked like a tea strainer compared to the five-foot-long halibut. So we went to Plan B.

Don rigged a half-inch mooring line into a slipknot and waited like a cowboy with a lariat, while slowly I led the fish on a course parallel to the swim deck. Somehow, Don managed to reach down, slip the noose around the halibut's tail and cleat the line off.

When she felt the pull (all halibut over 100 pounds are female), she dove for the bottom, actually towing *Forevergreen* backwards. But with a mooring line of 1,200-pound test, we were in control.

After a flurry of action, the fish lay limp, and Don and Scott managed to haul it out of the water over the swim deck and partially over the transom. A quick measurement showed a length of five and a half feet which—tables reveal—amounts to 157 pounds. I immediately understood the significance of this number. In sport angling there is a special distinction reserved for persons who have landed a fish ten times the test of their line or leader. For instance, a twenty-pound trout on a two-pound fly line tippet would qualify. And I was using twelve-pound test. "Heroics! National recognition!" I thought. "Take the fish into Klemtu for official weigh-in and eat halibut steak for two months!"

But as I knelt on the swim deck to unhook the tiny rubber jig, I looked directly into the two eyes on the topside of this flat bottomfish. They were yellow-green, flecked with brown, and about two inches wide, each. In them, I saw a wisdom acquired over perhaps fifty years of survival. Here was a microcosm of all the wildness that makes the thousand-mile coastline north of Puget Sound so wonderful. Here was a fellow traveller in the odyssey of evolution nearly as large and as old as I was.

So I unhooked the ridiculous orange lure from that huge lip, Don released the lasso, and the largest fish I have ever caught slipped back into the sea. She lay still a moment, then pumped her huge tail and slowly sank into her blue-green world of swaying kelp and scurrying baitfish. Don and I understood, without speaking, that this was a moment of planetary modesty—a small compensatory gesture against the massive environmental chaos our species is spreading over the earth.

Later that evening we anchored in Cougar Bay off Tolmie Channel and happily ate canned stew, instead of fresh halibut.

*(Continued on next page)*

(Continued from previous page)

The next morning, fog obscured even the cruising boat anchored a hundred feet away from us. We navigated with radar out into Finlayson Channel, and by the time we reached Oscar Pass the fog had dissipated. Don, manning the helm at the time, noticed a dark head on our course. Maybe a seal or an otter? No, it was a bear! The animal was about a quarter-mile from shore, and swimming north across our bow. Why, we wondered? Marital stress, technological unemployment, bad bear day? Or simply to reach the other side? But there he was, an old male with silver hairs on his muzzle—just like Don and me. And again, the eyes had it: we saw the terror in them as we approached, and so we veered off and went our separate ways in peace.

Big halibut and nautical black bears—you don't encounter them every day on the Inside Passage—but the magic of this place is that you still can. Up here, you are moved by ancient currents. That's why we cruise the Northwest!

Anchor as close to shore as practical in about 15 fathoms over an unrecorded bottom.

## **Meter Bight** (Zarembo Island)

Meter Bight is 4 miles north of Round Point.

Chart 17382
Position: 56°20.98′ N, 132°40.06′ W

*Meter Bight . . . is an open bight with sand flats at the head over 1 mile in extent that bares for about 500 yards offshore.* (CP)

Meter Bight and Fitter Cove, just north, are exposed to current and southeast chop. Roosevelt Harbor, 3 miles northeast, provides southeast protection.

## **Fritter Cove** (Zarembo Island)

Fritter Cove is one mile south of South Craig Point.

Chart 17382
Position: 56°22.58′ N, 132°38.56′ W

*Fritter Cove . . . is an open bight with rocks off the N point of the entrance. Depths inside Fritter Cove are generally too deep for anchorage.* (CP)

## **Roosevelt Harbor** (Zarembo Island)

Roosevelt Harbor is 0.7 mile northwest of South Craig Point.

Chart 17382
Entrance: 56°24.09′ N, 132°37.50′ W
Anchor: 56°23.75′ N, 132°38.16′ W

*Roosevelt Harbor . . . affords anchorage near the head for small craft in depths of 11 fathoms, mud bottom. In entering, leave the grass-covered rock at the entrance to the S. The channel S of the rock is reported foul.* (CP)

David Parker

*Eagle with dinner*

Locals report that Roosevelt Harbor offers very good protection from strong southeast winds. There are two USFS float cabins and a USFS dock at the head of the bay. This is a good staging point for timing your entry into Wrangell Narrows (allowing for the necessary time to transit Sumner Strait).

Anchor deep in the bay.

## Deep Bay (Zarembo Island)

Deep Bay is 1.1 miles north of South Craig Point Light.

**Chart 17382**
**Entrance: 56°24.48′ N, 132°37.68′ W**

> *Deep Bay is on the Zarembo Island side of the N end of Stikine Strait, about 1.1 mile N of south Craig Point Light. It is too deep for anchorage until near the head, although the bottom is rocky.* (CP)

We spent an afternoon rafted to M/V *Saccalaurie* (on her anchor) about 2/3 of the way toward the head of the bay without any problem. An inhabited float house was tied to the western shore.

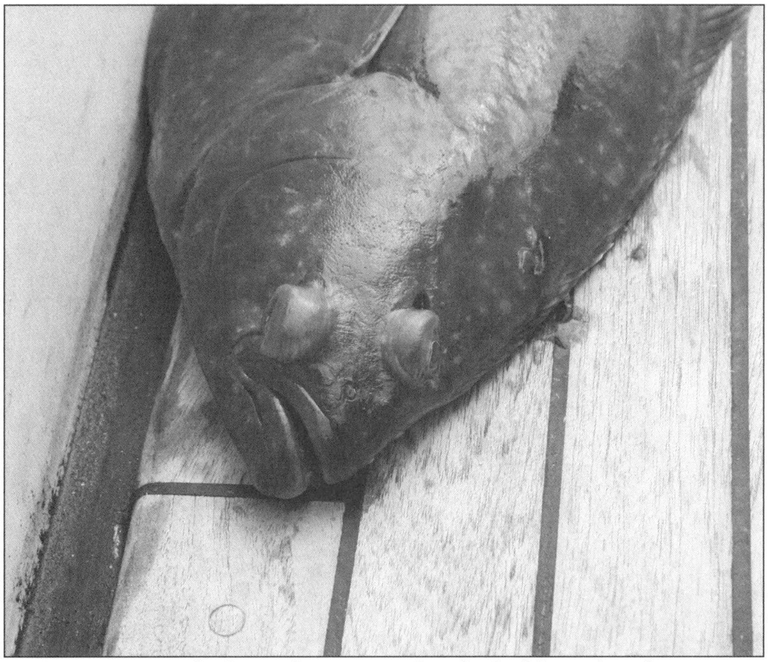
Linda Lewis
*Two eyes protrude from the same side of a halibut's head.*

## Chichagof Pass

Chichagof Pass, between Woronkofski and Etolin islands, connects Stikine Strait with the north part of Zimovia Strait.

**Chart 17382**
**East entrance (0.8 mile north of Young Rock): 56°22.47′ N, 132°23.55′ W**
**West entrance (0.5 mile south of Drag Island): 56°20.60′ N, 132°32.51′ W**

> [Chichagof Pass] *is clear except for Young Rock, with a depth of 2 fathoms, at the E end of Chichagof Pass in Zimovia Strait. . . . There is a small cove on the N side of East Point.* (CP)

David Parker
*Nature's art is everywhere.*

## Circle Bay (Woronkofski Island)

Circle Bay is 5.5 miles south of Wrangell.

**Chart 17382**
**Entrance (0.4 mile northwest of Hat Island Light): 56°22.81′ N, 132°25.93′ W**

> *Circle Bay is an open bight W of East Point.* (CP)

Circle Bay, the bight behind Hat Island, provides temporary anchorage close to shore in fair weather only.

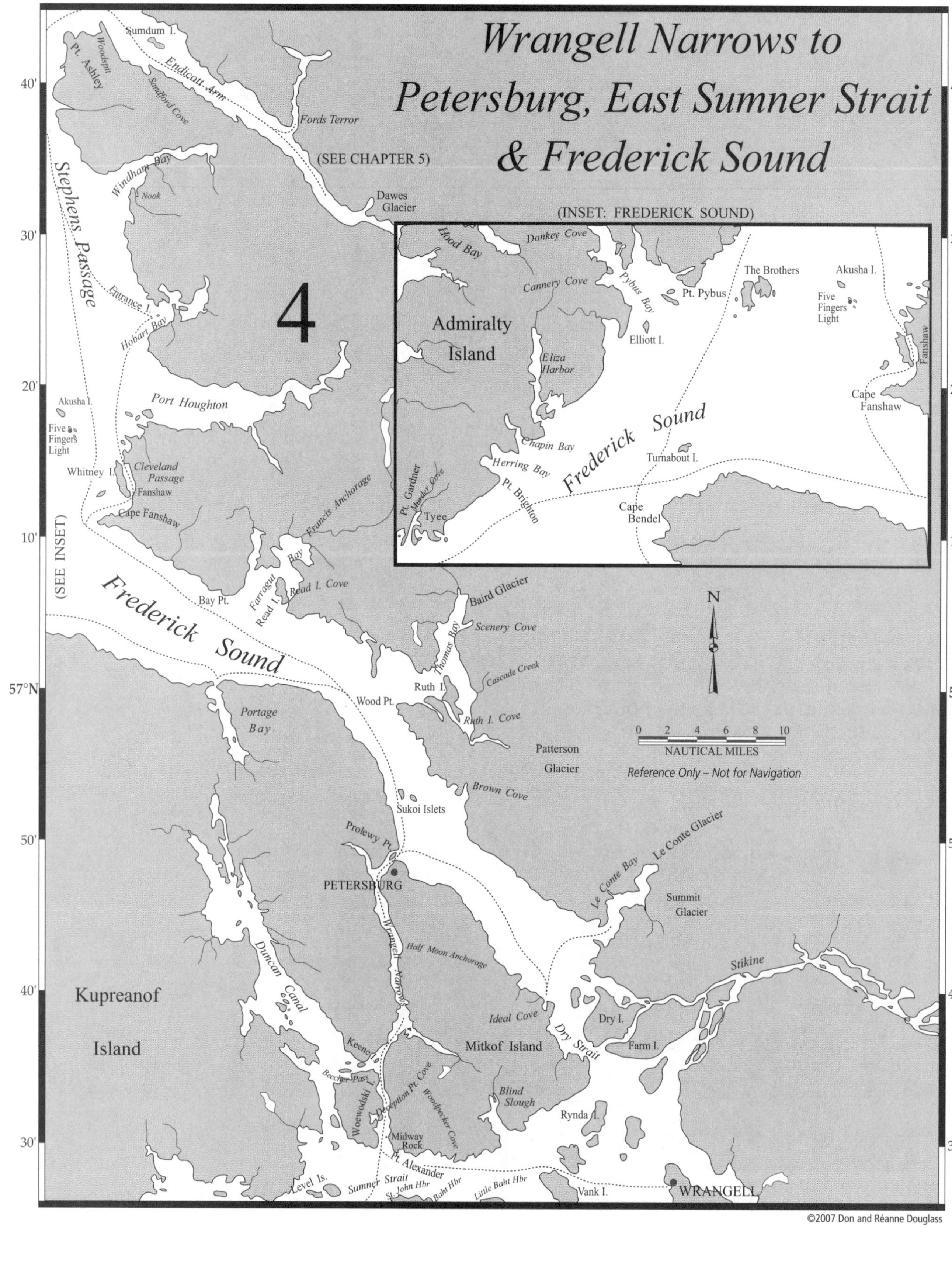
Wrangell Narrows to Petersburg, East Sumner Strait & Frederick Sound
4
(SEE CHAPTER 5)
(INSET: FREDERICK SOUND)
(SEE INSET)
Sumdum I.
Pt. Ashley
Woodspit
Endicott Arm
Sandford Cove
Fords Terror
Stephens Passage
Windham Bay
Nook
Dawes Glacier
Entrance I.
Hobart Bay
Port Houghton
Akusha I.
Five Fingers Light
Whitney I.
Cleveland Passage
Fanshaw
Cape Fanshaw
Francis Anchorage
Farragut Bay
Read I.
Read I. Cove
Bay Pt.
Frederick Sound
Baird Glacier
Scenery Cove
Thomas Bay
Cascade Creek
Ruth I.
Ruth I. Cove
Wood Pt.
Portage Bay
Patterson Glacier
Brown Cove
Sukoi Islets
Prolewy Pt.
PETERSBURG
Le Conte Bay
Le Conte Glacier
Summit Glacier
Duncan Canal
Wrangell Narrows
Half Moon Anchorage
Kupreanof Island
Ideal Cove
Dry Strait
Dry I.
Farm I.
Stikine
Mitkof Island
Keene I.
Beecher Pass
Woewodski I.
Deception Pt. Cove
Woodpecker Cove
Blind Slough
Rynda I.
Midway Rock
Pt. Alexander
Level Is.
Sumner Strait
St. John Hbr
Baht Hbr
Little Baht Hbr
Vank I.
WRANGELL
Hood Bay
Donkey Cove
Cannery Cove
Pybus Bay
Pt. Pybus
The Brothers
Akusha I.
Five Fingers Light
Admiralty Island
Eliza Harbor
Elliott I.
Fanshaw
Cape Fanshaw
Frederick Sound
Chapin Bay
Herring Bay
Turnabout I.
Pt. Gardner
Murder Cove
Tyee
Pt. Brighton
Cape Bendel
N
0 2 4 6 8 10
NAUTICAL MILES
Reference Only – Not for Navigation
40'
30'
20'
10'
57°N
50'

# 4

# SUMNER STRAIT AND FREDERICK SOUND VIA WRANGELL NARROWS AND PETERSBURG

## INTRODUCTION

Sumner Strait, the main outlet of the mighty Stikine River that flows from deep inside British Columbia, is one of the great inlets of Southeast Alaska. Running due west from Wrangell, Sumner Strait turns south at the northwestern tip of Prince of Wales Island and flows into the Gulf of Alaska. The eastern part of Sumner Strait has generally calm waters unless a strong easterly is blowing. South of Point Baker, the strait is subject to strong southerlies which—combined with a typical 4-knot ebb current off Point Baker—kick up a nasty chop.

Kuiu, Kupreanof and Mitkof islands lie along the northern shore of Sumner Strait, separating it from Frederick Sound and Chatham Strait. The standard northbound route from Wrangell or Clarence Strait leads through Wrangell Narrows to Petersburg. The alternatives are Keku Strait or Cape Decision to Chatham Strait.

Faced with these options, essentially all vessels choose the longer but easier and usually faster Wrangell narrows. Dry Strait, north of Wrangell, crosses the Stikine delta to reach the northern fork of the Stikine River. This route largely dries into a rippled 5-mile-long mud flat at 6 feet above zero tide.

Dry Strait is seldom used and then only by a few Wrangell locals who have intimate knowledge of the changing channels. Obviously it is not recommended for cruising boats.

Chatham Strait via Cape Decision is the deep-water route used by large ships heading to Sitka and Juneau. It is 50 miles longer than the route through Wrangell Narrows and it is subject to nasty chop during moderate southerly weather.

David Parker

*Whales—such as this pod of orcas—frequently can be spotted in Frederick Sound and Sumner Strait.*

Remote and beautiful, Keku Strait is becoming a more viable alternative for pleasure craft now that the navigation aids have been restored to Rocky Pass—the centermost 20 miles of the strait. Keku is a considerably shorter route for boats travelling between Ketchikan and Sitka. (Please see Chapter 8 for more detailed information on Rocky Pass.)

Rocky Pass is not a "piece of cake," and traversing it requires careful planning and diligent execution. Read our description and use your own judgment. The narrow 5-foot-deep dredged channel of the 1970s has slowly been filling in, and kelp abounds in some places. While we have heard of one or two boats of 50 feet that made the transit of Rocky Pass without problems, any vessel larger than a runabout needs to give serious thought before committing to a transit of Keku Strait. But the rewards are more than just the saving, in distance. This is pristine wilderness, almost completely protected by countless islands and islets. After a summer of experience with Alaskan tides, currents, narrows and other phenomena, using Keku Strait and Rocky Pass on a southbound passage can be a fitting conclusion to a world-class cruise.

Wrangell Narrows, the recommended north-south route, is used extensively by the Alaska ferry, small-to-medium cruise ships, barges, log rafts and fishing boats of all sizes and shapes. A transit of the narrows can be a bit harrowing to pleasure craft because these ships pass close alongside and, because of their size, may force you to the shallow margins.

The route is completely marked by navigation aids, but it is essential to carry and refer to Chart 17375 to keep you from getting confused in places. Although a nighttime transit is relatively easy, there are so many blinking red and green lights that you must use radar to determine which marker is ahead of, or behind, another.

Transiting Wrangell Narrows requires the crew to be alert and the person at the helm to look aft frequently to avoid being surprised and overtaken by a large ship travelling at high speed. One of the big advantages for using the narrows lies in the destination at its north end—Petersburg, the clean, friendly town with its Norwegian background and appearance. In summer it is a busy place. Salmon derbies and other festivals draw large crowds. This is a good place to launch your own expedition to see the floating ice from Le Conte Glacier or visit the glaciers in Tracy and Endicott arms.

The west end of Frederick Sound is renowned for its wildlife. In 10 annual trips to Alaska, we have seen some of the best displays of whales here and witnessed the greatest number of grizzly bears along shore. The eastern shore of Admiralty Island, from Point Gardner to Gambier Bay, has several well-protected inlets and coves where you can watch for grizzlies and spend time exploring.

Gary Luhm

*A prime specimen brown bear dining on the grass*

# Wrangell to Petersburg via Wrangell Narrows

## Vank Island

Vank Island is 2.1 miles northeast of Zarembo Island and 7 miles west of Wrangell.

Chart 17382
Anchor north end: 56°29.25′ N, 132°38.46′ W

*Vank Island . . . is timbered and has two prominent hills. The S shore is marked by cliffs 40 feet high in places; the N shore is low and strewn with rocks. A small church on the N end of the island is visible from N. A light is on Neal Point at the S end of the island. . . . The bight in the N end of Vank Island at times is used as a small-craft anchorage.* (CP)

In fair weather, boats find temporary anchorage in the bight off the north end of the island. This bight may provide some protection from southeast winds as well.

Anchor in 7 fathoms at the north end over an unrecorded bottom.

## Mud Bay (Vank Island)

Mud Bay is 0.3 mile northwest of Neal Point Light and 7.2 miles west of Wrangell Harbor.

Chart 17382
Entrance: 56°27.09′ N, 132°36.46′ W
Anchor: 56°27.22′ N, 132°36.21′ W

*Mud Bay . . . is deep at the entrance, shoals rapidly, and is not regarded as a favorable anchorage.* (CP)

On the southeast side of Vank Island, the small indentation called Mud Bay offers some protection from easterly williwaws, known locally as Stikine winds. Woodpecker Cove would be a better choice in Stikine winds.

## Sokolof Island Cove (Sokolof Island)

Sokolof Island Cove is 0.9 mile northeast of Two Tree Island Light and 7.5 miles northwest of Wrangell Harbor.

Chart 17382
Entrance: 56°29.98′ N, 132°36.94′ W
Anchor: 56°29.95′ N, 132°36.43′ W

*Sokolof Island, NE of Vank Island, is timbered. The center is low and is drained by a stream running W, which empties into a bay used as an anchorage by small boats except during W winds.* (CP)

"Sokolof Island Cove" (as we call it) provides good shelter for one or two boats in all but strong westerlies. Avoid the rock off the south entrance.

Anchor in 8 fathoms over a hard bottom with fair holding.

## Blind Slough (Mitkof Island)

Blind Slough, at the south end of Mitkof Island, is 2.8 miles northeast of Station Island Light.

Chart 17382
Entrance: 56°31.40′ N, 132°41.87′ W
Anchor: 56°32.18′ N, 132°43.51′ W

*Blind Slough . . . is too shallow to be of use as an anchorage except for small craft, and then local knowledge is desirable.* (CP)

Blind Slough is composed mostly of drying mud flats. Temporary anchorage can be found in the middle of the slough, but it is rather exposed.

Anchor in 3 fathoms just beyond the first old log storage area on the north shore.

## Woodpecker Cove (Mitkof Island)

Woodpecker Cove is 4 miles east of Point Alexander.

Chart 17382
Entrance: 56°29.86′ N, 132°49.69′ W
Anchor: 56°29.97′ N, 132°49.44′ W

*Woodpecker Cove is . . . close W of Point Howe. It affords anchorage for small craft with protection from Stikine winds.* (CP)

Woodpecker Cove, which offers good protection from easterlies, is used by local fishing boats. The head of the cove has a landing beach with a kayakers' campsite.

Anchored deep in the cove, you can get out of strong ebb currents and obtain shelter from all but southwest winds. However, if a major low-pressure front with strong southeast winds were approaching, the two Baht harbors on the north side of Zarembo Island might be better choices for less fetch.

Anchor in about 6 fathoms near the head of the cove over sand and gravel with fair-to-good holding.

## Little Baht Harbor (Zarembo Island)

Little Baht Harbor is 1 mile west of Craig Point.

**Chart 17382**
**Entrance: 56°27.44′ N, 132°45.87′ W**

> *Little Baht Harbor . . . affords anchorage for small craft in 11 fathoms, soft bottom, behind a wooded islet and off the mouth of a small creek. There is considerable current at the anchorage, and its use is recommended only in case of emergency.* (CP)

Little Baht Harbor is reported to offer some good shelter in most conditions. Be sure your anchor is well set when the current is strong.

## Baht Harbor (Zarembo Island)

Baht Harbor, on the north shore of Zarembo Island, is 6 miles east of St. John Harbor.

**Chart 17382**
**Entrance: 56°27.11′ N, 132°48.93′ W**
**Anchor: 56°26.61′ N, 132°48.69′ W**

> *Baht Harbor . . . about 3.5 miles E of Low Point is a broad, open bight, affording anchorage in SE winds. The anchorage is in the middle of the bight, in 12 to 15 fathoms, about 0.2 mile offshore. At high water, the navigator should not seek less than 15 fathoms.* (CP)

Baht Harbor offers temporary protection from southerly storms but is exposed to other weather. St. John Harbor, 6 miles west, is a superior small-craft harbor.

Anchor in about 8 fathoms close to shore as swinging room allows.

## St. John Harbor

St. John Harbor, on the northwest corner of Zarembo Island, is 4.2 miles south of the south entrance to Wrangell Narrows.

**Chart 17382**
**North entrance: 56°27.20′ N, 132°57.70′ W**
**Southwest entrance: 56°26.71′ N, 132°59.79′ W**
**Anchor: 56°26.39′ N, 132°57.68′ W**

> *Anchorage in about 14 fathoms, mud bottom, can be had midway between the middle of Southerly Island and the first bight in the opposite shore of Zarembo Island. Anchorage in 7 fathoms can be had farther in, but the currents are strong.*
>
> *Small craft can enter St. John Harbor SW of Northerly Island and Southerly Island, taking care to avoid a rock, awash at half tide, 200 yards SW of the S point of Northerly Island, and a similar rock that is 80 yards S of Southerly Island. A daybeacon is on the point about 1 mile E of Low Point.* (CP)

St. John Harbor is considered the best anchorage in the area; from inside the protected harbor, you can watch the current racing by outside at Vichnefski Rock. Entering is easiest from the west of Low Point. The southwest entrance requires careful piloting because of

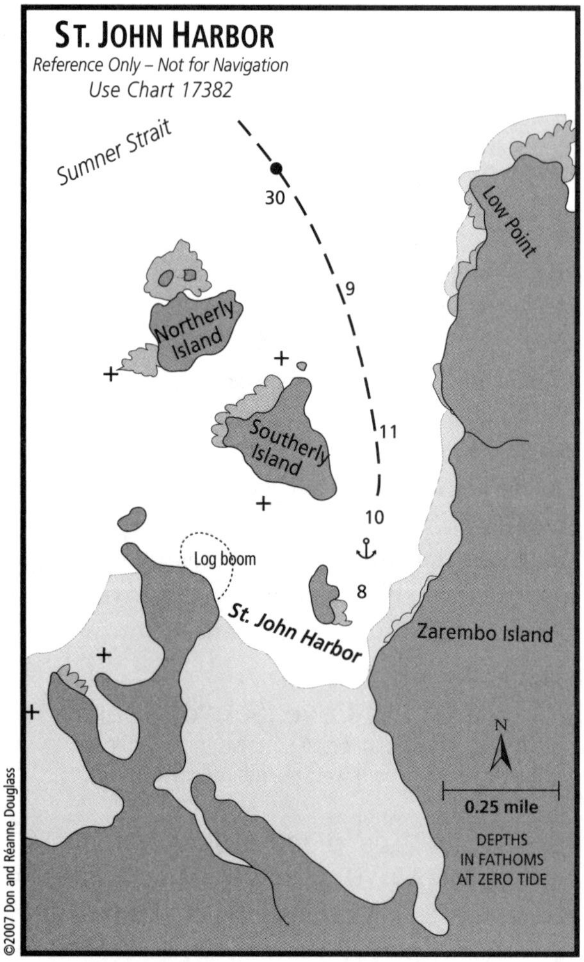

the narrow channel and irregular bottom. Some locals like to anchor deep in the harbor off the drying flat, while we prefer the area farther north that offers more swinging room.

A few summers ago, our daughter and son-in-law set out southbound in Cosmos from St. John, encountering 30-knot winds and 6-foot seas at Point St. John. Conditions worsened as they reached Stikine Strait, so they turned around and headed back to St. John.

The harbor has an interesting natural feature—a carbonated artesian spring found on the mud flats in the southwest corner of the bay, about a quarter mile past the house on the west side of the bay. The spring is visible only at low tide.

Gary Luhm

*This is my territory! Back off!*

Anchor between Southerly Island and the islet at the head of the harbor in 7 fathoms over sand with good holding.

## SUMNER STRAIT, WEST OF ZAREMBO ISLAND

### **Red Bay** (Prince of Wales Island)

Red Bay, on the north side of Prince of Wales Island, is 10.6 miles east of Point Baker and 33 miles southwest of Wrangell.

Chart 17381
Entrance: 56°19.89′ N, 133°18.23′ W
Anchor (outside, 0.5 mile northwest of Dead Island): 56°19.60′ N, 133°18.55′ W
Anchor (Flat Island): 56°18.80′ N, 133°19.38′ W
Anchor (head of bay): 56°16.63′ N, 133°19.87′ W

> [Red Bay] *is used extensively for anchorage during the fishing season.*
>
> *The entrance is through a narrow and rocky channel about 0.7 mile long, with depths of 1 to 4-1/2 fathoms. The narrowest part of the channel is between the SW side of Bell Island and a rock awash off the SE end of Danger Island.*
>
> *Vessels not wishing to enter or waiting for the proper stage of tide may anchor at the entrance to Red Bay in the bight W of Dead Island. . . . Inside the entrance the anchorage most used is the small bay E of Flat Island in 4 to 10 fathoms, mud bottom. This is good shelter in all weather.*
>
> *Tidal currents in the narrow entrance to the bay have velocities of 3 to 5 knots, with very short intervals of slack at times of high and low water.*
>
> *About 12 feet is the greatest draft that can be safely carried in at low water. The safest time to enter is at, or shortly before, high-water slack. All dangers are marked by kelp, but it is run under during the strength of the current.* (CP)

Red Bay, a large inlet with several choices for good protection in all kinds of weather, is a good place to head when you need to anchor in central Sumner Strait. Be sure you are using the large scale chart noted above. Anchorage can be taken at the west side of the entrance, near Flat Island; however the movements of the current on the uneven bottom all around you may demonstrate a "simmering pot" that makes you uneasy during your stay. You may find yourself much more comfortable deep in the inlet at the head of the bay where the water is shallow over a large area. There are a number of landing beaches and campsites

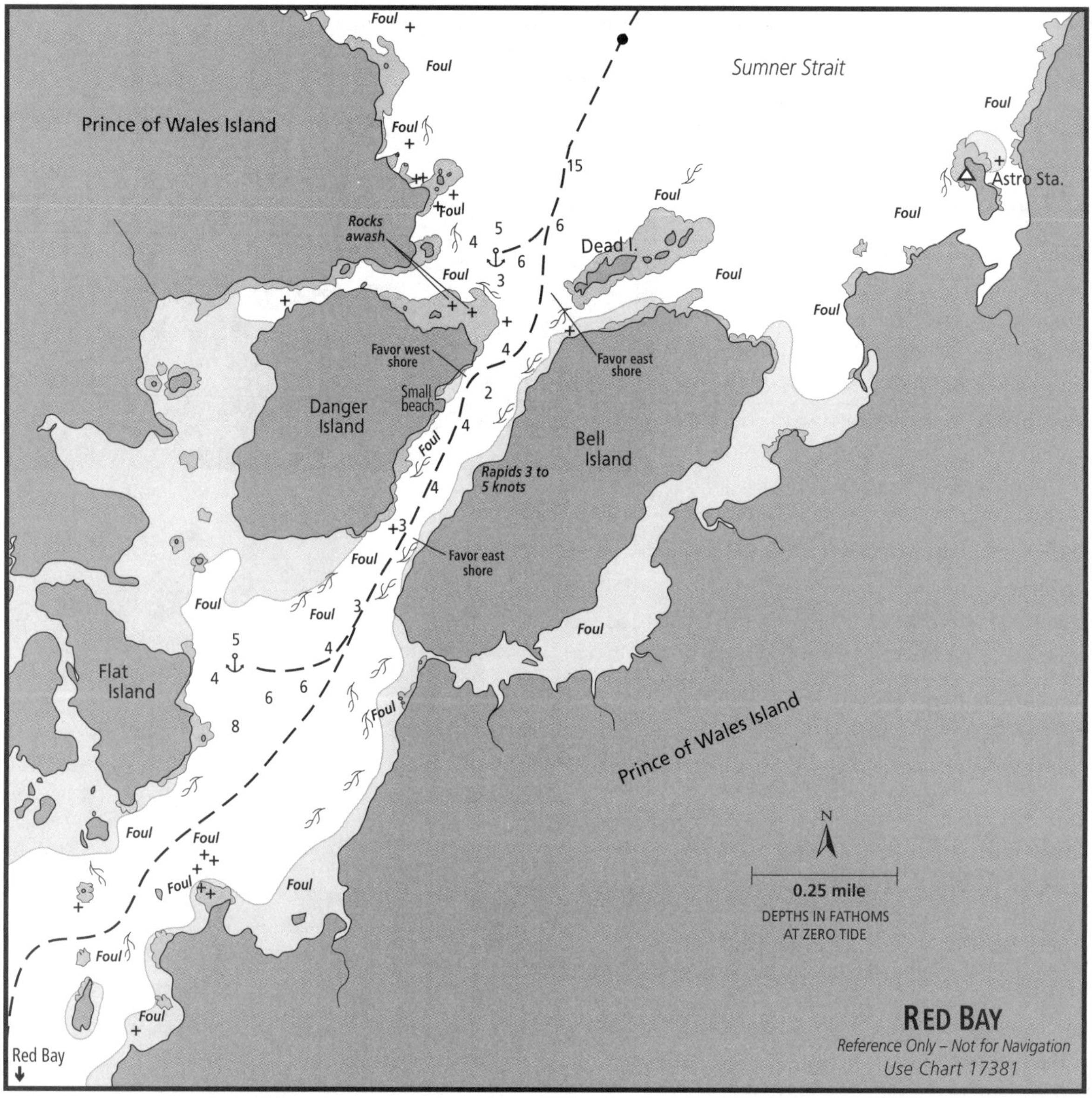




along the way. Avoid areas where the bottom has newspaper kelp; check that you set your anchor well.

The edges of the entrance channel are fouled with rocks and kelp, and large patches of kelp line the bottom. The current in the entrance channel reaches 3 to 5 knots, with the fastest water flowing through the deepest part of the narrow channel. Some cruisers consider this a favorite anchorage, but suggest entering and exiting the bay when the water is quietest, about 1-2 hours before or after slack. Entering in limited visibility or by radar is not advised.

Anchor (outside) in 4 fathoms over mud and shells with good holding.

Anchor (Flat Island) in 5 fathoms over a mud, gravel and kelp bottom with fair holding.

Anchor (head of bay) in 4 fathoms over gray mud with good holding.

## **Buster Bay** (Prince of Wales Island)

Buster Bay is 4 miles west of Red Bay and 6.5 miles east of Point Baker.

Chart 17360
Position: 56°20.30′ N, 133°25.51′ W

> *In Buster Bay . . . vessels may find anchorage with shelter from S winds in 10 fathoms, sand bottom, about 0.7 mile from shore.* (CP)

Buster Bay is an open roadstead offering little shelter except close to shore during strong southerlies.

## **Merrifield Bay** (Prince of Wales Island)

Merrifield Bay is 1 mile east of Point Baker.

Chart 17378
Entrance: 56°21.46′ N, 133°35.54′ W
Anchor: 56°21.03′ N, 133°35.33′ W

> *Merrifield Bay . . . is a good anchorage for small vessels in 8 to 10 fathoms, mud bottom, but is open to the N. On the W side at the entrance are several bare rocks, and a little W of the entrance about 0.55 mile E of Point Baker Light is East Rock, a large rock, awash at highest tides.* (CP)

Merrifield Bay has easy access and is little used. We like it during fair weather but we would use Point Baker in a storm.

## **Point Baker** (Prince of Wales Island)

Point Baker, on the northernmost tip of Prince of Wales Island, is 1.8 miles north of Port Protection.

Chart 17378
Entrance: 56°21.59′ N, 133°37.26′ W
Anchor: 56°21.16′ N, 133°37.25′ W

---

### Whale Songs

Excerpted from *Sea Stories of the Inside Passage*—Iain Lawrence

Every day we went a little farther south in Alaska, and every night we anchored somewhere new, in a different bay surrounded, like the last, by trees and rock. Kristin would settle under the skylight in the forward berth and say, "Put on a tape."

And I'd poke the cassette into its slot, start it going. I don't listen to a lot of music. In the last ten years, I've bought only one album, Judy Collins' Colors of the Day. So we played the same music in the same place, over and over and over again.

Then we ran into the whales. They were Orcas, going the same way we were, plowing in formation along a dead-straight line, rising together, falling together, steaming forward as purposefully as a naval task force. They passed us on each side, surrounded us ahead and astern and, for a moment, we might have been one of them, all heading south on a wonderful, mysterious voyage.

"Wow," said Kristin. We could hear them breathe, see the little flaps on their blowholes open and close. Without slowing, they pulled ahead and kept on going.

I don't know how it happened, but we decided that if we played music for them, the whales might stay around. So I went below and poked the cassette back in its slot. I turned up the volume and the music came blasting out, Farewell to Tarwathie, with its weird, haunting whale songs.

It thundered through the boat. It made the rigging vibrate like guitar strings; the cries of the whales screamed through inch-thick planks and blasted down into the sea twelve hundred feet deep. I twisted the knob until it wouldn't go any further.

I had to yell to Kristin over the music and the engine. "Is it working?"

She screamed back. "What?"

I said, "Is it working?" And the whales on the tape screeched and shrieked.

Kristin called through the hatch; I didn't have a clue what she said. I poked up my head, had a quick look around. I could almost see the music, shimmering like heat over the cockpit, the notes ricocheting in every direction. I said, "I can't hear you down there."

"What?" she said.

I yelled; I couldn't yell any louder than that. "I said I can't hear you."

"What?" She shook her head. "I can't hear a word you're saying."

"Oh, for God's sake," I said, and switched off the tape.

The Orcas were already half a mile away. Kristin said, "I think you scared them off."

We anchored that night in the same place again, right under the Dipper, just beside Cassiopeia. Kristin crawled into the berth, under the skylight. "Put on a tape," she said. "Anything but Judy Collins."

Linda Lewis

The dock at Point Baker

*Point Baker is a settlement . . . on the inner bay E of Point Baker and about 0.4 mile S of Point Baker Light. . . . A State-maintained 391-foot small-craft float with a seaplane float at its end is at Point Baker.*

*The shores of the bay are steep-to and lined with thick kelp. The mid-channel passage, with a controlling depth of 2-1/2 fathoms, leads to the float. The inner bay is restricted by several submerged off-lying dangers and is not recommended as an anchorage. This port is used extensively during the fishing season.* (CP)

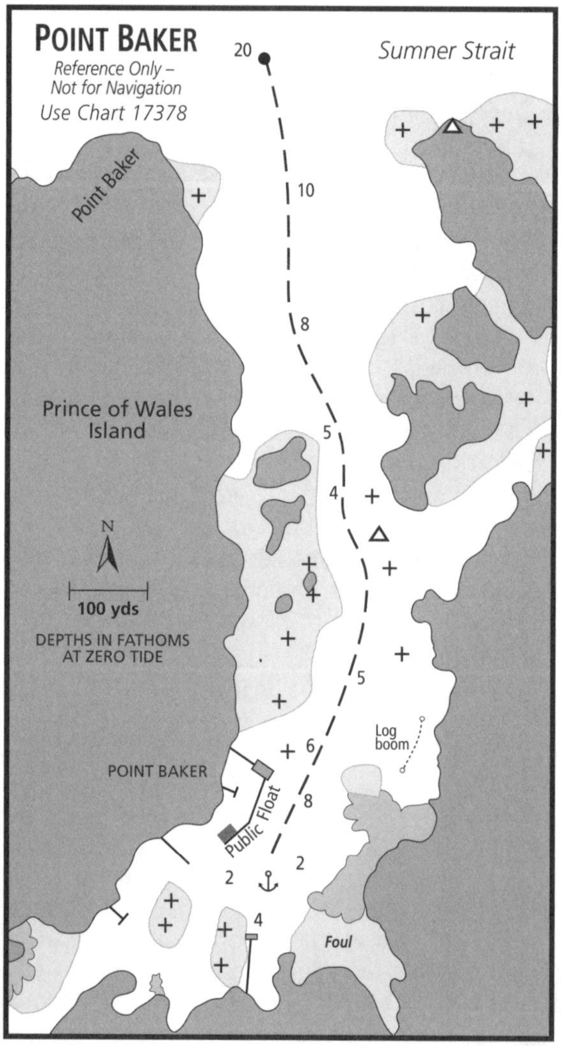




Point Baker, the fishing community in the small cove at the very northern tip of Prince of Wales Island, affords very good shelter from all weather. It's a good place to wait for optimum timing of Rocky Pass on a northbound trip.

The small public float is busy, and you may have to raft. Consult your chart carefully before approaching the float's south end. The water shallows markedly there (nine feet at zero tide) and numerous rocks lie just beyond the end of the dock. Although there is water, locals recommend boiling it for 10 minutes. The telephone on the dock may or may not be working. Point Baker Trading Post, open June through August, has very limited supplies.

Linda Lewis

The post office in the community building at Point Baker

The dock accommodations here are very spare so you should not expect anything fancy. However, the people are extremely friendly and generous about sharing local information with cruisers. They may even open the small restaurant for you if you ask.

The cove is busy with various floats and boats. Fuel is not available for cruisers; however, there is a fuel dock at nearby Port Protection (see Chapter 9). Temporary anchorage can be taken almost anywhere in the bay (except the south end) if you avoid existing floats and moorings.

David Parker

*A sure bet for seeing whales is found at Pt. Baker; beware the halitosis when up close to a spouting blow hole.*

Anchor off the public float in 3 fathoms over mud, gravel and some rocks with fair-to-good holding.

## SUMNER STRAIT, NORTH SHORE

### **Duncan Canal** (Kupreanof Island)

The entrance to Duncan Canal is 3 miles west of the entrance to Wrangell Narrows.

Chart 17360
Entrance (0.6 mile east of Lung Island): 56°30.52′ N, 133°02.96′ W
Anchor (0.3 mile northwest of south tip of Big Castle Island): 56°39.32′ N, 133°10.70′ W

*From its head, a low marshy valley, sometimes used as a portage, extends to Portage Bay. The soundings in the canal generally are less than 20 fathoms and somewhat irregular. Commercial crabbers and shrimpers operate in the canal.*

*Several good anchorages were found in Duncan Canal, usually in depths of 8 to 15 fathoms, sticky mud bottom, good holding ground.*

*The flood enters Duncan Canal with a velocity of 1 to 2 knots and runs in the direction of its axis, except at the W entrance of Beecher Pass, through which it passes into Wrangell Narrows, causing a crosscurrent in this immediate vicinity. The ebb flows in an opposite direction, and the same crosscurrent, with a W set, is found at Beecher Pass. The flood current has a W set in the vicinity of the rocks that are off the S end of Woewodski Island. Strong tide rips are found at the entrance to the canal.*

*Strangers should use caution when navigating this passage. The effect of the current diminishes inside the canal proper, but light to moderate tide rips have been noted in midchannel as far as Indian Point.*

*Enter Duncan Canal E of Lung Island, proceed in midchannel W of Butterworth Island, and follow midchannel courses. The known dangers are shown on the chart. Caution is needed in navigating it.* (CP)

Kupreanof Island is nearly cut in half by a low, marshy notch extending from Duncan Canal to Portage Bay on Frederick Sound.

There is no large-scale chart for entering Duncan Canal, so proceed slowly with alert lookouts.

Anchorage can be found in several sites avoiding rocky patches and shoals. Small craft may prefer the more intimate and shallow Little Duncan Bay.

Anchor (near Castle Island) in 5 fathoms over mud with good holding.

## **Little Duncan Bay** (Kupreanof Island)

Little Duncan Bay, on the west shore, is about 5 miles from the entrance to Duncan Canal.

Chart 17360
Entrance: 56°34.98′ N, 133°06.12′ W
Anchor: 56°36.03′ N, 133°07.93′ W

> *Little Duncan Bay, entering the W shore of Duncan Canal opposite Beecher Pass . . . is shallow, but affords protected anchorage for small craft. . . . Foul ground extends in a SE direction from the N point at the entrance.* (CP)

Little Duncan Bay is a narrow channel 6 to 10 feet deep at zero tide. Avoid rocks at the entrance and along the shore. Good shelter can be found west of Emily Islet.

Anchor in 6 to 10 fathoms over sand and mud with good holding.

## **Kah Sheets Bay** (Kupreanof Island)

Kah Sheets Bay is immediately west of the entrance to Duncan Canal.

Chart 17382
Entrance: 56°30.04′ N, 133°05.52′ W
Anchor: 56°30.72′ N, 133°06.72′ W

> *Kah Sheets Bay . . . is shoal and has many dangers. Three wooded islands are S of the N entrance point. Small fishing craft frequently anchor W of the S island in 1-1/2 fathoms, mud bottom.* (CP)

Kah Sheets Bay is a large, shallow mud flat filled with isolated islets and rocks. It is largely used for temporary anchorage by log tugs and fishing boats. The shallow 1-fathom bay west of the south island provides good anchorage in fair weather.

Anchor in 6 to 9 fathoms over mud with good holding.

## **Douglas Bay** (Kupreanof Island)

Douglas Bay, on the north side of Sumner Strait, is 4.7 miles north of Eye Opener Rock.

Charts 17382, 17360
Position: 56°27.67′ N, 133°16.55′ W

> *Douglas Bay is a bight, open S, about 4 miles N of The Eye Opener and E of Moss Island. It has depths of 5 to 6 fathoms, but is not important as an anchorage.* (CP)

Small craft may find temporary anchorage in fair weather in about 2 fathoms at the head of the bay, 0.8 mile north northeast of Moss Island.

## **Totem Bay** (Kupreanof Island)

Totem Bay is 11.7 miles west of Duncan Canal and 10.5 miles northeast of Point Baker.

Chart 17360
Entrance: 56°26.39′ N, 133°19.70′ W
Anchor: 56°29.30′ N, 133°24.02′ W

> *Totem Bay . . . is a large indentation on the N shore of Sumner Strait, midway between Point Barrie and Mitchell Point. A reef extends 1.2 miles E from the W point of the entrance. A shoal extends 0.2 mile off the E point at the entrance.*
>
> *To enter the bay, approach from E, keeping about 1 mile off Moss Island and about 0.5 mile off the E point at the entrance. The bay has depths of 7 to 8 fathoms, mud bottom, and is good protection except in S weather. Shoals extend over 0.2 mile from the shores of the bay.* (CP)

Totem Bay is a south-facing shore popular with the locals. While not secure in southerly weather, good protection from prevailing westerlies can be found at the head of the bay. Avoid all kelp, which hides rocks. This is a great place to explore.

Anchor in 5 to 10 fathoms over mud with good holding.

## **Wrangell Narrows**

Wrangell Narrows lies between Mitkof Island on the east and Woewodski and Kupreanof islands on the west.

Chart 17375
South entrance (Point Alexander Light brg 100°T at 0.50 Nm): 56°30.64′ N, 132°57.91′ W
North entrance: (100 yards west of Buoy "62"): 56°49.58′ N, 132°56.17′ W

> *Wrangell Narrows extends in a general N direction for 21 miles from near the E end of Sumner Strait to the E part of Frederick Sound. The channel is narrow and intricate in places, between dangerous ledges and flats, and the tidal currents*

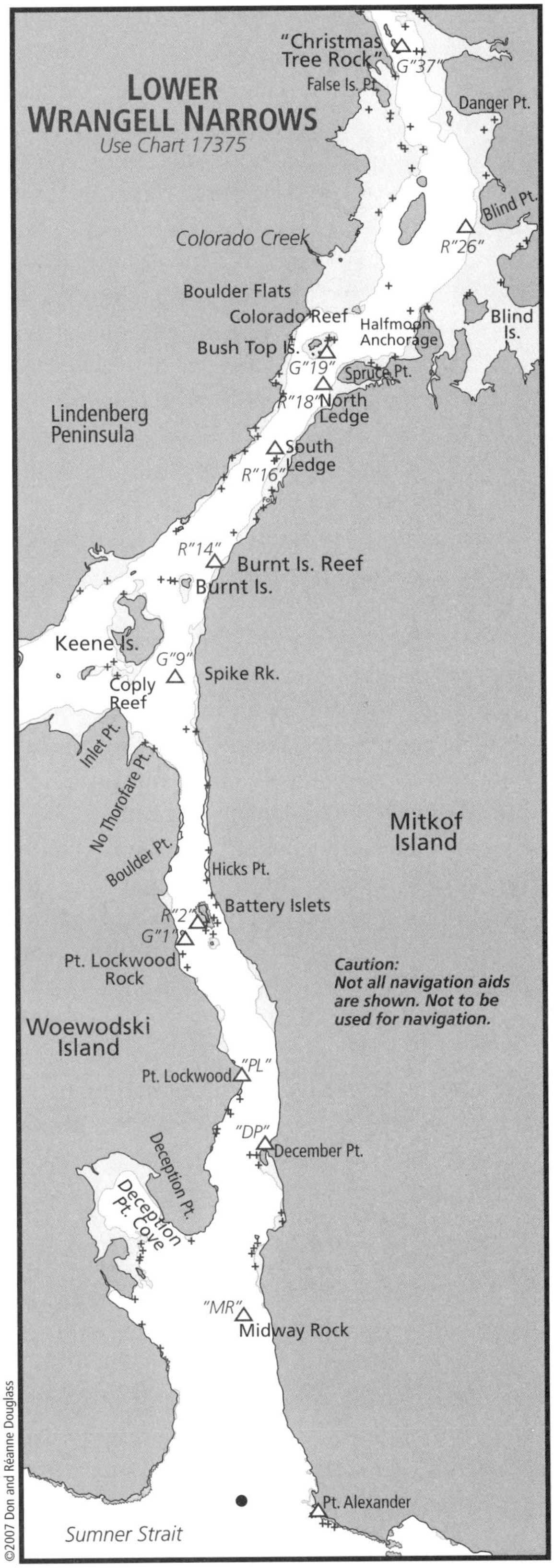

LOWER WRANGELL NARROWS
Use Chart 17375
"Christmas Tree Rock"
G"37"
False Is. Pt.
Danger Pt.
Blind Pt.
R"26"
Colorado Creek
Boulder Flats
Colorado Reef
Halfmoon Anchorage
Blind Is.
Bush Top Is.
G"19"
Spruce Pt.
R"18"
North Ledge
Lindenberg Peninsula
South Ledge
R"16"
R"14"
Burnt Is. Reef
Burnt Is.
Keene Is.
G"9"
Spike Rk.
Coply Reef
Inlet Pt.
No Thorofare Pt.
Mitkof Island
Boulder Pt.
Hicks Pt.
Battery Islets
R"2"
G"1"
Pt. Lockwood Rock
Caution: Not all navigation aids are shown. Not to be used for navigation.
Woewodski Island
Pt. Lockwood
"PL"
"DP"
December Pt.
Deception Pt.
Deception Pt. Cove
"MR"
Midway Rock
Pt. Alexander
Sumner Strait



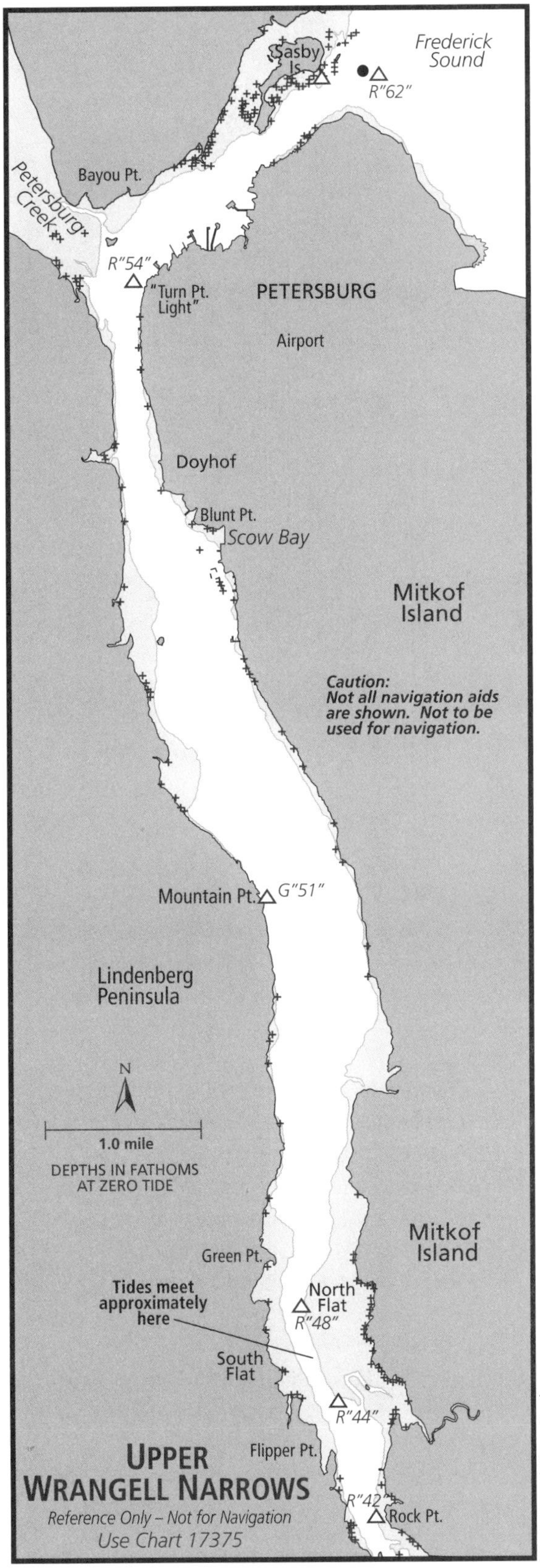

Frederick Sound
Sasby Is.
R"62"
Bayou Pt.
Petersburg Creek
R"54"
"Turn Pt. Light"
PETERSBURG
Airport
Doyhof
Blunt Pt.
Scow Bay
Mitkof Island
Caution: Not all navigation aids are shown. Not to be used for navigation.
Mountain Pt.
G"51"
Lindenberg Peninsula
N
1.0 mile
DEPTHS IN FATHOMS AT ZERO TIDE
Mitkof Island
Green Pt.
North Flat
Tides meet approximately here
R"48"
South Flat
R"44"
Flipper Pt.
UPPER WRANGELL NARROWS
Reference Only – Not for Navigation
Use Chart 17375
R"42"
Rock Pt.

Réanne Hemingway-Douglass

*Marker R"14" at the south end of Wrangell Narrows*

*are strong. It is marked by an extensive system of lights, lighted ranges, daybeacons, and buoys that, with the aid of the chart, renders the navigation of the narrows fairly easy for small craft, even without local knowledge. It is safest to enter either end late on a flood tide. Waterborne traffic through the narrows consists of cruise ships, State ferries, barges, and freight boats carrying lumber products, petroleum products, fish and fish products, provisions, and general cargo.*

*The strongest currents occur off Turn Point and off Spike Rock and South Ledge Light. The velocity of the current at times of strength at these points is between 4 and 5 knots. During spring and tropic tides, velocities of 6 to 7 knots may occur.*

*Specific courses for Wrangell Narrows would be of little help and could be confusing. The navigator should pay close attention to the chart as the narrows are well marked with aids to navigation that should be closely followed.*

*Low-powered vessels usually enter the narrows on the last of the flood and carry a favorable current all the way through. The currents meet about 8 miles from the N entrance and 12 miles from the S entrance.* (CP)

Nearly all north- and south-bound traffic in Southeast Alaska passes through Wrangell Narrows, and while it is sometimes a busy, congested passage, it is simple compared to the alternatives!

This passage can best be described as a "Piloting" challenge—one where looking out the window and navigating with landmarks and navigation aids (and your depth sounder) is paramount. You should do your work with your charts well before you begin the passage. When you make your actual transit through this 21 mile stretch of water your eyes must be directed out the window most of the time. You need to be looking for the next navigation aids and looking for traffic.

Wrangell Narrows is well marked throughout, with over 60 numbered navigational aids, including five sets of range markers. In preparation for your transit, review the chart carefully and note the placement, color and numbering of navigation aids; identify and note the spots that are especially challenging (see the following pages). Some cruisers making their first transit through Wrangell Narrows have created and printed out their own list of the navigation aids (name, color, number) in the order of approach when heading northward; a similar list for heading southward. During the transit, the crew would give the information on the upcoming navigation aid, call out the number of each aid as it was sighted, and then check off the nav aid (or note the time) on the list as it was passed.

The first of these navigational aids begins at Point Lockwood Rock at the south entrance. Here, where the dredged, 300-foot-wide channel begins, deep-draft vessels have little or no maneuvering room, and small craft must keep out of their way to avoid being run over! Shuffling for fairway position starts right here, in the stretch between Lockwood Rock and Battery Islets. Small vessels can use the narrow channel east of Battery Islets by keeping the green markers close to port on a northbound passage.

Dealing with the large flow of traffic will be one of your primary concerns on this passage. Make notes on your chart of some of the other areas where traffic issues are especially important. For example: Christmas Tree Rock, which larger ships must pass by very closely. During your entire transit of the Narrows, keep an eye out, both ahead and behind—commercial traffic tends to pass quite close at high speed, creating large wakes.

Make notations on your chart of the areas where you might expect the most turbulence. For example, when the current is running, the areas of the fastest and most turbulent water occur at Spike Rock Light G"9," South Ledge Light R"16," and Turn Point Light R"54."

Indicate on your chart the place where the currents generally meet (approximately just above the halfway mark, between R"44" and R"48") so you can make your plan for timing the start of your trip. If you enter on the last half of the flood tide, you can pick up the first of the ebb on the other side and have favorable currents the entire trip.

Wrangell Narrows is a convenient north-south route that can be readily planned for and transited by prudent mariners. For those new to Southeast Alaska, you will find it very satisfying to include a passage through Wrangell Narrows among your cruising accomplishments.

Réanne Hemingway-Douglass

*A tug shortens tow cables in Wrangell Narrows.*

## Midway Rock (Wrangell Narrows)

Midway Rock, inside the south entrance to Wrangell Narrows, is 1.3 miles north of Point Alexander.

Chart 17375
Midway Rock Light: 56°31.80′ N, 132°57.91′ W

> *Anchorage with protection from N and NE winds can be had near the W shore of the S end of the Narrows W of Midway Rock, in 6 to 12 fathoms, sticky bottom.* (CP)

Midway Rock marks the beginning of the narrows and strong currents. From this point on, you need to monitor VHF closely for announcements of larger vessels and tugs with slow-moving tows that are transiting the narrows.

Cruising boats that need a place to stay can tuck up deep in Deception Point Cove to avoid the area where commercial traffic sometimes waits for fog to clear, or where tugs usually adjust the length of their tow lines.

## Deception Point Cove (Woewodski Island)

Deception Point Cove, on the west side of Deception Point, is 2.3 miles northwest of Point Alexander.

Chart 17375
Entrance: 56°32.18′ N, 132°58.77′ W
Anchor: 56°32.55′ N, 132°59.19′ W

"Deception Point Cove" is the name we've given to the large, shallow cove northwest of

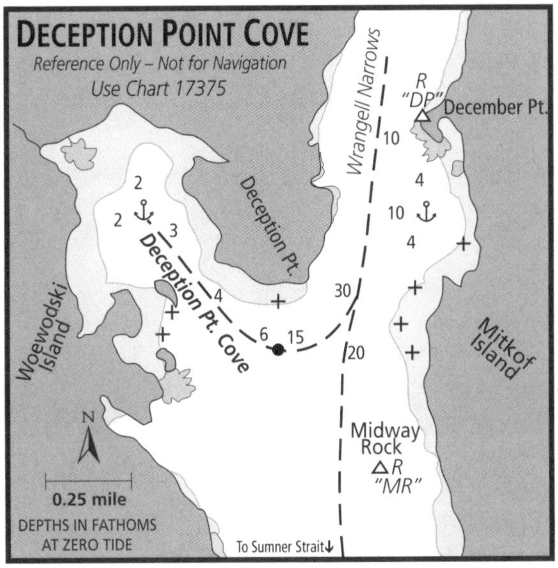

Linda Lewis

*Some of the 60 navigation aids to be found along Wrangell Narrows*

This shallow bight has a conveniently located 4-fathom patch out of the traffic lane along the eastern shore that allows temporary anchorage with relatively good shelter from southeast chop.

Cruising boats can wait here for optimum timing to transit Wrangell Narrows; however, you do notice the nearly constant traffic and feel the wake of other vessels.

Anchor in 4 fathoms over a mud, shell and rock bottom with good holding if well set.

Midway Rock. The cove offers good shelter from northerly winds as well as convenient anchorage in stable weather. Easy of access, it's a good place to wait for daylight, for the tide to change or for fog to lift.

Although this area is sometimes used as temporary storage for log rafts or other commercial operations, it can still accommodate a number of boats.

Should southeast chop develop, you can move to the bight just south of December Point to escape it, or in case of a major storm, move into Keene Island Bay for more complete protection.

When entering Deception Point Cove, favor the Deception Point shore and avoid the reef, rocks and shoals off the south and west sides.

Anchor in 2 to 3 fathoms over sticky mud with very good holding.

## December Point Bight (Mitkof Island)

December Point Bight is 0.29 Nm south of December Point Light.

Chart 17375
Entrance: 56°32.62′ N, 132°57.85′ W
Anchor: 56°32.58′ N, 132°57.57′ W

## Keene Island Bay
(Keene Island)

Keene Island Bay is on the west side of Keene Island at the northeast end of Beecher Pass.

Chart 17375
Southwest Entrance (No Thorofare Point brg 343°T at 0.20 Nm): 56°35.50′ N, 132°58.74′ W
Anchor: 56°36.12′ N, 132°59.60′ W

> *The bay between Keene Island and Big Saltery Island is good shelter and used extensively. A rock, which uncovers at extreme low tide, is about 0.2 mile E of Big Saltery Island. Anchor in 8 to 13 fathoms, mud bottom.* (CP)

The eastern side of what we call "Keene Island Bay," north of Coply Reef, is out of the current and away from traffic. Cruising boats can find good shelter here. (Notice on the chart that you will see your first set of range markers on your way towards the area of Keene Island.)

*Caution:* The entrance to Keene Island Bay— north and east of Inlet Point on the south side of Coply Reef—is narrow and shallow with numerous foul areas and strong currents. Study Chart 17375, check tide levels and stay alert while entering.

Anchor in 4 to 5 fathoms over a mixed bottom of mud and shells with good holding.

## Halfmoon Anchorage (Mitkof Island)

Halfmoon Anchorage is 7.5 miles north of Point Alexander.

Chart 17375
Entrance: 56°38.08′ N, 132°56.32′ W
Anchor: 56°38.05′ N, 132°56.06′ W

Halfmoon Anchorage—a bight on the eastern shore just above light R"18"—is shown on the chart, but is unmentioned in the *Coast Pilot*. If you want to get out of the traffic, this is a good place to do so.

Note the range markers that help guide you towards Bush Top Island, near Halfmoon Anchorage, then another set northeast of the anchorage. Also be alert to the possibility of a fishing opening in the adjacent Blind Slough area to the east; vessels intent on fishing may not be as courteous as you would like.

Réanne Hemingway-Douglass

*Lining up the range marks carefully will help to keep you on course in Wrangell Narrows.*

Anchor in 3 fathoms halfway between Spruce Point and Anchor Point, near the drying flat over a mud bottom with good holding.

## Christmas Tree Rock (Wrangell Narrows)

Christmas Tree Rock is 9.4 miles north of Point Alexander.

Chart 17375
Position: 56°39.97′ N, 132°55.93′ W

The rock on which light G"37" is placed has a finely shaped, 30-foot tree on its summit, so we call it "Christmas Tree Rock." Since ferryboats and cruise ships must pass very close to the rock, this is perhaps their most vulnerable spot.

## Papkes Landing (Mitkof Island)

Papkes Landing, on the east side of the narrows, is 0.25 mile north of Red Buoy "42."

Chart 17375
Position: 56°40.63′ N, 132°56.13′ W

> *Papkes Landing . . . is the site of a State-maintained small-craft float. . . . In 2002, the 100-foot-long float had a reported depth of 2 feet alongside. A lumber company bulkhead pier that runs dry at low water is close N of the float.*
>
> *The U.S. Forest Service maintains a log pond and rafting area just N of the pier.* (CP)

Papkes Landing has a public float used mainly as a dinghy dock. You may find temporary anchorage north of Papkes Landing, 0.70 mile north of Christmas Tree Rock.

Anchor in 5 fathoms, north of the skiffs and log boom storage area.

## Green Point Bight (Kupreanof Island)

Green Point is 0.4 mile north of Green Point.

Chart 17375
Anchor (0.24 mile northwest of light R"50"):
56°42.39′ N, 132°57.29′ W

> *From the light off Green Point the channel widens to almost the whole width of the narrows, and the water deepens to 15 to 20 fathoms.* (CP)

The currents generally meet just south of Green Point between lights R"44" and R"48." North of this point, Wrangell Narrows opens up for 5

## Haul-out Grids in Southeast Alaska

Q & A with Don Douglass

Don Douglass & Réanne Hemingway-Douglass

*Baidarka and Enetai on the perpendicular grid in Pelican.*

Linda Lewis

*Petersburg's parallel grid*

While cruising in Southeast Alaska you may need to get your boat out of the water for compelling reasons such as inspection or repairs. In larger places like Ketchikan or Sitka you will find the familiar travel lift. But in selected smaller towns your only option is something called a Tidal Haul-out Grid. Here are a few tips from Don Douglass on the use of these grids.

**Q:** *I have heard that the most likely way to get my boat out of the water in Southeast Alaska is by using a "Grid." What is that?*

**Don:** It's a series of carefully placed wooden beams (approx 6 x 6s placed about 6 feet apart) in the protected area of a harbor. At low tide these beams become exposed. You drive your boat onto this grid of beams at high tide; when the tide goes down, these beams become bare and you can inspect the boat or work on it.

**Q:** *Where can I find a grid?*

**Don:** Petersburg, Wrangell, Craig, Pelican, Elfin Cove and many other small coves. Don't look for them as much in the major ports; expect them in smaller towns where there are fishing vessels.

**Q:** *Can any boat be placed on a grid?*

**Don:** No! Grids are best used by boats with a flat keel—up to about 60 feet long. (Think: fishing vessels.) Sailing vessels or boats with fin or rounded keels risk tipping or damage. It can be done, but with great caution by someone who knows what they're doing. If in doubt, make local inquiries. If you are only changing a prop, you are better off hiring a diver.

**Q:** *I wonder if my boat is right for a grid.*

**Don:** Take pictures of your boat's bottom during your annual haul-out ... and carry the pictures with you. You'll be especially glad you did as you consider your careful placement on the grid. You need to know exactly what your keel looks like and whether anything (like a rudder) projects below your keel. You don't want your vessel

Linda Lewis

*Prop work on the grid in Petersburg*

Linda Lewis

*These keel configurations are what the grids were designed for.*

resting on your rudder. The flatter the "foot" of your keel, the more stable you will be on the grid.

**Q:** *Sounds tricky. Is anyone available to help me when I must do this?*

**Don:** You're pretty much on your own. Whenever you see a grid in use, watch carefully. Find someone to talk to who knows this particular grid. Ask questions; Alaska fishermen are very friendly.

**Q:** *Do you have to pay to use a grid?*

**Don:** They are usually free; might carry a nominal fee.

**Q:** *When I want to arrange to use a grid who do I talk to?*

**Don:** The harbormaster. There is usually a sign-up schedule—first come, first served. One tide cycle is usually the polite duration of stay.

**Q:** *OK. Here's the hard part: When and how do I drive onto the grid?*

**Don:** Considering your draft, go in at high tide when you will have about a 6- to 12-inch clearance. Grids have tide gauges posted, against which you can measure water depth. (Remember we have mixed-pattern tides on the West Coast.)

Pick the high tide carefully. Consider issues of current, spring/neap tides, and whether you will be leaving the grid in the dark. Make sure the exit tide will be as high or higher than when you went on the grid. Local weather or atmospheric conditions can change tide levels somewhat.

**Q:** *Can you give me more detail about driving onto the grid and securing my boat to it?*

**Don:** If the grid is perpendicular to the shore, just drive up onto it bow first. If the grid is parallel to the shore, make sure you check which end is for the bow and which for the stern; on some grids the beams are lower at one end than the other.

Have your lines and fenders in place. (Use sacrificial lines as the creosote on the pilings is very messy.) Remember your bottom configuration and position yourself accordingly. Be sure to span as many beams as possible to spread the weight of your vessel. Drive onto the grid until your cleats are more or less opposite the pilings and run your lines directly across (horizontal), then tie up securely. (The lines don't have to be super tight.)

**Q:** *A few more details, please. Is power available? And can I stay on my boat?*

**Don:** Make local inquiries. Power is not usually available; however you might be able to work something out with someone nearby. Yes, you can live aboard it if you wish. Be careful using the very steep ladders (vertical and slippery). Rig a line and bucket to lower and raise things you need to carry.

**Q:** *Can you tell me anything else to allay my anxieties?*

**Don:** It sounds scarier than it is! Take any opportunity to watch someone else doing it. Look at the grid timbers at low water when they are exposed. Carry your boat-bottom pictures with you. As the tide goes out or lifts you off you will be surprised how smooth the whole procedure is.

Linda Lewis

*Petersburg: Notice the tide gauge at the distant right and the very steep, slippery ladders along the left side.*

Réanne Hemingway-Douglass

*The Alaska Marine Highway (ferry) travelling south through Wrangell Narrows at R"42"*

miles before narrowing again a few miles south of the approach to Petersburg.

In severe fog, we have anchored overnight next to the west shore, north-northwest of light G"49," in 4 fathoms with good holding. Located on the north edge of South Flat, this site also makes a good lunch stop or a place to wait for the ebb to give you a free boost north.

Anchor in 4 fathoms over mud with good holding.

---

## Lessons from the Petersburg Birds

Linda Lewis—Journal Notes—
M/V *Royal Sounder*

I'm beginning to understand what the birds can teach me about the weather. The seagulls are thick on the roofs of the buildings here in Petersburg—all hunkered down, tucked in tight, solid and safe. They look like patches of tapioca pudding up there on the roofs. A big storm is coming and the birds are not flying. They're just waiting. Like us. I figure we must be doing the right thing.

Suddenly the winds come whistling through and I look back at the rooftops to see how the birds are reacting. What do I see? A gang of seagulls swirling and riding the wind. Dive-bombing. Doing wheelies. Rising on the gusts. (Just like some people I know.)

I realize that we are like these birds—living all out—tucking in and out of the winds. For me, that is the real lesson from the Petersburg birds.

---

### **Scow Bay** (Mitkof Island)

Scow Bay, on the east side of Wrangell Narrows, is 3 miles south of Petersburg.

Chart 17375
Position: 56°46.55′ N, 132°58.22′ W

> *Scow Bay, on the E side of Wrangell Narrows, is about 2 miles below Petersburg and immediately S of Blunt Point.* (CP)

### **Petersburg Creek** (Kupreanof Island)

Petersburg Creek enters the narrows from the west side opposite Turn Point.

Chart 17375
Entrance: 56°48.42′ N, 132°59.27′ W

> *Petersburg Creek . . . is navigable for small craft at high tide.* (CP)

Two sets of range markers near Petersburg Creek help guide you around this last corner to the town of Petersburg.

Réanne Hemingway-Douglass

*Spotting marker R"58" means you are nearing the north end of Wrangell Narrows.*

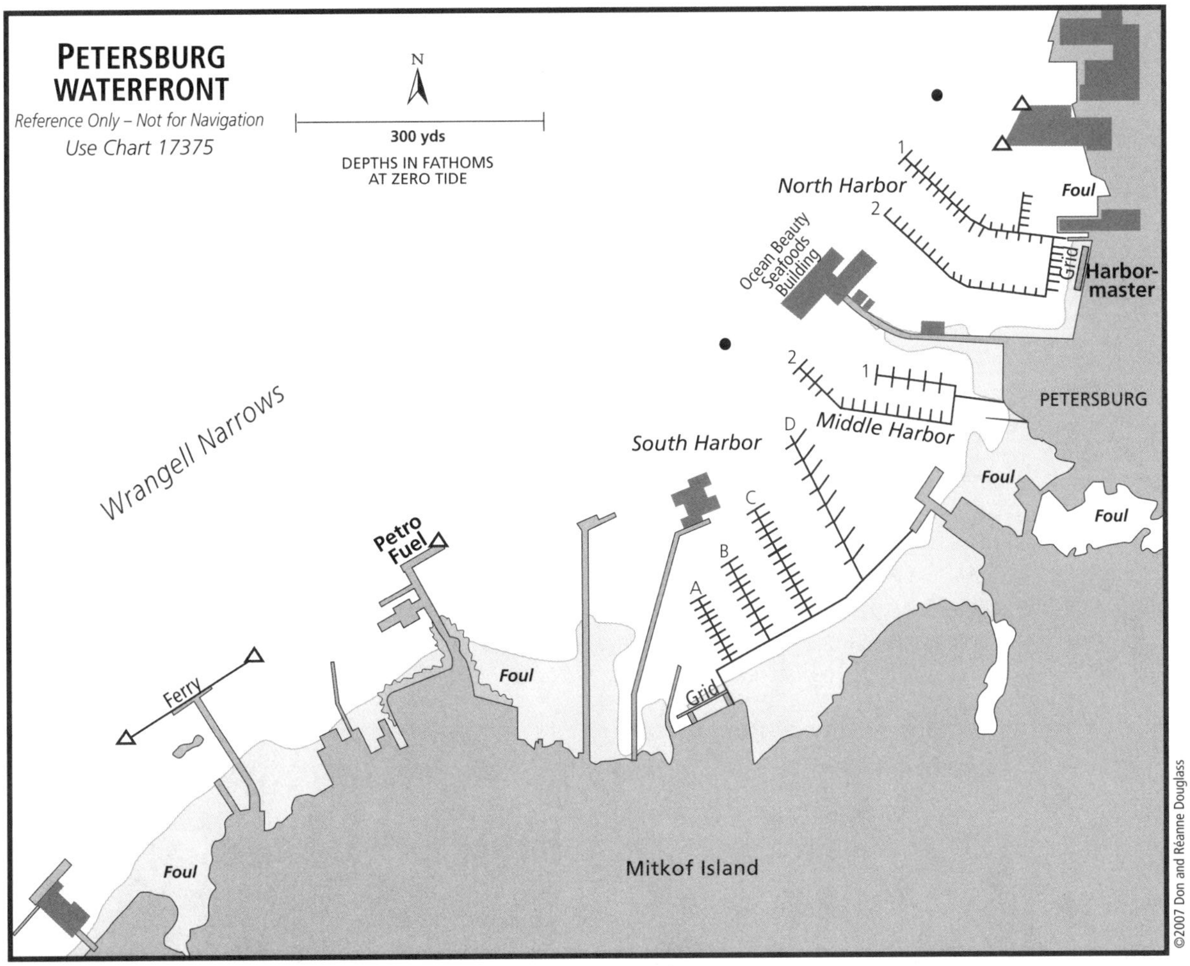


## **Petersburg** (Mitkof Island)

Petersburg is 1 mile inside the north entrance of Wrangell Narrows on the east side.

Chart 17375
North Harbor entrance: 56°48.84′ N, 132°57.79′ W
South Harbor entrance: 56°48.68′ N, 132°57.91′ W

> *Petersburg is the home port of over* [800] *fishing boats.*
>
> *Anchorages. The harbor affords excellent protection for small craft. Larger vessels may find protected anchorage 0.3 mile S of Scow Bay in 4 to 5 fathoms, mud bottom. . . The deepest draft of a commercial vessel calling at the port was 20 feet in 2003.*
>
> *The city of Petersburg operates a boat harbor immediately N of the Ocean Beauty Seafoods Wharf and two boat harbors immediately S of the* [Trident] *Seafoods Wharf.* (CP)

Petersburg (pop. about 3,500) has three boat harbors, which have been upgraded in the past few years, with moorage for transients located between the Petro Marine fuel dock and Trident Seafoods. They've added 100 new

*The Petersburg waterfront comes into sight after the last turn up Wrangell Narrows.*

## Petersburg

Don Douglass & Réanne Hemingway-Douglass

Named for its founder, Peter Buschmann, who built the first cannery and sawmill here in the late 1800s, clean, neatly laid-out Petersburg is famous for its Norwegian heritage. Because it lacks a deep-water port, large cruise ships do not call here, and the town has retained its friendly, unhurried atmosphere. Its popular Little Norway Festival, held the third weekend of May each year, draws locals and "outsiders" alike.

Known as the halibut capital of Alaska, Petersburg's economy depends on its fishing fleet and seafood processing plants—it is the major fish-processing center in Southeast Alaska. Plan to spend a few days here. Walk around the town and admire the brightly painted houses and the well-tended yards and gardens.

After you've done your marketing at Hammer and Wilken (and arranged for delivery of your groceries at the harbor) take the trail that leads downhill to town from the U.S. Forest Service building. The trail passes through muskeg, stunted pines and 100-foot-tall cedars and hemlock to a "peak" where you have a view of the snow-capped mountains across Frederick Sound—this is a real "photo op" hike. (But don't forget to wear boots!)

For further diversion, rent a bicycle and head south on Mitkof Highway, checking out additional hiking trails along the way; visit the shops that carry Norwegian sweaters and crafts; or spend an afternoon in the Clausen Memorial Museum, which features local history.

About 15 miles south of Petersburg, an observation blind that overlooks Blind Slough allows you to view one of the wintering areas of trumpeter swans, and if you arrive in April, you may be lucky enough to catch sight of these magnificent birds. Excursions to nearby Le Conte Glacier by boat or floatplane also can be arranged.

For further information about the harbor and the town, go to : ci.petersburg.ak.us/Harbor/ports.htm

Linda Lewis

*Petersburg is proud of its Norwegian heritage.*

Linda Lewis

*Petersburg's Norwegian Festival means parades and food and dancing.*

Linda Lewis

*The kids are a big part of the festivities.*

Mahina Expeditions

*Petersburg has an active commercial fishing fleet.*

Réanne Hemingway-Douglass

*South Harbor at Petersburg accommodates larger vessels.*

slips in South Harbor and now have a total of 750. There are toilets, water and power in all three harbors (South, Middle and North), but showers in North Harbor only. Power at South Harbor is 30, 50 and 100 amp; North Harbor is 30 amp only.

At the end of Wrangell Narrows, as you round the corner at Petersburg Creek, you will pass the Ferry dock and then the Petro Marine fuel dock. The first harbor you see is South Harbor (the floats are lettered A, B, C, D, south to north); next is Middle Harbor (floats are numbered 2, 1, south to north); then a good landmark: the complex of large, green Ocean Beauty Seafood buildings. To its immediate north is the North Harbor (floats are numbered 2, 1, south to north). On the immediate north side of North Harbor is the Trident Seafoods building. (North Harbor will be undergoing reconstruction in the coming years; anticipated completion is 2009.)

The harbormaster's office is located adjacent to North Harbor and is staffed 24 hours a day. Since all of the harbors are usually congested in summer months, the harbormaster suggests that you call on VHF Ch 16 at least 30 minutes before your arrival, then switch to Ch 9 to receive a mooring assignment. Despite crowded conditions, they do their best in Petersburg to find a place for pleasure boats, frequently by "hot berthing" (essentially, renting you the slip of a fisherman who is away). Current can be heavy in the outer harbors, so plan accordingly.

Water, telephone, garbage dumpster, waste oil disposal and showers are available at North Harbor. Propane can be purchased at Petersburg Bottled Gas (tel.: 907.772.4270; 8:30 a.m.–5:00 p.m.) at 3rd and Haugen Drive. Full repair services are available in town.

Linda Lewis

*View from harbormaster's office—North Harbor at Petersburg; large building in upper left is a good landmark.*

Réanne Hemingway-Douglass

*Cruise ship travelling west in Frederick Sound crosses the north entrance of Wrangell Narrows.*

(One year, we had *Baidarka*'s flux-gate compass properly adjusted after having exhausted other possibilities elsewhere.) A small-boat' 40 feet or less) tidal grid is located just beneath the harbormaster's office in North Harbor. A larger tidal grid is located at the south end of South Harbor. A travel lift, located south of the fuel dock, is also available.

Other services include Glacier Laundry (self-service open, Mon.–Sun.), located just a half-block from North Harbor; for groceries, The Trading Union, a block east of North Harbor. Hammer & Wilken, 14 blocks south of town, which has a larger selection, will pick you up and deliver your groceries to the dock—it's too far a walk to carry much more than one bag. The Trading Union, across from the grocery store, carries marine and hardware supplies.

In case you need to make a crew change, both the Alaska State Ferry and Alaska Airlines serve the town. FM station KFSK (91.1 MHz) gives public service announcements broadcasting to Southeast Central Alaska and it also has a service called "Muskeg Messages" for outlying areas that have no phones. Contact 907.772.3808 for information.

Search for a Wifi connection with your laptop and an area-owned service provider's sign-up screen may appear. You can purchase packets of time on this secured connection. (See Internet Resources in the Introduction of this book for a more complete explanation.) A likely location for picking up the signal is at the Northern Lights restaurant. The library in town also has computer time available via a sign-up process.

## Frederick Sound, East to West

Frederick Sound extends from the north outlet of the Stikine River west to Chatham Strait west of Kake.

Charts 17320, 17360

East entrance: Most vessels enter Frederick Sound via Wrangell Narrows.

West entrance (mid-channel between Kingsmill Point and Yasha Island): 56°53.95′ N, 134°29.06′ W

*Frederick Sound has its entrance from Chatham Strait between Kingsmill Point and Point Gardner and extends NE to The Brothers and Cape Fanshaw, at the entrance to Stephens Passage, and SE to Dry Strait, a high-water boat passage connecting it with the E end of Sumner Strait. The sound is open and clear of obstructions, and has few offshore dangers to navigation. The shores and islands of the sound are all high.*

*Strong flood and ebb currents were observed in the vicinity of Cape Fanshaw, Round Rock, and in the passage between Turnabout Island and Kupreanof Island. Standing waves were sometimes observed in the vicinity of Cape Fanshaw when strong winds shift rapidly from SE to N.*

*Glacial ice from Le Conte Bay is generally present in the E arm of Frederick Sound, and at times in large quantities. The ice generally follows the N shore of the sound as far as the entrance to Thomas Bay. Under certain conditions of wind and weather, ice may be expected as far as the Sukoi Islets, and it may also be found at Cape Strait and Turnabout Island. Occasionally a few stray pieces of ice work into Wrangell Narrows as far as Green Point, making navigation dangerous.*

*Yasha Island, about 3.5 miles SE of Point Gardner, is small, low, wooded, and surrounded by kelp to a distance of 200 yards. A rock with a depth of 1-3/4 fathoms over it is about 1 mile 318° from the N point of the island. A lighted buoy marks the NNW side of the rock.*

*Heavy tide rips will be found between Yasha Island and the buoy. These tide rips sometimes extend across to Point Gardner and along that shore E as far as Carroll Island, and are dangerous for small boats.* (CP)

The cold waters of Frederick Sound seem to attract humpback whales and orcas. We've seen them between Kake and Gambier Bay in sizes and numbers as great as those in Glacier Bay.

Frederick Sound and Stephens Passage, although less encumbered with logs and deadheads than the channels to the south, do have icebergs.

Glacier ice comes in all sizes and shapes, and like clouds, their shapes often resemble mammals, fish, birds, or ships. It's fun to observe them at close hand, but remember that since two-thirds of their mass lies below water,

Réanne Hemingway-Douglass

*These cruisers must have enjoyed the unusually calm waters they found in Frederick Sound.*

they are inherently unstable and subject to rolling without notice.

Le Conte Glacier, the southernmost tidewater glacier on the North American continent, is difficult to approach, and the bay is not recommended for cruising boats because its shallow and dangerous entrance bar typically is full of grounded and moving icebergs. However, if you're interested in visiting the glacier, guided tours are available from Petersburg or Wrangell. Le Conte Glacier is the source of floating ice in the southeast part of Frederick Sound, while Holkham Bay is the source of the ice floating in the central part of Stephens Passage. If you want to observe a non-tidal glacier, visit Thomas Bay and the flats off the face of Baird Glacier.

Between Petersburg and Juneau, with a few exceptions, you traverse an area that uses only small-scale Charts 17360 (1:217,828) and 17300 (1:209,978). You're on your own to find and explore the intimate gunkholes from Frederick Sound all the way up Lynn Canal to Skagway. Don't forget the added challenge of reduced visibility through the opaque water.

Réanne Hemingway-Douglass

*Hovercraft leaving Wrangell for a Stikine River trip*

Linda Lewis

*Glacier fields can be seen high above Frederick Sound.*

## Frederick Sound, East Section

### Stikine River

Stikine River flows northwest via Dry Strait 13 miles northwest of Wrangell Harbor.

Chart 17360
Position: (See Dry Strait north entrance below.)

*The Stikine River has its source in a small lake in British Columbia near 57°10'N., 128°00'W., and is about 200 miles long. It flows in a SW direction through glaciers and gorges; one of the latter, very narrow and about 30 miles long, is known as the Grand Canyon. The river freezes in the winter, and with the spring freshets the current builds up great force. The river is usually navigable from about May 1 to October 15. The highest water is generally in July. Vessels drawing 3 feet and less navigate the river to Telegraph Creek, B.C., about 143 miles above the mouth.*

*Stikine River empties by two mouths: one, the N channel, following the mainland W, enters the head of Frederick Sound; the other follows the mainland S and forms the only navigable entrance to the river. The N channel can be navigated only by small craft at high water. The S entrance has a least depth of about 2 feet at mean lower low water. The mean range of tide is about 11-1/2 feet, and the diurnal range is about*

Réanne Hemingway-Douglass

*The mighty Stikine drains snowfields and glaciers.*

*14 feet. The channel is from 0.2 to 0.5 mile wide. Tidal effects have been noted for a distance of about 17.4 miles above the mouth.* (CP)

The Stikine River, deep in the interior of British Columbia, flows northwest and south for 330 miles, finally entering the Pacific above Wrangell. Glacial effluent discolors the saltwater for many miles and creates strong ebb currents that mask much of the floods.

The river's name—a derivation of the Tlingit word meaning "Great River"—which it is!—has gone through many spelling adaptations (including that of John Muir's Stickeen).

## Dry Strait

Dry Strait, between Mitkof Island and the mainland, connects Sumner Strait to Frederick Sound.

Chart 17360

North entrance (0.25 mile northeast of green light "5" west of Dry Island):

56°38.45′ N, 132°36.63′ W

*Dry Strait, mostly bare at low water, affords passage for small craft at high water between the head of Sumner Strait and the head of Frederick Sound. It is extensively used by fishing boats and towboats operating between the towns of Wrangell and Petersburg. The channel requires local knowledge for safe navigation. Boats should attempt the passage only on the upper half of a rising tide. There are no abrupt changes in depth. The water is muddy at all times, and strong currents are experienced in places, 5 knots having been observed at times at Blaquiere Point.*

---

### Dry Strait—Good Judgment or Lack of Courage?

Don Douglass & Réanne Hemingway-Douglass

After a pleasant night anchored in Ideal Cove, we started a southbound passage of Dry Strait, but soon discovered that we lacked the courage to continue. Or had we acquired good judgment? We anchored quickly in 6 feet of water on the west side of Dry Island and launched the dinghy. The outboard wouldn't start and the current, flowing north at 3 knots, immediately carried us away. We barely managed to row back to *Baidarka. We* made a hasty decision—to turn back immediately.

The river is so opaque that we couldn't see a quarter-inch below its seething surface. Everything "disappeared" in the murky water—an oar, a hand—as if it were plunged into cement. Our echo sounder went nuts; bouncing off all the turbulence and changing densities, sending confusing messages about the depth. We wondered what the mud was doing to our prop and cooling system. Then we remembered what an old-timer had told us years earlier in Wrangell: If you get caught on a bar, just work the engine in reverse and forward many times until you dig a cradle in which the hull can sit, high and dry; failing that, your boat will lay over (in the current) and—when the tide and river meet at your gunnels—it will fill with water.

The mighty Stikine is a serious challenge, with strong fresh-water currents on the surface pushing and pulling you ever backwards. If exploring the Stikine really tempts you, we suggest contacting Stickeen Wilderness Adventures in Wrangell. The outfit has been guiding this type of expedition in the area for nearly two decades.

*The channel passes close E of Blaquiere Point and to the W of the small islet 0.9 mile N of the point. A light on the W shore, about 3.5 miles NW of the islet, marks the N end of the shoal water area through the strait.* (CP)

As mentioned previously, Dry Strait largely dries into a rippled 5-mile-long mud flat at 6 feet above zero tide. It is seldom used and then only by a few Wrangell locals who have intimate knowledge of the changing channels. Obviously it is *not* recommended for cruising boats.

## **Ideal Cove** (Mitkof Island)

Ideal Cove, on the south side of Frederick Sound, is 1.7 miles south of Coney Island and 13.8 miles southeast of Petersburg Harbor.

Chart 17360
Entrance: 56°40.35′ N, 132°38.03′ W
Anchor: 56°39.77′ N, 132°38.35′ W

*Ideal Cove . . .* [is] *1.2 miles S of Coney Island. . . . A well-defined rock awash is close to the E point of the entrance. A small islet is on the W side at the entrance.* (CP)

Réanne Hemingway-Douglass

*Approaching Le Conte Bay*

Ideal Cove is a wonderfully secluded anchorage far off the beaten path and an ideal place from which to explore Dry Strait (by dinghy) and Le Conte Bay.

Underwater visibility is limited due to glacial melt from the Stikine River.

Anchor in 6 fathoms over a mud bottom with good holding.

## **Le Conte Bay**

Le Conte Bay, on the north side of the head of Frederick Sound, is 15 miles southeast of Petersburg Harbor.

Chart 17377
Inner entrance (0.3 mile south of Indian Point): 56°44.66′ N, 132°31.81′ W
Outer entrance (3.3 mile west of Indian Point): 56°45.86′ N, 132°37.12′ W

*Le Conte Bay is entered from Frederick Sound through a very narrow passage just N of Stikine River flats. At the entrance, a reef that bares at low water extends from the N shore halfway across the passage.*

*Several groundings have occurred on this reef; extreme caution is advised. The bay is very shallow along its W edge from the mouth N to Timber Point. Boulders 1 to 3 meters in size are located in the narrow channel and are displaced about by ice bergs that sweep through the area. Strong currents have also been noted in this area.*

*Large icebergs from Le Conte Glacier are a menace to navigation from Camp Island to Frederick Point.* (CP)

Le Conte Bay and the Stikine River Delta are remote and rugged wilderness areas full of various kinds of water fowl: scoters, guillemots, mergansers, gulls and eagles. As the southernmost tidewater glacier in North America, Le Conte attracts special interest; however, its remoteness, difficult entrance and lack of navaids mean that it is seldom visited by cruising boats. The water is opaque, giving you no visual warning of depth or rocks.

We do not recommend it, except for expeditionary-type excursions. Tracy Arm, 60 miles to the north, is much easier to enter and has become the route of choice for cruising boaters who want to experience Alaska glaciers first hand.

A few years ago the entire face of Le Conte Glacier broke loose and the subsequent disintegration has made the approach to Le Conte Bay hazardous. The problem we found is this: you must favor the north shore to avoid the large drying mud flats that flow out of the Stikine River North Arm, while at the same time avoiding a line of rocks that extend from the north shore into the narrow, shallow channel for a few hundred yards about 1-3/4 miles west of Indian Point. It is important to identify and avoid this dike of rocks and the stationary icebergs—major obstacles!

We have found that the best time to approach the entrance bar is just after low water so you can identify the dike and rocks and have a rising tide for several hours if you should ground. At low water the bar can be plugged with grounded bergs. At the same time, a strong 3- to 5-knot flood current can put you and small bergie bits on a direct collision course with temporarily stranded, house-sized ice chunks, leaving you unsure of which side to pass. It is not unusual to see bergs 200 feet across, standing fast and several stories high while the small stuff crashes into them. You hear the bergs growling from all the contact and, needless to say, should avoid getting caught in between. (We have anchored here in the silt when we needed time to figure out exactly what to do.) We found the minimum depth in the fairway of the channel across the entrance bar to be between 3 and 4 fathoms just east of the south end of the rocky dike at about 56°44.70' N, 132°34.02' W. Once you reach deeper waters south of Indian Point, the current decreases and depths quickly drop to over 30 fathoms. A line of crab pots marks the 2-fathom lip of the Stikine delta in the direction of Camp Island; but beware, the mud flats on your south side are ever-changing and steep-to.

Réanne Hemingway-Douglass

*Ice on the Le Conte Bay bar*

## Brown Cove

Brown Cove, on the northeast side of Frederick Sound, is 7.1 miles northeast of Petersburg Harbor.

Chart 17360
Entrance: 56°53.23′ N, 132°48.83′ W

> *Brown Cove . . . affords indifferent anchorage in 11 to 12 fathoms at the entrance. The head of the cove bares at low water.* (CP)

## Sukoi Islets (Frederick Sound)

Sukoi Islets are 3.8 miles north of the entrance to Wrangell Narrows.

Chart 17360
Position: Sukoi Islet Light (brg 090°T at 0.25Nm): 56°53.76′ N, 132°57.12′ W

> *Sukoi Islets, locally known as Sockeye Islets, are two wooded islands, with a smaller one between. . . . The usual channel is W of the islets.* (CP)

## Thomas Bay

Thomas Bay, between Wood Point and Point Vandeput, is 12 miles north of Petersburg Harbor.

Charts 17367, 17360
Entrance (0.2 mile southwest of Buoy "2"): 56°59.09′ N, 132°58.24′ W

> *The entrance, marked by buoys, is about 10 miles N of the N entrance to Wrangell Narrows and 22 miles ESE of Cape Fanshaw. Good anchorage with protection from SE weather can be had off the S shore well inside Wood Point. Very good small-craft anchorage can be had in either of two small coves on the E shore of Ruth Island in depths of 3 to 10 fathoms, soft bottom.* (CP)

Réanne Hemingway-Douglass

*Icebergs make good vantage points for eagles.*

Thomas Bay, with Baird Glacier at its north end, is a classic example of an Alaskan fiord. Set at the foot of high snowy peaks, with glaciers towering above, this bay is well worth exploring. Like other fiords, the water, as you proceed to its head, changes from light green to a creamy, opaque color, with glacial silt that provides no through-water visibility. Ruth Island Cove, at the south end of the bay, which offers the best shelter, is a good base camp from which to do your exploring.

The entrance to Thomas Bay is narrow but well marked by buoys. Minimum depth over its bar is 5 fathoms, and the ebb current and turbulence can be strong for the first half-mile.

## **Bock Bight** (Thomas Bay)

Bock Bight is about 1.8 miles east of Wood Point.

Charts 17367, 17360
Position: 56°59.78′ N, 132°53.75′ W

> *Bock Bight . . . is a narrow and deep bight. The entrance to the bight is bare nearly 2 hours before low water, forming a dam with deep water inside that overflows with great force except at slack water.*
>
> *The NW entrance to the passage W of Ruth Island is shoal, but may be used by small vessels.* (CP)

Bock Bight brings a new meaning to the term "landlocked." (Perhaps "seaweed-locked" is a better term.) Although it might be worth fighting your way through for a bombproof anchorage, Ruth Island Cove is generally more convenient and easier to enter.

## **Ruth Island Cove** (Thomas Bay)

Ruth Island Cove is 5 miles east of the Thomas Bay entrance bar.

Charts 17367, 17360
Entrance: 56°58.71′ N, 132°48.73′ W
Anchor (Ruth Island Cove): 56°58.82′ N, 132°49.04′ W
Anchor (southern part of bay): 56°58.21′ N, 132°49.09′ W

Ruth Island Cove is the well-sheltered cove facing the drying mud flat formed by the terminal river of Patterson Glacier. The cove has little fetch so you can stay here protected from all but small chop. At times, williwaws from Patterson Glacier may funnel through the cove, but you can decrease the effects of

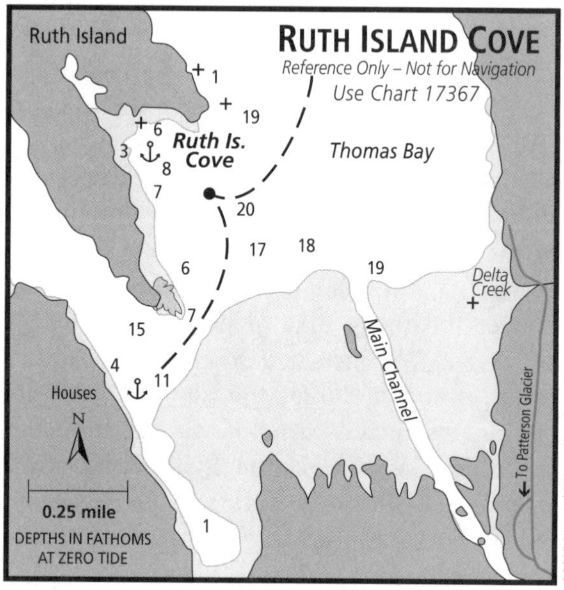

*This anchor check shows a mud bottom.*

these williwaws by anchoring farther south in the narrow channel that serves the houses in the southernmost part of the bay. (However, it has been reported that logging operations have been started up again in this location.) It may take a little longer to go around the east side of the island, but we find it easier and less congested with seaweed.

Off the easternmost tip of Ruth Island you must avoid a large drying rock just north of the cove. Although this cove is becoming a popular anchorage, it has enough room for several boats.

By kayak, we discovered that the main part of Patterson River now flows by the center islet, which has several small trees on it. Patterson Glacier has receded, and its snout cannot be seen from a boat.

Anchor in 7 fathoms over sand and mud with good holding.

## **Cascade Creek Bight** (Thomas Bay)

Spray Island Bight is 1.0 mile east of Ruth Island.

Charts 17367, 17360
North entrance: 57°00.32′ N, 132°47.80′ W

> *Anchorage for small boats may be had in 5 fathoms off the NW entrance of the passage between Ruth Island and the mainland. Anchorage for small vessels may be had in the bight E of Spray Island in 18 fathoms. The anchorage is close to the beach that is steep-to.* (CP)

You can explore the east shore of Cascade Creek Bight by following the overgrown skid road at Delta Creek, or take the waterfall trail at Cascade Creek. Some boats find temporary moorage on the red steel buoy or anchorage in the shallow bight off the cabin and beach at Cascade Creek.

The bottom is steep-to near shore, so a shore-tie may be a good idea when anchoring.

## **Scenery Cove** (Thomas Bay)

Scenery Cove is in the north part of Thomas Bay 7.5 miles from the entrance.

Charts 17367, 17360
Entrance: 57°04.63′ N, 132°49.24′ W
Anchor: 57°04.69′ N, 132°47.76′ W

> *Scenery Cove . . . does not afford anchorage except for small craft. Large vessels can anchor at the entrance to the cove in 7 to 15 fathoms.* (CP)

We have not been able to locate the anchor site mentioned in *Coast Pilot* at the entrance to Scenery Cove. All we've found is a small, 9-fathom rocky patch; however, we have anchored temporarily at the head of the cove off the steep drying beach. This truly scenic cove is a good place to wait while a shore party explores the base of Baird Glacier.

Anchor at the head of Scenery Cove with due regard for tide level and holding power. Maintain an anchor watch and remain in radio contact with any crew that go ashore. We did not record the bottom.

Anchor in 10 to 15 fathoms.

## Baird Glacier Mud Flats (Thomas Bay)

Baird Glacier mud flats are 8 miles from the entrance to Thomas Bay.

**Charts 17367, 17360**
**Position: 57°05.50′ N, 132°49.58′ W**

> *The moraine of Baird Glacier was reported to have encroached to a point about 900 yards S of Elephants Head in 1976.* (CP)

The glacier has retreated much farther north during the last of the twentieth century. It is a good long hike to the pool at the snout of Baird Glacier, but a rewarding one. It can be dangerous traversing the ice cold and rapidly flowing river that shoots under the glacier snout and erupts from the pool like a geyser. It is best to have someone drop you off since there is no place to store the dinghy.

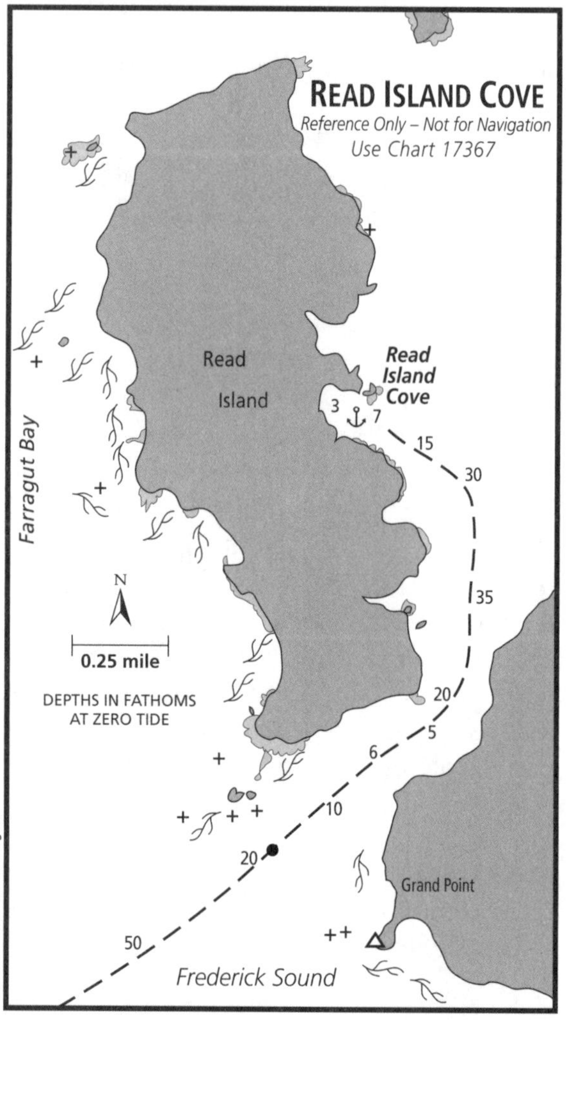




## Farragut Bay

Farragut Bay is 20 miles northwest of Petersburg.

**Charts 17367, 17360**
**Entrance: 57°05.95′ N, 133°14.87′ W**

> *The entrance, between Grand Point and Bay Point, is about 20 miles NW of the N entrance to Wrangell Narrows and 12 miles ESE of Cape Fanshaw.*
>
> *Read Island is just inside the entrance on the E side of Farragut Bay. A very narrow passage, which may be used by small craft, and with reported depths of 4 fathoms, leads between the island and Grand Point.*
>
> *A small vessel can make a temporary fair-weather anchorage between Grand Point and the S end of Read Island in 5 to 6 fathoms, hard bottom. Of the four coves or indentations making into the E side of Read Island, the third, leading N, is reported to provide the best anchorage for small vessels in 3 to 5 fathoms, rocky bottom.* (CP)

The third cove north on Read Island is said to offer the best protection; however, the bottom along the shoreline is rocky, so holding is variable and requires that you set your anchor well.

## Read Island Cove (Farragut Bay)

Read Island Cove is 1.3 miles north of Grand Point Light.

**Charts 17367, 17360**
**South entrance: 57°05.64′ N, 133°11.57′ W**
**North entrance: 57°08.11′ N, 133°10.38′ W**
**Anchor: 57°06.76′ N, 133°11.20′ W**

We have found the second cove on the east side of Read Island quite comfortable and its south entrance easily accessible.

Anchor in 4 fathoms over a mixed bottom of sand and rocks with fair holding.

## Francis Anchorage (Farragut Bay)

Francis Anchorage is north of Read Island.

**Charts 17367, 17360**
**Entrance: 57°08.58′ N, 133°11.08′ W**
**Anchor: 57°08.65′ N, 133°08.10′ W**

> *Farragut Bay has two arms. The E arm expands into a large bay known as Francis Anchorage.*

*SE winds are reported to draw through the anchorage with velocities up to 60 mph. Small craft may find anchorage with adequate protection in close to the E shore, just N of the projecting point, in 4 to 5 fathoms. The extensive tidal flats at the head of the bay were reported to be encroaching in 1976.* (CP)

Francis Anchorage is too deep for cruising boats and may be subject to blasts of williwaws. We have not explored the eastern part, which may provide interesting anchorage if the shoal water permits access.

*Making friends with reclusive fishermen is an art.*

## **Portage Bay** (Kupreanof Island)

Portage Bay, on the north side of Kupreanof Island, is 7 miles west of Cape Strait, 13 miles southeast of Cape Fanshaw, and 17 miles northwest of Petersburg Harbor.

Charts 17367, 17360
Entrance: 57°01.11′ N, 133°19.55′ W
Anchor north (0.15 mile southeast of East Point): 57°00.15′ N, 133°19.37′ W
Anchor south (0.9 mile northwest of Stop Island): 56°58.09′ N, 133°18.20′ W

*Portage Bay . . . is a secure anchorage, but its entrance is narrow. The tidal currents in the entrance have considerable velocity at spring tides. Ice forms in the bay during extreme cold weather.*

*The entrance channel has a controlling depth of 3-1/2 fathoms, but is constricted by shoals to a width of 150 yards. Shoals make out from the shores of the bay and also from the head to 0.8 mile N of Stop Island.*

*High-water slack is the best time to enter Portage Bay. Small boats have used the grass line of East Point, Hook Point, and a small hill in the background as an entrance range. Round East Point about 200 yards off and follow midchannel courses.*

*Anchor in 4 to 6 fathoms from 1 to 1.5 miles NNW of Stop Island. The water shoals gradually toward the shore; there are no dangers outside the 3-fathom curve.* (CP)

Portage Bay, located on the main route of the Inside Passage, makes a convenient stopover. The large bay has a feature that's hard to find as you go north—acres and acres of good, shallow holding ground with unlimited swinging room.

In stable weather, it's not necessary to go farther than the anchor site shown in the diagram, 0.35 mile due south of East Point Light, where you can find good shelter from prevailing winds. At times, however, the wind may whistle through the large U-shaped valley at the head of Portage Bay, and if this happens, you can minimize fetch by anchoring deep in the bay as close to Harrington Rock and Stop Island as safety allows.

The entrance to Portage Bay is restricted, with wide shoals on either side. We advise a mid-channel course. Minimum depth is about 3 fathoms. From outside, head due south for the East Point light, then pass midway between West Point and East Point navigational aids before turning south into the bay. Both sides of the bay dry, so stay near the center.

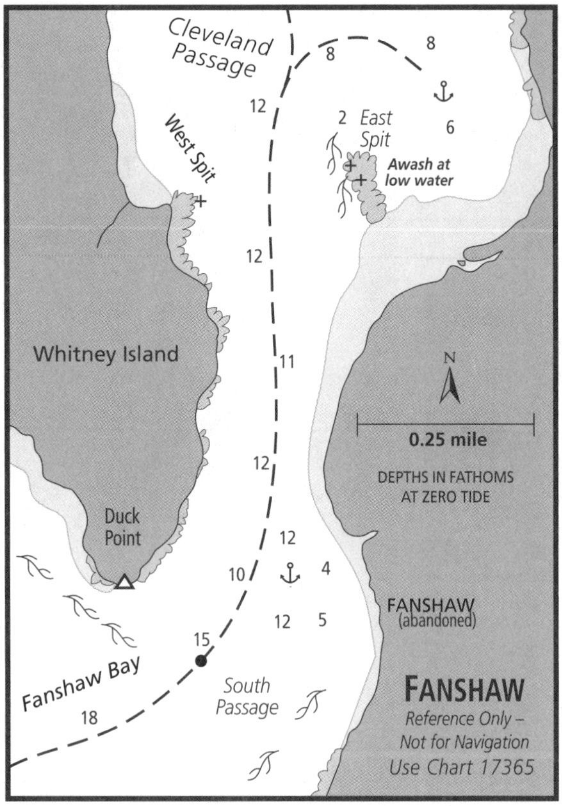




Anchor (East Point) in 6 fathoms over mud and rock with good holding.

Anchor (Stop Island) in 3 fathoms over mud and sand with good holding. Some boaters have reported difficulty anchoring in Portage Bay due to newspaper kelp.

## Cape Fanshaw

Cape Fanshaw, on the east side of the junction of Stephens Passage and Frederick Sound, is 30 miles northwest of Petersburg.

Charts 17365, 17360
Position: Cape Fanshaw Light (brg 090°T at 0.50 Nm): 57°11.12′ N, 133°35.38′ W

> *Cape Fanshaw . . . is a long, low, wooded point terminating in a sandspit, with a reef and rocks at the extreme end and deep water within 0.2 mile.* (CP)

Give Cape Fanshaw a wide berth—turbulent, shoal water extends over 600 yards off the light on the point.

## Fanshaw Bay (Cleveland Passage)

Fanshaw Bay is on the northeast side of Cape Fanshaw.

Charts 17365, 17360
Entrance (0.9 mile northwest of Cape Fanshaw): 57°11.93′ N, 133°35.19′ W
Anchor (south bay): 57°12.23′ N, 133°31.25′ W

> *Fanshaw Bay . . . is connected with Cleveland Passage by South Passage. Anchorage can be made in the SE side of the head, about 600 yards offshore and 0.5 mile SW of Whitney Island in 12 to 15 fathoms, sand and shell bottom, sheltered from NE and SE winds.* (CP)

## Cleveland Passage

Cleveland Passage separates Whitney Island from the mainland.

Chart 17365
South entrance: 57°12.49′ N, 133°30.83′ W
North entrance: 57°15.24′ N, 133°32.03′ W
Anchor (0.8 mile east of Duck Point Light): 57°12.69′ N, 133°30.50′ W
Anchor (East Spit): 57°13.39′ N, 133°30.20′ W

> *Cleveland Passage . . . is 0.5 mile wide and affords good anchorage near its SE end. The depths vary from 8 fathoms at its SE end to over 70 fathoms at the NW end. A rocky shoal, covered 1-1/4 fathoms, is reported about 250 yards off the W shore of the passage about 0.9 mile N of Duck Point. The anchorage is about 0.8 mile N of the narrowest part of South Passage, favoring the E shore, in 12 to 20 fathoms, soft bottom; take care to keep clear of East Spit. Small craft find anchorage in 4 to 8 fathoms E and N of East Spit. . . .*
>
> *Small boats can find anchorage E of Duck Point close to the mainland in 10 to 12 fathoms with protection from NE and SE blows.*
>
> *The tidal currents have a velocity of 1 to 2 knots in South Passage.* (CP)

You can extend your smooth-water route a few additional miles by using the very pleasant Cleveland Passage, which is straightforward and has two possible very nice anchor sites that afford fair-to-good protection depending on wind conditions.

Anchorage can be taken off the abandoned Fanshaw site east of Duck Point with protection from southeast and northeast winds.

Anchorage can be taken east of East Spit, 0.65 mile north of the Fanshaw site, with good protection in southeast weather and in prevailing weather. There will be some afternoon chop from the north. It is a short walk south to an old abandoned fox farm.

Anchor (south bay) in 10 fathoms over a soft bottom with good holding.

Anchor (East Spit) in 6 fathoms over a hard bottom with fair holding.

*Afternoon winds often bring chop.*

## Steamboat Bay

Steamboat Bay is 1 mile northeast of Whitney Island and has Foot Island on its north side.

Chart 17365
South entrance: 57°16.12′ N, 133°32.09′ W
North entrance (0.1 mile southwest of Ford Point): 57°16.70′ N, 133°31.71′ W

> *Steamboat Bay . . . has generally deep water except for a reef that uncovers, about 400 yards N of McNairy Point, and has an advantage as an anchorage near Cleveland Passage. . . . The narrow passage on the NE side of Foot Island might afford shelter to small craft in 7 to 10 fathoms, abreast the middle of the island.* (CP)

Steamboat Bay is exposed to westerly chop, so we prefer to anchor east of Foot Island. *Note:* Use the north entrance to avoid crossing the drying sandspit that connects to Foot Island.

Anchor in 7 fathoms over sand with good holding.

## Surprise Harbor (Admiralty Island)

Surprise Harbor, just east of Point Gardner, is on the southernmost extremity of Admiralty Island.

Chart 17336
Entrance: 57°00.30′ N, 134°35.21′ W

> *To enter* [Surprise Harbor}, *keep from 0.2 to 0.5 mile off the W shore, using caution and avoiding kelp. Anchor about midharbor in 7 fathoms, rocky bottom.* (CP)

Surprise Harbor is open to the south. It has much kelp and is not a good anchorage. It is, however, a good lee when the wind is blowing strong down Chatham Strait.

We prefer Murder Cove (Tyee) when the winds are blowing.

## Murder Cove (Admiralty Island)

Murder Cove is 1.5 miles northeast of Surprise Harbor.

Chart 17336
Entrance: 57°00.70′ N, 134°33.32′ W
Anchor: 57°02.82′ N, 134°32.69′ W

> *Murder Cove has its entrance between Bartlett Point and Walker Point, 2 miles E of Point Gardner. The channel narrows to 300 yards 0.4 mile inside the entrance, between a bare ledge on the E and two rocks, each with a clump of scrub, on the W. Above this point the channel has a width of about 200 yards between kelp-marked ledges, and it is best to enter at low water when the dangers show. The tide rips are sometimes heavy across the entrance when the wind is strong against the current.*
>
> *Fair anchorage, unprotected from SE winds, is in midchannel, in 8 to 11 fathoms, off the cannery site.* (CP)

We have found fair protection from all weather farther in off the new building in the cove at

*Whale sounding close to the boat*

the head of the narrow channel. Avoid all kelp patches, which mark rocks and reefs.

Anchor in about 5 fathoms over sand and mud with fair-to-good holding.

## **Rod's Cove** (Admiralty Island)

Chart 17320
Entrance: 57°01.99′ N, 134°28.42′ W
Anchor: 57°01.89′ N, 134°29.27′ W

> *Carroll Island, on the N side of Frederick Sound is a small island 4. 5 miles E of Point Gardner Light. The island is conspicuous, but appears as a point of the main shore.* (CP)

Roderick Nash told us of a small, snug anchorage behind Carroll Island, so we call it "Rod's Cove." We have found Rod's Cove a very pleasant place—quiet and intimate—for a temporary or overnight stop in fair weather. It provides strategic shelter and a place to wait for better conditions at the confluence of Chatham Strait and Frederick Sound. In serious weather, swells may enter the cove from the southeast.

At a distance, from any direction, Carroll Island appears as a peninsula. However, there is a 100-foot-wide channel on the north side of Carroll Island that connects to the small cove to the northwest. A narrow, unnamed island to the south provides additional protection. Entry is from the east, north of Carroll Island. It's a quiet anchorage and a good place to explore by dinghy.

Anchor in 3 fathoms over a sand bottom, shells with some kelp; good holding.

## **Herring Bay** (Admiralty Island)

Herring Bay is 10 miles northeast of Point Gardner Light.

Charts 17336, 17320
Entrance (0.50 mile east of Brightman Point): 57°05.91′ N, 134°21.38′ W
Anchor (200 yards off the drying mud flat): 57°06.52′ N, 134°23.81′ W

> *Herring Bay . . . has its entrance between Point Brightman and the point to the N that separates Herring Bay from Chapin Bay. A tongue of land, prolonged by rocks, reefs, and kelp patches, extends in a SE direction from the bay, dividing it centrally into two parts.*
>
> *A rock awash is about 225 yards W of the charted 3-fathom shoal in the middle of the NE arm of the bay.*
>
> *There is a fair anchorage, open to the SE, in the SW corner of the bay, about 0.8 mile from the head. To make this anchorage, follow the S shore at a distance of about 0.4 mile, the chart being the guide.* (CP)

Herring Bay provides quite easy-to-get-to anchorage in fair weather. Chapin Bay offers better protection.

Anchor in 4 fathoms over mud and pebbles with good holding if the anchor is well set.

## **Chapin Bay** (Admiralty Island)

Chapin Bay is on the north side of Frederick Sound, 12.4 miles northeast of Point Gardner.

Charts 17336, 17320
Entrance: 57°07.75′ N, 134°18.64′ W
Anchor: 57°08.91′ N, 134°20.41′ W

> *Chapin Bay is a small inlet . . . affording secure anchorage in 9 to 11 fathoms, sandy bottom.*

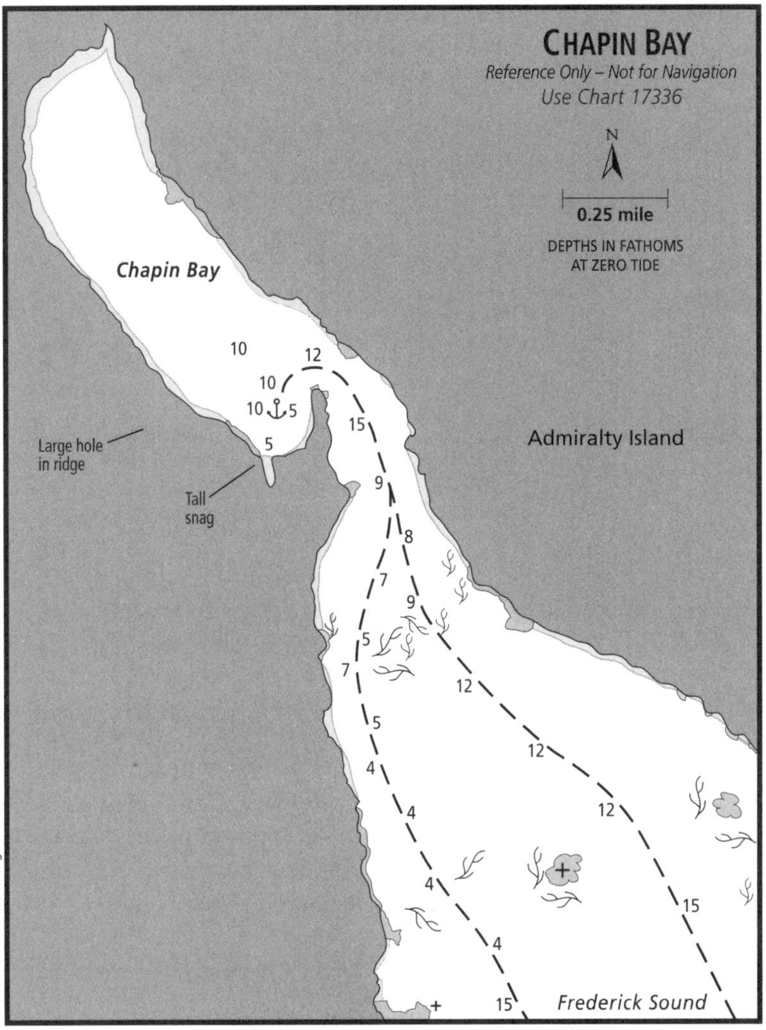


*A reef, marked by kelp, with a least depth of 1.8 fathoms in 57°07′47″N, 134°19′09″W, is 0.6 mile NE from the W point at the entrance. A ledge, bare at half tide, is 330 yards SW from the N point at the entrance, and kelp shows about 400 yards S of the ledge. There is also kelp in the middle of the channel, about 0.8 mile inside the entrance, and a shoal extends 150 yards E from the point on the W side of the S entrance to the narrows.*

*It is safest to enter Chapin Bay at low water. Enter about 400 yards SW of the half-tide ledge off the N point at the entrance and keep the N shore aboard at a distance of 200 yards until in the narrows. A midchannel course leads safely to the anchorage in the basin above the narrows.* (CP)

Chapin Bay is little used for log storage now and you may well see grizzlies along the shore north of the narrows. Avoid the reefs at the entrance. Good protection is found in the lee of the narrows spit.

Anchor in 9 fathoms over sand with good holding.

## Woewodski Harbor

(Admiralty Island)

Woewodski Harbor lies between Liesnoi Island and Deepwater Point.

Chart 17365
Entrance: 57°09.99′ N, 134°14.43′ W
Anchor (shallow draft vessels 0.5 mile west of Jaw Point): 57°10.17′ N, 134°15.90′ W

*Ledges and rocks, covered or awash at various stages of the tide and generally marked by kelp, extend NE from Liesnoi Island halfway across Woewodski Harbor. . . . Small vessels find temporary shelter off Bluff Point in 6 fathoms, and S of Polivnoi Rocks in 3 to 6 fathoms, soft bottom.* (CP)

Woewodski Harbor is not considered well sheltered; however, we like to anchor on the large shallow shelf between Jaw and Log points on Liesnoi Island. This avoids the currents of South Passage in Eliza Harbor. When entering, avoid the rocky patches marked by kelp. North Passage is passable but has strong currents on spring tides.

Anchor in 2 fathoms over sand, mud, pebbles and isolated rocks with fair-to-good holding.

## Eliza Harbor (Admiralty Island)

Eliza Harbor is 10 miles south of Pybus Bay.

Chart 17365
Entrance (0.4 mile south of Pin Point): 57°09.11′ N, 134°15.81′ W
Anchor (0.4 mile west of Saw Point): 57°09.51′ N, 134°17.84′ W

*Eliza Harbor is a deep inlet with generally bold shores. The only available anchorage is at the S end of the harbor, off the W side of Liesnoi Island in depths of 18 to 20 fathoms. On each side of Liesnoi Island are narrow passages called North and South Passage, leading to Eliza Harbor.*

*South Passage . . . is reduced by submerged rocks at its narrowest part to a width of 70 yards, has a sharp turn and strong tidal currents, and should not be attempted except at slack water and with local knowledge. The rocks are marked by kelp, which, however, does not show when the current is running. In N winds, an indifferent anchorage may be had in the entrance to South Passage in 6-3/4 fathoms. . . .* (CP)

Eliza Harbor is calm once past the shallow narrows off Saw Point. Strong currents flow through South Passage during spring tides, and transit during slack water is advised. Avoid the mid-channel reef extending out from Saw Point in South Passage by favoring the north shore. Avoid a mid-channel reef south of Thumb Point shown on Chart 17365.

North Passage has about a 3-knot current on flood. Favor the north shore to avoid mid-channel shoals along the south shore.

Protection can be found from wind and chop 0.4 mile west of Saw Point; however, getting a good anchor set is problematical. Grizzly bears can be seen roaming the western shore.

Anchor in about 7 fathoms over hard rocky bottom with newspaper kelp. Very poor holding unless your anchor is well set through the kelp.

## Little Pybus Bay
(Admiralty Island)

Little Pybus Bay is 3 miles south of Pybus Bay.

**Chart 17363**
**Entrance: 57°12.74′ N, 134°08.30′ W**

*Little Pybus Bay . . . is about 2.5 miles long and 1 mile wide at the entrance, and is open to the S. . . . Shoal water, with several islets and rocks, extends about 1.2 miles from the head of the bay.* (CP)

Little Pybus Bay is largely foul at its north end; however, small craft can find temporary anchorage in a narrow channel on its west shore. Pybus Bay offers better shelter.

## Pybus Bay (Admiralty Island)

Pybus Bay is 12 miles northeast of Chapin Bay and 12 miles southwest of Gambier Bay.

**Chart 17363**
**South entrance (1 mile north of Spruce Island): 57°13.87′ N, 134°05.00′ W**

*Pybus Bay is . . . about 3.5 miles WNW of Round Rock Light. . . . . The best anchorage in the bay is in Cannery Cove. Good anchorage is also available in the northeastern half of Pybus Bay between the San Juan Islands and Admiralty Island in 14 to 18 fathoms of water.* (CP)

Entrance to Pybus Bay is made through West Channel, between Grave Island Light and Elliott Island. Favor the western shore once you've cleared the reef extending 0.4 mile north of the light. Avoid the reef 0.74 mile due south of the light, and the rock and shoals one-half mile

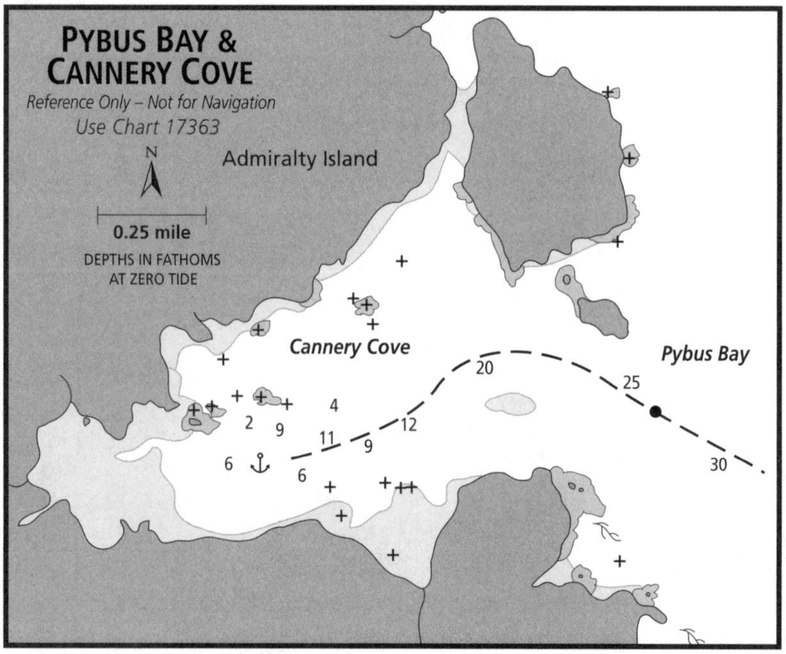

southeast of the south spit of Elliott Island.

Pybus Bay is well protected by all the islets at its entrance. You have three good coves to anchor in. The inner basin contains Sheldon Cove, one of our favorite coves.

*A playful bear in Cannery Cove puts on a real show.*

## Cannery Cove (Pybus Bay)

Cannery Cove, on the west shore of Pybus Bay, is 3.5 miles northwest of Elliott Island.

Chart 17363
Entrance: 57°18.51′ N, 134°07.38′ W
Anchor: 57°18.34′ N, 134°09.26′ W

> *The cove is nearly landlocked and affords secure anchorage in 6 to 15 fathoms, sticky bottom. A large island with an islet close to the S forms the N point at the entrance. A rock with 1⁄4 fathom over it is in the middle of the entrance.* (CP)

Cannery Cove, named after the cannery formerly located here, provides good protection from all weather and is one of the best anchorages in this part of Frederick Sound. At this site, locals say they can't wait to set their crab pots, anchor and let down a halibut line. (Chapin Bay, 12 miles to the southwest, is another well-protected anchorage in southerlies, as is Snug Cove 10 miles north.)

Access to Cannery Cove is easy; however, avoid the 1⁄4-fathom rock on the south side of the entrance.

Anchor in 8 fathoms over sticky mud with good holding.

## Donkey Bay (Pybus Bay)

Donkey Bay is on the west side of Pybus Bay and 1.8 miles north of Cannery Cove.

Chart 17363
Entrance: 57°20.41′ N, 134°08.81′ W

> *Donkey Bay . . . is an open bight that bares in its W part and is of no importance to navigation.*
>
> *Henrys Arm, the southernmost of the two coves opposite Donkey Bay, has depths of 1-1/4 to 6-3/4 fathoms.*
>
> *The channel between Point Pybus and the San Juan Islands is not recommended except for small craft with local knowledge.* (CP)

The southwest corner of Donkey Bay, called Sheldon Cove, is useful for small craft.

## Sheldon Cove (Donkey Bay)

Sheldon Cove is the southwest corner of Donkey Bay.

Chart 17363
Entrance: 57°20.08′ N, 134°09.57′ W
Anchor (inner basin): 57°19.98′ N, 134°09.85′ W

Sheldon Cove is the tiny 5-fathom anchor hole deep in Donkey Bay. It is suitable only for small craft (less than 40 feet). You can't beat this for a small intimate setting with lots of islets to explore.

Anchor in the corner off the 6-fathom hole.

## Henry's Arm

Henry's Arm is across Pybus Bay and opposite Donkey Bay.

Chart 17363
Entrance: 57°20.15′ N, 134°07.23′ W
Anchor: 57°20.78′ N, 134°06.44′ W

If Sheldon Cove is too small, try Henry's Arm, which is well sheltered with much more swinging room.

Anchor in 8 fathoms over mud and sand with good holding.

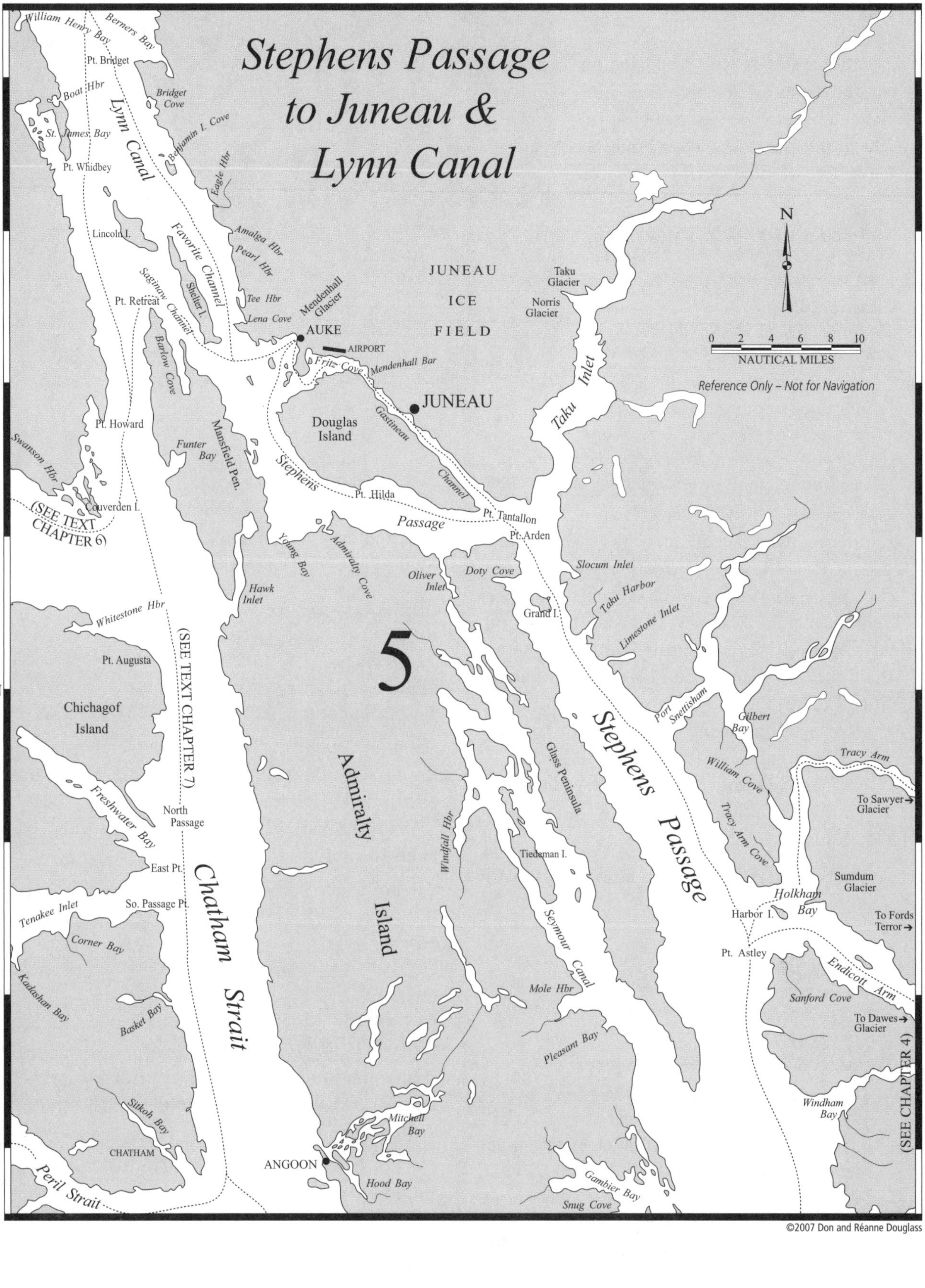
Stephens Passage
to Juneau &
Lynn Canal
N
0 2 4 6 8 10
NAUTICAL MILES
Reference Only – Not for Navigation
40'
30'
20'
10'
58°N
50'
40'
30'
William Henry Bay
Berners Bay
Pt. Bridget
Bridget Cove
Boat Hbr
St. James Bay
Benjamin I. Cove
Lynn Canal
Pt. Whidbey
Eagle Hbr
Lincoln I.
Favorite Channel
Amalga Hbr
Pearl Hbr
Saginaw Channel
Shelter I.
Tee Hbr
Pt. Retreat
Mendenhall Glacier
Lena Cove
AUKE
AIRPORT
Barlow Cove
Fritz Cove
Mendenhall Bar
JUNEAU
ICE
FIELD
Taku Glacier
Norris Glacier
JUNEAU
Douglas Island
Gastineau Channel
Pt. Howard
Funter Bay
Mansfield Pen.
Swanson Hbr
Stephens
Pt. Hilda
Couverden I.
(SEE TEXT CHAPTER 6)
Passage
Pt. Tantallon
Pt. Arden
Taku Inlet
Young Bay
Admiralty Cove
Hawk Inlet
Oliver Inlet
Doty Cove
Slocum Inlet
Taku Harbor
Grand I.
Limestone Inlet
Whitestone Hbr
(SEE TEXT CHAPTER 7)
Pt. Augusta
5
Chichagof Island
Port Snettisham
Gilbert Bay
Stephens Passage
Glass Peninsula
Tracy Arm
William Cove
To Sawyer Glacier
Admiralty Island
Freshwater Bay
North Passage
Windfall Hbr
Tracy Arm Cove
East Pt.
Tiedeman I.
Chatham Strait
Sumdum Glacier
Tenakee Inlet
So. Passage Pt.
Holkham Bay
Harbor I.
Seymour Canal
To Fords Terror
Corner Bay
Pt. Astley
Endicott Arm
Kadashan Bay
Mole Hbr
Sanford Cove
Basket Bay
To Dawes Glacier
Pleasant Bay
(SEE CHAPTER 4)
Windham Bay
Sitkoh Bay
Mitchell Bay
CHATHAM
ANGOON
Peril Strait
Hood Bay
Gambier Bay
Snug Cove

# 5

# STEPHENS PASSAGE, PORT HOUGHTON AND GAMBIER BAY TO JUNEAU AND LYNN CANAL SOUTH

## INTRODUCTION

The eastern portion of Stephens Passage gives you your first taste of the ABC islands (Admiralty, Baranof, Chichagof), where the great brown bear (grizzly) often appears along shore hunting for migrating salmon. These waters attract large numbers of humpback whales and orcas and, in summer, you can frequently catch some wonderful "exhibitions." Be aware, also, that in Stephens Passage you may encounter icebergs and "bergie bits," whose source is the glaciers in Tracy and Endicott arms.

One of the more exciting experiences in Southeast is navigating ice-choked waters and watching tidewater glaciers calve. Tracy and Endicott arms have outstanding tidewater glaciers that crack, dropping huge chunks of ice into the saltwater off their snouts; it's a thrill to see these primal forces at work. The glaciers of Holkham Bay and the narrow, deep-sided fiord at Fords Terror are second-to-none for their beauty and ease of access. Some boaters prefer these glaciers to those of Glacier Bay and, unlike the National Park and Preserve, Tracy Arm and Endicott Arm have, as yet, no controls for pleasure boaters regarding entry. However, because the area is not patrolled and there is little radio reception, you're on your own here. Please navigate safely and cautiously so all boaters can continue to enjoy this freedom.

The massive Juneau Ice Field, at the north end of Stephens Passage, marks the beginning of Lynn Canal, one of the longest fiords on the

Réanne Hemingway-Douglass

*The* Maple Leaf *about to pass* Baidarka *in Stephen's Passage*

North American continent. While this huge fiord has no tidewater glaciers, it does have magnificent hanging glaciers along the passage to Skagway.

Juneau, Alaska's state capital and second largest city, has one of the loveliest settings of any of the 50 state capitals. Built along a narrow strip of land at the foot of the stunning snow-capped Coast Range, the capital can be reached only by air and sea. The waterfront, which has been extensively renovated, makes a lasting first impression after visiting smaller ports of call. First-class art galleries, shops, restaurants, and an attractive downtown historic district are a real treat for the visitor. Cruise ship passengers dock in Juneau during the summer. Juneau is home to the State Legislature and hosts the Alaska State Museum, the six-story Capitol built in 1930, and the Governor's Mansion. Numerous attractive totems are scattered throughout this city, some of the more notable are the Four-Story Totem on Seward Street outside the Juneau-Douglas City Museum; the Friendship Pole in the lobby of the Court Building; and the Governor's Totem Pole in front of the Governor's Mansion.

For pleasure craft, the disadvantage in visiting Juneau is that the city receives more than half a million tourists who arrive by cruise ship during the summer season.

If you plan to moor in downtown Juneau, take Gastineau Channel to Harris Harbor or Aurora Basin. You can also find moorage at the upgraded Douglas Harbor facilities south and west of town or at the larger public floats located at Statter Harbor in Auke Bay, north of the city.

From Juneau, the recommended route to Auke Bay for cruising vessels leads south to Stephens Passage, then north via the west side of Douglas Island.

Mendenhall Bar is a mud flat that extends essentially from Aurora Basin northwest to Fritz Cove, south of Auke Bay. Only small, shallow-draft vessels with expert local knowledge should attempt transit of the bar. We *do not recommend* its use by cruising boats.

Although Lynn Canal is a popular area for salmon fishing and its waters are frequently quite benign, the seas can quickly reach alarming proportions under certain winds and currents. In cases like this, you should have an alternative plan ready and seek shelter quickly in a small cove en route. Vanderbilt Reef—11 miles north of Point Retreat Lighthouse—is the site of Alaska's own *Titanic* story. In 1918, 350 passengers lost their lives during a fierce storm that precipitated the Inside Passage's worst maritime disaster. The reputation of Canadian Pacific's coastal service was forever tarnished with the wreck of the steamship *Princess Sophia.*

## Stephens Passage

Stephens Passage extends 88 miles northward from Frederick Sound at Cape Fanshaw to Shelter Island, where it divides into Saginaw and Favorite channels and connects with Lynn Canal.

**Charts 17360, 17300**

**South entrance (6.3 miles northwest of Cape Fanshaw): 57°13.24′ N, 133°45.12′ W**

*Numerous islands are in both entrances to the passage, but otherwise it is open, deep, and generally free from dangers. . . .*

*The flood current enters Stephens Passage from both ends and meets in varying places W of Point Arden; the ebb current flows in the opposite direction. The velocity of the current is 0.5 to 2 knots. . . . The currents have considerable velocity in the entrance to all the larger bays and inlets that make off from Stephens Passage, causing tide rips and swirls.*

*The prevailing winds are SE throughout the year . . . SE gales may occur at any season, but they are more frequent and more severe in winter than in summer. . . .*

*Ice is discharged from glaciers in Tracy and Endicott Arms and is always found in Holkham Bay, and is prevalent in Stephens Passage off the entrance to that bay. Occasional pieces of ice may be expected in all parts of the passage. In daytime with clear weather it is not a serious menace to navigation, but it is dangerous at night or in thick weather.* (CP)

Stephens Passage is a wide channel that carries a lot of traffic. Since the winds generally follow the channel north or south, it doesn't take much south wind opposing a strong ebb current to kick up a nasty chop. (Chatham Strait and Lynn Canal both have the same problem.) Early morning transits are usually calm, and when afternoon breezes pick up, you can duck into a side inlet until conditions settle down. Unfortunately, except for a few inset charts, only small-scale charts exist for Stephens Passage, requiring extra caution along the shore and in small anchorages. Fortunately, NOAA has issued a large-scale chart for the popular glacier-viewing destination, Tracy Arm—Chart 17311.

Several good anchorages are available in Stephens Passage. The best ones are Cannery Cove in Pybus Bay, Snug Cove in Gambier Bay, Sandborn Canal in Port Houghton, Seymour Canal and Taku Harbor.

## Port Houghton

Port Houghton is 9 miles north of Cape Fanshaw.

Chart 17360
Entrance (1.5 mile northeast of Point Walpole): 57°19.98′ N, 133°30.13′ W

> *Port Houghton is an extensive bay. . . . A reef is reported to extend about 0.5 mile N from the N side of Walter Island. In 1971, rocks awash were reported off the unnamed point, on the S side of the bay about 3.5 miles ENE of Walter Island; caution is advised in this area because depths and character of bottom are not totally known.* (CP)

Port Houghton has two unusual features—the large tidal basin at the bitter end and beautiful Sandborn Canal.

## Sandborn Canal (Port Houghton)

Sandborn Canal is a long narrow arm southeast of Walter Island.

Chart 17360
Entrance: 57°17.75′ N, 133°15.57′ W
Anchor: 57°16.34′ N, 133°14.70′ W

> *A good small-craft anchorage may be found in Sandborn Canal, which is a long narrow arm SE of Walter Island, in 8 fathoms, soft bottom. This is a good winter anchorage if ice does not bother. . . .* (CP)

It is a pity that there is no large-scale chart for this area. Sandborn Canal is worth visiting even if it is out of the way for most cruising boats. We have seen more wildlife here, including bear and moose, than almost any place in Southeast Alaska. It should be protected as natural habitat and a well-sheltered anchorage. When *Cosmos* anchored here recently, they launched their kayaks and paddled up the stream about a mile, leaving the boat about an hour and a half before high tide. They recommend it as great fun!

When entering, watch for shoals on either side of the canal.

Anchor in about 5 fathoms over sand and mud with good holding.

## Hobart Bay (Entrance Island)

Hobart Bay, on the north side of Point Hobart, is 14 miles north of Cape Fanshaw.

Charts 17363, 17360
Entrance (0.5 mile southwest of Entrance Island): 57°24.42′ N, 133°27.67′ W
Entrance (Entrance Island cove): 57°24.68′ N, 133°26.17′ W
Entrance (inner bay): 57°25.30′ N, 133°25.99′ W
Northwest arm position: 57°26.58′ N, 133°26.72′ W
Salt Chuck entrance: 57°26.44′ N, 133°21.32′ W
Public float: 57°24.76′ N, 133°26.40′ W

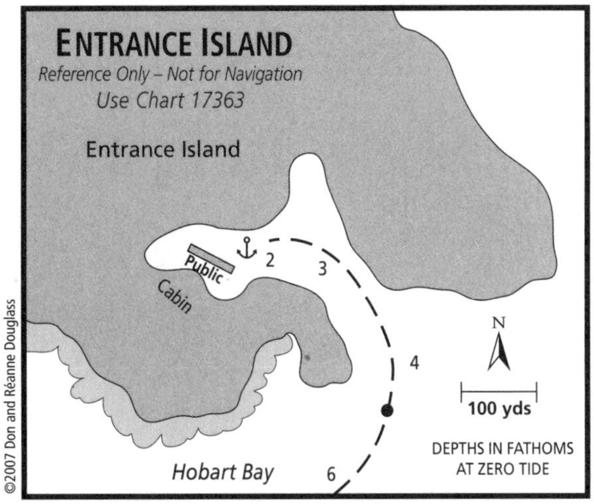

*A small bay, suitable for small craft, indents the SE side of* [Entrance Island] *for about 300 yards. . . . A State-maintained 100-foot-long small-craft and seaplane float is near the head of the small bay off the SW shore. . . . The float is used primarily as a weather layover facility. In 1976, depths of 15 feet were reported alongside the float. . . .*

*About 0.5 mile NE of Entrance Island, projecting points narrow the entrance into the inner bay. Bars, on which there are rocks, extend from the points of this entrance, leaving a navigable channel about 100 yards wide and 5-1/2 fathoms deep into the inner bay. A rock with 1 fathom over it has been reported about 0.5 mile NNE of the S point at the entrance to the inner bay.*

*Just within the entrance to the inner bay, a narrow arm leads NW to a basin, where a constricted anchorage in 10 fathoms may be found. In entering this basin, pass close E of the rocky islets just inside the entrance.*

*The channel leading to the basin at the head of the bay is very narrow. Heavy overfalls at the end of the narrow passage are dangerous for small craft, except during a short period at slack water.* (CP)

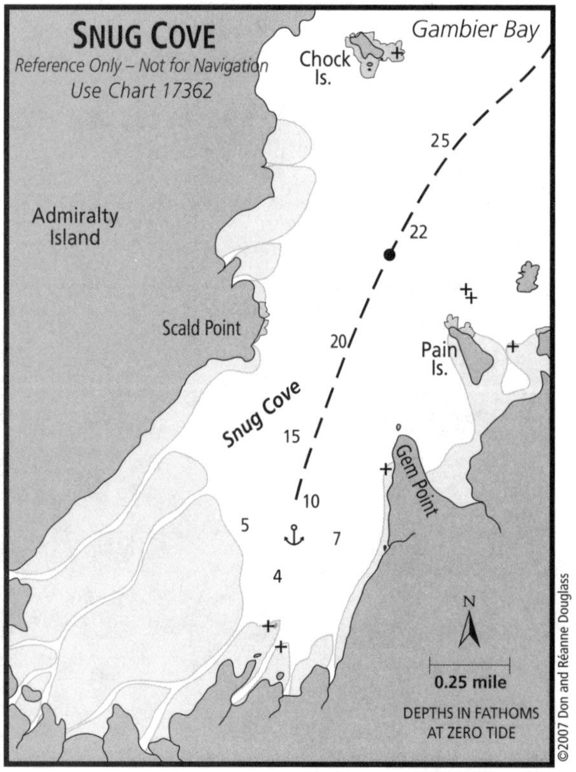


Entrance Island is quite small, and the inlet on its south side is almost tiny. But because it offers good shelter, it attracts a lot of northbound cruising boats.

There is a public float (12 by 100 feet) in the west part of the bay, but if you want to use it arrive early as it is usually very crowded. The inner side of the float is appreciably shallower than the outer side of the float. Know your draft and check the tide tables. You may want to avoid the inside of the float during minus tides.

In calm weather, we have successfully anchored in the tiny cove on the north side of the inlet, but there's little swinging room or scope here. Snug Cove in Gambier Bay to the west, described below, is a better anchorage.

The inner basin at Hobart Bay has major logging activity. The inner entrance is narrow with fast currents and encumbered with rocks. Secure anchorage can be found in its large northwest arm. The salt chuck at the east end is separated from the inner basin by tidal rapids.

## Gambier Bay—Snug Cove, North Cove, Good Island Nook, Good Island Inlet Basin, Last Chance Harbor

(Admiralty Island)

Gambier Bay, on the west side of Stephens Passage, is 8 miles north of The Brothers.

Charts 17362, 17360
Entrance (0.8 mile south of Gambier Island Light): 57°25.32′ N, 133°50.77′ W
Snug Cove entrance (Chock Island bearing 346°T at 0.5 Nm): 57°26.38′ N, 133°57.59′ W
Position (Last Chance Harbor): 57°28.16′ N, 133°52.43′ W
Anchor (Snug Cove): 57°25.37′ N, 133°58.18′ W
Anchor (Good Island Nook): 57°28.78′ N, 133°53.39′ W
Anchor (Good Island Inlet Basin): 57°31.93′ N, 133°56.62′ W
Anchor (unnamed cove 1.4 miles northwest of Gain Island): 57°28.84′ N, 133°56.43′ W

*The bay . . . is divided into two parts by a chain of narrow islands and reefs. The outer bay . . . extends from Point Gambier about 7*

Réanne Hemingway-Douglass

*This finely etched wolf track looks like it was recently made.*

*miles in a NNW direction. . . . Anchorage in 6 to 17 fathoms, mud bottom, can be had N of Good Island. . . . care should be taken to avoid the foul ground that extends off the NW point of Good Island.*

*Snug Cove, on the S side of the inner bay about 2 miles WSW of Church Point, has anchorage in 15 to 20 fathoms, soft bottom. Small craft find good protection here in 4 to 7 fathoms. Large vessels reach the cove by way of the channel close E of Church Point, Gain Island, and the unnamed island to the NW; two charted rocks are about 500 yards NNW of the unnamed island with a shoal of 8.9 fathoms between the south rock and the NNW end of the unnamed island. A S course can then be laid to pass about midway between the unnamed island and Muse Island, 0.7 mile to the SW. Only small boats can navigate the passage between Church Point and Gain Island because of the rocks.* (CP)

Gambier Bay is strategically located at the south end of Stephens Passage and the north end of Frederick Sound. (You won't find as good protection from southeast winds again until you reach Taku Harbor, 20 miles north on the east side of the passage.)

Many small coves among the islets and reefs guard the entrance to Gambier Bay. The tiny cove northwest of Last Chance Harbor to the east of Good Island offers good shelter for small craft and is easy to get to. However, if you're looking for shelter from south winds with lots of swinging room and good holding, consider anchoring in Snug Cove off the edge of its large drying mud flats.

In July 1999, *Tintagel* found Snug Cove exposed to williwaws and then, when the wind died, the mosquitoes swarmed in. They found what they considered a better site up the west shore of Snug Cove just beyond Chock Island, to the west of Hutchinson-Muse Island. They anchored in 6 to 9 fathoms with good holding.

We have also spent comfortable nights anchored in the unnamed cove bearing 325° true at 1.15 miles from the entrance light north of Gain Island. We also like the small basin at the head of Good Island Inlet.

If you're approaching from the north in limited visibility, the conservative approach to Snug Cove is to avoid the nasty shoal 2 miles northeast of Gambier Light on Gambier Island, then round the light, giving it a wide berth of 1⁄2 mile.

Head northwest 3 miles until you're almost due east of the entrance marker light on the reef northeast of Gain Island. Pass fairly close to this light (avoiding the small reef to the south), then head northwest and round by 300 yards the unnamed island mentioned in *Coast Pilot* before you head south, then southwest, into Snug Cove.

We have found that the passage between Church Point and Gain Island is fine for small craft; however, the current can be strong during spring tides. If in doubt, use the northwest entrance. When coming from the south we use the narrow passage west of Price and Chapel islands.

Anchor (Snug Cove) in 8 fathoms over soft mud with good holding.

Anchor (Good Island Nook) in 4 fathoms over mud and shells with good holding.

Anchor (Good Island Inlet Basin) in 6 fathoms over sand with good holding.

Anchor (unnamed cove) 1.4 miles northwest of Gain Island) in 4 fathoms over sand and mud with good holding.

## Windham Bay

Windham Bay, on the mainland side of Stephens Passage, is 7.5 miles north of The Twins and 17 miles north of Five Finger Light.

Charts 17363, 17360
Entrance (0.9 mile southeast of Point Windham): 57°33.17′ N, 133°32.76′ W
Entrance (nook, south side): 57°33.00′ N, 133°30.32′ W
Entrance (narrows): 57°35.15′ N, 133°27.11′ W
Anchor (entrance nook): 57°32.54′ N, 133°29.94′ W

> *Indifferent anchorage, in about 20 fathoms, may be had off the ruins of Windham N of the flat near the head of the bay. There is constricted anchorage in the cove just E of the S point of the entrance to the bay in 25 fathoms. Small craft anchor closer in.*
>
> *A fog bank of varying density frequently hangs over the upper part of Windham Bay, especially at night.*
>
> *From its 1.5-mile-wide entrance, Windham Bay narrows rapidly and connects with a deep inner basin about 4 miles long and 0.5 mile wide. This narrow connecting channel is constricted to about 100 yards by a ledge on its N side that bares. In passing through the narrows, great care should be exercised and the S shore kept aboard at a distance of about 50 yards. From the point on the S shore SE of the edge, a spur that bares extends about 20 yards . . . The extensive flat that extends from the SE side of Windham Bay leaves a passage about 0.2 mile wide close to the N shore up to within 0.4 mile from the head of the bay. Chuck River, entering the head of the bay, is reported to be navigable in a rowboat for about 1 mile.* (CP)

The head of Windham Bay is landlocked, offering almost total isolation from Stephens Passage. We have not used the nook on the south side of the Windham Bay entrance, but we have friends who weathered a strong southeasterly blow better than we did when, at the same time, we were tucked in behind Point Astley (Holkham Bay), 11 miles north. If you need shelter from strong southerly winds, go deep into the cove.

Depths in the bay are even greater than those depths marked on the chart, and it tends to be rather gloomy there. The bitter end of the bay at the delta of Chuck River is steep-to, and we have not found a good anchor site there.

## Seymour Canal (Admiralty Island)

Seymour Canal lies between Admiralty Island on the west and Glass Peninsula on the east.

Charts 17360, 17300
Entrance (2.3 miles south of Point Hugh): 57°31.98′ N, 133°49.89′ W

> *Seymour Canal has its entrance W of Point Hugh, 15.5 miles N of The Brothers. It extends . . . into Admiralty Island for about 38 miles. . . . The survey of the canal is old and incomplete, and dangers exist in addition to those shown on the chart, especially near the shores. The upper part of the canal* (chart 17300), *to a distance of about 21 miles from its head, is filled with islands, ledges, and rocks. . . . The waters of the canal are, in general, deep. . . . In the upper part of the canal . . . anchorage can be selected in places for which the chart is the guide. . . . Vessels transiting the canal N of Tiedeman Island should use caution and local knowledge.*
>
> *Currents in excess of 4 knots during both flood and ebb have been observed in the channel that approaches Fool Inlet in Seymour Canal.* (CP)

## Pleasant Bay (Seymour Canal)

Pleasant Bay, on the southwest side of Seymour Canal, is 7.1 miles northwest of Point Hugh.

Chart 17360
Entrance: 57°38.87′ N, 133°59.31′ W
Anchor: 57°38.57′ N, 133°59.49′ W

> *Pleasant Bay is a small cove . . . which affords anchorage for small craft. Two islets are in its entrance. The channel between the two islets is*

*foul. A reef extends about 150 yards N from the NW islet. The best channel to enter is between this reef and the very prominent point of broken rock resembling a breakwater on the NW side of the entrance. . . . Depths of about 6 fathoms are in the entrance and depths of 2 to 5 fathoms are inside the bay. Anchor in 4 fathoms about 300 yards SW of the NW islet.*

*The head of the bay bares except for a pool just W of the small point that projects from the NW shore. Small craft can pass into this pool at high water and have sufficient depth and swinging room for one or two boats at low water. This is an excellent shelter in N winds.* (CP)

Pleasant Bay is the first cove inside Seymour Inlet. Small craft can enter by finding the narrow channel on the north side of the entrance between a rocky ledge, which looks like a breakwater extending south from the point, and a reef extending northwest from the northernmost of the two entrance islets. Stay midchannel with about 6 fathoms in the fairway approximately 100 feet off the rocky ledge on your starboard hand.

Pleasant Bay offers good shelter in all weather if your anchor is well set. However, the shallow bay has only a thin layer of mud over a hard bottom and holding is poor-to-fair, unless you are lucky. Multi-anchors may be called for if strong winds are expected, or you can move to Mole Harbor.

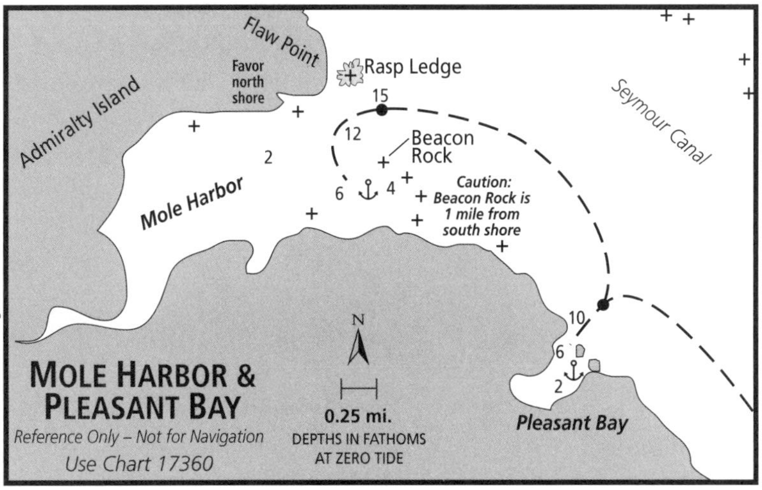


The head of the bay shoals to bare at low water, and one or two small craft are said to be able to anchor in the backwater behind the shoal on the west shore.

Anchor in 4 fathoms over a thin mud layer with poor-to-fair holding.

## **Mole Harbor** (Seymour Canal)

Mole Harbor, on the southwest shore of Seymour Canal, is 9.5 miles northwest of Point Hugh.

Chart 17360
Entrance: 57°40.50′ N, 134°02.00′ W
Anchor: 57°39.88′ N, 134°02.35′ W

*Beacon Rock, in the middle of the entrance, is part of a chain of rocky reefs extending from the S side of the entrance to the harbor to 400 yards NW of Beacon Rock. . . . Enter midway between Beacon Rock and Rasp Ledge; when abeam of Flaw Point, maintain a distance of 0.2 mile from the N shore and come to a W heading, using care to avoid the 2-1/4- and 3-fathoms shoals. . . . Small craft can find anchorage SW of Beacon Rock in 3 to 10 fathoms, mud bottom.* (CP)

Mole Harbor is entered north of a chain of rocky reefs extending nearly a mile from the south entrance point, avoiding Rasp Ledge off Flaw Point at the north entrance to the harbor. Beacon Rock, at the north end of the reefs, bares at low water. Small craft anchor a couple hundred yards southwest of Beacon Rock.

Anchor in 3 to 10 fathoms over mud with good-to-very-good holding and lots of swinging room.

## **Sore Finger Cove** (Seymour Canal)

Sore Finger Cove, on the east shore of the canal, is 4.5 miles north of Mole Harbor and 11.2 miles northwest of Point Hugh.

Chart 17360
Position: 57°43.64′ N, 134°00.13′ W

*Sore Finger Cove . . . offers good anchorage in 1 to 5 fathoms with shelter from all but W winds.* (CP)

Sore Finger Cove looks like an open bight on a small-scale chart but is reported to be useful in all winds except westerlies. *Note:* The S/V *Beltane* reported finding 14 fathoms with a sand and shell bottom. They could not locate the 1 to 5 fathoms mentioned in *Coast Pilot* and stated that it might be located on the east side, deep inside the cove. Another boat reported having spent *one month* inside the cove without any problems.

Anchor in 1 to 14 fathoms over sand and shells with good holding; little swinging room.

## **Short Finger Bay** (Seymour Canal)

Short Finger Bay, directly east of Faust Island, is 16 miles north of Point Hugh.

Charts 17360, 17300
Entrance: 57°48.67′ N, 134°02.45′ W
Anchor: 57°48.22′ N, 134°01.80′ W

> *Good shelter from S weather and anchorage in 5 to 10 fathoms, mud bottom, can be had here.* (CP)

Short Finger Cove is entered north of a series of rocks and reefs extending northwest 0.3 mile from the small peninsula forming the west shore of the bay.

Anchor in about 5 fathoms over mud with good holding.

## **Winning Cove** (Seymour Canal)

Winning Cove, on the east shore, is 19 miles north of Point Hugh.

Charts 17360, 17300
Entrance: 57°51.89′ N, 134°07.04′ W

> *Winning Cove . . . is a shallow inlet of no importance. . . .* (CP)

## **Windfall Harbor** (Seymour Canal)

Windfall Harbor, on the west side of Seymour Canal, is 23.5 miles north of Point Hugh.

Chart 17300
Entrance: 57°52.63′ N, 134°14.91′ W
Anchor: 57°50.25′ N, 134°17.75′ W

> *The entrance to Windfall Harbor is SE of Windfall Island between Late Point, the S end of the island, and Staunch Point, directly opposite on Admiralty Island. A 2-1/2-fathom shoal extends 0.3 mile S of Late Point. The passage on the NW side of Windfall Island is foul.*
>
> *Windfall Harbor should be approached only by the channel W of Tiedeman Island, which is about 0.8 mile wide. In using this passage keep in midchannel, except at a point 2 miles above the SE end of the island, where the W shore, which is bold, should be favored to avoid a patch of rocks about 700 yards off the E shore. . . . Enter the harbor SE of Windfall Island. . . .* (CP)

Gary Luhm

*Although they look serious, these two brown bear yearlings rough-housed like this for a long time.*

Windfall Harbor is known for the bear observatory at nearby Pack Creek.

Good shelter can be found near the head of the harbor over an oozy bottom of sticky mud.

The Pack Creek Bear Viewing Area is controlled by the U.S. Forest Service and is intended to give visitors a safe viewing experience of brown bears. (Pack Creek is located at approximately 57°54.3' N, 134°17.0' W.) Rangers are present at the arrival location and at the viewing area, which is at the end of a one-mile trail. This is a by-permit-only area with a per person fee.

Go to the following Website and click on "FAQ" for many important details; click on "Permits" to download the reservation form. Pay special attention to directions for boaters, such as the following:

"IMPORTANT NOTE: For the protection of Pack Creek's bears and the safety of all visitors, the Pack Creek mud flats are closed to boat traffic at all tides. These flats flood at approximately +12' tide."

Go to: http://www.fs.fed.us/r10/tongass/districts/admiralty/packcreek/index.shtml

Anchor in about 12 fathoms over sticky mud with very good holding.

### **King Salmon Bay** (Seymour Canal)

King Salmon Bay, on the west side of Seymour Canal near its head, is 8 miles north of Windfall Harbor.

Chart 17300
Position: 58°00.59' N, 134°15.97' W

> *King Salmon Bay . . . affords anchorage but the approach is difficult. The U.S. Fish and Wildlife Service patrol vessel BRANT reported grounding on a gravel bar that extends 100 yards W from the end of the long point forming the W side of the bay.* (CP)

### **Fool Inlet** (Seymour Canal)

Fool Inlet, on the east side of Seymour Canal, is 9 miles north of Windfall Harbor.

Chart 17300
Entrance: 58°01.43' N, 134°14.89' W

> *By passing W of Dorn and Faust Islands and E of Tiedeman Island and Swan Island, the canal may be navigated to the head of Fool Inlet, though above Tiedeman Island the passage is narrow and somewhat intricate.* (CP)

Fool Inlet is the bitter end of Seymour Inlet. A canoe/kayak portage trail leads from the upper

## Pack Creek Brown Bears

Steven Hannon—S/V *Beltane*

A visit to Pack Creek is well worth the 25-mile trip up Seymour Canal on Admiralty Island. Anchor immediately south of the dinghy haul-out lines that are marked by four florescent-orange buoys west of Windfall Island. The anchorage is tenuous on the little creek delta that drops off quickly into 15 fathoms. A more secure if exposed anchorage is south of Swan Island, a mile and a half east. The authorities do not want boats moored on the Pack Creek delta, which is north of the spit that separates the two creeks.

The weather report was benign for my visit so I perched on the delta at low tide. I was just getting my anchor sorted out when a brown bear came out of the woods and walked right along the waterline, not more than 40 yards away. She was very intent upon her clamming and paid me no apparent attention. A USFS ranger and an Alaska Fish and Game officer came right out to my boat to explain the procedure and collect the fee. I arranged to meet them the following morning.

Nine a.m. and I was on the beach being given a hand to haul my dinghy offshore on a continuous line. Leaving a dinghy on the beach would invite its being reduced to kindling or hypalon strips. Too many irresistible smells on a well used dinghy. The bears are habituated to people but great effort is made to avoid their getting any human food. All food must be left in a locker at the haul-out.

We walked around to the viewing area on the Pack Creek estuary. The ranger was carrying a spotting scope and a stainless steel .30/06. Immediately upon arrival we saw the same chocolate and cinnamon sow I had seen on the beach the evening before, but now in the company of a large male. It was mid-June and he had very obvious amorous intentions, but she was having none of it. She would sit down whenever he came very near. He had to be content with munching on sedges.

After watching her for a while the ranger said, "Watch this." The boar was not leaving her alone so she got up and ambled straight toward us. She was covering the 200 yards very quickly and was soon across the creek and heading up to our observation site.

The boar followed but was getting progressively more upset. He'd fall back and then tentatively catch up, all the while grunting and growling and making short, loud exhales that steadily increased in frequency. The ranger explained that the still-underage female had learned that she could get rid of him by getting near people!

About 40 to 50 yards away the boar could take no more. Proximity to people trumped his sex drive. He stood upright, whuffed loudly, then bolted for the far side of the sedge meadow. The female slowly made her way after him, and for the rest of our visit she didn't have to either sit down or come back to us. The whole episode was not unlike what one sees on a Friday night in the Hotel Alaska bar in Juneau.

end of Fool Inlet to Oliver Inlet on a nearly level track. The inlet is a rock pile with fast-moving currents, and since no large-scale chart exists for this area, you are on your own—as the name implies.

### **Point League Cove** (Stevens Passage)

Point League Cove is 7 miles northwest of Windham Bay.

Chart 17360
Entrance: 57°38.21′ N, 133°40.36′ W

*Anchorage has been obtained in the cove . . . by a vessel 150 feet long in 15 fathoms close to the entrance near the N shore, but it is not recommended. It is exposed to SW winds and is constricted by a shoal making out from the S shore and shoal water inside the cove.* (CP)

### Holkham Bay

Holkham Bay, on the east side of Stephens Passage, has two extensive arms—Tracy Arm and Endicott Arm.

Chart 17311
Entrance (2 miles west of Harbor Island):
57°45.43′ N, 133°42.37′ W

*The tidal currents have an estimated velocity of 4 knots at the entrances to Tracy Arm and Endicott Arm, forming swirls in these areas. Currents of much greater velocity are found in Fords Terror.*

*Glaciers discharge ice into both Tracy Arm and Endicott Arm. It is always present in Holkham Bay, sometimes in large quantities, and is prevalent in Stephens Passage off the entrance to the bay in greater or smaller quantities. This ice is dangerous at night or in thick weather, and in entering Tracy Arm or Endicott Arm care should be taken when near the ice, as the swirls are often dangerous.* (CP)

Réanne Hemingway-Douglass

*Iceberg rolls in front of* Baidarka.

Holkham Bay discharges large chunks of ice into Stephens Passage that originate from the calving tidewater glaciers in Tracy and Endicott Arms. While the average temperature of the water near the glaciers is 32°F, by the time it leaves Holkham Bay it has warmed to about 40°F.

Sumdum Glacier, high on the south side of Mt. Sumdum, is clearly visible from Stephens Passage. (According to John Muir, "sumdum" was the native word for the sound calving glaciers make.) The entrances to both Tracy and Endicott arms contain turbulent water and fast-moving icebergs, so use caution in these vicinities.

Pack ice off the glaciers usually keeps small boats at least a half-mile away. Although kayaks

---

**Meditations on Passing Sumdum Glacier**

Don Douglass

We are passing Sumdum Glacier to starboard on an unusually clear, calm day. Sumdum is one of the closest glaciers along the ferry route south of Juneau. The tongue of Sumdum has receded to about 1000 feet above sea level.

It is so clear that I believe that, as pre-historic man watched the islands grow out of the water ahead and sink into the sea astern, it was obvious to him that the world was at least curved, if not round. At first we see only a small blip of land on the horizon—the high point of a distant ridge—that rises to a peak. The peak grows taller and wider as we approach until it overtakes the land. As we continue away, we see the shoreline and then this land dance reverse as the land falls slowly behind us to a mere point, then disappears.

The curvature of the earth is such that a paddling kayaker can't see a log floating ahead in the water until the log is within a mile or so ahead and then, quickly, the log dips below the horizon. Early man must have known much more about how oceans worked than all the modern, city-dweller gents sunning in Central Park!

---

and dinghies can approach the glaciers at closer range, calving ice (some pieces as large as buildings) can cause high waves that present extreme hazards to boats of that size. In addition, icebergs often roll over without warning and can swamp a cruising boat. Since it's difficult to avoid all ice when you're cruising near glaciers, *Coast Pilot* suggests you carry a backup propeller if you intend to push deep into glacier country.

More and more cruise ships and day-tour boats are entering Holkham Bay and its two scenic arms. Some skippers of small local boats complain that the propellers of the larger vessels chew up bergie bits, leaving numerous smaller chunks that are difficult to avoid. We have found floating summer ice in Stephens Passage as far north as Point Anmer, 12 miles north of Holkham Bay.

## Point Astley, Wood Spit

Point Astley is the south point at the entrance to Holkham Bay, and Wood Spit extends 0.8 mile in a north direction from the south entrance point of Endicott Arm.

Chart 17311
Anchor (Wood Spit): 57°43.23′ N, 133°35.10′ W

> *An anchorage with shelter from SE winds may be had in the W bight between Point Astley and Wood Spit, in 20 to 30 fathoms, hard bottom.* (CP)

Following the recommendation quoted above, we anchored here once when the barometer had fallen a quarter-inch in 24 hours and Stephens Passage was kicking up a nasty southeast blow. We tucked into the bight just east of Point Astley, where we found good protection in 6 fathoms. We had a front row seat watching wild water blow out of Endicott Arm and up Stephens Passage. After the front passed, the wind backed to the northeast and screamed out of Tracy Arm. We spent the remainder of the night rolling and pitching uncomfortably off the rocky lee shore.

Boats anchored on the far east end of the bight, tucked next to Wood Spit, might escape some of the chop from the outflow of Tracy Arm. Although we consider Point Astley a marginal anchorage, we would use Wood Spit in stable conditions or in strong southerlies.

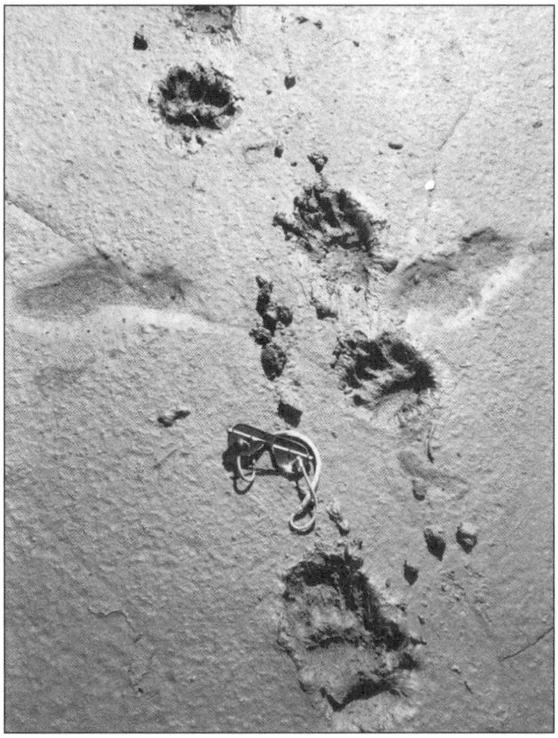
Réanne Hemingway-Douglass

*Fresh bear tracks in the mud*

Anchor (Wood Spit) in 10 to 15 fathoms over hard sand and pebbles with fair-to-good holding, depending on how well anchor is set.

## Harbor Island (Holkham Bay)

Harbor Island is in the middle of the entrance to Holkham Bay.

Chart 17311
Entrance (southwest): 57°44.92′ N, 133°37.15′ W
Anchor (0.15 mile west of Round Islet): 57°45.19′ N, 133°36.74′ W

> *In N weather the bight on the SE side of the island affords safe anchorage for small craft in 2 to 8 fathoms, hard bottom.* (CP)

We haven't used this anchorage, but we have seen other boats anchored between Harbor Island and Round Islet. The anchor site looks a little exposed to us but could be satisfactory in fair weather.

Jim Kyle

*Endicott Arm*

Anchor in 3 to 6 fathoms over hard clay and shells. Set anchor well since the area is subject to currents.

## **Endicott Arm** (Holkham Bay)

Endicott Arm is the south arm of Holkham Bay.

Chart 17311 (northwest end of Endicott Arm)
Chart 17360 (rest of Endicott Arm)
Entrance (mid-channel 0.48 mile north of Wood Spit Light): 57°44.74′ N, 133°34.56′ W

> *Sumdum Island is in midchannel, abreast Sanford Cove. Bushy Islands are two small islets midway between Sumdum Island and the NE shore.*
>
> *In approaching from S give the E shore of Stephens Passage a berth of 1 mile or more. From a position 0.8 to 1.0 mile NW of Point Astley steer for Sumdum Glacier, and pass in midchannel between Wood Spit Light and the Round Islet group, passing 0.44 mile of the light.*
>
> *In approaching from W, pass about 0.5 mile S of Point Coke and steer SE, leaving Harbor Island 0.2 mile or more to NE. Follow around the S side of Harbor Island and the Round Islet group at a 0.2-mile distance and pass midchannel between the latter and Wood Spit Light. The chart should be the guide.* (CP)

From Harbor Island, Endicott Arm extends southeast 30 miles to Dawes Glacier. Since this glacier calves great amounts of ice, it's often difficult to approach within more than a couple of miles.

The small bay in front of North Dawes Glacier may give some shelter from prevailing winds and massive ice in the main channel, but we have no details about any anchor sites.

There are no convenient anchorages for small cruising boats in Endicott Arm. Cruising boats generally stay overnight behind Wood Spit, in Tracy Arm Cove ("No Name Cove"), or in Taku Harbor.

## Sanford Cove (Endicott Arm)

Sanford Cove, on the south shore of Endicott Arm, is 5 miles inside the entrance to Endicott Arm.

Chart 17311
Entrance: 57°41.09′ N, 133°29.62′ W
Anchor: (approximate) 57°40.67′ N, 133°29.47′ W

> *Sanford Cove . . . is one of the two available anchorages in the arm. It has a depth of 36 fathoms and is protected except from N winds. Rock Point forms the NE side of the cove. A shoal with a depth of 4-1/2 fathoms extends 0.3 mile off the point. A flat extends out 300 yards in the S part of the cove. An occasional piece of ice drifts into the cove, but is of no danger to vessels at anchor.* (CP)

Sanford Cove appears to offer good protection from southeast winds but depths are too great for convenient anchoring. We generally favor Fords Terror due to its more moderate depths.

## Fords Terror (Endicott Arm)

Fords Terror is 15 miles from the entrance to Endicott Arm.

Chart 17360 (small-scale chart only)
Entrance: 57°36.64′ N, 133°11.15′ W
Entrance (east arm): (approximate) 57°41.38′ N, 133°08.71′ W
Temporary anchor (outer basin): (approximate) 57°38.24′ N, 133°10.23′ W

> *Fords Terror is a narrow inlet that extends 5 miles in a N direction. Its entrance, dangerous except at high water slack, is on the N side of Endicott Arm . . . Tidal currents rush through the narrowest part of the inlet with great velocity. The controlling depth through the narrows is 1/4 fathom. Fords Terror has magnificent scenery and affords a relatively safe anchorage.*
>
> *Brown Glacier, at the head of Fords Terror has receded, and the shoreline is about 0.5 mile E of the former charted position of the edge of the glacier.* (CP)

Although Fords Terror shows up on the chart as an unsurveyed indentation on the north side of Endicott Arm, skippers with a penchant for exploring can hardly resist its call. (Fords Terror was reportedly named in 1889 for a crew member of the *Patterson* who entered the narrows, got caught inside and spent a terrifying six hours until the tide reversed.)

Not much hard data exists on Fords Terror, and since it's extremely remote and has negligible radio reception, cruising boats seldom visit it.

We find the surroundings of Fords Terror spectacular—high granite mountains with snow bowls and hanging glaciers, vertical cliffs and, in the basin south of the rapids, a spectacular waterfall.

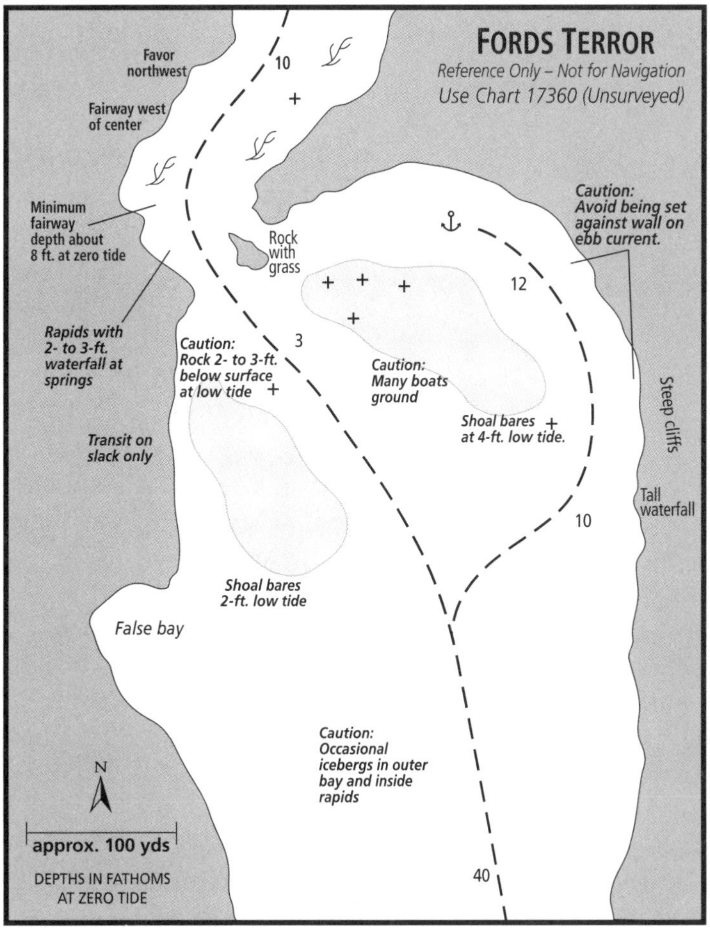

Ben Kyle

*Fords Terror*

The outer bay is deep to the outlet of the rapids, where there are large shoals dotted with glacial erratics (rocks) on either side. The shoals dry near low water and present a hazard due to the opaqueness of the water.

A channel that begins just off the high waterfall on the east wall leads to a temporary anchor site north of the northernmost shoal (see diagram) where you can wait for proper slack water to transit the rapids. *Navigate very cautiously here.* The diagram of the outer bay and rapids in Fords Terror comes from a hand sketch in our logbook. Use it only as a rough guide, with the utmost caution and verification on your part.

The rapids in Fords Terror, which form a 2- to 3-foot waterfall during spring tides, have a straight length of about 100 feet. Where the narrows turn north, the whitewater quickly subsides. Passage can be made easily near high-water slack with 3 to 4 fathoms in the fairway. As noted below, we have also transited this passage several times at low water slack.

With the exception of a few hundred yards, the water on either side of the rapids is quite deep, and for the most part, the cliffs are steep-to and can be approached closely. Small icebergs from Dawes Glacier occasionally make their way into the mile-long outer bay, and sometimes even inside the rapids on flood tides.

We have not been able to locate the shoal with 1⁄4 fathom over it at zero tide mentioned in *Coast Pilot.* On 14 September 1992—when the tide tables predicted a low tide of 1.5 feet for 0922 at Juneau—we waited 200 yards north of the rapids, anchored midstream in 3 knots of ebb current.

Joined by Ron Storro-Patterson, skipper of *Delphinus,* we plumbed the rapids for an hour and found the bottom quite level and the water adequate for passage. Long strings of kelp near our anchorage did not start to stream northward (indicating the start of the flood) until 1050 hours. We motored through the rapids at 1106 on the beginning flood at fast idle with good control, favoring the west side of the center channel, where we found a minimum depth of 12 feet. By the Rule of Twelfths, we estimate that Juneau tide at 1106 was 5 feet. Therefore, the minimum tide level behind the *rapids* in Fords Terror on that tide was about 5 feet, not 1.5 feet as listed for Juneau. (Proprietary tide books, based on NOAA data, include Table 3 for use in estimating the "Height of Tide at Any Time." Please consult *Tide Tables* [year] *West Coast of North and South America* for an explanation.)

These findings indicate to us that the time of each slack water varies with the change in tide level on the south side of the rapids. The

Don Douglass

*Maintain a bow watch when exiting Fords Terror at low water.*

larger the tide, the later the slack, and it probably varies from one to a little over two hours behind that of Juneau. We surmise that the water behind the narrows has a much smaller dynamic tide range—perhaps as little as half the Juneau range (i.e., 7.5 feet when Juneau has 15 feet)—and that ebb currents are stronger, on an average, than floods.

We estimate that the fairway through Fords Terror Rapids carries 8 feet at zero tide (as measured in Juneau tide level), and shallow-draft boats do not have to limit their transit to high-water slack only.

## Fords Terror

Mary Fox—M/V *Hannah Jane*

From our anchorage in Tracy Arm Cove, we left to explore Endicott Arm and Dawes Glacier at its end before returning to Fords Terror to await slack water. Basing our transit of the "rapids" in Fords Terror on the 3:02 P.M. Juneau tide, we arrived early, anchored near the waterfall outside the entrance, and watched the water rip around the rocks as it headed around the corner and into the rapids area. Here, slack water was about 40–45 minutes after high water in Juneau.

With binoculars, I could watch the rapids slow down and eventually flatten out as the white water subsided. Aligning the thin waterfall with our stern, we headed for the "flat" rapids. It was quite a thrill for us as this has been a long-held dream of ours. Six years ago we explored Alaska in our 27-foot Sea Ray but didn't have the cruising range to enter Fords Terror and Tracy Arm.

Gliding past Forevergreen Nook, we headed for the West Arm Anchorage and anchored in front of the waterfall in 22 feet of water. Since the Douglasses' book, *Exploring Southeast Alaska,* says there is a drop off, I was somewhat concerned about the 22-foot depth, thinking we might be over the shoal. My husband Al thought we were okay.

Once the boat was secured, we launched our dinghy and explored Forevergreen Nook on a falling tide. We scooted past the shallow spit as we hugged the south wall. We slowly motored past cascading waterfalls up to the head of the nook where there is another cascading waterfall and a good-size stream. As we cut between two grassy knolls, a raven swooped down over our heads, screeching at us and making dive bomb attacks until it finally flew away, confident it had scared off the intruders.

Returning to our boat, we were dismayed to clearly see the bottom off the stern! Though the depth sounder showed plenty of water, we had swung back over the shoal and the aft part of the keel was hitting bottom. I started the engine as Al headed forward to begin pulling in the chain anchor rode.

I put the engine in forward, but the boat wouldn't move as we are sitting on the mud. "More power," Al screamed. Slowly, I added more power fearing the boat would burst apart. Nothing. "MORE POWER," Al screamed again! Finally, I gave it the last thrust and I could feel the transom fishtailing off the mud. With a slight scrape, *Hannah Jane* was floating once again and we pulled in the rest of the anchor. This time we set the anchor in about 70 feet of water!

It is hard to adequately describe the beauty of Fords Terror with its majestic soaring granite mountains, waterfalls cascading everywhere, and such stillness. Because of the remoteness and isolation, few people come. We were the only people in all of Fords Terror for two days. It was like having Yosemite National Park in California all to ourselves!

*Authors' Note: We've received reports that mini-cruise ships have been anchoring in the outer section of the bay and ferrying their passengers into Fords Terror by tender, leaving little space for the smaller private cruising boats. Be aware that, in high season, you may find wall-to-wall boats.*

## Glacier Ice Cruising—Keeping it Safe and Enjoyable

Captain Richard M. Friedman - M/V *Explorer* & M/V *Alaskan Song*
Crewed Yacht Charters in Southeast Alaska

One of the most spectacular and beautiful places to visit in Southeast Alaska is the Sawyer Glacier complex in Tracy Arm. By taking some simple precautions, knowing the current patterns and making judicious choices of anchorage and timing, you can safely navigate what otherwise can be hazardous waters.

Richard Friedman

*Yacht charter vessel* Explorer *at North Sawyer Glacier*

As one cruises through Stephens Passage, approaching the entrance to Holkham Bay, it is not uncommon to see larger ice bergs that have escaped over the two terminal moraines or bars of Tracy and Endicott Arms. That should signal the prudent mariner to keep a closer lookout for small "bergie bits" or pieces of ice that could damage a hull or a boat's running gear. Larger ice is occasionally seen as far as ten miles north or south of the entrance but the smaller bits are usually no more than a mile or two north or south.

The most hazardous pieces are the smaller, denser bits of ice, just a few feet in diameter that can be extremely difficult to see depending upon sea conditions and the angle of the sun. The denser ice that breaks off from the lower part of the glacier is heavier, floats lower on the surface, and, because any air content has been compressed out of it, is more transparent, making it much more difficult to spot. Wearing polarized sun glasses, even if it is cloudy, can greatly enhance the mariner's ability to see this low floating, clear ice.

From Holkham Bay into the arms, one must cross what is referred to as the Tracy Arm or Endicott Arm bar. These are actually the terminal moraines, the point of greatest advance of the glaciers during the last ice age, where the glaciers pushed a wall of scree, boulders and gravel, receding and leaving the "bar" behind. Both ebb and flood currents can run at up to six knots across the Tracy Arm bar but diminish quite quickly once you have crossed. The current ebbs down Tracy Arm at all times, even on a rising tide, however the velocity increases on the ebb. It only actually switches direction near the entry bar.

This author likes to anchor in "No Name Cove" just 1.5 nm NNW of the Tracy Arm Bar in time for dinner and then make an early morning departure up the arm. This helps to avoid the go-fast tour boats that run day trips out of Juneau. A 7 A.M. departure will allow you to make the 23 nm cruise up Tracy Arm, arriving at the head by the glacier with very few, if any, other boats to spoil your experience. An hour or two spent in the area and then the cruise back out the arm will have you passing the bulk of the day's traffic on its way in.

Moving up the arm, the ice will get thicker the closer you get to the glaciers. Just how much ice depends on the volume of recent calving activity, while the ice's distribution will depend on the wind and current. Typically, the ice is thicker on the wide side of the channel's turns. Again, this can vary given stronger winds but this is the general pattern with the influence of currents only. Ice can be more readily avoided by taking a "race-course" path, hugging the inside corner of each bend in the channel. As the ice thickens, you should slow down; use your binoculars to find your clearest path up to a half mile ahead and get one or two shipmates to keep a watch for ice as well.

An increasingly large number of cruise ships have been coming into Tracy Arm over the past few years. While they clearly detract from the experience of the place, they can offer some help to the yachtsman in clearing a path through the ice in what might have been a difficult or otherwise hazardous approach. They will leave small bits in their wake so proceed with caution.

There are times when the sheer volume of ice will force a prudent mariner to make the tough decision to turn back before the glaciers even come into view. There is no radio contact from inside the arm as the high granite cliffs of the canyon limit VHF radio propagation except with other boats in the immediate vicinity.

Should you be successful in getting up near the glacier, bear in mind that the currents move ice about quite vigorously near the glaciers in the two "armlets" that make the final approach to the North and South Sawyer glaciers. It is quite possible to easily find your way deep into the arm and be just ½ mile away from the glacier's face and then have the ice shift, effectively blocking you in until it clears back out. Be on the watch for this, looking behind you once in a while, as you are watching and listening to the glacier.

This is a passage of a lifetime. It is akin to cruising up the Yosemite Valley in a boat. Knowing how to move through the ice, proceeding with caution and prudence and being willing to turn back, if necessary, are key to avoiding problems and being able to continue on your cruise without having to stop for costly repairs.

Linda Lewis

*Pushing the smaller bergie bits away in Tracy Arm*

Linda Lewis

*First you hear it, then you see it—calving ice at South Sawyer Glacier*

## **Forevergreen Nook** (Fords Terror)

Forevergreen Nook is 4 miles northeast of Fords Terror.

Chart 17360 (small-scale chart only)
Entrance (east arm): (approximate) 57°41.38′ N, 133°08.71′ W
Anchor: 57°41.47′ N, 133°07.94′ W

The eastern arm of Fords Terror has a shallow spit at its entrance that extends from its north side more than halfway to its south wall, and you can enter it only on the upper half of the rising tide. Rocks and kelp are present from this spit to the south wall, and there are two rocks about 30 feet off the south wall. At normal low tides, there is a 100-foot channel of unknown bottom. It is largely filled with kelp and has a depth of about one fathom between the two rocks. It is possible that this bar nearly dries on minus tides.

According to Rod Nash, (of M/V *Forevergreen*), you can find snug anchorage inside the eastern arm, just east of the gravel spit on the north side of a whale-shaped islet. To reach this site, circle around the south side of the islet and approach from the east. Near mid-tide, Rod found 15 feet minimum through the narrow entrance of the arm.

Ben Kyle

*Dawes Glacier, in Endicott Arm*

Anchor southeast of the gravel spit in 2 to 3 fathoms over mud with good holding.

### **West Arm Anchorage** (Fords Terror)

West Arm Anchorage is at the head of the west arm, just off a steep-to shoal near the stream.

Chart 17360
Entrance: 57°41.42′ N, 133°09.69′ W
Anchor: (approximate) 57°41.90′ N, 133°11.00′ W

We found relatively safe anchorage at the head of the west arm, just off a steep shoal near the stream. A steep bank, with depths that rise from 12 fathoms to 2 fathoms within just 20 yards, lies off this shoal. If you choose this site, set your anchor well in case of williwaws.

Anchor northeast of the large waterfall just south of the river's outlet in 12 to 14 fathoms; bottom is sand, gravel and rock with fair holding. Move out into deeper water with more scope if an easterly picks up.

### **Dawes Glacier** (Endicott Arm)

Dawes Glacier, at the head of Endicott Arm, is 26 miles from the entrance to Endicott Arm.

Chart 17360
Position: 57°30.06′ N, 132°53.99′ W
Position (North Dawes Glacier): 57°32.08′ N, 133°00.55′ W

*Dawes Glacier . . . extends to the water's edge. This glacier occasionally calves off enough ice into the arm to hamper navigation seriously.* (CP)

North Dawes Glacier is 4.3 miles northwest of Dawes Glacier in a small inlet walled by two mile-high peaks.

### **Tracy Arm** (Holkham Bay)

Tracy Arm, the north arm of Holkham Bay, extends north and east for 22 miles to its head and North Sawyer and South Sawyer glaciers.

Charts 17311
Entrance (start of mid-channel range): 57°46.59′ N, 133°38.06′ W

*The arm is often clogged by small icebergs for several miles, and great care is needed in navigating the ice field. Both glaciers,* [North] *Sawyer Glacier and South Sawyer Glacier, can be very active, and huge blocks of ice fall off their faces into very deep water. These can generate waves that have been observed as high as 25 feet; however, a small boat can ride the waves safely if it keeps a few miles distance from the glacier face and avoids getting packed in the ice flow. It is recommended that vessels use extreme caution and avoid navigating in proximity to the glacier faces.*

*In the N branch of Tracy Arm, which extends from Sawyer Island (57°52′45″N., 133°11′25″W.)*

*to Sawyer Glacier, there is a shoal area on the E side of the arm which reaches a minimum depth of 0.8 fathom at MLLW and extends to 57°53'40"N., 133°10'51"W., about 250 yards from a waterfall on shore. Caution is advised in this area. Tracy Arm, with its deep water, numerous waterfalls, and bold shores, is one of the outstanding fjords of SE Alaska.*

*The entrance to the arm is about 1.75 miles wide. The navigable channel, only 0.3 mile wide, has a depth of 6-1/2 fathoms and is marked by two unlighted buoys and a mariner activated sector light (57°49'23"N., 133°34'27"W.) on the E shore of the arm, and heavy kelp beds in the summer on the SE side. To activate the sector light, mariners should transmit 5 carrier pulses in 5 seconds on VHF-FM channel 65. The aid will remain lighted for 10 minutes. The buoys and lights are seasonal. The buoys may become submerged during periods of strong current. Tidal swirls, in conjunction with very strong currents, will be met in the entrance except at slack water. Caution should be used when transiting this area due to large pieces of grounded ice or moving through the entrance with the current.* (CP)

Gary Luhm

*A plaintive face; do not disturb this harbor seal pup.*

Tracy Arm, a beautiful fiord, has deep water and impressive vertical granite walls. At the head of the arm, two scenic tidewater glaciers, North Sawyer and South Sawyer, generate the blue-and-white icebergs you encounter in the fiord. Magnificent glacier-polished peaks of up to 5,000 feet flank Tracy Arm, and classic U-shaped valleys run between the ridges. Because of its high, steep sides, you lose all radio reception and, from time to time, you lose GPS signals as well.

Within recent years, large cruise ships have made Tracy Arm one of their calls, decreasing the enjoyment for pleasure craft. While, as yet, no restrictions have been placed on the numbers and types of vessels that can enter Tracy Arm, we predict that some sort of government regulation will eventually be imposed.

At the entrance bar to Tracy Arm, you pass red buoy N"2" to starboard. Although this buoy is a helpful navigational aid, its position should *not* be relied upon—it is sometimes moved or carried away by icebergs! Green buoy C"1" is generally more dependable, but it is also subject to being moved off position. As your best guides, use the range marks behind you on Harbor Island and the sector light located to the northeast.

It is possible to anchor temporarily in 8 fathoms off a stream frequently covered by a snow bridge on the south shore of Tracy Arm at about 133°20' W longitude, facing a major U-shaped valley and 50 yards from a waterfall.

Réanne Hemingway-Douglass

*Navigate gently around seal pups in Fords Terror and Tracy Arm.*

## Tracy Arm Cove (Tracy Arm)

Tracy Arm Cove is 2.5 miles from Harbor Island.

Chart 17311
Entrance: 57°47.64′ N, 133°37.09′ W
Anchor (west shore): 57°48.50′ N, 133°38.11′ W
Anchor (north shore): 57°48.61′ N, 133°37.98′ W

> *An anchorage for small boats in 5 fathoms, rocky bottom, is reported available in the small bight on the W side of the arm, about 2 miles above the entrance. A rock awash is about 0.2 mile SE of the entrance to the small bight.* (CP)

The cove we call "Tracy Arm Cove" is unnamed on the nautical chart. Some locals call it "No Name Cove." Whatever name you choose, it is the best anchorage in Holkham Bay and makes a good base camp from which to explore Tracy Arm and Endicott Arm.

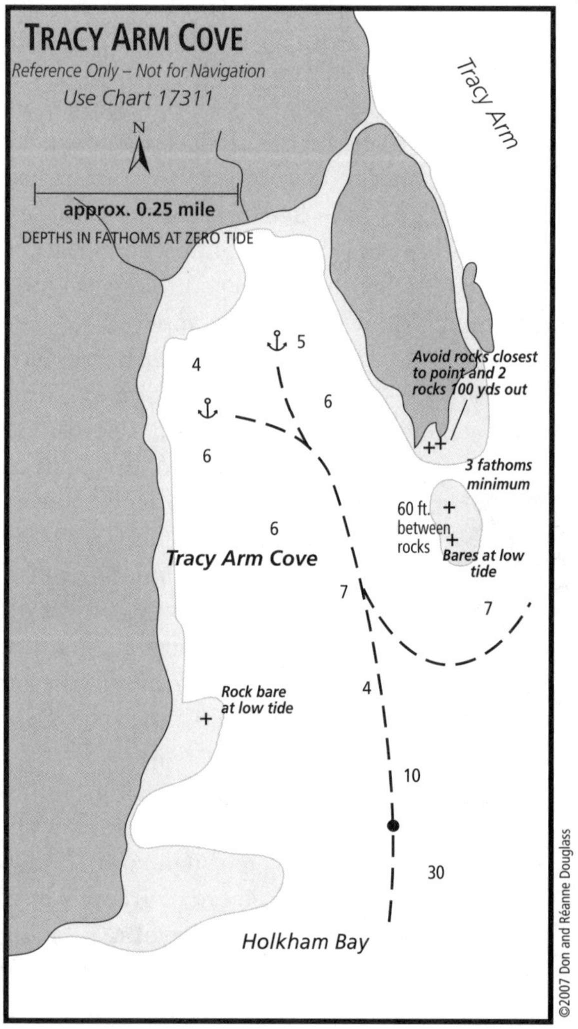


*Caution:* Before entering the cove, study your chart for the location of the 2-fathom bar that extends from the cove opening's west side in a generally northeast direction. (This is a lateral moraine from the glacier.) Note on our diagram's schematic route for entering the cove that you will be going across this 2-fathom (at mean lower low water) bar. Be sure you know the stage of the tide and adjust your course to the east (closer to the "60-ft. between rocks" notation on our diagram) when you are transiting the cove at lower tides, especially on Spring Tides.

The cove is relatively flat, but holding varies due to its mixed bottom. Although it's well protected from northerly winds, it is open to the south. In anything stronger than light southerlies, it receives quite a chop, and icebergs enter it on flood tide with gusto!

To avoid some of the chop and ice, old-timers anchor near the west shore, as indicated on the diagram. We have spent several comfortable nights here. (The exception was a night when a large berg entered the cove, broke in two, and circled around our boat.) The shallower you can anchor, the more chance the bigger bergs will ground before hitting you. However, the 2-4-fathom bar and shoals at the entrance do a pretty good job of keeping out house-sized monsters.

When leaving the cove for Sawyer glaciers, avoid the submerged rocks extending a quarter-mile or more from the south tip of the east island. It is recommended to pass well south of this reef with its two drying rocks. A small channel inside this major reef and two smaller rocks close to the point has 3 fathoms in the fairway. However, boats have had trouble staying in the narrow fairway and have lost props in the process. The North shore of Tracy Arm entrance is riddled with sea caves.

Anchor in about 4 fathoms over a mixed bottom with good holding if your anchor is well set.

Réanne Hemingway-Douglass

*An iceberg corridor in Tracy Arm beckons; resist the temptation to get too close to these unstable bergs.*

*5 fathoms, rocky bottom, is reported available in the small bight on the W side of the arm, about 2 miles above the entrance. A rock awash is about 0.2 mile SE of the entrance to the small bight. . .* (CP)

We haven't found a good place to anchor in William Cove yet. The clay bottom is hard, and bergs fill the bay on southerly winds.

However in 2004, *Non-Pareil* reported finding good anchorage in 2 fathoms off the small creek in William Cove. Swinging room within the cove is restricted.

## William Cove (Tracy Arm)

William Cove, on the west side of the arm, is 6 miles north of the entrance to the arm.

Charts 17311, 17300
Entrance: 57°50.86′ N, 133°36.89′ W

> *William Cove* [is] *a deepwater anchorage with constricted swinging room and hard bottom with patches of mud . . . An anchorage for small boats in*

## North Sawyer and South Sawyer Glaciers (Tracy Arm)

North and South Sawyer glaciers are at the head of Tracy Arm.

Charts 17311, 17300
North Sawyer Glacier arm entrance: (approximate) 57°53.39′ N, 133°11.20′ W
South Sawyer Glacier dog-leg position: (approximate) 57°51.72′ N, 133°08.11′ W

---

### Hypnotic Icebergs!

Don Douglass & Réanne Hemingway-Douglass

"Move in closer," I shouted to Don over the noise of the engine. "I want to get a close-up photo of the ice dripping down."

Our two crew members had just taken off in Don Kyte's amphibious, *Seabee,* for a flight over Tracy Arm and the glaciers, and we were motoring slowly near the head of the arm, admiring the various shapes of the icebergs. A berg the size of a two-story house, but much wider, caught my eye. Its shape reminded me of a dolmen perched on four huge, squat legs, and its translucent blue captivated me.

I had already shot a roll of slide film from different views—the full "table," its underneath curving edge, through its "legs," the two gulls sitting atop; telephoto, wide-angle, regular lens. I changed the film quickly. This was too good to pass up.

"Closer!" I yelled again. The shades of turquoise were stunning and I had lost all sense of the boat and its safety. All I wanted was to get more shots of this beautiful creature. "That's perfect!" I shouted. I could almost touch the overhanging lip, and I snapped shot after shot.

Suddenly, water started streaming down the side of the berg. "Back up. Back up!" I yelled. "It's rising!"

Don stared at the iceberg, seemingly hypnotized, without paying attention to me.

"REVERSE!" I screamed.

He suddenly came to his senses and jammed the throttle into full reverse. The prop cavitated wildly, and we quickly drew back 100 yards. The iceberg rose from the water then fell, time and time again, sending swells in all directions—a giant sea monster teeter-tottering, cracking and growling. It continued to rise slowly until the lip and legs towered more than 25 feet above the water. It rocked back and forth for twenty minutes, then slowly stabilized.

We looked at one another and rolled our eyes, sighing almost simultaneously, "That was close! We'd better not try that again."

Réanne Hemingway-Douglass

*The North Sawyer Glacier appears off your port as you are approaching South Sawyer Glacier.*

You can approach North Sawyer Glacier by carefully avoiding the large icebergs in the main channel. This glacier has receded remarkably in recent decades and is currently mostly landbound.

To reach South Sawyer Glacier, the much bigger tongue, you must make a dogleg for about two miles to the north and east. However, it's difficult to approach due to the icebergs.

Calving glaciers may create 25-foot-high waves, and although they quickly die down, they can be dangerous to within a half-mile. Local excursion boats from Juneau arrive just after noon, and you can study the path they take through the ice. We have found the pack ice so thick at South Sawyer, and the channels along either shore so changeable, that we couldn't get to where we could see the glacier. Once, when the wind changed, we were surrounded by chunks of ice, and the channel behind us closed. At such times, we keep a boat hook handy to push away chair-sized bergs. In addition to admiring the bergs, you can watch hundreds of seals floating on slabs of ice near the glacier.

For the trip of a lifetime, hire a floatplane from Juneau to rendezvous with you in the main channel off North Sawyer Glacier and take you for a spin. From the air you can view the indescribable raw beauty of the huge ice fields, with giant seracs and frozen lakes stretching to the Canadian border and beyond. The coloration of the different glacier arms, the crevasses and overfalls are spectacular. On one flight, we saw mountain goats working their way along rocky ridges that seemed encased in a sea of ice.

Richard Friedman

*South Sawyer Glacier—Look for the clearest path through the pack ice and proceed very slowly.*

Gary Luhm

*M/V* Homeshore *cruises close to the face of South Sawyer Glacier.*

Mahina Expeditions

*S/V* Mahina Tiare *chooses to do its glacier-viewing under full sail.*

## Port Snettisham

Port Snettisham, on the east side of Stephens Passage and 13 miles north of Holkham Bay, has two arms—Speel Arm and Gilbert Bay.

Charts 17313, 17300
Entrance: 57°57.46′ N, 133°52.73′ W

> *The shores of Port Snettisham are steep and wooded. Because of the great depth, it is not suitable as an anchorage. . . .*
> *Moderately heavy tide rips are sometimes found at the entrance to Port Snettisham.*
> *A* [private] *barge dock and a small-craft float are in the basin at the head of Speel Arm.* (CP)

Port Snettisham is a classic fiord with high steep sides and deep water throughout. The port itself is at the head of Speel Arm where a large hydroelectric plant that supplies much of the Juneau area is located. The channel leading to the power plant and its private float is very narrow and shallow and is not much use except in an emergency. *Note:* Extreme magnetic disturbances of 78° or more have been observed at the entrance to Port Snettisham. Mallard Cove, 0.5 mile west of Fannie Island, is a fair-weather anchorage only.

## Southeast Cove (Port Snettisham)

Southeast Cove is 1.7 miles inside Port Snettisham.

Charts 17313, 17300
Position: 57°58.24′ N, 133°49.24′ W

> *Anchorage can be had directly across from Mist Island, on the southeast side of Port Snettisham in a small cove in 5 to 15 fathoms, hard bottom.* (CP)

The small cove just inside Port Snettisham, which we call "Southeast Cove," can be useful as a place to hide when a nasty southerly chop occurs in Stephens Passage. Gilbert Bay, however, has more swinging room than Southeast Cove.

## Gilbert Bay (Port Snettisham)

Gilbert Bay is the south arm of Port Snettisham.

Charts 17313, 17300
Entrance: 58°00.06′ N, 133°44.50′ W
Anchor: 57°56.73′ N, 133°42.25′ W

> *Gilbert Bay . . . is 3.5 miles long to the flat that extends 1 mile from its head. . . .* (CP)

Anchorage can be found at the head of Gilbert Bay off the drying mud flat at the mouth of Sweetheart Creek. The bay is useful in fair-to-moderate weather, but it is exposed to Tracy

Arm weather that spills over a shallow divide and may receive strong williwaws.

Anchor in about 8 fathoms over mud (the bottom is steep-to) with fair to-good holding.

## Limestone Inlet

Limestone Inlet, on the east side of Stephens Passage, is 2 miles southeast of Taku Harbor.

**Charts 17314, 17300**
**Entrance: 58°01.82′ N, 133°59.84′ W**
**Anchor: 58°02.14′ N, 133°58.25′ W**

> *The depths are 13 to 30 fathoms in the lower half of the inlet, and a vessel may anchor anywhere in midchannel, but the holding ground is not very good. With the close proximity of Taku Harbor, vessels seldom find it necessary to enter. The upper half of the inlet is filled by a flat, most of which covers at high water. An overhead power cable with a clearance of 95 feet crosses the inlet about 0.3 mile above the mouth. The maximum safe clearance under this 138,000-volt line is 80 feet.* (CP)

Anchorage may be found off the large grassy meadow in 10 fathoms or less over a gravel bottom. A small private float and buoy lie near the head of the bay.

## Taku Harbor

Taku Harbor, on the east shore of Stephens Passage, is 19 miles southeast of Juneau.

**Charts 17314, 17300**
**Entrance: (Grave Point Light bearing 305°T at 0.48 Nm): 58°03.45′ N, 134°02.32′ W**
**Public float: 58°04.11′ N, 134°00.80′ W**
**Anchor (south end of harbor): 58°03.82′ N, 134°01.05′ W**

> *The entrance is between Stockade Point and the SE tangent of Grave Point. In the approach from the S, its position is readily known by the projecting highland of Grave Point and Taku Mountain rising behind the point. . . .*
>
> *The anchorage is in about 13 fathoms, soft bottom, favoring the E shore. A slight eddy current in Taku Harbor from Stephens Passage is sometimes noticed on the flood and, with large tides, swirls are produced that cause a vessel to surge somewhat on her cable at times.* (CP)

Taku Harbor, a popular and well-placed anchorage, offers some of the best protection between Juneau and the south end of Stephens Passage. It has easy access and can be entered without trouble using radar. A short boardwalk trail that wraps around the shore off the float, can be used to stretch your legs. An additional detached 200-foot public float is located in the south end of the harbor.

Taku, named for a sub-division of the Tlingit tribe once living in the vicinity, was once the site of a Hudson's Bay trading post established in 1840. In the 1900s, a commercial cannery, now in decay, was located here. Remains of piers, boilers, bunkhouses, and electrical generators are being overtaken by dense brush. Bear continue to fish for salmon in the stream north of the old cannery, so remain alert if you explore the area when the salmon are running. If you moor to the float, do not leave any food or garbage outside on your deck—you may be boarded by a black

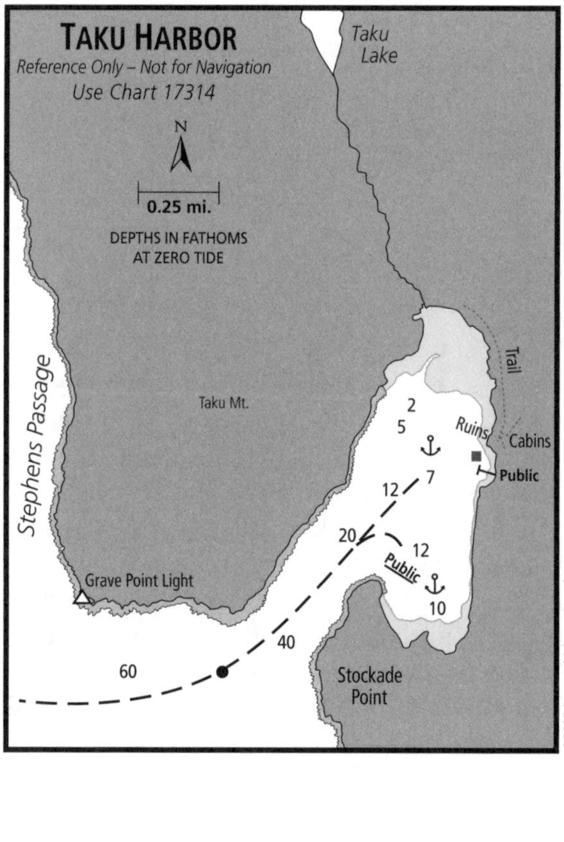

bear! River otters roam the dock area at all hours. The dock is also a Seaplane Base.

You can anchor along the east shore in shallow water off the stream outlet to watch for bears. However, as you are maneuvering here be sure you don't stray north beyond our indicated anchorage into the quickly shallowing area. In southeast weather, anchor on the south side for best protection. Most people anchor in the south-east bight in shallow water, as there are frequently crab pots in the northern part of the harbor. A heavy southeast wind can whip across the westerly point with violent force.

Frank Sjolie

*Looking at the detached public float—south end of Taku Harbor*

Anchor (south end) in 8 to 10 fathoms over hard gravel and soft sand with good holding if well set.

## **Doty Cove** (Admiralty Island)

Doty Cove, on the west side of Stephens Passage, is 13.5 miles south of Juneau.

Chart 17300
Entrance: 58°06.82′ N, 134°10.86′ W
Anchor: 58°07.21′ N, 134°12.69′ W

> *Doty Cove, S of Cove Point, is deep. Flats at the head of the cove drop off rapidly to 20 fathoms.* (CP)

Known to local fishermen, Doty Cove offers good protection in fair weather only. There is a 4-fathom shoal near its head which makes a reasonable anchor site.

## Suicide Cove

Suicide Cove is 1 mile south of Slocum Inlet.

Charts 17314, 17300
Entrance: 58°06.89′ N, 134°04.33′ W
Anchor: 58°07.00′ N, 134°04.15′ W

Protection from Taku winds is available in Suicide Cove, a shallow tiny bight just south of 1,060-foot Butler Peak. This site is sheltered from outflow winds but rocky. In winter, Taku Inlet is subject to violent storms, known locally as "Taku winds." Confused seas caused by conflicting currents can make it extremely treacherous. Juneau skipper Kent Fagerstrom has used this site many times on his return from fall deer-hunting trips. Although open to the south, it is protected from the winds that blast down the inlet.

Temporary anchorage can be found in 5 fathoms over a rocky bottom.

## Slocum Inlet

Slocum Inlet, on the east shore of Stephens Passage, is 15 miles southeast of Juneau.

Charts 17314, 17300
Entrance: 58°08.10′ N, 134°04.58′ W
Anchor: 58°07.86′ N, 134°04.02′ W

> [Slocum Inlet] *is almost filled with flats. The water is deep close to the flats, but it does afford convenient anchorage.* (CP)

Slocum Inlet will give protection from southerlies behind Circle Point if you get a good bite with your anchor. However, we generally opt for Taku Harbor or the run to Juneau.

Anchor close to the steep-to mud flat in the southeast corner over sand with fair holding if well set.

## Taku Inlet

Taku Inlet, on the northeast side of Stephens Passage, extends about 15 miles to Taku Glacier at its head.

**Chart 17315**
**Entrance: (Bishop Point bearing 303°T at 1.08 Nm): 58°11.47′ N, 134°07.29′ W**

*In Taku Inlet, currents have greater velocity on the ebb than on the flood. At Taku Point, the ebb current has an estimated velocity of 3 to 4 knots at times. At the entrance to Taku Inlet the velocity of the ebb current does not exceed 2 knots. (See the Tidal Current Tables for daily predictions.)*

*Large vessels should not venture N of Flat Point because of the extensive shoaling at the head of Taku Inlet. It is reported that the deepest water between Flat Point and Scow Cove is 4 feet in the channel about 100 yards off the W shore of the inlet.* (CP)

On one trip, we headed up Taku Inlet for a view of the glacier. We got as far as the anchorage east of Jaw Point, and instead of a view of the glacier, we were greeted by nasty, opaque chop.

Taku Inlet is famous for its dangerous winds and breaking seas that start at Greely Point northward or from southward if a downslope Taku wind is blowing. Opaque glacier water makes for spooky navigation. A short airplane ride from Juneau is a far faster way to see this large impressive waterway that drains the Juneau Ice Field and upper British Columbia.

## Sunny Cove (Taku Inlet)

Sunny Cove, on the west side of the inlet, is 4 miles north of Cooper Point.

**Chart 17315**
**Position: 58°18.14′ N, 134°08.16′ W**

*In a small bight between Sunny Cove and Flat Point about 1.3 miles NE of Sunny Cove is the Annex Creek Power Station, which furnishes electric power to Juneau. . .The power station constitutes a good landmark.*

*Small craft should exercise caution when maneuvering in shoal water especially off Sunny Cove, Annex Creek Power Station, and off Turner Creek on the E side of Taku Inlet. These areas have scattered boulders that stand 2 to 5 feet above the surrounding bottom. Because of the discoloration of the water it is impossible to see them even when covered by only a foot of water. This area should be avoided by small boats except at high water. . .* (CP)

Sunny Cove is only accessible by small craft in fair conditions.

## Gastineau Channel

Gastineau Channel separates Douglas Island from the mainland.

**Chart 17315**
**Entrance (south): 58°12.05′ N, 134°14.24′ W**

*Gastineau Channel, separating Douglas Island from the mainland, extends NW for 13 miles from Stephens Passage, and then W for 2.5 miles to Fritz Cove. The channel is marked by lights, lighted and unlighted buoys, and daybeacons. The section of the channel from Salmon Creek NW for about 2 miles is marked by seasonal buoys. Juneau, 8 miles above the SE entrance, is the head of deep-draft navigation. The channel from Juneau to Fritz Cove, a distance of 7.5 miles, crosses Mendenhall Bar and is navigable only by small craft with local knowledge. This part of the channel is subject to considerable shoaling; mariners are advised to obtain the latest local information concerning channel conditions.* (CP)

Gastineau Channel has easy access from the south, but it is extremely busy and you must keep a sharp eye at all times for cruise ships, floatplanes taking off and landing and kayakers. To reach Harris Harbor or Aurora Basin, you pass under Douglas Bridge, which has a minimum height of 50 feet. The float south of the bridge is reserved for cruise ship tenders and tour boats and is off limits to pleasure craft. Moorage in all Juneau harbors is assigned by the harbormaster's office, which monitors Ch 16 and 73. If you plan to remain in Juneau for any length of time, make prior arrangements with the Harbor authorities.

Harris and Aurora harbors in downtown Juneau have transient moorage, as does Douglas Harbor, south of the Douglas Bridge on the west side of Gastineau Channel. Statter Harbor, in Auke Bay, 12 miles north of Juneau, is a transient-only harbor and the largest of the facilities in the greater Juneau area.

*One of the many cruise ships you may see approaching Juneau*

## **Juneau** (Gastineau Channel)

Juneau, on the northeast side of Gastineau Channel, is 8 miles north of Stephens Passage.

Chart 17315
Entrance (Harris Harbor): 58°18.01′ N, 134°25.76′ W
Entrance (Aurora Basin): 58°18.20′ N, 134°26.04′ W

*Juneau is well within the area of maritime influences that prevail over the coastal areas of southeastern Alaska, and is in the path of most storms that cross the Gulf of Alaska. Consequently, the area has little sunshine, generally moderate temperatures, and abundant precipitation. The surrounding rugged terrain causes considerable variation in the weather within relatively short distances.*

*Harris Harbor and Aurora Basin . . . are small-boat basins just N of Juneau-Douglas Bridge, and Juneau City Float, immediately NW of the City Wharf and Ferry Terminal. All three facilities are operated by the city of Juneau. The harbormaster monitors VHF-FM channels 16 and 73 and can be contacted by telephone (907.586.5255) or FAX (907.586.5367).*

*Harris Harbor, immediately N of the bridge, has a 12-foot project depth and is protected by two rock-mound breakwaters. In June 2005, depths of 8 to 12 feet were available in the harbor with shoaling to 6.1 feet along the SE edge. A light at the end of the N breakwater marks the entrance. The harbor floats can accommodate over 275 vessels. Berths for transients are available. A seaplane hangar and float are in the SE part of the harbor, and a 450-foot grid is in the NW part. Water and metered electricity are available at the floats.*

*Aurora Basin, 0.5 mile NW of Harris Harbor . . . has a project depth of 14 feet in the SE half and 12 feet in the NW half. The basin is protected on the NW side by a breakwater, marked by a light, and by a detached breakwater on the channel side. In April 2002, depths of 6.5 to 12.0 feet were*

*Juneau's Gastineau Channel; Harris and Aurora Harbors are on the northeast side of the bridge (lower center part of the photo).*

*available in the N part of the basin and 13.4 to 14.0 feet in the S part. The basin can be entered at either end of the detached breakwater. The SE end of the detached breakwater is marked by a light. The basin can accommodate approximately 457 vessels. Water and metered electricity are available at the floats. A 100-foot-long float with facilities for fueling small craft is at the SE end of the basin. In 2002, 12 feet (3.7 m) was reported alongside the float. Gasoline, diesel oil, and lubricating oils and greases are available.* (CP)

Réanne Hemingway-Douglass

*Bagpipes and drums celebrate the Veendam's arrival in Juneau.*

Juneau, Southeast's largest city and Alaska's State capital, is the most cosmopolitan of the cities along the Inside Passage; nevertheless, it's a friendly community where you can see people in slickers and rubber boots (called Juneau sneakers by locals) meeting with friends dressed in business suits. An estimated half of its 31,000 residents are involved in government; the rest work in tourism, fishing, mining, transportation, consulting and construction.

The city sits along a narrow strip of land, flanked on either side of Gastineau Channel by magnificent snow-clad mountains. In addition to its lovely site, the city offers wonderful gift shops, espresso bars and several supermarkets. Engine parts are available, but other parts may have to be ordered from Seattle. If you're interested in history, the Alaska State Museum and the Alaska State Library are musts. (Pick up the Juneau Walking Tour brochure from the Visitor's Bureau for ideas on what to see.) Bus service from the city center to Auke Bay is frequent and there are shopping centers in between, as well. There are tours to Mendenhall Glacier, you can rent kayaks to tour the harbor or nearby areas or you can rent a car at the airport and do your own touring.

The area around Juneau has hundreds of trails, ranging from beach walks to mountain trails and boardwalks. Point Bridget Trail is

Réanne Hemingway-Douglass

*The bronze effigy of Patsy Ann greets Juneau tourists.*

one of our favorite hikes. The easy 7-mile trail begins at milepost 39 north of Juneau on Glacier Highway and leads through a variety of ecosystems—muskeg, beaver ponds, wet meadows and spongy tundra with stunted forest—on its way to Point Bridget beach.

Transient moorage in Juneau is available at Douglas Harbor, Harris Harbor and Aurora Basin. Visiting vessels should call the harbormaster on VHF Ch 73 for assignment to slips and transient floats. Water and power is available at most spaces. A 14-day limitation

## Juneau

Don Douglass & Réanne Hemingway-Douglass

Juneau is a place of glaciers, gold and government. Conifer-covered hills provide a green backdrop to Alaska's bustling capital city. Although gold mining was Juneau's first industry, it has slipped in importance since World War II. Now, government accounts for the most jobs, followed by tourism, fishing, retail and mining. Juneau's population is just under 31,000 people, but when as many as five cruise ships tie up, it can swell by more than 13,000. Happily, most sail away in the evening.

### Around town

Tourists from cruise ships flock to souvenir and jewelry stores on Franklin Street and eat lunch at the Red Dog Saloon. Near the docks the streets are filled with tour buses and yellow minivan taxis. But traffic fumes and crowds thin out as you stroll in residential areas. You'll see Victorian homes as well as quirky houses in pastel colors, flower gardens, streets so steep that some of them have metal or wooden stairways, and an atmosphere that says artists and rugged individualists live here.

See the Governor's House at 716 Calhoun Avenue and the 1894 St. Nicholas Russian Orthodox Church on 5th St. Walk to the end of 6th St. and step from the city into the forest at the Mt. Roberts Trailhead. If prepared for a hike, keep going five more miles to Roberts Peak.

Learn about Juneau by touring the Alaska State Capitol, the Juneau-Douglas City Museum and the Alaska State Museum.

### What to do

Kiosks lining the dock offer a variety of day and half-day tours. Salmon bakes, helicopter and float plane rides can be arranged, as well as fishing or hiking excursions. Or book a boat trip to see waterfalls, wildlife and the twin Sawyer Glaciers in Tracy Arm Fiord.

The spectacular Mendenhall Glacier is only 13 miles from downtown along the Gastineau Channel. Buses and taxis will take you there, or you can rent a car. Or visit the glacier via a short but dramatic helicopter ride through the "Back Door of Suicide," looking down at the Suicide Ice Fall. You can do a quick turnaround, stay for a 2-hour hike or ride a dogsled.

The Mt. Roberts Tramway, located at the dock, offers a five-minute ride to the top of Mt. Roberts, where you can take in the views, shop and eat. Watch artists carving, beading or creating totems before you ride back down.

You can tour the Alaska-Juneau Mine to learn about mining and its role in Juneau's history. Or pan for gold in Gold Creek.

Juneau is home to places of more specialized interests, including the Mendenhall Golf Course, the Perseverance Theater, the Macaulay Salmon Hatchery and the Alaskan Brewing Company.

### Museums

The Juneau-Douglas City Museum is small but interesting. On display are recently-recovered photos of mining operations and a large fish trap as well as exhibits that recall mining and pioneer days.

Spending time at the Alaska State Museum at 395 Whittier St. will give you a good working knowledge of the state's history, art and natural resources. Its galleries house contemporary artwork and objects from the Haida, Tglingit, Tsimshian as well as Aleut and Athabascan cultures. You'll see clothing, baskets, ivory billikens, totems and maritime and Russian artifacts.

Before you leave Juneau, pet Patsy Ann. She was a well-loved bull terrier who used to frequent the docks whenever a ship would arrive and now her bronze effigy sits on the waterfront.

Two interesting shops are Hearthside Books and Toys for Alaskana (245 Front St.) and Observatory for rare books (200 N. Franklin St.).

For visitor information go to the Juneau Convention & Visitors Bureau at Centennial Hall Convention Center, 101 Egan Dr. (tel.: 888.581.2201; www.traveljuneau.com).

Juneau harbormaster: 907.586.5255.

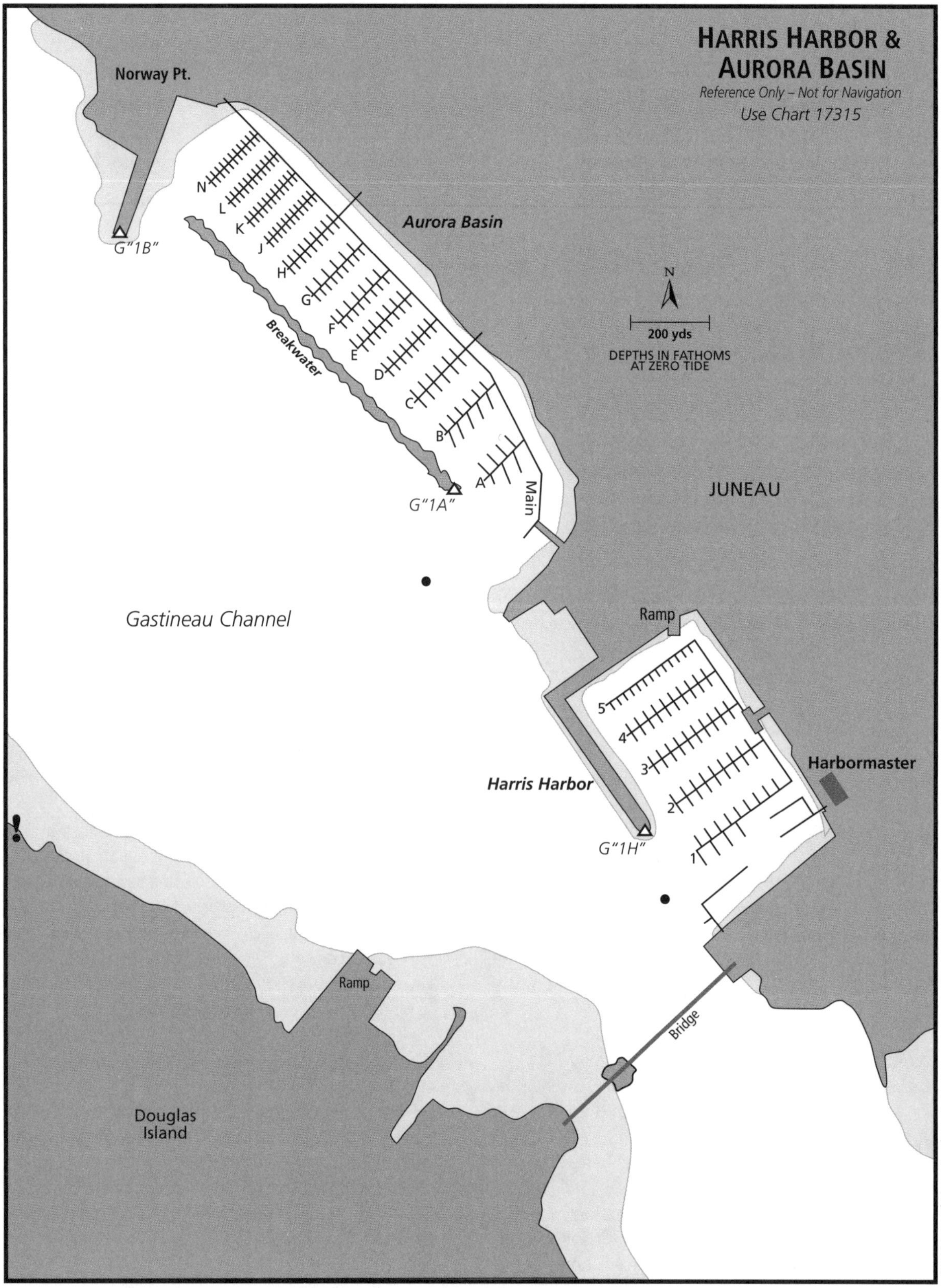
HARRIS HARBOR &
AURORA BASIN
Reference Only – Not for Navigation
Use Chart 17315
Norway Pt.
G"1B"
Aurora Basin
N
L
K
J
H
G
F
E
D
C
B
A
Breakwater
G"1A"
Main
200 yds
DEPTHS IN FATHOMS
AT ZERO TIDE
JUNEAU
Gastineau Channel
Ramp
5
4
3
2
1
Harbormaster
Harris Harbor
G"1H"
Ramp
Bridge
Douglas
Island
©2007 Don and Réanne Douglass

Réanne Hemingway-Douglass

*The road north from Juneau leads to a dead end.*

is enforced on the transient floats. The harbormaster is available from 0700 to 2330 during summer months. Statter Harbor in Auke Bay has only shower facilities.

Fuel can be obtained at Taku Fuels, on the southeast corner of the Juneau Harbor Basin, or at Petro Marine, on the west side of Gastineau Channel, just south of the Juneau-Douglas bridge.

## **Douglas** (Douglas Island)

Douglas Harbor, on the southwest side of Gastineau Channel, is 1.9 miles south of the Juneau-Douglas Bridge.

Chart 17315

Entrance (small-craft harbor): 58°16.63′ N, 134°23.23′ W

*Douglas Boat Harbor, on the inshore side of Juneau Isle, has a Federal project depth of 12 feet. The basin is protected by a 105-foot-long jetty, marked by a light, that extends from the westernmost end of the isle. In June 2004, the controlling depths in the basin were 6.5 to 12 feet. Enter the basin between the jetty and the Douglas City Dock.*

*The small-craft floats in Douglas Boat Harbor, operated by the city of Juneau, can accommodate about 135 craft including transients.* (CP)

Réanne Hemingway-Douglass

*This sign points out the seriousness of driving the road to nowhere.*

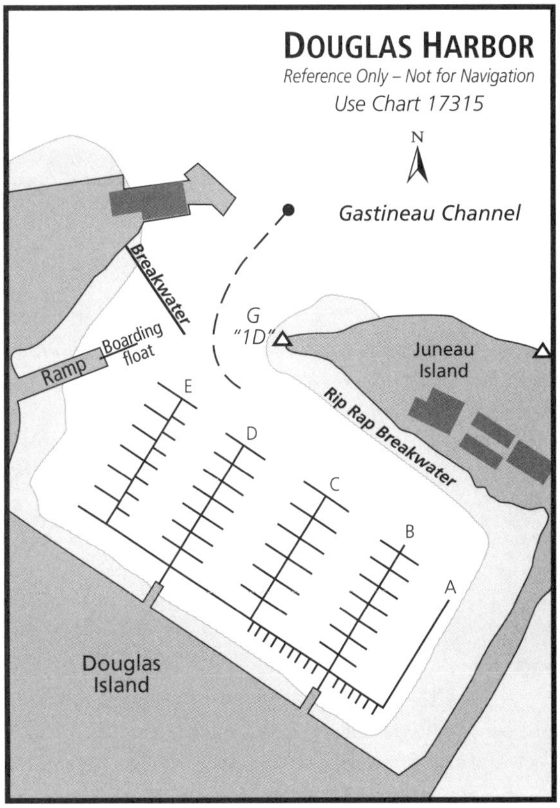


©2007 Don and Réanne Douglass

Douglas Harbor facilities have been upgraded with new floats and electricity. The basin has a double-lane boat launching ramp and a new pump-out station. A grid, formerly located in the basin, was removed. Power and water are available on the floats. The harbor is dredged to 12 feet, with adequate maneuvering room in the new section. The old harbor section has limited maneuvering room; however, transient vessels are normally assigned available moorage in the newer section. The old section of the harbor is scheduled to be upgraded in 2007.

Fuel can be obtained at Petro Marine, on the west side of Gastineau Channel, just south of the Juneau-Douglas bridge or at Taku Fuels, on the southeast corner of the Juneau Harbor Basin.

For availability of pleasure craft moorage, check with the Juneau harbormaster, VHF Ch 73 (tel.: 907.586.5255). There are no showers or other services in the harbor. For easy access to downtown Juneau, the City Transit System runs along Savikko Road, adjacent to the harbor.

Registration can be made at Harris Harbor.

---

### White Knuckles
Réanne Hemingway-Douglass

The captain, with tongue in cheek, tells me he considers the Mendenhall Bar a pre-requisite to attempting either Dry Strait or Dry Pass. While we've tried all three, we've had varying degrees of success.

Years ago, we made the transit across Mendenhall Bar in our first *Baidarka*, bumping our keel twice on the sandy, muddy bottom—a high-adrenaline experience! We navigated Dry Pass (Chichagof Island) successfully in our 32-foot Nordic Tug (west to east), but the two attempts we've made to transit Dry Strait from either end turned our knuckles white and we reversed course each time.

Now, after years of too much excitement, we heed our own printed recommendations and can attest to the fact that Dry Strait is definitely for a few knowledgable locals! (See Chapter 4 for Dry Strait details.)

---

## Mendenhall Bar

Mendenhall Bar is the drying mud flat between Juneau and Fritz Cove and Auke Bay.

### Chart 17315 and USCG diagram

> [Gastineau Channel] . . . *from Juneau to Fritz Cove, a distance of 7.5 miles, crosses Mendenhall Bar and is navigable only by small craft with local knowledge. This part of the channel is subject to considerable shoaling; mariners are advised to obtain the latest local information concerning channel conditions.* (CP)

The route across Mendenhall Bar is sometimes used as a shortcut to Auke Bay by small, shallow-draft boats with expert local knowledge. (Vessels with a draft of 3 feet or less can cross on a 15-foot tide.) The center of the bar dries at 10 feet above MLLW, and many boats still ground. This is a tricky passage with poor underwater visibility and is not advised for visiting cruising boats, which should use Stephens Passage along the west of Douglas Island to reach Auke Bay.

If you insist on a challenge with your dinghy or a skiff, check with the harbormaster first. It's a good idea, also, to follow a local small boat that has first-hand knowledge. The narrow channel changes from year to year and is full of silt. The city has not dredged the channel for a number of years and has no future plans to do so. Because of the silting, it's easy to get off course. The approach from the northwest through Fritz Cove and Mendenhall Bar is narrow, shallow and seasonally marked. *It is not recommended for use without local knowledge.*

Tide gauges at either end of the channel indicate the present amount of water over the shallowest part of the bar. But remember, tide tables are only approximate and can be influenced by wind and barometric pressure. Actual high tide levels are frequently lower than the predicted levels, and locals enjoy watching boats ground on the mud flats along the channel.

## Fritz Cove

Fritz Cove is northeast of Outer Point, the northwest extremity of Douglas Island.

Chart 17315
West entrance (midway between George and Gibby rocks): 58°19.29′ N, 134°41.64′ W
East entrance (Mendenhall Bar west entrance): 58°19.92′ N, 134°37.02′ W

> *Fritz Cove . . . affords anchorage and shelter from S and E winds. A boat-launching ramp is along the S shore at Fritz Cove about 1.6 miles inside the entrance.* (CP)

## Auke Bay

Auke Bay is 3.5 miles north of Fritz Cove.

Chart 17315
Entrance (mid-channel between Battleship Island and Indian Point): 58°22.00′ N, 134°40.77′ W

> *Auke Bay is a community with general stores, a ferry terminal, and seasonal small-craft facilities on the NE shore at the head of Auke Bay. The National Marine Fisheries Service has a biological laboratory at Auke Bay. Auke Lake and Mendenhall Glacier are about 0.3 mile and 3.6 miles inland, respectively, from the community.* (CP)

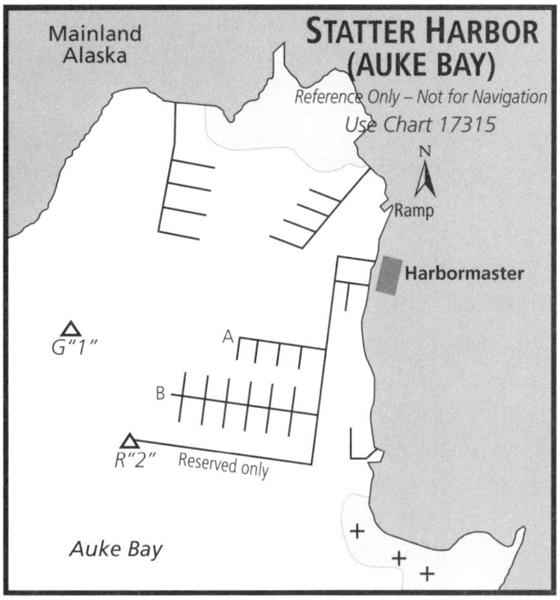


©2007 Don and Réanne Douglass

Statter Harbor in Auke Bay, 12 miles north of Juneau, is the largest of the facilities in the greater Juneau area. Facilities include 7,672 lineal feet of open moorage space (there are no slips). Reservations are accepted for vessels larger than 50 feet in length overall on the float-

Réanne Hemingway-Douglass

*Approaching Auke Bay; Mendenhall Glacier in sight*

ing concrete breakwater. All other moorage space is on a first-come, first-served basis.

The harbor, which is very busy during summer months, has a 10-day transient vessel limitation, after which the vessel must depart for a minimum of six hours before returning. (This limitation does not apply to vessels requesting reserved moorage.) Be sure that you leave the dock by 1100 on your check out date or you will be charged for another day's moorage.

*Auke Bay's Statter Harbor at sunrise*

The harbormaster's office, located at the head of the dock, has restrooms, showers, pay telephones and a weather service squawk box. A seasonal snack bar located in the parking lot has great sandwiches and fries and is a popular place with tourists and boaters. Kayaks can be rented at a kiosk in the harbor parking lot. A convenience store with wine and beer is located just uphill from the harbor office; a self-serve laundromat is a block uphill, and the Auke Bay post office is nearby.

Auke Bay has two fuel docks: Petro Marine at DeHart's Marina and Tesoro Fuel at Fisherman's Bend.

For major provisioning and marine supplies, you must go to Juneau. Although there is bus or taxi service to town, we find it more convenient to rent a car for a day or two. The drawback to having your own vehicle is that parking space at Statter is limited and the hourly limits strictly monitored.

The harbormaster monitors VHF Ch 73. The telephone for the Auke Bay office is 907.789.0819. Boaters can register at either Auke Bay or Harris Harbor.

*Larger vessels can moor at Statter Harbor's concrete breakwater.*

Réanne Hemingway-Douglass

*You can rent a kayak right from Statter's parking lot!*

## NORTHERN STEPHENS PASSAGE

(See the following chapter for Lynn Canal north of Benjamin Island.)

### **Oliver Inlet** (Admiralty Island)

Oliver Inlet, on the south side of Stephens Passage, indents the north end of Admiralty Island.

Chart 17300
Entrance: 58°08.96′ N, 134°19.94′ W
Anchor: 58°06.54′ N, 134°18.37′ W

> *Oliver Inlet has its entrance . . . through a narrow channel 1 mile long and 200 yards wide. The inlet is accessible only at high water to boats and small craft. . . . At high-water slack, small vessels drawing not over 6 feet can enter. The currents in the entrance have a velocity of 6 to 8 knots, forming heavy swirls. A portage of about 0.5 mile long connects this inlet with the head of Seymour Canal.* (CP)

Oliver Inlet is a quiet and peaceful anchorage surrounded by moss-covered trees in which wind and chop never seem to enter. Time stands still here. A breaking twig seemingly reverberates for minutes. Being narrow and 3 miles long, the inlet has an almost spooky quality to it.

The entrance, however, takes some planning to traverse it near slack water with an adequate tide level. On a 13.2-foot slack tide we found a minimum of 8 feet under the keel. During neap tides entering is fairly easy for small craft. However, during spring tides currents are dangerous to small craft.

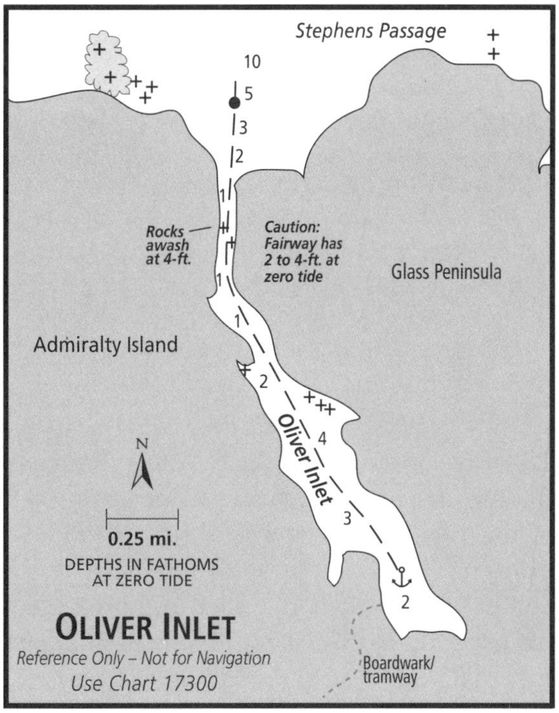



Anchorage can be taken anywhere in the inlet once south of the narrows since the bottom is quite flat and composed of sand, mud and decaying matter with good sticky holding.

The tramway/boardwalk on the west shore leads to Seymour Inlet and a State Parks cabin, a mile to the south. The tramway was rebuilt in 2000 and 50 yards of track were removed. Do not plan on packing a skiff to the other side. This short, narrow and level land mass is all that connects Glass Peninsula to Admiralty Island. Brown and black bears swim across what's called "The Very Berry Zone." On the Seymour Canal side, a 15-foot tide is needed to launch a kayak or skiff.

Anchor in 2 to 3 fathoms over sand and mud with very good holding.

### **Admiralty Cove** (Admiralty Island)

Admiralty Cove, on the south side of Stephens Passage, is just east of Young Bay and 7.8 miles west of Oliver Inlet.

Charts 17315, 17300
Entrance: 58°10.84′ N, 134°36.32′ W
Anchor (south of island): 58°10.70′ N, 134°35.70′ W

Anchor (east of island): 58°11.16′ N, 134°34.90′ W

*Admiralty Cove . . . does not afford anchorage except for small craft because of shallow water. A small vessel can anchor in the cove S of the island on the SW side of Admiralty Cove, in 3 to 6 fathoms, mud bottom. This is a favorite anchorage for small craft but is open to W winds. A conspicuous trail-marker on the SE shore marks the end of a good trail maintained by the U.S. Forest Service. The trail extends 4.5 miles to Admiralty Lake and is much used by trout fishermen and hunters in season.* (CP)

The cove marked on Chart 17300 is largely filled with a mud flat, but a smaller cove south of the island connected to shore offers good protection in all but westerly winds, as noted above. We have anchored about 50 yards east of the north tip of this island in a small 4-fathom hole. The cabin on shore is one of many recreational cabins maintained by the USFS; a permit is required to use these cabins.

Anchor (south of island) in 3 to 6 fathoms over mud with good holding.

Anchor (east of island) in 4 fathoms over mud and sand with good holding.

## Young Bay (Admiralty Island)

Young Bay is 11 miles west of Oliver Inlet.

Chart 17315
Position: 58°10.41′ N, 134°40.71′ W

*Anchorage with shelter from SE winds can be had about 0.5 mile from the SE side of the bay, between Point Young and the head, in 18 to 22 fathoms, soft bottom. Small vessels may anchor closer in shore in desired depths.*

*A good foot trail maintained by the U.S. Forest Service extends from the SW side of Young Bay to the shore of Hawk Inlet.* (CP)

Young Bay is rather deep and exposed for convenient anchorage for small craft. A private dock in the southwest corner of Young Bay is used by a power catamaran that makes daily round trips to Juneau. The cat hauls personnel who work at Green's Creek Mine in Hawk Inlet.

## Saginaw Channel

Saginaw Channel, between Mansfield Peninsula and Shelter Island, joins Stephens Passage with Lynn Canal.

Chart 17316
South entrance (Strauss Rock buoy bearing 053°T at 0.76 Nm): 58°21.22′ N, 134°49.40′ W
North entrance: (Point Retreat Light bearing 158°T at 1.2 Nm): 58°25.82′ N, 134°58.18′ W

*This channel is used by vessels going from Stephens Passage to Chatham Strait or Icy Strait.* (CP)

Some small vessels coming out of Auke Bay pass north of Strauss Rock over a 1- to 2-fathom shoal avoiding the many sport fishing boats frequenting here.

## Adams Anchorage (Shelter Island)

Adams Anchorage is off the south end of Shelter Island and 5 miles west of Auke Bay.

Chart 17316
Position: 58°22.16′ N, 134°49.25′ W

*Adams Anchorage . . . offers good anchorage in 11 fathoms and very good anchorage for small craft in less depth, close to the shore during N weather.* (CP)

Adams Anchorage, a favorite for sport fishing boats during openings of fishing season, is a fair-weather anchor site; however, a lot of wake from passing boats is felt here.

## Barlow Cove (Mansfield Peninsula)

Barlow Cove is on the northeast side of the north tip of Mansfield Peninsula.

Chart 17316
Entrance: 58.24.11′ N, 134°55.42′ W

*A light on Point Retreat . . . marks the W point of the entrance and the Barlow Islands form the E point of the entrance. The waters throughout the cove are deep.* (CP)

According to locals, small craft can anchor at the southeast head of the cove in less than 10 fathoms, mud bottom with good holding.

## Favorite Channel

Favorite Channel, between Shelter Island and the mainland, joins Stephens Passage with Lynn Canal.

Chart 17316
South entrance: 58°22.27′ N, 134°46.60′ W
North entrance (Little Island Light bearing 250°T at 1.65 Nm): 58°33.00′ N, 135°00.85′ W

> [Favorite Channel] *is the channel used by vessels going from Stephens Passage to upper Lynn Canal points and Skagway.* (CP)

Favorite Channel contains Lena, Tee, Pearl, Amalga and Eagle harbors on its east shore.

## **Lena Cove** (Favorite Channel)

Lena Cove is 3.3 miles northwest of Auke Bay.

Chart 17316
Entrance: 58°24.13′ N, 134°46.35′ W

> *Lena Cove is . . . about 2 miles NE of Shelter Island Light. . . . It affords a SE lee, but the bottom is rocky and is not a good anchorage for large vessels. Rocks awash are close to the NE shore, N of the N point of the entrance.* (CP)

## **Tee Harbor** (Favorite Channel)

Tee Harbor is 4.2 miles northwest of Auke Bay.

Chart 17316
Entrance: 58°25.46′ N, 134°46.19′ W
Anchor (south): 58°24.75′ N, 134°45.63′ W
Anchor (north): 58°25.79′ N, 134°45.83′ W

> *Tee Harbor . . . affords anchorage in the middle just within the points at the entrance, in 12 to 14 fathoms. During SE weather, williwaws are severe at times. Small craft avoid these by anchoring in 6 to 9 fathoms at the S end of the S arm close to the beach. Winter N winds can be avoided by small craft by anchoring in the N arm, close to the beach, in 4 to 9 fathoms. Tee Harbor has telephone and highway connections with Juneau.* (CP)

The marina in Tee Harbor is used mainly by sport fishing boats. There is a "No Trespassing" sign at the dock as you enter. A parking area several hundred yards up from the dock has space for boat trailers. The water in the harbor is partially discolored due to the glacier-fed creeks entering the harbor; visibility through the water is limited to 3–4 feet. Fuel is available at the float. If you enter the harbor, avoid the rock marked by buoy R"2."

Réanne Hemingway-Douglass

*Fuel is available at Tee Harbor's sports-fishing floats*

## **Pearl Harbor** (Favorite Channel)

Pearl Harbor is 7.4 miles northwest of Auke Bay.

Chart 17316
Entrance: 58°28.60′ N, 134°47.40′ W

Pearl Harbor is a small indentation where some temporary shelter can be found from south winds in the lee of the south islet. Avoid the shoal on the north side of the islet when entering.

## **Amalga Harbor** (Favorite Channel)

Amalga Harbor is 0.8 miles north of Pearl Harbor.

Chart 17316
Entrance: 58°29.26′ N, 134°47.58′ W

> *Amalga Harbor, a small landlocked cove . . . affords good small-craft anchorage in 3 to 4 fathoms, rocky bottom. The harbor has a State-maintained surfaced boat-launching ramp.* (CP)

Amalga Harbor is a tiny coastal opening sheltered by several islands on its north and west sides.

## **Eagle Harbor** (Favorite Channel)

Eagle Harbor is 8.5 miles northwest of Auke Bay.

Chart 17316
Entrance: 58°29.73′ N, 134°48.10′ W

> *Eagle Harbor . . . affords anchorage in moderate weather. Good holding ground is found in depths of 14 fathoms near midharbor.* (CP)

Locals report temporary anchorages, close in, over 5 to 7 fathoms and good holding. Avoid the charted mid-channel rock north of the island northwest of Amalga Harbor.

## Lynn Canal

Lynn Canal extends northward from the junction of Chatham Strait and Icy Strait for about 58 miles to Seduction Point, where it divides into Chilkat and Chilkoot inlets.

### Charts 17300, 17317
### South entrance (Point Couverden bearing 270°T at 2.5 Nm): 58°11.50′ N, 134°58.67′ W

*The canal is nearly free of dangers, and the water is generally very deep. The shores as a rule are very high and wooded, with many bare mountain peaks and small glaciers in nearly every ravine.*

*Anchorage can be had in Funter Bay, William Henry Bay, W of Sullivan Island, Portage Cove (Chilkoot Inlet), and Lutak Inlet. Temporary anchorage can also be had in St. James Bay, Berners Bay, and at Skagway. Small craft can find anchorage in several coves.*

*The high shores of Lynn Canal tend to guide winds along its axis while the narrowing to N intensifies winds blowing from S or SE. Southerlies often reach 16 knots or more.* (CP)

Lynn Canal—named by George Vancouver for his birthplace in England—leads north to Haines and picturesque Skagway along a route of alpine splendor. The high, jagged peaks, snowfields and hanging glaciers along the canal are magnificent.

Winds kick up a nasty chop in this long fiord, so plan for alternative shelter should you need it. It is not always bleak, however—the entire 85-mile trip from Juneau to Haines has been made in fair weather by jet skis.

---

## Treacherous Waters

**Don Douglass & Réanne Hemingway-Douglass**

Lynn Canal extends from Chatham and Icy Straits in the south to Skagway, 84 miles to the north. The deep fiord has steep shores that reach to bare alpine summits, and hanging glaciers in canyons along the route are visible from the canal on a clear day.

Due to its north-south orientation, and because so many large rivers feed into it from the interior, strong winds are a common occurrence in Lynn Canal. Southerly winds are particularly dangerous because the canal gradually narrows toward the north, intensifying the winds. The length of the canal provides a long fetch where seas can build quickly to alarming heights. Williwaw winds (katabatic winds dropping from the hanging glaciers), of an intensity that covers the canal with spray, create poor visibility and make navigation difficult.

Considered an iron-bound coast, the steep rocky shores of Lynn Canal offer little if any protection from the elements. Small craft transiting the area are left to find what shelter they can in small indentations along the mainland shore or in the lee of small islands.

Approximately 3 miles northwest of Benjamin Island lurks Vanderbilt Reef (58°35.45′ N, 135°01.13′ W), awash on a 12-foot tide. Since tides in the area frequently reach 20 feet on springs (twice each month), the reef lies below the surface about half the time.

This reef marks Alaska's greatest maritime tragedy. On a stormy night in October 1918, the Canadian Pacific steamer, *Princess Sophia,* on its last southbound voyage of the year, ran aground on the reef at near full-speed. The ship, which was carrying 350 miners, businessmen, civil servants, their families and crew, did not sink at the time. In fact it appeared to have only minor damage. Rescue vessels, dispatched from Juneau the next day, waited for an opportunity to remove the passengers and crew, but by late afternoon the storm had worsened and the rescue vessels were forced to seek shelter behind Sentinel and Benjamin islands and in Bridget Cove. When they were able to return the following morning, all they found of the *Princess Sophia* was 20 feet of her mast extending above the water. The only survivor was a dog that managed to swim to the mainland and was found in Tee Harbor several days later. For a good account of the accident and its effect on post-gold rush Alaska, read *The Final Voyage of the Princess Sophia* by Betty O'Keefe and Ian Macdonald.

Linda Lewis

*Ships are the transport life-line in Southeast Alaska, bearing all kinds of goods.*

## Howard Bay (Lynn Canal)

Howard Bay is northwest of Howard Point.

Chart 17316
Entrance: 58°16.40′ N, 135°03.49′ W
Anchor: 58°17.68′ N, 135°04.49′ W

> *Good anchorage in 15 to 25 fathoms, soft bottom, may be found in Howard Bay. . . . Anchor with the tip of Point Howard ESE at a distance of about 0.7 mile.* (CP)

Howard Bay provides shelter from westerlies and outflow winds but it is open to southeast gales.

Anchor in 10 fathoms over hard mud with fair holding.

## St. James Bay (Lynn Canal)

St. James Bay, on the west shore of Lynn Canal, is 11 miles northwest of Point Retreat.

Chart 17316
Entrance (Point Whidbey bearing 016°T at 0.7 Nm): 58°34.02′ N, 135°08.76′ W
Anchor: 58°37.37′ N, 135°10.58′ W

> *St. James Bay . . . extends about 4.5 miles in a N direction to its head, where a large stream enters, forming extensive mud flats. A temporary anchorage, in 20 fathoms, soft bottom, may be selected on the E side of the bay. The anchorage is open to SE winds.* (CP)

St. James Bay, and adjacent Boat Harbor and the surrounding shorelines, comprise St. James Bay State Marine Park. The anchorage shown in the diagram is located in the northeast corner of the bay. Since you may find crab pots set in this area during summer, you may need to anchor in deeper water.

Avoid the rocks and foul ground south of Point Whidbey. Steer east of the reef and rock that extend approximately 1/2 mile southeast from the island in the northeast corner of the bay.

Anchor approximately opposite the small islet in 3 to 7 fathoms; good holding.

## Boat Harbor (Lynn Canal)

Boat Harbor, on the west side of Lynn Canal, is 3.5 miles north of Point Whidbey.

Chart 17316
Entrance: 58°38.24′ N, 135°09.33′ W
Anchor: 58°37.78′ N, 135°09.96′ W

> *Boat Harbor,* [is] *a basin with depths up to 14 fathoms. It can be entered by small craft only*

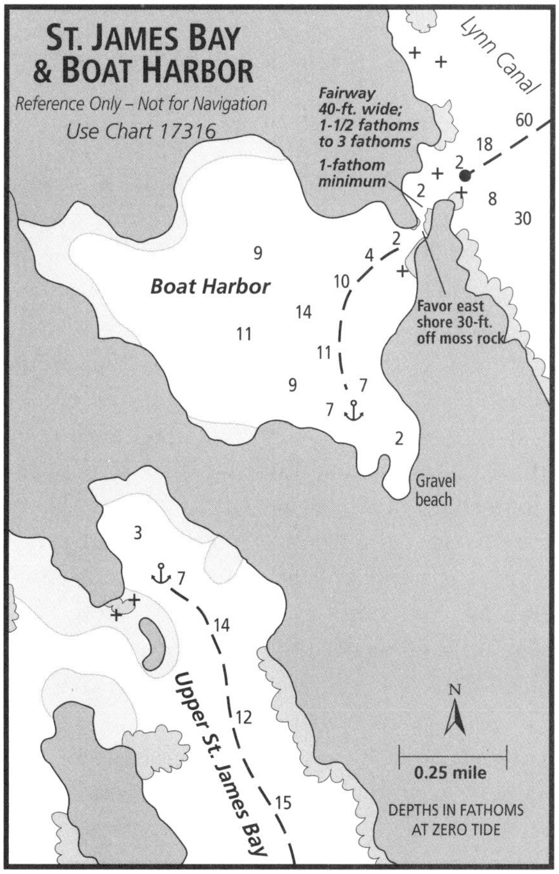

Réanne Hemingway-Douglass

*Boat Harbor's entrance, viewed from inside*

*because of its contracted entrance, which is about 60 feet wide in its narrowest part. In 1993, the channel was reportedly well-defined at low water, but boulders along the bottom of the entrance reduce the controlling depth. In 2000, the controlling depth was 1-1/4 fathoms. The currents have considerable velocity through the entrance and the period of slack water on low tide reportedly lasts less than normal. Boat Harbor is also reported to have a delayed tidal flow and will continue to ebb 30 to 40 minutes after low tide.* (CP)

While Boat Harbor is very inviting, it should only be utilized with great care and preferably with a reconnoitering first with a dinghy. Once you're inside, Boat Harbor is an excellent anchorage for cruising boats. Since its entrance is almost invisible from the south, you can completely miss it when you're only a quarter-mile from shore. The harbor is totally landlocked, and lack of driftwood along shore indicates a calm anchorage. There are landing beaches and potential campsites along the sand and gravel shore, and a few crab pot floats on the west side of the harbor. Midsummer water temperatures frequently reach 62°F.

The tiny, somewhat difficult entrance is the price you pay for a near-perfect shelter. Boats without local knowledge should reconnoiter by dinghy before entering the harbor, since strong currents make steering difficult. One reason Boat Harbor is seldom mentioned in guidebooks is that its entrance is much narrower and shallower than that stated in *Coast Pilot.*

We estimate the fairway to have a width of about 40 feet and a minimum depth of from 1 to 1.5 fathoms at zero tide. It is safest to enter at high-water slack. The fairway has an irregular bottom with reefs that extend from either side. Favor the east shore once you're inside the narrows. We have not seen the rock or kelp noted on the chart at the 2-fathom flat bar outside the narrows.

Anchor in 7 fathoms over hard sand and gravel with fair-to-good holding.

## Benjamin Island Cove and Benjamin Island Bight

(Benjamin Island)

Benjamin Island is 14 miles north of Auke Bay.

Chart 17316
Entrance (Benjamin Island): 58°34.17′ N, 134°54.69′ W
Anchor (Benjamin Island Cove): 58°33.93′ N, 134°54.60′ W
Anchor (Benjamin Island Bight): 58°33.21′ N, 134°54.28′ W

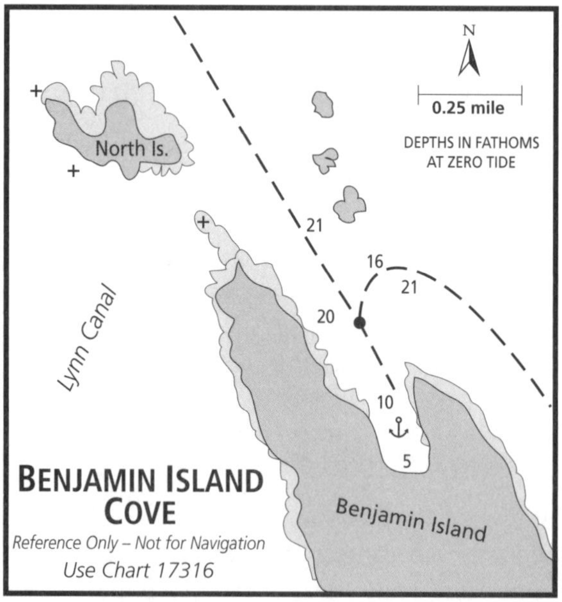


©2007 Don and Réanne Douglass

*Temporary anchorage, with protection against severe winds, may be had in the bight on the S side of Benjamin Island.* (CP)

From the south, vessels can travel up Favorite Channel, Saginaw Channel, and through North Pass between Shelter and Lincoln islands, or up the main trunk of Lynn Canal until north of Little Island.

The bight on the south end of Benjamin Island is reported to offer some shelter from strong outflow winds whistling down Lynn Canal.

The cove on the north end of Benjamin Island provides shelter from southeast gales and is entered from the channel between the island and the mainland. Although the channel between Benjamin and North islands is suitable for kayaks and skiffs, cruising boats should probably not attempt the passage. You can enter the cove under radar in limited visibility, although you should post a crew member to look out for the small rocky islets northeast of the cove. Enter the cove in mid-channel and move close to the head where suitable depths for anchoring can be found. The head of the cove has a cobble beach, and there is a campsite there.

Anchor at the head of the cove in 6 to 8 fathoms.

## **Vanderbilt Reef** (Lynn Canal)

Vanderbilt Reef is 3.2 miles northwest of Benjamin Island.

Chart 17316
Position (Vanderbilt Reef Light): 58°35.42′ N, 135°01.15′ W

*Vanderbilt Reef . . . is a rock that uncovers 12 feet. It is marked by Vanderbilt Reef Light. . . .* (CP)

Vanderbilt Reef is the site of the tragic grounding and sinking of *Princess Sophia* in 1918, when 350 people lost their lives. See *The Final Voyage of the Princess Sophia* for this Alaskan *"Titanic"* story.

If you drive the highway, there's a pull-out above the water where you have a good view of the reef.

On the eastern shore, due east of Vanderbilt Reef, there is a series of north-south islets and a half-moon stony beach at its head with few, if any storm drift logs (indicating shelter) that may offer a temporary anchor site.

## **Yankee Cove** (Lynn Canal)

Yankee Cove, on the east side of Lynn Canal, is 1.2 miles northeast of North Island.

Chart 17316
Position: 58°35.29′ N, 134°54.15′ W

Yankee Cove is too exposed for use other than sport fishing boats.

## **Bridget Cove** (Lynn Canal)

Bridget Cove is 3.2 miles northeast of Vanderbilt Reef and 18 miles north of Auke Bay.

Chart 17316
South entrance: 58°37.53′ N, 134°57.22′ W
North entrance: 58°38.56′ N, 134°57.97′ W
Anchor: 58°38.47′ N, 134°57.38′ W

*Bridget Cove . . . is behind Mab Island, affording anchorage for small craft in 4 to 7 fathoms, with scant swinging room. A 1.3 fathom shoal in 58°38′06″N., 134°57′06″W. is in the middle of the passage between Mab Island and the mainland. Small boats may secure better protection by anchoring inside the cove opposite the N end of Mab Island* [known locally as Akiyama Bight] . . . (CP)

Bridget Cove, which is within the 2,800-acre Point Bridget State Park, provides reasonable shelter. The highway north from Juneau lies a short distance inland to the east. The cove can be entered by the passages north or south of Mab Island. If you enter from the south, favor the Mab Island side, watching for rocks and a reef that extend south from the south point of the island. A reef parallel to the mainland shore extends north from the outer south point of Bridget Cove.

If you enter from the north end of Mab Island, avoid the rocky reefs that extend short distances from either shore.

We have observed vessels of up to 60 feet (seiner tenders) anchored in the channel between the island and the mainland. Except for the cobbled shores in the southeast and northeast bights, the shorelines of the cove are rocky. You can land a dinghy at the head of the northeast bight. If you rent a car and drive north from Juneau, Point Bridget State Park has a trail that leads from the road southwest to the cove. The boardwalk trail is unmarked except by a post.

Anchor in the northeast bight in 5 to 7 fathoms over mud with good holding.

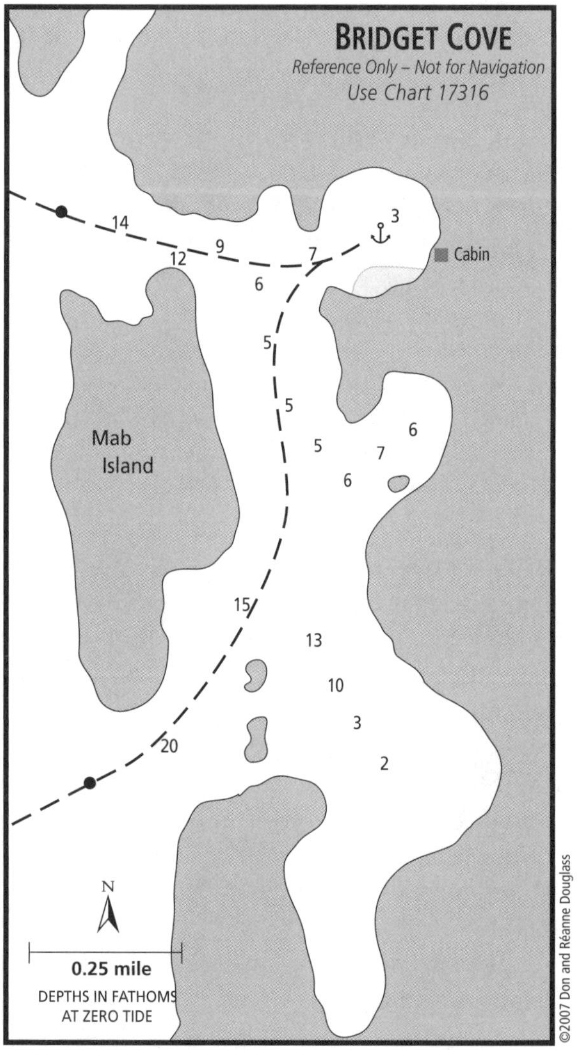


## Berners Bay (Lynn Canal)

Berners Bay is 23 miles north of Auke Bay.

**Chart 17316**
**Entrance: 58°42.43′ N, 135°00.44′ W**

> *The bay is open to S winds, but in fine weather temporary anchorage in 16 to 25 fathoms may be selected near the head . . .* (CP)

Berners Bay is rather deep and exposed for small craft, but it does offer relief from downslope winds. Small craft will find more secure anchorage in Echo Cove on the southeast side of the bay.

## Echo Cove (Berners Bay)

Echo Cove is the second bight 2 miles east of Pt. Bridget.

**Chart 17316**
**Entrance (1.8 miles northeast of Pt. Bridget): 58°41.28′ N, 134°56.06′ W**
**Anchor: 58°39.86′ N, 134°54.80′ W**

> *The entrance is nearly blocked by a flat making out from the W point, leaving a very narrow channel that follows the E shore at a distance of 150 yards and has a controlling depth of 1 fathom. Inside, the depths are 3 to 12 fathoms, and small vessels using caution can enter and find secure anchorage.* (CP)

The entrance to Echo Cove is narrow and shallow, but the cove, which is well protected from all weather, is a favorite of local fishing boats.

There are primitive campsites on shore; The absence of drift logs along shore indicates good protection. Above the cove, there is parking lot and a good boat launch ramp.

Anchor in 4 to 8 fathoms over a soft bottom.

## William Henry Bay (Lynn Canal)

William Henry Bay is 9 miles north of Point Whidbey.

**Chart 17316**
**Entrance: 58°43.44′ N, 135°13.81′ W**
**Anchor: 58°42.66′ N, 135°14.40′ W**

> *William Henry Bay . . . is easy of access and is the best anchorage from S weather in this vicinity. According to local reports, N winds are felt with considerable force. Enter in midchannel,*

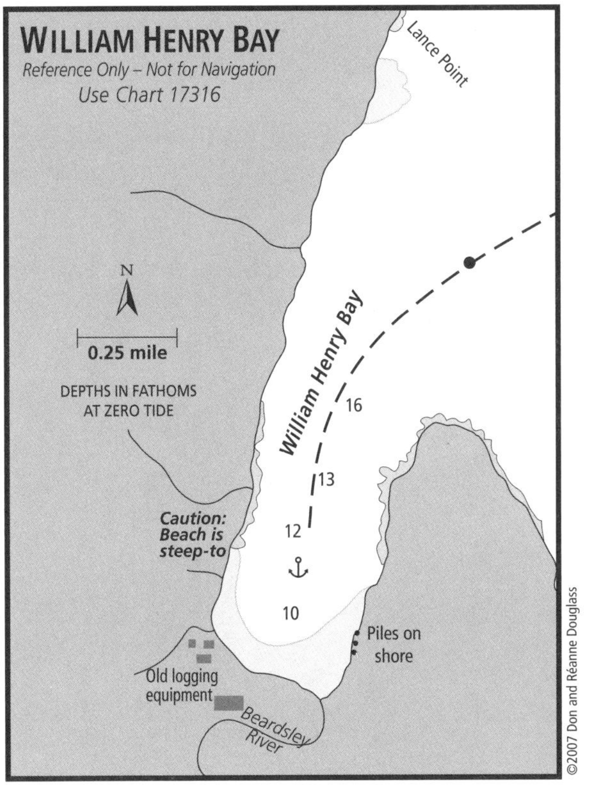


*and when the second waterfall on the W shore of the bay is abeam, anchor in 12 fathoms, soft bottom, about 0.4 mile from the head.* (CP)

William Henry Bay provides easy access and excellent protection from southerlies, and when southeast storms are raging outside, it is dead calm inside the bay. The entire bottom is flat, and there is swinging room for several boats. The best anchorage is off the Beardsley River outlet. The beach, which can be approached by dinghy, is mostly gravel. The bay offers good views of snowfields to the south and a verdant valley to the west.

Entrance can be made easily in limited visibility with radar. Avoid the rocky, kelp-covered reef that extends from Lancer Point; it dries at 3 feet.

Anchor in 12 fathoms over sand and mud with good holding.

*Réanne and Don admiring a massive piece of driftwood on the beach.*

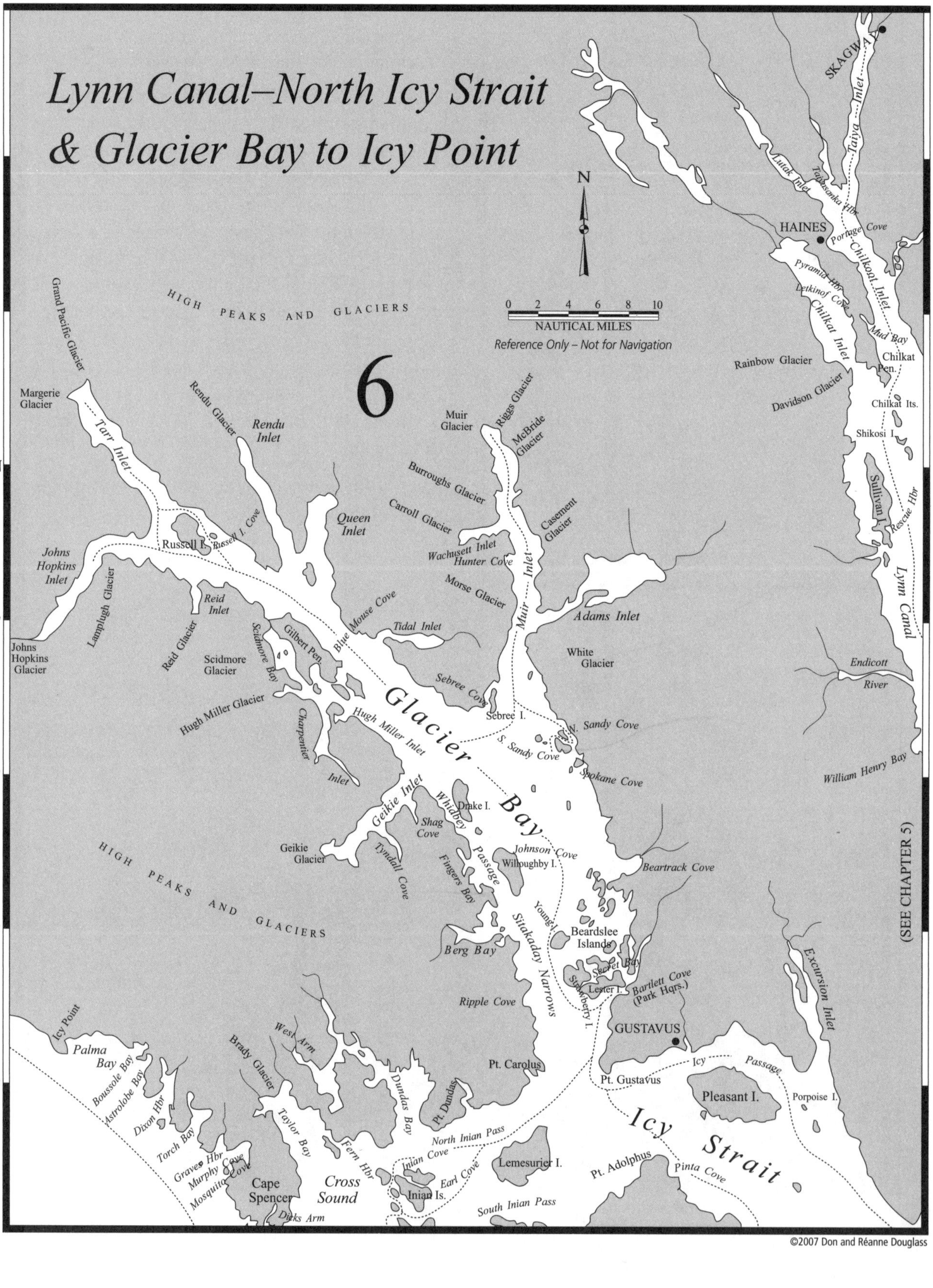
Lynn Canal–North Icy Strait
& Glacier Bay to Icy Point
6
N
0 2 4 6 8 10
NAUTICAL MILES
Reference Only – Not for Navigation
HIGH PEAKS AND GLACIERS
HIGH PEAKS AND GLACIERS
SKAGWAY
Taiya Inlet
Lutak Inlet
Taiyasanka Hbr
HAINES
Portage Cove
Chilkoot Inlet
Pyramid Hbr
Letkinof Cove
Chilkat Inlet
Mud Bay
Chilkat Pen.
Rainbow Glacier
Davidson Glacier
Chilkat Its.
Shikosi I.
Sullivan I.
Rescue Hbr
Lynn Canal
Endicott River
William Henry Bay
(SEE CHAPTER 5)
Excursion Inlet
Grand Pacific Glacier
Margerie Glacier
Tarr Inlet
Rendu Glacier
Rendu Inlet
Johns Hopkins Inlet
Johns Hopkins Glacier
Russell I.
Russell I. Cove
Queen Inlet
Lamplugh Glacier
Reid Inlet
Reid Glacier
Scidmore Bay
Scidmore Glacier
Gilbert Pen.
Blue Mouse Cove
Hugh Miller Glacier
Hugh Miller Inlet
Charpentier Inlet
Muir Glacier
Riggs Glacier
McBride Glacier
Burroughs Glacier
Carroll Glacier
Casement Glacier
Wachusett Inlet
Hunter Cove
Morse Glacier
Muir Inlet
Adams Inlet
Tidal Inlet
White Glacier
Sebree Cove
Sebree I.
Glacier Bay
N. Sandy Cove
S. Sandy Cove
Spokane Cove
Geikie Inlet
Geikie Glacier
Drake I.
Whidbey Passage
Shag Cove
Tyndall Cove
Fingers Bay
Johnson Cove
Willoughby I.
Beartrack Cove
Young I.
Beardslee Islands
Sitakaday Narrows
Berg Bay
Secret Bay
Lester I.
Strawberry I.
Bartlett Cove (Park Hqrs.)
Ripple Cove
GUSTAVUS
Icy Point
Palma Bay
Boussole Bay
Astrolabe Bay
Dixon Hbr
Torch Bay
Graves Hbr
Murphy Cove
Mosquito Cove
Cape Spencer
Dicks Arm
West Arm
Brady Glacier
Taylor Bay
Dundas Bay
Pt. Dundas
Pt. Carolus
Fern Hbr
Cross Sound
North Inian Pass
Inian Cove
Earl Cove
Inian Is.
South Inian Pass
Lemesurier I.
Pt. Adolphus
Pt. Gustavus
Icy Passage
Pleasant I.
Porpoise I.
Icy Strait
Pinta Cove
59°N
59°N
10'
20'
30'
40'
50'

# 6

# LYNN CANAL NORTH, ICY STRAIT AND GLACIER BAY, CROSS SOUND TO ICY POINT

## INTRODUCTION

Mountains covered with massive icefields, hanging glaciers and stunning scenery—you find all of this and more as your proceed north in Lynn Canal and then south and west into Icy Strait and Glacier Bay National Park. This is a remote region of high-latitude, frigid waters, limited radio reception and extreme tides, so be well prepared!

From Point Retreat at the northern tip of Admiralty Island (28 miles northwest of Juneau), Lynn Canal continues north for 60 miles, where it breaks into three inlets: Chilkat, Chilkoot and Taiya. The landscape along the canal becomes increasingly more dramatic; the mountainsides that rise steeply from the water's edge are filled with snowbowls and hanging glaciers.

The craggy Cathedral Peaks behind Haines provide a spectacular and classic Alaskan backdrop for the town. The Alaska State Ferry drops many passengers here who continue north on the Haines Highway that connects to the Alaska Highway. Haines itself is worth a visit, and cruising boaters will find it a friendly community, with an excellent museum, totems and art galleries. In addition to the many events put on for summer tourists—including performances by the Chilkat Dancers—Haines is also the site of the popular Southeast Alaska State Fair, held in August. Twenty miles north of Haines is the Chilkat Bald Eagle Preserve, where over 3,000 eagles make their winter home.

Linda Lewis

*Glacier Bay in all its magnificence*

Linda Lewis

*A perfect bird ice sculpture in Glacier Bay*

Skagway, at the bitter north end of Taiya Inlet, nestles in the beautiful Skagway River delta. Famous for its gold rush history, the main part of the town was set aside as the Klondike Gold Rush National Historical Park. The Chilkoot Trail, originally an Indian trail that leads over the 3,500-foot Chilkoot Pass, gained its reputation in the late 1800s as prospectors flocked to the Klondike gold fields beyond the Canadian border. Photos of the period can be seen in many of the local establishments.

West of the southern end of Lynn Canal lies Glacier Bay National Park and Preserve, a gem covering 3.3 million acres of wilderness. Famous for its concentration of tidewater glaciers, the park contains miles of austere land recently revealed by receding glaciers. When Captain George Vancouver and his men first explored the area in 1794, they found Icy Strait choked with "solid mountains of ice." But by the time John Muir visited Glacier Bay from Wrangell by canoe 85 years later (1879), he found that the ice had retreated 48 miles up the bay. Muir was the first to document the topography of Glacier Bay, and his writings have become part of classical literature. Current Park Service maps show the limits to which the glaciers have retreated during the past 200 years—the most rapid retreat known in the world.

Vegetation in the park ranges from the mature rainforest in Bartlett Cove, which is about 200 years old, to successively younger species as you proceed northward in Glacier Bay. The land in the upper reaches is still raw, the rock scraped and ground to glacial till where just small plants and lichens can establish themselves. In addition to its magnificent glaciers, the park is renowned for its wildlife—nearly 200 species of birds have been sighted here; whales, orcas and seals frequent the waters, and bear can sometimes be spotted along shore.

The park boundaries encompass not only Glacier Bay proper, but also the area west of Icy Strait in Cross Sound, all the way along the outer coast to Dry Bay, 90 miles north of Cape Spencer. Between June 1 and August 31, a permit is required to enter Glacier Bay National Park north of a line between Points Gustavus and Carolus. The number of boats allowed within the permit area is limited to 25 a day (which means just three or four per day may enter).

The remote and beautiful park areas to the west of Glacier Bay proper have no permit requirements. It is worth spending a week exploring Dundas Bay, Fern Harbor, Dicks Arm and Graves Harbor. Lituya Bay, 47 miles north of Cape Spencer, is not only exceptionally beautiful, but it has an awesome history that includes earthquake-induced avalanches and colossal waves.

## LYNN CANAL NORTH

### **Rescue Harbor** (Sullivan Island)

Rescue Harbor, on the southeast side of Sullivan Island, is 2.2 miles north of Sullivan Rock. Sullivan Island, on the W side of Lynn Canal, is about 6 miles NW of Point Sherman.

Chart 17317
Entrance: 58°56.09′ N, 135°17.95′ W
Anchor: 58°56.43′ N, 135°18.47′ W

*Anchorage for small boats, with protection against N winds, may be had in the small bight on the E shore of Sullivan Island near the SE end. In entering avoid the reef that extends about 0.2 mile off the NE entrance point.* (CP)

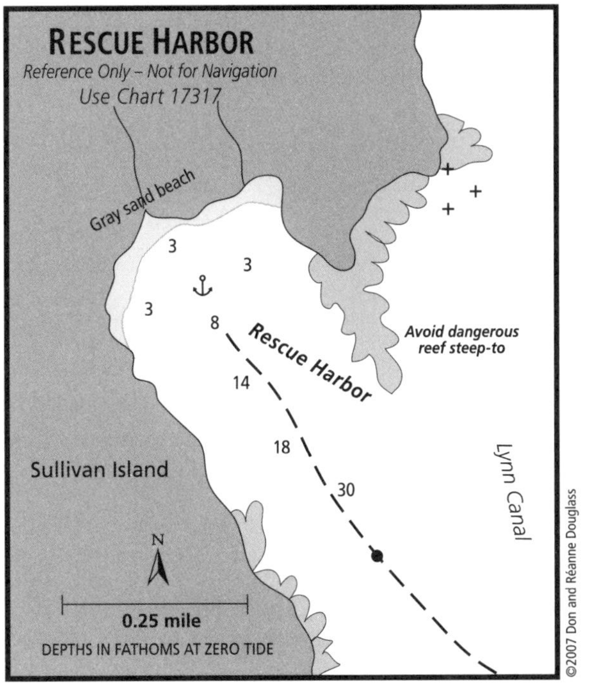


Rescue Harbor, the second bight on the southeast side of Sullivan Island, provides very good shelter from winds from southwest through north to northeast. Its beach, gray sand with gravel, becomes steep-to about 100 yards offshore.

You can enter Rescue Harbor by radar in limited visibility, but be careful to avoid the reef on the east side, which is steep-to with depths of 30 fathoms 150 feet off its south edge. This reef extends over 400 yards offshore.

Do not confuse Rescue Harbor with the first bight north of Sullivan Rock.

Rescue Harbor is exposed to the southeast. For protection from southerlies, see Sullivan West Bight below.

Anchor in 3 to 5 fathoms over sand and mud with excellent holding.

## Shikosi Island Bight (Shikosi Island)

Shikosi Island Bight is on the north side of Shikosi Island, one of the four islands in the Chilkat Islands chain.

Chart 17317
Entrance: 59°02.31′ N, 135°16.36′ W
Anchor: 59°02.08′ N, 135°16.32′ W

> *Shikosi Island, N of Kataguni Island, has a bight in its N side that affords anchorage for small craft with shelter from moderate S winds. A shoal with depths of as little as 1 fathom, and terminating with a rock that bares, extends over 0.2 mile N of the E point of the bight. Favor the W point of the bight in entering.* (CP)

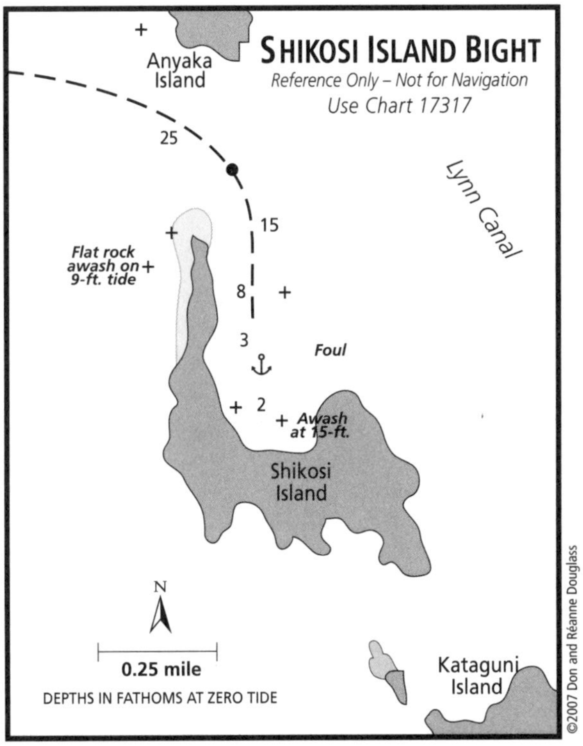


Shikosi Island Bight, small and picturesque, offers fair-weather anchorage with great views of the snowy massifs bordering Lynn Canal. At times, the rocks scattered around Shikosi and Kataguni islands are covered with seals. Moderate protection from southerlies can be obtained here.

The entrance to the bight requires caution due to an irregular bottom, numerous rocks and a foul area. The small-scale chart is inadequate for navigation.

Anchor in about 2 fathoms over gravel and rocks with poor-to-fair holding.

## Sullivan West Bight

Sullivan West Bight is 1 mile west of Sullivan Island and 2.6 miles northwest of Sullivan Rock.

**Chart 17317**
**Entrance (south): 58°54.10′ N, 135°18.78′ W**
**Anchor: 58°55.57′ N, 135°22.06′ W**

> *Anchorage may be had in 16 fathoms, sticky bottom, in the bight in the W shore, W of the S end of Sullivan Island. Vessels entering from the S should favor the islands.* (CP)

"Sullivan West Bight" is our name for the bight 2.6 miles northwest of Sullivan Rock. This site is tucked below the snowfields and glaciers on the west side of Lynn Canal and offers some protection in the lee of Sullivan Island off the drying mud flat in sticky mud. Pass south of Sullivan Rock and avoid both the foul area at the tip of Sullivan Island and the rock 400 yards offshore, 0.6 mile north of the bight.

Anchor in 12 fathoms over sticky mud with very good holding.

## Chilkat Inlet (Lynn Canal)

Chilkat Inlet, at the head of Lynn Canal, lies west of Chilkat Peninsula.

**Chart 17317**
**Entrance (Seduction Point bearing 083°T at 0.83 Nm): 59°04.74′ N, 135°20.12′ W**

> *The arm is narrowed to 0.8 mile by Glacier Point, 2.5 miles from Seduction Point; it then expands to 2.5 miles and maintains this width for some distance, narrowing to 2 miles at its head.*
>
> *The E shore of Chilkat Inlet is very irregular. . . . There are several bights that furnish fair weather anchorage for small boats.* (CP)

Chilkat Inlet is 9 miles long and largely shoal with opaque water. Small craft can find shelter in Letnikof Cove, but most boats visiting Haines use the harbor in Portage Bay.

## Kalhagu Cove (Chilkat Inlet)

Kalhagu Cove, on the southwest side of Chilkat Peninsula, is 7.8 miles southeast of Haines.

**Chart 17317**
**Position: 59°06.42′ N, 135°21.34′ W**

> *A ledge that bares extends 0.2 mile S from* [Glacier Point] *on the W shore of Kalhagu Cove.* (CP)

## Letnikof Cove (Chilkat Inlet)

Letnikof Cove, on the east shore of Chilkat Inlet, is 4 miles southeast of Haines.

**Chart 17317**
**Entrance: 59°10.59′ N, 135°24.21′ W**
**Anchor: 59°10.33′ N, 135°23.26′ W**

> *Letnikof Cove . . . affords anchorage for small craft, exposed to NW winds near the head of the cove, in 6 to 10 fathoms.*
>
> *The State-maintained seasonal small-craft floats are across the cove. . . .* (CP)

Letnikof Cove, which is popular for locals in the summer, offers shelter from southeast gales; however, it is open to downslope winds.

This location has no electricity, water or fuel.

## Chilkoot Inlet (Lynn Canal)

Chilkoot Inlet, the east arm of Lynn Canal, extends northward 12.6 miles, where it divides. The east arm of Chilkoot—Taiya Inlet—terminates at Skagway.

**Chart 17317**
**South entrance (Seduction Point bearing 270°T at 1.7 Nm): 59°04.86′ N, 135°15.11′ W**

> *Chilkoot Inlet has on its E side, and the Taiya Inlet on both sides, lofty mountain glaciers in their gorges. The midchannel depths are great throughout. Katzehin River Flat and Indian Rock are the only dangers in Chilkoot Inlet.* (CP)

## Mud Bay (Chilkoot Inlet)

Mud Bay is about 4 miles northwest of Seduction Point.

**Chart 17317**
**Entrance: 59°08.73′ N, 135°19.99′ W**
**Anchor: 59°09.05′ N, 135°20.67′ W**

> *Mud Bay is a small cove . . . from which low land extends across the peninsula to Letnikof Cove, and is connected with Haines by a gravel road.* (CP)

Mud Bay offers excellent protection from all but southeast winds. There are several cabins around the bay and a three-story house on the south entrance point. To the west the bay offers good views of rugged peaks and Rainbow Hanging Glacier.

Avoid the rocks off the south point and

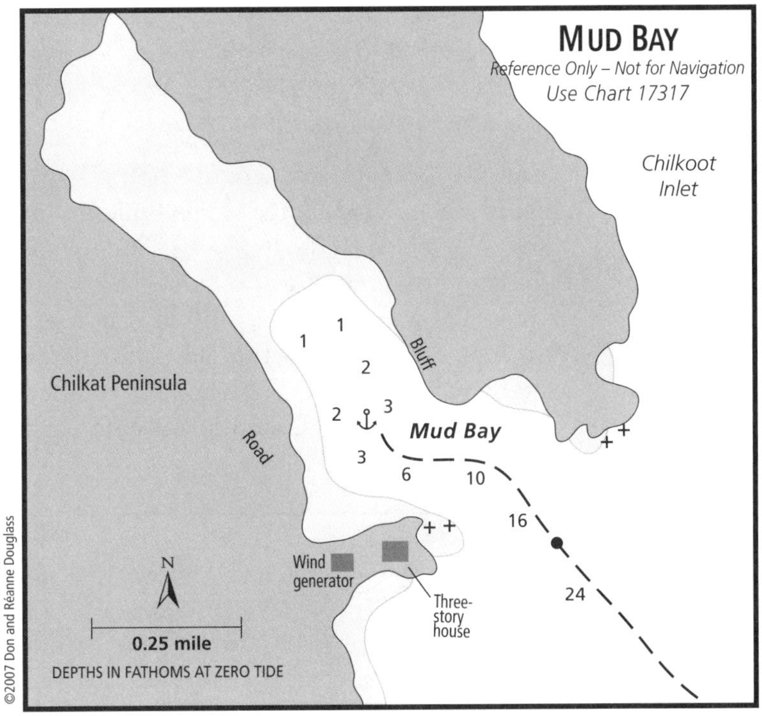


the numerous crab pot floats spread over the large, shallow inner bay. The water has a milky appearance due to the outflow of Katzehin River.

Anchor in 2 to 3 fathoms over soft mud with good holding.

## Kelgaya Bay (Chilkoot Inlet)

Kelgaya Bay is 2.5 miles southeast of Haines Harbor.

**Chart 17317**
**Position: 59°12.75′ N, 135°22.20′ W**

*Kelgaya Bay is a small cove on the N side of Battery Point.* (CP)

## Portage Cove (Chilkoot Inlet)

Portage Cove is about 2.5 miles northwest of Battery Point.

**Chart 17317 (inset)**
**Entrance: 59°14.04′ N, 135°24.82′ W**
**Anchor: 59°13.83′ N, 135°26.29′ W**

*Portage Cove . . . affords the best anchorage and shelter in Chilkoot Inlet. The anchorage is about 0.2 mile off the wharf in 12 to 15 fathoms, soft bottom. N winds blow home and bring in some sea.* (CP)

Open anchorage can be found between the small-craft basin and the first pier south. This can be a bouncy anchorage due to chop from both north and south and traffic in the basin. Skippers prefer to anchor southeast of the second pier just west of the point.

Anchor in 6 fathoms over soft mud with good holding.

## Haines (Chilkoot Inlet)

Haines, at the outlet of the Chilkat River, lies on the west side of Portage Cove, 59 miles north of Auke Bay.

**Chart 17317**
**Entrance (small-craft basin): 59°13.94′ N, 135°26.32′ W**

*Haines is a* [borough] *with several hotels, motels, machine shops, and general stores. . . . It is 950 miles from Seattle and 88 miles from Juneau, and is at the S end of a highway running along the Chilkat River and . . . connecting with the Alaska Highway.*

*The city of Haines operates a small-craft basin that is protected on its N side by a breakwater and on its E side by a detached breakwater. . . . The harbormaster controls the use of the grid and*

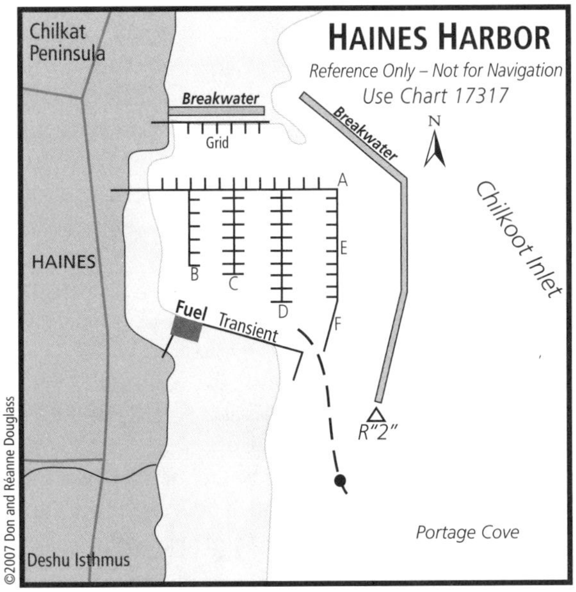

Réanne Hemingway-Douglass

*Small-boat harbor at Haines*

*makes berthing assignments. The harbormaster's office, at the small-craft basin, monitors VHF-FM channel 16. The harbormaster can be contacted by telephone (907-776-2448).* (CP)

Haines, a borough of about 2,300 inhabitants, is surrounded by ice-capped mountains whose glaciers spill down sheer granite walls into Lynn Canal and Chilkat Inlet. The paved Haines Highway, originally built during World War II, roughly follows the old trading trail used by native Alaskans to reach the interior.

The 48,000-acre Alaska Chilkat Bald Eagle

---

## Haines

Don Douglass & Réanne Hemingway-Douglass

Approaching Haines via Lynn Canal, you'll notice how the white, pitched-roof buildings of Fort William H. Seward echo the snowy mountain peaks in the background. Built in 1902 because of border disputes with Canada, the fort was decommissioned in 1947 and now houses galleries, restaurants and the Hotel Hälsingland.

Haines, named for Presbyterian missionary Francina Haines, is located on a peninsula between the Inside Passage and the Chilkat River. The Haines Highway connects to the Alaska Highway at Haines Junction, Yukon, 155 miles north of Haines.

Over 2,000 residents live in this pocket of civilization in the wilderness. It's a haven for artists who create ceramics, woodcarvings, jewelry, sculptures and paintings and display their handiwork in galleries and shops.

In winter, the 48,000-acre Chilkat Bald Eagle Preserve is home to the greatest concentration of bald eagles anywhere. Plenty stick around in summer, too. To watch them, book a float trip on the Chilkat River, take a guided tour of the preserve or rent a car and drive up the Haines Highway where you can view the birds from pullouts.

Haines residents party all summer long, starting in May with Fort Seward Days and the King Salmon Derby. In June the Summer Solstice Celebration is held, and in July there's the Independence Day Celebration and the Southeast Alaska State Fair and Bald Eagle Music Festival.

Opportunities for hiking, birding, photography, hunting, fishing, mountain biking and other outdoor activities mean you won't get bored while you're in port.

### Places of Interest

Sample the local beers at the Haines Brewing Company, 108 White Fang Way in Dalton City at the Southeast Alaska Fairgrounds. Dalton City was the movie set for *White Fang.* (tel.: 907.766.3823).

The Hammer Museum, 108 Main St., (tel.: 907.766.2374), is a unique museum that tells the story of man's most basic tool, the hammer. You can see a collection of 1,400 hammers; Website: www.hammermuseum.org.

At the Tsirku Canning Company, located at Fifth and Main, you can see an antique salmon canning line in action (tel.: 907.766.3474; Website: www.cannerytour.com).

The Sheldon Museum and Cultural Center, 11 Main St., (tel.: 907.766.2366), houses displays on pioneer history, as well as Tlingit art and cultural practices such as the potlatch; Website: www.sheldonmuseum.org.

For more information, contact the Haines Convention and Visitors Bureau, 122 Second Ave., (tel.: 907.766.2234 or 800.458.3579; Website: www.haines.ak.us).

### Moving On

It would be a shame to be so close to Skagway and not visit. You could rent a car and drive the 350 road miles via the Golden Circle route (see: www.goldencircleroute.com).

Or go by water, which is much shorter. If you want to take a break from navigating your own vessel, hop on the *Fairweather* Express for a 35-minute ride to Skagway. For tickets and reservations (tel.: 907.766.2100 or 888.766.2103; Website: www.chilkatcruises.com).

Preserve along the Chilkat River boasts a winter eagle population of nearly 4,000—the largest gathering of bald eagles in the world. In stretches of the Chilkat River, warm water upwellings remain ice-free during winter, attracting chum salmon from all over the Northwest, thus providing food for the eagles.

Sport fishing, camping, and hiking are popular among tourists here, and native crafts and dancing can be viewed during summer months.

The town has a laundromat, showers, bakery, restaurants and a well-stocked market. Fuel and water can be obtained in the harbor. The Alaska ferry terminal is located in Lutak Inlet, 3 miles north of town, and several air services fly to and from Juneau.

Haines has a small, compact boat basin, and the harbormaster says they "will try to find a hole for cruising boats." Somehow they manage to do it. If they can't find a place for you, you can also anchor in Portage Cove (see Portage Cove, above) between the basin entrance and the first wharf south. Telephone the harbormaster at 907.776.2448 or 907.766.2231.

Be sure to check your chart and follow the dredged channel into the boat basin, staying well clear of the shoaling area from the west that extends to the south side of the transient dock.

## Tanani Bay (Chilkoot Inlet)

Tanani Bay is 2 miles north of Haines.

**Chart 17317**
**Position: 59°15.82′ N, 135°26.26′ W**

Tanani Bay is a shallow bight on the south side of the tank farm on Tanani Point.

## Lutak Inlet (Chilkoot Inlet)

Lutak Inlet is the west arm of Chilkoot Inlet.

**Chart 17317**
**Entrance: 59°16.91′ N, 135°25.50′ W**

> *Lutak Inlet . . . is 5 miles long. Taiya Point is the NE entrance point, and Tanani Point, the SW. . . . Anchorage with good holding ground for large vessels can be had in a depth of 40 fathoms about 2.5 miles from the head of the inlet, to 20 fathoms about 0.8 mile from the head. In winter, Lutak Inlet offers the only good protection on Lynn Canal from N winds, although small boats will experience icing.* (CP)

The half-mile-wide Chilkoot River drains Chilkoot Lake at the head of the inlet. An Alaska State Ferry terminal is located in Lutak Inlet at approximately 59°16.92' N, 135°27.72' W.

## Taiyasanka Harbor

Taiyasanka Harbor, at the foot of the Ferebee River valley, is 4 miles north of Haines.

**Chart 17317**
**Entrance: 59°17.72′ N, 135°26.03′ W**

> *The harbor has a narrow entrance that is protected from S, but exposed to winter winds drawing down the Ferebee Glacier. There is 12 fathoms in the narrow entrance, which is 100 yards wide and close to the W side. A rock spit extends over halfway across the entrance from the W end of the narrow neck of land. . . . Log storage takes up the SE end of the basin. Small craft tie up to the booms for moorage.* (CP)

Taiyasanka Harbor can provide welcome shelter from southerly weather.

## Taiya Inlet (Chilkoot Inlet)

Taiya Inlet is the north arm of Chilkoot Inlet.

**Chart 17317**
**Entrance (Taiya Point bearing 270°T at 0.5 Nm): 59°17.23′ N, 135°23.03′ W**

> *A prominent waterfall, locally called Cavanaugh Falls, is on the E side of Taiya Inlet, about 1.5 miles N of Low Point.* (CP)

Réanne Hemingway-Douglass

*Some cruisers avoid the time-consuming Lynn Canal passage by taking the Fast Ferry from Juneau to Skagway.*

Taiya Inlet has the Taiya River on its north shore, the town of Skagway and Skagway River on its northeast shore.

## **Skagway** (Taiya Inlet)

Skagway is 13.5 miles north of Haines.

**Chart 17317 (inset)**
**Entrance (small-boat basin): 59°26.91′ N, 135°19.43′ W**

> *Skagway* [is] *a city on the delta formed by the Skagway River at the N terminus of the Inside Passage to Alaska. . .*
>
> *The Skagway Small-Boat Basin, protected by a breakwater marked by a light, is just northward of the White Pass and Yukon Route railway wharf. . . . A launching ramp, grid, and seaplane float are in the basin. Water (during summer), electricity, and gasoline are available at the floats.*
>
> *The White Pass and Yukon Route is a railway of 3-foot gage, 111 miles long, that extends from tidewater up the Skagway Valley to White Pass and across the international boundary to Whitehorse, the head of navigation on the Yukon River. The railway maintains daily service with Whitehorse from May to September.* (CP)

The historic town of Skagway is nestled in the V-shaped Skagway River Valley, between majestic mountain ranges. The town (pop. 800) now swells dramatically in summer as thousands of tourists descend from cruise ships.

In the late 1890s, the town was home to over 20,000 people as thousands of miners trudged north over the White Pass or the Chilkoot trails during the Klondike gold rush. During its heyday, Skagway supported over 80 saloons, as well as numerous other businesses. Nowadays, you can tour the boardwalks of the restored historic district, browse its shops, galleries and saloons, visit its museums, take in its daily shows and ride the famous White Pass and Yukon Railroad (twice-daily runs in summer season).

If you'd like to stretch your hiking muscles and take in the views from above the town, trails lead out and around Skagway. Or—if you're so inclined and can spare the time—you can hike for several days along the Chilkoot Pass Trail. (Advance reservations required!)

One of the most intriguing sites near Skagway was a rock wall along the south side of the bay where names of crew members of visiting ships were painted over the years. In late 1994, however, a large chunk of rock dropped off the wall into the bay, removing some of these colorful landmarks.

The Skagway small-boat basin has about 14 feet of water (at zero tide) at its entrance and a capacity for about 165 boats. The harbor monitors Ch 16, or you can telephone 907.983.2628. The electrical system was upgraded in early

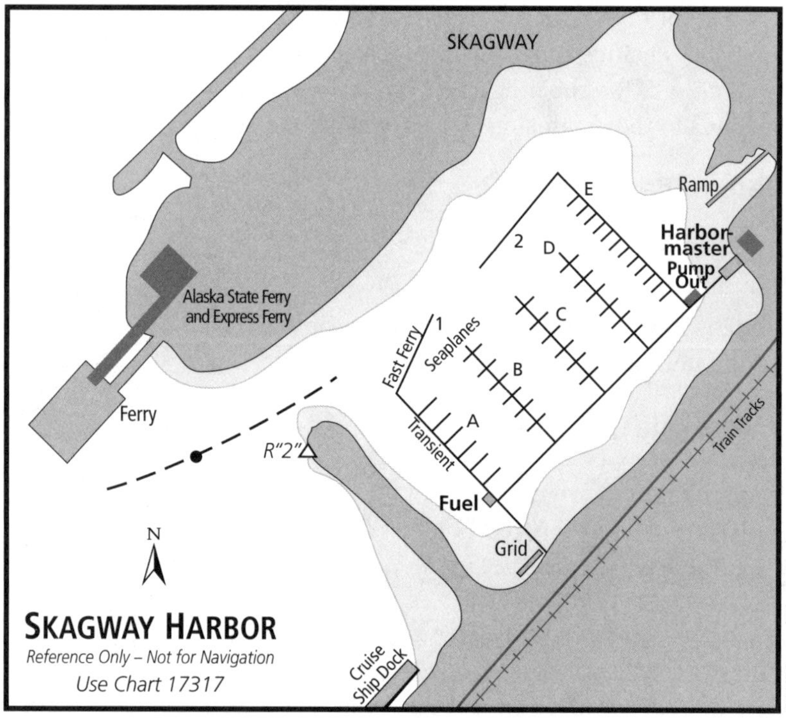

2007 to include 30- and 50- amp power. There is a 60-foot, small-craft grid in the southeast corner of the basin; a pump-out is located at the foot of the gangway that leads to the harbormaster's office.

Nearby facilities include a large market, laundromat, liquor store, medical clinic, bank and a variety of restaurants. Showers and bathrooms are located at the harbormaster's building at the head of the dock. Ice can be purchased at the seafood company above the dock. The town is serviced by air from Juneau, by motor vehicle

Claudia Herrick

*The entrance to Skagway's small-boat basin is at the top left.*

## Skagway

Don Douglass & Réanne Hemingway-Douglass

Skagway comes from the Tlingit word "skagua," meaning "home of the north wind." In 2000 the population was 862, but a century earlier thousands of men passed through on their quest for gold. That's why the town is called "Gateway to the Gold Rush of '98." It's the northernmost port of the Inside Passage, and Alaska's largest town in area, covering 453 square miles.

You can learn about local history at the Klondike Gold Rush National Historical Park. Rangers lead tours of the Skagway Historic District, a collection of 15 restored buildings, including a cigar store, bakery and dry goods store. See www.nps.gov/klgo for details. The Trail Center will give you information on the many hiking trails nearby, including the 33-mile Chilkoot Trail. If you're up for a strenuous, multi-day hike you can recreate the miners' trek to gold country.

The waning years of the nineteenth century were wild times. Outlaw Jefferson "Soapy" Smith and his gang prevailed until Frank Reid, fed-up citizen, shot him in 1898. Reid was wounded in the fray and died 12 days later. Both men are buried in Gold Rush Cemetery.

Nowadays, the stampede of visitors is from cruise ships. Tourists shop in Skagway's many gift shops and explore the area via tours that include flights over glacier country, hiking trips, bus trips to Carcross (short for Caribou Crossing) in the Yukon Territory and Dyea at the head of Taiya Inlet, trailhead for the Chilkoot Trail. You can pan for gold at the Liarsville Trail Camp. Other activities include Jeep tours and sled dog rides, rock climbing and canoeing.

Skagway offers a range of lodging from cabins and hostels to bed & breakfast inns and motels. Downtown is the Skagway Inn, established in 1897 as a brothel. It's more respectable now and houses Olivia's Restaurant. There are also pubs, cafes and saloons.

### Attractions

The Skagway Museum outlines local history and is located at Seventh and Spring in the McCabe College Building (tel.: 907.983.2420; Website: www.skagwaymuseum.org).

At Jewell Gardens, mile 1.1 on the Klondike Highway, you can see the flowers of Alaska and sip afternoon tea in the conservatory (tel.: 907.983.2111; Website: www.jewellgardens.com).

The White Pass and Yukon Route Railroad, completed in 1900, runs sightseeing tours on vintage trains. You can chug up to the summit of White Pass via tunnels and trestles, seeing spectacular scenery on the way. The office is at Second Ave. and Spring St. (tel.: 907.983.2217 or 800.343.7373; Website www.whitepassrailroad.com).

For further information, contact the Skagway Convention & Visitors Bureau, P.O. Box 1029, Skagway, AK 99840 (tel.: 907.983.2854 or 888.762.1898; Website: www.skagway.com).

Claudia Herrick

*Start exploring Skagway's rich history here in the historic district.*

along the Klondike Highway, and by the Alaska ferry.

Pleasure craft that do not want to make the long slog up Lynn Canal can leave their boats in Juneau and take the Alaska State Ferry's "Express Ferry" for an overnight trip to Haines or Skagway.

### Nahku Bay (Taiya Inlet)

Nahku Bay is 2 miles northwest of Skagway at the head of Taiya Inlet.

Chart 17317 (inset)
Entrance: 59°27.72′ N, 135°20.45′ W

> *Good anchorage is available in midchannel in 30 fathoms about 0.5 mile from the head. The bottom is sticky mud; it shoals gradually. During the summer with prevailing S winds, there is little protection from the short choppy seas coming in from Taiya Inlet.* (CP)

Réanne Hemingway-Douglass

*Boat names and a skull "decorate" Skagway's rock wall.*

The Taiya River flows into Nahku Bay.

### Long Bay and Taiya River

Long Bay is 1 mile northwest of Skagway.

Chart 17317 (inset)
Long Bay (entrance): 59°27.79′ N, 135°21.42′ W

> *Taiya River . . . is navigable for small boats and canoes as far as high water can be carried, a short distance above the mud flats. Canoes can be poled or towed by line for a greater distance.* (CP)

Long Bay is deep and exposed to southerlies. Protection from northwesterlies can be found at its head in 10 to 15 fathoms.

## Icy Strait to Cross Sound

### Icy Strait

Icy Strait extends northwest 27 miles from Chatham Strait to Point Adolphus, then west 16 miles to the Inian Islands.

Charts 17300, 17302
East entrance (Hanus Reef Light bearing 090°T at 1.8 Nm): 58°07.84′ N, 135°03.43′ W
West entrance: (North Inian Pass Light bearing 142°T at 0.9 Nm): 58°16.94′ N, 136°25.11′ W

> [Icy Strait] *averages 6.5 miles wide, but in places this is reduced by islands. Glacial ice from Glacier Bay may be found in the strait in small quantities mainly in winter.* (CP)

Icy Strait is the main east-west route connecting Chatham Strait and Cross Sound to Glacier Bay and the Gulf of Alaska.

Upper Chatham Strait, between Admiralty and Chichagof islands, extends southward from Icy Strait and Lynn Canal to Peril Strait.

### Funter Bay (Mansfield Peninsula)

Funter Bay is on the east side of Chatham Strait at its junction with Lynn Canal.

Charts 17316 (inset), 17300

Suzanne Steel

*A humpback breaches near a favorite whale-watching location in Icy Strait: Pt. Adolphus, on the northern tip of Chichagof Island.*

Entrance: 58°14.29′ N, 134°55.77′ W
Public float: 58°14.64′ N, 134°53.05′ W
Anchor (Coot Cove): 58°15.32′ N, 134°54.32′ W
Anchor (Crab Cove): 58°15.32′ N, 134°52.87′ W

*Funter Bay . . . is about 10.5 miles S of Point Retreat and 5.5 miles NE of Rocky Island.*

*Coot Cove, at the NW end of the bay, has extensive beaches at its head. Crab Cove, with depths of 3-3/4 fathoms to 12 fathoms, is at the NE end of the bay.*

*A State-maintained 100-foot small-craft float . . . extends E from the head of the wharf in ruins. . . . A rock ledge is off the SE side of the wharf. Caution is advised.*

*A State-maintained 150-foot-long small-craft float is on the SE side of the bay E of Funter Bay Entrance Light 1.*

*Anchorage in Funter Bay can be made about 0.2 mile SW of the cannery ruins.* (CP)

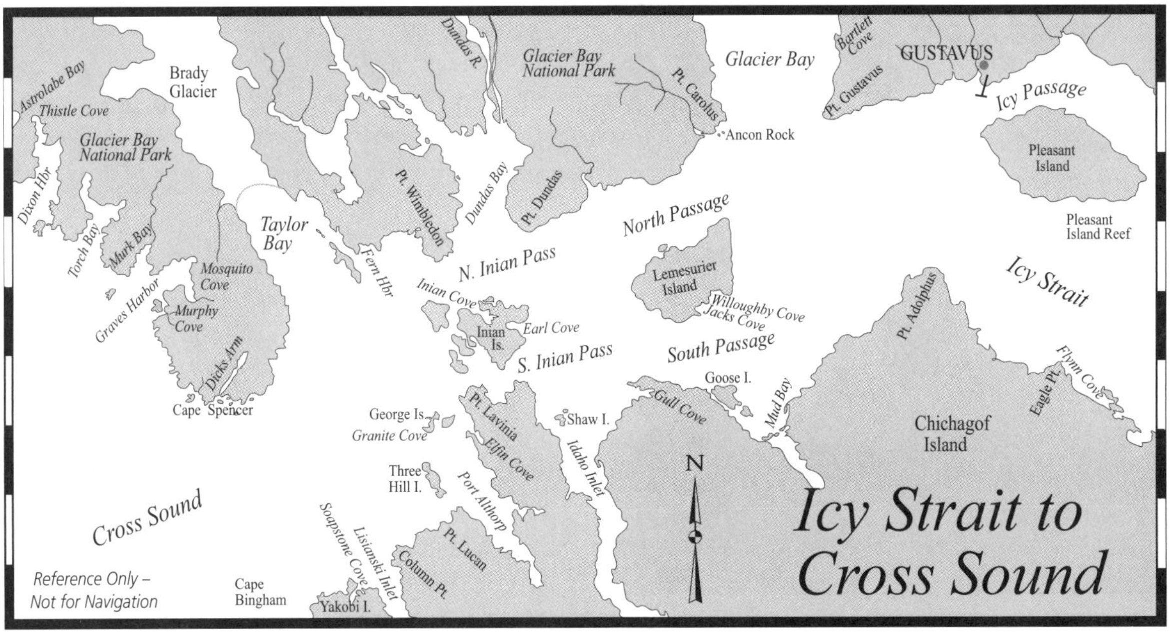

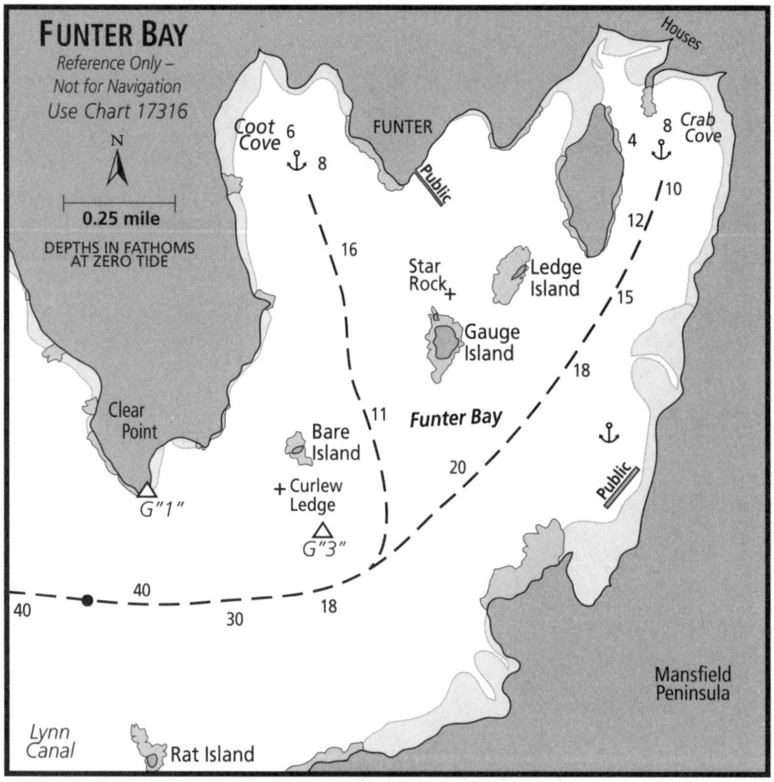


©2007 Don and Réanne Douglass

Funter Bay, like Swanson Harbor, provides good protection at the critical southern end of Lynn Canal. Space at the public float on the southeast corner of the bay is often taken, but good anchorage can be found in either Coot Cove or Crab Cove.

This is a low point across Admiralty Island, so east and west winds whistle across here and in Hawk Inlet to the south.

Anchor (Crab Cove) in 8 to 10 fathoms over soft mud with good holding.

Anchor (Coot Cove) in 6 to 10 fathoms over sticky mud with very good holding.

Réanne Hemingway-Douglass

*Two public floats are available in Swanson Harbor.*

## Swanson Harbor

Swanson Harbor is 18 miles southwest of Auke Bay and 30 miles southeast of Glacier Bay.

**Chart 17316**
**Entrance (Swanson Harbor Entrance Light "2" bearing 340°T at 0.35 Nm) 58°11.27′ N, 135°04.48′ W**
**Public float: 58°12.79′ N, 135°06.59′ W**
**Anchor (harbor): 58°12.85′ N, 135°07.47′ W**

> *Swanson Harbor is formed by a group of islands and reefs off the extreme SE point of the mainland. . . .*
>
> *Anchor with the NE side of Entrance Island just open from the E side of Ansley Island, and with the NW end of Ansley Island bearing S, distant 0.3 mile, in 14 to 16 fathoms, soft bottom. Small vessels anchor close in the head of the bay or to the E side of the head behind No Use Ledge.* (CP)

Swanson Harbor, strategically located at the intersection of Icy Strait, Chatham Strait and Lynn Canal, provides good shelter for cruising and fishing boats. Two detached concrete public floats in the east side of the bay are used by

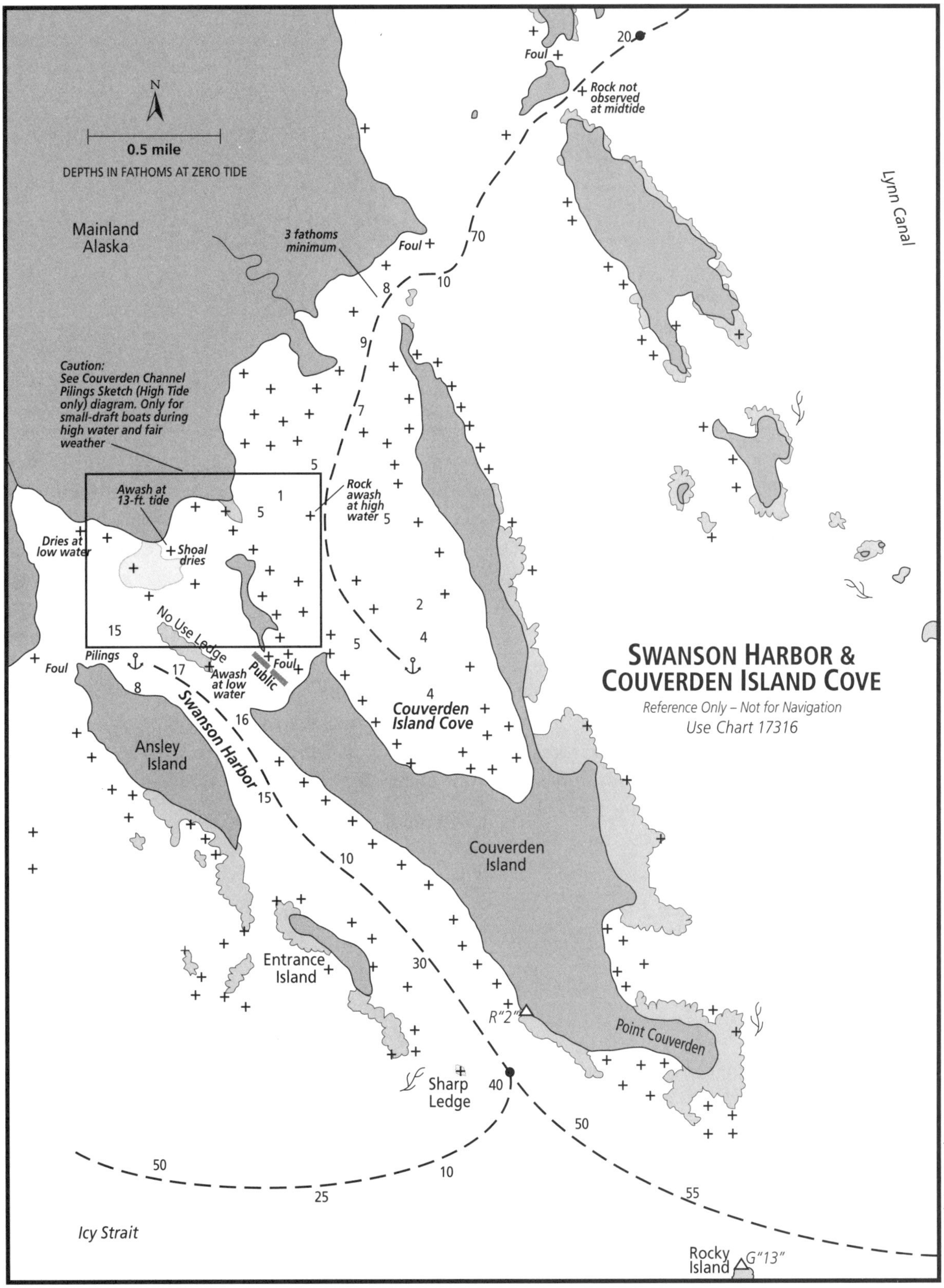

SWANSON HARBOR & COUVERDEN ISLAND COVE
Reference Only – Not for Navigation
Use Chart 17316
N
0.5 mile
DEPTHS IN FATHOMS AT ZERO TIDE
Mainland Alaska
3 fathoms minimum
Foul
Rock not observed at midtide
Lynn Canal
Caution: See Couverden Channel Pilings Sketch (High Tide only) diagram. Only for small-draft boats during high water and fair weather
Awash at 13-ft. tide
Rock awash at high water
Dries at low water
Shoal dries
No Use Ledge
Pilings
Foul
Awash at low water
Public
Swanson Harbor
Ansley Island
Couverden Island Cove
Couverden Island
Entrance Island
R"2"
Point Couverden
Sharp Ledge
Icy Strait
Rocky Island
G"13"

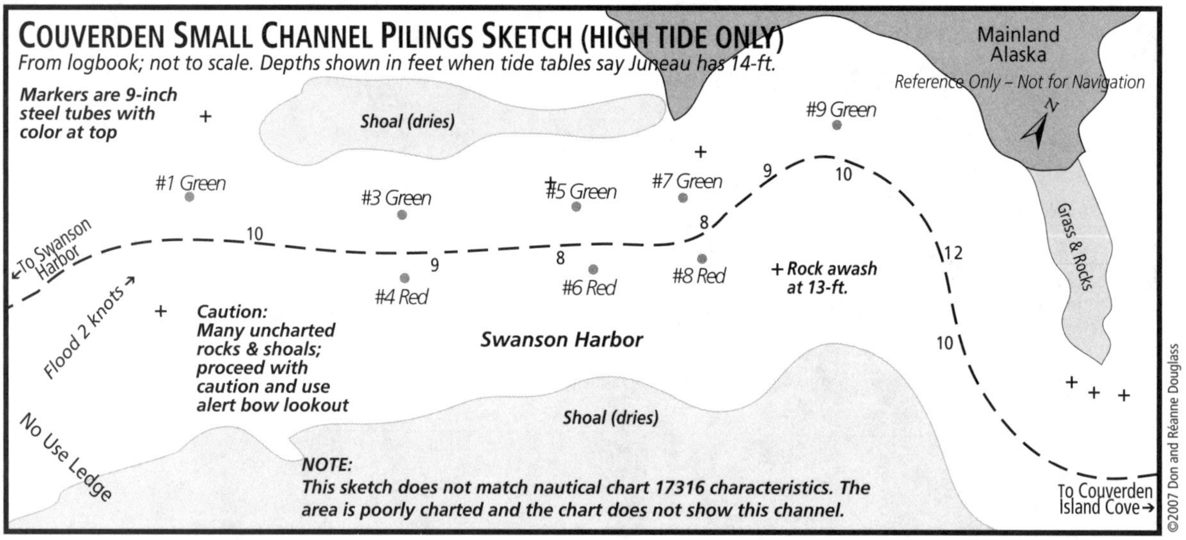

COUVERDEN SMALL CHANNEL PILINGS SKETCH (HIGH TIDE ONLY)

sport fishing boats and for vessels preparing to enter Glacier Bay. A fish-cleaning station is located on one of the floats.

Enter Swanson Harbor from the south via the channel west of Point Couverden. Avoid Sharp Ledge, which extends a half-mile or more southeast of Entrance Island. Watch carefully for submerged rocks along both shores. As you proceed deeper into the channel watch for No Use Ledge on the east; some of this area is marked by kelp. There is a rock awash at low water about 150 yards SSE of the obvious No Use Ledge shoal area. The best anchorage for small craft is in the bight on the northeast end of Ansley Island.

## Couverden Island Cove

(Couverden Island)

"Couverden Island Cove" is what we call the indentation on the north side of Couverden Island.

Chart 17316
Northeast entrance: 58°14.28′ N, 135°05.24′ W
Anchor: 58°12.77′ N, 135°05.43′ W

Couverden Island Cove is a favorite of local fishing boats and others who want solid protection from all weather. Extra caution is required in this area, which is very poorly charted and shoal with many rocks. The entrance route to Couverden Island Cove is made from the northeast tip of the island's long, thin eastern peninsula with about 3 fathoms minimum in the narrow fairway. Some professional skippers caution against using this anchorage and advise using the Swanson Harbor anchorage (above) instead. Consider your abilities carefully in choosing this anchorage and proceed cautiously.

Avoid the shoals and rocks in the center of Couverden Island Cove. A dangerous charted rock, awash at high water, lies at 58°13.35'N, 135°06.20'W.

Anchor in 4 fathoms over sand and mud with very good holding.

## Couverden Channel

Chart 71316

*A small narrow channel, marked by piles between the small island N of Couverden Island and No Use Ledge, leads E from Swanson Harbor to a cove on the N side of Couverden Island; this channel should only be used by small craft at high water.* (CP)

Shallow-draft boats *only* can transit Couverden Channel, a small, very narrow channel (between mainland Alaska and an un-named island northeast of Couverden Island) via a shallow bar not shown on Chart 17316. Transit should be made *only on high water slack* and only in fair weather. Note C on Chart 17316 states: "The highwater channel between Swanson Harbor and the cove behind Couverden Island is marked by pilings. Tide boards at each end show least channel depth."

For a suggested pathway through this channel, see our Couverden Channel Pilings Sketch (High Tide Only) on previous page. Tide boards show depths in feet when Juneau tide tables show 14 feet, as derived from notes in our logbook. *Use the channel at your own risk.*

On June 25, 2004, the S/V *Merlin* of Southampton, England, a 40-foot centerboard sailboat drawing 3'6" with the centerboard up, transited this channel using our sketch and verified that the depth in the channel was the predicted tide level in Juneau minus 6 feet.

The channel has a flat, sandy bottom that requires an alert bow watch, careful monitoring of a depth sounder and a visual approach to ensure safe passage. We advise reconnoitering this channel by dinghy before attempting a passage.

Don Douglass

*Boots are a necessity on the rainforest trails.*

## **Spasski Bay** (Chichagof Island)

Spasski Bay is 9 miles southwest of Swanson Harbor.

Chart 17316
**Entrance (Neck Point bearing 305°T at 0.6 Nm): 58°06.71' N, 135°18.31' W**
**Anchor: 58°06.95' N, 135°19.97' W**

> *Several submerged rocks are about 700 yards N of Neck Point; the least depth over the rocks is 1-1/2 fathoms. Rocks, usually marked by kelp, extend E of Neck Point. A 1-3/4-fathom shoal is about 0.6 mile ESE of Neck Point. An opposing wind and current causes treacherous sea conditions in the entrance to the bay; exercise caution when entering the bay. . . . The shores of the bight at the W end of the bay are wide sand and gravel beaches.*
>
> *The anchorage, exposed to the NE, is in 9 to 10 fathoms in the middle of the W end of the bay, with Neck Point bearing NE.* (CP)

Spasski Bay entrance is surrounded by rocks and shoal, and strong currents here cause turbulence. A good anchor site in prevailing northwest winds can be found at the head of the bay, out of the current and turbulence. Most southeast winds appear to pass up Icy Strait with little effect on Spasski Bay.

Anchor in 4 fathoms over mud, sand and gravel with fair holding.

## **Port Frederick** (Chichagof Island)

Port Frederick is on the south side of Icy Strait between Crist Point and Point Sophia.

Chart 17302
**Entrance (Pinta Rock buoy bearing 000°T at 0.6 Nm): 58°09.38' N, 135°27.28' W**

> *Port Frederick . . . has no known dangers other than those charted. It offers several very good anchorages with good holding ground and shelter.*
>
> *Small craft approaching from W use Gedney Channel.*
>
> *If bound for Hoonah, give Cannery Point and the shore to E a berth of 200 yards or more.* (CP)

Port Frederick extends 15 miles southeast from Pinta Rock. Hoonah lies along its northeastern shore, and there are intriguing bights and lagoons at its head. This is a good place to anchor when waiting to enter Glacier Bay.

*A sailboat at Hoonah's transient dock*

## **Hoonah** (Port Frederick)

Hoonah, inside the east entrance to Port Frederick, is 25 miles southeast of Bartlett Cove in Glacier Bay.

Chart 17302

Note: *There is a 200-yard or more offset between latitude/longitude on Chart 17302 and Chart 17316 for the Hoonah area. Also, charted depths may be off by a fathom or more due to the 1958 Alaska earthquake.*

Entrance: 58°06.72′ N, 135°27.24′ W
Float: 58°06.42′ N, 135°26.85′ W

*The anchorage is between, or a little inside, the NW end of Pitt Island and the W end of the city of Hoonah, in 11 to 14 fathoms, soft bottom. The anchorage is not well protected from SW, but the holding ground is good.*

*The city-operated small-craft floats, about 120 yards NNW of the Hoonah Cold Storage Dock, has berthing space for approximately 61 vessels; contact the harbormaster on VHF-FM channel 16 or telephone (907-945-3670). Depths alongside were reported at 17 feet in 2002. It is recommended that only small craft and skiffs moor on the inshore side of the float. A seaplane float extends from shore about 200 yards NW of the city float approach pier.*

*A boat basin, known locally as the Inner Harbor, operated by the Hoonah Harbormaster is close S of Hoonah. In April 2002, the controlling depth was 15 feet (17 feet at midchannel) in the entrance channel with*

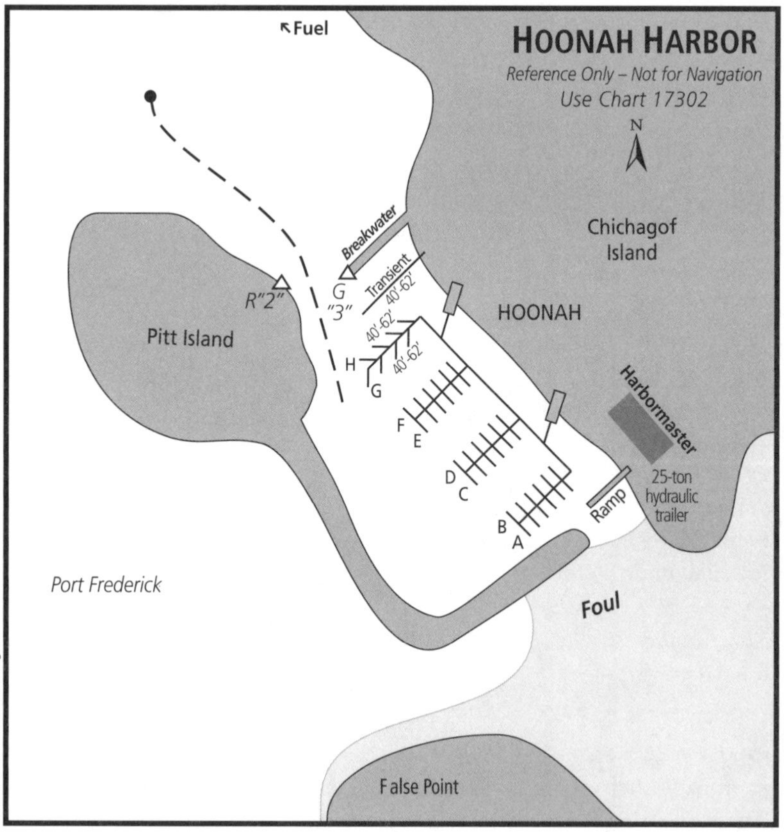

*depths of 10 to 18 feet in the basin. Floats in the basin provide berthing space for approximately 239 vessels.* (CP)

Linda Lewis

*Hoonah Harbor—some cruisers store their boat here over the winter.*

Hoonah, the largest Tlingit settlement in Southeast Alaska, is a popular spot for cruising boats waiting for entry to Glacier Bay. In the past few years, Hoonah has been "discovered" by the cruise ship industry. What was once an economy based on logging and fishing has recently become dependent on tourism. The former cannery was renovated and is now a cultural center where local artisans sell their crafts and Tlingit dancers, in their colorful red button blankets, perform for the tourists. At present, the village has limited the number of ships that may call on the harbor to one or two a week; however, the numbers may increase in the future, creating a double-edged sword for the community.

Cruising boaters are still welcomed, and the harbormaster, who is efficient and friendly, does his best to accommodate pleasure craft. Moorage can be found inside the harbor breakwater beyond Hoonah Cold Storage dock by calling the harbormaster on Ch 16 to arrange for a slip; change to 09 or 14. In 2007, the harbor added additional floats to accommodate 40-foot vessels.

Linda Lewis

*The large Trading Company store in Hoonah surprises many cruisers.*

Some cruisers choose Hoonah Harbor for storing their boat over the winter, in part because Hoonah is located closer to the Pacific Ocean, resulting in more temperate winter weather. Add to this a harbormaster who does a truly excellent job and you can see why this spot is selected.

Laundry, showers, power and water are available within the harbor, as well as a 35-ton hydraulic trailer; there is no pump-out station (2007). Telephone the harbormaster at 907.945.3670. (Cell phone connection is possible in Icy Strait, but is lost upon entering Port Frederick; at press time no cell connection could be made within the harbor itself.)

Hoonah Trading Company (monitors Ch 11), in the outer harbor, sells groceries, hardware, and fuel (gasoline, diesel and propane).

You can stretch your legs along the road between the cultural center and the end of the road to the south.

In 2007 the outer harbor (city) floats were being renovated with an additional drive-down ramp added; there is no power or water at this site, and the area is subject to strong northwesterlies; a fee is charged for moorage.

As you enter Port Frederick on your way to Hoonah Harbor, watch for the possible appearance of an Alaska State Ferry. The ferry terminal is located northwest of the breakwater entrance to the harbor at approximately 58°06.95' N, 135°27.40' W.

The harbor has a 5-knot, no-wake zone that begins off the ferry terminal. Boaters are asked to respect this limit.

For a quieter anchorage, consider Neka Bay, 7.5 miles southwest.

### **Neka Bay** (Port Frederick)

Neka Bay, on the west side of Port Frederick, is 9 miles from the entrance.

Chart 17302
Neka Bay (Entrance, Neka Island bearing 213°T at 0.5 Nm): 58°02.51' N, 135°37.71' W
Anchor (Neka Bay): 58°03.08' N, 135°40.01' W
Entrance (North and South Bight, Neka Island bearing 300°T at 0.4 Nm): 58°01.79' N, 135°37.59' W
Anchor (North Bight) 58°02.35' N, 135°40.94' W

*Neka Bay . . . is divided into three arms.*

*From Neka Island, the N arm follows a WNW direction . . . terminating in a large basin. The greater part of the basin is navigable at high water for vessels of 2- or 3-foot draft; it dries at low water. About 0.4 mile inside the entrance to the N arm are private mooring buoys, used for barge transfer. . . . On the S side of the channel, 0.3 mile from the entrance to the narrow part, is a small wooded island with a bight to the SSW. A depth of 2-3/4 fathoms was found in the S channel leading to the bight; a rock is in the W channel.*

*North Bight, the middle arm of Neka Bay, with the entrance S of Neka Island, has depths of 6 to 12 fathoms, sticky bottom.*

*The entrance to South Bight is constricted to a width of about 100 yards by a long narrow point that projects from the S shore.* (CP)

The north arm of Neka Bay has excellent shelter for cruising boats, however this anchorage is very open and can be subject to windy conditions at times. Anchor west of the tugboat buoys on the north side of the small islet. You can also find excellent protection in North Bight. From here we've enjoyed exploring the drying reef by dinghy and watching humpback whales surface, spout and breach nearby. Lots of bears have been seen in the area west of the North Bight anchorage. Avoid the charted rocks off the entrance to North Bight. South Bight has a 4-fathom hole and is very

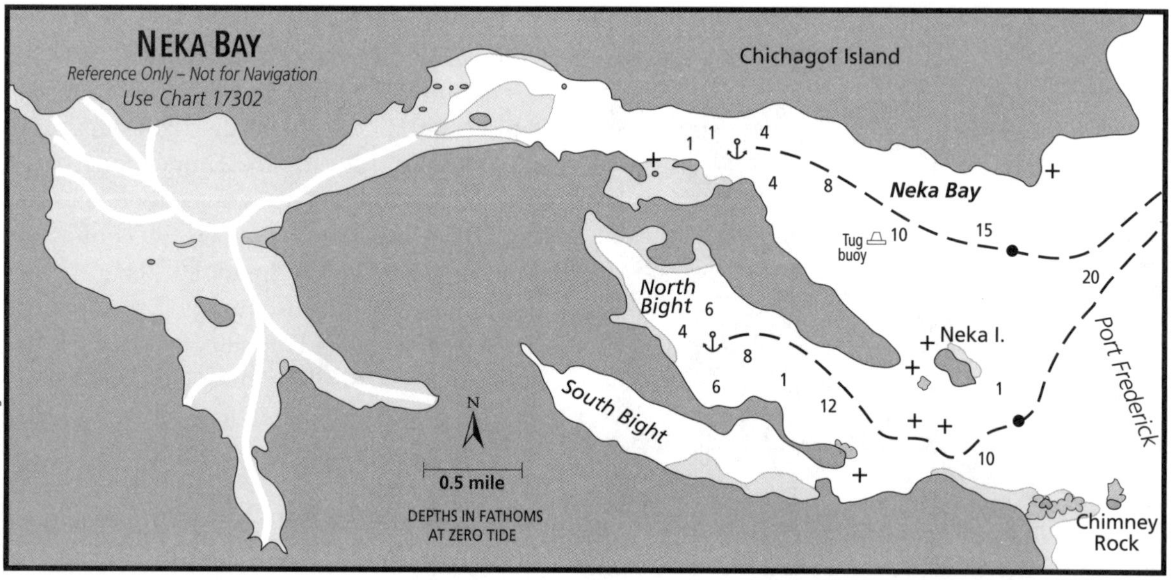

well protected, but its entrance is shallow and constricted.

Anchor (Neka Bay) in about 4 fathoms over mud with excellent holding.

Anchor (North Bight) in 6 fathoms over green mud with good holding.

## **Salt Lake Bay** (Port Frederick)

Salt Lake Bay, at the south end of Port Frederick inside The Narrows, is 4 miles south of Neka Bay.

Chart 17302
Entrance: 57°58.55′ N, 135°39.58′ W
Entrance (Salt Chuck): 57°57.52′ N, 135°39.24′ W

> *Salt Lake Bay . . . extends in a south direction, with depths of 43 fathoms at the entrance to 9 fathoms off the flats, which extend about 0.2 mile from the SE corner. The bay then extends SW to a lagoon. . . . The opening to Salt Chuck has swift currents and riptides during maximum tides; local knowledge is advised.*
>
> *A logging camp with a small pier and a float is on the E side of the entrance to Salt Lake Bay.* (CP)

Salt Lake Bay is too deep for convenient anchorage. However, Salt Chuck has a center depth of 10 fathoms and should be bombproof if the tiny entrance can be safely negotiated. (We have no local knowledge to share about Salt Chuck.)

## **Eight Fathom Bight** (Port Frederick)

Eight Fathom Bight is 11 miles southwest of Hoonah.

Chart 17302
Position: 58°00.35′ N, 135°44.27′ W

> *Anchorage may be had in 5½ to 12 fathoms in Eight Fathom Bight which indents the N shore about 3 miles WNW of The Narrows. A logging camp with a small pier is on the W side of Eight Fathom Bight. The camp monitors VHF-FM channel 16.* (CP)

## **Southwest Arm at Head of Port Frederick** (Port Frederick)

The southwest arm at the head of Port Frederick is 2 miles southwest of Eight Fathom Bight.

Chart 17302
Entrance: 57°59.58′ N, 135°45.96′ W
Anchor: 57°59.31′ N, 135°48.30′ W

> *The S inlet is long and narrow with several bends and has depths of 6 to 11 fathoms in the widest part, except near the shores. The channel to the two arms at the head of this inlet leads between the point and the rock and has depths of 5-1/2 fathoms. . . . The SW arm has depths of 3 to 5 fathoms, sticky bottom.* (CP)

The head of Southwest Arm appears to be a remote getaway with excellent shelter over a grassy, sticky bottom. Tenakee Inlet is only a few hundred yards to the southwest over land, but many miles by water!

## **Flynn Cove** (Chichagof Island)

Flynn Cove is 7 miles southeast of Point Adolphus and 15 miles from the entrance to Glacier Bay.

Chart 17302
Entrance: 58°13.10′ N, 135°37.03′ W
Anchor: 58°12.34′ N, 135°35.20′ W

> *A shoal extends 300 yards NW from the NW extremity of Burger Point, the high wooded peninsula forming the NE side of the cove.* (CP)

Réanne Hemingway-Douglass

Baidarka *anchored in Flynn Cove*

Flynn Cove is one of our favorite anchor sites when we're waiting to enter Glacier Bay. The large cove has a fairly consistent bottom with grassy shores where you can stretch your legs. When entering the cove, stay well north of Harry Island and the rocks and shoals on its west side before turning south. Pass a grassy islet and a 200-yard-long reef awash on a 12-foot tide. Once past the reef, favor the northeast shore avoiding a ledge awash on a 15-foot tide. You can anchor toward the head of the bay being careful to monitor your depth sounder.

Anchor in about 9 fathoms over sticky mud with good holding.

## **Pinta Cove** (Chichagof Island)

Pinta Cove, immediately southeast of Point Adolphus, is 13.7 miles northwest of Hoonah.

Chart 17302
Position: 58°16.21′ N, 135°45.90′ W

> *Pinta Cove . . . has been used as a temporary anchorage, but is not recommended. A 1/2-fathom rock is near the center of the cove.* (CP)

## **Excursion Inlet** (Sawmill Bay)

Excursion Inlet is 16 miles east of the entrance to Glacier Bay.

Charts 17316, 17318
Entrance: 58°22.04′ N, 135°27.03′ W

Réanne Hemingway-Douglass

*A cruise ship appears out of the fog in Icy Strait.*

Anchor (Sawmill Bay): 58°28.31′ N, 135°29.78′ W

> *Excursion Inlet, a deep, clear, narrow inlet, . . . has its entrance N of Porpoise Islands.*
>
> *Vessels will find indifferent anchorage near the head of the E arm, 0.2 mile from the E shore, in about 30 fathoms. Small craft can select anchorage in about 10 fathoms in the coves at the head of the W arm.*
>
> *Excursion Inlet, a small settlement on the E shore about 3.3 miles above the entrance, is the site of a cannery. . . . A seaplane float and a seasonal small-craft float are just N of the wharf. In 1999, 10 feet was reported alongside the small-craft float.* (CP)

Excursion Inlet, which was cut out of the towering peaks by glaciers long ago, is too deep for convenient anchoring. However, fair shelter at reasonable depths can be found in the eastern bight of Sawmill Bay. The area around the dock and cannery were used as a prisoner-of-war camp for Germans in World War II. Cruisers have reported that it is possible to moor at the Cannery Town docks. The western arm of the inlet is called Sawmill Bay.

Anchor in (Sawmill Bay) in about 10 fathoms.

## **Icy Passage and Pleasant Island Cove**

Icy Passage lies 8 miles east of the entrance to Glacier Bay, between Pleasant Island and the mainland.

Chart 17302
Anchor (Pleasant Island Cove): 58°23.02′ N, 135°37.16′ W
Anchor (south of Gustavus): 58°22.80′ N, 135°42.30′ W

> *Icy Passage Light 2, . . . off the N shore of Pleasant Island, marks the S side of Icy Passage. . . . Mudflats extend off the N shore to within 0.8 mile of the N shore of Pleasant Island. The shallow cove on the N shore of Pleasant Island, SE of the light, offers fair shelter in 1 to 8 fathoms, mud bottom.* (CP)

Icy Passage has Gustavus on its north shore. Temporary anchorage can be found in shallow

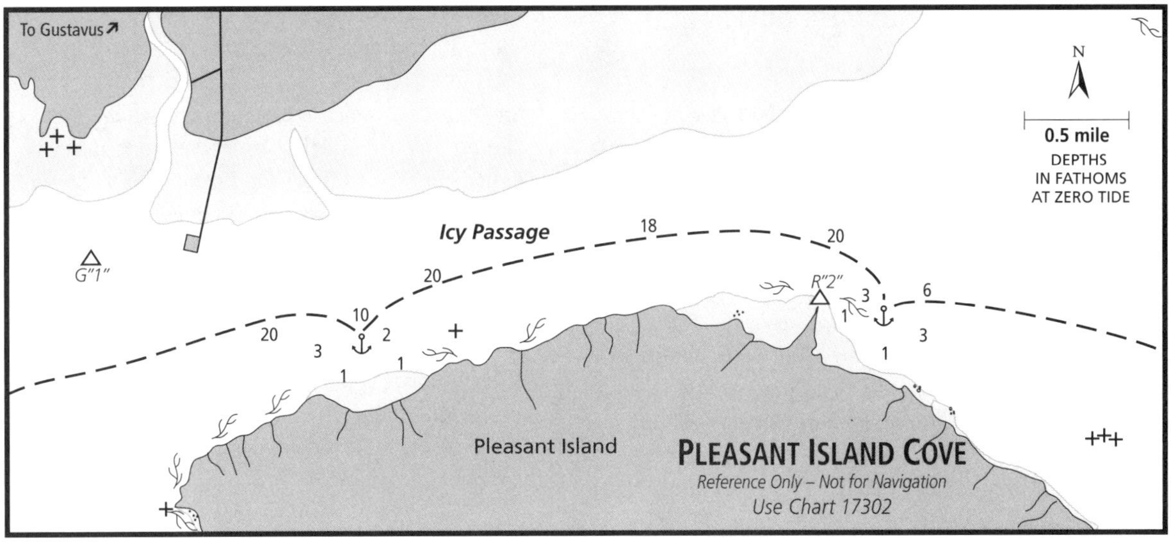



water along either its north or south shore. Pleasant Island Cove is a convenient anchorage with easy access by radar. The large flat, 1-1/2 to 2 fathoms, east of the Icy Passage spit is well protected from most summer winds and is out of the westerly chop sometimes found off Gustavus. There is room here for quite a few boats. We prefer to anchor immediately east of the lone tree on the spit, avoiding the numerous crab pot floats. We have found the bottom to be hard blue-gray clay packed with clam shells, not mud, as mentioned in the *Coast Pilot*. This makes setting your anchor difficult—you must set it slowly or it will break out before burying itself. The last of the flood tide flows west, and we have measured currents to 2 knots on spring tides.

---

### Orcas Finish Moose

Don Douglass

In June '92, while *Baidarka* was in Icy Passage, the first recorded attack and kill of a moose by orcas occurred off Pleasant Island.

Two moose were swimming Icy Passage when they were attacked by a pod of orcas. One moose was killed outright; the other died when he swam into a kelp bed, apparently got tangled up, exhausted himself and drowned.

---

In a serious southeast blow, consider anchoring on the west side of the spit. Alternately, you can anchor on a shoal on Pleasant Island, south of Gustavus pier and 2.5 miles west of Icy Passage Light over a steep-to, rocky bottom.

Anchor in 2 fathoms over hard blue-gray clay, sea grass and clamshells with poor-to-fair holding. Holding is good if your anchor is well dug in.

## **Gustavus** (Icy Passage)

Gustavus is on the north side of Icy Passage.

Chart 17302
Float: 58°23.23′ N, 135°43.77′ W

> *A State-owned pier, with a 48-foot face and 12 to 15 feet reported alongside in 2002, is about 0.3 mile E of the entrance to Salmon River. Seasonal small-craft floats extend E off the end of the pier. A W swell makes the pier and float a poor moorage for small craft.* (CP)

Gustavus is the village that serves Glacier Bay National Park. It has an airport, located 2 miles north of the public float, and it is a busy transportation hub in the summer. The float is frequently crowded in tourist season. Local or visiting boats anchor or tie to moorings on either side of the float.

## Glacier Bay National Park and Preserve

The entrance to Glacier Bay, between Point Gustavus and Point Carolus, is 16 miles northeast of Elfin Cove and 23 miles northwest of Hoonah.

### Chart 17318
### Entrance: 58°22.73′ N, 135°58.84′ W

> [Glacier Bay] *is about 50 miles long to the head of Muir Inlet, 54 miles to the head of John Hopkins Inlet, and 62 miles to the head of Tarr Inlet. . . . above Willoughby Island both shores of the bay are steep and foul, and should be avoided. All the shoals of less than 6-fathom depth are covered with kelp part of the year, but this kelp cannot be depended upon to indicate the dangers as the strong current tows the kelp under most of the time.*
>
> *Glacier Bay National Park and Preserve, 4,400 square miles in area, comprises all of Glacier Bay. It has over 20 tremendous glaciers and many others almost equally impressive. They illustrate all stages, from actively moving ice masses to those that are nearly stagnant and slowly dying.*
>
> *Humpback whales frequent Glacier Bay. . . . All motor vessels are prohibited from pursuing or approaching within 0.25 mile of humpback whales.*
>
> *Currents. The tidal currents from Point Gustavus to Willoughby Island at times attain a velocity of 6 knots or more. Heavy tide rips and swirls occur abreast Beardslee Islands. . . .*
>
> *Ice. Numerous discharging glaciers enter the bay, and glacial ice is always present, sometimes in enormous quantities in Muir Inlet, Tarr Inlet, and Johns Hopkins Inlet. . . . When the ice falls from the faces of the glaciers, it may create waves 30 feet high. Therefore, small boats should not approach closer than 0.5 mile to active glaciers. Icebergs are unstable and should not be approached closely because, if disturbed by swell from the small boat passing, they may roll over or break apart at any time. . .*
>
> *Caution. The navigation of Glacier Bay outside of the main channels is not considered safe without local knowledge. . . .*
>
> *Ocean liners and other vessels that cruise the bay are advised to watch for kayaks and canoes in the area.*
>
> *Vessels are advised to carry extra propellers aboard when navigating Glacier Bay, and single-screw vessels should not attempt to navigate the bay at all.* (CP)

Glacier Bay National Park is a place where the word "awesome" was appropriate long before it became a cliché, and what better way to experience it than on your own boat! Between June 1 and August 31, a permit is mandatory to enter Glacier Bay north of a line between Point Gustavus and Point Carolus. There are still many places within park boundaries where you can enter without a permit and find beautiful and remote anchor sites—to the east in Excursion Inlet, and to the west in Dundas Bay, as well as north of Cape Spencer. (You may enter Glacier Bay National Park before June 1 and after August 31 without a permit. However, park authorities ask that you call them on VHF Ch 16 to inform them of your entrance and exit. All park rules must be followed during this non-permit period.)

Linda Lewis

*Glacier Bay ice sculpture—could it be a sea otter clad in ice?*

Pleasure craft can obtain a permit by contacting the Superintendent, Glacier Bay National Park and Preserve, P.O. Box 140, Bartlett Cove, Gustavus, Alaska 99826 (tel.: 907.697.2627, May–September; 907.697.2230, October–April.) Full permit information and a permit form download can be found on the park's Website at www.nps.gov/glba. An Advance-notice Permit application is not accepted more than 60 days in advance of your requested date. Just 25 pleasure craft are allowed in the permit area at one time. You may reserve up to seven consecutive days. (An extension of this stay may be permitted on a space-available basis.) This means that just three to four new boats are allowed to enter the permit area per day. These permits must be confirmed with the park within 48 hours of scheduled arrival or they will be cancelled.

Linda Lewis

*At anchor in the glory that is Glacier Bay National Park*

A new permitting process, implemented in 2007, allocates 10 of the 25 daily permits to the Advance-notice Permits (described above). Fourteen of the 25 daily permits are allocated as Short-notice Permits and may be reserved

## Glacier Facts

Herb Nickles, Certified Alaska Naturalist

How many tidewater glaciers remain in Glacier Bay? How fast are the glaciers retreating?

The glaciers seen in Glacier Bay today are remnants of the Little Ice Age that began about 4,000 years ago and reached its maximum extent in Glacier Bay around 1750, when general melting began. In 1794, Captain George Vancouver and his crew described what we now call Glacier Bay as just a small five-mile indent in a gigantic glacier that stretched to the horizon. That massive glacier was 4,000 feet thick, 20 miles wide, and extended more than 100 miles to the St. Elias mountain range. In 1879, when naturalist John Muir visited Glacier Bay, the ice had retreated more than 30 miles forming an actual bay. By 1916, the Grand Pacific Glacier, the primary glacier responsible for carving the bay, had melted back 60 miles to the head of Tarr Inlet.

Glacier Bay contains both tidewater and non-tidewater glaciers. According to the National Park Service, Glacier Bay National Park boundaries today include 11 tidewater glaciers, glaciers that flow out of the mountains and terminate in tidal waters. Eight of these tidewater glaciers flow into Glacier Bay. Many of the tidewater glaciers that Muir first observed in 1879 have been reduced to small glaciers that terminate on land.

In general, tidewater glaciers in Glacier Bay have been in a state of retreat since the 1750. However, between 1920 and 1930, the Johns Hopkins and Grand Pacific Glaciers began to advance. In 2004, the Johns Hopkins Glacier was advancing at the rate of 8 feet per day but the Grand Pacific was receding at approximately 4 feet per day. The most active tidewater glacier is McBride that is retreating at the rate of 3,000 feet per year.

Since tidewater glaciers follow their own cycles that are independent of climate changes, individual tidewater glaciers may recede, advance, or remain stable at any given time. There is one thing you can be certain—a glacier's face you see today will be changed by tomorrow and even more significantly 20 years from now.

### Additional Resources:

Glacier Bay National Park and Preserve at http://www.nps.gov/glba/

Used with permission from author: http://www.insidepassagenews.com/AlaskaFAQ/FAQ_6.html

up to 48 hours in advance of arrival at Glacier Bay National Park. These Short-notice Permits are meant to accommodate local residents as well as those with limited advanced destination planning. For pleasure boaters this means that if you are not able to arrange for an Advance-notice Permit you can call and try for a Short-notice Permit when you are within two days travel-distance from the park.

Entry into the Park headquarters at Bartlett Cove is not permitted even if a boat is on the stand-by list. (Boats have been fined for entering without a mandatory permit.) There is no cell phone coverage inside the bay.

All boaters are required to call on VHF Ch 16 and then switch to Ch 12 immediately upon entering the bay. Proceed directly to the Visitor Information Station in Bartlett Cove for a required boater orientation prior to continuing in the bay. (Visitor Information Station tel.: 907.697.2627.) Cell phone connection is possible in Icy Strait but is lost approximately two miles southeast of the entrance to the park.

As you enter, take a mid-channel course, 1 mile offshore and, upon approaching the docks, turn 90 degrees toward the floats. Watch for the wake of high-speed charter boats that may pass close by you inside the bay. You can tie up at the dock for up to 3 hours.

*Please note:* Pets are not allowed on shore anywhere in Glacier Bay National Park except on a leash at Bartlett Cove.

Weather in Glacier Bay during summer is usually cool and rainy with temperatures that average about 50°F, but clear, windless days that cause short-term heat waves do occur. (On our many visits to the park we have had extraordinary luck with the weather.) Nevertheless, saltwater temperatures remain frigid enough to keep the humpback whales and orcas returning to the region.

The most picturesque glaciers, in our opinion, are Margerie and Grand Pacific in Tarr Inlet, Johns Hopkins in Johns Hopkins Inlet, Reid in the west arm of the bay, and Riggs and Muir glaciers in Muir Inlet.

Glacier Bay has wide tidal ranges (up to approximately 20 feet), with floating ice of different depths and drift rate. Williwaws sometimes blow off the glaciers bringing threatening

## A High-Latitude Emergency

Lachlan and Becky McGuigan, S/V *Xephyr*

It was getting dark, which in Glacier Park, Alaska is almost tomorrow. Crab pots littered the anchorage. The engine gave a strangled cough and died. The pots were catching more than crabs tonight. A morning dive was a chilling prospect.

Making do with what I had, I donned a thin wet suit (1/8 of an inch is not enough), a light jacket, quilted hood, boots, and sailing gloves. My accessories included mask, snorkel and a fanny-pack of zinc weights.

We rigged a guide-line under the boat, rafted the dinghy as a work float, taped a hose to the snorkel, and went in. The water was the temperature of a martini with visibility like milk. Scary stuff. The snorkel kinked. No air. Straighten the snorkel and try again. No air. Shorten the hose. Still can't get air below 2 feet. Bag the snorkel.

The guide-line curves into the darkness. No prop here. We move the line three times before a shadowy prop materializes. Dive, search the murk for the rope end, unwrap a loop. One dive per wrap. After each dive the crew dumps very hot water (feels lukewarm) inside my wetsuit. Finally there is enough line free to bring the end to the surface. Heavy duty, expensive stuff; just like on our boat. Funny they would use it for crabbing. Hello??!! This isn't a crab pot float line. We ran over our own gib sheet. Crab fishermen aren't so bad after all. More hot water. Back down. I fantasize about hot showers. Only icebergs are comfortable here. My average dive lasts 10 seconds. Up on the dinghy, hot water down the wetsuit, drag myself down the guide-line. My lungs tell me to stop. Back to the dinghy for more blessed water. Only six more wraps to go. Last wrap. Warm up the champagne. Let's celebrate!

ice or making an anchorage insecure. While we do not agree with *Coast Pilot* that single-screw vessels shouldn't enter Glacier Bay, we do feel that cautious, prudent navigation is essential, especially around floating ice or in opaque waters.

Anchor sites in Glacier Bay—which are relatively few for the hundreds of miles of shoreline—are deep, with hard bottoms and poor-to-fair holding, making holding marginal. The channels are steep-to, and the shoals along shore inadequate for swinging room. It is also almost impossible to get an anchor to bite, well—understandable when you consider that these fiords were carved by ice out of solid rock. Mud and silt on the bottom tend to form a thin layer, adding to the difficulty of anchoring.

In this guidebook we have researched and documented many new, small sites to give you additional choices. Since the time when over 4,000 crab pots were no longer permitted, and commercial Dungeness crabbing was no longer permitted within the park's permit area, many of the small coves and shoals located off creeks have become more feasible as anchor sites.

*Note:* Since few anchor sites are located near glaciers, you may consume more fuel than expected as you sightsee, so it's a good idea to check your fuel levels, both at entry and upon exit of Glacier Bay.

The area west of Glacier Bay to Cape Spencer, then north 90 miles to Dry Bay—although within the Park boundaries—lies outside the mandatory permit area. Later in this chapter, we describe anchor sites on both sides of Cape Spencer for boaters who want to experience some of the rugged backcountry to the south and west of the Fairweather Range.

Réanne Hemingway-Douglass

*Approach the Bartlett Cove dock after a 90-degree turn from mid-channel.*

## **Bartlett Cove** (Glacier Bay)

Bartlett Cove, on the east side of Glacier Bay, is 4 miles north of Point Gustavus.

Chart 17318 (inset)
Entrance: 58°26.44′ N, 135°55.25′ W
Public float: 58°27.31′ N, 135°53.30′ W
Anchor: 58°27.47′ N, 135°53.18′ W

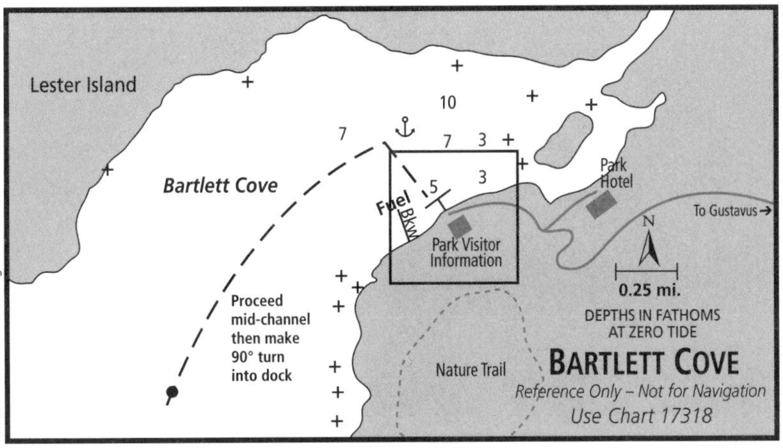




*The best anchorage in the cove is about 0.2 mile off the SE side in 7 to 10 fathoms, mud bottom. Take care not to approach too close to the head of the cove. In S weather small boats can anchor close inshore on the SE side of the cove. . . . Anchorage for large vessels is recommended in the center of the cove in 8 to 16 fathoms.* (CP)

Bartlett Cove is the headquarters of Glacier Bay National Park. Cruising boats are re-

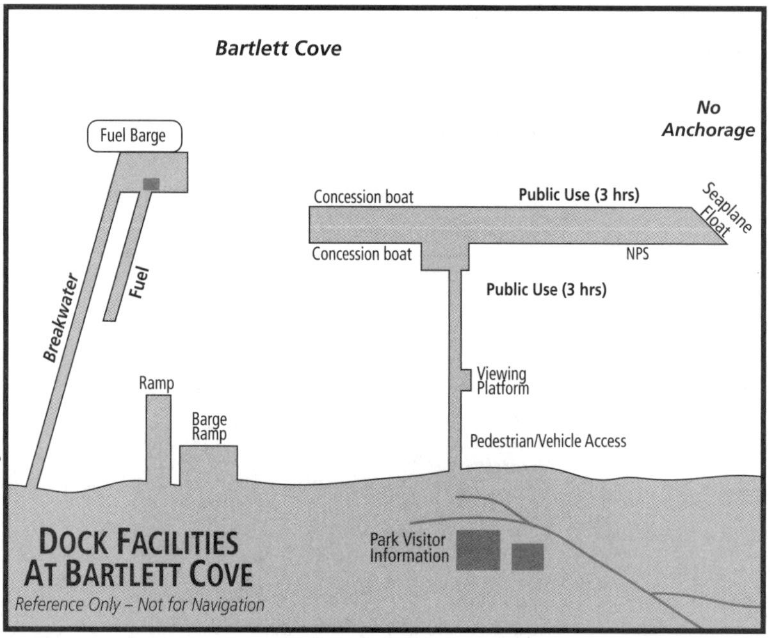


©2007 Don and Réanne Douglass

quired to check in here and receive their orientation; however, any boat entering the area north of Point Gustavus must have its permit or it is subject to a fine. The park has programs that include slide presentations and nature walks. Please do your part to keep this special environment pristine by observing all park regulations. (For details on park regulations, go to: www.nps.gov/glba.) Since the number of kayakers and self-propelled travelers is growing, please watch your wake!

Glacier Bay Lodge, a short distance east of park headquarters, has pay telephones, showers and laundry facilities for campers and boaters, as well as comfortable lodging, a restaurant, gift shop and interpretive center. Gas and diesel are sold at the fuel dock (operated by Glacier Bay Lodge) from approximately May 20 to September 10. Call the lodge ahead of time on Ch 16 to arrange for fuel.

An interesting nature trail circles around a small lake to the west of the lodge. Bartlett Cove is connected by road to Gustavus (the last hint of civilization before you head deeper into the fiords).

Larger docks were placed in Bartlett Cove in 2000. Space on the docks is limited and use is restricted to 3 hours. Read the signs carefully and park only in a designated space. Water is available on the floats. Cruising boats may anchor outside the no-anchoring area to the north and take a dinghy to the dock.

Réanne Hemingway-Douglass

*Bartlett Cove's transient dock*

For a less lumpy night, shallow-draft boats can also anchor in Bartlett River, to the east on the south side of Lagoon Island. However, the entrance is shallow, with changing levels that may prevent your entering or leaving at anything but high water. Ask for details at the dock.

Anchor in 6 fathoms, 200 yards north of the dock, over mud with good holding.

*The fuel dock at Bartlett Cove, as viewed looking west from the vehicle ramp*

*For those who choose to anchor at Bartlett Cove, there is an excellent dinghy dock.*

## **Ripple Cove** (Glacier Bay)

Ripple Cove, on the west side of Glacier Bay, is 6.2 miles west of Bartlett Cove.

Chart 17318
Entrance: 58°27.06′ N, 136°04.19′ W
Anchor: 58°27.17′ N, 136°05.08′ W

While not mentioned in *Coast Pilot*, Ripple Cove is a good temporary anchorage in fair weather. We use it as a lunch stop or a place to wait for favorable currents or to get organized before heading up into Glacier Bay. The approach is simple and it is out of nearly all the current of Sitakaday Narrows.

Anchor in 2 to 3 fathoms over sand and mud with good holding.

## **Beardslee Islands** (Glacier Bay)

Beardslee Entrance, the approach to Beardslee Islands is 4.9 miles northwest of Bartlett Cove.

Chart 17318
Entrance (George Point bearing 000°T at 0.7 Nm): 58°29.63′ N, 136°00.45′ W

> *The shoals at the entrance, although they have comparatively deep water over them, cause numerous swirls and the tide rips. Among the islands are a number of anchorages, but local knowledge is necessary for their approach.* (CP)

The Beardslee Islands are a labyrinth of islands and islets connected by tiny channels with many rocks and foul bottoms—an exciting place to explore by small craft at slow speed and perfect for a kayak. The Beardslee Islands are closed to motorized travel from May 15 to September 15.

## **Secret Bay** (Beardslee Islands)

Secret Bay is 2.3 miles northwest of Bartlett Cove.

Chart 17318
Position: 58°29.11′ N, 135°56.35′ W

## **Hutchins Bay** (Beardslee Islands)

Hutchins Bay is 5.4 miles north of Bartlett Cove.

Chart 17318
Position: 58°32.46′ N, 135°52.22′ W

## **Berg Bay** (Glacier Bay)

Berg Bay is 8.9 miles northwest of Bartlett Cove.

Chart 17318
South entrance: 58°31.89′ N, 136°07.74′ W
Anchor (west arm): 58°31.08′ N, 136°13.55′ W
Anchor (Nifty Nook): 58°32.75′ N, 136°10.25′ W

> *Two channels enter the bay. The passage N of Netland Island is not recommended. . . .*
>
> *Anchorage is good in about 18 fathoms about 1 mile inside the entrance. Small craft can anchor farther inshore for protection from S winds. Good anchorage, with protection from N winds, can be had in the N arm. Small craft also have good anchorage in the W arm.* (CP)

Berg Bay is the site of John Muir's first camp as he explored Glacier Bay. We find it interest-

Réanne Hemingway-Douglass

*Berg Bay Lagoon is especially attractive for its bird-watching opportunities.*

ing and well sheltered. However, entering is difficult due to rocky bars and poor charting. The bottom is generally irregular and an alert

Réanne Hemingway-Douglass

*The entrance to Berg Bay is over a shallow, rocky bar seen here at low tide.*

bow watch is required. The small entrance north of Netland Island is choked with kelp and has a large mid-channel rock awash on an 8-foot tide. The main entrance is south of Netland Island by way of a shallow rocky bar that has a broken area near mid-channel that dries on about zero tide.

*Baidarka* follows an entrance track close to Netland Island and south of the rock pile, but avoiding detached rocks off the south coast of the island. Current can be quite strong across the bar and passage near high-water slack is recommended.

A fine intimate anchor site that we call "Nifty Nook" can be found behind the small unnamed island in the far northwest corner of the bay. Once you have successfully crossed the Berg Bay entrance bar, turn north to find the nook by carefully crossing a small bar with about 9 feet of water. The anchor site then opens into a very well protected hole of about five fathoms.

Anchor over a mud bottom with limited swinging room.

The main bay has a well-sheltered anchorage at its western head with room for many boats. The two west ends of this bay are interesting to explore, as is the lagoon entered 0.5 mile south of Netland Island and southwest of Lars Island.

The entrance to the lagoon is a raging torrent on a spring tide, but entry can be made by a small, shallow-draft vessel, a skiff or dinghy at high-water slack. The lagoon, which harbors extensive bird life, is a special place to investigate. Very well sheltered anchorage can be found inside the lagoon in about two fathoms. The bottom of the lagoon is very irregular and should be reconnoitered by dinghy before entry. Avoid the shallow rock pile in the center of the "fairway" just inside the entrance channel to the lagoon

Anchor in the far west corner of the main bay in 10 fathoms over sand, mud and shale with fair-to-good holding.

Anchor in Nifty Nook in about 1 to 2 fathoms over sand, mud and shale; fair-to-good holding with very limited swinging room.

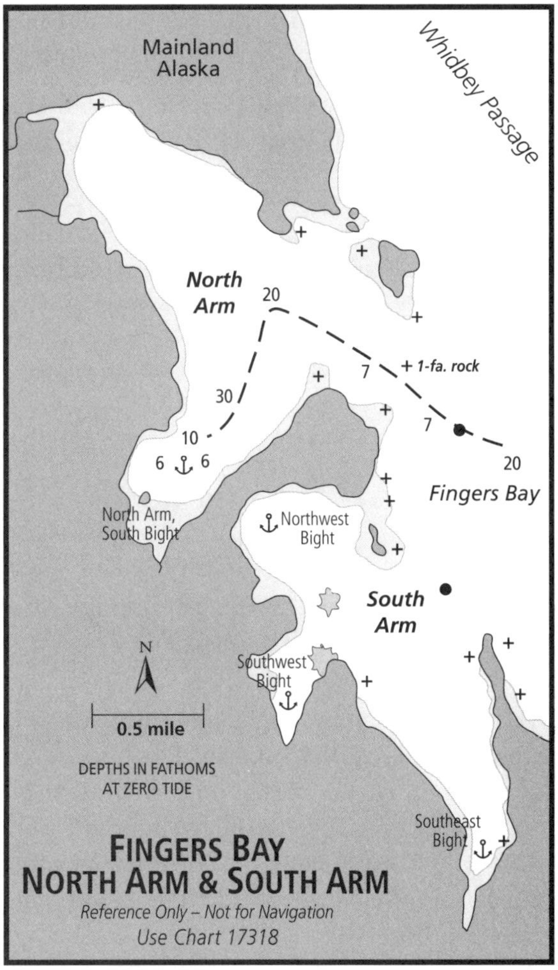




## Fingers Bay—North Arm

(Whidbey Passage)

Fingers Bay, on the west side of Whidbey Passage, is 12.3 miles north of Bartlett Cove and approximately 1 mile west of Willoughby Island.

Chart 17318
North entrance: 58°35.19′ N, 136°11.14′ W
Anchor (North Arm, South Bight): 58°34.95′ N, 136°12.91′ W

> *Whidbey Passage, a well-defined and deep passage, separates Willoughby Island from the mainland to the W.* (CP)

Although Fingers Bay does not appear in *Coast Pilot*, we have found good shelter in the South Bight of the north arm. The entrances to both the north arm and the south arm of Fingers Bay are shallow with an irregular bottom, so keep a sharp bow watch as you approach. With the removal of crab pot floats, Fingers Bay is much more useful for small pleasure craft, and it is also a good place to watch for bear.

Anchor in the South Bight in 6 to 10 fathoms over sand and mud with fair-to-good holding.

## Fingers Bay—South Arm

The south arm of Fingers Bay is approximately 1 mile west of Willoughby Island.

Chart 17318
Entrance: 58°34.62′ N, 136°11.02′ W
Anchor (Northwest Bight): 58°34.78′ N, 136°12.28′ W
Anchor (Southwest Bight): 58°34.21′ N, 136°12.10′ W
Anchor (Southeast Bight): 58°33.66′ N, 136°10.79′ W

The south arm of Fingers Bay is smaller than the north arm and has three sheltered anchor sites. Its entrance is narrow and requires careful studying of the chart to avoid the hazards. *Caution:* the bottom is somewhat irregular and is poorly charted.

When entering the bay, avoid the unnamed center reef awash on an 11-foot tide.

The first anchor site can be found in the Northwest Bight. Southwest Bight, the second anchor site, has a shallow bar at its entrance and you must once again maneuver around the center reef (awash on an 11-foot tide), and avoid rocks that extend halfway out from the eastern shore. The third anchor site is found in the Southeast Bight.

Remember that to enter and exit the south arm of Fingers Bay, you must avoid the center reef and rocks.

Anchor (Northwest Bight) in 7 fathoms over a bottom of silt over gravel; fair-to-good holding.

Anchor (Southwest Bight) in 8 to 11 fathoms over an irregular bottom with silt over gravel; fair holding.

Anchor (Southeast Bight) in 10 fathoms over a bottom of silt and gravel; fair-to-good holding.

## Beartrack Cove

Beartrack Cove, on the east side of Glacier Bay, is 7.6 miles north of Bartlett Cove.

Chart 17318
Entrance: 58°37.24′ N, 135°57.06′ W
Anchor: 58°35.17′ N, 135°52.30′ W

> *Beartrack Cove . . . is very deep throughout, and the bottom slopes steeply from the shore. . . . To anchor in 20 fathoms or less a vessel must lie about 175 yards off the low-water line. Strong W winds bring swells into the cove.* (CP)

We found a shallow bight one mile south of Beartrack Island that affords fair anchorage, subject to northwest chop, on the south shore close to the Beardslee Islands Wilderness non-motorized area. It can be used in fair weather as a kayak home base. For better shelter, consider Beartrack Island.

## Beartrack Island

Beartrack Island is 8.6 miles north of Bartlett Cove.

Chart 17318
Anchor: 58°36.15′ N, 135°52.07′ W

The tiny cove on the north side of Beartrack Island provides very good shelter. Because swinging room is limited, a stern-tie can be used to good advantage.

## Johnson Cove (Willoughby Island)

Johnson Cove is 11.3 miles northwest of Bartlett Cove.

Chart 17318
Entrance: 58°36.25′ N, 136°06.30′ W
Anchor: 58°36.35′ N, 136°06.90′ W

> *Johnson Cove . . . is partially protected from wind and waves by the small islets and affords some protection for small boats in all but SE weather.* (CP)

Tiny Johnson Cove can provide welcome shelter in blowing northerlies. This is a perfect lunch stop during prevailing northwest winds. It is open to southeast chop and is not recommended as an anchorage in gales. Swinging room is limited in the cove.

Anchor in 2 to 4 fathoms over sand with fair holding.

## Spokane Cove (Glacier Bay)

Spokane Cove is 14.5 miles north of Bartlett Cove.

Chart 17318
Entrance: 58°41.03′ N, 135°58.42′ W
Anchor: 58°41.88′ N, 135°57.45′ W

> *In entering, care must be taken to pass S of the rock off the N shore and to avoid the boulders which fringe the shore of the mainland. The entrance channel has a depth of 10 fathoms. This cove is used by fishing boats with local knowledge but is open to winds from the NW. Anchorage can be had in 5 to 8 fathoms, mud and sand bottom.* (CP)

We have found that Spokane Cove provides fair shelter deep in the cove off the bluff on its south shore.

Anchor in about 6 fathoms over sand with fair holding.

## South Sandy Cove (Glacier Bay)

South Sandy Cove is 15.4 miles north of Bartlett Cove.

Chart 17318
Entrance: 58°42.05′ N, 135°59.82′ W
Anchor (west): 58°42.63′ N, 135°59.76′ W
Anchor (east): 58°42.49′ N, 135°58.59′ W

> *South Sandy Cove . . . is used by fishing vessels with local knowledge. Excellent anchorage can be had any place in the cove, including the bight at the SE side of the head, in 5 to 8 fathoms, mud and sand bottom. This anchorage is almost always free of ice, but is open to winds from the SW.* (CP)

Offering easy access, Sandy Cove is one of the more popular anchorages in Glacier Bay. While South Sandy Cove is not as good an anchorage as North Sandy Cove, it does provide two anchor sites. The west site is usually preferred over the east site, because it is more protected from northerly chop and the bottom gives a better anchor bite. Although formerly crab pots limited swinging room, with their removal, this cove is a much safer place to anchor. If a strong southerly is expected, North Sandy Cove provides better shelter.

It's interesting to note that, as late as 1855, the terminus of the glacier later named after John Muir covered 15-mile-wide Glacier Bay north of Sandy Cove from east to west.

Anchor (west) in 6 fathoms over a mixed bottom of sand and mud with good holding.

Anchor (east) in 5 fathoms over a hard rocky bottom with poor-to-fair holding.

## **North Sandy Cove** (Glacier Bay)

North Sandy Cove is 16.2 miles north of Bartlett Cove.

Chart 17318
Entrance (west of Puffin Island): 58°43.58′ N, 136°01.03′ W
Entrance (east of Puffin Island): 58°44.01′ N, 136°00.16′ W
Anchor: 58°43.14′ N, 135°59.19′ W

*North Sandy Cove . . . affords anchorage in 4 to 6 fathoms, good holding ground, and good protection form winds from any quarter. Ice rarely drifts* into the cove. (CP)

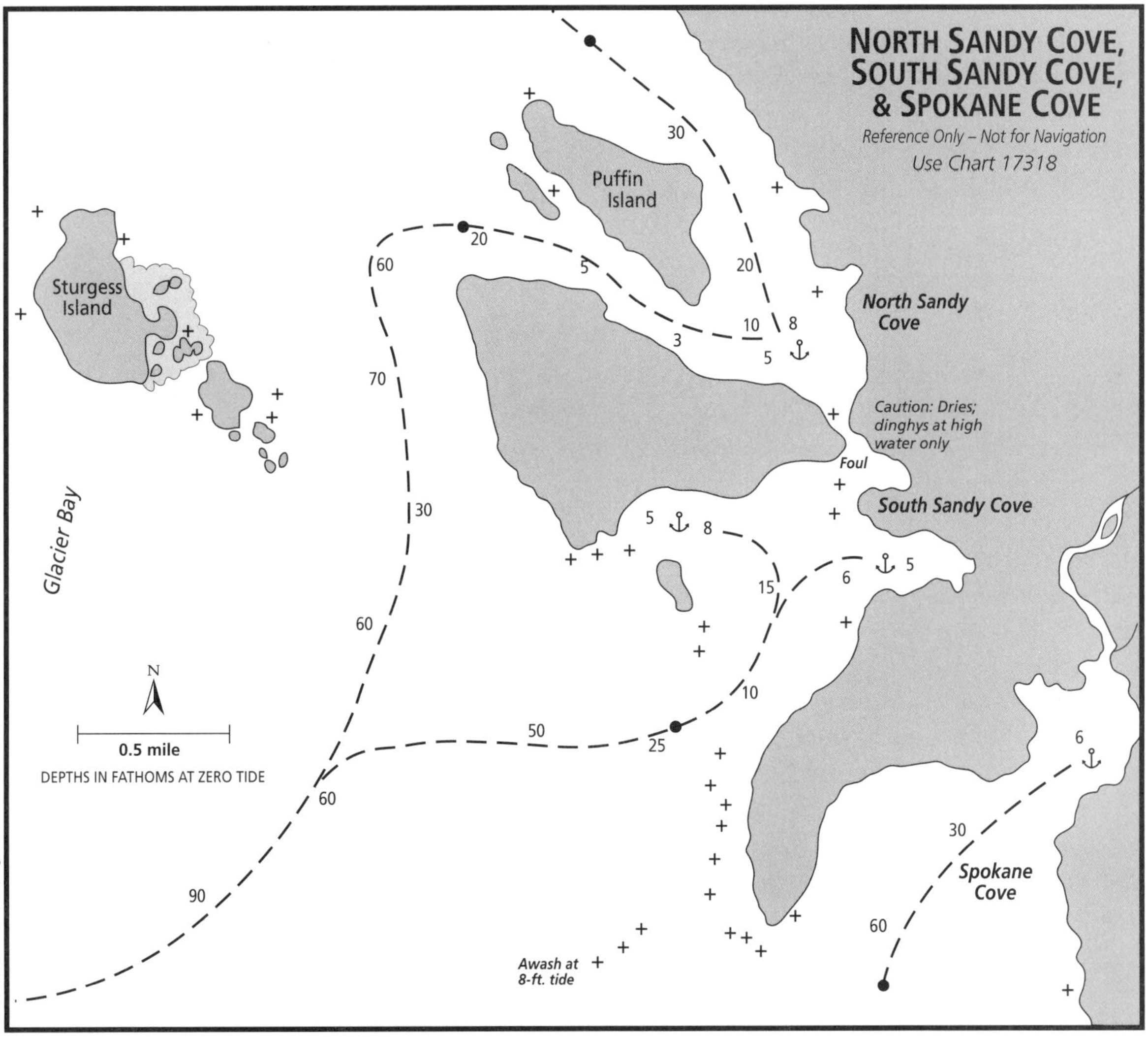

North Sandy Cove is our choice for easy anchoring with good protection and holding. It is safe to enter the cove from either the west or the north, and possible anchor sites are available over a relatively large area. This is a good place to view wildlife while relaxing on grassy meadows.

Anchor in 5 fathoms in the south corner, or further north in 10 fathoms over sand with good holding.

### Geikie Inlet (Glacier Bay)

Geikie Inlet is 19 miles northwest of Bartlett Cove.

Chart 17318

**Entrance (Geikie Rock bearing 037°T at 0.8 Nm): 58°40.91′ N, 136°19.76′ W**

> *Geikie Inlet extends 8 miles SW from the S shore of Glacier Bay. Midchannel depths range from 40 to 80 fathoms with unobstructed depths greater than 10 fathoms that extend to within 200 yards of shore.* (CP)

### Shag Cove (Geikie Inlet)

Shag Cove is 1 mile inside the entrance to Geikie Inlet on the south shore.

**Chart 17318**
**Entrance: 58°39.44′ N, 136°20.09′ W**
**Anchor: 58°37.46′ N, 136°18.74′ W**

> *Protected anchorage may be had in 5 to 20 fathoms at the head of the cove, soft bottom.* (CP)

Shag Cove is a classic U-shaped alpine valley. Glacier-polished granite walls rise 1,000 feet; numerous waterfalls tumble down these walls, and small bowls that hold year-round snow nestle here and there. The water throughout the cove is turquoise blue glacier wash.

Shag Cove offers good shelter in all weather. It also provides a good home base from which you can explore wildlife and nature's beauty away from the main route. Frequently, you'll spot a bear or two along the beach, flipping over rocks in search of shellfish.

Marble Mountain, on the north side of the cove, rises 3,366 feet above the water and is less than a half-mile away. This mountain has one of the sharpest vertical rock walls within the park.

Réanne Hemingway-Douglass

*Cascades tumble down Shag Cove's walls.*

Anchor near the head of the bay in about 13 fathoms where there is good, almost landlocked protection, over a bottom of a thin layer of mud over sand and gravel; good holding.

### Tyndall Cove (Geikie Inlet)

Tyndall Cove is 2 miles southwest of Shag Cove.

**Chart 17318**
**Entrance: 58°37.65′ N, 136°23.80′ W**
**Anchor: 58°35.69′ N, 136°21.52′ W**

> *Anchorage may be made in 10 to 20 fathoms at the head of the cove, soft bottom.* (CP)

Tyndall Cove, like Shag Cove, provides good shelter and more sun at its narrow head. Although it has less swinging room than Shag Cove, it offers a more intimate feeling below the towering peaks.

Anchor in about 10 fathoms over sand and mud with good holding.

## **Wood Lake Creek Outlet** (Geikie Inlet)

Wood Lake Creek Outlet is 8 miles southwest of the entrance to Geike Inlet.

Chart 17318
Anchor: 58°35.32′ N, 136°28.31′ W

Temporary anchorage surrounded by spectacular scenery can be found off the outlet to Wood Lake. This is a good base from which to explore the nearby streams and mud flats.

Anchor in 5 to 10 fathoms over sandy gravel with fair holding.

## **Muir Inlet** (Glacier Bay)

Muir Inlet extends north and then west for over 24 miles from Glacier Bay.

Charts 17318
Entrance (Caroline Shoal bearing 270°T at 0.75 Nm): 58°46.45′ N, 136°05.90′ W

> *Numerous shifting glacial streams line the moraines, and a number of glaciers empty into the inlet. Good depth is found in midchannel.* (CP)

Muir Inlet has two accessible tidewater glaciers—Muir and Riggs. Both are worth a visit by kayak, or by motor vessel when no entry restrictions exist.

## **Sebree Cove** (Muir Inlet)

Sebree Cove is 10.1 miles north of Bartlett Cove and 10 miles southeast of Blue Mouse Cove.

Chart 17318
Entrance: 58°44.79′ N, 136°10.07′ W
Anchor: 58°45.56′ N, 136°10.20′ W

> *Small vessels can anchor in Sebree Cove, between Tlingit Point and the S part of Sebree Island; the holding ground is good.* (CP)

Sebree Cove, strategically located at the south end of Muir Inlet, provides excellent protection during westerlies. Since it is open to the south, however, it is a fair-weather anchorage only. The wind frequently changes direction to the northeast in early morning. (Before removal of the 100 crab pot floats in the cove, *Baidarka* fouled a prop here.)

Anchor in 5 fathoms over a good sand/mud bottom with fair-to-good holding.

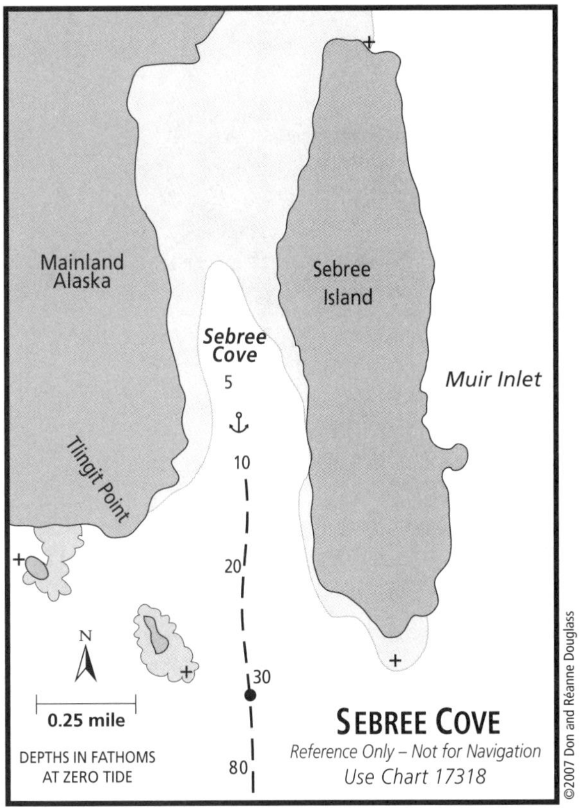


## **Adams Inlet** (Muir Inlet)

Adams Inlet is 24.1 miles north of Bartlett Cove.

Chart 17318
Wilderness entrance: 58°50.70′ N, 136°03.47′ W

> *Adams Inlet, on the lower E shore of Muir Inlet, is deep at the entrance. However, the remainder of the inlet is dangerous to enter without local knowledge.*
>
> *The waters are very muddy, and submerged shoals cannot be seen except for those marked by turbulent currents.* (CP)

Adams Inlet, like the Beardslee Islands, cries out for exploration but it is now restricted to non-motorized boats.

## **Maquinna Cove** (Muir Inlet)

Maquinna Cove is 25 miles north of Bartlett Cove.

Chart 17318
Position: 58°51.71′ N, 136°03.34′ W

Maquinna Cove is the small bight on the north side of the entrance to Adams Inlet. It is exposed to all weather and is useful only as a temporary stop in fair weather.

Ellie Sharman

*Seen in Wachusett Inlet; "Hey Skipper, did you check the tide tables last night?"*

## Hunter Cove (Muir Inlet)

Hunter Cove is 28 miles north of Bartlett Cove.

Chart 17318
Entrance: 58°54.21′ N, 136°06.96′ W
Anchor: 58°54.62′ N, 136°07.54′ W

> *Hunter Cove . . . is a bight formed by the recession of Plateau Glacier; the cove is a good temporary anchorage. When using this bight, take care to avoid two rocks, which uncover 2 feet, close E of the bold point at the N entrance.* (CP)

Hunter Cove, while exposed to the southeast, does provide good downslope protection if you tuck in close to shore.

Anchor in less than 10 fathoms over sand and mud with fair holding.

## Wachusett Inlet (Muir Inlet)

Wachusett Inlet is 28 miles north of Bartlett Cove.

Chart 17318
Entrance: 58°56.54′ N, 136°07.70′ W

> *A shoal with a depth of 3-1/2 fathoms is near the middle of the entrance; large icebergs frequently ground on this shoal.*
>
> *Wachusett Inlet extends over 9 miles from its entrance, W to the terminus of Plateau Glacier.* (CP)

Wachusett Inlet has a stunning hanging glacier that towers above. The head of the inlet is a restricted entry area. We have taken overnight anchorage east of the two rocks, but the sand is very thin over a hard rocky bottom with poor holding. The photo gives you an idea of tidal swing and the care needed in transiting and anchoring in Glacier Bay.

## Goose Cove (Muir Inlet)

Goose Cove is 30.9 miles north of Bartlett Cove.

Chart 17318
Entrance: 58°57.37′ N, 136°06.51′ W

> *Small fishing vessels can anchor in Goose Cove, the small cove E of* [Sealers Island]. *The cove is narrow and shoal, but generally free from ice during the summer.* (CP)

We have not anchored in Goose Cove, but it appears to be sheltered from downslope winds and drift ice. It is tiny with limited swinging room. Entry restrictions may apply.

## Nunatak Cove (Muir Inlet)

Nunatak Cove is 32 miles north of Bartlett Cove.

Chart 17318
Position: 58°58.52′ N, 136°06.78′ W

Nunatak Cove is largely a drying sand flat offering little protection.

## Stump Cove (Muir Inlet)

Stump Cove is 32.3 miles north of Bartlett Cove.

Chart 17318
Position: 58°58.60′ N, 136°09.36′ W

Stump Cove, southwest of Westdahl Point, gets some protection from downslope winds close to shore. It can provide temporary anchorage only.

## Riggs Glacier (Muir Inlet)

Riggs Glacier is 37.9 miles north of Bartlett Cove.

Chart 17318
Position: 59°04.14′ N, 136°11.04′ W

Riggs Glacier, which has restricted entry, is a good area to explore by kayak. We have found temporary anchorage in fair weather along the north shore off the glacier in about 10 fathoms.

## Muir Glacier (Muir Inlet)

Muir Glacier is 41 miles north of Bartlett Cove.

Chart 17318
Position: 59°05.42′ N, 136°22.47′ W

> *Muir Glacier, at the head of Muir Inlet, is no longer a tidal glacier. Recent warming has caused the glacier to retreat out of the waters of Muir Inlet. The face of Muir Glacier is now blocked by a series of low moraines. Ice rarely reaches the waters of the inlet.* (CP)

Muir Glacier has restricted entry. We have found temporary anchorage in fair weather off the steep-to shore on the east side.

## **Hugh Miller Inlet** (Glacier Bay)

Hugh Miller Inlet is one mile southwest of Blue Mouse Cove.

Chart 17318

Wilderness entrance: 58°45.18′ N, 136°28.79′ W

> *Safe passage may be had into Hugh Miller Inlet by staying 100 to 600 yards off the S shore, from the prominent point 3.5 miles NW of Geikie Rock to a small unnamed cove on the S shore just within the mouth of the inlet. . . . Anchorage may be had in 5 to 35 fathoms in the cove, soft bottom.*
>
> *Division Island separates Charpentier Inlet and upper Hugh Miller Inlet. No attempt should be made to enter the head of Hugh Miller Inlet between Division Island and Gilbert Peninsula without local knowledge; numerous rocks and foul areas exist in this area. The SW shore of Hugh Miller Inlet between the unnamed cove and Division Island should be kept at least 500 yards to port when passing from the unnamed cove to the NW part of Charpentier Inlet.*
>
> *To pass through Hugh Miller Inlet into Charpentier Inlet, follow a midchannel course until the N and westernmost low rocky island is abeam to port and then follow a SW course so as to pass midchannel between the SE end of Division Island and the rocky island about 500 yards S of the southeast point of Division Island. Take care to pass well clear of the islands, which are fringed by reefs and shoal areas.* (CP)

Hugh Miller Inlet is a Wilderness Area with entry restricted to non-motorized boats between May 1 and September 15. By anchoring in Blue Mouse Cove, you can easily take a kayak or row your dinghy into the inlet.

## **Charpentier Inlet** (Hugh Miller Inlet)

Charpentier Inlet is 27 miles northwest of Bartlett Cove.

Chart 17318

Position (Hugh Miller Inlet position at head): 58°40.26′ N, 136°27.16′ W

> *Charpentier Inlet extends about 6 miles SSE from the SSW end of Division Island. . . . Anchorage may be had in soft bottom anywhere in the inlet. The SE arm is navigable to its head where anchorage may be had in 10 to 20 fathoms.* (CP)

Linda Lewis

*Don't forget to scoop up some of the longest-lasting cocktail ice you'll ever get.*

Charpentier Inlet is a Wilderness Area with entry restricted to non-motorized boats between May 1 and September 15.

## **Scidmore Bay** (Glacier Bay)

Scidmore Bay is 3 miles west of Blue Mouse Cove.

Chart 17318

Position: 58°48.30′ N, 136°37.26′ W

> *Strong NW and SE winds blow though the bay, and best anchorage is made in 10 to 20 fathoms in the lee of the islands, soft bottom. To enter Scidmore Bay, hold a midchannel course from Charpentier Inlet.* (CP)

Scidmore Bay is now a Wilderness Area with entry restricted to non-motorized boats between May 1 and September 15.

## **Blue Mouse Cove** (Gilbert Peninsula)

Blue Mouse Cove is 27.3 miles northwest of Bartlett Cove.

Chart 17318
Entrance: 58°47.30′ N, 136°28.95′ W
Anchor (southeast): 58°46.69′ N, 136°29.13′ W
Anchor (southwest): 58°47.00′ N, 136°30.41′ W

> *Unobstructed depths greater than 5 fathoms extend to within 150 yards of the shore, with central depths from 15 to 30 fathoms good holding ground.* (CP)

Blue Mouse Cove is perhaps the most popular anchorage in Glacier Bay proper, but we find the bottom somewhat marginal. Protection from both north and south winds is good here, and there is generally little concern about drifting ice. The Park Service maintains a seasonal float cabin here. The south side of the cove offers satisfactory anchorage. You can often sight wolves and bear along shore and, occasionally, humpback whales visit the cove. The bottom is irregular with a mixture of silt, mud, gravel and rocks.

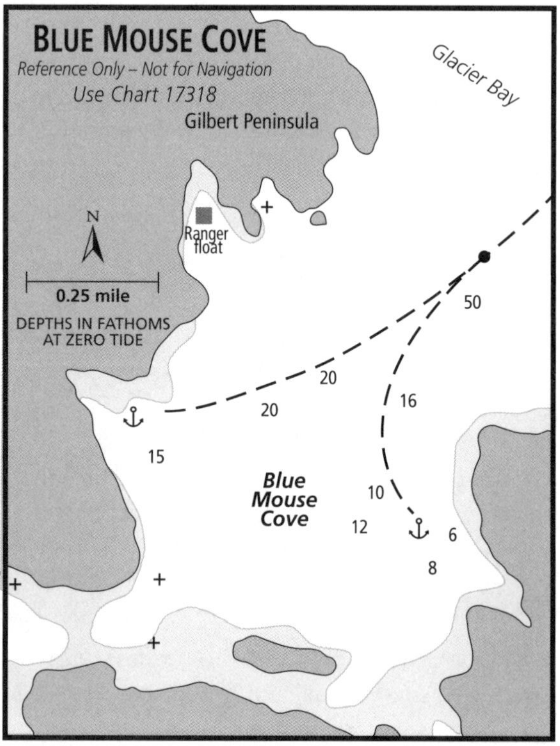




Anchor (southeast) in 6 to 10 fathoms over a thin layer of silt on top of a hard rocky bottom with poor-to-fair holding. Be sure to test the set of your anchor.

## **Tidal Inlet** (Glacier Bay)

Tidal Inlet is 3.5 miles northeast of Blue Mouse Cove.

Chart 17318
Entrance: 58°48.90′ N, 136°24.37′ W
Anchor: (cove northwest of entrance):
58°49.40′ N, 136°26.00′ W

> *Anchorage is best in 5 to 20 fathoms off the S shore, 2.6 miles from the entrance, and 100 yards NW of a prominent reef 100 yards from the apparent shoreline; anchorage in other areas is difficult, because of excessive depths.* (CP)

We prefer to anchor in the small cove 1 mile northwest of the entrance to Tidal Inlet, which is a fair-weather site only but with good views to the west.

Anchor in about 8 fathoms over a rocky bottom with poor-to-fair holding.

## **Queen Inlet** (Glacier Bay)

Queen Inlet is 34.4 miles northwest of Bartlett Cove.

Chart 17318
Entrance (Composite Island bearing 297°T at 0.7 Nm): 58°52.38′ N, 136°32.04′ W

> *Neither Rendu Inlet nor Queen Inlet offers safe anchorage, because of the steeply sloping bottom and excessive depths. Take care to avoid*

Linda Lewis

*You can hike right up to the face of Reid Glacier—one of the few opportunities to do this.*

Linda Lewis

*Approaching the Reid Inlet anchorage; Reid Glacier*

*the rapidly building bars at the heads of these inlets.* (CP)

## Rendu Inlet (Glacier Bay)

Rendu Inlet is 35 miles northwest of Bartlett Cove.

Chart 17318
Wilderness entrance: 58°53.91′ N, 136°36.45′ W

*Rendu Inlet, 7 miles long, is NW of Composite island. . . .* (CP)

Rendu Inlet is a Wilderness Area with restricted entry.

## Reid Inlet (Glacier Bay)

Reid Inlet is 11 miles northwest of Blue Mouse Cove.

Chart 17318 (inset)
Entrance: 58°52.37′ N, 136°48.92′ W
Anchor (west): 58°51.70′ N, 136°49.24′ W

*Anchorage may be had in 10 to 20 fathoms 500 yards past the entrance to either the NE or SW.*

*To enter Reid Inlet, go W past the entrance; turn and steer 135°* [true] *parallel to and about 300 yards off the shoreline NW of the entrance. Approach is best made at low tide when the channel is well marked by the bars on either side.* (CP)

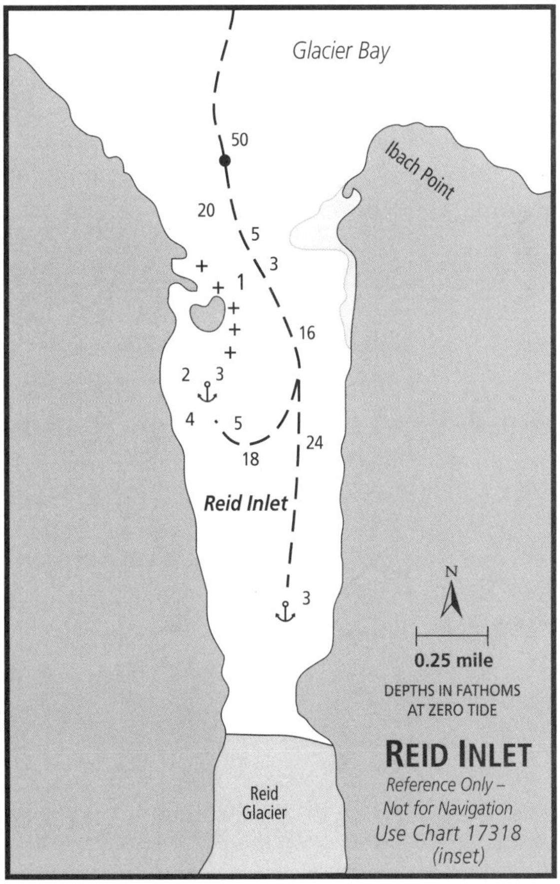

Linda Lewis

*A grizzly bear paw print spotted on a Reid Glacier hike*

David Parker

*Our editor catches the water dripping from an ice boulder—a real thirst-quencher.*

Reid Inlet is a good cruising boat destination because large cruise ships don't enter it. The inlet is not as overwhelming as other nearby fiords, and its proximity to Johns Hopkins Inlet and the glacier in Tarr Inlet make it a convenient overnight anchorage. You can approach Reid Glacier, land a dinghy on either side and explore the glacier's snout, which no longer reaches tidal water. If you do, however, use caution.

The entrance to Reid Inlet is somewhat narrow and shallow, but you can usually find 3 to 6 fathoms across the bar. We have anchored overnight in the inlet when the iceberg situation is not threatening. You can anchor on either the west or east shore, the eastern being significantly deeper.

Linda Lewis

*Wandering among the ice boulders at Reid Glacier*

The area near the west shore, inside the entrance, is the most commonly-used anchor site. It is also a good place to get ashore. You can walk all the way from the north point, where you can explore an old miners' site. Be aware that winds can blow off the glacier at night, making the anchor site marginal.

Anchor (west) in 3 to 10 fathoms over silt and sand with fair holding.

Linda Lewis

*Lamplugh Glacier cave spewing water and ice*

Linda Lewis

*Lamplugh Glacier*

## Lamplugh Glacier
(Johns Hopkins Inlet)

Lamplugh Glacier is 15.5 miles northwest of Blue Mouse Cove and 42.5 miles northwest of Bartlett Cove.

**Chart 17318 (inset)**
**Position: 58°53.81′ N, 136°56.29′ W**

Lamplugh Glacier is a tidewater glacier and good spot for photo opportunities. It's also a good place to fill your ice chest with long-lasting glacial ice.

Kayakers frequently camp on the east side of the glacier snout.

## Johns Hopkins Inlet
(Glacier Bay)

Johns Hopkins Inlet is 44.7 miles northwest of Bartlett Cove.

**Chart 17318 (inset)**
**Entrance (north of Lamplugh Glacier):**
**58°54.48′ N, 136°55.71′ W**

*Several smaller glaciers feed into the inlet at various places . . . . Rock and ice falls are very common along the SE shore in the lower section of the inlet. The inlet has no anchorages.* (CP)

North-facing Johns Hopkins Inlet is frequently choked with several square miles of floating ice and pack ice near its head. Entry to the inlet is restricted due to the presence of seal pups. A small ice tongue that tumbles steeply into the east side of the bay can be viewed from just inside the entrance. It is interesting to note that as recently (in geologic time) as 1892, Johns Hopkins Glacier extended nearly to the entrance to Reid Inlet.

## Russell Island Passage (Russell Island)

Russell Island Passage is 40.3 miles northwest of Bartlett Cove.

**Chart 17318 (inset)**
**South entrance: 58°54.59′ N, 136°46.08′ W**
**North entrance: 58°57.33′ N, 136°52.00′ W**
**Anchor: 58°55.48′ N, 136°48.36′ W**

*Anchorage is in mud with grave and cobbles anywhere from the islet due N of the easternmost point of Russell Island up to the north easternmost point of Russell Island.*

*Anchorage may* [also] *be found on the NW side of Russell Island between the northernmost and the westernmost points, about 0.4 mile offshore. Depths are 5 to 20 fathoms in mud bottom with gravel and cobbles.* (CP)

Russell Island Passage is now in designated whale waters with entry restricted to 1 Nm offshore between June 1 and August 31.

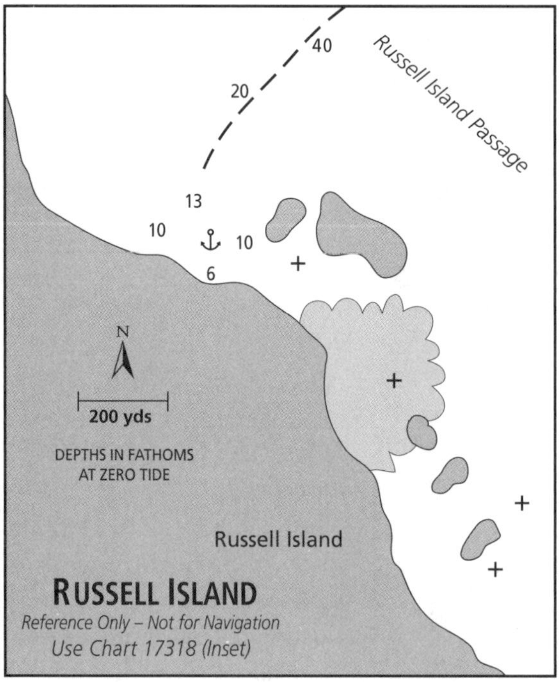


©2007 Don and Réanne Douglass

While we loved watching the orcas cruise though the passage, our experience anchoring at the north corner of Russell Island was somewhat marginal. However, our friend, Rod Nash, found a secure anchorage just west of the small islets on the northeast-central part of Russell Island, as indicated in the diagram. This is one of the better up-bay anchorages, but it is restricted, as indicated above.

Anchor in 6 to 10 fathoms over sand and mud with fair holding.

### **Tarr Inlet** (Glacier Bay)

Tarr Inlet is 43 miles northwest of Bartlett Cove.

Chart 17318 (inset)
Entrance (Russell Island bearing 090°T at 1.0 Nm): 58°56.33′ N, 136°53.62′ W
Anchor (cove): 59°01.04′ N, 137°01.78′ W

*Tarr Inlet leads NW from Russell Island for about 9 miles to Grand Pacific Glacier. . . . The*

Linda Lewis

*Margerie Glacier—the sounds of cracking ice combined with its stunning beauty make this a favorite for many cruisers.*

*NE shore has several alluvial fans of gravel, cobbles, and boulders. The SW shore is steep bare rocks except for one gently sloping valley leading S from a cove about 7 miles NW of Russell Island. . . . Ice collects in the cove in sufficient quantity to interfere with small vessels attempting anchorage. Depths greater than 10 fathoms can be carried to within 200 yards of shore throughout Tarr Inlet. . . .* (CP)

The cove in Tarr Inlet provides temporary anchorage with shelter from southerly winds. It is exposed to ice calving from the nearby glaciers and you must guard against moving icebergs at all times. The cove is also used by kayak mother ships that frequently create an uncomfortable wake for small craft.

Anchor in 5 to 10 fathoms over silt with fair holding.

Linda Lewis

*The Grand Pacific Glacier was not so grand in this 2005 photo.*

## Margerie Glacier (Tarr Inlet)

Margerie Glacier is 23 miles northwest of Blue Mouse Cove and 50.5 miles northwest of Bartlett Cove.

**Chart 17318 (inset)**
**Position: 59°02.48′ N, 137°03.54′ W**

*Margerie Glacier is on the SW shore of* [Tarr] *inlet and adjacent to Grand Pacific.* (CP)

Margerie Glacier offers the quintessential tidewater glacier experience with 200-foot-high cliffs of ice that calve into the deep bay creating large waves that, at times, may pose danger for small craft. To prevent prop damage, watch out for the build-up of ice as the wind changes direction.

This is the destination glacier for many large cruise ships in Glacier Bay, as well as the Grand Pacific Glacier. Be alert for traffic.

## Grand Pacific Glacier (Tarr Inlet)

Grand Pacific Glacier is 24 miles northwest of Blue Mouse Cove and 51.1 miles northwest of Bartlett Cove.

Chart 17318 (inset)
Position: 59°03.32′ N, 137°03.33′ W

*Grand Pacific Glacier* [is] *the largest glacier entering Glacier Bay. The glacier has advanced slowly for the past few years, and the face was 0.7 mile SE of the United States–Canadian border in 1972.* (CP)

Grand Pacific Glacier, at the far north end of Glacier Bay at the head of Tarr Inlet, is a wall

---

### When Big Brother Can't Do the Job
**(From the First Mate's Diary)**
**Réanne Hemingway-Douglass**

A voice came over Ch 16, low and deliberate, without identifying itself. "Does anyone know what conditions are off Yakobi Island?"

We had been trying to rouse Juneau Coast Guard ourselves to ask the same question, but there was no contact in Cross Sound.

Another voice came on: "S'posed to be winds west 26 knots."

A pause, then a third voice: "Winds southwest, 17 knots, seas 6 feet."

Ten minutes later a woman's voice announced, Okay, for those of you who haven't heard the weather, go to Channel 67. . . . Here it is. From Yakutat: winds east 20, seas 6 feet. Outlook: winds southeast 15, seas 7 feet."

The voice went off without identifying itself, without signing off, and one by one male voices came on. "Thank you . . . " "Thank you . . ." "Thank you . . ."

*Baidarka*'s first mate picked up the microphone and added a feminine thank you.

"That's Alaska for you," said the skipper. "When Big Brother can't do the job, the fishermen take care of one another."

of ice a mile and a half wide. The glacier has its source in the Saint Elias Mountains on the U.S.-Canadian border north of Mt. Fairweather which, at 15,300 feet, is the highest peak in the range. It is difficult to approach the snout of the Grand Pacific because the inlet is so chock-full of ice; careful navigation is necessary to prevent prop damage. Watch out for the build-up of ice as the wind changes direction, and stay well clear of cruise ships whose turning radius may be greater than you imagine.

## **Lemesurier Island—East Coast** (Icy Strait)

Lemesurier Island is in the middle of Icy Strait, 4 miles east of the Inian Islands and 5 miles southwest of the entrance to Glacier Bay.

Chart 17302
Anchor: 58°17.51′ N, 136°01.52′ W

> *North Passage is more often used, furnishing a more direct passage to sea. A 5.3-fathom reef is in the entrance to North Passage, 2.3 miles 033°* [True] *from Lemesurier Island Light 4. South Passage is clear, but the S shore should be given a berth of at least 0.8 mile to avoid the reef and submerged rocks off Goose Island.* (CP)

Fair anchorage can be found on the east side of Lemesurier Island over a large, shallow area sheltered from west wind and chop. This is the closest place to anchor temporarily when you are waiting for clearance to enter Glacier Bay. We have sometimes sighted as many whales around the island as we have inside the park.

Anchor in 7 fathoms over sand with fair holding.

## **Willoughby Cove and Jacks Cove** (Lemesurier Island)

Willoughby Cove is on the southeast side of Lemesurier Island.

Chart 17302
Position: 58°16.03′ N, 136°03.60′ W

> *Willoughby Cove . . . affords anchorage in 8 to 10 fathoms in the E part of the cove about 0.2 mile off the beach; a strong eddy occasionally sweeps in a small iceberg.* (CP)

The bight east of Iceberg Point on Lemesurier Island is known as Willoughby and Jacks coves and provides temporary anchorage over a sand and pebble bottom in 5 to 10 fathoms. Avoid the rocks along the shore.

## **Mud Bay** (Chichagof Island)

Mud Bay, on the southeast side of South Passage, is 10 miles south of the entrance to Glacier Bay.

Chart 17302
Entrance: 58°13.64′ N, 135°59.95′ W
Anchor: 58°12.09′ N, 135°59.40′ W

> *Anchorage may be had in 5 to 9 fathoms, 1 mile from the head of Mud Bay, but is exposed from W to NE, and at times ice is encountered. In entering from the W, give the N shore of Goose Island a berth of at least 0.8 mile and Quartz Point a berth of 0.5 mile.* (CP)

Mud Bay, a large open roadstead filled with mud along its shore, is somewhat sheltered from southerlies and has easy entry. It is a good place to wait for favorable currents in passages to the west. Mud Bay is shallow throughout and anchorage can be taken in depths as needed off the drying mud flats.

Anchor temporarily in about 6 fathoms over mud with fair holding.

## **Idaho Inlet** (Chichagof Island)

Idaho Inlet, southeast of the Inian Islands, is 5 miles northeast of Elfin Cove.

Chart 17302
Entrance (South Inian Pass Light R"6" bearing 278°T at 1.5 Nm): 58°13.64′ N, 136°12.73′ W
Anchor (head of inlet): 58°04.86′ N, 136°08.31′ W

> *A shoal extends about 0.2 mile W from the E point at the entrance to Idaho Inlet. . . .*
>
> *A midchannel course leads safely to the head of the inlet, where there is anchorage in 18 fathoms, mud bottom, in the middle about 0.4 to 0.5 mile WNW of a wooded islet. Container barges often use this anchorage during foul weather. Small craft find anchorage closer to the head of the bay in 5 to 10 fathoms. A marker at the head of the bay marks a trail that extends inland for about 8 miles to the head to Tenakee Inlet. The trail is maintained by the U.S. Forest Service.* (CP)

Some cruisers have reported wonderful halibut fishing in this inlet.

## Gull Cove (Idaho Inlet)

Gull Cove is on the east side of the entrance to Idaho Inlet.

Chart 17302
Entrance: 58°12.82′ N, 136°10.24′ W

*Anchorage can be made in 15 fathoms in the entrance to Gull Cove, on the E shore of the inlet. . . . At low water a small vessel can select an anchorage closer in, with better shelter from N winds in depth of 15 fathoms.* (CP)

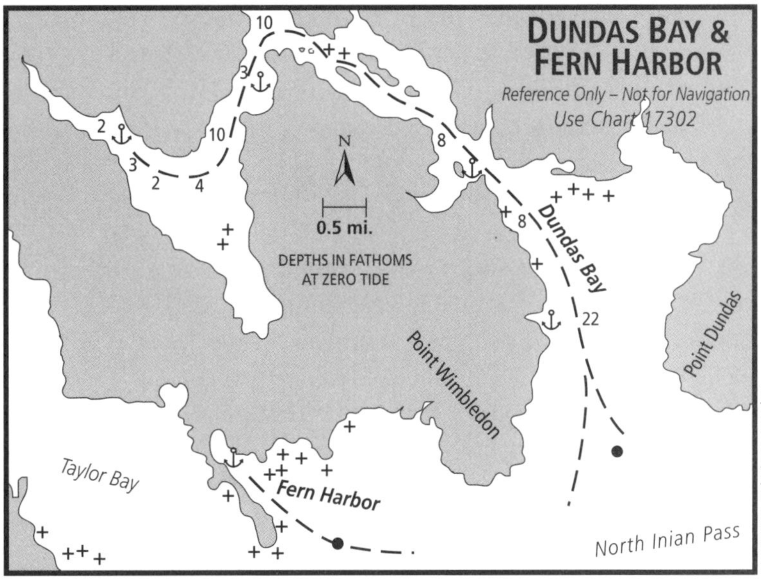




## Dundas Bay, Horsefly Bay and Mickey's Arm

Dundas Bay, on the northwest side of Icy Strait, is north of the Inian Islands.

Chart 17302
Entrance: 58°18.63′ N, 136°19.92′ W
Anchor (cannery site): 58°20.18′ N, 136°21.72′ W
Anchor (SE gale): 58°21.04′ N, 136°29.68′ W
Anchor (Horsefly Bay): 58°22.15′ N, 136°23.74′ W
Anchor (Mickey's Arm): 58°22.86′ N, 136°32.81′ W
Anchor (southwest arm): 58°23.34′ N, 136°29.11′ W

*Anchorage in 8 to 12 fathoms, sticky bottom, can be had about 0.3 mile off the SW shore, opposite a wooded islet, about 3 miles N of Point Wimbledon. The only danger is the flat about 0.8 mile NE of the islet. The anchorage is exposed to the SE, and heavy ice drifting with the current is sometimes troublesome.* (CP)

Dundas Bay, which lies outside the required permit area of Glacier Bay National Park, is seldom visited by small cruising boats. The area has Wilderness Area designation, allowing explorers to avoid the "madding crowd" of large cruise ships and tour boats and find some solitude and quiet.

The 1989, 15th edition of Chart 17302 gave no depths in Dundas Bay, other than for the outer bay. An updated edition of the chart for the area was issued in 2002 with depths given throughout Dundas Bay, making the bay safer to navigate. Additional hazards have been identified on this newer edition; nevertheless, you must exercise extreme caution when entering this primitive area.

The outer bay is deep, with strong currents. As you head into the west arm, west of Dundas River, keep a mid-channel course, favoring the south shore. Temporary anchorage can be found in the drying bight on the south shore, south of the small island. (We named this site

*Dundas Bay is a wonderful alternative for cruisers who do not have a park permit.*

"Horsefly Bay" because of the large horseflies that appeared after the wind died down.) The entrance to this shallow cove is on the south side of the island; the areas west and north of the island are foul.

The upper part of this west arm is filled with a number of small islands and islets. The fairway lies between the two major islands, then favors the north shore until the division occurs between the northwest and southwest arms. Good anchorage, with fair protection from southeast winds, can be found in the first part of the southwest arm, favoring the east shore in about 7 fathoms. Anchorage can also be found at the head of the northwest arm, avoiding the dangerous mid-channel rock near the head of the arm by favoring the west shore.

Our favorite Dundas Bay anchor site lies in the far west end of the southwest arm. Once past the small islets and rocks west of the anchor site noted above, we follow the north shore around the point to just below a terminal moraine from a chute of the Brady Glacier, two miles away. We call this site, "Mickey's Arm" in honor of Frenchwoman Michèle Demai, skipper of *Nuage*—a cutter-rigged, steel-hulled sailboat—who first told us about this place. (Mickey and a companion spent the winter of 1996–97 in *Nuage,* ice-bound in Gut Bay.)

We like to anchor off the small islet off a small bight with a drying mud flat. There is some fetch at this site in southeast weather and, in a southeast gale, we would anchor southeast of the small island, in the shallow southern part of the bay to minimize fetch.

Anchor temporarily (Horsefly Bay) in 1 to 2 fathoms south of the island in sand and gravel off a drying mud flat; fair holding.

Anchor (Mickey's Arm) in 2 fathoms over sand and mud with good holding.

## **Fern Harbor** (Taylor Island)

Fern Harbor is on the east side of Taylor Island.

**Chart 17302**
**Entrance: 58°17.36′ N, 136°28.29′ W**
**Anchor: 58°18.37′ N, 136°30.16′ W**

*Fern Harbor . . . extends about 1 mile in a NW direction and is about 0.3 mile wide. Depths of 25 fathoms were found at the entrance and depths of 9 to 11 fathoms, sticky bottom, within the cove. A boulder reef closes the head of the bay except a narrow high-water channel near the Taylor Island shore. The harbor affords anchor-*

---

## **John Muir's *Stickeen***

**Don Douglass & Réanne Hemingway-Douglass**

In the summer of 1880, John Muir set out from Fort Wrangell in a canoe to continue his exploration of Southeast Alaska. He was joined by a native American crew and by his friend and companion, the Reverend S.H. Young with his little black mongrel, Stickeen. Although Muir had tried to dissuade his friend from taking the dog, Stickeen soon became a fixture of the group, taking part not only in the exploration, but in the hunting as well.

Near the head of Taylor Bay at the foot of Brady Glacier, the group made camp in a grove of spruce. The next morning, in a raging storm, Muir set off from camp. "I made haste to join [the storm]; for many of Nature's finest lessons are to be found in her storms, and if careful to keep in right relations with them, we may go safely abroad with them, rejoicing in the grandeur and beauty of their works and ways . . . "

Mr. Young and the crew were still asleep, but not Stickeen who, despite numerous scoldings from Muir, refused to return to camp.

". . . The pitiful little wanderer just stood there in the wind, drenched and blinking, saying doggedly, 'Where thou goest I will go.' So at last I told him to come on if he must, and gave him a piece of the bread I had in my pocket; then we struggled on together, and thus began the most memorable of all my wild days."

For the full and humorous story, see *Stickeen,* by John Muir, first published in 1897. [Quotes are taken from the Heyday Books illustrated edition, ISBN 0-930588-48-7.]

*age for small craft.* (CP)

Fern Harbor is frequently a safe haven when strong current and nasty chop occur at the east end of Icy Strait. It is not as sheltered as Inian Cove in southeast gales. We like Fern Harbor and so do large numbers of sea otters.

Anchor in 5 to 7 fathoms in sand, mud and silt with fair-to-good holding.

## Taylor Bay (Cross Sound)

Taylor Bay, on the northwest side of Cross Sound, is 6 miles northeast of Cape Spencer.

Chart 17302
Entrance: 58°16.45′ N, 136°30.70′ W

> *Taylor Bay . . . is open to the SE. . . . The flat at the face of the glacier is extending rapidly down the bay. Vessels proceeding up the bay should use caution and keep sounding. Extensive shoaling has been reported in the upper half of the bay with bare spots in some places. The bottom is mud. . . .* (CP)

Taylor Bay, which lies at the base of large Brady Glacier, was the setting for John Muir's story, *Stickeen,* which is an all-time favorite to be read aloud.

An interesting small cove lies 0.5 mile northwest of Taylor Island; however, Taylor Bay is uncharted, and several once-potential anchor sites are now filled with silt. Fern Harbor is the best place from which to explore the area.

## North Inian Pass

North Inian Pass lies between the Inian Islands and Point Wimbleton.

Chart 17302
East entrance (Point Dundas bearing 008°T at 1.4 Nm): 58°17.56′ N, 136°17.30′ W
West entrance (Taylor Island bearing 311°T at 1.25 Nm): 58°16.22′ N, 136°27.06′ W

North Inian Pass is generally preferred over South Inian Pass. Strong current runs through North Inian Pass, reaching 8 to 10 knots on spring ebbs, and large waves, dangerous to small craft, develop when winds oppose the currents. Inian Cove (see below) offers good, convenient shelter, out of the current, and is well protected from southeast gales.

## Inian Islands

The Inian Islands, 4 miles north of Elfin Cove, separate Icy Strait from Cross Sound.

Chart 17302 (inset)

> *The Inian Islands, consisting of five principal islands, five smaller islets, and a few rocks, are between Point Wimbledon and Point Lavinia. . . . They are close together, mountainous, and wooded.* (CP)

Since the Inian Islands have frequent summer fog, encountering huge cruise ships here can be spooky. The current is very strong on either side of the islands. Excellent shelter can be found in Inian Cove (see below).

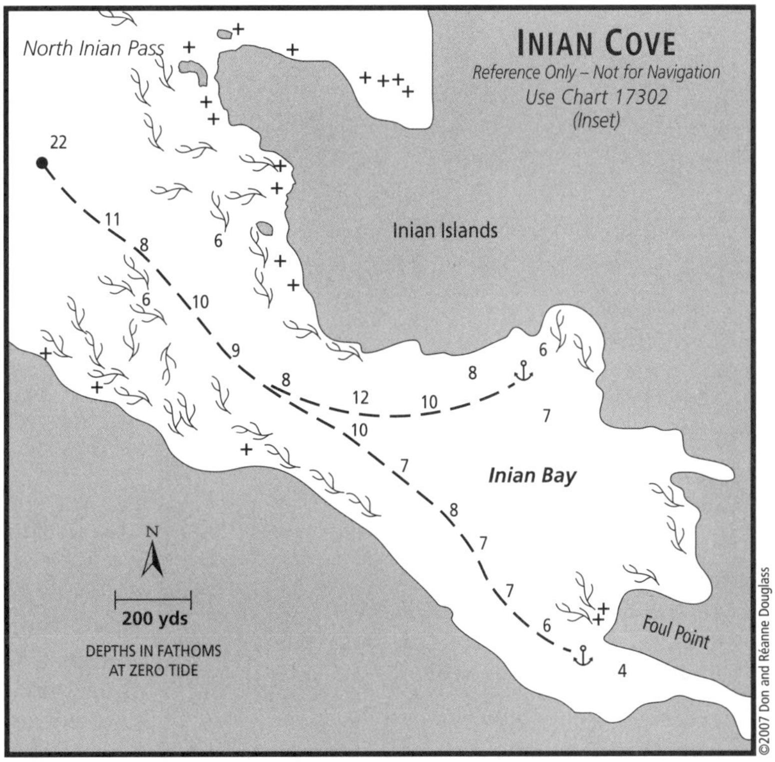

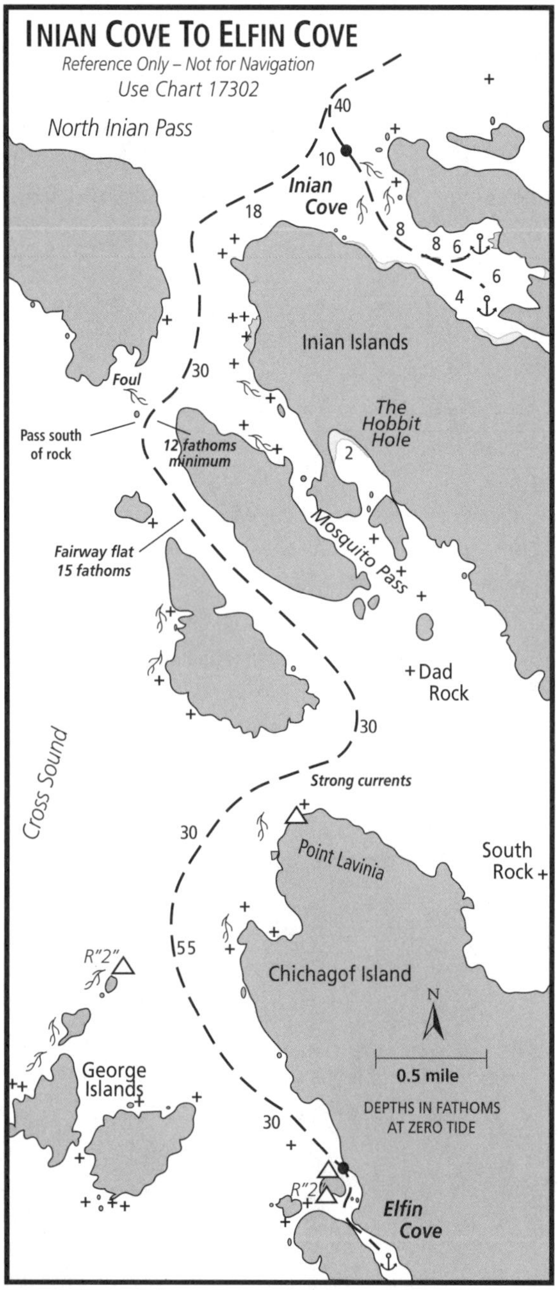




## **Inian Cove** (Inian Islands)

Inian Cove is 4 miles north of Elfin Cove.

Chart 17302 (inset)
Entrance: 58°16.15′ N, 136°21.01′ W
Anchor (southeast): 58°15.50′ N, 136°19.64′ W
Anchor (northeast): 58°15.89′ N, 136°19.80′ W

*A dangerous rock awash is about 0.6 mile ENE from the NE entrance point of Inian Cove, and about 0.2 mile offshore; a bare rock is between this shoal spot and the shore.*

*Inian Cove . . . is a secure anchorage with a clear width of about 600 yards. . . . Ice drifts into the cove, usually along the SW side, but is not considered dangerous to vessels at anchor.*

*Anchor in the wide part of the cove in 4-1/2 to 6-1/2 fathoms, soft bottom.* (CP)

Deep within Inian Cove, cruising boats can find excellent shelter in two places, as indicated on the diagram. Extensive kelp patches at the entrance reduce summer chop and swell to a minor surge, and entering does not present a problem as long as you avoid these kelp patches. Depths are moderate, but the bottom is irregular. Be alert for uncharted rocks in the area.

Anchor (southeast) in 4 to 6 fathoms over sand, mud, pebbles and some kelp, with very good holding.

Anchor (northeast) in 6 to 8 fathoms over mud and pebbles with good holding.

## **Earl Cove** (Inian Islands)

Earl Cove is 1 mile southeast of Inian Cove.

Chart 17302
Entrance: 58°15.34′ N, 136°17.25′ W
Anchor: 58°15.44′ N, 136°18.13′ W

*Earl Cove . . . is clear, and a small vessel may anchor here temporarily in 8 to 16 fathoms, but it is exposed E and generally has considerable ice.* (CP)

Ice in Earl Cove is not generally a problem in summer these days, and the cove offers good shelter from northwest winds and current.

Anchor in about 4 fathoms at the head of the cove over mud with fair holding.

## **South Inian Pass**

South Inian Pass, south of the Inian Islands, connects Cross Sound and Icy Strait.

Chart 17302
East entrance (Idaho Inlet Light bearing 180°T at 0.5 Nm): 58°14.38′ N, 136°15.45′ W
West entrance (Point Lavinia Light bearing 112°T at 0.5 Nm): 58°13.48′ N, 136°22.16′ W

*Two shoal spots are off the point on the S side of the pass at the E entrance; the N one, a rock awash, is marked by a lighted bell buoy; the S spot is covered by 2 fathoms at low water.* (CP)

South Inian Pass has strong currents with dangerous turbulence, especially during spring tide and gale winds. Both North and South Inian Pass are very picturesque, with a steep-sided, iron-bound coast that houses many sea caves.

Note that the tide in South Inian Pass turns to ebb about 1.5 hours before the tide table.

## Cross Sound

Cross Sound, southwest of the Inian Islands, separates Chichagof and Yakobi islands from the mainland.

Charts 17302, 17301, 17300
West entrance (Cape Spencer Light bearing 000°T at 3.8 Nm): 58°08.11′ N, 136°38.48′ W

*Cross Sound and Icy Strait are the northernmost sea connections for the inland passages of southeastern Alaska. . . .*

*Caution. From Cross Sound to Excursion Inlet, shoalings amounting to as much as 6 feet in several critical areas were disclosed during 1959. . . . Accordingly, mariners are urged to use caution in navigating over or near critical depths.*

*Cross Sound is exposed to wind and weather off the Gulf of Alaska. . . . It is more exposed to winds and seas from SW through NW. These winds are most frequent in summer and fall; fall conditions are roughest. . . . Poor visibilities are most frequent in summer and winter.* (CP)

During the summer, southwest swells in Cross Sound can heap up to dangerous proportions when strong ebbs meet southwest winds. In seasonal fogs, the sound is generally calm.

## Elfin Cove (Chichagof Island)

Elfin Cove is east of the George Islands at the entrance of Port Althorp.

Chart 17302 (inset)
Entrance (entrance light bearing 200°T at 0.75 Nm): 58°11.88′ N, 136°21.03′ W
Fuel float: 58°11.71′ N, 136°20.85′ W

*The main entrance to* [Elfin Cove]*, SW of the large islet, is marked by Elfin Cove Entrance Light 2* (58°11.7'N., 136°21.1'W.), *48 feet above the water, shown from a small house with a red triangular daymark on the S entrance.* (CP)

Réanne Hemingway-Douglass

*Elfin Cove's transient dock (at right)*

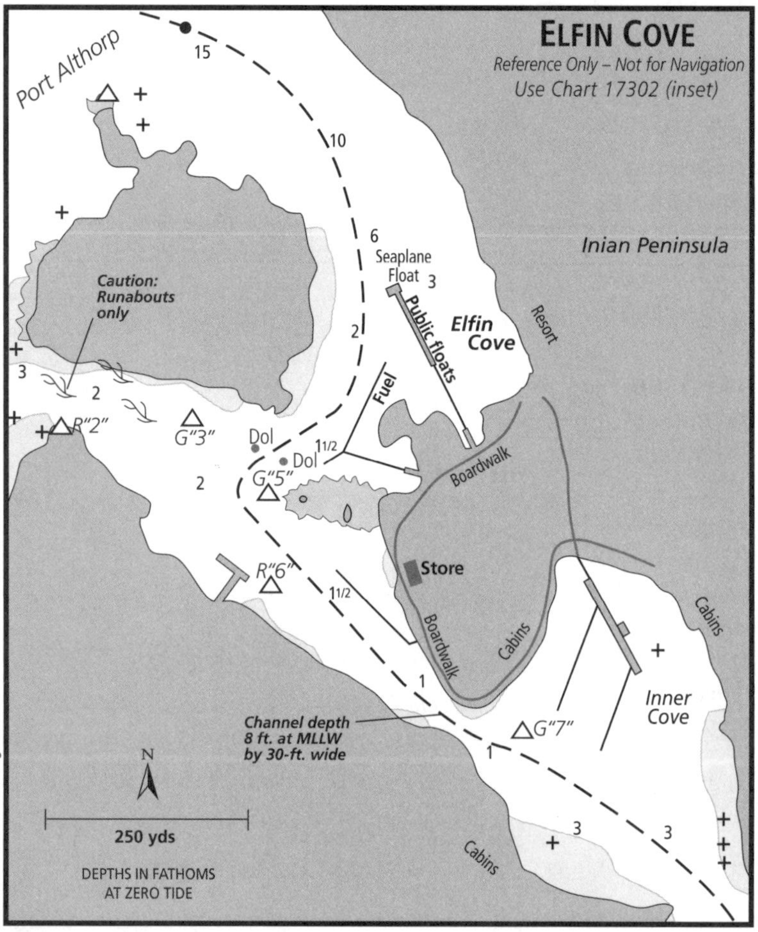




Elfin Cove, a quaint community perched along the sides of the harbor, is a favorite stop among cruising boaters. A 200-foot-long float in the outer harbor has limited space for transient vessels with moorage on either side of the float. The fuel dock, south of the float, sells gasoline, diesel and propane (tel.: 907.239.2208; monitors VHF Ch 16). Water is available at the fuel dock and the inner harbor floats.

A boardwalk that begins at the head of the transient dock and encircles the community (see diagram) leads to the village where there's a general store, laundromat, postal service, café and public pay phones.

The inner cove (south) is reached by a narrow passage whose fairway at low tide has a maximum width of about 30 feet and a minimum depth of about 8 feet. The two floats in the inner cove are used mainly by locals. Underpowered boats should enter the south cove on a flood and exit on an ebb. A tidal grid is located in the inner cove. In the past, cruising vessels have entered and anchored in the inner cove, however locals do not recommend that visitors do so.

From Elfin Cove to Lisianski Inlet, high cliffs with crevices and craggy towers line the way; along the waterline, there are wind-sculpted caves.

*The inner cove at Elfin Cove*

## Granite Cove (George Island)

Granite Cove, on the south side of George Island, is 1.4 miles west of Elfin Cove.

**Chart 17302**
**Position: 58°11.74′ N, 136°23.61′ W**

> *Granite Cove . . . is open to the S. The sides of the cove are irregular cliffs, and the head is a shingle beach.* (CP)

Granite Cove is used by fishermen wanting convenient shelter during fair weather.

Linda Lewis

*Elfin Cove's transient dock at right; looking across the outer cove*

## Port Althorp (Chichagof Island)

Port Althorp, on the southeast side of Cross Sound, lies between Point Lucan and Point Lavinia.

Chart 17302
Entrance (Althorp Rock Light bearing 175°T at 0.75 Nm): 58°10.70′ N, 136°21.69′ W
Entrance (cove): 58°08.68′ N, 136°17.58′ W
Anchor: 58°06.27′ N, 136°17.00′ W

> *On the NE shore of Port Althorp, about 5 miles SSE of Point Lavinia, is a cove with a small island near the N shore and a small islet with rocks close-to near the E shore. . . . From the N part of the cove an inlet extends E for about*

---

### Elfin Cove

Linda Lewis—Journal Notes—M/V *Royal Sounder*

So often when you have heard about a place for years it can be less than you expected once you arrive. Not so Elfin Cove. It is enchanted. What is it about a tiny, wandering-fairways, many-coves place that I find so endearing? I wonder if it is about being womb-snug in full beauty.

This is a place of meandering boardwalks going in multiple directions, lined by homes, a few shops and friendly people. A bird is scolding in my ear as I sit here writing this, kids across the water play and splash. This is a rare chance among our stops to walk and walk and walk. This tiny village nearly sings out the attention and love and care it has been given. The word "charming" really means something when you gaze around in Elfin Cove.

Linda Lewis

*A wooden sentry along the boardwalk at Elfin Cove*

Linda Lewis

*Elfin Cove's boardwalk magic*

*0.3 mile to a bight about 0.3 mile in diameter; flats extend for a considerable distance off the N shore. Depths of 1 fathom were found in the bight and in the channel.*

*Anchorage may be had in 15 to 20 fathoms, mud bottom, at the head of Port Althorp. Small craft anchor closer in, near the head in 5 fathoms, soft bottom.* (CP)

Port Althorp Cove, 2.5 miles southeast of Althorp Rock, is a tiny, landlocked cove suitable for shallow-draft small craft. Good shelter can also be found at the southern end of Port Althorp.

Anchor in 5 fathoms over soft mud with good holding.

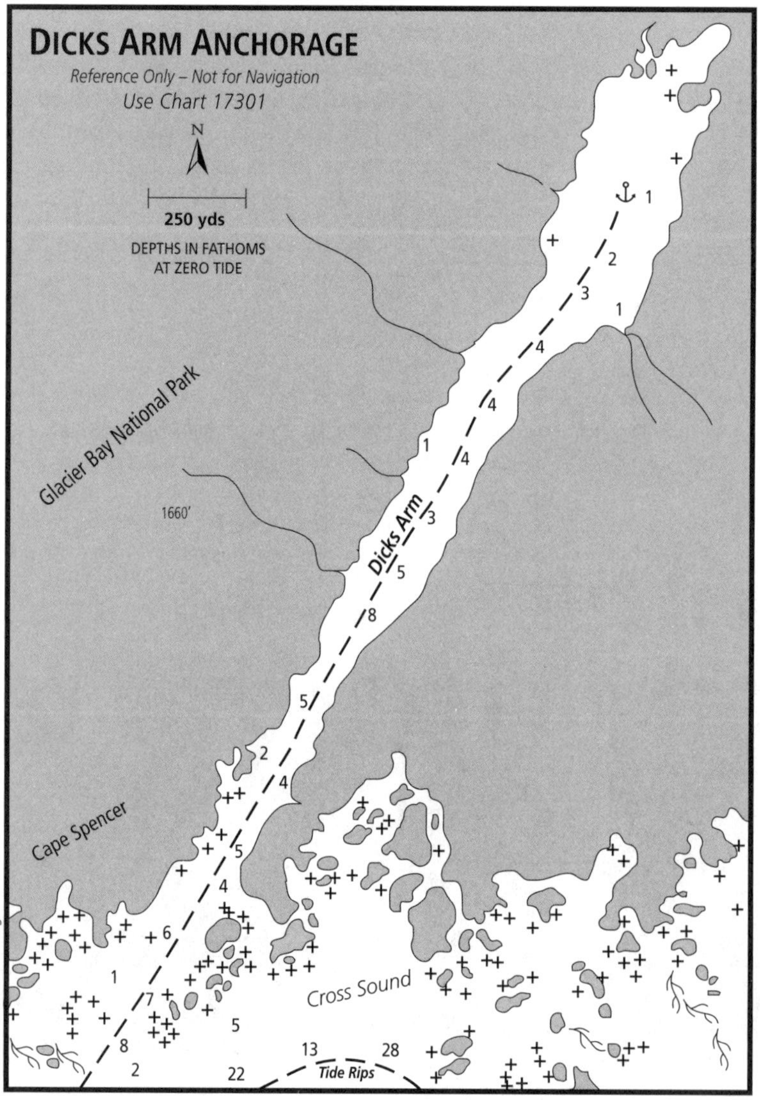




## Cape Spencer

Cape Spencer Light, the northwest entrance point to Cross Sound, is 9.3 miles west of Elfin Cove.

**Charts 17301, 17302**
**Cape Spencer Light position: 58°11.94′ N, 136°38.43′ W**

*Extending from the cape for about 1.2 miles in a S direction is a large shoal area in which there are rocky islets, some of the inner ones wooded, and rocks, the outer ones usually showing as breakers. From the shoreline the cape rises rapidly to timbered ridges.* (CP)

Cape Spencer marks the passage from the sheltered inside waters to the open Pacific Ocean and Gulf of Alaska. Glacier Bay National Park extends 55 miles to the northwest, past Lituya Bay and Cape Fairweather to Dry Bay. Good shelter for small craft can be found in Dicks Arm.

## Dicks Arm (Cross Sound)

Dicks Arm anchor site is 2.3 miles north of Cape Spencer Light.

**Charts 17301, 17302**
**Main entrance: 58°12.04′ N, 136°40.04′ W**
**Alternative entrance (east of Cape Spencer Light: 58°12.01′ N, 136°37.42′ W**
**Anchor: 58°14.04′ N, 136°37.36′ W**

*Dicks Arm . . . is a narrow inlet . . . that extends in a N direction for about 2 miles. . . . A narrow channel, with depths of 2-1/2 to 12 fathoms leads E of Zip Rock, 20 feet high and bare, through the off-lying rocks and islets to the inlet. Depths of 3/4 to 8 fathoms are found in the inlet to within 0.5 mile of the head, where it is shoal.* (CP)

Dicks Arm provides good shelter for small craft when the sound is heaping up off Cape

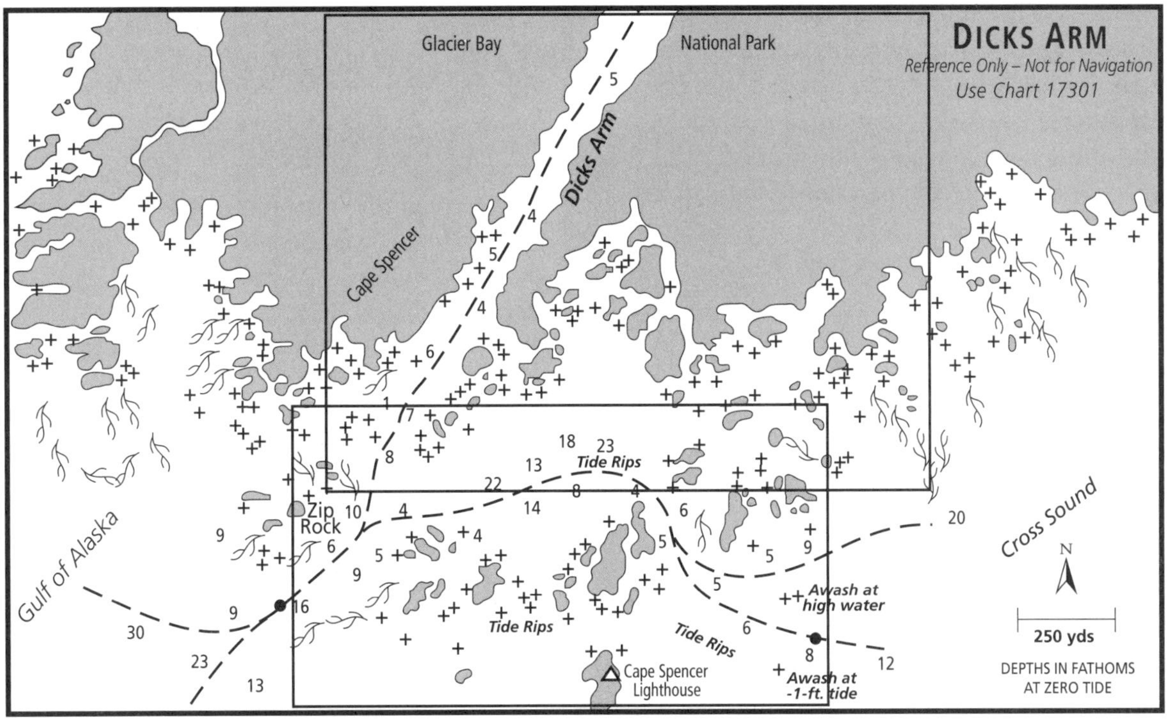
DICKS ARM
Reference Only – Not for Navigation
Use Chart 17301
Glacier Bay
National Park
Dicks Arm
Cape Spencer
Tide Rips
Zip Rock
Gulf of Alaska
Cross Sound
Awash at high water
Tide Rips
Tide Rips
Cape Spencer Lighthouse
Awash at -1-ft. tide
250 yds
DEPTHS IN FATHOMS AT ZERO TIDE



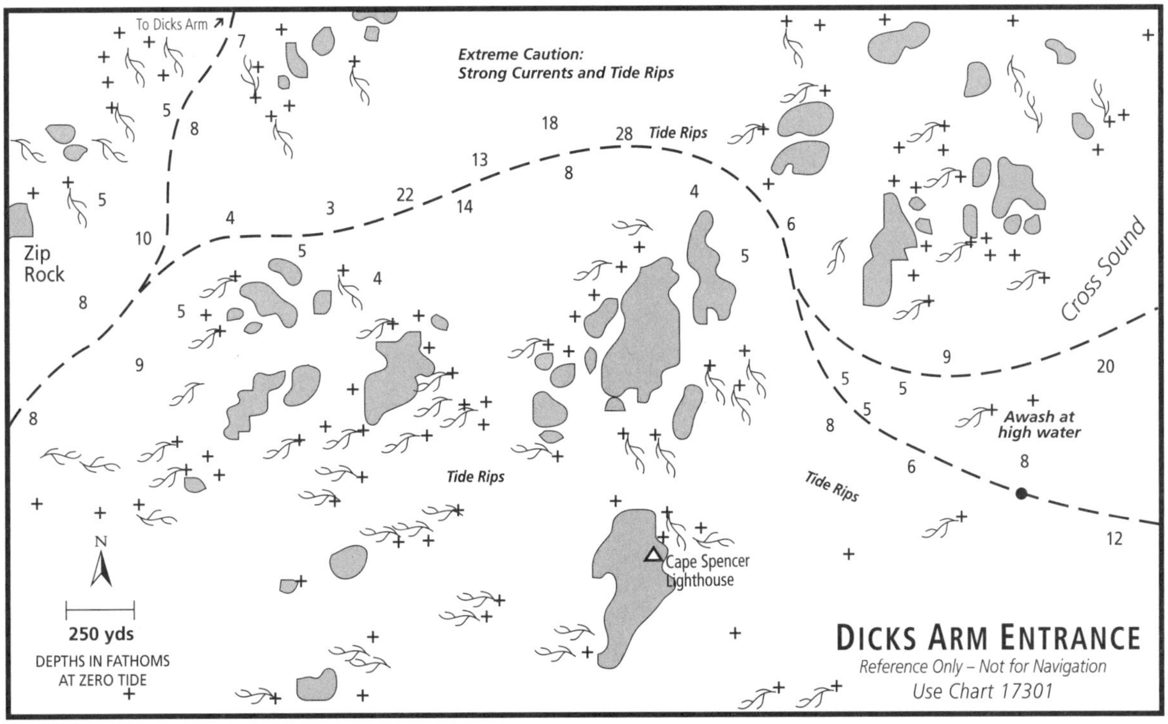
To Dicks Arm
Extreme Caution:
Strong Currents and Tide Rips
Tide Rips
Zip Rock
Cross Sound
Awash at high water
Tide Rips
Tide Rips
Cape Spencer Lighthouse
250 yds
DEPTHS IN FATHOMS AT ZERO TIDE
DICKS ARM ENTRANCE
Reference Only – Not for Navigation
Use Chart 17301

Spencer. The entrance to the inlet is somewhat daunting and requires careful piloting. It is essential to give this place a wide berth in stormy weather. The numerous rocks off the entrance give remarkable protection to the narrow inlet, and the head of the arm is snug and quiet.

## Graves Harbor

Graves Harbor, entered between Graves Rocks and Libby Island Light, is 5 miles northwest of Cape Spencer.

Charts 17301, 17302
Entrance: 58°15.52′ N, 136°46.50′ W
Anchor (south arm): 58°16.60′ N, 136°41.24′ W

> *Graves Harbor . . . extends inland for about 3 miles. Depths in the harbor are 11 to 79 fathoms. The unnamed cove, which makes off to the S from the head of Graves Harbor, affords good landlocked anchorage in 7 to 15 fathoms and is easily entered. . . .* (CP)

Protected anchorage can be found at the head of Graves Harbor. However, for a more intimate setting, you might want to anchor in what is known locally as Mosquito Cove (in the southeast corner of the south arm of the harbor). From Graves Rocks you can begin to see the edge of La Pérouse Glacier behind Icy Point.

Graves Rocks are a major haul-out spot for sea lions. You can transit inside Graves Rocks with a minimum of 8 fathoms in the fairway. Please do not disturb the sea lions; their numbers have been decreasing in recent years.

Anchor (south arm) in 7 to 12 fathoms over mud with good holding; good swinging room.

## Murphy Cove (Graves Harbor)

Murphy Cove is on the southeast side of Graves Harbor, about 1.7 miles above Graves Rocks.

Charts 17301, 17302
Entrance: 58°16.55′ N, 136°43.57′ W
Anchor: 58°16.27′ N, 136°43.11′ W

> *Murphy Cove . . . has depths of 11 fathoms or more in its outer part and affords snug anchorage for small vessels.* (CP)

Murphy Cove, inside Graves Harbor, is a popular anchorage for fishing boats and boats heading north. The site provides fairly comfortable anchorage in stable weather and is a good place to watch the weather of the outer waters. For a landlocked anchorage during stormy weather, Mosquito Cove at the southeast head of Graves Harbor offers bombproof protection; however, you cannot tell the weather conditions in the Gulf from this site.

Anchor (off the lagoon entrance) in 4 to 6 fathoms over sand and mud with good holding.

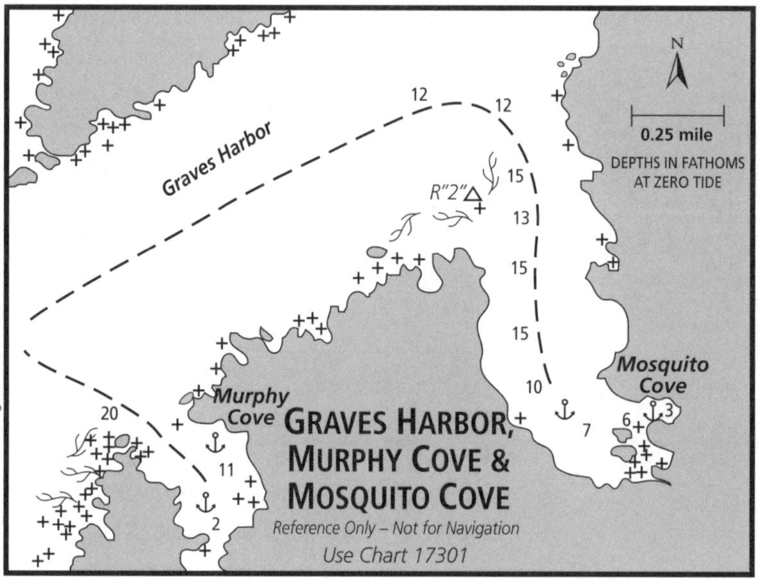




## Mosquito Cove (Graves Harbor)

Mosquito Cove is at the southeast corner of the south arm of Graves Harbor.

Chart 17301
Anchor: 58°16.53′ N, 136°40.63′ W

Mosquito Cove is a wonderful landlocked cove, but yes, there are mosquitoes. However, for such shelter and stillness close to the Gulf of Alaska, it's a small price to pay. You can find steep-to anchorage northwest of the islets, or in the cove south of the islets in shallower water. Swinging room is limited at both sites. A ranger float previously located here has been removed.

Anchor in 3 fathoms over brown mud and shells with good holding.

## Murk Bay (Graves Harbor)

Murk Bay is opposite Murphy Cove.

Chart 17301
Entrance: 58°17.17′ N, 136°45.02′ W

> *Murk Bay . . . is clear but too deep and open for good anchorage.* (CP)

## Torch Bay

Torch Bay is 7 miles northwest of Cape Spencer.

Chart 17301
Entrance (Venisa Point bearing 112°T at 0.7 Nm): 58°17.89′ N, 136°48.88′ W
Anchor (east cove): 58°19.37′ N, 136°46.50′ W

Don Douglass

*Réanne, hard at work, grabs a snack.*

> *Torch Bay . . . extends inland more than 2 miles in a N direction and varies in width from 1 mile at the entrance to 0.3 mile at the head of the W arm. Rocks, which uncover 7 feet and always marked by breakers, are 1 mile S of Venisa Point, on the W side of the entrance; vessels can pass on either side of these rocks when entering the bay. The bay has depths of 13 to 56 fathoms; . . . small vessels can find protected anchorage in the NE arm.* (CP)

When you approach Torch Bay, avoid the outlying shoals. Reasonable shelter can be found in the small cove on the east shore near the head of the bay. The bottom of the cove is somewhat irregular, indicating many rocks, so be careful to check the set of your anchor. This bay is a favorite of sea otters, and you can have a great time watching the mothers taking their babies for a ride.

Anchor (east cove) in 4 to 6 fathoms over a hard bottom with poor-to-fair holding.

## Dixon Harbor, Hankinson Cove

Dixon Harbor, 11 miles northwest of Cape Spencer, is entered between Sugarloaf Island and Astrolabe Point.

Chart 17301
Entrance: 58°19.52′ N, 136°53.37′ W
Anchor: 58°19.91′ N, 136°50.90′ W

> *Dixon Harbor . . . has depths of 60 to 20 fathoms over an average width of 0.8 mile for 2 miles N of Thistle Cove, the NW arm. Depths of 13 to 18 feet are just W of the middle of the entrance. A glacier above the head of the harbor is visible from the entrance.* (CP)

Dixon Harbor, the large bay 1.1 miles northeast of Sugarloaf Island, is wide and deep, with turquoise-colored water whose source originates from Brady Glacier. From inside the bay, you can still view the ramparts of this rapidly receding glacier, which will eventually disappear from view at this site.

A small cove on the south side of Dixon Harbor, inside a hook on the southwest side of Hankinson Peninsula, provides good anchorage in stable weather. (We call this site “Hankinson

Linda Lewis

*Feast on the magnitude of the landscape in Icy Strait.*

Cove.") Depths along a mainly flat bottom range from 10 to 6, making anchoring reasonable. The cove is surrounded by granite rock formations striated throughout with white. There is a small, but rocky landing beach at the head of the cove. Logs along shore indicate that winter storms curve around into the bay at this site but, during stable summer weather, the cove offers very good protection from the southwest to the southeast and fair-to-good from prevailing northwesterlies and no swell is felt in these conditions.

Several dangerous rocks lie along the east side of the cove. Stay mid-channel as you choose your anchor site.

Anchor in 5 to 10 fathoms over sand, rocks and kelp; fair-to-good holding.

## **Thistle Cove** (Dixon Harbor)

Thistle Cove, the northwest arm of Dixon Harbor, is 1 mile long in a north direction.

**Chart 17301**

**Entrance: 58°21.53′ N, 136°51.87′ W**

> *Thistle Cove is 1 mile long in a N direction. At the point on the NE side of the entrance is a grass-covered rock, 20 feet high. In June 1998, it was reported that a shoal extended across the entrance to the cove. As* [a] *result, Dixon Harbor does not offer a secure anchor*[age] *in S or W weather.* (CP)

Although many small boaters and fisherman remember anchoring in Thistle Cove with great fondness prior to 1997, the cove has shoaled as Brady Glacier recedes and is no longer viable as an anchorage.

In 2005, we did extensive sounding of the

cove in *Baidarka*'s tender and could find no channel or areas where depths would allow good anchoring. This is unfortunate, because this is a beautiful cove.

## Palma Bay

Palma Bay, between Astrolabe and Icy points, is 16 miles northwest of Cape Spencer.

Chart 17301
Entrance: 58°22.01′ N, 136°59.59′ W
Anchor (off Kaknau Creek 1.0 mile northeast of Icy Point): 58°23.73′ N, 137°04.21′ W

> *This large body of water, sometimes called Icy Bay, has depths of 20 to 60 fathoms; large vessels have anchored close inshore in 15 to 20 fathoms.*
>
> *Another anchorage, which affords some protection for small craft in W weather, is off the mouth of Kaknau Creek, a large stream which empties into Palma Bay on the NE side of Icy Point; recommended anchorage is close inshore in 6 to 10 fathoms, sand bottom.* (CP)

Palma Bay is a large, open bay with a lovely 3-mile-long sandy shore that looks inviting until you watch the huge swells breaking heavily onto the beach. The wreckage of several fishing boats can be seen along the beach, a further sign of its openness. Boussole and Astrolabe bays are moderately more sheltered in fair weather. Some temporary protection from westerlies can be found off Kaknau Creek 1.0 mile northeast of Icy Point. Avoid the rocks 200 yards or more from the west shore.

Anchor (Kaknau Creek) in 6 to 10 fathoms over sand with fair holding.

## Boussole Bay (Palma Bay)

Boussole Head is in the east part of Palma Bay, between Astrolabe and Boussole bays.

Chart 17301
Entrance: 58°23.12′ N, 136°56.21′ W
Anchor (Boussole Head): 58°23.30′ N, 136°54.89′ W

> *Boussole Head . . . is a prominent wooded 650-foot-high peninsula which extends about 1 mile into the bay. The outer end of the head is a natural arch which rises 60 feet above the water. . . . Alder Rock, 0.3 mile S of Boussole Head, uncovers 4 feet.* (CP)

Boussole Head is remarkable for its magnificent arch, which was certainly noticed by French explorer La Pérouse when he explored this coast in the late 1700s. (Both Boussole and Astrolabe bays were later named for La Pérouse's two ships.) Although we haven't yet taken *Baidarka* through the arch, it's a challenge that might be possible in calm weather!

Temporary anchorage can be found along Boussole Head in fair weather.

Anchor in 8 fathoms over sand with fair holding.

Réanne Hemingway-Douglass

*Natural arch at Boussole Bay*

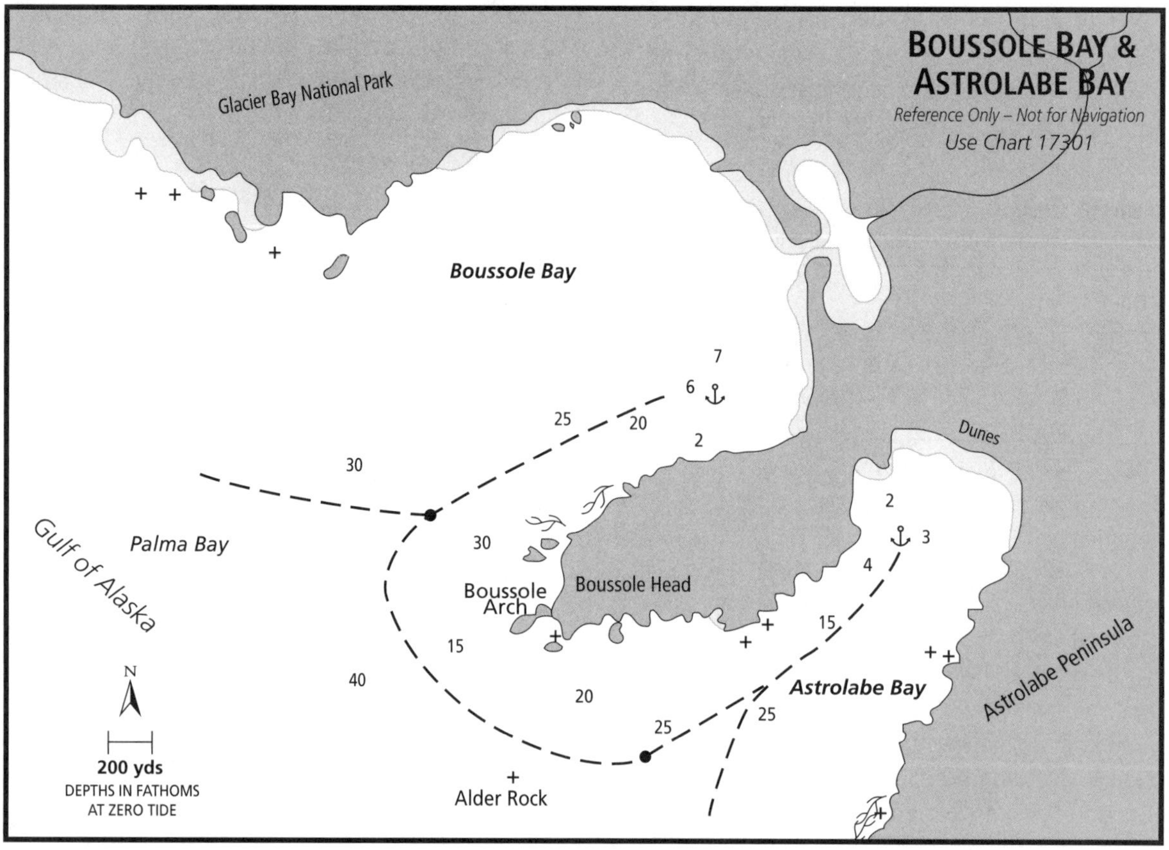


## Astrolabe Bay (Palma Bay)

Astrolabe Bay is southeast of Boussole Head.

**Chart 17301**
**Entrance (Alder Rock bearing 292°T at 0.38 Nm): 58°22.26′ N, 136°55.15′ W**
**Anchor (bay): 58°22.97′ N, 136°54.08′ W**

> *Astrolabe Bay . . . and Boussole Bay . . . are open to the S but afford protection to small vessels in N or E weather. Anchorage is possible in 6 to 8 fathoms, sand bottom, near the head of each bay; the best is Boussole Bay.* (CP)

Astrolabe Bay is ringed by grassy dunes above a light sandy beach, giving it the appearance of a well-manicured golf course. In good weather, it's fairly easy to land a dinghy at the northwestern end of the beach and, from there, hike to the dunes and a lagoon in Boussole Bay, 0.25 mile to the north. Be aware, though, that this is bear country and use caution when you go ashore. Remember to leave a responsible crew member aboard while a shore party does its exploring. (It's a good idea always to carry a hand-held VHF with you in this territory.)

Astrolabe Bay is a fair-weather anchorage only and, even in good weather, swells may

*Delicate creatures of the sea*

Ben Kyle

*Jim Kyle measures the 6'4" Bob Duke who is hugging his prize halibut, caught in Lituya Bay.*

Linda Lewis

*Most cruisers use electronic charting these days, but don't forget to always have your paper charts out and open—ready for the day's travel.*

enter, creating uncomfortable rolling at night. During heavy southwesterly weather, swells create a dangerous lee shore.

Anchor in 3 fathoms over sand with fair-to-good holding.

## Icy Point

Icy Point, on the west side of Palma Bay, is 17 miles northwest of Cape Spencer.

**Chart 17301**
**Position (Icy Point bearing 052°T at 0.5 mile): 58°22.63′ N, 137°06.26′ W**

> *Icy Point . . . is low and wooded; from S La Perouse Glacier can be seen over the point. Many rocks fringe the point but deep water is only 0.3 mile offshore.* (CP)

Rocks extend nearly a half-mile south from the tree line on Icy Point. Entering or exiting Palma Bay, give wide clearance to the point.

Lituya Bay, part of Glacier Bay National Park, lies 22.5 miles northwest of Icy Point.

For more information on Glacier Bay National Park north of Icy Point, including Lituya Bay, go to www.nps.gov/glba.

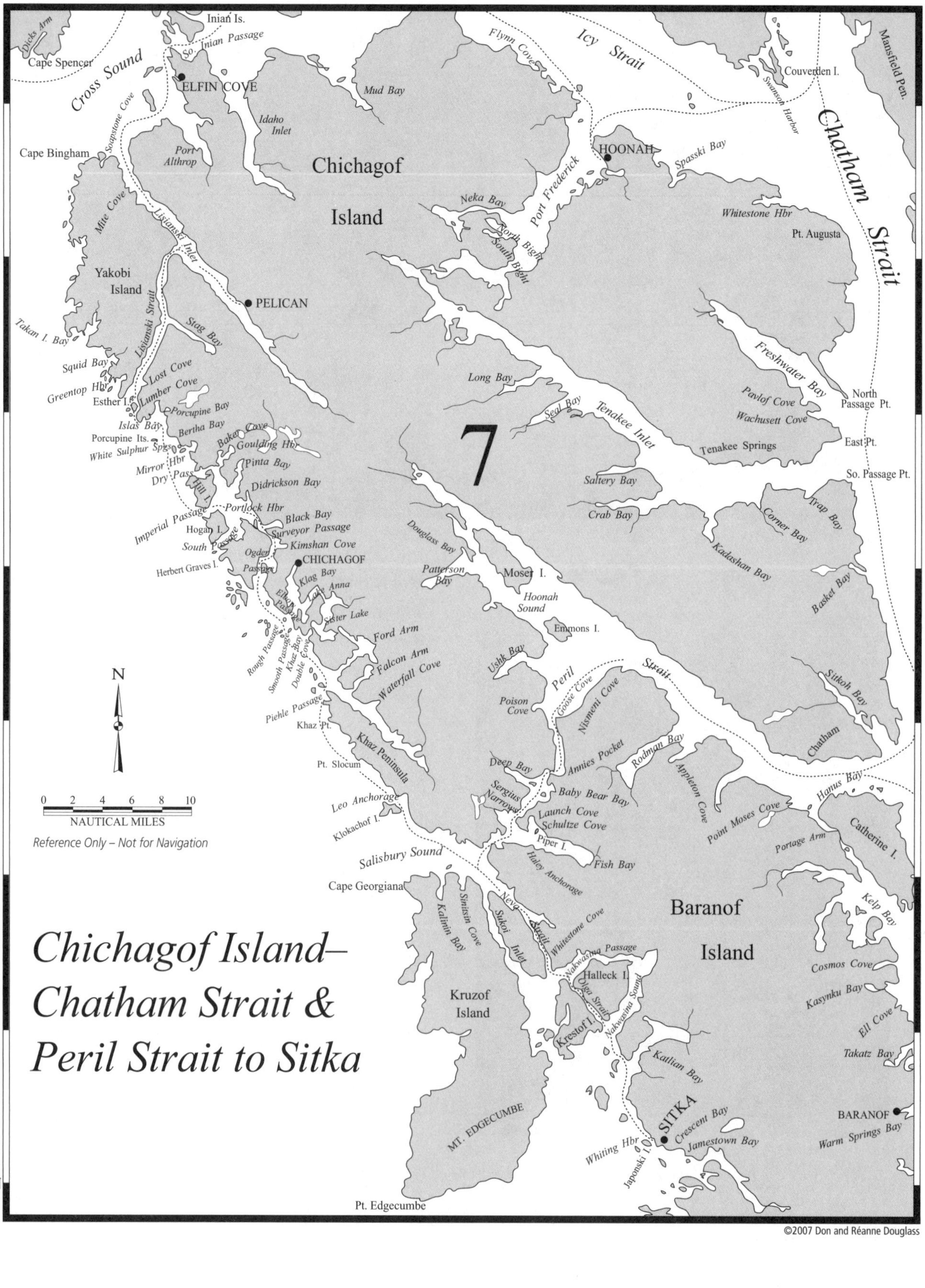
Chichagof Island–
Chatham Strait &
Peril Strait to Sitka
7
Chichagof
Island
Baranof
Island
Kruzof
Island
Yakobi
Island
Icy Strait
Chatham Strait
Cross Sound
Peril Strait
Inian Is.
So. Inian Passage
Dicks Arm
Cape Spencer
ELFIN COVE
Soapstone Cove
Cape Bingham
Port Althrop
Idaho Inlet
Mud Bay
Flynn Cove
Couverden I.
Mansfield Pen.
Swanson Harbor
HOONAH
Spasski Bay
Port Frederick
Neka Bay
North Bight
South Bight
Whitestone Hbr
Pt. Augusta
Mite Cove
Lisianski Inlet
Lisianski Strait
PELICAN
Takan I. Bay
Stag Bay
Squid Bay
Greentop Hbr
Lost Cove
Lumber Cove
Esther I.
Porcupine Bay
Islas Bay
Bertha Bay
Porcupine Its.
White Sulphur Spgs
Baker Cove
Goulding Hbr
Mirror Hbr
Dry Pass
Pinta Bay
Hill I.
Didrickson Bay
Imperial Passage
Portlock Hbr
Black Bay
Hogan I.
Surveyor Passage
South Passage
Kimshan Cove
Herbert Graves I.
Ogden Passage
CHICHAGOF
Klag Bay
Lake Anna
Sister Lake
Rough Passage
Smooth Passage
Double Cove
Ford Arm
Falcon Arm
Waterfall Cove
Piehle Passage
Khaz Pt.
Khaz Peninsula
Pt. Slocum
Leo Anchorage
Klokachof I.
Salisbury Sound
Cape Georgiana
Long Bay
Seal Bay
Tenakee Inlet
Freshwater Bay
North Passage Pt.
Pavlof Cove
Wachusett Cove
Tenakee Springs
East Pt.
So. Passage Pt.
Saltery Bay
Crab Bay
Trap Bay
Corner Bay
Kadashan Bay
Douglass Bay
Patterson Bay
Moser I.
Hoonah Sound
Emmons I.
Basket Bay
Ushk Bay
Poison Cove
Goose Cove
Nismeni Cove
Sitkoh Bay
Chatham
Deep Bay
Annies Pocket
Rodman Bay
Appleton Cove
Sergius Narrows
Baby Bear Bay
Launch Cove
Schultze Cove
Piper I.
Fish Bay
Haley Anchorage
Point Moses Cove
Hanus Bay
Portage Arm
Catherine I.
Kelp Bay
Sinitsin Cove
Kalinin Bay
Neva Strait
Sukoi Inlet
Whitestone Cove
Nakwasina Passage
Halleck I.
Olga Strait
Nakwasina Sound
Krestof I.
Cosmos Cove
Kasynku Bay
Ell Cove
Takatz Bay
Katlian Bay
MT. EDGECUMBE
SITKA
Crescent Bay
Jamestown Bay
Whiting Hbr
Japonski I.
BARANOF
Warm Springs Bay
Pt. Edgecumbe
N
0 2 4 6 8 10
NAUTICAL MILES
Reference Only – Not for Navigation
10'
58°N
50'
40'
30'
20'
10'
57°N

# 7

# CHICHAGOF ISLAND, CHATHAM STRAIT AND PERIL STRAIT TO SITKA

## INTRODUCTION

Chichagof Island—the "C" of the ABC islands that also include Admiralty and Baranof, home to the coast brown bear (grizzly)—lies south of Glacier Bay across Icy Strait. Yakobi Island and the northwestern part of Chichagof (as well as the southern part of Baranof and Pleasant, Lemesurier and Inian islands) are designated Wilderness Areas. The rugged west coasts of Chichagof and Yakobi are indented with many coves and gunkholes that show few signs of human presence. Except for a handful of navigation aids, a ruin here and there, a trail and a cabin or two, the area is unspoiled; we consider it some of the finest wilderness cruising we have experienced.

Just offshore of this coastline lie hundreds of small, unnamed islands, islets and rocks that provide semi-protected passages through which a cruising boat can thread its way in waters that face the Gulf of Alaska!

Most boaters who plan to visit Sitka after Glacier Bay head east to Chatham Strait then down to Peril Strait and west again. This is generally the less exposed way and requires less demanding navigation.

However, a shorter and more interesting route—what we call the "Outer Passage"—leads south via Lisianski Inlet and Lisianski Strait to Sitka. As it snakes along the west coast of Chichagof Island, this route keeps a number of islands and rocks to windward. During fair weather the waters along this route are reasonably smooth.

We like the Outer Passage for its scenic charm and solitude and its intricate passages and coves with complex entrances that challenge our navigational skills. Although this route is shorter in mileage, it is so much more

Jim Kyle

*Column Pt. at the west end of Lisianski Inlet, looking north towards the Fairweather Mountain range*

Ben Kyle

*Jock Sutherland and Ling Cod—an awesome pair!*

picturesque and wild that you will probably want to linger, exploring the little coves and inlets along the way and adding to the length of time it takes to get to Sitka. If you have large-scale charts of the area, consider using this Outer Passage. When the weather is fair—and when you have time to ride out any heavy weather that comes along—this is an exquisite route!

Set among countless islands on the west side of Baranof Island, Sitka—one of the jewels of Southeast Alaska—looks out toward the southern tip of Kruzof Island and the striking volcanic cone, Mt. Edgecumbe (3,271 feet). Once the proud capital of Russian Alaska, Sitka has a long and interesting history. The Russian influence is still seen in the Orthodox Church and Bishop's House, open daily for tours. Sheldon Jackson Museum houses one of the finest collections of Alaskan native art in North America. The town—whose economy is supported by commercial fishing, sport fishing, tourism and two colleges (Sheldon Jackson and University of Alaska-Southeast)—has become increasingly accommodating to visiting yachts with new, larger port facilities (breakwaters and floats) and a responsive staff in the harbormaster's office. Convenient air and ferry connections make it easy to arrange for pick-up of guests or crew. Full outfitting services and repair experts are available here. (Sitka and Ketchikan are the only two towns in Southeast with facilities for prop repair!)

Peril Strait, which separates Chichagof and Baranof islands, connects Sitka to Chatham Strait. This is the route taken by the Alaska ferry, as well as most commercial and recreational vessels. Sergius Narrows, at the west end of Peril Strait, is a narrow "rapids" that must be transited at, or near, slack water. There are several good anchor sites on either side of the narrows where vessels can wait to time the currents.

Tenakee Springs, on Chatham Strait, is a quaint settlement lining the shores of Tenakee Inlet. In addition to the residents, the hot sulfur springs draw scores of Juneau boaters or visitors who arrive by ferry to partake of the baths or to see a community that has remained "Alaska rustic."

*Note:* The difference in charted positions between Charts 17302 and 17303 is approximately 300 feet. Use caution in accepting waypoints along this coast, and visually check all critical positions.

## **Lisianski Inlet** (Chichagof Island)

Lisianski Inlet, on the northwest side of Chichagof Island and south of Cross Sound, is about 21.5 miles long.

**Chart 17303 (inset)**
**Entrance (buoy G"1" bearing 087°T at 0.5 Nm): 58°06.91′ N, 136°28.44′ W**

> *Good anchorage and shelter may be had at the head of Lisianski Inlet in 15 fathoms, soft, sticky bottom. Small boats anchor along shore where the depths are not too great, particularly in Mite Cove, off Miner Island, and off the flats along shore.* (CP)

Lisianski Inlet is the north entrance to the smooth-water, outside route to Sitka, which uses Lisianski Strait to reach the Gulf of Alaska. Both the inlet and strait were named after Russian Captain Urey Theodorovich Lisianski, who explored the area in 1804 aboard the Neva. The northern entrance to Lisianski Strait leads south about a third of the way down the inlet. Once inside the inlet, you lose cell phone coverage. Lisianski Inlet continues southeast to its head, passing the village of Pelican.

## Soapstone Cove (Lisianski Inlet)

Soapstone Cove, on the west side of the entrance to Lisianski Inlet, is 7 miles southwest of Elfin Cove.

**Chart 17303**
**Entrance: 58°06.27′ N, 136°29.21′ W**
**Anchor (outside): 58°06.14′ N, 136°29.14′ W**
**Anchor (inside): 58°05.65′ N, 136°29.84′ W**

> *E* [of Soapstone Point] *is Soapstone Cove, a narrow inlet that has at its head a valley with a stream. Depths shoal rapidly from 25 fathoms at the entrance to less than 1 fathom 0.5 mile within Soapstone Cove.* (CP)

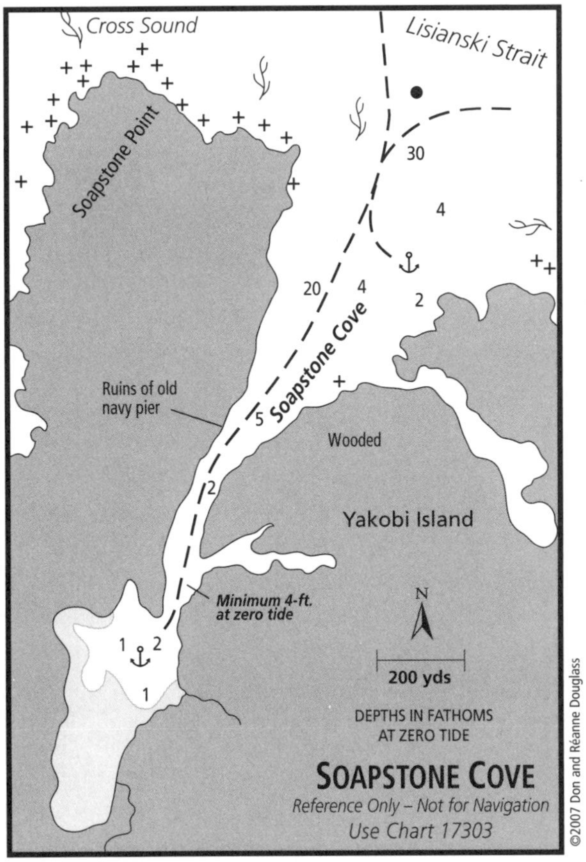


Small boats of 40 feet or less can pass in or out of inner Soapstone Cove at half-tide or more, with a minimum depth of 4 feet at zero tide. Be careful to avoid a rock near the center of the narrow channel. You can often spot brown bear along the shore.

During World War II, this cove was the site of a secret naval operation. A piling located on the west side of the entrance to the inner cove and a bomb shelter, still in good condition, are reminders of that era.

Anchor in a 1-1⁄2-fathom hole on the east side of the inner cove over mud with good holding.

## Mite Cove (Lisianski Inlet)

Mite Cove, 2.5 miles inside the entrance to Lisianski Inlet, is 8 miles south of Elfin Cove.

**Charts 17303, 17302 (inset)**
**Entrance: 58°04.39′ N, 136°26.21′ W**
**Anchor: 58°04.09′ N, 136°26.55′ W**

> *Mite Cove . . . is the best anchorage for small craft. . . . Protected anchorage may be had in 11 to 12 fathoms, soft bottom, in the center of the cove.* (CP)

Mite Cove offers protection from most winds for several boats over a flat bottom. Old-

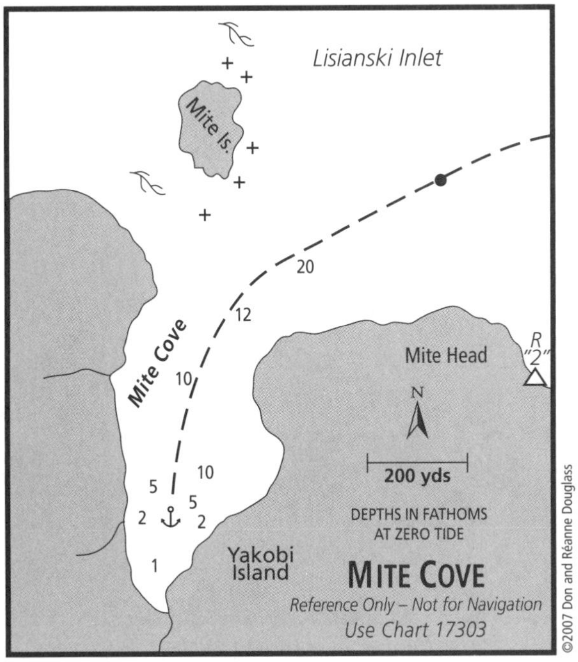

growth trees line the shore, and there is a gravel beach near a stream at the head of the cove where you can land a dinghy. Newspaper kelp along the bottom of the cove may make setting your anchor a little difficult. If you have trouble, just pull your anchor up, remove the kelp, and try again. Once your anchor is set, it should hold well.

Anchor in 6 fathoms over gravel and kelp with poor holding unless your anchor is well set.

Réanne Hemingway-Douglass

*One of the newest docks in Pelican*

## **Pelican** (Lisianski Inlet)

Pelican is 15 miles south of Elfin Cove.

Chart 17303 (inset)
Entrance: 57°57.51′ N, 136°14.05′ W
Float: 57°57.55′ N, 136°13.70′ W

> [Pelican's] *city-operated small-craft floats close SE of the fuel pier provide about 3,600 feet of float space. In May 2003, 12 feet was alongside the floats except for lesser depths along the floats on the N and E outer parts of the harbor. A seaplane float is at the W end of the second float E of the fuel pier. Water and electricity are available at the floats. . . . the small-craft floats are partially protected from SE winds by the breakwater and the rocky islets.*
>
> *Vessels up to 75 feet long can be handled at one of the city-operated grids in the mudflats E of the fuel pier. Two other city-operated grids, capable of servicing three vessels, are between the fuel pier and small-boat basin. A nearby machine shop is available to small craft for minor engine repairs.* (CP)

Linda Lewis

*Approaching the harbor at Pelican*

Located midway down Lisianski Inlet's east shore, Pelican profits from a beautiful setting. To the west, across the inlet, precipitous, snow-covered peaks discharge melting snow that cascades down granite flanks into the inlet across from the boardwalk village.

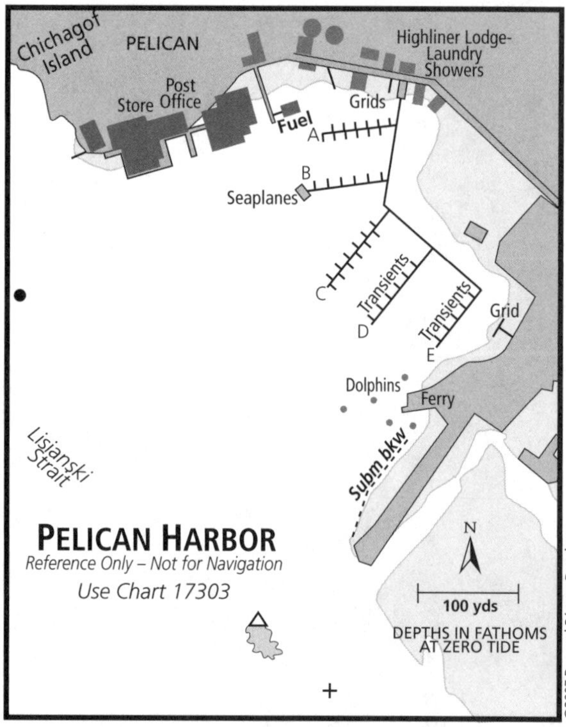

Réanne Hemingway-Douglass

*Pelican is an all-boardwalk town; this is "Main Street."*

Réanne Hemingway-Douglass

*This is the only form of motorized-transportation allowed on the boardwalk.*

Since the closure of the cold storage facilities in 2004, the village has encouraged the development of tourism, albeit in a small way. The harbor itself has undergone many upgrades and improvements, and Pelican has become a cruising destination not only for boaters from Juneau and Sitka but for "outsiders" as well, who vie for space during the annual Boardwalk Boogy held in May, the Fourth of July activities or the Salmon Derby.

In 2005, the old floats and the electrical outlets were upgraded, and two new floats were installed, making room for local fishing vessels, along with cruising vessels. Several new businesses geared to tourism have also taken hold. Harbormaster, David Duffy, does a masterful job of finding space for visiting boats, and for making everyone feel welcome. David runs the town's only authorized motor vehicle—the garbage truck. Quads are the only other motorized vehicles permitted along the boardwalk.

The new Highliner Lodge at the top of the harbor gangway has showers, laundry, liquor store, the latest in fish-cleaning and freezing facilities, B & B accommodations, Internet access and custom fishing packages. There are two tidal grids on the north side of the harbor gangway and another at the south side of the harbor. Lisianski Inlet Café, well-known for great breakfasts and fish and chips lunches, received State authorization to serve their own freshly caught fish and crab.

A library where you can get Internet access, a post office, pay telephones (above the docks and at the post office) and two cafés—that include the infamous Rosie's Bar—round out the town's other amenities. For a fee of around $50, large grocery orders can be shipped by floatplane from Costco in Juneau. (There is almost daily service by floatplane.)

Kayaking along the inlet from Pelican is pleasant and there are several short hikes along the shore. Bear share Lisianski Inlet with people here, as well as in many other

Jim Kyle

*An island marks the junction of Lisianski Inlet and Lisianski Strait.*

areas of Chichagof Island, so be cautious if you wander!

Harbormaster (tel.: 907.735.2212) monitors VHF Ch 16. During busy summer holidays it's best to call ahead to inquire about space at the floats. City Office (tel.: 907.735.2202).

## Lisianski Strait

Lisianski Strait, 4.5 miles northwest of Pelican, connects Lisianski Inlet with the Gulf of Alaska.

**Chart 17303**
**North entrance (Rock Point Light bearing 238°T at 0.3 Nm): 58°00.31′ N, 136°20.74′ W**
**South entrance (bell buoy GR bearing 306°T at 0.38 Nm): 57°49.56′ N, 136°27.54′ W**

> *From the SW end NNE, the strait is clear until 1.2 miles to the SW of the junction with Lisianski Inlet, where there are two small islands. . . . Kelp extends from the islands to the Chichagof Island shore.*
>
> *The S entrance channel to Lisianski Strait is about 125 yards wide, with a reef on the E side with 2-1/2 fathoms over it, and rocks on the W side. Favor the W side, especially if the current is ebbing, because there is a SE set then.* (CP)

Lisianski Strait marks the entrance to West Chichagof-Yakobi Wilderness area. The area from Soapstone Cove on the north end of Yakobi Island to Sergius Narrows in Peril Strait is dedicated wilderness supervised by the Sitka Ranger District of the Tongass National Forest (tel.: 907.747.4220). This wilderness has some of the most spectacular terrain and rainforest of the Inside Passage, with little evidence of man's penetration. Hazards to navigation are not marked by manmade means, and aids are few and far between.

Lisianski Strait's south entrance and the west coast of Yakobi Island have countless islets, rocks and reefs up to a mile or more offshore. Navigation in this area is recommended only in fair weather with good visibility.

Except for a small shoal northwest of the entrance to Stag Bay, Lisianski Strait is deep. In fair weather, local boats avoid the chop off the strait's south entrance and most of the swell from the Gulf of Alaska by taking what is called the "Inside Passage" east of Esther Island and Urey and Threenob Rocks.

## Stag Bay (Lisianski Strait)

Stag Bay, on the east side of Lisianski Strait, is 4 miles southwest of Pelican.

**Chart 17303**
**Entrance: 57°55.76′ N, 136°21.56′ W**

> *The shores* [of Stag Bay] *are steep and precipitous. . . . At the head of the bay is an extensive tide flat, the greater part of it bares at lowest tides and the approach is very steep.*
>
> *Along each shore are mountain streams at the mouths of which banks have been formed that extend offshore for 100 to 150 yards. In entering follow midchannel courses. There is an anchorage at the head of the bay off the flats in 40 fathoms, with restricted swinging room; this anchorage is not recommended.* (CP)

Stag Bay is steep-sided and picturesque with snow patches on its sides. Cruisers have reported bear sightings in this bay. There is a triangular island that sits as a sentinel on the east side of the entrance to Stag Bay. Note that the head of the bay shallows very quickly.

## Lost Cove (Lisianski Strait)

Lost Cove is 2.5 miles northeast of the south entrance buoy of Lisianski Strait.

Chart 17303
Entrance: 57°51.70′ N, 136°25.13′ W
Anchor (northeast): 57°51.73′ N, 136°24.53′ W
Anchor (southeast): 57°51.55′ N, 136°24.59′ W

> *Lost Cove . . . affords anchorage for small vessels in 11 to 17 fathoms, mud bottom. The anchorage is about 300 yards wide. Midway between the entrance points is a rock that uncovers 5 feet and is marked by kelp during the summer and fall. Water may be had at the head of the arm near the end of the cove.* (CP)

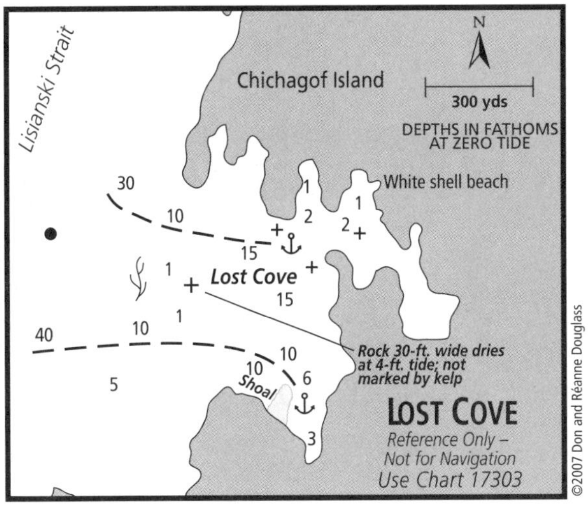


Several small back bays that form Lost Cove provide good shelter in fair weather. In foul weather, however, the north coves are open to southwest chop. In stable weather, boats of less than 30 feet can anchor in either the northwest or northeast cove in 2 fathoms; one vessel can anchor in 4 fathoms at the north entrance to the inner coves. Since swinging room is limited, we suggest using a shore tie. Be on the lookout for sea otters—this is one of their favorite cruising grounds.

When entering the outer cove, beware of a 30-foot-wide rock mid-bay that dries on a 4-foot tide; it is not well marked by kelp. We do not advise a radar approach. Visibility of the water is about 10 feet. In summer, you often see small moon jellyfish and huge orange sea nettles wafting their way across the cove.

*Rough seas off the west coast of Yakobi Island*

The southeast corner of the outer cove is protected from southerlies, allowing more swinging room for longer vessels.

Anchor (northeast) in 4 fathoms over mud, shells, and gravel with heavy kelp; good holding with a well-set anchor.

Anchor (southeast) in 6 fathoms over a mixed bottom with kelp; good holding if your anchor is well set.

## Yakobi Island's West Coast

Yakobi Island's west coast extends 10 miles southward from Cross Sound to Lisianski Strait.

Chart 17303

> *The W coast of the island is broken by many islands and off-lying rocks into numerous bays and bights, forming frequent shelter for small craft.* (CP)

Yakobi's West Coast is rugged and wild. The shelter that the *Coast Pilot* mentions is largely hidden by a labyrinth of rocks and islets requiring very careful navigation. We recommend following the route only in fair weather and good visibility—approaching closer than one mile in foul weather and in depths less than 10 to 15 fathoms can subject a boat to breaking seas. Although we find Greentop Harbor to offer the best shelter from heavy weather along Yakobi's west coast, entering is a navigator's challenge. (See below.)

Linda Lewis

*Exploring the many inlets along Chichagof Island*

## **Bingham Cove** (Yakobi Island)

Bingham Cove is on the south side of Cape Bingham.

Chart 17303
Entrance: 58°05.48′ N, 136°32.92′ W
Anchor: 58°04.89′ N, 136°32.74′ W

> *Bingham Cove . . .* [requires] *local knowledge to enter. . . . The cove is open to the W, but has a well-sheltered S arm. It is reported that local fishing boats use Bingham Cove as a foul weather anchorage.* (CP)

Bingham Cove has its south arm fairway constricted by rocks and a shoal. If you want to use the cove, either follow a local fishing boat or contact one on Ch 16 for local knowledge. Our designated anchor site is best for shallow draft-boats only.

Anchor in 9 feet.

## **Hoktaheen Cove** (Yakobi Island)

Hoktaheen Cove is about 1.2 miles south of Cape Bingham.

Chart 17303
Entrance (Yakobi Rock bearing 030°T at 0.98 Nm): 58°04.32′ N, 136°34.74′ W
Anchor: 58°04.30′ N, 136°32.93′ W

> *Hoktaheen Cove, a small, open, and exposed cove . . . is suitable only for small craft, and local knowledge is required for its entry.* (CP)

Chart 17303 is the best guide to entering Hoktaheen Cove. The entrance requires a circuitous route avoiding the rocks and kelp. Entry is not advised in foul weather or during poor visibility.

Anchor in about 2 fathoms near the head of the cove.

## **Surge Bay** (Yakobi Island)

Surge Bay is 4.1 miles north of Cape Cross.

Chart 17303
Entrance (high rocky islet bearing 053°T at 0.50 Nm): 57°58.89′ N, 136°34.35′ W

> *Surge Bay . . . is an open bight with numerous rocks, and is suitable only for small vessels with local knowledge. The small bights on the E side of the bay are open W. . . . In about the center of the bay is a high rocky islet. . . . The best entrance to the bay is S and E of the islet; the entrance NNW of it is through kelp, and in W weather breakers extend clear across the entrance.* (CP)

The recommended entrance to Surge Bay, noted above, passes close to three tiny islets to avoid the rocks that cover at high water 0.28 Nm southwest of these islets.

This part of the coast is subject to breaking waves any time depths are less than 10 to 15 fathoms. Once inside the numerous rocks and reefs, swells flatten out. However, surge may be felt anywhere in the bay.

Good shelter is reported at the north end of the bay in the lee of the small islands by avoiding numerous rocks en route.

## **Deer Harbor** (Yakobi Island)

Deer Harbor is 1.7 miles northwest of Cape Cross and 7.7 miles northwest of the entrance to Lisianski Strait.

Chart 17303
Entrance (buoy G"1" bearing 133°T at 0.1 Nm): 57°56.23′ N, 136°34.75′ W
Anchor: 57°56.46 N, 136°33.13′ W

> *Two miles N of Cape Cross is a large bight. . . . there is no protected anchorage even for small boats in the main part of the bight. . . . In the S part of the bight, E of the large wooded island, is an inner bight called Deer Harbor. It is entered only on the upper half of the tide. Vessels should pass*

*S of the large wooded island. Sheltered anchorage may be had in either the N or S arm of Deer Harbor in 4 to 7 fathoms, mud bottom.* (CP)

The entrance to Deer Harbor is narrow and shallow and should not be attempted on the lower half of the tide or during foul seas when seas break or limit steering control. Once you are inside, you may not be able to get back across the bar if the weather worsens. Inside the landlocked harbor, the shelter is good. *Enetai*, *Saratoga* and *Baidarka* spent several days anchored inside the harbor in 2005 and enjoyed good fishing and calm waters. *Deception* reports that the harbor is known locally as "The Fishmarket" and is especially known for its excellent king salmon fishing. However, when heavy seas are running outside, surge can be felt inside. *Black Tie*, a 112-foot vessel, with a 6-foot draft, anchored inside Deer Harbor in 2004 and used a stern-tie to limit swinging room. Deer Harbor reminds us of tiny Depot Bay on the coast of Oregon.

Anchor in 5 to 6 fathoms over sand and gravel with some kelp; fair to good holding.

## **Takanis Bay** (Yakobi Island)

Takanis Bay is 1.4 miles southeast of Cape Cross and 5 miles northwest of Lisianski Strait.

**Chart 17303**
**Entrance (Cape Cross bearing 325°T at 1.4 Nm): 57°53.50′ N, 136°32.11′ W**
**Anchor (northwest branch): 57°55.47′ N, 136°31.40′ W**

[Takanis Bay] *is exposed to the S, but small craft can usually find protected anchorage in its branches.*

*The usual anchorage for small craft is in the NW branch, which contains a small, wooded island near its head. There is ample swinging room S of this island in 6½ fathoms, mud and rock bottom. Very small craft anchor N of this island, which affords more protection but limited swinging room, the best approach being E of the island.*

*Small craft with local knowledge sometimes anchor in the lagoon E of the upper end of Takanis Bay. . . . passage should not be attempted except at high-water slack and with good local knowledge. Anchorage exposed to the S can be found in the middle of the bay in 8 fathoms, mud and rock bottom, about 0.5 mile above the large flat rock on the E side of the bay just inside the entrance.* (CP)

Takanis Bay, although open to the south, offers fairly good protection in its northwest arm. On a southbound route, you must clear a number of rocks, reefs, and islets south of Cape Cross before rounding up into Takanis Bay. Carefully work northward to the northwest arm of the bay, using your depth sounder and a bow watch. Despite its small scale, Chart 17303 can be of assistance in helping you thread your way. Numerous rocks and reefs lie at the entrance to the northwest arm, which give it protection from southerly weather. For maximum shelter, anchor north of the islet at the head the arm. Enter east of the islet; west of the islet two large rocks extend half way from the shore to the islet. Depths surrounding the islet in the cove vary from 6 to about 3 fathoms. Boats over 40 feet can anchor south of the islet. Swinging room is more limited north of the islet, so a shore tie may be useful.

The lack of drift logs on shore at this site indicates a fair amount of protection.

Anchor (northwest branch) in about 6 fathoms, brown sand, rocks and kelp with fair-to-good holding.

## **Squid Bay** (Yakobi Island)

Squid Bay is 3 miles northwest of Lisianski Strait.

**Chart 17303**
**Entrance: 57°52.55′ N, 136°30.25′ W**
**Anchor: 57°53.13′ N, 136°27.98′ W**

*The anchorage* [in Squid Bay] *here in 5 to 17 fathoms, soft bottom, is exposed to S. The entrance is clear and is bounded to SE by the high, wooded shoreline, and to the NW by a large area of foul ground that extends to Point Satchrun. All vessels should keep well away from this foul area. In entering, favor the SE shore.* (CP)

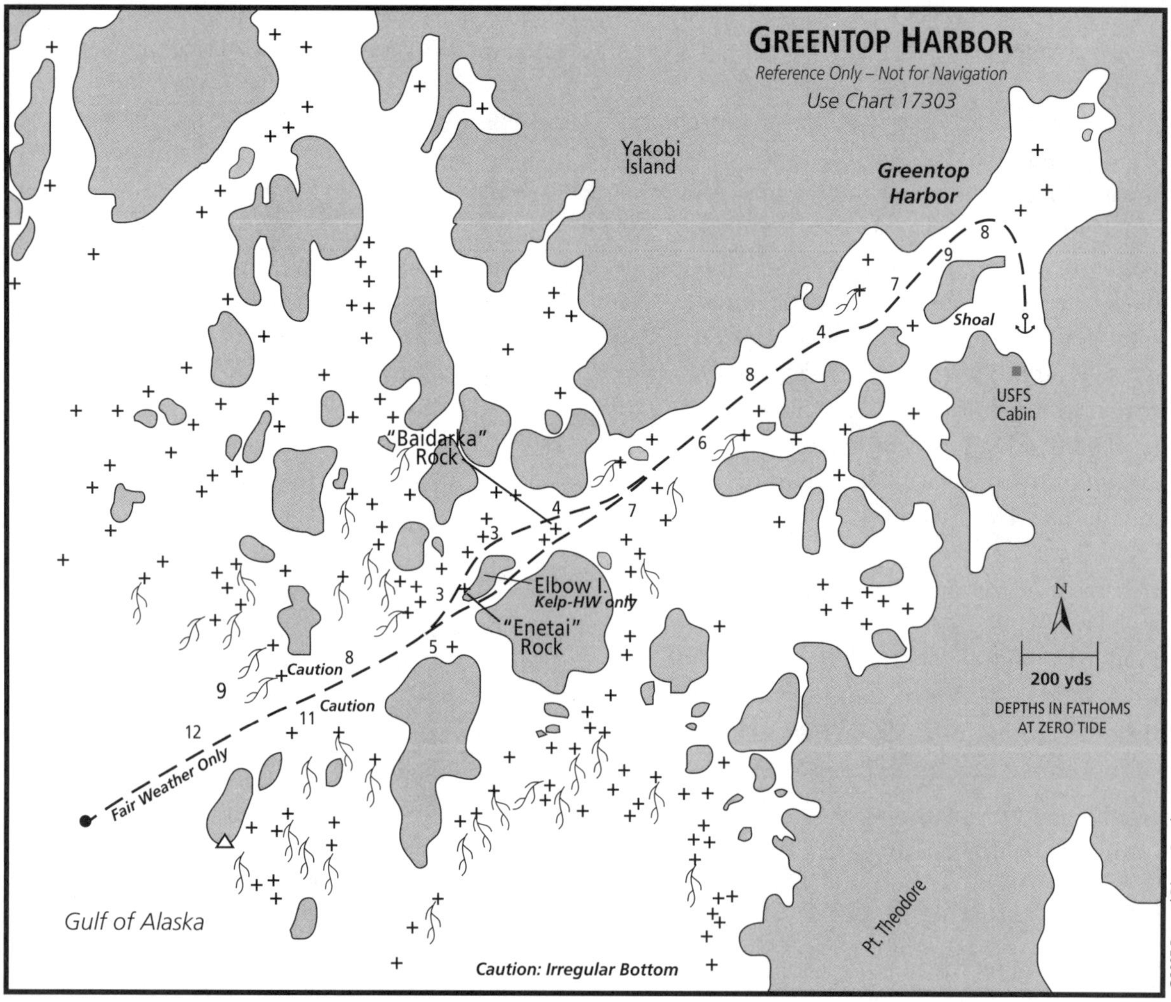



Although we anchored temporarily in Squid Bay at the coordinates listed above, we did not care for the site. Temporary relief can be obtained from southeast and southwest weather, but there's little else to recommend it due to uncharted rocks and the fact that foam blows into the inner bay from the northwest.

Anchor (if you wish) in 7 fathoms over a soft bottom with kelp; poor-to-fair holding.

## **Greentop Harbor** (Yakobi Island)

Greentop Harbor entrance is 1.7 miles northwest of the Lisianski Strait entrance buoy.

Chart 17303
Entrance (entrance light bearing 097°T at 0.2 Nm): 57°51.33′ N, 136°29.46′ W
Anchor: 57°52.01′ N, 136°27.01′ W

*Enter the harbor N of Greentop Island, passing N of the two large islands and the small elbow-shaped island. Favor the N shore of the harbor, being careful to avoid the rock near the N shore.*

*Secure anchorage may be had in the harbor in 4 to 7 fathoms, mud bottom, about 0.3 mile from the head. A large anchorage is on the E side of the harbor. This anchorage has a depth of 5 to 8 fathoms, mud bottom, but there are rocks that bare in the entrance, and caution is required in entering. The other passages among the islands are foul and should not be attempted except by very small craft with local knowledge.* (CP)

Greentop Harbor is one of our favorite harbors for kayaking. With a larger boat, however, we find entering a more difficult experience. Shelter at the bitter end of the harbor is bomb-

Réanne Hemingway-Douglass

Baidarka *approaching Greentop Island*

proof and the scenery is lovely. During heavy seas, we do not recommend attempting to enter Greentop. The entire west coast of Yakobi Island is irregular, with many uncharted rocks, and Greentop is no exception. Its entrance is very narrow and intricate, and both sides of the fairway are choked with kelp. In 2005 (our fourth visit), *Baidarka* hit a charted rock at the north end of Elbow Island; during the same time, *Enetai* hit an uncharted rock close ashore off its southwest corner, causing minimal damage to both vessels, as confirmed during a grid haul-out later in Pelican.

If you want to risk entering Greentop, be sure to identify Greentop Island correctly in advance; it is 70 feet high, has a grassy top and a navigation light on its summit. The M/V *Royal Sounder* entered Greentop in June 2005 and stated that it was one of the worst entrances they had experienced in years.

There are several homesites and a U.S. Forest Service cabin on the east shore at the far end of the bay. The cabin, built on land homesteaded by Joe Scott, who lived there until 1985, is a favorite stop for hard-core kayakers whose comments you may be interested in reading in the Forest Service guest book inside the cabin. You can anchor in several places, but we prefer the small cove off the USFS cabin where the water is perfectly smooth and the setting primeval.

Anchor in 4 fathoms over sand and mud with good holding.

## CHICHAGOF ISLAND'S WEST COAST

Chichagof Island's west coast extends 38 miles from Cape Cross to the west end of Klokachef Island.

Chart 17320

*An inside passage for small vessels extends along the greater part of this coast. . . . From Portlock Harbor to Lisianski Strait, the route leads outside, thence through Lisianski Strait and Inlet to Cross Sound.* (CP)

David Frisby

*The author stands on Baidarka Rock at a minus tide—north of Elbow Island*

### Lisianski Inside Passage

Charts 17303, 17321
North entrance: 57°50.93′ N, 136°25.88′ W
South entrance: (Point Urey bearing 015°T at 0.64 Nm) 57°48.55′ N, 136°25.32′ W

*Esther Island . . . is heavily timbered. . . . The E shore of Esther Island is on the W side of what is known locally as the Inside Passage. Rocks extend for about 0.5 mile NNE of the N end of Esther Island.* (CP)

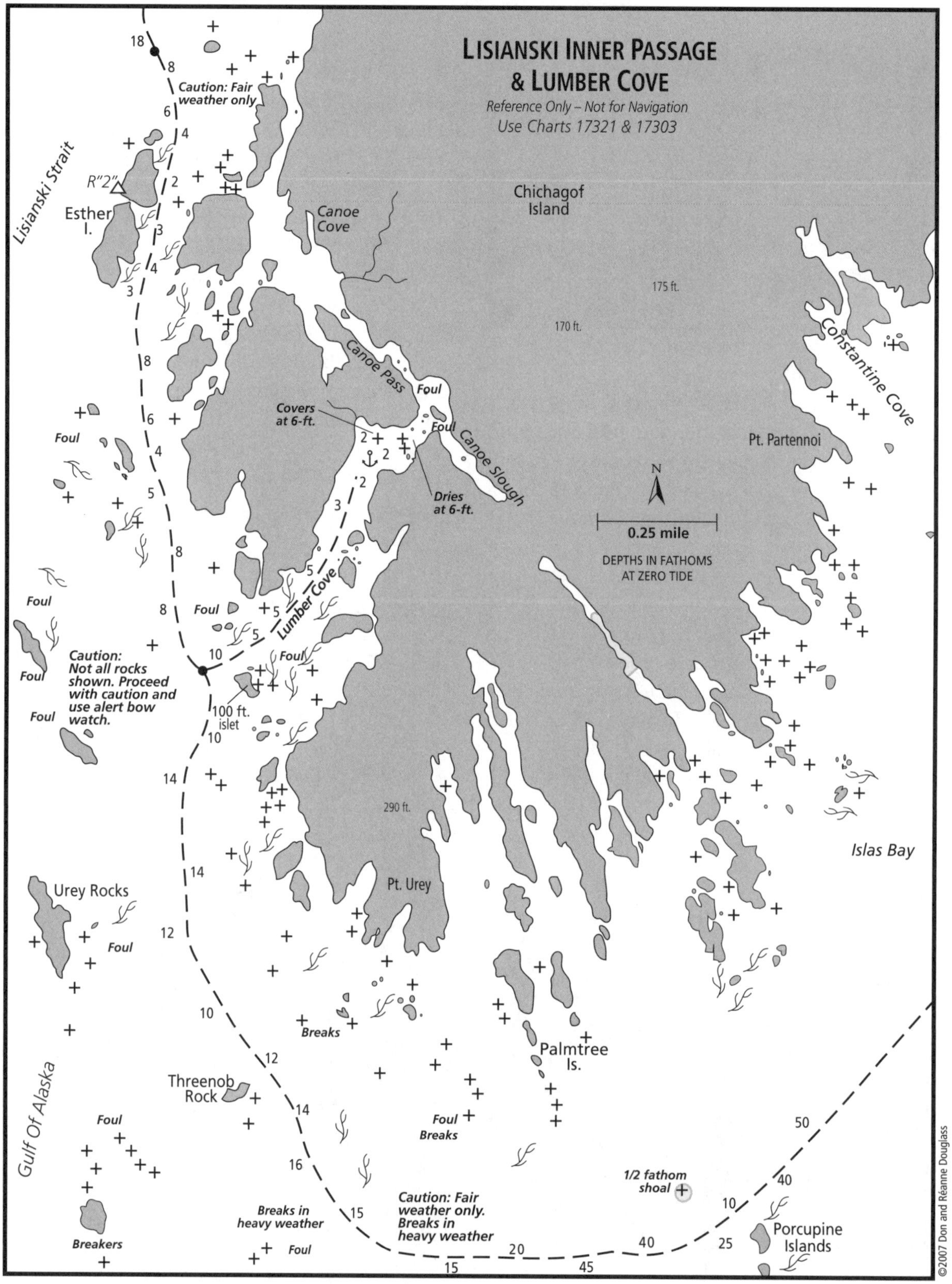
LISIANSKI INNER PASSAGE
& LUMBER COVE
Reference Only – Not for Navigation
Use Charts 17321 & 17303
Chichagof Island
Canoe Cove
Canoe Pass
Canoe Slough
Foul
Covers at 6-ft.
Dries at 6-ft.
Lumber Cove
Lisianski Strait
Esther I.
R"2"
Caution: Fair weather only
Caution: Not all rocks shown. Proceed with caution and use alert bow watch.
100 ft. islet
175 ft.
170 ft.
290 ft.
Constantine Cove
Pt. Partennoi
0.25 mile
DEPTHS IN FATHOMS AT ZERO TIDE
Islas Bay
Pt. Urey
Urey Rocks
Palmtree Is.
Threenob Rock
Gulf Of Alaska
Breaks
Breakers
Foul Breaks
1/2 fathom shoal
Breaks in heavy weather
Caution: Fair weather only. Breaks in heavy weather
Porcupine Islands
©2007 Don and Réanne Douglass

The Lisianski "Inside Passage"—the smooth-water route between Lisianski Strait and Islas Bay (at the southern end of Lisianski Strait)—provides welcome shelter from the open Pacific but requires skillful and vigilant navigation. Be aware that the entire coast of Yakobi and Chichagof islands has an irregular seabed with patches of rocks that extend two miles or more offshore. The south entrance to Lisianski Strait is full of rocks and reefs where seas heap up and break during spring ebb tides, as well as in areas of less than 10 to 15 fathoms exposed to the Gulf of Alaska. Such conditions cause hazards to cruising boats.

Navigating along this coast or entering Lisianski Strait from the south is not recommended in foul weather, limited visibility, or if you are an inexperienced navigator.

Cruising boats (travelling down Lisianski Strait) can avoid much of the Gulf of Alaska swell that occurs at the southern entrance of Lisianski Strait by taking the 3.5-mile, smooth-water Inside Passage. Because this route is so intricate, threading through many islets, rocks and reefs, it should not be taken during periods of foul weather or poor visibility. Swells here are cut to a minimum, and rocks are well marked by kelp or turbulent water.

Follow the Inside Passage south, first by staying close to the east shore of Esther Island, then favoring the west shore of the large island located west of Lumber Cove. Avoid kelp and surging water. From a point off the entrance to Lumber Cove, follow the deep channel south, heading roughly for Threenob Rock (avoiding rocks on your port hand). Pass east of Urey Rocks, then turn southeast to pass close north of Threenob Rock. Continue southeast, avoiding the rocks to the west and the shoals to the east. If you're heading for Porcupine Bay, turn east at about 57°48.55' N, and pass close north of the unnamed islets. If you're headed for Bertha Bay and Mirror Harbor, turn east-southeast and pass north of Beric and Winfred islands.

Along the Inside Passage, you can expect minimum depths to run 3 to 4 fathoms along Esther Island, and 4 to 5 fathoms 0.3 mile south of Esther Island. Otherwise, the depths are irregular and range from 8 to 15 fathoms minimum.

Fishing boats, with stabilizer poles extended, anchor close east of Esther Island in 3 to 4 fathoms.

## **Canoe Cove** (Lisianski Strait)

Canoe Cove is one mile southwest of Lost Cove and 1.4 miles north of Point Urey.

Chart 17303
Position: 57°50.61′ N, 136°25.53′ W

*Canoe Cove . . . furnishes anchorage for small boats in 4 to 5 fathoms, sticky bottom. The anchorage is small, about 250 yards wide. It has two entrances . . . North Pass and the West Pass; both are narrow. At low water North Pass bares for a short distance while West Pass has about 1 foot at its shoalest part. At the seaward end of West Pass is a heavy growth of kelp.*

*Lumber Cove and Canoe Cove are connected at high water by narrow Canoe Pass.* (CP)

Canoe Cove hides its charms behind a fortress of rocks, shoals and a reef. Until a large-scale chart becomes available, visit only with a canoe or kayak.

## **Lumber Cove** (Chichagof Island)

Lumber Cove is 0.7 mile northwest of Point Urey and 2 miles south of Lost Cove.

Chart 17303
Entrance: 57°49.75′ N, 136°25.85′ W
Anchor: 57°50.15′ N, 136°25.17′ W

*Lumber Cove is a small-boat anchorage. . . . Midway in the entrance is a small steep island that is covered with trees. In entering, pass close to the island, leaving it to S. When clear of the island, pass in midchannel and anchor near the head of the cove in 5 to 6 fathoms, sticky bottom.* (CP)

Lumber Cove offers surprisingly good protection in all but the foulest weather. It is entered from the Inside Passage, 0.5 mile northwest of

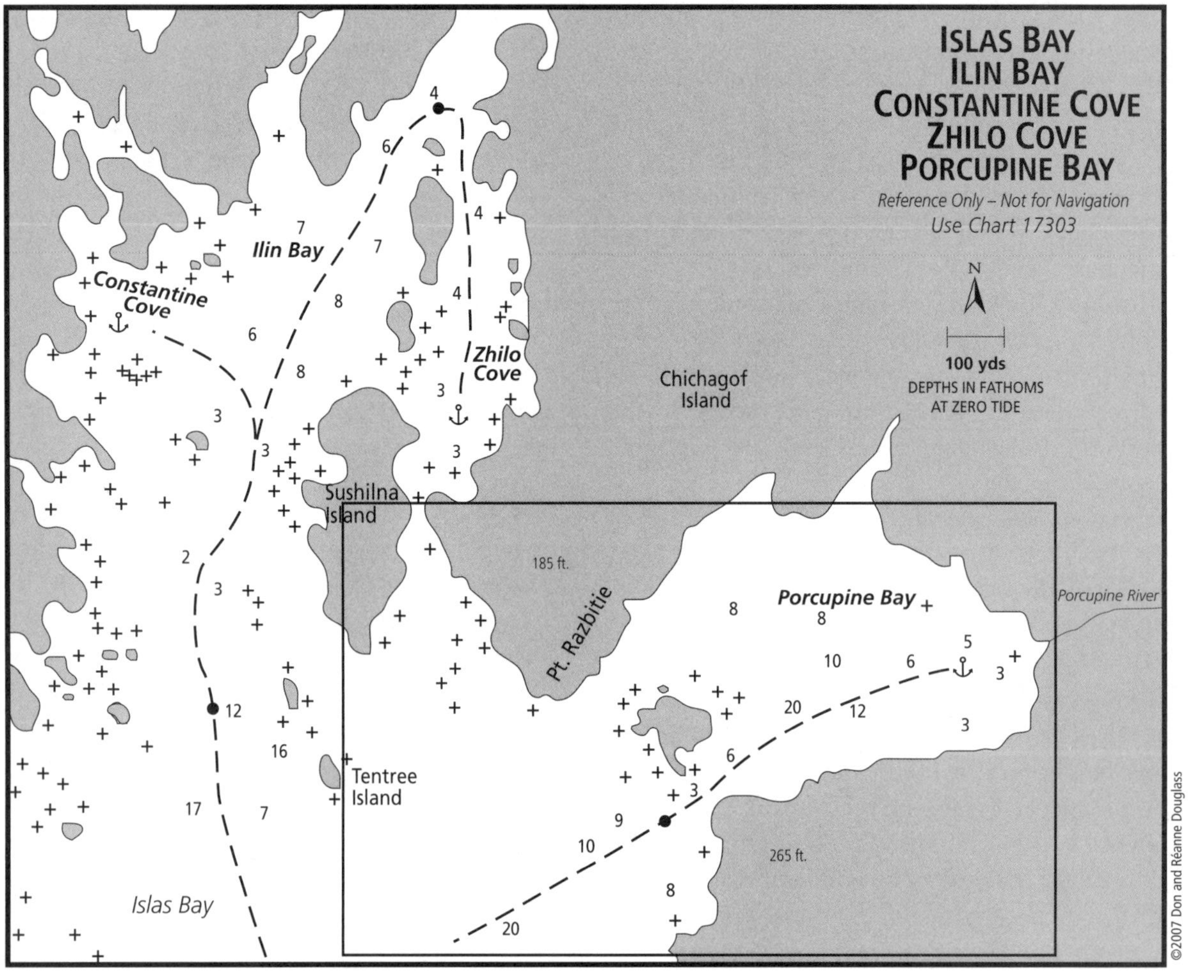


Point Urey. A peninsula to the southeast and south, islets and large kelp beds to the southwest keep the north basin essentially landlocked. The basin has a wide, flat bottom of 2 to 3 fathoms that can handle several boats.

Enter northwest of the 100-foot islet covered with trees and proceed northeast with a clear mid-channel. Depths decrease slowly from 10 fathoms to 2 fathoms as you enter. The inner basin has a flat bottom, and visibility through the water is about 6 feet.

This is an attractive anchorage where you can watch seals and sea otters. The entrance to Canoe Pass is foul but it is usable by kayak at high water.

Anchor in 2 to 3 fathoms over mud and clamshells with good holding.

## Islas Bay

(Chichagof Island)

Islas Bay is 2.2 miles southeast of Lisianski Strait and 7 miles northwest of Portlock Harbor.

**Charts 17321, 17303**

**West Entrance: (Beric Island bearing 160°Tat 0.40 mi) 57°48.59′ N, 136°24.04′ W**

*On its NW side are numerous inlets, most of which have shoal water and rocks at the entrances. Ilin Bay and Porcupine Bay branch off from the N end.* (CP)

Islas Bay, in the lee of Porcupine Islands, is part of the smooth-water route south. Watch for dangerous, unmarked rocks and shoals north of Porcupine Islands and along the shore. The bay has several well-sheltered coves along its northern and eastern shore.

## Ilin Bay and Constantine Cove

(Islas Bay)

Ilin Bay is the north part of Islas Bay.

Charts 17321, 17303
Entrance (Tentree Island bearing 115°T at 0.14 Nm): 57°49.84′ N, 136°23.09′ W
Position (Constantine Cove): 57°50.35′ N, 136°23.34′ W

> *Ilin Bay* [is] *narrow, rocky, and suitable for small craft only. . . . An anchorage in 8 fathoms, mud bottom, is in the upper half of the bay, but this anchorage is exposed to the S.* (CP)

Large yachts may find anchorage in the middle of Ilin Bay or in Porcupine Bay 0.8 mile to the southeast. Constantine Cove, on the west shore looks interesting, but we have no local knowledge to offer. We find Zhilo Cove very comfortable and quiet.

## Zhilo Cove (Ilin Bay)

Zhilo Cove, in Ilin Bay, is 0.5 mile northwest of Porcupine Bay.

Charts 17321, 17303
Entrance: 57°50.57′ N, 136°22.55′ W
Anchor: 57°50.25′ N, 136°22.44′ W

> *A more protected anchorage is in Zhilo Cove, behind the islands, on the E side of the bay in 3 to 4 fathoms, mud bottom. The S and W entrances between the islands leading to this anchorage are foul, but the N entrance at the head of the bay is clear.* (CP)

Zhilo Cove offers very good shelter in a wilderness setting. Its foul south entrance breaks most of the southerly chop.

Anchor in 4 fathoms, sand and mud with fair-to-good holding.

## Porcupine Bay (Islas Bay)

Porcupine Bay is 2 miles northeast of Porcupine Islands and 2 miles east of Point Urey.

Charts 17321, 17303
Entrance: 57°49.71′ N, 136°22.05′ W
Anchor: 57°49.87′ N, 136°21.37′ W

> *Porcupine Bay is about 0.3 mile in diameter and has general depths of 8 to 12 fathoms. A wooded island, 90 feet high, is in the W part of the entrance. The entrance SE of this island is clear. The entrance NW is shoaler and narrower. A waterfall at the E end of the bay shows from the entrance. The harbor affords protected anchorage.* (CP)

Porcupine Bay, a well-sheltered anchorage with lots of swinging room, is lovely and quiet. Steep, green peaks that resemble the fog-shrouded peaks of the South Pacific, tower above the bay. You may have some difficulty setting your anchor; otherwise this bay and Zhilo Cove are good places to wait for better weather.

To enter, use the south entrance. From the islets north of Porcupine Islands, head for 2,215-foot Pinnacle Mountain. We found a minimum of 3 fathoms in the fairway, not the 6½ fathoms shown on the chart. The bottom of the bay is somewhat irregular; however, there is a fine 3- to 6-fathom shoal in the southeast corner where you have a good view of the waterfall. The bottom is very soft over a hard bottom, and it takes a light hand on the rode to set your anchor.

Anchor in 3 to 4 fathoms over a hard bottom covered with a thin layer of soft sand and coarse, broken shells. Holding is poor unless you set your anchor well; then it is fair.

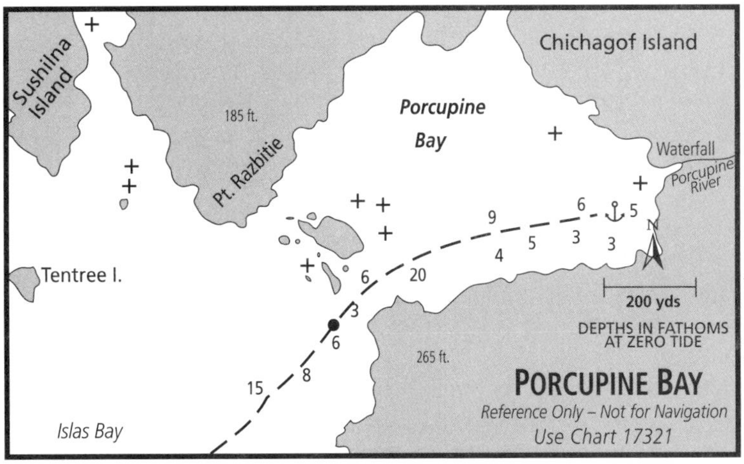

Réanne Hemingway-Douglass

*View of Bertha Bay from White Sulphur Hot Springs*

Kristin Hoelting

*Whale sounding in Bertha Bay*

## **Bertha Bay** (Chichagof Island)

Bertha Bay is 2 miles southeast of Porcupine Bay.

Chart 17321
Position: 57°47.93′ N, 136°20.78′ W

> *The bay is rocky at the head and is very foul; it affords little protection from the ocean swell.* (CP)

The north shore of Bertha Bay is home to beautiful White Sulphur Hot Springs. Bertha Bay itself is foul and you should not attempt to anchor here.

After crossing the rolly Bertha Bay and the foul area west of Skinner Island, you can enter the perfectly smooth waters of Mirror Harbor by following a very narrow, intricate channel southeast of Post Island.

## **White Sulphur Springs, West Arm, and Mirror Harbor** (Bertha Bay)

White Sulphur Springs, 1 mile northwest of Mirror Harbor, is 55 miles northwest of Sitka.

Chart 17321; 55 miles NW of Sitka; 2.5 miles SE of Porcupine Bay
Position (hot springs): 57°48.33′ N, 136°20.70′ W
Entrance Mirror Harbor (Fairway Reef bearing 000°T at 0.12 Nm): 57°47.03′ N, 136°19.85′ W
Anchor (Mirror Harbor): 57°47.73′ N, 136°19.09′ W

---

### Mirror Harbor—A Piece of Cake?

Don Douglass & Réanne Hemingway-Douglass

The skipper was confident. He'd been into Mirror Harbor several times. "Piece a cake," he told our crew. "But we need all of you at the bow to help negotiate the dogleg."

The three of us headed forward on deck. (One of us, like the skipper, had previous experience in the area.)

The tide was exceptionally low. "No way," I muttered to the others. "There's not enough room to maneuver. . . . Look! You can see the bottom right under the bow."

"I don't think it'll go, Don," Herb shouted.

"We'll give it a try," came the answer as we idled slowly forward.

"Reverse! Reverse! Rock! Rock!" we screamed in unison, gesturing excitedly so the skipper would understand.

We came to a slow halt, just a foot or two away from the rock.

The skipper came out of the pilothouse and looked over the bow pulpit. "Oooh, I see what you mean," he said, unperturbed. "Yeah, we might be able to make the turn if we had a bow thruster. Maybe we'd better anchor over there," he motioned with his head toward West Arm, . . . "'til the tide comes up."

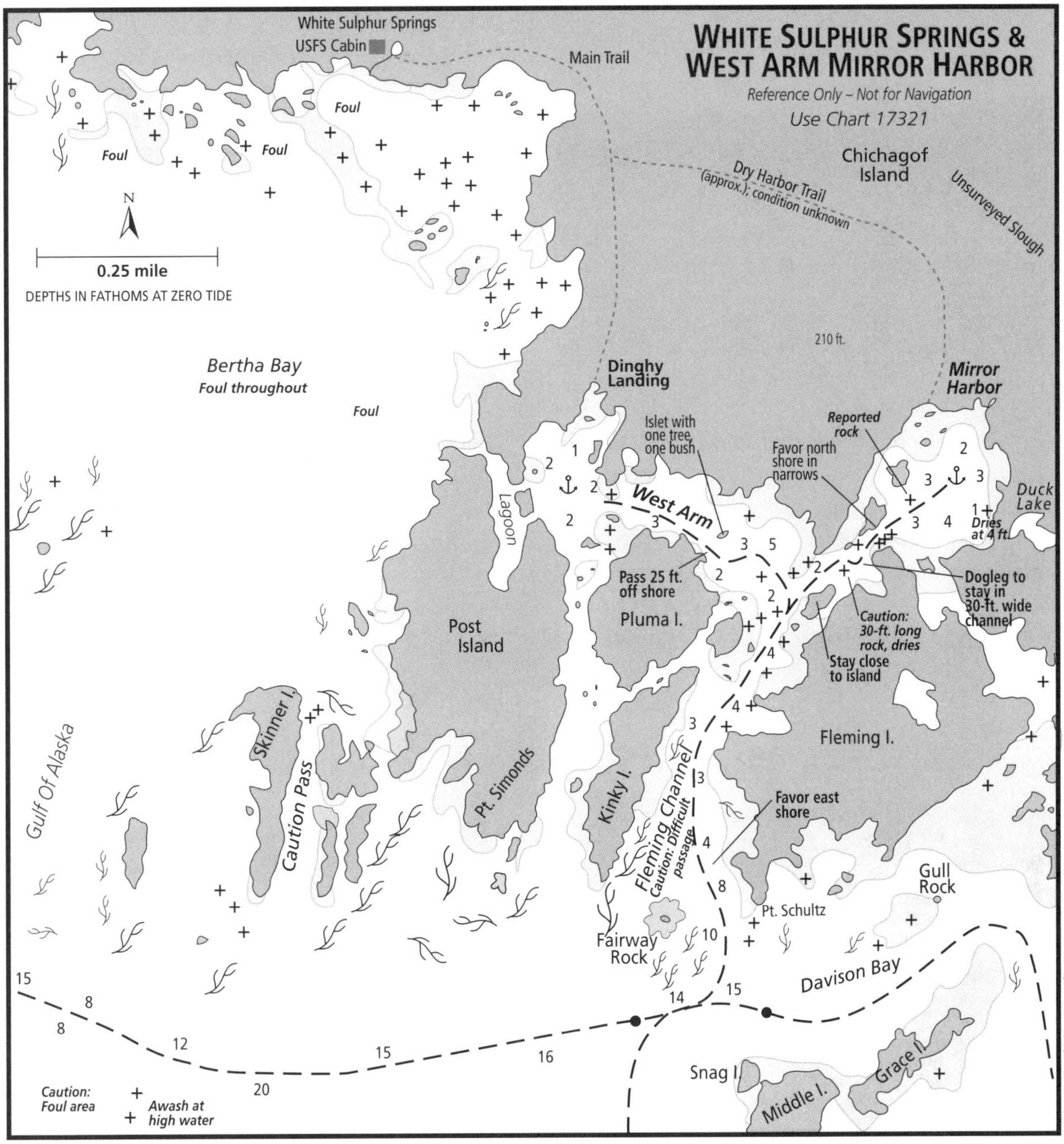


Anchor (West Arm): 57°47.65′ N, 136°19.53′ W
Position (West Arm trailhead): 57°47.86′ N, 136°19.97′ W

*Small craft usually anchor in West Arm, and users of the White Sulphur Springs follow a trail, about 0.5 mile long, to the springs. Local knowledge is advised.*

*Mirror Harbor . . . has depths of 3 to 4 fathoms in the middle. In 1972, the harbor was reported to be a good anchorage for small craft with excellent protection and holding qualities, soft bottom. The channel leading to the harbor is between Fleming Island and the group to the W. It is intricate, narrows to about 10 yards, and in places has depths of about 1 fathom. Local knowledge is required for safe passage.*

*West Arm, N of Pluma Island, is foul, but limited anchorage for small craft is available.* (CP)

Mirror Harbor, one of the most isolated and intricate places imaginable, offers excellent

Réanne Hemingway-Douglass

*South entrance to the Mirror Harbor complex*

protection from all weather and seas. It is also one of the most difficult harbors to enter. The challenge you experience in entering, however, is offset by wonderful White Sulphur Hot Springs nearby, where you can soak your body in perfect quiet. We prefer to anchor in Mirror Harbor and take a dinghy to the trailhead in West Arm for the 15-minute boardwalk to White Sulphur Hot Springs. The boardwalk

Réanne Hemingway-Douglass

*Wendy and Herb enjoy White Sulphur Hot Springs.*

passes through rainforest where Sitka spruce and skunk cabbage thrive and water lilies bloom in small ponds.

The springs fill a comfortable, covered pool that looks out over Bertha Bay. There are changing rooms and an area to rinse your clothes. Swimsuits are sometimes worn. There is also a very nice natural pool outside under a tree to the southeast. A USFS cabin is located next to this outside pool with primitive campsites to the east. During the summer, the cabin is often occupied by local vacationers or kayakers.

Entering Mirror Harbor should be attempted only at high-water slack. Boats much over 30 feet will have trouble making the dogleg unless they have a bow thruster. We have taken our 40-foot *Baidarka* inside the harbor at both low tide and high tide. At low tide, we were unable to make the dogleg despite using our bowthruster. At high tide, we had no problem.

On earlier visits in our single-screw, 32-foot Nordic Tug (without a bowthruster), we were unable to make the dogleg on a minus one-foot tide, although we could maneuver fairly easily on an 8-foot tide. We have talked to skippers on sailboats with drafts varying from 6 to 8 feet and lengths to 50 feet who made the dogleg successfully at high tide.

Chart 17321 is inadequate for entering Mirror Harbor, so we have used local knowledge resources, as well as our own experience, to try to create a meaningful diagram and route instructions. *Use them at your own risk!* Be sure to post a bow watch so you don't ground like so many boats have. You should enter Mirror Harbor just before high-water slack.

This is the route we follow:

Carefully locate Fairway Rock at the entrance and pass well to its south. Turn north when you're abeam Snag Island, and favor the east shore where the water is deeper along Point Schultz. Once you are inside Fleming Channel along Kinky Island, the swell dies off.

Avoid the kelp and shoal to your port side. Keep a mid-channel course until you have

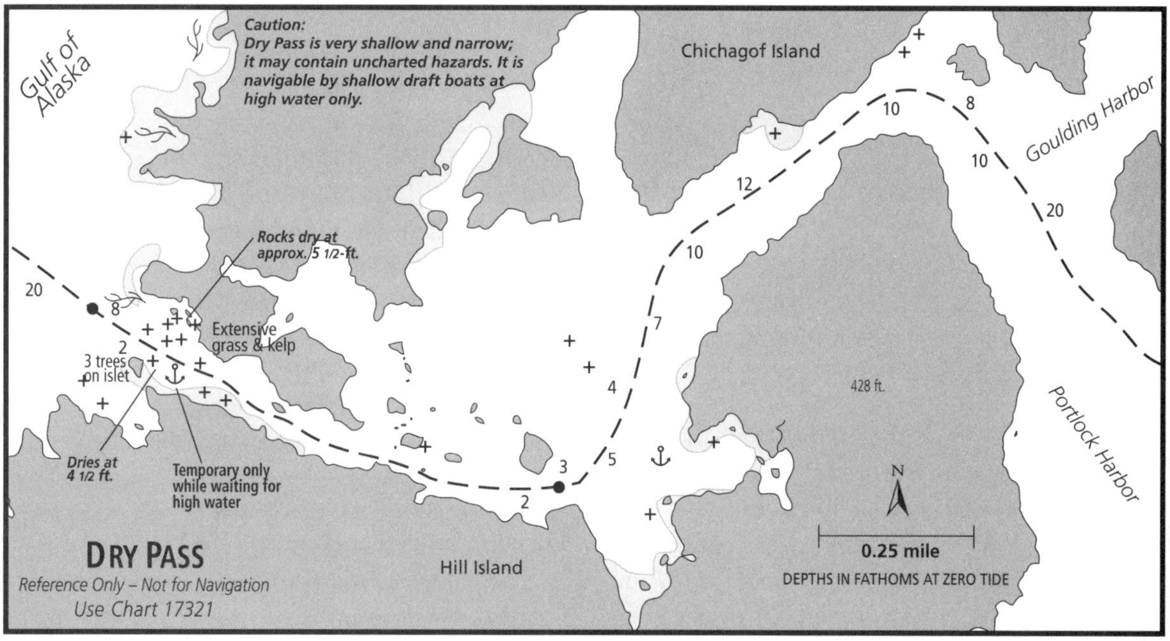


passed the several rocks on your port side that mark the entrance to the West Arm. At this point, stay close to the unnamed island with gnarled trees on the northwest side of Fleming Island.

Continue northeast, heading straight for a small islet that has a dangerous, mid-channel, submerged rock immediately to the east. You must make a very definite dogleg to the east just before you reach the steep-to islet (a few feet off!) to avoid a 30-foot-wide submerged rock (its tip dries on a 6-foot tide) on your starboard. This submerged rock defines the south side of the narrow channel. On this dogleg you are pointed toward a shallow cove on the north end of Fleming Island.

Réanne Hemingway-Douglass

*Pond along trail to White Sulphur Hot Springs*

Réanne Hemingway-Douglass

*Critical dogleg with Mirror Harbor in the background*

Once clear of the large submerged rock to starboard (and islet to port), turn left (northeast) again and enter Mirror Harbor over a shallow bar. We found this bar to have approximately 3 feet over it at low water. Avoid the rocks on the east side of the bar by favoring the west shore.

Once you've crossed the bar, proceed to anchor as desired. Avoid two rocks close to

Gary Luhm

*Everywhere! The sea otters are everywhere along the west side of Chichagof Island*

the east shore of Mirror Harbor that dry at 4 feet, avoid also the northwest end of the bay, which shoals and has small rocks. The rock in the west center of the bay was reported as submerged, and we have not located it. When you're figuring tides, remember that Sitka reports tides as low as minus 3 feet.

The West Arm, in some ways, is more difficult to enter since you cannot pinpoint certain of the submerged hazards. Visibility is also decreased by eel grass and primeval-looking scum that floats along the top of the stagnant waters. Before you enter or anchor in this arm, it's a good idea to check it out first by dinghy.

Continuing south from Mirror Harbor you must pass outside Hill Island and re-enter the smooth water at Imperial Passage 4.5 miles to the south. If you're up for another challenge and have a shallow-draft boat less than 32 feet in length, and the tide conditions are right, you could try Dry Pass, 1.5 miles southeast. (We have not transited Dry Pass, other than by dinghy, since we acquired our 40-foot *Baidarka*.)

## **Davison Bay** (Chichagof Island)

Davison Bay is east of Mirror Harbor entrance and 1.2 miles northwest of Dry Pass.

Chart 17321
West entrance: 57°47.05′ N, 136°19.52′ W
East entrance: 57°46.94′ N, 136°18.95′ W

> *Cormorant Island, Shag Rock, Grace Island, Middle Island, and Snag Island form a group about 1.7 miles N from Cape Dearborn. Fern rock, Gull Rock, and a rock awash midway between the two, are 270 yards N of Grace Rock. Davison Bay, the bight E and NE of this group, has depths of 3-1/2 to 15 fathoms.* (CP)

Davison Bay is a smooth-water route that leads from Mirror Harbor, around several small islands, to Little Bay and Dry Pass. The bay can be used for temporary anchorage while you wait for high water to enter either Mirror Harbor or Dry Pass. The shallow bar in the center of the bay requires a careful transit.

## **Little Bay** (Chichagof Island)

Little Bay is 1.5 miles northeast of Cape Dearborn.

Chart 17321
Entrance: 57°46.52′ N, 136°18.22′ W
Anchor: 57°46.80′ N, 136°17.83′ W

> *The entrance to the bay is wide and clear, except near the shores, and has a depth of about 11 fathoms decreasing to 2-1/2 fathoms near the head of the bay where it is foul.* (CP)

Quiet anchorage can be found deep in the head of this narrow inlet. Little weather appears to penetrate the head of the bay.

Anchor in 2 to 4 fathoms over sand and gravel with fair holding.

## **Dry Pass**

Dry Pass, 1.5 miles south of the entrance to Mirror Harbor, separates Hill and Chichagof islands.

Chart 17321
West entrance: 57°45.96′ N, 136°18.42′ W
East entrance: 57°45.69′ N, 136°17.10′ W
Anchor (east entrance): 57°45.72′ N, 136°16.87′ W

> *Dry Pass, the N passage from Portlock Harbor to the Pacific Ocean, is N of Hill Island. For 0.4 mile from the W end,* ***the pass is less than 0.1 mile wide and is foul*** [Authors' emphasis].
>
> *Anchorage in Dry Pass is reported in the cove on the N shore back of a large island in 6 fathoms, sticky bottom, and also in the cove on the SE shore in 4 to 7 fathoms.* (CP)

Dry Pass is just that at low water—*dry*—which creates an adrenaline-rush that explorers live for. However, in addition to shallow depths, it is chock-full of eel grass and a few patches of kelp, confusing a depth sounder and adding to the excitement. The pass should be attempted only by smaller boats under proper conditions, and during the last few hours of a sufficiently-high flooding tide. Most boats find it more convenient to pass west of Hill Island and re-enter the sheltered waters of the Outer Passage using Imperial Pass.

The northwest entrance to Dry Pass is tiny and encumbered with rocks, but once you've passed the first grass-covered bar, there is no ocean swell. Do not approach this northwest entrance from sea during heavy weather, when this shore becomes a dangerous lee. The sea bottom for two miles west of Dry Pass is irregular with rocky patches where the sea breaks during heavy swells—the same is true for much of the coast.

The narrows of Dry Pass are a good half-mile long, requiring that you find a suitable route between and around the shoals, avoiding grass, kelp and . . . who knows what else! We recommend Dry Pass *only* if you truly want to explore an off-the-beaten route.

The bottom throughout the pass is flat sand for the most part and, where the eel grass does not obscure visibility, the water is quite clear. (We have made it through in our 32-foot Nordic Tug, which draws 4 feet, with 2 or 3 feet to spare, on approximately a 6-foot Sitka tide.) We favor the south shore in the narrows, south of the islets, three-quarters of the way through. This is one of the shallowest parts and has considerably *less water* than that shown on Chart 17321.

When we first did Dry Pass on a southbound route, we anchored temporarily just inside the entrance in 6 feet (on a 4.5-foot flooding tide in Sitka) where the eel grass begins so that we could reconnoiter by dinghy, which is a good idea. The anchor site we used lies just off a small, rocky cave on the south shore fronted by a pin-shaped rock that—we calculate—covers at a 6.5-foot Sitka tide. (A 4-foot draft boat should wait until Pin Rock is awash before proceeding.) We took our dinghy into the narrows to probe the bottom and waited an hour for another foot of water.

Past the narrows, the bay opens up into a large, well-sheltered basin where Rod Nash, who was transiting Dry Pass from south to north on *Forevergreen,* once sighted 30 to 40 humpback whales.

On a northbound passage, transiting Dry Pass from the east end is easier. There are more anchoring options at low water, and you don't have the winds and swells to your back, as you do off the west entrance.

The scenery is just as rugged and untouched as it must have been when early Russian explorers visited this coast. You can safely anchor anywhere in the bay once you've passed through the narrows. It's probably faster to go around Hill Island and re-enter smooth water at Imperial Passage, but much less exciting!

Once you are anchored, enjoy the great kayaking in this bay. Also note that you are only a short dinghy ride away from White Sulphur Hot Springs in West Arm.

Secure anchorage can be found east of the east entrance to Dry Pass with lots of swinging room. (A professional skipper we know likes to anchor between the feet of the rabbit-shaped island in the bay in about 40 feet of water. You might check that out and see if it is to your liking.)

Anchor at the east entrance site in 4 fathoms over sand and mud with fair-to-good holding.

## Imperial Passage

Imperial Passage, the main entrance into Portlock Harbor, lies between Hill and Hogan islands, giving access to another part of the smooth-water Outer Passage.

Chart 17321
West entrance: 57°43.61′ N, 136°17.89′ W
East entrance: 57°43.91′ N, 136°15.33′ W

The passage is easy to enter with good protection from swells and is the beginning of the smooth water route.

## Portlock Harbor (Chichagof Island)

Portlock Harbor is surrounded by Hill, Hogan, Herbert Graves, and Chichagof islands.

Chart 17321
North entrance (Dry Pass): 57°46.20′ N, 136°15.79′ W

> *Portlock Harbor is used chiefly by boats going through the inside waters to Ogden Passage. It has three entrances from the sea: South Passage, Imperial Passage, and Dry Pass. Imperial Passage is used by most vessels, although South Passage is equally good. Dry Pass is foul and is used only by small boats.* (CP)

Portlock Harbor is a large harbor with calm waters and many heavily wooded islets where limbs hang low to the water's edge. At this point you begin to pick up the Coast Guard on Ch 16 and Ch 22A, after essentially no reception since Icy Strait. Some of these radio deadspots are slowly being improved by added repeater stations. Call Juneau Coast Guard for more information.

The harbor was named for Captain Nathaniel Portlock, the leader of a two-ship expedition to Alaska in 1787. Portlock, who anchored here for several weeks, subsequently published a sketch of the harbor. The captain of his second vessel was George Dixon, whose name appears on many geographic locations in Alaska—the most famous of which is Dixon Entrance. (Both men had been officers under James Cook.)

## Goulding Harbor (Portlock Harbor)

Goulding Harbor is at the northwest end of Portlock Harbor and has two branches.

Chart 17321
Entrance: 57°46.23′ N, 136°15.48′ W

> *The NE branch terminates in a shallow cove, bordered with sand and gravel flats. With local knowledge it is possible to take launches of 4 feet or less draft to the head of the cove. . . . Small craft can anchor near the flat at the head of the cove. Soundings taken at the entrance to the NE branch show a depth of 1 fathom on a reef of considerable size that extends from the S point of the entrance to the arm.* (CP)

The northeast branch of Goulding Harbor needs more exploration since good shelter may be available there. Goulding Harbor is poorly charted, so caution is required.

## Baker Cove (Goulding Harbor)

Baker Cove is the north arm of Goulding Harbor.

Chart 17321
Entrance: 57°47.11′ N, 136°15.12′ W
Anchor: 57°47.42′ N, 136°14.96′ W

Baker Cove is the easiest place to anchor in lovely Goulding Harbor; the lack of driftwood along the grassy shore indicates excellent shelter. At low water, the east side at the head of the bay becomes landlocked.

Entrance can be made by radar if needed. A 4-fathom bar lies across the middle (not charted). The basin off the head of the cove is deeper and the shore steep-to. When we hauled up our anchor, we discovered a brittle star attached to it—the first we'd seen in these waters.

Anchor in 8 fathoms over dark mud, shells and wood debris with good holding.

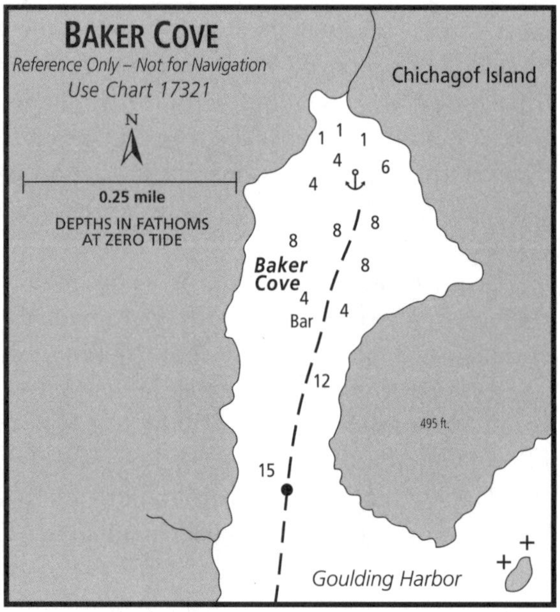

## **Pinta Bay** (Portlock Harbor)

Pinta Bay extends 2.1 miles north from Portlock Harbor)

Chart 17321
Entrance: 57°45.04′ N, 136°12.88′ W
Anchor: 57°46.79′ N, 136°12.31′ W

> *Two small, wooded islands on the W side of the entrance are joined by a reef that bares. E of these islands the entrance is clear.* (CP)

Anchorage can be found in about 6 fathoms at the head of the bay. The bottom is unknown.

## **Didrickson Bay** (Portlock Harbor)

Didrickson Bay is on the east side of Portlock Harbor.

Chart 17321
Entrance: 57°43.98′ N, 136°11.39′ W
Anchor (west shore): 57°44.54′ N, 136°11.57′ W
Anchor (head of bay): 57°44.77′ N, 136°11.38′ W

> *Between submerged rocks and reefs on each side, the entrance is deep and clear. A 6-foot waterfall at the head of the bay can be seen from the entrance. Good anchorage can be had near the head of the bay in 5 to 16 fathoms, mud bottom.* (CP)

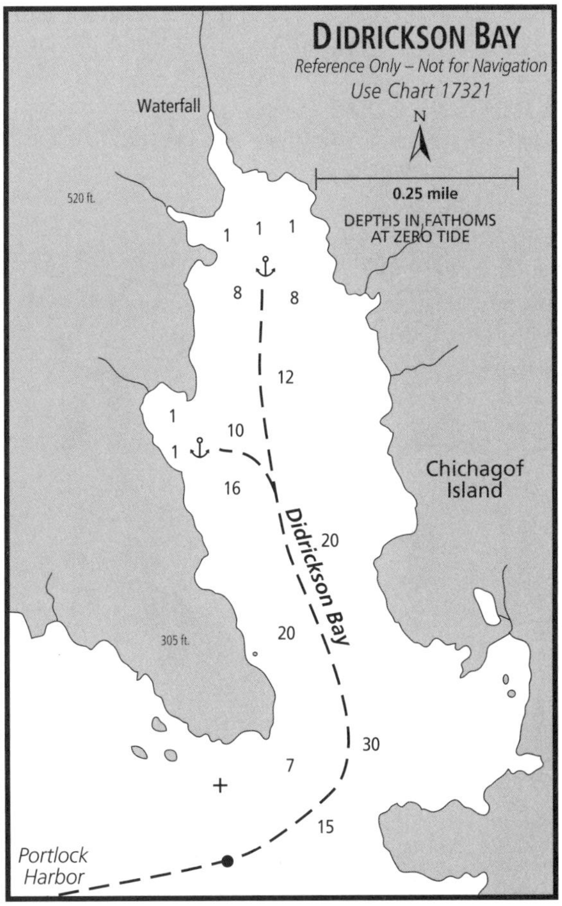




Didrickson Bay is well sheltered and easy to enter by favoring its east side. The head and sides of the bay are steep-to and we have not been able to locate the 5-fathom patch mentioned in *Coast Pilot.* The grassy shores here show no signs of driftwood; sea otters play in the bay and, in late summer, salmon can be seen trying to head up creek.

Anchor off the waterfall at the head of the bay, or off to the side as indicated in the diagram (a favorite spot of local fishing boats). Both shores are steep-to.

Anchor in about 8 fathoms along the west shore, or at the head of the bay over soft mud and hard bottom. Holding is good if you set your anchor well.

---

### Lessons from Adverse Experiences

Don Douglass

Alaska-bound cruisers can learn important lessons from the adverse experiences of others. Keep these things in mind:

1. High-tech doesn't mean immunity from disasters or the ability to be able to communicate directly with authorities during emergencies.
2. Charts—especially in Alaska—are old, mostly small-scale and are replete with various errors or omissions. Even new charts and guidebooks must be used with skepticism and caution.
3. Be seriously prepared and self-sufficient when cruising in wilderness waters.
4. There are many radio blackout areas along the Pacific Coast and within fiords.
5. It's always good policy to keep an alert bow watch in any tight quarters or when the bottom is uneven.
6. Reduce speed to slow or dead-slow if you don't know that it is safe to proceed.
7. Cruising boaters are a friendly lot and are willing to lend a hand in emergencies. You can do the same when you're privileged to travel in these beautiful and remote areas.

## Troller Anchorage (Lydonia Island)

Troller Anchorage is on the north side of Lydonia Island.

Chart 17321
Anchor: 57°42.91′ N, 136°10.60′ W

"Troller Anchorage," which seems to be a favorite of local trollers, is our name for the cove on the northwest corner of Lydonia Island. Some protection from southerlies is reported.

Anchor in 6 fathoms over a mixed bottom.

## South Passage

South Passage lies between Hogan and Herbert Graves islands.

Chart 17321
West entrance: 57°40.98′ N, 136°16.44′ W
Northeast entrance: 57°42.02′ N, 136°13.58′ W

> *South Passage is between Cape Edward and Point Hogan, which is the S point on Hogan Island. Reefs extend for 0.3 mile S from Point Hogan.* (CP)

## Surveyor Passage

Surveyor Passage extends from Portlock Harbor to Ogden Passage.

Chart 17321
North entrance: 57°43.22′ N, 136°10.28′ W
South entrance: 57°41.83′ N, 136°08.18′ W

> *Many submerged rocks are in the passage. A daybeacon marks a reef, that uncovers about 7 feet, on the NE side of the passage 0.4 mile SE of Lydonia Island. A rock awash is 50 yards off the NE shore in the narrow part of the passage about 0.5 mile SE of the daybeacon.* (CP)

Narrow Surveyor Passage is bordered by high, snowy peaks that form the south flanks of Mt. Lydonia. Small slab avalanches are evident along the north wall of the passage. The waters throughout this short passage are calm, without any swell. The fairway through the passage is about 20 yards wide. Anchorage can be found along the shoals in a number of places.

*Note:* on a southbound passage, take the green day beacons to starboard, the red to port.

## Black Bay (Chichagof Island)

Black Bay extends east from Surveyor Passage for 1.2 miles.

Chart 17321
Entrance: 57°42.55′ N, 136°09.46′ W

> *Black Bay . . . has two islands obstructing its entrance. The best passage into the bay is between Point Lydonia and the northernmost of these islands, although small boats can pass between them . . . Strong winds draw through the bay from the head, and it is not recommended for shelter.* (CP)

Black Bay is truly landlocked but, in most places, the depths are too great for convenient small-craft anchorage. However, larger, deep-draft vessels can find moderate depths off the grassy margins at the head of the bay.

South of Point Lydonia, along the east side of Surveyor Passage, two islets partially block the entrance to Black Bay. On entering the bay, stay close under Point Lydonia, but favoring the northern islet, to avoid a ridge that extends about 50 feet off the point.

## Kimshan Cove (Chichagof Island)

Kimshan Cove is east of Fitz Island at the junction of Ogden and Surveyor passages.

Chart 17321
Entrance: 57°41.46′ N, 136°07.29′ W
Anchor: 57°41.27′ N, 136°07.17′ W

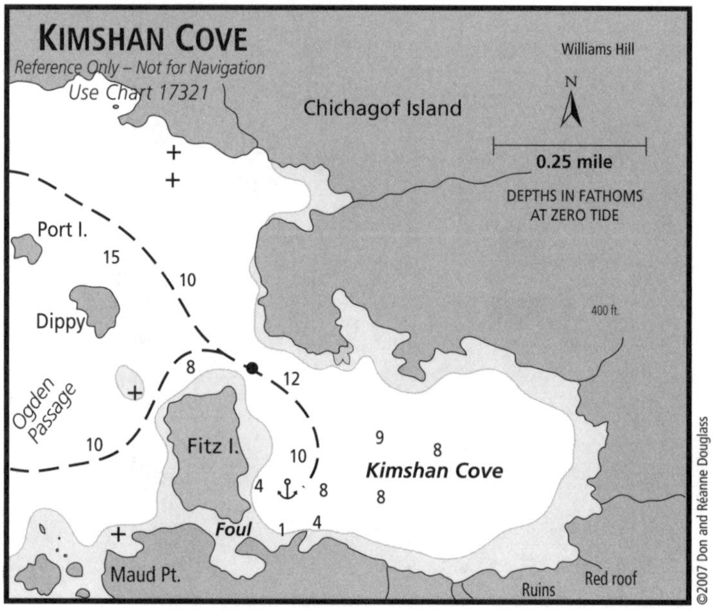

*Kimshan Cove . . . has depths of 6 to 11 fathoms. Anchorage can be selected anywhere in the cove, being careful to avoid the pile ruins of a wharf on the SE side of the cove.* (CP)

Landlocked Kimshan Cove provides excellent shelter and calm waters. Seals and sea otters like these waters and, in the fall, you see salmon jumping constantly here. Kimshan is said to be Chinese for "gold mountain," after the old gold mines in the vicinity.

Although the shoreline is flat, the underwater contour is steep-to—8 fathoms just 200 feet from the beach.

Anchor in 6 to 8 fathoms over mud and grass with very good holding.

## Ogden Passage

Ogden Passage extends southward from Surveyor Passage to Khaz Bay.

Chart 17322
North entrance: 57°41.53′ N, 136°07.51′ W
South entrance at Smooth Channel: 57°36.81′ N, 136°07.82′ W

*The depths in Ogden Passage are generally good and the dangers are charted . . .* (CP)

Ogden Passage is calm, smooth, quiet and so untouched that it seems to take you back to prehistoric times. Inquisitive sea otters pass close by your boat, as if to say, "Who are you and what are you doing here?" This is a great place to reduce your RPM and enjoy the beautiful, natural environment.

*Caution:* Several years ago the skipper of a 77-foot, state-of-the-art sailing vessel with a 14-foot draft found an uncharted rock in the narrow, middle section of Ogden Passage, on the west side of the channel at 57°39.329' N, 136°10.281' W. Several people were seriously injured; nearby boaters and the USCG came to their rescue. Be sure you are using up-to-date, corrected charts as this rock is now indicated and noted on the chart as "Rep (2003)."

Ogden Passage is a unique part of the Outer Passage and not easily forgotten. But as always, maintain your vigilance for uncharted hazards.

Linda Lewis

*Ogden Passage sea otter checking out the disturbance*

## Elkugu Bay (Herbert Graves Island)

Elkugu Bay lies to the east of Cape Edward along the southeast side of Elkugu Island.

Chart 17322
Entrance: 57°40.57′ N, 136°15.15′ W

*Elkugu Bay . . . is exposed to the S and is of no importance.* (CP)

## Kukkan Bay (Herbert Graves Island)

Kukkan Bay is 2 miles southeast of South Passage.

Chart 17322
Entrance: 57°39.88′ N, 136°13.88′ W

[Kukkan Bay] *is poorly protected and is used only as a passage into Ogden Passage through Kukkan Passage. . . . The spot shown as 2 fathoms, on the N end of the shoal area off Pole Point, breaks in heavy weather and may have less than 2 fathoms on it. It should be avoided by all vessels.* (CP)

## Kukkan Passage

Kukkan Passage is on the southwest side of Herbert Graves Island.

Chart 17322
North entrance (Pole Point bearing 058°T at 0.7 Nm): 57°39.28′ N, 136°14.97′ W
South entrance (Snipe Rock G"1" bearing 170°T at 0.08 Nm): 57°38.33′ N, 136°10.73′ W

*Kukkan Bay is connected with Ogden Passage by Kukkan Passage and is used by fish packers of about 12-foot draft at all stages of the tide; however, the spot shown as 2 fathoms, on the N end of the shoal area off Pole Point, breaks in heavy weather and may have less than 2 fathoms on it. It should be avoided by all vessels. . . .*

*Ittar Rock is a bare rock 12 feet high in the middle of the entrance to Kukkan Passage.* (CP)

Kukkan Passage is a shortcut for boats wanting to enter the south end of Ogden Passage from the outer waters.

## Tawak Passage and Gig Pass

Tawak Passage and Gig Pass are 4 miles north of Khaz Bay.

Chart 17322
South entrance (Tawak Passage): 57°37.19′ N, 136°11.61′ W
Position (Gig Pass): 57°37.11′ N, 136°11.40′ W

*Tawak Passage . . . affords a protected, although intricate, passage for small boats along the coast. The N end of the passage is foul and should not be used without local knowledge.* (CP)

Gig Pass is a narrow passage that connects the south part of Ogden Passage to Tawak Passage.

## Elbow Passage

Elbow Passage is the west entrance to Klag Bay.

Chart 17322
Entrance: 57°37.08′ N, 136°07.74′ W

Réanne Hemingway-Douglass

*Lining up these two markers helps keep you in The Gate's channel; then make the turn to starboard into Elbow Passage.*

*The W part of this passage has a midchannel depth of 2-3/4 fathoms and is constricted in places to a width of about 75 yards by kelp-marked shoals. . . . The pass W of Klag Island is almost blocked at the N end and is suitable only for small boats and launches.*

*Caution. The last of the ebb sets out of Elbow Passage W with great velocity through the W entrance, forming heavy swirls, and the passage should be attempted only at slack water, preferably low-water slack.* (CP)

## The Gate

The Gate is the main entrance to Klag Bay.

Chart 17322
South entrance: 57°36.51′ N, 136°06.20′ W
North entrance: 57°36.82′ N, 136°06.01′ W

*The Gate . . . has its entrance 1 mile N of Guide Rock. It has a depth of 4-3/4 fathoms and a width of 50 yards at its narrowest part, between a daybeacon on the E side of Vorota Island and a rocky 1-fathom shoal 20 yards off a sparsely wooded islet on the E side of the entrance. A 008°* [true] *unlighted range marking the centerline of the channel clears the 1-fathom shoal.* (CP)

Most cruisers headed for Klag Bay use the Smooth Channel route, then turn northward to pass through The Gate. Note in the accompanying picture the markers (GW Bn "A" and RW Bn "B") used for making your way through The Gate's channel safely. After transiting The Gate, make a starboard turn toward the eastern end of Elbow Passage, while staying alert to the effects of the current. Then easily follow Elbow Passage as it turns northward into Klag Bay—still minding the current.

## Klag Bay, Chichagof Village Site (Chichagof Island)

Klag Bay is at the head of Khaz Bay.

Chart 17322 (inset)
South entrance (Rose Point bearing 200°T at 0.13 Nm): 57°37.74′ N, 136°05.36′ W
Anchor (Chichagof site): 57°39.73′ N, 136°05.52′ W

Linda Lewis

*A few buildings remain at this once-prosperous mining village at Klag Bay, a place that offers endless fascinating exploring.*

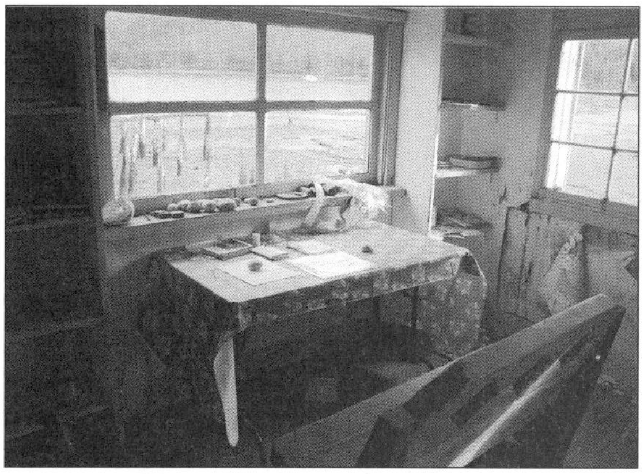

Linda Lewis

*A note on the table invites explorers to make an entry into the diary.*

Linda Lewis

*This Alaska State Library photograph (found on the table) shows what the mining camp looked like in its working prime.*

Linda Lewis

*The rusted remains of mining equipment*

Linda Lewis

*The story of the mining camp tells itself with sights like this.*

Linda Lewis

*A walk up the hill brings you to the mine shaft; you can do your own panning for gold in the nearby stream.*

Linda Lewis

*Radio Transmitter license found in an abandoned building at Klag Bay*

> *The two entrances to* [Klag Bay] *lead through narrow crooked channels, with foul shores and strong currents, which are difficult except for small vessels at slack water.*
>
> *Anchorage can be found in the bay above Klag Island in depths of from 3 to 20 fathoms.* (CP)

Chichagof, at the head of Klag Bay, was the site of a gold and silver mining village during the first half of the twentieth century. More than $13,000,000 in gold was brought out of area mines between 1905 and the late 1930s. On a nearby small island ("Radioville"), a retired signal corps operator ran a radio station, delivering messages from the outside world to the village site.

Inside Klag Bay, it is perfectly still, while outside boaters complain via VHF of 5-foot southeast seas and a rough ride. The abandoned site of Chichagof is fun to explore.

Many structures and all kinds of fascinating mill equipment lie rusting along shore, sprouting moss or colorful wild flowers or young shoots of hemlock. One cruiser found a note at the kitchen table inviting them to make an entry in the diary; a picture of the original mining camp was placed nearby. For many cruisers, Klag Bay is a highlight of their Chichagof Island trip.

The bay is fairly flat at 4 fathoms over a long stretch and anchorage can be taken toward the head, avoiding rocks and a foul area from the islet to the eastern shore. This area is awash on low water and almost forms a breakwater.

Anchor in 4 fathoms over gray, sticky mud, clam shells and sand, with very good holding.

## Lake Anna and Sister Lake (Klag Bay)

Lake Anna is entered through a narrow channel on the east side of the north end of Elbow Passage. Sister Lake is joined to the northeast end of Lake Anna by a narrow, foul passage.

Chart 17322
Entrance (Lake Anna): 57°37.45′ N, 136°05.00′ W
Entrance (Sister Lake): 57°38.34′ N, 136°02.46′ W
Anchor (Lake Anna): 57°38.79′ N, 136°02.76′ W

> *There is anchorage at the S end of* [Lake Anna] *in 6 to 15 fathoms. . . . At the N end of the lake is an anchorage in 5 to 12 fathoms. Lake Anna should only be entered by those with local knowledge because of its narrow entrance and extreme currents, except at slack water.*
>
> *Passage* [into Sister Lake] *should be made at slack water only. It is reported that slack water occurs about 2-1/2 hours after slack water at Sitka, and that the currents reach a maximum strength of 12 knots. . . . The lake is reported to be deep, with good anchorage in the coves. The lake should be navigated with caution.* (CP)

Lake Anna and Sister Lake are remote and poorly surveyed, but are worth entering at the proper tide. We entered and spent the night at the north end of Lake Anna, off a creek. The depths inside the lake are substantial until toward the head, where they shallow to about 5 or 6 fathoms.

The passage joining Sister Lake to Lake Anna has extremely dangerous currents on ebb tides. There is a 0.25-mile portage trail from the southeast end of Sister Lake to Ford Arm.

Anchor in about 5 fathoms over mud and sand with good holding.

## Rough Channel

Rough Channel, west of Quit Point and Gray Rock, connects Ogden Passage to Khaz Bay.

Chart 17322
North entrance: 57°36.82′ N, 136°08.06′ W
South entrance: 57°35.00′ N, 136°07.62′ W

[Rough Channel's] *N end has rocks above and under water that contract the channel to about 200 yards. Because it generally has heavy swell, the channel should be avoided except possibly at low water with a smooth sea.* (CP)

## Smooth Channel

Smooth Channel connects Ogden Passage to Khaz Bay.

Chart 17322
North entrance: 57°36.81′ N, 136°07.82′ W
South entrance: 57°35.59′ N, 136°05.73′ W

> *Smooth Channel, the best entrance to Ogden Passage, is protected from ocean swell by a chain of wooded islands and ledges. . . . Smooth Channel also forms the approach to Klag Bay and connecting bodies of water.* (CP)

As its name implies, Smooth Channel is more protected than Rough Channel to the west.

## Khaz Bay (Chichagof Island)

Khaz Bay is the entrance to Slocum Inlet and Klag Bay.

Chart 17322
Entrance (Ninefoot Shoal buoy bearing 034°T at 1.9 Nm): 57°33.31′ N, 136°07.72′ W

> *Khaz Bay . . . is 2.2 miles wide at its entrance between Ramp Island and Outer Rocks, and extends N about 2 miles to Quit Point. Here it divides into an extensive system of inland passages that extend E, N, and W. . . .*
>
> *Khaz Bay . . . is a navigable route for small vessels.* (CP)

Although some guidebooks suggest using Khaz Bay to enter the Gulf of Alaska, then passing west of the buoy at Khaz Breakers, 4 miles offshore, we prefer to prolong the smooth-water route of the Outer Passage and, instead, have some fun making our way into the Gulf of Alaska at Khaz Point via Piehle Passage.

## Double Cove, Khaz Bay (Chichagof Island)

Double Cove is at the northeast end of Khaz Bay.

Chart 17322
Entrance: 57°35.50′ N, 136°03.90′ W
Anchor: 57°35.96′ N, 136°03.62′ W

Double Cove provides excellent shelter and is a good base from which to explore Khaz Bay

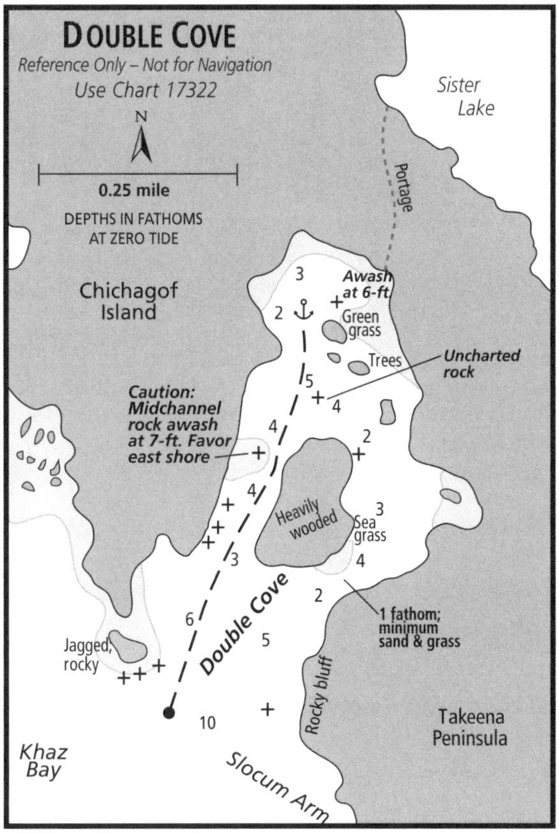



and Klag Bay by inflatable. The area offers outstanding sport fishing and an unspoiled environment.

You can anchor with landlocked protection behind the point in the northwest corner or east of the heavily wooded island. Avoid the dangerous rock awash on a 7-foot tide in mid-channel on the west entrance; this rock, which is poorly charted, extends almost to the center of the channel with a shoal on its west side. You may want to consider using a stern-tie in this small anchorage. Prevailing swell dies once you're abeam the island and, inside, it is perfectly calm.

A beach of small shale and grass that is free of driftwood lies at the head of the cove. The water is somewhat stagnant, with just 6-foot visibility; summer water temperature averages about 60°F.

Anchor in 3 fathoms over black mud with clamshells and pieces of shale; excellent holding.

Linda Lewis

*A homesteader's fireplace with name engraved—Chichagof Island*

## **Slocum Arm** (Chichagof Island)

Slocum Arm extends southeast from Khaz Bay.

Chart 17322
Entrance: 57°34.77′ N, 136°04.11′ W

> *The arm is free from dangers, with the exception of a rock, bare at half tide, 300 yards from the NE shore.* (CP)

Slocum Arm was named after one of the naval officers in the original survey party at the end of the nineteenth century, no relation to America's famous first circumnavigator, Joshua Slocum.

## **Ford Arm** (Chichagof Island)

Ford Arm is northeast of Khaz Head and Slocum Arm.

Chart 17322
Entrance: 57°33.04′ N, 136°00.43′ W
Anchor (northwest arm): 57°36.04′ N, 136°00.17′ W
Anchor (southeast arm): 57°34.14′ N, 135°55.62′ W
Position (Rocky Bay): 57°34.01′ N, 135°58.53′ W

> *Ford Arm . . . is constricted in places by islands and rocks. At its head is an expansion . . . from which arms extend SE and NW. The SE arm has some islets . . . there is anchorage for vessels NW of the islets in desired depths up to 15 fathoms. The NW arm has anchorage for small craft at its head in 6 to 15 fathoms.*
>
> *The entrance to Ford Arm is marked on the SE side by a group of small wooded islands that should not be approached closely.* (CP)

Linda Lewis

*Inside an abandoned cabin on Chichagof Island*

Anchorage can be found in Elf Cove or at the head of either the southeast or northwest arm of Ford Arm.

## **Elf Cove** (Ford Arm)

Elf Cove is 2.9 miles inside Ford Arm.

Chart 17322
Anchor: 57°35.45′ N, 135°57.41′ W

> *Small craft can also anchor in Elf Cove . . . in 5 to 8 fathoms; a ledge bare at half tide is close to the N side of the cove.* (CP)

Anchor in about 6 fathoms with some exposure to southeast winds. Swinging room is limited.

## **Falcon Arm** (Slocum Arm)

Falcon Arm is 1.4 miles southeast of Ford Arm.

Chart 17322
Entrance: 57°32.04′ N, 135°58.32′ W
Anchor: 57°33.42′ N, 135°55.96′ W

*A rock with 1 foot over it is 0.4 mile inside the bay, in the middle. Favor the NW shore for 0.5 mile from the entrance to avoid this rock and then keep in midchannel . . . A good anchorage is in an expansion above a point on the NW side 1.5 miles from the entrance in 11 to 14 fathoms,* soft bottom. (CP)

You may find that the rock location (noted in the *Coast Pilot* text above) is reported differently on electronic charts and paper charts. This is common along the coast and skippers need to be cautious in this area. They must also be sure to keep their electronic charts updated. It has been reported that in one major vendor's electronic charting program, the rock is indicated in the vector view, but is not seen at all in the raster view. (Even though the raster chart properties dialog indicates a 1:40,000 scale, the raster chart does not display at this scale.) Electronic charting has become standard on cruising boats but it does have its problems. Paper charts should *always be simultaneously in use.*

Small craft can find good anchorage at the head of the bay in 6 fathoms over a soft bottom.

## Waterfall Cove (Slocum Arm)

Waterfall Cove is 1.8 miles southeast of Falcon Arm.

Chart 17322
Entrance: 57°31.15′ N, 135°55.92′ W
Anchor: 57°31.49′ N, 135°55.30′ W

*Waterfall Cove . . . is identified by a large waterfall about 1 mile above its head. Two bights are at the head; the E one dries and the W one, which has 4 to 11 fathoms, affords anchorage for small craft.* (CP)

Waterfall Cove is an attractive anchorage offering good shelter behind the heavily wooded spit formed by the outlet of the river. It is protected from most winds and chop. Here, leaping salmon, soaring eagles and squawking ravens greet your arrival. The water is 60°F and visibility is 10 feet. The 500-foot vertical waterfall, about one mile inland, falls from a saddle, and the rugged granite outcropping of

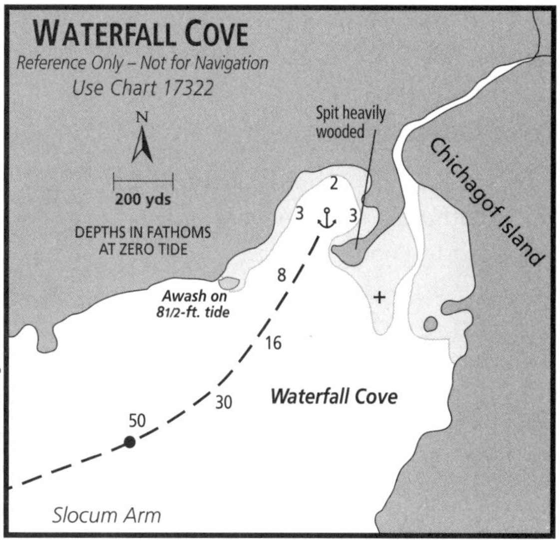


©2007 Don and Réanne Douglass

2,700-foot Khaz Peak is topped with a green velvet crown. Deer and grizzlies can sometimes be sighted along the river's outlet.

Anchor in 4 fathoms over black mud, clamshell and shale chip with some kelp; good holding.

## Island Cove and Wooded Knoll Cove (Slocum Arm)

Island Cove is 4.5 miles southeast of Falcon Arm.

Chart 17322
Entrance (Island Cove): 57°28.95′ N, 135°52.01′ W
Anchor (Island Cove): 57°28.89′ N, 135°51.58′ W
Anchor (Wooded Knoll Cove): 57°28.73′ N, 135°53.41′ W

*The anchorage is in the SE end of the cove in about 16 fathoms. Favor the SE point of the cove when entering and avoid a flat that extends about 300 yards from the N shore of the anchorage.*

*On the SW shore of Slocum Arm, opposite Island Cove, is a small point with a wooded knoll 80 feet high. Anchorage for small craft is in the cove W of this point in 6 to 10 fathoms.* (CP)

Island Cove is somewhat open to prevailing upslope winds; however, larger boats can get good protection from downslope winds here. Smaller boats may find what we call "Wooded Knoll Cove" more intimate, less open to chop, with more moderate depths.

Anchor (Island Cove) in about 15 fathoms over sticky mud with good holding. There is plenty of swinging room in this area.

Anchor (Wooded Knoll Cove) in 6 to 10 fathoms over mud and gravel with fair-to-good holding.

*Piehle Passage—a smooth-water transit that avoids six miles of open ocean.* Caution: *careful piloting is required.*

## **Flat Cove** (Slocum Arm)

Flat Cove, on the northeast side of Slocum Arm, is 6 miles southeast of Falcon Arm.

Chart 17322
Entrance: 57°28.30′ N, 135°50.23′ W

> *Flat Cove . . . has depths of 12 to 32 fathoms to the flat that extends 700 yards from its head.* (CP)

Flat Cove is steep-to and open to westerlies. Hidden Cove is preferable as an anchorage.

## **Hidden Cove** (Slocum Arm)

Hidden Cove is 1 mile north of the head of Slocum Arm.

Chart 17322
Entrance: 57°27.64′ N, 135°49.12′ W
Anchor: 57°27.93′ N, 135°49.07′ W

> *Good anchorage is 0.5 to 0.6 mile from the head of Slocum Arm in 16 to 18 fathoms. A flat extends about 0.2 mile from its head.* (CP)

Although *Coast Pilot* does not mention Hidden Cove by name, the cove is reported to offer secluded, well-sheltered anchorage. However, it may be subject to williwaws.

Anchor in 5 fathoms over an unrecorded bottom.

## **Piehle Passage**

Piehle Passage leads from Slocum Arm to west of Khaz Point.

Chart 17322
North entrance: 57°32.13′ N, 136°01.08′ W
South entrance: 57°30.06′ N, 136°01.67′ W
Entrance (alternative N entry): 57°32.94′ N, 136°02.25′ W

> *This passage is extensively used by small craft with local knowledge, but is difficult for strangers. The entrance at Khaz Point is closed by breakers in heavy weather. Good protected anchorage for small craft can be had in the bight at the NW end of Khaz Head on the SE side of Piehle Passage. Anchorage can be selected at the head of the bight in 8 to 10 fathoms, mud and gravel bottom.* (CP)

Piehle Passage, another of our favorite areas along the Outer Passage, requires careful piloting in good visibility and fair weather only. It is not recommended for larger vessels or those with limited maneuverability. But, if you feel confident using Piehle Passage, you can avoid about 6 miles of open water and have a good time doing it. We feel our diagram, in conjunction with Chart 17322, is the correct route, but we offer you *no* guarantees! Our information checks with the ubiquitous white paint so often splashed on rocks by locals at critical turning points.

If you have a small-to-moderate-sized cruising boat, you can use Piehle Passage without problems in good visibility, as long as you're cautious. It's best to go through at low tide when hazards are easier to spot and, of course, always post lookouts on your bow. Remember that—like all explorers—if you give this passage a try, *you* alone are responsible for your own decisions and safety. You can always turn around and retrace your steps if you get confused.

On a *southward* transit, head west from Slocum Arm, north of Khaz Head and south of island (215). Follow the deep-water channel until you have passed the small islet on your port side, southwest of island (215). At this point, turn south-southeast and pass close starboard to another islet (5 fathoms minimum). Continue deep into the cove in Khaz Head until you are almost to the westernmost peninsula of the head. The cove below Khaz Head provides good shelter in 8 to 9 fathoms. After passing two islets to starboard, turn west around these two islets and head for three small islands covered with trees 0.5 mile offshore—the northernmost of which is marked (120). Depths in this vicinity are 6 fathoms minimum.

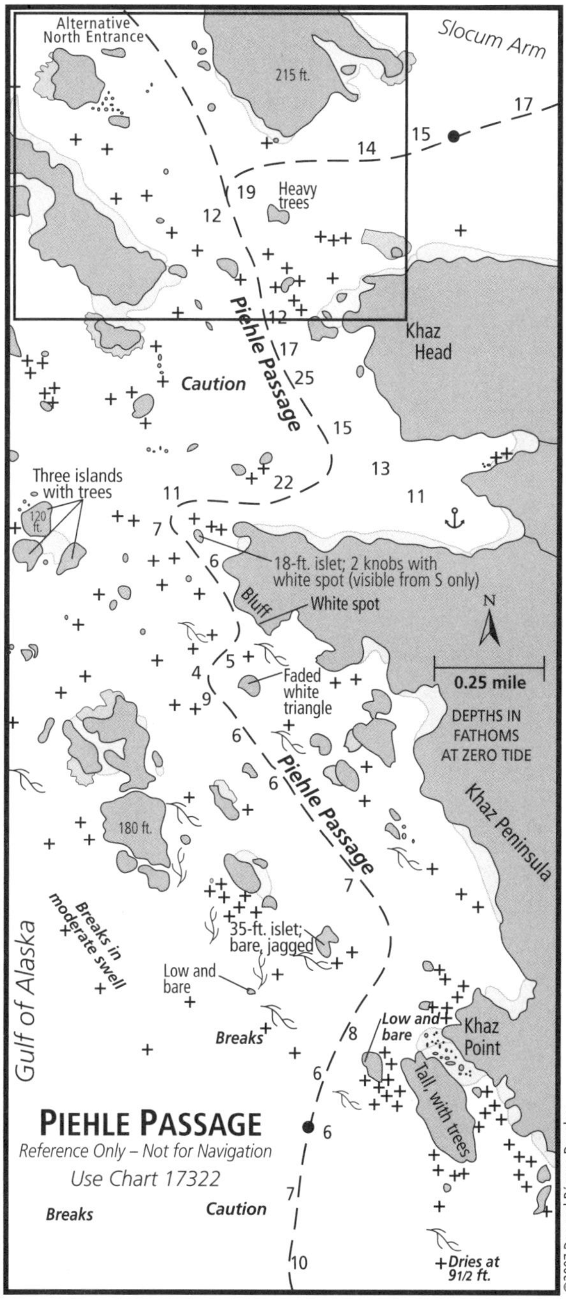



Just past a 25-foot-high islet off the peninsula to port (identified by two light-colored knobs), turn southeast and remain close to the peninsula, east of the rocks and kelp patches. Stay about 60 feet from the bluff and 30 feet from the kelp to starboard.

When you are able to see the faded white paint on the peninsula to your port (minimum 4 fathoms—do not overshoot into the 2-fathom kelp patch north of the islet ahead), turn to the southwest, working your way in clear channels between the kelp patches and covered rocks (minimum 5 fathoms in the fairway). This is the trickiest part of the passage. Once you have cleared the kelp and rocks, turn southeast, passing to port the islet which is about 0.35 mile south of the white spot on the bluff; the islet has a white triangle on its south side. There are several more islets and kelp patches to pass on the port hand before you approach the northeast corner of Khaz Point.

Don Douglass

*Consider making your transit through Piehle Passage at low water when the rocks throughout are more visible to your bow watch*

*Khaz Point and south entrance to Piehle Passage*

Réanne Hemingway-Douglass

About 400 yards off the peninsula at Khaz Point, the channel opens to the south-southwest. When you have passed the bare, jagged, 35-foot-high islet to starboard, turn southwest and pass west of Khaz Point, avoiding the breaking rocks to starboard. At what we judge to be the south entrance point (57°30.06' N, 136°01.67' W), depths in the fairway are 6 fathoms minimum. From this entrance point, turn south until you reach the 12- to 15-fathom curve, then turn southeast and parallel the coast, giving Point Slocum rock pile a wide berth of at least a mile.

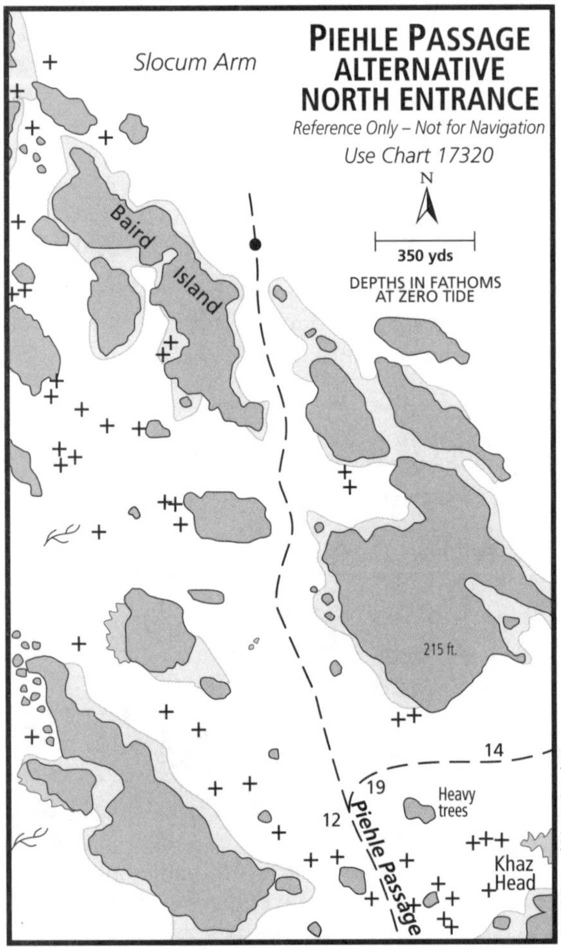




As an alternative North Entrance to Piehle Passage when transiting *southbound*, you can enter further north in Slocum Arm, near the center point of Baird Island's eastern shore. Pass carefully the easternmost points of the southern portion of Baird Island, favoring the west side of this passage and avoiding the charted 1-fathom shoal that extends west from the large unnamed island north of Khaz Head. (Northbound, reverse the directions. See diagram for route.)

---

## Piehle Passage—A Real Challenge for Experienced Mariners

Linda Lewis & Dave Parker
M/V *Royal Sounder*

We made it through Chichagof's Piehle Passage with the help of your diagram (very slowly with a very vigilant bow watch [Dave] —at low water and in good visibility as you advised), Don and Réanne. And you were so right about the tricky part. It was very confusing when the chart and the world outside the window didn't match. We saw no rocks or kelp dead ahead where you made the point that we were *not* supposed to go, but *lots* of rocks and kelp on our starboard where you referred to the white spot on the peninsula and said to turn to the Southwest (to our starboard).

Based on what we were both seeing outside the boat, I decided that instead of turning to starboard at that moment, I would proceed *very slowly* ahead a few feet. That quickly didn't feel right based on what Dave could now see. Stop the boat. Assess. I reminded myself of the point you had made to not overshoot past the white spot painted on the bluff. So we carefully backed up a bit, and when I was abeam the white spot, we made the right angle turn to starboard, staying with the course as I had laid it out from your notes. That did the trick! Just like you said.

On a *northbound* passage, head for the entrance point west of Khaz Point before turning north-northeast into Piehle Passage. Then reverse the procedure described above.

*Note 1:* The white spot on the bluff and the white triangle mentioned above have faded in recent years.

*Note 2:* In our previous edition we asked readers to comment about our documentation of Piehle Passage and, since then, have received only positive responses. In 2005, on *Baidarka's* southbound passage from Lituya Bay, we again verified our waypoints—this was about the tenth time we've transited Piehle Passage.

From Khaz Point southward for about 6.5 miles, you are subject to the prevailing northwest swells of the Gulf of Alaska until you enter Fortuna Strait and the calmer waters of Salisbury Sound.

## Khaz Head Anchorage

**Chart 17332**
**Anchor: 57°31.30′ N, 136°00.95′ W**

We have anchored inside Khaz Head several times in recent years and found the site to offer protection from northwest swells. During southeast weather conditions we have experienced some gusts at this site, but no swell. Fish and Game vessels frequently use this site as a refuge, also.

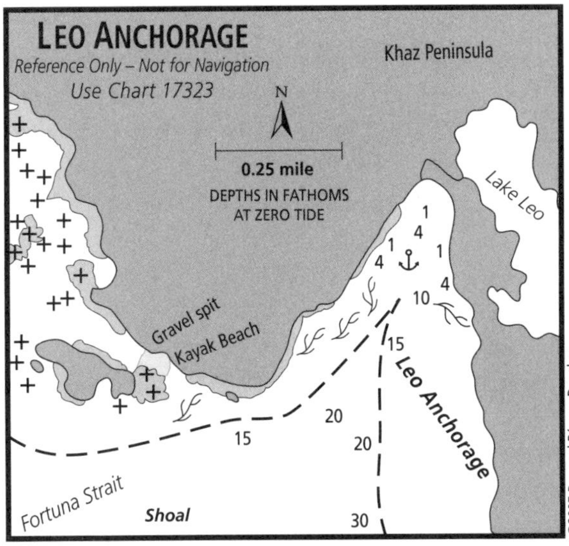




Anchor in 6 to 9 fathoms over brown mud and shell with very good holding.

## Fortuna Strait

Fortuna Strait lies between Chichagof and Klokachef islands.

**Chart 17323**
**North entrance: 57°25.71′ N, 135°54.85′ W**
**South entrance: 57°23.84′ N, 135°51.70′ W**

> *Fortuna Strait is used, especially by small craft, when bound to Khaz Bay from Salisbury Sound.* (CP)

Leo Anchorage on Fortuna Strait's north shore is a good lunch stop.

## Leo Anchorage (Chichagof Island)

Leo Anchorage, on the northeast side of Fortuna Strait, is 5.5 miles northwest of Kalinin Bay.

**Chart 17323**
**Anchor: 57°25.50′ N, 135°51.67′ W**

> [Leo] *anchorage affords a fair shelter from N winds, but it is not recommended in S weather. . . . The anchorage . . . for small craft* [is] *near the head in 5 to 7 fathoms. The bottom is hard with sticky patches.* (CP)

Leo Anchorage provides good shelter in stable conditions, and it's a welcome relief from the swell encountered a few miles to the north. The head of the bay has old-growth trees along its shore and a gray stone beach. In the fall, salmon swarm off the outlet to the stream, waiting for rains to swell the stream so they can reach their spawning grounds. Seals feed off the salmon and, farther off the beach, huge white and orange sea nettles float by. The bottom is steep-to and hard. Set your anchor well and test it.

On the west point of the bay, just east of the wooded islet, there is a gravel spit, kayak beach and a 1-fathom anchor site surrounded by kelp. You can wait here temporarily and watch conditions to the northwest if you're heading northward. For shelter in southeast gales, we recommend Kalinin Bay.

Anchor in 4 to 10 fathoms over a hard bottom with kelp; good holding only if well set.

*Salisbury Sound sea otters*

## Salisbury Sound

Salisbury Sound, bounded by Chichagof, Kruzof and Baranof islands, leads to the west entrance to Peril Strait and the northwest entrance to Neva Strait.

Chart 17323
West entrance (Point Kruzof bearing 183°T at 1.4 Nm): 57°21.70′ N, 135°50.57′ W
East entrance (Kakul Rock Light bearing 033°T at 0.55 Nm): 57°21.27′ N, 135°42.45′ W

> *The shores of the sound are foul, especially the N side, which is studded with islands, rocks, and reefs with some kelp. It is open to the prevailing wind and sea, and generally a SW swell rolls in and breaks along the N shore, sometimes reaching Baranof Island. There are no dangers through the middle of the sound, but the depths are irregular. . . .*
>
> *Approaching Salisbury Sound from seaward, especially from W, it is sometimes difficult for a stranger to recognize the entrance until close-to.*
>
> *The current from the sea sets E on the flood into Salisbury Sound, Peril Strait, and Neva Strait. The ebb current sets W. The current velocity is 1 to 1.5 knots.* (CP)

As you approach the east end of Salisbury Sound and fall into the lee of Kruzof Island, the Gulf of Alaska swells gradually subside. Goloi Island is home to several dozen sea otters, and you can pass close by for a good look.

Salisbury Sound was named by Captain Portlock in honor of the Bishop of Salisbury; nine years earlier, Captain James Cook had called it Bay of Islands.

# SALISBURY SOUND TO SITKA—EAST SIDE OF KRUZOF ISLAND

## Kalinin Bay (Kruzof Island)

Kalinin Bay, on the north side of Kruzof Island, is 2.5 miles inside the west entrance to Salisbury Sound.

Chart 17323
Entrance: 57°20.37′ N, 135°47.00′ W
Anchor: 57°19.15′ N, 135°47.28′ W

> *Kalinin Bay . . . has anchorage near its head that is used by fishing craft, but its narrow entrance is obstructed by rocks.*
>
> *Large craft should favor the SW shore in approaching the entrance in order to avoid a 3¼-fathom kelp-marked shoal off the entrance. Favor the W shore in entering until up to the first bend, then steer midchannel courses. A large rock awash is about 100 yards off the E shore at the narrowest part of the channel, just before the bay widens to form the main anchorage. Another rock awash is close E.*
>
> *A submerged rock with 1 fathom over it, and usually marked by a halibut float during the summer, is 100 yards off the W shore and about 100 yards NW of the large rock awash. Also marking this site is the ruins of a building with stub piling that extends 10 yards offshore. Strangers should enter at half tide or low water, passing about 30 yards W of the large rock.*
>
> *Well-protected anchorage . . . can be found near the head of the bay in 4 to 5 fathoms, soft mud bottom.* (CP)

Kalinin Bay, on the south side of Salisbury Sound, is a popular anchorage for both sport fishing and cruising boats. Its proximity to the rich fishing grounds in Salisbury Sound as well as to Peril Strait—the usual pleasure boater's route south to Sitka—make it a convenient place to wait for proper tides or weather conditions. Although it is one of the best anchorages in the area, it is not the most secluded.

The entrance channel is a mile long, and care should be taken to remain mid-channel to avoid rocks along either shore. A large rock awash at high water at the narrowest part of the entrance channel, is essentially part of a

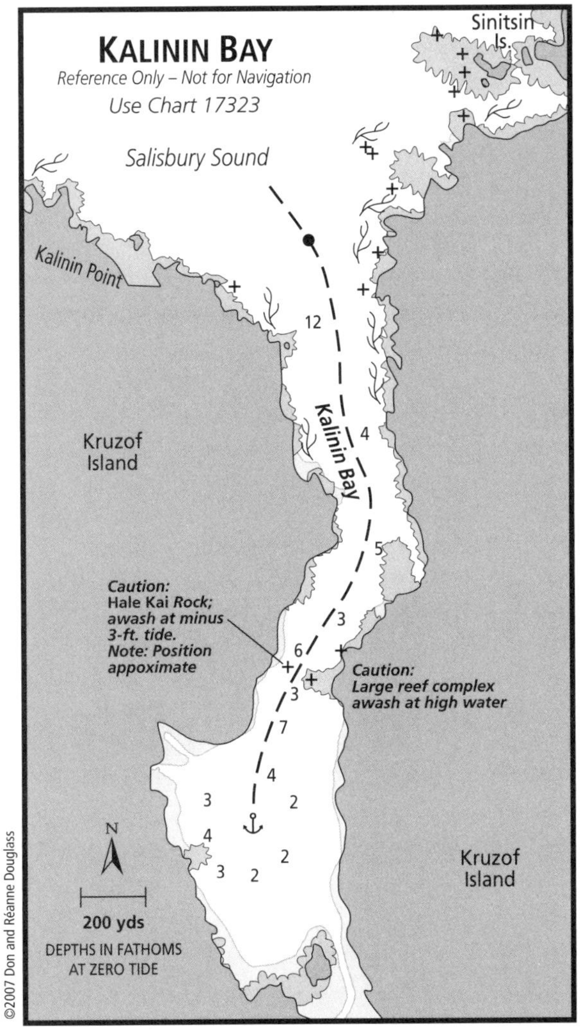


reef complex charted as extending from the eastern shore to near mid-channel.

*Caution:* About 100 yards to the northwest of the western edge of the reef complex, and 100 yards off the west shore, there is a large uncharted rock awash on a minus 3-foot tide which we call "Hale Kai (pronounced hah-lay-kie) Rock" after the vessel that grounded here, in 2005. The 2006 edition of *Coast Pilot* suggests that the preferred entrance route is about 30 yards west of the large rock awash at high water (see *Coast Pilot* quote above). Some skippers with local knowledge place the uncharted rock slightly more west than northwest.

[*Editor's Note:* The accompanying diagram shows the ***approximate position*** of the uncharted rock based on the *Coast Pilot* description.]

*Baidarka* has always followed a route close to the far western shore in about 1 fathom. However, several boaters have stated they prefer to pass *between* the large rock at the western end of the reef and the sometimes-marked (with a small float) Hale Kai Rock. A professional charter skipper who frequently uses the bay has seen numerous boats hit this rock; he advises hugging the reef complex on the east side as closely as you safely can in

## A Whale's Tale

*(From the First Mate's Diary, July 1997)*

Réanne Hemingway-Douglass

We were snuggly anchored in Kalinin Bay after a choppy four-hour passage down the coast. Earlier in the day, we had heard a broadcast over Ch 16 asking anyone who had sighted a whale trailing a line to contact the USCG. There were no other details, and it wasn't until our arrival in Sitka that we heard the full story:

Two Sitka men were out fishing in Icy Strait in a 17-foot Boston whaler when they sighted a whale with a crab pot line and buoy wrapped around its tail. Thinking they could just cut the rope and free the whale, they decided to go to its rescue. But as they approached, the line snagged and caught on their prop.

The whale sounded, pulling the boat stern-under and dumping the two men into the icy waters. As the men struggled to stay afloat, the whale and the boat disappeared completely under water.

Suddenly the boat shot up again out of the water, intact, without the whale, without the line.

Fortunately, another boat witnessed the scene and sped to the rescue of the two men. "They were more astonished than anything," we were told. "They might have lost their lives, but that didn't seem to cross their minds."

Whatever happened to the whale, no one knows. Perhaps the poor creature is still out there in the Gulf of Alaska trailing a line behind its tail.

order to stay well clear of the uncharted rock. This route, between the Hale Kai Rock and the reef complex, appears to follow a deeper channel than *Baidarka*'s route. In any case, you should approach this narrowest part of the entrance channel *very carefully*, paying attention to avoid the uncharted rock.

Once you have passed south of these hazards, you enter a wide basin that has ample swinging room for a number of various-sized boats over a flat bottom.

An interesting hiking trail, recently maintained, leads from the southwest end of the bay and heads west to Sea Lion Cove on the outer shore of Kruzof Island via some rugged grizzly country. We have heard varying reports of the trail's difficulty.

Anchor in 4 fathoms over soft black mud and shells with very good holding. *Note:* the south half of the bay shoals to bare.

## **Sinitsin Cove** (Kruzof Island)

Sinitsin Cove, on the north shore of Kruzof Island, is 1.5 miles east of Kalinin Bay.

Chart 17323
Entrance: 57°20.43′ N, 135°44.50′ W

> *Sinitsin Cove . . . 1 mile SE of Sinitsin Island, has deep water, an irregular, rocky bottom; its shores are fringed with ledges. In bad weather the swell rolls heavily into this cove.* (CP)

Sinitsin is used by seiners that want a deep-water anchorage.

## **Sukoi Inlet** (Kruzof and Partofshikof islands)

Sukoi Inlet's north entrance is about 0.8 mile west of Kane Islands.

Chart 17324
North entrance: 57°19.47′ N, 135°41.42′ W
Anchor: 57°16.60′ N, 135°40.50′ W

> *Sukoi Inlet . . . affords good anchorage. At its head it connects at high water by a canoe passage with Krestof Sound. . . . Anchorage may be selected in any place desired, according to depths of water and swinging room required. The best anchorage is about 2.5 miles inside the entrance, opposite a small stream and flat on the W side, in 7 to 10 fathoms. Only small craft should go into the narrow part of the inlet beyond this point.* (CP)

Sukoi Inlet, like Kalinin Bay to the west, is another bombproof anchorage for cruising boats; however, it is 3.5 miles to shallow water, which is a bit of an inconvenience.

Anchor in 6 fathoms over a thin layer of sand and mud over a hard bottom; good holding if your anchor is well set.

## **Neva Strait**

Neva Strait, between Baranof and Partofshikof islands, with Olga Strait, connects Salisbury Sound with Sitka Sound.

Chart 17324 (inset)
Northwest entrance (Scraggy Islands bearing 232°T at 0.34 Nm): 57°20.67′ N, 135°41.82′ W
South entrance (Neva Point Light bearing 081°T at 0.2 Nm): 57°14.02′ N, 135°33.49′ W

> *The strait is narrow throughout and foul and requires careful piloting especially in Whitestone Narrows. . . . The flood current sets generally S and ebb current N. The current velocity is about 1.4 knots.* (CP)

Neva Strait, the route to Sitka, is a scenic and busy passage. Be on the lookout for fast-moving vessels, especially ferries, since the passage is too narrow to pass safely, particularly in foul weather or poor visibility. The buoy colors read from south to north in Neva Strait, so keep the red markers to port on a southbound transit, and to starboard on a northbound tran-

Linda Lewis

*The fast ferry* Fairweather *pops out of the north end of Neva Strait.*

sit. *Note: Baidarka's* flux-gate compass has registered a 3-degree or more shift in Neva Strait off Zeal Point, requiring a correction of about 5 degrees.

## Gilmer Cove (Neva Strait)

Gilmer Cove is 1.2 miles northwest of Entrance Island.

Chart 17324
Entrance: 57°18.19′ N, 135°38.28′ W
Anchor: 57°18.06′ N, 135°38.22′ W

> *Gilmer Cove is . . . 250 yards long by 75 yards wide, with a flat 150 yards wide at the head, and is a fit anchorage only for small craft in 7 fathoms.* (CP)

Gilmer Cove is a tiny cove on the west shore of Neva Strait, 1.5 miles southeast of Kane Islands Light. Although just large enough for one or two boats, with limited swinging room, the cove does provide shelter from southeast winds and chop. The bottom of the cove is steep-to until near its head, where it begins to shallow. We find Gilmer to be a good temporary lunch stop.

Anchor in 6 fathoms over sand, gravel and newspaper kelp; fair holding with a well-set anchor.

## St. John Baptist Bay (Baranof Island)

St. John Baptist Bay is east of Zeal Point and 2.5 miles southeast of Kane Islands.

Chart 17324
Entrance: 57°17.79′ N, 135°36.25′ W
Anchor: 57°17.16′ N, 135°33.68′ W

> *A timbered islet is 200 yards off the SW shore and 0.6 mile SE of Entrance Island . . . S of the islet the bight is clear, furnishing good anchorage for small craft in 7 fathoms.*
>
> [St. John Baptist Bay] *is open to the sea through Salisbury Sound. . . . In SE weather the bay is said to be subject to severe williwaws that make the anchorages undesirable.* (CP)

St. John Baptist Bay, strategically located at the north end of Neva Strait, provides good swinging room for larger boats.

Anchor in 10 fathoms over a soft bottom.

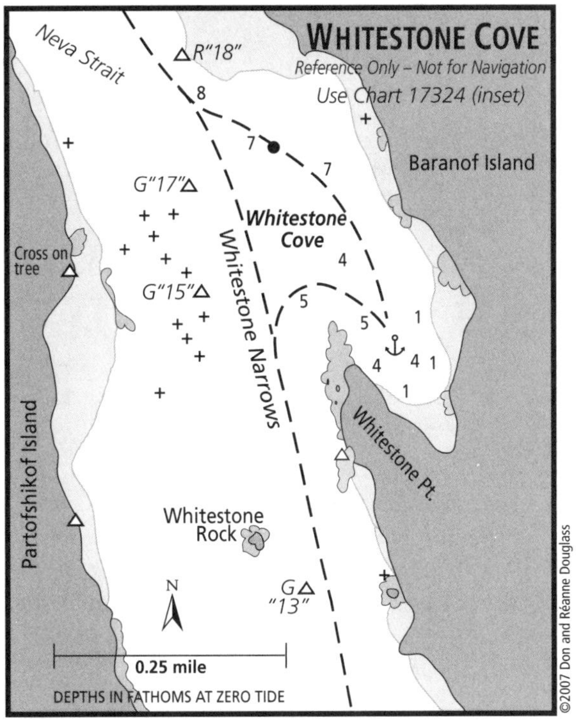


## Whitestone Cove (Baranof Island)

Whitestone Cove is on the east side of Neva Strait, near the south entrance.

Chart 17324 (inset)
Entrance: 57°14.95′ N, 135°33.86′ W
Anchor: 57°14.76′ N, 135°33.64′ W

> *Whitestone Cove . . . is a good anchorage with depths from 5 to 7 fathoms.* (CP)

Whitestone Cove is a small bight that provides temporary anchorage at its head. Although it is partially out of the current and the wake of passing vessels, it can hold just one or two small vessels. The cove gives good protection from southeast winds. Water temperatures range in the high forties here and, in summer, the cove is filled with sea nettles.

Anchor deep in the cove in 4 fathoms over mud, shells and grass with good holding.

## Nakwasina Passage

Nakwasina Passage separates the north side of Halleck Island from Baranof Island.

Chart 17324
West entrance: 57°14.14′ N, 135°31.30′ W
East entrance: 57°14.70′ N, 135°22.80′ W

Jim Kyle

*These Pigeon Guillemots have bright red-orange feet.*

> *The navigable channel is winding and constricted in places to 30 yards by extensive flats. The limits of the channel are distinguishable at low water. The controlling depth in the best channel is about 10 feet; this passage is suitable only for small craft.* (CP)

## Olga Strait

Olga Strait separates Halleck and Krestof islands.

Chart 17324
Northwest entrance (Olga Point Light bearing 217°T at 0.31 Nm): 57°13.96′ N, 135°31.83′ W
Southeast entrance: 57°10.76′ N, 135°26.83′ W

> *Olga Strait . . . forms a part of the inside route from Sitka to Salisbury Sound. It is in general clear, with a controlling depth of 4 fathoms in midchannel. . . . The current sets NW on the flood and SE on the ebb. . . .* (CP)

Navigational aids mark Middle Shoal in the center of Olga Strait.

## Nakwasina Sound, Beehive Island Cove

Nakwasina Sound extends from the south entrance of Olga Strait and connects with Nakwasina Passage.

Chart 17324
South entrance (Nakwasina Sound): 57°10.45′ N, 135°25.40′ W
Entrance (Beehive Island Cove): 57°10.97′ N, 135°26.26′ W
Anchor (Beehive Island Cove): 57°11.17′ N, 135°26.30′ W

> *The sound is contracted at its S end to about 0.2 mile by Crosswise Islands and Beehive Island. Small vessels can anchor in the cove W of Beehive Island in 5 to 6 fathoms.* (CP)

Beehive Island Cove is tiny and landlocked, just large enough for one or two small craft to anchor north of Krugloi Point.

Anchor in 6 fathoms with limited swinging room.

## Krestof Sound

Krestof Sound connects Neva Strait, through Hayward Strait, with Sitka Sound.

Chart 17324
North entrance (Partof Point bearing 282°T at 0.24 Nm): 57°13.61′ N, 135°33.70′ W
Northwest entrance (Sukoi Inlet): 57°14.74′ N, 135°38.66′ W
South entrance (meets Hayward Strait, West and East channels): 57°09.25′ N, 135°33.80′ W

> *At its NW end* [Krestof Sound] *connects by a high-water passage with Sukoi Inlet. At its S end the sound is filled by Magoun Islands, with a narrow channel E and W of them and a boat channel through them.* (CP)

Krestof Sound is a small inland "sea," bounded by Kruzof Island on the west, Partofshikof Island on the north and Krestof Island on the east. It is entirely landlocked, offering very good shelter, but it is seldom visited. It is an interesting place to explore by small craft. The shore is free of signs of stress or logs. While most of the sound is unobstructed, the shores on the south end have numerous rocks and shoals that create navigational challenges, *so proceed slowly.* DeGroff Bay and Magoun Islands are our favorites for secluded anchorages.

## Mud Bay (Krestof Sound)

Mud Bay is west of the Magoun Islands.

Chart 17324
Position: 57°10.68′ N, 135°36.72′ W

> *A better anchorage* [than Port Krestof] *can be had in Mud Bay, . . . taking care to avoid the 3-foot shoal about 130 yards off the SE point of the bay. Two private mooring buoys are in Mud Bay.* (CP)

Good protection from southerly weather can be found in Mud Bay near the southern buoy against the west shore, or off the cabin on the north shore near the trailhead to Shelikof Bay. The trail, which is about 5 miles long, heads due west to the north side of Shelikof Bay.

## Port Krestof (Krestof Sound)

Port Krestof is on the south side of West Channel.

Chart 17324
Anchor: 57°09.14′ N, 135°35.30′ W

> *Port Krestof is a broad bight . . . ; an anchorage can be had in 6 to 13 fathoms, taking care at high water not to get on the flat that fills the S end of the port to a distance of about 0.5 mile out to an islet 12 feet high.* (CP)

We have found satisfactory anchorage in Port Krestof off the extensive drying mud flat. The current here is moderate and the pleasant, well-protected area is fun to explore by kayak.

A more sheltered anchorage with little or no current can be found in De Groff Bay.

Anchor in 4 to 6 fathoms over sand and mud with shells and fair-to-good holding. (Be advised that a professional skipper who anchors here frequently reports also finding numerous areas that have a rocky bottom.)

## West Channel (Krestof Sound)

West Channel is between Kruzof Island and the Magoun Islands.

Chart 17324
East entrance: 57°09.25′ N, 135°33.80′ W
North entrance: 57°09.61′ N, 135°35.44′ W

> *West Channel should not be attempted except by small craft.* (CP)

Southwest swell quickly dies down in West Channel north of Brown Point. In this area, numerous, small coves provide anchor sites. West Channel is easily transited by cruising boats by staying mid-channel in about a 4- to 13-fathom fairway, avoiding rocks along both shores.

## East Channel (Krestof Sound)

East Channel is between Krestof Island and the Magoun Islands.

Chart 17324
North entrance (mid-channel between Brady and Mills islands): 57°11.12′ N, 135°33.76′ W
South entrance: 57°09.25′ N, 135°33.80′ W

> *East Channel is clear in midchannel; the dangers are shown on the chart.* (CP)

East Channel, which leads into DeGroff Bay, is the shortest route between Krestof Sound and Sitka Sound. Good anchorage can be found on the southeast side of the Magoun Island complex or in the central bay.

Avoid the charted shoals, especially during spring tides when strong currents are flowing.

## De Groff Bay (Krestof Island)

De Groff Bay is northeast of Magoun Islands.

Chart 17324
Entrance: 57°10.42′ N, 135°32.66′ W
Anchor: 57°11.05′ N, 135°31.33′ W

> [De Groff Bay's] *entrance is narrow, has a depth of 3-3/4 fathoms, is overgrown with kelp, and should only be attempted by small craft.* (CP)

De Groff Bay is a special place where you find solitude and lots of wildlife. Its entrance is narrow and intricate, requiring skillful navigation near slack water. Favor the west shore at the inner narrows. Inside, it is totally landlocked and protected from all weather. There is plenty of swinging room for many boats, although we've never seen another vessel here. Avoid the kelp patches, which may hide rocks. Temporary anchorage might be found in the basin between the narrows, but the bottom may be rocky there.

Anchor in 3 to 5 fathoms over soft mud with good holding.

## Hayward Strait

Hayward Strait, at the south end of Krestof Sound, separates Krestof and Kruzof islands.

Chart 17324
South entrance: 57°08.31′ N, 135°32.25′ W
North entrance: 57°09.25′ N, 135°33.80′ W

*Hayward Strait, connecting East Channel with Sitka Sound, has a good channel through it, but the shores are fringed with rocks and reefs, especially at its S entrance.* (CP)

Hayward Strait connects Sitka sound to Krestof Sound. Freds Creek, where there is a U.S. Forest Service cabin, located 0.5 mile south of Point Brown.

## **Promisla Bay** (Krestof Island)

Promisla Bay is 7.3 miles northwest of Sitka.

Chart 17324
Position: 57°09.28′ N, 135°31.22′ W

*The depths in the bay are 15 to 21 fathoms, and a fair anchorage can probably be had near its head in 16 fathoms, mud bottom, with good protection in almost any weather.* (CP)

## **Eastern Bay** (Krestof Island)

Eastern Bay is 7 miles northwest of Sitka.

Chart 17324
Position: 57°09.80′ N, 135°28.30′ W

Eastern Bay is sheltered by Siginaka Islands, which can be explored by kayak. Anchorage can be found in shallow water close to shore.

## **Katlian Bay, Cedar and Mosquito Coves** (Baranof Island)

Katlian Bay is 5 miles north of Sitka.

Chart 17324
Entrance (Cedar Cove): 57°10.90′ N, 135°21.06′ W
Position (Mosquito Cove): 57°08.60′ N, 135°22.44′ W

*At 2.5 miles within the entrance to the bay an arm extends NW; fair anchorage can be had in this arm NW of the group of islands on the N side in 11 to 20 fathoms, and very small vessels can anchor in Cedar Cove, the narrow part at the head of this arm, in 4-1/4 to 7 fathoms.* (CP)

Katlian Bay has been used by the logging industry and, at this time, is of little interest to pleasure craft.

## **Starrigavan Bay** (Baranof Island)

Starrigavan Bay is 4.5 miles north of Sitka.

Chart 17324
Position: 57°08.04′ N, 135°22.52′ W

*"Old Sitka," now a State Historical Monument, is on the point dividing the two coves on the E side of the bay. The N cove is filled by a flat, and a rock that bares is 150 yards off the N shore W of the end of the flat. The anchorage is abreast the S cove, about 400 yards from shore, in 18 to 20 fathoms, soft bottom. W winds and some sea have a fair sweep into this bay.* (CP)

The Alaska State Ferry terminal is located on the south shore of Starrigavan Bay.

## **Whiting Harbor** (Japonski Island)

Whiting Harbor is 0.5 mile west of Sitka Harbor.

Chart 17327
North entrance: 57°03.47′ N, 135°22.49′ W
West entrance: 57°03.21′ N, 135°23.07′ W
Anchor (southeast corner): 57°02.75′ N, 135°22.08′ W

*Whiting Harbor . . . affords anchorage in about 12 fathoms, mud bottom. . . . This anchorage is exposed to W and NW winds and swells and is seldom used, because most vessels prefer the Eastern Anchorage at Sitka.* (CP)

If a major southerly blow is expected or if you arrive at night after the harbormaster's office

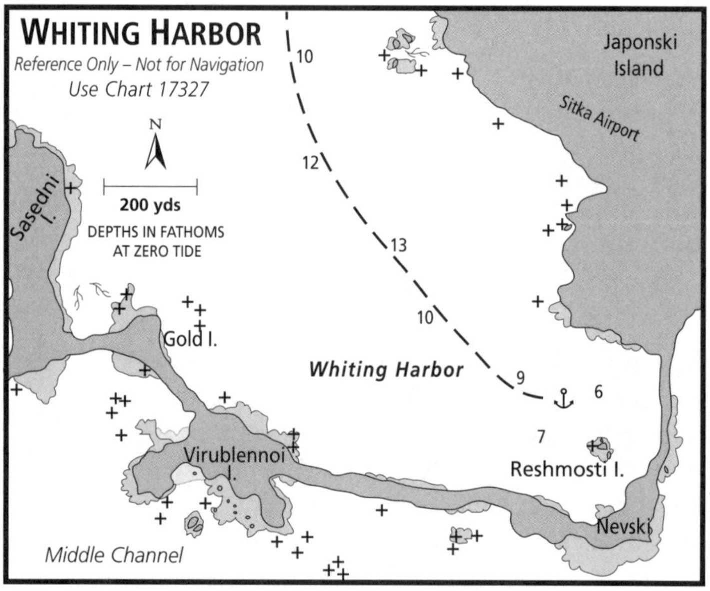

## Unexpected Creatures

Linda Lewis—Journal Notes—M/V *Royal Sounder*

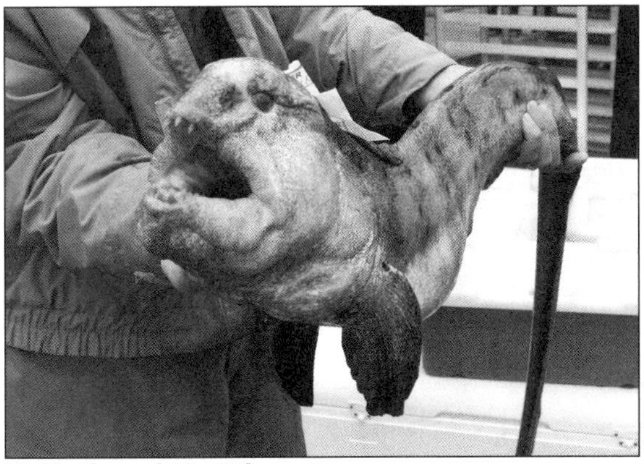
Linda Lewis

*Wolf eel caught in Sitka waters*

David Parker

*Halibut caught in crab trap*

The most unexpected creature sightings can happen when you're cruising in Southeast Alaska.

This wolf eel was caught in the waters near Sitka. About six feet long, this creature is my idea of a nightmare in the flesh. However, in Sitka the wolf eel is considered a prize catch and this one was destined for someone's fireplace wall. Another unexpected creature sighting occurred in Glacier Bay when I pulled the crab trap up and saw two eyes on the same side of a head staring up at me. Now how did that halibut manage to get into my crab trap?

On one of our hikes I looked down into the crystal clear streams and saw a carpet of salmon literally at arm's length. And somewhere during our trip we spotted a hapless deer in the water frantically trying to avoid the wakes of not just one, but two boats. The deer went in circles for a while, then he managed to swim back the way he had come and find land safely.

Seeing the unexpected is part of the gift of cruising in these waters.

David Parker

*A carpet of salmon at arm's length*

Linda Lewis

*Deer trying to avoid wakes of two boats. A near miss.*

has closed, Whiting Harbor is a good choice for anchoring. You can select your site according to the chop and depth. The site shown in the diagram is good for southerly winds. Transient moorage is open after hours at the south floating breakwater in Eliason Harbor.

Anchor in about 8 fathoms over a mixed bottom with fair-to-good holding. Be sure to check that your anchor is well set, since parts of the bottom are rocky.

## **Sitka** (Baranof Island)

Sitka is on the east side of Sitka Sound.

Chart 17327

West entrance (at breakwaters): 57°03.74′ N, 135°21.96′ W

*Sitka, the site of an early Russian settlement and once the capital of Alaska, is a major fishing port* [and] . . . *the main distribution point for the settlements in the NW section of SE Alaska.*

*The city operates* [five] *small-boat basins* [and two grids]. [The] *harbormaster with an office at* [Old Thomsen Harbor] *enforces a 3-knot speed limit and a no-wake law in the city basins and a 5-knot speed limit in the main harbor channel makes berth assignments in the city basins, and controls the use of the grids. The harbormaster can be contacted on VHF-FM channel 16 (156.80 MHz) and by telephone (907-747-3439).* (CP)

[*Editor's Note:* The *Coast Pilot* has excellent color photographs of the Sitka Harbor from several different viewpoints.]

Réanne Hemingway-Douglass

*The Sitka Pioneers' Home*

Sitka (Tlingit for "by the sea") is perhaps the most popular of Southeast Alaska destinations. Its lovely setting, native culture, Russian history, museums and shops draw thousands of tourists who arrive by air, small cruise ships or pleasure craft. The town of 8,800, whose economy thrives on tourism, lost one of its major employers when its large pulp mill closed down in 1997.

Réanne Hemingway-Douglass

*Sitka Harbor looking north*

Eliason Harbor (formerly known as New Thomsen Harbor) is the northernmost harbor inside the Rubblemound Breakwater and the designated harbor for transient pleasure-craft vessels. (In late 2006, New Thomsen Harbor was renamed after Senator Richard I. Eliason Sr. to honor the former state senator and first Alaskan to be nominated to the Wild Salmon Hall of Fame.) The harbor personnel do an excellent job of finding moorage for

# Sitka

Don Douglass & Réanne Hemingway-Douglass

Sitka's natural beauty will captivate you even before you arrive. You'll take in views of jagged peaks topped with snow, forested islands, many with homes and docks, and fishing boats going to and fro in Sitka Sound.

When you dock you'll notice Sitka's Russian influence. Sitka was the center of the fur trade and home base to the Russian-American Company in the nineteenth century. It was the first capital of territorial Alaska until the honor was ceded to Juneau in 1906. Its current population is just under 8,900 people.

A walk around downtown gives you shopping opportunities galore, plus a view of important historical sites. Most prominent is St. Michael's Cathedral with its wealth of icons, many of which were saved from a 1966 fire that destroyed the original structure built in the 1840s. It's still an active Russian Orthodox Church. At the corner of Lincoln and Katlian Streets, you'll find the stately Pioneers' Home, and nearby is the Russian Cemetery and Block House. Walking the opposite direction on Lincoln, you'll soon arrive at the restored 1843 Russian Bishop's House, a National Historic Landmark.

Further out is the 100-acre Sitka National Historical Park on the site of the 1804 battle between Russians and Kiksadi. Now it provides a tranquil path through towering trees and past Tlingit and Haida totems, with views of the bay peeking through the foliage. Inside you can talk to local artists as they carve wooden masks or craft silver jewelry.

Walking back to town, stop in the Sheldon Jackson Museum, an absolute gem. It is named for its founder, a Presbyterian missionary who came to Sitka in 1877. He collected artifacts from many Alaskan cultures and built the concrete octagonal building to house them in 1885-87. You'll see well-lit displays of masks, watercraft and clothing, as well as argillite and ivory carvings. Allow plenty of time to slide open all of the exhibit drawers, where you'll find hundreds more tiny treasures.

Learn more about Sitka's history at the Isabel Miller Museum in Harrigan Centennial Hall at Crescent Harbor.

Cultural opportunities include the New Archangel Dancers who perform Russian folk dances at Harrigan Centennial Hall and native Naa Kahidi dancers appearing at the Sheet'ka Kwaan Naa Kahidi Community House. The annual Sitka Music Festival, featuring classical performers from around the world, is held each June.

Réanne Hemingway-Douglass

*St. Michael's Cathedral, Russian Orthodox Church, Sitka*

In the surrounding forests and waters you can bike, hike, kayak, snorkel and fish. If up-close wildlife interests you, visit the Alaska Raptor Center, which cares for injured eagles, hawks, owls and other birds. Then learn about marine life at the Sheldon Jackson Aquarium. Or, even better, take an excursion boat to the offshore St. Lazaria Island NWR, whose twisted volcanic cliffs harbor hundreds of puffins, murres and petrels.

Before you leave Sitka, climb to the top of Castle Hill to enjoy the views of the harbor and city. Think about how different Alaska, the U.S. and world history would have been if Russia had not decided to sell this chunk of land. You are standing right where the transfer took place in a ceremony on October 18, 1867.

For visitor information contact the Sitka Convention & Visitors Bureau, located in the Lahmeyer Building in downtown Sitka (tel.: 907.747.5940 www.sitka.org) or the harbormaster (tel.: 907.747.3439 or VHF Ch 16).

pleasure craft during the summer season, but accommodations are made on a first-come, first-served basis; call on VHF Ch 16, then switch to Ch 14 as you enter the Rubblemound Breakwater. Vessels of 100 feet or more are asked to call ahead for information about accommodations. Telephone the harbormaster's office at 907.747.3439. Summer office hours are 0700 to 1800; assignments may be made until 2330 each night in high season. After-hours transients may moor to the south floating breakwater.

Be forewarned that you may have to move your vessel several times during your stay if a reserved stall owner returns. Eliason has water and 30-amp power on the docks. (There are some 50-amp and a few 3-phase stalls.) Showers and restrooms are located above the covered harbor gangway. The South Floating Breakwater (see diagram) has no electricity.

In 2007, renovations were underway in (Old) Thomsen Harbor, which may eventually have pleasure craft moorage. Moorage in Sealing Cove (see below) is limited to boats of less than 40 feet, and at present the harbor is filled mostly with local vessels.

Many cruise ships visit Sitka during the summer months; however, there are no cruise ship docks in Sitka. The cruise ships approach Sitka through Middle Channel, just south of Sitka, and anchor in the eastern anchorage area off Crescent Bay.

Crescent Harbor (see below), near Sitka's Convention Center, does not have transient moorage. The use of the lightering float in Crescent Harbor, and the float to the west near the bridge, are strictly reserved for use by cruise ships.

All services and supplies are available for pleasure craft. Lakeside Grocery (tel.: 907.747.3317) is a block above the harbormaster's office, and Sea Mart (tel.: 907.747.6266) about two miles north of New Thomsen. (Sea Mart will pay the taxi fare when you buy groceries.) In summer, Chelan Produce Company brings a truck to town several times a month stocked with fresh produce (they station their truck a block above the harbormaster's office)—plan to arrive early for the best choices.

Réanne Hemingway-Douglass

*Propeller work in Sitka*

A self-serve and wash-and-fold laundry is located at 906 Halibut Point Road, just a block uphill from Thomsen Harbor. Diesel, gasoline and propane are available at the Sitka Petro Dock near Eliason Harbor (previously known as New Thomsen Harbor) (tel.: 907.747.8460); diesel and gasoline at Sitka Petro Marine, near the bridge (907.747.3414); Sitka Service Transfer, 321 Lincoln sells propane (tel.: 907.747.3276). For repair service call Halibut Point Marine (tel.: 907.344.4999), located at the north end of Sitka, opposite Old Sitka Rocks. *Note:* Sitka and Ketchikan are the only two towns in Southeast where you can have a propeller repaired.

The center of town is just a 10- to 15- minute walk from Eliason Harbor. Other businesses of interest to cruising boaters are as follows: for nautical supplies, books and charts—Murray Pacific on Katlian Street, two blocks south of the harbor (tel.: 907.747.3171); Sitka electronics, 232 Katlian (tel.: 907.747.6570); Old Harbor Books, 201 Lincoln (tel.: 907.747.8808), which has one of the largest selections of books on Alaska! For boaters staying in Eliason, the U.S. Postal substation on Lincoln, a block east of St. Michael's Cathedral, is closer than the main station.

Réanne Hemingway-Douglass

*Sitka Harbor with airport bridge in background*

We'll leave it to you to find your favorite restaurant. Ask around, since quality varies from year to year and from owner to owner. However, there's everything from continental to Japanese and Chinese and dynamite hamburgers.

## **Eliason Harbor** (Sitka)
## (previously New Thomsen Harbor)

Eliason Harbor is located on the northwest side of Sitka, inside the breakwater.

Chart 17327

West end of floats: 57°03.52′ N, 135°21.47′ W

> [Eliason Harbor, formerly] . . . *New Thomsen Harbor the most northerly basin on the E side of Sitka Harbor, is protected by a floating breakwater. . . . Approximately* [320] *vessels can be accommodated. Transient vessels berth at the breakwater.* (CP)

Eliason Harbor (previously called New Thomsen Harbor) can accommodate up to 320 fishing and pleasure vessels. Moorage is on a first-come, first-served basis, and the harbormaster does an excellent job of making "hot berth" assignments in land-accessible stalls during the summer season. Water and power (30- and 50-amp, as well as some stalls with 3-phase) are available, as are showers. Moorage

Réanne Hemingway-Douglass

*Our editor, Linda Lewis, brings the* Royal Sounder *to the dock at Eliason Harbor in Sitka.*

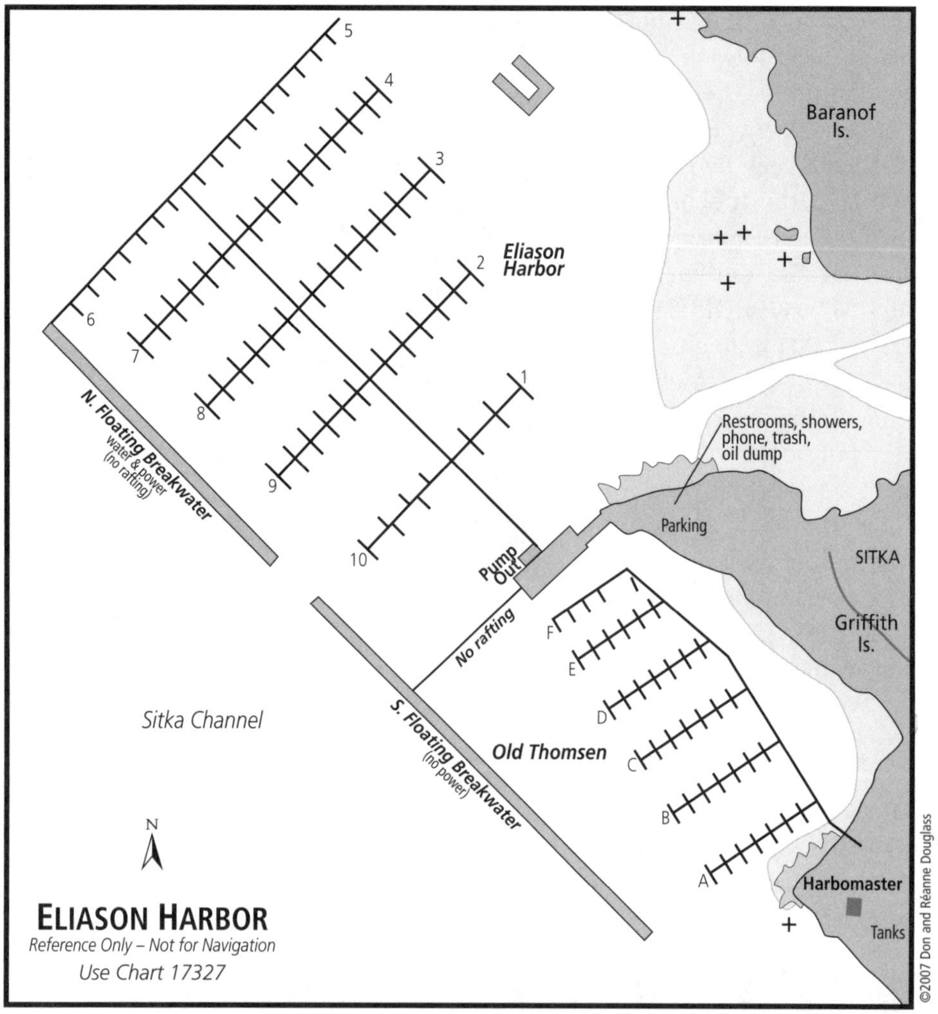


is also available on the North and South Floating breakwaters (water and power on the North Floating Breakwater; no power on the South Floating Breakwater). A pump-out facility is located in Eliason Harbor.

The center of town is about a 10-to-15 minute walk from the harbor; marine supply stores are also located along the waterfront between the harbor and town. Sitka also has a marine ways for vessel haul-out and repair. Call on VHF Ch 16 before you enter the harbor for an assignment. Harbor personnel will then assist you in docking your boat. (See above for services and fuel suppliers.)

Sitka is an extremely popular destination for pleasure craft and moorage can be tight, particularly the week before and the week following the Fourth of July. Plan accordingly!

## Sealing Cove (Japonski Island)

Sealing Cove is 0.5 mile west of the bridge.

Chart 17327

Entrance: 57°02.68′ N, 135°20.59′ W

*A light and daybeacons mark the entrance channel. Transient berths, electricity, water, and a launching ramp are available in the basin.* (CP)

Berthage in Sealing Cove is strictly regu-

*These eagles are in a feeding frenzy near a fish-cleaning station where the waste is being cast onto the beach.*

lated by the harbormaster. As mentioned above, moorage in Sealing Cove is limited to boats of less than 40 feet, and at present the harbor is filled mostly with local vessels.

Réanne Hemingway-Douglass

*Don't try to tie up your dinghy here! This dock at Crescent Harbor is only for use by cruise ship tenders.*

## Crescent Harbor (Sitka)

Crescent Bay Boat Basin is on the east side of Sitka.

Chart 17327
Entrance (boat basin):
57°02.92′ N, 135°19.79′ W

> *The floats can accommodate 413 small craft. Electricity is available, but water can be had only in the summer.* (CP)

Crescent Bay has no moorage for transient vessels and the harbormaster's office tightly controls these restrictions. Use of the lightering floats is strictly reserved for cruise ship tenders.

## Jamestown Bay (Baranof Island)

Jamestown Bay is 1.5 miles east of Sitka.

Chart 17327
Entrance: 57°02.49′ N, 135°17.87′ W
Anchor (southeast): 57°02.48′ N, 135°17.14′ W

> *Jamestown Bay . . . affords anchorage in 9 to 12 fathoms, mud bottom, about 400 yards offshore and 300 yards W of the rocks, awash at high water, in the NE part of the bay.* (CP)

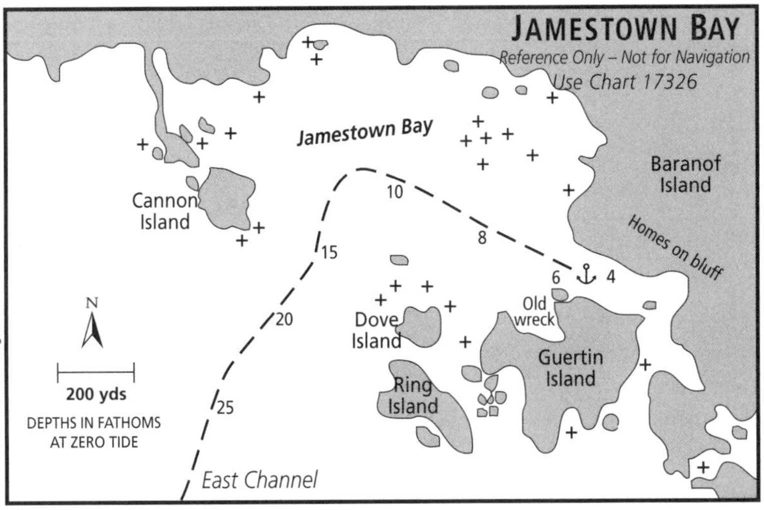



Some boats anchor in Jamestown Bay and commute the 2 miles to Sitka. The bay offers good protection from southerly storms in several of its small coves.

Anchor in about 4 fathoms over mud and sand with fair-to-good holding.

# OUTER PASSAGE SOUTH OF SITKA

*Note:* Due to potential exposure to the Gulf of Alaska weather and the lack of well-documented cruising-boat anchorages, the coastline south of Sitka along the west coast of Baranof Island has been essentially ignored. Most pleasure craft departing Sitka use Peril Strait for destinations east or south. In settled weather, however, the Outer Passage south of Sitka offers great exploring and a lot of wonderful surprises! This section of the coast is documented in Chapter 8.

Réanne Hemingway-Douglass

*The Outer Passage continues south from Sitka.*

## WEST COAST OF KRUZOF ISLAND

Charts 17325, 17320

> *There are no hidden outlying dangers until Cape Georgiana is reached. Submerged rocks do exist in the bays and bights along this coast. The 100-fathom curve is 8 miles from shore abreast Cape Edgecumbe, 12 miles abreast Cape Georgiana. . . .*
>
> *The shore from Cape Edgecumbe to Neva Bay rises in a precipitous cliff of brown lava and forms a prominent landmark. Numerous large caves or blowholes are to be seen in this lava cliff. The shore between Cape Edgecumbe and Beaver Point is fringed with ledges . . . and shoal water, marked by thick kelp. . . .* (CP)

### **Sealion Cove** (Kruzof Island)

Sealion Cove is 2 miles southeast of Cape Georgiana.

Chart 17325
Entrance: 57°18.26′ N, 135°51.49′ W

> *A sand beach at the head is almost 1 mile long. A small peninsula forms its S point.* (CP)

Sealion Cove has one of the most beautiful sandy beaches along the outer coast. Although the cove is exposed to northwest swells that crash onto its long, shallow beach, in stable, calm weather it's worth making a temporary stop here. However, be extremely careful to pick the proper tide level if you take a dinghy to shore or you may find yourself stranded for hours. We do not recommend anchoring overnight in Sealion Cove. Sea lions like this cove as they commute back and forth from the nearby Sealion Islands.

A fairly strenuous trail leads east from the cove to Kalinan Bay. Most hikers make a round-trip from the east side of Kruzof in order to leave their vessel in sheltered water. This trail passes through serious bear country, so be prepared if you attempt the trail.

### **Gilmer Bay** (Kruzof Island)

Gilmer Bay is 13 miles north of Cape Edgecumbe.

Chart 17325
Entrance: 57°12.91′ N, 135°50.35′ W
Anchor (Reef Cove): 57°13.83′ N, 135°48.72′ W
Anchor (NE of Reef Cove): 57°14.15′ N, 135°48.31′ W
Anchor (upper inlet): 57°15.17′ N, 135°48.27′ W
Anchor (Gilmer Cove): 57°18.06′ N, 135°38.22′ W

> *About 1 mile inside Point Amelia the bay contracts to 0.6 mile wide; it then expands to 1 mile, and terminates in a narrow arm.* (CP)

The shoreline of Gilmer Bay is surrounded by peaks that rise to 2,300 feet whose flanks hold steep-sided granite cliffs and ledges with many avalanche areas. Several sites in the bay can be used for anchoring, depending on the weather.

The site we call "Reef Cove" is open to northwest chop and whitecaps that blow into the cove, but it is protected from the southeast. A pinnacle rock, located at 57°12.05'N, 135°49.98'W and marked on the chart as 7 fathoms, is actually 2.4 fathoms.

The site northeast of Reef Cove does not receive chop from the northwest and is preferable in northwesterlies. Although it may also be acceptable in southeast weather, it is open to the southwest and should be avoided in weather from that quadrant.

The upper inlet appears not to be subject to northerly winds; the prevailing northwest winds curl into the inlet, but die out at its head. Shore landing can be made on a small beach south of the stream that flows into the northernmost part of the inlet.

The last site, Gilmer Cove, is good in southeasterly weather. The cove is steep-to, but anchorage can be found in the middle in about 6 fathoms, slightly favoring the west shore.

Visibility through the water is good at all sites.

Anchor (Reef Cove) in about 4 fathoms over hard sand and some kelp; fair-to-good holding.

Réanne Hemingway-Douglass

*Goleta Cove*

Anchor (NE of Reef Cove) in 4 fathoms over hard sand with stone and some kelp; fair-to-good holding.

Anchor (upper inlet) in 7 fathoms over brown sand and mud; good holding.

Anchor (Gilmer Cove) in 6-8 fathoms over thin sand, gravel and newspaper kelp; fair holding with a well-set anchor.

## **Shelikof Bay** (Kruzof Island)

Shelikof Bay is 8.5 miles north of Cape Edgecumbe.

**Chart 17325**
**Entrance: 57°08.54′ N, 135°49.74′ W**

> *Shelikof Bay, with depths ranging from 10 to 20 fathoms, is open W, and is not recommended as an anchorage.* (CP)

Shelikof Bay offers good anchoring in Goleta and Cuvacan coves. Goleta is popular with local fishing boats. Cruising boats without local knowledge should reconnoiter by dinghy before attempting to enter either cove.

## **Goleta Cove** (Shelikof Bay)

Goleta Cove, on the north side of Shelikof Bay, is 1.1 miles east of Point Mary.

**Chart 17325**
**Entrance: 57°10.11′ N, 135°47.82′ W**
**Anchor: 57°10.32′ N, 135°47.76′ W**

> [Goleta Cove] *affords protected anchorage for small craft and is much used by local fishermen. . . . To enter, pass very close W of the large bare rock and E of the rock that bares at half tide.* (CP)

Goleta Cove has a very narrow, shallow entrance. Entry should be made to the west of the islet that has about six trees and east of a rock that is awash on a 6-foot tide. Once past the hazards, the cove opens to a flat sandy bottom that can hold more than a half-dozen vessels.

Anchor in about 3 fathoms near the center of the cove over sand with fair-to-good holding.

## **Cuvacan Cove** (Shelikof Bay)

Cuvacan Cove, on the north side of Shelikof Bay, is 1.6 miles east of Point Mary.

**Chart 17325**
**Entrance: 57°09.68′ N, 135°46.70′ W**
**Anchor: 57°10.16′ N, 135°46.88′ W**

> *Small vessels can find partially protected anchorage in the bight called Cuvacan Cove . . . east of a group of islands. . . . To enter the cove, pass S and E of the group of islands and anchor in 3 to 4 fathoms, sand bottom.* (CP)

Cuvacan Cove offers good protection inside the northernmost islet of a series of islets and reefs. However, it has a very tricky entrance and should be entered only with local knowledge or by reconnoitering by dinghy first.

Anchor in 3 fathoms over sand with fair holding.

## **Port Mary** (Shelikof Bay)

Port Mary is at the head of Shelikof Bay.

Chart 17325
Entrance: 57°08.81′ N, 135°45.70′ W
Anchor: 57°08.78′ N, 135°44.53′ W

> *Port Mary . . . has general depths of 3 to 5 fathoms except at its N end where it is shoaler. The only known danger in Port Mary is a rock awash 300 yards off the SE shore and 0.7 mile NE of the S entrance point. Small craft can find protected anchorage in S weather in the small bight, with a high rock in its center, on the SE side of the port.* (CP)

Port Mary is open to the west and southwest, but can be used as an anchorage in winds with an easterly component. A series of islets on the northwest side of the cove offer some protection from northwesterly swells. The coastline along this stretch is full of rocky outcroppings and sea caves, but the anchorage has a fairly flat, wide bottom.

Anchor in about 5 fathoms over a hard bottom; fair-to-good holding with a well-set anchor.

Réanne Hemingway-Douglass

*Geologic formations on the west side of the Kruzof Islands*

## **Neva Bay** (Kruzof Island)

Neva Bay is 2.4 miles north of Cape Edgecumbe.

Chart 17325
Entrance: 57°02.28′ N, 135°51.18′ W

Neva Bay is a small indentation guarded by thick kelp beds and we have not found a suitable anchor site.

Ben Kyle

*Mount Edgecumbe on Kruzof Island*

## **Cape Edgecumbe Light** (Kruzof Island)

Cape Edgecumbe is the southwest tip of Kruzof Island.

Chart 17325
Position (Light bearing 050°T at 0.50 Nm): 56°59.57′ N, 135°52.16′ W

> *Mount Edgecumbe . . . is the prominent landmark for Sitka Sound. From any point seaward, it is easily distinguished by its isolated position, its flat top, its peculiar streaked appearance, and its reddishness. The upper part is a bare volcanic cone, usually snow-covered.* (CP)

Mount Edgecumbe is 4.7 miles northeast of Cape Edgecumbe

Light at the northwest corner of Sitka Sound.

*The St. Lazaria Islands are west of Sitka—just off the south end of Kruzof Island.*

## PERIL STRAIT (West to East)

Peril Strait, which connects Salisbury Sound to Chatham Strait, separates Chichagof Island from Baranof Island.

Chart 17320
West entrance (Kakul Rock Light bearing 127°T at 0.23 Nm): 57°21.85′ N, 135°42.22′ W
East entrance (Morris Reef Buoy bearing 036°T at 0.9 Nm): 57°27.02′ N, 134°49.47′ W

> *Peril Strait is important as affording a frequently used passage from Salisbury Sound, and the waters S to Chatham Strait. Its total length is about 39 miles.* (CP)

Peril Strait is used by essentially all vessels that navigate to and from Sitka, so careful piloting is critical at all times. Strong current reacting with the wind creates large "square" waves, especially during southeast gales that blow through Peril Strait from east to west. Several coves along the south side of the strait afford good shelter.

### Kakul Narrows (Peril Strait)

Kakul Narrows forms the entrance to Peril Strait from Salisbury Sound.

Chart 17323
South entrance (Kakul Rock Light bearing 127°T at 0.23 Nm): 57°21.85′ N, 135°42.22′ W
North entrance (Channel Rocks Light bearing 152°T at 0.11 Nm): 57°22.52′ N, 135°41.09′ W

> *The narrows are deep, the dangers are marked by aids, and they are easily navigated.* (CP)

### Salmonberry Cove (Chichagof Island)

Salmonberry Cove is on the northwest side of Kakul Narrows.

Chart 17323
Position: 57°22.36′ N, 135°42.04′ W

> *Salmonberry Cove is a small bight . . . where small craft can find indifferent and partially protected anchorage.* (CP)

Salmonberry Cove is exposed to traffic wake and southerly chop.

### Louise Cove (Baranof Island)

Louise Cove is east of Kakul Narrows.

Chart 17323
Entrance: 57°22.14′ N, 135°40.06′ W

Louise Cove is an open bight too deep for convenient anchorage.

### Bradshaw Cove (Chichagof Island)

Bradshaw Cove is 0.5 mile north of Channel Rock Light.

Chart 17323
Entrance: 57°22.98′ N, 135°40.62′ W

Bradshaw Cove, on the north side of Struya Narrows, provides good shelter from north winds, but the cove is not shallow enough to offer convenient anchorage. We suggest you travel 2.5 miles northeast to Schulze Cove, which offers more swinging room.

### Fish Bay (Baranof Island)

Fish Bay is south of Sergius Narrows and extends eastward into Baranof Island.

Chart 17323
Entrance (Haley Rocks bearing 202°T at 0.27 Nm): 57°22.92′ N, 135°37.92′ W

> *Sand and gravel beaches show along the shores at low water, and at its head is a flat nearly 0.5 mile in extent. The easternmost of the Haley Rocks in the entrance are covered 4 feet and they*

*are surrounded by kelp. A rock awash is 250 yards W of Haley Rocks.* (CP)

Because Fish Bay has been used for log storage, we prefer the shelter of Schulze Cove (see below).

## Haley Anchorage (Fish Bay)

Haley Anchorage is 1.2 miles southeast of Fish Point.

Chart 17323
Anchor: 57°22.31′ N, 135°36.74′ W

> *Haley Anchorage, 300 yards from the S shore, has depths of 18 to 20 fathoms, sand bottom, and affords fair shelter in S weather.* (CP)

Haley Anchorage is somewhat protected from south winds and is frequently used by cruising boats to time their transit of Sergius Narrows. Since the anchorage is an open roadstead, we prefer the more protected Schulze Cove on the west side of Piper Island. Avoid Haley Rocks and anchor about 0.25 mile west of Haley Point.

Anchor in 10 fathoms over sand and gravel with poor-to-fair holding.

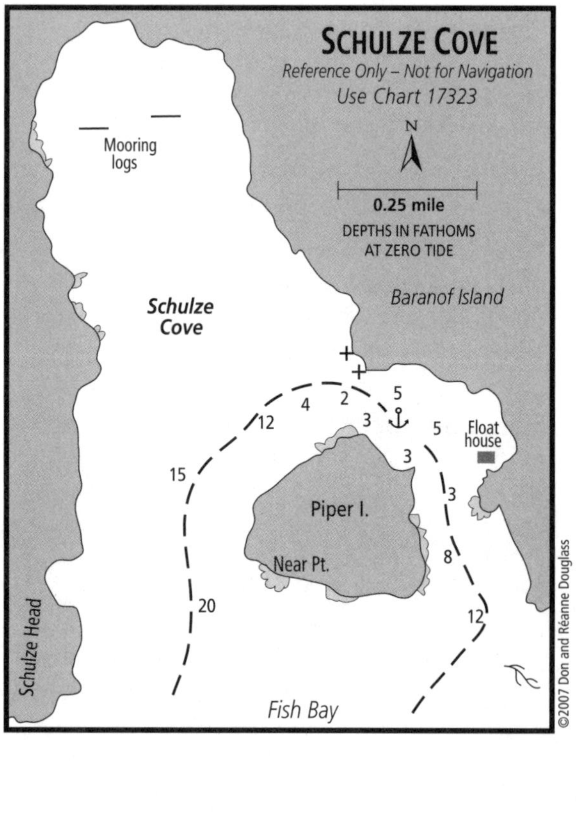


## Schulze Cove, Piper Island (Fish Bay)

Schulze Cove, with Piper Island in its entrance, is on the north side of Fish Bay.

Chart 17323
Entrance: 57°23.07′ N, 135°35.80′ W
Anchor: 57°23.61′ N, 135°35.30′ W

> *Piper Island* [is] *low and wooded . . . the navigable channel, about 0.2 mile wide, is between it and the W shore; the channel on the E side of the island should not be attempted. The only danger in the approach to the cove is Haley Rocks. It is reported that SE winds draw through the cove with considerable force.* (CP)

Our preferred anchorage in Schulze Cove is at the northeast side of Piper Island. It offers very good protection in shallow water with a flat bottom and good swinging room. The channel at the north end of Piper Island is narrow with 2 to 3 fathoms in the fairway. While the site can be subject to heavy northerly winds, it is otherwise quite comfortable and conveniently located close to Sergius Narrows.

Anchor in 4 fathoms over mud and sand with good holding.

## Suloia Bay (Chichagof Island)

Suloia Bay is west of the south entrance to Sergius Narrows.

Chart 17323
Entrance: 57°24.31′ N, 135°40.37′ W

> *Suloia Bay . . . has anchorage for small craft near its head in 18 to 22 fathoms, rocky bottom. The shores are foul near the anchorage, contracting it somewhat, and it is not recommended.* (CP)

Suloia Bay is too deep, exposed and filled with gravel and kelp for convenient anchorage.

## Sergius Narrows (Peril Strait)

Sergius Narrows has a channel 450 feet wide, dredged to a depth of 21 feet.

Chart 17323 (inset)
West entrance: 57°24.29′ N, 135°38.60′ W
East entrance: 57°24.49′ N, 135°37.34′ W

> *Vessels should pass through the narrows only at or near slack water, especially with the large tides, and preferably at high-water slack. At the strength of the current it is not safe for any ves-*

Réanne Hemingway-Douglass

*Orcas charge through Peril Strait near Sergius Narrows.*

> *sel bound either way . . . the maximum velocity* [of the strongest currents] *is 8 to 9 knots on the flood and 8 to 9 knots on the ebb, creating standing waves.*
>
> *With the smallest tides those with local knowledge pass through at all stages of the current.*
>
> *A small-craft channel that passes S of East Francis Rock and Rapids Island is narrow. The channel is used extensively by local fishermen and should only be used with local knowledge.* (CP)

See *Current Tables* for predictions since slack in Sergius Narrows does not coincide with Sitka high and low water. At ebb tide, Sergius Narrows is dangerous, with tide rips and turbulence, except near slack water—which is when you should plan your transit.

The tilt of the channel buoys is an excellent measure of the strength and direction of the current. Avoid transiting the Narrows when a large vessel has given a Sécurité announcement. You may wish to make a Sécurité call yourself on Ch 16 when there is limited visibility or heavy traffic or strong current that might impede steerage. This is especially important at the most restricted part of the channel, which is approximately 145 yards wide for a length of approximately 0.3 nm. Commercial vessels have priority, so you may have to wait your turn. Be mindful of the effect of your wake on other boats.

Small boats frequently use Canoe Pass. However, while the current is less than in Sergius Narrows, it can still be very strong—with tide rips. These conditions can be especially troublesome at the center of Canoe Pass (center: 57°24.12' N, 135°37.92' W), where a sharp turn is required. A Sécurité call on Ch 16 is advised. Avoid East Francis Rock.

## **Launch Cove** (Baranof Island)

Launch Cove lies immediately southeast of Sergius Narrows.

Chart 17323
Anchor: 57°23.93′ N, 135°37.37′ W

To wait for slack water, small craft can find temporary anchorage in the far west corner of Launch Cove. Strong back eddies sometimes enter the cove.

## **Bear Bay and Baby Bear Bay** (Baranof Island)

Bear and Baby Bear bays are northeast of Point Siroi Light.

Chart 17323
Entrance (Bear Bay): 57°25.25′ N, 135°34.93′ W
Anchor (Bear Bay): 57°25.13′ N, 135°34.56′ W
Entrance (Baby Bear Bay): 57°25.87′ N, 135°34.26′ W
Anchor (Baby Bear Bay): 57°26.28′ N, 135°33.50′ W

> *Bear Bay . . . has anchorage for small vessels only, but is convenient if awaiting slack water in Sergius Narrows. Enter in midchannel and anchor with Arthur Island in line with the SW side of Bear Bay Island, bearing N, in 13 to 18 fathoms, soft bottom.* (CP)

Baby Bear Bay, one of the best anchorages in this entire area, is sheltered from all weather and chop. Its shores are lined with beautiful, old, silvery cedar snags. However, its entrance channel is intricate and requires careful navigation. It is not recommended in foul weather or poor visibility.

Because its entrance is narrow and circuitous and full of rocks, caution is required. Pass about 75 feet east of the islet on the north side of Bear Bay Island to avoid the dangerous "shark teeth" rocks to the northeast, which appear to dry on a 6-foot tide in

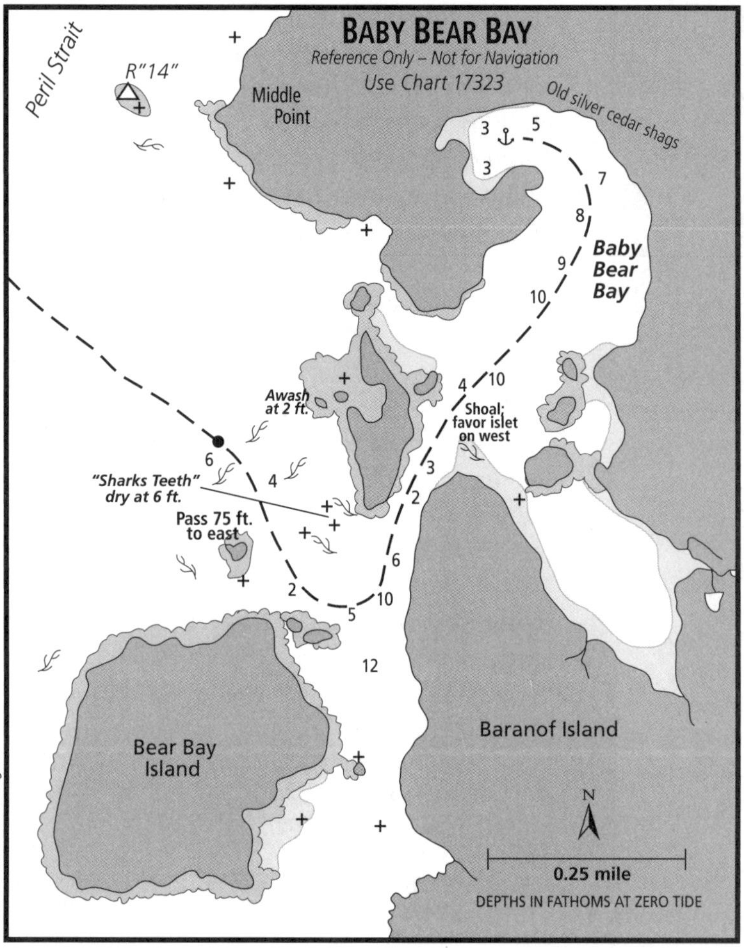




Sitka. Once you are clear of these rocks, turn north-northeast and pass through the narrow, shallow channel between Baranof Island and the unnamed island to port. Stay mid-channel, then favor the west shore as the narrows open up.

Continue to the northeast, and circle into the northwest corner of the small landlocked bay. Nothing man-made is visible from inside, and traffic passes by outside without disturbing Baby Bear's waters—it's completely calm here!

Deep Bay, across the channel, is easier to enter and has more swinging room.

Anchor in 4 fathoms over gravel with fair holding.

## **Deep Bay** (Chichagof Island)

Deep Bay is 2.5 miles n. of Sergius Narrows.

**Chart 17323**
**Entrance: 57°25.78′ N, 135°35.17′ W**
**Anchor: 57°26.76′ N, 135°38.04′ W**

*Deep Bay . . . is a good anchorage. To enter, keep the S side of Big Island aboard at a distance of 100 yards in passing Grasstop Rock, then follow a midchannel course into the bay and anchor 0.2 to 0.8 mile beyond the wooded islet on the N side, W of Big Island in 10 to 12 fathoms, soft bottom.* (CP)

Deep Bay is much easier to enter than Baby Bear Bay but it has more fetch in southeast weather.

Anchor in 8 fathoms over a soft bottom with good holding.

## **Annie's Pocket** (Baranof Island)

Annie's Pocket is 3.5 miles northeast of Sergius Narrows.

**Chart 17323**
**Entrance: 57°26.89′ N, 135°32.95′ W**
**Anchor: 57°26.79′ N, 135°33.01′ W**

"Annie's Pocket" is a small bight out of the traffic and current at the south end of Adams Channel. This is also a good place to watch for a pod of orcas ripping down Rose Channel (west of Rose Islands) at flank speed.

Don named this strategically located bight after his first mate. This is an excellent place to wait for proper conditions at Sergius Narrows, and it makes a good overnight anchorage in stable conditions.

Annie's Pocket is out of the current, sheltered from all winds except northerlies. When there is no wind, you can slowly drift in circles if you don't want to drop your hook while waiting.

Avoid the large shallow sandbar to the east, off the outlet of Range Creek, and anchor off the gray pebble beach.

Anchor in 3 fathoms over sand and shells with good holding.

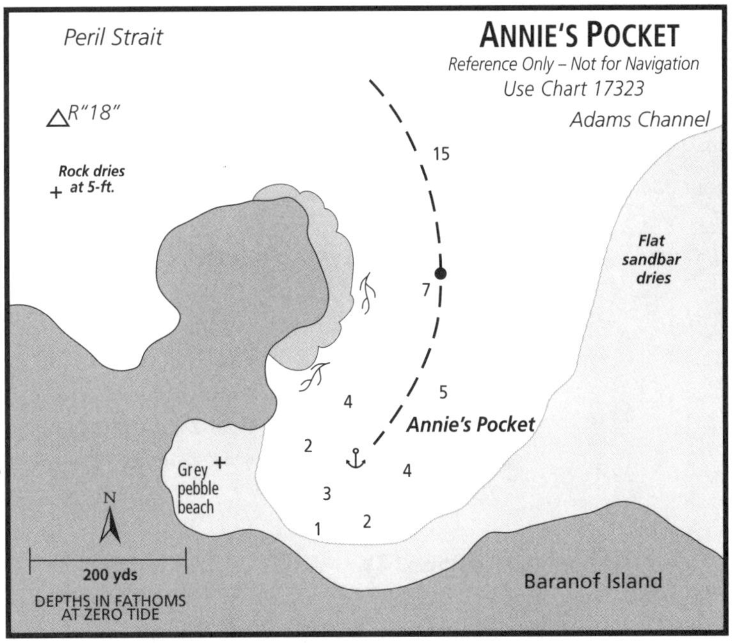

©2007 Don and Réanne Douglass

Don Douglass

*Annie enjoys a sunny afternoon in Peril Strait.*

## Poison Cove (Chichagof Island)

Poison Cove is 1.5 miles northeast of Goose Bay.

Chart 17323
Entrance: 57°31.16′ N, 135°34.41′ W

*Poison Cove has its entrance W of Povorotni Island. Anchorage for small craft is available throughout the cove.* (CP)

## Goose Cove (Baranof Island)

Goose Cove is 6.5 miles northeast of Sergius Narrows.

Chart 17323
Anchor: 57°30.56′ N, 135°32.64′ W

Goose Cove, an open bight subject to some chop but out of the strong current of Sergius Narrows, is protected from southerlies. It is a good place to wait for the proper timing of the narrows if you're westbound. To enter Goose Cove from the west, you can pass southeast of Povorotni Island; the passage has 2 to 3 fathoms with a sandy bottom.

Anchor in 10 fathoms over a soft bottom; fair holding.

## Ushk Bay (Chichagof Island)

Ushk Bay is 2.5 miles southwest of Emmons Island.

Chart 17323
Entrance: 57°33.73′ N, 135°34.38′ W

*Secure anchorage may be found in the bay, in 17 to 22 fathoms, soft bottom. Caution is advised during the periods of reduced visibility.* (CP)

Deep anchorage may be found behind the peninsula near the head of the bay.

## Hoonah Sound (Chichagof Island)

Hoonah Sound is northwest of Peril Strait.

Chart 17323
Position: 57°37.98′ N, 135°32.31′ W
East entrance (North Arm, Pedersen Point Light bearing 251°T at 0.6 Nm): 57°39.77′ N, 135°34.38′ W
East entrance (South Arm, White Cliff Point bearing 023°T at 0.52 Nm): 57°37.83′ N, 135°37.59′ W

*A midchannel reef, baring 5 feet, obstructs the passage between Emmons Island and the Vixen Islands. Ledges and shoal areas fringe the NW shore of Emmons Island. Small craft may make the passage in 3 to 10 fathoms by holding the wooded Vixen Islands close aboard at about 200 yards and staying well clear of the ledge that extends about 150 yards NE of the wooded and rocky northernmost island.*

*North Arm is comparatively clear to within 2 miles of its head. . . .*

*South Arm extends NW about 5.5 miles along the S shore of Moser Island.* (CP)

## **Fick Cove** (Chichagof Island)

Fick Cove is 1 mile within the entrance to the South Arm of Hoonah Sound.

Chart 17323
Entrance: 57°38.17′ N, 135°40.01′ W

*On the S side of the arm, . . . just west of a wooded islet, is Fick Cove; the head and W edge of the cove are shoal. . . . Anchorage with minimum depths of 15 fathoms is found within the cove, E of a line running NW from the cabins on its E edge.* (CP)

## **Patterson Bay and Point Reynard Inlet** (Chichagof Island)

Patterson Bay is the south branch of the South Arm of Hoonah Sound.

Chart 17323
Entrance (Patterson Bay): 57°40.00′ N, 135°42.51′ W
Entrance (Point Reynard Inlet): 57°40.60′ N, 135°42.58′ W

*Patterson Bay . . . has shoals fringing its NW side and a flat at its head. Near its entrance on the N, adjacent to Point Reynard, is a small, NW trending inlet, about 0.3 mile long, that offers anchorage for small craft in 3 to 8 fathoms in its center.* (CP)

## **Douglass Bay** (Patterson Bay)

Douglass Bay is on the north shore of Patterson Bay west of Point Reynard.

Chart 17323
Entrance: 57°40.68′ N, 135°43.68′ W
Anchor: 57°41.10′ N, 135°43.92′ W

*Douglass Bay . . . affords anchorage in 5 to 12 fathoms. To enter, keep the E shore aboard at a distance of 200 yards to avoid the reef to the W, and anchor in the middle of the bay about 0.4 mile from the head. . . .* (CP)

Douglass Bay has a reef that extends to mid-channel from its south shore.

Anchor in 6 fathoms off the drying mud flat over sand, gravel and green mud with fair-to-good holding.

Linda Lewis

*The best crab catch these cruisers ever had was right here, locally known as "Half-tide Neck," on the north tip of Moser Island, at half tide.*

## **Nismeni Cove** (Baranof Island)

Nismeni Cove lies on the east side of Nismeni Point.

Chart 17338
Entrance: 57°33.76′ N, 135°23.66′ W
Anchor: 57°33.59′ N, 135°24.78′ W

*Nismeni Cove . . . affords anchorage for small craft, with protection from S*

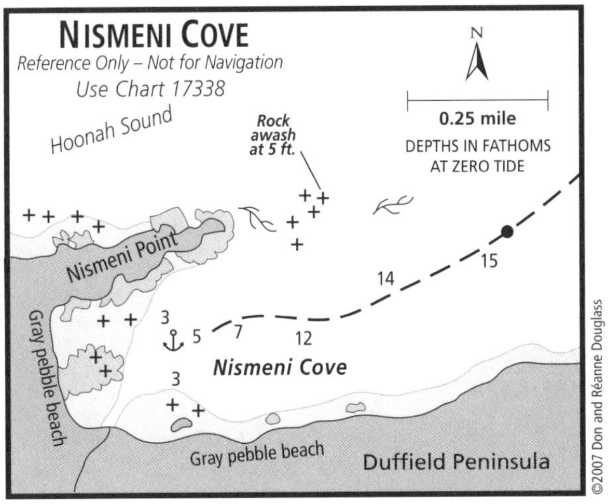


*winds. To enter, keep the S shore aboard at a distance of about 200 yards to avoid the reef off Nismeni Point, and anchor in the middle of the cove about 0.3 mile from the head, in 6 fathoms, fair holding ground.* (CP)

Nismeni Cove offers good protection from westerlies, but it is somewhat exposed to easterlies. You can enter from the west by using the channel south of Otstoia Island, staying 0.3 mile east of Nismeni Point before you turn south into the cove. The reef mentioned above in *Coast Pilot* is awash on about a 5-foot tide and is very dangerous. Chop from southeast winds may enter the cove.

Anchor in 4 fathoms over a mixed sand bottom with good holding.

## **Rodman Bay** (Baranof Island)

Rodman Bay is 6 miles southeast of Nismeni Point.

Chart 17338
Entrance (Rodman buoy G"1" bearing 105°T at 0.39 Nm): 57°29.87′ N, 135°15.08′ W
Anchor: 57°26.91′ N, 135°23.76′ W

*Rodman Bay . . . offers good anchorage at its head. The wide mouth of the bay contains several shoal areas. . . . Safe passage to the head of the bay may be gained by passing 0.2 mile to the N and W of Rodman Rock Buoy 1 until SW of the buoy; continuing, stay 0.6 mile off the S shore until S of Point Elizabeth, and follow a midchannel course up the narrow part of the bay to its head.* (CP)

Anchorage can be found in Rodman Bay south of Lauf Islands in about 10 fathoms over a soft bottom.

## **Appleton Cove** (Rodman Bay)

Appleton Cove is 1.5 miles inside Rodman Bay on the south shore.

Chart 17338
Entrance: 57°28.88′ N, 135°16.28′ W
Anchor: 57°28.25′ N, 135°17.33′ W

*Appleton Cove . . . affords good anchorage and lee from seas for small craft though winds may be quite strong. . . . Care should be taken to avoid a reef and foul area about 0.2 mile S of the SE corner of Prince Island.* (CP)

Appleton Cove offers very good shelter behind the western reef, north of what was once a

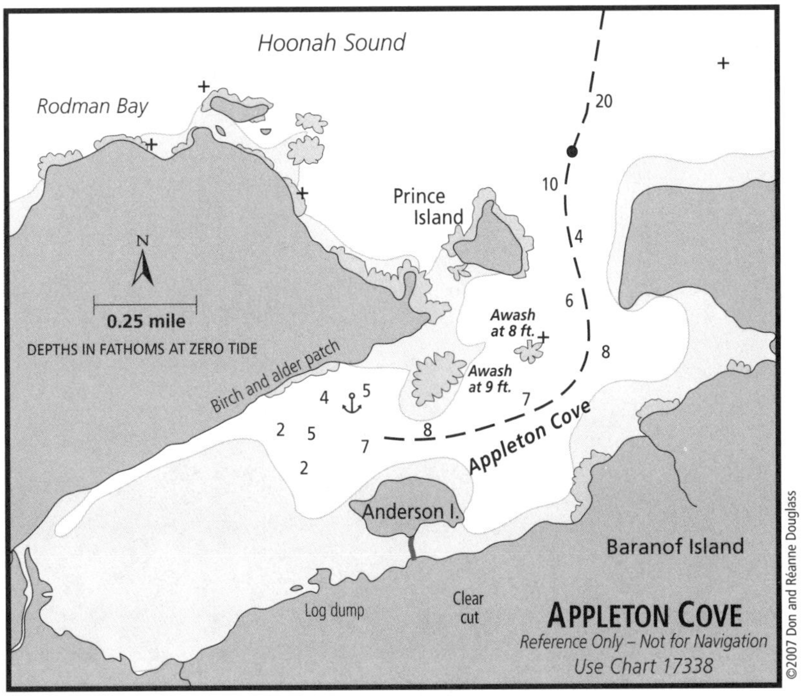

busy logging operation located on its south shore. The cove is one of the most protected anchorages in Peril Strait. Favor the east side of the entrance channel about 200 yards off the east shore. Avoid the reef in the center of the entrance, which is awash at 8 feet, as well as the reef north of Andersen Island. A professional skipper notes that the small cove to the east of the reefs also affords good anchorage. (Stay alert to the shoaling bottom in this suggested anchorage.)

Anchor in 5 fathoms over a soft bottom with good holding

## **Saook Bay** (Baranof Island)

Saook Bay, on the south side of Peril Strait, is 4 miles southeast of Rodman Bay.

Chart 17338
Entrance: 57°27.17′ N, 135°08.99′ W

> *The bay affords a good and convenient anchorage with shelter from all winds.* (CP)

Saook Bay is too deep to be a convenient small-craft anchorage except along its steep-to shore.

## Hanus Bay and Point Moses Cove
(Baranof Island)

Hanus Bay is on the south side of Peril Strait.

Chart 17338
East entrance (Hanus Bay): 57°25.06′ N, 135°00.28′ W
West entrance: (Hanus Bay): 57°25.18′ N, 135°03.12′ W
Anchor (Hanus Bay):
57°24.25′ N, 135°01.06′ W
Anchor (Pt. Moses Cove): 57°25.04′ N, 135°04.09′ W

> *At the W end of* [Hanus Bay] *are two coves . . . the N one has anchorage for small craft . . . Small craft frequently anchor in the cove at the SE side of the bay in 3 fathoms, mud bottom.* (CP)

Cruising boats can find protection from southerly weather in Hanus Bay, south of Dead Tree Island and west of the logging operation located on its east shore. Depths are quite shallow.

A log boom once located south of Dead Tree Island has been removed. Avoid the temptation to make your entrance through the center

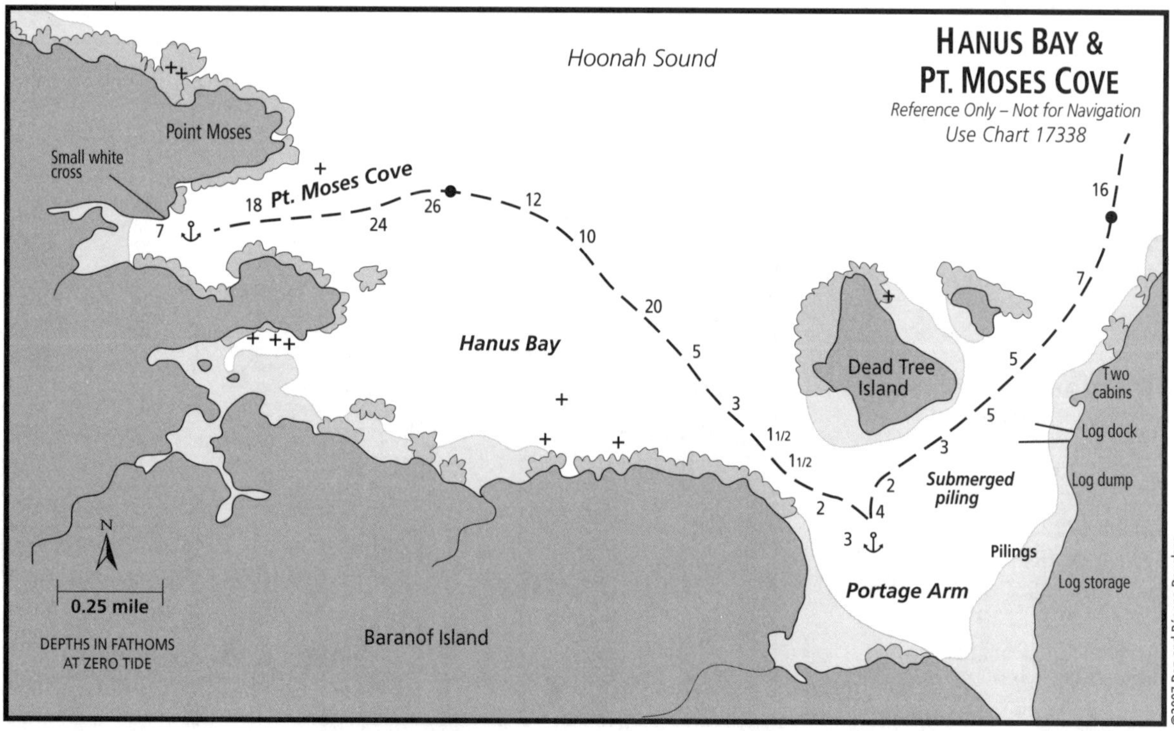

of this east entrance to Hanus Bay as there is an uncharted area of shoal/drying sandbar in the middle, at about the area we note on the diagram as "submerged piling." Consult your charts carefully; you may find that you want to transit the more easterly, deeper 4- and 3-fathom areas to make your way to the anchorage. There may still be old submerged pilings or submerged logs in the vicinity, so enter cautiously, paying attention to Chart 17338 and your depth sounder.

Although easterly winds can howl though the opening to the southeast, fetch is relatively short, and there is enough swinging room to allow good scope. The creek outlet located at the lower center of the diagram is a popular brown bear viewing site.

You can also tuck in behind Point Moses immediately west to find good protection from westerlies.

Anchor (Hanus Bay) in 3 fathoms over mud with good holding.

Anchor (Pt. Moses Cove) south of the white cross located on the north shore, in 8 fathoms over a mixed bottom with unrecorded holding.

### Lindenberg Harbor

Lindenberg Harbor is on the west side of Lindenberg Head, 3 miles north of Hanus Bay.

Chart 17338
Position: 57°27.50′ N, 135°01.83′ W
Anchor: 57°27.57′ N, 135°01.55′ W

> *Lindenberg Harbor is a small cove . . . and affords protection from N and E. The anchorage is in the middle of the cove in 12 to 15 fathoms, with indifferent holding ground. . . .* (CP)

Lindenberg Harbor provides good protection from northwest to easterly weather; it is open to the south and southwest. Moorage can be found deep in the harbor, north of the old pier complex ramp at the head of the cove. In heavy southeast weather, Appleton Cove is recommended.

Be aware that, because this site was formerly used for log-loading, the bottom may contain debris.

Anchor in about 7 fathoms over sand and gravel with newspaper kelp; fair-to-good holding with a well-set anchor.

### Sitkoh Bay (Chichagof Island)

Sitkoh Bay is northwest of the east entrance to Peril Strait.

Chart 17338
Entrance: 57°27.82′ N, 134°50.97′ W

> *The bay is deep throughout in midchannel, but there are several flats at the mouths of streams, and an extensive one, 1 mile wide, at its head.*
>
> *Chatham, on the southwest side of Sitkoh Bay, about 2.1 miles inside the entrance, is the site of a privately-owned inactive cannery.* (CP)

Sitkoh Bay is open to the southeast and is deep and steep-to. Avoid rocks on the west shore near the marker.

### Florence Bay (Sitkoh Bay)

Florence Bay is inside Sitkoh Bay on the north shore.

Chart 17338
Position: 57°30.03′ N, 134°52.96′ W

Florence Bay is exposed to the southeast and is useful as temporary protection in strong northerly winds. Tuck in close to shore at the head of the bay.

## UPPER CHATHAM STRAIT

### Hawk Inlet (Admiralty Island)

Hawk Inlet, on the east side of Chatham Strait, lies 0.75 mile west of Young Bay on Stephens Passage.

Charts 17312, 17316, 17300
Entrance (Hawk Point bearing 025°T at 0.48 Nm): 58°05.38′ N, 134°47.47′ W
Anchor (head of inlet): 58°10.50′ N, 134°44.67′ W

> *Hawk Inlet has its entrance . . . 10 miles SE of Rocky Island Light 13. It has a N direction for a distance of 5 miles from its mouth. It then contracts and changes to a NE direction, terminating in a basin about 1 mile in diameter.*
>
> *Anchorage for shallow-draft vessels can be*

Linda Lewis

*This is the size of the shrimp you can catch in these waters.*

*had in 4 to 6 fathoms in the basin at the head of the inlet. The channel leading to the basin has a least depth of 2-1/2 fathoms. To make the channel, keep off the E shore by about 0.1 mile. The channel is winding with strong currents and should not be attempted without local knowledge.* (CP)

The entrance is reported to have moderately swift currents. Green's Creek Mine marine terminal is located about 2 miles above the entrance at the former cannery site, and nav-aids mark the route. Favor the west shore at the narrows 0.3 mile northeast of Hawk Point. Anchorage in the basin at the head of the inlet is remote and bombproof. However, the entrance is shallow and narrow with a mid-channel rock and mud flats in all quarters. Favor the east shore. Currents add to the hazard. Use the most recent Chart 17312 as your guide.

Anchor (head of inlet) in 6 fathoms over mud and gravel with broken shells; fair-to-good holding.

## **Piledriver Cove** (Hawk Inlet)

Pile driver Cove is just inside Hawk Inlet on the south shore.

Charts 17312, 17316, 17300
Position: 58°05.19′ N, 134°46.44′ W

*Piledriver Cove, which dries, is on the S side of the inlet at the entrance. Two small islets are on the W side of the entrance to the cove; submerged pilings are in the entrance . . .* (CP)

## **No Name Cove** (Admiralty Island)

No Name Cove is 0.6 mile southwest of Piledriver Cove.

Charts 17312, 17300
Entrance: 58°04.80′ N, 134°47.42′ W
Anchor (No Name Cove): 58°04.52′ N, 134°47.38′ W

*A small cove, about 0.6 mile SW of Piledriver Cove and SW of Hawk Inlet, offers good anchorage for small craft in all but NW winds in 9 to 13 fathoms. A ledge extends 0.2 mile NW from the SW entrance point; another ledge, bare at half tide, is in the middle of the entrance. A deep channel is on each side of the ledge in the middle of the entrance, but the channel on the NE side is better. The anchorage is in the middle of the cove, about 300 yards SE of the ledge.* (CP)

"No Name Cove" is located 0.5 mile south of the entrance to Hawk Inlet. Enter east of the islet where you can find good anchorage between the islet and the head of the bay. The cove offers good protection from southeasterly weather, but it is open to northwest chop.

Anchor in about 10 fathoms, over sand and shells with fair holding.

*Note:* Chart 17300 is a small-scale chart covering a large area with inadequate detail for coastal navigation.

## **Game Cove** (Admiralty Island)

Game Cove is 1.6 miles south of the entrance to Hawk Inlet.

Chart 17300
Entrance: 58°03.84′ N, 134°48.46′ W

## **Square Cove** (Admiralty Island)

Square Cove is 2 miles north of Point Hepburn, 13.1 miles northeast of Tenakee Inlet.

Chart 17300
Entrance: 57°58.95′ N, 134°46.27′ W

*Square Cove, on the E side of Chatham Strait . . . 7 miles SE of Point Augusta, is on the N side of Cube Point. It affords anchorage for small craft with protection from SE winds. The cove is about 500 yards long and about half that wide. It has a depth of about 3 fathoms within 200 yards of its head and deeper water farther out. There are no dangers. A stream enters at each end of the sand beach at its head; the E one forms a cascade.* (CP)

## Point Hepburn Cove (Admiralty Island)

Point Hepburn Cove is 11.4 miles northeast of Tenakee Inlet.

Chart 17300
Entrance: 57°56.79′ N, 134°45.42′ W

> *The bight on the N side of Point Hepburn . . . about 26 miles N of Kootznahoo Head* (chart 17320), *affords anchorage for small craft in 5 fathoms with shelter from SE winds. A stream enters the head of the bight. A logging camp is at the base of the stream. Deadheads and floating logs were reported in the area.* (CP)

## Whitestone Harbor (Chichagof Island)

Whitestone Harbor is on the south side of Icy Strait and northeast corner of Chichagof Island.

Chart 17300
Entrance: 58°04.03′ N, 135°03.73′ W
Anchor: (approximately) 58°04.11′ N, 135°06.48′ W

> *The SW arm of the harbor is foul. . . . Enter the harbor at midchannel, thence favor the N shore to avoid a reported boulder that bares just S of the center of the harbor. Anchorage for small craft is in the arm on the N side of the harbor, in sand and gravel bottom.* (CP)

## False Bay (Chichagof Island)

False Bay is 10.1 miles north of Tenakee Inlet.

Chart 17300
Entrance: 57°57.31′ N, 134°55.84′ W

> *False Bay, 5 miles N of Iyoukeen Cove, is an open bight with deep water. Fair emergency anchorage for small craft may be found in its S part in 3 to 5 fathoms, rocky bottom.* (CP)

## Iyoukeen Cove (Chichagof Island)

Iyoukeen Cove is 6.5 miles north of Tenakee Inlet.

Chart 17300
Position: 57°53.35′ N, 134°59.36′ W

> *Iyoukeen Cove is close N of the entrance to Freshwater Bay, from which it is separated by a long, narrow, wooded peninsula, terminating in North Passage point. It does not afford shelter except from offshore winds, but can be used temporarily by anchoring about 0.5 mile from the S shore in 23 fathoms.* (CP)

## Freshwater Bay (Chichagof Island)

Freshwater Bay, on the west side of Chatham Strait, is 4 miles north of Tenakee Inlet Entrance Light 1.

Chart 17300
Entrance: 57°49.85′ N, 134°56.48′ W

> *Freshwater Bay . . . extends 11 miles NW, terminating in a sand flat with a large stream. . . . The main bay has no anchorages, but small vessels may find temporary anchorage at the head of the bay or off the flats at mouths of streams, of which there are several.* (CP)

## Wachusett Cove (Freshwater Bay)

Wachusett Cove, on the southwest side of Freshwater Bay, is 2.1 miles southwest of North Passage Point.

Chart 17300
Entrance: 57°49.85′ N, 134°59.05′ W
Anchor: 57°49.86′ N, 134°59.75′ W

> *The cove is almost filled with a flat and has a small stream at its head. A fair-weather anchorage may be made between the points at the entrance to the cove in 4 to 10 fathoms.* (CP)

Wachusett Cove is somewhat exposed to Chatham Strait weather but it is useful in fair weather. Pavlof Harbor is the preferred shelter.

Anchor in about 5 fathoms.

## Pavlof Harbor (Freshwater Bay)

Pavlof Harbor is 3 miles west of North Passage Point.

Chart 17300
Entrance: 57°50.95′ N, 135°01.41′ W
Anchor: 57°50.60′ N, 135°01.64′ W

> *A reef, covered at half tide, extends about 100 yards from the E point at the entrance, and the entire E side of the bay is bordered by a flat 250 yards wide. A pinnacle rock, covered at half tide, is 200 yards from the W side halfway up the bay. Anchorage may be made outside the rock in about 15 fathoms and in the middle between the rock and the SE shore. The clear anchorage is 350 yards wide in 5 to 12 fathoms, sand and rock bottom. The shelter is good, and the harbor is easily entered, though in strong W or N weather the wind draws down the bay with considerable force.* (CP)

Pavlof Harbor offers convenient shelter along this section of Chatham Strait.

Anchor southeast of the pinnacle rock in about 7 fathoms.

## **Cedar Cove** (Freshwater Bay)

Cedar Cove, on the south side of Freshwater Bay, is 4 miles northwest of North Passage Point.

**Chart 17300**
**Entrance: 57°52.33′ N, 135°03.75′ W**
**Anchor: 57°51.73′ N, 135°03.00′ W**

> *Cedar Cove . . . affords good shelter for small craft drawing less than 10 feet, but its entrances are very narrow and foul.* (CP)

Cedar Cove, which is almost landlocked, must be carefully entered west and south of the shoals extending northwest from the island that provides a natural breakwater. Avoid kelp patches and foul areas. Inside the cove there are depths of 10 fathoms. A number of years ago, there was a float house and boat settlement in the southeast bight.

## **Tenakee Inlet** (Chichagof Island)

Tenakee Inlet, on the west side of Chatham Strait, is 97 miles north of Cape Ommaney.

**Charts 17320, 17300**
**Entrance: 57°47.25′ N, 134°56.50′ W**

> *The depths in the inlet are great, and the dangers easily avoided. A number of bays on the S side afford anchorage.*
>
> *Anchorage may be made at the head of Tenakee Inlet near the sand flat in 7 to 10 fathom; hard gravel and shell bottom.* (CP)

## **Trap Bay** (Tenakee Inlet)

Trap Bay is 2.8 miles southwest of Tenakee Inlet Entrance Light.

**Charts 17320, 17300**
**Entrance: 57°45.14′ N, 135°01.06′ W**

> *A 2-3/4-fathom shoal is in Trap Bay about 3 miles WSW from Tenakee Inlet Entrance Light 1.* (CP)

## **Corner Bay** (Tenakee Inlet)

Corner Bay is 6.3 miles west of Tenakee Inlet Entrance Light.

**Charts 17320, 17300**
**Entrance: 57°44.64′ N, 135°07.44′ W**

> *In 1980, a logging camp was operating on the W side of Corner Bay, about 6.9 miles W of Tenakee Inlet Entrance Light 1. A log storage area is on the E side of the bay. The camp has a 60-foot small-craft and seaplane float, and, also mooring buoys.* (CP)

## **Kadashan Bay** (Tenakee Inlet)

Kadashan Bay, on the south side of Tenakee Inlet, is opposite Tenakee Springs.

**Charts 17320, 17300**
**Entrance: 57°44.01′ N, 135°13.50′ W**

> *Kadashan Bay . . . is filled with a flat that bares.* (CP)

## **Tenakee Springs** (Tenakee Inlet)

Tenakee Springs lies on the north side of Tenakee Inlet, 9 miles inside the entrance.

**Charts 17320, 17300**
**Tenakee Boat Harbor Light G"1": 57°46.64′ N, 135°12.40′ W**

> *Tenakee Springs . . . is a community with a general store and warm springs. A 51-foot grid is on the E side of the approach pier to the small-craft floats.* (CP)

Tenakee Springs, a popular getaway for Juneau residents and cruising vessels, is a quaint village of approximately 100 people. It is best known for its hot springs, located in a bathhouse at the center of the village, which are free. (Contributions for its upkeep are appreciated.) Hours for use of the hot springs are posted on the bathhouse door. *Note:* women and men bathe separately without bathing suits!

The main street of town is a 6-foot-wide path. The fire and fuel trucks, both 3/4-ton pickups, are the largest and just about the only motor vehicles here. Tenakee Springs often serves as the beginning or end of kayak trips to and from Hoonah.

The harbor, protected by two floating breakwaters, is located approximately 1/2 mile east of the center of the community. A light on the north shore, approximately 0.1 mile east of the harbor, marks a small islet close to the north shore. The harbor is easily entered from either end of the main breakwater that runs parallel to the shore. There is both assigned and open

Linda Lewis

*The colorful harbormaster in Tenakee Springs; his vest says: "Heaven doesn't want me. Hell is afraid I will take over."*

moorage in the harbor. Except on holiday weekends, like the 4th of July, finding space is not generally a problem. There is a telephone at the head of the trail from the harbor to town and there are other telephones in town. No sewage facilities exist at the harbor. Because the town has no solid waste management facilities, boaters are encouraged to keep their solid waste aboard.

Fuel and water (untreated) are available at the community pier. The pier has a 64-foot-long face, and if you tie to it for fuel, be sure to use batter boards or fenders and lines that you don't mind being coated with creosote.

You can find limited supplies at the general store in town, as well as meals and accommodations. The Alaska Marine Highway System ferry stops in Tenakee on runs between Juneau and Sitka, and floatplane air service to Juneau is available. The ferry docks are immediately adjacent to the pier.

## **Crab Bay** (Tenakee Inlet)

Crab Bay, on the south side of Tenakee Inlet, is 4 miles southwest of Tenakee Springs.

Charts 17320, 17300
Entrance: 57°45.11′ N, 135°18.82′ W

> *The S side and the head of* [Crab Bay] *have streams and mudflat areas. The N side of the bay is deep, with steep banks. Anchorage is available in the bay in 5 to 25 fathoms. A . . . logging jetty and a private seasonal mooring buoy are at the S side of the entrance to the bay. A 2-1/2-fathom spot is immediately E of the mooring buoy.* (CP)

## **Saltery Bay** (Tenakee Inlet)

Saltery Bay is 3 miles northwest of Crab Bay.

Charts 17320, 17300
Entrance: 57°46.80′ N, 135°22.30′ W

> *The entrance is narrow but deep. Near the head,* [Saltery Bay] *opens into a small basin with depths ranging from 5 to 15 fathoms. A mudflat extends 1.2 miles from the head of the bay. Anchorage is available in the basin area in a soft mud and gravel bottom.* (CP)

## **Seal Bay** (Tenakee Inlet)

Seal Bay, on the south side of Tenakee Inlet, is 10 miles northwest of Tenakee Springs.

Charts 17320, 17300
Entrance: 57°51.06′ N, 135°30.45′ W

> *A 6-3/4-fathoms shoal and a 1-1/2-fathom shoal are in the entrance to Seal Bay. A 5-3/4-fathom shoal is E of the 6-3/4-fathom shoal. . . . A flat extends 0.8 mile from its head, and a rock, covered at high water, is near the middle of the bay 1.5 miles inside the entrance.* (CP)

## **Long Bay** (Tenakee Inlet)

Long Bay, on the southwest side of Tenakee Inlet, is 2.5 miles northwest of Seal Bay.

Chart 17300
Entrance: 57°52.70′ N, 135°33.17′ W

> *From the NW point at the entrance a reef, covered at half tide, extends E about 0.5 mile. A 3-1/2-fathom spot is in about the middle of the entrance to Long Bay. . . . The bay has depths of 5 to 15 fathoms, mud bottom, affording good anchorage.* (CP)

## **Basket Bay** (Chichagof Island)

Basket Bay, on the west side of Chatham Strait, is 11 miles north of Point Hayes.

Chart 17338
Entrance: 57°39.54′ N, 134°53.54′ W

> *The bay is exposed to the SE, has a rocky bottom and depths of 12 to 40 fathoms, and is not recommended as an anchorage. The midchannel course up the bay is clear.* (CP)

## **Little Basket Bay** (Chichagof Island)

Little Basket Bay is 1.4 miles south of Basket Bay.

Chart 17338
Position: 57°38.17′ N, 134°53.00′ W

Little Basket Bay is a small, shallow bight used for temporary stops in fair weather.

## **Kootznahoo Inlet** (Admiralty Island)

Kootznahoo Inlet, on the east shore of Chatham Strait, is 7.5 miles northeast of Peril Strait.

Chart 17339
Entrance: 57°31.25′ N, 134°36.26′ W

> *Kootznahoo Inlet is an intricate group of narrow passages, lagoons, and bays. . . . It is full of rocks and reefs, and through the narrow passages the tidal currents rush with great velocity. The navigation of Kootzhahoo Inlet is such that it should not be attempted except by small craft of short length and ready turning qualities, and then only at slack water and with local knowledge.*
>
> *The southernmost arm continues in a SE direction to Favorite Bay; the northernmost extends NE to Mitchell Bay; the middle arm, also extending E, leads among the islands, is obstructed at its entrance, and is navigable only by small craft. The lagoons between the islands are full of rocks and reefs, and are not navigable except by small craft.*
>
> *Caution. The navigation of Kootznahoo Inlet should not be attempted by strangers. A guide can be obtained at Angoon, Petersburg, and Sitka.* (CP)

## **Angoon and Kootznahoo Inlet Inner Harbor** (Admiralty Island)

Angoon is bordered on its west side by Chatham Strait and on its east side by Kootznahoo Inlet.

Chart 17339
Entrance (Danger Point Light bearing 195°T at 0.32 Nm): 57°31.25′ N, 134°36.26′ W

Réanne Hemingway-Douglass

*Floatplane dock in Kootznahoo Inlet, Angoon's inner harbor*

*Angoon, is a village with a general store, a seasonal hotel . . .*

*The village pier, a 525-foot-long T-headed pier . . . extends into Chatham Strait. In 2002, a depth of 30 feet was reported along the outer face.* [Editor's Note: This pier was condemned in 2006 and is no longer in use.]

[In] *Kootznahoo Inlet* [the inner harbor], *a seaplane float is in the small cove about 800 yards SE of the daybeacon W of Rose Rock. The city of Angoon maintains small-craft floats about 300 yards SE of the seaplane float. Berthing is on both sides of the floats. A fueling float, 185-feet long, is close NW to the small-craft floats. In 2002, a least depth of 10 feet was reported along the floats. The harbormaster assigns berths.* [Telephone 907.788.3960 or VHF Ch 14 or 16.] *A tidal drydock is available. A 72-foot-long grid is on the SE side of the approach pier to the small-craft floats. Water and electricity are at the small-craft floats.* (CP)

The Tlingit village of Angoon, population about 400, lies within the Admiralty Island National Monument and is the only settlement on the island. Although the *Coast Pilot* (above) refers to the village pier in Chatham Strait, this pier is now condemned and most services in Angoon are located in the inner harbor, inside Kootznahoo Inlet.

The entrance to the inner harbor, which lies between Danger Point and Kootznahoo Head, has numerous rocks and reefs. Transit to the inner harbor should be made at slack tide. Distance from the light at Danger Point to the inner harbor marina is 1.9 miles. Proceed into Kootznahoo Inlet past R"6" where you will see on your starboard first the seaplane float, then the Angoon Oil fuel dock, then the inner harbor floats.

*Note:* Boaters without expert local knowledge should not go beyond the waters of the inner harbor to Stillwater Anchorage, Mitchell Bay or Kanalku Bay, as these areas are uncharted and full of hazards.

Since Kootznahoo Inlet drains a large portion of west Admiralty Island, currents at the narrow entrance run to 7 knots. (Stillwater, itself, is just the opposite—only 40-45 minutes of "still water.") Follow the chart carefully to avoid the many hazards. Boats over 60 feet are discouraged from entering. Night entry for any pleasure craft is not advisable.

The inner harbor floats, which have room for just a couple of transient boats, are essentially filled with local vessels and are limited in length to 40 feet; vessels over 40 feet must anchor across from the floats and take a dinghy to the dock. Occasionally, the harbormaster can accommodate up to two 58-foot vessels at the inner harbor; call ahead to inquire about availability. Vessels over 60 feet are advised to anchor on the outside in Killisnoo Harbor, in Chatham Strait. For space availability, it's a good idea to call the harbormaster on VHF Ch 16 or 14 (tel.: 907.788.3960) or city hall (tel.: 907.788.3653) before you enter Kootznahoo Inlet.

Water and garbage disposal are the only services provided at the harbor floats. Diesel, gasoline and propane can be purchased at the Angoon Oil fuel dock (tel.: 907.788.3436). The fuel dock is normally open during the summer season from Monday through Friday, 1000 to 1700. However, if you call the fuel dock or the harbormaster, special arrangements can be made. Groceries can be obtained at the small general store.

Frequently passed up by cruising boats, the villagers do everything possible to make your visit pleasant, and the area has now become particularly popular with kayakers and canoeists.

The village is serviced by daily air service and the State Ferry which calls twice a week year-round (once southbound, once northbound). The Ferry terminal is located in Killisnoo Harbor, approximately 1.9 miles SSE of Angoon, in Chatham Strait.

Killisnoo Harbor can provide convenient anchorage in stable weather, but it is not advisable in southeast weather.

Réanne Hemingway-Douglass

*Angoon's small craft harbor inside Kootznahoo Inlet*

Several lodges have also become popular for their cuisine, but phone well in advance for reservations. Shuttle service to and from Killisnoo Harbor, near the ferry dock, is usually provided by these lodges.
Kootznahoo Inlet Lodge (tel.: 907.788.3501).
Favorite Bay Sportfishing Lodge (French chef) (tel.: 907.788.3344; www.favoritebay.com).
Whalers Cove Lodge in Killisnoo Harbor (tel.: 907.788.3123; www.whalerscovelodge.com).

Anchor sites can be found in 5 fathoms, mid-channel east of the marina in Kootznahoo Inlet, avoiding the many rocks; or deep in Favorite Bay, 2.2 miles southeast of the marina in about 6 fathoms.

## **Favorite Bay** (Kootznahoo Inlet)

Favorite Bay is southeast of Angoon.

**Chart 17339**
**Entrance (Sullivan Point bearing 015°T at 0.2 Nm): 57°29.70′ N, 134°33.72′ W**

*Favorite Bay has anchorage in 10 to 17 fathoms near the SW shore anywhere NW of a high bluff marking the end of the flat that extends 1 mile from its head. The bay is used as a fishing ground for herring.*

*The passage to Favorite Bay is obstructed at its NW end by a series of rocks that bare. . . . The SE end of the passage is obstructed by a rock in midchannel about 0.2 mile NW of the NW end of Favorite Bay.* (CP)

## **Killisnoo Harbor** (Admiralty Island)

Killisnoo Harbor, on the east side of Chatham Strait, is on the north side of the entrance to Hood Bay.

**Charts 17339 (inset), 17320**
**Entrance (Light G"3" bearing 331°T at 0.11 Nm): 57°27.86′ N, 134°33.86′ W**
**Anchor: 57°27.97′ N, 134°33.01′ W**

*The anchorage is in mid-harbor off the E end of Killisnoo Island, in 14 to 15 fathoms. The harbor is somewhat exposed to SE gales, but no considerable sea makes into this anchorage.*

*An Alaska State Ferry Terminal, with 26 feet reported alongside, is on the NW shore of Killisnoo Harbor, about 0.15 mile NE of Killisnoo Harbor Light 7. A steel transfer bridge . . . is immediately NE of the terminal. A small-craft grid is immediately N of the steel transfer bridge.* (CP)

The Alaska State Ferry dock that serves the Angoon region is located in this harbor.

Anchorage can be found on the east side of the harbor, northeast of the rocky kelp patch.

Anchor in 3 to 4 fathoms over a hard bottom with fair holding.

## **Hood Bay** (Admiralty Island)

Hood Bay, on the east side of Chatham Strait, is 25 miles north of Point Gardner.

**Chart 17339**
**Entrance (mid-channel between buoys G"1" and R"2"): 57°25.29′ N, 134°33.13′ W**

*Hood Bay has its entrance . . . between Distant Point and Killisnoo Island. . . . The bay is about 7 miles long from the entrance to the junction with both arms.* (CP)

## **North Arm** (Hood Bay)

North Arm is 6 miles from the entrance to Hood Bay.

Chart 17339
Entrance: 57°22.74′ N, 134°23.86′ W

> *North Arm has a flat 0.5 mile wide at its head. . . . Small craft find anchorage at the head of each arm in 5 to 10 fathoms, mud bottom. Winds of considerable force are reported in the North Arm.*
>
> *Pile ruins of two wharves are on the N side of the entrance to North Arm. Caution is advised.* (CP)

The head of the bay is reported to have a great combination of good anchoring and very good bear watching.

## **South Arm** (Hood Bay)

South Arm is immediately south of North Arm.

Chart 17339
Entrance: 57°22.47′ N, 134°24.36′ W

> *South Arm is free from midchannel dangers inside its entrance.* (CP)

## **Chaik Bay** (Admiralty Island)

Chaik Bay, on the east side of Chatham Strait, is 19 miles north of Point Gardner.

Charts 17339, 17341
Entrance: 57°19.50′ N, 134°35.48′ W
Entrance (north arm): 57°20.06′ N, 134°31.59′ W
Entrance (south arm): 57°19.74′ N, 134°31.63′ W

> *About 2 miles from the entrance . . .* [Chaik Bay] *divides into two arms.*
>
> *The N arm has good anchorage in 12 fathoms, sticky bottom, but is open SW. The S arm has considerable foul ground and should be avoided by strangers.*
>
> *Caution. Numerous uncharted rocks have been reported in Chaik Bay. A submerged rock has been reported on the bar across the entrance to the S arm midway between the two small islets.* (CP)

Note D on the paper chart warns: "There are numerous uncharted rocks in Chaik Bay which are a hazard to navigation. The mariner should use caution when navigating in this area." We have a report of a vessel going aground in this bay in an area that was indicated as 60 feet deep on the chart. It is worth saying again that the waters of Southeast Alaska are poorly charted. You must proceed slowly with an alert bow watch in areas like this. And read the notes on your paper and/or electronic raster charts.

## **Whitewater Bay** (Admiralty Island)

Whitewater Bay is 15 miles north of Point Gardner.

Charts 17341, 17320
Entrance: 57°15.84′ N, 134°38.35′ W
Anchor: 57°13.83′ N, 134°33.16′ W

> *Whitewater Bay has its entrance on the E side of Chatham Strait between Point Caution and Woody Point . . . The bay at the head connects by a narrow passage with a lagoon, bare at low water. Secure anchorage can be had near the head of the bay.*
>
> *Caution. No recent surveys have been made of the bay. The bottom is very irregular, and there is not certainty that all dangers are charted. In 1975, a 1-1/2-fathom spot was reported in the entrance to the bay, about 0.6 mile E of Lone Tree Islet.* (CP)

Whitewater Bay requires vigilant piloting, as noted above. Well-sheltered anchorage is reported at the head of the bay about 0.18 Nm northeast of East Point. Note that all hazards are not charted and a skipper should verify that there is adequate swinging room. Avoid all kelp areas. The bottom is hard.

## **Wilson Cove** (Admiralty Island)

Wilson Cove, the east side of Chatham Strait, is immediately north of Point Wilson.

Chart 17320
Entrance: 57°09.16′ N, 134°38.61′ W

> *The entrance has an extensive reef covered at highest tides. Wilson Cove should be avoided, as it affords no protection as an anchorage, except from E winds. The bottom of the cove is foul with depths of 4 to 8 fathoms in places. But should it be necessary to enter the cove, stand in parallel to the S shore, pass S of the reef in the mouth of the cove, keep clear of the kelp on both sides, and anchor in 8 fathoms.* (CP)

Although Wilson Cove is useful in easterly weather, we prefer Murder Cove, 8 miles to the south or Whitewater Bay, 7 miles north.

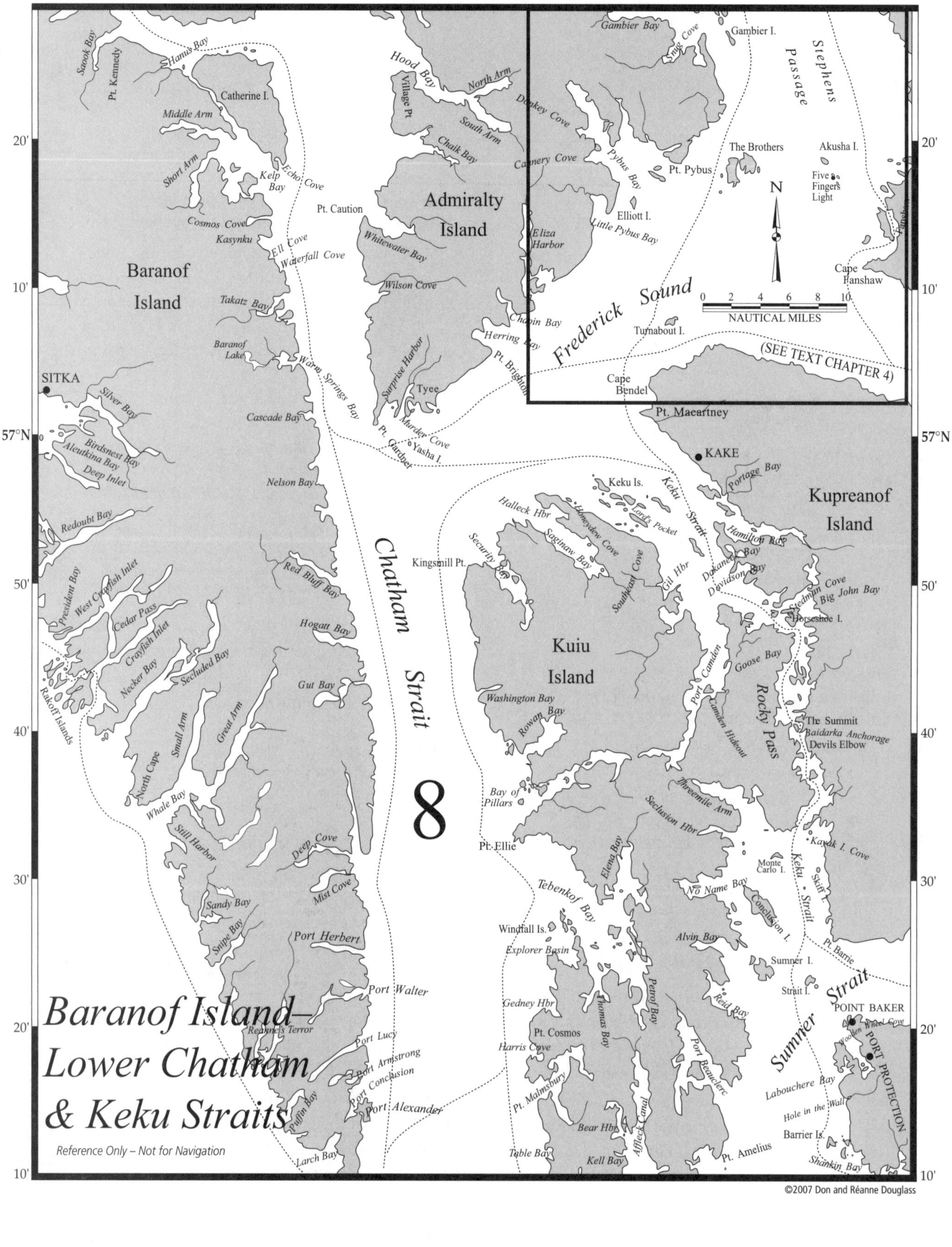
Baranof Island–
Lower Chatham
& Keku Straits
Reference Only – Not for Navigation
8
Chatham Strait
Baranof Island
Admiralty Island
Kuiu Island
Kupreanof Island
Frederick Sound
Stephens Passage
Sumner Strait
Keku Strait
Rocky Pass
(SEE TEXT CHAPTER 4)
NAUTICAL MILES
0 2 4 6 8 10
N
SITKA
KAKE
POINT BAKER
PORT PROTECTION
Saook Bay
Pt. Kennedy
Hanus Bay
Catherine I.
Middle Arm
Short Arm
Kelp Bay
Echo Cove
Cosmos Cove
Kasynku
Ell Cove
Waterfall Cove
Pt. Caution
Takatz Bay
Baranof Lake
Warm Springs Bay
Silver Bay
Birdsnest Bay
Aleutkina Bay
Deep Inlet
Cascade Bay
Nelson Bay
Redoubt Bay
President Bay
West Crayfish Inlet
Cedar Pass
Crayfish Inlet
Necker Bay
Secluded Bay
Rakoff Islands
Red Bluff Bay
Hogatt Bay
Gut Bay
Small Arm
Great Arm
North Cape
Whale Bay
Still Harbor
Deep Cove
Mist Cove
Sandy Bay
Snipe Bay
Port Herbert
Port Walter
Reanne's Terror
Port Lucy
Port Armstrong
Port Conclusion
Port Alexander
Puffin Bay
Larch Bay
Hood Bay
Village Pt.
North Arm
South Arm
Chaik Bay
Donkey Cove
Cannery Cove
Whitewater Bay
Wilson Cove
Surprise Harbor
Tyee
Murder Cove
Pt. Gardner
Yasha I.
Chapin Bay
Herring Bay
Pt. Brightman
Gambier Bay
Snug Cove
Gambier I.
Pybus Bay
Pt. Pybus
The Brothers
Akusha I.
Five Fingers Light
Elliott I.
Little Pybus Bay
Eliza Harbor
Cape Fanshaw
Turnabout I.
Cape Bendel
Pt. Macartney
Keku Is.
Portage Bay
Halleck Hbr
Honeydew Cove
Lord's Pocket
Saginaw Bay
Security Bay
Southeast Cove
Gil Hbr
Kingsmill Pt.
Hamilton Bay
Dakaneek Bay
Davidson Bay
Stedman Cove
Big John Bay
Horseshoe I.
Goose Bay
Port Camden
Camden Hideout
Washington Bay
Rowan Bay
The Summit
Baidarka Anchorage
Devils Elbow
Bay of Pillars
Threemile Arm
Seclusion Hbr
Pt. Ellie
Elena Bay
Monte Carlo I.
Kayak I. Cove
Skiff I.
Tebenkof Bay
No Name Bay
Conclusion I.
Windfall Is.
Explorer Basin
Alvin Bay
Pt. Barrie
Sumner I.
Strait I.
Gedney Hbr
Thomas Bay
Petrof Bay
Reid Bay
Pt. Cosmos
Harris Cove
Port Beauclerc
Woolen Wheel Cove
Labouchere Bay
Pt. Malmsbury
Hole in the Wall
Barrier Is.
Bear Hbr
Affleck Canal
Pt. Amelius
Table Bay
Kell Bay
Shakan Bay
57°N
10'
20'
30'
40'
50'

# 8

# BARANOF ISLAND, SOUTH OF SITKA; LOWER CHATHAM STRAIT & KEKU STRAIT

## INTRODUCTION

South Baranof Island's west and east coasts, Kuiu Island's west coast, and Keku Strait include some of the most stunningly beautiful and seldom-visited parts of Southeast Alaska. As an example of the remoteness of this vast cruising area, the number of public telephones to be found can be counted on one hand, with fingers left over! If you are well prepared and ready for adventure, then venture forth to the most pristine part of Southeast.

Southward of Sitka, hundreds of small offlying islands and reefs give protection along the first 40 percent of the way to Cape Ommaney, continuing the smooth-water route. Careful navigation is required to find your way among the islets and submerged rocks, and large-scale charts are a must for safe transit of this coast.

Goddard Hot Springs, with its wooden hot tubs provided by the U.S. Forest Service, is well worth a stop. Dorothy Narrows, a small, intricate route that opens up a large sheltered area for exploration, marks the end of navigational aids until Cape Ommaney. The Necker and Rakof islands offer some outstanding anchor sites that make perfect places for launching kayak and dinghy expeditions to the rugged west coast surroundings.

South of Aspid and North capes you are exposed to the full fury of whatever the Gulf of Alaska is dispensing, and you must pick your weather windows to transit to the next safe anchorage. Fortunately, the distances are short and you can choose from a number of well-protected anchor sites—our favorites are found

Ben Kyle

*Humpbacks in classic bubble-feeding activity*

in Necker Bay, Still Harbor, the small unnamed inlet we call Réanne's Terror, Redfish Bay and Puffin Bay. Port Alexander, at the southern tip of Chatham Strait, is a small Alaska frontier village that caters to fishing vessels and occasional pleasure craft.

Although the east coast of Baranof Island has smaller inlets, they are no less striking. The mountains are higher and more precipitous and their peaks covered with more snow than those of the west coast. Countless gullies are packed with snow to sea level into late summer; beautiful waterfalls and unnamed rivers and creeks make this coast unusual.

Breathtaking Red Bluff Bay and Gut Bay are "quintessential Southeast," where secure anchorage can be found deep within their bounds. The public float at Warm Springs Bay is a popular stop among pleasure boaters. From your boat or one of the hot tubs above the float you have a striking view of the beautiful falls.

The west coast of Kuiu Island, now largely included within the Tebenkof Wilderness, has wonderful unspoiled bays and portages to explore. Wildlife is abundant and sport fishing is good.

Keku Strait connects Sumner Strait to Frederick Sound via the infamous Rocky Pass. Kake, on the northeast corner of Keku Strait, is a thriving native community with public moorage floats, a fuel dock and grocery store. The Alaska Ferry, which calls here frequently, brings kayakers who want to explore the waters of Rocky Pass.

Between the years 1977 and 1982—after a narrow 5-foot-deep channel was dredged in Rocky Pass and marked with a system of poles set in concrete drums—many boats were lost or damaged; the poles were subsequently removed and the passage "closed." In the early 1990s, we spent many days reconstructing the route and found it a delightful area for exploration by small craft. In 1996, the U.S. Coast Guard reestablished a marker system that opened up this pristine area for those willing to meet its challenges. In more recent years, the USCG has added additional makers in the two most intricate areas in Rocky Pass. Today, more than ever, pleasure boat skippers with good navigation skills venture through Rocky Pass. This is a rare opportunity for boaters to see true wildness.

## BARANOF ISLAND'S WEST COAST, SOUTH OF SITKA

Most small vessels enter and exit Sitka via Peril Strait and Salisbury Sound. Very few small craft venture down Baranof Island's west coast because of its remoteness and direct exposure to the Gulf of Alaska. We have found good shelter and smooth sailing for a large part of the distance. Passages with exposure to the open Pacific, such as Aspid and North capes and south of Point Lander to Ommaney Point, should be attempted only in fair weather.

### Eastern Channel

Eastern Channel is the main entrance to Sitka from the Gulf of Alaska.

**Charts 17327, 17326**
**West entrance (Kulichkof Rock Light R"2" bearing 090°T at 1.2 Nm): 56°59.90′ N, 135°29.21′ W**
**East entrance (The Twins Light G"9" bearing 270°T at 0.2 Nm): 57°02.07′ N, 135°18.45′ W**

> *From the sea, three natural channels lead to Sitka among islands and reefs on the NE side of Sitka Sound. Eastern Channel is the widest . . . the principal dangers are marked by buoys.* (CP)

### Eastern Anchorage (Baranof Island)

Eastern Anchorage is 0.4 mile southwest of Jamestown Bay.

**Chart 17327**
**Position: 57°02.32′ N, 135°18.46′ W**

> *Anchorage in 7 to 20 fathoms, mud bottom, can be had at the Eastern Anchorage. . . . The swell from outside makes this anchorage uneasy in S weather.* (CP)

Eastern Anchorage is used by cruise ships, but it is too exposed for small craft. Jamestown Bay, just north, is more protected (see Chapter 7).

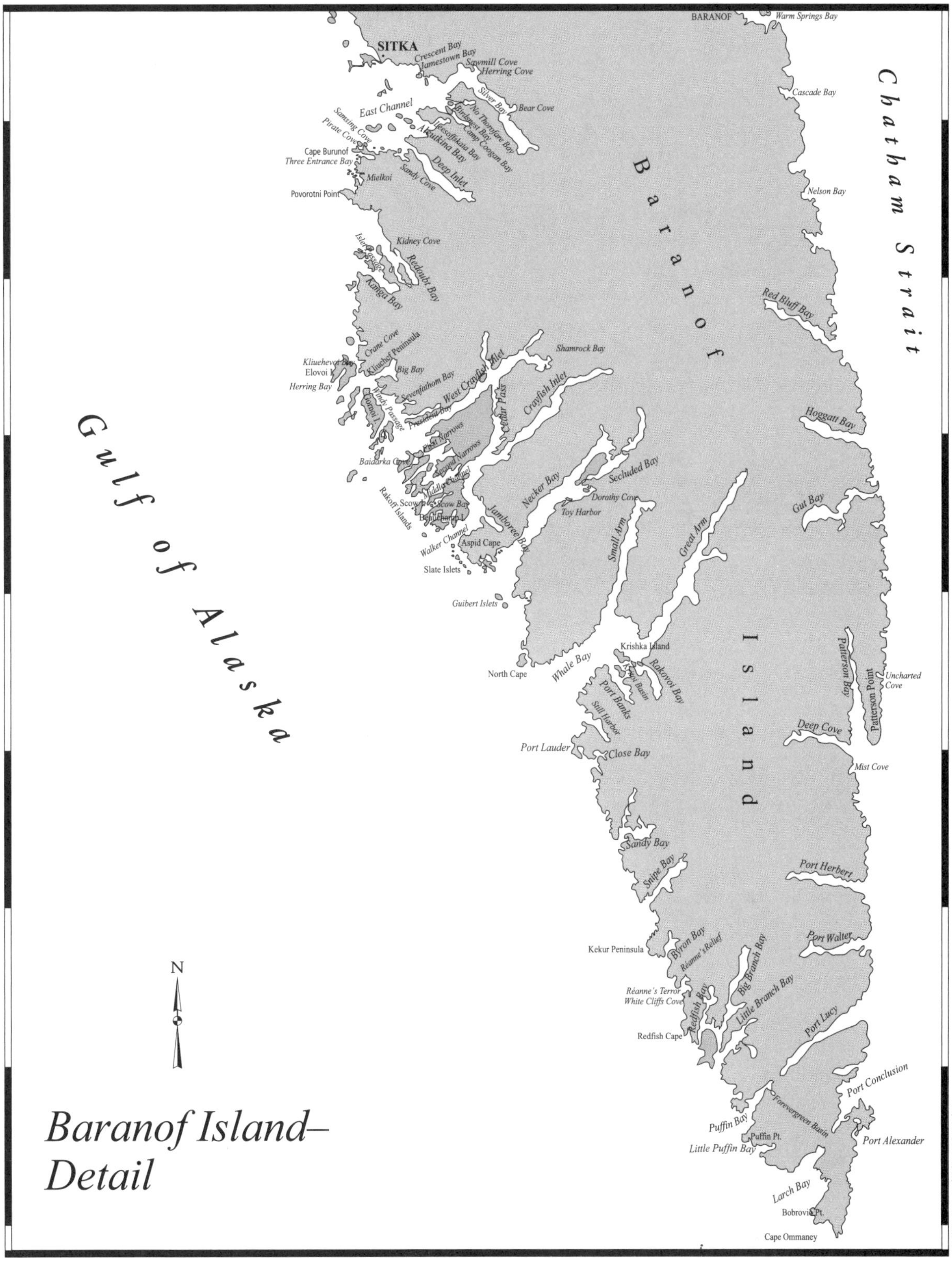
Baranof Island
Chatham Strait
Gulf of Alaska
SITKA
BARANOF
Warm Springs Bay
Crescent Bay
Jamestown Bay
Sawmill Cove
Herring Cove
Silver Bay
Bear Cove
East Channel
Samsing Cove
Pirate Cove
Cape Burunof
Three Entrance Bay
Mielkoi
Povorotni Point
Deep Inlet
Sandy Cove
Cascade Bay
Nelson Bay
Kidney Cove
Redoubt Bay
Kanga Bay
Crane Cove
Big Bay
Kliuchef Peninsula
Kliuchevoi Bay
Elovoi I.
Herring Bay
Sevenfathom Bay
West Crawfish Inlet
Cedar Pass
Crawfish Inlet
Shamrock Bay
Red Bluff Bay
Hoggatt Bay
Windy Passage
Baidarka Cove
Rakoff Islands
Scow Bay
Walker Channel
Aspid Cape
Slate Islets
Guibert Islets
Jamboree Bay
Necker Bay
Secluded Bay
Dorothy Cove
Toy Harbor
Small Arm
Great Arm
Gut Bay
Krishka Island
North Cape
Whale Bay
Rakovoi Bay
Port Banks
Still Harbor
Port Lauder
Close Bay
Patterson Bay
Patterson Point
Uncharted Cove
Deep Cove
Mist Cove
Sandy Bay
Snipe Bay
Port Herbert
Kekur Peninsula
Byron Bay
Réanne's Relief
Port Walter
Big Branch Bay
Little Branch Bay
Réanne's Terror
White Cliffs Cove
Redfish Bay
Redfish Cape
Port Lucy
Port Conclusion
Puffin Bay
Puffin Pt.
Little Puffin Bay
Forevergreen Basin
Port Alexander
Larch Bay
Bobrovoi Pt.
Cape Ommaney
N
Baranof Island–
Detail

*Whales close to the boat in Sitka Sound*

## **Silver Bay** (Baranof Island)

Silver Bay, at the east end of Eastern Channel, is 3 miles southeast of Sitka.

Chart 17326
Entrance: 57°01.77′ N, 135°14.86′ W

> *A light on Entry Point on the W side, marks the entrance to the bay. Unlighted log rafts, moored close to shore, extend about 2.2 miles from Sugarloaf Point. On the opposite side of the bay log rafts extend from Herring Cove to Bear Cove.* (CP)

As the logging industry retrenches, parts of Silver Bay, such as Herring Bay, may open up for recreational uses.

## **Sawmill Cove** (Silver Bay)

Sawmill Cove is 1 mile above the entrance to Silver Bay at its north end.

Chart 17326 (inset)
Entrance: 57°02.53′ N, 135°13.47′ W

> *Sawmill Cove . . . was the site of a large pulpmill with wharves on the W side of the cove.* (CP)

## **Herring Cove** (Silver Bay)

Herring Cove is 0.7 mile east of Sawmill Cove.

Chart 17326
Entrance: 57°02.38′ N, 135°12.35′ W

> *In 1976, the entire bay was used for log storage. At times, small craft can tie up to the log storage booms. Mariners should pass with caution the 1-1/2-fathom spot in the middle of the entrance.* (CP)

Herring Cove may have potential for pleasure craft as the healing process from logging operations proceeds.

## **Bear Cove** (Silver Bay)

Bear Cove is 3 miles southeast of Sawmill Cove.

Chart 17326
Entrance: 57°00.85′ N, 135°09.84′ W

> *Most of this cove, in 1976, was used for log storage, and like Herring Cove, small craft at times can tie up to the log storage booms.* (CP)

## **No Thorofare Bay** (Baranof Island)

No Thorofare Bay is north of Camp Coogan Bay.

Chart 17326
Entrance: 57°01.27′ N, 135°14.97′ W

> *No Thorofare Bay . . . is composed of two landlocked bodies of water connected by narrow, shallow channels. Only small boats can enter and then only at high-water slack, because of strong currents in the outer narrows. . . . Shoal depths of 3/4 fathom are off the entrance and in the outer narrows, and a rock awash at high water is on the S side of the outer narrows near the inner end.* (CP)

## **Birdsnest Bay** (Baranof Island)

Birdsnest Bay is between Camp Coogan Bay and No Thorofare Bay.

Chart 17326
Entrance: 57°00.58′ N, 135°14.47′ W

> *A small foul passage connects with Camp Coogan Bay, but can be used only by small boats at half tide or more. Use this passage only with local knowledge.* (CP)

It is preferable to enter through the narrow channel from the west. Only enter with high tide. There is good shelter with narrow swinging room. Camp Coogan Bay is much easier to enter than Birdsnest Bay.

Anchor in 4 fathoms.

## **Camp Coogan Bay** (Baranof Island)

Camp Coogan Bay is 3.5 miles southeast of Sitka.

Chart 17326
Entrance: 57°00.93′ N, 135°15.63′ W
Anchor: 57°00.21′ N, 135°13.51′ W

> *Camp Coogan Bay . . . has a narrow, but clear entrance, and a landlocked anchorage inside for small vessels in 6-3/4 to 14 fathoms, mud bottom.* (CP)

Camp Coogan Bay, easily entered through a 100-yard-wide channel, offers very good protection with lots of swinging room over a large flat bottom. (Favor the south shore.)

Anchor in 8 fathoms over soft mud with fair-to-good holding.

## **Aleutkina Bay** (Baranof Island)

Aleutkina Bay is 2 miles west of Camp Coogan Bay.

Chart 17326
West entrance: 57°00.45′ N, 135°19.72′ W
East entrance: 57°00.82′ N, 135°18.31′ W
Anchor (large boats): 56°59.79′ N, 135°17.28′ W

> *Aleutkina Bay . . . offers fair anchorage in 15 to 17 fathoms, mud bottom. The bay has two entrances. The W entrance, between Emgeten Island and Error Island, is clear, and a midchannel course will lead to the anchorage. The E entrance is between Fassett Island and Silver Point, and a midchannel course will likewise lead safely to the anchorage.* (CP)

Small craft will prefer the more sheltered and intimate Leesoffskaia Bay.

Anchor (large vessels) in 15 fathoms, mud bottom with fair holding.

*The channel on the north side of Entrance Island, Leesoffskaia Bay*

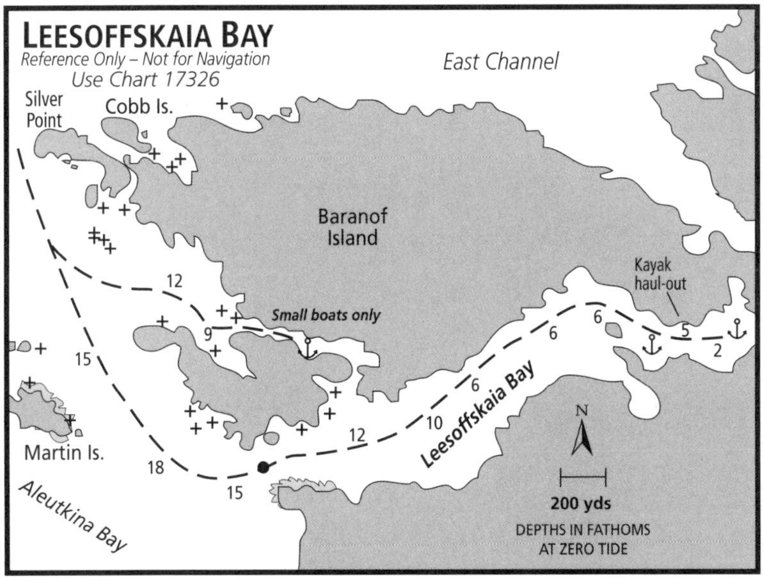



## **Leesoffskaia Bay** (Aleutkina Bay)

Leesoffskaia Bay is the east basin of Aleutkina Bay.

Chart 17326
Entrance: 56°59.97′ N, 135°17.08′ W
Anchor (Site #1): 57°00.25′ N, 135°15.23′ W
Anchor (Site #2): 57°00.30′ N, 135°14.94′ W

> *Leesoffskaia Bay . . . affords anchorage for small vessels in any desired depth. . . . Vessels desiring to make use of this well-sheltered anchorage should follow the N shores close-to in order to avoid the extensive sand and mudflats bordering the S shores. The bottom is mud in the middle of the bay, but rocky near the shores.* (CP)

Leesoffskaia Bay is a good example of an intimate cove tucked

Réanne Hemingway-Douglass

*Fish packer at Sandy Cove*

back behind a group of islands. It is an excellent landlocked, safe anchorage. We have also seen small boats anchored in the narrow channel on the north side of the entrance island (very intimate!) or deep in the bay.

When you enter the bay, favor the north shore as the drying mud flat to the south nearly closes the entrance channel.

Anchor (Site #1): Anchor in 5 to 6 fathoms over mud and shells with good holding.

Anchor (Site #2): Anchor in 2 to 3 fathoms over mud and clamshells with good holding.

## **Deep Inlet** (Baranof Island)

Deep Inlet has a narrow entrance southeast of The Eckholms and the entrance to Eastern Channel.

Chart 17326
Entrance: 56°59.27′ N, 135°18.57′ W

> *Deep Inlet . . . has no anchorage. A large flat rock with 3/4 fathom over it is on the S side and partly blocks the entrance.* (CP)

Either Sandy Cove, at the entrance to Deep Cove, or Samsing Cove to the west are preferred anchor sites.

## **Sandy Cove** (Baranof Island)

Sandy Cove is 4.5 miles south of Sitka.

Chart 17326
Entrance: 56°59.30′ N, 135°19.26′ W
Anchor: 56°58.80′ N, 135°18.97′ W

> *Sandy Cove . . . is a protected anchorage for small craft in 5-1/4 to 9-1/4 fathoms, mud and sand bottom.* (CP)

There is good shelter in Sandy Cove. Fish buyers anchor here during gill net season.

The bottom is covered with newspaper kelp, so holding is poor unless you set your anchor well.

Anchor in 7 to 10 fathoms over sand, some rocks and kelp with poor holding.

## **Samsing Cove** (Baranof Island)

Samsing Cove is 4 miles south of Sitka.

Chart 17326
Entrance: 56°59.32′ N, 135°21.75′ W
Anchor: 56°59.01′ N, 135°21.60′ W

> *Samsing Cove . . . is a well-protected anchorage for small boats with easy access from the W side*

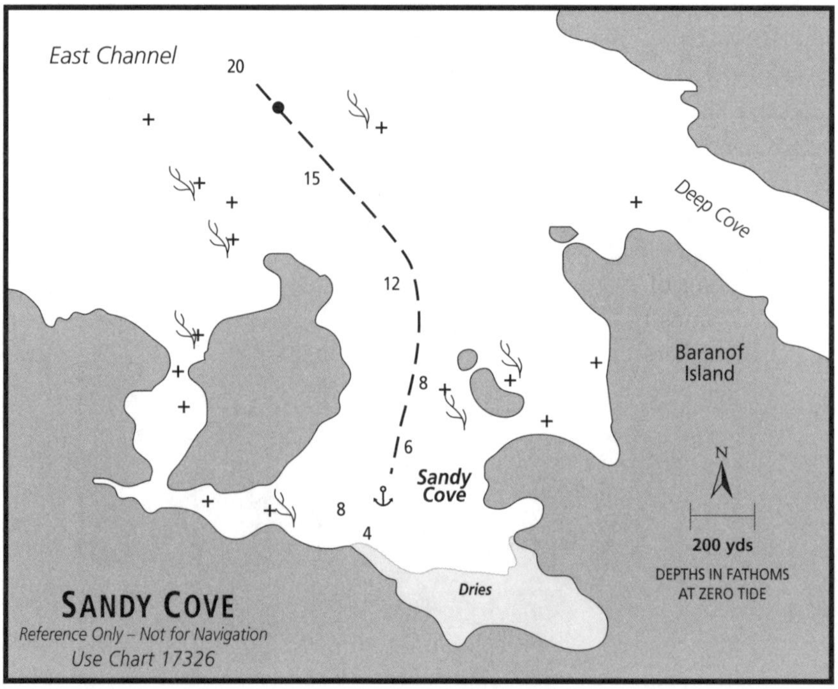

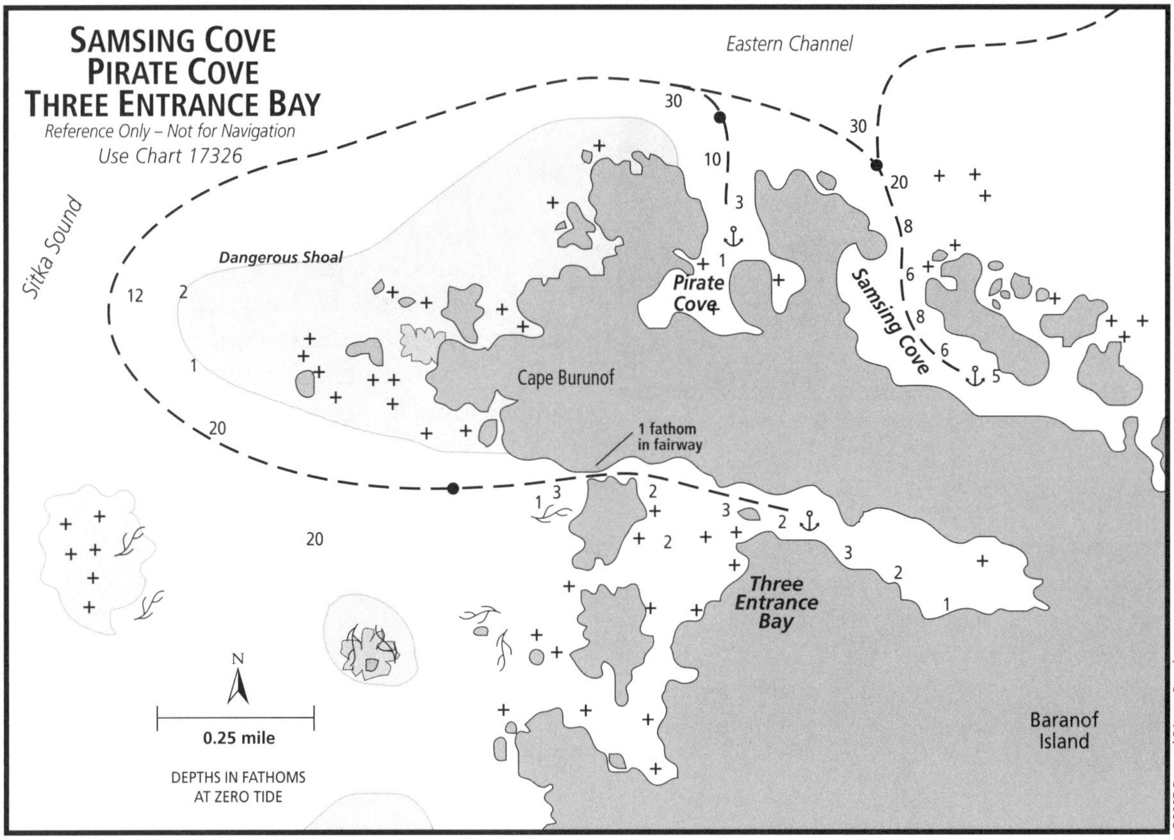



*and good holding ground of mud and sand in 2 to 8-1/2 fathoms.* (CP)

Samsing Cove, the first of the three coves in the vicinity of Cape Burunof, is well sheltered in all winds. It is small and cozy with a flat bottom for the most part. It is also fairly easy to enter if you keep a mid-channel course until you are inside Easter Island, avoiding the off-lying rocks.

[*Editor's Note:* The word *burunof* is not a misspelling of Baranof, as one might think; rather, it comes from the Russian *mys burunof* (cape of breakers).]

Anchor in 5 fathoms over mud and sand with good holding.

## **Pirate Cove** (Baranof Island)

Pirate Cove is 4 miles south of Sitka.

Chart 17326
Entrance: 56°59.36′ N, 135°22.26′ W
Anchor: 56°59.22′ N, 135°22.26′ W

*Pirate Cove . . . is a protected anchorage at the head, but is constricted and shoals. Two to three small boats can anchor.* (CP)

Pirate Cove, the second of the three small scenic coves in the vicinity of Cape Burunof, has less protection and swinging room than Samsing Cove and is open to northwest chop. Temporary anchorage is somewhat marginal.

Anchor mid-bay in 2 fathoms over mud and sand with fair holding.

## **Three Entrance Bay** (Baranof Island)

Three Entrance Bay is south of Cape Burunof.

Chart 17326
North entrance: 56°58.84′ N, 135°23.12′ W
Anchor: 56°58.76′ N, 135°22.10′ W

*Three Entrance Bay . . . is a protected anchorage for small boats, but is seldom used. The N entrance is the best and will carry 11/4 fathoms. In W weather, all entrances are exposed to the open sound. Do not use this bay without local knowledge.* (CP)

*North entrance to Three Entrance Bay*

Three Entrance Bay, the third of the Cape Burunof coves, is well sheltered and has a wild aspect with an intricate entrance. This is a narrow, fair weather entrance only, requiring good visibility to avoid major offshore rocks. Of the three entrances, we prefer the northern one. The south and middle entrances are foul.

Favor the north shore in the narrows, go slowly, and watch for rocks—this part of the coast is one big rock pile!

Anchor as you choose in 2 to 3 fathoms over sand and gravel with fair holding.

## **Mielkoi Cove** (Baranof Island)

Mielkoi Cove is 1 mile south of Three Entrance Bay.

Chart 17326
Entrance: 56°58.24′ N, 135°23.19′ W

Mielkoi Cove is surrounded by islets and rocks and is uncharted. We have not explored the cove, but it does look like an interesting place.

## **Koka Island Passage**

Koka Island Passage is 8 miles south of Sitka.

Chart 17326
North entrance: 56°55.09′ N, 135°22.93′ W
South entrance: 56°54.19′ N, 135°23.48′ W

> *Koka Island Passage . . . is part of the inside route for small vessels between Sitka and Hot Springs Bay.* (CP)

## **Redoubt Bay** (Baranof Island)

Redoubt Bay is 3 miles southeast of Povorotni Point.

Chart 17326
Entrance: 56°54.98′ N, 135°20.72′ W

> *The head of the bay has two arms, which are deep.* (CP)

Redoubt Bay has Redoubt Lake at its far end. The rapids and warm falls are impressive. We found depths on the north side of the rapids to be greater than those charted. This is a good place to watch for spawning salmon jumping and heading upstream.

## **Kidney Cove** (Redoubt Bay)

Kidney Cove is on the north shore of Redoubt Bay.

Chart 17326
Entrance: 56°54.27′ N, 135°19.27′ W
Anchor: 56°54.55′ N, 135°19.46′ W

Kidney Cove, which provides a calm anchorage in west winds, is a good place to anchor if you want to visit Redoubt Lake. There is a good view of 3,200-foot Mt. Dainishnikof from here and you can see bear roaming the shores. Kidney Cove is exposed to southerly weather; otherwise, it is sheltered.

Anchor in about 8 fathoms.

## **Redoubt Lake** (Redoubt Bay)

Redoubt Lake empties into the east arm of Redoubt Bay.

Chart 17326
Position (rapids): 56°53.19′ N, 135°17.81′ W

> *The entrance to Redoubt Lake is not navigable by any type craft. . . . A boat lift has been built along*

*Rapids at Redoubt Lake*

Réanne Hemingway-Douglass

North entrance to Redoubt Bay

*the N side of the entrance so that small boats up to 16 feet can be lifted into the lake.* (CP)

The falls from 10-mile-long Redoubt Lake make a roaring noise and create a lot of foam. There is a public mooring buoy in a nook on the west side of the falls out of the bulk of the current. The water is deeper than charted. The stairs leading to the lake are east of the buoy. *Caution:* We had a large offset to the east when we charted our GPS position.

## Islet Passage

Islet Passage is 0.5 mile west of Redoubt Bay.

Chart 17326
North entrance: 56°54.66′ N, 135°21.36′ W
South entrance: 56°53.44′ N, 135°21.16′ W

*Islet Passage, in which depths of 11 to 29 fathoms are found, leads from Kanga Bay to Redoubt Bay.* (CP)

## Kanga Bay (Baranof Island)

Kanga Bay is 1 mile southwest of Redoubt Bay.

Chart 17326
West entrance: 56°53.88′ N, 135°22.92′ W
Anchor: 56°52.82′ N, 135°19.53′ W

*The entrance to Kanga Bay is about 1.9 miles E of Peisar Island, and the inner bay has depths of 10 to 21 fathoms.* (CP)

The inner basin of Kanga Bay provides good anchorage for larger boats with lots of swinging room.

Anchor in 12 to 15 fathoms over soft mud with good holding.

## Crane Cove (Baranof Island)

Crane Cove is 0.4 mile southeast of Calligan Island.

Chart 17326
Entrance: 56°51.00′ N, 135°23.07′ W

Crane Cove is a tiny shallow cove more suited to sandhill cranes than small craft.

## Goddard Hot Springs Bay (Baranof Island)

Goddard Hot Springs Bay is 15 miles south of Sitka.

Chart 17326
North entrance (Torsar Island bearing 270°T at 0.35 Nm): 56°50.98′ N, 135°24.59′ W
South entrance (north entrance of Dorothy Narrows): 56°49.48′ N, 135°22.81′ W
Entrance (Goddard Hot Springs): 56°50.25′ N, 135°23.46′ W
Anchor (Goddard Hot Springs): 56°50.13′ N, 135°22.81′ W

Réanne Hemingway-Douglass

*U.S. Forest Service cabin with hot tub at Goddard Hot Springs Bay*

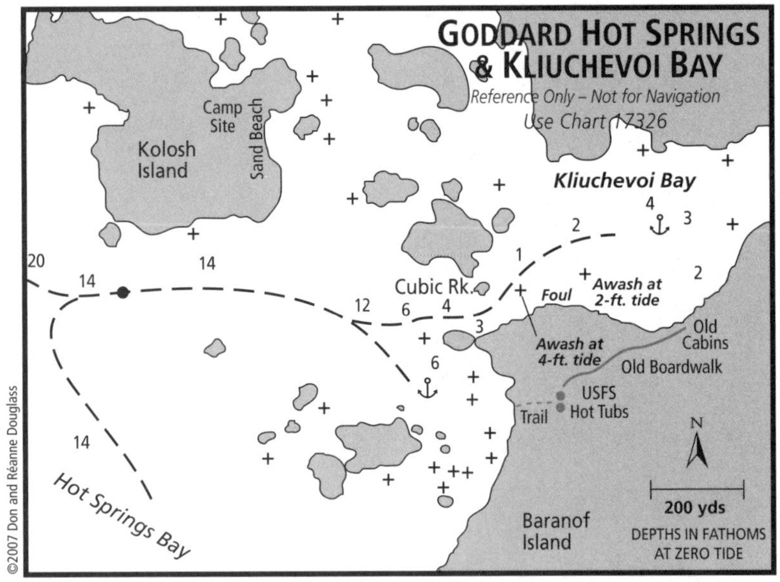


*The best route into Hot Springs Bay from the S or SW is to pass 0.4 mile E of North Rock in a N direction, passing W of Elovoi Island and the three small wooded islands about 400 yards off its shore and E of Fragrant Island. Keep midway between visible objects.*

*The hot springs on the NE side of the bay have a temperature of about 145°F., and the water contains chlorine, iron, magnesia, and sulphur.* (CP)

Goddard Hot Springs are a real treat for all those exploring Baranof Island's west coast. Don't miss this inviting call. The USFS has installed wooden hot tubs inside wooden shelters with a large open window to seaward. You have a choice of two valves to regulate temperature—hot or very hot! A boardwalk leads to the tubs from the sand and gravel beach where you can easily land your dinghy; there is an outhouse on the trail to the north, with an old open cement pool with a bathtub further up the hill.

*Heading for a dip in the hot tub*

The cove is small and foul with a rocky bottom and marginal holding (mud is reported in deeper water). The cove in front of the tub is used by local fishing boats from late afternoon to very early in the morning.

Anchor in 5 to 10 fathoms over sand, mud and kelp with fair holding. Set your anchor well so you can enjoy your hot tubbing. Kliuchevoi Bay to the northeast has better holding and shelter, but your boat is out of view while tubbing.

## Kliuchevoi Bay (Baranof Island)

Kliuchevoi Bay is 0.3 mile north of Goddard Hot Springs.

Chart 17326
Entrance: 56°50.25′ N, 135°22.85′ W
Anchor: 56°50.32′ N, 135°22.32′ W

Kliuchevoi Bay, northeast of Goddard Hot Springs, is a small bay protected by islets and rock piles with very good shelter and holding over a largely mud bottom with many clam shells. Its entrance, however, is narrow and shallow with numerous uncharted rocks. Pass south of "Cubic Rock" where you must make a dogleg, as shown on the diagram. The passage, at this point, is about 40 feet wide, and a foul area lies along the southeast shore. Be extra cautious making this entrance; post a bow watch and proceed very slowly.

Anchor in 3 to 4 fathoms over mud with clamshells; very good holding.

Réanne Hemingway-Douglass

*Approaching Dorothy Narrows . . .*

Réanne Hemingway-Douglass

*. . . while maintaining a sharp lookout!*

## Dorothy Narrows

Dorothy Narrows, between Windy Passage and Hot Springs Bay, separates Baranof and Elovoi islands.

Chart 17326
North entrance: 56°49.48′ N, 135°22.81′ W
South entrance: 56°48.88′ N, 135°22.71′ W

> *Dorothy Narrows . . . has 1-1/4 fathoms of water at lowest tides. . . . Coming from the S, keep midchannel through the narrowest part, then swing right to avoid the rock. When past Elovoi Island rock, swing left to avoid a rock awash at half tide, 250 yards NE of the daybeacon. Local knowledge is essential.* (CP)

Réanne Hemingway-Douglass

*Green marker, G"1," north end of Dorothy Narrows*

Dorothy Narrows is the first of several narrows that allow cruising boats to enjoy the southwest coast of Baranof Island using a smooth-water route. Small craft will have no problem maneuvering provided they post an alert bow watch and transit these channels slowly.

On a transit at zero tide, we found 1 fathom in the fairway from marker G"1" to the narrows, then a gradual deepening to 2-1/2 fathoms, except for a 1-fathom shoal at the south entrance. Dorothy Narrows is not well charted, but you can see the soft bottom of sand, clam shells and newspaper kelp, with lots of starfish.

The fairway in the narrows is about 60 feet wide. The biggest danger lies in cutting the corner north of marker G"1." Do not hug the marker, and stay east until you have passed the last of a series of rocks on the west shore. Favor the east shore a bit at the south entrance.

## Necker Islands

Necker Islands are located west of Goddard Hot Springs and north of West Crawfish Inlet.

Chart 17326

> *Between the islands are many passages. An inside passage for small craft leads through Windy Passage, Dorothy Narrows, and Hot Springs Bay. . . .* (CP)

Réanne Hemingway-Douglass

*Necker Islands provide beautiful shelter.*

We like to stay in wild-looking yet secure Herring Bay when visiting the Necker Islands. These islands are fun to explore by kayak.

## **Herring Bay** (Elovoi Island)

Herring Bay indents the south side of Elovoi Island and is 2 miles south of Goddard Hot Springs.

Chart 17326
Entrance: 56°48.11′ N, 135°24.54′ W
Anchor: 56°49.07′ N, 135°23.80′ W

> *The approach W of Kirbas island is impassable . . . . Excellent anchorage can be had for small craft in 2 to 3 fathoms, mud bottom.* (CP)

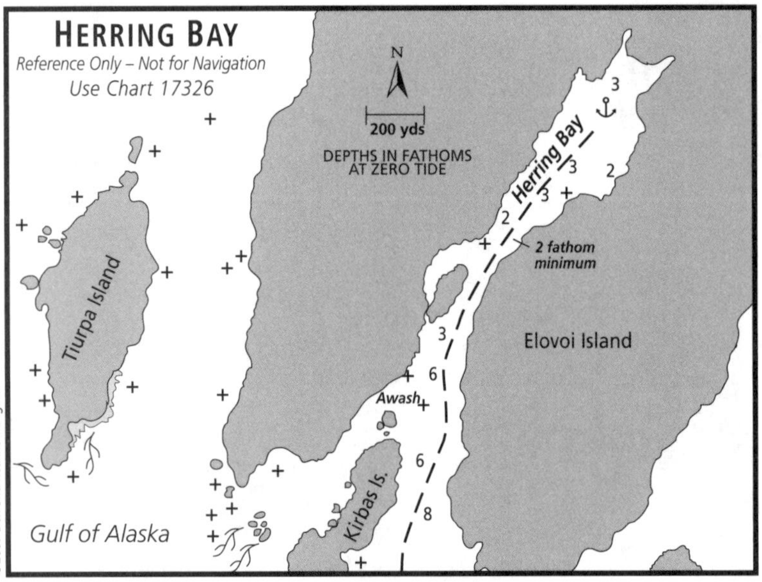




The head of Herring Bay offers very good protection. Note the absence of logs on the beach. While close to the Gulf of Alaska, in fair weather this little inlet makes a good base camp from which to explore a great variety of islets, rocks and tidepools. Avoid foul areas and kelp when entering the bay. Once inside, you are landlocked and surrounded by old cedar forest.

Anchor in 3 fathoms over mud, sand, shells and kelp patches with good to very good holding.

## **Symonds Bay and Rocky Cove** (Biorka Island)

Symonds Bay is the cove on the north side of Biorka Island.

Chart 17326
Entrance: 56°51.98′ N, 135°31.09′ W
Anchor: 56°51.39′ N, 135°31.05′ W
Entrance (Rocky Cove): 56°50.53′ N, 135°33.04′ W

> *Symonds Bay . . . is sometimes a convenient anchorage for small vessels deterred from entering the sound by thick weather.*
>
> *The bay is open N, but affords anchorage with shelter from S winds, sand and shell bottom. The best shelter is near the head inside the 1/4-fathom rock in 4-1/2 to 6-1/4 fathoms, but it is suitable only for small craft.*
>
> *A U.S. Government wharf, a mooring buoy, and a seaplane float are on the W side near the head of Symonds Bay.* (CP)

Biorka Island has a large aero beacon and antenna "farm." Symonds Bay offers good shelter from southerly weather with easy entry and good swinging room. Rocky Cove is uncharted and too exposed for anchorage.

Anchor (Symonds Bay) in 5 fathoms over sand with fair holding.

## Big Bay (Baranof Island)

Big Bay is at the northwest end of Windy Passage.

Chart 17326
Entrance: 56°48.80′ N, 135°21.46′ W
Anchor: 56°48.96′ N, 135°19.62′ W

> *Anchorage is good in 5 to 10 fathoms, mud bottom, 0.3 mile off the stream at the SE end of the bay.* (CP)

Big Bay, well sheltered in the south arm, has easy entry and a lot of swinging room for large boats.

Anchor in 5 fathoms over mud with fair holding.

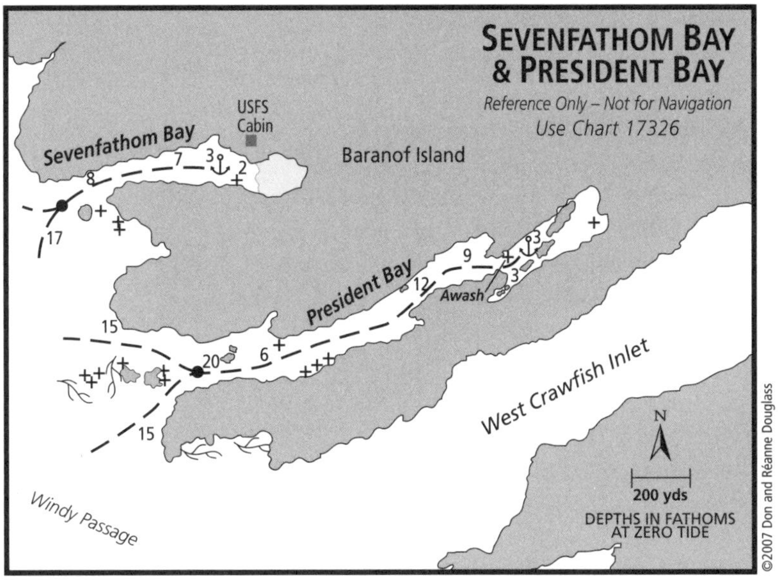


## Windy Passage

Windy Passage lies between Gornoi and Baranof islands.

Chart 17326
North entrance: 56°48.47′ N, 135°21.65′ W
South entrance: 56°46.44′ N, 135°19.09′ W

> *Windy Passage is the S approach to Hot Springs Bay from West Crawfish Inlet.* (CP)

Windy Passage gets its name from the strong southeast winds that blow down its 5-mile length. VHF Weather Ch 1 fades in and out in this area.

## Sevenfathom Bay (Windy Passage)

Sevenfathom Bay, on the east side of Windy Passage, is 0.7 mile north of President Bay.

Chart 17326
Entrance: 56°47.52′ N, 135°19.10′ W
Anchor: 56°47.62′ N, 135°18.23′ W

> *Sevenfathom Bay . . . affords better anchorage than President Bay. When entering, keep in mid-channel until near the head of the bay. . . . Good anchorage for small craft in 51/2 to 8 fathoms, mud bottom, can be found in the bay.* (CP)

Sevenfathom Bay and President Bay both offer very good anchorage for small craft at their head. In Sevenfathom Bay there is a USFS A-frame hut on the north shore and a public mooring buoy off the drying mud flat.

*Note:* The flat is much more extensive than indicated on the chart. For example, there is grass growing where the chart shows 2 fathoms!

Anchor in 6 fathoms over mud, sand, clam-shells and some kelp.

## President Bay (Windy Passage)

President Bay is on the east side of Windy Passage, just inside the south entrance.

Chart 17326
Entrance: 56°46.90′ N, 135°18.37′ W
Anchor: 56°47.30′ N, 135°16.21′ W

> *Good anchorage, with mud bottom, is afforded small craft well toward the head of the bay. A basin at the head of the bay is accessible only to skiffs.* (CP)

We find good shelter at the head of President Bay in the small basin west of the islets and lagoon. We anchor north of a window between the islets and west of a rock pile. Avoid the rock awash on a 6-foot tide off the north entrance point to the inner basin.

Anchor in 3 to 4 fathoms over mud and clam shells with good holding.

## West Crawfish Inlet (Baranof Island)

West Crawfish Inlet is 5 miles south of Goddard Hot Springs.

**Chart 17326**
**Entrance: 56°46.35′ N, 135°17.43′ W**

> *West Crawfish Inlet extends NE for about 8 miles where it divides into two arms. The N arm, opposite Cedar Pass, is clear in midchannel except for a landslide shoal with 41/2 fathoms over it, which is off the W shore about 0.8 mile from the entrance. . . . The inlet and bays are too deep for good anchorage.* (CP)

## Shamrock Bay (West Crawfish Inlet)

Shamrock Bay is 6 miles from the entrance to West Crawfish Inlet.

**Chart 17326**
**Entrance: 56°49.82′ N, 135°08.46′ W**

> *Shamrock Bay leads E from a point near the head of the inlet.* (CP)

Shamrock Bay may provide good shelter, except for williwaws that sweep down the peaks towering overhead.
Anchor behind the islet at the head of the bay in 6 to 9 fathoms over gravel.

## Cedar Pass

Cedar Pass, between Lodge and Baranof islands, connects West Crawfish Inlet to Crawfish Inlet.

**Chart 17326**
**North entrance: 56°48.53′ N, 135°11.20′ W**
**South entrance: 56°45.38′ N, 135°11.58′ W**

> *Cedar Pass . . . is suitable only for small craft. In using the pass, favor the W shore up to the narrows, then keep a midchannel course.* (CP)

We prefer the outside, smooth-water passage using First and Second Narrows west of Lodge Island.

## First Narrows (Rakof Islands)

First Narrows is between Lodge Island and Rakof Islands.

**Chart 17326**
**Position: 56°45.40′ N, 135°17.00′ W**

> *An inside passage furnishes protection for small craft bound for Sitka. Pass E of Scow Island, avoiding the rock in midchannel, and through Cameron Pass. Favor the SE shore of Middle Channel until up to Second Narrows. Pass E of a large rock off the point, then favor the S shore, and take a midchannel course through the narrows. A shoal of 2-1/2 fathoms is in the Second Narrows. Head N until up to an opening leading NW. Favor the NE shore of this opening, passing a rock near the shore and avoiding a submerged rock in the center. Then head NE for about 0.6 mile and turn W around a point, passing in midchannel through First Narrows. Cross West Crawfish Inlet and enter Windy Passage.* (CP)

First and Second Narrows provide a secure route south to Walker Channel. We find a little less than 3 fathoms at zero tide in the fairway through the first narrows. Avoid an uncharted rock marked by kelp on the east shore of the northern entrance.

*Note:* the *Coast Pilot* instructions read from south to north, whereas our data is given from north to south. Plan your route with this note in mind.

## Baidarka Cove (Rakof Islands)

Baidarka Cove is 6 miles south of Goddard Hot Springs.

**Chart 17326**
**Entrance: 56°45.20′ N, 135°17.00′ W**
**Anchor: 56°44.89′ N, 135°17.61′ W**

Baidarka Cove is formed by the three northernmost unnamed islands of the Rakof Islands.

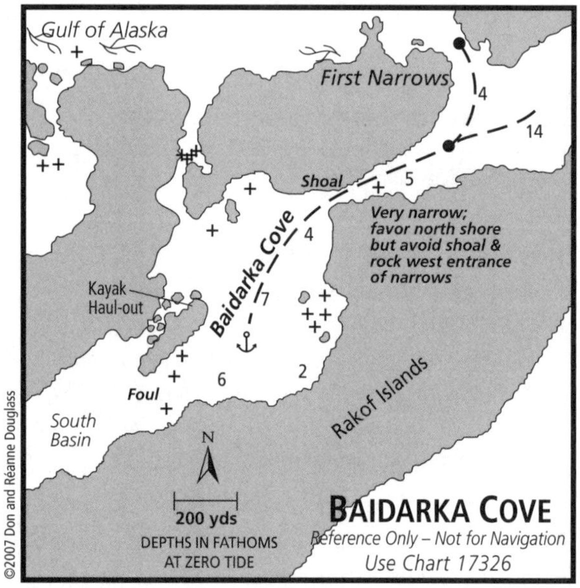

Réanne Hemingway-Douglass

*Outer passage through the Rakof Islands*

The cove offers good shelter in a rugged west coast setting. On entering the very narrow entrance, favor the north shore to avoid a dangerous rock awash on an 18-inch tide that extends over halfway from the south shore. The fairway carries a minimum of 3 fathoms.

Entry to the southwest basin is advised only by dinghy or kayak. It is separated from the north basin by a foul line of mussel-covered rocks. Enter only at high water by favoring the south shore about 45 feet off a bold white rock.

Weather reports on VHF Ch 1 can be heard from Baidarka Cove, so named for its appropriateness as a natural base for kayaking.

Anchor in 6 fathoms over mud with good holding.

## Second Narrows (Rakof Islands)

Second Narrows is between the southwest side of Lodge Island and Rakof Islands.

Chart 17326
Position: 56°44.08′ N, 135°16.33′ W

*A shoal of 2-1/2 fathoms is in Second Narrows.* (CP)

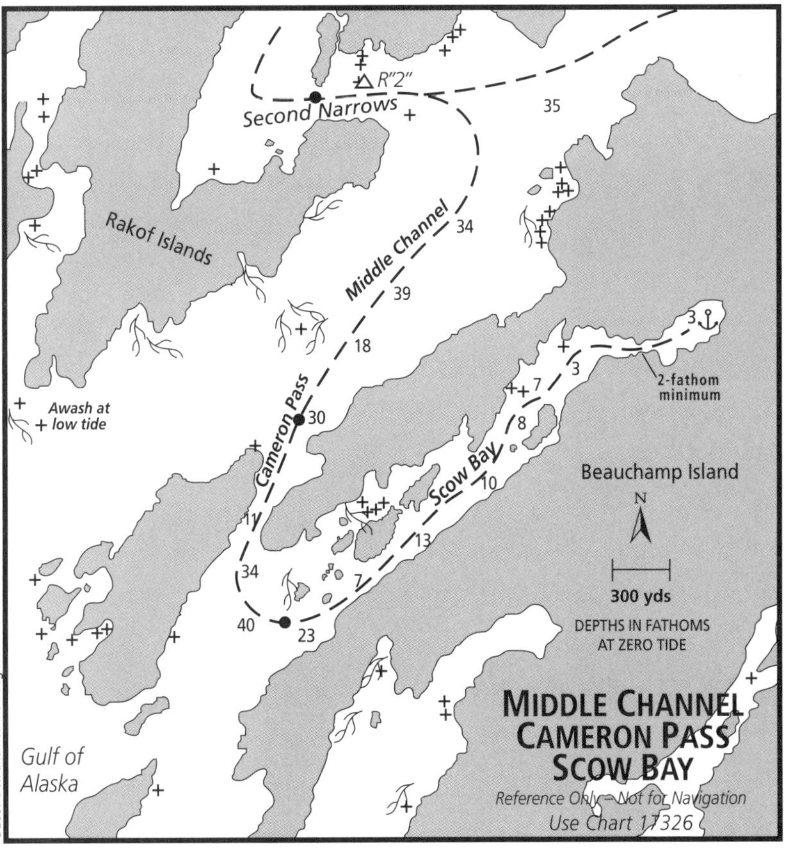




## Middle Channel (Rakof Islands)

Middle Channel, north of Beauchamp Island, leads to Crawfish Inlet, midway between Walker Channel and West Crawfish Inlet.

Chart 17326
Northeast entrance:
56°44.70′ N, 135°12.98′ W
Southwest entrance:
56°43.04′ N, 135°17.77′ W

*Setting a course from SW, to pass close to the NW side of Scow Island, then adjusting course as necessary to clear the island, islets, and rocks N of Scow Island will lead clear of the dangers up to this entrance. One mile inside this entrance, near midchannel, is a sub-*

*Inlet on Baranof's west coast*

*merged rock with 1-1/2 fathoms over it and marked by kelp, which should preferably be passed to the S.* (CP)

Middle Channel provides access to Scow Bay, another of our favorite "West Coast" coves.

## Cameron Pass

Cameron Pass cuts across the northwest side of Beauchamp Island to Middle Channel.

Chart 17326
Northeast entrance: 56°43.20′ N, 135°16.49′ W
Southwest entrance: 56°41.80′ N, 135°17.23′ W

Cameron Pass connects Middle Channel to Scow Bay.

## Scow Bay (Beauchamp Island)

Scow Bay is on the west shore of Beauchamp Island.

Chart 17326
Entrance: 56°42.70′ N, 135°16.46′ W
Anchor (northeast cove): 56°43.47′ N, 135°14.53′ W

*Scow Bay . . . is much used by local fishermen as an anchorage. . . . It is reported that the safe channel in the narrows leading to a basin at the head of the bay is very close to the S shore. . . . There is good anchorage off the point about 0.8 mile above the entrance on the N shore of the bay in 10 fathoms, mud bottom; also in the basin in 2-1/2 to 3-1/4 fathoms, mud bottom.* (CP)

Scow Bay is a bombproof anchorage separated from the Gulf of Alaska by just a few low-lying islets and rocks. Shelter is good here and the contrast between the rugged coast and the cedar-lined shores with many silver snags impressive.

Avoid the bad rocks on the north shore as you enter the inner basin; these rocks extend 60 percent of the way into the basin. Stay hard against the south shore about 5 to 10 feet off the tree limbs.

Anchor in 3-1⁄2 fathoms over brown mud, clamshells and some twigs with very good holding.

## Walker Channel

Walker Channel is the southeast entrance to Crawfish Inlet.

Chart 17326
West entrance: 56°41.41′ N, 135°14.99′ W
Northeast entrance: 56°44.60′ N, 135°12.57′ W

*Aspid Cape . . . forms the SE point at the entrance.* (CP)

Walker Channel takes you out into the Gulf and your progress southward depends on hopping from one sheltered inlet to the next by rounding some imposing capes all the way to Cape Ommaney.

## Crawfish Inlet (Baranof Island)

Crawfish Inlet is 2.5 miles northeast of Scow Bay.

Chart 17326
Entrance: 56°45.09′ N, 135°11.40′ W

*Crawfish Inlet is deep and clear except for a rock that uncovers 3 feet in midchannel, about 3.5 miles from its junction with Walker Channel, Middle Channel, and Cedar Pass. The inlet can be entered from seaward through Walker Channel or Middle Channel; the former is safer.* (CP)

## Jamboree Bay (Walker Channel)

Jamboree Bay extends southeast from the head of Walker Channel.

**Chart 17326**
**Entrance: 56°42.62′ N, 135°11.62′ W**
**Anchor: 56°41.91′ N, 135°10.37′ W**

> *In entering, keep in midchannel, and anchor near the head of the bay in 10 to 17 fathoms with good holding ground. SE winds sweep through the anchorage with considerable force.* (CP)

Anchored at the head of Jamboree Bay, you have little fetch in southeast winds. However, the bottom is rocky and of marginal holding.

Anchor in 10 fathoms over mud with marginal holding.

## Necker Bay (Baranof Island)

Necker Bay is 35 miles northwest of Cape Ommaney.

**Chart 17328**
**Entrance: 56°39.37′ N, 135°10.50′ W**

> *A rocky patch where 10 fathoms were found is about 0.5 mile N of the northernmost of the Guibert Islets in the middle of the bay; it is reported to break in extremely heavy weather. . . .* (CP)

Necker Bay has several remote, but good anchorages.

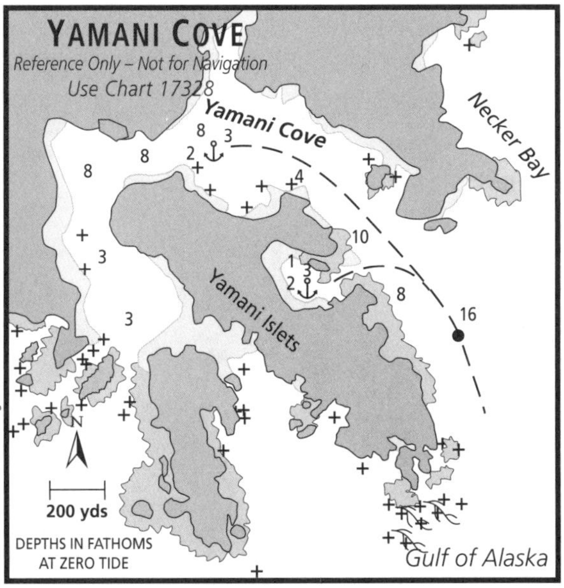


## Yamani Cove (Necker Bay)

Yamani Cove is on the north side of the entrance to Necker Bay and north of the Yamani Islets.

**Chart 17328**
**Entrance: 56°40.30′ N, 135°10.65′ W**
**Anchor (east cove): 56°′40.32 N, 135°11.09′ W**
**Anchor (north cove): 56°40.53′ N, 135°11.35′ W**

> *Good anchorage for small craft can be had N of the islets in Yamani Cove.* (CP)

Yamani Cove is another small cove with good shelter and an "outside feel." Enter east of the larger of the Yamani Islets and proceed to the cove on the islet's eastern side. From this site you have an excellent view of the Gulf of Alaska—including blowing foam! For the most protection, anchor along the north side of this islet.

Anchor (east cove) in about 2 fathoms over sand, gravel and newspaper kelp; holding is marginal unless you set your anchor well.

Anchor (north cove) in 2 to 8 fathoms over sand, gravel and kelp; fair-to-good holding with a well-set anchor.

## Toy Harbor (Necker Bay)

Toy Harbor, south of Dorothy Cove, is 5 miles above the entrance to Necker Bay.

**Chart 17328**
**Entrance: 56°43.27′ N, 135°04.84′ W**
**Anchor: 56°43.07′ N, 135°05.15′ W**

> *Toy Harbor . . . is reported to afford shelter for small boats.* (CP)

Toy Harbor is very well sheltered, but its 200- to 300-foot-wide channel limits swinging room. However, two anchors or a shore tie can be useful.

Anchor in 4 fathoms over a mixed bottom.

## Dorothy Cove (Necker Bay)

Dorothy Cove is 6 miles above the entrance to Necker Bay.

**Chart 17328**
**Entrance: 56°43.56′ N, 135°03.51′ W**
**Anchor: 56°43.78′ N, 135°02.52′ W**

> *Dorothy Cove . . . affords excellent anchorage for small craft in depths of about 6 to 10 fathoms E of the largest islet near the head of the cove.* (CP)

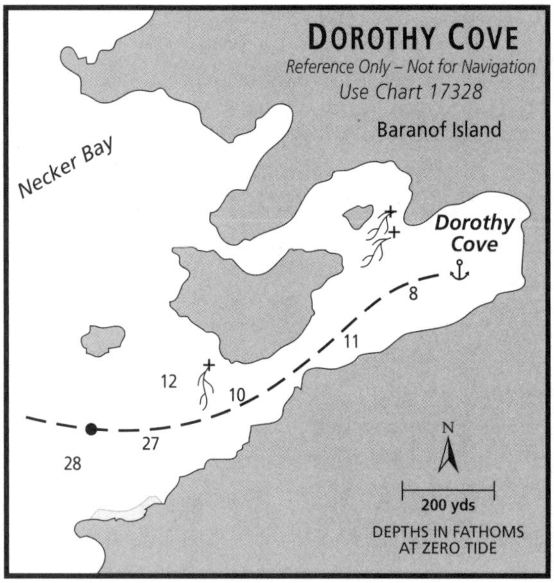


Dorothy Cove is a cozy anchorage in Necker Bay. Although the preferred anchorage is at the head of the bay, the site north of the islet may be even more snug.

Anchor in 7 fathoms over sand and gravel with good holding if anchor is well set.

## **Secluded Bay** (Necker Bay)

Secluded Bay is 0.7 miles north of Dorothy Cove.

Chart 17328
Entrance: 56°44.01′ N, 135°03.72′ W
Anchor: 56°44.43′ N, 135°02.87′ W

> *The S entrance is extremely narrow . . . with least known depth of 6-1/2 fathoms. The N entrance, N of the island . . . is obstructed by a ledge that extends NE about 100 yards from the N point of the island, leaving a clear channel of about 100 yards with a depth of 3-1/2 fathoms. . . . Small craft can find anchorage in 6 fathoms in the S part of the bay.* (CP)

Secluded Bay is isolated and remote. It has an almost hidden south entrance. Call on Ch 16 or sound your horn if you think there might be opposing traffic. Passing and turning room is tight.

Anchor snuggled up against the unnamed islet in 4 fathoms over sand, mud and rocks with fair holding.

## **North Cape** (Baranof Island)

North Cape is 6 miles south of Aspid Cape and 30.5 miles northwest of Cape Ommaney.

Chart 17328
Position: (approximate) 56°35.75′ N, 135°08.29′ W

> *North Cape . . . the NW point of entrance to Whale bay, 4 miles NW of Point Lauder, is an island close to shore with three hills on it. The middle hill is the highest.* (CP)

North Cape is exposed to the fury of southern storms from the Gulf of Alaska, as indicated by rocks washed bare of soil to a height of 150 feet. Still Harbor, 4 miles southeast of North Cape, provides very good shelter.

## **Whale Bay** (Baranof Island)

Whale Bay is 18 miles southeast of Goddard Hot Springs and 29 miles northwest of Cape Ommaney.

Chart 17328
Entrance: 56°34.38′ N, 135°05.79′ W

> *Whale Bay . . . extends in a NE direction for about 4 miles, where it divides into two arms, Great Arm and Small Arm.* (CP)

Whale Bay is roughly halfway between Sitka and Cape Ommaney. While anchorage can be found along the south shore of Whale Bay, we favor Still Harbor for both protection and convenience.

## **Still Harbor** (Whale Bay)

Still Harbor, at the entrance to Whale Bay, is 4 miles southeast of North Cape.

Chart 17328
Entrance: 56°33.91′ N, 135°03.49′ W
Anchor: 56°32.50′ N, 135°00.96′ W

*Entrance Islets protect Still Harbor.*

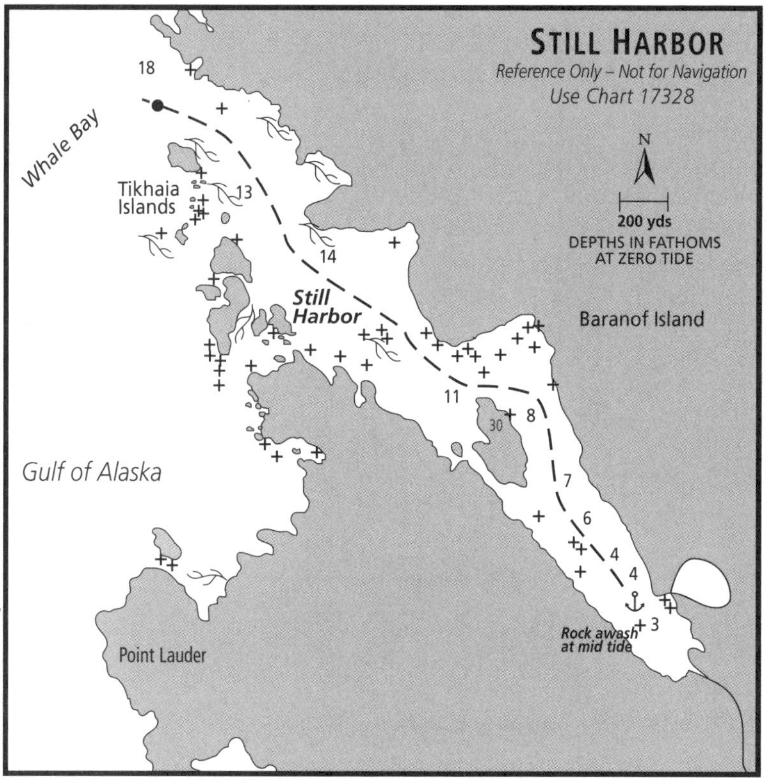




*Still Harbor . . . is about 1.5 miles N of Point Lauder. . . . The NE shore at the entrance is foul.*

*The only anchorage is at the head of the harbor, and even there the swell is felt in heavy weather; this anchorage is not recommended.* (CP)

Still Harbor is indeed still; the entrance islets, reefs and rocks do a good job of knocking down the swells and dispersing their energy. (Our Petersburg fishing friend loves to anchor here.) We found no signs of shore stress from swell or chop and would feel free to call this a "summer home." Good anchorage can be found anywhere from north of island (30) to the head of the bay. We saw lots of wildlife here. Avoid the rocks on the

## Still Harbor Disaster

Don Douglass & Réanne Hemingway-Douglass

In 1979, Ward Eldridge, a Sitka shipright, fell in love with a derelict 73-foot Herreshoff schooner he'd seen in a Florida boatyard and felt he could restore the 1888 *Merlin*. He bought her and spent the next six years rebuilding her from the keel up. Eleven years later, he brought her through the Panama Canal and up the West Coast to Sitka.

In 1999, Ward and his soon-to-be spouse, Kathy, set out a weekend for some R & R on *Merlin*. They anchored the schooner in Still Harbor, 35 miles south of Sitka, and launched their kayaks to do some exploring. When they returned several hours later, the masts were the only part of the vessel visible—the hull and superstructure lay below water. How could a boat of that size possibly just sink without warning?

Ward wondered if a seacock had failed; Kathy wondered if she'd forgotten to turn off the valve to the propane stove and an explosion had occurred.

Ward was devastated. Everything he owned, except what he'd taken in the kayak, was gone. With his VHF handheld, he made contact with a boat that took them back to Sitka. The next day, a friend took Ward back to Still Harbor where they dove the boat and recovered some of his belongings.

The community rallied around Ward, offering help and money. But when a second diver discovered a 5-foot round hole near the bottom of the hull, Ward speculated that a whale might have rammed *Merlin*. "Naively, I told people about my theory," he said, "and they thought I was nuts. I felt horrible."

Eventually, help outweighed the negative comments and, in a monumental community effort, the vessel was raised and towed to Sitka and set up in a boatyard where Ward and Kathy began the task of cleaning out *Merlin*'s interior. Imagine his relief when he discovered a piece of baleen, four by sixteen inches, wedged in the hull near the hole. Ward was exonerated, and *Merlin* was replanked and donated to the Sitka Maritime Heritage Society.

[*Note:* In the ensuing years, *Merlin* has passed into private hands. Ward and Kathy still live in Sitka and, in summers, cruise on their more modern *S/V Blue Merlin*.]

west shore; the southernmost rock extends farther from shore than charted!

The fishing boat, *Mary Gene,* rode out a 95-knot storm here in July 1996, proving that, when a storm is blowing in the Gulf, this anchorage may be underrated. Once again, we like the outside environment, where we can hear the surf pounding, yet we feel safe where there is no evidence of storm damage along shore—no logs at the head of the bay—and where the bottom is shallow, flat and sticky mud!

Anchor in 4 to 8 fathoms over sticky brown mud with very good holding.

## Port Banks (Whale Bay)

Port Banks is 2.5 miles east of Still Harbor.

Chart 17328
Entrance: 56°36.03′ N, 135°00.70′ W
Anchor: 56°34.15′ N,
134°58.91′ W

> *It is recommended that vessels bound for Port Banks steer midchannel courses until clear of the off-lying dangers, then head into Port Banks, favoring the E shore. . . . Good anchorage in depths from 8 to 20 fathoms, mud bottom, may be had in Port Banks which is used extensively during the fishing season.* (CP)

Réanne Hemingway-Douglass

*Salmon for dinner again!*

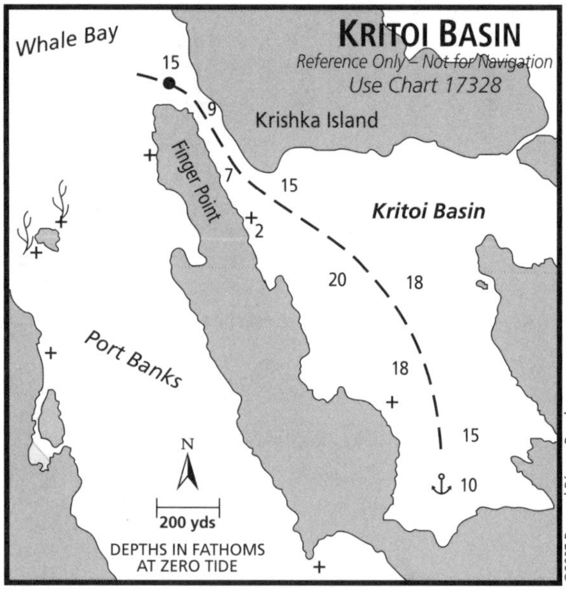

©2007 Don and Réanne Douglass

We prefer Still Harbor or landlocked Kritoi Basin to Port Banks.

## Kritoi Basin (Whale Bay)

Kritoi Basin is between Rakovoi Bay and Port Banks.

Chart 17328
Entrance: 56°36.14′ N, 135°00.35′ W
Anchor: 56°35.38′ N,
134°59.31′ W

> *Kritoi Basin* [is] *used extensively during the fishing season. . . . The bay affords excellent shelter, but is used mostly by small craft, because of its narrow entrance. . . . The entrance between Finger Point and Krishka Island is deep and clear except for a depth of 2-1/4 fathoms about 0.3 mile inside the entrance. . . . Good anchorage in desired depths from 5 to 20 fathoms, mud bottom, can be had in the basin.* (CP)

We like completely landlocked Kritoi Basin. While the basin is a little deep, good, well-sheltered anchorage can be found anywhere along its shore. However, there is some shale bottom with poor holding. We prefer the south shore.

Anchor in about 10 fathoms over brown mud, cobble and shale; fair-to-good holding if your anchor is well set.

## Rakovoi Bay (Whale Bay)

Rakovoi Bay is immediately east of Kritoi Basin.

Chart 17328
Entrance: 56°35.58′ N, 134°58.23′ W

The channel E of the island is foul and suitable only for small boats. Anchorage may be found S of the island at the entrance in about 18 fathoms or farther up the bay in 20 fathoms.

Rakovoi Bay is a little deep for our comfort.

## Small Arm (Whale Bay)

Small Arm is on the northwest side of Whale Bay.

Chart 17328
Entrance: 56°37.67′ N, 135°01.46′ W

> *The depths in Small Arm are too great to afford anchorage.* (CP)

Small Arm may offer reasonable anchorage for small craft at its bitter end in 6 fathoms over mud and shells.

## Great Arm (Whale Bay)

Great Arm is the northeast arm of Whale Bay, northeast of Rakovoi Bay.

Chart 17328
Entrance: 56°36.60′ N, 134°58.52′ W
Entrance (Small Bay): 56°39.27′ N, 134°54.20′ W
Anchor (Small Bay): 56°38.79′ N, 134°53.67′ W

> *An excellent anchorage with sand and mud bottom is in the small bay on the E side of the arm about 3.5 miles above the entrance to the arm. However, in the arm proper depths are too great for anchorage.* (CP)

Depths in Great Arm and Small Bay, 3.5 miles inside, are too great (20 to 30 fathoms) for small-craft anchorage.

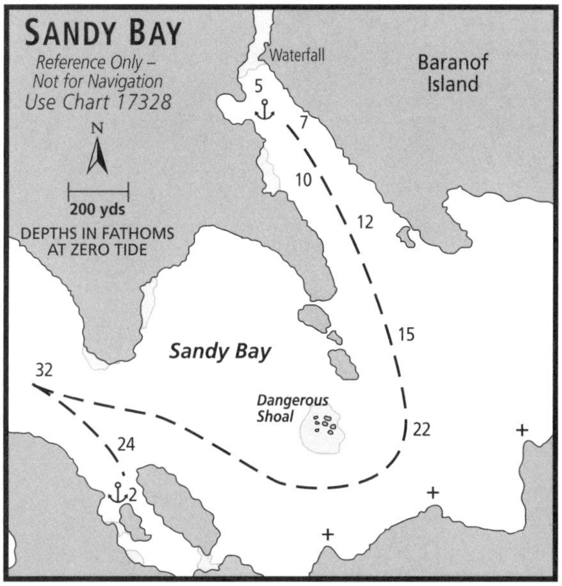


## Close Bay (Baranof Island)

Close Bay is 2.5 miles south of Still Harbor.

Chart 17328
Entrance: 56°31.19′ N, 135°02.20′ W

> *Close Bay consists of an open bight and a lagoon that can only be entered on the flood.* (CP)

Close Bay has an interesting lagoon and two small coves useful only under very limited conditions.

## Sandy Bay (Baranof Island)

Sandy Bay is 6.5 miles south of Still Harbor and 21 miles north of Cape Ommaney.

Chart 17328
Entrance: 56°27.49′ N, 134°59.96′ W
Anchor (south shore, East Arm): 56°28.03′ N, 134°58.43′ W
Anchor (north shore, East Arm): 56°28.68′ N, 134°57.90′ W

> *Sandy Bay . . . divides into two arms 0.8 mile from the entrance. . . .*
>
> *Good anchorage may be had in 22 to 24 fathoms at the NE head of the E arm off the waterfall. About 0.8 mile within the arm a group of islets extends off the N shore. Pass well S of these to avoid a 1-1/2-fathom spot . . . which is about 0.1 mile S of the islands. Anchorage may be had either in the bight W of the islands or in the arm that extends NW from the E arm.*
>
> *A 7-1/2-fathom spot in the middle of the entrance causes the seas to pile up dangerously in SE weather.* (CP)

The entrance to Sandy Bay is pure rock-bound coast. The picturesque sides of the cliffs are washed bare to a height of about 50 feet, and the waterfall is lovely.

The east arm of Sandy Bay has two anchor sites; however, neither would be considered secure in a gale. Swells dissipate at East Arm.

The south shore is the more protected spot, but the fairway into the inner basin is only about 20 feet wide and is shoal with kelp.

Anchor (south shore, East Arm) in 6 fathoms over mud, sand, clams, rocks and kelp; fair holding.

Anchor (north shore, East Arm) in 4 to 6 fathoms over mud, sand and shells with good holding.

## **Snipe Bay** (Baranof Island)

Snipe Bay is 3 miles south of Sandy Bay.

Chart 17328
Entrance: 56°24.82′ N, 134°57.46′ W

> *The bay is deep and clear except for the rocks close to the shore at the entrance. . . . About 1.4 miles within the entrance in the SE shore is a sheltered bight with 35 fathoms in the middle. At the head of Snipe Bay are two short branches. . . . Depths of 31 fathoms were obtained in the small bight S of the NE branch.* (CP)

Snipe Bay appears too deep for our taste.

## **Byron Bay** (Baranof Island)

Byron Bay lies east of Kekur Peninsula.

Chart 17330
Entrance: 56°22.33′ N,
134°55.36′ W
Anchor (second cove east):
56°23.30′ N, 134°54.49′ W

> *Byron Bay . . . is apparently clear, but too deep for secure anchorage. . . . Close to the W shore, near the head, is a small island above which small craft can find anchorage.* (CP)

The anchor site above the small island, mentioned above in *Coast Pilot,* has no swinging room and is a marginal anchorage at best. We prefer the second cove to the east.

Anchor in 4 to 6 fathoms over gravel, brown mud and clamshells; fair holding.

## **Réanne's Terror** (Baranof Island)

Réanne's Terror is 2.6 miles northwest of Redfish Cape.

Chart 17330
West entrance: 56°21.10′ N, 134°54.51′ W
South entrance: 56°20.94′ N, 134°54.33′ W
Entrance (Réanne's Relief): 56°21.47′ N,
134°53.87′ W
Anchor (Réanne's Relief): 56°21.50′ N,
134°53.59′ W
Entrance (White Cliffs Cove): 56°21.13′ N,
134°53.45′ W
Anchor (White Cliffs Cove): 56°20.85′ N,
134°53.33′ W

> *The small bay . . . furnishes good shelter for small boats, but the entrance is so narrow and the turns so sharp that a vessel of any size cannot enter, especially if there is any swell.* (CP)

At last, an unnamed cove with a suitable description to name after *Baidarka*'s intrepid Cape Horner and first mate. Entering from the north appears to be a formidable task, as we discovered on our first visit to this bay. Heavy southwest swells were breaking on the

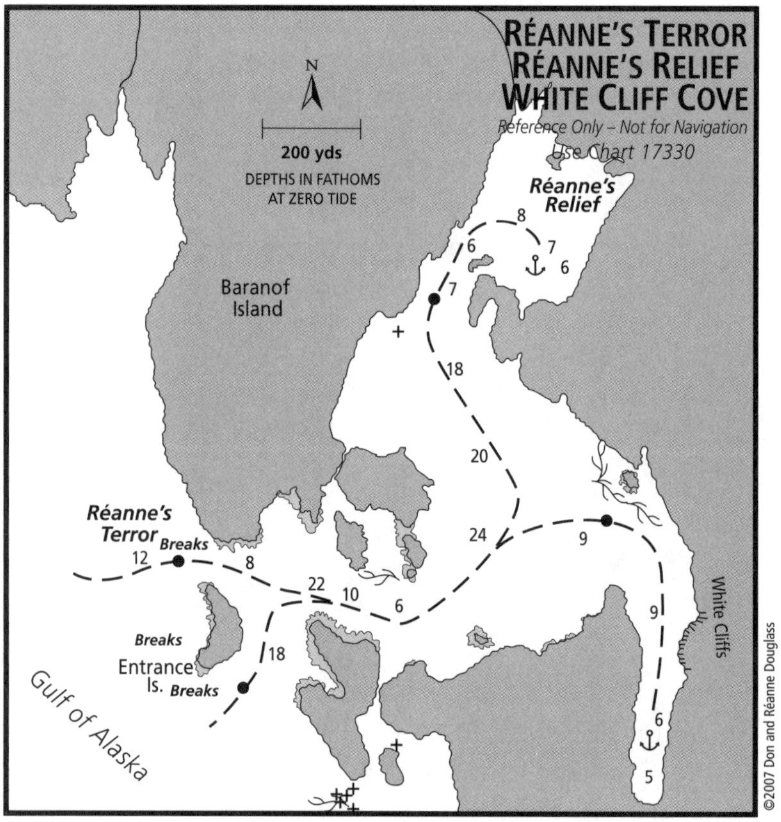

*Entrance to Réanne's Terror*

Since that first time in the early 1990s, we have entered what we call "Réanne's Terror" many times in stable weather without fear on the first mate's part.

Under moderate conditions, you can enter either the north or the south side of the entrance island; the south entrance is wider and has less foam. Both entrances are deep, but can be dangerous when large seas are running. The north entrance has 8 fathoms minimum in its fairway; the south has 15 fathoms minimum. Pleasure craft should have little trouble negotiating the turns required to enter Réanne's Terror. Note that we have found less water than Chart 17330 indicates.

entrance island, as well as along the north shore of Baranof Island, and foam spewed across the opening. With a large northwest swell running, the swells heap up near the entrance island and threaten to break, making the entrance appear worse than it may be. Réanne held tight on that first visit, and we scooted through the north opening in grand style.

Once inside the bay—what relief! It is perfectly calm and the beauty stunning—this is pristine wilderness at its best. You can anchor with complete shelter in the southeast cove, which we call "White Cliffs Cove," or

*The photo says it all.*

Don Douglass

*The terror lessening*

Don Douglass

*Réanne's Relief at last*

in the north cove we call "Réanne's Relief." *Deception* reports this to be excellent anchorage that easily holds seven boats.

The bottom in Réanne's Relief is a thin layer of mud, so fair holding is about the best you can get. Using a shore tie in either of the two coves would make the anchorage more comfortable and secure.

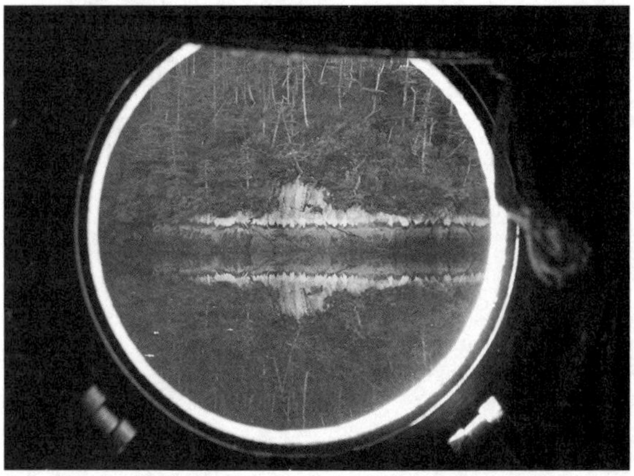

Benson Isley

*Looking through the port hole at the perfect calm in Réanne's Relief*

Anchor (Réanne's Relief) in 7 fathoms, soft brown mud bottom; fair-to-good holding.

Anchor (White Cliffs Cove) in about 8 fathoms over brown mud and clam shells with fair holding.

## **Redfish Bay** (Baranof Island)

Redfish Bay is 3 miles south of Réanne's Terror.

Chart 17330
Entrance (Redfish Point bearing 326°T at 0.25 Nm): 56°17.86′ N, 134°52.28′ W
Anchor (Granite Point Cove): 56°20.66′ N, 134°51.98′ W

> *Between Redfish Point and Big Branch Rock are the entrances to Little Branch Bay, Big Branch Bay, and Redfish Bay.*
>
> *Redfish Bay has its entrance between Redfish Cape and Beavertail Island. . . . The channels are probably safe, but too narrow for safe steering; there is no certainty that dangers do not exist. The use of the bay by vessels other than small craft is not recommended.* (CP)

The north arm of Redfish Bay leads to a good anchorage north of Granite Point. The first narrows is 100 yards wide; the second narrows is 25 yards wide.

Anchor in 8 to 10 fathoms over mud with fair holding.

Easier anchorage in all but a serious blow can be found in Tenfathom Anchorage.

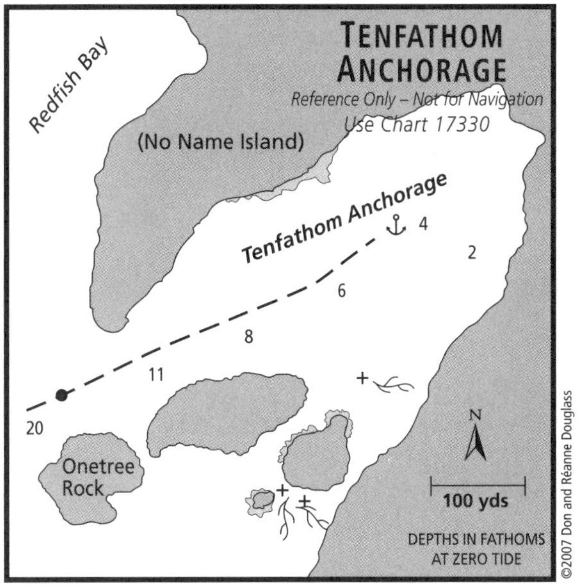


## Tenfathom Anchorage (Redfish Bay)

Tenfathom Anchorage is 0.6 mile east of Redfish Cape.

Chart 17330
Entrance: 56°18.80′ N, 134°51.88′ W
Anchor: 56°18.91′ N, 134°51.43′ W

> *Tenfathom Anchorage . . . furnishes secure anchorage for small craft.* (CP)

Tenfathom Anchorage is well sheltered and easy to enter. Some southerly swell enters the anchorage at high water via the south window.

Anchor in 10 to 12 fathoms over hard sand and mud with fair-to-good holding.

*Heading inside Big Branch for a lunch stop*

## Big Branch Bay (Baranof Island)

Big Branch Bay is just east of Redfish Bay.

Chart 17330
Entrance (light bearing 063°T at 0.2 Nm):
56°18.14′ N, 134°51.07′ W

> *Big Branch Bay* [is] *separated from Little Branch Bay by a high narrow neck of land. . . .* (CP)

## West Cove (Big Branch Bay)

West Cove is 1 mile north of the light at the mouth of Little Branch Bay.

Chart 17330
Entrance: 56°19.19′ N, 134°50.96′ W
Anchor: 56°19.61′ N, 134°51.21′ W

> *An arm indenting the W shore about 0.9 mile from the W entrance point has depths from 9 to 20 fathoms, where small boats can find good shelter.* (CP)

"West Cove" is what we call the anchor site in the west arm of Big Branch Bay; it is calm and well protected.

Anchor in 10 fathoms over sand and some newspaper kelp with fair holding if you set your anchor well.

## Little Branch Bay (Baranof Island)

Little Branch Bay is just east of Big Branch Bay.

Chart 17330
Entrance: 56°17.96′ N, 134°50.61′ W
Entrance (lagoon): 56°18.40′ N, 134°49.51′ W

*Little Branch Bay is about 1.9 miles long to the narrows . . . and widens into a basin. . . . Mid-channel depths in the bay range from 81 fathoms near the entrance to . . . 17 fathoms in the middle of the basin at the head. About 0.8 mile within the entrance, a narrow channel in the SE shore, entered only at high water, leads to a lagoon that has depths of 1 to 71/2 fathoms.* (CP)

The lagoon in Little Branch Bay is on our list of "worth exploring."

## **Driftwood Cove** (Baranof Island)

Driftwood Cove is 1 mile northwest of Puffin Bay.

Chart 17330
Entrance: 56°16.27′ N, 134°49.55′ W

*Driftwood Cove is . . . 1.2 miles N of Sealion Rocks; its entrance is obstructed by reefs marked by kelp patches. The cove is exposed.* (CP)

## **Puffin Bay** (Baranof Island)

Puffin Bay's entrance is east of Sealion Rocks and 7 miles northwest of Cape Ommaney.

Chart 17330
Entrance: 56°15.00′ N, 134°48.59′ W

*A small bight in the NW shore, 1 mile within the bay, furnishes temporary anchorage with limited swinging room for small craft. The entrance to the anchorage has a depth of 11 fathoms in a channel about 60 yards wide between shoals that extend from both points of the entrance. The cove furnishes little protection from S.* (CP)

We don't like the small bight in Puffin Bay mentioned above since it is full of logs, indicating heavy pounding in southerly gales. We find far superior anchorage further up the bay in Forevergreen Basin.

## **Forevergreen Basin** (Baranof Island)

Forevergreen Basin is 2 miles inside Puffin Bay.

Chart 17330
Entrance: 56°16.62′ N, 134°46.28′ W
Anchor: 56°16.45′ N, 134°46.11′ W

*The small cove in the SE shore near the head of the bay furnishes anchorage for small craft in 5 to 8 fathoms in the middle of the cove. The very narrow entrance channel has depths of 12 fathoms. Williwaws blow with considerable force during SE gales.* (CP)

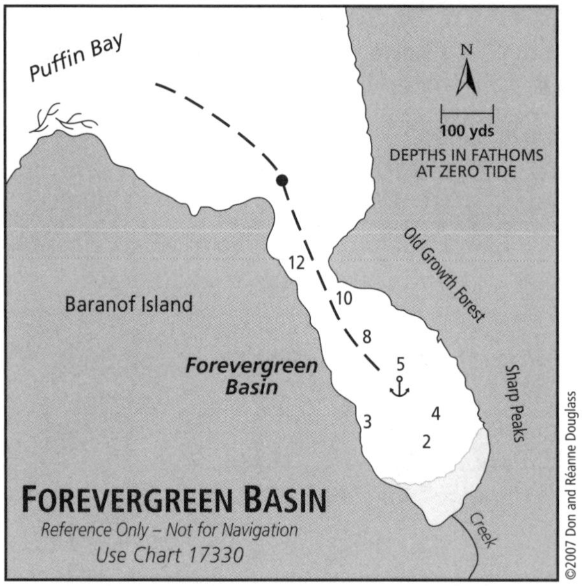


The head of "Forevergreen Basin," our name for the unnamed basin south of Puffin Bay, has excellent anchorage. We call this basin Forevergreen because we had such a good time here with our friend and fellow explorer, Professor Roderick Frazer Nash, owner of *Forevergreen*, who has crewed with us.

We consider this to be an excellent and secure anchor site. Williwaws may be strong at times, but the basin has little fetch and good holding. Wildlife viewing is good and fishing excellent. West winds, deflected down the high ridge to the east, become gentle breezes. Old-growth trees lie along the east shore below high sharp peaks.

Anchor in 6 fathoms over mud with good holding.

## **Little Puffin Bay** (Baranof Island)

Little Puffin Bay is 1.5 miles south of Puffin Bay.

Chart 17330
Entrance: 56°13.75′ N, 134°47.47′ W

*Exposed anchorage for small vessels may be had in 6 to 7 fathoms, hard bottom. In entering, favor the N shore to avoid rocks awash and breakers off the S shore near the entrance.* (CP)

Little Puffin Bay is open to the west and should be considered a fair-weather anchorage only. The bottom appears to be a thin layer of sand over rocks with marginal holding.

## **Larch Bay** (Baranof Island)

Larch Bay is 3 miles north of Cape Ommaney.

Chart 17330
Entrance: 56°12.10′ N, 134°43.37′ W

> *Larch Bay is a large open bay with an arm that extends in a NE direction. Anchorage may be found in about 20 fathoms in this arm. Small launches use this arm during the fishing season when fair weather prevails. Rocks extend about 500 yards off the W point of the entrance to the bay.* (CP)

## **Ommaney Bay** (Baranof Island)

Ommaney Bay is 1 mile northwest of Cape Ommaney.

Chart 17330
Position: 56°10.36′ N, 134°41.39′ W

> *Ommaney Bay . . . is of no importance to navigation.* (CP)

## **Cape Ommaney** (Baranof Island)

Cape Ommaney is the south tip of Baranof Island.

Chart 17330
Position (0.25 Nm south of cape, Wooden Island Light bearing 057°T at 0.44 Nm): 56°09.38′ N, 134°40.32′ W

> *Cape Ommaney . . . is a remarkable promontory terminating in Ommaney Peak, a bluff, rugged, rocky mountain, detached from the higher land N by a low depression running through from Port Conclusion.* (CP)

*Caution:* Tide rips and turbulent seas are found off Cape Ommaney and Wooden Island.

# CHATHAM STRAIT AND BARANOF ISLAND'S EAST COAST (North to South)

The east coast of Baranof Island, which is infrequently visited, is well worth exploring. Some excellent, well-sheltered coves and inlets run deep into the island's interior with high snowy peaks that tower above. Port Alexander, 5

David Parker

*Humpback in Chatham Strait showing "stove bolt" markings on its head and the white underside of its long pectoral fin.*

Linda Lewis

*A whale research boat in Chatham Strait...*

Linda Lewis

*...with transponder for listening to whale sounds.*

miles north of Cape Ommaney, has a public telephone and limited services. The hot tubs at Baranof Warm Springs and the raw beauty of Red Bluff Bay are particularly inviting.

## **Kelp Bay** (Baranof Island)

Kelp Bay, on the northeast corner of Baranof Island, is 10.5 miles south of Peril Strait.

Chart 17337
Entrance (mid-channel South and North Point): 57°16.87′ N, 134°50.65′ W

> *The main bay extends about 3.5 miles NW where it divides into three arms. . . .*
>
> *Anchorages in the bay are few, the best being in the SE corner of The Basin. . . .*
>
> *Dangers. The survey of the bay is old and incomplete, and dangers may exist in addition to those shown on the chart.* (CP)

We prefer the excellent shelter and ease of entry found in Cosmos Cove, 2 miles south of Kelp Bay.

Chart 17337 carries the following cautionary note: "Exercise extreme caution when transiting the areas adjacent to Pond Island and southeast of Portage Point. Previously uncharted shoals and dangerous rocks have been located and others may exist."

## **Echo Cove** (Catherine Island)

Echo Cove is north of the entrance to Kelp Bay.

Chart 17337
Entrance: 57°17.25′ N, 134°49.13′ W
Anchor: 57°18.45′ N, 134°49.72′ W

> *Point Lull, the SE extremity of Catherine Island, forms the E side of Echo Cove, a narrow bight, which extends in a NNW direction. The cove is open to the S and affords temporary anchorage for small craft only. A submerged reef, marked by kelp, extends 0.6 mile S of Point Lull. Vessels transiting Echo Cove and The Basin in Kelp Bay should use caution or seek local knowledge.* (CP)

Pay attention to the cautions mentioned above in *Coast Pilot* on entering Kelp Bay. Echo Cove is convenient to Chatham Strait for temporary anchorage in fair weather. However, we prefer Cosmos or Ell coves.

## **Portage Arm** (Kelp Bay)

Portage Arm extends northwest between Catherine and Baranof islands.

Chart 17337
Entrance: 57°19.53′ N, 134°53.64′ W

> *Portage Arm, which extends in a NW direction, is reported to connect with Hanus Bay, in Peril Strait, by an overgrown portage.*
>
> *A small vessel can find temporary anchorage in Portage Arm about 2.7 miles above the entrance in midchannel, in 10 fathoms, but this anchorage has scant swinging room and is exposed to SE winds that draw through the arm.* (CP)

## **Middle Arm** (Kelp Bay)

Middle Arm extends in a west direction.

Chart 17337
Entrance: 57°19.67′ N, 134°56.31′ W

> *Another* [anchorage] *is in Middle Arm about 0.8 mile from its head in 22 to 25 fathoms, soft bottom.* (CP)

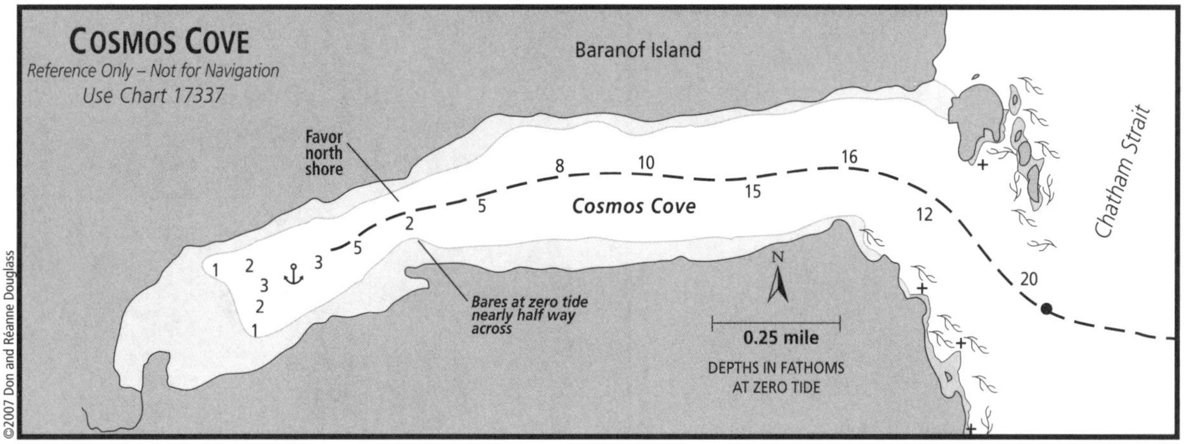




## **South Arm** (Kelp Bay)

South Arm extends in a southwest direction.

Chart 17337
Entrance: 57°18.79′ N, 134°57.52′ W

## **The Basin** (Kelp Bay)

The Basin is in the south part of Kelp Bay.

Chart 17337
Entrance (mid-channel Plover and Yellow Rocks): 57°18.66′ N, 134°55.20′ W

> *The Basin . . . is bordered on the E by two groups of islands. . . .*
>
> *Zubof Rock* [is] *in the middle of the entrance to The Basin, and extensive shoal areas with depths as little as 1 fathom* [are] *in the E and SE parts of The Basin.* (CP)

*Note:* See cautionary note for Chart 17337 under Kelp Bay (page 384). The same dangers exist here.

## **Cosmos Cove** (Baranof Island)

Cosmos Cove, on the west side of Chatham Strait, is 2 miles south of Kelp Bay.

Chart 17337
Entrance: 57°14.41′ N, 134°50.23′ W
Anchor: 57°14.48′ N, 134°52.79′ W

> *The cove affords anchorage with good shelter in 10 to 15 fathoms, soft bottom, for small vessels.* (CP)

Cosmos Cove is one of several coves on Baranof Island's east side. It is a large cove with a flat bottom that can be easily entered in all weather. When entering, favor the north shore midway into the cove; a shoal extends nearly halfway from the south side. A southerly wind can reduce the holding appreciably in this anchorage.

Anchor in 3 fathoms over soft mud, gravel, shell and grass with good holding.

## **Kasnyku Bay** (Baranof Island)

Kasnyku Bay, on the west side of Chatham Strait, is 1.5 miles south of Cosmos Cove.

Chart 17337
Entrance: 57°12.89′ N, 134°50.07′ W

> *Kasnyku Bay . . . has deep water and no secure anchorage.* (CP)

The small basin off Hidden Falls may provide temporary anchorage in 6 fathoms over a sticky bottom. Ell Cove, 0.5 mile south of Round Island, provides excellent shelter.

## **Ell Cove** (Baranof Island)

Ell Cove is 2.5 miles south of Cosmos Cove.

Chart 17337
Entrance: 57°12.14′ N, 134°50.42′ W
Anchor: 57°11.96′ N, 134°51.02′ W

Although Ell Cove is not mentioned in *Coast Pilot*, we consider it one of the best coves along Chatham Strait. Its name comes from its L-shape, which gives it full protection in all weather. It can be entered carefully in limited visibility by using radar.

The small cove has steep granite sides with cascades that descend from snowy ridges

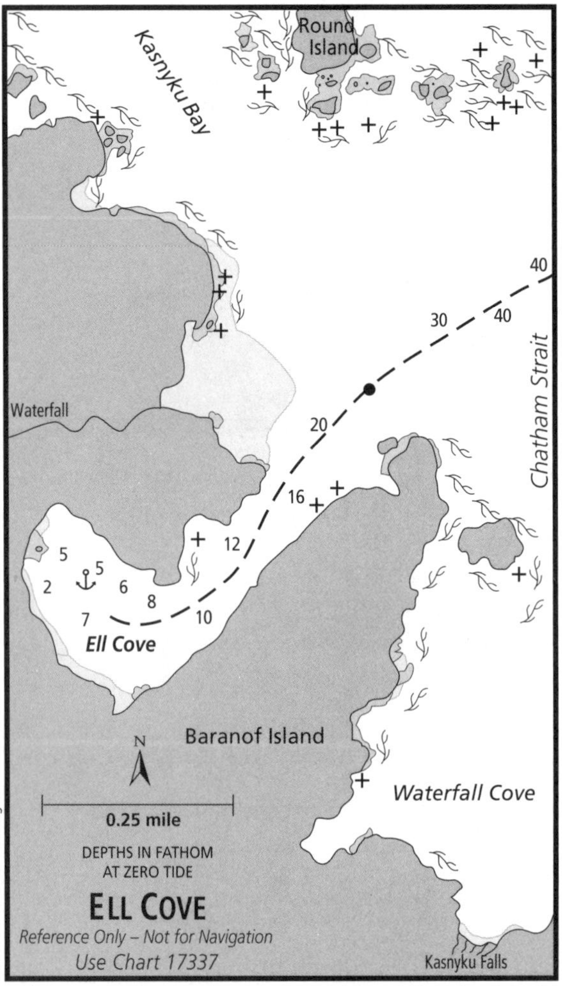

*Takatz Bay fish hatchery*

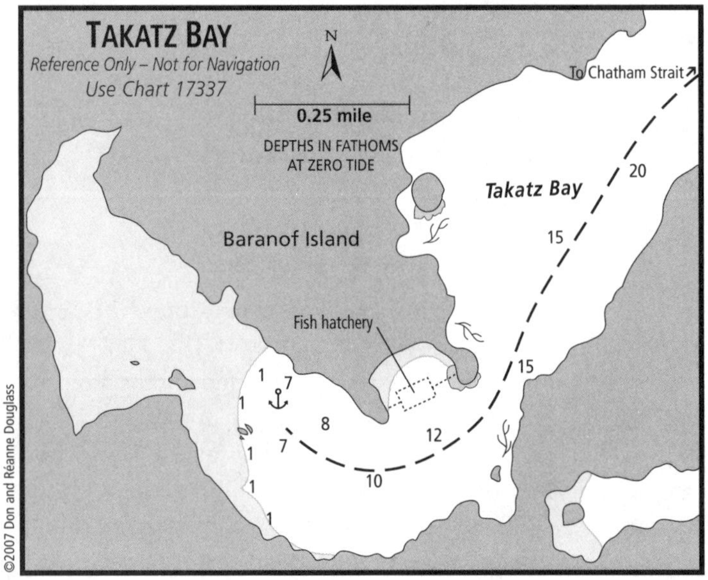


above. Old-growth spruce, cedar and hemlock cover its slopes. Immediately north of Ell Cove is a beautiful waterfall with a large sandy beach. Beware of the shoal that extends much farther from shore than what is shown on the chart.

The direction of the wind felt inside the cove is not indicative of that blowing outside; inside the cove the wind tends to blow in circles without strength. There is no driftwood or any evidence of seas entering Ell Cove. Water temperature is about 50°F.

A half-mile south is Kasnyku Falls with its outstanding high cascade.

Anchor in 6 fathoms over soft mud with good holding.

## Waterfall Cove (Baranof Island)

Waterfall Cove is 6 miles north of Warm Springs Bay.

Chart 17337
Entrance: 57°11.82′ N, 134°49.84′ W
Anchor: 57°11.64′ N, 134°50.41′ W

Waterfall Cove is a good place to turn off your engine and take a short break to enjoy the outstanding view of the 300- to 400-foot cascade, Kasnyku Falls, which drops into the bay. The tiny cove at the head of the bay is marginal and too small

Linda Lewis

*Fish hatchery tanks*

for anchorage unless you use a shore tie. It is, however, an excellent temporary anchorage in fair weather because it provides you the opportunity to dinghy over to the falls and truly appreciate their magnitude, up close.

## **Takatz Bay** (Baranof Island)

Takatz Bay is 4 miles north of Warm Springs Bay.

Chart 17337
Entrance: 57°09.39′ N, 134°48.09′ W
Anchor: 57°08.11′ N, 134°51.44′ W

*Takatz Bay . . . terminates in a flat about 0.4 mile in extent, formed by a mountain stream emptying as a waterfall.*

*Small craft may pass through the narrows in midchannel and anchor 0.2 to 0.4 mile beyond them, but should not pass the largest islet 0.5 mile beyond the narrows, as the flat at the head begins there.* (CP)

David Parker

*A person waving at the lower left gives perspective to the towering Kasnyku Falls in Waterfall Cove.*

Deep in landlocked Takatz Bay, you can find excellent shelter from all weather. The basin, a large granite bowl surrounded by snowy peaks, shows evidence of avalanches. A fish hatchery operates in the bight on the north side of the basin. The bay has easy access and a flat bottom.

The shoal at the head of the bay is steep-to and has been creeping eastward over time, so proceed slowly and carefully to the anchorage. The water is a translucent glacier melt with a visibility of less than 6 feet; summer water temperature is a cool 44° F.

Anchor north of the first small islet.

Anchor in 6 to 8 fathoms over soft mud with very good holding.

## Warm Springs Bay

(Baranof Island)

Warm Springs Bay is 7 miles northwest of Point Gardner.

Chart 17337
Entrance: 57°05.01′ N, 134°46.54′ W
Public float: 57°05.34′ N, 134°49.99′ W
Anchor (southwest arm): 57°04.46′ N, 134°49.65′ W
Anchor (Schooner Cove): 57°05.34′ N, 134°48.04′ W

> *Two small bights in the S shore afford anchorage for small craft. The W one is preferable, because of shoaler water, from 12 to 15 fathoms.*
>
> *Care should be taken to avoid the reef that makes out 60 yards from the N shore at a point about 200 yards E of Baranof.* (CP)

Linda Lewis

*It's a roaring waterfall at Warm Springs Bay.*

Warm Springs Bay has a huge, beautiful 100-foot waterfall at its head that once provided hydropower for the residents of the tiny community of Baranof, and you can still see remnants of this system. Equally impressive are the natural hot springs, an easy half-mile walk from the public float. Rubber boots are recommended. Three natural hot pools tumble down the hillside adjacent to the river. The temperature in the pools is hot and hotter.

The main trail to the natural hot springs, mostly boardwalk with muddy spots, continues past the hot pools a short distance west to Lake Baranof through stunted forest and tundra. Ground dogwood, salmonberry, wild violets and skunkweed cover the alpine tundra in summer. The USFS maintains one of its recreational cabins at the far west end of the lake.

Water from the hot

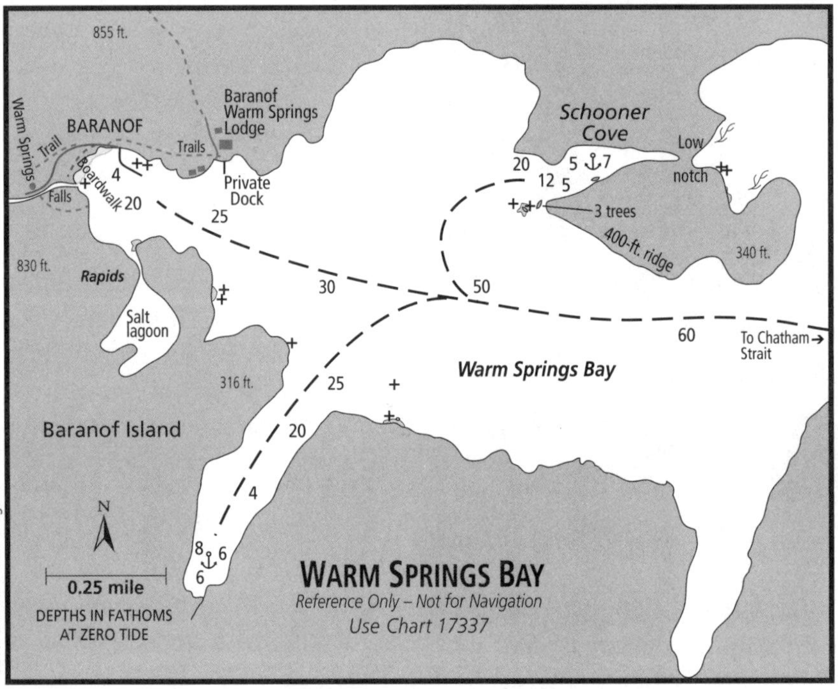

Linda Lewis

*The approach to the dock at the head of Baranof Warm Springs Bay*

Jim Kyle

*The natural hot pools right next to the waterfall*

Linda Lewis

*The boardwalk at Warm Springs Bay, Baranof Is.*

springs, a half-mile uphill from the public float, is piped to the more private, metal-tub bathhouses above the dock. The bathhouses are open on the water side and have a magnificent view of the falls. Please respect the instructions and limit your soak to give others their turn.

This is an increasingly popular stop for cruisers, so plan to arrive early in the day if you want a spot at the dock. Boats often anchor nearby and dinghy in for the hot tubbing.

The 250-foot public float at the head of the bay receives strong east-flowing current from the river, so use caution when you dock. Avoid the large submerged rock approximately 6 feet

Réanne Hemingway-Douglass

*The dock at Warm Springs Bay can become crowed very quickly; this is a very popular spot.*

Don Douglass

*The author checks out one of the individual tubs in the bath house.*

off the east end of the float. There is untreated water at the float. A small store with sundries, canned foods, ice cream, locally made gifts and a coffee bar is located along the boardwalk above the bay.

You can probably get a cell phone connection while in Chatham Strait, outside the entrance to Warm Springs Bay. (Note the nearby MICRO tower.) However, once you proceed deep into the bay the signal weakens because of the topography.

The salt lagoon across the bay to the south is fun to explore by dinghy or kayak. The opening is about 15 feet wide and carries 6 feet of water through its fairway at slack on a 14-foot tide. At other times, it is a waterfall! Inside the lagoon we have spotted seals, harlequins, loons, and many other birds.

If our suggested anchor sites are full, try the bight just to the east of the lagoon. This anchorage has room for four or five boats.

Anchor (southwest arm) in 7 fathoms over gravel and kelp with fair holding.

Anchor (Schooner Cove) in 6 fathoms over a hard bottom; good holding with a well-set anchor.

## Cascade Bay (Baranof Island)

Cascade Bay is 3.4 miles south of Warm Springs Bay.

**Chart 17320**

**Entrance: 57°01.56′ N, 134°45.24′ W**

> *Cascade Bay . . . has deep water, rocky bottom, and no good anchorage. . . . At its head is a prominent cascade seen from a distance in Frederick Sound.* (CP)

Cascade Bay is a beautiful anchorage with a huge waterfall in its northwest corner. The

---

### Bears—Where to Find Them

Herb Nickles, Certified Alaska Naturalist

What types of bears can you see and what are the best islands or best reserves for viewing them?

Three species of bear are native to Alaska. Brown Bears, also known as Grizzly Bears, can be found from Southeast Alaska to the arctic. Black Bears are found throughout Alaska's forests and Polar Bears are only found in extreme northern and western Alaska.

Cruisers to Southeast Alaska are most likely to see the Black Bear (*Ursus americanus*). Although the species is primarily black in color, some individuals can be chocolate, red-brown or cinnamon. Black Bears with a creamy white fur occur on Kermode Island in Northern British Columbia. The Black Bear is generally solitary, except for a female with cubs, and primarily nocturnal. In Southeast Alaska, Black Bears occupy most islands with the exceptions of Admiralty, Baranof, Chichagof, and Kruzof. The best opportunity for viewing Black Bears from your vessel is on forested island beaches at sunset.

The Brown Bear (*Ursus Arctos*) is much larger than the Black Bear, ranging from 6 to 8 feet in length and weighing between 500 and 900 pounds. Brown Bear have a distinctive hump between their front shoulders. Brown Bears occur throughout Southeast Alaska except on the islands south of Frederick Sound. They are abundant on islands with easily available food sources like Admiralty, Baranof, Chichagof, and Kruzof. The Brown Bear is most readily observed on Admiralty Island where the population density is as high as one bear per square mile. The Pack Creek viewing area in Admiralty Island National Monument is a popular location to view Brown Bears but requires a permit and fee paid in advance of your visit.

#### Additional Resources:

Tongass National Forest—Bear Facts at:
http://www.fs.fed.us/r10/tongass/forest_facts/safety/bearfacts.htm

Stan Price State Wildlife Sanctuary on Admiralty Island at: http://www.wildlife.alaska.gov/index.cfm?adfg=refuge.pack_ck

Admiralty Island National Monument at:
http://www.fs.fed.us/r10/tongass/districts/admiralty/packcreek/index.shtml

Used with permission from author: http://www.insidepassagenews.com/AlaskaFAQ/FAQ_16.html

## Musings on Infinity in Southeast Alaska

Linda Lewis—Journal Notes—M/V *Royal Sounder*

Linda Lewis

*Shades of shadows on the west side of Prince of Wales Island*

I have been on watch alone on the ocean during a gray dawn when I could see absolutely nothing but gray water for a full circle of the horizon. It was like being in a broad, flat pan, with just the edges curled up a bit—for 360 degrees. Why didn't I feel as though I was staring at infinity? Paradoxically, I felt closed in.

In Southeast Alaska, however, "infinity" means something. Because here there is perspective. I see multitudes of mountain peaks. I see shades of shadows—like a visual glissando. I see sky, and snow, and trees, and water. Now looking at this is something to set the mind afire.

Looking at ***this*** is musing on infinity.

Linda Lewis

*Multitudes of mountain peaks in Glacier Bay National Park*

Linda Lewis

*Mysterious, strange light shows*

Linda Lewis

*A forest fire of fog creeps over the hill.*

cove has a flat bottom of 25 fathoms nearly all the way to shore. There are rocks off the cascade, some of which bare at high water. A small shelf, below a large snow bowl and avalanche chute, provides a good kayak haul-out and campsite.

You can find temporary anchorage off this site below the snow bowl. The bottom is rocky with poor holding, so if you plan to spend any time here, it's a good idea to use a shore tie. Although southerly winds curl around the cove, there is little chop near shore. Until late June, you often see snow along the high-tide line on shore.

## **Nelson Bay** (Baranof Island)

Nelson Bay is 8 miles south of Warm Springs Bay and 7 miles north of Red Bluff Bay.

Chart 17320
Entrance: 56°57.16′ N, 134°44.06′ W

> *Between Red Bluff Bay and Cascade Bay . . . are four small bays where small craft may find a depth suitable for anchorage in smooth weather, but only one, Nelson Bay, has protection.*
>
> *Nelson Bay . . . is an open bight at the head of which is a circular cove having two islets across the entrance. The entrance to the cove is between the N islet and the point N of it, and is 75 yards wide with a depth of 5 fathoms. The cove is 250 yards in diameter between the 10-fathom curves, and the general depth is 15 fathoms, soft bottom. This cove is suitable only for small craft.* (CP)

We have explored all four small bays mentioned in the *Coast Pilot* and found them all delightful, but uncharted. It is a pity that no large-scale chart exists of this area to allow common use without high risk.

## **Red Bluff Bay** (Baranof Island)

Red Bluff Bay is 6.8 miles south of Nelson Bay and 10 miles west of Kingsmill Point.

Chart 17336
Entrance: 56°50.37′ N, 134°41.88′ W
Anchor: 56°52.29′ N, 134°47.06′ W

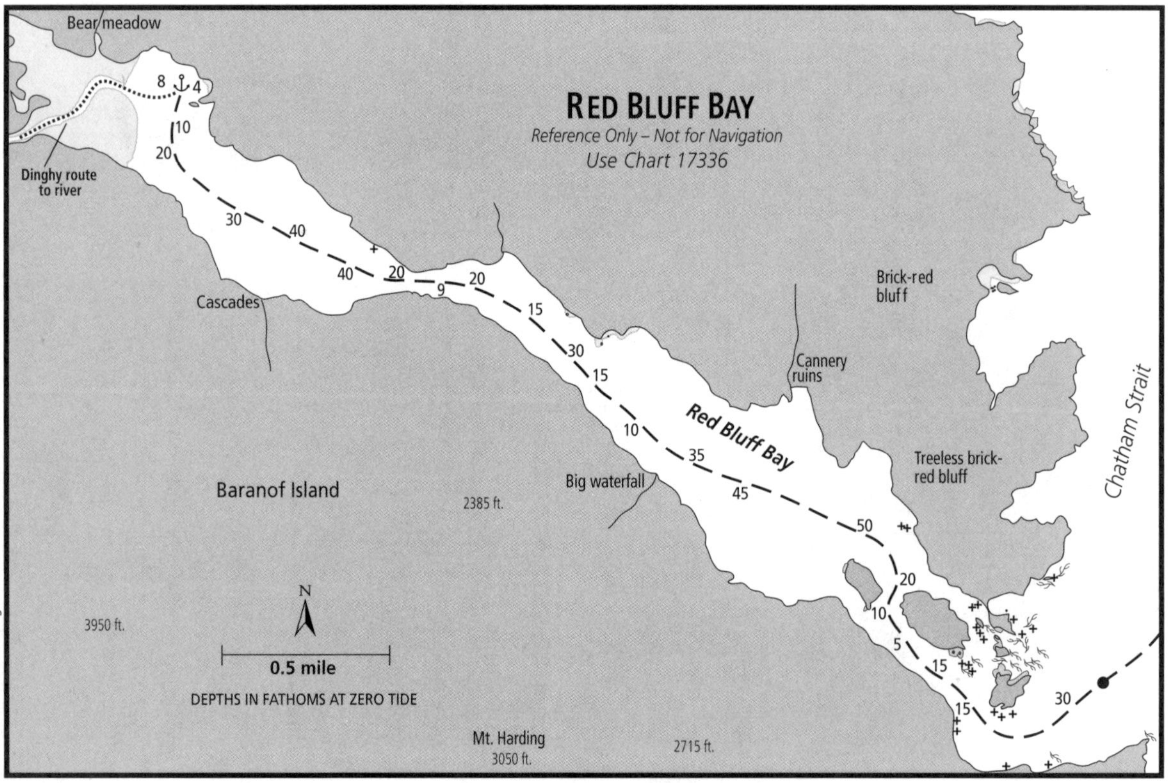

Réanne Hemingway-Douglass

Copasetic *enters Red Bluff Bay*

*The small islands in the entrance to the bay almost close it. The bay extends back into the mountains. About the middle it chokes to about 100 yards between high cliffs, but the channel is good. On the S side at the head of the bay is a large stream; a flat extends about 0.4 mile from the head and 0.3 mile E from the mouth of the stream.*

*At the head, favoring the N shore and NNE of the flat at the mount of the stream, is a good anchorage in 12 to 16 fathoms with soft bottom and perfect protection.* (CP)

Red Bluff Bay is perhaps the most spectacular combination of mountains, waterfalls and ice-fields in Southeast Alaska. From the entrance, the view of the high peaks of Baranof Island is breathtaking. Within this one bay we have counted nine waterfalls cascading off the surrounding massif. The entrance to the bay is unmistakable for the prominent, treeless red bluff on the north side of the fiord. Entry is made south of the islands, as indicated on the diagram. The bay is totally landlocked and shows no effect of outside chop or evidence of storm damage or logs along shore. (Red Bluff receives more sunlight in the summer than Gut Bay.)

You can find anchorage off the ruins of the old cannery on the north shore opposite the large waterfall, in the double bight west of the cannery, or at the head of the inner basin. We prefer to anchor on the north side of a small islet at the head of the bay, opposite the large drying mud flat known locally as Bear Meadow. A large stream flowing out of a glacier-carved valley meanders across the grassy, sandy flats of this meadow. The lake upstream has great cutthroat fishing, but you need to watch out for brown bears along the riverbanks—this is their turf.

Linda Lewis

*A bucket full of shrimp caught in Red Bluff Bay*

Linda Lewis

*Waterfall in Red Bluff Bay*

Some pleasure boaters report finding consistently excellent shrimping along the NW corner of the island marked with the number 85.

Red Bluff Bay shows no signs of human intrusion. This is pure wilderness—no logging, no urban noises, just the sound of the water cascading down the sides of the mountain.

Anchor in 4 fathoms over mud with good holding.

## **Hoggatt Bay** (Baranof Island)

Hoggatt Bay is 4.5 miles south of Red Bluff Bay.

**Chart 17336**
**Entrance: 56°46.27′ N, 134°39.58′ W**

> *Hoggatt Bay . . . extends back into the mountains of Baranof Island. The sides are steep and bold and the water deep, over 100 fathoms through the middle.* (CP)

Hoggatt Bay is reported to have excellent shrimping and sport fishing. The data on Chart 17336 from the survey done in 1897 is a good example of why you should use extreme caution in these areas where no modern large-scale charts exist.

## **Gut Bay** (Baranof Island)

Gut Bay is 7 miles south of Red Bluff Bay.

**Chart 17336**
**Entrance: 56°43.97′ N, 134°38.36′ W**
**Entrance (Mickie's Winter Basin): 56°42.59′ N, 134°41.29′ W**
**Anchor (Mickie's Winter Basin): 56°42.42′ N, 134°41.36′ W**
**Anchor (head of bay): 56°42.30′ N, 134°44.45′ W**

> *At 0.3 mile E of the narrow entrance and 300 yards from the S side is a rocky patch with 41/2 fathoms; vessels should pass N of it. . . . On the S side, 2.5 miles from the entrance, is the narrow opening of a little bay, between high ridges, with a depth of 3/4 fathom. Small craft can enter this bay at high water and anchor in about 3 fathoms.*
>
> *A fair anchorage can be had near the head in 10 to 20 fathoms.* (CP)

Gut Bay is a beautiful place, well worth a visit by cruising boats that want a remote, quiet

---

### **Icebound in Gut Bay**

**Réanne Hemingway-Douglass**

Somewhere in Michèle (Mickie) Demai's background lay a thirst for unusual adventure. You wouldn't have suspected it, though, if you had met her in Paris where she spent 15 years as a TV journalist, specializing in health problems. Her "secret garden," as she calls it, had always been the sea, and a dream to discover the last frontier of Alaska called to her. Not only to explore, but to experience a winter—a winter icebound—on *Nuage*, her 42-foot steel hulled sailboat!

Mickie had studied the charts of Alaska and discovered a little fjord on Baranof Island's east side—Gut Bay—well-sheltered and its waters fed by freshwater streams cold enough to ice over. She and her companion, Thomas, fell in love with the bay, and in September 1995, they sailed to Juneau to prepared *Nuage* for a long winter's night. Mickie prepared 120 jars of food; they took on extra water and fuel; propane; firewood; mountaineering equipment; they added insulation; they built a funny-looking cabin of plywood over the cockpit. Three months of preparations for five months in an icy retreat.

Every day in Gut Bay brought new fears—williwaws gusted to more than 80 miles an hour; avalanches roared down the mountainsides above the bay; ice cracked and groaned against the hull; the deck iced over.

But every day brought new delights, as well—the iridescent colors of the high-latitude winter sky; the pristine snow; the river otters that played on the ice near the boat. Mickie and Thomas reveled in their sanctuary. They maintained the boat; they read; they wrote; they chopped wood from the mountainsides; they skied across the frozen surface of the bay; they watched the wildlife—deer, ptarmigans, mink, bald eagles. The days sped by; they felt privileged to be a part of this wilderness.

April came. The ice began to melt and soon *Nuage* floated free again. Mickie and Thomas returned to sea, with a heightened sense of awareness, having tested their emotional strength. Gut Bay and Alaska captured the heart of a woman; a charming and unusual woman!

*Note:* We have called the anchorage where *Nuage* spent the winter "Mickie's Winter Basin" in honor of this unusual French woman.

---

and protected anchorage. The entire bay is landlocked and rather poorly charted. Except for occasional williwaws that blow off the surrounding snow-covered peaks (3,000 to 4,000 feet high) in unsettled weather, shelter is almost complete. Only the isolation—there is no VHF radio reception inside Gut Bay—and a deep, rocky bottom keep the bay from becoming a popular destination.

Mickie's Winter Basin is the best anchor site; the other is the narrow tongue of water at the far southwest corner of the bay. The entrance to Mickey's Winter Basin is shallow and narrow. We figure the fairway, which is roughly 30 feet wide, carries about 4 feet. Tidal range in the basin is less than that found outside, but due to restricted flow it occurs about an hour later than that listed for Sitka.

The shores are surrounded by thick forest to the water's edge. Steep bluffs and granite slopes rise abruptly to snow-filled cirques and avalanches chutes. To the south, Mt. Ada's stark pinnacles tower 4,500 feet above.

We found just two disadvantages to Mickey's Winter Basin. The first is that the surrounding peaks limit the duration of direct sunlight, causing the basin to be a chilly 42° F during the day (in late June). The second is that without radio reception, it is difficult to know what conditions exist outside in Chatham Strait.

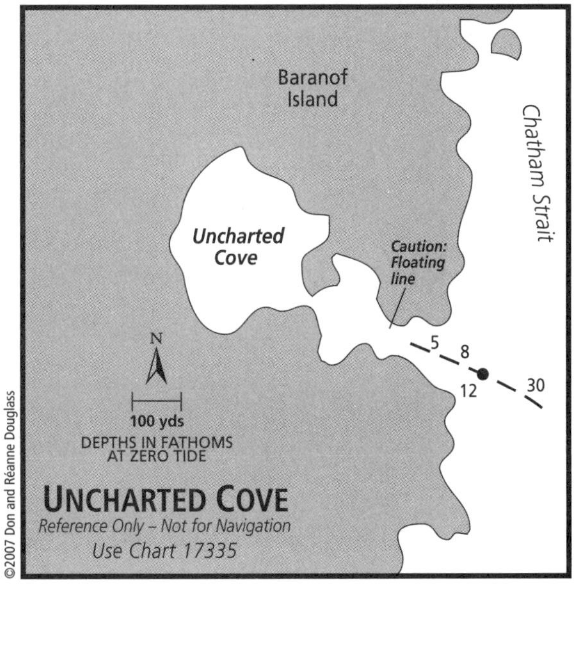


There is a large grassy meadow at the head of the basin beyond a drying mud flat. Inside, the basin narrows (about 100 yards long) and depths increase to 4 to 5 fathoms before rising at the mud flats.

Anchor (Mickey's Winter Basin) in 3 to 4 fathoms over brown mud with roots and grass; fair-to-good holding. (Use a shore tie if williwaws are expected. You could also anchor outside the basin with more swinging room in 6 to 8 fathoms, soft mud bottom.)

The tiny inlet at the far southwest end of Gut Bay has limited swinging room, but we have found that the current from the stream and the gentle breezes keep a boat lined up with the 150-foot wide channel. The view from this spot is similar to Mickie's Winter Basin—high granite bluffs with snow patches and cascades and little direct morning sun.

Anchor (head of bay) in 4 to 5 fathoms over soft brown mud with very good holding.

## **Uncharted Cove** (Baranof Island)

Uncharted Cove is 3.25 miles north of Patterson Point and 15 miles south of Red Bluff Bay.

**Chart 17335**
**Entrance: 56°35.56′ N, 134°37.43′ W**

Uncharted Cove has an interesting geological feature—an almost perfectly round crater with high, sloping sides and a tiny opening to the sea. On Chart 17335, this cove shows only vague dashed lines and no depths.

We started to explore the entrance and found that someone had secured a large, yellow floating line across the cove, east of the narrows. Perhaps the cove is a perfectly sheltered spot for small craft . . . *or* perhaps the yellow line is there to prevent a rock pile from snaring an unwary boat.

The narrows appears to be about 30 feet wide at high water. An irregular bottom at the entrance indicates a potential rock pile.

## **Patterson Bay** (Baranof Island)

Patterson Bay is 12 miles south of Gut Bay and 23 miles north of Cape Ommaney.

Chart 17335
Entrance: 56°32.44′ N, 134°39.29′ W

> *Patterson Bay has its entrance W of Patterson Point. Constricted anchorage in 22 to 24 fathoms can be made below the wooded islet at the head and abreast a small green point on the W side. . . .* (CP)

Patterson Bay is a stunning, narrow fiord with steep snowy peaks on all sides. The 3,200-foot Mt. Cecil towers above the end of the bay. We have not explored the bay, but the stream outlet from Brentwood Lake seems to have created a sizeable flat area that could provide a good anchorage. The upper end of the bay is essentially landlocked, but this is williwaw terrain, so be careful in unstable weather!

## **Deep Cove** (Baranof Island)

Deep Cove is 1.1 miles west of Patterson Point.

Chart 17335
Entrance: 56°32.29′ N, 134°40.21′ W

> [A] *stream with a waterfall empties at the head of Deep Cove. Anchorage can be made near the small flat below this waterfall in 20 to 25 fathoms, soft bottom. The water in the cove is otherwise too deep for anchorage.* (CP)

Deep Cove has beautiful peaks along its south shore and a snowy ridge on its north shore. Although it is sheltered, we did not find any convenient anchor sites for small craft.

## **Mist Cove** (Baranof Island)

Mist Cove is 1.5 miles southwest of Patterson Point

Chart 17335
Entrance: 56°31.39′ N, 134°39.87′ W
Anchor: 56°30.98′ N, 134°40.22′ W

> *Mist Cove . . . is an open bight too deep for anchorage. A waterfall on the SW side of the cove is visible from well N in Chatham Strait.* (CP)

Mist Cove takes its name from the stunning high, thin cascade enveloped in blowing mist on its southwest side.

There is a small shelf with temporary anchorage below the falls. However, we have found better temporary anchorage deep in the south corner of the cove off the creek which has its source in Fawn Lake. The current here keeps you facing in one direction.

Anchor in 5 to 10 fathoms over sand and gravel with fair holding.

Réanne Hemingway-Douglass

*Entrance to Mist Cove*

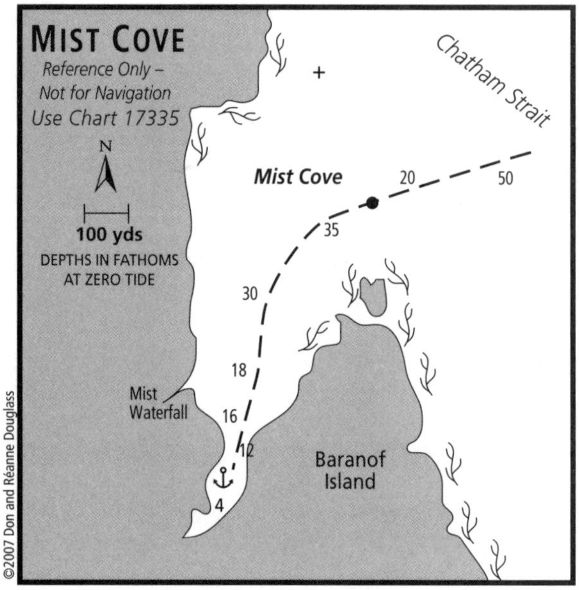

## **Port Herbert** (Baranof Island)

Port Herbert is 6.5 miles south of Patterson Point

Chart 17333
Entrance: 56°25.98′ N, 134°38.94′ W

*The water is too deep for anchorage, and there are apparently no dangers.* (CP)

## **Codfish Cove** (Baranof Island)

Codfish Cove is 0.7 mile south of Port Herbert.

Chart 17333
Entrance: 56°25.40′ N, 134°38.62′ W

Codfish Cove is a small bight, too deep and steep as an acceptable anchorage.

## **Port Walter** (Baranof Island)

Port Walter is 9 miles south of Patterson Point and 14 miles north of Cape Ommaney.

Chart 17333
Entrance: 56°23.49′ N, 134°38.16′ W

*Near the head of Port Walter, a little S of midchannel, is a wooded islet. A high-water rocky islet, from which a reef extends in a N direction into the channel, is 50 yards N of the wooded islet. Anchorage in 11 to 14 fathoms, sandy bottom, can be had between the islet and the N shore.* (CP)

## **Little Port Walter** (Port Walter)

Little Port Walter is west of the south entrance point to Port Walter.

Chart 17333
Entrance: 56°23.34′ N, 134°38.22′ W
Anchor: 56°22.88′ N, 134°38.88′ W

*Little Port Walter . . . consists of an inner and outer harbor with a narrow connecting channel.*

*The narrow channel . . . has a width of about 30 yards with a depth of 3-1/4 fathoms and is subject to shoaling. Vessels should enter the port between half and high tide only and preferably on a rising tide. They should pass along the SE side of the channel and make a slow turn to enter the inner harbor. . . .*

*Good protected anchorage for small craft can be had in the inner harbor in 6 to 8 fathoms, mud bottom.* (CP)

*NOAA Building at Little Port Walter*

Little Port Walter (inner harbor) is a very good cruising boat anchorage with a beautiful setting. The inner harbor, which is landlocked, has excellent shelter in all weather.

To enter the inner harbor, favor the west shore over a bar of about 3 fathoms at zero tide. The west shore has a three-story NOAA building with floats and a flag pole. Across a low lush valley, there are views of Baranof Island's snowy peaks.

Anchor in 7 fathoms on the middle of the inner harbor (avoiding the fish floats) over brown mud with good holding. The bottom is flat over a large area.

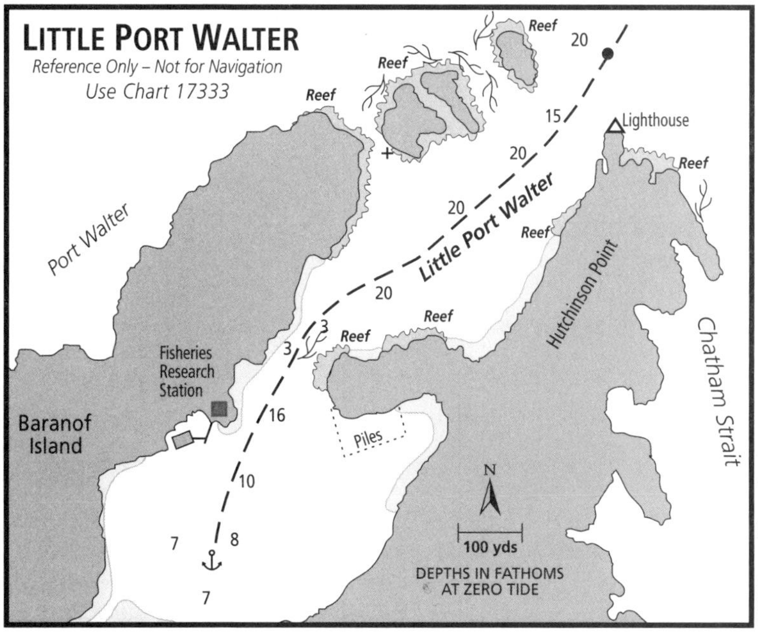

## **New Port Walter** (Port Walter)

New Port Walter, on the north side, is 0.8 mile from the entrance to Port Walter.

Chart 17333
Position: 56°23.55′ N, 134°39.62′ W

> *New Port Walter is at the head of a small cove . . . A rock, bare at extreme tide, is close to the E entrance point to the cove. A rock, bare at high water, is off the W point of the cove, with a reef that extends part way from the shore.* (CP)

## **Denmark Cove** (Port Walter)

Denmark Cove is just east of Port Walter Narrows.

Chart 17333
Entrance: 56°22.89′ N, 134°41.27′ W
Anchor: 56°22.85′ N, 134°41.23′ W

Anchorage for small craft is reported in Denmark Cove at the southwest corner of Port Walter, sheltered by Clam Island and nearby islands.

Anchor in 6 to 8 fathoms over an unknown bottom.

## **Big Port Walter** (Port Walter)

Big Port Walter extends west from Port Walter.

Chart 17333
Entrance: 56°22.95′ N, 134°41.36′ W

> *Big Port Walter, a basin with depths 22 to 55 fathoms, is entered through a narrow passage 0.4 mile long leading from the anchorage W of the wooded islet. . . . The shores are steep-to. . . . The basin is too deep for good anchorage.* (CP)

An abandoned saltery plant lies at the head of Big Port Walter.

## **Lovers Cove** (Big Port Walter)

Lovers Cove is on the north shore of Big Port Walter.

Chart 17333
Entrance: 56°23.28′ N, 134°43.15′ W

Anchorage is reported in Lovers Cove off the drying mud flat that fills the northeast side of the cove.

## **Toledo Harbor** (Baranof Island)

Toledo Harbor is 0.9 mile south of Port Walter Light 5.

Chart 17333
Entrance: 56°22.35′ N, 134°37.86′ W

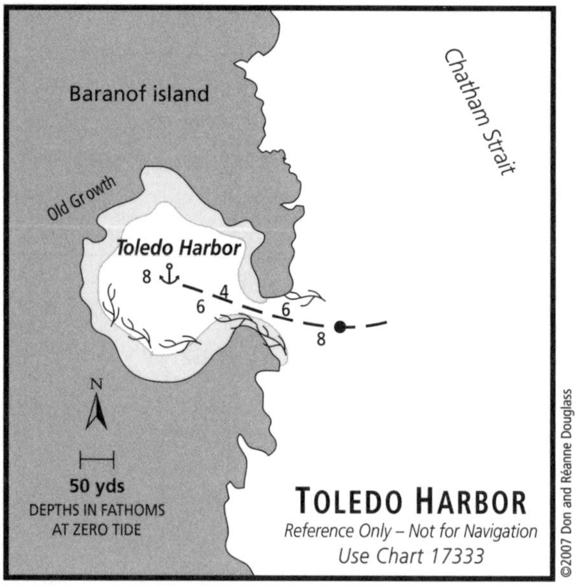


Anchor: 56°22.40′ N, 134°38.13′ W

> *Toledo Harbor is a small, horseshoe-shaped bay with depths of 3-1/4 to 8 fathoms, mud bottom. . . . It is used considerably by small local fishing craft.* (CP)

Toledo Harbor is a good pleasure-craft anchorage, close to Chatham Strait. The name for this tiny round cove may have come from someone who poked the nose of their boat inside and said, "Holy Toledo!"

The cove provides good protection for small craft in all weather, but swinging room is limited. Inside the basin, it is perfectly calm when a northerly is blowing. The narrow entrance lies between patches of kelp on both shores; minimum depth in the fairway is about 3 fathoms.

Anchor in 7 fathoms over mud, avoiding the shoals; good holding.

## **Port Lucy** (Baranof Island)

Port Lucy is 10.5 miles north of Cape Ommaney.

Chart 17333
Entrance: 56°20.34′ N, 134°38.64′ W
Anchor: 56°17.38′ N, 134°45.24′ W

> *The anchorage for large vessels is near the head, abreast a deep gulch on the NW side, in about 20 fathoms. Small vessels can go farther in and anchor in about 10 fathoms. From the head of*

*the port low land extends through to the W side of Baranof Island at Puffin Bay, and winds from those quarters may draw through. . . .* (CP)

Protected anchorage can be found at the bitter end of Port Lucy over a large flat area.

Anchor in about 7 fathoms over a soft bottom.

## Miner Cove (Baranof Island)

Miner Cove is 1 mile north of Port Armstrong.

Chart 17331
Entrance: 56°18.51′ N, 134°38.14′ W

*Miner Cove . . . is an open bight that might afford temporary anchorage for small craft.* (CP)

Port Armstrong, 1 mile south of Miner Cove, provides complete protection.

## Port Armstrong (Baranof Island)

Port Armstrong is 3.5 miles north of Port Alexander.

Charts 17331
Entrance: 56°17.82′ N, 134°38.60′ W
Anchor: 56°17.50′ N, 134°39.56′ W

*About 0.3 mile W of Point Eliza is the narrowest part of the channel with bold shores, leading to the inner landlocked basin of Port Armstrong. This basin affords the best anchorage in the vicinity. The anchorage is in the W end of the basin in 11 to 20 fathoms, soft bottom. A mid-channel course carries in safely.* (CP)

Port Armstrong has very good shelter from all weather. The entrance is fairly shallow, but the mid-channel fairway is clear and well protected. A resort is located on the creek on the

---

## A Wilderness Friend

Réanne Hemingway-Douglass

Along the coast of Kuiu Island lives my new friend. We met by chance as *Baidarka* was slowly navigating a narrow, rock-filled inlet. I was on the bow, pointing the way through the rocks, when a shadow crossed my periphery vision.

"Don, look!" I yelled, stunned to see a woman standing on shore.

We'd been exploring for days without seeing another human. A few passing fishing boats here and there, but no houses, no structures. Imagine—in all this wilderness a human being!

"Do you live here? I asked.

"Yes, for 20 years."

"Just summers?"

"No, all year."

My friend, who shall remain nameless, moved to Petersburg with her young daughter after the death of her first husband. They spent 12 months in town and "hated it." Too many people!

She moved back to the secluded home with her daughter and second husband and his son, where they raised and home-schooled their combined family.

I imagined the response city teen-agers would have to their life, and the proverbial comment, "How boring!" No malls, no television, no movies, no Seven-Eleven to run to. Electricity and hot showers regulated by their generator; mail once a month when her husband crosses the strait by boat to the nearest village—much longer periods without mail in the winter.

"What do you do?" would be the next typical response.

And in her quiet, unassuming, almost shy manner, she would run down the list of things she does: Dig and can over 3,000 clams; make liverwurst and sausage out of the left-over venison; can the vegetables she grows in the summer; freeze the halibut and salmon they catch during the season (their quota is 700 lbs.). Before the winter sets in, she buys 350 lbs. of popping corn so she'll be able to feed the Canada geese that winter over every year. She knows them all by sight and has a name for each one. (One couple, a small male and a huge female, returned every season for five years.) She has a pet ferret to care for, too. He has white fur and pink eyes. "It's like having a permanent two-year old living with us," she comments.

And unlike city folk, my friend is decidedly attuned to nature. She knows all the habits of the wolves, the deer, the bear, the mink, the ferrets, the sea otters, the orcas and other whales. She can tell us all about the plants and the trees and the edible sea creatures. She sews and reads in her spare time, but she doesn't have much of that. Life is full and busy and, when the winter darkness sets in, she finds time to write me a long letter. In the spring, when the storms have abated, she'll mail it to me.

"Do you keep a journal?" I once asked her. Her ingenuousness struck me as refreshing.

"Yes, and someday I'd like to write a book . . . but I don't yet know how it ends."

north shore, with an oyster farm, private floats and a fish hatchery where the old charted wharf was once located.

Our preferred anchor site is in the southeast corner of the basin off a small pebble beach where there are two rusted tanks. Avoid the large rock awash on a 5-foot tide that extends from the north point of the basin.

Anchor in 6 to 10 fathoms over mud with good holding.

## **Port Conclusion** (Baranof Island)

Port Conclusion is 2.5 miles north of Port Alexander.

**Chart 17331**
**Entrance: 56°16.77′ N, 134°38.77′ W**
**Position (Graveyard Cove): 56°16.20′ N, 134°38.49′ W**
**Position (John Bay): 56°16.67′ N, 134°40.57′ W**

> *The only ship anchorage in Port Conclusion is in midchannel, about 0.3 mile N of Ship Cove and S of the 53/4-fathom spot, in 13 to 20 fathoms, rocky and uneven bottom. The holding ground is poor, and its use is not recommended. . . . John Bay, on the W side opposite Point Conclusion, is a deep bight of no importance.*
>
> *Graveyard Cove is an open bight on the SE side of the point.* (CP)

Port Conclusion was named by George Vancouver in 1793 as he concluded his exploration of the Northwest Coast. The best anchorage in Port Conclusion for small craft is Ship Cove.

## **Ship Cove** (Port Conclusion)

Ship Cove is 1.2 miles southwest of Point Conclusion.

**Chart 17331**
**Entrance: 56°15.31′ N, 134°40.04′ W**
**Anchor: 56°15.37′ N, 134°39.79′ W**

> *On the SE shore of the port, 0.3 mile SSW of Point Conclusion, is a cove about 0.2 mile long with a sandy beach at its head. About 0.9 mile farther SW, on the same shore, is Ship Cove where Vancouver . . . moored his vessels. . . . The cove affords protected anchorage for small craft in 2-1/2 to 4 fathoms.* (CP)

Ship Cove provides shelter for small craft over a flat, shallow bottom. A small plaque on the

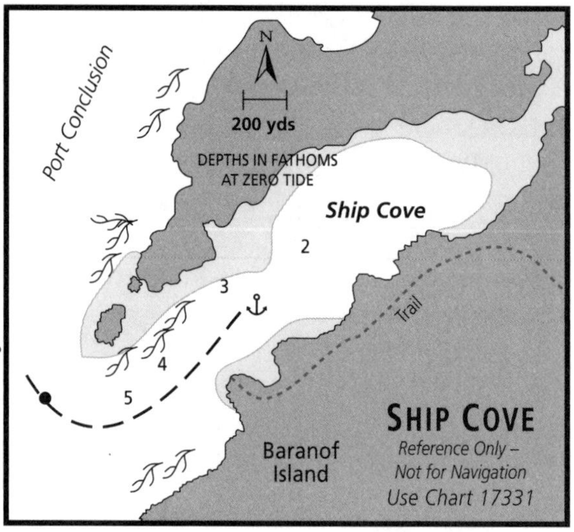


©2007 Don and Réanne Douglass

northwest side of this cove commemorates Vancouver's historic visit. A half-mile trail of unknown condition connects Ship Cove to the upper bay of Port Alexander.

Anchor in 2 to 3 fathoms, avoiding the kelp and shoals, over sand, gravel and mud with fair holding.

## **Port Alexander** (Baranof Island)

Port Alexander, near the south entrance to Chatham Strait, is 5 miles north of Cape Ommaney.

**Chart 17331**
**Entrance (range): 56°14.39′ N, 134°38.88′ W**
**Public float: 56°14.80′ N, 134°38.92′ W**

> *Port Alexander is a small-boat harbor. . . .*
>
> *A Federal project provides for a 150-foot-wide channel, 15 feet deep, that leads through ledge rock at the main entrance and a 40-foot-wide channel that is 6 feet deep at the entrance to the inner harbor. In May 2005, the controlling depth was 14.9 feet in the main entrance channel except for shoaling and heavy kelp buildup in the W quarter of the channel.*
>
> *The channel to the inner harbor is no longer maintained, and local knowledge is necessary for safe entry.*
>
> *Port Alexander, a fishing settlement with a general store, is on the E side of the harbor. It has a public wharf and two State-maintained small-craft floats. . . . The second small-craft float is on the E side of the inner harbor.* (CP)

Port Alexander offers shelter for boaters working and cruising in the area of Cape Ommaney. The entrance is very narrow with only 2 fathoms in the fairway. The incorporated townsite has a public phone at the head of the gangway, a post office, a school, a small supply store and a few gift boutiques that sell handmade items. Some supplies can be obtained along the boardwalk. You may be able to purchase fuel for pleasure craft in season, but don't count on it. A 48-foot grid is west of the approach pier to the small-craft float. Several lodges cater to sport fishing enthusiasts.

The public float is frequently crowded with fishing boats and live-aboards. Water at the float is untreated and must be boiled or treated for drinking; the water supply is also subject to shortages. The upper bay, which is filled with shoals, is used exclusively by locals in small boats. (We do not recommend entering it.)

In early summer 1996, severe 80-knot winds blew into the bay, causing the public float to undulate 6 feet and preventing anyone from walking on it.

## KUIU ISLAND'S WEST COAST

The west coast of Kuiu Island is a great place to view whales and sea otters and get a vantage point of the mountains of Baranof Island.

### Washington Bay (Kuiu Island)

Washington Bay, on the east side of Chatham Strait, is 9.5 miles south of Security Bay.

Chart 17370
Entrance: 56°42.99′ N, 134°23.56′ W

> *The bay is deep and has high, steep sides. . . . Submerged pilings extend about 50 yards off the N shore, about 0.5 mile from the head of the bay; caution is advised in the area. Temporary anchorage can be had in the middle of the bay about 0.7 mile from the head.*
>
> *The head of the bay is not recommended as an anchorage because of insufficient swinging room. . . . Mariners should follow a mid-channel course when entering the bay.* (CP)

Réanne Hemingway-Douglass

*A ghostly derelict*

Washington Bay is easy to enter and use as an escape from the chop of Chatham Strait. However, it is too deep for convenient anchoring. The shore is steep-to and you would need to consider using a shore-tie. Both Rowan Bay, 5.5 miles to the south, and Security Bay, 9 miles to the north, offer better anchorage.

### Rowan Bay (Kuiu Island)

Rowan Bay is 5.5 miles south of Washington Bay and 5 miles north of the Bay of Pillars.

Chart 17370
Entrance: 56°38.41′ N, 134°18.14′ W

> *Rowan Bay . . . is suitable only for small vessels. Strangers should preferably enter at low water and exercise care, because there are many charted and uncharted shoals in the bay and at its entrance.*
>
> *A rock awash, with deep water around it, is about 0.8 mile SW of the narrow entrance to Rowan Bay. It is marked by kelp. A rock, covered 3-1/2 fathoms in 56°37′40″ N, 134°20′13″ W, is about 1.1 miles SW of the rock awash. Another danger spot, covered 1.8 fathoms, is about 220 yards SW of the 3-1/2-fathom covered rock in about 56°37′35″N, 134°20′24″W. Mariners are advised to exercise caution in this area.*
>
> *At 1.2 miles within the entrance there is an island in the middle. . . . E of the island, the bay has a NE direction with depths of 3 to 15 fathoms, and is a secure anchorage.*
>
> *In 1981, a logging camp was operating in Rowan Bay on the NW shore on both sides of*

*the point about 0.6 mile NNE of the island. A small-craft and seaplane float is about 0.2 mile W of the point. . . .* (CP)

The entrance to Rowan Bay has an irregular bottom with many surprises. Entering requires careful piloting and good visibility. Avoid the three dangerous rocks in the center of the entrance, and keep a sharp lookout as not all shoals and rocks are charted! The bay provides good shelter and comfortable anchorage on its south shore; carefully avoid, the numerous rocks. (The Bay of Pillars is more secluded and even more sheltered.) After all these negatives, you may ask, "Why enter Rowan Bay?" The answer: you stand a good chance of sighting bears, whales and sea otters.

Réanne Hemingway-Douglass

*Sea Ranger Resort in Bay of Pillars*

Anchor in 6 fathoms over mud, shells and gravel with fair-to-good holding.

## Bay of Pillars and Honeymoon Basin

(Kuiu Island)

Bay of Pillars is 18 miles south of Security Bay and 23 miles northeast of Port Alexander.

**Chart 17370**
**Entrance: 56°34.87′ N, 134°19.61′ W**
**Anchor (inside first islands): 56°36.73′ N, 134°12.88′ W**
**Anchor (inner bay at portage trail): 56°38.71′ N, 134°05.49′ W**
**Entrance (Honeymoon Basin): 56°38.28′ N, 134°06.37′ W**
**Anchor (Honeymoon Basin): 56°37.63′ N, 134°06.65′ W**

*Islands, islets, reefs, and bare and covered rocks are on the N side of the entrance to the Bay of Pillars; kelp is in the area.*

*Bay of Pillars . . . is comparatively clear for 4.5 miles. Above this the bay is foul and must be navigated with caution.*

*Temporary anchorage for small boats can be had in a cove about 2.1 miles NE of Point Ellis in 10 to 20 fathoms, mud and shell bottom.*

*Four small islands are on the SE side of the bay, about 4.5 miles above Point Ellis. Secure anchorage for small vessels can be found about 400 yards E of the islands and the same distance from the shore, in 10 to 11 fathoms. It is safer for a stranger to enter at low water. . . .*

*The narrow entrance to the inner bay has strong tidal currents and should only be entered at slack water or with local knowledge. . . .*

*Anchorage can be found in the cove to the SW corner of the inner bay in 4 to 10 fathoms, mud bottom. A 1-1/2-fathom spot is near the center of the cove. Good anchorage in 2 to 7 fathoms, mud bottom, is found in any part of the arm leading S at the head of the bay.* (CP)

The Bay of Pillars offers very good shelter along the south shore behind the group of five small islands. Upon entering, avoid the large shoal off the south entrance, northwest of Point Ellis. There are numerous rock pillars throughout the bay that give it its name.

Excellent protection can be found in the inner bay; however, don't try entering without Chart 17370 and without reconnoitering first by dinghy. *The narrows should be attempted only near slack water and with utmost caution and skill.* The rewards are great—wilderness and solitude with excellent shelter.

The narrows are poorly charted, requiring constant vigilance as you transit. We found 3 knots or more of ebb current and 2 knots of flood. The change of direction is delayed 60 to 90 minutes from high or low water on the outside.

Minimum fairway depths on a 5-foot tide were 4 fathoms at the west end of the narrows and the same amount as you approach the two islands at the east end of the narrows. The best route favors the north shore, north of those two islands, avoiding the islet with one tree on it and a rock just to the northeast that is awash at high water. Avoid the charted 1-fathom shoal by favoring the north shore until you reach the 10-fathom contour.

Once inside the inner basin, you discover true wilderness with eagles, blue herons, spotted harbor seals, sea otters and black bear.

Anchorage in the inner basin can be found off the east end at the Bay of Pillars portage trail #6M, marked by a board nailed to a tree. The mile-long trail leads to the bitter end of Port Camden on Keku Strait.

The most secure anchorage is found in the basin on the south side, which we call "Honeymoon Basin." This site is remote, quiet and wild, with a nice shallow bottom of brown mud with good holding and lots of swinging room. The shore is covered with old-growth forest backed by a high granite ridge. The rugged ridge to the east has a peak in the shape of an equilateral triangle, and there are snowy peaks to the south. Two creeks flow into the head of the basin; the westernmost of which flows through a low saddle.

Kayakers will find a good haul-out spot on a knoll on the eastern shore at the entrance to Honeymoon Basin.

Anchor (inside first islands) in 10 fathoms over a bottom of mud and clam shells; fair-to-good holding.

Anchor (inner basin at portage trail) in 9 fathoms over mud with shells; good holding.

Anchor near the head of Honeymoon Basin (east of a large silver snag) in 4 fathoms, brown mud with good holding.

## **Tebenkof Bay** (Kuiu Island)

Tebenkof Bay, just south of the Bay of Pillars, is entered between Point Ellis on the north and Swaine Point on the south.

Chart 17376
Entrance: 56°31.07′ N, 134°16.82′ W

*The bay extends inland for about 7 miles and branches into three arms of irregular shape. . . .*

*Davis Rock is a bare rock in the entrance to Tebenkof Bay, about 0.9 mile NW from Troller Point. It forms an excellent landmark for entering the bay. SW from the rock are a number of shoals and submerged pinnacle rocks as shown on the chart. A rock, 15 feet high, similar to Davis Rock in appearance, is off Troller Point.*

*The entrance to Tebenkof Bay N of Davis Rock is clear and may be navigated easily with the aid of the chart. In approaching this entrance from S, take care to avoid the dangers SW of Davis Rock. Small craft can enter the bay via Explorer Basin and Helianthus Passage.* (CP)

Tebenkof Bay, surrounded by the Tebenkof Bay Wilderness area, holds wonderful surprises for exploring cruising boaters and kayakers. The entire bay is worth a week's stay in itself.

## **Piledriver Cove** (Tebenkof Bay)

Piledriver Cove is on the north side of Tebenkof Bay.

Chart 17376
Entrance: 56°32.42′ N, 134°12.18′ W

Piledriver Cove is a small indentation just south of Piledriver Mountain. Temporary anchorage can be found north of the mid-cove islet. The site is exposed to southwest winds.

## **Happy Cove** (Tebenkof Bay)

Happy Cove, on the north side of the Tebenkof Bay, is 1.2 miles north of Gap Point.

Chart 17376
Entrance: 56°29.97′ N, 134°09.13′ W
Anchor: 56°30.32′ N, 134°08.74′ W

*Happy Cove . . . is well sheltered. . . . The inner cove, separated from the lower part by a narrow channel, has sand bottom and beach.* (CP)

Happy Cove, a tiny uncharted indentation with pleasant anchorage in all but southerly gales, has room for a couple of boats. The nar-

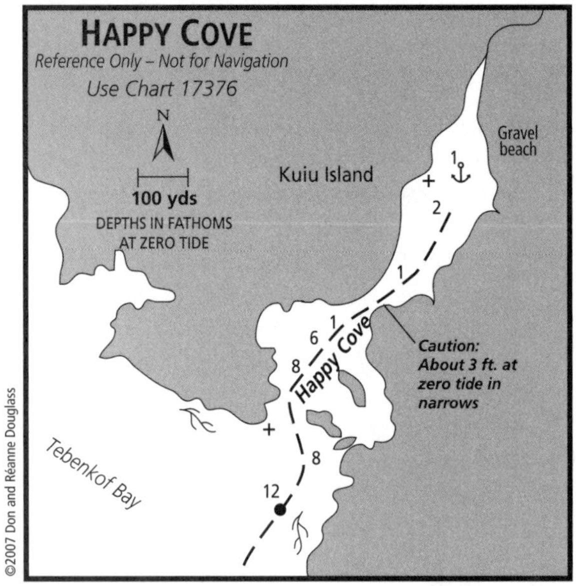


rows has only 3 feet of water at zero tide, but the basin on the north side makes for happy anchoring.

Anchor in 2 to 3 fathoms over thick brown mud with very good holding if you set your anchor slowly.

## **Elena Bay** (Tebenkof Bay)

Elena Bay is the north arm of Tebenkof Bay.

Chart 17376
Entrance: 56°29.53′ N, 134°06.33′ W
Anchor (east side) : 56°30.50′ N, 134°03.89′ W

> *Elena Bay . . . affords good anchorage at various places.* (CP)

The head of Elena Bay, which is shallow, provides unlimited anchor sites for small craft. We prefer the east shore, north of island (70), avoiding rocks in the entrance.

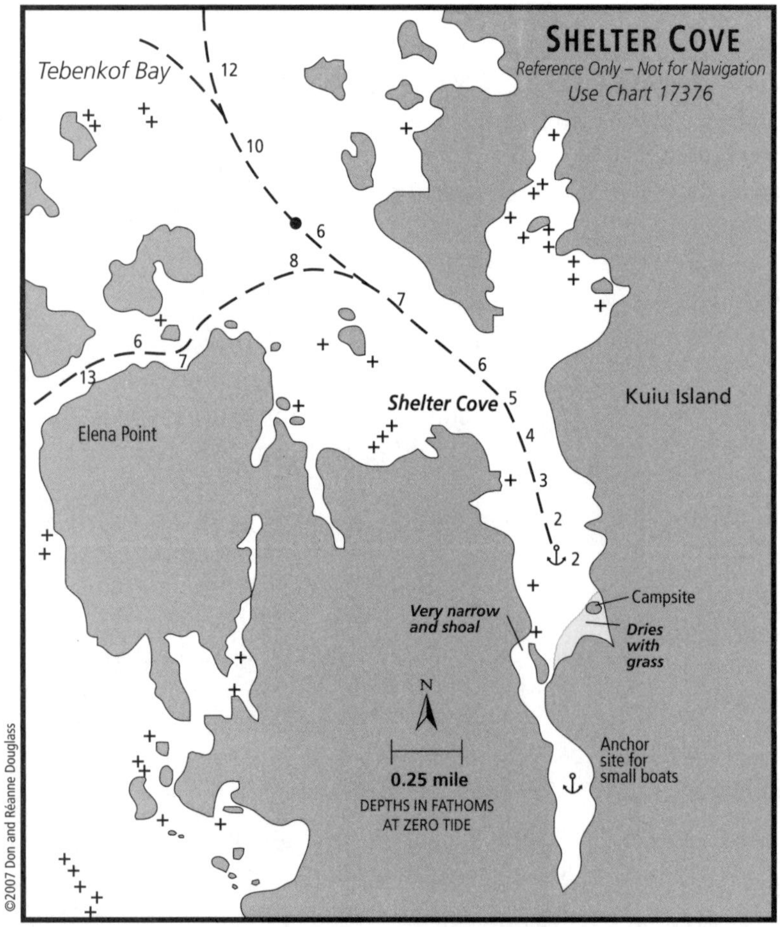


Anchor in 4 fathoms over mud and sand with good holding.

## **Shelter Cove** (Tebenkof Bay)

Shelter Bay lies on the southeast side of Elena Bay.

Chart 17376
Entrance: 56°29.72′ N, 134°04.09′ W
Anchor: 56°28.82′ N, 134°02.60′ W
Anchor (inner basin): 56°27.94′ N, 134°02.41′ W

We find Shelter Bay very well sheltered, and wild and remote. The south part of the bay has a large flat bottom with plenty of swinging room.

The inner basin to the south has a difficult entrance and is "Really far out!" as the captain says. Reconnoiter the entrance to the basin before you enter. It is narrow and winding, with moderate current and about a half-fathom at zero tide. The channel starts close to the drying mud flat to avoid a rock awash at zero tide 100 yards from the west shore. Once you are a quarter-mile south of the rock, the basin opens up with 1 to 3 fathoms to the south end.

Anchor in 2 fathoms over soft brown mud with clam shells; good holding.

Anchor (inner basin) in 1 to 2 fathoms over brown mud with good holding.

## **Eye of the Needle** (Tebenkof Bay)

Eye of the Needle is 1.25 miles south of Elena Point.

Chart 17376
Entrance: 56°27.80′ N, 134°05.22′ W
Anchor (Site #1): 56°25.95′ N, 134°03.00′ W
Anchor (Site #2): 56°25.70′ N, 134°02.85′ W

"Eye of the Needle" is what we call a 2.5-mile-long narrow channel that leads through primeval wilderness—a passage in time. This is a special rainforest environment, a 5-mile round trip with optional anchor sites. This passage is best done in a smaller cruising vessel (under 35 feet) or one with a bow-thruster—most of the needle is too narrow to turn around. If you do attempt this channel, proceed at dead-slow speed and in whispered voices.

Here, the branches of old-growth trees laden with green moss sag nearly to the water's edge. It is so peaceful that even the bald eagles seem content just to perch in the tree branches above watching your every movement. The mud in the shoals is slowly being covered with thick green lichen.

The average width of the channel is about 100 feet, with less in the narrows. Favor the west shore until you near a dangerous rock halfway through the narrows; then use the center of the channel. After the first narrows, the channel widens. Continue to favor the west shore to avoid a large rock in the center that dries on a 6-foot tide. Anchor Site #1 is on the south side of that rock.

Anchor (Site #1) in 8 fathoms over mud and gravel with good holding.

Continuing south, you pass through the second narrows (60 feet wide), avoiding rocks on both shores, before you come to the *eye* of the needle. Favor the west shore to avoid both a big rock awash on a 4-foot tide and a bushy islet. South of this islet is anchor Site #2.

Anchor (Site #2) in 2 to 4 fathoms over mud and clam shells with good holding. At this point the channel shoals, so you need to turn around and retrace your route.

(We went to the bitter end on a minus 2-foot tide, which allowed us a good view of bright red starfish and reflections of what we saw as "faces" on the rocks. Minimum depths in the fairway were 1-1/2 fathoms in both the first and second narrows, and between 3 to 8 fathoms elsewhere.)

## **Petrof Bay and Cedar Bight** (Tebenkof Bay)

Petrof Bay is the southeast arm of Tebenkof Bay.

Chart 17376
Entrance (Petrof Bay): 56°24.14′ N, 134°03.72′ W
Anchor (Petrof Bay): 56°22.09′ N, 134°03.09′ W
Entrance (Cedar Bight): 56°23.73′ N, 134°04.61′ W
Anchor (Cedar Bight): 56°22.97′ N, 134°04.82′ W

> *The entrance to Petrof Bay . . . is endangered by numerous reefs and shoals. . . .*
>
> *Good anchorage can be selected in various parts of Petrof Bay; the chart is the best guide.* (CP)

Petrof Bay and the smaller bay to the west (Cedar Bight) offer good shelter over a flat, shallow bottom. The head of Petrof Bay is seldom used for anchorage because of its remoteness. However, if you choose this site, you may get a view of the elusive sandhill cranes that nest along the creek. A trail—reportedly a good 2-mile walk—connects with Affleck Canal to the south.

For more coziness we prefer what we call "Cedar Bight"—the cove to the west—which has stands of cedar along its east shore, with hemlock and spruce on its west shore. Avoid the 1-fathom shoal and two mid-channel rocks not marked by kelp. The rapids in this cove are great for kayaking.

Anchor (Petrof Bay) in 3 fathoms over soft mud with very good holding.

Anchor (Cedar Bight) in 2 fathoms over brown mud with shells and small rocks; holding is good if you set your anchor well.

## **Thetis Bay** (Tebenkof Bay)

Thetis Bay is the southwest arm of Tebenkof Bay.

Chart 17376
Entrance: 56°25.03′ N, 134°09.26′ W
Anchor: 56°22.18′ N, 134°10.30′ W

> *Thetis Bay . . . affords excellent anchorage near its head in 9 to 10 fathoms, mud bottom.* (CP)

Thetis Bay, surrounded by high ridges and peaks, offers very good protection from all weather. Tidal rapids flow in and out of the lagoon on the west shore and may be a place for kayakers to practice some whitewater techniques.

Anchor in 6 fathoms over sticky mud with very good holding.

## **Orel Anchorage** (Tebenkof Bay)

Orel Anchorage is 3 miles southeast of Explorer Basin.

Chart 17376
Entrance: 56°25.30′ N, 134°08.34′ W
Anchor: 56°24.86′ N, 134°08.05′ W

Orel Anchorage is a small landlocked anchorage, easy to get to, with good protection from southerlies. Avoid the rocks on both sides of the entrance channel.

Anchor in 5 to 6 fathoms over mud in the center of the anchorage; good holding.

## **Explorer Basin**

Explorer Basin lies on the south side of Tebenkof Bay between Kuiu Island and the off-lying Windfall and Troller islands.

Chart 17376
West entrance (Swaine Point Passage): 56°26.14′ N, 134°15.13′ W
East entrance (Helianthus Passage): 56°26.96′ N, 134°11.44′ W
Anchor (southeast corner): 56°24.75′ N, 134°11.18′ W

Linda Lewis

*Sometimes the kelp is so thick you need to use the boat hook to get it off the anchor.*

> *Explorer Basin . . . affords fair anchorage during S weather. The entrance is obstructed by shoals off Swaine Point and the southernmost Windfall Island.* (CP)

Explorer Basin is well named. It's a great place to explore by kayak or dinghy. We have seen many sea otters here, two humpback whales and numerous sea lions. Enter south of Windfall Islands or via Helianthus Passage, known locally as Mail Boat Pass.

Anchorage can be found in the center of the Troller Islands or in the coves on the south side and southeast corner. Several small beaches on the islands are good for kayak haul-outs or camping.

Anchor (southeast corner) in 5 fathoms over a soft bottom with fair-to-good holding.

## **Gedney Harbor** (Kuiu Island)

Gedney Harbor is 2 miles northeast of Point Cosmos.

Chart 17376
Entrance: 56°22.26′ N, 134°15.12′ W
Anchor: 56°22.64′ N, 134°14.25′ W

> *The entrance to the harbor is on either side of a ledge about 400 yards long. . . . The channels on each side of the ledge are clear in midchannel. . . .*
>
> *The harbor is used extensively by fishermen during the season. Anchorage is available in most parts of the harbor in 6 to 12 fathoms, mud bottom.*

*A fish-buying scow is usually anchored in the harbor during the summer. Water, ice, gasoline, diesel fuel, limited provisions, and fishing supplies are available on the scow.* (CP)

Gedney Harbor is well protected in all weather by an island on its west side. This is a quiet place with no sign of chop. When you reach the head of the entrance channel, turn north and anchor in the lee of the large island on your port side.

Anchor in about 5 fathoms over soft sticky mud and sand with very good holding.

## Harris Cove (Kuiu Island)

Harris Cove is between Gedney Harbor and Port Malmesbury.

Chart 17376
Entrance: 56°19.12′ N, 134°17.90′ W

*Harris Cove . . . extends to the basin at the NW end of Port Malmesbury, with low land between. This bight is used by small craft for anchorage in all but W weather.* (CP)

We have not found a good anchor site in Harris Cove yet, although shelter can be found on the south side next to the shore. We much prefer Gedney Harbor, 3.5 miles to the north (described above). At high water, a dinghy can enter the lagoon to the east of Harris Harbor from either the north or south end.

## Port Malmesbury (Kuiu Island)

Port Malmesbury is 13 miles east of Port Alexander.

Chart 17376
Entrance: 56°16.47′ N, 134°17.48′ W
Anchor (bitter end): 56°17.49′ N, 134°09.60′ W

*On the SE side of the port are two arms; one about 1.7 miles inside the entrance and the other near the head. The NW side has a short arm about halfway between the entrance and the head of the port.*

*. . . A reef extends about 350 yards off the point on the N side of the port about 1.5 miles E of Point Harris. The bight W of this reef affords fair-weather anchorage, protected from N winds, in 15 fathoms, soft bottom.*

*. . . The head of the first arm on the S side affords anchorage in 12 fathoms. Favor the SW side near the head. . . .*

*In the second arm on the S side, anchorage may be had in 7 to 17 fathoms, mud bottom.* (CP)

We feel that the best shelter for cruising boats in Port Malmesbury is in the first arm to the northwest—the place we call the "Mud Hole." We also like the basin at the far eastern end that has high peaks streaked by avalanche paths; this site offers good shelter, too, but it may be subject to williwaws in unsettled weather. Favor the southwest shore when entering the bitter end as a rocky patch extends 100 yards from shore. The scenery here is spectacular, with large old-growth trees and many giant silver snags. A striking, high peak towers above the head of the basin.

Anchor (bitter end) in 8 to 10 fathoms over soft brown mud with very good holding.

## Mud Hole (Port Malmesbury)

Mud Hole is 2.5 miles northeast of Point Harris Light in Port Malmesbury.

Chart 17376
Entrance: 56°18.57′ N, 134°13.99′ W
Anchor: 56°18.21′ N, 134°14.58′ W

*The small arm on the NW side has a narrow entrance channel with dangers on both sides.*

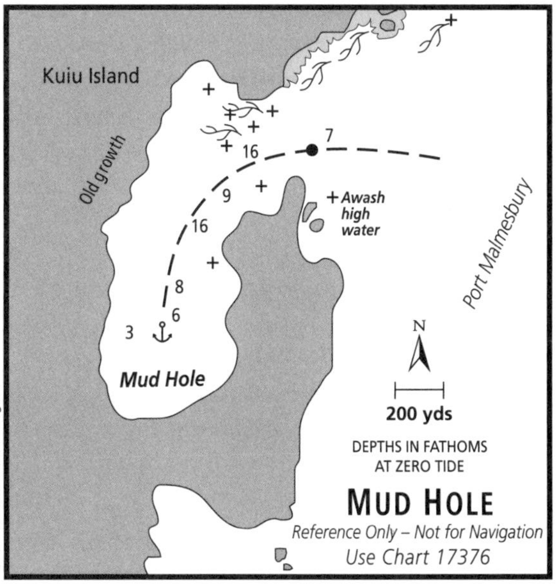

*Vessels entering should favor the S shore in the narrow entrance. Good anchorage is inside the arm in 7 to 10 fathoms, mud bottom.* (CP)

Landlocked Mud Hole offers very good shelter from all weather, with adequate swinging room for several boats. The entrance has 4 fathoms in the fairway. Avoid rocks extending to mid-channel from the north shore. The swells from the southwest die off at a reef on the southeast side of the peninsula forming Mud Hole. We call this "Nursery Reef" because a dozen or more mother sea otters gathered to show off their babies as we slowly motored in.

Anchor in 6 to 8 fathoms over mud with very good holding.

### **Table Bay** (Kuiu Island)

Table Bay is 2 miles north of Point Crowley Light.

Chart 17386
Entrance: 56°08.96′ N, 134°15.44′ W
Entrance (landlocked cove): 56°10.02′ N, 134°14.72′ W

*The N entrance point of Table Bay, about 2 miles N of Point Crowley, consists of an island close to a tongue of lowland, which affords some shelter from the swell in the N arm of the bay. Temporary anchorage may be had in 13 to 16 fathoms, mud bottom. . . . At high water small craft can enter the land-locked cove on the W side of the N arm by passing between the wooded island on the N side of the cove and the rocky islet S of this island. At low water this entrance has bare rocks.* (CP)

The east side of Table Bay is only a half-mile from Kell Bay in Affleck Canal. We prefer Port Malmesbury to those bays south of here.

### **Crowley Bight** (Kuiu Island)

Crowley Bight is 1.5 miles southeast of Point Crowley Light.

Chart 17386
Entrance: 56°06.10′ N, 134°14.83′ W

*Crowley Bight, a fair-weather anchorage, is an indentation in the shoreline between Point Howard and Point Crowley. It is exposed and affords poor holding ground.* (CP)

Crowley Bight is exposed in all but calm weather. (See Mud Hole above.)

### **Howard Cove** (Kuiu Island)

Howard Cove is 5 miles southeast of Point Crowley Light and 3 miles northwest of Cape Decision.

Chart 17386
Entrance: 56°02.39′ N, 134°11.77′ W

*Howard Cove . . . is open to the W and is not considered a secure anchorage. The temporary use of the cove is recommended only for small craft of not over 6-foot draft with local knowledge.* (CP)

Howard Cove is full of kelp and useful only to boats fishing off Cape Decision in fair weather.

### **Cape Decision** (Kuiu Island)

Cape Decision is the south tip of Kuiu Island.

Chart 17386
Cape Decision (light brg 000°T at 0.50 Nm): 55°59.59′ N, 134°08.16′ W

*Cape Decision . . . is a low, bare, rocky point, from which the land rises gradually to an irregular, timbered ridge. . . . Avoid the large kelp patches 1.5 and 2 miles NW from the cape and about 0.8 mile off the Kuiu Island shore.* (CP)

Cape Decision connects Chatham Strait to Sumner Strait. Beware of breakers and strong tide rips south and east of the light.

## KEKU STRAIT FROM CONCLUSION ISLAND TO SUMNER STRAIT

***Note:*** Please see West Sumner Strait in Chapter 9 for coves along Kuiu Island between Cape Decision and Reid Bay.

### **Keku Strait**

Keku Strait separates the west shore of Kupreanof Island from Kuiu Island and connects Sumner Strait with Frederick Sound via Rocky Pass.

Charts 17360, 17368, 17372

***Note:* Chart 17372 measures depths in feet.**

South entrance (1.0 mile east of Conclusion Island and 3.6 miles northwest of Point Barrie): 56°27.83′ N 133°45.03′ W
North entrance (2.1 miles southwest of Pt. Macartney Light; 4.8 miles west of Kake): 56°59.57′ N, 134°05.22′ W

*The strait consists of three parts: a large bay at the S and N ends, and a narrow, intricate pas-*

*sage, about 18 miles long, known as Rocky Pass, that connects the two bays.*

*The bay forming the S entrance to the strait is very foul, particularly the E and NE shore. Navigation through any part of the bay should be with caution. The entrance to the bay is between Sumner Island and Point Barrie.*

*The N bay of Keku Strait is about 13 miles long from the entrance to Point Camden where the bay branches, the W branch forming Port Camden and the E branch forming Rocky Pass. . . . The entrance from Frederick Sound is between Point Macartney and Cornwallis Point.* (CP)

Keku Strait is an interesting alternative to busy Wrangell Narrows for small craft transiting from Sumner Strait to Frederick Strait or vice versa. Although Keku Strait can be considered a complex rock pile through which saltwater flows, it represents quite a short cut for small craft heading between Ketchikan and Sitka. The large bays at either end of Keku Strait have some primitive and isolated anchorages that are well protected and seldom visited.

The middle 20 miles of Keku Strait, called Rocky Pass, involves a variety of technical challenges to anyone who attempts it. In our earlier book, *Exploring the Inside Passage to Alaska*, we wrote that "Rocky Pass is an explorer's dream and a marginal navigator's nightmare." This comment related to the period between 1982 and 1996 when there were no navigational aids to help you find your way through this "rock pile," surrounded by hidden mud flats and surging saltwater.

Don Douglass

*A sunny day brings a smile to the author's face!*

Now there are route markers in place with a few new ones added in recent years and the uncertainty of the route is greatly diminished. However, Rocky Pass remains a wild, remote area requiring superior piloting skills. It is not recommended for all boats, since the route, despite being marked, still involves considerable risk. The channel is shallow with numerous mud flats on all sides and with strong currents in the narrows at Devils Elbow and The Summit. Thick kelp patches are found in many places.

We do not recommend Rocky Pass for larger boats or for skippers unsure of their piloting skills. Vessels over 30 feet may want to scout out the narrow parts of the route by dinghy before attempting a passage. Since you can easily anchor almost anywhere in Rocky Pass, this scouting can be fun!

Why would anyone want to go to such a place? For its charm, its lack of visitors and its pristine wilderness, which has been open to boaters for just a little over a decade. You will still be one of only a handful of boats to experience the challenges of Rocky Pass.

In August 2003, we met Ben Kyle (son of Jim Kyle and co-skipper of the charter vessel M/V *Home Shore*) in the middle of Rocky Pass. He told us that he had been dropped off in Chatham Strait with his kayak two weeks before, and that we were the first humans he had seen in 13 days.

Traffic has increased in the last few years, and you will most likely see another boat or two in the Narrows. It's a good idea to give a Securité call when transiting the areas of limited visibility—especially The Summit and Devils Elbow.

Stories abound of good skippers who grounded or ruined their boats in Rocky Pass. Even when we first wrote about Rocky Pass, the USCG buoy tender, *Elderberry*—which was responsible for the area—had not visited the pass in over a decade, and they stated they would not be of help to stranded boats. During the early 1990s, in the several transits we made initially, we could find only one skipper (from Kake) who had ever been through.

Yes, more boats are trying it now, but Rocky Pass still remains a part of untouched Southeast Alaska—no clearcuts, no signs of civilization. More than 40 nav-aids is all you have, but if you have a chance to try it, by all means do so.

### **No Name Bay** (Kuiu Island)

No Name Bay is 3 miles west of Conclusion Island.

Chart 17360
Entrance: 56°29.85′ N, 133°53.76′ W
Anchor: 56°30.19′ N, 133°57.55′ W

> *No Name Bay . . . is constricted at its head by several wooded islets. Near the head is anchorage suitable for small craft.* (CP)

No Name Bay has a narrow channel lined with islets and rocks and about a 2-fathom minimum in the fairway. Alvin Bay, west of Sumner Island, is considered the first choice by local fishermen for shelter along this part of Kuiu Island; No Name Bay follows as their second choice.

Anchor in 3 to 4 fathoms over a mixed bottom.

### **Seclusion Harbor** (Kuiu Island)

Seclusion Harbor is 4 miles northwest of Conclusion Island.

Chart 17360
Entrance: 56°32.94′ N, 133°51.35′ W

> *Seclusion Harbor is a small inlet . . . . A chain of islands is E of its entrance.* (CP)

Seclusion Island has no large-scale chart. It has a tiny opening that appears to restrict its use. Locals recommend No Name Bay or Alvin Bay for shelter in foul weather.

### **Threemile Arm** (Kuiu Island)

Threemile Arm is 10 miles north of Alvin Bay.

Chart 17360
Entrance: 56°35.04′ N, 133°49.37′ W

> *Threemile Arm . . . makes off to the W at the NW end of the bay. Its entrance is obstructed by rocks. By proceeding with care, vessels can enter passing NE of the islet in the middle of the entrance, and find good protected anchorage in the middle of the arm in 5 to 8 fathoms, soft bottom.*
>
> *In 1974, a survey revealed a rock awash in the middle of the arm in 56°35′45″ N, 133°50′10″ W.* (CP)

Threemile Arm is the northwest corner of the intricate islet/rock area north of Conclusion Island. Note the cautions above. We have not entered this area.

### **Kayak Island Cove** (Keku Strait)

Kayak Island Cove is on the west side of the islets at the south end of Rocky Pass.

Chart 17372 (depths measured in feet)
Entrance (1.6 miles northeast of Monte Carlo Island): 56°32.45′ N, 133°43.01′ W
Anchor: 56°32.87′ N, 133°43.04′ W

Kayak Island Cove, formed by a group of small islets and sandy beaches at the south end of Rocky Pass, is an almost complete circle that offers temporary shelter for a lunch stop or a chance to explore the area. Primitive campsites lie along shell beaches among the islets, making it a great place for kayaks. We have used this cove as a temporary stop on several occasions and would consider it as an overnighter in calm conditions only. The bottom is irregular and hard, with poor holding, and we once dragged anchor, here, on a stiff southerly breeze.

If you need shelter near the south entrance to Keku Strait, Point Baker fishermen have told us they prefer Alvin Cove first and No Name Bay second. Both Port Protection and Point Baker on the south side of Sumner Strait (Prince of Wales Island) have excellent shelter

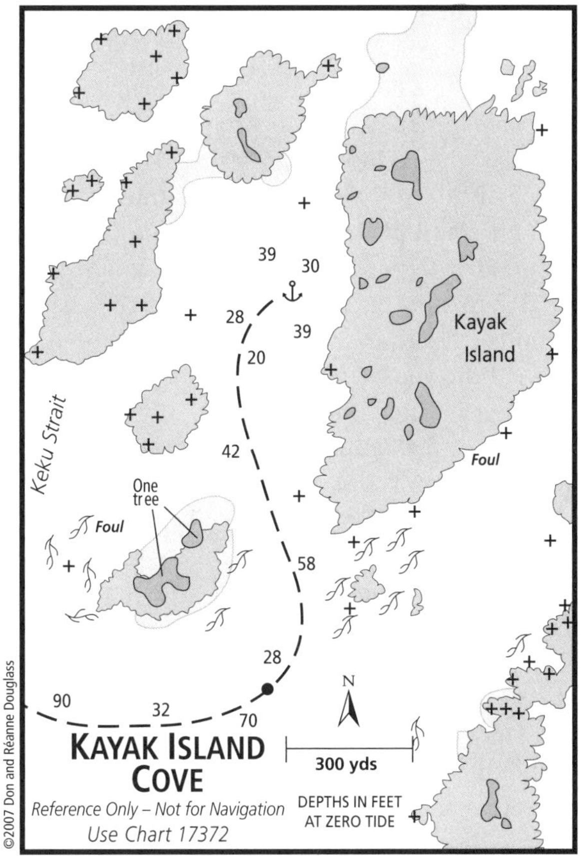


and are good places to wait for proper conditions, if you're northbound.

Strong ebb currents flowing south from Sumner Strait between Sumner Island and Point Baker can make for a rough-water crossing if the wind is blowing from the south. In this case, a short stop in either the recommended Alvin Cove or No Name Bay would be prudent.

Anchor in 30 to 40 feet on the west side of the islets over a hard mixed bottom with poor holding.

## **Rocky Pass** (Keku Strait)

Rocky Pass lies between Kupreanof and Kuiu islands.

Chart 17372.

***Note:* Chart 17372 gives all depths in feet; our two diagrams on Rocky Pass also use feet.**

South entrance (marker R"2" brg 025°T at 0.53 Nm) 56°33.43′ N, 133°43.84′ W

North entrance: (Entrance Island light brg 060°Tat 0.18 Nm): 56°48.54′ N, 133°48.11′ W

*Rocky Pass has its S entrance about 8 miles N of Point Barrie.*

*Because of strong currents, narrow channel, and sharp turns, it is advisable to make passage at or near high-water slack.*

*The depths through Rocky Pass are generally shallow, and small craft can anchor practically anywhere with the aid of the chart.*

*A Federal project provides for a channel dredged to a depth of 5 feet through Devils Elbow and The Summit, the shallowest parts of the pass.*

*Devils Elbow, about 14 miles N of Point Barrie, is the most dangerous part of the pass. The channel here makes a full right-angle turn. It had a controlling depth of 5 feet in April 2001.*

*The Summit is the narrow passage, W and NW of Summit Island, through which a channel has been dredged. The channel had a controlling depth of 3.5 feet (4.1 feet at midchannel) in April 2001. Passage through The Summit should be attempted only with local knowledge.*

*Tides. The range of tide at The Summit is about the same as at Ketchikan, but the time of tide occurs about 1/2 hour later than at Ketchikan. In the S and N bays of Keku Strait, the range of tide is about 0.8 of that at Ketchikan, and the time of tide is about the same as at Ketchikan. When proceeding in either direction, it is best to enter Rocky Pass about 1-1/2 to 2 hours before high water. There are many places at each end of Rocky Pass where vessels waiting for the tide can anchor. Strangers should make passage on a rising tide and be careful to remain in the channel because of the many unmarked dangers close to the channel edge. . . .*

*Currents. The flood current enters Keku Strait at both ends and meets in varying places between High Island and The Summit. At the entrance to Rocky Pass the tidal current has a velocity at strength of 0.9 to 1.2 knots.*

*At Devils Elbow the velocity of current is 1.8 to 2.4 knots, this being the strongest current encountered in the pass. Slack water occurs at practically high and low water. The period of slack at low water lasts only 5 or 10 minutes, and the current attains considerable velocity within a half hour of this time. The high-water slack lasts considerably longer, and passage through Devils*

*Elbow can easily be made within an hour before and after the high-water slack.*

*At The Summit strong currents set in within 1 hour of high-water slack attaining a velocity of about 2.6 knots. Through The Summit and the passages N of The Summit, the currents are quite variable because of frequent shallow depths and the intricate topography. High-water slack occurs near high water, but the ebb current runs for a considerable time after low water.* (CP)

*Authors' Note*: The Coast Guard re-marked Rocky Pass with all new navigation aids some time ago and they continue to add markers or change the position of markers. It is essential that you use the most recent edition of Chart 17372 (dated no earlier than 2003), with up-to-date corrections.

Rocky Pass is a special place enjoyed by more and more boaters with each passing season. In the past year or two, we have talked with skippers of boats as large as 50 feet who successfully passed through Rocky Pass at high-water rising tide, and after having reconnoitered both Devils Elbow and The Summit by dinghy first. With the dredged channels slowly silting in, you have as little as 2 feet depth at low water. We recommend that, before you commit to a passage of Rocky Pass, you talk with someone who has already made the trip in a boat similar to yours. The pass should be attempted only in good visibility and in fair weather.

Linda Lewis

*Remember that on a* southbound *trip through Rocky Pass, as in this picture, the green markers must be kept to starboard.*

With the additional navigation aids now in place, much of the uncertainty of the exact route is gone. However, a transit is still not a piece of cake. It is a risky venture that requires careful small-boat handling in close quarters, coupled with good judgment. You should post alert lookouts on the bow, one on the depth sounder, then proceed slowly, preferably on a rising tide, and be ready to stop or anchor on a moment's notice if need be.

On a *northbound* trip, you need to watch for mud banks along both sides of the route and avoid the rocks and heavy kelp in the fast flowing Devils Elbow. The southern end of The Summit is frequently choked with kelp, and the dredged sections are shallow and slowly filling in. Avoid kelp when possible, and glide through slowly when you can't.

On a *southbound* trip, it is still somewhat difficult to find the north entrance to The Summit; the kelp is thick in many places. Using electronic charting or pre-setting a GPS waypoint here will help. Care should be taken on a flood tide not to get too close to the small island to the east near the south end of The Summit. When approaching Devils Elbow, it is easy to overshoot the sharp left turn required at the northwest entrance.

When making this almost-due-east dogleg, keep both G"17" and G"15" close to your starboard hand and R"14" on your port hand to avoid nasty rocks on the north side of the Narrows. Slow down and monitor your position carefully.

A transit of Rocky Pass should not be attempted without a copy of Chart 17372 (2003 or later), which shows the location of the navaids, including some newer aids that have been added at The Summit and at Devils Elbow.

We have noticed a flood current of an estimated 4 knots flowing north at Devils Elbow, and a flood of about 6 knots flowing south at The Summit along the edge of Summit Island.

Réanne Hemingway-Douglass

*Working our way through the kelp in Rocky Pass*

(This information is contrary to *Coast Pilot*, but it has been confirmed in conversation with U.S. Coast Guard personnel.) These currents can cause high closing-speeds or a loss of steerage. Otherwise, except for these short stretches, currents are moderate and the water is smooth.

As a tool, GPS and electronic charting can help you identify turning points and make your transit of Rocky Pass feasible. A pre-drawn course line and waypoints on the latest edition of Chart 17372 are useful aids to prevent getting lost, as well as quick checks against your depth sounder readings. However, GPS variations and magnetic abnormalities are still too great to allow precisely following a GPS route. Added to these issues is the fact that the horizontal datum *of the chart insets* for The Summit and for Devils Elbow are NAD 27, not WGS 84 as for the rest of Chart 17372. If you are using paper charts and working with latitude and longitude from your GPS you should ideally re-set your GPS to NAD 27 for these sections. In reality, there is little time to do this, so paper-chart navigators working in conjunction with GPS coordinates should be extra cautious in these areas. Reaching The Summit at high tide and using good piloting skills (visual cues) are the critical elements for making this passage a safe one.

Réanne Hemingway-Douglass

*You can anchor almost anywhere in Rocky Pass.*

Rocky Pass is a wild place, so keep an alert bow watch and one eye on your depth sounder. Proceed accordingly and enjoy your explorations!

## **Tunehean Creek Bight** (Rocky Pass)

Tunehean Creek Bight is 2.4 miles northeast of the south entrance to Rocky Pass.

Chart 17372 (depths in feet)
Anchor (off Tunehean Creek): 56°35.19′ N, 133°41.01′ W

> *Larger craft can enter the S end of the pass for a distance of 2 miles until opposite Tunehean Creek and select anchorage according to draft, either to N or S of the midchannel reef off the mouth of the creek.* (CP)

## **Devils Elbow** (Rocky Pass)

Devils Elbow is 5 miles north of the south entrance to Rocky Pass.

Chart 17372 (depths in feet)
South entrance: 56°37.89′ N, 133°41.11′ W
North entrance: 56°38.21′ N, 133°42.16′ W

> *Devils Elbow . . . is the most dangerous part of the pass. The channel here makes a full right-angle turn. It had a controlling depth of 5 feet in April 2001. . . A Federal project provides for a channel dredged to a depth of 5 feet through Devils Elbow and The Summit, the shallowest parts of the pass.* (CP)

When in Rocky Pass, use extra caution transiting the Devils Elbow. Upon entering Rocky Pass, northbound, favor the Kuiu Island shore in a broad sweeping turn to the northeast. Favor the east shore to avoid the shoals southeast of

Eagle Island. Passing G"11," maintain a mid-channel course and pass close to green markers G"13," G"15," and G"17" on your port side, keeping the red marker R"14" off to your starboard. Avoid the rocks on the foul north shore and all kelp patches by following a mid-channel course. Turn north as soon as the channel behind the peninsula opens up to avoid mid-channel rocks west of the tip of the peninsula.

## **Baidarka Anchorage** (Rocky Pass)

Baidarka Anchorage is 0.35 mile south of Brown Bear Head Island.

Chart 17372 (depths in feet)
Anchor: 56°39.00′ N, 133°43.24′ W

You can anchor anywhere in Rocky Pass and should be prepared to do so quickly if conditions require it. Our favorite site is the small basin halfway between The Summit and Devils

---

## Rocky Pass Conquered!

Linda Lewis & Dave Parker—M/V *Royal Sounder*

I finally got to accomplish what I considered my number one SE AK navigation challenge. As many things go, the anticipation was more nerve-wracking than the actual event. Everything went very smoothly on this 21 mile rocky, winding and shallow transit. We followed the Douglass guidebook's advice throughout. Because it was my holy grail, I was at the helm most of the trip. Dave did bow watch through the tricky parts, using the kelp for guidance and keeping a lookout for unanticipated rocks.

The number one issue for Rocky Pass is being in the right sections of the transit at the right times. Otherwise, the water is definitely too skinny and too fast. On our southbound trip—at high water slack—the lowest depth we encountered was 18 feet. We encountered that in the trickiest and shallowest sections (The Summit & Devils Elbow), as expected. We were happy with that depth.

We agree with Douglass that the currents run considerably faster than the *Coast Pilot* says. Our STWs and SOGs showed us a 3-4-knot current at the north entrance when we started down and I'll bet it was running 4-6-knots at that same time in the tricky places down the road. By the time we arrived at those sections it was high water slack at The Summit and running about 1 knot at Devils Elbow. As planned. We were happy that we got the timing right.

We were kept really busy. Eyes flicking from looking outside the boat, to spotting markers, to shifting to the depth sounder, to watching for kelp and unanticipated rocks, to following the course on the electronic chart, then back through the whole routine again. Even at a SOG of only 5 knots, I felt really busy at the helm.

We encountered considerable traffic during our passage on a Saturday in June, 2005. Four fishing boats popped out at The Summit and we encountered one pleasure boat after we started through. He was smaller than we were so he decided to beat a retreat and let us go through. The navigable channel is so narrow through places like The Summit and Devils Elbow that it would be very difficult to share—sort of like a one-lane road. I forgot to do a Sécurité call to warn that we were coming through; next time I won't forget. From our experience, it seems that more people may be using this passage.

It was a challenging and fun experience. In truth, we would not want to do it without using electronic charts. There is so much to look at to decide where you are that to pilot through using only visual cues for where to steer would be extremely difficult, if not downright hair-raising. The electronic charting was a great asset. (But we also always have our paper-chart backups sitting open and in the order of the day's trip.)

We found some additional extremely helpful markers have been put in place since the first edition of your book was published. Two are located in the area of the Summit (R"28" and R"24"), and one at Devils Elbow (R"14"). We also discovered that while our recently updated electronic chart collection (from a major vendor) had provided us with the newer edition raster chart of the area, the vector chart for this area did not get updated. The newer markers showed up on the raster view, but not the vector view. There is also a section right at The Devils Elbow where chart quilting problems appeared: the edges of the inset pieces of the chart don't line up nicely with the general chart. Electronic charting is wonderful, but also brings its challenges.

We jokingly said to each other that if they add a few more markers Rocky Pass will be like a mini Wrangell Narrows—only *lots* shallower. The markers are excellent. Transiting only at high water is no joke; we're believers. But with electronic charts, good timing, and good mariner's-eye watchfulness, this is a go-for-it transit for experienced cruisers. Other cruisers said it was doable and enjoyable. Now we can agree—from experience.

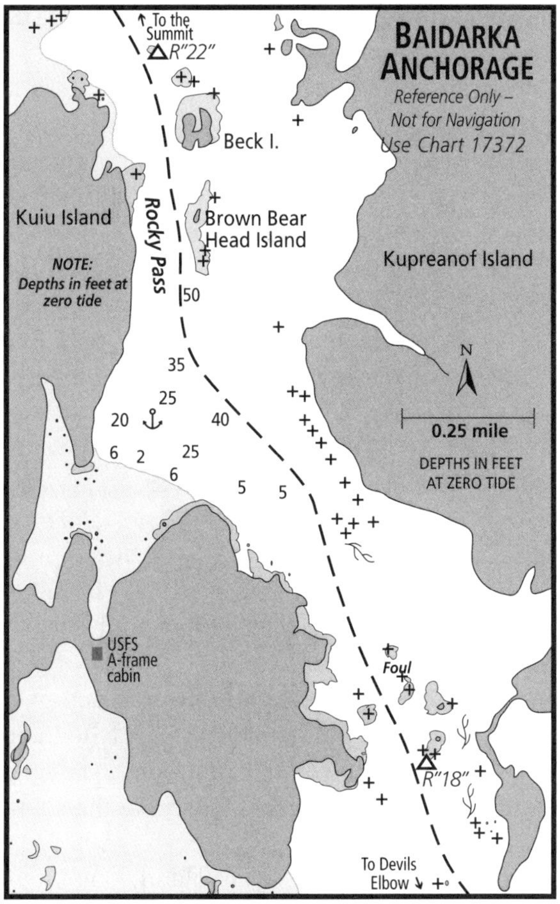


©2007 Don and Réanne Douglass

Réanne Hemingway-Douglass

*An earlier* Baidarka *in Baidarka Anchorage*

Elbow. What we call "Baidarka Anchorage" is a good place to anchor while you reconnoiter ahead, wait for the correct tide or even remain overnight. We named this site after our trusty trawler, which has poked its bow (sometimes wrongly!) into the many excellent channels of Rocky Pass. So far, we have not grounded or left any paint in Rocky Pass, but some of our transits have been rather exciting!

Baidarka Anchorage is protected from all weather and is out of the strong currents found in the channels to the north and south. At high water, you can take a dinghy trip to the USFS Devils Elbow cabin in the cove directly south. The nice A-frame cabin, used primarily by deer hunters in autumn, is quite often available in the summer. This is an excellent spot for photographing wild ducks, geese, mink, marten, wolves, and black bear.

Leaving Baidarka Anchorage heading north, we have passed Brown Bear Head Island on either side. If you use the west passage, stay close to the island for the deepest water.

Anchor off the steep-to flat in 25 feet over sand, mud and some gravel; holding is good if you set your anchor well.

## **The Summit** (Rocky Pass)

The Summit is 2.5 miles northwest of Devils Elbow.

Chart 17372 (depths in feet)
South entrance (100 yards northeast of G"23"): 56°39.98′ N, 133°43.79′ W
South entrance of dredged channel: 56°40.16′ N, 133°44.01′ W
North entrance (0.2 mile north of G"27"): 56°41.25′ N, 133°44.16′ W
North entrance (100 yards north of G"35," 0.6 mile south of High Island): 56°42.72′ N, 133°44.13′ W

> *The Summit is the shallowest part of the pass.* [It is] *a narrow passage, W and NW of Summit Island, through which a channel has been dredged. The channel had a controlling depth*

*of 3.5 feet (4.1 feet at midchannel) in April 2001. Passage through The Summit should be attempted only with local knowledge.* (CP)

The tides generally meet between Devils Elbow and The Summit, so Baidarka Anchorage is a good place to stay and reconnoiter the challenges ahead. This section of Rocky Pass is fully protected from outside influences; it has limited fetch, so there are no swells and little chop. For the most part, the waters are very calm and it is extremely quiet and peaceful.

As mentioned above, when heading north from Baidarka Anchorage, you can pass Brown Bear Head on either side. We prefer the west side, staying close to the island to avoid a 5-foot shoal off the west shore.

As you approach the south end of The Summit, you find a lot of kelp that hides numerous rocks and boulders. Stay close to G“23” to avoid the rocks near R“24.” Turn north where the kelp opens up revealing a channel that points toward G“25.”

There is generally less kelp on the surface at high water than at low water, and increased traffic is helping to keep the channels open. If you worry that the kelp you must pass through hides dangerous rocks, anchor for a few minutes and do some probing with your dinghy.

*Caution:* Rocks extend southeast from G“25,” and across the fairway, north of G“23.” Your route should follow an S-shaped curve in this area. Avoid the kelp patch at G“25;” there are underwater rocks close by on the east side. (This is one of the shallowest and most kelp-ridden places in Rocky Pass.) The channel through The Summit favors the east shore until you approach the north entrance.

On a southbound transit, the north entrance to The Summit is somewhat difficult to locate, but it can be identified by the dredged material thrown up on either side of the channel on the west side of the reef marked “awash at 1⁄2 tide” southeast of R“30.”

Once inside the old dredged channel, you can generally see the bottom even in rainy weather. If you are passing through The Summit with a strong flood current flowing, be careful not to let your boat get set against the small islet on the west side of Summit Island. This is where we've found maximum current (up to 6 knots) and you will have little steerage as you try to motor slowly through.

Continuing northbound, once you pass the long thin reef marked “awash at 1⁄2 tide,” keep the entire reef to your starboard until you pass R“30.” You are then out of the dredged section of The Summit.

From here north, stay in the deep-water channel as indicated on the chart, then favor the Kuiu Island shore north of G“35,” and pass the reef off 560-foot High Island. After passing Stadia Rock, favor Horseshoe Island shore. Stedman Cove is well sheltered and a good overnight anchorage.

Continuing westbound, favor Cucumber Reef to avoid the bad reef southwest of Stedman Cove entrance, then favor Entrance Island to avoid the long reef that extends from the south shore.

Once clear of Entrance Island, you leave Rocky Pass and can find good shelter in Dakaneek Bay, or head for the village of Kake. You can also head south into remote Port Camden or steam out through the Keku Islands to Frederick Sound.

Don't rush through this wonderful area. We encourage you to anchor overnight in Baidarka Anchorage and enjoy this special passage. Stopping for awhile can decrease your anxieties about timing The Summit and the Devils Elbow correctly and can increase your pleasure factor enormously.

## **Stedman Cove** (Horseshoe Island)

Stedman Cove, on the southwest shore of Horseshoe Island, is just inside the north entrance of Rocky Pass.

**Chart 17372 (depths in feet)**
**Entrance (0.3 mile northeast of Cucumber Reef): 56°47.45′ N, 133°45.18′ W**
**Anchor: 56°48.04′ N, 133°44.53′ W**

Réanne Hemingway-Douglass

*A labyrinth of islands*

*Stedman Cove . . . affords the best anchorage in the vicinity for small craft; it is well protected from almost every direction, particularly from SE and from N to NW. It is a convenient place to await favorable tidal conditions before proceeding S through the pass.* (CP)

Stedman Cove, the site of an oyster farm, is a landlocked anchorage that offers excellent shelter from all weather. Avoid the shoal water off both the north and south sides of the cove. Be on the lookout for old floats and fishing platforms moored here, as well as for kelp patches on an otherwise soft bottom.

Anchor in 12 feet over soft sand and mud with very good holding.

## **Big John Bay** (Kupreanof Island)

Big John Bay is 2 miles east of Stedman Cove.

**Chart 17372 (depths in feet)**
**Entrance (0.5 mile north of Beacon Island): 56°47.21′ N, 133°43.25′ W**
**Anchor: 56°47.93′ N, 133°40.77′ W**

*Passage E of Beacon Island leads into Big John Bay, a large bay that extends N and E of Horseshoe Island. Fishing vessels often anchor in the SE arm of Big John Bay in 18 to 24 feet, soft bottom.* (CP)

Anchor in 3 fathoms over sand and mud with isolated rocks.

## **Davidson Bay** (Kupreanof Island)

Davidson Bay is 2.5 miles north of the north entrance to Rocky Pass.

**Chart 17368**
**Entrance: 56°50.45′ N, 133°51.00′ W**
**Anchor: 56°50.99′ N, 133°51.00′ W**

Davidson Bay, a large bay just east of Salt Point, is easy to enter, but it is open to southwest winds. The eastern section is a drying mud flat. Anchorage can be found in the corner of the bay off the drying mud flats, but better shelter can be found in Dakaneek Bay.

Anchor in 4 fathoms over sand with fair-to-good holding.

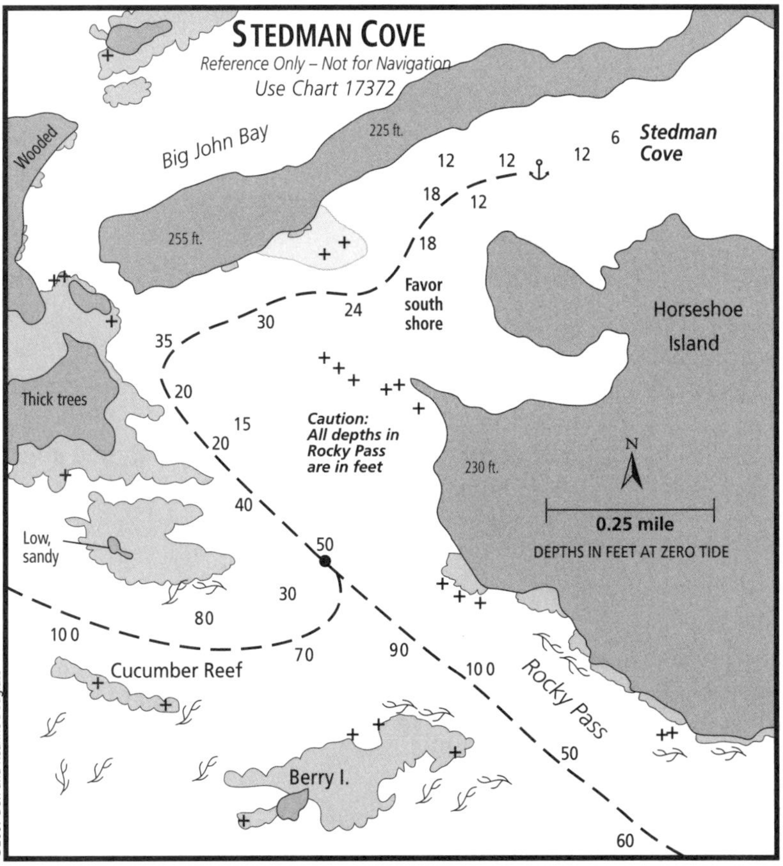

## Dakaneek Bay
(Kupreanof Island)

Dakaneek Bay is 5 miles south of Kake at the head of Port Camden and 5 miles north of the north entrance to Rocky Pass.

**Chart 17368**
**Entrance: 56°51.36′ N, 133°52.27′ W**
**Anchor 56°51.87′ N, 133°51.00′ W**

Dakaneek Bay, a small inlet on Kupreanof Island, is not listed in *Coast Pilot*. We find its shelter good and its access easy. You need to avoid two charted, isolated rocks in the entrance. (If you are southbound, this is a good place to stay while you're timing your approach to Rocky Pass.) Both Dakaneek and Davidson bays are good for crabbing.

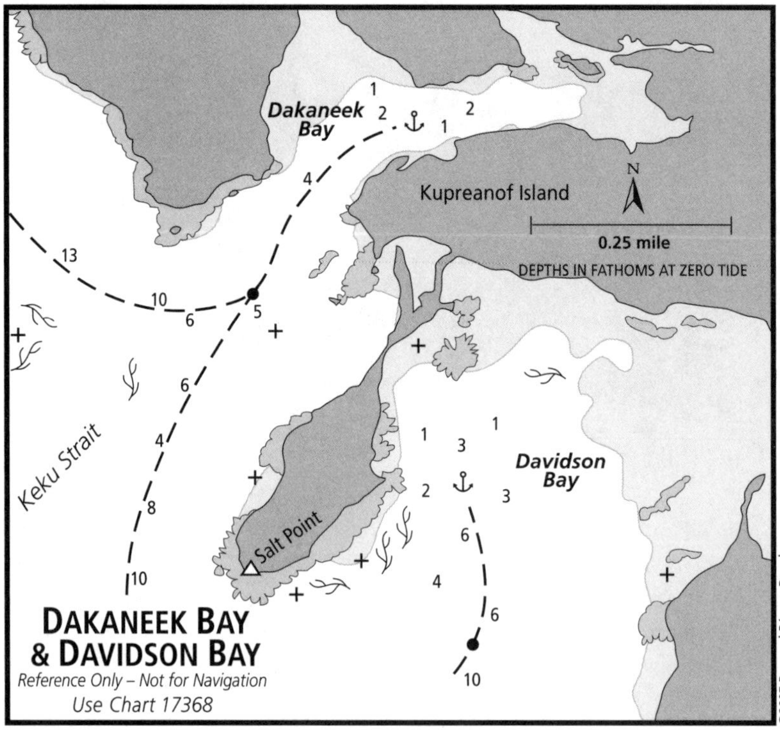

**DAKANEEK BAY & DAVIDSON BAY**
*Reference Only – Not for Navigation*
*Use Chart 17368*



Anchor off the drying mud flats in 2 fathoms over mud with good holding.

## Port Camden (Kuiu Island)

Port Camden, the large inlet west of Rocky Pass, is 10 miles south of Kake.

**Chart 17368**
**Entrance: 56°48.41′ N, 133°55.01′ W**

> *Port Camden, the entrance to which is on the W side of Pup Island and 14 miles from Point Macartney, is an inlet 13 miles long and 1.5 miles wide for a distance of 5 miles from its entrance. . . . A good anchorage can be found in 20 fathoms in the wide part of Port Camden SW of Cam Island, favoring the SW shore of the inlet. Good anchorage, protected from all directions but the N, is available in 4 to 10 fathoms in the cove SE of Cam Island. Favor the W shore of the cove to avoid a large reef and a 3-fathom shoal to the N on the E side of the cove. An excellent anchorage for small boats can be had in a small cove on the E shore E of Cam Island. The entrance shoals to 2 1/2 fathoms. Keep close to the W shore of the entrance. Beware of the reefs on the N side of the entrance to this cove. Anchorage in 4 fathoms, well protected on all sides, can be had.* (CP)

## Goose Bay (Port Camden)

Goose Bay is about 6 miles south of Point Camden.

**Chart 17368**
**Entrance: 56°44.15′ N, 133°52.65′ W**
**Anchor: 56°44.65′ N, 133°52.14′ W**

Goose Bay, the attractive landlocked bay on the east side of Port Camden Inlet, offers excellent protection from all weather. It is close enough to Rocky Pass to allow an early-morning start on a southbound transit. We named this "Goose Bay" for a Canadian honker family that lives along the shore. Port Camden is full of black bear and, in addition to Goose Bay, an excellent place to photograph them. The area from Goose Bay to the head of Port Camden is reported to have very good "dungie" crab fishing.

There is plenty of swinging room in the bay, but avoid the rocks off the peninsula and the drying shoal to starboard at the entrance narrows.

Anchor in 4 fathoms over black mud and clamshells with excellent holding.

## **Camden Hideout** (Port Camden)

Camden Hideout is 2.5 miles southwest of Goose Bay.

Chart 17368 (inset)

Entrance: 56°43.14′ N, 133°53.99′ W

Anchor: 56°42.54′ N, 133°54.96′ W

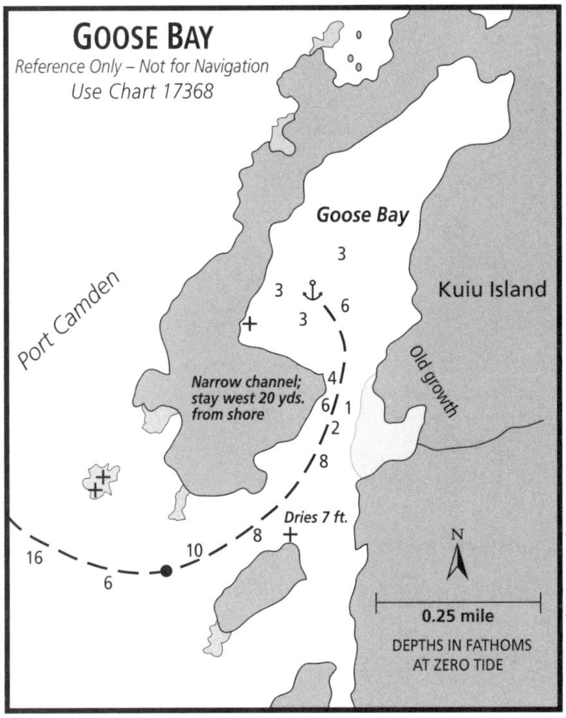


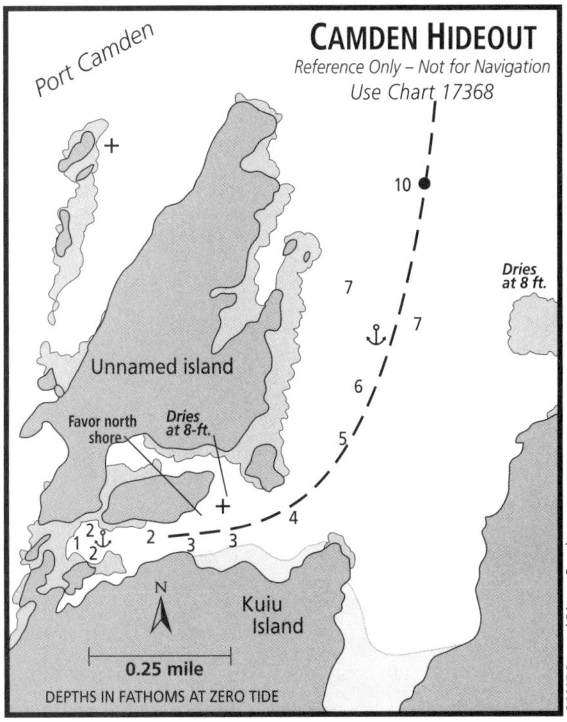


If you like true old Alaska, Camden Hideout is a classic off-the-beaten-path with no signs of weather. The entrance and basin are narrow and there is little turning room.

Favor the north shore inside the narrows. A small, 15-foot-deep basin at the head of the channel has enough room for one small boat. Although there is almost no swinging room, you hardly need to worry because it is so protected in here, but a stern-tie is a good idea. The water temperature is in the low-to-mid-sixties. You can anchor in the outer basin in 7 fathoms if a blow is expected.

Anchor in 2 fathoms over a mixed bottom with very good holding.

## **Kadake Bay** (Kuiu Island)

Kadake Bay is 2.2 miles southwest of Pup Island.

Chart 17368

Position: 56°48.59′ N, 133°57.38′ W

Kadake Bay is almost entirely filled with a drying mud flat. Some temporary anchorage can be found in its entrance channel.

## **Gil Harbor** (Kuiu Island)

Gil Harbor is 3.3 miles northwest of Pup Island.

Chart 17368

Entrance: 56°50.11′ N, 133°59.06′ W

Anchor: 56°49.64′ N, 133°59.77′ W

Gil Harbor is not mentioned in *Coast Pilot*, but fishing boats use it for anchorage, especially in southeast weather.

Anchor deep in the harbor avoiding the numerous rocks in the northwest corner.

Anchor in 3 fathoms over sand and shells with good holding.

## **Keku Islands** (Keku Strait)

Keku Islands are on the southwest side of Keku Strait and 5 miles west of Kake.

Chart 17368

> *Keku Islands . . . comprise a group of wooded islands, with outlying reefs, between which are no practicable channels. . . . Between Keku Islands and the reefs on the NE side is a chan-*

*nel about 1.5 miles wide and 8 miles long to Point Hamilton, with depths of 7 to 50 fathoms. S of Eva Island the channel is about 1 mile wide, between Point Hamilton and Hound Island, and leads between kelp-marked rocks and shoals on both sides.* (CP)

The enchanted Keku Islands are full of surprises — a ridge of land uplifted in deep water provides a playground of islands, islets, reefs, and isolated rocks all rising steeply, unmarked with navigational aids and ready to explore.

Réanne Hemingway-Douglass

*Going ashore at Lord's Pocket*

Check Chart 17368 carefully and notice how quickly the depths of the water change without warning. The Keku Islands and Keku Strait have a warm and pleasant micro-climate that is quite agreeable for exploration. It is seldom visited by cruising vessels, so you're likely to see more whales than boats in this vicinity.

## Kuiu Island Southeast Cove
(Kuiu Island)

Kuiu Island Southwest Cove is 6 miles southwest of Kake.

**Chart 17368**
**Position: 56°52.87′ N, 134°01.77′ W**

"Southeast Cove," a local name, is easy to get to and offers good protection in southeast weather. There are two large buoys here used by tugs to park barges and rafts. The cove is rather deep for small craft, except close to shore.

## Lord's Pocket (Payne Island)

Lord's Pocket is 5.5 miles southwest of Kake.

**Chart 17368**
**West entrance: 56°56.47′ N, 134°08.76′ W**
**East entrance: 56°56.20′ N, 134°05.50′ W**

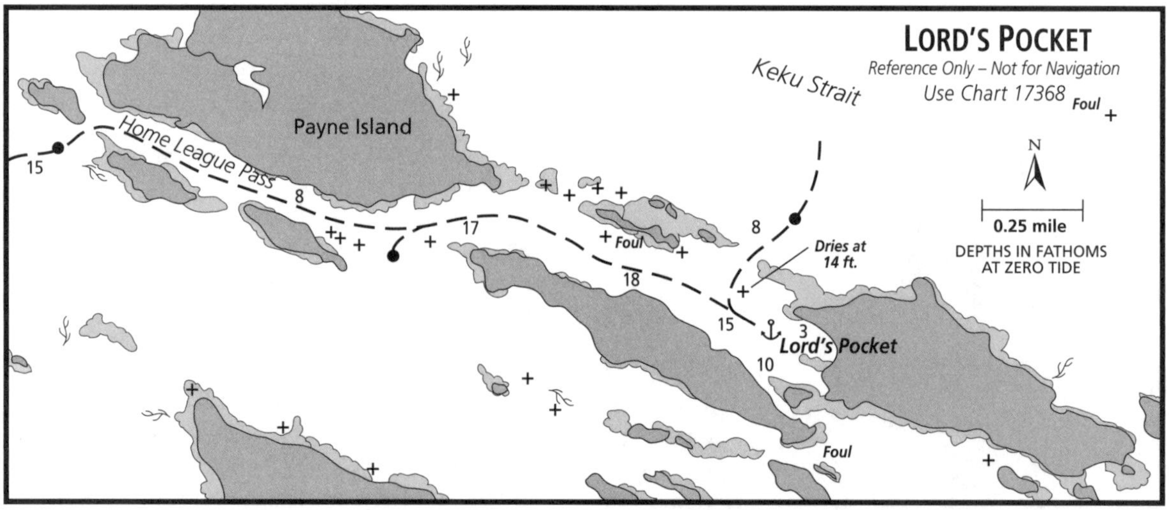

South entrance: 56°56.16′ N, 134°07.20′ W
Anchor: 56°55.95′ N, 134°05.41′ W

"Lord's Pocket" is the local name for a centrally located anchorage on the southeast side of Payne Island. Skipper Paul Martin of Kake first told us about the anchorage, which offers good protection from all weather. Entry is via Home League Pass on the south side of Payne Island, or through a window to the northeast. We have received reports that the anchorage can be somewhat uncomfortable in strong northeast winds, especially at high tides.

Anchor in the southeast corner in 3 to 10 fathoms over mixed gravel with fair holding.

## **Honeydew Cove** (Kuiu Island)

Honeydew Cove, on the northeast corner of Kuiu Island, is due east across the peninsula from Halleck Harbor and 3 miles west of Lord's Pocket.

Chart 17368
East entrance: 56°55.01′ N, 134°10.53′ W
North entrance: 56°55.19′ N, 134°11.00′ W
Anchor: 56°54.96′ N, 134°10.86′ W

"Honeydew Cove," a small unnamed bight, provides a picturesque anchorage with good protection in summer conditions, as well as good fishing and exploring. It is somewhat shallow and protected by kelp.

This cove is the favorite Southeast cove of Honeydew Murray, first mate on *Forevergreen*. The sandy beach gives her a chance to stretch her legs and explore the rocky bluffs, sculptured headlands, caves and shoreline of this remote, quiet spot.

Bull kelp (some strands 60 feet long or more) keeps the surface of the water calm. The water is so clear you can see the sandy, grassy bottom. As you row around, you can't help noticing the striking natural rock pillar, 15 feet high and equally wide, that has a single small tree hanging onto it for dear life. Overhead, bald eagles soar while puffins scurry about the cove.

If Honeydew Cove is already taken, consider anchoring one mile northwest, between the small wooded island and Kuiu Island, where there are sandy, shell beaches and high bluffs with shallow caves.

Anchor in 2 fathoms over sand and grass, avoiding the kelp patches and small rocks close to shore.

Anchor in about 4 fathoms over sand with good holding.

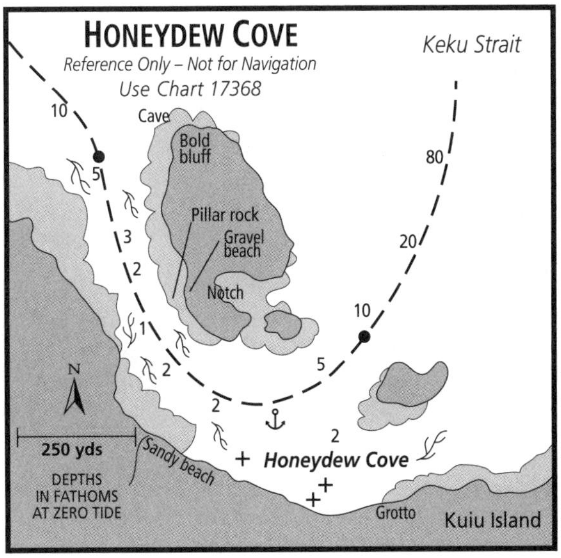




## **Hamilton Bay** (Kupreanof Island)

Hamilton Bay, on the southeast side of Point Hamilton, is 5 miles southeast of Kake.

Chart 17368
Entrance (0.6 mile northeast of Point Hamilton): 56°54.50′ N, 133°53.08′ W
Anchor (0.4 mile southeast of Little Hamilton Island): 56°53.33′ N, 133°47.65′ W

> *Hamilton Bay . . . is a secure anchorage for vessels of any size. The entrance is clear in mid-channel, and extensive bare flats are at the head of the bay. Two large streams enter near the head.* (CP)

Anchor in 5 fathoms over mud and shells with good holding.

## **Portage Pass Bay** (Kupreanof Island)

Portage Pass Bay is 1.2 miles south of the Kake ferry docks.

Chart 17368
Northwest entrance (0.1 mile south of ferry docks): 56°57.53′ N, 133°55.34′ W
West entrance (0.5 mile northwest of Hamilton Island): 56°56.68′ N, 133°56.41′ W

Portage Pass Bay is a drying mud flat that connects Portage Bay to Hamilton Bay. Public floats are found on the north side of Portage Bay.

## **Kake** (Kupreanof Island)

Kake is 5 miles southeast of Point Macartney.

Chart 17368 (inset)
South entrance: 56°58.22′ N, 133°56.83′ W
West entrance: 56°58.30′ N, 133°57.18′ W
Public float: 56°58.37′ N, 133°56.75′ W
Fuel dock: 56°57.76′ N, 133°55.49′ W

*The best approach to Kake harbor is from the NW on a SE course from between Point White and the light about 1.1 miles to the SSW. The approach to the City Pier is marked by a light and a daybeacon. If bound for the piers 1 to 1.5 miles SE of Kake, pass SW of the buoys marking the reefs off the village and the flats SE of it; when clear and S of the southeasternmost buoy, head for the piers, taking care to avoid the tidal flats to the N and the reef marked by a light about 0.3 mile SSW of the Alaska State Ferry Terminal.*

*Small craft coming from the W usually pass 100 yards off Payne Island, . . . and head for Kake Harbor Light on Grave Island, course 088°* [true], *until within 0.5 mile of it, and then pass N of the light. Small fishing vessels approaching Kake and the cannery from the S often pass through the reef N of Hamilton Island. The channel is marked by daybeacons but may be dangerous and should only be attempted with local knowledge, preferably on a rising tide.*

*A small-craft and seaplane float branches NW from the approach to the City Pier. City-maintained floats with 30-to 48-foot stalls, provides berthing for approximately 140 vessels, are connected to shore by a 307-foot approach pier and extends into Portage Bay, about 2.3 miles SE of Kake. In 2002, 5 to 15 feet was reported alongside the float, but caution should be exercised during periods of extreme spring tides that sometimes reach minus 4 feet. A light and a daybeacon mark the approach from the N. An L-shaped floating breakwater is W of the floats. The S end of the breakwater is marked by a light.* (CP)

Kake, a Tlingit community of 715, boasts Alaska's tallest totem pole (132.5 feet). The approaches to downtown Kake, as well as the tribal fuel dock, one mile southeast of town, and Portage Bay, all lead through shallow waters, so monitor your depth sounder carefully. See *Coast Pilot* for additional information on routes and lists of hazards.

Avoid the shoal patch directly in line with the city pier and the very large shoal

Linda Lewis

*Kake boasts the tallest totem pole in southeast Alaska; public float is at right.*

Linda Lewis

*This large, well-stocked store in Kake is a welcome stop after wilderness cruising.*

that extends from shore one-third of a mile between the city pier and the fuel dock.

Neither the city float nor the larger public floats in Portage Bay have water or power. The fuel dock, however, does have water. (It's a good idea to contact the fuel dock on Ch 16 before you enter the bay to be sure it is open.) The only accessible public telephone is located above the city dock near the post office. If you plan to fuel up or buy provisions, it's a three-quarter mile walk to Value Mart. The Alaska State Ferry calls here in Kake. There is also excellent cell phone coverage in the Kake vicinity.

Jill Princehouse on M/V *Passages* writes, "We were in Kake twice. The first time we stayed at the dock south of town. The second time we anchored out behind the islands. We enjoyed the anchorage and a gorgeous sunset but, both times we used our dinghy to get around. The best place to hide a dinghy is behind the ferry dock because it's a short walk from there to the grocery store, south of the dock. For the post office and main village, the city dock is better."

## WEST FREDERICK SOUND FROM KEKU STRAIT (KAKE) TO KINGSMILL POINT

### **Saginaw Bay** (Kuiu Island)

Saginaw Bay is 11.7 miles west of Kake.

Chart 17368

Entrance: 56°55.37′ N, 134°17.43′ W

*Saginaw Bay indents the N shore of Kuiu Island for about 7 miles in a SE direction.* (CP)

Saginaw Bay, entered south of Cornwallis Point, has a number of islets and isolated rocks. Anchorage can be found at its head near the drying mud flats or, more conveniently, along the north shore of Halleck Harbor.

Linda Lewis

*The fuel dock at Kake*

### **Halleck Harbor** (Saginaw Bay)

Halleck Harbor, on the northeast side of Saginaw Bay, is about 1.5 miles southeast of Cornwallis Point.

Chart 17368

Entrance: 56°54.96′ N, 134°14.29′ W

Anchor: 56°54.60′ N, 134°12.36′ W

*Halleck Harbor . . . is the best anchorage in Saginaw Bay, but is open W, and the bottom is generally hard and in places uneven. . . . The best channel to enter is 0.4 mile wide between the 3-1/2-fathom rock in the entrance and the NW point. The bight at the NW end of the harbor dries. Anchorage can be had in the middle of the harbor in 8 to 12 fathoms.*

*Anchorage in 9 to 10 fathoms, with protection from the prevailing SE winds, can be had about 300 yards SW of the small craft float.* (CP)

*This NOAA ship home bases in Petersburg.*

Halleck Harbor has good protection from southerly weather in its southeast corner with room for several boats. We hear it's also a good place to jig for halibut.

Anchor in 10 fathoms over hard sand and pebbles with fair-to-good holding.

## Security Bay (Kuiu Island)

Security Bay is 4.2 miles southwest of Saginaw Bay.

**Chart 17368 (inset)**
**Entrance (0.25 mile west of Roadstead Island Light): 56°52.40′ N, 134°22.90′ W**
**Anchor (0.5 mile southeast of Cleft Island): 56°50.21′ N, 134°19.34′ W**

*Security Bay, about 4.5 miles SW of Cornwallis Point, is a secure anchorage. Numerous islands and ledges obstruct the entrance and bay, which should be entered with caution because of the possibility of unknown dangers.*

*The usual entrance to the bay is between Roadstead Island and Paralysis Point. It is marked by Security Bay Light 1. . . .*

*The best anchorage in Security Bay is about 0.5 mile SE of Cleft island in 9 to 11 fathoms, midway between the large island on the NE side and a wooded islet and some bare rocks near the SW side. Anchorage can also be had between the W end of Cleft Island and Harbor Island, in 11 to 16 fathoms, clear of the 1-1/4-fathom rock 0.2 mile SE of Harbor Island. The head of the bay is foul with several reefs, some of which cover at high water.* (CP)

The entrance to Security Bay is in a narrow channel west of Roadstead Island. Avoid the dangerous shoals and kelp patches north of Roadstead Island Light.

Good shelter can be found deep in the bay, avoiding numerous foul areas, or in Cedar Bight.

Anchor in 10 fathoms over a hard mixed bottom with fair holding.

## Cedar Bight (Security Bay)

Cedar Bight is east of Cleft Island.

**Chart 17368**
**Entrance: 56°51.30′ N, 134°20.76′ W**
**Anchor: 56°50.88′ N, 134°19.26′ W**

*Its entrance, between Cleft Island and Retaliation Point, is obstructed by a ledge bare at lowest tides and surrounded by kelp. The SE part of the bight is shoal and rocky; otherwise the depths are 4 to 6 fathoms, rocky bottom.* (CP)

The entrance ledge at Cedar Bight can be passed on either the north or south side.

*Whale spouts can be seen from a long distance.*

Sheltered anchorage can be found deep in the bight, avoiding the ledges on the north shore north and east of Expedition Point.

Anchor over a hard mixed bottom with fair holding.

## Christmas Cove (Security Bay)

Christmas Cove is 0.6 Nm south of Roadstead Island Light.

Chart 17368
Entrance: 56°51.85′ N, 134°22.57′ W
Anchor: 56°51.54′ N, 134°22.29′ W

"Christmas Cove" is the local name for a tiny nook on the south end of Christmas Island. It is appropriate only for one or two small trawlers (under 30 feet). The entrance is via a very narrow, kelp-lined channel on the east side of Paralysis Point.

Christmas Cove is close to Frederick Sound and secure when you are well anchored inside, but is marginal for most cruising boats.

Anchor in 1-1/2 fathoms over sand and mud with fair holding and very limited swinging room.

## Band Cove (Kuiu Island)

Band Cove, just west of Security Bay, is between Paralysis and Hourigan points.

Chart 17368
Entrance: 56°51.83′ N, 134°23.23′ W

> *A small vessel can anchor in the entrance in about 6 fathoms, but the cove is not clear and is open from the NW to SW. With Security and Saginaw Bays available, the cove is not recommended as an anchorage.* (CP)

When entering Band Cove, avoid Bibb Shoal off the entrance. The bottom is reported to be rocky with kelp.

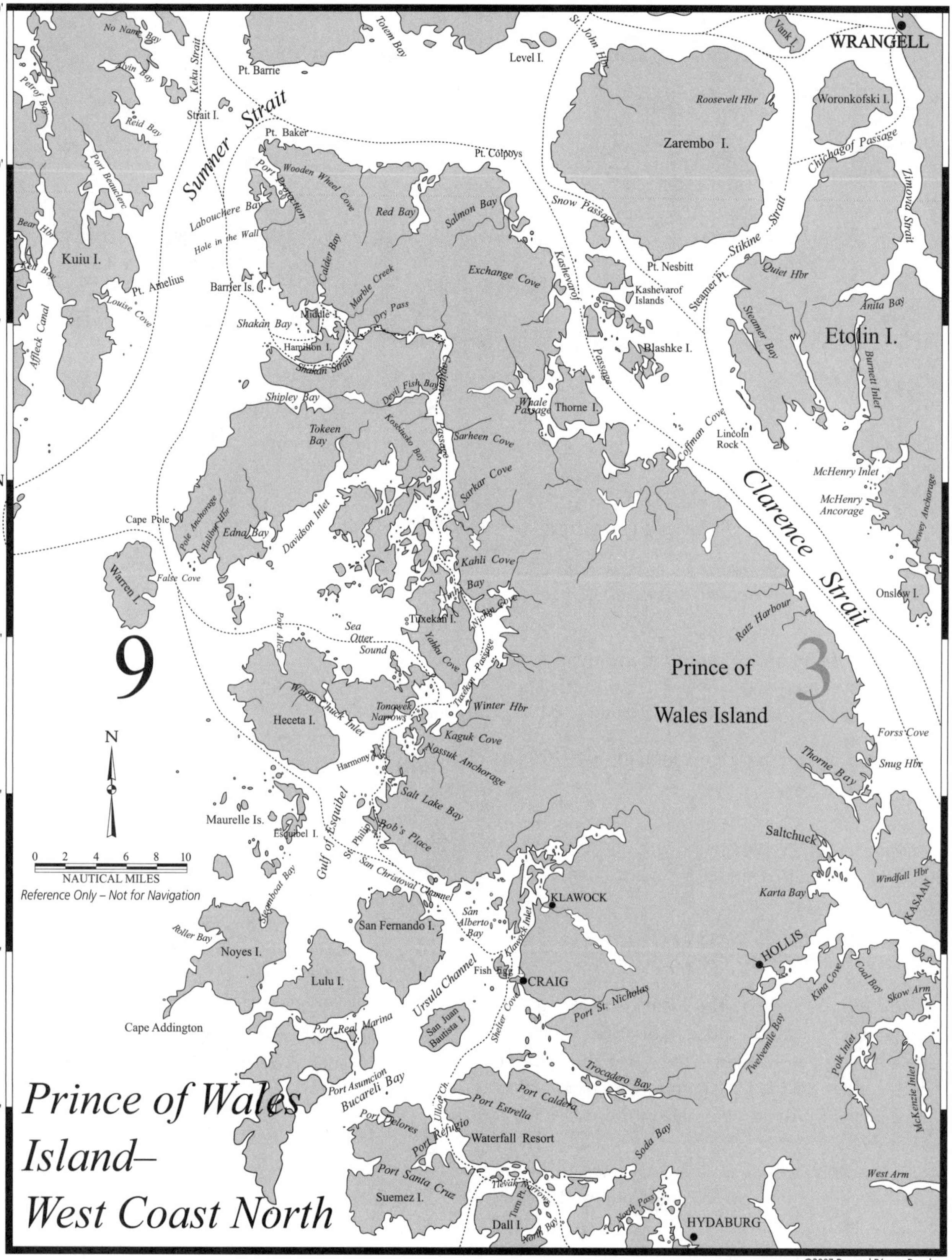
Prince of Wales Island–
West Coast North
9
3
N
0 2 4 6 8 10
NAUTICAL MILES
Reference Only – Not for Navigation
30'
20'
10'
56°N
50'
40'
30'
20'
WRANGELL
Vank I.
Woronkofski I.
Zarembo I.
Roosevelt Hbr
St. John Hbr
Level I.
Totem Bay
Pt. Barrie
No Name Bay
Alvin Bay
Petrof Bay
Keku Strait
Strait I.
Reid Bay
Sumner Strait
Pt. Baker
Pt. Colpoys
Port Beauclerc
Port Protection
Wooden Wheel Cove
Red Bay
Salmon Bay
Snow Passage
Chichagof Passage
Zimovia Strait
Stikine Strait
Labouchere Bay
Hole in the Wall
Bear Hbr
Kell Bay
Kuiu I.
Pt. Amelius
Louise Cove
Barrier Is.
Calder Bay
Marble Creek
Exchange Cove
Kashevarof Passage
Pt. Nesbitt
Kashevarof Islands
Steamer Pt.
Quiet Hbr
Anita Bay
Etolin I.
Steamer Bay
Burnett Inlet
Afflect Canal
Shakan Bay
Middle I.
Dry Pass
Hamilton I.
Shakan Strait
El Capitan Passage
Blashke I.
Devil Fish Bay
Shipley Bay
Whale Passage
Thorne I.
Coffman Cove
Lincoln Rock
Tokeen Bay
Kosciusko Bay
Sarheen Cove
McHenry Inlet
McHenry Ancorage
Dewey Anchorage
Clarence Strait
Sarkar Cove
Cape Pole
Pole Anchorage
Halibut Hbr
Edna Bay
Davidson Inlet
Kahli Cove
Warren I.
False Cove
Tuxekan I.
Nichin Cove
Onslow I.
Ratz Harbour
Port Alice
Sea Otter Sound
Yaktu Cove
Tuxekan Passage
Prince of Wales Island
Warm Chuck Inlet
Tonowek Narrows
Winter Hbr
Heceta I.
Kaguk Cove
Forss Cove
Nossuk Anchorage
Thorne Bay
Snug Hbr
Harmony Is.
Salt Lake Bay
Maurelle Is.
Esquibel I.
Gulf of Esquibel
St. Philip I.
Bob's Place
Saltchuck
San Christoval Channel
Steamboat Bay
Windfall Hbr
KASAAN
KLAWOCK
Karta Bay
San Alberto Bay
Klawock Inlet
San Fernando I.
Roller Bay
Noyes I.
HOLLIS
Fish Egg I.
CRAIG
Lulu I.
Ursula Channel
Kina Cove
Coal Bay
Skow Arm
Port St. Nicholas
Cape Addington
Port Real Marina
San Juan Bautista I.
Shelter Cove
Twelvemile Bay
Polk Inlet
McKenzie Inlet
Trocadero Bay
Port Asumcion
Bucareli Bay
Ulloa Ch.
Port Caldera
Port Estrella
Port Delores
Port Refugio
Waterfall Resort
Soda Bay
West Arm
Port Santa Cruz
Tlevak Narrows
Turn Pt.
Suemez I.
Dall I.
North Pass
North Bay
HYDABURG

# 9

# WEST SUMNER STRAIT & PRINCE OF WALES ISLAND WEST COAST TO CRAIG

## INTRODUCTION

The west coast of Prince of Wales Island is one of the most beautiful regions in Southeast Alaska and perhaps the least explored. Hundreds of small islands lie off this west coast, creating their own "Outer Passage," smooth-water route through beautiful wilderness waters. Several of these islands—Coronation and Warren islands and the Maurelle group—are now designated Wilderness areas. The entire Prince of Wales Island, which stretches from Sumner Strait to Dixon Entrance, is 135 miles long with almost 1,000 miles of coastline. Heavy logging over the years has been a mixed blessing for the island: more than a thousand miles of logging roads that denuded much of the terrain are now used by tourists and visitors who come to the island to fish, camp, kayak, mountain bike or just sightsee by vehicle. Fortunately, a portion of the island has been set aside as South Prince of Wales Wilderness to preserve a truly pristine environment.

Increasingly, cruising boaters are discovering the wonderful opportunities to get away from the more travelled waterways and enjoy the quiet beauty along the Prince of Wales west coast. Wildlife viewing along these shores is excellent and you may spot black bear, wolves, beaver, whales, seals, marten or mink, as well as eagles and abundant species of waterfowl.

Heading south along the northwestern side of Prince of Wales, you come to Shakan Strait, whose waters curve around an arm of mountainous Kosciusko Island; from either side of the strait you have stunning views of high walls and rounded peaks.

Kurt Baumann

*Sea lion dining on squid*

Linda Lewis

*One of the many fisherman active in the Pt. Baker area*

turn-of-the-century gold mining town and logging camp; it has limited facilities. However, there is a paved road between Hollis and Craig. If you want to go hiking or see this island up close, you can rent a vehicle in Craig to head deep into the island. Driving the island's extensive system of dirt roads can be an explorer's delight, but remember these are rough logging roads; be sure to give way to the logging trucks and check the fuel availability on your route.

Archaeological evidence suggests that the island has been inhabited for at least 7,500 years. Two native tribes—the Tlingits and the Haida—are more recent inhabitants in historical terms. Klawock, pop. 854, is a Tlingit Village and the site of the island's only airport. Here it is possible to drop off or pick up crew. The town is home to an impressive collection of area totem poles and is the site of Alaska's first salmon fishery, which opened in 1878. From Klawock, it's a short cruise to the public float at neighboring Craig, the largest community on Prince of Wales Island, where you will find plenty of commercial services—groceries, stores, banks, restaurants, shops and bars. For those who have time, the Haida community of Hydaburg (see next chapter), has a wonderful totem park.

Dry Pass, which connects Shakan Strait to El Capitan Passage, leads to perhaps the most spectacular area along this coast—high granite walls with rounded domes that evoke a comparison to Yosemite Valley. Numerous limestone caves have been discovered near the north end of El Capitan Passage; cataloging of these caves and exploration of new caves is an ongoing process. El Capitan, the largest of these caves, is reported to be the deepest (about 600 feet) in the United States.

From Shakan Bay through Sea Otter Sound to Craig, there are miles of wonderful cruising and sport fishing grounds. Prince of Wales Island is a sport fisherman's delight and you will find plenty of salmon and halibut along the coast as well as rainbow, steelhead and cutthroat trout in the island's many lakes and streams.

During the summer, temperatures range from 45°F to 70°F; winter temperatures are moderated by cloud cover and warm marine waters and range from 32°F to 42°F. Precipitation around the island ranges from 60 to over 200 inches per year in this cool, moist climate.

The Alaska Marine Highway provides a 2.5-hour ferry ride from Ketchikan to Hollis—its only terminal on Prince of Wales. Hollis, on the east side of Prince of Wales Island, is a

## WEST SUMNER STRAIT FROM PORT PROTECTION TO CORONATION AND WARREN ISLANDS

*Note:* No large-scale charts exist for most of this coast, so navigate with due caution.

### Port Protection (Prince of Wales Island)

Port Protection is 1.5 miles south of Point Baker.

Chart 17378
Entrance: 56°20.21′ N, 133°39.00′ W

*There is good anchorage for large craft 1.8 miles in from the daybeacon and SW of the chain of*

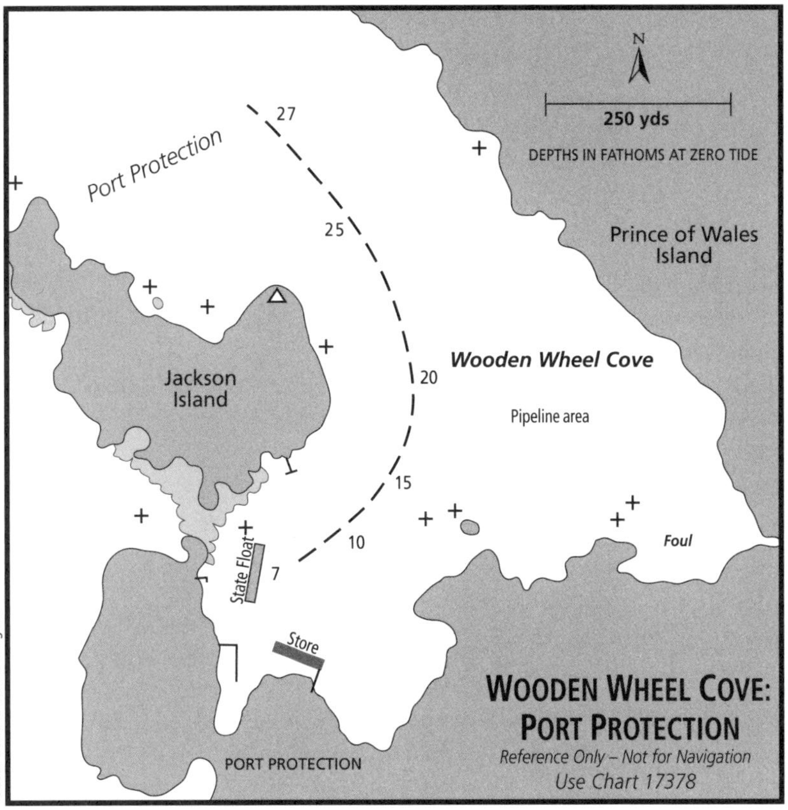




*small wooded islands in the upper half of the bay in 6 to 18 fathoms, mud and sand bottom. A more sheltered anchorage may be had E of the chain of islands.*

*Depths in the passage between the islands are 6 to 11 fathoms. Good anchorage in 10 fathoms, mud bottom, is directly ahead and about halfway between the island passed on the right and the E shore of the bay. . . . Small vessels may find anchorage in 5 to 8 fathoms a little farther in.* (CP)

Port Protection, named by George Vancouver, is a small settlement with a State float that offers good shelter from all weather as its name implies.

## **Wooden Wheel Cove** (Port Protection)

Wooden Wheel Cove is 1 mile inside the entrance to Port Protection.

Chart 17378
Entrance: 56°19.77′ N, 133°36.92′ W
Public float: 56°19.40′ N, 133°36.79′ W

*Port Protection is a small settlement on the NE side of the port in Wooden Wheel Cove and S of Port Protection Light. . . . A 250-foot State-maintained small-craft float is anchored on the W side of the cove with 4 to 8 fathoms reported alongside in July 2005.* (CP)

The public float (detached from shore) in Port Protection (Wooden Wheel Cove) is busy when the fishing fleet is in, and rafting is encouraged; there is also a fish-loading pier. Wooden Wheel Trading Post (seasonal) has some provisions, fuel, showers and a laundry.

## **Alvin Bay** (Kuiu Island)

Alvin Bay, northwest of Sumner Island, is 11 miles northwest of Point Baker.

Chart 17360
Outer entrance (south tip Sumner Island brg 066°T at 0.80 Nm): 56°23.40′ N, 133°49.93′ W
Inner entrance (0.30 Nm east of channel): 56°26.12′ N, 133°53.61′ W
Anchor: 56°26.12′ N, 133°55.46′ W

*Alvin Bay . . . is clear of dangers except for a depth of 1-3/4 fathoms in the center near where it starts to narrow. . . .*

*To enter, pass N of the islet leaving the detached rocks on the starboard side. Good anchorage may be had inside in 41/4 fathoms, mud bottom. With caution, this entrance can be made easily. The bay is used extensively for anchorage during the fishing season.* (CP)

Alvin Bay is considered one of the more sheltered anchorages on the west side of Sumner Strait. The entrance passage north of Sumner Island is possible but is encumbered with rocks. *Caution:* There is no large-scale chart for Alvin Bay and much of this coast. Avoid the entrance channel rocks and anchor near the center of the 1⁄4-mile-wide bay.

Anchor in about 5 fathoms over mud and shell bottom with good holding.

## **Reid Bay, Peninsula Cove** (Kuiu Island)

Reid Bay is 3 miles southwest of Sumner Island and 8 miles west of Point Baker.

Chart 17360
Entrance: 56°22.34′ N, 133°51.46′ W
Anchor (Peninsula Cove): 56°21.86′ N, 133°52.64′ W

> *Reid Bay is on the W side of Sumner Strait, 3 miles N of Boulder Point. it has two islets and several outlying rocks along its NW shore and rocks awash S of the islets in midchannel. Small craft may anchor in the cove on the W side of the Peninsula point at the S side of the entrance to the bay in 5 to 6 fathoms, mud bottom. There are dangers off the points at the entrance to this cove, and it should be entered with caution. A kelp-marked reef with rocks awash is 1.8 miles WSW from the S end of Sumner Island.* (CP)

Reid Bay is exposed to southeast winds and the chop of Sumner Strait. Its shores are ringed with submerged rocks, but small craft can find fair anchorage at the shore in what we call "Peninsula Cove." Anchor near the head of the cove, but avoid the rocks along shore.

Anchor (Peninsula Cove) in 5 to 8 fathoms over mud with rocks and kelp.

## **Labouchere Bay** (Prince of Wales Island)

Labouchere Bay is 4 miles south of Point Baker.

Chart 17378
Entrance: 56°18.12′ N, 133°40.45′ W
Anchor (south side of bay): 56°17.12′ N, 133°39.16′ W

> *There is sheltered anchorage for small vessels just inside the bay on the S side . . . in depths of 3 to 21 fathoms, mud and sand bottom. Three detached rocks that cover at half tide are near the head of the anchorage. Small fishing craft anchor SE of the rocks and near the sand beach in 2 to 5 fathoms.*
>
> *There are a small-craft float, a seaplane float, and log storage in the cove.* (CP)

Labouchere Bay is a landlocked bay with a number of islands, reefs and back bays to explore. The Forest Service says that this area of Prince of Wales has the largest number of bears on the island. Within the many nooks and crannies of this marvelous area, you can find a number of well-sheltered anchor sites. The most convenient anchorage is located on the south shore behind the largest of the islands. The bottom in Labouchere is highly irregular with isolated reefs.

Anchor (south side of bay) in 2 to 5 fathoms over sand, gravel and kelp with fair holding.

## **Hole in the Wall** (Prince of Wales Island)

Hole in the Wall is 1.8 miles south of Labouchere Bay.

Chart 17378
Entrance: 56°15.62′ N, 133°38.74′ W
Anchor: 56°16.06′ N, 133°37.60′ W

> *The entrance is through a very narrow passage 0.5 mile long, between high bluffs, and opens into a basin 400 yards in diameter. Two rocks that bare are in the narrow entrance. Depths in the basin are from 1/2 to 7 fathoms; it may be used for anchorage, but is subject to strong winds drawing through the entrance. The bottom is sand and mud. Small craft pass through the narrow entrance only at half tide or higher water.* (CP)

A breathtaking passage through clear aquamarine water, Hole in the Wall is a gem of the west coast of Prince of Wales Island. Threads of green moss and black lichen crisscross the fissured, convoluted base of granite that rises vertically along the entrance. Devil's claw, old-growth spruce, hemlock and cedar hang tenaciously to ledges high above, while deli-

Réanne Hemingway-Douglass

*Entrance to Hole in the Wall*

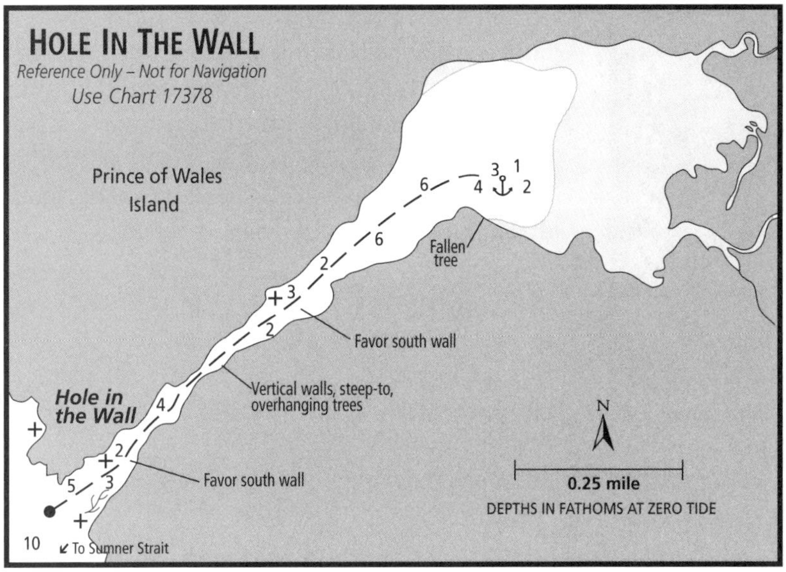


cate purple flowers line diagonal cracks in the rock.

The basin is landlocked and provides very good protection. Anchorage can be found tucked in behind the point in the southeast corner of the inner bay between the fallen log in the water and a nearby sandbar.

*Looking back at the entrance to the narrow Hole in the Wall*

Anchor in 3 fathoms. Because the bottom is such soft black mud, use an extra light touch in setting your anchor; once set, it holds well.

## Port Beauclerc (Kuiu Island)

Port Beauclerc, on the west side of Sumner Strait, is 10 miles southwest of Point Baker.

Chart 17360
Entrance (Kuiu Island):
56°15.85′ N, 133°52.88′ W
Anchor (south arm):
56°15.65′ N, 133°59.17′ W

*Small-boat anchorage is available in the small cove W of the charted rock awash on the S side of this island, or in the cove on the Kuiu Island side S of the E end of Edwards Island.*

*Anchorage may also be had in the S arm in 4 or 6 fathoms, mud bottom. Enter by the narrow passage S of Edwards Island and slightly favor the E shore of the arm to avoid a sunken rock, marked by kelp, 1 mile W of the W end of the narrow passage S of Edwards Island. On the E shore of the arm, 1 mile SE from the narrow passage, is a point close to a 3-1/2-fathom spot.*

*Caution: Where local knowledge is lacking, caution is advised in entering Port Beauclerc.* (CP)

Port Beauclerc was named by Vancouver after Englishman, Amelius Beauclerk. (Somewhere along the centuries the port received its French spelling.) No large-scale chart exists for Port Beauclerc, so take precautions if you enter.

Anchorage is reported off the islands northwest of Edwards Island, or deep in the south arm, which offers the most protection. Favor slightly east of mid-channel when entering the south arm to avoid the rock marked by kelp on the west shore.

Anchor (south arm) in 6 fathoms, mud bottom with fair holding.

Linda Lewis

*A box from far across the ocean washes up on a remote beach on Prince of Wales Island.*

## **Louise Cove** (Kuiu Island)

Louise Cove is on the west side of Point Amelius.

Chart 17386
Entrance: 56°11.49′ N, 133°56.89′ W

> *Louise Cove . . . affords anchorage for small vessels in 3-1/2 fathoms.* (CP)

Use the larger-scale Chart 17386 available for this cove.

## **Shakan Bay** (Prince of Wales and Kosciusko islands)

Shakan Bay is 12 miles south of Point Baker.

Chart 17379
Entrance: 56°09.79′ N, 133°39.60′ W

> *The bay, including Shakan Strait, is circular in shape. . . . The center of the bay is almost filled with islands. At the E extremity of Shakan Strait, the bay connects with El Capitan Passage.*
>
> *The N shore of the bay is foul for about 1.5 miles offshore and should be avoided. The E part of the outer bay is extremely foul.* (CP)

The addition of Chart 17379 (1st Ed. in 2002) brings a welcome large-scale (1:10,000) view of Shakan Bay and Shakan Strait. However, *please note* the misleading notation for the location of the entrance to El Capitan Passage. The correct Passage is south of the narrow drying slough and island shown on the chart! (This misleading notation will likely be revised in a future edition of this chart.)

Shakan Strait, along the south side of Shakan Bay, takes you just to the north-end entrance of the increasingly popular El Capitan Passage. Most cruisers travelling the west side of Prince of Wales Island would not think of bypassing the beautiful, well-marked transit through El Capitan Passage.

## **Shipley Bay** (Kosciusko Island)

Shipley Bay is 4 miles south of Shakan Bay.

Chart 17387
Entrance: 56°05.87′ N, 133°38.72′ W
Anchor: 56°04.65′ N, 133°32.13′ W

> *Shipley Bay . . . has good anchorage available at the head. . . .*
>
> *The best anchorage is near the S shore at the head of the bay, just E of the point 1 mile from the head of the bay, in depths of 15 fathoms, mud bottom, and good holding ground. A small cove just W of the point is suitable for small craft; depths are 3 to 5 fathoms, mud and sand bottom.* (CP)

When entering Shipley Bay, avoid the rocks and shoals extending from north to mid-channel. You can find good shelter in the cove. Avoid rocks and kelp on the north side of the cove.

Anchor (cove west of point) in 3 fathoms over sand and mud with fair holding.

## **Affleck Canal** (Kuiu Island)

Affleck Canal, 14 miles long, is entered west of Point St. Albans and northwest of Fairway Island.

Chart 17386
Entrance: 56°04.86′ N, 134°03.31′ W

> *The depths in general are great but very irregular, especially near the shores and at the head of the canal.*
>
> *A dangerous rock, covered 1 fathom, is in Affleck Canal, 1,300 yards 150°* [true] *from the center of Bush Islets.* (CP)

*Note:* Affleck Canal has a rocky bottom and only small-scale charts are available for the area.

The west arm of Affleck Canal is called Kell Bay; the northwest arm is Bear Harbor.

## **Kell Bay** (Affleck Canal)

Kell Bay, on the west side of Affleck Canal, is 7 miles north of Fairway Island.

Chart 17386
Entrance: 56°09.35′ N, 134°06.64′ W
Entrance (southwest arm): 56°08.50′ N, 134°09.84′ W
Anchor (southwest arm): 56°08.29′ N, 134°09.36′ W
Anchor (southwest arm basin): 56°07.62′ N, 134°10.34′ W

*At the head of the bay are two arms that extend in a NW and SW direction. The NW arm is about 1.5 miles long. . . . Vessels entering this arm should proceed with caution. . . .*

*The SW arm is separated from the main body of Kell Bay by three wooded islands. To enter, pass midchannel between the islands and the SW shore, follow the SW shore at a distance of 150 yards until the S point of the W island has passed abeam. Then stand in midchannel, taking care to round the S side of the island at a distance of 200 yards so as to avoid the ledge that extends about 150 yards offshore. Anchorage may be had in 9 to 12 fathoms, soft bottom.*

*The basin at the head of the SW arm affords excellent anchorage for small craft in depths of 4 to 5 fathoms, soft bottom. The entrance is constricted, being only 30 to 35 yards wide, and vessels entering are advised to proceed with caution keeping close to the W shore, which is abrupt and steep-to.* (CP)

The southwest shore of Kell Bay has a small landlocked arm that provides very good shelter to small craft behind the entrance islands or in the small basin at its head. Favor the west shore when you enter the basin.

Anchor (southwest arm behind the entrance islands) in 8 fathoms over mud with fair holding.

Anchor (southwest basin) in 4 to 6 fathoms over sand and gravel with fair-to-good holding.

## **Bear Harbor** (Affleck Canal)

Bear Harbor, on the west side of Affleck Canal, is 4 miles north of Kell Bay.

Chart 17386
Entrance: 56°13.51′ N, 134°05.96′ W
Entrance (middle arm): 56°13.89′ N, 134°06.51′ W
Anchor (west arm): 56°13.60′ N, 134°07.32′ W
Anchor (middle arm): 56°14.78′ N, 134°06.67′ W

*The harbor has three arms; the E is deep and open to the S; the middle and W arms are sheltered and afford suitable anchorage for small vessels. The approach to these two arms is S of the island at the entrance. The deepest part of the channel, about 5-1/4 fathoms, is 100 yards off the shore of the island. Favor the shore of this island in entering and navigate with caution. After the E tip of the island is passed abeam by 100 yards, a midchannel course will lead over a 1/2-fathom spot marked by kelp. This spot is the end of a reef making out from the S shore.*

*After the entrance is passed, midchannel courses lead into the W arm that is deep except along the S shore near the head.*

*A midchannel course is followed in the middle arm until about 1 mile from the entrance when the E shore is followed at a distance of about 200 yards. This arm is deep to within 0.5 mile of its head where it shoals gradually to the tidal flats off the mouth of the principal streams that empty into Bear Harbor.* (CP)

Bear Harbor, like Kell Bay above, has very protected waters reached by narrow passages. The middle arm is landlocked (protected by small islands); very good anchorage can be found near the head of the arm.

Anchor (west arm) in 16 fathoms over mud with fair holding.

Anchor (middle arm) in 5 to 10 fathoms over sand, mud and gravel with fair holding.

## **Port McArthur** (Kuiu Island)

Port McArthur is 4.5 miles north of Cape Decision.

Chart 17386
Entrance (Lemon Point Rock brg 246°T at 0.3 Nm): 56°04.48′ N, 134°06.26′ W
Anchor: 56°03.55′ N, 134°07.12′ W

*Port McArthur . . . is protected at the entrance by a group of islands and reefs, and it affords anchorage that is not secure because large swells run to the head of the bay. For small craft the most secure anchorage is in 4 fathoms behind South Island.* (CP)

Anchor in 5 fathoms over mud, sand, gravel and kelp with fair holding

## Fishermans Harbor (Kosciusko Island)

Fishermans Harbor is 22 miles southwest of Port Protection

Chart 17402
Entrance: 55°58.62′ N, 133°48.55′ W

*Fishermans Harbor, a bight NE of Pole Anchorage, is used extensively by small fishing craft. . . .*

*Fishermans Harbor light . . . 17 feet above the water, is shown from a skeleton tower with a red and white diamond-shaped daymark on the edge of a reef on the SE side of the harbor. A daybeacon is on a reef on the E side of the entrance to the harbor.* (CP)

To enter Fishermans Harbor, please refer to the detailed directions in *Coast Pilot.*

## Pole Anchorage (Kosciusko Island)

Pole Anchorage is 1 mile south of Fishermans Harbor.

Chart 17402
Entrance: 55°58.23′ N, 133°48.97′ W
Anchor: 55°57.49′ N, 133° 48.50′ W

*Pole Anchorage, on the E side of the S end of Sumner Strait, affords an anchorage for small vessels, protected from NE and SE winds; it is exposed to W winds and swells. The SW point of the entrance is a large mass of grassy-topped rocks, about 10 feet high, that extend about 0.6 mile N of Cape Pole; the passage between them and the cape has many bare rocks and almost dries. There is considerable kelp for some distance N of the grassy-topped rocks. The N point at the entrance is a wooded islet close to shore; kelp extends some distance NW of it, also about 100 yards W.*

*Anchorage can be had in 10 to 11 fathoms, mud bottom, with the N end of Warren Island showing about midway between Cape Pole and the grassy-topped rocks. Small fishing vessel may find suitable anchorage SE of Cape Pole, E of a large kelp patch, in any desired depth.* (CP)

Anchor in 10 fathoms over sand and mud surrounded by rocks and kelp, with fair holding.

## Coronation Island

Coronation Island is 5 miles south of Cape Decision and 20 miles southeast of Cape Ommaney.

Chart 17402

*Coronation Island, west of Warren Island, is . . . divided into three peninsulas by Windy Bay on the W side and Aats Bay on the N side, the heads of which are separated by a range 1 mile in the center of the island.* (CP)

Coronation Island, due south of Cape Decision, and Warren Island directly east of Coronation Island both lie within designated Wilderness areas and are less frequently visited than other

---

### Exploring Coronation Island Wilderness

Barb Davis—S/V *Antares*

Egg Harbor is dominated by a 1,600-foot rock peak on its west side. A white sand beach that spreads out around the shore at the head of the bay is backed by magical, moss-covered forest. We explored the forest, climbing through 3-foot-deep moss that gave way under our feet like sponge. The island appears uninhabited except for evidence of deer and mountain goats. We spent a morning exploring the caves along the rocky shore, then began a climb to the peak, hand-over-foot, clawing our way up a mossy cliff toward the summit.

After bushwhacking through primitive forest, we found ourselves at the top of a moon-like peak with crystal-clear views in every direction. We could see west to the Gulf of Alaska, north to the islands from which we had come, and east and south to the islands we had yet to explore, and we sighted a humpback whale feeding in the bay below.

By the time we got back to shore, we were exhausted and hungry, and all we could think about was what we'd have for dinner. But when we returned to the boat, we found it partially flooded with sea water from the head which had overflowed. (One of the cats must have dislodged the shut-off valve.) We spent the next hour bailing and mopping up with towels. After that, all we could think of was relaxing with a big glass of wine—forget dinner!

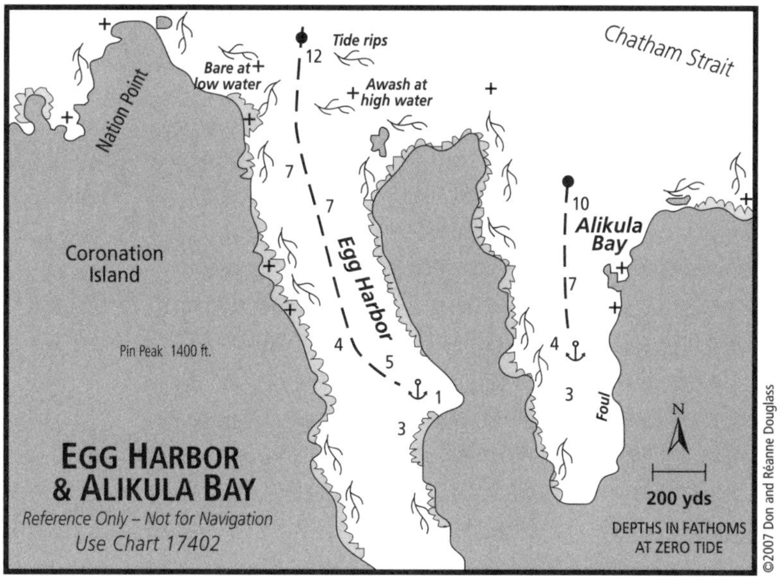


islands to the north and east. Coronation Island is strategically located between Sumner and Chatham straits, but the area is subject to strong turbulent currents from Cape Decision through the Spanish Islands to Coronation Island, which may discourage some boaters.

The island was named more than two centuries ago by George Vancouver in honor of King George III's coronation—the very king against whom American waged its Revolutionary War.

While fishermen have long sought shelter along Coronation Island, pleasure craft are just beginning to discover its beauties—white sand beach (Egg Harbor), pointed peaks, primitive forest untouched by chain saws and sea caves. Animal life abounds here, too, both ashore and in the surrounding waters—deer and mountain goats, orcas, humpback whales and sea otters. One professional skipper who frequently takes guests here says Coronation Island ". . . is not to be missed!" We agree.

## Egg Harbor (Coronation Island)

Egg Harbor, on the east side of Nation Point, is 22 miles from Port Alexander.

**Chart 17402**
**Entrance (Nation Point brg 285°T at 0.45 Nm): 55°55.63′ N, 134°19.38′ W**
**Anchor: 55°54.77′ N, 134°18.87′ W**

[Egg Harbor] *. . . is a secure anchorage, except from N winds. . . . Off the E point of the entrance is a rock about 10 feet high. About 160 yards to the NW of this rock is a rock awash at high water.*

*The channel between the rocks off the* [east] *point is about 500 yards wide, and a midchannel course leads to safe anchorage in 5 to 7 fathoms, sand bottom. During SE gales, williwaws sweep down with considerable force and heavy ground tackle is necessary to prevent dragging. On the E side of the bay, halfway to the head, is a small bight used by fishing craft, as it affords better protection.* (CP)

Egg Harbor, a lovely anchorage in a deep cove on the northwest side of Coronation Island, provides very good anchorage in most summer weather. The sandy bottom gradually shoals toward the head of the cove, and boats can anchor almost anywhere over the large flat bottom. A broad sandy beach backed by a lovely forest affords excellent combing, and the steep hills promise good climbs and excellent views. When S/V *Tintagel* was approaching Coronation Island on a beam reach from

*Fishing boats at anchor in Egg Harbor*

Chatham Strait one recent summer, they had an unforgettable experience—a pod of orcas swam up to and right under their hull!

Entering Egg Harbor, avoid the charted rocks, especially the rock on the east side of the channel awash at high water. During heavy northwesterlies (30 knots) the cove can become rolly, and it is not recommended during northerly storms. In northerly winds, Windy Bay offers the best protection on Coronation Island. Note that strong currents flowing out of Sumner Strait cause strong tide rips off all the islands south of Cape Decision.

Anchor in 3 fathoms over mud with fair-to-good holding.

## **Alikula Bay** (Coronation Island)

Alikula Bay is 0.75 mile east of Egg Harbor.

**Chart 17402**
**Entrance: 55°55.36′ N, 134°18.12′ W**
**Anchor: 55°54.72′ N, 134°18.15′ W**

> *Alikula Bay . . . is free of dangers, and anchorage can be selected according to size of vessel in either the outer or inner part of the bay.* (CP)

Alikula Bay is much like Egg Harbor—good anchorage but exposed to northerly gales and with more kelp.

Anchor is 5 fathoms over sand with fair holding.

## **Aats Bay** (Coronation Island)

Aats Bay is 2.5 miles east of Egg Harbor.

**Chart 17402**
**Entrance: 55°55.11′ N, 134°14.60′ W**
**Anchor: 55°53.76′ N, 134°13.94′ W**

> *Aats Bay . . . has two arms. The W arm is too deep for secure anchorage; the E arm affords anchorage in 6 to 8 fathoms, sand and mud bottom. The entrance of the E arm has a 1-1/2-fathom rock marked by kelp. . . . Favor the E shore in entering. . . . The bay is exposed to N weather.* (CP)

Aats Bay is useful only for temporary anchorage in fair weather.

## **Gish Bay** (Coronation Island)

Gish Bay is 4 miles east of Egg Harbor.

**Chart 17402**
**Entrance: 55°54.84′ N, 134°12.52′ W**

> *The bay is full of kelp and has depths of 3 to 7 fathoms; shoal water extends 0.3 mile from its head. It is not suitable as an anchorage.* (CP)

## **Windy Bay** (Coronation Island)

Windy Bay, on the west side of Coronation Island, is 3.2 miles south of Egg Harbor.

**Chart 17402**
**Entrance: 55°51.78′ N, 134°20.91′ W**
**Anchor: 55°52.35′ N, 134°17.53′ W**

> *Windy Bay . . . is well protected from the sea by rocks and reefs that extend from the N shore of the entrance to within 0.3 mile of the S shore.*
>
> *The entrance is S of the reefs. Follow the general trend of the S shore about 0.2 mile off. When approaching the S inner point where the bay narrows, change course so as to pass about 220 yards off the point; beyond, the bay is clear. . .*
>
> *Anchorage may be had in 22 fathoms, mud and sand bottom, off the stream on the S side of the bay or near the head. . . . Fishing boats and other small craft may anchor in shoaler water closer in.* (CP)

From a half-mile offshore Windy Bay's entrance looks daunting. A series of reefs that stretch nearly two-thirds of the way from north to south to block the entrance. The reefs, which act as a sort of breakwater, provide good shelter from the outside seas. However, on extreme high tides, swells break high over the reefs and surge can be felt all the way to the easternmost end of the bay.

Upon entering Windy Bay, favor the south shore to avoid the reefs and head to the southeastern end of the bay. Although depths throughout the entire bay are great and the shores steep-to, anchor sites can be found in 6 to 10 fathoms.

The view to the outside from behind the breaking reefs is spectacular and the steep rocky shores are lined with old-growth forests. We spotted deer and mountain goats from our anchor site, and sea otters constantly peeked out at us from nearby kelp beds.

Anchor in 8 to 10 fathoms over a bottom of hard sand and rocks; fair-to good holding with a well-set anchor.

## False Cove (Warren Island)

False Cove is 1.5 miles north of Warren Cove.

Chart 17402
Entrance: 55°53.76′ N, 133°50.29′ W
Anchor: 55°53.82′ N, 133°51.04′ W

*False Cove . . . affords anchorage in depths of 4 to 5 fathoms, sand bottom, behind the kelp-marked rocks awash that extend across the N half of the entrance.* (CP)

False Cove provides reasonable anchorage in fair weather during prevailing northwesterly wind. However, we prefer Warren Cove.

Anchor in 4 to 5 fathoms over sand with some kelp, fair holding.

## Warren Cove (Warren Island)

Warren Cove is on the east shore of Warren Island.

Chart 17402
Entrance: 55°52.36′ N, 133°50.35′ W
Anchor: 55°52.78′ N, 133°51.66′ W

*In entering, favor the S shore and give it a berth of at least 300 yards until inside the entrance, thereby avoiding a shoal covered 1-1/2 fathoms that extends about 250 yards N from the S point at the entrance. . . . There is a small gravel beach just inside the entrance on the S side of the cove. . . .*

Réanne Hemingway-Douglass

*Shipwreck in Warren Cove*

Réanne Hemingway-Douglass

*Pilothouse sits in sand at Warren Cove.*

*Anchorage may be had in 7 fathoms, sand bottom, in the center of Warren Cove. A heavy swell enters the cove during SE weather.* (CP)

Warren Cove's wide beach backed by rainforest is a delight to explore.

Anchor in 4 fathoms over sand with fair holding.

## Shakan Bay and El Capitan Passage

(Kosciusko and Hamilton Islands)

Shakan Bay is 12 miles south of Point Baker.

Charts 17379 (Shakan Bay) & 17387 (El Capitan Passage)
West entrance (Shakan Strait): 56°07.95′ N, 133°34.75′ W
El Capitan Cave USFS Dock (1.4 miles northwest of Aneskett Point): 56°09.66′ N, 133°19.28′ W

*Shakan Strait . . . is about 4.6 miles long, averages 0.4 mile in width, and is semicircular in shape. It affords a clear and safe route to El Capitan Passage. The W entrance, marked by a daybeacon on an islet off the SW end of Hamilton Island, is 0.3 mile wide, but between the 5-fathom curves is constricted to about half that, by reefs on both sides. About midway of its*

## Prince of Wales Underground—El Capitan Cave

Don Douglass & Réanne Hemingway-Douglass

The cliffs above El Capitan Passage on the northwest coast of Prince of Wales Island hide the most extensive karst (limestone) caves in Alaska. The caves, which were discovered as recently as the mid-1990s, cover thousands of square feet, over 2 miles of which have been mapped by paleontologists and archeologists. The most exciting discovery has been the perfectly preserved remains of a brown bear dating back 45,000 years. Indications of human habitation dating back 10,000 years give promise that this cave system will be a center of intense exploration for years.

Linda Lewis

*The Forest Service dinghy dock—for access to the El Capitan Cave*

Linda Lewis

*It's a steep climb, but worth it.*

A small float where you can tie up to visit the caves is located at about 55°09.66′ N, 133°19.28′ W. Fortunately, 370 wooden steps leading up to the cave entrance will prevent this wild cave from becoming a Disney attraction. The U.S. Forest Service conducts three (six-person) guided tours per day (Memorial Day through Labor Day) through a major portion of the cave. To visit the caves, call the USFS ranger in Thorne Bay at least two days in advance of your arrival to make reservations (tel.: 907.828.3304). Hard hats are provided—and you need them—we know! Take along your own flashlight, wear boots and carry a rain jacket—temperatures inside the cave run about 40°F and it drips. (Note: Children under seven are not admitted.) You can find more cave details online and you can even take a virtual tour of the cave. Go to: www.fs.fed.us/r10/tongass/districts/pow/discover/caves/tour/tour.shtml.

Linda Lewis

*Linda and Dave use the requisite hard hats, provided by the cave personnel.*

Linda Lewis

*This caver* really *got into the spirit!*

*length is a 5-1/4-fathom rocky shoal in midchannel about 0.2 mile E of the daybeacon marking the SE end of Hamilton Island.*

*In entering Shakan Strait, favor the N point slightly. When 1.2 miles inside the entrance to the strait, favor the N shore slightly, otherwise follow a midchannel course to the anchorage, about 0.8 mile SSW of the entrance to El Capitan Passage, a distance of 4 miles. Anchor about 0.3 mile offshore in 7 to 9 fathoms, mud bottom.* (CP)

Shakan Bay, with its number of shoals and rocks, requires alert piloting; however, kelp marks most of these hazards. As mentioned previously, the newer Chart 17379 (1st Ed. in 2002) provides a large-scale (1:10,000) view of Shakan Bay.

There is a small-boat passage to the inner bay north of Hamilton Island and west of Divide Island, which is a shortcut to Marble Creek Cove or Calder Bay. This passage requires careful navigation. Shakan Strait, although longer, has easier access to El Capitan Passage and can be navigated in limited visibility by radar.

El Capitan Cave, reported to be the deepest cave in the U.S., is located on the southern flank of 2,500-foot El Capitan Peak, on the north shore of El Capitan Passage east of Dry Pass. (See above for the coordinates of the USFS dinghy dock associated with the cave.) Cruising boaters can tie up at the USFS dock, walk across a parking lot and take a short but steep trail of stairs to the mouth of the cave. (See accompanying sidebar on Prince of Wales Underground—El Capitan Cave.)

Note that the buoys in El Capitan Passage follow the standard color convention (red right returning) from *south to north*. In other words, if you are southbound, you must keep all red buoys to port and green ones to starboard.

## **Marble Creek Cove** (Prince of Wales Island)

Marble Creek is 8 miles southeast of Hole in the Wall.

**Chart 17379**
**Entrance: 56°10.55′ N, 133°28.83′ W**
**Anchor: 56°10.58′ N, 133°28.45′ W**

Surrounded by the huge, smooth granite domes of Mt. Calder to the northwest and the peaks towering on the north side of the strait, it's impossible not to compare the inner waters of Shakan Strait to Yosemite Valley. But here, there are no tourists, no roads, and if you're lucky, you'll see no more than one or two small boats. Aside from occasional clearcuts and the marble quarry on the north side of the bay, no evidence of man mars this area. Unfortunately, Marble Creek no longer looks like a park, but a large mining complex.

Anchorage with fair protection can be taken off the ramp once used in logging operations. Due to soft mud, you must set your anchor with a light touch. Avoid the shoal that separates the north side of the bay from the creek outlet. Small boats can tuck in east of the ramp in 1 to 2 fathoms near the head of the bay with better protection from south and west winds.

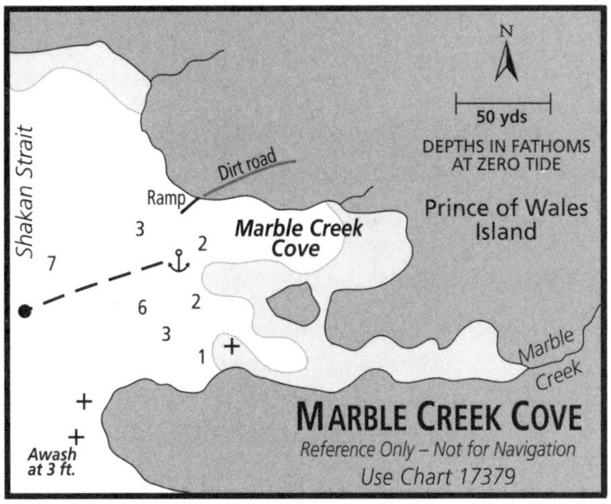

©2007 Don and Réanne Douglass

Réanne Hemingway-Douglass

*Entrance to Marble Creek Cove*

Anchor off the ramp in 5 fathoms over soft black mud with good holding.

## **Calder Bay** (Prince of Wales Island)

Calder Bay is 2 miles northwest of Marble Creek.

Chart 17379 & 17387
Entrance: 56°11.15′ N, 133°31.61′ W
Anchor: 56°11.42′ N, 133°31.44′ W

> *Calder Bay is on the N side of Shakan Bay N of Middle Island. Depths shoal gradually from about 9 fathoms at its entrance to the tidal flat about 0.6 mile from the entrance.* (CP)

Calder Bay, at the base of Mt. Calder, has a large area for easy anchoring. It is somewhat exposed to south winds but the surrounding area is generally quiet and calm and cruisers have reported watching seven bears feeding in the large grassy area at its head. We have entered Calder Bay via the narrow passage north of Hamilton Island and west of Divide Island, which is shorter than Shakan Strait but requires caution and good visibility.

Anchor in 4 fathoms over sand with fair holding.

## **El Capitan Passage** (from Shakan Strait to Sea Otter Sound)

El Capitan Passage, between Kosciusko and Prince of Wales islands, extends about 18 miles from Shakan Strait to Sea Otter Sound.

Chart 17387 (inset)
West entrance (R"28" brg 000°T at 0.04 Nm):
56°09.14′ N, 133°27.68′ W

> *The S part of the passage is 1 to 4 miles wide, forming a bay about 7 miles long with numerous rocks and islets. To the N of this section the passage is 0.3 to 1 mile wide and is comparatively clear to Aneskett Point. The shoreline should not be approached too closely, as numerous rocks, awash at various stages of the tide, are close-to.*
>
> *. . . a Federal project about 2.8 miles long . . . provides for a 12-foot channel dredged through seven shoals, including Dry Pass, to the W entrance of El Capitan Passage at Shakan Strait. Daybeacons mark the dredged sections of the channel. In April 2005, the controlling depth was 9.1 feet in the dredged sections of the channel with 3.6 feet in the right outside quarter at Daybeacon 9 and 5.3 feet in the left outside quarter about 235 yards W of Daybeacon 2.*
>
> *Local knowledge is desirable for safe navigation through the channels in El Capitan Passage. This applies in particular to the section between Aneskett Point and Shakan Strait, including Dry Pass. . . . The charts are the guide for safe navigation.*
>
> *In Dry Pass, the current floods E with a velocity of 1.8 knots and ebbs W with a velocity of 0.9 knot.*
>
> *All of El Capitan Passage is protected. . . . Small craft can usually find anchorage in the bights and inlets that indent the shores of the passage.* (CP)

El Capitan Passage, the beautiful smooth-water route east of Kosciusko Island, is well marked and gives little trouble to cruising boats that carefully monitor their progress on Chart 17387 at all stages of the tide.

Note that the *Coast Pilot* entry above gives information from south to north while our text outlines a north to south passage. Note also that when you are *southbound*, the port-hand buoys are all red and count down from R"28" to R"2." *Caution:* Watch for shoals and mud flats on either side.

Small craft can find secure anchorage among a number of coves along either shore, or in the center of Dry Pass.

Linda Lewis

*Transiting El Capitan southward; keeping all red buoys to port and all green buoys to starboard*

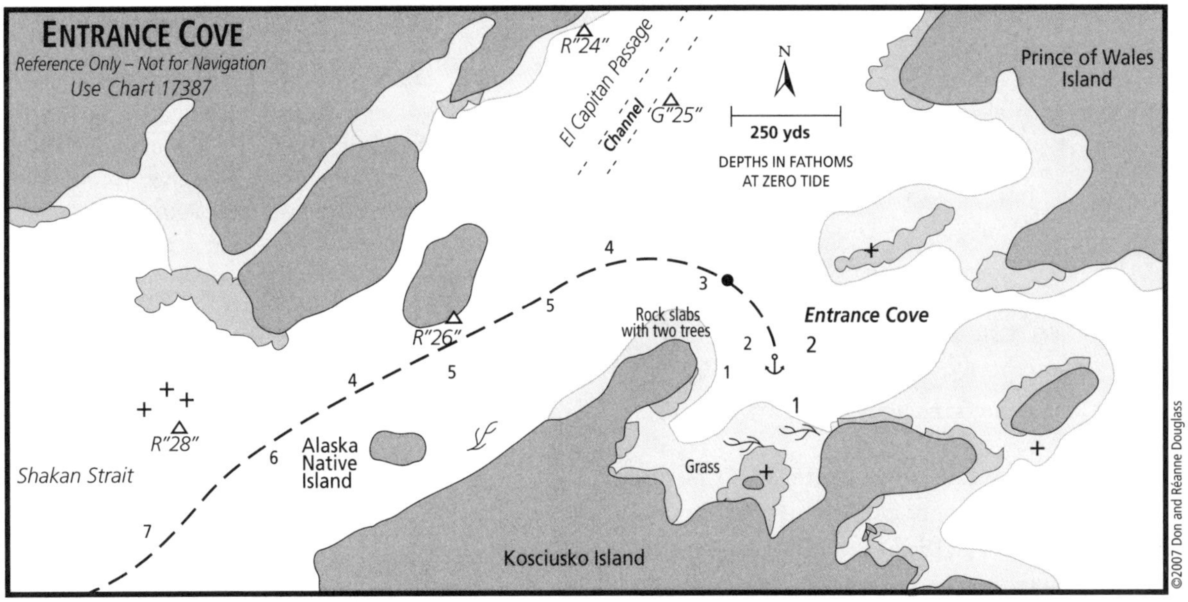


## **Entrance Cove** (El Capitan Passage)

Entrance Cove, on the south side of the passage, is just inside the entrance to El Capitan Passage and past a small islet.

**Chart 17387 (inset)**
**Entrance: 56°09.25′ N, 133°27.17′ W**
**Anchor: 56°09.21′ N, 133°27.18′ W**

"Entrance Cove" is what we call this small shallow cove that offers very good protection from seas in any direction. The cove is located just east of what we call "Alaska Native Island" and south of green channel marker G"25." To get to the anchor site, turn at the rock spit that has two trees on it—a good place to stretch your legs.

*Smooth water at Entrance Cove*

Anchor in 1 to 2 fathoms over sand with kelp and grass with fair holding.

## **Dry Pass Anchorage**

(El Capitan Passage)

Dry Pass Anchorage is 2.2 miles east of West Entrance.

**Chart 17387 (inset)**
**Anchor: 56°09.63′ N, 133°23.80′ W**

Dry Pass Anchorage, an excellent and very well-protected

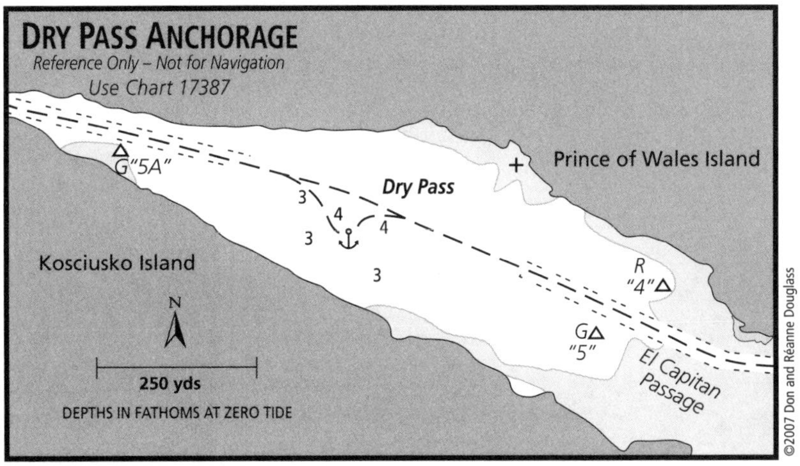

David Parker

*Heron fishing in the eel grass*

site, can be found in the center of El Capitan Passage, midway between the two easternmost dredged channels. (See *Coast Pilot* notes above for dredged channel depths.) This 500-yard-long lagoon is shallow throughout and offers plenty of swinging room. Or you can anchor in the larger basin, 0.3 mile west of the entrance to Dry Pass. This anchorage is the closest to the El Capitan Cave dinghy dock.

Anchor in 3 fathoms over mud with very good holding.

## **Devilfish Bay** (El Capitan Passage)

Devilfish Bay, on the west side of El Capitan Passage, is 3.5 miles south of Aneskett Point.

Chart 17387
Entrance: 56°05.31′ N, 133°18.70′ W
Anchor: 56°05.12′ N, 133°22.68′ W

*Devilfish Bay . . . consists of two parts connected by a narrows. . . .*

*The narrows, about 170 yards wide, expands into an arm with depths of 7-1/2 to 18 fathoms at midchannel to within 0.8 mile of the head. About 0.5 mile from the head of the arm, in mid-channel, is a submerged rock with 3/4 fathom over it. The narrows is constricted by a rock in midchannel, awash at high water. Depths of 3-1/2 fathoms W and 5 fathoms E of the rock were found, but the channel should not be attempted until seen at low water. Currents of 2 to 3 knots were observed in the vicinity of the rock.* (CP)

Devilfish Bay, a quiet, smooth, landlocked anchorage whose shores are covered with old-growth forest, provides excellent protection from all sectors. When the wind is blowing from the south in El Capitan Passage, just a slight wind is felt from the west inside Devilfish Bay.

Some cruisers anchor in Devilfish Bay and then dinghy approximately 4.5 miles north to the USFS dock to tour El Capitan Cave.

An Indian legend recounts that a giant devilfish rose out of the bay and washed away an entire village. When a group of researchers visited the bay in 1975, they were so overcome with "supernatural feelings of oppression, depression and alarm" that they fled, convinced the area was cursed. However, we found the bay just the opposite—charming and lovely, with a touch of magic added when a great blue heron

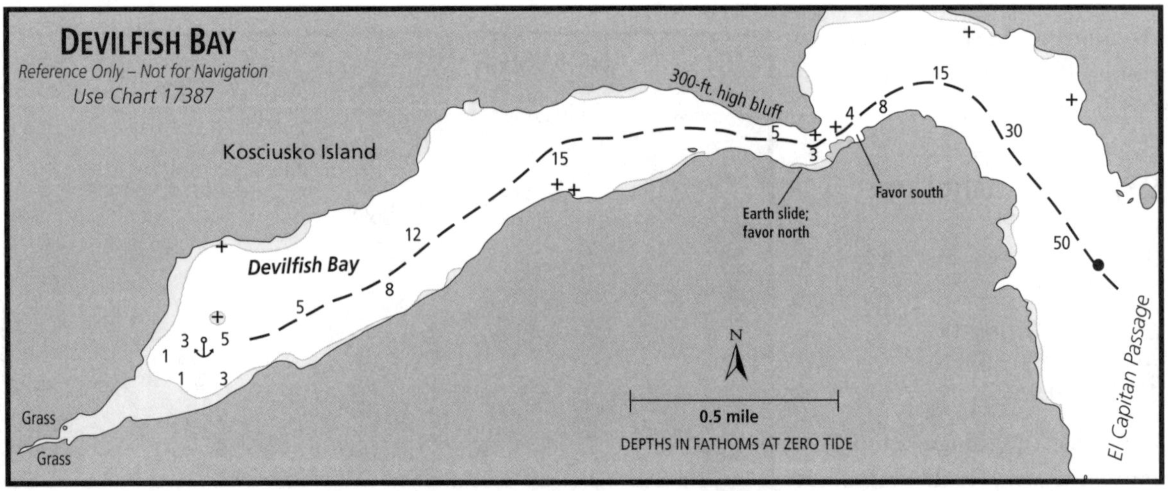

## Devilfish Bay—A Different Perspective

### Brian Pemberton, NW Explorations

What a great cruise we were having exploring the west side of Baranof Island, using *Exploring Southeast Alaska* as our only cruising guide, which had been spot-on. We had a great time at Réanne's Relief, then continued south along the coast, past Cape Ommaney, to seldom-visited Coronation Island, where we spent a wonderful couple of days.

On leaving Windy Bay we crossed Sumner Strait and set our course for Devilfish Bay in El Capitan Passage. I had chosen the site for the evening because the Douglass book reported it to be a good anchorage, and I was also intrigued by the interesting detail in their book about the superstitions natives held about Devilfish Bay.

After all seven of our boats were at anchor, we had a reception on our boat. By 1730, the wind was blowing consistently over 35 knots and gusting upward, so we started ferrying people back to their boats. Fortunately, we had our Grady White 22-foot boat with us, so despite the 2-3-foot seas, a lot of foam and wind, we delivered everyone safely to their boats.

Some of the boats that were rafted together started to drag after the winds reached a steady 50 knots. At that point, they split up and each set their anchor. Since we had a 46-foot Grand Banks rafted alongside our 49 foot, I decided now would be a good time to let out all the 500 feet of chain I'd been carrying all summer in my chain locker. So, with 10X scope, 500 feet of 3/8-foot chain, a 60-lb CQR, and an anchor bridal, we rode out the 55+ knots gale. Strangely, 100 yards north on the other side of the bay, there was virtually no wind at all.

When we raised our anchor the next morning, it took us over an hour to wash all the mud off the chain. We understood why we did not drag at bit—we had a great set!

So the lessons learned: 1) A lot of chain and scope is good! 2) Maybe the native folklore about mysteries we don't understand has merit. I know for sure that I will always use 10X scope in Devilfish Bay!

landed on our bow after we anchored. We spotted more leaping salmon in Devilfish Bay than we had seen anywhere else on the entire west coast. We like the bitter end of the bay, but the center has more swinging room.

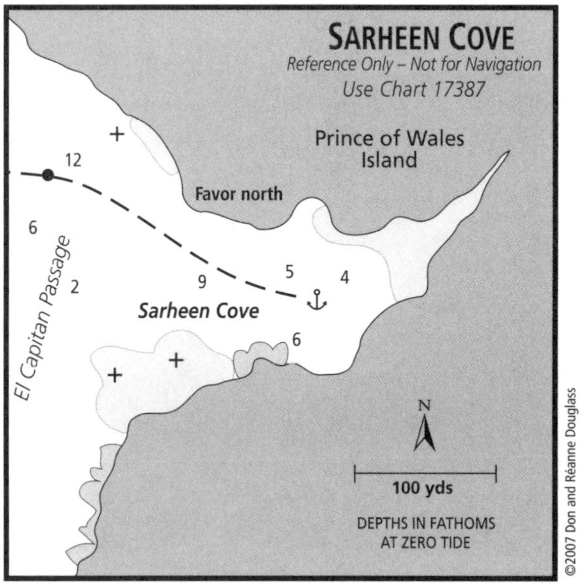


Anchor in 3 fathoms at the head of the bay over mud and clam shells with very good holding.

## Sarheen Cove (El Capitan Passage)

Sarheen Cove, on the east shore of El Capitan Passage, is 3 miles southeast of Devilfish Bay.

**Chart 17387**
**Entrance: 56°03.11′ N, 133°16.14′ W**
**Anchor: 56°03.00′ N, 133°15.73′ W**

> *Depths of 8 to 10 fathoms were found within the cove except toward the head where it is shoal.* (CP)

## Sarheen Cove

### From the First Mate's Diary

### Réanne Hemingway-Douglass

A Clark's nutcracker flies from treetop to treetop noisily warning the other birds of our approach. Soon a chorus of nutcrackers is clicking. Salmon cruise off the stream at the head of the cove, jumping—their silver bodies gleaming and curved—waiting, waiting for the rains to flood the creeks so they can head upstream to their natal ground.

Sarheen Cove, a small indentation on Prince of Wales Island near the south end of El Capitan Passage, is a good overnight anchor site. The cove offers protection in most weather; southerlies generally blow by its entrance. By favoring the north shore on entering, you can avoid the large shoal on the south entrance point. The best protection is found close to the east shore.

Anchor in 5 fathoms over mud, rocks, shells and grass with good holding.

## **Kosciusko Bay** (Kosciusko Island)

Kosciusko Bay is 3 miles southwest of Sarheen Cove.

Chart 17403
Entrance: 56°00.53′ N, 133°18.62′ W

Kosciusko Bay has very good shelter, but the entrance is mostly foul and the bay has an irregular rocky bottom. Favor the north shore when entering the bay but make sure you have adequate water for your draft. We don't recommend this bay as an anchorage.

## **Rocky Cove** (Prince of Wales Island)

Rocky Cove is 3.5 miles south of Sarheen Cove.

Chart 17403
Position: 55°59.42′ N, 133°15.98′ W

> *The cove is foul.* (CP)

## **Clam Cove** (Prince of Wales Island)

Clam Cove is 0.4 mile south of Rocky Cove.

Chart 17403
Entrance: 55°58.98′ N, 133°15.96′ W

> *Clam Island and rocks block the S part of the entrance. The head of the cove is shoal. Mariners should navigate with caution, referring to the latest edition of the chart.* (CP)

## **Tunga Inlet** (Prince of Wales Island)

Tunga Inlet is 0.6 mile north of Sarkar Cove.

Chart 17403
Entrance: 55°58.34′ N, 133°15.92′ W

> *Salt Water Lagoon . . . is connected to Tunga Inlet by short rapids. Water ebbs from the lagoon for about 2-1/2 hours after low water. At slack water, about 2-1/2 hours after high water, a launch drawing 4 feet may pass through the entrance into the lagoon.* (CP)

## **Sarkar Cove** (Prince of Wales Island)

Sarkar Cove, on the east side of El Capitan Passage, is 6 miles from Sea Otter Sound.

Chart 17403
Entrance: 55°57.76′ N, 133°15.84′ W
Anchor: 55°57.44′ N, 133°15.02′ W

> *Sarkar Cove . . . is entered about 1.3 miles SE of Burnt Island Light 5, and . . . about 18 miles from Shakan Strait. The cove affords good anchorage in 6 to 8 fathoms, mud bottom.*
>
> *A large lake empties into the head of the cove through a series of rapids. . . . The lake is an important spawning ground for red salmon.* (CP)

Good protection from winds of all directions can be found in Sarkar Cove. El Capitan Lodge on the south shore provides sport fishing opportunities on nearby Sarkar Lake. Watch for float planes taking off and landing at the lodge. The Lodge management is willing to talk with you about chartering one of their float planes for your guests to fly in or out.

Anchor deep in the cove in 6 fathoms over mud with good holding.

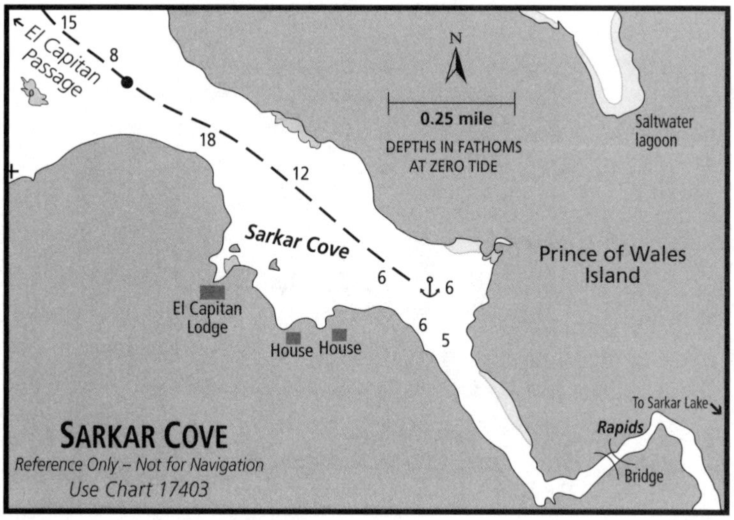

## New Tokeen (El Capitan Island)

New Tokeen is a small settlement on the west side of El Capitan Island near the south end of El Capitan Passage.

Chart 17403
Entrance: 55°56.15′ N, 133°19.79′ W

> *A mooring float 180 feet long is anchored in the bight for the use of fishing vessels. Limited amounts of ice, gasoline, diesel fuel, water, and provisions can be had during the fishing season.* (CP)

## Tuxekan Passage

Tuxekan Passage is on the east side of Tuxekan Island.

Charts 17403, 17404
North entrance (west of Kassan Islands):
55°55.47′ N, 133°17.64′ W
South entrance: 55°46.00′ N, 133°15.25′ W

> *Tuxekan Passage has its S entrance on the SE side of Karheen Passage, and extends N along the E side of Tuxekan Island for about 10 miles to El Capitan Passage. The shores are heavily wooded throughout its length, and are indented with numerous bights, coves, and bays that provide anchorage in any desired depth.* (CP)

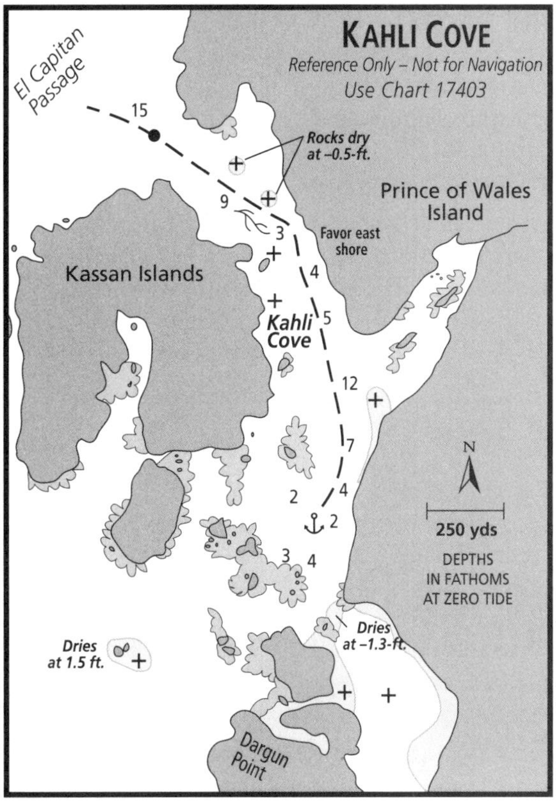


©2007 Don and Réanne Douglass

## Kahli Cove (Prince of Wales Island)

Kahli Cove is 2 miles east of El Capitan Island.

Chart 17403
Entrance: 55°55.89′ N, 133°16.08′ W
Anchor: 55°55.27′ N, 133°15.63′ W

> *Kahli Cove . . . provides suitable anchorage for small craft. The SW entrance is constricted by rocks and reefs, but a narrow winding channel is open. The NW entrance is less winding and has fewer rocks.* (CP)

Kahli Cove is an intimate, well-protected anchorage west of Kassan Islands. Numerous islets and reefs at the south end provide total protection in a calm, quiet setting. Entry requires careful navigation and should not be attempted in poor visibility or by radar. When there is sufficient water, you can continue south through the narrow exit, but beware of the rock piles.

Anchor in 3 fathoms over a rocky bottom with poor-to-fair holding.

Réanne Hemingway-Douglass

*Kahli Cove looking south*

## **Jinhi Bay** (Tuxekan Island)

Jinhi Bay is 3 miles south of Kahli Cove.

Chart 17403

Entrance (via Kwati Point): 55°53.15′ N, 133°16.46′ W

> *Jinhi Bay extends SW from Village Rock. This bay shoals gradually to mud flats that bare in its SW extremities. It is studded with small islets and numerous rocks that bare at various stages of tide. Only those with local knowledge should attempt to enter this bay.* (CP)

An old float house is anchored in the east side of the bay.

## **Cyrus Cove** (Orr Island)

Cyrus Cove is 5.5 miles northwest of Tuxekan Narrows and 7.5 miles east of Edna Bay.

Chart 17403

Entrance: 55°54.15′ N, 133°25.19′ W

Anchor (small vessels): 55°55.04′ N, 133°24.34′ W

Anchor (large vessels): 55°55.08′ N, 133°24.96′ W

> *Cyrus Cove . . . is an excellent anchorage for small boats. The best anchorage in depths of 5 to 11 fathoms, good holding ground, mud bottom, is in the center of the N part where the cove branches to E. Five fathoms can be carried through midchannel to this anchorage. Smaller vessels may anchor in shoaler water in midchannel in the E arm of the cove . . . The passages between Owl Island, Hoot Island, and Orr Island should be used only with local knowledge.* (CP)

Cyrus Cove provides welcome shelter in one of the more remote and challenging navigation areas on the north coast of Prince of Wales Island. It is essentially landlocked, but is easy to enter in all conditions as Owl Island provides a good lee.

When entering Cyrus Cove, favor the east shore at the narrows 0.5 miles inside the entrance to avoid a shoal that extends over half way out from the west shore.

Larger boats will find very good anchorage with adequate swinging room in the center of the cove in 8 to 12 fathoms, black mud bottom, with very good holding.

Smaller vessels will want to curl around east into the landlocked east basin. Favor the

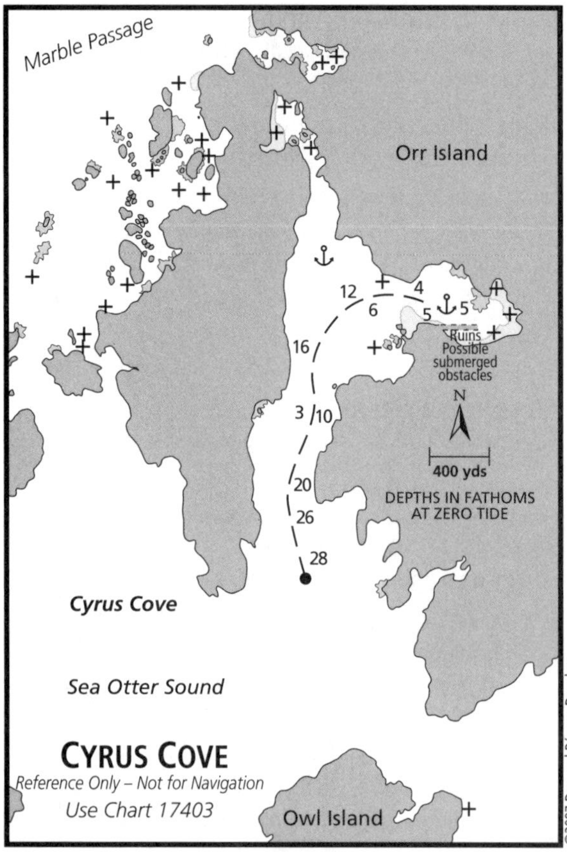

*A passenger on the anchor chain*

north shore of the basin to avoid the rocks in the basin entrance on both shores, which narrow the entrance considerably. There is adequate swinging room for one or two boats, but avoid the rock pile and reef extending south near the head of the basin. The charted wharf ruins are no longer visible and you might want to avoid this spot because of possible submerged obstacles. Orr Island is fairly low so you might experience some wind but no significant williwaws.

Anchor (inner basin) in 5 fathoms over a mud and shell bottom with very good holding.

## Tuxekan Narrows

Tuxekan Narrows lies between Tuxekan and Prince of Wales islands.

Chart 17403
North entrance (Village Rock "VR" brg 074°T at 0.28 Nm): 55°53.28′ N, 133°15.79′ W
South entrance: 55°51.73′ N, 133°13.07′ W

> *The width* [of Tuxekan Passage] *varies from a maximum of about 2 miles N of Staney Island to about 225 yards in Tuxekan Narrows.* (CP)

The safest route through Tuxekan Narrows passes south and west of Village Rock at the north entrance to the narrows. The currents are weak—less than one knot—with flooding to the north and ebbing to the south.

## Little Naukati Bay (Prince of Wales Island)

Little Naukati Bay is on the east side of Tuxekan Narrows.

Chart 17403
Entrance: 55°52.63′ N, 133°13.75′ W

> *Little Naukati Bay . . . is not recommended as a small-boat anchorage. At low water its entrance is almost closed by rocks and reefs. The best water into it is the N channel.* (CP)

## Nichin Cove (Tuxekan Island)

Nichin Cove is just south of Tuxekan Narrows.

Chart 17403
Entrance: 55°51.18′ N, 133°13.42′ W
Anchor: 55°50.94′ N, 133°13.69′ W

> *Nichin Cove . . . about 1.3 miles WSW of Klinau Island, affords good small-craft anchorage. . . . A ramp and float . . . are on the W side of the cove near the entrance.* (CP)

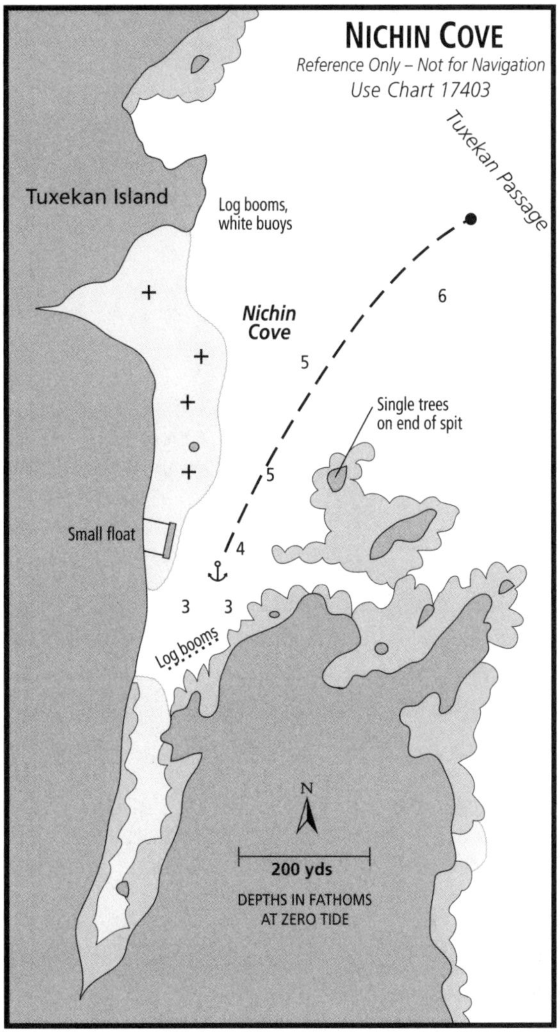



Nichin Cove provides convenient shelter from southerly winds. (North of this point, the effect of southerlies is nil because of the many islands.) In previous years Nichin Cove has been occupied by a large logging operation. Excellent temporary shelter from chop can be found deep in the cove just off the small float where swinging room is limited. Avoid the commercial operations and the large steel buoys marking the booming operation on the northwest side of the cove.

Anchor in 4 fathoms over sticky mud with very good holding.

## Naukati Bay (Prince of Wales Island)

Naukati Bay is on the east shore of Tuxekan Passage.

Chart 17403
Entrance: 55°51.23′ N, 133°10.77′ W

> *Its entrance . . . is constricted by rocks and kelp. . . . In the narrow winding channel, 3 fathoms can be carried well in toward the head of the bay.* (CP)

# Naukati Bay Coves

## Kaikli Cove

Kaikli Cove is on the northwest corner of Naukati Bay.
Entrance: 55°53.00′ N, 133°10.25′ W

## Kaigao Cove

Kaigao Cove is just east of Kaikli Cove.
Entrance: 55°53.13′ N, 133°10.10′ W

## Gutchi Cove

Gutchi Cove is on the east side of Naukati Bay.
Entrance: 55°52.85′ N, 133°09.13′ W

## Surku Cove (Prince of Wales Island)

Surku Cove is southeast of the entrance to Naukati Bay.
Entrance: 55°50.73′ N, 133°10.00′ W

## Chusini Cove (Prince of Wales Island)

Chusini Cove is 1 mile southeast of Stanley Island.
Chart 17403
Entrance: 55°49.44′ N, 133°11.00′ W

## Yahku Cove (Tuxekan Island)

Yahku Cove is on the west side of Tuxekan Passage.

Chart 17403
Entrance: 55°47.55′ N, 133°14.49′ W
Anchor: 55°47.86′ N, 133°14.52′ W

> *Yahku Cove . . .* [is] *not recommended for small-boat anchorages. . . . A rocky reef that is uncovered at high water constricts the entrance to Yahku Cove.* (CP)

Yahku Cove, although tiny, deserves a better mention than *Coast Pilot* gives it. (*Baidarka*'s first mate called this cove "a Douglass find!") The rocky reef off the eastern entrance point acts, in effect, as a breakwater for the cove, and the moderate southerly chop from Tuxekan

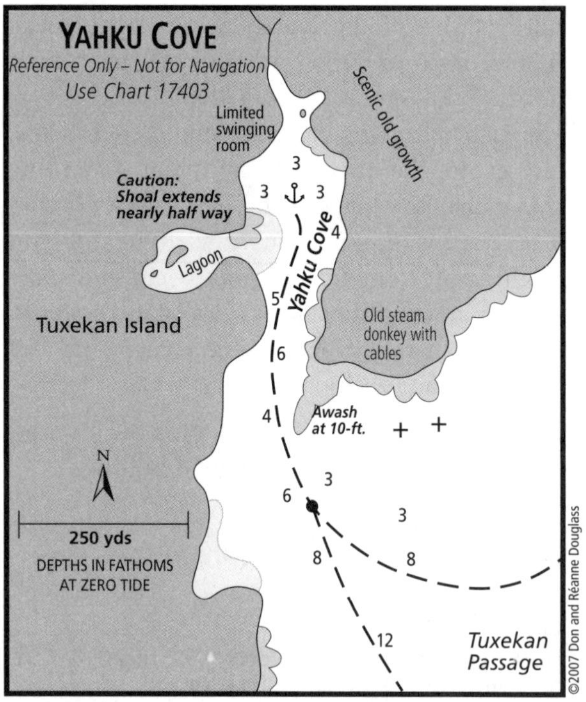


Passage does not enter the cove. If a strong southerly storm is expected, consider Winter Harbor or Kaguk Cove.

Almost landlocked, Yahku is surrounded by old-growth, mixed forest of spruce, cedar, hemlock and alder. Anchor just beyond the opening to the lagoon; swinging room is limited.

Anchor in 3 fathoms over sticky brown mud and clam shells with excellent holding.

## Nundei Cove (Prince of Wales Island)

Nundei Cove, on the east side of Tuxekan Passage, is opposite Yahku Cove.

Chart 17403
Entrance: 55°47.38′ N, 133°13.00′ W

> *Nundei Cove . . .* [is] *not recommended for small-boat anchorages.* (CP)

## Davidson Inlet

Davidson Inlet is between Heceta and Kosciusko islands.

Chart 17403
Entrance (Surf Point Light brg 098°T at 1.10 Nm): 55°50.24′ N, 133°39.87′ W

> *Davidson Inlet is the W part of a large expanse of water. . . . The E part, Sea Otter Sound, is sepa-*

*rated from it by a chain of islands that extend SW from Marble Island and Orr Island.*

*The entrance to Davidson Inlet is . . . between Whale Head and Surf Point, the NW extremity of Heceta Island.* (CP)

## **Holbrook Arm** (Kosciusko Island)

Holbrook Arm is at the north end of Davidson Inlet.

Chart 17403
Entrance: 56°00.29′ N, 133°29.51′ W

Once the home of the village of Holbrook (abandoned), Holbrook Arm offers anchorage in moderate depths but is open to the south.

## **Tokeen Bay** (Kosciusko Island)

Tokeen Bay, on the east side of Davidson Inlet, is 12 miles northeast of Whale Head.

Chart 17403
West entrance (Holbrook Point brg 025°T at 0.4 Nm): 55°59.92′ N, 133°28.92′ W

[Tokeen Bay's] *E side is connected with El Capitan Passage by a high-water boat passage. . . .*

*Anchorage can be found in the middle of Tokeen Bay, about 0.5 mile E from the N point at the entrance in 14 to 16 fathoms; also at the N end, NE side, and SE end of the bay. There are several sheltered anchorages for small craft, one of which is at the head of the bay behind the small islet in 4 fathoms, mud bottom. The area E of the small wooded islands in the SE part of the bay also offers good anchorage in 4 to 10 fathoms, mud bottom.* (CP)

## **Tokeen Cove** (Tokeen Bay)

Tokeen Cove is on the northwest end of Marble Island.

Chart 17403
Entrance: 55°59.76′ N, 133°28.76′ W
Anchor: 55°59.47′ N, 133°28.33′ W

*Anchorage can be had W of the ruins of a wharf, on the E side of the cove, in 14 to 18 fathoms. Small craft can find anchorage in 4 to 8 fathoms, soft bottom. The cove is shoal S of the wharf site. A rock that uncovers 6 feet is 300 yards W from the NE point of the cove.* (CP)

Anchor in about 6 fathoms over a soft bottom with good holding.

## **Edna Bay** (Kosciusko Island)

Edna Bay, on the west side of Davidson Inlet, is 5.5 miles north of Whale Head.

Chart 17403 (inset)
Entrance (Limestone Point Light brg 015°T at 0.15 Nm): 55°56.16′ N, 133°36.99′ W
Anchor: 55°56.81′ N, 133°39.53′ W

*Edna Bay . . . has good anchorage about 0.3 mile from the S shore in 14 to 17 fathoms, soft bottom.*

*In September 1986, an uncharted reef, covered 5 feet, was reported about 50 feet SW of the face of a T-float at the N end of Edna Bay. A dangerous shoal area near the float is marked by buoys.* (CP)

M/V *Passages* reports that in addition to the rock noted in the *Coast Pilot*, above, there is an unmarked rock under the moorage area on the west end of the T-float, possibly extending into the area between the breakwater and the dock. They caution against trying to moor in Edna Bay.

Anchorage in Edna Bay can be found southwest of the T-float, at the far west end of the bay. The inner entrance is marked by buoys.

Anchor in 4 fathoms over mud with good holding.

## **Van Sant Cove** (Kosciusko Island)

Van Sant Cove is 4 miles northeast of Edna Bay.

Chart 17403
Entrance: 55°59.17′ N, 133°32.11′ W

*Van Sant Cove is a small open bight. . . . A reef is off the S point of the entrance.* (CP)

Van Sant Cove is exposed to southerlies and its bottom is steep-to.

## **Sea Otter Sound**

Sea Otter Sound extends west of Tuxekan Island and Karheen Passage to Davidson Inlet.

Chart 17403
Position (Gas Rock brg 247°T at 1.1 Nm): 55°51.17′ N, 133°32.15′ W

*The* [south] *entrance to El Capitan Passage is at the NE end of Sea Otter Sound.*

*The sound has few desirable anchorages. With the assistance of the chart, depths suitable for anchorage can be found on its E side, but care is required because of submerged rocks that are generally marked by kelp during summer.* (CP)

Sea Otter Sound is comparable to an inland sea, surrounded by an intricate group of islands, rocks and reefs. While secure anchor sites are somewhat scarce, the region is interesting to explore.

## **Port Alice** (Heceta Island)

Port Alice is on the south side of Davidson Inlet.

Chart 17403
Entrance: 55°49.97′ N, 133°36.76′ W
Anchor: 55°47.98′ N, 133°35.73′ W

*Port Alice . . . is a secure anchorage. . . . To enter, give the points at the entrance a berth of about 0.5 mile and enter in midchannel. Follow the W shore at a distance of about 250 yards, passing W of the ledge until about 0.5 mile from the head of the port, where good anchorage will be found in the middle in 14 to 18 fathoms, soft bottom.* (CP)

Well-sheltered anchorage can be found at the head of the bay near the old log booms.

Anchor in 9 fathoms over mud and clam shells with good holding.

## **Cone Bay** (Heceta Island)

Cone Bay is northeast of Cape Lynch.

Chart 17403
Entrance: 55°48.05′ N, 133°41.26′ W

*Cone Bay . . . is open and exposed to the W. The bottom is irregular, and kelp extends well into the bay along the S shore.* (CP)

## **Squam Bay** (Heceta Island)

Squam Bay is southwest of Karheen Passage.

Chart 17403
Entrance: 55°46.94′ N, 133°19.83′ W

Squam Bay is sheltered from northwest winds, but its bottom is irregular with unknown holding.

## **Karheen Passage** (Tuxekan Island)

Karheen Passage, on the southwest side of Tuxekan Island, extends from Tonowek Narrows to Sea Otter Sound.

Chart 17403
Northwest entrance: 55°50.35′ N, 133°22.29′ W
Southeast entrance (Kauda Point brg 012°T at 0.4 Nm): 55°46.03′ N, 133°15.78′ W

*The SE part of the passage is characterized by islets, ledges, and generally broken ground, surrounded by comparatively deep water. . . . The channel is marked by a daybeacon, buoys, and an unlighted range as far as Karheen Cove and is used by vessels with a draft of about 17 feet.* (CP)

## **Karheen Cove** (Tuxekan Island)

Karheen Cove is on the northeast side of Karheen Passage at its northwest end.

Chart 17403
Entrance: 55°48.65′ N, 133°18.94′ W

*A bare rock is off the S point at the entrance. A buoy marks the outer end of the ledge that extends about 400 yards SW from the S point.* (CP)

## **Winter Harbor** (Prince of Wales Island)

Winter Harbor is 1.5 miles from Yahku Cove on the east shore of Tuxekan Passage.

Chart 17403 & 17404
Entrance: 55°46.44′ N, 133°14.08′ W
Anchor: 55°46.22′ N, 133°13.83′ W

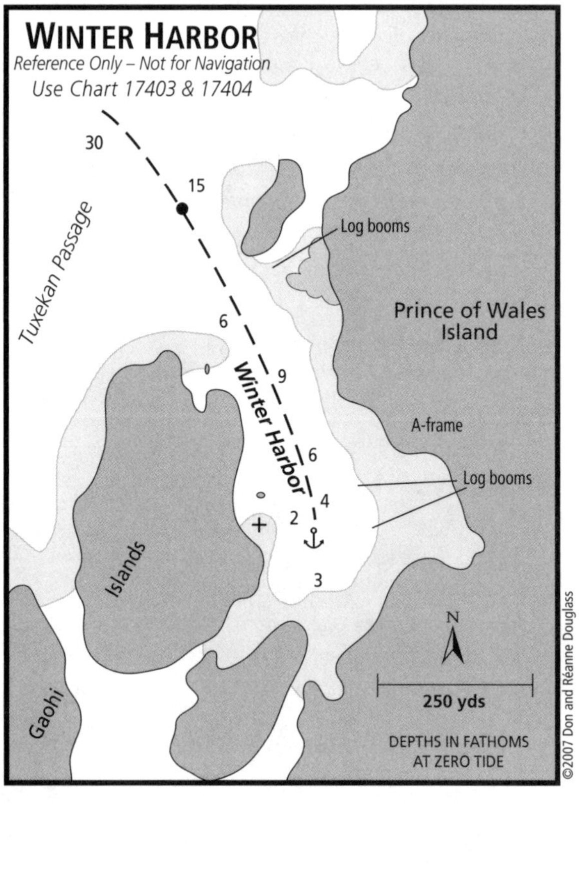

*Gaohi Islands, across the passage from Kauda Point, form the SW shore of Winter Harbor . . .* [and] *are difficult to identify when approaching from the W.* (CP)

Winter Harbor provides very good shelter in strong southerlies. Like Nichin Cove, there has been an active logging operation in Winter Harbor. Temporary anchorage can be found nearby, but avoid the commercial operations at the head of the harbor. Larger cruising boats may find better southerly shelter in Kaguk Cove, 3 miles to the south.

Anchor in 3 fathoms over soft mud with shells; holding is good with a well-set anchor.

## Kaguk Cove (Prince of Wales Island)

Kaguk Cove, at the south end of Tuxekan Passage, is 2 miles southwest of Kauda Point.

Chart 17404
Entrance: 55°44.89′ N, 133°16.96′ W
Anchor: 55°44.35′ N, 133°17.63′ W

*Kaguk Cove . . . affords a well-protected anchorage in depths of 4 to 8 fathoms, with a gentle sloping bottom.* (CP)

Kaguk Cove offers excellent shelter for all sizes of cruising boats.

Anchor in 5 fathoms over mud with good holding.

Réanne Hemingway-Douglass

*Word has it that this totem is no longer visible here on the west shore of Tonowek Narrows.*

## Indian Garden Bay (Heceta Island)

Indian Garden Bay is at the north end of Tonowek Narrows.

**Chart 17404**
**Entrance: 55°46.13′ N, 133°19.79′ W**

Indian Garden Bay looks interesting and may provide good shelter. However, the cove is not well charted and it appears to have a rocky, irregular bottom.

## Tonowek Narrows

Tonowek Narrows, between Prince of Wales and Heceta islands, joins Tonowek Bay and Karheen Passage.

**Chart 17404**
**North entrance (Green buoy "5" brg 300°T at 0.1 Nm): 55°47.11′ N, 133°17.22′ W**
**Southwest entrance: 55°45.22′ N, 133°20.80′ W**

*Tonowek Narrows* [is] *locally known as Little Skookum Chuck. . . . It has a least width of 100 yards between the 10-fathom curves.*

*The currents in Tonowek Narrows set NE on the flood and SW on the ebb. The velocity of the current is 3.0 knots.*

*Two totem poles and a gravesite can be seen on an island about 0.4 mile W of Point Swift, on the W side of Tonowek Narrows.* (CP)

We have found that the flood current at Tonowek Narrows runs a snappy 4 to 6 knots. We have heard reports that the weathered totem pole at the southern tip of the island on the west side of the narrows is no longer visible. Avoid Point Swift Rock that dries at about 5 feet by following the marked channel immediately north.

The channel where Karheen Passage and Tuxekan Passage meet Tonowek Narrows is a rock pile. Substantial current and kelp patches require alert navigation. The flood flows north and the ebb flows south.

## Nossuk Anchorage (Prince of Wales Island)

Nossuk Anchorage, in the north part of Nossuk Bay, is 0.7 mile south of Tonowek Narrows.

**Chart 17404**
**Entrance: 55°44.60′ N, 133°21.04′ W**

*Nossuk Anchorage . . . affords excellent anchorage in 10 fathoms, soft bottom. The N entrance is narrow; the chart shows the least depths.* (CP)

Nossuk Anchorage provides good shelter from chop, but contrary to *Coast Pilot*, we found that it has very irregular soundings, indicating a sharp rocky bottom. We would not risk fouling an anchor here and don't recommend it. If someone has located the soft bottom, we would like to know where it is! (We anchored in Nossuk Bay, instead.)

## **Nossuk Bay** (Prince of Wales Island)

Nossuk Bay, in the northeast part of Tonowek Bay, is 1.5 miles south of Tonowek Narrows.

Chart 17404
Entrance: 55°44.35′ N, 133°22.02′ W

> *Nossuk Bay . . . is largely filled with islands and shoals.* (CP)

Nossuk Bay has lots of shallow anchorages with tons of swinging room, but watch for isolated rocks.

## **No Name Cove** (Nossuk Bay)

No Name Cove is the first cove on the southwest shore as you enter the bay.

Chart 17404
Entrance: 55°43.82′ N, 133°22.01′ W
Anchor: 55°43.68′ N, 133°22.32′ W

No Name Cove provides good anchorage in most weather.

Anchor in 6 fathoms over sand and gravel with fair holding.

## **Tonowek Bay** (Prince of Wales and Heceta islands)

Tonowek Bay extends northeast for 6 miles from the Gulf of Esquibel to Tonowek Narrows.

Chart 17404
South entrance (Desconocida Reef Light brg 300°T at 1.3 Nm): 55°40.66′ N, 133°29.37′ W

> *Tonowek Bay . . . borders the SE side of Heceta Island.* (CP)

## **Warm Chuck Inlet** (Heceta Island)

Warm Chuck Inlet is on the northwest side of Tonowek Bay.

Chart 17404
Entrance: 55°43.96′ N, 133°27.41′ W
Anchor: 55°47.12′ N, 133°30.63′ W

> *Warm Chuck Inlet . . . has considerable foul ground. . . . A rock, with 1/2 fathom over it, is in midchannel, 0.5 mile E of a well-defined point on the SW shore.* (CP)

Warm Chuck Inlet may offer small craft shelter in its far northwest arm.

## **Harmony Islands Passage** (Harmony Islands)

Harmony Islands Passage is the channel east of the Harmony Islands and east of the islands to the south, off the entrance to Salt Lake Bay.

Chart 17404
North entrance: 55°43.45′ N, 133°23.77′ W
South entrance (Blanquizal Island brg 125°T at 0.25 Nm): 55°37.16′ N, 133°24.64′ W

> *Harmony Islands are a group of high, wooded islands. There are channels between the islands of this group, but they are made difficult by numerous dangers. Rocks that cover are off the S and W points of the group.*
>
> [Harmony Islands Passage] *. . . is used extensively by small craft plying between San Christoval Channel and Tonowek Narrows. The midchannel is safe and partially protected.* (CP)

"Harmony Islands Passage" is our name for the excellent smooth-water route described above in *Coast Pilot*. To follow the passage, continue due south almost to the peninsula before turning west to Culebra Islands; the shoal south of the smallest Harmony Islands is larger than the area shown on the chart. The sheltered route continues inside St. Philip Island, but it is encumbered with mid-channel rocks near its south end and requires careful navigation.

## **Salt Lake Bay** (Prince of Wales Island)

Salt Lake Bay, on the southeast side of Tonowek Bay, is 2 miles northeast of the Culebra Islands.

Chart 17404
Entrance (south shore): 55°41.03′ N, 133°23.41′ W

> *The entrance is choked by a group of wooded islands. Two channels are used, one N of the group with a depth of 1-1/2 fathoms, the other S of the group with a depth of 2-1/2 fathoms. The*

*NE and SW ends of the bay are shoal; depths of 7 to 15 fathoms are found in the center.* (CP)

Salt Lake Bay is another possible anchorage, but the bottom may be hard and irregular. More research is necessary.

## **Bobs Place** (St. Philip Island)

Bobs Place is on the southeast corner of St. Philip Island.

Chart 17404
Anchor: 55°38.30′ N, 133°24.36′ W

*At the SE end of St. Philip Island is an old Native American village, known locally as Bobs Place. Fair anchorage for moderate-sized vessels can be had in midchannel off the village.*

*Small craft with local knowledge pass inside all the islands of the St. Philip and Culebra groups. A rock awash and a submerged rock are about 300 yards SE and ESE, respectively, of the 130-foot island off the SE end of St. Philip Island.* (CP)

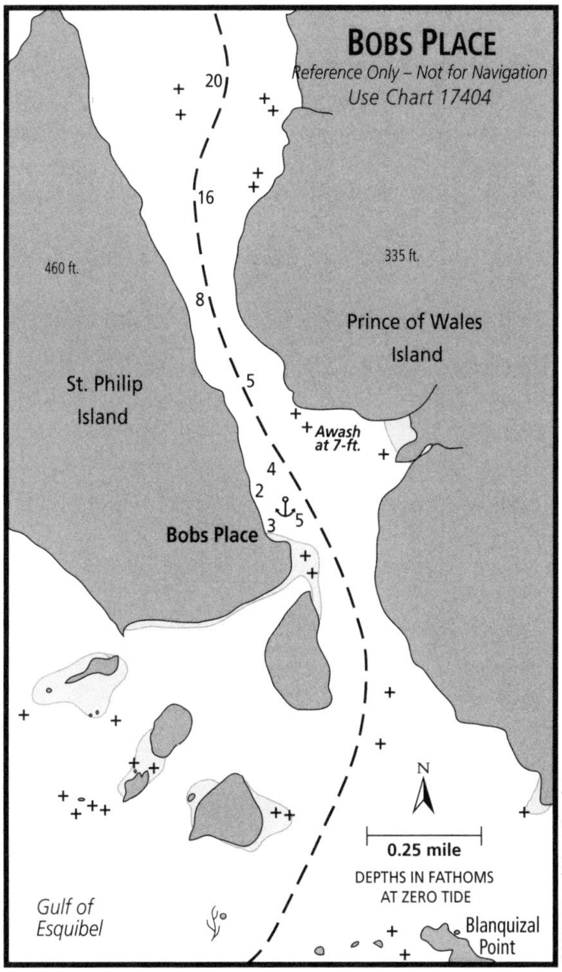




Cruising boats can find additional shelter from southerly and westerly winds by passing inside St. Philip Island. Picturesque Bobs Place affords shelter, from all but a hard north or south blow, tucked behind the little hook on St. Philip Island, off the gravel and shell beach. There are some newspaper kelp patches here, so check your anchor set. Unfortunately, on our most recent visit, we were unable to get our anchor to set, so we ventured on.

Anchor in 2 to 3 fathoms over soft sand with shell, kelp and grass; fair holding if you can get a set.

## **Bocas de Finas**

Bocas de Finas, the passage between the southwest coast of Heceta Island and the northeasternmost islands of the Maurelle group, leads from the junction of the Gulf of Esquibel with Tonowek Bay to Iphigenia Bay and the Pacific Ocean.

Chart 17404
Northwest entrance (Cape Lynch Light brg 058°T at 0.5 Nm): 55°46.59′ N, 133°42.90′ W
Southeast entrance (Desconocida Reef Light brg 025°T at 0.6 Nm): 55°40.77′ N, 133°31.94′ W

*The SW side of the passage is foul for about 0.3 mile off the Anguilla Island shore, and should be avoided.*

*There is secure anchorage in the W bight on the N side of Anguilla Island, about 0.5 mile S of Bushtop Island. When entering, pass about 200 yards E of Bushtop Island and stand in on a S course. Anchor in 11 to 15 fathoms, soft bottom. Kelp and broken ground are on the W side of the anchorage.* (CP)

## **Maurelle Islands**

The Maurelle Islands lie on the northwest side of the Gulf of Esquibel.

Chart 17404

*The Maurelle Islands are a group of islands, rocks, reefs, and breakers forming the W side of the Gulf of Esquibel, covering an area about 12.5 miles long in a NNW direction and about*

Don Douglass

*Entering Launch Passage, Maurelle Islands*

*9 miles wide. . . . Caution. Without local knowledge, navigation among these islands, except in small craft, is dangerous.* (CP)

The Maurelle Islands are a designated Wilderness. Within these islands, during stable weather, you can find surprisingly smooth waters and many small anchor sites. It is a perfect place to explore by kayak and dinghy. Our favorite anchor site in the region is Nagasay Cove on the north side of Esquibel Island.

## **Anguilla Bay** (Anguilla Island)

Anguilla Bay is on the south side of Bocas de Finas.

Chart 17404
West entrance: 55°39.51′ N, 133°36.38′ W

*Anguilla Bay . . . is foul at its head.* (CP)

Anguilla Bay is largely a rock pile, but we like the shelter and isolation found in Nagasay Cove. Use caution when plying the channels.

## **Launch Passage**

Launch Passage lies between Anguilla and Esquibel islands.

Chart 17404
East entrance: 55°39.05′ N, 133°32.81′ W

*Launch Passage . . . is frequently used. In making passage from the Gulf of Esquibel, keep S of the rocks awash at half tide and the submerged rocks just inside the entrance. When abeam the inner rock, change course to pass close to and just S of the two islands in midchannel. Keep close to the islands. From here the channel is clear to the anchorage in Nagasay Cove . . . the chart is the best guide for mariners without local knowledge.* (CP)

Narrow Launch Passage has some current and lots of kelp. Favor the south shore and use caution. If exiting Launch Passage by Anguilla Bay, avoid two dangerous rocks off the south tip of Anguilla Island that bare on a 2-foot tide.

## **Nagasay Cove** (Esquibel Island)

Nagasay Cove is on the north side of Esquibel Island.

Chart 17404
Anchor: 55°38.66′ N, 133°33.93′ W

*An anchorage for small craft is on the W side of Nagasay Cove . . . in 4 fathoms, mud bottom.* (CP)

Nagasay Cove, one of our favorites in this area, offers very good shelter in intimate, landlocked surroundings. Beware of the two large submerged rocks on the northeast side of the anchorage.

Anchor in 3 fathoms over sand and mud with good holding.

## **San Lorenzo Islands, Hole in the Wall**

San Lorenzo Islands, at the northeast end of Arriaga Passage, lie between Noyes Island and the Maurelle Islands.

Chart 17404
North entrance (Hole in the Wall): 55°36.24′ N, 133°37.24′ W
South entrance (Hole in the Wall): 55°35.25′ N, 133°36.77′ W

*San Lorenzo Islands . . . consists* [sic] *of two timbered islands separated by a narrow channel. This channel is locally known as Hole in the Wall.*

*A submerged rock, which covers 4 feet, is about 150 feet off the W shore, opposite the vertical bluff. A depth of 3 fathoms can be carried past the rock on its NE side.* (CP)

Here is another Hole in the Wall experience for cruisers. Favor the east shore.

## Gulf of Esquibel

The Gulf of Esquibel is 8 miles long from Tonowek Bay to Noyes Island and 6 miles wide from the Maurelle Islands to San Fernando Island.

Chart 17404
Position: 55°35.00′ N, 133°30.01′ W

> *The known dangers are shown on the chart; the principal one, Curacao Reef, is marked by a buoy. Small craft with local knowledge pass inside all the islands of the St. Philip and Culebra groups.* (CP)

The gulf is a large bay sheltered by many islands from the Gulf of Alaska. It can get brisk from westerly winds and chop. Garcia Cove on San Fernando Island is well protected.

## Ulitka Bay (Noyes Island)

Ulitka Bay is 0.5 mile southeast of Cape Ulitka Light.

Chart 17404
Entrance: 55°33.58′ N, 133°43.07′ W
Anchor: 55°33.30′ N, 133°43.29′ W

> *Ulitka Bay . . . affords fair-weather anchorage for fishing boats in depths of 6 to 8 fathoms. The head of the cove should not be approached too closely as the shores are foul.* (CP)

## Steamboat Bay (Noyes Island)

Steamboat Bay is 3 miles east of Cape Ulitka Light.

Chart 17404
Entrance: 55°33.21′ N, 133°38.16′ W
Anchor: 55°32.00′ N, 133°38.10′ W

> *At low water, a sand and gravel beach extends several hundred yards from the head of the bay. Small boats anchor close to the head of the bay. The bay is open to the N; during N blows it affords little protection. It is reported that the ocean swells enter the bay.*
>
> *A 75-foot small-craft float extends N from the 285-foot wharf. During the fishing season, the facility for fishing vessels has fishing supplies, limited provisions, gasoline, diesel fuel, lubricating oils, greases, water, and ice.* (CP)

Anchor in about 12 fathoms over sand and gravel with fair holding.

## San Christoval Channel

San Christoval Channel, between Prince of Wales Island and San Fernando Island, connects San Alberto Bay to the Gulf of Esquibel.

Charts 17405, 17404
West entrance: 55°35.74′ N, 133°23.49′ W
Entrance (Larzatita Island brg 047°T at 0.2 Nm): 55°34.61′ N, 133°20.31′ W

---

### Learning to Carve

Barb Davis—S/V *Antares*

With our last load of laundry in the dryer in Craig, Bill and I ventured across the street where we had seen a lean-to with a couple of people inside. As we neared, we noticed Alaska native people carving a totem pole. We hesitated a bit, not wanting to bother them, when the young women saw us and invited us to come in and take a look at their work. The pole, being carved from a 300-year-old cedar, was about 30 feet long and 36 inches in diameter and would be dedicated to the elders of Hydaburg.

Stan Rosen, a well-known carver, had been working on the pole for close to a year, and the raising was less than two weeks away. He had recruited his daughter and some friends to help, but they still had quite a bit of work left to do.

After spending some time talking with them, Stan asked us if we would like to help. He gave us the handmade tools and a quick lesson and away we went! I carved out the teeth of a raven while Bill planed the dorsal fin of a killer whale.

As we worked, Stan told us about another pole they had raised the previous year in Craig. It was in memory of his son who had died of a drug overdose. The entire town was involved in the carving and, on the day of the raising, 100 people helped carry it down the street to the park where it was to be raised. A three-day celebration was held, and everyone was invited. Stan explained that bringing everyone together for this event helped mend long-standing ill feelings.

As we were leaving, Stan invited us to attend the raising of the pole. We felt honored to be asked. Later when we walked down the street to view the other pole, it was the first time we understood the meaning behind the totem. It was a touching experience, and undoubtedly the most beautiful totem we had ever seen.

Southeast entrance (San Christoval Rock buoy R"8" brg 300°T at 0.14 Nm): 55°33.61′ N, 133°17.71′ W

*There are numerous islands, reefs, and shoals with three passages between them, all of which present difficulties for vessels of any size, because of the narrowness of the passages and the strength of the currents. The dangers, mostly marked by kelp in summer, are shown on the charts.* (CP)

In transiting San Christoval Channel, we prefer to use the route along the south side of Larzatita Island, which is marked by mid-channel buoy "SC" and the range marks on Hermanos Islands. Cruising boats should experience few problems. We have found 3 knots of current, but we don't know where the upper limit lies. If you have a low-powered boat, wait for appropriate current.

## **Garcia Cove** (San Fernando Island)

Garcia Cove, at the northwest end of San Fernando Island, is 0.4 mile east of Point Garcia.

Chart 17404
Entrance: 55°33.82′ N, 133°26.02′ W
Anchor: 55°33.28′ N, 133°25.83′ W

*In December 1983, a rock, which bares at low water, was reported in the approach to Garcia Cove. . . . Anchorage with restricted swinging room may be found in 9 fathoms, mud bottom about 150 yards S of the 9-foot rock in the center of the cove.* (CP)

Anchorage with good shelter is reported in 8 fathoms over mud, sand and gravel with fair holding.

## **Aquirre Bay** (San Fernando Island)

Aquirre Bay is just south of Point Aguirre.

Chart 17404
Entrance: 55°33.26′ N, 133°27.59′ W

*Aguirre Bay is an open bight. . . . Rocks awash extend part way across the entrance.* (CP)

## **San Alberto Bay**

San Alberto Bay is east of San Fernando Island.

Chart 17405
Position: 55°30.00′ N, 133°15.01′ W

*San Alberto Bay, with numerous shoals and broken areas, extends about 7 miles N from Bucareli Bay to San Christoval Channel.* (CP)

A marked channel in the southeast part of San Alberto Bay leads to Klawock Inlet and village.

## **Shinaku Inlet** (Prince of Wales Island)

Shinaku Inlet, at the north end of San Alberto Bay, connects with Big Salt Lake and Klawock Inlet.

Chart 17405
West entrance: 55°34.25′ N, 133°12.03′ W
South entrance: 55°32.70′ N, 133°10.51′ W

*The inlet has much foul ground, and the passages leading to Big Salt Lake and Klawock Inlet are only good for small craft with local knowledge.* (CP)

## **Klawock Inlet** (Prince of Wales Island)

Klawock Inlet has the city of Craig at its south entrance and Big Salt Lake at its north end.

Chart 17405
West entrance (buoy G"1" brg 075°T at 0.12 Nm): 55°30.52′ N, 133°11.42′ W
South entrance (Craig Harbor, buoy G"3" brg 326°T at 0.1 Nm): 55°28.34′ N, 133°09.52′ W

*The inlet has two entrances. The entrance from Bucareli Bay is SE of Fish Egg Island; the entrance from San Alberto Bay is N of Fish Egg Island.* (CP)

## **Klawock Harbor** (Prince of Wales Island)

Klawock Harbor is 5 miles north of Craig.

Chart 17405
Entrance: 55°33.51′ N, 133°06.50′ W
Public floats: 55°33.26′ N, 133°06.14′ W

Réanne Hemingway-Douglass

*Public floats at Klawock*

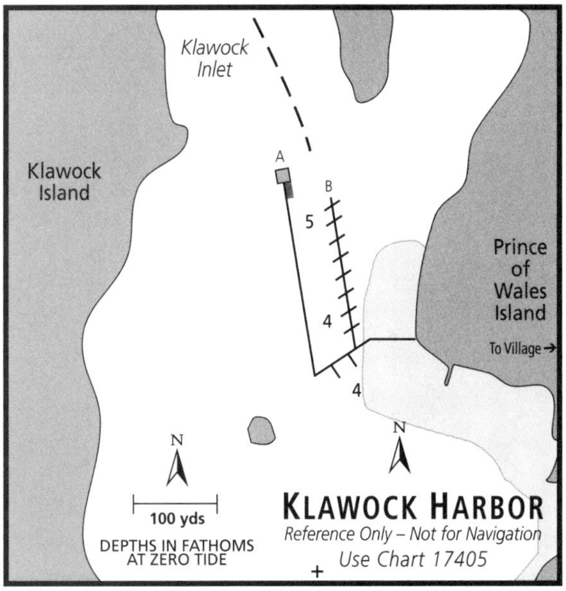




*Klawock Harbor separates Klawock Island from the W shore of Prince of Wales Island.*

*Klawock is a community on the E shore of Klawock Harbor. Two general stores, an airstrip, a sawmill, and a cannery are here.*

*The approach to Klawock Harbor is rocky and narrow. Depths of 3-1/2 to 8 fathoms can be made with local knowledge.*

*A small anchorage is in the bight S of the community. The S end of the anchorage has a high-water pass for canoes to Klawock Inlet.*

*The community of Klawock operates 792 feet of small-craft floats with a seaplane float at the N end of the W float, about 0.2 mile S of Klawock Dock.* (CP)

*They're all upside down!*

Klawock village—the site of Southeast's first cannery established in 1878—has a small park with a remarkable collection of totems. If you do nothing else here, you should take a walk uphill from the harbor to visit the park. The totems, brought from abandoned communities on Prince of Wales Island, are beautiful examples of Northwest art. Some of them are quite unusual.

Klawock Harbor has two public floats with electricity; fuel and water can be obtained at the cannery. Supplies are available at the village store (no alcohol). A paved road connects Klawock to Craig, just seven miles south.

*The totem park at Klawock includes this interesting combination.*

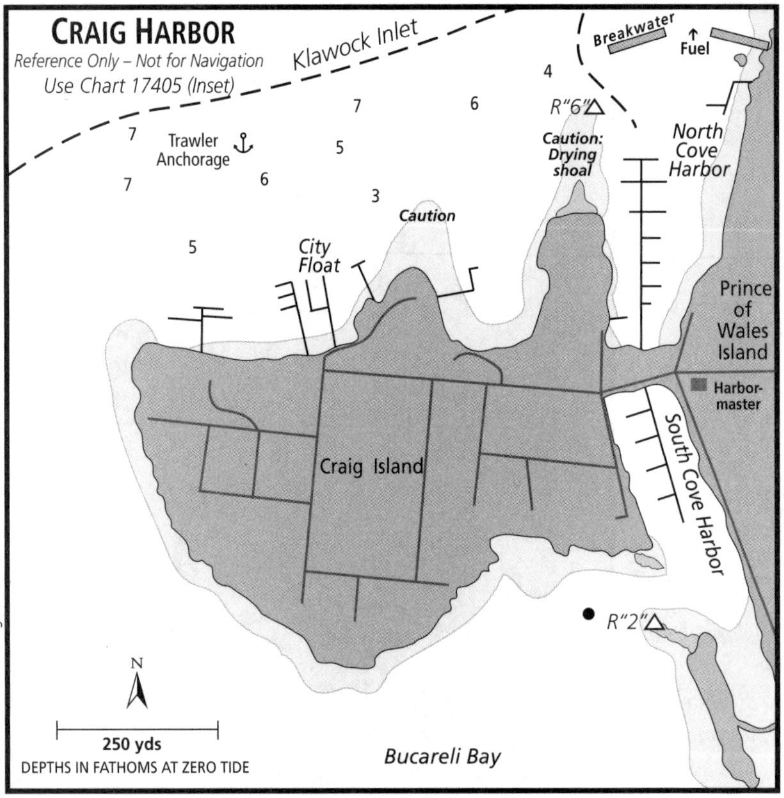




## Craig (Prince of Wales Island)

Craig is 55 miles southeast of Point Baker and 61 miles northwest of Cape Chacon. (Shelter Cove, known locally as South Cove, is on the southeast side of Craig Island.)

Chart 17405 (inset)
Position: (City float): 55°28.69′ N, 133°09.10′ W
Entrance (North Cove): 55°28.90′ N, 133°08.64′ W
Entrance (South Cove): 55°28.42′ N, 133°08.70′ W
Floats (North Cove): 55°28.71′ N, 133°08.64′ W
Floats (South Cove): 55°28.50′ N, 133°08.59′ W

> *Craig is an incorporated settlement on the island at the S end of Klawock Inlet and close SE of Fish Egg Island. . .*
>
> *A Federal project provides for a mooring basin and a 100-foot-wide entrance channel, protected by two breakwaters, in Shelter Cove. . . . The project depth for the entrance channel and basin is 11 feet. In April 2003, the entrance channel had a controlling depth of 9.0 feet (10 feet at midchannel), thence 10.0 feet in the basin except for lesser depths along the edges.*
>
> *The community of Craig operates a small-craft basin and floats at Shelter Cove* [North and South Cove Harbors]. *Water and electricity are available at the floats. . . A depth of 8 feet was reported alongside the floats W of the City Dock. . . Additional public float space is on the W side of North Cove, about 500 yards E of the City Dock. This 1,025 foot float had 14 feet reported alongside in 2002. . . . A seaplane float is on the W side of the Cove W of North Cove.* (CP)

Craig, the largest town on Prince of Wales Island, is the major supply center for the southern end of the island. It is 31 miles by paved road from the ferry terminal at Hollis. The city has expanded its harbor facilities in recent years and welcomes visiting pleasure craft. There are two public marinas—South Cove Harbor and North Cove Harbor—both with power and water. The City Float at the foot of town has room for just 12 boats; it is quite crowded in fishing season and has no water. The town has full services: a marine supply store, cafés and a bank (just above the City

*The breakwater at the north end of North Cove Harbor is a barge, actively used for storage of fishing gear.*

Linda Lewis

*Stay close to the breakwater (far left) and hug the docks as you come into the North Harbor; avoid the drying shoal marked R"6" just to the left of this picture.*

Float). Thompson House Market (a good mile from the City Float, or 1⁄4 mile from South and North Cove Harbors) has film and kitchen supplies, in addition to a nice selection of groceries. With advance notice they will deliver you and your purchases to the harbor. The post office and public telephones are next door to the market, as is the liquor store. You can find good anchorage anywhere in the bay north of Craig Island. *Note:* Most stores close on Sunday; Thompson's and the liquor store are exceptions.

Most transients use the North Cove Harbor. The fuel dock is located outside the North Cove Harbor area, to the north beyond the breakwater. There is a large, drying shoal east

---

## Craig

### Michael Kampnich—Craig Harbormaster

Are you considering a trip to Southeast Alaska by boat? Maybe you're interested in getting a bit off the beaten track and away from the cruise ships? Then you may want to take a look at Craig and the west coast of Prince of Wales Island.

Craig, a community of 1,200 people, is the largest community on Prince of Wales Island. It is home-port and service center to the recreational and local commercial fishing fleet. Craig and the west coast area of POW Island also have much to offer anyone visiting the area, whether by boat or vehicle.

The west coast of Prince of Wales is a boating visitor's paradise. With hundreds of smaller islands scattered along the western shore, opportunities for cruising and exploring the many bays and passages are almost unlimited. Marine wildlife is abundant and viewing opportunities abound.

If you want to tie up and take a break, Craig has three harbors with over 200 slips that can be hot berthed along with designated transient moorage available and all the services expected. Vessels up to 150 feet can be accommodated with advance notice. On the floats you'll find a friendly, accommodating harbor staff. All basic accommodations are available at the harbors. The Craig Harbor Department is staffed seven days a week, year round, and monitors VHF 16 for all harbormaster calls. Shore side services include a laundromat, marine hardware stores, outboard and marine repair facilities, grocery stores, a post office, a library with Internet service for the public, a medical clinic, a dental office, two banks and an ATM, clothing stores, sport fish processing facilities and many other stores and shops that are all located within a 10-minute walk of the harbors.

There are also a number of smaller communities on the island that offer an opportunity to sample some of the different life styles of the island. Klawock, Hydaburg, Thorne Bay, Coffman Cove and Whale Pass are all accessible by road. Vehicle rentals are available in Craig. The native communities of Klawock (the Tlingit tribe) and Hydaburg and Kasaan (the Haida tribes) each have totem parks for interested visitors. Two new totems have been carved by local resident, Stan Marsden. One was raised in the Hydaburg totem park and the other, the Healing Heart Totem Pole, was raised here in Craig. Over the past 15 years a significant number of caves have been discovered in the northwestern area of the island. The Forest Service has daily tours during the summer of one of the most accessible caves, El Capitan. Craig has a number of 4th of July festivities and fireworks the evening of the 3rd., as do many of the communities on the island.

So stop in and see us. We'll meet you on the floats, catch a line and give ya a hand tying up. If you'd like more information give us a call at 907.826.3404 or send us an email at: craighm@aptalaska.net. You can also learn more about Craig at www.craigak.com.

Linda Lewis

*The purse seiner* Misty Moon *works on its net at the dock in Craig.*

and south of R"6." Avoid this hazard by staying close to the docks. Enter the harbor slowly due to limited vision and turning room. This is a tricky spot, so stay alert.

The harbormaster monitors Ch 16 (tel.: 907.826.3404; Website: www.craigak.com).

## **Crab Bay** (Prince of Wales Island)

Crab Bay is immediately northeast of Craig.

Chart 17405
Entrance: 55°28.97′ N, 133°08.48′ W

## **Port Bagial** (Prince of Wales Island)

Port Bagial lies on the east side of Cape Suspiro.

Chart 17405
Entrance: 55°27.59′ N, 133°08.01′ W

> *Port Bagial . . . has depths of 4 to 5 fathoms W of the islands on the E side.* (CP)

### Dolphin Courage
Don Douglass

A pod of dolphins swim in *Baidarka*'s bow wake, cheered on by our boisterous encouragement. One brave soul can't help but hover on either side of our stem, as if testing his nerve. He slows ever so slightly, until he makes gentle contact with our keel. Then, proving his superior control in touching a 50,000-pound bouncing trawler, he speeds off, perpendicular, performing a precision ritual few other dolphins have the courage to try.

Linda Lewis

*Sitting up high on land, this is a fitting landmark for Craig's North Harbor.*

Port Bagial is open to southerly weather.

## **Port St. Nicholas** (Prince of Wales Island)

Port St. Nicholas is 3 miles southeast of Craig.

Chart 17405
Entrance: 55°25.45′ N, 133°06.04′ W
Anchor: 55°27.13′ N, 133°00.66′ W

> *Coronados Islands . . . are midway in the entrance, and rocks and reefs, with two channels between, extend to the N. Rancheria Island is SSW of and close to Point Miraballes, the S point at the entrance to Port St. Nicholas. Dangers are shown on the chart.* (CP)

Port St. Nicholas is reported to provide anchorage near the head of the bay.

Anchor in about 8 fathoms over a soft bottom.

Réanne Hemingway-Douglass

*Craig has a very active fishing fleet.*

## Port Caldera (Prince of Wales Island)

Port Caldera is 6 miles south of Craig.

Chart 17405
Entrance: 55°22.86′ N, 133°10.06′ W
Anchor: 55°21.86′ N, 133°09.68′ W

> *Port Caldera . . . is open to the N. It affords anchorage for small craft. A 6-1/2-fathom spot is in the center near the entrance.* (CP)

Port Caldera is steep-to and useful only in strong southerlies or as a temporary anchorage for one or two small craft.

Anchor in about 10 fathoms over an unknown bottom.

## Doyle Bay (Prince of Wales Island)

Doyle Bay is just south of Port St. Nicholas.

Chart 17405
Position: 55°24.80′ N, 133°02.98′ W

## Trocadero Bay (Big Harbor) (Prince of Wales Island)

Trocadero Bay is 5 miles southeast of Craig.

Chart 17405
Southwest entrance (mid-channel between Point Iphigenia and Madre de Dios Island): 55°23.10′ N, 133°08.98′ W
Northwest entrance (Culebrina Island brg 017°T at 0.45 Nm): 55°24.26′ N, 133°04.93′ W

> *The bay is locally known as Big Harbor. . . . From the head of the bay is an easy portage to Twelvemile Arm, Kasaan Bay, on the E side of Prince of Wales Island. In entering Trocadero Bay, the chart is the guide.* (CP)

Much of Trocadero Bay is a cable area, but good anchorage may be found along the south shore, 0.9 and 1.8 miles from the head of the bay.

We have not made the portage to Kasaan Bay, which follows a 5-mile-long canyon between two 2,000-foot peaks, and have no knowledge of its difficulty.

## Port Estrella (Prince of Wales Island)

Port Estrella is south of San Juan Bautista Island and east of Cape Flores.

Chart 17405
Entrance: 55°21.42′ N, 133°17.00′ W
Anchor: 55°21.20′ N, 133°14.39′ W

> *Anchor near the head of the bay in 7 to 9 fathoms. Caution is necessary on entering, as shoal water makes out from each side of the bay.* (CP)

Port Estrella is reported to offer excellent protection from southerlies, but it is open to prevailing westerlies.

## Bucareli Bay

Bucareli Bay, about 50 miles northwest of Dixon Entrance, extends about 20 miles northeast from its southwest entrance between Cape Bartolome and Cape Felix.

Chart 17400, 17406
Entrance (Cape Bartolome Light brg 280°T at 2.9 Nm): 55°13.48′ N, 133°31.95′ W

> *Baker, St. Ignace, Lulu and San Fernando Islands form* [Bucareli Bay's] *W shore, and Suemez and Prince of Wales Islands form its E shore. The passages between these islands connect the bay*

Linda Lewis

*Shall we turn to port, where it's clear? Or starboard into the fog?*

*with the sea, the Gulf of Esquibel, or Cordova Bay. They are used by small vessels and small craft as a protected route when proceeding along the outer coast between Dixon Entrance and Sumner Strait.* (CP)

## **Cape Bartolome Light** (Baker Island)

Cape Bartolome Light is 14 miles southwest of Port Estrella.

Chart 17406
Position (light brg 000°T at 1.0 Nm): 55°12.84′ N, 133°36.92′ W

*Cape Bartolome Light . . . marks the entrance to Bucareli Bay.* (CP)

## **Fortaleza Bay** (Baker Island)

Fortaleza Bay is on the west side of Bucareli Bay and about 4.5 miles north of Cape Bartolome.

Chart17406
Entrance: 55°17.96′ N, 133°35.52′ W

*Fortaleza Bay . . . is a small open deepwater bight. Lake Fortaleza, with an elevation of about 12 feet, empties into the bay.* (CP)

## **Port San Antonio** (Baker Island)

Port San Antonio is about 2.0 miles north of Fortaleza Bay.

Chart 17406
Entrance (Point San Roque brg 043°T at 0.5 Nm): 55°19.72′ N, 133°33.31′ W
Entrance (north arm): 55°21.41′ N, 133°35.48′ W
Entrance (south arm): 55°21.06′ N, 133°35.93′ W
Anchor (north arm): 55°22.06′ N, 133°35.32′ W
Anchor (south arm): 55°20.14′ N, 133°36.88′ W

*Port San Antonio . . . has two arms at the head. . . . The midchannel is clear, but a shoal with rocks that uncovers 7 feet is about 0.3 mile WSW from Point San Roque, the N point at the entrance. . . . Small craft can find anchorage in the N arm in 5 to 7 fathoms, and in the S arm in 10 fathoms, mud bottom.* (CP)

Port San Antonio has two arms, both surrounded by 2,000-foot peaks, which provide the best shelter on Baker Island for small craft. Williwaws may be present when gales blow outside, but little chop or fetch enters the port. Avoid the dangerous mid-channel rock at the entrance that bares on a 1-foot tide. The north arm has a good, shallow bottom, but the south arm may be better in southeast winds.

Anchor (north arm) in 5 fathoms over mud with fair-to-good holding.

Anchor (south arm) in 10 fathoms over mud with good holding.

## **Port Santa Cruz** (Suemez Island)

Port Santa Cruz is 4.5 miles north of Cape Felix.

Chart 17406
Entrance (Labandera Rock brg 180°T at 0.25 Nm): 55°17.18′ N, 133°27.54′ W
Entrance (Indiada Cove): 55°16.51′ N, 133°27.21′ W
Anchor (Agueda Cove): 55°16.35′ N, 133°25.98′ W
Anchor (head of cove): 55°17.10′ N, 133°24.65′ W

> *Labandera Rock, a kelp-marked submerged rock covered 2-3/4 fathom, is midway between Point Rosary and Point San Jose. . . .*
>
> *In entering, round Point Rosary or Point San Jose at a distance of 0.2 mile and head for the point on the N side of the bay 1 mile inside the entrance. Round this point at a distance of 300 yards and select anchorage as desired in 12 to 17 fathoms, mud bottom. . . . The channel to the N of Labandera Rock is preferable.* (CP)

Small craft can find protection from southeast winds in Agueda Cove or in the head of the cove. Indiada Cove appears to be full of kelp.

Anchor (Agueda Cove) in 6 to 10 fathoms over mud.

Anchor (head of cove) in 15 fathoms over mud.

## **Port Dolores** (Suemez Island)

Port Dolores is 4 miles northwest of Port Santa Cruz.

Chart17406
Entrance: 55°20.21′ N, 133°24.97′ W
Anchor: 55°19.61′ N, 133°23.47′ W

> [Port Dolores] *has generally broken bottom with a rocky reef, about 400 yards in extent, in its center about 0.4 mile inside the entrance. Its use is recommended only for small craft, and they can find anchorage in about 11 fathoms 0.4 mile from the head. The anchorage is exposed to W winds.* (CP)

Note the difference in spelling on the chart and in *Coast Pilot*. Be forewarned: *Dolores* means "much pain" in Spanish.

Anchor 0.4 mile southeast of mid-bay islet in 10 fathoms over mud, sand, gravel with kelp; fair holding if you set your anchor well.

## **Port Asumcion** (Baker Island)

Port Asumcion is about 2.5 miles northeast of Port San Antonio.

Chart 17406
Entrance: 55°21.64′ N, 133°30.13′ W
Anchor: 55°22.32′ N, 133°33.05′ W

> *Port Asumcion . . . offers protected anchorage in 12 to 21 fathoms, sand bottom, near its head. The midchannel is clear.* (CP)

Port Asumcion offers good protection in all weather and is easy to enter. The bay is deep, however.

Anchor in 10 fathoms over sand with fair holding.

## **Port Mayoral** (Baker Island)

Port Mayoral lies between Baker Island and San Ignace Island.

Chart 17406
Entrance (south): 55°23.00′ N, 133°27.13′ W

> *Port Mayoral, the passage between St. Ignace Island and Baker Island, has depths of 6 to 12 fathoms, with irregular bottom. Cristina Island, small and wooded, and a cluster of high-water islets are W of midchannel at the entrance, with a deepwater passage on either side. Foul ground extends 300 yards off the S end of the island and for 550 yards of Canal Point. The N entrance is obstructed by the Santa Rita group is islands between them, and the St. Ignace shore is a narrow channel less than 50 yards wide with a least depth of 3-1/4 fathoms.* (CP)

*Please note:* Port Mayoral, Port Real Marina and Portillo Channel all lie in a wild, west-coast environment between Baker and San Fernando islands. This is an island area of many reefs, rocks and kelp beds. While it may offer excellent exploration and fishing, we can add nothing to Chart 17406 at this time.

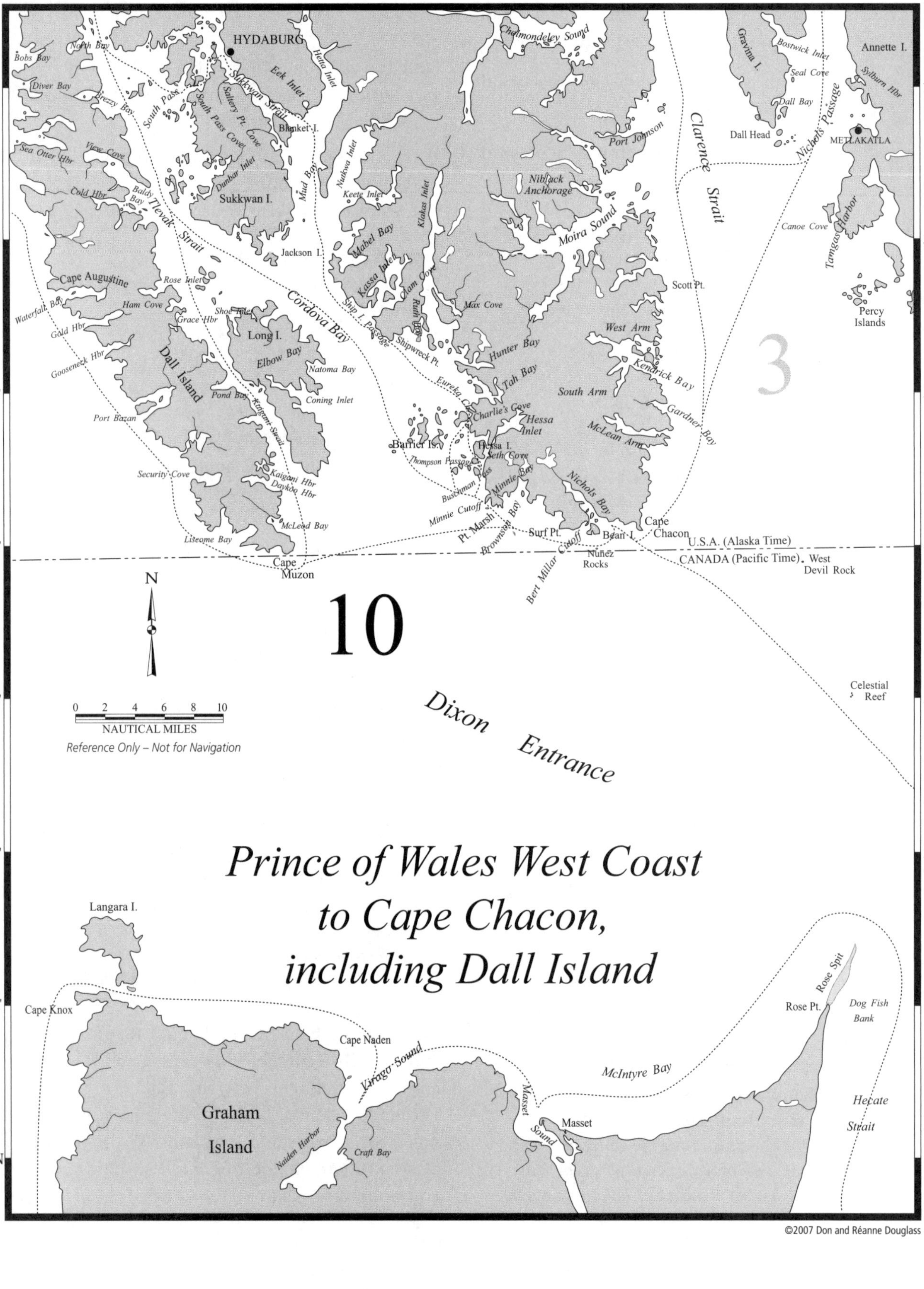
Prince of Wales West Coast
to Cape Chacon,
including Dall Island
10
3
HYDABURG
METLAKATLA
Annette I.
Gravina I.
Bostwick Inlet
Seal Cove
Dall Bay
Dall Head
Sylburn Hbr
Nichols Passage
Tamgas Harbor
Canoe Cove
Percy Islands
Clarence Strait
Cholmondeley Sound
Port Johnson
Niblack Anchorage
Moira Sound
Scott Pt.
West Arm
Kendrick Bay
South Arm
Gardner Bay
McLean Arm
Nichols Bay
Cape Chacon
Bean I.
Nuñez Rocks
West Devil Rock
U.S.A. (Alaska Time)
CANADA (Pacific Time)
Bert Millar Cutoff
Surf Pt.
Brownson Bay
Pt. Marsh
Minnie Cutoff
Minnie Bay
Buschman Pass
Hessa I.
Seth Cove
Hessa Inlet
Charlie's Cove
Thompson Passage
Barrier Is.
Eureka Chan
Tah Bay
Hunter Bay
Max Cove
Ruth Bay
Clam Cove
Shipwreck Pt.
Ship I. Passage
Kassa Inlet
Mabel Bay
Klakas Inlet
Keete Inlet
Nutkwa Inlet
Mud Bay
Hetta Inlet
Eek Inlet
Sukkwan Strait
Blanket I.
Saltery Pt. Cove
South Pass Cove
South Pass
Dunbar Inlet
Sukkwan I.
Jackson I.
Cordova Bay
Long I.
Elbow Bay
Natoma Bay
Coning Inlet
Shoe Inlet
Grace Hbr
Kaigani Strait
Kaigani Hbr
Daykoo Hbr
McLeod Bay
Liscome Bay
Cape Muzon
Pond Bay
Dall Island
Tlevak Strait
Rose Inlet
Cape Augustine
Ham Cove
Waterfall Bay
Gold Hbr
Gooseneck Hbr
Port Bazan
Security Cove
Baldy Bay
Cold Hbr
View Cove
Sea Otter Hbr
Breezy Bay
Diver Bay
Bobs Bay
North Bay
N
0 2 4 6 8 10
NAUTICAL MILES
Reference Only – Not for Navigation
Dixon Entrance
Celestial Reef
Langara I.
Cape Knox
Cape Naden
Virago Sound
Naiden Harbor
Craft Bay
Graham Island
Masset Sound
Masset
McIntyre Bay
Rose Spit
Rose Pt.
Dog Fish Bank
Hecate Strait
10'
55°N
50'
40'
30'
20'
10'
54°N

# 10

# PRINCE OF WALES ISLAND WEST COAST TO CAPE CHACON, INCLUDING DALL ISLAND

## INTRODUCTION

The southwestern tip of Prince of Wales Island, as well as Dall and Long islands, are remote and seldom visited by either pleasure craft or small fishing boats. This is a region you can explore to your heart's content and feel as if you are the first visitor since the early sailing ships encountered the mighty Haida 200 years ago. In many cases, either there are no large-scale charts or the charts are inadequate or inaccurate. You must be skeptical and careful when entering these waters.

The route south of Craig, following the Prince of Wales shore, is a smooth-water route all the way to Point Marsh at the southwest tip of the island, with many islands that afford comfortable and quiet anchor sites for cruising boats. Hydaburg, with its magnificent totems and lovely setting, is a delightful place to visit. South of Hydaburg, you are on your own and should be as self-sufficient as possible. Then, as you round Point Marsh, the open seas of Dixon Entrance predominate. The VHF radio weather repeater at Craig means that you are not quite as isolated from outside contact as previously.

Once you are south of Kassa Point, you enter the South Prince of Wales Wilderness, which preserves, in their wild state, islands and inlets nearly all the way to Bert Millar Cutoff. It is difficult to imagine a more complex and isolated region to explore than that found from Hunter Bay and Hessa Inlet to Little Brownson Bay.

South of Tlevak Strait, the east shore of Dall Island and Kaigani Strait offer exciting waters all the way to Cape Muzon. This raw, undeveloped coastline is worth exploring; however, you

David Parker

*A perfect picture of tranquility*

need to watch for chart inaccuracies. The west coast of Dall Island is exposed to the full fury of the Gulf of Alaska when the winds blow, but in fair summer weather you can find a number of beautiful and sheltered inlets to explore.

So, in the spirit of expeditionary cruising, we offer what information we have found on this delightful area of the southwest corner of Southeast Alaska. We hope that those who visit this coast will help us add to the storehouse of knowledge for future boaters who seek the same beauty and solitude.

## WEST COAST PRINCE OF WALES TO CAPE CHACON

### Ulloa Channel

Ulloa Channel, 10 miles south of Craig, extends 9 miles from Bucareli Bay to Tlevak Narrows.

Chart 17407
North entrance (buoy R"2" bearing 072°T at 0.5 Nm): 55°21.28′ N, 133°18.57′ W
Southeast entrance (buoy R"4" bearing 000°T at 0.13 Nm): 55°15.90′ N, 133°08.18′ W

*The flood current in the channel sets SE, and the ebb NW. . . .*

*Anchorage in 10 to 15 fathoms, soft bottom, near Tlevak Narrows, can be had in Ulloa Channel, at the entrance to a small passage that is on the NW side of the largest island N of Ulloa Island, between it and the main shore of Prince of Wales Island.* (CP)

Ulloa Channel is the smooth-water route connecting Klawock and the Craig area to the cruising grounds of Hydaburg, Tlevak Strait, and Cordova Bay to the south.

### Adrian Cove (Suemez Island)

Adrian Cove is 11 miles southwest of Craig.

Chart 17407
Entrance: 55°20.21′ N, 133°18.77′ W

*Adrian Cove . . . is open to N and is of no importance.* (CP)

Adrian Cove offers temporary shelter tucked in close to shore in southeast winds. Port Refugio offers complete protection and is generally recommended because it has more swinging room.

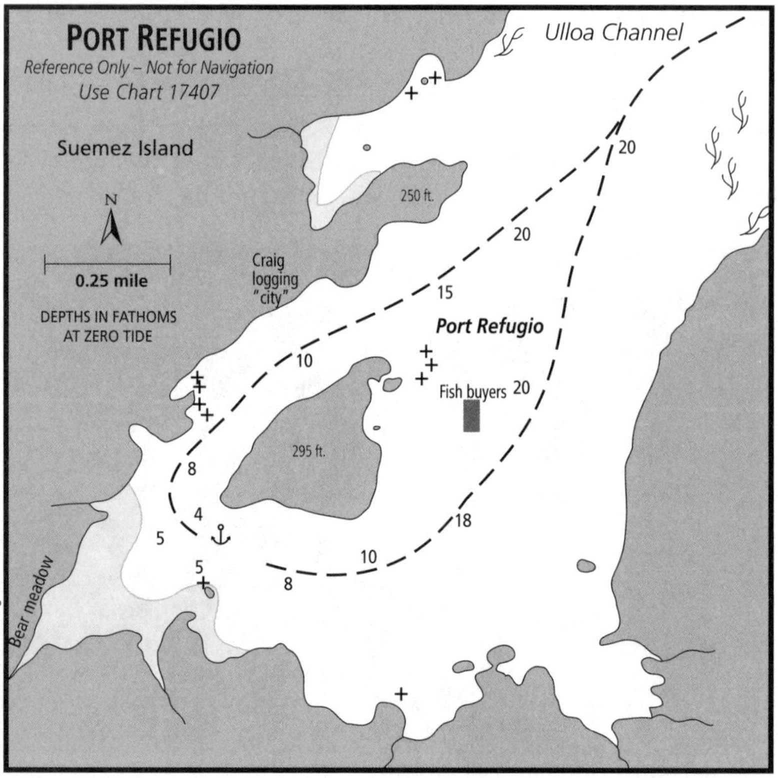




### Port Refugio (Suemez Island)

Port Refugio, on the west side of Ulloa Channel, is opposite Waterfall.

Chart 17407
Entrance: 55°18.01′ N, 133°17.90′ W
Anchor: 55°16.91′ N, 133°19.77′ W

*Port Refugio is a large bay, with two arms. . . . Its SE arm, inside of Bocas Point, is 1 mile long and about 0.2 mile wide, and near its head affords anchorage for small craft in about 12 fathoms.* (CP)

Excellent shelter from all weather can be found behind the island at the head of the bay. Large fish-buying vessels use the bay during the season, and floating logging communities sometimes moor here to harvest timber on Suemez Island.

This is a good place to watch black bear that comb the tidal flats along the stream at the head of the bay.

Anchor in 5 fathoms over mud and gravel with fair-to-good holding.

## Waterfall (Prince of Wales Island)

Waterfall is 11.5 miles south of Craig.

Chart 17407
Entrance: 55°18.26′ N, 133°14.86′ W

> *Waterfall . . . is the site of a fishing resort. Vessels waiting for berthage at Waterfall can find temporary anchorage in 61/2 to 10 fathoms, rocky bottom, on a shoal about 0.3 mile NW of the fishing resort. . . . Gasoline, diesel fuel, and water are available at the main dock. A nearby store sells limited supplies and provisions. A seaplane and a small-craft float are close N of the main dock.* (CP)

Waterfall is a busy resort that is not set up to accommodate cruising boats.

## Tlevak Narrows (The Skookum Chuck)

Tlevak Narrows, The Skookum Chuck, is 13 miles south of Craig and joins Ulloa Channel and Tlevak Strait.

Chart 17407
North entrance (Dall Island): 55°16.02′ N, 133°07.59′ W
South entrance (Lively Island Light bearing 000°T at 0.6 Nm): 55°13.11′ N, 133°05.11′ W

> *Tlevak Narrows, locally known as The Skookum Chuck, is a narrow and comparatively deep passage. . . . A 1/2-fathom shoal 0.4 mile NW of Turn Point is marked on its S side by a buoy that is reported to tow under during large tides. The channel S of the buoy is the one generally used. Currents in the vicinity of Tlevak Narrows run*

### Paralytic Shellfish Poisoning

Amanda Swan-Neal

Paralytic Shellfish Poisoning is one malady no boater needs to get. Eating personally-harvested shellfish can be a risky business. In Alaska, microscopic single-celled dinoflagellate algae produce toxins, which are a main source of food for the shellfish. Paralytic Shellfish Poisoning (PSP) results from these toxins that accumulate in algae-eating clams, mussels, oysters, scallops, and whelks. The toxins are then consumed by humans in life-threatening concentrations. PSP episodes in Alaska tend to be seasonal and occur most often during late spring or summer, although they can occur year around.

Symptoms of PSP include tingling and numbness that starts around the lips and mouth and spreads to the face and neck. Prickly sensations occur in the fingertips and toes and are accompanied with headache and dizziness. Muscle weakness, nausea and vomiting can also occur. Severe poisoning can produce tingling or burning in the arms and legs, incoherent speech, lack of coordination and breathing difficulties.

When you suspect that someone has PSP, you should seek immediate medical attention. There is no antidote for PSP.

To reduce your risk of getting PSP, you should not eat self-harvested shellfish but purchase it from a reputable seafood retailer or shellfish farm that is required to sell only tested products. Cooking does not eliminate PSP from shellfish because these toxins are heat stable.

Even when pressure cooked at a temperature of 250° F for 15 minutes, PSP remains toxic.

You should listen regularly for local PSP alerts on the weather channel. If you consider harvesting shellfish, you should, at a minimum, take into account: the recent history of PSP in the area; the species harvested and their ability to concentrate and retain toxin; the season of the year; the method of cleaning and preparing the shellfish. You should also be aware that water color is not a reliable indicator of PSP. Just because red tide is not present does not mean absence of danger.

Do not under estimate the seriousness of PSP. Once you suspect PSP, induce vomiting by sticking a finger down the victim's throat, by having him drink warm salt water or take Syrup of Ipecac to expel shellfish from the stomach. Treat for shock and transport the victim as quickly as possible to a medical facility. Life support services may be necessary to sustain the victim's life. Once treated, the reduction of symptoms usually occurs within nine hours, with complete recovery within 24 hours.

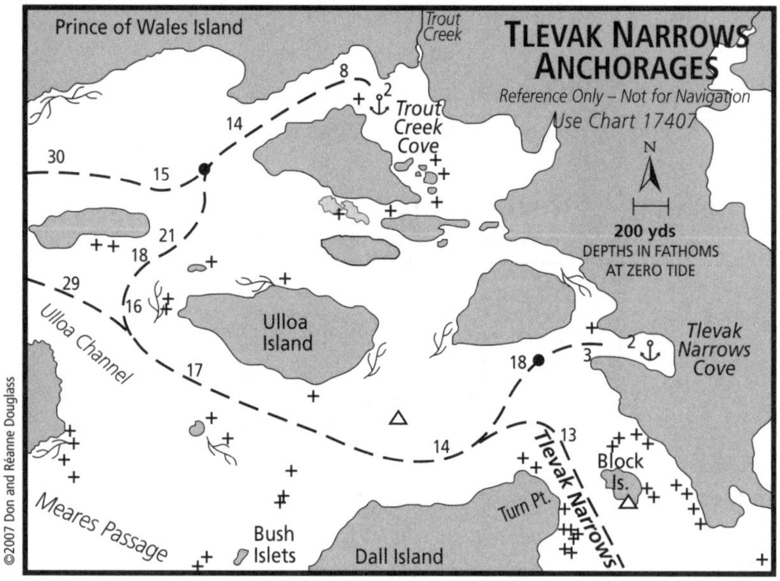


*very strong during large tides; in the narrowest part the velocity is over 4 knots.* (CP)

Tlevak Narrows runs at well over 5 knots at spring tides, with significant rips; flood currents flow east.

## Tlevak Narrows Anchorages

(Prince of Wales Island)

Tlevak Narrows Anchorages are 1 mile north of the north entrance of Tlevak Narrows.

**Chart 17407**
**Entrance (Trout Creek Cove): 55°16.78′ N, 133°09.33′ W**
**Anchor (Trout Creek Cove): 55°16.95′ N, 133°08.37′ W**
**Entrance (Tlevak Narrows Cove): 55°16.20′ N, 133°07.38′ W**
**Anchor (Tlevak Narrows Cove): 55°16.22′ N, 133°06.82′ W**

*Good anchorage for small craft can be had in 3-1/4 fathoms, soft bottom, in the small cove on the N side of Tlevak Narrows; the entrance to it is about 0.5 mile N of Turn Point.* (CP)

Tlevak Narrows anchorages are well-sheltered coves out of the current of the narrows. Both coves are quiet with good trout fishing in the creek on the north shore. If you should dredge up a nice rubber bucket here, with a yellow nylon strap attached, please return it to the rightful owners. We miss it.

Anchor (Trout Creek Cove) in 1-1/2 fathoms over sand and mud with very good holding.

Anchor (Tlevak Narrows Cove) in 3 fathoms over sand with good holding.

## Soda Bay

(Prince of Wales Island)

Soda Bay is 2 miles east of Tlevak Narrows.

**Chart 17407**
**Entrance: 55°14.55′ N, 133°02.73′ W**
**Anchor (inner basin): 55°16.59′ N, 132°55.75′ W**

*Anchorage can be found in Soda Bay about 0.5 mile E of Shelikof Island in about 20 fathoms, mud and shell bottom. The low surrounding land offers little protection from the wind.* (CP)

Soda Bay, a large bay tucked in behind Shelikof Island, is out of both the current and chop. The

*The* Coast Pilot *notes that this buoy (R"4") in Tlevak Narrows tows under during large tides.*

half-mile-long inner basin is particularly safe and sheltered and has a large flat, shallow and sandy bottom. The basin has a complex entrance with about 5 fathoms carried through the narrow fairway channel. Two mini-coves are also west of the basin on the south shore. *Caution:* Avoid isolated rocks throughout the bay and survey the anchor site to verify that you have adequate swinging room.

Anchor in 3 fathoms over sand and mud and some gravel with fair holding.

Don Douglass

*Réanne admiring a boat builder's work in Hydaburg*

## North Pass

North Pass is 4 miles west of Hydaburg.

Chart 17407
Southwest entrance (Goat Island): 55°12.35′ N, 132°56.74′ W
East entrance (Goat Island): 55°13.70′ N, 132°52.49′ W

> *North Pass . . . is navigable by shallow draft vessels at high-water slack with local knowledge. Numerous rocks and reefs must be passed close aboard until clear of North Pass to the W. Tidal currents are estimated at 3 to 4 knots. Surveys indicate a least depth of 1/2 fathom at the shallowest point of the pass.* (CP)

North Pass is an intricate waterway connecting North Tlevak Strait to Natzuhini Bay and Hydaburg. South Pass has fewer restrictions and is the recommended route to Hydaburg.

## Natzuhini Bay (Prince of Wales Island)

Natzuhini Bay is 3 miles north of Hydaburg.

Chart 17407
Position: 55°15.42′ N, 132°50.88′ W

> *Natzuhini Bay, N of Hydaburg and Sukkwan Narrows, is navigable for large fishing vessels. However, strangers should not attempt it because of the many reefs and shoals in it and the lack of aids to navigation.* (CP)

Natzuhini Bay is a large, landlocked rock pile better explored by kayak or dinghy.

## Goat Mouth Inlet (Goat Island)

Goat Mouth Inlet is north of the west entrance to South Pass.

Chart 17407
Entrance: 55°10.11′ N, 132°54.23′ W
Anchor: 55°11.43′ N, 132°53.90′ W

Goat Mouth Inlet appears to offer reasonable shelter at its head in fair weather but is partially exposed to southerly weather.

Anchor (deep in the inlet) in 8 to 10 fathoms over a mud bottom.

## South Pass

South Pass extends 3.5 miles northeast from Tlevak Strait to Sukkwan Narrows.

Chart 17407
West entrance: 55°10.07′ N, 132°53.84′ W
East entrance (at Sukkwan Narrows): 55°12.22′ N, 132°50.20′ W

> *South Pass . . . has good depths in the middle of a channel that has many turns between islands, islets, and rocks.* (CP)

South Pass is the standard route to and from Hydaburg. Many small anchor sites can be found on the east side of Goat Island. *Caution:*

As you transit this rocky, narrow passage, be extremely vigilant. Keep buoys R"2" and R"4" to starboard as you make a northbound passage through South Pass to Hydaburg.

*Looking west from Hydaburg towards Sukkwan Narrows, which has a 13-foot depth at zero tide; check your tide tables and proceed carefully through here.*

## South Pass Cove
(Sukkwan Island)

South Pass Cove is 1 mile east of the west entrance to South Pass.

**Chart 17407**
**Anchor: 55°10.00′ N, 132°52.27′ W**

> *Small craft can find good anchorage in South Pass in the small bay on the SE side, about 2.4 miles SSW of Sukkwan Narrows.* (CP)

South Pass Cove offers good shelter as shown in the diagram. Tucked in near the south shore, you avoid the back eddy that flows clockwise, outside, on flood currents. There is a small landing beach on the south shore and a canoe pass to the west.

Anchor in 4 fathoms over sand, gravel and kelp with fair holding.

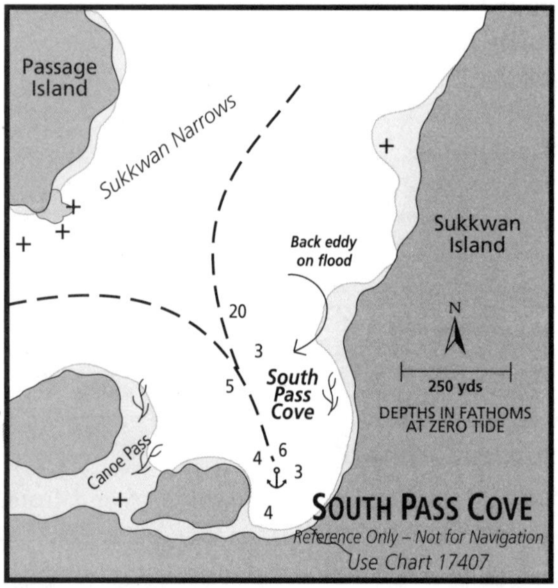


## Hydaburg (Prince of Wales Island)

Hydaburg is 19 miles southeast of Craig.

**Chart 17407**
**Public floats: 55°12.68′ N, 132°49.79′ W**

> *Hydaburg is an incorporated Native American village. . . . The village has an airport, a post office, school, and church.*
>
> *A small-craft basin . . . provide[s] about 160 berthing spaces. In 2002, depths of 15 to 25 feet*

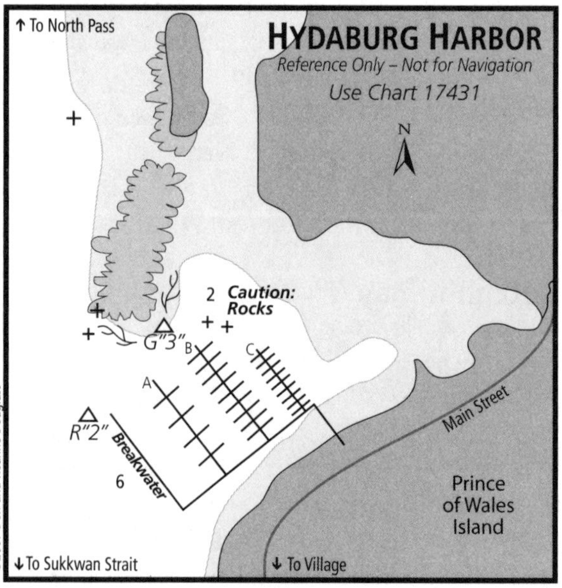

Réanne Hemingway-Douglass

*Artistic expertise seen in a Hydaburg totem*

*were reported alongside. Water and electricity are available at some of the floats. A 100-foot by 39-foot grid is inshore of the floats.* (CP)

Hydaburg, the main native Haida settlement of in Southeast, is connected by road to Craig and the ferry terminal at Hollis. Facilities for cruising boats are few, but the village warrants a stop—particularly when the salmon are running. From the dock you can watch the residents bringing in their subsistence catches and filleting them to smoke for their winter food stock. From the bridge over Hydaburg River, you can look down upon swarms of salmon fighting to head upstream to their spawning grounds, and you can watch schoolchildren dropping lines along the river's edge to snag fish.

Above the floats there is a fine stand of old and well-cared-for totems, perhaps the best designs we've seen anywhere. A small store about 1/2 mile south of the harbor has limited supplies. In 2005, the floats in the harbor were

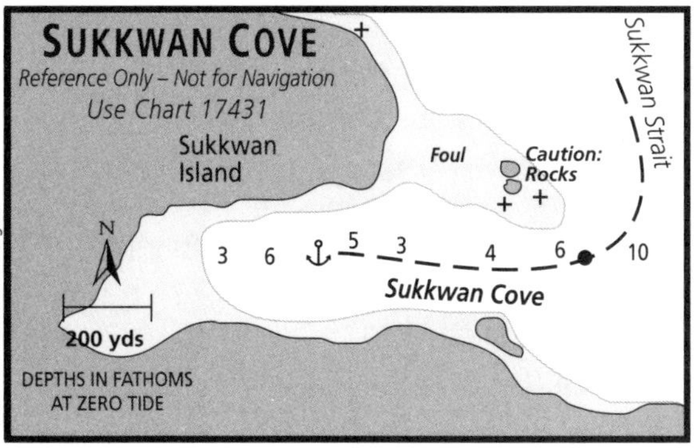

©2007 Don and Réanne Douglass

not being maintained and were a bit hazardous, and a few derelict boats were almost sinking in their slips. Fuel is not available and we recommend against taking on water at the floats. There are two pay telephones in town, one at the south side of the bridge, the other above the store at the foot of a microwave antenna.

## Sukkwan Strait

Sukkwan Strait extends 7 miles southeast from Hydaburg.

**Chart 17431**
**North entrance: 55°12.22′ N, 132°50.20′ W**
**Southeast entrance: 55°07.87′ N, 132°40.61′ W**

*Sukkwan Strait has its SE entrance between Eek Point on the NE and Round Point, the E extremity of Blanket Island, on the SW. . . . It has good depths and few dangers and is entered by vessels of considerable size as far as the village of Hydaburg.* (CP)

Sukkwan Strait connects Hydaburg to Cordova Bay to the south.

## Sukkwan Cove (Sukkwan Island)

Sukkwan Cove is 2.2 miles south of Hydaburg.

**Chart 17431**
**Entrance: 55°10.55′ N, 132°48.53′ W**
**Anchor: 55°10.56′ N, 132°49.14′ W**

"Sukkwan Cove" is what we call the unnamed cove on the northeast corner of Sukkwan Island, west of Saltery Point. The cove offers fair protection in southeast winds and very good protection in all other winds.

Entry is easy, but the shoal at the north entrance, which has several rocks, extends a quarter-mile out. Although the bay may be full of crab pot floats, it is shallow and has good swinging room.

Anchor in 4 fathoms over mud with good holding.

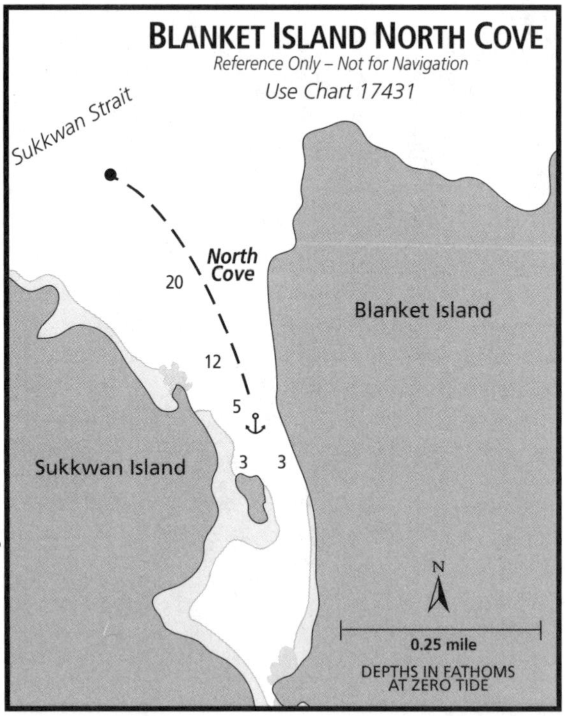


## **Blanket Island North Cove** (Blanket Island)

Blanket Island North Cove is on the north side of Blanket Island.

Chart 17431
Entrance: 55°08.53′ N, 132°44.23′ W
Anchor: 55°08.12′ N, 132°43.98′ W

You can find anchorage in what we call "Blanket Island North Cove." To avoid a southerly chop in Hetta Inlet, duck into the cove where it narrows just north of the first islet. The narrow passage is peaceful and fun to explore by kayak.

Anchor in 2 to 4 fathoms over sand, pebbles, shells and kelp with poor-to-fair holding.

## **Hetta Inlet** (Prince of Wales Island)

Hetta Inlet extends 5 miles north from Lime Point to the entrance of Sukkwan Strait, then 11 miles to Gould Island.

Chart 17431
Entrance (Lime Point bearing 090°T at 0.6 Nm): 55°03.24′ N, 132°39.22′ W

> *Considerable fishing for salmon is done in the inlet in season, and boats may be found in all of its parts.* (CP)

Hetta Inlet is the site of a number of abandoned mining operations; we prefer to anchor in Eek Inlet, at its south end.

At the head of Hetta Inlet (11 miles away), Gould Island nearly closes the inlet. However, you can pass through Sulzer Passage to get to Portage Bay–a spot not to be missed. See further description below under Sulzer Passage and Gould Passage and under Portage Bay.

Baidarka *and friend cruising past Hydaburg*

## **Eek Inlet** (Hetta Inlet)

Eek Inlet is 0.6 mile north of Eek Point.

Chart 17431
Entrance: 55°08.72′ N, 132°39.24′ W
Anchor: 55°09.17′ N, 132°39.69′ W

> *Eek Inlet . . . may be used by fishermen with local knowledge. A midchannel course leads to an anchorage in 8 fathoms, midway in the inlet, about 0.3 mile NW of the narrow entrance.* (CP)

Despite it name, Eek Inlet offers good protection from all weather and is conveniently located at Hetta Inlet north of Cordova Bay. The inner basin on the east side is the best anchorage.

Enter Eek Inlet by passing east of the island and its off-lying rock, a half-mile east of Eek Point, as indicated in the diagram. This can be done carefully by radar if necessary.

Anchor in 5 fathoms over sand and gravel with fair holding.

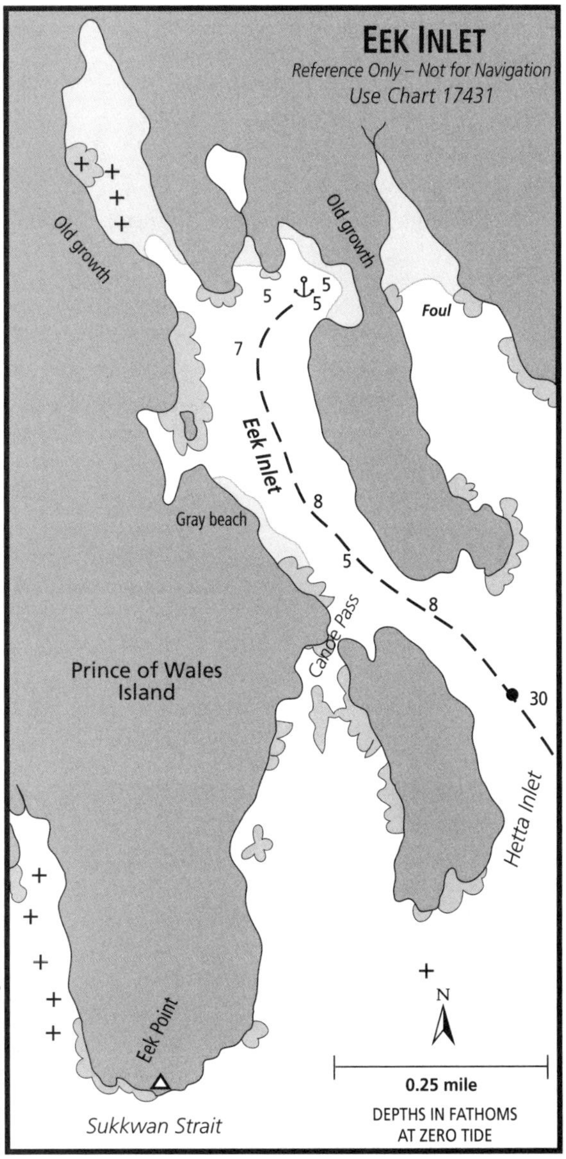

Linda Lewis

*Local fishermen sometimes run their nets almost all the way across the fairway in places like Eek Inlet.*

## Mud Bay (Hetta Inlet)

Mud Bay is 2 miles north of Lime Point.

Chart 17431
Entrance: 55°05.15′ N, 132°38.14′ W
Anchor: 55°04.91′ N, 132°37.86′ W

> *Mud Bay . . . is used extensively for anchorage during the fishing season. The anchorage has a depth of 4 to 10 fathoms with mud bottom.* (CP)

We have a problem with *Coast Pilot* on this one—the name Mud Bay seems like someone's joke. We tried the bottom in several places and found it only hard and rocky; in addition, it is deep and steep-to. The anchorage offers protection from southerly winds only; anchor, if you must, just east of the small islet.

Anchor in 6 to 10 fathoms over a hard, rocky bottom with poor-to-fair holding. Better yet, head for Mabel Bay.

## Alder Cove (Hetta Inlet)

Alder Cove is 1 mile north of Mud Bay.

Chart 17431
Entrance: 55°06.09′ N, 132°37.70′ W

> *Alder Cove . . . is used by small craft for anchorage in 4 to 8 fathoms, mud bottom, during the fishing season. The cove has no known dangers.* (CP)

Alder Cove looks deep and very steep-to to us. Take care!

Linda Lewis

*Hiking the trail made smooth by the game in Hetta Cove; don't forget to make noise to keep the bears away (clap, sing, whistle).*

## **Hetta Cove** (Hetta Inlet)

Hetta Cove is 3 miles northeast of Eek Inlet.

Chart 17431
Entrance: 55°10.16′ N, 132°35.41′ W

> *The cove E of the point* [Hetta Point] *affords anchorage for small craft having local knowledge of the area. The cove has numerous reefs and shoal soundings.* (CP)

Hetta cove has an inner basin that looks secure, but we have no further knowledge to add about anchoring here. However, cruisers report to us the hiking is wonderful following the game trails or bushwhacking along the stream to Hetta Lake above the cove.

Linda Lewis

*Coming upon this utterly beautiful scene took a lot of bushwhacking effort, as the hikers made their way towards Hetta Lake.*

## **Copper Harbor** (Hetta Inlet)

Copper Harbor is 4 miles northeast of Eek Inlet.

Chart 17431
Entrance: 55°12.56′ N, 132°37.89′ W

> *A midchannel course leads to the head of the harbor, where there is anchorage in 10 to 20 fathoms.* (CP)

Copper Harbor looks a little deep for convenient anchorage, but a shoal may be found off one of the creeks at the head of the bay.

## **Deer Bay** (Hetta Inlet)

Deer Bay is 2 miles northwest of Copper Harbor.

Chart 17431
Entrance: 55°14.06′ N, 132°40.55′ W
Anchor: 55°14.41′ N, 132°41.19′ W

> *Deer Bay . . . affords good anchorage in 5 to 16 fathoms; the midchannel course is clear.* (CP)

Deer Bay, on the west shore of Hetta Inlet, is a good place to anchor while exploring the bit-

Linda Lewis

*Two deer swimming across the bow as if to greet these cruisers in Deer Bay*

*Climbing out on the other side*

*One last look back to check on the visitors*

ter end of the inlet and Portage Bay. The M/V *Royal Sounder* found the bay to be true to its name. During their approach, two deer swam across the mouth of the bay as if they were official greeters.

Anchor in about 5 fathoms over mud and gravel with fair holding.

## Sulzer Passage and Gould Passage (Hetta Inlet)

Sulzer Passage is north of Gould Island; Gould Passage is south of Gould Island.

Chart 17431
West entrance (Sulzer Passage): 55°17.03′ N, 132°37.68′ W
East entrance (Sulzer Passage): 55°17.00′ N, 132°35.46′ W

> *Sulzer Passage . . . is navigable for small craft, but foul for 1 mile above the entrance, and the tidal currents have considerable velocity. It should be navigated only by those having thorough local knowledge.*
>
> *Gould Island practically closes the inlet for a distance of about 1.4 miles. Gould Passage . . . runs dry at about half tide and should not be attempted at any stage of the tide as a through passage into Portage Bay because of tidal currents and numerous rocks and dangers at the E end of the passage.* (CP)

## Portage Bay (Hetta Inlet)

Portage Bay is the area north of Gould Island.

Chart 17431
Position: 55°16.80′ N, 132°33.76′ W

> *Portage Bay . . . is about 1.5 miles long, with depths of 9 to 27 fathoms. A trail leads from its head to the head of Cholmondeley Sound, about 2.8 miles.* (CP)

Portage Bay must be carefully entered via Sulzer Passage, as noted in the *Coast Pilot.*

*Portage Bay—at the head of Hetta Inlet*

*Looking through crystal clear water to see lots of salmon only inches away*

David Parker

*A wolf print in Portage Bay*

Linda Lewis

*This entrance to the lagoon at Nutkwa Inlet needs to be transited only at high water slack, by shallow-draft boats.*

We have no local knowledge about anchoring here.

Prince of Wales Island is nearly cut in half by two deep inlets at this point. An old skid road that at one time supplied all the abandoned mill sites along this coast leads across 2.5 miles to the east side of Prince of Wales in the west arm of Cholmondeley Sound.

Cruisers using our book dinghied from their anchorage in nearby Deer Bay to Portage Bay to look for the remains of the skid road we report—but could not find it. What they did find, however, was wonderful broad vistas, a crystal clear mountain stream filled with fish, and animal prints in the mud. "Pristine" was the word they used for this fascinating place.

Linda Lewis

*The anchorage at Nutkwa Inlet*

## **Nutkwa Inlet** (Prince of Wales Island)

Nutkwa Inlet, at the head of Cordova Bay east of Lime Point, is 4.5 miles north of Point Webster.

**Chart 17431**

**Entrance: 55°02.55′ N, 132°36.58′ W**

> *Nutkwa Inlet . . . is 1.5 miles wide at the entrance and extends about 5 miles NNE.*
>
> *Nutkwa Falls, at the head of Nutkwa Inlet, obstructs passage into the lagoon; on the higher water slacks, drafts of 3 or 4 feet can be carried into the lagoon, but this passage should not be attempted without local knowledge.* (CP)

Nutkwa Inlet, and its 3-mile-long lagoon, are ripe for exploration. It appears that temporary anchorage can be found out of the current at the head of the inlet west of the falls.

## **Keete Inlet** (Prince of Wales Island)

Keete Inlet is entered 2.5 miles east of Lime Point.

**Chart 17431**

**Entrance: 55°03.36′ N, 132°33.35′ W**

> *Keete Inlet . . . has depths of more than 10 fathoms throughout, except for several scattered shoal spots with depths of 4 to 8 fathoms. . . . Good anchorage in 20 fathoms, mud bottom, can be had S of the small island at the bend in the inlet.* (CP)

The east shore or the bitter end of Keete Inlet looks promising for anchor sites. If you want more shallow water, our preference is Mabel Bay, 4 miles to the south.

## **Hassiah Inlet** (Prince of Wales Island)

Hassiah Inlet lies on the east side of Cordova Bay.

Chart 17431
Entrance: 55°00.65′ N, 132°36.10′ W

> *Hassiah Inlet . . . is about 2 miles long to the head of its NE and E arms; the latter is a landlocked anchorage known as Mabel Bay.* (CP)

We prefer to anchor in the south basin of Mabel Bay.

## **Mabel Bay** (Hassiah Inlet)

Mabel Bay is 16 miles southeast of Hydaburg.

Chart 17431
West entrance: 54°59.73′ N, 132°36.86′ W
North entrance: 54°59.98′ N, 132°35.12′ W
Anchor (south basin): 54°58.36′ N, 132°35.56′ W
Anchor (east basin): 54°59.10′ N, 132°33.12′ W

> *To enter Mabel Bay pass N and E of Mabel Island, giving it a berth of 0.2 mile, and steer for the E end of Helen Island. Follow a careful midchannel course, passing NE of Helen Island, and anchor about 0.3 mile from the islet at the head in 10 to 12 fathoms.* (CP)

Scenic and landlocked, Mabel Bay offers excellent southerly protection. You can choose

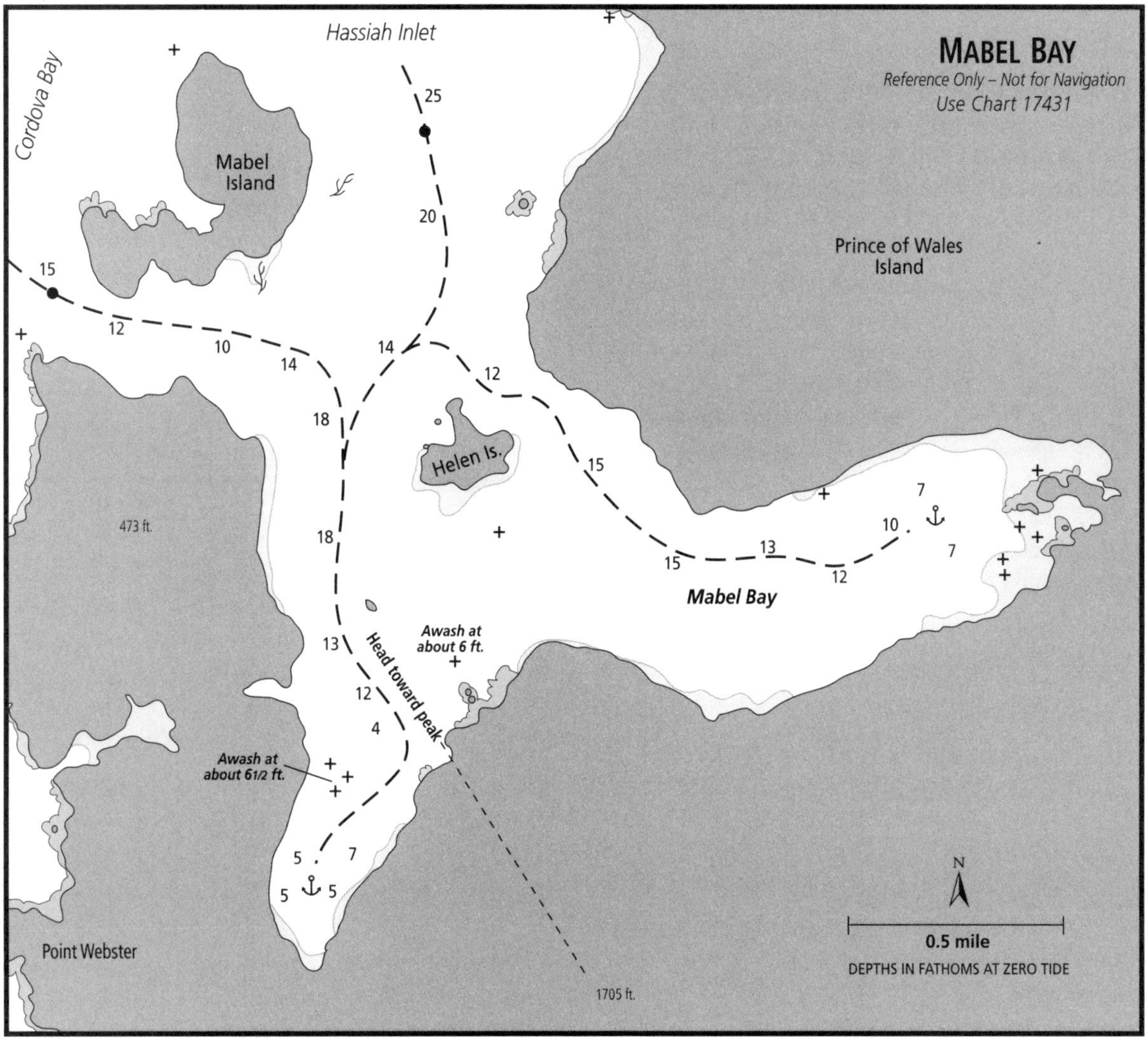

between the east basin, which is slightly easier to enter, or the southern basin (avoid the rocky shoal off the west shore). In a southeast storm, the wind may whistle across the trees in the southern basin, but it's a snug anchorage with plenty of swinging room.

A giant 40-foot white cross is located on the coast outside of Mabel Bay, southeast of Point Webster and just north of Abalone Island.

Anchor (south basin) in 5 fathoms over a mixed bottom with fair-to-good holding.

Anchor (east basin) in 7 fathoms over a mixed bottom with fair-to-good holding.

## Cordova Bay

Cordova Bay extends from Lime Point to the northwest side of Dixon Entrance.

**Chart 17400**
**North entrance (Mellen Rock Light bearing 270°T at 1.0 Nm): 55°01.59′ N, 132°38.13′ W**
**South entrance (Cape Muzon Light bearing 253°T at 5.5 Nm and Point Marsh bearing 082° at 8.5 Nm): 54°43.18′ N, 132°33.62′ W**

*The best* [south] *entrance to the bay is between Barrier Islands and Long Island, but Eureka Channel, E of Barrier Islands, is sometimes used by vessels with local knowledge. . . . Small craft ply from Ketchikan to Cordova Bay, Hetta Inlet, and other points on the W coast of Prince of Wales Island.*

*The E side of the* [south] *entrance to Cordova Bay, from Point Marsh to Shipwreck Point, is very broken and abounds with islands, reefs, shoals, and pinnacles in random pattern. . . . Currents and eddies about the islands, large tides, and exposure to ocean swells make the running of straight courses difficult.* (CP)

Since Cordova Bay is open to the southeast, gales that blow with full force can create nasty chop.

## Dova Bay (Long Island)

Dova Bay is 2 miles northwest of Elbow Bay and 6 miles west of Kassa Inlet.

**Chart 17431**
**Entrance: 54°55.74′ N, 132°42.27′ W**

*Dova Bay . . . appears to be well protected at its head, but because of the configuration of the surrounding hills, SE and NW winds draw across it with considerable force.* (CP)

Dova Bay is deep and steep-to with a rocky bottom. We would recommend staying in Elbow Bay.

## Elbow Bay (Long Island)

Elbow Bay is 4.5 miles west of Kassa Inlet.

**Chart 17431**
**Entrance: 54°54.41′ N, 132°39.02′ W**
**Anchor (southeast arm): 54°53.79′ N, 132°39.15′ W**

*Good anchorage for small vessels can be had in the SE arm in 13 fathoms, mud bottom. The anchorage is about 250 yards wide. A large lagoon extends S from the W end of the bay, where it is connected by a narrow rocky channel. Rapids make this channel impassable except at high water.*

*To enter Elbow Bay, pass in midchannel SE of the wooded islets in the entrance and avoid the reefs making off to S of the islets. The submerged rock in the middle of the bay can be passed on either side; the W side has the best water.* (CP)

Elbow Bay offers very good shelter, deep in the largely landlocked bay. The entrance islands and reef off the north entrance point

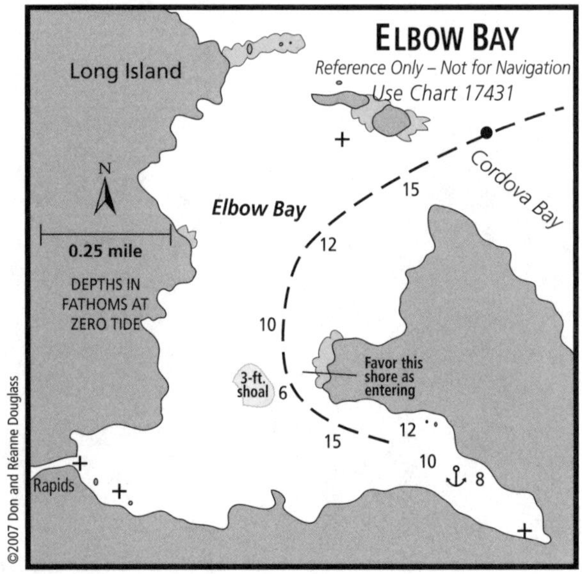

act as a natural breakwater in northerly winds. The south peninsula provides complete shelter from southeast chop sometimes found in Cordova Bay. The lagoon and tidal rapids on the west shore provide a dynamic display of natural forces at work.

Long Island was once home to some of the largest cedars in Southeast Alaska. They are now a thing of the past as the clear cutting of Long Island is essentially complete.

Linda Lewis

*A rare, close encounter with Alaska's commanding eagle*

Favor the south entrance point as you enter, and avoid the 3-foot shoal in the middle of the bay. Anchor deep in the southeast arm. The depths in Elbow Bay are somewhat irregular, and the bottom may be rocky with kelp in many places, so set your anchor well.

Anchor in 8 to 10 fathoms over a mixed bottom with fair-to-good holding.

### **Natoma Bay** (Long Island)

Natoma Bay is 3 miles south of Elbow Bay.

Chart 17409
Entrance: 54°51.01′ N, 132°37.10′ W
Anchor: 54°52.27′ N, 132°38.02′ W

> *Natoma Bay . . . is about 1 mile in diameter and open to E and SE. Partially protected anchorage can be had in the N part of the bay in 11 to 20 fathoms, mud bottom. . . . A 5-1/4-fathom shoal is about 0.6 mile NW of the islets* [in the middle of the entrance]. *The shores of the bay are foul and should be given a good berth.* (CP)

Natoma Bay is a good lee when strong north-

## Bald Eagles

**Is the bald eagle still an endangered species?**

**Herb Nickles, Certified Alaska Naturalist**

Claims by fox farmers and fishermen of marauding eagles caused the Alaska Territorial Legislature in 1917 to impose a bounty on eagles. These claims were later found to be mainly false, but over 100,000 eagles were killed before the bounty was removed in 1953. However, the bald eagle's decline during the past half century was primarily due to reproductive failure caused by pesticides, such as DDT. Habitat destruction also contributed to shrinking populations in the Lower 48 states.

With statehood in 1959, the bald eagle in Alaska received federal protection under the Bald Eagle Protection Act of 1940. This act makes it illegal to kill or possess an eagle, alive or dead, or to possess any part of an eagle, including feathers. In 1972, the Alaska State Legislature established a stretch of the Chilkat River as critical bald eagle habitat to ensure protection of the large numbers found there in winter. In 1982, a portion of the surrounding area was established as the Alaska Chilkat Bald Eagle Preserve.

The bald eagle is well on its way to recovery in Alaska and is no longer considered as threatened or endangered. In the lower 48 states this uniquely American bird is still classified as threatened and endangered. However, the U.S. Fish and Wildlife Service is moving forward on the process to remove the bald eagle from the endangered list nationwide. Today, of the estimated 50,000 bald eagles found in the United States, approximately 80 percent live in Alaska.

### Additional Resources:

U.S. Fish & Wildlife Service—Bald Eagle Website: http://www.fws.gov/migratorybirds/BaldEagle.htm

Alaska Chilkat Bald Eagle Preserve: http://www.dnr.state.ak.us/parks/units/eagleprv.htm

Alaska Department of Fish & Game—Endangered Species: http://www.wc.adfg.state.ak.us/index.cfm?adfg=endangered.main

Used with permission from author: http://www.insidepassagenews.com/AlaskaFAQ/FAQ_15.html

westerlies are blowing, but anything more than a moderate southerly makes for an exposed, rolly anchorage. The bay is shaped like a large crater, and isolated rocks and erratics litter the shoreline.

Anchor in 10 fathoms over mud with shells and rocks with fair holding. Be sure you set your anchor well.

## Coning Inlet (Long Island)

Coning Inlet is 4.5 miles south of Elbow Bay.

Chart 17409
Entrance: 54°49.51′ N, 132°37.72′ W

> *Coning Inlet . . . is open to E and does not afford good anchorage. A lagoon is at the head of the inlet, where it is connected to saltwater rapids.* (CP)

Coning Inlet is exposed to southeasterly weather like Natoma Bay. The lagoon at the head of Coning Inlet reaches to within 0.25 mile of Bolles Inlet on the other side of Long Island. (Nina Cove is the preferable place to anchor in Coning Inlet.)

## Nina Cove (Coning Inlet)

Nina Cove is on the south side of Coning Inlet at the entrance.

Chart 17409
Entrance: 54°49.44′ N, 132°39.39′ W
Anchor: 54°49.40′ N, 132°40.58′ W

> *Nina Cove . . . affords secure anchorage for small craft in 3 to 4 fathoms, sticky bottom. The anchorage is about 200 yards in extent and S of the small islet in the center of the cove at its head.* (CP)

Nina Cove is a small landlocked cove offering excellent shelter in all weather. This is a good place to stay while exploring the intricate system of lagoons that nearly cuts Long Island in half.

The entrance to Nina Cove is restricted; avoid the submerged rock off the small islet by favoring the east shore. The bottom of the cove is rocky sand and mud, so set your anchor well.

Anchor in 4 fathoms over sand, mud and some rocks with fair-to-good holding.

## Kassa Inlet (Prince of Wales Island)

Kassa Inlet is 4.5 miles northeast of Elbow Bay.

Chart 17431
Entrance: 54°55.62′ N, 132°32.32′ W

> *Kassa Inlet, just N of the northernmost of the Ship Island group, has an entrance about 0.8 mile wide.* (CP)

Kassa Inlet is a landlocked waterway with a couple of large islands in its center. Good protection is available at Clam Cove or northwest of Kassa Island.

## Clam Cove (Kassa Inlet)

Clam Cove is 2 miles inside Kassa Inlet.

Chart 17431
Anchor: 54°56.38′ N, 132°28.63′ W

> *Good anchorage for small craft is available at Clam Cove and several places in the upper reaches. A mooring buoy is about in the middle of the entrance to Clam Cove.* (CP)

Although it appears to be an open roadstead, Clam Cove provides good shelter from all quarters. Hook in behind the point; you will find it calm, even when a southwest wind blows outside in Cordova Bay. Anchor close to shore, avoiding the pile at unknown depth noted on the chart.

Interesting to visitors, and visible from boats in the bight of the cove, is a great silvery white snag sporting a bright blue and white

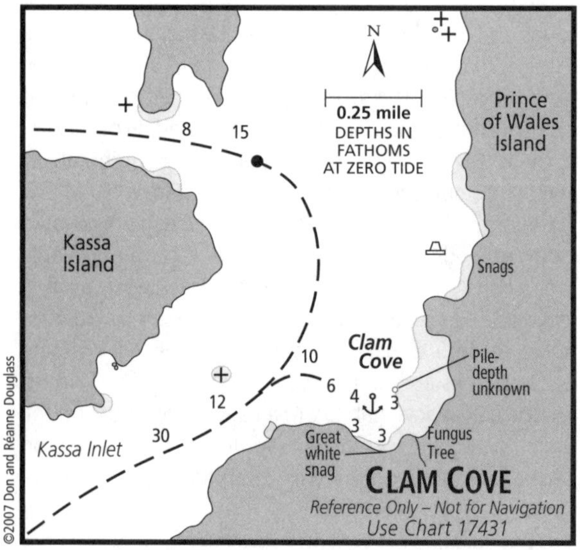

fungus known as Dryad's Saddle. This cove is also a favorite haunt of bald eagles. Note: In 2005, the mooring buoy shown on the chart seemed to be charted south of its actual position.

The landlocked bay northwest of Kassa Island offers complete shelter during storms.

Anchor in 4 fathoms over sand, shells and grass with good holding.

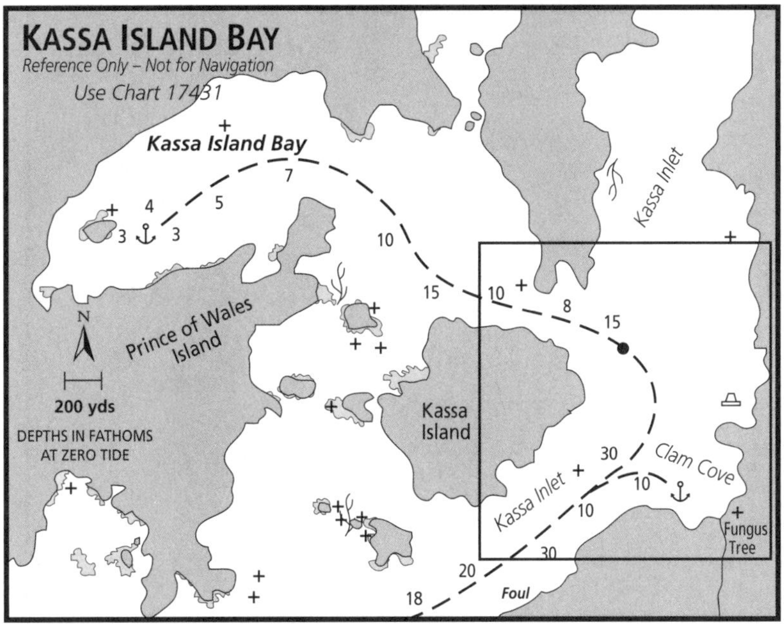


©2007 Don and Réanne Douglass

## Kassa Island Bay

(Kassa Inlet)

Kassa Island Cove is 1 mile northwest of Clam Cove.

Chart 17431
Entrance: 54°56.92′ N, 132°29.19′ W
Anchor: 54°57.24′ N, 132°31.79′ W

Kassa Island Bay, our name for the protected bay northwest of Kassa Island, offers great shelter over a large, mostly-flat bottom with unlimited swinging room. Avoid the kelp patches that indicate rocks. The intricate area immediately west of Kassa Island may offer a more cozy anchor site for small craft.

Anchor in 3 to 5 fathoms over sand and mud with fair-to-good holding.

## Ship Island Passage

(Prince of Wales Island)

Ship Island Passage is 1 mile south of Kassa Inlet.

Chart 17431
North entrance: 54°55.20′ N, 132°31.99′ W
South entrance (Barbara Rock bearing 056°T at 0.26 Nm): 54°53.40′ N, 132°30.12′ W

*Small craft from Turn Point pass N of Bird Rocks and between Shipwreck Point and the island close-to. The narrow channel has a submerged rock. The pass to the W of the inner island is preferable; avoid the rock in the middle of the entrance.* (CP)

Linda Lewis

*A stately parade of Mergansers, with one riding on mama . . .*

Linda Lewis

*. . . but when they get spooked, they all try to pile on.*

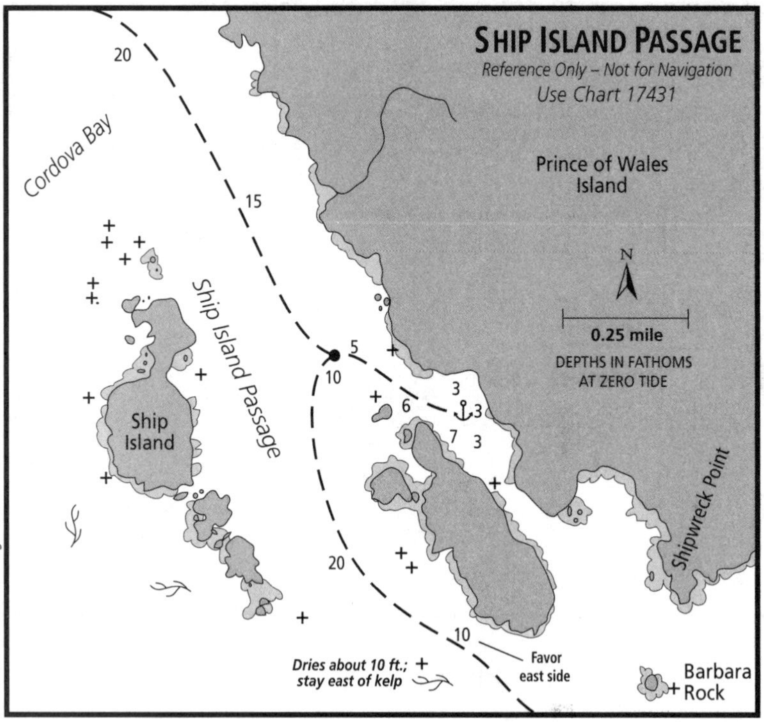


Barbara Rock. On the west side of the passage, avoid the rock and kelp patch southwest of the unnamed island. The rock dries on about a 10-foot tide.

Anchor in 3 to 5 fathoms over a mixed bottom with poor-to-fair holding.

## Klakas Inlet
(Prince of Wales Island)
Klakas Inlet is 9.5 miles east of Elbow Bay.

**Chart 17431**
**Entrance (mid-channel between Turn Island and Turn Point): 54°52.28′ N, 132°22.87′ W**
**Entrance (cove northeast of Klakas Island): 54°54.20′ N, 132°23.00′ W**
**Anchor (cove northeast of Klakas Island): 54°54.94′ N, 132°22.13′ W**

*The main entrance to Klakas Inlet is E of Klakas Island; the deepest water favors the W side of the entrance. . . .*

*Good anchorage in a depth of about 16 fathoms can be found E of a small wooded island about 1.5 miles ENE of the N end of Klakas Island.* (CP)

The anchor site for Klakas Inlet mentioned above in *Coast Pilot* is a little exposed for our

Ship Island Passage is a short, smooth-water route between Kassa Inlet and the entrance to Klakas Inlet. Temporary anchorage can be found near its south end. This marks the northern limit of the south Prince of Wales Wilderness Area.

## Ship Island Passage Cove (Ship Island)
Ship Island Passage Cove is 0.7 mile inside the south entrance to the passage.

**Chart 17431**
**Entrance: 54°54.26′ N, 132°30.84′ W**
**Anchor: 54°54.14′ N, 132°30.47′ W**

Ship Island Passage Cove is our name for the cove that makes a good rest stop or temporary anchorage in fair weather only. However, it can receive some chop, especially from the northwest. The bottom is a combination of rocks, sand, crushed shell and large kelp; holding may vary from extremely poor to good, so check the set of your anchor carefully.

The southern exit to Ship Island Passage is narrow, and you should favor the east side next to the unnamed island located northwest of

*Remnants of the past can be found all over the southeast forests.*

taste. We prefer Ruth Bay or Max Cove for more intimacy.

Anchor in about 7 fathoms over mud and shells with some rocks.

## **Ruth Bay** (Klakas Inlet)

Ruth Bay is west of Klakas Island and 1.5 miles northeast of Bird Rocks.

Chart 17431
Entrance: 54°53.62′ N, 132°25.68′ W
West entrance (Ruth Cutoff): 54°54.37′ N, 132°25.08′ W
Anchor: 54°55.03′ N, 132°26.39′ W

> *Local fishermen frequently use Ruth Cutoff, the narrow pass N of Klakas Island that has a controlling depth of 1-3⁄4 fathoms and extends from Ruth Bay to Klakas Inlet.* (CP)

Ruth Bay offers fair anchorage for small craft off the small basin at the head of the bay or in the landlocked cove south of the peninsula to the basin. A more sheltered anchorage with more swinging room can be found in Max Cove.

## **Max Cove** (Klakas Inlet)

Max Cove is 2.5 miles north of the entrance to Klakas Inlet.

Chart 17431
Entrance: 54°57.40′ N, 132°24.37′ W
Anchor: 54°55.64′ N, 132°21.93′ W

> *Max Cove . . . offers good anchorage for small craft near the SE end in 8 fathoms, mud bottom.* (CP)

Max Cove is a long, narrow indentation with several islets and a foul shore, good for exploring with a dinghy. Although the cove lies in a southeast direction, fetch is minimized if you anchor near the head of the cove.

Anchor in 8 fathoms over mud and shells with good holding.

## **Hunter Bay** (Prince of Wales Island)

Hunter Bay extends 2.5 miles east of Turn Point.

Chart 17433
Entrance (Turn Point bearing 090°T at 0.3 Nm): 54°52.62′ N, 132°22.33′ W
Anchor: 54°52.23′ N, 132°18.57′ W

> *About 1 mile above the entrance, the bay contracts . . . with a large bare rock in the middle. The best channel is between this rock and a rock awash about 200 yards N of it. About 0.4 mile E of the bare rock is an arm leading NNE about 1 mile to Biscuit Lagoon.*
>
> *Hunter Bay has good anchorage about 1.8 miles E from the entrance in 10 to 15 fathoms. The anchorage, however, is subject to strong williwaws. . . . Velocities up to 78.2 knots have been experienced here.* (CP)

Hunter Bay, with Biscuit Lagoon, is a narrow, intriguing waterway leading to an isolated salt chuck at the head of its north arm. If southeast gales are forecast, set your anchor accordingly or use a stern-tie west of the islet, close in, on the south shore. All anchorages below peaks are subject to williwaws in gales or storms, and this place is no exception. Williwaws notwithstanding, Hunter Bay is a well-protected spot.

The features of Hunter Bay beg to be explored; if you do, be careful of tidal currents and avoid the mid-channel rocks on entering.

Anchor in 6 fathoms over mud and shells with good holding.

## **Klinkwan Cove** (Hunter Bay)

Klinkwan Cove is first cove on the north shore of Hunter Bay.

Chart 17433
Entrance: 54°52.83′ N, 132°21.46′ W

> *Klinkwan Cove . . . should be avoided as it contains many rocks.* (CP)

Klinkwan Cove is a natural for exploring by kayak.

## **Biscuit Lagoon** (Hunter Bay)

Biscuit Lagoon is at the head of the northeast arm of Hunter Bay.

Chart 17433
Entrance: 54°52.38′ N, 132°19.78′ W

> *Passage into this lagoon is through a narrow pass that is partially obstructed by several rocks. Small craft of 3-foot draft can clear these rocks at high water. Tidal currents are strong, and passage should be attempted only on the high-water slack.* (CP)

Don Douglass

*That looks scary; did we make it out safely? (Dinghy exit from Biscuit Lagoon)*

Don Douglass

*You bet we did; look at that smile on Réanne's face!*

Biscuit Lagoon is nearly cut off by a small island. It is passable only as noted above in *Coast Pilot.* A large quantity of water passes through this narrow opening and to enter you need to time your passage at high water slack or you may be facing a waterfall. Avoid the rocks on the east side of the small entrance channel. Depths within the lagoon are great, but the salt chuck at its head dries at low water. The shores of Biscuit Lagoon attract sandhill cranes as well as bear.

Don Douglass

*Exploring the rocky shoreline in Biscuit Lagoon*

## **Barrier Islands** (Cordova Bay)

Barrier Islands lie 1 to 5 miles east of Round Islands Light and 4 to 8 miles northwest of Point Marsh.

**Chart 17433**
**Position (Round Island Light): 54°46.68′ N, 132°30.42′ W**

Approach courses to seldom-used channels through the Barrier Islands pass about 0.5 mile both E and W of Black Rock. These two passages, Rocky Pass and Kelp Passage, continuing E and W, respectively, of Middle Island, are useful only to small craft. It is possible to carry 2 fathoms of water through the W passage and 7 fathoms through the E.

The Barrier Islands provide a substantial break for you before you enter the southerly swell of Dixon Entrance. Covered with stubby, old-growth cedar, these numerous, low islands are alive with Clark's nutcrackers that raise a shrill cry upon your arrival. There are many

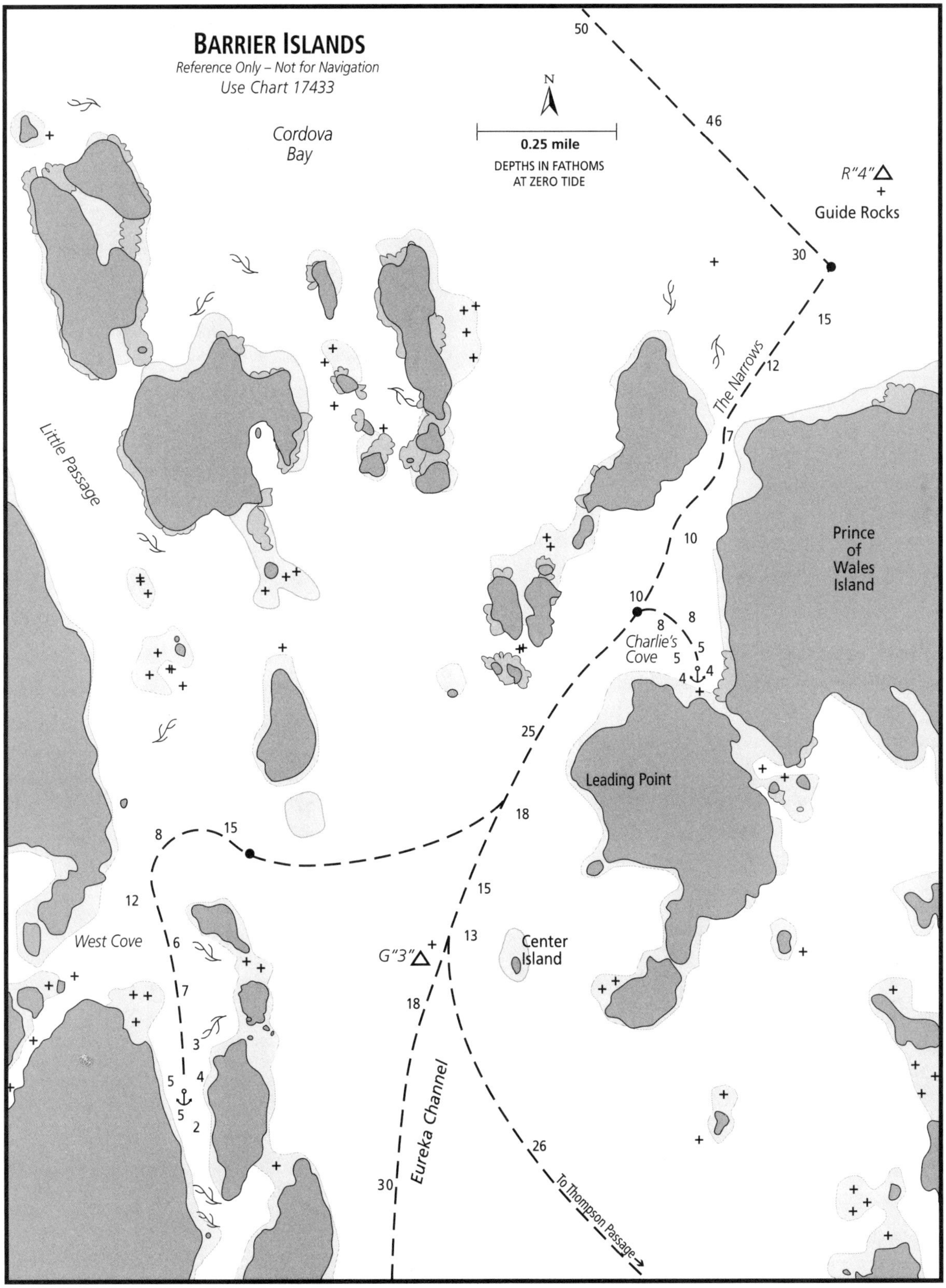
BARRIER ISLANDS
Reference Only – Not for Navigation
Use Chart 17433
N
0.25 mile
DEPTHS IN FATHOMS
AT ZERO TIDE
Cordova Bay
R"4"
Guide Rocks
The Narrows
Little Passage
Prince of Wales Island
Charlie's Cove
Leading Point
West Cove
G"3"
Center Island
Eureka Channel
To Thompson Passage
50
46
30
15
12
7
10
10
8
8
5
5
4
4
25
18
8
15
12
15
13
6
7
18
3
4
5
5
2
26
30

beautiful inlets and bays to explore in this remote area.

## Eureka Channel

Eureka Channel is between Barrier Islands and Prince of Wales Island.

Chart 17433
North entrance (Guide Rocks R"4" bearing 060°T at 0.2 Nm): 54°49.43′ N, 132°21.78′ W
South entrance (Mexico Point bearing 142°T at 0.8 Nm): 54°46.02′ N, 132°23.37′ W

> *Eureka Channel . . . affords a short cut to Klakas Inlet and is suitable for moderate-sized craft with local knowledge; large vessels should use the passage W of Dewey Rocks and Barrier Islands. The depths in Eureka Channel are good, but it is narrow and has several dangers that are generally marked by kelp in the summer.*
>
> *The Narrows has a least width of 125 yards. Good depths are found through The Narrows except for narrow ledges close to the W shore. About 480 yards N of the N end of The Narrows is a submerged rock that is awash at extreme low tides.* (CP)

Eureka Channel is the scenic, smooth-water route heading south. The marker R"4" at Guide Rocks is the north entrance for this route. If Eureka Channel is used in conjunction with Thompson Passage or Buschmann Pass in fair weather, you should find smooth water until just north of Point Marsh, where you begin a turn east to Nichols Bay and Cape Chacon.

Linda Lewis

*The Barrier Islands offer some of the most beautiful scenery along the west side of Prince of Wales Island.*

Réanne Hemingway-Douglass

*Charlie's Cove, Barrier Islands*

Southwest swell and chop greatly diminish north of the Barrier Islands, but pick up quickly south of the islands. It's unwise to head south from Eureka Channel in the face of a southeast gale; there is no reliable shelter you can safely enter until you're on the east side of Prince of Wales Island. Shelter along Eureka Channel is marginal because the bottom tends to be rocky with poor holding. A shore tie will improve holding among the beautiful Barrier Islands.

### **Charlie's Cove** (Eureka Channel)

Chart 17433
Entrance: 54°48.77′ N, 132°22.18′ W
Anchor: 54°48.67′ N, 132°22.07′ W

We named "Charlie's Cove" after Charles E. Wood, author of the famous guides, *Charlie's Charts,* who made this unnamed cove known to cruising boats with his original *Charlie's Charts North to Alaska* description. Charlie's Cove is a convenient stopover offering good southerly protection when you tuck up against the small opening to the east.

Anchor in 4 fathoms over rock, gravel and kelp with poor-to-fair holding. Holding can be good if you set your anchor well.

### **West Cove** (Eureka Channel)

West Cove is 1 mile southwest of Charlie's Cove.

Chart 17433
Entrance: 54°48.28′ N, 132°23.39′ W
Anchor: 54°47.96′ N, 132°23.72′ W

Snug little West Cove is located on the west side of Eureka Channel west of marker G"3." This cove is not as charted and is choked with kelp that allows little chop to enter. The bottom is poor, however, so check your anchor set.

Anchor in 5 fathoms over rock, gravel and kelp with poor-to-fair holding.

## **Hessa Inlet** (Prince of Wales Island)

Hessa Inlet is 5 miles east of the Barrier Islands.

Chart 17433
West entrance (northwest tip of Hessa Island bearing 150°T at 0.3 Nm): 54°47.37′ N, 132°20.34′ W

> *Hessa Inlet . . . is about 3.5 miles long and has depths up to 32 fathoms. The best approach to the inlet is through the passage N of Hessa Island, but it can be approached from the S via Buschmann Pass; only small craft with local knowledge should attempt this pass, which is narrow and full of rocks. In Hessa Narrows the tidal currents attain a reported velocity of 6 to 7 knots.* (CP)

Réanne Hemingway-Douglass

*Waterfall from High Lake, Hessa Inlet*

Hessa Inlet is a remote, landlocked waterway to explore where few boats will be found. In many ways, this southern tip of Prince of Wales Island is the ultimate frontier of expeditionary cruising in Southeast Alaska. Only highly maneuverable, small craft with experienced crew should consider this exciting type of experience.

## **Thompson Passage**

Thompson Passage is 0.5 mile west of Hessa Island.

Chart 17433
North entrance (Eureka Channel marker G"3" bearing 316°T at 0.8 Nm): 54°47.58′ N, 132°22.03′ W
South entrance (Seagull Island bearing 121°T at 0.3 Nm): 54°44.88′ N, 132°19.93′ W

> *Thompson Passage, used extensively by fishing craft, extends between the islands from 1.2 to 1.5 miles N and NE of Mexico Point. Although 8 fathoms can be carried through it, this passage is not suitable for large vessels.* (CP)

By taking Thompson Passage, you put off entering the swell off Mexico Point. In fair weather Thompson Passage lines up well with Minnie Cutoff to further avoid the swells off Point Marsh; however, you must be careful to avoid the many submerged and exposed rocks between these two points. The north entrance to Minnie Cutoff is encumbered with several breaking rocks; the entrance *looks* and is formidable in foul weather or when sizable swell is running.

If you have time to spare or you are seeking intimate surroundings, consider Buschmann Pass, which can be approached through the channel on the south side of Hessa Island. These small passages are fun and exciting to explore, but should be done with great care and in fair weather with good visibility. Avoid the mid-channel rock near the south end of Thompson Passage by favoring the east shore.

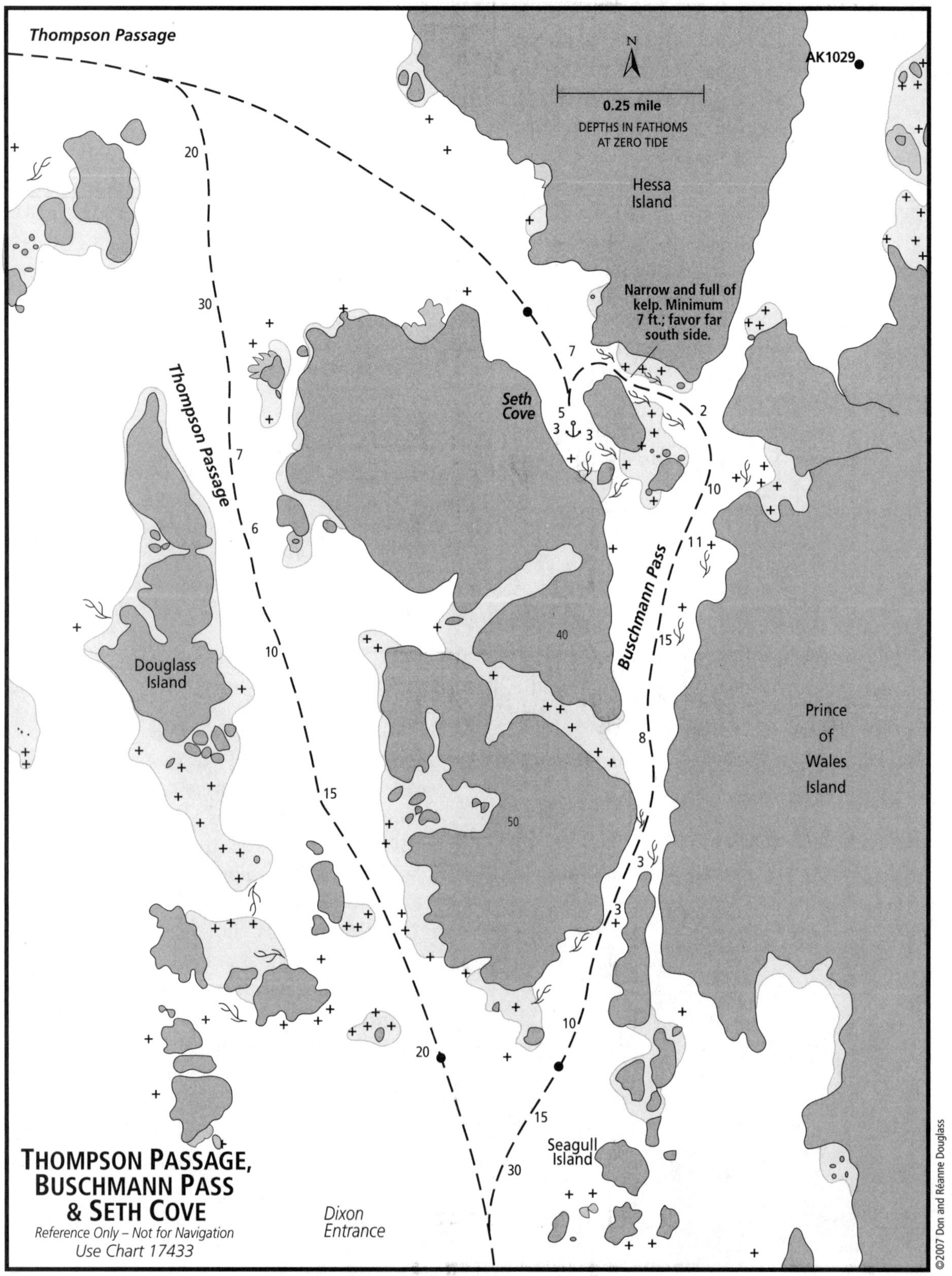
Thompson Passage
N
0.25 mile
DEPTHS IN FATHOMS
AT ZERO TIDE
AK1029
Hessa
Island
Narrow and full of
kelp. Minimum
7 ft.; favor far
south side.
Seth
Cove
Thompson Passage
Buschmann Pass
Douglass
Island
Prince
of
Wales
Island
Seagull
Island
Dixon
Entrance
THOMPSON PASSAGE,
BUSCHMANN PASS
& SETH COVE
Reference Only – Not for Navigation
Use Chart 17433
©2007 Don and Réanne Douglass

## Buschmann Pass

Buschmann Pass connects Point Marsh to Hessa Inlet.

**Chart 17433**
**North entrance (Whirlpool Point bearing 027°T at 0.3 Nm): 54°46.56′ N, 132°18.80′ W**
**South entrance (Seagull Island bearing 164°T at 0.16 Nm): 54°44.88′ N, 132°19.54′ W**

> *. . . only small craft with local knowledge should attempt this pass, which is narrow and full of rocks.* (CP)

Buschmann Pass is inadequately charted. It is narrow, very remote and with many rocks and strong, uncertain currents. Use extreme caution during a transit of Buschmann Pass.

You can enter the north end of Buschmann Pass from Hessa Inlet south of Whirlpool Point. The north end is quite narrow and favors the Hessa Island shore. A moderate flood tide may be the best time to use Buschmann Pass if you are southbound, as you will have more steering control.

If you are entering Buschmann Pass south of Hessa Island east of what we call Seth Cove, reconnoiter the narrow, shallow pass before you attempt it. The bar is choked with kelp, and rocks awash on a 2-foot tide extend from the north shore to mid-channel. We found a tiny opening that favors the far south shore (stay about 30 feet from the south island). Let a moderate, east-flowing flood current carry you through the kelp and across the bar.

Buschmann Pass is a calm channel compared to the outside; however, it has considerable current flow at times. The pass has an enchanted feeling to it as it passes forested islets and heads directly for Dixon Entrance.

## Seth Cove (Barrier Islands)

Seth Cove is off the southwest tip of Hessa Island.

**Chart 17433**
**Entrance: 54°46.07′ N, 132°19.66′ W**
**Anchor: 54°45.91′ N, 132°19.59′ W**

"Seth Cove" is the small cove we named after our dedicated crew member, Seth Nickles, and the base from which we reconnoitered this area. It is protected from all southerly weather and is a calm place to stay until tides are favorable for an attempt to enter Buschmann Pass.

Anchor in 5 to 6 fathoms over rocks, clamshell and kelp with poor-to-fair holding; check your anchor set.

## Minnie Cutoff

Minnie Cutoff is just east of Point Marsh and 10 miles west of Cape Chacon.

**Chart 17433**
**South entrance: 54°42.68′ N, 132°18.09′ W**
**North entrance: 54°43.74′ N, 132°19.41′ W**

> *Small fishing vessels bound between Point Marsh and Eureka Channel frequently pass through Minnie Cutoff, then run between the reefs close inshore along the SW coast of Prince of Wales Island, and thence through Thompson Passage to Eureka Channel.* (CP)

Minnie Cutoff, occasionally used by experienced fishermen in small boats, is not a place for the faint-hearted!

Entering Minnie Cutoff from the south on a northbound route is easier than on a southbound route. The northern entrance has several breaking rocks that are difficult to identify precisely. From the north, one glance and you know this is not a cutoff to try in poor visibility or in foul weather when swells are running and whitewater breaks over the rocks and islets. The south entrance is less encumbered with rocks and has a navigation light.

We have entered from the north several times and, on our latest passage (in stable weather), we found Minnie Cutoff so choked with kelp and submerged rocks that we had only about 30 feet on either side of *Baidarka*. Depth in the fairway east of island 90 is about 2 fathoms. Across from the entrance to Minnie Bay just south of island (90), there is a dangerous rock in the center of Minnie Cutoff awash on a 9-foot tide.

"Note B" on Chart 17433 states that all of Brownson Bay (and apparently Minnie Bay) is shallower than that stated on the chart, so beware! If you're in doubt about using this cutoff, do the safest thing: round Point Marsh on the outside by staying a mile west and give a wide berth to the rocks off the point's northwest, southwest and south sides before you turn east. Only Bert Millar Cutoff, 7 miles to the east, has a more intimidating entrance.

## Minnie Bay (Prince of Wales Island)

Minnie Bay lies 1 mile northeast of Point Marsh.

Chart 17433
Entrance: 54°43.26′ N, 132°18.62′ W
Anchor: 54°43.46′ N, 132°18.36′ W

> *Minnie Bay . . . is much used by local fishermen and affords excellent anchorage for small craft. Enter the bay W of the small charted islets inside the entrance and run fairly close-to in order to avoid a reef extending 30 feet out from the W shore opposite the southernmost islet. Heavy kelp covers much of the shoreline during the summer, but the center of the bay is clear.* (CP)

Minnie Bay is a lovely little cove with a restricted entrance choked with kelp (as is Minnie Cutoff). Entrance to the bay is made just south of island (90) by turning almost due east, avoiding kelp and rocks, then passing to the west side of three islets.

Depths throughout the entire bay do not exceed more than about one-and-a-half fathoms at zero tide, so it is appropriate only for boats with drafts of less than 4 feet. The bottom of the bay is rocky and irregular with patches of sand and kelp. No swell is felt within the bay.

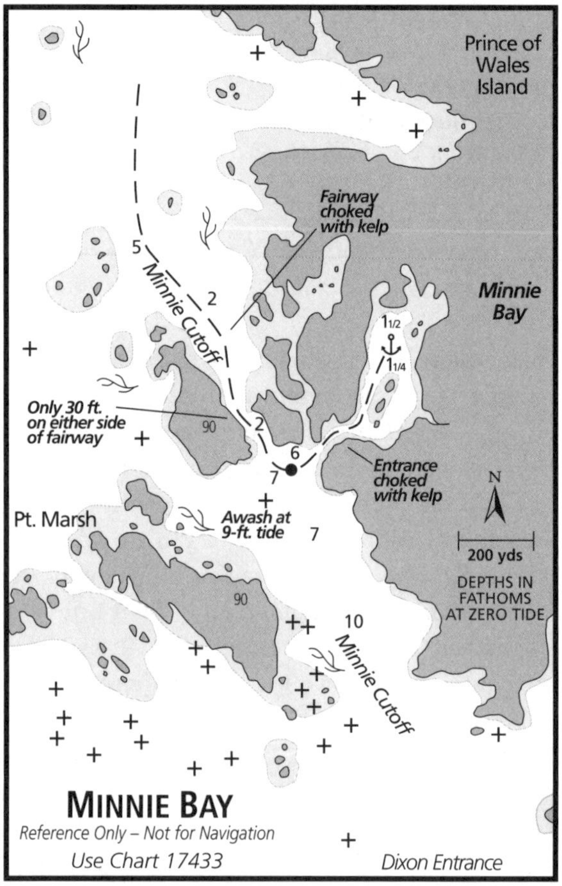


©2007 Don and Réanne Douglass

Don Douglass

*Threading our way through Minnie Bay*

Minnie Bay has not been adequately surveyed, and Chart 17433 is helpful only for an overall view.

## Brownson Bay (Prince of Wales Island)

Brownson Bay is 1.5 miles northeast of Point Marsh Light.

Chart 17433
Entrance: 54°42.72′ N, 132°15.42′ W

> *Brownson Bay . . . is narrow, and its entrance is somewhat obstructed by islets and rocks. It affords indifferent anchorage in about 11 fathoms, 0.2 mile S of the rock awash near the head of the bay.*
>
> *In 1968, it was reported that the depths in Brownson Bay were considerably less than the charted depths; caution is advised.* (CP)

If shelter is needed, we would use Nichols Bay, 6 miles to the east, or Barrier Islands, 8 miles northwest.

## Little Brownson Bay

(Prince of Wales Island)

Little Brownson Bay is on the east shore of Brownson Bay.

**Chart 17433**
**Entrance: 54°43.11′ N, 132°14.35′ W**

> *Little Brownson Bay, on the E side of the entrance to Brownson Bay, affords anchorage for small craft. The bay is entered from the S, but local knowledge is required; the N passage can only be used by very small boats. Williwaws sweep across the bay during SE gales.* (CP)

Little Brownson Bay is another uncharted area, so beware. We have no local knowledge of Little Brownson Bay, but we would consider carefully entering it in an emergency.

## Bert Millar Cutoff (Prince of Wales Island)

Bert Millar Cutoff, a tiny passage to Nichols Bay, is west of Bean Island and 3 miles west of Cape Chacon.

**Chart 17433**
**South entrance: 54°41.15′ N, 132°07.71′ W**
**North entrance: 54°41.88′ N, 132°06.51′ W**

> *Bert Millar Cutoff . . . forms a bight at each end, narrowing at the center to a channel about 30 yards long and 10 yards wide. A depth of about 1-3/4 fathoms is in the narrow part of the channel, and submerged rocks are in the bight at the N end. At times the current through the channel is very swift.* (CP)

Bert Millar Cutoff is used by sport fishing skiffs or small shallow draft runabouts with local knowledge. Entering from Dixon Entrance is particularly challenging with foam and breakers rolling in toward the cutoff.

Bert Millar Cutoff is a stunt passage for anything but a high-powered dinghy. Its entrance is considerably narrower than that described in *Coast Pilot*. We estimate the fairway to be only 18 feet wide between the rock walls. (Scott Davis, in his high-tech rowing craft, found it too narrow to row through, and let the current carry him through instead.) There is zero margin of safety if any current is running or if anything goes wrong!

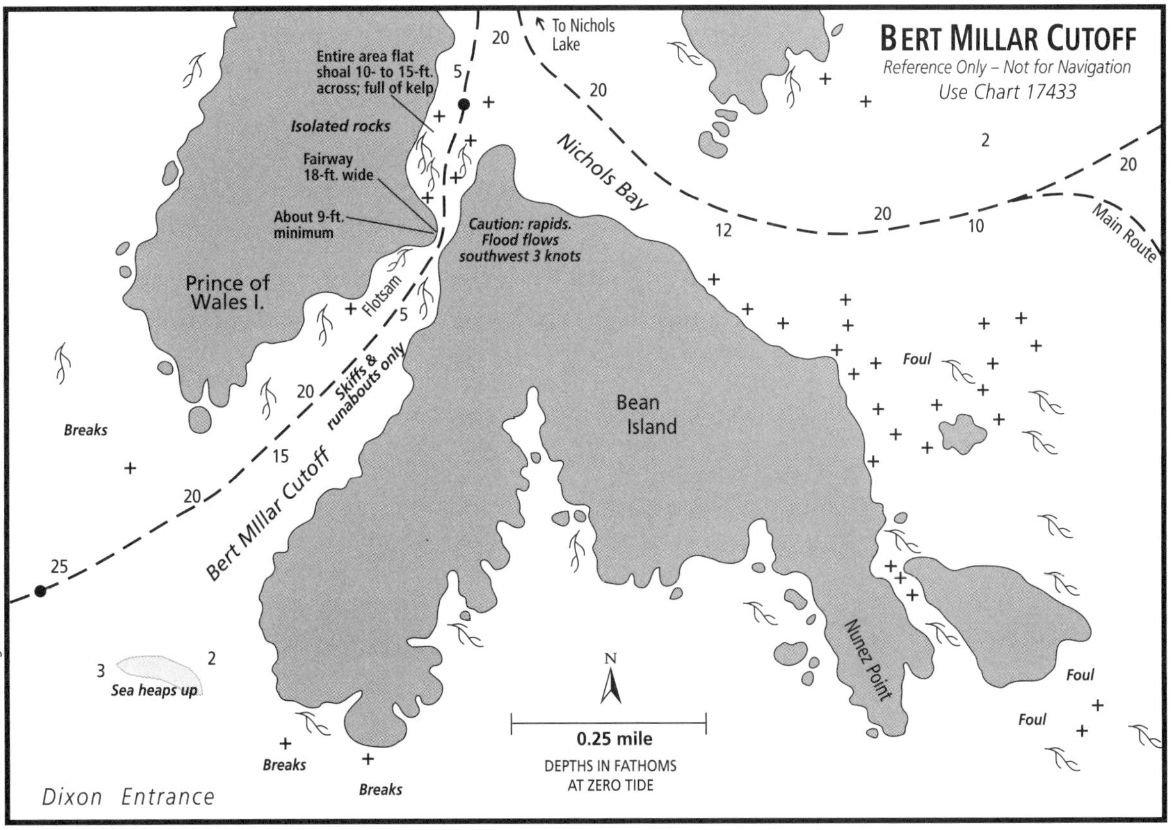

The current through the channel is mysterious. We went through Bert Millar in our 32-foot Nordic Tug, northbound on a flood and found ourselves face-to-face with a 6- to 9-inch waterfall flowing *south!* (Off Cape Chacon and Nichols Bay, apparently, there is a significant back eddy that runs for a couple of hours of flood.) With all hands poised to fend off, and with big fenders out on both sides of our 11-foot beam, we managed to squeak through with just a couple of feet to spare. Our depth sounder was useless in the kelp, but our bow crew said it appeared that we had 8 feet under the keel, which means we doubt there is 1-3⁄4 fathoms at zero tide in the tiny fairway. (Scott Davis reported he could see bottom all the way.) The narrows is full of kelp, suggesting that few propeller boats of any size use Bert Millar Cutoff.

As we headed into Nichols Bay, we turned around to study the tiny entrance and saw a great blue heron standing on kelp in the center

Réanne Hemingway-Douglass

*The Bert Millar Cutoff is a stunt passage for small, high-powered skiffs.*

## Whale and Dolphin Types

### What types of whales and dolphins can you see and how do you view them responsibly?

Herb Nickles, Certified Alaska Naturalist

Whales begin their northbound migration to Alaska in February with most cows and calves migrating between April and May. Cruisers who visit Southeast Alaska between June and early September are most likely to see Humpback Whales, Minke Whales, Orcas (Killer Whales), Pacific White-Sided Dolphins, Dall's Porpoises and Harbour Porpoises. Whales will begin their southbound trek in late October and continue through December.

The Marine Mammal Protection Act prohibits harassment of all marine mammal species in U.S. waters. Harassment means any act of pursuit, torment, or annoyance which has the potential to injure a marine mammal, or has the potential to disturb a marine mammal by causing disruption of behavioral patterns, including migration, breathing, nursing, breeding, and feeding. Boaters must remain 100 yards from marine mammals and should keep clear of the whales' path. Limit observation times to 30 minutes. Whales should not be encircled, trapped between vessels, or trapped between a vessel and the shore. You may not place your vessel in the path of on-coming whales causing them to surface. You should reduce speed to less than 7 knots when within 400 yards of a whale. If approached by a whale, put your engine in neutral and allow the whale to pass.

To safely observe porpoises and dolphins, observe all guidelines for watching whales. Do not steer through groups of porpoises or dolphins to encourage them to bow ride. Should a porpoise or dolphin choose to ride your bow wave, reduce speed gradually and avoid sudden course changes.

### Additional Resources:

Sea World—Killer Whale Behavior at: http://www.seaworld.org/infobooks/KillerWhale/behaviorkw.html.

Alaska Marine Mammal Viewing Guidelines and Regulations at: http://www.fakr.noaa.gov/protectedresources/mmv/guide.htm.

Used with permission of author from: http://www.insidepassagenews.com/AlaskaFAQ/FAQ_20.html.

of the channel we'd just come through and a fisheries skiff heading pell-mell *out* through the cutoff. If you want to see what Bert Millar is all about, we recommend that you enter Nichols Bay from the main route east of Bean Island and check it out by dinghy. Bert Millar is one of the only places we know of in Southeast Alaska to be honored with a full name.

## **Nichols Bay** (Prince of Wales Island)

Nichols Bay is 2.5 miles west of Cape Chacon.

Chart 17433
Entrance: 54°41.34′ N, 132°03.89′ W
Anchor (south): 54°42.87′ N, 132°07.68′ W
Anchor (central): 54°43.25′ N, 132°08.12′ W
Anchor (north): 54°44.45′ N, 132°09.55′ W

> *During severe S gales seas pile up heavily at the entrance and are reported to break entirely across it at times.*
>
> *The bay has three anchorages, one in each of the three bights on the SW shore. In entering the first bight keep well off the NW end of the N island to avoid rocks. Anchor in 16 fathoms, mud bottom, 250 yards offshore. The second anchorage is to the NW of the peninsula, in depths of 15 fathoms, 300 yards offshore. The third anchorage is about 0.7 mile to the NW of the second anchorage and about 0.6 mile from the head of the bay, in depths of about 13 fathoms, soft mud bottom, 350 yards offshore.*
>
> *Nichols Lake, a large freshwater lake, empties into the head of the bay through a stream. Small boats anchor off the flats at the mouth of this stream.* (CP)

When entering Nichols Bay, we use the deeper channel on the south and west side of the three unnamed islands that nearly choke the entrance to the bay. The bay has three anchor sites, as indicated on the diagram. Our favorite is the south site, which is calm when 8-foot seas are running in Dixon Entrance. If a serious southeasterly blow were approaching, we would anchor at the central site just north of the peninsula that juts out on the west side of the bay; it appears to offer complete shelter. (We have received a report that this site is occupied by a busy fishing resort.) The far north site has driftwood at its head, indicating that, at times, southeast winds carry all the way up the bay. This northern anchor site is favored by boaters who like to explore the creek that drains Nichols Lake three-quarters of a mile upstream.

*Checking out a classic Grumman that landed in Nichols Bay*

Anchor (south) in 6 fathoms over sand and mud with fair-to-good holding.

Anchor (central) in 5 fathoms over sand and gravel with fair holding.

Anchor (north) in 5 fathoms over sand and mud with good holding.

## **Nunez Rocks**

Nunez Rocks are about 1.4 miles south of Nunez Point.

Chart 17433
Position: 54°39.67′ N, 132°05.37′ W

> *Nunez Rocks . . . are bare at half tide and usually show as a breaker. . . . The channel between Nunez Rocks and Nunez Point is clear. The rocks when passed to the S should be given a berth of 0.8 mile.* (CP)

Nunez Rocks are now also known as Zopilote's Rocks.

## **Cape Chacon** (Prince of Wales Island)

Cape Chacon, the southeast point of Prince of Wales Island, is 23 miles east of Cape Muzon.

Chart 17433
Position (light bearing 335°T at 0.5 Nm):
54°40.91′ N, 132°00.60′ W

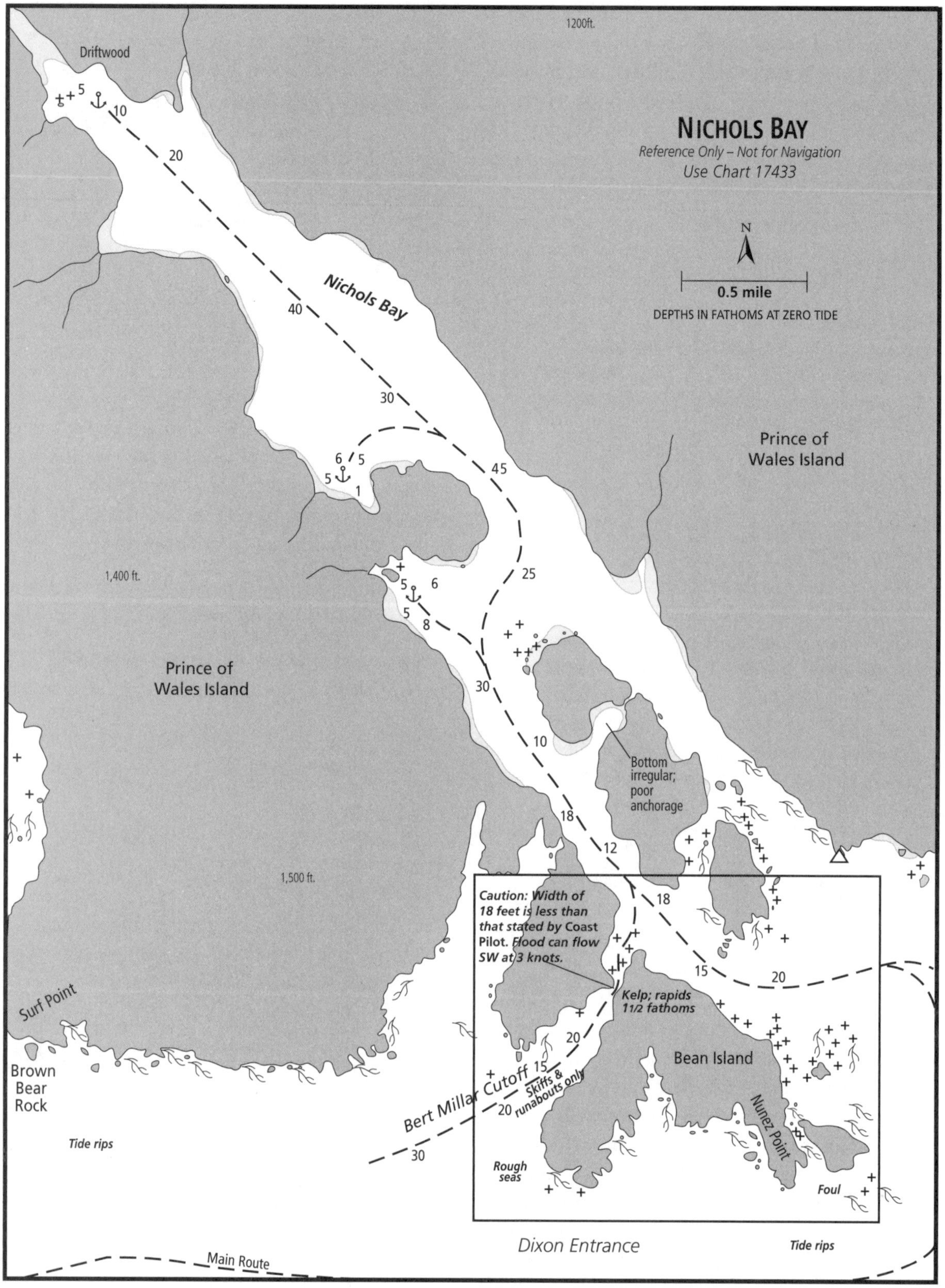
NICHOLS BAY
Reference Only – Not for Navigation
Use Chart 17433
N
0.5 mile
DEPTHS IN FATHOMS AT ZERO TIDE
Driftwood
1200ft.
Nichols Bay
Prince of Wales Island
Prince of Wales Island
1,400 ft.
1,500 ft.
Bottom irregular; poor anchorage
Caution: Width of 18 feet is less than that stated by Coast Pilot. Flood can flow SW at 3 knots.
Kelp; rapids 11/2 fathoms
Bean Island
Nunez Point
Bert Millar Cutoff
Skiffs & runabouts only
Surf Point
Brown Bear Rock
Tide rips
Rough seas
Foul
Dixon Entrance
Tide rips
Main Route

*Cape Chacon Light, 50 feet above the water, is shown from a frame with a red and white diamond-shaped daymark on the S extremity of the cape.*

*A rock, awash at extreme low water and usually showing as a breaker, is 260 yards SE from the cape. The pass between the rock and the cape has depths of 5 fathoms and is used by small craft. For a distance of about 0.5 mile from the cape, tide rips are likely to be severe for small craft.* (CP)

In addition to the back eddy off Cape Chacon mentioned for Bert Millar Cutoff, you may encounter tide rips along the south tip of Prince of Wales Island. Most fishing boats pass between Nunez Rocks and Nunez Point. Larger fishing boats return from Cordova Bay to Ketchikan via Cape Chacon, but because of Dixon Entrance's reputation for rough seas, most smaller fishing boats from the Craig area prefer to return to Ketchikan via El Capitan Passage and the north end of Prince of Wales Island. If you are unable to get U.S. weather on VHF, try the Canadian channels, as reception may be better from this area.

## TLEVAK AND KAIGANI STRAITS TO CAPE MUZON

### Tlevak Strait

Tlevak Strait extends 24 miles from Tlevak Narrows to Cordova Bay.

**Chart 17400**
**North entrance (Lively Island Light bearing 000°T at 0.6 Nm): 55°13.11′ N, 133°05.11′ W**
**Southeast entrance (Shoe Island Light bearing 270°T at 1.7 Nm): 54°57.02′ N, 132°41.71′ W**

*The direction of maximum flood current (and ebb) varies considerably as one progresses through the 24-mile-long Tlevak Strait. Maximum average currents range from 1.5 to 3.0 knots on the flood and 1.5 to 4.3 knots on the ebb; the strongest currents occurring in Tlevak Narrows.* (CP)

We have seen the flood current at 5 to 6 knots on spring tides in the narrows and, at times, it may even be higher! The current is much more moderate in the southern part of the bay.

Unfortunately, the northeast side of Dall Island above Farallon and Breezy bays was clear-cut in the past few decades, detracting greatly from the beauty of the shoreline.

---

## Clear-cutting Facts

**Is clear-cutting still practiced in Southeast Alaska? How much is done by helicopter? How long does it take clear-cut areas to become harvestable?**

**Herb Nickles, Certified Alaska Naturalist**

Clear-cutting is still the most economical method of harvesting timber, especially in steep terrain. The Southeast Alaska Conservation Council estimates that 4 percent of the Tongass National Forest contains the biggest, most productive, old-growth forest. The lush valley-bottom and beach fringe areas are most in demand for logging due to economies of harvesting. However, these same areas provide critical habitat for fish and wildlife. In the past 50 years, over half of this habitat has been clear-cut. Compounding the problem is that 1.7 million acres of prime old-growth forest is on private land in the hands of Alaska Native corporations. These lands are exempt from many of the laws and are being clear-cut at an alarming rate.

Helicopters are used as an alternative to clear-cutting, by harvesting selected individual trees and leaving 75 percent of the trees in a given area. But helicopter operations can be as much as five times more expensive than conventional logging.

Conservationists estimate that full recovery of an old-growth forest requires 200 years, but that will rarely happen since most secondary growth forests will be harvested after 100 years.

Additional Resources:
Southeast Alaska Conservation Council—The Tongass: http://www.seacc.org/index.php?section=14

Alaska Rainforest Campaign: http://www.akrain.org/

Used with permission from author: http://www.insidepassagenews.com/AlaskaFAQ/FAQ_11.html

## North Bay (Dall Island)

North Bay is 2.8 miles south of Tlevak Narrows.

Chart 17407
Entrance: 55°13.12′ N, 133°05.86′ W
Anchor: 55°12.29′ N, 133°07.61′ W

> *When entering North Bay, favor the SE side and anchor near the head of the bay in 12 to 15 fathoms, soft bottom, with the high-water islet at the head, bearing about W. SE winds draw around Cayman Point and blow directly into the bay with severe squalls and williwaws.*
>
> *The N side of the bight* [on the north side of Hassler Point] *is formed by a wooded island; between it and the main shore is a cove with depths of 1 to 4 fathoms.* (CP)

Anchorage can be found in the southwest corner of North Bay.

Anchor in 8 fathoms over sand and gravel with fair holding.

## Farallon Bay (Dall Island)

Farallon Bay, on the west side of Tlevak Strait, is 1.5 miles southeast of North Bay.

Chart 17407
Entrance: 55°11.66′ N, 133°04.62′ W

> *The bottom is rocky and very broken; SE winds draw through it, and it is not recommended as an anchorage.* (CP)

Avoid the dangerous reef on the north entrance to Farallon Bay shown on the chart as a submerged rock.

## Breezy Bay (Dall Island)

Breezy Bay is 4 miles south of Tlevak Narrows.

Chart 17407
Entrance: 55°09.58′ N, 133°03.32′ W
Anchor: 55°09.52′ N, 133°06.43′ W

> *Breezy Bay . . . is 2 miles wide between Eolus and Boreas Points. It is divided into two arms. . . . It does not appear to afford an anchorage.* (CP)

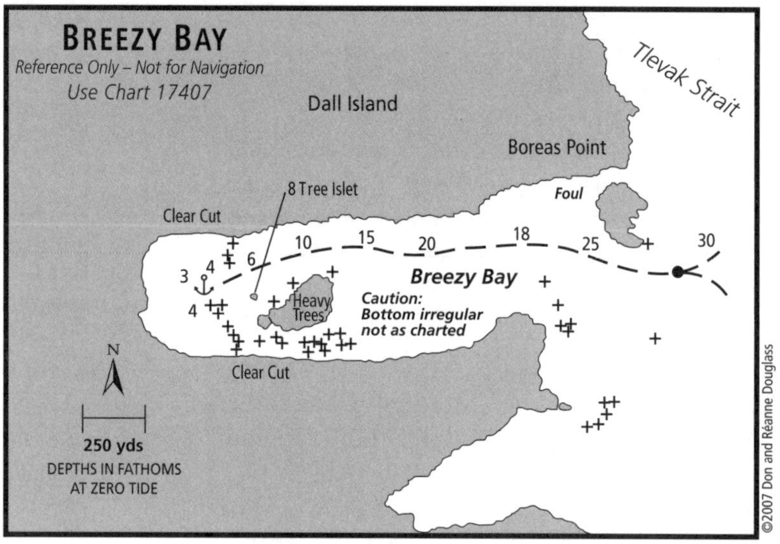


We have found good fair-weather anchorage here and would consider it as an emergency shelter under some circumstances. The head of the bay in the lee of the large island is nearly landlocked. However, you need to avoid many charted and uncharted isolated rocks. Like much of Dall Island, the charting in these bays is incomplete or inaccurate, requiring vigilant piloting when entering. The beach is relatively log-free even though the clear-cut logging left the shore in shambles.

Anchor in 4 fathoms over an irregular rocky mixed bottom; fair-to-good holding with a well-set anchor.

## Island Bay (Sukkwan Island)

Island Bay is just north of Dunbar Inlet.

Chart 17408
Entrance: 55°05.57′ N, 132°52.23′ W
Anchor (north basin):
55°05.65′ N, 132°51.40′ W
Anchor: 55°05.32′ N, 132°51.15′ W

> *Island Bay . . . affords well-protected anchorage from all winds, except W, in depths of 6 to 7 fathoms, sticky to hard bottom. Swinging room is limited. . . .* (CP)

Island Bay has a nice, intimate feel and anchor sites are limited only by your imagination.

Anchor (north basin) in 6 fathoms over a thin layer of mud with fair holding.

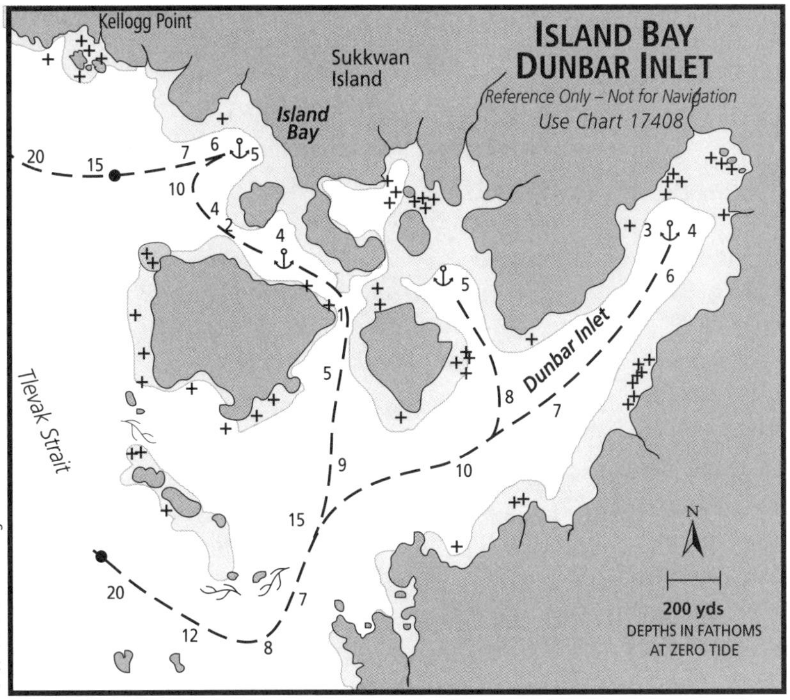




## Dunbar Inlet (Sukkwan Island)

Dunbar Inlet is 15 miles southeast of Tlevak Narrows.

Chart 17408
Entrance: 55°04.41′ N, 132°52.32′ W
Anchor (head of bay): 55°05.40′ N, 132°48.95′ W
Anchor: 55°05.20′ N, 132°50.18′ W

*Dunbar Inlet . . . has numerous rocks and islets at the entrance, but a clear channel, . . . with least depths of 5 to 6 fathoms, leads to a protected anchorage inside. Small craft can find good anchorage in the passage between Dunbar Inlet and Island Bay.* (CP)

Dunbar Inlet has a somewhat tricky entrance. However, the effort is well worth it. There is good shelter from all weather and plenty of swinging room over a flat bottom. This is one of the better anchor sites in a southeast gale for the greater Tlevak Strait/Cordova Bay area.

Anchor (head of bay) in 4 fathoms over sand and mud with good holding.

*Stellar Sea Lion*

## Baldy Bay (Dall Island)

Baldy Bay is 2 miles southwest of the McFarland Islands.

Chart 17409
Entrance (View Cove Entrance Light bearing 000°T at 0.5 Nm): 55°02.65′ N, 132°57.89′ W

*Baldy Bay . . . is easily approached when coming from Cordova Bay. The entrance is between High Point and Reef Point. It has two large arms known as View Cove and Coco Harbor. High Point, bold and rounded, is the S point of the entrance to the bay.* (CP)

Baldy Bay is the largest inlet on the east shore of Dall Island. The large northwest arm is called View Cove. Coco Harbor is the well protected but deep arm to the west. Windy Cove, the south arm, is surrounded by high ridges.

Baldy Bay and its main arms are entered north of Reef Islands. Entrance Island can be passed on either side, but a mid-channel approach is required to avoid the off-lying rocks surrounding the island and along both shores. The anchorages in Baldy Bay are mostly deep and not strongly recommended. Because of the low pass in View Cove leading to the west side of Dall Island, winds rip through the area. We would recommend Dunbar Inlet, 6 miles northeast, as a more satisfactory anchorage for small craft.

## View Cove (Dall Island)

View Cove is in Baldy Bay.

**Chart 17408**
**Entrance: 55°03.42′ N, 132°59.52′ W**

> *View Cove . . . extends about 4.5 miles inside Reef Point and is practically free of obstruction. The shores are generally steep-to. . . . A good anchorage, with protection from all but W to NW winds, is about 0.25 mile from the head of the bay in 15 to 20 fathoms.*
>
> *Pile ruins of a wharf are on the N shore of View Cove about 2 miles from Reef Point; caution is advised.* (CP)

View Cove is open to the southeast and gales rip through the cove and into Manhattan Arm on the west side of Dall Island. Turn inside the reef light, north of a 7.5 fathom shoal, and find 10 fathoms. There is an old wharf on the north side below the clear-cut area. Karst formations are visible along the north shore.

## Green Inlet (View Cove)

Green Inlet is on the south shore of View Cove.

**Chart 17408**
**Entrance: 55°03.92′ N, 133°01.91′ W**
**Anchor: 55°03.52′ N, 133°02.23′ W**

> *Green Inlet . . . offers good anchorage, with sticky bottom, for small craft, but the entrance is shallow, running dry on minus tides, and large mudflats extend a long distance from the head; also there are heavy williwaws.* (CP)

A sand bar awash at zero tide obstructs the entrance to Green Inlet, but inside is a well-protected anchorage for several small craft. Avoid the rocks at the inlet entrance.

Anchor in 3 fathoms over grass, mud and shells with fair-to-good holding.

## Coco Harbor (Dall Island)

Coco Harbor is the west arm of Baldy Bay.

**Chart 17408**
**Entrance: 55°02.45′ N, 133°01.45′ W**

> *Off this* [entrance] *island are numerous rocks and islets that must be avoided when entering Coco Harbor.*
>
> *Near the head of Coco Harbor are anchorage depths of 12 to 20 fathoms, soft bottom, but heavy williwaws prevail.* (CP)

## Windy Cove (Dall Island)

Windy Cove is 2 miles west northwest of High Point.

**Chart 17408**
**Entrance: 55°02.15′ N, 133°01.58′ W**

> *Windy Cove . . . is narrow, clear, and deep. Its entrance is scarcely 100 yards wide with a depth of 1 fathom. Strong tidal currents prevail through this entrance.* (CP)

Windy Cove is a landlocked cove and, despite its name suggesting the presence of williwaws, we would consider it for anchorage. The water is deep once you have passed the entrance bar. A mud shoal extends from the head of the cove to where 2.3 fathoms is shown on Chart 17408. A stern-tie to shore may be required.

## Reef Islands Inlet (Baldy Bay)

Reef Islands Inlet lies south of Reef Islands west of High Point.

**Chart 17408**
**Entrance (View Cove Entrance Light bearing 000°T at 0.5 Nm): 55°02.65′ N, 132°57.89′ W**
**Entrance (West Arm, Reef Island Inlet): 55°01.57′ N, 132°58.81′ W**
**Anchor (East Arm): 55°00.91′ N, 132°58.90′ W**
**Anchor (West Arm, Reef Island Inlet): 55°00.82′ N, 132°59.85′ W**

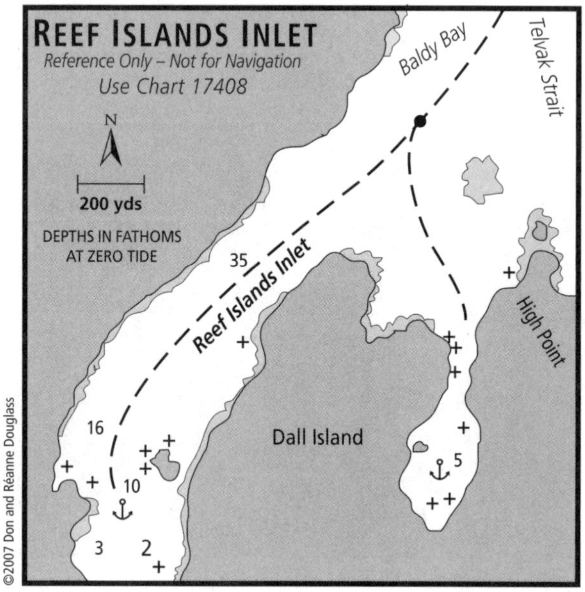

*S of Reef Islands and just inside High Point is a small inlet with two arms at the head. The W arm is rather deep and clear, but the anchorage area is suitable only for small vessels; it is exposed to williwaws. The E arm offers fairly good anchorage for small vessels. The entrance is very narrow and partially obstructed by rocks awash. Anchor in the center in 5 fathoms, sticky bottom. A 1/4-fathom spot is about 600 yards N of the entrance.* (CP)

Reef Islands Inlet is the unnamed inlet south of Reef Islands and to the west of High Point. The *Coast Pilot* suggests this inlet may hold the better anchor sites in Baldy Bay for small craft.

The East Arm can accommodate just one or two small boats, and a shore tie may be needed. West Arm has slightly more swinging room. As you enter East Arm, favor the eastern shore to avoid the bad mid-channel rock in the center of the entrance.

Anchor (west arm) in 5 to 10 fathoms over mud with good holding.

Anchor (east arm) between the west islet and the avalanche chute in about 5 fathoms over mud with good holding. (Limited swinging room available.)

## Kaigani Strait

Kaigani Strait, south of Tlevak Strait, separates Long Island and the island groups to the northwest of it from Dall Island.

Charts 17408, 17400
North entrance: 55°00.28′ N, 132°55.92′ W
South entrance: 54°43.89′ N, 132°39.09′ W

## Rose Inlet (Dall Island)

Rose Inlet is 20 miles north of Cape Muzon.

Chart 17408
Entrance: 54°57.89′ N, 132°56.09′ W

*Two groups of islands are in the entrance with the entrance channel between.*

*A rock, awash at spring low water, is about 50 yards SE of the prominent point on the N shore* [of Rose Inlet], *about 1.6 miles WNW of Vesta Point. An unmarked ledge, about 300 yards long with a rock awash at lowest tides on its E end, is 0.7 mile W of the prominent point on the N shore. Submerged pile ruins are 100 yards N of the ledge; caution is advised.* (CP)

Réanne Hemingway-Douglass

*A classic fishing boat on the west side of Prince of Wales Island*

Rose Inlet is well sheltered and may have anchorage for small craft near its head.

## Vesta Bay (Dall Island)

Vesta Bay, on the west side of Kaigani Strait, is entered between Luke and Vesta points.

Chart 17408
Entrance: 54°56.24′ N, 132°54.05′ W
Anchor: 54°55.83′ N, 132°55.76′ W

*Vesta Bay . . . appears to be clear in midchannel. . . . There is anchorage near the head of the bay in 12 to 15 fathoms, soft bottom, with scant swinging room.* (CP)

## Grace Harbor (Dall Island)

Grace Harbor is 1.5 miles south of Vesta Bay.

Chart 17408
Entrance: 54°54.87′ N, 132°54.62′ W
Anchor: 54°54.65′ N, 132°55.40′ W

*When entering, give Luke Point . . . a berth of over 0.2 mile to avoid the rocks that extend SE from that point. . . . Anchor near the middle of the basin in 10 to 16 fathoms, soft bottom, taking care to avoid a ledge that extends 150 yards from the N shore. SW winds draw through a low divide from the ocean.* (CP)

Grace Harbor appears to offer good shelter, but we have no local knowledge.

## **Cleva Bay** (Long Island)

Cleva Bay is 1 mile east of Shoe Inlet.

Chart 17431
Entrance: 54°55.91′ N, 132°46.43′ W

> *Cleva Bay . . . is of no importance as an anchorage.* (CP)

## **Shoe Inlet** (Long Island)

Shoe Inlet indents the northwest end of Long Island.

Chart 17431
Entrance: 54°55.90′ N, 132°49.00′ W
Anchor: 54°54.49′ N, 132°47.79′ W

> *Shoe Inlet . . . is clear except near the shore. Anchorage for small vessels can be had near its head.* (CP)

Shoe Inlet has been used intensively for logging operations and the bottom may be covered with debris. We would consider it only as temporary shelter in southerly weather.

Anchor in 8 fathoms over a rocky bottom with poor holding.

## **Touchit Cove** (Shoe Inlet)

Touchit Cove is on the northeast side of Shoe Inlet, just inside the entrance.

Chart 17431
Entrance: 54°55.53′ N, 132°48.21′ W

> *Touchit Cove is a foul bight. . . .* (CP)

## **Howkan Narrows**

Howkan Narrows lies at the south end of Kaigani Strait.

Chart 17409
North entrance (Howkan Narrows): 54°52.90′ N, 132°50.00′ W
South entrance (Howkan Narrows): 54°51.59′ N, 132°48.34′ W

> *The channel is 300 yards wide between Howkan Reef and an extensive kelp patch about 600 yards in diameter on the W side of Howkan Narrows. Mill Reef, between the kelp patch and the shore W of it, shows at high water. There is no safe channel between the kelp patch and the W shore.* (CP)

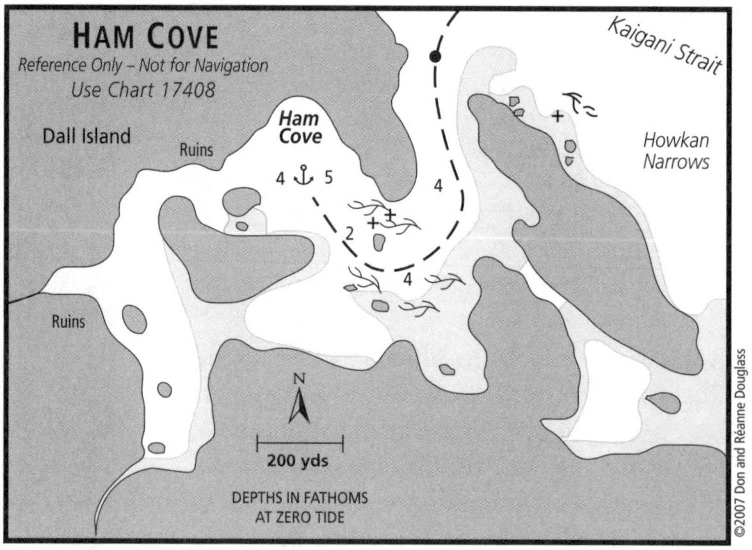


Kaigani Strait and Howkan Narrows are small-craft waterways. The currents are moderate; watch for isolated shoals and turbulent water.

## **Ham Cove** (Dall Island)

Ham Cove is 0.8 mile west of the Channel Islands.

Chart 17408
Entrance: 54°53.09′ N, 132°50.88′ W
Anchor: 54°52.86′ N, 132°51.25′ W

> *Ham Cove . . . has a very narrow entrance and can be entered only by small craft.* (CP)

Ham Cove is a small, rocky site with shallow water for small craft. We like its shelter; however, swinging room is limited and finding the right place can be a challenge.

Anchor in 5 fathoms over sand, gravel and newspaper kelp with poor holding unless well set.

## **Mission Cove** (Long Island)

Mission Cove, on the east side of Kaigani Strait, is 4.5 miles southeast of Grace Harbor.

Chart 17409
Entrance: 54°52.43′ N, 132°48.36′ W
Anchor: 54°52.38′ N, 132°48.18′ W

> *Small craft can anchor here in 6 to 8 fathoms, although there is considerable kelp in the cove.*

*A submerged rock is close off the S shore just inside the entrance.* (CP)

Mission Cove is too small and exposed for our taste.

Anchor in 8 fathoms over a rocky bottom with poor holding and limited swinging room.

## **American Bay** (Dall Island)

American Bay is 12 miles north of Cape Muzon.

Chart 17409
Entrance: 54°51.05′ N, 132°48.46′ W
Anchor (east of Bay Islands): 54°51.10′ N, 132°49.13′ W
Anchor (west of Bay Islands): 54°50.99′ N, 132°49.73′ W

*Small craft may find good anchorage in 5 fathoms near the N shore in the cove just E of the group of islands.* (CP)

American Bay is somewhat sheltered by Howkan Narrows and anchorage can be found close-in along the north shore.

Anchor (either side of Bay Islands) in 5 to 10 fathoms.

## **Bolles Inlet** (Long Island)

Bolles Inlet is 2 miles east of American Bay.

Chart 17409
Entrance: 54°50.30′ N, 132°44.48′ W

*The entrance is very narrow, and rapids occur here; the currents are estimated to be at least 8 knots. It is reported that the inlet once had a logging camp and small craft used the entrance at high-water slack.* (CP)

Bolles Inlet is uncharted and looks quite interesting to explore. The east shore is just 1⁄4 mile from Coning Inlet on the east side of Long Island.

## **Pond Bay** (Dall Island)

Pond Bay is 9 miles north of Cape Muzon.

Chart 17409
Entrance: 54°48.77′ N, 132°44.76′ W
Anchor: 54°48.49′ N, 132°46.66′ W

*A wooded island is halfway toward the head of the bay with a clear channel on the N side. Anchorage may be had W of this island in desired depths up to 10 fathoms, soft bottom. However, a strong wind blows up the bay in SE weather and, because of the danger from dragging, it is not recommended for anchorage.* (CP)

Réanne Hemingway-Douglass

*The sad remains of better days*

Pond Bay appears to provide good anchorage, except for southeast winds, but it is poorly charted. Its south shore, in the lee of the second or third island, may provide adequate shelter. The bottom appears rocky and lined with kelp, so more exploring is required. A stern-tie to shore would be advisable.

Anchor in about 10 fathoms over a thin layer of sand and mud with poor-to-fair holding.

## **New Prop Cove** (Dall Island)

New Prop Cove is 7 miles north of Cape Muzon.

Chart 17409
Entrance: 54°46.67′ N, 132°43.41′ W

*The small bight about 0.8 mile N of North Kaigani Harbor has an entrance difficult even for small vessels. Good anchorage may be had here in 5 to 10 fathoms. Very small vessels may anchor near the head in about 3-1/2 fathoms.* (CP)

"New Prop Cove" is our name for this small bight. The chart for the area is very poorly drawn and, to our dismay, we found a rocky pile lurking just below the surface on the north side of the entrance islet (110). We had to limp into Ketchikan for repairs to our prop. The extensive reefs and kelp seem to provide good shelter for small craft along its south shore, but we will avoid New Prop Cove until it is more adequately charted. South Kaigani Harbor is a better choice.

## **North Kaigani Harbor** (Dall Island)

North Kaigani Harbor is 6 miles north of Cape Muzon.

Chart 17409
Entrance: 54°45.44′ N, 132°43.33′ W

> *North Kaigani Harbor . . . is entirely exposed to SE weather and the ocean swell, and is of no use as an anchorage.* (CP)

## **South Kaigani Harbor** (Dall Island)

South Kaigani Harbor is 5.5 miles north of Cape Muzon.

Chart 17409
Entrance: 54°45.18′ N, 132°43.41′ W
Anchor: 54°45.39′ N, 132°44.88′ W

> *South Kaigani Harbor . . . is constricted at the entrance by reefs on the N side and a rock that uncovers 5 feet on the S side. . . . During fishing season a fish-buying scow may be anchored in the harbor. The scow sells gasoline, diesel fuel, water, provisions and fishing supplies. In 1968, it was reported that anchorage for small craft was available in depths of about 5 fathoms, mud bottom, in the cove on the S side of the harbor about 0.7 mile above the entrance. In 1971, submerged pilings were reported in about the middle of the cove; caution is advised.* (CP)

The south basin of South Kaigani Harbor offers good shelter for two or three small vessels. Don't count on the fish-buying scow mentioned above in *Coast Pilot*; the south cove has been used as a fly-in fishing resort and has a private float, buoy and pilings.

Locals say that the cove is secure in 40-knot southeast winds. We found anchoring near the center of the cove quite satisfactory.

Anchor in 6 fathoms over mud with good holding.

## **Datzkoo Harbor** (Dall Island)

Datzkoo Harbor is 5 miles north of Cape Muzon.

Chart 17409
Entrance: 54°44.41′ N, 132°43.17′ W
Anchor: 54°44.73′ N, 132°45.89′ W

> *The entrance is clear and is N of two wooded islands. Anchorage can be had in 15 to 20 fathoms, soft bottom.* (CP)

An anchorage can be found 200 yards east of the small islet at the head of the bay.

Anchor in 10 to 12 fathoms over a soft, thin bottom with fair holding.

## **Little Daykoo Harbor** (Dall Island)

Little Daykoo Harbor is 2.5 miles north of Cape Muzon.

Chart 17409
Entrance: 54°42.35′ N, 132°41.95′ W

> *Little Daykoo Harbor* [is] *a small-boat harbor . . .* (CP)

Little Daykoo Harbor may offer good shelter to small boats, but it looks like a rock pile to us.

## **McLeod Bay** (Dall Island)

McLeod Bay is 2 miles north of Cape Muzon.

Chart 17409
Entrance: 54°41.62′ N, 132°41.90′ W

> *Temporary anchorage in 5 to 9 fathoms, exposed to all E winds, may be had in this bay, about 0.5 mile NW of a green landslide. The chart and the lead are the best guides. . . . At the head of the bay is a small stream of freshwater and a sand and gravel beach for about 200 yards.* (CP)

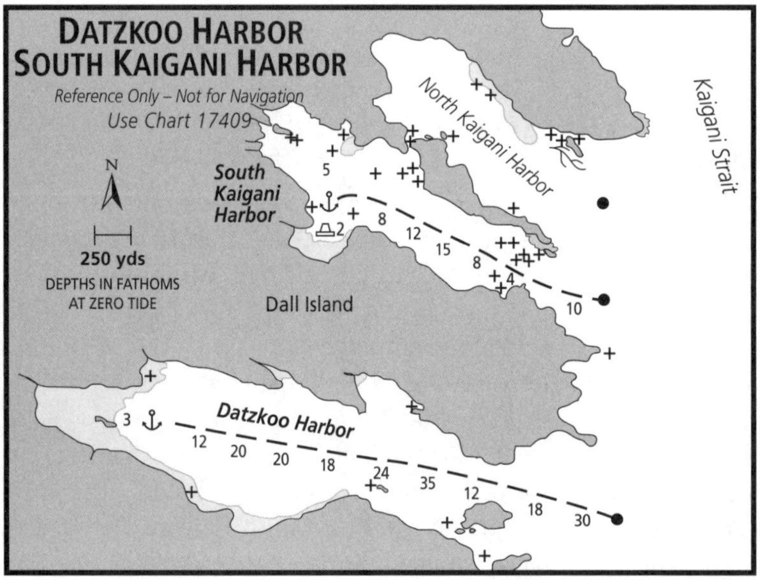

The chart indicates that the bay is an unused submarine cable area. Being totally open to southeast winds and chop, this bay cannot be recommended.

### Cape Muzon (Dall Island)

Cape Muzon is the south extremity of Dall Island.

Charts 17409, 17400
Position (Muzon Light brg 000°T at 1.0 Nm): 54°38.82′ N, 132°41.51′ W

*Cape Muzon . . . forms the NW headland of Dixon Entrance. . . . Off the E end of the cape is a group of small islands and rocks. A breaker is 0.3 mile off the S shore of the cape. Vessels should give the cape a berth of at least 1 mile.* (CP)

## DALL ISLAND WEST COAST, FROM NORTH TO SOUTH

Dall Island is about 40 miles long from Eagle Point, its northwest extremity in Meares Passage, to Cape Muzon.

Chart 17400

*Both the E and W coasts of the island are indented by numerous bays, coves, and inlets, some of which are excellent harbors of refuge.*

*The W coast of Dall Island . . . is rugged with prominent partially wooded peaks ranging in elevation to about 3,000 feet.* (CP)

The west coast of Dall Island is exposed to the full force of the Gulf of Alaska, but its unique topography is similar to that of south Baranof Island. Bold headlands with karst formations here and there can be spotted through the trees along shore. Dall's many deep inlets surrounded by high peaks and ridges remain some of the least frequented cruising grounds and are an "undiscovered treasure." However, navigating along this coast is a constant challenge.

### Meares Passage (Dall Island)

Meares Passage, at the northwest end of Dall Island, lies between Dall and Suemez islands.

Chart 17407
North entrance (between Suemez and Dall islands): 55°16.58′ N, 133°11.69′ W
South entrance (Diver Islands Light bearing 090°T at 0.9 Nm): 55°10.68′ N, 133°17.52′ W

*Meares Passage . . . affords passage from the sea to Tlevak Narrows and the E part of Ulloa Channel. The approach to Meares Passage from W is foul in places for about 2 miles from the Suemez Island shore.* (CP)

Meares Passage connects Craig to the 40-mile-long west coast of Dall Island. Ocean swells are not prevalent until you are south of Millar Rocks and Divers islands. Meares Passage has obstructions at both ends as noted on the chart.

### Bobs Bay (Dall Island)

Bobs Bay is 4 miles south of Meares Island.

Chart 17407
Entrance: 55°11.15′ N, 133°14.73′ W
Entrance (east arm): 55°11.64′ N, 133°11.93′ W
Anchor (east arm): 55°11.78′ N, 133°10.12′ W

*The bay is divided into three arms. The northernmost arm is deep and clear and the middle arm is foul and not navigable except by small boats. The easternmost arm affords good anchorage*

Linda Lewis

*The very beautiful Bobs Bay*

*for moderate sized craft in 6 to 10 fathoms, soft bottom.* (CP)

Bobs Bay at the northwest end of Dall Island is an almost landlocked bay offering very good shelter deep in the East Arm.

Anchor in 4 to 8 fathoms over mud bottom with good holding.

## Diver Bay (Dall Island)

Diver Bay is 6 miles south of Meares Island.

Chart 17407
Entrance: 55°10.54′ N, 133°14.45′ W

*The bay is clear except for a kelp-marked rock, with 1/2 fathom over it, that is 650 yards from the N shore about in midchannel. . . . Small craft can find excellent anchorage in the Hole in the Wall, an indentation in the N shore . . . .* (CP)

## Hole in the Wall (Diver Bay)

Hole in the Wall is on the north side of Diver Bay.

Chart 17407
Entrance: 55°10.32′ N, 133°12.39′ W
Anchor: 55°10.50′ N, 133°11.95′ W

*. . . the entrance is narrow, but has a least depth of 4-1/4 fathoms. Pass either side of the 1/2-fathom rock in entering.* (CP)

Hole in the Wall is a quintessential bowl-shaped Alaskan anchorage, fully protected from outside weather. Swells that decrease as you enter Diver Bay do not enter Hole in the Wall. As you traverse Diver Bay, watch carefully to avoid crab pots.

The entrance fairway to Hole in the Wall is about 40 feet wide with shallowest depths approximately 4 fathoms at its east end. Favor the north shore slightly to avoid a rocky spit at the east end. We prefer to anchor deep in the cove near the south shore in 2 to 3 fathoms, while local fishing boats tend to anchor along the north shore, closer to the entrance.

Anchor in 3 to 5 fathoms over sticky, soft, brown mud and sand with shells; very good holding.

Linda Lewis

*Approaching Hole in the Wall*

## Foul Bay (Dall Island)

Foul Bay is 8 miles south of Meares Island.

Chart 17407
Entrance: 55°08.42′ N, 133°13.50′ W

*In the center of the bay near the entrance is a cluster of submerged rocks. The shores of the bay are foul where the bay narrows; reefs extend from either shore almost to midchannel, leaving a narrow passage 50 to 100 feet wide through which very small boats pass to a secure anchorage in 3 to 5 fathoms near the head of the bay. Only those with local knowledge should enter the bay.* (CP)

Although some shelter may be available behind the reefs in Foul Bay, its entrance, which opens directly to the west, is intimidating and not often used even by local fishermen due to its threatening lee shore.

## Sea Otter Harbor (Dall Island)

Sea Otter Harbor is 9 miles south of Meares Island.

Chart 17408
Entrance: 55°07.02′ N, 133°14.39′ W

*Sea Otter Harbor . . . divides into two branches about 1.4 miles from the entrance.*

*In entering Sea Otter Harbor, small boats, with local knowledge, frequently use a channel to the E of Entrance Island, passing close to Cape Lookout.* (CP)

## Hook Arm (Sea Otter Harbor)

Hook Arm is the north arm of Sea Otter Harbor.

Chart 17408
Entrance: 55°06.86′ N, 133°11.89′ W
Anchor (Channel Island bight): 55°07.74′ N, 133°09.89′ W

*Hook Arm . . . is well protected from wind and sea. Small vessels can anchor in 8 to 15 fathoms at the head of the arm or in the bight N of Channel Island. A small sand and gravel beach is at the head of this bight.* (CP)

Hook Arm, surrounded by high ridges 3 miles northeast of Cape Lookout, is a convenient shelter for exploring this part of the coast.

Anchor in 8 to 12 fathoms on the north side of Channel Island over a mixed bottom; fair-to-good holding.

## **Manhattan Arm** (Sea Otter Harbor)

Manhattan Arm is the southeast branch of Sea Otter Harbor.

Chart 17408
Entrance: 55°06.57′ N, 133°11.71′ W

*Manhattan Arm . . . is exposed to the force of the wind and sea and is too deep for secure anchorage.* (CP)

Manhattan Arm lines up with View Cove on the east side of Dall Island to funnel southeast winds with great velocity.

## **Sakie Bay** (Dall Island)

Sakie Bay is 13 miles south of Meares Island.

Chart 17408
Entrance: 55°04.10′ N, 133°13.35′ W

*The channel, about 300 yards wide, is to the S of Table Rock. Tide rips, severe for small craft, are experienced at the entrance. The bay has not been thoroughly surveyed.* (CP)

Sakie Bay gets the full blast of northwesterlies, but it appears to offer fair shelter in southerly winds. Tide rips suggest an irregular bottom that has not been adequately surveyed. We would use Hook Arm or Waterfall Bay.

## **Fisherman Cove** (Dall Island)

Fisherman Cove is 15 miles south of Meares Island.

Chart 17408
Entrance: 55°01.23′ N, 133°10.57′ W
Anchor: 55°01.77′ N, 133°10.05′ W

*At the entrance is a small island. . . . In entering, pass the S point of this island at a distance of about 100 yards and steer for the left or W edge of the sand beach at the head of the cove. The anchorage is about 170 yards wide, with depths of 3 to 6 fathoms, mud bottom, and is large enough for four or five small fishing vessels.* (CP)

Fisherman Cove has temporary anchorage in fair summer weather only. We can't help wondering how it fares in southwest gales.

## **Camp Cove** (Dall Island)

Camp Cove is 5 miles south of Sakie Bay.

Chart 17408
Entrance: 54°59.50′ N, 133°09.96′ W

*The S shore of the cove is foul.* (CP)

Camp Cove is another rock pile with kelp that is poorly surveyed. It may be useful for small craft as temporary anchorage in fair weather.

## **Welcome Cove** (Dall Island)

Welcome Cove is 1.5 miles north of Cape Augustine.

Chart 17408
Entrance: 54°58.38′ N, 133°09.95′ W

*Off the entrance the ground is foul, but there is a narrow channel into the cove, where anchorage may be had for small boats in 2 to 5 fathoms, mud bottom. The entrance should not be attempted without local knowledge.* (CP)

Welcome Cove is a misnomer as far as we are concerned. Not only is the cove poorly charted, but its entrance is so encumbered with rocks that, upon an attempt to reconnoiter in *Baidarka*, the bow watch (first mate) screamed, "Get out of here; it's too shallow!" Pass it up and leave it to small, local runabouts.

## **Augustine Bay** (Dall Island)

Augustine Bay is 18.5 miles south of Meares Island.

Chart 17408
Entrance: 54°57.57′ N, 133°09.89′ W

*Kelp and rocks extend offshore; depths of 8 to 16 fathoms are found near the center of the bay. It is open and exposed and is not suitable for anchorage.* (CP)

Augustine Bay is open to the full force of Gulf of Alaska weather and is poorly charted. We do not recommend it as an anchorage.

## **Waterfall Bay** (Dall Island)

Waterfall Bay is 20 miles south of Meares Island.

**Chart 17408**
**Entrance (Gourd Island bearing 070°T at 0.35 Nm): 54°56.54′ N, 133°07.76′ W**
**Anchor (north of north island): 54°57.04′ N, 133°06.85′ W**
**Anchor (east bight): 54°56.83′ N, 133°03.08′ W**

> *Dangers are shown on the chart. The bay has two prominent waterfalls: one at the head and the other on the N shore close to the N island and several islets.*
>
> *The bay may be entered NW or SE of Gourd Island.*
>
> *Small craft anchor in 10 fathoms on the NW side of the bay, just N of the N island. There is anchorage for small craft, 50 feet long or less,* [Author's note: We would say 30 feet or less] *in 5 fathoms, mud bottom, in the small bight at the extreme head of the bay.* (CP)

Waterfall Bay, immediately south of Cape Augustine, is ringed by high peaks with steep-sided shores. Waterfall Bay is one of the most stunning inlets along Dall Island's west coast and deserves a stop. However, depths are so great that vessels under 70 feet may have trouble finding a good place to drop anchor. We have taken rest breaks here but, despite its beauty, we prefer not to remain overnight. The small bight at the head of the bay is suitable only for one vessel under 30 feet.

## **Gold Harbor** (Dall Island)

Gold Harbor is 21.5 miles south of Meares Island.

**Chart 17408**
**Entrance: 54°54.73′ N, 133°05.71′ W**

> *Gold Harbor . . . is reported clear in midchannel.*
>
> *The small cove W of the NW point of the entrance to Gold Harbor is foul.* (CP)

Gold Harbor is too deep for convenience, but anchorage may be found up against the bowl at the head of the bay using a stern-tie. The bottom is rocky. The entrance is marked by a long gray scar that runs from the top of the ridge to about two-thirds of the way to shore.

## **Gooseneck Harbor** (Dall Island)

Gooseneck Harbor is 18 miles northwest of Cape Muzon and 23.5 miles south of Meares Island.

**Chart 17408**
**Entrance: 54°53.01′ N, 133°03.19′ W**
**Anchor: 54°53.53′ N, 133°00.50′ W**

> *The upper half of the harbor is mostly obstructed by bare rocks and ledges, and the head is especially foul. . . . In entering, follow the N shore at a distance of about 250 yards until about 1 mile inside. After rounding the point on the N side, find anchorage for small craft 100 yards off the N shore, 1.5 miles within the entrance.* (CP)

Gooseneck Harbor looks like our kind of place—landlocked by dozens of islets and rocks that cut down the swell, yet provide a scenic and vital view of what is occurring outside. High ridges surround the harbor bowl, deflecting the winds in unusual directions. Gooseneck Harbor is a lovely "bay of islands" and rocks topped with tufts of shrubs and small trees, but its entrance is daunting and depths do not agree with those shown on the chart. (We found 3.2 fathoms where the chart shows 7 fathoms.)

In addition, the bottom is so rocky and irregular we could not get our 110-pound Bruce anchor to set despite several attempts. On our final try, we decided to move south to Port Bazan.

Anchor in about 7 fathoms over a very hard bottom with poor holding.

## **Port Bazan** (Dall Island)

Port Bazan is 14 miles northwest of Cape Muzon and 28 miles south of Meares Island.

**Chart 17409**
**Northwest entrance: 54°49.57′ N, 133°00.15′ W**
**Anchor (in the lee of north center island): 54°50.63′ N, 132°56.48′ W**

> *Port Bazan affords good anchorage N and NE of the islands that stretch across the E part of the bay. The anchorage is well protected from the swell and is generally free of williwaws. It can be entered either SE or NW of Dolgoi Island, but the NW entrance is more often used. . . . Rocks*

*that cover are a considerable distance from the shores of the narrow channels, presenting elements of danger to those without local knowledge. The chart shows known dangers.*

*Anchorage may be had NE of the islands in the center of the bay in 11 to 19 fathoms, mud bottom, or in the bight N of the N island in 11 to 13 fathoms. A rock, bare at low water, is close to the NE end of the N island. A small 6-1/4-fathom shoal is 0.2 mile NE from the N island. The small bight at the head of the bay is foul.* (CP)

Port Bazan, on the south side of Cape Magdalena, is landlocked by large Dolgoi Island at its entrance. You can enter the port by passages on either the north or south side. A careful mid-channel course is required to avoid the submerged rocks lying along the route.

Once you are east of Dolgoi, the swells drop to nil, and very good shelter can be found on the north side of the north island.

Anchor in about 10 fathoms over brown, sticky (and stinky!) mud, with very good holding.

## **Essowah Harbor** (Dall Island)

Essowah Harbor is 10 miles northwest of Cape Muzon.

Chart 17409
Entrance: 54°46.44′ N, 132°54.34′ W

*Essowah Lakes empty into the head of Essowah Harbor. A small lake, 0.5 mile S of Essowah Lakes, empties near the entrance to Essowah Harbor.* (CP)

Essowah Harbor and lakes look interesting, but the area is uncharted and choked with kelp.

## **Security Cove** (Dall Island)

Security Cove is 8 miles northwest of Cape Muzon.

Chart 17409
Entrance: 54°44.99′ N, 132°52.62′ W

*In the bight on the N side, close inside the narrowest part of the entrance, small craft have found temporary anchorage in depths from 6 to 22 fathoms. A small lake, about 0.5 mile inshore . . . empties into the head of Security Cove.* (CP)

## **Liscome Bay** (Dall Island)

Liscome Bay is 5 miles northwest of Cape Muzon.

Chart 17409
Entrance: 54°41.38′ N, 132°48.78′ W
Anchor: 54°42.65′ N, 132°48.94′ W

*Liscome Bay . . . affords an anchorage for small vessels, but is exposed to S weather and swell. A submerged rock is about 100 yards off the E shore, about 1.1 miles within the entrance, where the bay narrows. . . . Depths of 8 to 10 fathoms are found at the head of the bay.* (CP)

Liscome Bay is sheltered from northwest weather, but it is open to the full effects of the

---

### Port Bazan

*(First Mate's Diary)*

Réanne Hemingway-Douglass

The weather was picking by mid-afternoon today so, after passing up Welcome Cove (a shallow rock pile), we ran into Waterfall Bay, which is absolutely gorgeous. There's a lovely, high waterfall along the north side of the inlet and another smaller one at the head of the bay—hidden from view into until you're practically on it. The little bight of the bay into which this second cascade drops is where *Coast Pilot* says small craft could anchor. It was way too small for us, though, and we guess only a boat smaller than 30 feet could possibly fit.

We would have loved to spend the night there, soothed by the sound of the two falls, but the depths are too great for us to anchor conveniently. Our next try was Gooseneck Harbor, whose rock-infested entrance is harrowing. By the time we'd made three attempts to set anchor, williwaws were sending gusts of 30 to 35 knots and setting *Baidarka* toward the rocks. "I don't like this!" I shouted to Don. "Let's go on to Port Bazan."

So we raised anchor for the last time and brought up a 200-pound rock that took us 30 minutes to dislodge. When we finally anchored in Bazan it was 1608. Ten hours of work today. It's amazing how much mental energy we expend in a day like this. We had a Cup O' Soup tonight. I was too exhausted to cook.

south. Temporary anchorage for small craft is reported at the head of the bay.

Anchor in about 8 fathoms over an unrecorded bottom.

## **Wolk Harbor** (Dall Island)

Wolk Harbor is about 3.5 miles west of Cape Muzon.

Chart 17409
Entrance: 54°40.73′ N, 132°47.25′ W

> *Wolk Harbor . . . is deep throughout and is open and exposed. . . . There are tide rips off Wolk Point between Chickwan Bight and Wolk Harbor.* (CP)

Wolk Harbor has an unused submarine cable area marked on the chart.

## **Chickwan Bight** (Dall Island)

Chickwan Bight is 2 miles west of Cape Muzon.

Chart 17409
Entrance: 54°40.22′ N, 132°45.80′ W

> *Chickwan Bight . . . is open and exposed and has depths of about 30 fathoms at the entrance, decreasing to 12 fathoms near the head.* (CP)

Chickwan Bight is useful only as a lunch stop in fair weather.

Ben Kyle

*Blow holes and flukes—the mighty whales are in action*

# Appendices and References

## APPENDIX A
## Suggested Itineraries for the Inside Passage to Alaska

Although this cruising guide begins in northern British Columbia and includes all of Southeast Alaska, we want to give you our suggested itineraries for cruising the Inside Passage all the way from Seattle, Washington, through Southeast Alaska. We hope you will consider this an added bonus to the book.

These itineraries are just examples of many possible schedules. The length of time you have available, your average cruising speeds and your choice of actual anchor sites will depend on the weather, as well as your own needs and values. We offer these ideas as a planning tool, not as something to follow rigidly.

The more time you can allow for your cruise, the better. Most boaters we've talked to wish they had allowed more time for the passage; many intend to, or actually do, return year after year.

As examples of some of the speediest passages possible, Alaska tugs run twenty-four hours a day, making the Seattle-Juneau-Seattle round-trip in fewer than ten days. A professional skipper who delivers small vessels from Anacortes to Juneau typically takes eight days, running at 10 knots during daylight hours.

For pleasure cruising, we find that less strenuous round-trips of four, six, eight and twelve weeks are most common, with average daily runs of 30 to 75 nautical miles the norm. Add more time if you have a slow boat, a small sailboat with an outboard, or if you simply want a more leisurely trip.

These suggested itineraries give typical daily runs and anchor sites, but they do not include layover days for shore activities, bad weather, or crew needs. You should plan for these contingencies, and adapt your schedule to the particular situation.

When conditions are favorable, you can frequently extend a day's run and accumulate layover days for the future. Then, if conditions deteriorate during a day's run, you can duck into a nearby cove without jeopardizing the overall pace of your trip. The lengthy daylight hours on the Inside Passage in summer (see Duration of Daylight in Appendix E) usually give you time to stop for a few hours to fish, to go ashore or to take a rest at midday before you push on in the afternoon.

## "Ultra Marathon" Itinerary

**Rapid out-and-back trip to Juneau and Sitka**
**Four weeks (28 days) minimum**

*Features:*
Direct ferry route to Juneau with side trips to Tracy Arm to visit glaciers and icebergs, and to Sitka and major hot springs

*Total distance:*
2,030 miles

*Average daily run:*
75 miles

*Advantages:*
For fast boats having minimal time to "do Alaska"

*Feasibility:*
Suitable for well-equipped offshore cruising boats with a cruising speed in excess of 10 knots; good radar and GPS are mandatory.

*Best time:*
Mid-June to mid-July (longest days, least fog); requires stable weather conditions (see notes below under Planning Tips).

*Anchoring required:*
One-third of the time or less; this route offers the possibility of staying at marinas, government float docks or public mooring buoys a majority of the time.

| | | |
|---|---|---|
| Day 1 | Anacortes to Nanaimo | 78 mi. |
| Day 2 | to Campbell River | 84 mi. |
| Day 3 | to Port McNeill | 93 mi. |
| Day 4 | to Inner Warrior Cove | 85 mi. |
| Day 5 | to Goat Harbour | 78 mi. |
| Day 6 | to Lowe Inlet | 67 mi. |
| Day 7 | to Prince Rupert | 65 mi. |
| Day 8 | to Ketchikan | 85 mi. |
| Day 9 | to Wrangell | 95 mi. |
| Day 10 | to Entrance Island, Hobart Bay | 92 mi. |
| Day 11 | to Taku Harbor via Tracy Arm, Sawyer Glacier | 94 mi. |
| Day 12 | to Auke Bay via Juneau | 35 mi. |
| Day 13 | layover | |
| Day 14 | to Tenakee Hot Springs | 63 mi. |
| Day 15 | to Sitka via Peril Strait | 90 mi. |
| Day 16 | to Little Bear Cove | 32 mi. |
| Day 17 | to Baranof Warm Springs | 55 mi. |
| Day 18 | to Petersburg | 77 mi. |
| Day 19 | to Meyers Chuck via Wrangell Narrows | 79 mi. |
| Day 20 | to Ketchikan | 33 mi. |
| Day 21 | to Prince Rupert | 85 mi. |
| Day 22 | to Bishop Bay Hot Springs | 93 mi. |
| Day 23 | to Oliver Cove | 85 mi. |
| Day 24 | to Millbrook Cove | 78 mi. |
| Day 25 | to Port Neville | 97 mi. |
| Day 26 | to Campbell River | 50 mi. |
| Day 27 | to Nanaimo | 84 mi. |
| Day 28 | to Anacortes | 78 mi. |

## "The Highlights" Itinerary

**Fast round-trip to Juneau, Sitka and Glacier Bay**
**Six weeks (42 days) minimum**

*Features:*
Conventional ferry/cruise ship route including Tracy Arm and Glacier Bay to visit tidewater glaciers and icebergs, hot springs and Sitka

*Total Distance:*
2,156 miles

*Average daily run:*
53 miles

*Advantages:*
A fast trip for most small boats. Gives highlights of the Inside Passage for those with limited time; an introduction to scenic and historical opportunities.

*Feasibility:*
Suitable for well-equipped cruising boats with a cruising speed of 7 to 8 knots or more; radar necessary; GPS recommended.

*Best time:*
Early June to late-July (long days; least fog); requires stable weather conditions.

*Anchoring required:*
60 percent of the time

| | | |
|---|---|---|
| Day 1 | Anacortes to Montague via Pender Island | 47 mi. |
| Day 2 | to Scottie Bay | 65 mi. |
| Day 3 | to Campbell River | 48 mi. |
| Day 4 | to Port Neville | 50 mi. |
| Day 5 | to Port Hardy | 61 mi. |
| Day 6 | to Fury Island Cove | 55 mi. |
| Day 7 | to Oliver Cove | 62 mi. |
| Day 8 | to Goat Harbour | 41 mi. |
| Day 9 | to Bishop Bay Hot Springs | 52 mi. |
| Day 10 | to East Inlet | 56 mi. |
| Day 11 | to Prince Rupert | 57 mi. |
| Day 12 | to Foggy Bay | 50 mi. |
| Day 13 | to Ketchikan | 34 mi. |
| Day 14 | to Santa Anna Inlet | 55 mi. |
| Day 15 | to Deception Cove via Wrangell | 57 mi. |
| Day 16 | to Entrance Island, Hobart Bay | 70 mi. |
| Day 17 | to Tracy Arm Cove via Sawyer Glacier | 48 mi. |
| Day 18 | to Juneau | 42 mi. |
| Day 19 | layover | |
| Day 20 | to Swanson Harbor | 51 mi. |
| Day 21 | to North Sandy Cove, Glacier Bay via headquarters | 59 mi. |
| Day 22 | to North Sandy Cove via Muir Glacier | 46 mi. |
| Day 23 | to Swanson Harbor | 51 mi. |
| Day 24 | to Appleton Cove | 65 mi. |
| Day 25 | to Sitka | 51 mi. |
| Day 26 | to Ell Cove | 68 mi. |
| Day 27 | to Portage Bay | 61 mi. |
| Day 28 | to St. John Harbor | 48 mi. |
| Day 29 | to Meyers Chuck | 54 mi. |
| Day 30 | to Ketchikan | 34 mi. |
| Day 31 | to Foggy Bay | 33 mi. |
| Day 32 | to Prince Rupert | 50 mi. |
| Day 33 | to Lowe Inlet | 60 mi. |
| Day 34 | to Goat Harbour | 61 mi. |
| Day 35 | to Oliver Cove | 38 mi. |
| Day 36 | to Fury Island | 55 mi. |
| Day 37 | to Blunden Harbour | 50 mi. |
| Day 38 | to Minstrel Island | 45 mi. |
| Day 39 | to Turn Island Cove | 45 mi. |
| Day 40 | to Sandy Island Marine Park | 57 mi. |
| Day 41 | to Pirates Cove | 62 mi. |
| Day 42 | to Anacortes | 62 mi. |

## "The Classic" Itinerary

**The full round-trip route to most scenic areas and introduction to the Outer Passage**
**Eight weeks (60 days) minimum**

*Features:*
Includes scenic routes such as Fiordland, Misty Fiords, Tracy Arm and Glacier Bay, Lynn Canal and Skagway; north portion of the Outer Passage from Glacier Bay to Milbanke Sound.

*Total distance:*
2,507 miles

*Average daily run:*
42 miles

*Advantages:*
Less hurried, but still a quick pace with a chance to explore some scenic, historic and out-of-the-way places; allows a wider choice of favorable transit times

*Feasibility:*
Suitable for well-equipped cruising boats with a cruising speed of 6 knots or more; radar and GPS recommended.

*Best time:*
Early June to late August (best weather, long days)

*Anchoring required:*
One-third of the time with a few nights at marinas or public floats

| | | |
|---|---|---|
| Day 1 | Anacortes to Stuart Island | 32 mi. |
| Day 2 | to Pirates Cove | 36 mi. |
| Day 3 | to Scottie Bay | 43 mi. |
| Day 4 | to Mitlenatch Island | 37 mi. |
| Day 5 | to Turn Island Cove | 33 mi. |
| Day 6 | to Cutter Cove | 47 mi. |
| Day 7 | to Blunden Harbour | 45 mi. |
| Day 8 | to Millbrook Cove | 38 mi. |
| Day 9 | to Warrior Cove | 37 mi. |

| | | | |
|---|---|---|---|
| Day 10 | to | Oliver Cove | 45 mi. |
| Day 11 | to | Windy Bay | 42 mi. |
| Day 12 | to | Bishop Bay Hot Springs | 51 mi. |
| Day 13 | to | Lowe Inlet | 45 mi. |
| Day 14 | to | Lawson Harbour | 43 mi. |
| Day 15 | to | Prince Rupert | 19 mi. |
| Day 16 | to | Tongass Island Cove | 43 mi. |
| Day 17 | to | Ketchikan | 52 mi. |
| Day 18 | to | Shoalwater Pass via Misty Fiords | 40 mi. |
| Day 19 | to | Yes Bay via Saks Cove | 60 mi. |
| Day 20 | to | Moser Bay | 40 mi. |
| Day 21 | to | Vixen Harbor | 41 mi. |
| Day 22 | to | Wrangell | 45 mi. |
| Day 23 | to | Ruth Cove | 63 mi. |
| Day 24 | to | Entrance Island, Hobart Bay | 47 mi. |
| Day 25 | to | Tracy Arm Cove via Sawyer Glacier | 70 mi. |
| Day 26 | to | Juneau | 42 mi. |
| Day 27 | to | Auke Bay | 15 mi. |
| Day 28 | to | Sullivan Island, Lynn Canal, Rescue Harbor | 43 mi. |
| Day 29 | to | Skagway | 32 mi. |
| Day 30 | to | Boat Harbor or St. James Bay | 48 mi. |
| Day 31 | to | Pleasant Island Bight | 47 mi. |
| Day 32 | to | North Sandy Cove, Glacier Bay | 38 mi. |
| Day 33 | to | North Sandy Cove via Muir Glacier | 45 mi. |
| Day 34 | to | North Inian Island | 38 mi. |
| Day 35 | to | Lost Cove, Lisianski Strait | 33 mi. |
| Day 36 | to | Double Cove | 26 mi. |
| Day 37 | to | Sitka | 44 mi. |
| Day 38 | to | "Annie's Pocket" | 34 mi. |
| Day 39 | to | Baranof Warm Springs | 53 mi. |
| Day 40 | to | Stedman Cove via Kake | 42 mi. |
| Day 41 | to | Port Protection via Rocky Pass | 38 mi. |
| Day 42 | to | Kahli Cove | 42 mi. |
| Day 43 | to | Craig | 42 mi. |
| Day 44 | to | Eek Inlet | 43 mi. |
| Day 45 | to | Charlie's Cove | 26 mi. |
| Day 46 | to | Nichols Bay | 20 mi. |
| Day 47 | to | Prince Rupert | 68 mi. |
| Day 48 | to | Captain Cove | 38 mi. |
| Day 49 | to | Patterson Inlet | 33 mi. |
| Day 50 | to | Helmcken Island Cove | 52 mi. |
| Day 51 | to | Kynumpt Harbour via Higgins Passage | 53 mi. |
| Day 52 | to | Goldstream Harbour | 41 mi. |
| Day 53 | to | Millbrook Cove | 30 mi. |
| Day 54 | to | Blunden Harbour | 38 mi. |
| Day 55 | to | Cutter Cove | 45 mi. |
| Day 56 | to | Turn Island Cove | 47 mi. |
| Day 57 | to | Sandy Island Marine Park | 53 mi. |
| Day 58 | to | Nanaimo | 49 mi. |
| Day 59 | to | Friday Harbor (or Roche Harbor) | 55 mi. |
| Day 60 | to | Anacortes | 20 mi. |

## "Dream" Itinerary

**Off-the-beaten-path round-trip with exposure to full Outer Passage**
**Three months (97 days or more) minimum**

*Features:*
Ultra-scenic route includes Nakwakto Rapids, the top hot springs, Fiordland, Misty Fiords, Tracy Arm and Glacier Bay, Lynn Canal and Skagway; full West Coast Outer Passage, including Vancouver Island's West Coast

*Total distance:*
3,006 miles

*Average daily run:*
31 miles

*Advantages:*
Self-paced immersion trip for those who want to do the Inside Passage to Alaska "right," with time to explore the West Coast Outer Passage and to visit the Northwest's secluded spots and major scenic and historical places; can be undertaken by most well-equipped cruising boats

*Feasibility:*
Suitable for boats equipped for extended travel with a cruising speed of 5 knots or more; radar and GPS recommended

*Best time:*
Mid-May to early September

Anchoring required:
80 percent or more of the time in secluded coves, off the beaten path; balance as desired at public mooring buoys or public floats

| | | |
|---|---|---|
| Day 1 | Anacortes to Stuart Island | 32 mi. |
| Day 2 | to Princess Bay, Wallace Island | 25 mi. |
| Day 3 | to Nanaimo | 28 mi. |
| Day 4 | to Scottie Bay | 33 mi. |
| Day 5 | to Copeland Islands | 35 mi. |
| Day 6 | to Thurston Bay via Yuculta Rapids | 43 mi. |
| Day 7 | to Port Neville | 34 mi. |
| Day 8 | to Mamalilaculla | 37 mi. |
| Day 9 | to Cypress Harbour | 25 mi. |
| Day 10 | to Blunden Harbour | 30 mi. |
| Day 11 | to Goose Point Cove (Nakwakto Rapids) | 18 mi. |
| Day 12 | to Miles Inlet via Seymour Inlet | 13 mi. |
| Day 13 | to Millbrook Cove via Indian Island Cove | 29 mi. |
| Day 14 | to Joe's Bay, Fish Egg Inlet | 26 mi. |
| Day 15 | to Codville Lagoon | 33 mi. |
| Day 16 | to Ocean Falls via McKenzie Rock | 46 mi. |
| Day 17 | to Troup Narrows (Deer Passage) | 24 mi. |
| Day 18 | to Rescue Bay | 38 mi. |
| Day 19 | to Windy Bay via waterfall and Fiordland | 40 mi. |
| Day 20 | to Swanson Bay | 23 mi. |
| Day 21 | to Bishop Hot Springs | 36 mi. |
| Day 22 | to Sue Channel via Weewanie Hot Springs | 25 mi. |
| Day 23 | to Coghlan Anchorage | 28 mi. |
| Day 24 | to East Inlet | 33 mi. |
| Day 25 | to Lawson Harbour | 33 mi. |
| Day 26 | to Prince Rupert | 19 mi. |
| Day 27 | to Tongass Island Cove | 43 mi. |
| Day 28 | to Foggy Bay via Very Inlet | 28 mi. |
| Day 29 | to Ketchikan | 37 mi. |
| Day 30 | to Carp Island | 32 mi. |
| Day 31 | to Manzanita Bay via Rudyard Bay | 40 mi. |
| Day 32 | to Yes Bay | 48 mi. |
| Day 33 | to Meyers Chuck | 48 mi. |
| Day 34 | to Frosty Bay | 25 mi. |
| Day 35 | to Wrangell | 30 mi. |
| Day 36 | to Petersburg | 40 mi. |
| Day 37 | to Fanshaw | 38 mi. |
| Day 38 | to Tracy Arm Cove | 40 mi. |
| Day 39 | to Tracy Arm Cove via Sawyer Glacier | 40 mi. |
| Day 40 | to Taku Harbor | 25 mi. |
| Day 41 | to Juneau | 20 mi. |
| Day 42 | to Auke Bay | 19 mi. |
| Day 43 | to Rescue Harbor | 43 mi. |
| Day 44 | to Skagway | 32 mi. |
| Day 45 | to Boat Harbor or St. James Bay | 48 mi. |
| Day 46 | to Swanson Harbor | 29 mi. |
| Day 47 | to Pleasant Island | 19 mi. |
| Day 48 | to N. Sandy Cove | 40 mi. |
| Day 49 | to N. Sandy Cove via Muir Glacier | 45 mi. |
| Day 50 | to Russell Island Cove via Grand Pacific Glacier and Margerie Glacier | 52 mi. |
| Day 51 | to Blue Mouse Cove via Hopkins Glacier | 37 mi. |
| Day 52 | to North Inian Island | 46 mi. |
| Day 53 | to Lost Cove, Lisianski Strait | 33 mi. |
| Day 54 | to Mirror Harbor, White Sulphur Springs | 12 mi. |
| Day 55 | to Double Cove | 20 mi. |
| Day 56 | to Whitestone Cove | 28 mi. |
| Day 57 | to Sitka | 15 mi. |
| Day 58 | to "Annie's Pocket" | 34 mi. |
| Day 59 | to Ell Cove | 46 mi. |
| Day 60 | to Baranof Warm Springs | 13 mi. |
| Day 61 | to "Honeydew Cove" | 22 mi. |
| Day 62 | to "Baidarka Anchorage" via Kake | 34 mi. |
| Day 63 | to Hole in the Wall (Prince of Wales Island) | 28 mi. |
| Day 64 | to Devilfish Bay | 28 mi. |
| Day 65 | to Bob's Place | 38 mi. |
| Day 66 | to Craig via Klawock | 24 mi. |
| Day 67 | to South Pass Cove | 33 mi. |
| Day 68 | to Charlie's Cove | 37 mi. |
| Day 69 | to Nichols Bay | 20 mi. |
| Day 70 | to Prince Rupert via Duke Island and Foggy Bay if necessary | 68 mi. |
| Day 71 | to Captains Cove | 38 mi. |
| Day 72 | to Patterson Inlet | 33 mi. |
| Day 73 | to Weinberg Inlet | 27 mi. |
| Day 74 | to Helmcken Island Cove | 30 mi. |
| Day 75 | to Oliver Cove | 45 mi. |
| Day 76 | to Rock Inlet Cove | 42 mi. |
| Day 77 | to Millbrook Cove (return to San Juans Islands via east or west coast of Vancouver Island. We suggest West Coast of Vancouver Island. | 40 mi. |
| Day 78 | to Bull Harbour | 33 mi. |
| Day 79 | to Sea Otter Cove | 32 mi. |
| Day 80 | to Winter Harbour | 26 mi. |
| Day 81 | to Klaskino Inlet | 19 mi. |
| Day 82 | to Klaskish Inlet | 12 mi. |

## "Dream" Itinerary *(Continued)*

| | | | |
|---|---|---|---|
| Day 83 | to | Baidarka Cove | 23 mi. |
| Day 84 | to | Gay Passage | 10 mi. |
| Day 85 | to | Petroglyph Cove | 17 mi. |
| Day 86 | to | Queen Cove | 23 mi. |
| Day 87 | to | Friendly Cove (Yuquot) | 30 mi. |
| Day 88 | to | Hot Springs Cove | 30 mi. |
| Day 89 | to | Little White Pine Cove | 19 mi. |
| Day 90 | to | Adventure Cove via Tofino | 20 mi. |
| Day 91 | to | Ucluelet | 32 mi. |
| Day 92 | to | Broken Group | 12 mi. |
| Day 93 | to | Dodger Pass via Broken Group | 15 mi. |
| Day 94 | to | Port San Juan | 42 mi. |
| Day 95 | to | Victoria | 53 mi. |
| Day 96 | layover | | |
| Day 97 | to | Anacortes | 40 mi. |

## "Maxi-Dream" for Boats with Unlimited Time

Additional stops in British Columbia might include Smith and Rivers Inlets, Fish Egg Inlet, the west and east coasts of Prince of Wales Island, Queen Charlotte Islands, Queens Sound and the "backcountry" of Vancouver Island's West Coast. Consider adding these to your next trip.

## Fuel Stops from Washington to Southeast Alaska for Cruising Boats

(Other fuel supplies may be available during fishing season—make local inquiry. Water is available at all stops and most have provisions.)

- Anacortes
- Friday Harbor
- Victoria
- Nanaimo
- Comox
- Lund
- Campbell River
- Blind Channel
- Port McNeill
- Alert Bay
- Port Hardy
- Bella Bella & Shearwater
- Klemtu
- Hartley Bay
- Prince Rupert
- Ketchikan
- Wrangell
- Prince of Wales east coast, Thorne Bay
- Petersburg
- Juneau
- Haines
- Skagway
- Hoonah
- Glacier Bay: Bartlett Cove
- Elfin Cove *(commercial diesel only)*
- Pelican
- Sitka
- Kake
- Point Baker
- Craig

# APPENDIX B
# Distances Table

## Inside Passage—Seattle, Washington, to Cape Spencer, Alaska

From *United States Coast Pilot,* Vol. 8. 2006

| | Cape Spencer, AK | Gustavus, AK | Skagway, AK | Haines, AK | Juneau, AK | Pelican, AK | Sitka, AK | Petersburg, AK | Port Alexander, AK | Cape Decision, AK | Wrangell, AK | Craig, AK | Ketchikan, AK | Metlakatla, AK | Cape Chacon, AK | Hyder, AK | Dixon Entrance, B.C. | Victoria, B.C. | Seattle, WA |
|---|---|---|---|---|---|---|---|---|---|---|---|---|---|---|---|---|---|---|---|
| Seattle, WA 47°36.2'N., 122°20.3'W. | 976 | 938 | 962 | 950 | 879 | 989 | 883 | 771 | 812 | 788 | 749 | 716 | 659 | 660 | 640 | 690 | 664 | 72 | - |
| Victoria, B.C. 48°25.0'N., 123°28.5'W. | 924 | 886 | 910 | 898 | 827 | 937 | 832 | 719 | 761 | 737 | 697 | 664 | 608 | 608 | 588 | 638 | 612 | - | |
| Dixon Entrance, AK 54°28.0'N., 132°52.0'W. | 319 | 290 | 371 | 359 | 288 | 332 | 221 | 180 | 150 | 126 | 157 | 77 | 79 | 66 | 34 | 169 | - | | |
| Hyder, AK 55°54.2'N., 130°00.6'W. | 451 | 423 | 447 | 435 | 364 | 464 | 368 | 256 | 297 | 273 | 234 | 212 | 144 | 148 | 136 | - | | | |
| Cape Chacon, AK 54°40.6'N., 131°59.7'W. | 318 | 289 | 337 | 325 | 254 | 331 | 220 | 146 | 149 | 125 | 123 | 76 | 45 | 32 | - | | | | |
| Metlakatla, AK 55°07.8'N., 131°34.2'W. | 321 | 293 | 317 | 305 | 235 | 334 | 238 | 126 | 167 | 143 | 104 | 109 | 16 | - | | | | | |
| Ketchikan, AK 55°20.5'N., 131°38.7'W. | 307 | 278 | 303 | 291 | 220 | 320 | 224 | 112 | 153 | 129 | 89 | 121 | - | | | | | | |
| Craig, AK 55°28.7'N., 133°09.7'W | 242 | 213 | 264 | 253 | 206 | 255 | 144 | 113 | 73 | 49 | 111 | - | | | | | | | |
| Wrangell, AK 56°28.2'N., 132°23.2'W. | 235 | 208 | 231 | 219 | 148 | 248 | 170 | 40 | 99 | 75 | - | | | | | | | | |
| Cape Decision, AK 55°59.4'N., 134°08.1'W. | 193 | 164 | 215 | 204 | 157 | 206 | 95 | 76 | 24 | - | | | | | | | | | |
| Port Alexander, AK 56°14.8'N., 134°38.8'W. | 173 | 147 | 198 | 186 | 140 | 186 | 82 | 100 | - | | | | | | | | | | |
| Petersburg, AK 56°48.9'N., 132°57.8'W. | 195 | 166 | 191 | 179 | 108 | 207 | 159 | - | | | | | | | | | | | |
| Sitka, AK 57°03.1'N., 135°20.5'W. | 85 | 136 | 187 | 176 | 162 | 79 | - | | | | | | | | | | | | |
| Pelican, AK 57°57.6'N., 136°13.8'W. | 18 | 45 | 148 | 136 | 123 | - | | | | | | | | | | | | | |
| Juneau, AK 58°17.9'N., 134°24.7'W. | 110 | 82 | 100 | 88 | - | | | | | | | | | | | | | | |
| Haines, AK 59°13.8'N., 135°26.1'W. | 124 | 96 | 14 | - | | | | | | | | | | | | | | | |
| Skagway, AK 59°26.8'N., 135°19.3'W. | 136 | 106 | - | | | | | | | | | | | | | | | | |
| Gustavus, AK 58°23.3N., 135°43.6'W. | 32 | - | | | | | | | | | | | | | | | | | |
| CAPE SPENCER, AK 58°10.0'N., 136°38.3'W. | - | | | | | | | | | | | | | | | | | | |

# APPENDIX C
# Key VHF Radio Channels

## Emergency

16 Calling and Distress
When making emergency calls on Ch 16, please use the following guidelines:
**Mayday:** Vessel is threatened by grave danger; request immediate assistance.
**Securité:** Urgent; vessel- or person-safety issue.
**Pan Pan:** Navigation safety issue or meteorological warning.
06 Ship-to-ship safety; Search & Rescue
22A U.S. Coast Guard working frequency
70 Digital Selective Calling

Search & Rescue:
Calling by telephone in an emergency is discouraged —use VHF Ch 16 to report an emergency. To talk with Search & Rescue personnel, call the number of the nearest U.S. Coast Guard station.

## Weather Channels

**Southeast Alaska**
WX1 and WX 2
Scroll through your VHF radio WX frequency channels until you pick up the best signal. See the "Mariner's Weather Guide" in the Introduction of this book to locate the transmitter stations as you listen.

**Seattle through B.C.**
WX1—Seattle, Alert Bay, Comox, Klemtu
WX2—Calvert Island, Dundas Island
WX3—Bowen Island, Mt. Helmcken
WX4—Puget Sound, San Juan Islands

**Marinas & Yacht Clubs—Port Operations**
66—All marinas are being encouraged to use this frequency

## Working Channels

13 Vessel bridge to vessel bridge
09, 67 Intership and Ship-to-shore: all vessels
66 Port Operations
68, 69 Intership and Ship-to-shore: pleasure vessels
72 Intership: all vessels
73 Intership and ship-to shore

## Vessel Traffic Services

05A Seattle—Northern Puget Sound & Western Strait of Juan de Fuca
11 Victoria
12 Vancouver Harbor
71 Comox
11 Prince Rupert—Cape Caution to Hecate Strait
71 Prince Rupert Harbour and approaches, Dixon Entrance
74 Fraser River; Sand Heads to Shoal Point; New Westminster

## Marine Telephone Operators

Washington and Alaska waters marine telephone service was discontinued in 2000.
Canadian waters: the Coast Guard does not service telephone calls; a special marine telephone account can be set up by calling Telus at 800.663.0640 (while in B.C.) or 604.432.2574 (outside B.C.)

## Marine Operator Channels in B.C.

01 Kyuquot, Denny Island
02 Cape Caution, Noble Mountain
03 Rivers Inlet
23 Chatham Point, East Thurlow, Estevan Point, Calvert Island
24 Port Hardy, Grenville Channel
25 Bella Bella
26 Alert Bay (& Ch 86)
27 Bamfield, Swindle Island
28 King Island, Sayward (Newcastle Ridge)
60 Trutch Island, Gil Island, Holberg, Pearse Island
85 Dundas Island, Coast Cone/Smith Sound, Griffin Point

## APPENDIX D
## Summer Wind Reports

The following wind report shows percentages of wind speeds for May through September for the area of East Dixon Entrance:

**Triple Island**

*East Dixon Entrance, south of Dundas Island*

**May winds**

| | |
|---|---|
| less than 20 knots | 84 % |
| 20 to 30 knots | 15 % |
| greater than 34 knots | 1 % |

**June winds**

| | |
|---|---|
| less than 20 knots | 87 % |
| 20 to 30 knots | 13 % |
| greater than 34 knots | nil |

**July winds**

| | |
|---|---|
| less than 20 knots | 92 % |
| 20 to 30 knots | 8 % |
| greater than 34 knots | nil |

**August winds**

| | |
|---|---|
| less than 20 knots | 91 % |
| 20 to 30 knots | 9 % |
| greater than 34 knots | nil |

**September winds**

| | |
|---|---|
| less than 20 knots | 85 % |
| 20 to 30 knots | 14 % |
| greater than 34 knots | 1 % |

## APPENDIX E
## Duration of Daylight

Typical duration of daylight at 58° North (Juneau and Glacier Bay)

**June 15**

*(Daylight Time at 135° W)*

| | | |
|---|---|---|
| Nautical (morning) | twilight | — |
| Civil | twilight | 0241 |
| Sunrise | | 0356 |
| | | |
| Sunset | | 2205 |
| Civil | twilight | 2320 |
| Nautical (evening) | twilight | — |

Hours of daylight: 18 hours, 09 minutes
Hours of daylight and civil twilight:
20 hours, 39 minutes
Hours of daylight and nautical twilight: 24 hours

**August 15**

*(Daylight Time at 135° W)*

| | | |
|---|---|---|
| Nautical (morning) | twilight | 0327 |
| Civil | twilight | 0434 |
| Sunrise | | 0521 |
| | | |
| Sunset | | 2046 |
| Civil | twilight | 2133 |
| Nautical (evening) | twilight | 2239 |

Hours of daylight: 15 hours, 25 minutes
Hours of daylight and civil twilight:
16 hours, 59 minutes
Hours of daylight and nautical twilight:
19 hours, 12 minutes

### Notes on Duration of Daylight Tables

1. *Civil twilight* is defined as that time when the sun is six degrees below the nominal horizon. At this time, the horizon is clearly visible, as are the brightest stars.
2. *Nautical twilight* is defined as that time when the sun is twelve degrees below the nominal horizon. At this time, the horizon is barely visible or fading from view.
3. Factors of local terrain, fog or moonlight can influence usable daylight or twilight hours.
4. See the Nautical Almanac for the formula to interpolate for exact times for various latitudes and longitudes.

## APPENDIX F
## Sources for Fishing Regulations

Southeast Alaska is home to some of the most productive fishing waters in the world, and opportunities for quality fishing are endless for small craft.

The Alaska Department of Fish and Game publishes a yearly pamphlet entitled *Sport Fishing Regulations Summary for Southeast Alaska*, which includes a summary of regulations that become effective in April of each year. These can be obtained by contacting Alaska Department of Fish and Game, Sportfish Division, 2030 Sea Level Drive, Suite 205, Ketchikan, Alaska, 99901, or by calling 907.225.2859. A pamphlet is also available on line at www.sf.adfg.state.ak.us.

Toxic paraplegic shellfish warnings, as well as local fishing closures/openings, are broadcast on VHF weather channels.

---

## APPENDIX G
## Documenting Local Knowledge

1. Coves, bays or bights that seem to offer full or limited protection from different weather conditions are identified and visited by the authors.
2. Routes are sketched and photographed.
3. Perusal of a possible anchor site is made with a dual-frequency recording echo sounder; major underwater obstacles are identified; depth and flatness of the bottom over the expected swinging area are checked; depths are then recorded on the sketches.
4. A sample test of the bottom is made by using a small "lunch hook" attached to light line and six feet of chain for maximum responsiveness and feel of the bottom.
5. The response of the anchor to the bottom is noted (i.e., soft or hard mud, sand, gravel, rocky, etc.; also, digging power, bounce, foul with kelp, pull out, etc.)
6. Additional line is let out to fully set the anchor.
7. A pull-down, with the engine in reverse, is made against the anchor to test holding power of the bottom.
8. Upon retrieving the anchor, we inspect the residue on its flukes to verify bottom material, as well as the type of grass, kelp, etc.
9. Discussions are held with local residents and fishermen about anchorages, names, etc., and their comments noted on the sketches. In some cases rough drafts of the manuscript are sent to experts for review.
10. The information gathered from our tests or that submitted by local experts is consolidated and edited and becomes the local knowledge we have presented in our diagrams and text.

---

## APPENDIX H
## Sources of Books and Nautical Charts

Titles published by Fine Edge Nautical & Recreational Publishing can be found at most ship's chandlers and nautical bookstores. For a current list of titles, please go to www.FineEdge.com

# APPENDIX I
## Provincial and Federal Agencies; Guides and Air Transportation; Visitors Centers: Prince Rupert, B.C., and Alaska

**Admiralty Island National Monument**
8461 Old Dairy Road
Juneau, AK 99801
Tel.: 907.586.8790

**Alaska Marine Highway (Juneau and Prince Rupert)**
Tel.: 800.642.0066
Web (to make reservations): www.ferryalaska.com

**Alaska Marine Highway (Prince Rupert)**
Tel.: 250.627.1744
Fax: 250.624.9554
Web (to make reservations): www.ferryalaska.com

**Alaska Natural History Association**
750 W. 2nd Avenue
Anchorage, AK 99501
Tel.: 907.274.8440

**Glacier Bay National Park and Preserve**
P.O. Box 140, Gustavus, AK 99826
Tel Visitor Information Station (May through September): 907.697.2627
Tel (after hours; emergency): 907.697.2322
Tel (October through April): 907.697.2230
Fax: 907.697.2654
Web (for Permit form, park regulations, maps): www.nps.gov/glba

**Haines Convention and Visitors Bureau**
Box 530
122 Second Ave.
Haines, AK 99827
Tel.: 907.766.2234
Web: www.haines.ak.us

**Juneau Convention and Visitors Bureau**
101 Egan Drive
Juneau, AK 99801
Tel.: 907.586.2284
Web: www.traveljuneau.com

**Ketchikan Visitors Bureau**
131 Front Street
Ketchikan, AK 99901
Tel.: 907.225.6166
Web: www.visit-ketchikan.com

**Mendenhall Glacier Visitor Center**
8465 Old Dairy Road
Glacier Spur Road
Juneau, AK 99801
Tel.: 907.789.0097

**Misty Fiords National Monument**
Ketchikan/Misty Fiords Ranger District
3031 Tongass
Ketchikan, AK 99901
Tel.: 907.225.2148
Fax: 907.225.8738
Web: www.fs.fed.us\r10\tongass\index.shtml

**Petersburg Visitor Information Center**
P.O. Box 649
Petersburg, AK 99833
Web: www.petersburg.org

**Prince Rupert Convention and Visitors Bureau**
215 Cow Bay Road, Suite 100
Prince Rupert, B.C. V8J 3S1 Canada
Tel.: 250.624.5637
Fax: 250.624.6105

**Sitka Convention and Visitors Bureau**
Box 1226
303 Lincoln Street
Sitka, AK 99835
Tel.: 907.747.5940
Fax: 907.747.3739
Web: www.sitka.org

**Skagway Convention and Visitors Bureau**
Box 1029
Skagway, AK 99840
Tel.: 907.983.2854
Fax: 907.983.3854
Web: www.skagway.com

**Southeast Alaska Visitor Center**
50 Main Street
Ketchikan, AK 99901
Tel.: 907.228.6220
Fax: 907.228.6234
email: kvb@ktn.net
Web: www.ketchikanonline.com/info.html

**Stickeen Wilderness Adventures**
P.O. Box 934
Wrangell, AK 99929
Fax: 907.874.2997
Email: info@alaskavistas.com
Web: www.alaskavistas.com

**Taquan Air**
1007 Water Street
Ketchikan, AK 99901
Tel.: 907.225.8800 or 800.770.8800
Email: reservations@taquanair.com
Web: www.taquanair.com

**Tongass National Forest—Craig**
Craig Ranger District
900 9th St., P.O. Box 500
Craig, AK 99921
Tel.: 907.826.1600

**Tongass National Forest—Juneau**
Summer Recreation Activity and Cabin Reservations
101 Egan Dr.
Juneau, AK 99801
Tel.: 877.444.6777

**Tongass National Forest —Ketchikan**
Misty Fiords Ranger District
3031 Tongass Ave
Ketchikan, AK 99901
Tel.: 907.225.2148

**Tongass National Forest—Sitka**
204 Siginaka Way
Sitka, AK 99835
Tel.: 907.747.4218

**U.S. Forest Service Information Center**
101 Egan Drive
Juneau, AK 99801
Tel.: 907.586.8800

**Wrangell Chamber of Commerce**
Box 49
Wrangell, AK 99929
Tel.: 907.874.3901

# Bibliography & References


*Alaska-Yukon Wild Flowers Guide.* Anchorage: Alaska Northwest Publishing Company, 1974.

Ashenfelter, Pete & Nancy. *Row to Alaska by Wind & Oar.* Anacortes, WA: Anderson Publishing Inc., 1994.

Bohn, Dave. *Glacier Bay, the Land and the Silence,* edited by David Brower, San Francisco: Sierra Club, 1967.

Burch, David. *Radar for Mariners.* San Francisco: International Marine/McGraw Hill, 2005. [Very complete and accessible information; includes CD for radar simulation practice.]

Calder, Nigel. *Boatowner's Mechanical and Electrical Manual,* 2nd Ed. San Francisco: International Marine/ McGraw-Hill, 2005. [No serious boater leaves port without it.]

Caldwell, Francis E. *Land of the Ocean Mists.* Annapolis: Lighthouse Press, 1986; Second Printing 2003. [Probably the best book to date about Lituya Bay.]

Caldwell, Francis E. *Pacific Troller: Life on the Northwest Fishing Grounds.* Victoria: Trafford Publishing, 1978. [Reissue 2005. Short true adventures from Caldwell's fishing days in the Gulf of Alaska.]

DeArmond, R.N. & Patricia Roppel. *Baranof Island's Eastern Shore: The Waterfall Coast.* Sitka: Arrowhead Press, 1998. [Descriptions and historical details of Baranof's East Coast by two well-known Alaskan authors.]

Douglass, Don & Réanne Hemingway-Douglass. *Exploring the North Coast of British Columbia* , 2nd Edition. Anacortes, WA: FineEdge.com, 2002.

Douglass, Don & Réanne Hemingway-Douglass. *Exploring the San Juan and Gulf Islands.* 2nd Edition, Anacortes, WA: FineEdge.com, 2003.

Douglass, Don & Réanne Hemingway-Douglass. *Exploring the South Coast of British Columbia,* 2nd Edition, Anacortes, WA: FineEdge.com, 1999.

Douglass, Don & Réanne Hemingway-Douglass. *Exploring Vancouver Island's West Coast,* 2nd Edition. Anacortes, WA: FineEdge.com, 1999.

Duke, Bob. *Cruising To Alaska: Tips and Tactics.* Bellingham: Good Enough Publishing, 2004. [Interviews with seasoned Alaska boaters.]

Eppenbach, Sarah. *Alaska's Southeast, Touring the Inside Passage.* Guilford, CT: The Globe Pequot Press, 2004. [The best all-around general guide to Southeast Alaska; frequently updated since its 1st Edition in 1983.]

Fox, William T. *At the Sea's Edge.* New York: Prentice Hall Press, 1983.

Hale, Robert, Ed. *Waggoner Cruising Guide.* Bellevue: Robert Hale & Co. Inc., published annually. [Excellent for getting a boater as far as Prince Rupert.]

Hinz, Earl R. *The Complete Book of Anchoring and Mooring.* Maryland: Cornell Maritime Pres, 2001 reprint. [Highly recommended by Don Douglass as the best all-around book on anchoring.]

Horn, Elizabeth L. *Coastal Wildflowers of the Pacific Northwest.* Missoula, Montana: Mountain Press Publishing Company, 1994.

Jensen, Susan Clark, Ed. *Beating the Odds on the North Pacific: A Guide to Fishing Safety,* 2nd Edition. Sitka: Alaska Marine Safety Education Association (AMSEA), 1994. [Although written for the fishing industry, the information on Alaska weather is excellent.]

Kirchhoff, M. J. *Baranof Island.* Juneau: Alaska Cedar Press, 1990. [An illustrated history by one of the island's residents.]

Kozloff, Eugene N. *Plants and Animals of the Pacific Northwest.* Seattle: University of Washington Press, 1976. [Still one of the classic references for flora & fauna.]

Maloney, Elbert S. *Chapman Piloting, Seamanship & Small Boat Handling.* New York: Hearst Marine Books. [Another classic that boaters should carry as a standard on board their vessel.]

Miller, Robert H. *Kayaking The Inside Passage.* Woodstock: Countryman Press, 2005.

Monahan, Kevin. *Local Knowledge-—A Skipper's Reference—Tacoma to Ketchikan*, Anacortes, WA: FineEdge.com, 2005.

Monahan, Kevin. *The Radar Book: Effective Navigation and Collision Avoidance.* Anacortes, WA: FineEdge.com, 2004. [One of the best books on how to use your radar effectively.]

Monahan, Kevin & Don Douglass. *Proven Cruising Routes, Seattle to Ketchikan*, Vol. 1. Anacortes, WA: FineEdge.com, 2000.

Monahan, Kevin & Don Douglass. *GPS Instant Navigation*, 2nd Edition. Anacortes, WA: FineEdge.com, 2000.

Morton, Alexandra. *Listening to Whales—What the Orcas Have Taught Us.* New York: Ballantine Books, 2002.

Naske, Claus-M. & Herman E. Slotnick. *Alaska: A History of the 49th State,* 2nd Edition. Norman, OK: University of Oklahoma Press, 1987. [Good resource for boaters interested in Alaska's history and political and environmental issues.]

*Northwest Boat Travel.* Woodinville: Vernon Publishing Company, published annually. [Covers the entire Inside Passage, as well as Southeast Alaska.]

O'Clair, Rita M., Robert H. Armstrong, and Richard Carstensen. *The Nature of Southeast Alaska, A Guide to Plants, Animals, and Habitats.* Anchorage: Alaska Northwest Books, 2004.

Peterson, Dale R. *Day By Day to Alaska.* Victoria, B.C.: Trafford, 2000. [Good reading for boaters with a vessel less than 28 feet in length.]

Raban, Jonathan, *Passage to Juneau—A Sea and Its Meanings.* New York; Vintage Books, 2000.

Roppel, Patricia. *Misty Fiords National Monument Wilderness.* Wrangell: Farwest Research, 2000.

NOTE: In 2002, the Canadian Hydrographic Service replaced the *Sailing Directions Volume 2* with: *Sailing Directions PAC 200—General Information-Pacific Coast* (for all B.C. areas) and several publications detailing specific geographical areas within B.C. For Inside Passage cruisers, the areas of interest in northern B.C. waters can be found in: PAC 205, and PAC 206.

*Sailing Directions—British Columbia Coast (PAC200) General Information—Pacific Coast,1st Ed.* Minister of Fisheries and Oceans: Canada, Latest edition. [Entire BC Pacific coast includes nav-aids, hazards, buoyage, port facilities.]

*Sailing Directions—British Columbia Coast (PAC205) Inner Passage—Queen Charlotte Sound to Chatham Sound, 1st Ed.,* Minister of Fisheries and Oceans: Canada, Latest edition. [North coast from Queen Charlotte Sound to Prince Rupert area.]

*Sailing Directions—British Columbia Coast (PAC206) Hecate Strait, Dixon Entrance, Portland Inlet & Queen Charlotte Islands 1st Ed.* Minister of Fisheries and Oceans: Canada, 2002.

*Sailing Direction B.C.—S Portion, Volume 1,* Minister of Fisheries and Oceans: Canada, (2004—check for latest edition)

Snively, Gloria. *Exploring the Seashore in British Columbia, Washington and Oregon. A Guide to Shorebirds and Intertidal Plants and Animals.* West Vancouver: Gordon Soules Book Publishers Ltd., 1978, sixth printing, 1985.

Sweet, Bob. *The Weekend Navigator.* San Francisco: International Marine/McGraw-Hill, 2005. [Excellent, straight forward how-to book for GPS and electronics.]

Terdal, Leif G. *Small-Boat Cruising to Alaska.* Seattle: Hara Publishing, 2000. [Required reading for anyone attempting an Alaska cruise in a vessel less than 28 feet.]

*United States Coast Pilot,* Number 8. Washington, D.C.: U.S. Department of Commerce, NOAA, [Latest Edition].

Upton, Joe. *Journeys through the Inside Passage.* Anchorage: Alaska Northwest Books, 1992.

Upton, Joe. *The Coastal Companion: A Guide for the Alaska-bound Traveler.* Bainbridge Island, 1995. [A mile-post guide interspersed with descriptions of Upton's experiences as an Alaskan fisherman.]

Upton, Joe. *Alaska Blues: A Season of Fishing the Inside Passage.* 2nd Edition. Seattle: Sasquatch Books, 1998. [Perhaps Upton's best of his true adventures.]

Wing, Charlie. *How Boat Things Work.* San Francisco: International Marine/ McGraw-Hill, 2004. [Wonderfully clear explanations; particularly good book for the First Mate.]

Wise, Ken C. *Cruise of the Blue Flujin.* Fowlerville, Michigan: Wilderness Adventure Books, 1987. [Account of four Sea Scouts that canoed to Alaska in 1937.]

Wood, Charles E. *Charlie's Charts North to Alaska,* 3rd Edition. Surrey, B.C.: Charlie's Charts, 2000.

## Acknowledgments

When it comes to exploring new horizons, we all stand on the shoulders of those who preceded us. This has been true since the first humans paddled down the coast of Southeast Alaska from Asia and since Cook, Quadra, Vancouver and others started their historic explorations. In doing our research of the harbors and coves of this beautiful water wilderness, we have those earlier explorers to thank, as well as those who have helped us along the waterways for decades.

We would like to express our thanks to the intrepid explorer-friends who've assisted us in collecting data for Southeast Alaska, either as crew on our vessel Research Vessel *Baidarka*, as companion boaters, or as "local knowledge" experts who have shared their "secrets" or photographs with us: Rod Nash, Herb and Wendy Nickles, Dave and Evie Frisby, Greg and Ilse Hine, Jean and Joel Gillingwators, Jean and Geneviève Doudeau, Barb and Bill Davis, Jack and Linda Shreiber, Carl and Carol Cederberg, Jill and Doug Princehouse, John Leone, Henry Wendt, Larry Johnson, Ward Eldridge and Kathy Kyle, Kevin Monahan, Bill Stanley, Frank and Margy Fletcher, Mike Youngblood, Mike and Claudia Herrick, Pat Roppell, Art and Linda Forbes, Larry Calvin, John Neal and Amanda Swan-Neal, Jim Kyle, Bruce and Margaret Evertz, Brian and Carol Pemberton, Chara Stewart, Clyde Ford, Bob Duke, David J. Shuler, Bob Berto, Dave Scott, Richard Friedman, David Parker, Dick and Nancy White, Carolyn and Tim De Cook, Jordan Roderick, and John Grinter.

Our thanks go, also, to the many harbormasters, park rangers and their staff, who have given freely of their time to help keep us abreast of changes throughout the years: Ray Majeski, Lou McCall, John Stone, Mike Kampnich, Bob Clausen, David Duffey, Paul Dybdahl, Matt O'Boyle, Chris Brewton, Robert Venables and Chuck Young.

Our appreciation, also, to the myriad unnamed readers who have shared their tips or findings with us and who have given us encouragement to "keep exploring." And last, special thanks to our editor, Linda Lewis, whose critical eye and thoughtful suggestions have helped us bring this lengthy project together, and to our "home crew," Kelly Heiberg.

## About the Authors

*Réanne Hemingway-Douglass and Don Douglass*

Don Douglass and Réanne Hemingway-Douglass have logged more than 170,000 cruising miles over the past 30 years—from South America to Dutch Harbor in the Aleutians. They consider Alaskan waters as some of the finest in the world and they spend many of their summers there on their research vessel, *Baidarka.*

Don, who began exploring Northwest waters in 1949 as a youth, has sailed the Inside Passage on everything from a 26-foot pleasure craft and commercial fishing boats to a Coast Guard icebreaker. He holds a BSEE degree from California State University and a Masters in Business Economics from Claremont Graduate University. Don holds honorary membership in the International Association of Cape Horners and, as a founding father of the International Bicycling Association, was elected to the Mountain Biking Hall of Fame.

Réanne Hemingway-Douglass holds a BA degree in French from Pomona College. She attended Claremont Graduate University and the University of Grenoble, France. Her classic, *Cape Horn: One Man's Dream, One Woman's Nightmare*, describes pitchpoling in the Great Southern Ocean. She is the first woman to have bicycled across Tierra del Fuego.

Together, the Douglasses have documented over 8,000 anchor sites between Mexico and the Gulf of Alaska, and their six highly acclaimed "Exploring" series guidebooks, published by FineEdge.com, and their cruising planning maps cover the waters from Baja, California, to the Gulf of Alaska.

# Index

*Please Note: When multiple page numbers are listed, the page for the major text is in bold; italicized names and page numbers refer to Sidebars.*

*Please Note: When multiple page numbers are listed, the page for the major text is in bold; italicized names and page numbers refer to Sidebars.*

*Please Note: When multiple page numbers are listed, the page for the major text is in bold; italicized names and page numbers refer to Sidebars.*

*Please Note: When multiple page numbers are listed, the page for the major text is in bold; italicized names and page numbers refer to Sidebars.*

*Please Note: When multiple page numbers are listed, the page for the major text is in bold; italicized names and page numbers refer to Sidebars.*

*Please Note: When multiple page numbers are listed, the page for the major text is in bold; italicized names and page numbers refer to Sidebars.*

*Please Note: When multiple page numbers are listed, the page for the major text is in bold; italicized names and page numbers refer to Sidebars.*

*Please Note: When multiple page numbers are listed, the page for the major text is in bold; italicized names and page numbers refer to Sidebars.*

# Enjoy these other publications from Fine Edge

## Exploring the Pacific Coast—San Diego to Seattle

**Don Douglass and Réanne Hemingway-Douglass**

All the places to tie up or anchor your boat from the Mexican border to Victoria/ Seattle. Over 500 of the best marinas and anchor sites, starting from San Diego to Santa Barbara—every anchor site in the beautiful Channel Islands, the greater SF Bay Area, the lower Columbia River, and the greater Puget Sound.

## Exploring the San Juan and Gulf Islands—2nd Ed.

*Cruising Paradise of the Pacific Northwest*

**Don Douglass and Réanne Hemingway-Douglass**

All the anchor sites in the paradise that straddles the U.S.-Canadian border, bounded by Deception Pass and Anacortes on the south, Nanaimo on the north, Victoria on the west, and Bellingham on the east.

## Exploring Vancouver Island's West Coast—2nd Ed.

**Don Douglass and Réanne Hemingway-Douglass**

With five great sounds, sixteen major inlets, and an abundance of spectacular wildlife, the largest island on the west coast of North America is a cruising paradise.

## Exploring the South Coast of British Columbia—2nd Ed.

*Gulf Islands & Desolation Sound to Port Hardy & Blunden Harbour*

**Don Douglass and Réanne Hemingway-Douglass**

"Clearly the most thorough, best produced and most useful [guides] available . . . particularly well thought out and painstakingly researched." — *NW Yachting*

## Exploring the North Coast of British Columbia

*Blunden Harbour to Dixon Entrance, Including Queen Charlotte Islands*

**Don Douglass and Réanne Hemingway-Douglass**

Describes previously uncharted Spiller Channel and Griffin Passage, the stunning scenery of Nakwakto Rapids and Seymour Inlet, Fish Egg Inlet, Queens Sound, and Hakai Recreation Area. Helps you plot a course for the beautiful South Moresby Island of the Queen Charlottes.

## Exploring the Virgin Islands

**Joe Russell and Mark Bunzel**

This cruising guide for the British and U.S. Virgin Islands features all the well-known anchorages, as well as many you have not seen before. Most shown with aerial photos, anchorage diagrams and GPS waypoints to make navigation in this cruising paradise easy.

## Exploring the Marquesas Islands

**Joe Russell**

Russell, who has lived and sailed in the Marquesas, documents the first cruising guide to this beautiful, little-known place. Includes history, language guide, chart diagrams, mileages and heading tables and archaeology. "A must reference for those wanting to thoroughly enjoy their first landfall on the famous Coconut Milk Run."—Earl Hinz, author, *Landfalls of Paradise—Cruising Guide to the Pacific Islands*

## Inside Passage Maps *North and South portions*

Now, for the first time, our maps include an index to all harbors and coves in this superb wilderness allowing you to customize your own routes.

## Exploring the Pacicific Coast Planning Map, *North & South*

## San Juan and Gulf Islands Nautical and Recreational Planning Map

# Enjoy these other publications from Fine Edge

## THE DREAMSPEAKER SERIES

BY ANNE & LAURENCE YEADON-JONES

Volume 1: Gulf Islands & Vancouver Island
ISBN 978-1-932310-13-9

Volume 2: Desolation Sound & Discovery Islands
ISBN 978-1-932310-14-6

Volume 3: Vancouver, Howe Sound & the Sunshine Coast
ISBN 978-1-932310-15-3

Volume 4: The San Juan Islands
ISBN 978-1-932310-16-0

Volume 5: The Broughtons
ISBN 978-1-932310-17-7

***Ann and Laurence Yeadon-Jones' Dreamspeaker series are not only valuable resources filled with delightful hand-drawn maps, photos and important cruising information, they're also infused with a little bit of fun which makes them stand out from the others.***
—Peter A. Robson, editor, *Pacific Yachting Magazine*

ANNE & LAURENCE YEADON-JONES are experienced offshore and inshore sailors who voyaged from Southampton, England, in 1985 on their first adventure across the Atlantic Ocean. Over the last 17 years they have logged thousands of cruising hours charting, recording and photographing their travels, and exclusively along the beautifully rugged coastline and islands of the Pacific Northwest. Through their writing, charting and photography they endeavour to promote safe and enjoyable boating while profiling the uniqueness of coastal life.

Available at nautical bookstores, West Marine and www.FineEdge.com

**FINE EDGE**

*Nautical & Recreational Publishing*

# The Nautical Knowledge Series from Fine Edge

## Local Knowledge: A Skipper's Reference

*Tacoma to Ketchikan*

**Kevin Monahan**

A must-have reference for the skipper of any boat traveling the Inside Passage! Includes over 50 pages of handy distance tables and strategies for managing tides and currents in Johnstone Strait and Cordero Channel, time, distance and speed tables, weather data and much, much more!

## The Radar Book

**Kevin Monahan**

The complete picture on how to maximize the use of your marine radar system. By using practical examples, illustrated with screen displays and the corresponding charts, the newcomer to radar as well as the experienced mariner will learn how to tune a radar system, interpret the display in a variety of conditions, take advantage of all of the built-in features and use radar effectively as a real-time navigational tool.

## Keeping Your Boat Legal

*The Boating Legal Guide*

**Curt Epperson**, JD, LLM

This practical guide, written in a FAQ format, makes it easy to read and easy to find the information you need. It will help to understand today's legal requirements, insurance contract language and coverage, and to develop a system to organize your boats documents, maintain the proper records for insurance purposes and manage border crossings to Canada, Mexico or the Bahamas.

## GPS Instant Navigation, 2nd Edition

*A Practical Guide from Basics to Advanced Techniques*

**Kevin Monahan and Don Douglass**

In this clear, well-illustrated manual, mariners will find simple solutions to navigational challenges. Includes 150 detailed diagrams, which illustrate the many ways you can use GPS to solve classic piloting and navigation problems.

# For Your Reading Enjoyment

## Cape Horn

*One Man's Dream, One Woman's Nightmare—2nd Ed.*

**Réanne Hemingway-Douglass**

"This is the sea story to read if you read only one."—McGraw Hill, *International Marine Catalog* "Easily the hairy-chested adventure yarn of the decade, if not the half-century."
—Peter H. Spectre, *Wooden Boat*

## Unsinkable

**Dee Saunders**

Sunk by a freighter on their way to paradise, a cruising couple's strength and perseverance help them to rebuild their life and dreams.

## *Trekka* Round the World

**John Guzzwell**

Long out-of-print, this international classic is the story of Guzzwell's circumnavigation on his 20-foot yawl, *Trekka.* Includes previously unpublished photos and a foreword by America's renowned bluewater sailor-author Hal Roth.

## Destination Cortez Island

*A sailor's life along the BC Coast*

**June Cameron**

A nostalgic memoir of the lives of coastal pioneers—the old timers and their boats, that were essential in the days when the ocean was the only highway.

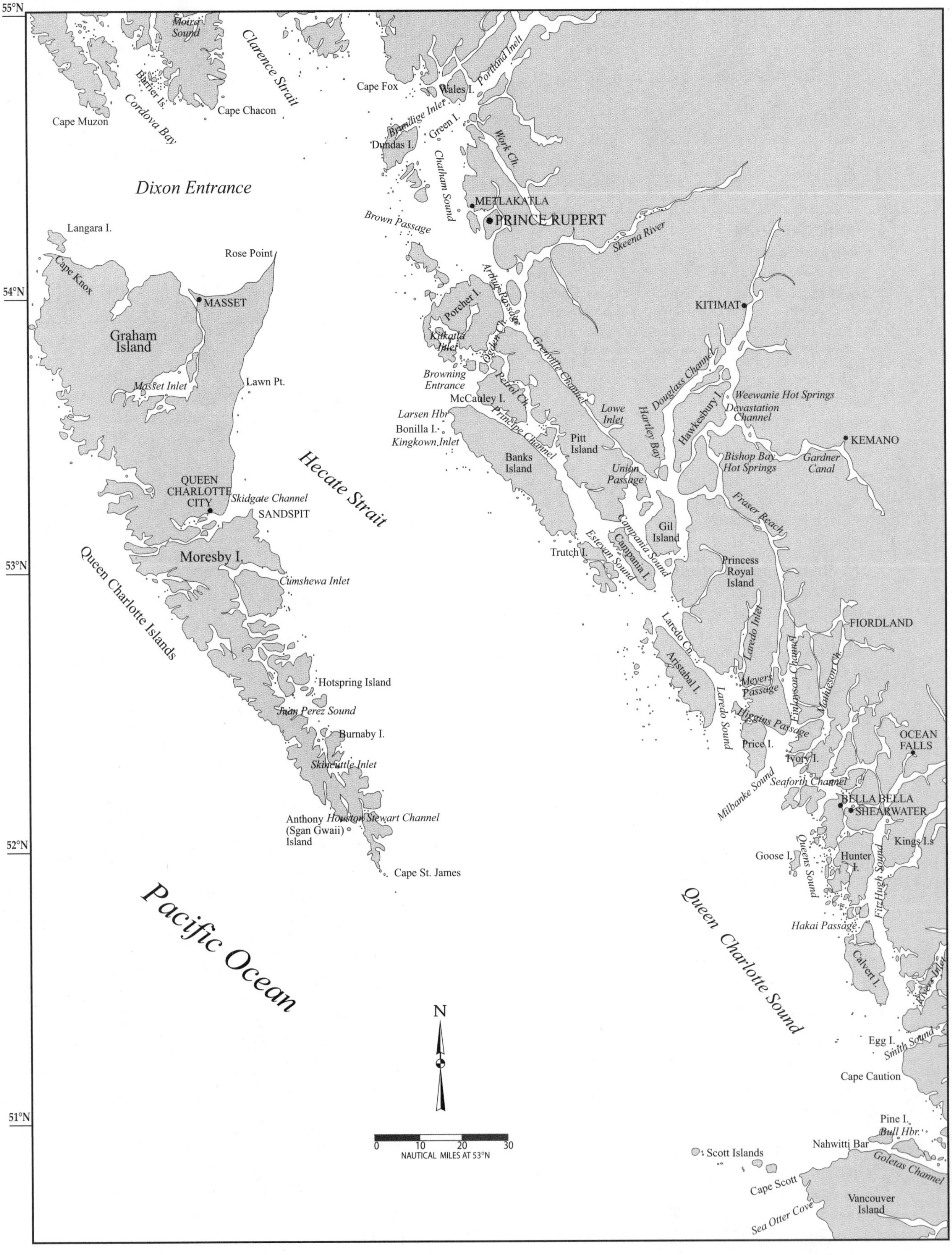
55°N
54°N
53°N
52°N
51°N
Moira Sound
Clarence Strait
Barrier Is.
Cordova Bay
Cape Chacon
Cape Muzon
Cape Fox
Wales I.
Portland Inlet
Brundige Inlet
Green I.
Dundas I.
Work Ch.
Chatham Sound
Dixon Entrance
METLAKATLA
PRINCE RUPERT
Brown Passage
Skeena River
Langara I.
Rose Point
Cape Knox
MASSET
Graham Island
Masset Inlet
Lawn Pt.
Arthur Passage
Porcher I.
Kitkatla Inlet
Ogden Ch.
Browning Entrance
Grenville Channel
KITIMAT
Douglass Channel
Lowe Inlet
Hartley Bay
Hawkesbury I.
Weewanie Hot Springs
Devastation Channel
KEMANO
Gardner Canal
Bishop Bay Hot Springs
McCauley I.
Petrol Ch.
Larsen Hbr
Bonilla I.
Kingkown Inlet
Principe Channel
Pitt Island
Banks Island
Union Passage
Hecate Strait
QUEEN CHARLOTTE CITY
Skidgate Channel
SANDSPIT
Fraser Reach
Gil Island
Campania Sound
Campania I.
Estevan Sound
Trutch I.
Princess Royal Island
Moresby I.
Queen Charlotte Islands
Cumshewa Inlet
FIORDLAND
Laredo Ch.
Laredo Inlet
Aristabal I.
Laredo Sound
Meyers Passage
Finlayson Channel
Mathieson Ch.
Higgins Passage
Hotspring Island
Juan Perez Sound
Burnaby I.
Skincuttle Inlet
Price I.
Ivory I.
OCEAN FALLS
Milbanke Sound
Seaforth Channel
BELLA BELLA
SHEARWATER
Anthony (Sgan Gwaii) Island
Houston Stewart Channel
Kings I.s
Goose I.
Queens Sound
Hunter I.
Fitz Hugh Sound
Cape St. James
Hakai Passage
Calvert I.
Rivers Inlet
Pacific Ocean
Queen Charlotte Sound
N
Egg I.
Smith Sound
Cape Caution
0
10
20
30
NAUTICAL MILES AT 53°N
Pine I.
Bull Hbr.
Nahwitti Bar
Scott Islands
Goletas Channel
Cape Scott
Vancouver Island
Sea Otter Cove